AF520042

ACCOUNTING FOR MANAGEMENT

ACCOUNTING FOR MANAGEMENT

Dr. JAWAHAR LAL

Ex-Head, Department of Commerce,
Ex-Dean, Faculty of Commerce and Business
Professor, Department of Commerce,
Delhi School of Economics,
University of Delhi,
Delhi 110 007.

First Edition : 2001
Second Revised Edition : 2002
Third Edition : 2003
Fourth Edition : 2004
Fifth Revised Edition : 2009
Edition : 2010, 2012, 2013, 2017, 2018, 2019, 2020
Edition : 2022
Edition : 2023
Edition : 2025

Published by : Mrs. Meena Pandey
for **HIMALAYA PUBLISHING HOUSE PVT. LTD.,**
"Ramdoot", Dr. Bhalerao Marg, Girgaon, Mumbai - 400 004.
Phone: 022-23860170, 23863863; **Fax:** 022-23877178
E-mail: himpub@bharatmail.co.in; **Website:** www.himpub.com

Branch Offices :

New Delhi : "Pooja Apartments", 4-B, Murari Lal Street, Ansari Road, Darya Ganj, New Delhi - 110 002. Phone: 011-23270392, 23278631; Fax: 011-23256286

Nagpur : Kundanlal Chandak Industrial Estate, Ghat Road, Nagpur - 440 018. Mobile: 09325409992, 09325908881

Bengaluru : Plot No. 91-33, 2nd Main Road, Seshadripuram, Behind Nataraja Theatre, Bengaluru - 560 020. Phone: 080-41138821; Mobile: 09379847017, 09379847005

Hyderabad : No. 3-4-184, Lingampally, Besides Raghavendra Swamy Matham, Kachiguda, Hyderabad - 500 027. Phone: 040-27560041, 27550139

Chennai : No. 34/44, Motilal Street, T. Nagar, Chennai - 600 017. Mobile: 09380460419

Pune : "Laksha" Apartment, First Floor, No. 527, Mehunpura, Shaniwarpeth (Near Prabhat Theatre), Pune - 411 030. Phone: 020-24496323, 24496333; Mobile: 09370579333

Cuttack : Plot No. 5F-755/4, Sector-9, CDA Markat Nagar, Cuttack - 753 014, Odisha. Mobile: 09338746007

Kolkata : 3, S.M. Bose Road, Near Gate No. 5, Agarpara Railway Station, North 24 Parganas, West Bengal - 700 109. Mobile: 09674536325

DTP by : HPH, Editorial Office, Bhandup **(Krunali)**.

Printed at : Geetanjali Press Pvt. Ltd., Nagpur, on behalf of HPH.

In Memory of My Parents

PREFACE TO THE FIFTH EDITION

It is my immense pleasure to present to the readers and students the thoroughly revised edition of the text, Accounting for Management.

The book discusses the principles, practices and uses of accounting in making business decisions. It is oriented towards providing useful and adequate knowledge in the two components of accounting information, viz., Financial Accounting, Cost and Management Accounting. It is obvious that if one understands how accounting information is prepared and presented, he can take appropriate decisions based on accounting information. Since the accounting information is used in business decisions, accountants have an important role in all aspects of management through supplying useful information to managers. Due to this, there is a need to develop utmost coordination between the managers and accountants and increase understanding between them about their respective functions and responsibilities. Managers of Indian Companies need to make business decisions with sound familiarity and understanding of use of accounting information.

The book presents a comprehensive coverage of important topics in Financial, Cost and Management Accounting in a clear, concise and logical manner. The book is intended primarily for those who are pursuing management and business courses in Indian Universities and Management Institutes and need to possess requisite accounting knowledge. The text does not assume a prior knowledge or understanding of accounting discipline.

The book is divided into two Parts. Part one deals with Financial Accounting and covers Financial and Management Accounting: An overview; Accounting Postulates, Concepts and Principles; Accounting Equation and Transaction Analysis; Accounting Mechanics: Journals; Cash Book and Subsidiary Books; Ledger Posting and Trial Balance; Bank Reconciliation Statement; Errors and Their Rectifications; Preparation of Financial Statements; Depreciation Accounting; Inventory Valuation; Statement of Changes in Financial Position (SC FP); Cash Flow Statement; Financial Statement Analysis.

Part Two deals with Cost and Management Accounting and covers Nature of Cost Accounting; Cost Concepts and Classification; Materials Control; Labour Cost Accounting and Control; Overheads: Distribution; Job, Contract and Batch Costing; Process Costing; Service Costing; Marginal (Variable) Costing; Alternative Choices Decisions; Standards Costing; Budgeting; Responsibility Accounting, Divisional Performance Measurement and Transfer Pricing; Activity-Based Costing.

This revised edition has many pedagogical features to give a judicious blend of conceptual analysis, accounting concepts and techniques and use of accounting information. Some such features are:

- Up-to-date coverage of the subject
- Clear and logical presentation
- Inclusion of more latest solved numerical problems and exercises and problems taken from the university and professional examinations
- Thought provoking and real-life theory questions
- Inclusion of cases at the end of the book in the Appendix.

All the chapters in the revised edition have been thoroughly rewritten to add new concepts and inputs and materials which are not relevant, have been deleted.

The book has been primarily written for MBA and similar programmes of Indian Universities and Management/Business Institutes. It will be equally useful for specialized management programmes such as MIB, MHROD, MFC and comparable programmes.

Any suggestion and views to improve the quality of the book and make it more useful are welcome.

Professor Jawahar Lal

CONTENTS

PART II: COST AND MANAGEMENT ACCOUNTING

Part One
Financial Accounting

Financial and Management Accounting: An Overview

EVOLUTION OF ACCOUNTING

Accounting has evolved in a manner similar to law, medicine and most other fields of human activity, in response to the social and economic needs of society. Book-keeping and accounting did not emerge as chance phenomena, but as a pragmatic response to a specific world need.[1] This is true not only of the days of Paciolo[2] but also important for present-day accounting survival. For centuries after the system of double-entry book-keeping appeared, accounting was practised without a uniform methodology or any form of theory. It was only during the 19th century that a distinct move from book-keeping to accounting — a move from relatively simple recording and analysis of transactions towards a comprehensive accounting information system — was effected. The close of 19th century was marked by the most extraordinary expansion of business.

Company form of organisation, a phenomenon which was becoming increasingly common in business world, grew at a great speed. Books about business transactions were written, conventions were followed and accounting was recognised as a system of analysing and maintaining records of business transactions.

Modern business is marked by continuity, a never-ending flow of economic activities. Therefore, accounting has grown to meet a social requirement and to guide the business and industry accordingly. Accounting is moving away from its traditional procedural base, encompassing

1. Maurice, Moonitz and A.C. Littleton, *Significant Accounting Essays,* Prentice Hall, 1965, p. 12.
2. Francisan Monk, Paciolo, is looked upon as the father of modern accounting. His *Summa,* published in 1494, comprised the first text reference on book-keeping. Later book-keeping spread throughout the world through a series of Paciolo imitations.

record-keeping and such related work as the preparation of budgets and final accounts, towards the adoption of a role which emphasises its social importance. Welsch and Anthony[3] comment:

> "The growth of business organisations in size, particularly publicly-held corporations, has brought pressure from stock-holders, potential investors, creditors, governmental agencies, and the public at large, for increased financial disclosure. The public's right to know more about organisations that directly and indirectly affect them (whether or not they are shareholders) is being increasingly recognised as essential. An open society is one that has a high degree of freedom at the individual level and typically evidences an effective commitment to measuring the quality of life attained. These characteristics make it essential that the members of that society be provided adequate, understandable, and dependable financial information from the major institutions that comprise it."

Further, refinements in cost and management accounting followed later on in the 20th century along with large-scale production and high-capital investment. These developments created a need to allocate costs correctly over the units of production, and also to provide a measure of productivity and efficiency. Thereafter, cost accounting evolved naturally to meet recognized managerial requirements of pricing and costing for competitive purposes, and towards determining and setting forth of operational information for decision-making purposes.

Traditionally, governmental accounting was linked to taxation and revenue control, and to the recording of, and accountability for, receipts and expenditure. Development in budgeting in the 20th century created a much larger scope for government accounting. The national budget became a managerial and policy-making instrument and developed into a mechanism for the forward planning of receipts and expenditure. Budgeting has now developed to form one of the bases of — and is closely associated with — economic planning and programming.

Accounting, thus, has gone through many phases — simple double-entry book-keeping, enterprise, government, and cost and management accounting, and recently, social accounting. These phases have largely been a product of changing economic and social environments. As business and society have become more complex over the years, accounting has developed new concepts and techniques to meet the ever increasing needs for financial information.

DEFINITION OF ACCOUNTING

What is accounting? This basic question has never been answered precisely and many definitions of the term are available.

Back in 1941, the Committee on Terminology of the American Institute of Certified Public Accountants (AICPA) formulated the following definition[4] which was widely quoted for many years:

> "Accounting is the art of recording, classifying and summarising in a significant manner, and in terms of money, transactions and events which are, in part at least, of a financial character, and interpreting the results thereof."

In 1966, The American Accounting Association (AAA), in order to emphasise the broader perspective of accounting, provided the following definition of accounting:[5]

3. Glenn A. Welsch and Robert N. Anthony, *Fundamentals of Financial Accounting,* Richard D. Irwin, 1971 p. 19.
4. Accounting Terminology Bulletin No. 1: *Review and Resume,* AICPA, 1953, para 9.
5. American Accounting Association, *A Statement of Basic Accounting Theory,* 1966, p. 1.

> "Accounting is the process of identifying, measuring and communicating economic information to permit informed judgements and decisions by users of the information."

In 1970, the AICPA of the USA defined accounting with reference to the concept of information.[6]

"Accounting is a service activity. Its function is to provide quantitative information, primarily financial in nature, and about economic activities, that is intended to be useful in making economic decisions."

The term, 'quantitative information' used in the above definition is wider in scope than financial or economic information. Both the definitions, AAA (1966), and AICPA (1970) emphasise on using the information for the purposes of decision-making.

Modern accounting, therefore, is not merely concerned with record-keeping but also with a whole range of activities involving planning, control, decision-making, problem solving, performance measurement and evaluation, coordinating and directing, auditing, tax determination and planning, cost and management accounting.

The managers within an organisation and interested outside parties use accounting information in making decisions that affect the organisation. Today's accounting focusses on the ultimate needs of those, who use accounting information, whether these users are inside or outside the busines itself.

ACCOUNTING AND BOOK-KEEPING

Book-keeping should be distinguished from accounting which has been defined earlier. Book-keeping is a process of accounting concerned merely with recording transactions and keeping records. Book-keeping is a small and simple part of accounting. It is mechanical and repetitive while dealing with business transactions.

Accounting, on the other hand, aims at designing a satisfactory information system which may fulfil informational needs of different users and decision makers. Accounting primarily focuses on measurement, analysis, interpretation and use of information. It highlights the relevance and relationship of the information produced by the accounting process and effects of different accounting alternatives. Accounting includes budgeting, strategic planning, cost analysis, auditing, income-tax preparation, performance measurement, evaluation, control, preparing managerial reports for decision making, etc.

ACCOUNTING AS AN INFORMATION SYSTEM

The term 'system' may be defined as a set of elements which operate together in order to attain a goal. A system does not consist of random sets of elements but elements which may be identified as belonging together because of a common goal. A system contains three activities: (*i*) input, (*ii*) processing of input, and (*iii*) output. A business organisation is regarded as an open system which has a dynamic interplay with its environment from which it draws resources, and to which it consigns its product and services.

Accounting comprises a series of linked activities. These a counting activities form a progression of steps, beginning with observing, then collecting, recording, analysing, and finally communicating information to users. In other words, the accounting process involves the accumulation,

6. Accounting Principles Board, Statement No. 4, *Basic Concepts and Accounting Principles Underlying Financial Statements of Business Enterprises,* 1970, para 40.

analysis, measurement, interpretation, classification, and summarisation of the results of each of the many business transactions that affected the entity during the year. After this processing, accounting then transmits or projects messages to potential decision makers. The messages are in the form of financial statements, and the decision makers are the users. Accounting generally does not generate the basic information (raw financial data), rather the raw financial data results from the day-to-day transactions of the enterprise.

Figure 1.1 displays how accounting as an information system aids business and economic decisions made by user-decision-makers, In this service activity, as shown in Fig. 1.1, accounting assumes a link between business activities and transactions and the decision makers. First, accounting measures business activities and transactions through recording data. Second, the recorded data is processed and stored until needed. Processing can be done in such a manner or format as to become useful information. Alteratively, sometimes, the processed data are further processed or prepared to provide the required information to the user. Thirdly, processed and prepared information is communicated to users and decision makers in the forms of financial statements, other statements, reports, etc. In this accounting system, business transactions and activities are the input and statements and reports generated for the decision makers comprise the output.

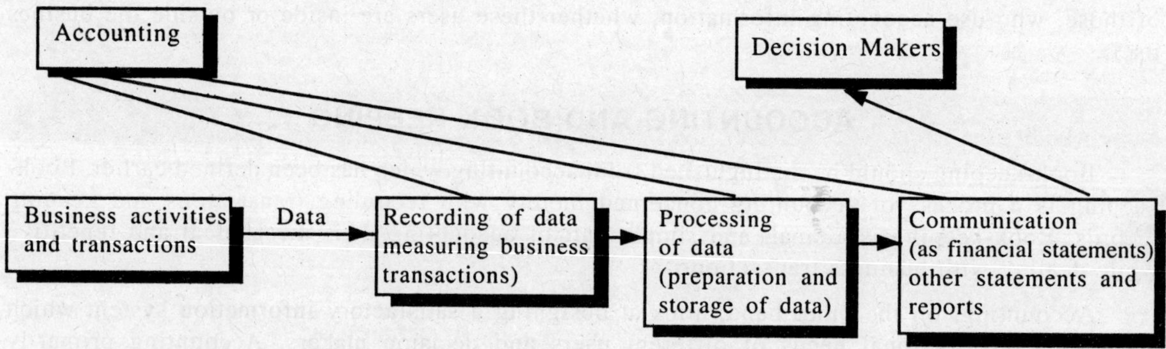

Fig. 1.1 Accounting as an information system in business and economic decision-making

ACCOUNTING AS A LANGUAGE

Accounting is often called the 'language of business.' It is one means of communicating information about a business. As a new language is to be learnt to converse and communicate, so also accounting is to be learnt and practised to communicate vis-a-vis business events. Many accounting writers and researchers, as well as the accounting profession have referred to accounting as the language of business. For instance, Yuji Ijiri[7] observes:

> "As the language of business, accounting has many things in common with other languages. The vaious business activities of a firm are reported in accounting statements using accounting language, just as news events are reported in newspapers; in English or another Language. To express an event in accounting or in English we must follow certain rules. Without following certain rules diligently, not only does one run the risk of being misunderstood but also risks a penalty for misrepresentation, lying or perjury. Comparability of statements is essential to the effective functioning of a language whether it is in English or in accounting. At the same time, language has to be flexible to adapt to a changing environment.

7. Yuji Ijiri, *Theory of Accounting Measurement,* Accounting Research Study No. 10, AAA, 1975, p. 14.

There are important similarities between a language and accounting. A language broadly has two components: (*i*) symbols, and (*ii*) rules to make it purposeful. Symbols are the meaningful units or words identifiable in any language, known as linguistic objects and which are used to convey particular meanings or concepts. The arrangement of symbols in a systematic manner becomes a language. The rules which influence the usage and pattern of the symbols are known as the grammar of the language or grammatical rules.

In accounting too, there are two components (*i*) symbols, and (*ii*) grammatical rules. In accounting, numerals and words and debits and credits are accepted as symbols which are unique to the accounting discipline.[8] The grammatical rules in accounting refer to the general set of procedures followed to create all manners of financial data for business. Anthony and Reece[9] draw the following parallel between accounting and language:

> "Accounting... resembles a language in that some of its rules are definite whereas others are not. Accountants differ as to how a given event should be reported, just as grammarians differ as to many matters of sentence structure, punctuation and choice of words. Nevertheless, just as many practices are clearly poor English (language), many practices are definitely poor accounting. Languages evolve and change in response to the changing needs of society, and so does accounting."

USERS OF ACCOUNTING INFORMATION

Accounting provides useful information about the activities of an entity to various individuals or groups for their use in making informed judgements and decisions. The users of accounting information can be broadly divided into three categories:

1. Management or managers
2. Users with direct financial interest
3. Users with indirect financial interest

Fig. 1.2 shows different users of accounting information and different decisions made by them.

1. Management: Management is a group of people who are responsible for using the resources and managing the affairs of an entity to achieve certain predetermined goals and objectives. Managers perform many managerial functions such as planning, controlling, directing, measuring, evaluating and taking corrective action. Business managers need to decide continuously what to do, how to do it and whether the actual results tally the original plans and targets. Accounting provides timely and useful information to the management for planning, control, performance measurement, decision making and for performing many activities and functions in the company. Thus, management is one of the most important users of accounting information and a major function of accounting is to provide useful information to the managers and management.

2. Users with Direct Financial Interest: Users who have direct financial interest in a company include existing and potential investors and creditors. These users do not participate in the actual management of the company but have interest in how a business has performed because they have invested, or are thinking of investing in a company. Existing and potential investors are obviously interested in the past performance of a company and its earning potential and growth prospects in

8. Daniel L. McDonald, *Comparative Accounting Theory,* Addison Wesley, 1972.
9. Robert N. Anthony and James S. Reece, *Accounting Principles,* Richard D. Irwin, 1991, p. 14.

the future. For this, the company's financial statements and other information should be analysed to decide and select a profitable investment opportunity.

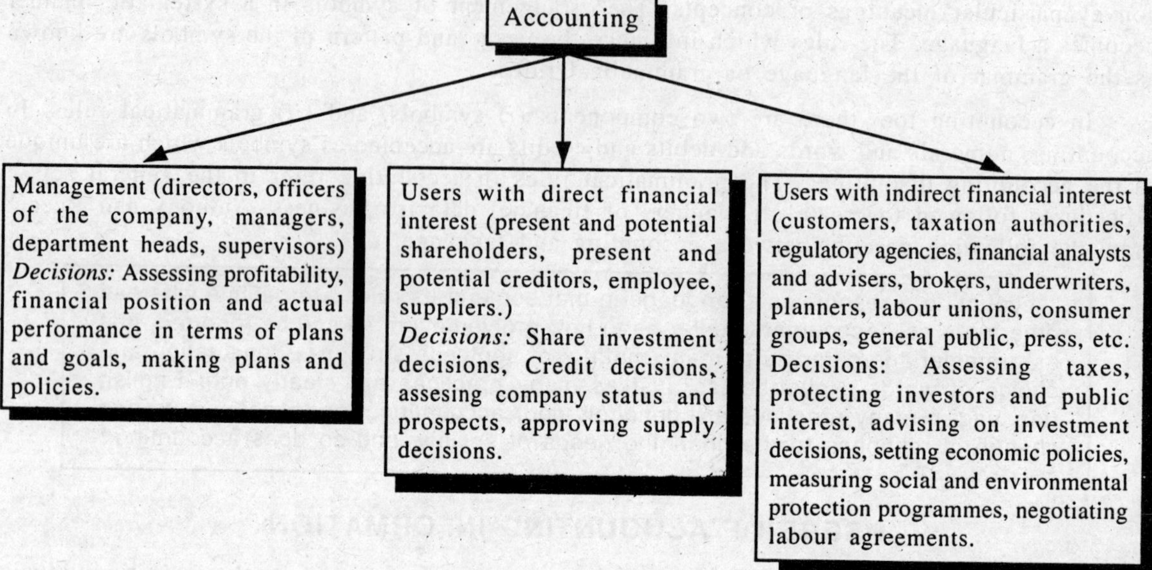

Fig. 1.2 Different Users of Accounting Information

Similarly, the existing and potential creditors require accounting information to make sound credit decisions, *i.e.,* whether to lend money to a company. The creditors are interested in knowing whether the company will have enough cash to pay interest charge and repay the debt at the due date. For this, the company's liquidity and cash flow position should be analysed. Banks, finance companies, mortgage companies, investment and insurance concerns, individual creditors and other similar individuals and groups who lend money need accounting information to analyse a company's profitability, liquidity and financial position before making a loan to the company.

Besides the investors and creditors, there are other users such as employees, and suppliers who have direct financial interest in a company and accounting information as well. Employees' decisions may be based on perceptions of company's economic status acquired through financial statements. In particular, prospective and present employees may use the financial reports to assess risk and growth potential of a company, therefore job security and future promotional possibilities.

To suppliers, a business enterprise is a source of cash in the form of payment for goods or services supplied. Suppliers are also interested in a company's ability to generate adequate cash flows towards the payment of goods and services supplied which in turn, can be decided on the basis of the company's financial statement.

3. Users with an Indirect Financial Interest: There are some other users who have indirect interest in a company's business or who use accounting information to help others having direct interest in a company's profitability and financial position. Such users are customers, taxation authorities, governmental and regulatory agencies, labour unions, financial analysts and advisers; stock exchanges and brokers, underwriters, economists; planners; consumers groups; general public and the financial press.

Customers may use financial statement data to forecast the likelihood and/or timing of a firm going bankrupt or being unable to meet its commitments. This information may be important in estimating the value of a warranty or in predicting the availability of supporting services or continuing supply of goods over an extended period of time.

Taxation authorities require financial statements to ascertain tax liability of a company, Governmental and regulatory agencies are concerned with the financial activities of business organisations for purposes of regulation to protect the public interest. Labour unions are also vitally interested in the stability and the profitability of the organisation that hires them or in which the employees are working. Stockbrokers, financial analysts, investment advisers have an indirect interest in the financial performance and prospects of a company as they advise investors and creditors in their investment and lending decisions.

Economic planners use accounting information to set economic policies, to forecast economic activities and to evaluate economic programmes undertaken in the country. The other users such as consumers groups, economists, financial press and the general public have become more concerned about business enterprises as well as with the effects that these enterprises have on the environment, social problem, inflation, and the quality of life.

FINANCIAL AND MANAGEMENT ACCOUNTING

As stated earlier, accounting is an information system that measures, processes and communicates information that is useful to decision-makers and interested users. The field of accounting is divided into two parts: (*i*) financial accounting, and (*ii*) management accounting.

Financial Accounting

Financial accounting is concerned with providing information to external users. It refers to the preparation of general purpose reports for use by persons outside a business enterprise, such as shareholders (existing and potential), creditors, financial analysts, labour unions, government authorities, and the like. Financial accounting is oriented towards the preparation of financial statements which summarise the results of operations for selected periods of time and show the financial position of the business at particular dates. It involves recording, classifying and summarising of the effects of internal events and external transactions. The following are important to understand the scope and nature of financial accounting.

(i) Contents

The end product of the financial accounting process comprises financial statements that communicate useful information to decision makers. The financial statements reflect a combination of recorded facts, accounting conventions and personal judgements of the preparers. There are three primary financial statements for a profit-making entity in India, viz., the income statement (statement of revenues, expenses and profit), and the balance sheet (statement of assets, liabilities and owner's equity), Cash Flow Statement as per AS 3 issued by the Institute of Chartered Accountants of India.

(ii) Accounting System

The accounting system includes various techniques and procedures used by the accountant (preparer) in measuring, describing and communicating financial data to users. Journals, ledgers, trial balance, financial statements are prepared using double entry accounting system.

(iii) Accounting Principles

Financial accounting follows a set of ground rules or accounting principles which are generally known as Generally Accepted Accounting Principles (GAAP). GAAP helps in the preparation of financial statements and in the choice of accounting methods, procedures and techniques.

(iv) Measurement Unit

Financial accounting measures all business transactions in terms of monetary unit of a society in which it operates. The common denominator or yardstick used for accounting measurement is say, rupee in India and dollar in the US.

(v) Users of Financial Accounting Information

As stated earner, financial accounting information is intended to primarily serve external users. The Financial Accounting Standards Board of the USA observes that financial accounting should provide information that is useful to present and potential investors and creditors and other users for making rational investments, credit and similar decisions.[10] Financial accounting information is used by a variety of groups, and for diverse purposes. Some users have direct interest in reported information. Examples of such users are owners, creditors and suppliers, potential owners, management, employees, customers. Some users need financial accounting information to help those who have direct interest in a business enterprise. Examples of such users are financial analysts and advisers, stock exchanges, financial press and reporting agencies, trade associations, labour unions. These user groups having direct/indirect interest have different objectives and diverse information needs. The emphasis in financial accounting has been on general-purpose information which, obviously, is not intended to satisfy any specialised needs of individual users or specific user groups.

Limitations of Financial Accounting

Financial accounting is significant for management as it helps them direct and control the firm activities. It also helps business management in determining appropriate managerial policies in different areas, such as production, sales, administration and finance. However, financial accounting does not provide adequate and useful information regarding different segments or divisions of the firm. Financial accounting suffers from the following limitations which have been responsible for the emergence of cost and management accounting:

1. Financial accounting does not provide detailed cost information for different departments, processes, products, jobs in the production divisions. Similarly, separate cost data are not available for different services and functions in the administration division. Management may need information about different products, sales territories and sales activities which are also not available in financial accounting.

2. Financial accounting does not set up a proper system of controlling materials and supplies. Undoubtedly, if material and supplies are not controlled in a manufacturing concern, they will lead to losses on account of misappropriation, misutilisation, scrap, defectives, etc. They may, in turn, influence the reported net income of a business enterprise.

3. Recording and accounting for wages and labour is not carried out for different jobs, processes, products, departments. This creates problems in analysing the cost associated with different activities. This also does not provide a basis for rewarding workers and employees for the above-average performance.

10. Financial Accounting Standards Board, *Objectives of Financial Reporting by Business Enterprises,* Statements of Financial Accounting Concepts No. 1, FASB, 1978, Para 34.

4. It is difficult to know the behaviour of costs in financial accounting as expenses are not assigned to the product at each stage of production. Expenses are not classified into direct and indirect, and therefore, cannot be classified as controllable and uncontrollable. Control of cost which is the most important objective of all business enterprises, cannot be achieved with the aid of financial accounting alone.

5. Financial accounting does not possess an adequate system of standards to evaluate the performance of departments and employees working in the departments. Standardisation is now applied to all elements of business. Standards need to be developed for materials, labour and overheads so that a firm can compare the work of labourers, workers, supervisors and executives with what should have been done in an allotted period of time.

6. Financial accounting contains historical cost information which is accumulated at the end of the accounting period. This accounting does not provide day-to-day information about costs and expenses. This is the reason why much dissatisfaction has been shown with external financial reporting. Historical cost is not a reliable basis for predicting future earning, solvency, or overall managerial effectiveness. Historical cost information is relevant but not adequate for all purposes. It is now rightly contended that current cost information should be reported along with historical cost information.

7. Financial accounting does not provide information to analyse the losses due to various factors, such as idle plant and equipment, seasonal fluctuations in volume of business, etc. It does not help management in taking important decisions about expansion of business, dropping a product line, starting with a new product, alternative methods of production, improvement in product, etc. Managerial decisions about these business matters have now become vital for the survival and growth of business enterprises.

Despite the above limitations, financial accounting has utility and will continue to be used in the future also. It is an important and conceptually rich area. Because of growing business complexities and advances in knowledge of human behaviour and decision processes, the scope and methods of financial accounting are changing and can be expected to continue to change. In the light of these developments, financial accounting theory and practice will probably be broadened considerably in the future.

Management Accounting

Management accounting refers to all types of accounting information and reports for the internal use of managements. Management accounting is concerned with providing information to managers to carry out their managerial responsibilities and functions such as planning, execution, control and decision making. The Institute of Management Accountants (US) defines management accounting as:

> "...the process of identification, measurement, accumulation, analysis, preparation and communication of financial information used by management to plan, evaluate and control within the organisation and to assure appropriate use and accountability for its resources."

Management accounting provides both historical and estimated data which the management uses in evaluating and controlling performances, and in planning future operations. For instance, accounting information may be used by top management in determining the selling price of a new product. A finance manager may use a statement of projected cash receipts and disbursements in deciding if short-term borrowing is necessary. Production managers, by comparing past performances with planned objectives, can take steps to reduce wastages, unfavourable trends, and to increase productivity and induce favourable trends.

A sales manager may use a report and compare cost of producing and selling different products and then recommend to the top management the prices to be charged and the products to be pushed through by the sales force. The different users (managers) within an enterprise can specify the types of information they need for their decisions and management accounting accordingly may prepare or supply information to satisfy their needs.

Management accounting uses the information and statements prepared in financial accounting plus it prepares and provides additional information and reports to the management. In providing this additional information, management accounting is not governed by any definite set of accounting principles. Since the additional data are used only by management, the management accounting provides the data in the format that is most useful for management.

Financial Accounting vs. Management Accounting

Before discussing the differences between financial accounting and management accounting, it would be correct to say that there are some similarities between the two accounting systems. Both financial accounting and management accounting are part of the total accounting information system. Both deal with economic events. Both try to quantify the results of economic activity and transactions. Both are concerned with financial statements, revenues, expenses, assets, liabilities and cash flows.

The accounting information system that accumulates and classifies information, generates financial statements is the same system that is used for most of the reports and analyses which are prepared under management accounting. Further, the reports prepared in management accounting and financial accounting are based on the same database. This is the reason why the accounting system in an organisation, when it collects and classifies information, does so in a manner and format which can be appropriate for both the accounting systems. To achieve this dual purpose in developing the database, many business enterprises, expand this database so as to fulfil adequately the informational needs of their managers and decision makers.

For example, investors and other users are primarily interested in the overall profitability of a company. However, the managers within the company are more interested in the profitability of individual products. In this situation, the accounting system can be developed and designed so as to provide both total company profits as well as profits from individual products. The vital point about an accounting system is its flexibility.

More specifically, financial accounting and management accounting are also similar with respect to determination and measurement of costs, their assignment to different accounting periods and allocation of costs to different departments and segments. The concepts and principles which are used in the area of financial accounting for the purposes of cost accumulation and cost allocation may also be suitable for management accounting. It means any method, principle or concept which is developed for financial accounting, can also be used for preparing reports and analyses falling under management accounting.

In spite of the above similarities, financial and management accounting differ in the following respects:

1. Primary Users of Information: The users of financial accounting statements are mainly external to the business enterprise. The financial statements prepared under financial accounting show how the resources have been used by a business enterprise during a specific period of time and are useful to external users in making sound economic decisions. These financial statements are relevant to managements but are not adequate for the purpose of planning, control and decision-making. External users include shareholders, creditors, financial analysts, government authorities, stock exchanges, labour unions, etc.

Management accounting prepares reports and supplies information to the management for planning, controlling and decision making. The information generated under the management accounting system is used by members of management at different levels in conformity with their information requirements for analysing business operations and for planning and control purposes. Thus, different sets of information could be developed under management accounting and supplied to different persons responsible for various activities in the organisation.

2. Accounting Method: Financial accounting follows the double-entry system for recording, classifying and summarising business transactions. This accounting process results in aggregate balances of all accounts maintained in a firm's books.

Management accounting is not based on the double-entry system. The data under management accounting may be gathered for small or large segments or activities of an organisation and monetary as well as other measures and, information can be used for different activities in the firm. The only constraint regarding accounting principles and methods is that they should be useful for managerial purposes.

3. Accounting Principles: Financial accounting data is primarily meant for external users. The Generally Accepted Accounting Principles (GAAP)* are important in financial accounting, and are used extensively while recording, classifying, summarising, and reporting business transactions. The use of GAAP adds credibility and reliability to financial statements and creates confidence among the financial statement users.

On the contrary, management accounting is not bound to use GAAP. It can use any accounting technique or practice which generates useful information. Besides, data developed in management accounting may comprise facts, estimates, projections, analyses, etc.

4. Unit of Measurement: All information under financial accounting is in terms of money. That is, transactions measured in terms of money have already occurred. In comparison, management accounting applies any measurement unit that is useful in a particular situation. Besides the monetary units, the management accountant may find it necessary to use measures such as number of employees, labour hours, machine hours and product units for the purpose of analysis and decision making. The common objective in all measurement, reporting and data analysis in management accounting is usefulness for a particular, and mostly 'in house', purpose. Historical costs and past transactions are essential to financial accounting but may be secondary to management accounting as they are not of much use to management.

5. Time Span: Financial accounting data and statements are developed for a definite period, usually a year. It requires that financial statements be developed and presented at regular time intervals. Company annual reports may be prepared semi-annually or quarterly but the important point is that they are prepaid on a regular basis.

Management Accounting reports and statements are prepared as and when they are needed. Reports may be prepared on a monthly, weekly or even a daily basis. Frequency of reports is determined by the planning, controlling and decision-making needs.

---

* Generally Accepted Accounting Principles (GAAP) includes conventions, rules and procedures used in financial accounting to process financial information and to define accepted accounting practice at a particular time.

6. General Purpose Report vs. Specific Purpose Report: Financial accounting produces information and reports which are general purpose in nature in order to serve the informational needs of many external users such as shareholders, creditors, potential investors, customers, suppliers, regulatory authorities, employees and the general public. Financial accounting is concerned with overall firm performance rather than individual segments or departments.

On the contrary, the reports and data developed under management accounting are known as specific purpose reports designed for a particular user (manager) or particular decision. Management accounting uses internal reports to evaluate the performance of entities, product lines, departments and managers.

7. Historical vs. Futuristic Data: Financial accounting has a historical orientation and records and reports what has happened. Financial accounting concentrates on the results of past decisions. Management accounting has a futuristic orientation and concentrates on what is likely to happen in the future. This is due to the fact that management accounting emphasises on developing information for planning, control and decision-making purposes. Therefore, management accounting focusses on the future more than the financial accounting.

8. Use of Disciplines: Management accounting uses other disciplines to prepare the most useful reports and analyses for the managers. Some such disciplines are economics, finance, management information system, industrial engineering, operations research, marketing, computer science, production management, statistics, psychology and sociology, etc. In this way, management accounting is much broader in scope compared with financial accounting.

PRINCIPAL FINANCIAL STATEMENTS

The end product of the financial accounting process is a set of reports that are called financial statements. The following constitute the financial statements:

1. Profit and loss account
2. Balance sheet
3. Statement of Changes in Financial Position (SCFP)

Profit and loss account, also known as income statement, presents the results of operations of a business enterprise for a period of time. This statement shows net profit or net income of an entity for a period of time. Net profit or income is the difference between revenues and expenses. The profit and loss account indicates how successful a business enterprise has been in achieving its profit goal for a given time span. It also gives the sources and amounts of revenues earned and the different types and amounts of expenses. Net profit indicates an enterprise's accomplishments (revenues) in relation to the efforts required (expenses) in pursuing its operating activities. When expenses exceed revenues for a period, a business enterprise incurs a net loss.

Balance sheet shows the financial position of a business on a certain date. For this reason, it is often called the statement of financial position. Balance sheet indicates the investing and financing activities of a business enterprise at a point of time and shows a firm's assets, liabilities and equity capital usually at the close of the last day of a month or a year. Assets are economic resources and provide future benefits to a firm such as cash, inventories, building, plant, patent, goodwill, etc. Liabilities are outsiders' claims on the assets of a business enterprise such as creditors, account payables, salaries payable, income-tax payable, debentures. Liabilities include shareholders' equity as well which is in the forms of ordinary shares, preference shares, retained earnings. Shareholders' equity is the shareholders' or owners' claim on the assets of a firm. The shareholders' claims are only residual, *i.e.,* shareholders have claims against the assets of a company only after all creditors' claims have been met.

A Statement of Changes in Financial Position (SCFP) shows where the financial resources (funds) have come from (sources) and where they have gone (uses). SCFP is generally prepared on working capital basis and cash basis. Working capital-based SCFP explains increase or decrease in working capital for a specified period of time. It reports:

(*a*) amount of changes in working capital associated with the operating activities of a firm.

(*b*) long-term financing or other sources that cause an increase in the working capital.

(*c*) long-term investment activities or other uses that cause a reduction in the working capital.

Cash basis SCFP, popularly known as cash flow statement, summarises the flow of cash in and out of the firm over a period of time. It focusses on various items which bring out changes in the cash balance between two balance sheet dates. Cash flow statement covers all items which increase or decrease the cash of a business enterprise. In USA, UK and other countries, statement of cash flows is legally required to be prepared by companies alongwith income statement and balance sheet. In India also, cash flow statement is required to be given in published company annual reports by the Indian companies as per AS3 Cash Flow Statement whose securities are listed on the Stock Exchanges.

Among the above statements, balance sheet is considered a status or stock report and the other two statements — income statement and statement of changes in financial position — are known as flow reports. Balance sheets, as stocks reports, show the information about the resources of an organisation at a specified moment of time. The income statement and statement of changes in financial position (working capital and cash basis), as the flow reports, show the activities of the enterprises over a period of time, say for a year, half-year, or a quarter. Figure 1.3 summarises the information provided by the financial statements.

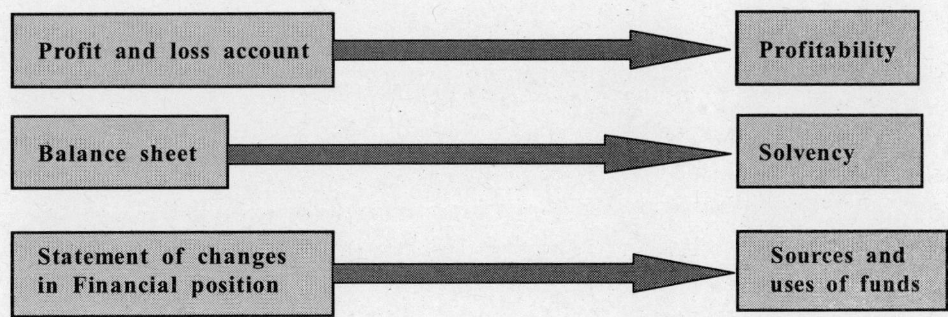

Fig. 1.3 Information provided by the financial statements

THEORY QUESTIONS

1. What are the objectives of accounting, financial accounting and management accounting?
2. Distinguish between management accounting and financial accounting.
3. Which decision-makers use accounting information?
4. What objectives does management seek to achieve by using accounting information?
5. Why are investors and creditors interested in the financial statements of a business enterprise?
6. What groups besides managers, investors and creditors use accounting information?
7. What are the main financial statements obtained through the financial accounting process?
8. Why is balance sheet sometimes called the statements of financial position?
9. Contrast the purposes of the balance sheet from those of the income statement?
10. Suggest reasons why the format and content of financial accounting statements and reports tend to be more standardised than is the case for management accounting reports?
11. "Accounting is an information system." Explain this statement.
12. List and briefly describe the main audiences for financial accounting information.
13. Accounting is said to be the language of business. What does it try to communicate and how?
14. Rajan is the accountant of a small company making two or three different types of household tools. He systematically and accurately collects and records all the transactions of the company, and prepares statements, so that the management knows the annual profit and the financial position. "What more can a good accountant do?" ponders Rajan. From your understanding of the scope of accounting, advise him in what other ways he might be of service to the management.
15. Discuss the limitations of financial accounting.
16. Explain different users and their informational requirements.

Accounting Postulates, Concepts and Principles

POSTULATES, CONCEPTS AND PRINCIPLES

Terms such as postulates, concepts, principles (and others such as procedures, rules) are widely used, but with no general agreement as to their precise meaning. Often, what is referred to as 'postulates' by some writers, are termed as 'concepts' or 'principles' by others and vice-versa. To give a few examples of such conflicting opinions, the views of Belkaoui, Anthony and Reece, and the Financial Accounting Standards Board (US) have been provided:

Accounting Postulates

1. Entity postulate
2. Going-concern postulate
3. Unit of measure postulate
4. Accounting period postulate

Accounting Principles

1. Cost principle
2. Revenue principle
3. Matching principle
4. Objectivity principle
5. Consistency principle
6. Full disclosure principle
7. Conservatism principle
8. Materiality principle
9. Uniformity and comparability principle

Source: Ahmed Belkaoui, *Accounting Theory,* Harcourt Brace Jovanovich, San Diego. 1985 Chapter 6.

Accounting Concepts

1.	Money measurement	2.	Entity
3.	Going concern	4.	Cost
5.	Dual-aspect	6.	Accounting period
7.	Conservatism	8.	Realisation
9.	Matching	10.	Consistency
11.	Materiality		

Source: Robert N. Anthony and James S. Reece, *Accounting Principles,* Richard D. Irwin, 1991. p. 22.

Fundamental Concepts of Accounting

(A) *Assumptions of Accounting*	(B) *Principles of Accounting*
1. Separate-entity assumption	1. Cost principle
2. Continuity assumption	2. Revenue principle
3. Unit-of-measure assumption	3. Matching principle
4. Time-period assumption	4. Full-disclosure principle

Source: Financial Accounting Standard Board, USA, Statement of Financial Accounting Concepts, No. 6, *Elements of Financial Statements,* December 1985.

Note: Financial Accounting Standards Board (FASB), US, refers to assumptions and principles of accounting as 'Fundamental Concepts of Accounting.'

Thus it can be observed that finding a precise terminology has always been one of the most difficult task in accounting. Further, the lack of agreement about precise meaning has affected, to some extent, the attempts made towards developing a theory for financial accounting.

The purpose of this chapter is not to engage the readers in a debate of suitable terminology but to explain terms which are widely accepted as of greatest importance and widest applicability, whether as postulates, concepts or principles. But before this, an attempt has been made to define the terms postulates, concepts and principles.

Postulates

Accounting postulates are basic assumptions which are generally accepted as self-evident truths in accounting. Postulates are established or general truths which do not require any evidence to prove them. They are the propositions taken for granted.

Belkaoui[1] defines accounting postulates

"as self-evident statements or axioms, generally accepted by virtue of their conformity to the objectives of financial statements, that portray the economic, political, sociological and legal environments in which accounting must operate."

American Institute of Certified Public Accountants (US) observes:

"Postulates are few in number and are the basic assumptions on which principles rest. They necessarily are derived from the economic and political environment and from the modes of thought and customs of all segments of the business community. The profession, however, should make clear their understanding and interpretation of what they are, to provide a meaningful foundation for the formulation of principles and the development of rules or other guides for the application of principles in specific situations."[2]

1. Ahmed Belkaoui, *Accounting Theory,* 1985, p. 220.
2. American Institute of Certified Public Accountants, *The Basic Postulates of Accounting,* Accounting Research Study No. 1, AICPA, 1961, p. 7.

According to Hendriksen[3]

"Postulates are basic assumptions or fundamental propositions concerning the economic, political, and sociological environment in which accounting must operate. The basic criteria are: (*i*) they must be relevant to the development of accounting logic, *i.e.,* they must serve as a foundation for the logical derivation of further propositions, and (*ii*) they must be accepted as valid by the participants in the discussions; as either being true or providing as useful starting point as an assumption in the development of accounting logic."

Concepts

Accounting concepts are also self-evident statements or truths. Accounting concepts are so basic that people accept them as valid without any questioning. Accounting concepts provide the conceptual guidelines for application in the financial accounting process, *i.e.,* for recording measurement, analysis and communication of information about an organisation. These concepts provide help in resolving future accounting issues on a permanent or a longer basis, rather than trying to deal with each issue on an ad-hoc basis. The concepts are important because they (*a*) help explain the 'why' of accounting (*b*) provide guidance when new accounting situations are encountered, and (*c*) significantly reduce the need to memorise accounting procedures when learning about accounting.[4]

Principles

Accounting principles are general decision rules derived from the accounting concepts. According to AICPA (US), a principle means "a general law or rule adopted or professed as a guide to action: a settled ground or basis of conduct or practice." Accounting principles are characterised as 'how to apply' concepts. Anthony and Reece[5] comment:

"Accounting principles are man-made. Unlike the principles of physics, chemistry and other natural science, accounting principles were not deducted from basic axioms, nor can they be verified by observation and experiment. Instead, they have evolved. This evolutionary process is going on constantly; accounting principles are not eternal truths."

A principle is an explanation concisely farmed in words to compress an important relationship among accounting ideas into a few words. Principles are concise explanations. Accounting principles do not suggest exactly as to how each transaction will be recorded. This is the reason that accounting practices differ from one enterprise to another. The differences in accounting practices is also due to the fact that GAAP provides flexibility in the recording and reporting of business transactions.

Accounting principles influence and guide the development of accounting techniques which are specific rules to record specific transactions and events in an organisation.

ACCOUNTING POSTULATES

1. Entity Postulate: The entity postulate assumes that the financial statements and other accounting information are for the specific business enterprise which is distinct from its owners. Attention in financial accounting is focussed on the economic activities of individual business enterprises. Consequently, the analysis of business transactions involving costs and revenue is expressed in terms of the changes in the firm's financial conditions. Similarly, the assets and

3. Eldon S. Hendriksen, *Accounting Theory,* Richard D. Irwin, 1984, p. 61.
4. Glewn A. Welsch and Daniel G. Short, *Fundamentals of Financial Accounting,* Irwin. 1987, p. 144.
5. Robert N. Anthony and James S. Reece, *ibid.,* p. 15.

liabilities devoted to business activities are entity assets and liabilities. The transactions of the enterprise are to be reported rather than the transaction of the enterprise's owners. This concept, therefore, enables the accountant to distinguish between personal and business transactions. The concept applies to sole proprietorship, partnership, companies, and small and large enterprise. It may also apply to a segment of a firm, such as division, or several firms, such as when interrelated firms are consolidated.

The distinction between the business entity and outside interests is a difficult one to make in practice in those businesses in which there is a close relationship between the business and the people who own it. In the case of small firms where the owners exert day-to-day control over the affairs of the business and personal and business assets are intermingled, definition of the business activity is more difficult for financial as well as management accounting purposes.

However, in the case of a company, the distinction is often quite easily made. A company has a separate legal entity, separate from persons who own it. Owners, creditors, banks and others entrust funds to management and management is expected to use these funds effectively. Financial accounting reports are one of the principal means to show how well this responsibility, or stewardship, has been discharged.

2. Going Concern Postulate: An accounting entity is viewed as continuing in operation in the absence of evidence to the contrary.* Because of the relative permanence of enterprises, financial accounting is formulated assuming that the business will continue to operate for an indefinitely long period in the future. The going-concern postulate justifies the valuation of assets on a non-liquidation basis and it calls for the use of historical cost for many valuations. Also, the fixed assets and intangibles are amortised over their useful life rather than over a shorter period in expectation of early liquidation.

The significance of going-concern postulate can be indicated by contrasting it with a possible alternative, namely, that the business is about to be liquidated or sold. Under the later assumption, accounting would attempt to measure at all times what the business is currently worth to a buyer; but under the going-concern concept, there is no need to do this, and it is, in fact, not done. Instead, a business is viewed as a mechanism for creating value, and its success is measured by the difference between the value of its outputs (*i.e.,* sales of goods and services) and the cost of resources used in creating those outputs.

3. Money Measurement Postulate: A unit of exchange and measurement is necessary to account for the transactions of business enterprises in a uniform manner. The common denominator chosen in accounting is the monetary unit. Money is the common denominator in terms of which the exchangeability of goods and services, including labour, natural resources and capital are measured. Money measurement concept holds that accounting is a measurement and communication process of the activities of the firm that are measurable in monetary terms.

Money measurement postulate implies two limitations of accounting. First, accounting is limited to the production of information expressed in terms of a monetary unit: it does not record and communicate other relevant but non-monetary information. Accounting does not record or communicate the state of chairman's health, the attitude of the employees, or the relative advantages of competitive products or the fact that the sales manager is not on speaking terms with the production manager. Although accounting is a discipline concerned with measurement and communication of monetary activities, it has been expanding into areas previously viewed as qualitative in

* A related proposition is that if liquidation appears imminent, financial information may be prepared on the assumption that liquidation will take place.

nature. *In fact, a number of empirical studies refer to the relevance of non-accounting information compared with accounting information.*

4. Accounting Period Postulate: Financial accounting provides information about the economic activities of an enterprise for specified time periods that are shorter than the life of the enterprise. Normally, the time periods are of equal length to facilitate comparison.

The time period is identified in the financial statements. The time periods are usually of twelve months. Sometimes quarterly or half-yearly statements are also issued. These are considered interim and different from annual statements. For managerial use, statements covering shorter periods such as a month or a week may also be prepared. Dividing business activities into specific time periods creates a number of measurement problems in financial accounting such as allocation of the cost of an asset to specific periods, determining income and costs associated with long-term contracts covering several accounting periods, treatment of R & D costs, etc.

ACCOUNTING CONCEPTS AND PRINCIPLES

I. Cost Principle: The cost principle requires that assets be recorded at the exchange price, i.e., acquisition cost or historical cost. Historical cost is recognised as the appropriate valuation basis for recognition of the acquisition of all goods and services, expenses, costs and equities. In other words, an item is valued at the exchange price at the date of acquisition and shown in the financial statements at that value or an amortised portion of it. For accounting purposes, business transactions are normally measured in terms of the actual prices or costs at the time the transaction occurs, i.e., financial accounting measurements are primarily based on exchange prices at which economic resources and obligations are exchanged.

The historical cost concept implies that since the business is not going to sell its asset as such there is little point in revaluing assets to reflect current values. In addition, for practical reasons, the accountant prefers the reporting of actual costs to market values which are difficult to verify. By using historical costs, the accountant's already difficult task is not further complicated by the need to keep additional records of changing market value. Thus, the cost concept provides greater objectivity and greater feasibility to the Financial statements.

2. Dual-Aspect Principle: This principle lies at the heart of the whole accounting process. The accountant records events affecting the wealth of a particular entity. The question is — which aspect of this wealth are important? Since an accounting entity is an artificial creation, it is essential to know to whom its resources belong to or what purpose they serve. It is also important to know what kind of resources it controls, *e.g.*, cash, buildings or land. Accounts recording systems have therefore developed so as to show two main things: (*a*) the source of wealth, and (*b*) the form it takes.

Suppose Mr. X decides to establish a business and transfers Rs. 1,00,000 from his private bank account to a separate business account. He might record this event as follows:

Business Entity Records

Liabilities	*Assets*
Source of wealth X's capital Rs. 1,00,000	Form of wealth Cash at bank Rs. 1,00,000

Clearly, the source of wealth must be numerically equal to the form of wealth. Since they are simply different aspects of the same thing, *i.e.*, in the form of an equation: S (sources) must equal F (forms)

Moreover, any transaction or event affecting the wealth of entity must have two aspects recorded in order to maintain the equality of both sides of the accounting equation. If business has acquired an asset, it must have resulted in one of the following:

(*a*) Some other asset has been given up.

(*b*) The obligation to pay for it has arisen.

(*c*) There has been a profit, leading to an increase in the amount that the business owes to the proprietor.

(*d*) The proprietor has contributed money for the acquisition of asset.

This does not mean that a transaction will affect both the source and form of wealth. There are four categories of events affecting the accounting equation:

(*a*) Both, sources and forms of wealth, increase by the same amount.

(*b*) Both, sources and forms of wealth, decrease by the same amount.

(*c*) Some forms of wealth increase while others decrease without any change in the source of wealth.

(*d*) Some sources of wealth increase while others decrease without any change in the form in which wealth is held.

The example given above illustrates category (*a*) since the commencing transaction for the entity results in the source of wealth and form of wealth, cash, both increasing from zero to Rs. 1,00,000. By contrast, X might decide to withdraw Rs. 20,000 cash from the business. Then financial position of business entity would result in —

Liabilities	*Assets*
Source of wealth	Form of wealth
X's capital Rs. 80,000	Cash Rs. 80,000

It is essential to appreciate why both sides of the equation decrease. By taking out cash, X automatically reduces his supply of private finance to the business by the same amount.

Suppose now that Mr. X buys stocks of goods for Rs. 30,000 with the available cash. His supply of capital does not change, but the composition of the business assets does.

Source of wealth		*Form of wealth*	
X's capital	Rs. 80,000	Stock	Rs. 30,000
		Cash	Rs. 50,000
	Rs. 80,000		Rs. 80.000

The two aspects of this transaction are not in the same direction but compensatory, an increase in stocks of setting a decrease in cash. Similarly, sources of wealth also may be affected by a transaction. Thus, if X gives his son Y, a Rs. 20,000 share in the business by transferring part of his own interest, the effect is as follows:

Source of wealth		*Form of wealth*	
X's capital	Rs. 60,000	Stocks	Rs. 30,000
Y's capital	Rs. 20,000	Cash	Rs. 50,000
	Rs. 80.000		Rs. 80,000

If however, X gives Y Rs. 20,000 in cash privately and Y then puts it into the business, both sides of equation would be affected. Y's capital of Rs. 20,000 being balanced by an extra Rs. 20,000 in cash, X's capital remaining at Rs. 80,000.

3. Accrual Principle: According to Financial Accounting Standards Board (US): "Accrual accounting attempts to record the financial effects on an enterprise of transactions and other events and circumstances that have cash consequences for the enterprise in the periods in which those transactions, events and circumstances occur rather than only in the periods in which cash is received or paid by the enterprise. Accrual accounting is concerned with the process by which cash expended on resources and activities is returned as more (or perhaps less) cash to the enterprise, not just with the beginning and end of that process. It recognises that the buying, producing, selling and other operations of an enterprise during a period, as well as other events that effect enterprise performance often do not coincide with the cash receipts and payments of the period."

A business enterprise's economic activity in a short period seldom follows the simple form of a cycle from money to productive resources to product to money. Instead, continuous production, extensive use of credit and long-lived resources, and overlapping cycles of activity complicate the evaluation of periodic activities. As a result, non-cash resources and obligations change in time periods other than those in which money is received or paid. Recording these changes is necessary to determine periodic income and to measure financial position. This is the essence of accrual accounting.

Thus, accrual accounting is based not only on cash transaction but also on credit transactions, barter exchanges, changes in prices, changes in the form of assets or liabilities, and other transactions, events and circumstances that have cash consequences for an enterprise but involve no concurrent cash movement. Although it does not ignore cash transactions, accrual accounting is primarily accounting for non-cash assets, liabilities, revenues, expenses, gains and losses.

4. Conservatism Principle:* This principle is often described as "anticipate no profit, and provide for all possible losses." This characterisation might be viewed as the reactive version of the minimix managerial philosophy, *i.e.,* minimise the chance of maximum losses.

Accounting conservatism does not mean intentionally understating income and assets; it applies only to situations in which there are reasonable doubts. For example, inventories are valued at the lower ends of cost or current replacement value.

In its application to the income statement, conservatism encourages the recognition of all losses that have occurred or are likely to occur but does not acknowledge gains until actually realised. The procedure of reducing inventory values when market has declined below cost but the failure to countenance 'writeups' under reverse conditions can be attributed to conservatism. The early amortisation of intangible assets and the restrictions against recording appreciation of assets have also, at least to some extent, been motivated by conservatism. Failure to recognise revenue until a sale has transferred is still another manifestation of conservatism.

5. Matching Principle: The matching principle in financial accounting is the process of matching (relating) accomplishments or revenues (as measured by the selling prices of goods and services delivered) with efforts or expenses (as measured by the cost of goods and services used) to a particular period for which the income is being determined. This concept emphasises which

---

* According to some writers 'prudence' is a better word than conservatism. Uncertainties inevitably surround many transactions and this should be recognised by exercising prudence in preparing financial statements. Prudence does not, however, justify the creation of secret or hidden reserves.

items of cost are expenses in a given accounting period. That is, costs are reported as expenses in the accounting period in which the revenue associated with those costs is reported. For example, when the sales value of some goods is reported as revenue in a year, the cost of those goods would be reported as an expenses in the same year.

Matching concepts needs to be fulfilled only after realisation (accrual) concept has been completed by the accountant: first revenues are measured in accordance with the realisation concept and then costs are associated with these revenues. *Costs are matched with revenues, not the other way around.* The matching process, therefore, requires cost allocation which is significant in historical cost accounting. Past (historical) costs are examined and despite their historic nature, are subjected to a procedure whereby elements of cost regarded as having expired service potential are allocated or matched against relevant revenues. The remaining elements of costs which are regarded as continuing to have future service potential are carried forward in the historical balance sheet and are termed as assets. *Thus, the balance sheet is nothing more than a report of unallocated past costs waiting expiry of their estimated future service potential before being matched with suitable revenues.*

6. Consistency Principle: This principle requires that once an organisation has decided on one method, it should use the same method for all subsequent transactions and events of the same nature unless it has sound reasons to change methods. If accounting methods are frequently changed, comparison of financial statements for one period with those of another period would be difficult. The consistent use of accounting methods and procedures over time will check the distortion of profit and loss account and the balance sheet and the possible manipulation of these statements. Consistency is necessary to help external users in comparing financial statements of a given firm over time and in making sound economic decisions.

7. Materiality Principle: Materiality concept implies that the transactions and events that have immaterial or insignificant effects should not be recorded and reported in the financial statements. It is argued that the recording of insignificant events cannot be justified in terms of its subsequent poor utility to users.

There is no agreement as to the meaning of materiality and what can be said to be material or immaterial events or transactions. It is for the preparer of accounts to interpret what is and what is not material. Probably the materiality of an event or transaction can be decided in terms of its impact on the financial position, results of operations, changes in the financial position of an organisation and on evaluation or decisions made by users.

8. Full-disclosure Principle: The principle of full disclosure requires that a business enterprise should provide all relevant information to external users for the purpose of sound economic decisions. This concept implies that no information of substance or of interest to the average investors will be omitted or concealed from an entity's financial statements.

GENERALLY ACCEPTED ACCOUNTING PRINCIPLES

Financial accounting follows a set of ground rules or accounting principles (discussed earlier) in presenting financial information which are known as Generally Accepted Accounting Principles (GAAP). In fact, to be useful, financial accounting information should be collected, classified, summarised and reported objectively. Those who use such information and rely on such data have a right to be assured that the data are reliable, free from bias and consistencies, whether deliberate or otherwise. For this reason, financial accounting depends on certain guidelines or standards that have proved useful over the years in accounting and reporting information. In this task, GAAP plays a vital role and financial accounting information can be meaningful only when prepared according to some agreed upon standards and procedures, *i.e.,* Generally Accepted Accounting Principles.

Accounting Principles Board[6] of the USA observes:

"Generally Accepted Accounting Principles incorporate the consensus at a particular times as to which economic resources and obligations should be recorded as assets and liabilities by financial accounting, which changes in assets and liabilities should be recorded, when these changes are to be recorded, how the assets and liabilities and changes in them should be measured, what information should be disclosed and which financial statements should be prepared."

GAAP are simply guides to action and may change over time. Sometimes specific principles must be altered or new principles must be formulated to fit changed economic circumstances of changes in business practices. Accounting principles originate from problem situations such as changes in the law, tax regulations, new business organisational arrangements, or new financing or ownership techniques.

Certain accounting techniques or procedures are tried in response to the effect such problems have on financial reports. Through comparative use and analysis, one or more of these techniques are judged most suitable, obtain substantial authoritative support and are then considered a generally accepted accounting principle.[7]

Walgenbach, et al. comment

"Because no basic natural accounting law exists, accounting principles have developed on the basis of their usefulness. Consequently, the growth of accounting is more closely related to experience and practice than to the foundation provided by ultimate law. As such accounting principles tend to evolve rather than be discovered, to be flexible rather than precise and to be subject to regular evaluation rather than be ultimate or final."

In India, organisations such as the Accounting Standards Board (ASB), Institute of Chartered Accountants of India, Department of Company Affairs (Government of India), Securities and Exchange Board of India (SEBI), Institute of Costs and Works Accountants of India, Institute of Company Secretaries, Stock Exchanges, and the literature each of these publishes, are instrumental in the development of most accounting principles. In the US, Financial Accounting Standards Board (FASB), American Institute of Certified Public Accountants (AICPA), Securities and Exchange Commission (SEC), Internal Revenue Service and the American Accounting Association are instrumental in the formulation of accounting principles.

Selection of Accounting Principles

Generally Accepted Accounting Principles are primarily relevant to financial accounting. In management accounting, the main objective of using GAAP is to help management in making decisions and in operating effectively. Therefore, in the area of management accounting it is frequently useful to depart from accounting principles used in financial accounting. On many occasions, financial accounting data are reassembled or altered to be more useful in solving internal business problems and in making decisions. Similarly, different accounting principles may need to be used in accordance with income tax regulations for determination of income (taxable income) which may differ from income acceptable for financial accounting, business

6. Accounting Principles Board. Statement No. 4, AICPA 1970.
7. Paul H. Walgenbach, Ernst I., Hanson and Norman K. Dittrich, *Financial Accounting: An Introduction,* Harcourt Brace Jovanovich, 1988, p. 443.

reporting purposes. This does not necessarily mean that business enterprises may keep more than one set of records to satisfy the different requirements. In most cases, certain items taken for financial accounting purposes may have to be omitted and certain other items may have to be included for determining taxable income and tax liability. Even if an organisation maintains different set of records and books, one for financial reporting purposes and the other for income-tax reporting purposes, this practice cannot be termed as illegal or unethical. In fact, there is nothing wrong or illegal about keeping separate records to fulfill separate needs, so long as all the records and books are open to examination by the appropriate parties. But, as stated earlier, business enterprises attempt to meet the different requirements of shareholders and investors (through financial reporting) and tax authorities (through tax reporting) using the same set of data.

DEFINITION OF ACCOUNTING STANDARDS

The term 'accounting standard' is defined as written statements issued from time to time by institutions of the accounting profession or institutions in which there is sufficient involvement and which are established expressly for this purpose. Such accounting institutions or bodies are currently found in many countries of the world, e.g., Accounting Standards Board (India), Financial Accounting Standards Board (US), Accounting Standards Committee (UK), Accounting Standards Committee (Canada), etc.

At the international level, International Accounting Standards Board (IASB) (earlier IASC) has been created "to formulate and publish, in the public interest, basic standards to be observed in the presentation of audited accounts and financial statements and to promote their worldwide acceptance and observance."

Accounting standards mainly deal with financial measurements and disclosures used in producing a set of fairly presented financial statements. In this respect, accounting standards can be thought of as a system of measurements and disclosure. They also draw the boundaries within which acceptable conduct lies and in that and many other respects, they are similar in nature to laws.

BENEFITS OF ACCOUNTING STANDARDS

Accounting standards have evolved to curb the abuse of flexibility in adoption of accounting policies by business enterprises. Standards help accounting practitioners to apply those accounting practices regarded as the most suitable for the circumstances covered. Further, they help individual companies and their managements to justify the adoption of certain practices when producing their financial statements. The benefits of accounting standards may be listed as follows:

1. To Improve the Credibility and Reliability of Financial Statements: Financial statements of business enterprises are used by a diverse group of users for making sound economic decision. The users are shareholders (existing and potential), trade creditors, customers, suppliers, employees, taxation authorities and other interested parties. It is necessary, therefore, that the financial statements the users use and upon which they rely, present a fair picture of the position and progress of the enterprises. It is the function of accounting (and auditing) standards to create this general sense of confidence by providing a framework within which credible financial statements can be produced. Accounting standards are required in order to meet a basic need of managers, investors and creditors to compare results and financial conditions of different segments of firms, different periods of a firm, different firms and different industries. In the absence of standards, there would be no incentives to encourage an enterprise to conform to any particular model for the sake of comparison. Thus, the main aim of accounting standards is to protect users' interest by providing them with information in which they can have confidence.

2. Benefits to Preparers and Auditors: Preparers and auditors, with the passage of time and changing climate of opinion, have to work in an environment where they face the threat of stern sanctions and a bad name to their professions. These result partly from changed penalties and remedies available under the company law and partly from the greater willingness of aggrieved parties to take their causes before the courts. The risk of these developments are considerable to auditors whether in terms of uncovered financial exposure to liability or adverse effects on professional reputation resulting from unfavourable publicity.

Particularly dangerous are causes of undetected fraud, and audited accounts, which are held to be misleading due to insufficient disclosure or use of inappropriate accounting principles. Given the increasing risks, the accounting profession realised that it needed to have the accounting standards for their own benefits.

3. Determining Managerial Accountability: Accounting standards facilitate in determining specific corporate accountability and regulation of the company. They help in assessing managerial skill in maintaining and improving the profitability of the company, depicting the progress of the company, its solvency and liquidity.

Generally they are important factors in assessing the effectiveness of management's performance of its duties and leadership. Standards aim to ensure consistency and comparability in place of (imposed) uniformity in financial reporting to permit better comparisons in profitability, financial position, future prospects and other performance indicators associated with different business firms. Management's basic purpose should be to opt for the best method (standards) available. Accounting standards should significantly reduce the amount of manipulation of reported net profit that is likely to occur in the absence of standards.

ACCOUNTING STANDARDS IN INDIA

The Institute of Chartered Accountants of India constituted the Accounting Standard Board (ASB) in April 1977, recognising the need to harmonise the diverse accounting policies and practice in India and keeping in view the international development in the field of accounting. The ASB is entrusted with the following functions:

1. To formulate accounting standards which may be established by the Council of ICAI in India. While formulating standards, the ASB is required to take into consideration the applicable laws, customs and usages and business environment; it is also required to give due consideration to International Accounting Standards Issued by IASB and to integrate them, to the extent possible, in the light of the conditions and practices prevailing in India.
2. To propagate the Accounting Standards and persuade the concerned parties to adopt them in the preparation and presentation of financial statements.
3. To issue guidance notes on the Accounting Standards and give clarifications on issues arising therefrom.
4. To review the accounting standards at periodic intervals.

The date from which a particular standard will come to effect, as well as the class of enterprises to which it will apply, will also be specified by the Institute. Unless otherwise stated, no standard will have retrospective application. Normally, before formulating the standards, ASB will hold discussions with the representatives of the government, public sector undertakings, industry and other organisations, for ascertaining their views. An Exposure Draft of the proposed standard will be prepared and issued for comments by members of the institute and the public at large. After considering the comments received, the draft of the proposed standard will be finalised by ASB and submitted to the Council which will study it, modify it if necessary and issue it under its own authority.

Auditor's Duties in Relation to Accounting Standards: In case the company does not conform to any of the mandatory accounting standards, the auditor will have to qualify his report. In case he fails to do so the ICAI can take disciplinary action against him on the grounds of professional misconduct.

ACCOUNTING STANDARDS ISSUED BY ASB

The Accounting Standards Board (ASB) of the Institute of Chartered Accountants of India, has in line with the International Standards, issued thirty two standards so far to be followed by its members while auditing the accounts of the companies. These are:

1. Disclosures of Accounting Policies (AS 1)
2. Valuation of Inventories (AS 2)
3. Cash Flow Statements (AS 3)
4. Contingents and Events Occurring After the Balance Sheet Date (AS 4)
5. Net profit or Loss for the period, prior period Items and Changes in Accounting Policies (AS 5)
6. Depreciation Accounting (AS 6)
7. Accounting for Construction Contract (AS 7)
8. Accounting for Research and Development (AS 8)
9. Revenue Recognition (AS 9)
10. Accounting for Fixed Assets (AS 10)
11. Accounting for the Effects of Changes in Foreign Exchange Rates (AS 11)
12. Accounting for Government Grants (AS 12)
13. Accounting for Investments (AS 13)
14. Accounting for Amalgamation (AS 14)
15. Accounting for Retirement Benefits in the Financial Statement of Employers (AS 15)
16. Borrowing Cost (AS 16)
17. Segment Reporting (AS 17)
18. Related Party Disclosures (AS 18)
19. Leases (AS 19)
20. Earnings Per Share (AS 20)
21. Consolidated Financial Statements (AS 21)
22. Accounting for taxes on income (AS 22)
23. Accounting for Investments in Associates in Consolidated Financial Statements (AS 23)
24. Discontinuing Operations (AS 24)

25. Interim Financial Reporting (AS 25)
26. Intangible Assets (AS 26)
27. Financial Reporting of Interest in Joint Venture (AS 27)
28. Impairment of Assets (AS 28)
29. Provisions, Contingent Liabilities and Contingent Assets (AS 29)
30. Financial Instruments: Recognition and Measurement (AS 30)
31. Financial Instruments: Presentation (AS 31)
32. Financial Instruments: Disclosures (AS 32).

In addition to these standards, the Institute of Chartered Accountants of India has issued Statements, Guidance Notes and Opinions which seek to bring uniformity in corporate accounting and reporting practices.

AS 1, DISCLOSURE OF ACCOUNTING POLICIES

The Institute of Chartered Accountants of India (ICAI) issued AS 1 titled 'Disclosure of Accounting Policies' in November 1979. This standard is now mandatory and deals with the disclosure of significant accounting policies followed in preparing and presenting Financial Statements.

In general accounting policies are not at present regularly and fully disclosed in all financial statements. Many enterprises include in the Notes on the Accounts, description of some of the significant accounting policies.

Even among the few enterprises that presently include in their annual reports a separate statement of accounting policies, considerable variation exists. The statement of accounting policies forms part of the accounts in some cases while in others it is given as supplementary information.

The purpose of this statement is to promote better understanding of financial statements by establishing through an accounting standard the disclosure of significant accounting policies and the manner in which accounting policies are disclosed in the financial statements. Such disclosure would also facilitate a more meaningful comparison between financial statements of different enterprises.

AS 1 contains explanations on following points:

1. Fundamental Accounting Assumptions

Certain fundamental accounting assumptions underlie the preparation and presentation of financial statements. They are usually not specifically stated because their acceptance and use are assumed. Disclosure is necessary if they are not followed.

The following have been generally accepted as fundamental accounting assumption:

(a) *Going Concern:* The enterprise is normally viewed as a going concern, that is, as continuing in operation for the foreseeable future. It is assumed that the enterprise has neither the intention nor the necessity of liquidation or of curtailing materially the scale of the operations.

(b) *Consistency:* It is assumed that accounting policies are consistent from one period to another.

(c) *Accrual:* Revenues and costs are accrued, that is, recognised as they are earned or incurred (and not as money is received or paid) and recorded in the financial statements of the periods to which they relate. (The considerations affecting the process of matching costs with revenues under the accrual assumption are not dealt with in this Statement).

2. Nature of Accounting Policies

(*i*) The accounting policies refer to the specific accounting principles and the methods of applying those principles adopted by the enterprise in the preparation and presentation of financial statements.

(*ii*) There is no single list of accounting policies which are applicable to all circumstances. The differing circumstances in which enterprises operate in a situation of diverse and complex economic activity make alternative accounting principles and methods of applying those principles acceptable. The choice of the appropriate accounting principles and the methods of applying those principles in the specific circumstances of each enterprise calls for considerable judgment by the management of the enterprise.

(*iii*) The various statements of the Institute of Chartered Accountants of India combined with the efforts of government and other regularity agencies and progressive managements have reduced in recent years the number of acceptable alternatives particularly in the case of corporate enterprises. While continuing efforts in this regard in future are likely to reduce the number still further, the availability of alternative accounting principles and methods of applying those principles is not likely to be eliminated altogether in view of the differing circumstances faced by the enterprises.

3. Areas in which differing Accounting Policies are encountered

The following are examples of the areas in which different accounting policies may be adopted by different enterprises:

- Method of depreciation, depletion and amortisation
- Treatment of expenditure during construction
- Conversion of translation of foreign currency items
- Valuation of inventories
- Treatment of goodwill
- Valuation of investments
- Treatment of retirement benefits
- Recognition of profit on long-term contracts
- Valuation of fixed assets
- Treatment of contingent liabilities.

The above list of examples is not intended to be exhaustive.

4. Considerations in the Selection of Accounting Policies

The primary consideration in the selection of accounting policies by an enterprise is that the financial statements prepared and presented on the basis of such accounting policies should represent a true and fair view of the state of affairs of the enterprise as at the balance sheet date and of the profit or loss for the period ended on that date.

For this purpose, the major considerations governing the selection and application of accounting policies are:

(*a*) *Prudence:* In view of the uncertainty attached to future events, profits are not anticipated but recognised only when realised though not necessarily in cash. Provision is made for all known liabilities and losses even though the amount cannot be determined with certainty and represents only a best estimate in the light of available information.

(*b*) *Substance over Form:* The accounting treatment and presentation in financial statements of transactions and events should be governed by their substance and not merely by the legal form.

(*c*) *Materiality:* Financial statements should disclose all "material" items, *i.e.*, items the knowledge of which might influence the decisions of the user of the financial statements.

5. Disclosure of Accounting Policies

(*i*) To ensure proper understanding of financial statements, it is necessary that all significant accounting policies adopted in the preparation and presentation of financial statements should be disclosed.

(*ii*) Such disclosure should form part of the financial statements.

(*iii*) It would be helpful to the reader of financial statements if they are all disclosed as such in one place instead of being scattered over several statements, schedules and notes.

(*iv*) Examples of matters in respect of which disclosure of accounting policies adopted will be required are contained in point No. 3. This list of examples is not, however, intended to be exhaustive.

(*v*) Any change in an accounting policy which has a material effect should be disclosed. The amount by which any item in the financial statements is affected by such change should also be disclosed to the extent ascertainable. Where such amount is not ascertainable, wholly or in part, the fact should be indicated. If a change is made in the accounting policies which has no material effect on the financial statements for the current period but which is reasonably expected to have a material effect in later periods, the fact of such change should be appropriately disclosed in the period in which the change is adopted.

(*vi*) Disclosure of accounting policies or of changes therein cannot remedy a wrong or inappropriate treatment of the item in the accounts.

6. Accounting Standard in AS 1

(*i*) All significant accounting policies adopted in the preparation and presentation of financial statements should be disclosed.

(*ii*) The disclosure of the significant accounting policies as such should form part of the financial statements and the significant accounting policies should normally be disclosed in one place.

(*iii*) Any change in the accounting policies which has a material effect in the current period or which is reasonably expected to have a material effect in later periods should be disclosed. In the case of a change in accounting policies which has a material effect in the current period, the amount by which any item in the financial statements is affected by such change should also be disclosed to the extent ascertainable. Where such amount is not ascertainable, wholly or in part, the fact should be indicated.

(*iv*) If the fundamental accounting assumptions, *viz.*, Going Concern, Consistency and accrual are followed in financial statements, specific disclosure is not required. If a fundamental accounting assumption is not followed, the fact should be disclosed.

THEORY QUESTIONS

1. Distinguish between postulates, concepts, principles.
2. Explain the following accounting terms:
   (*a*) Entity postulate
   (*b*) Going-concern postulate
   (*c*) Dual-aspect principle
   (*d*) Matching principle
   (*e*) Accrual principle
   (*f*) Cost principle.
3. Explain the significance of separate entity postulate in recording transactions and events of an entity.
4. Why is the going-concern postulate central to accounting practice?
5. What limitations does the money measurement postulate impose on accounting?
6. Mr. Johnson, the managing director of Alpha Co., purchased a new truck for delivery service. Alpha Co. is organised as a company with Mr. Swaminathan as the sole shareholder. The truck was purchased for Rs. 5,00,000 cash from Evons Ltd. According to the Business entity concept which of the entities (Johnson, Alpha Co., Swaminathan, Evans Ltd.) should record this transactions in their records.
7. "Many important events that influence the prospects for the entity are not recorded in the financial records." Comment and give examples.
8. Would an accountant record the personal assets and liabilities of the owners in the account of the business. Explain.
9. A company charges to expense all items (appearing like assets) that cost Rs. 1,000 or less. Which principle supports this policy?
10. "It is not important to know when cash is received and when payment is made." Comment.
11. What are accounting standards? Explain their significance.
12. In what way accounting standards are helpful to accountants, auditors and managers ?
13. Write an explanatory note on accounting standards setting in India.
14. Explain the progress made by ASB in standards setting.
15. Financial statements are prepared using generally accepted accounting principles. What does this term mean? Why are these principles necessary?
16. Discuss the guidelines suggested in AS1 Disclosure of Accounting Policies issued by ICAI.
17. Explain accounting assumptions as per AS1.
18. What are the considerations in selection of accounting policies?
19. Discuss the recommendations of AS1 on Accounting Policies.

Accounting Equation and Transaction Analysis

ACCOUNTING EQUATION

The end result of the accounting process for a business entity is the financial statements such as balance sheet, profit and loss account, statement of changes in financial position. These statements are presented in a condensed (highly summarised) form and cannot be prepared until the financial transactions of the business entity have been recorded, classified and summarised. The framework of the financial statements and the elements shown in these statements rests on important and basic relationship, referred to as basic or fundamental accounting equation, basic accounting model. This basic equation is expressed by the balance sheet equation, and therefore, is known as the balance sheet equation also. The balance sheet equation indicates that

Sources of Funds = Uses of Funds Or Equities = Assets Or Proprietor's Equity (Capital) + Outside Liability = Assets

The above accounting equation signifies that assets of a business are always equal to the total of outside liabilities and proprietor's equity. It means that the accounting equation should always be in balance. This fundamental equality is always true because the left side of the equation is simply another view of the right side. This is because whatever funds are raised by the business, either through capital or business operations or from outsider will be tied up in one or other form of uses (assets). Assets represent resources owned by the business entity; equity represents the claims of those who supplied the assets. Thus, the fundamental accounting equation emphasises accounting equivalence or duality concept, *i.e.,* each financial transaction has a dual nature and affects both the assets and liabilities side of the balance sheet.

Algebraically the equations can be expressed as:

$$A = L + P$$

Where A = Assets

L = Outside liabilities

P = Proprietor's equity

The above equation can also be expressed as

$$P = A - L \qquad \dots (1)$$

$$L = A - P \qquad \dots (2)$$

$$A - L - P = \text{Zero} \qquad \dots (3)$$

ASSETS AND LIABILITIES

The aforesaid Accounting Equation is concerned with assets and equities (outside liabilities and proprietor's equity). Following is the list of some assets and equities:

Assets:

1. Cash
2. Cash at Bank
3. Bills Receivable
4. Prepaid expenses
5. Debtors or accounts receivable
6. Stock (stock of raw materials, work-in-progress, finished goods etc.)
7. Loose tools
8. Office equipments and furniture
9. Patents, copyrights
10. Machinery
11. Buildings
12. Land
13. Goodwill

Equities (Outside liabilities and Proprietor's equity).

(a) Outside liabilities

1. Bank overdraft
2. Outstanding expenses
3. Bills payable
4. Creditors on accounts
5. Loan — short-term as well as long-term
6. Debentures

(b) Proprietorship equity

(*i*) Capital (Plus additions less withdrawals)

(*ii*) Reserves and surplus of profits/accumulated profits.

EFFECTS OF FINANCIAL TRANSACTIONS ON ACCOUNTING EQUATION

Every business transaction can be analysed by or expressed in terms of its effect on the balance sheet equation. A business transaction results into a change in all or any of the components of the equation. Whatever may be the change, the Accounting Equation remains in balance. Different types of business transactions may result into a maximum of nine possible effect combinations on the components of accounting equation.

These nine possible combinations of changes or effects are:

(*i*) Increase in one asset; decrease in another asset.

(*ii*) Increase in one liability; decrease in another liability.

(*iii*) Increase in one item of proprietor's equity; decrease in another item of proprietor's equity.

(*iv*) Increase in one item of proprietor's equity; decrease in liability.

(*v*) Increase in a liability; decrease in proprietor's equity.

(*vi*) Increase in asset; increase in liability.

(*vii*) Increase in asset; increase in proprietor's equity.

(*viii*) Decrease in asset; decrease in liability.

(*ix*) Decrease in asset; decrease in proprietor's equity.

Transaction Analysis

Determining the effect of a business transaction on assets, liabilities and equities of the accounting equation is called transaction analysis. A transaction analysis shows increases and decreases in the assets, liabilities or proprietor's equity of a business entity. Where these effects are presented in an account form, they are shown by a simultaneous debit and credit in the relevant accounts of assets, liabilities and/or equities.

Some illustrations are given to explain the transaction analysis and the effects of business transactions on the accounting equation.

Illustration 1:

Transaction 1-X starts business and invests Rs. 1,00,000 as his capital.

(Amt. in Rs.)

Assets		=	**Liabilities + Proprietor's equity**	
	Cash	=	–	X's capital
Effect of transaction	1,00,000	=	–	1,00,000
New Balance	1,00,000	=	–	1,00,000

Transaction 2:

On April 2, the firm purchases furniture for Rs. 40,000 for cash.

Assets	=	Liabilities + Proprietor's equity
Cash + furniture	= –	X's capital
Old Balance 1,00,000	= –	1,00,000
Effect of Transaction – 40,000 + 40,000	= –	1,00,000
New Balance 60.000 + 40.000	= –	1.00.000

Transaction 3:

On April 3, the firm purchases merchandise (goods) costing Rs. 30,000 for cash.

Assets		=	Liabilities + Proprietor's equity
Cash + furniture + Merchandise		= –	X's capital a/c
Old Balance	60,000 + 40,000	= –	1,00,000
Effect of transaction	– 30,000 + 30,000	= –	1,00,000
New Balance	30,000 + 40,000 + 30,000	= –	1 00.000

Transaction 4:

On April 4, the firm purchases merchandise costing 40,000 on credit.

Assets		=	Liabilities + Proprietor's equity	
Cash + furniture + Merchandise		=	Creditors	+ X's capital
Old Balance	30,000 + 40,000 + 30,000	=		+ 1,00,000
Effect of transaction	+ 40,000	=	+ 40.000	
New balance	30,000 + 40,000 + 70,000	=	40,000 + 1,00,000	

Transaction 5:

On April 6, the firm sells merchandise for Rs. 30,000 on credit to Mr. A, costing Rs. 20,000

Assets	=	Liabilities + Proprietor's equity	
Cash + Debtors + Merchandise + Furniture	=	Creditors + X's capital + surplus Profit	
Old Balance 30,000 + – + 70,000 + 40,000	=	40,000 + 1,00,000	
Effect of transactions + 30,000 – 20,000	=	–	10,000
New Balance 30,000 + 30,000 + 50,000 + 40,000	=	40,000 + 1,00,000 + 10,000	

Transaction 6:

On April 15, the firm receives 20,000 cash from Debtor.

Assets	=	Liabilities + Proprietor's equity
Cash + Debtor + Merchandise + Furniture	=	Creditor + X's Cap + surplus profit
Old Balance 30,000 + 30,000 + 50,000 + 40,000	=	40,000 + 1,00,000 + 10,000
Effect of transaction + 20,000 – 20,000	=	–
New Balance 50,000 + 10,000 + 50,000 + 40,000	=	40,000 + 1,00,000 + 10,000

Transaction 7:

On April 16, the firm pays Rs. 40,000 to its creditors.

Assets	=	Liabilities + Proprietor's equity
Cash + Debtors + Merchandise + Furniture	=	Creditors + X's capital + Surplus/Profit
Old Balance 50,000 + 10,000 + 50,000 + 40,000	=	40,000 + 1,00,000 + 10,000
Effect of Transaction – 40,000	=	– 40,000
New Balance 10,000 + 10,000 + 50,000 + 40,000	=	1,00,000 + 10,000

Transactions 8:

On April 17, the firm pays Rs. 2,000 as rent.

Assets	=	Liabilities + Proprietor's equity
Cash + Debtors + Merchandise + Furniture	=	Creditor + X's Cap + Surplus/Profit
Old Balance 10,000 + 10,000 + 50,000 + 40,000	=	+ 1,00,000 + 10,000
Effect of Transaction – 2000	=	– 2,000
New Balance 8,000 + 10,000 + 50,000 + 40,000	=	1,00,000 + 8,000

Profit and Loss A/c for the year ending ...

	Rs.		*Rs.*
To purchase a/c	30,000	By Sales a/c	30,000
To purchase a/c	40,000	By closing stock	50,000
To G/P c/d	10,000		
	80,000		80,000
To Rent a/c	2,000	By Gross profit b/d	10,000
To Net profit	8,000		
	10,000		10,000

Balance Sheet as on ...

Liabilities	*Rs.*	*Assets*	*Rs.*
Capital	1,00,000	Cash	8,000
Profit	8,000	Furniture	40,000
		Debtors	10,000
		Closing Stock (merchandise)	50,000
	1,08,000		1,08,000

Illustration 2:

Shows the Accounting equation on the basis of the following transactions:

(*i*) I started business with cash Rs. 1,00,000

(*ii*) Purchased goods on credit from Mohan – Rs. 40,000

(*iii*) Sold goods for cash Rs. 26,000 (Cost Rs. 22,000)

Solution:

(Amt. in Rs.)

Transaction	Assets	= Liabilities	+	Proprietor's equity
1. X started business with cash	Bank + Goods = Rs. 1,00,000 + 0	Creditors 0	+ +	Capital Rs. 1,00,000
Beginning Equation	1,00,000 + 0	= 0	+	Rs. 1,00,000
2. Purchased goods on Credit from Mohan	(+) 40,000	= (+) 40,000		
New Equation	1,00,000 +40,000	= 40,000	+	1,00,000
3. Sold goods for cash Rs. 26,000 (cost Rs. 22,000)	(+) 26,000 (–) 22,000	=	+	4,000
Ending Equation	1,26,000 + 18,000	= 40,000	+	1,04,000

Illustration 3:

On January 1, 2008, a company Super Consultants India Ltd. was incorporated. The following transactions occurred during January 2008.

January

1 Business was started with capital of Rs. 1,00,00 cash.

4 Equipment was rented (and paid) for the month at a cost of Rs. 12,000.

8 Paper stationery purchased on credit Rs. 8,000.

15 The company charged Rs. 30,000 as consulting fees from the customers during January. This amount is due to be received next month.

20 Miscellaneous expenses of Rs. 6,000 were paid.

29 Land was purchased by borrowing Rs. 4,00,000 from a bank. The loan is due to be repaid in five years. Interest payments are due at the end of each month beginning July 31.

30 Salaries of Rs. 7,000 for the month were paid.

31 Lesson fees were billed to customers in the amount of Rs. 28,000. (They are due to be received next month).

Prepare a summary of the preceding transactions. Determine balances after each transaction to show that the basic equation is in balance.

Prepare an income statement, a statement of retained earnings, balance sheet for January 2008.

Solution:

Super Consultants India Ltd.
Summary of Transactions
January 2008

(Amt. in Rs.)

Date	*Cash +*	*Assets* *Accounts + receivables*	*Land*	*= Liabilities* *= A/c payables +*	*+ Equity* *Loan*	*Capital +*	*Profit or Retained Earning*
1	1,00,000		–				1,00,000
4	–12,000						– 12,000
	88,000					1,00,000	– 12,000
8				+ 8,000			– 8,000
	88,000			8,000		1,00,000	– 20,000
15		+ 30,000					+ 30,000
	88,000	30,000		= 8,000		1,00,000	+ 10,000
20	– 6,000						– 6,000
	82.000	30,000		= 8,000		1,00,000	+ 4,000
29			+ 4,00,000		+ 4,00,000		
	82,000	30,000	4,00,000	= 8,000	4,00,000	1,00,000	4,000
30	– 7,000						– 7,000
31	75,000	30,000 + 28,000	4,00,000	= 8,000	4,00,000	1,00,000	– 3,000 + 28,000
	75,000	58,000	4,00,000	= 8,000	4,00,000	1,00,000	25,000

Income Statement for the Month Ended January 31, 2008

		(Rs.)
	Revenues:	
	Consulting fees	30,000
	Lesson Fees	28,000
	Total Revenues	58,000
Less:	Expenses:	
	Rent expense	12,000
	Paper & Stationery	8,000
	Salaries	7,000
	Misc. expenses	6,000
	Total expenses	33,000
	Net Income	25,000

Statement of Retained Earnings

Retained earnings as on January 1...	Nil
Add: Net Income for January 2008	Rs. 25,000
Total	25,000
Less: Dividends	Nil
Retained earnings, January 31	25,000

Balance Sheet as on January 31, 2008

Liabilities	*Rs.*	*Assets*	*Rs.*
Capital	1,00,000	Cash	75,000
Retained earnings	25,000	Account Receivable	58,000
Accounts payables	8,000	Land	4,00,000
Loan	4,00,000		
	5,33,000		5,33,000

Illustration 4:

Prove that accounting equation is satisfied in all the following transactions of Mr X.

(*i*) Commenced business with cash — Rs. 80,000

(*ii*) Purchased goods for cash — Rs. 40,000 and on credit Rs. 30,000

(*iii*) Sold goods for cash — Rs. 40,000 costing Rs. 25,000

(*iv*) Paid salary — Rs. 2,000, and salary outstanding Rs. 1,000

(*v*) Bought scooter for personal use for cash at Rs. 20,000.

Solution:

(Amt. in Rs.)

Transaction	*Assets* Cash	*Assets* Goods	=	*Liabilities* Creditors	+ *Owners' Equity* + Salary outstanding	+ Capital
(*i*) X commenced business with cash, beginning equation	80,000	—	=	—	—	80,000
(*ii*) Purchased goods for cash and on credit	– 40,000	+ 70,000	=	– 30,000		
(*iii*) Sold goods for cash Rs. 40,000 (costing Rs. 25,000)	40,000	– 25,000	=			+ 15,000
New equation	80,000	+ 45,000	=	30,000	—	+ 95,000
(*iv*) Paid salary of Rs. 2,000 and salary outstanding is Rs. 1,000	– 2,000	—	=	—	+ 1,000	– 3,000
New equation	78,000	+ 45,000	=	30,000	1,000	+ 92,000
(*v*) Bought scooter for personal use for cash	– 20,000					– 20,000
Ending equation	58,000	+ 45,000	=	30,000	+ 1,000	+ 72,000

Illustration 5:

Show the accounting equation on the basis of the following transactions:

		Rs.
(*i*)	Y started business with cash	90,000
(*ii*)	Purchased goods on credit	50,000
(*iii*)	Purchased furniture for cash	10,000
(*iv*)	Sold goods costing Rs. 20,000 for	40,000
(*v*)	Sold goods costing Rs. 20,000 on credit for	42,000
(*vi*)	Bought goods worth Rs. 20.000 (Rs. 15,000 paid in cash and balance on credit)	
(*vii*)	Drawn for personal use	5,000
(*viii*)	Paid as rent	1,000
(*ix*)	Paid for salaries	3,000
(*x*)	Paid for creditors	40,000
(*xi*)	Received from debtors	12,000

Solution:

(Amt. in Rs.)

Transaction	*Cash*	*+ Goods*	*+ Debtors*	*+ Furniture*	=	*Creditors*	*+ Y's Capital*
	Assets				*= Liabilities + Owners' Equity*		
1. Y started business with cash							
Beginning equation	90,000				=		90,000
2. Purchased goods on credit	—	+ 50,000	+ –	+ –	=	50,000	+ –
New equation	90,000	+ 50,000	+ –	+ –	=	50,000	+ 90,000
3. Purchased furniture for cash	– 10.000	+ –	– + –	+ 10,000	=	–	+ –
New equation	80,000	+ 50,000	+ – +	+ 10,000	=	50,000	+ 90,000
4. Sold goods costing Rs. 20,000 for Rs. 40,000	+ 40,000	– 20,000	+ –	+ –	=	– +	20,000
New equation	1,20,000	+ 30,000	+ – +	10,000	=	50,000	+ 1,10,000
5. Sold goods costing Rs. 20,000 for Rs. 42,000 on credit	–	– 20,000	+ 42,000	+ –	=	– +	22,000
New equation	1,20,000	+ 10,000	+ 42,000	+ 10,000	=	50,000	1,32,000
6. Bought goods worth Rs. 20,000 (Rs. 15,000 paid in cash, balance on credit)	– 15,000	+ 20,000	+	– +	=	+5,000	
New equation	1,05,000	– 30,000	+ 42,000	+ 10,000	=	55,000	+ 1,32,000
7. Drew for personal use	–5,000	+	+	–	=	– –	– 5,000
New equation	1,00,000	+ 30,000	+ 42,000	+ 10,000	=	55,000	+ 1,27,000
8. Paid as rent	–1,000	+	– +	–	=	–	– 1,000
New equation	99,000	+ 30,000	+ 42,000	+ 10,000	=	55,000	+ 1,26,000

9. Paid for salaries	-3,000	+	– +	–	=	–	– 3,000
New equation	96,000	+ 30,000	+ 42,000	+ 10,000	=	55,000	+ 1,23,000
10. Paid to creditors'	40,000	+	+	– +	= –	40,000	+ –
New equation	56,000	+ 30,000	+ 42,000	+10,000	=	15,000	+ 1,23,000
11. Received from Debtors	+12000	+	–12,000	+	=	–	+ –
Ending equation	68,000	+ 30,000	+ 30,000	+ 10,000	=	15,000	+ 1,23,000

Illustration 6:

Show the accounting equation on the basis of the following transactions and present a balance sheet on the basis of the ending equation.

		(Rs.)
(i)	Mohan commenced business with cash	70,000
(ii)	Purchased goods on credit	14,000
(iii)	Withdrew for private use	3,000
(iv)	Goods purchased for cash	10,000
(v)	Paid wages	2,000
(vi)	Paid to creditors	10,000
(vii)	Sold goods, on credit (Cost price - Rs. 10,000)	15,000
(viii)	Sold goods for cash (Cost price - Rs. 3,000)	6,000
(ix)	Purchased furniture for cash	2,000

Solution:

(Amt. in Rs.)

Transaction	*Cash*	*+ Goods*	*+ Debtors*	*+ Furniture*	*=*	*Creditors+*	*Mohan's Capital*
			Assets =	*Liabilities +*		*Owners' Equity*	
1. Mohan commenced Business with cash	70,000	+ –	+ –	+ –	=	–	+ 70,000
Beginning equation	70,000	+ –	+ –	+ –	=	–	+ 70,000
2. Purchased goods on credit	–	+ 14,000	+ –	+ –	=	14,000	+ –
New equation	70,000	+ 14,000	+ –	+ –	=	14,000	+ 70,000
3. Withdrawn for private use	– 3,000	+ –	+ –	+ –	=	–	– 3,000
New equation	67,000	+ 14,000	+ –	+ –	=	14,000	+ 67,000
4. Goods purchased for cash	– 10,000	+ 10,000	+ –	+ –	=	–	+ –
New equation	57,000	+ 24,000	+ –	+ –	=	14,000	+ 67,000
5. Paid wages	– 2,000	+ –	+ –	+ –	=	14,000	+ – 2,000
New equation	55,000	+ 24,000	–	–	=	14,000	+ 65,000
6. Paid to creditors	– 10,000	+ –	+ –	+	=	– 10,000	+ –
New equation	45,000	+ 24,000	+ –	+ –	=	4,000	+ 65,000
7. Sold goods on credit for Rs. 15,000 (Cost Rs. 10,000)		– 10,000	+15,000	+ –	=	–	+ 5,000
New equation	45,000	+ 14,000	+15,000	+ –	=	4,000	+ 70,000

8. Sold goods for cash Rs. 6,000 costing Rs. 3,000	+ 6,000	− 3,000	+ −	+ −	=	−	+ 3,000
New equation	51,000	+ − 11,000	+ 15,000	+	=	4,000	+ 73,000
9. Purchased furniture for cash	− 2,000	+	+ −	+2,000	=	−	+ −
Ending equation	49,000	+ 11,000	+15,000	+2,000	=	4000	+ 73,000

Balance Sheet

Liabilities	*Rs.*	*Assets*	*Rs.*
Creditor	4,000	Cash	49,000
Mohan's capital	73,000	Goods	11,000
		Debtors	15,000
		Furniture	2,000
	77,000		77,000

THEORY QUESTIONS

1. What is the fundamental accounting equation? Express it in two different forms.
2. What are the two classification of equities in a balance sheet?
3. What do you understand by transaction analysis? Illustrate.
4. Each business transaction has two elements. Explain.
5. Indicate whether each of the following would increase, decrease or have no effect on owner's equity:
   - (*a*) Purchased supplies for cash
   - (*b*) Withdrew supplies for personal use
   - (*c*) Paid salaries
   - (*d*) Purchased equipment for cash
   - (*e*) Invested cash in business
   - (*f*) Rendered service to customers, on account
   - (*g*) Rendered service to customers, for cash
6. Give one suitable transaction that would result into each of the following:
   - (*i*) Increase in an asset and decrease in another asset
   - (*ii*) Increase in one liability and decrease in another liability
   - (*iii*) Increase in liability and decrease in proprietor's equity
   - (*iv*) Increase in one asset and increase in liability
7. Certain generally accepted accounting principles or concepts have been violated in each of the situations described below.

   Indicate for each situation which concept or principle has been violated.
   - (*a*) When the Alpha company acquired its branch office building for Rs. 50,000, the total amount of cash outlay was recorded as rent expense.
   - (*b*) The personal automobile of Rajiv Dhawan, major shareholder of a company, is listed among the company assets.
   - (*c*) Land acquired at a cost of Rs. 2,50,000 in 2005 is upto Rs. 4,25,000.

(*d*) Equipment acquired on January 15, for Rs. 70,000 is recorded on December 31 balance sheet at Rs. 84,000. Mr. Ashok Johnson, the managing director of the company explains that since at the date of acquisition, the consumer price index was 100 and had increased to 120 by year-end, the appropriate value for financial statement presentation would accordingly be Rs. 84,000.

(*e*) A calculator purchased in early March for Rs. 1,150 can be purchased at year-end for Rs. 925. The company has used the later value on the balance sheet date.

(*f*) Land bought on July 1 for Rs. 5,15,000 is valued on the December 31 balance sheet at Rs.7,05,000, a value obtained by considering recent land sales in the vicinity.

(*g*) A lawnmower used by Mr. Rakesh, the managing director of the company, for his residence is included among the December 31 assets of the company.

8. What is an accounting equation? Explain with suitable examples.
9. "All transactions are subject to accounting equation." Comment on this statement.
10. Give the example of different transactions which may influence assets, liabilities and owner's funds.
11. "Assets and liabilities both are claims, one in favour of business, the other against business." Explain this statement.
12. What is transaction analysis. Explain with suitable examples.
13. Explain with examples as to how accounting equation is not influenced by occurrence of some transactions.

EXERCISES AND PROBLEMS

1. Show the Accounting Equation on the basis of the following transactions:

	Rs.
1. Ravi started business with cash	40,000
2. Purchased goods on credit	10,000
3. Received commission	250
4. Paid rent	1,000
5. Purchased goods for cash	14,000
6. Withdrew cash for private use	1,500
7. Sold goods on credit (Cost price Rs. 15,000)	20,000
8. Purchased furniture for cash	3,000
9. Paid to creditors	7,500

(*Ans.:* Assets Rs. 45,250; Liabilities Rs. 2,500; Capital Rs. 42,750).

2. Show the Accounting Equation on the basis of the following transactions:

	Rs
1. Mohan commenced business with cash	15,000
2. He purchased goods on credit	5,000
3. He sold goods for cash (costing Rs. 2,500) for	3,000
4. Purchased furniture for cash	1,500
5. Sold goods to Rakesh on credit (costing Rs. 400) for	500
6. Paid salaries	250
7. Received cash from Rakesh	500
8. Withdrew cash for private use	1,200
9. Received rent from tenants	1,500
10. Purchased goods from Mukesh for cash	500

(*Ans.:* Assets = Rs. 20,650; Liabilities Rs. 5,000; Capital Rs. 15,650).

3. Prove that Accounting Equation is satisfied in all the following transactions of Manu:
    1. Commenced business with cash Rs. 3,00,000
    2. Paid rent in advance Rs. 2,500
    3. Purchased goods for cash Rs. 1,50,000 and credit Rs. 1,00,000
    4. Sold goods for cash Rs. 1,50,000 costing Rs. 1,00,000
    5. Paid salary Rs. 2500 and salary outstanding Rs. 500
    6. Bought motorcycle for personal use Rs. 25,000

(*Ans.:* Asset Rs. 4,22,500; Liabilities Rs. 1,00,000; capital Rs. 3,22,500).

4. Prepare Accounting Equation from the following:
    1. Started business with cash Rs. 1,00,000 and goods Rs. 40,000
    2. Bought goods for cash Rs. 30,000 and credit for Rs. 20,000
    3. Goods costing Rs. 48,000 sold at a profit of 33 1/3%. Half the payment received in cash
    4. Purchased furniture for office use Rs. 12,000 and for household use of Sudhir Rs. 8,000

(*Ans.:* Assets Rs. 1,68,000; Liabilities Rs. 20,000, Capital Rs. 1,48,000)

5. Show the effect of the following transactions on assets, liabilities and capital using the Accounting Equation:
    1. Started business with cash Rs. 60,000
    2. Rent received Rs. 2,000
    3. Accrued interest Rs. 500
    4. Commission received in advance Rs. 1,000
    5. Amount withdrawn Rs. 5,000

(*Ans.:* Assets Rs. 58,500; Liabilities Rs. 1,000; Capital Rs. 57,500).

6. Anu has following transactions in an accounting year:
    1. Commenced business with cash Rs. 25,000.
    2. Paid wages Rs. 1,000
    3. Salaries outstanding Rs. 100
    4. Prepaid Insurance Rs. 350
    5. Interest due but not paid Rs. 50
    6. Rent paid in advance Rs. 75

(*Ans.:* Assets Rs. 24,000; Liabilities Rs. 150; Capital Rs. 23,850)

7. Prove that the accounting equation is satisfied in all the following transactions:
    1. Started business with cash Rs. 1,20,000
    2. Purchased a typewriter for cash for Rs. 8,000 for office use
    3. Purchased goods for Rs. 50,000 for cash
    4. Purchased goods for Rs. 40,000 on credit
    5. Goods costing Rs. 60,000 sold for Rs. 80,000 on credit
    6. Paid for Rent Rs. 1,500 and for salaries Rs. 2,000
    7. Received Rs. 800 for commission
    8. Withdrew for private use Rs. 5,000 in cash

(*Ans.:* Assets Rs. 1,72,300; Liabilities Rs. 40,000; Capital Rs. 1,32,300).

8. Develop accounting Equation for the following transactions:

	(*Rs.*)
1. Rohit started business with cash	1,50,000
2. He Purchased goods from Ram on credit	50,000
3. Paid carriage	500
4. Sold goods for (profit Rs. 3,000)	9,000
5. Received security deposits from tenants	1,500
6. Invested in shares (personal)	50,000

7. Introduced fresh capital 25,000
8. Goods destroyed by fire 2,500

(*Ans.:* Assets Rs. 1,76,500; Liabilities Rs. 51,500; Capital Rs. 1,25,000).

9. Prepare Accounting Equation from the following:
   1. Invested Rs. 3,00,000 in cash
   2. Purchased on old car for Rs. 56,000 cash
   3. Received cash as salary Rs. 72,000
   4. Purchased a home for Rs. 3,00,000, giving Rs. 1,00,000 in cash and balance through a loan
   5. Purchased securities for cash Rs. 1,50,000
   6. Received cash for dividend on securities Rs. 4,000
   7. Paid cash for household expenses Rs. 6,000
   8. Paid cash Rs. 10,000 for loan and Rs. 6,000 for interest
   9. Sold securities costing Rs. 20,000 for Rs. 30,000

(*Ans.:* Assets Rs. 5,64,000; Liabilities Rs. 1,90,000; Capital Rs. 3,74,000).

10. Prakash started a business with a cash investment of Rs. 70,000. Following transactions took place:
    1. Paid three months' advance rent for office accommodation Rs. 4,200
    2. Bought office car Rs. 42,000
    3. Purchased office furniture Rs. 14,000
    4. Bought office typewriter from Alpine Supply Company Rs. 6,000
    5. Sold extra office furniture at cost to Ajay for Rs. 2,000. Ajay paid Rs. 1,200 in cash and accepted a bill at three months for the balance
    6. Ajay paid the amount of the bill at maturity and Prakash paid half the amount he owed to Alpine Supply Company
    7. Collected Rs. 1,20,000 as commission
    8. Paid telephone bill amounting to Rs. 300.

    Develop Accounting Equation.

Accounting Mechanics-I: Journals

In the previous chapter, it was explained that, within the framework of basic accounting equation and duality concept, sources of funds must always equal uses of funds. That is,

Total Liabilities = Total Assets Or Owners' Equity + Outside Liability = Assets

It is also evident from the earlier discussions that any of the following is a source of funds in business:

— Incurring Liability (including owners equity)

— Earning Revenue

— Making Profits

It stands to reason that a decrease in liability, revenue or profit must be a use of funds being the opposite of a source. Similarly, any of the following is a use of funds:

— Acquiring Assets

— Incurring Expenses

— Incurring Losses

Also a decrease in assets, expenses or losses must be a source of funds, being the opposite of a use.

Thus, no matter what event transpires in the business, it must be possible to capture that event in the balance sheet in such a way that the liabilities (sources) and assets (uses) remain equal.

THE ACCOUNT

The account is the basic building block of any accounting system. An account is a standardised format used to maintain separate record and to accumulate data for each of the individual items in order to facilitate the preparation of periodic financial statements and to provide a continuous check on the accuracy of the recording of transactions. An account exists, therefore, for each asset, liability, owner capital, revenue and expense item. The account is used to record increases and decreases in these items (asset, liability, owner capital, revenue and expense) resulting from business transactions. The account (of an item) shows the following things:

1. The account title, which is the name of a particular accounting element, such as Cash Account.
2. A place to record increases in the monetary amounts in the account.
3. A place to record decreases in the monetary amounts in the account.
4. Dates and descriptive notations.
5. Cross-references to other accounting records.

To illustrate the nature of the account, an example of Cash Account is given below:

Cash Account

Debit *Credit*

Date	*Particulars*	*Ledger Folio*	*Amount (Rs.)*	*Date*	*Particulars*	*Ledger Folio*	*Amount (Rs.)*
2008				2008			
Jan. 1	To Balance b/d		50,000	Jan. 12	By Salaries		11,000
Jan. 15	To Debtors		21,000	Jan. 27	By Rent		17,000
Jan. 25	To Sales		35,000	Jan. 31	By Balance c/d		78,000
	Total		1,06,000		Total		1,06,000
Feb. 1	To Balance b/d		78,000				

On the left side of the Cash Account, there are three accounting entries, one representing the beginning balance and the other two entries representing increases to this account. On the right side there are three accounting entries, two entries representing decreases to this account and the third entry representing the closing balance. The left-side entries begin with the prefix "to" and right-side entries begin with the prefix "by." One may notice that the total of the left side of the cash account is Rs. 1,06,000 and the total of the right side is Rs. 28,000. The net difference between increases and decreases in the cash account is an increase and that is why the balance, of Rs. 78,000 is located on the increases in cash side. In the account plus (+) and minus (–) signs are not needed. Of course, total decreases in cash could not have exceeded total increases; as we cannot spend more cash than we have. The balance in an account is the difference between increases and decreases. The cash account (or any other account) thus, shows the four money elements:

1. Beginning balance
2. Increases or additions
3. Decreases or deductions
4. Closing balance

The form of the account looks like the letter T. For this reason it is referred to as a T-Account. The T-Account form is used by accountants for preparing accounts, actual record keeping, analysing accounting problems and by accounting teachers for teaching accounting.

DEBIT AND CREDIT

As stated earlier, accounts are prepared to provide help in the preparation of financial statements and to check the correctness of transactions recorded by a business enterprise. It is obvious that the financial statements can be prepared only after accounts for different elements (transactions) have been prepared which have to be reported on the financial statements.

Checking the accuracy of recorded transactions and the accounting system is done in terms of basic accounting equation (discussed in the previous chapter) and rules of debit and credit.

The terms debit and credit are used to describe the left-hand and the right-hand sides of an account, as shown below. The verb "to debit" means to make entry in the left-hand side of an account and the verb "to credit" means to make an entry in the right-hand side of an account. The terms debit and credit have no other meaning in accounting.

(Any Type of Account)

Debit	*Credit*
Always the left-side	Always the right-side

The abbreviations Dr. and Cr. are used in place of Debit and Credit. An entry made on the left-hand side is a debit to the account and entry recorded on the right-hand side is a credit to the account. About the debit and credit, a writer has commented in the following manner:

"When the book lies open in front of you and you look at the book (not the book at you) then the side where you have your heart is the left or Debit side. The side away from your heart is the right side and is called Credit."[1]

All accounts show entries recording increases and decreases. In some accounts (such as Cash Account illustrated earlier), increases are recorded on the left-hand side (Debit side) of the account and decreases are recorded on the right-hand side (credit side) of the account. In other accounts, the reverse is true. It means debits and credits by themselves do not indicate increases or decreases. Reference must be made to a specific account to determine if the debits or credits represent increases or decreases.

The five major categories of accounts are illustrated below showing debits and credits related to increases or decreases.

1. Asset Accounts

Debit Side	*Credit Side*
Shows increases Normal Balance-Debit	Shows Decreases

1. Paul H. Walgenbach, Ernest I., Hanson and Norman E. Dittrich, *Financial Accounting,* Harcourt Brace Jovanovich, 1988, p. 42.

2. Liabilities Account

Debit Side	*Credit Side*
Shows decreases	Shows increases Normal balance-Credit

3. Owners' Equity Account

Debit Side	*Credit Side*
Shows decreases	Shows increases Normal balance-Credit

4. Revenue Account

Debit Side	*Credit Side*
Shows decreases	Shows increases Normal balance-Credit

5. Expenses Account

Debit Side	*Credit Side*
Shows increases Normal balance-Debit	Shows decreases

Normal balance refers to positive balance of an account. For any account, generally speaking, the total of the increases to the account exceeds the total of the decreases to the account. The resulting balance is a positive balance rather than a negative balance. For example, a typical asset account (such as Plant Account) have total debits in excess of total credits and consequently have a normal debit balance. After observing the above five types of account, the following inferences are drawn:

1. Debit is always the left-side of all account, and credit is always the right-side of the account.
2. Increases in assets and expenses accounts are always debit entries.
3. Increases in liabilities, Owner's equity and revenue accounts are always credit entries.
4. Decreases are always recorded on the side opposite increases.
5. The normal balance of any account is on the side on which increases are recorded.
6. Assets and expense accounts normally have debit balances. The liabilities, owners' equity and revenue accounts generally have credit balances.

It should be understood that all the above types of accounts are part of the basic balance sheet equation, Assets = Liabilities + Owner's Equity. That is, each financial transaction has two parts, as observed in chapter 3. For example, if an asset is increased, then if the balance sheet equation is to remain in balance, something else must happen, namely, one of the following:

1. Another asset must decrease, or
2. A liability must increase, or
3. Owners' equity must increase.

In all the above situations, debit will always equal the credit and the basic balance sheet equation will remain in balance.

Illustration of Debit and Credit Rules and Recording of Transactions in the Accounts

The following illustrations are taken to explain the application of debit and credit rules (entries) in the various accounts, using T accounts for simplicity and understanding. Prior to making debit and credit entries, a transaction should be analysed to determine which accounts must be increased or decreased. After this has been determined, the rules of debit and credit are applied to record the appropriate increases and decreases to the accounts.

Transaction 1:

Ashok invested Rs. 80,000 of his funds in a new business entitled Alpha Co. Ltd.

(Amt. in Rs.)

Asset (increase)

Cash A/c

Debit			*Credit*
(1)	80,000		

Equity (increase)

Capital A/c

Debit			*Credit*
		(1)	80,000

This transaction increases both the assets and equities of the firm. According to rules of debit and credit, debits will increase assets and credits will increase equity accounts of the firm.

Transaction 2:

Alpha Co. Ltd. purchased the following assets for cash: Supplies Rs. 9,000, office equipment Rs. 7,000, Tools Rs. 6,000.

Assets (increases)

Supplies A/c

Debit			*Credit*
(2)	9,000		

Office Equipment A/c

Debit			*Credit*
(2)	7,000		

Tools A/c

Debit			*Credit*
(2)	6,000		

Assets (decrease)

Cash A/c

Debit			*Credit*
(1)	80,000	(2)	22,000

Three assets — supplies, office equipment and tools are purchased by the firm in cash, reducing the asset cash by Rs. 22,000. Assets are increased by debits and reduced by credits. Therefore, the three asset accounts — supplies, office equipment and tools are debited, each for its respective amount and cash is credited for the total of Rs. 22,000.

Transaction 3:

Alpha Co. acquired land for Rs. 75,000 for storing purposes, paying Rs. 15,000 in cash and issuing bills payable for the difference.

Asset (Increase, decrease)

Debit	*Cash A/c*		*Credit*
(1)	80,000	(2)	22,000
		(3)	15,000

Debit	*Land A/c*		*Credit*
(3)	75,000		

Liability (Increases)

Debit	*Account Payable A/c*		*Credit*
		(3)	60,000

The asset land account is debited by Rs. 75,000 (increases) and the asset cash account is credited by Rs. 15,000 (decrease). Bills payable account is credited by Rs. 60,000 (increase in liabilities). This transaction shows that increases in assets are recorded by debits, decreases in assets by credits and increases in liabilities by credits.

Transaction 4:

Alpha Co. paid Rs. 12000 for three months' rent in advance

Asset (increase)

Debit	*Prepaid Rent A/c*		*Credit*
(4)	12,000		

Assets (decrease)

Debit	*Cash A/c*		*Credit*
(1)	80,000	(2)	22,000
		(3)	15,000
		(4)	12,000

Rent paid in advance (or any expense paid in advance) is an asset or resource having future economic benefit as it gives right to the firm to occupy the rented property. As increases in assets are recorded by debits and decreases in assets are recorded by credits, prepaid rent is debited for Rs. 12,000 and cash is credited for Rs. 12,000.

Transaction 5:

Alpha Co. received Rs. 9,500 as payment for consultancy services rendered by the firm to the customers.

Assets (Increase)

Debit	*Cash A/c*		*Credit*
(1)	80,000	(2)	22,000
		(3)	15,000
(5)	9,500	(4)	12,000

Equity (Increases)

Debit	*Consultancy Services A/c*	*Credit*
		(5) 9,500

This transaction increases the asset cash and equity of the firm by the revenue received for services rendered. Assets are increased by debits and revenues are increased by credits. Therefore, a debit of Rs. 9,500 to cash and a credit of Rs. 9,500 to Receipts for consultancy services are made to record the transaction.

Transaction 6:

Alpha Co. rendered consultancy services to its customers for Rs. 13,500 on credit and the customers will pay later.

Assets (Increases)

Debit	*Account Receivable*	*Credit*
(6) 13,500		

Equity (Increases)

Debit	*Consultancy Services*	*Credit*
		(5) 9,500 (6) 13,500

The firm has given consultancy services to the customers who will pay in future. Since the services have been completed, revenue is earned. A future economic benefit has been received and therefore an asset account — Accounts Receivable — is created in exchange for the services rendered. Assets are increased by debits. Revenues are increased by credits.

Transaction 7:

Alpha Co. paid Rs. 12,000 for the land earlier purchased on credit for Rs. 60,000

Assets (decrease)

Debit	*Cash A/c*	*Credit*
(1) 80,000 (5) 9,500		(2) 22,000 (3) 15,000 (4) 12,000 (7) 12,000

Liabilities (decrease)

Debit	*Accounts Payable A/c*	*Credit*
(7) 12,000		(3) 60,000

The asset cash and liability bills payable are reduced by Rs. 12,000 each by this transaction. Assets are decreased by credits; liabilities are decreased by debits.

Transaction 8:

Additional tools are purchased on credit, for Rs. 1,500.

Assets (Increase)

Debit		*Tools A/c*	*Credit*
(2)	6,000		
(8)	1,500		

Debit	*Accounts Payable A/c*		*Credit*
		(8)	15,000

This transaction increases the asset Tools and the liability Accounts Payable each by Rs.1,500. Assets are increased by debits. Liabilities are increased by credits.

Transaction 9:

Alpha Co. paid utilities expense of Rs. 1,000.

Assets (decrease)

Debit		*Cash A/c*		*Credit*
(1)	80,000		(2)	22,000
(5)	9,500		(3)	15,000
			(4)	12,000
			(7)	12,000
			(9)	1,000

A separate expense account is created for each expense item. This transaction increases the utility Expense and reduces the asset cash by Rs. 1000. Expenses are increased by debits and assets are decreased by credits.

Transaction 10:

Alpha Co. received Rs. 7,500 in cash from customers for whom consultancy services was earlier rendered (transaction 6).

Asset (Increase)

Debit		*Cash*		*Credit*
(1)	80,000		(2)	22,000
(5)	9,500		(3)	15,000
(10)	7,500		(4)	12,000
			(7)	12,000
			(9)	1,000

Asset (decrease)

Debit		*Accounts Receivable*		*Credit*
(6)	13,500		(10)	7,500

Payments by customers reduce the asset accounts receivable and increase the asset cash. Assets are increased by debits and decreased by credits.

Transaction 11:

Depreciation of Rs. 7,500 is recorded on the office equipment.

Assets (decrease)

Debit	***Depreciation***	***Credit***
	(12)	7,500

Debit	***Equity (decrease)***	***Credit***
(12)	7,500	

Depreciation expense is recorded by increasing an expense and reducing an asset. The reduction of the asset is accomplished by the use of a contra-asset account. Expenses are increased by debits. Assets are reduced by credits.

Transaction 12:

Ashok withdrew Rs. 2,000 from the firm for personal use.

(Assets (decrease)

Debit		***Cash A/c***	***Credit***
(1)	80,000	(2)	22,000
(5)	9,500	(3)	15,000
(10)	7,500	(4)	12,000
		(7)	12,000
		(9)	1,000
		(12)	2,000

Equity (decrease)

Debit	***Drawing A/c***	***Credit***
(12)	2,000	

This transaction reduces cash and decreases equity of the firm by Rs. 2,000. Assets are reduced by credits and liabilities are reduced by debits. For withdrawals made by the proprietor, a separate account — Drawing Account — is opened. Drawing is a contra account because its balance represents a reduction of equity (capital) account. Debiting the drawing account to reflect the reduction in owner's equity has the same effect as debiting the owner's capital account directly because, at the end of the period, after net profit is added to the owner's capital account, the debit balance in the drawing account is deducted to arrive at the ending amount of owner's capital.

Transaction 13:

Rs. 4,000 of the prepaid rent (Rs. 12,000) had expired; as mentioned in transaction 4.

Assets (decrease)

Debit	***Prepaid Rent A/c***	***Credit***
(4) 12,000		(13) 4,000

Equity (decreases)

Debit	***Rent Expense A/c***	***Credit***
(13) 4,000		

In transaction 4 the firm paid Rs. 12,000 for three months' rent in advance. At the end of one month. Rs. 4,000 rent has expired and no longer represents an asset. Assets are decreased by credits and liability is decreased by debits. Expenses reduce the equity of the firm.

TYPES OF ACCOUNTS

The accounts maintained by a business organisation are classified into three types as shown in the following figure:

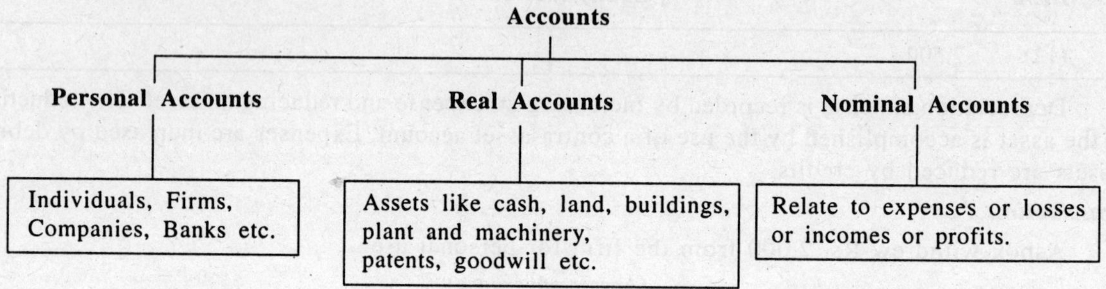

Personal Account: It deals with accounts of individuals like creditors, debtors, bank etc. It shows the balance due to these individuals or due from them on a particular date.

Real Account: It represents assets like plant and machinery, land and buildings, goodwill etc. As on a particular date, this account shows the worth of the asset.

Nominal Account: It consists of different types of expenses or incomes or loss or profit. These accounts show the amount of income earned or expenses incurred for a particular period say a month, a year etc.

LEDGER

Ledger contains a classified summary of all transactions recorded in the cash book and journal. A ledger is not an independent record. The transactions recorded in a ledger are derived from either the cash book or the journal.

JOURNALISING THE TRANSACTIONS

Recording the dual aspects of a transaction is known as journalising. Normally, in a business it is impossible to record every transaction as a journal entry. Hence, special journals such as purchases book, sales book etc. are used. Only certain special transactions are recorded in the journal book. However, for a clear understanding of the readers, the journal entries for various transactions are explained below. Let us apply the rules of debit and credit for a few sample transactions after ascertaining dual aspects.

Transaction (1)	*Aspects* (2)	*Account Debited* (3)	*Reason for the Debit* (4)	*Account Credited* (5)	*Reason for the Credit* (6)
ABC Ltd. received Rs. 5,000 from Gupta & Company	Aspect 1 Cash of Rs. 5,000 is received. Aspect 2 The amount is given by Gupta & Co.	Cash A/c	Cash A/c is a real A/c. The rule of 'Debit what comes in' applies	Gupta & Co.	Gupta & Co. A/c is a personal A/c. The rule of 'credit the giver' applies.
PQR Ltd. purchased Rs. 6,000 worth of goods from X Co.	Aspect 1 Goods worth Rs. 6,000 is received Aspect 2. The goods are supplied by X Co.	Purchases A/c	Purchases A/c is a real A/c. The rule of 'Debit what comes in' applies.	X Co. A/c	X Co. A/c a personal A/c. The rule of 'credit the giver' applies.
XYZ Ltd. paid the salaries of Rs. 15,500 to its staff for the month through bank transfer.	Aspect 1 Payment of an expense of Rs. 15,500 Aspect 2 Bank balance is reduced by Rs. 15,500.	Salaries A/c.	Salaries A/c is a nominal A/c. The rule of 'Debit all expenses' applies.	Bank A/c	Bank A/c here is a Real A/c the rule of 'credit what goes out' applies.

Illustration 1:

Journalise the following transactions in the books of Basu:

(a) Basu sold goods to Chowdhary for Rs. 75,000 against cheque.
(b) Received as commission Rs. 40,000.
(c) Bank paid Rs. 30,000 directly for insurance premium of Basu.
(d) Cash deposited into Bank Rs. 50,000.
(e) Withdrawn cash from Bank for personal expenses Rs. 85,000.

Solution:

Journal Entries

S. No.	*Particulars*		*L.F.*	*Amount Dr. (Rs.)*	*Amount Cr. (Rs.)*
(*a*)	Bank A/c To Sales A/c (Being the goods sold to Chowdhary against a cheque)	Dr.		75,000	75,000
(*b*)	Cash A/c To Commission A/c (Being the commission received)	Dr.		40,000	40,000
(*c*)	Insurance Premium A/c To Bank A/c (Being the Insurance Premium paid directly through Bank)	Dr.		30,000	30,000
(*d*)	Bank A/c To Cash A/c (Being the cash deposited in the bank)	Dr.		50,000	50,000
(*e*)	Drawings A/c To Bank A/c (Being the cash withdrawn from bank for personal use)	Dr.		85,000	85,000
	Total			2,80,000	2,80,000

Illustration 2:

Journalise the following transactions in the books of Shri Shiv Kumar Gupta.

2008		*(Rs.)*
Jan. 1	Commenced business with	50,000
Jan. 2	Goods purchased for cash	30,000
Jan. 3	Paid freight	2,000
Jan. 7	Goods sold to Rajani Kant on credit	13,000
Jan. 8	Paid for stationery	1.000
Jan. 9	Paid for Rent	5,000
Jan. 10	Cash received from Mohan Das	15,400
	Allowed him discount	600
Jan. 17	Paid Premium	4,000
Jan. 19	Paid postage	100
Jan. 20	Rakesh was declared insolvent, fifty paise in the rupee was received from his estate, total debt being Rs. 10,000	
Jan. 29	Paid for Salaries	8,000

Solution:

Journal

Date 2008	*Particulars*		*L.F.*	*Dr. Amount (Rs.)*	*Cr. Amount (Rs.)*
Jan. 1	Cash a/c	Dr.		50,000	
	To Capital a/c				
	(Started business with Rs. 50,000)				
Jan. 2	Purchases a/c	Dr.		30,000	
	To Cash				30,000
	(Being the amount of Cash purchases)				
Jan. 3	Freight a/c	Dr.		2,000	
	To Cash				2,000
	(Being the payment for freight)				
Jan. 7	Rajani Kant	Dr.		13,000	
	To Sales a/c				
	(Being the sales of Goods on credit)				
Jan. 8	Stationery a/c	Dr.		1,000	
	To Cash a/c				1,000
	(Being the amount of stationery paid)				
Jan. 9	Rent a/c	Dr.		5,000	
	To cash a/c				5,000
	(Being the amount of rent paid)				
Jan. 10	Cash a/c	Dr.		15,400	
	Discount a/c	Dr.		600	
	To Mohan Das				16,000
	(Being the cash received from Mohan Das)				
Jan. 17	Premium a/c	Dr.		4,000	
	To cash				4,000
	(Being the payment for premium)				

Jan. 19	Postage a/c Dr. To cash (Being the payment for postage)		100	100
Jan. 20	Cash a/c Dr. Bad debts a/c Dr. To Rakesh (Being the recovery of 50 paise in the rupee from Rakesh, total debt being Rs. 10,000)		5,000 5,000	10,000
Jan. 29	Salaries a/c Dr. To cash (Being the payment for salaries)		8,000	8,000
	Total		1,39,100	1,39,100

Illustration 3:

Journalise the following transactions:

2008		(Rs.)
July 1	X started business with cash	80,000
July 3	Goods purchased for cash	30,000
July 5	Goods purchased from A	5,000
July 7	Goods sold for cash	10,000
July 10	Goods sold to P	30,000
July 12	Cash paid to A	3,000
July 15	Cash received from P	10,000
July 21	Paid for wages	1,500
July 25	Purchased furniture from Sunil Kumar for cash	5,000
July 28	Paid rent	5,000
July 31	Paid for salaries	2,000

Solution:

Journal

Date 2008	*Particulars*	*L.F.*	*Dr. (Rs.)*	*Cr. (Rs.)*
July 1	Cash a/c Dr. To Capital a/c (Started business with cash)		80,000	80,000
July 3	Purchases a/c Dr. To Cash (Being the purchase of goods for cash)		30,000	30,000
July 5	Purchases a/c Dr. To A (Being goods purchased from A)		5,000	5,000
July 7	Cash a/c Dr. To Sales a/c (Being goods sold on cash)		10,000	10,000

Date	Particulars			Dr. (Rs.)	Cr. (Rs.)
July 10	P To Sales a/c (Being cash paid to A)	Dr.		30,000	30,000
July 12	A To Cash a/c (Being cash paid to A)	Dr.		3,000	3,000
July 15	Cash a/c To P (Being cash received from P)	Dr.		10,000	10,000
July 21	Wages a/c To Cash a/c (Being wages paid)	Dr.		1,500	1,500
July 25	Furniture a/c To Cash a/c (Being furniture purchased from Sunil Kumar)	Dr.		5,000	5,000
July 28	Rent a/c To Cash (Being rent paid)	Dr.		5,000	5,000
July 31	Salaries a/c To Cash (Being salaries paid)	Dr.		2,000	2,000

Illustration 4:

Journalise the following transactions in the books of Khanu and Co.

2008		*(Rs.)*
Jan. 2	Started the business with	8,00,000
Jan. 3	Bought furniture for	1,20,000
Jan. 6	Bought stationery for	5,000
Jan. 7	Purchased goods for cash at	2,00,000
Jan. 9	Sold goods for cash worth	50,000
Jan. 11	Sold to R. Desai goods worth	1,00,000
Jan. 14	Bought goods from Mundra Bros at	80,000
Jan. 18	Paid office cleaning charges	1,500
Jan. 20	Bought goods from Hari worth	1,00,000
Jan. 22	Sold to Sharma and Co. goods worth	60,000
Jan. 24	Received from R. Desai	50,000
Jan. 25	Paid to Hari	90,000
Jan. 28	Bought typewriter for	80,000
Jan. 31	Paid house rent of	7,500
Jan. 31	Paid light charges of	5,000
Jan. 31	Paid salary amounting to	50,000
Jan. 31	Received commission to	15,000

Solution:

Journal

Date 2008	*Particulars*		*L.F.*	*Dr.*	*Cr.*
Jan. 2	Cash	Dr.		8,00,000	
	To capital a/c				8,00,000
	(Started business with Rs. 8,00,000)				
Jan. 3	Furniture a/c	Dr.		1,20,000	
	To cash				1,20,000
	(Purchased furniture)				
Jan. 6	Stationery a/c	Dr.		5,000	
	To cash				5,000
	(Purchased stationery)				
Jan. 7	Purchases a/c	Dr.		2,00,000	
	To cash a/c				2,00,000
	(Being the purchase of goods)				
Jan. 9	Cash a/c	Dr.		50,000	
	To sales a/c				50,000
	(Being the sale of goods)				
Jan. 11	R. Desai	Dr.		1,00,000	
	To sales a/c				1,00,000
	(Being the sale of goods to R. Desai)				
Jan. 14	Purchases a/c	Dr.		80,000	
	To Mundra Brothers				80,000
	(Being the purchases of goods from Mundra Bros.)				
Jan. 18	Office cleaning charges a/c	Dr.		1,500	
	To cash				1,500
	(Being the office cleaning charges paid)				
Jan. 20	Purchases a/c	Dr.		1,00,000	
	To Hari				1,00,000
	(Being the purchase of goods)				
Jan. 22	Sharma & Co.	Dr.		60,000	
	To Sales a/c				60,000
	(Being the sale of goods)				
Jan. 24	Cash a/c	Dr.		50,000	
	To R. Desai				50,000
	(Being amount received from R. Desai)				
Jan. 25	Hari	Dr.		90,000	
	To Cash a/c				90,000
	(Being the amount paid to Hari)				
Jan. 28	Typewriter a/c	Dr.		80,000	
	To cash a/c				80,000
	(Being the purchase of typewriter)				
Jan. 31	Rent a/c	Dr.		7,500	
	Lighting a/c	Dr.		5,000	
	Salary a/c	Dr.		50,000	
	To cash				62,500
	(Being the payment made for rent, lighting and salary)				
Jan. 31	Cash a/c	Dr.		15,000	
	To Commission a/c				15,000
	(Being the amount of commission received)				

THEORY QUESTIONS

1. Explain the nature of an account. What information is recorded in an account ? Illustrate with an example.
2. Explain the meaning of the terms debit and credit.
3. What are the rules of debit and credit for different accounts?
4. Debits and credits are used to increase and decrease accounts. How is it possible for one of these items, say, debits, to be able to both increase and decrease accounts?
5. What are normal balances? How are they determined.
6. Identify the following as asset, liability, owner's equity, revenue or expense accounts and indicate whether a debit entry or credit entry increases the balance of the account.

   Accounts receivable
   Accounts payable
   Cash
   Professional fees
   Owner's capital
   Advertising expense
   Supplies on hand
   Plant
   Owners' drawings
7. What is the justification for using a separate owner's drawing account?
8. "During the year the total owner's equity of Alpha Co. increased from Rs. 1,00,000 to Rs. 1,50,000. Therefore, the annual earnings must have been Rs. 50,000." Is this statement necessarily true? Explain.
9. "Every journal entry made to the journal in a financial accounting system must have atleast one debit and one credit." Do you agree or not, explain.
10. For accounting purposes, what is an account? Explain why accounts are used in an accounting system?
11. Complete the following matrix by entering either debit or credit in each cell.

Item	Increases	Decreases
Assets		
Liabilities		
Owner's Equity		
Revenue		
Expenses		

12. Complete the following matrix by entering either increases or decreases in each cell

Item	Debit	Credit
Assets		
Liabilities		
Owner's Equity		
Revenues		
Expenses		

13. What is a journal entry?
14. Explain the Rules of debit and credit.
15. What do debits and credits mean in different types of accounts?
16. What is an account? How would you classify different accounts maintained by a business enterprise?
17. Give the rules of debit and credit and explain them with suitable examples.
18. "All transactions have double aspects." Comment giving examples.
19. What is double entry system? What are its benefits? Give examples.
20. "All transactions have debit as well as credit." Explain with illustrations.
21. Indicate the nature (debit or credit) of normal balance in the following accounts:
    (*i*) Personal accounts of a debtor (*ii*) Furniture a/c (*iii*) Merchandise a/c (*iv*) Salaries a/c (*v*) Rent payable a/c (*vi*) Bills payable a/c.
22. What are the usual entries that are passed through Journal proper?

EXERCISES AND PROBLEMS

1. Journalise the following transactions in the books of Hari.

2008		*Rs.*
April	1. Hari started business with cash	60,00,000
	2. Purchased furniture for cash	10,00,000
	4. Purchased goods for cash	25,00,000
	5. Bought goods from Kamlesh	1,50,000
	6. Sold goods for cash	36,00,000
	8. Sold good to Ram	30,00,000
	10. Paid cash to Kamal	15,00,000
	14. Received cash from Ram	18,00,000
	16. Purchased goods from Sohan	6,00,000
	18. Purchased goods from Sohan for cash	8,00,000
	20. Paid rent for the office	1,00,000
	26. Received commission	75,000
	27. Paid Salary to Gopal	1,20,000
	28. Received cash from Ram	12,00,000
	29. Withdrew cash from office for personal use	4,00,000
	30. Wages paid	7,20,000

2. Journalise the following transactions in the books of Sumit:

2008		
Jan.	1. Sumit started business with cash	10,00,000
	2. Paid into bank	6,00,000
	3. Bought goods from Mohan on credit	2,00,000
	4. Purchased furniture	20,000
	purchased adding machine	80,000
	purchased typewriter	60,000
	6. Paid for postage	1,500
	8. Sold goods for cash	40,000
	9. Sold goods on credit to Mahesh & Co.	1,00,000
	15. Paid to Mohan	1,95,000
	Discount allowed by them	5,000
	25. Sold goods to Ray & Co.	56,000

26. Received cheque from Mahesh & Co. in full settlement of amount due to them — 97,500
31. Paid for electric charge — 1,000
    Paid rent by cheque — 20,000

3. Pass Journal Entries in the books of Onkar Nath from the following transactions:

2008

Jan. 1. Onkar Nath started business with cash Rs. 40,000; Goods Rs. 40.000 and furniture Rs. 10,000
2. Sold goods to Ramlal for cash Rs. 10,000
4. Ramlal returned goods worth Rs. 2,000
8. Received from Ramlal Rs. 7,990 in full settlement of his account
10. Purchased goods from Brij of the list price of Rs. 10,000 at 15% trade discount
13. Returned goods to Brij of the list price of Rs. 1,000
16. Settled the account of Brij by paying cash, under a discount of 10%
18. Bought a 'Table fan' for Rs. 1,200 for the domestic use of Onkar Nath
25. Paid Trade Expenses Rs. 700 and Travelling Expenses Rs. 380

4. Record the following transactions:

1. Gee commences business with a capital of Rs. 25,00,000 trading under the name of Jain General Store.
2. Paid into State Bank of India Rs. 5,00,000.
3. Bought goods from Chandra for Rs. 10,00,000.
4. Bought furniture from Sharda and Co. for Rs. 3,00,000.
5. Sold goods to Paras for Rs. 50,000.
6. Received a sum of Rs. 1,00,000 being rent for the portion of a building let out.
7. Gee contracted with Deep Construction Co. for the renovation of the building at an estimated cost of Rs. 5,00,000.
8. Bought Shares in Siyaram Ltd. for Rs. 5,00,000.
9. Paid Gee's life insurance premium Rs, 15,000.
10. Bank collected dividends on our investments Rs. 50,000.

5. Pass Journal Entries for the following transactions:

1. Provide depreciation on Furniture Rs. 500 and on Machinery Rs. 2,000
2. Received cash Rs. 1,000 for bad debts written off last year
3. Ajay Singh was declared bankrupt. He owed Rs. 2,500 to us. This amount was written off as bad
4. Rs. 20,000 for wages and Rs. 4,000 for salaries are outstanding
5. Purchased furniture for Rs. 6,000 for the proprietor and paid the amount by cheque

6. Journalise the following:

1. Bought goods from Kapil for Rs. 40,000 at a trade discount of 10% and cash discount of 2%, paid 60% of the amount immediately.
2. Received a cheque from Y for Rs. 8,000, this cheque was deposited into bank the next day.
3. Cheque received from Y was dishonoured.
4. Old newspapers sold Rs. 50.
5. Purchased goods from X and paid by cheque Rs. 7,000.
6. Sold half of the above goods to P at a profit of 30% on cost.

7. Journalise the following transactions:

2008

Jan 1. Mohan Bros. commenced business with capital of Rs. 50,000 and goods worth Rs. 30,000.
Jan 11. Sold old machinery to Nathu for Rs. 2,500.
Jan 15. Goods worth Rs. 5,000 given as charity.
Jan 20. Proprietor withdrew for private use Rs. 2,000 from office and Rs. 3,000 from bank.

Jan 25. Cash purchases were of Rs. 10,000, cash Sales of Rs. 8,000.

Jan 30. Rent due has been decided to pay in the next accounting year amounting to Rs. 1,000. Interest on capital Rs. 500.

8. Journalise the following transactions:

   1. Amit is declared insolvent. Received from his official Receiver a first and final composition of 60 paise in the rupee on a debt of Rs. 4,000.
   2. Paid Rs. 250 in cash as wages on installation of a machine.
   3. Provided 10% depreciation on furniture costing Rs. 5,000.
   4. Sold goods to Manu list price Rs. 4,000, trade discount 10% and cash discount 5%. He paid the amount on the same day and availed the cash discount.
   5. Out of rent paid this year, Rs. 1,000 is related to next year.

9. Pass Journal Entries:

   1. Received Rs. 980 from Viru in full settlement of debt to his account for Rs. 1,000.
   2. Received interest on loan from the debtor Rs. 150.
   3. Rs. 550 due from Ram is a bad debt.
   4. Provide interest on capital (Rs. 50,000) at 6% for six months.
   5. Supplied goods costing Rs. 600 to Kunti, issued invoice at 10% above cost less 5% trade discount.
   6. Bought goods from Om and Co. goods worth Rs. 30,000 at 15% trade discount and 2% cash discount and paid them half the amount in cash.

10. Journalise the transactions:

   1. Goods for Rs. 2,500 were given away as charity.
   2. Goods worth Rs. 2,500 were distributed as free samples.
   3. Goods worth Rs. 5,000 and cash Rs. 4,000 were stolen by an employee.
   4. Goods worth Rs. 1,000 were destroyed by fire. Half of money received from Insurance Co.
   5. Interest charged on drawings @ 5% when total drawings were Rs. 10,000.

Cash Book and Subsidiary Books

CASH BOOK

Cash Book records all receipts of and payments in cash. Usually the deposits into bank accounts maintained by a business firm, withdrawals from such accounts and cheque payments are also recorded in the Cash Book. Sometimes a separate book for recording receipts and payments by cheques/DDs etc., is kept, known as the Bank Book. A cash Book which is used to record both cash and bank transactions is referred to as a Two-column Cash Book. The format of this cash book is given below:

Cash Book of Ramesh & Co.

Dr. *Cr.*

Date	*Receipts*	*Cash (Rs.)*	*Bank (Rs.)*	*Date*	*Payments*	*Cash (Rs.)*	*Bank (Rs.)*
2008				2008			
April 1	To Balance b/d	1,500	13,000	April 2	By Wages	50	
6	To Sales	800		5	By Electricity		400
7	To Arvind Co.		2,000	8	By Plumbing repairs	400	
11	To Bela Corporation		2,350	15	By Y Ltd.		10,800
20	To Sales	500		30	By Balance c/d	2,350	6,150
		2,800	17,350			2,800	17,350

Cash Discounts

Sometimes, in order to encourage early payments due from customers, a company may offer a certain percentage of the amount as a discount. For example, if a customer owes the company Rs. 1,000 the company may allow 2% discount if the payment is made before a certain date. In such a case, the customer would pay an actual cash of Rs. 980 only (Rs. 1,000-2% of Rs. 1,000) and Rs. 20 would be treated as discount expense by the company. In the same way, a company might be given some discounts by its creditors for early payment of the amounts payable by it. A cash discount may be distinguished from a trade discount which is given on the invoice price, especially when orders for large quantities are placed. The trade discount is therefore reflected as a reduction in the sale price itself.

A Cash Book can also be used to record the Cash discounts that are allowed to customers for prompt payments and the cash discounts that are received on payments made to suppliers within a stipulated time period. Since discounts will be allowed to customers at the time of receipt of money and received from suppliers at the time of payment of dues, it is convenient to maintain the column for discounts allowed on the receipts side of the Cash book and the column for discount received on the payments side. A Cash book in which the cash and bank transactions and the details of cash discounts are recorded is referred to as a Three-column Cash Book. An illustrative format of this type of Cash Book is given below:

Cash Book of Ramesh & Co.

Dr. *Cr.*

Date	*Receipts*	*Dis.*	*Cash*	*Bank*	*Date*	*Payment*	*Dis.*	*Cash*	*Bank*
2008					2008				
April 1	To Balance b/d		1,500	13,000	April 2	By Wages		50	
6	To Sales		800		5	By Electricity			400
7	To Arvind Co.	50		2,000	8	By Plumbing repairs		400	
11	To Bela Corporation	60		2,350	15	By Y Ltd.	150		10,800
20	To Sales		500		30	By Balance c/d		2,350	6,150
		110	2,800	17,350			150	2,800	17,350

The Cash Book normally also carries Columns for Cash Memo No., Ledger Folio, Vouchers No. etc.

The unique feature of the Cash Book is that it performs the functions of a Journal and the General Ledger with regard to the Cash and Bank transactions. In other words, Cash Book is the book of first entry for all such transactions and the ledger accounts for cash in hand and cash at bank will not be maintained in the General Ledger.

Petty Cash Book

When the petty cash fund is operated as an imprest fund, the recording of the petty expenses paid will be made in the petty cash book. This would also avoid recording too many small value transactions in the main cash book. The petty cash book would contain a number of analytical columns for grouping the various expenses under a few classifications which would facilitate subsequent posting into the General Ledger; A specimen petty cash book is given below:

Analytical Petty Cash Book of Ramesh & Co.

Amt. Recd. Rs.	*Date*	*Particulars*	*Total Amount Rs.*	*Postage & Stationery Rs.*	*Carriage Rs.*	*Travelling Rs.*	*Sundry Expenses Rs.*
	2008						
3000	April 1	To Bank a/c (cheque encashed)					
	April 17	By Postal stamps	800	800			
	April 10	By Stationery	320	320			
	April 15	By Carriage	160		160		

Receipts	Date	Particulars	Total				
	April 20	By Auto fare of salesman	200			200	
	April 22	By Telegram	50	50			
	April 27	By Tea to customers	150				150
	April 30	By Stationery	360	360			
		Total	2040	1530	160	200	150
	April 30	By Balance c/d	960				
3,000			3,000				
	2008						
960	May 1	To Balance b/d					
2040	May 1	To Bank a/c (Cheque encashed)					

The Imprest System

When an analytical petty cash book is maintained for recording the petty expenses, it will be practically more convenient to consider the petty cash as a separate account and take cheques issued for the petty cash imprest as a debit to petty cash account and all petty expenses paid as credits in petty cash account. The journal entries in the months of April and May, 2008 in the books of Ramesh's Co. will be as follows:

			(Rs.)	*(Rs.)*
April, 1	Petty cash a/c	Dr.	3,000	
	To Bank Account			3,000
	(Being the imprest amount released for petty expenses)			
April, 30	Postage and stationery a/c	Dr.	1,530	
	Carriage Account	Dr.	160	
	Travelling Expenses Account	Dr.	200	
	Sundry Expenses Account	Dr.	150	
	To petty Cash Account			2,040
	(Being the petty expenses incurred during April)			
May, 1	Petty Cash Account	Dr.	2,040	
	To Bank Account			2,040
	(Being the reimbursement of petty expenses)			

If credit for all the expenses is also given in the Cash Account (or Bank a/c) then the Cash a/c will be understated (due to two credits — one in respect of release of imprest and the other in respect of actual expenses), and to counter balance the understatement, the balance in Petty Cash Account must be added to that of the Cash Account.

JOURNAL

The Books of Accounts maintained by an organisation other than the cash book may be classified into Journals and Ledgers. The Journal is used as the book of first entry for all transactions which cannot be recorded in the Cash Book. In other words, all non-cash transactions should be recorded in the journal. For practical convenience the journal is maintained by using a number of books called the subsidiary books. For example, the following subsidiary books may constitute the journal for an enterprise.

(*i*) Purchase Book

(*ii*) Purchase Returns Book

(*iii*) Sales Book
(*iv*) Sales Returns Book
(*v*) Bills Receivable Book
(*vi*) Bills Payable Book
(*vii*) Journal Proper.

Specimen formats of these books and brief explanations regarding their use are given in the following sections.

Purchases Book

Also known as the Purchases Journal, this book is used to record credit purchases of goods only. The term 'goods' covers only the items procured by the business for resale.

Purchase Book of Johnson Co.

Date	*Name of Supplier*	*Ledger Folio*	*Inward Invoice No.*	*Amount Rs.*
2008				
April 12	Y Limited		3,354	10,95,000
12	Sharp Enterprises		401	2,70,000
20	Best and Company		5,542	3,90,000
	Total			17,55,000

Purchase Returns Book

This subsidiary book is used to record the goods purchased on credit and sent back to suppliers as they are found not conforming to specifications or for any other reason.

Purchase Returns Book of Johnson Co.

Date	*Name of Supplier*	*Ledger Folio*	*Debit Note No.*	*Amount Rs.*
2008				
April 15	Sharp Enterprises		80	1,00,000
25	Best and Company		81	90,000
	Total			1,90,000

Sales Book

Also known as the Sales Journal, this subsidiary book is used to record all sale of goods on credit.

Sales Book of Johnson Co.

Date	*Name of Customer*	*Ledger Folio*	*Outward Invoice No.*	*Amount Rs.*
2008				
April 3	Beta Corporation		1001	2,41,000
5	Zeta Company		1002	3,94,000
6	Quality Dealers		1003	4,90,000
15	Sooraj Traders		1004	1,80,000
25	Star Enterprises		1005	19,50,000
	Total			32,55,000

Sales Returns Book

This book is used to record the transactions relating to goods sold on credit and received back from the customers as not conforming to the specifications or for any other reason.

Sales Returns Book of Johnson Co.

Date	*Name of Customer*	*Ledger Folio*	*Credit Note No.*	*Amount Rs.*
2008				
April 10	Zeta Company		10	54,000
27	Star Enterprises		11	2,00,000
	Total			2,54,000

Bills Receivable Book

The Bills Receivable of an enterprise consist of all Promissory Notes given by or Bills of Exchange accepted by customers in respect of amounts due from them.

Bills Receivable Book of Johnson Co.

Date	*From whom recd.*	*Acceptor*	*Date of Bills*	*Term*	*Date of Maturity*	*Where payable*	*Amt. Rs.*	*How disposed*
April 12	Quality Dealers	Quality Dealers	8-4-08	90 days	10-7-08	Bank of India Mumbai	4,90,000	Discounted on 20-4-08
18	Sooraj Traders	Sooraj Traders	16-4-08	60 days	19-6-08	Union Bank of Bombay	1,80,000	
							6,70,000	

Bills Payable Book

The Bills Payables consist of all Promissory Notes given or Bills of Exchange accepted by the business in respect of amounts owing to its suppliers. The Bills Payable Book is used to record all such Promissory Notes given or Bills of Exchange accepted by the business.

Bills Payable Book of Johnson Co.

Date	*Name of the the drawer*	*Payee*	*Date of bill*	*Term*	*Date of maturity*	*Where payable*	*Amount Rs.*	*Remark*
2008								
April 25	Best & Co.	Best & Co.	25.4.2008	90 days	27.7.2008	Canara Bank, Mumbai	3,00,000	

Journal Proper

This Book is used to record all transactions which cannot be included in the cash book or any of the other six subsidiary books discussed above. The transactions that will be recorded in Journal Proper are, purchase or sale of fixed assets and investments on credit, adjusting entries, rectification entries etc.

Journal Proper of Johnson Co.

Date	Particulars	Ref.	Ledger Folio	Debit Rs.	Credit Rs.
April 10	Furniture and Fittings A/c To Furniture Mart A/c (being the purchase of furniture on credit)	Dr.		4,00,000	4,00,000
30	Repairs to Machinery A/c To Machinery A/c (being the rectification of a wrong posting of a repair expense to asset A/c)	Dr.		5,00,000	5,00,000

Illustration 1:

From the following transactions of M/s. J. Choudhary, write up his cash book (three column form) bringing down the balance as on May 31, 2008.

May 1	Balance at bank	1,50,000
May 2	Drew from bank for office use	50,000
May 3	Bought office furniture for cash	32,000
May 8	Paid wages in cash	15,000
May 14	Drew from bank for office use	25,000
May 16	Sold goods for cash	22,000
May 19	Received a cheque from B Batliwala & Co in settlement of their account of Rs. 75,000 less 5 per cent	
May 23	Bought goods for cash	45,000
May 25	Drew cheque for self	40,000
May 31	Paid Agrawals's account Rs. 40,000 by cheque less 2½ per cent	

Solution:

Cash Book

Date	Particulars	L.F. Rs.	Dis. Rs.	Cash Rs.	Bank	Date	Particulars	L.F.	Dis. Rs.	Cash Rs.	Bank Rs.
2008						2008					
May 1	To Balance b/d				1,50,000	May 2	By Cash a/c	C			50,000
May 2	To Bank a/c	C		50,000		May 3	By Furniture a/c			32,000	
May 14	To Bank a/c	C		25,000		May 8	By Wages a/c			15,000	
May 16	To Sales a/c			22,000		May 14	By Cash a/c				25,000
May 19	To Batliwala & Co.		3,750		71,250	May 23	By Purchases a/c			45,000	
						May 25	By Drawing a/c				40,000
						May 31	By Agarwala		1,000		39,000
						May 31	By Balance c/d			5,000	67,250
			3,750	97,000	2,21,250				1,000	97,000	2,21,250
June 1	To Balance b/d			5,000	67,250						

Illustration 2:

Enter the following transactions in the purchase day book.

January 2008

Jan. 2 Bought of G Saha and Co. 60 yards of longcloth @ Rs. 140 per yard.

Jan. 8 Purchased from B Chandra & Co. piece goods for Rs. 20,000

Jan. 16 Purchased from A Basu & Co. 100 yards of shirting @ Rs. 300 per yard less trade discount @ 2%

Jan. 28 Bought of SK Sarkar and Sons, 200 yards of terycot at Rs. 1,200 per yard less 2½ per cent trade discount.

Solution:

Purchase Book

Date	*Particulars*	*L.F.*	*Details*	*Amount Rs.*
2008	G. Saha & Co.			
Jan. 2	60 yds. of longcloth @ Rs. 140 per yard			8,400
Jan. 8	B. Chandra & Co. piece goods			20,000
Jan. 16	A. Basu & Co. 100 yards of shirting @ Rs. 300 per yard		30,000	
	Less: trade discount @ 2½%		600	
				29,400
Jan. 28	S.K. Sankar & Sons 200 yards of terycot @ Rs. 1,200 per yard		2,40,000	
	Less: trade discount @2½%		6,000	2,34,000
	Total			2,91,800

Illustration 3:

Prepare a sales day book from the following transactions:

Jan. 2 2008 Sold to Nilima, spices worth Rs. 80,000 less 10 % trade discount.

July 4 2008 Sold to Sadhana, sugar worth Rs. 40,000, extra charges Rs. 1,000.

July 5 2008 Sold to Mohan, wheat worth Rs. 20,000 forwarding expenses Rs. 1,500.

Solution:

Sales Book

Date	*Particulars*	*L.F.*	*Details Rs.*	*Amount Rs.*
2008				
July 2	Nilima			
	Spices		80,000	
	Less: trade discount 10%		8,000	72,000
	(Sales of spices to Nilima worth Rs. 80,000 *less* 10% trade discount)			
July 4	Sadhana			
	Sugar		40,000	
	Add: Extra charges		1,000	41,000
	(Sales of sugar worth Rs. 40,000 to Sadhana, extra charges being Rs. 1,000)			

July 5	Mohan Wheat *Add* forwarding charges (Sale of wheat to Mohan for Rs. 20,000 forwarding charges being Rs. 1,500)	20,000 1,500	21,500
	Total		1,34,500

Illustration 4:

Prepare the sales day book from the following transaction.

2008

Feb. 1 Sold goods to Ram, 200 meters cloth @ Rs. 100 per meter less trade discount 7 %

Feb. 3 Sold to Rahim, 500 metres cloth @ Rs. 200 per meter *less* trade discount 5%, packing charges Rs. 3,000

Feb. 4 Sold to Shyam, 2,000 metres cloth @ Rs. 200 per meter *less* trade discount 5%, other charges made of Rs. 2,500.

Feb. 7 Sold to Jadu, 300 metres cloth @ Rs. 250 per meter less trade discount of 10%.

Solution:

Sales Book

Date	*Particulars*	*Details (Rs.)*	*Amount (Rs.)*
2008 Feb. 1	Ram 200 meters cloth @ Rs. 100 per meter *Less:* Trade discount 7%	20,000 1,400	18,600
Feb. 3	Rahim 500 meters cloth @ Rs. 200 per meter *Less:* Trade discount 5%	1,00,000 5,000	
		95,000	
	Add: Packing charges	3,000	98,000
Feb. 4	Shyam 2000 meters cloth @ Rs. 200 per meter *Less:* Trade discount 5%	4,00,000 20,000	
		3,80,000	
	Add: other charges	2,500	3,82,500
Feb. 7	Jadu 300 meters cloth @ Rs. 2,50 per meter *Less*: Trade discount 10%	75,000 7,500	67,500
	Total		5,66,600

Illustration 5:

Prepare purchase returns book (returns outward) from the following particulars:

July 1 Returned to Sumit Prakash 50 m of cloth @Rs. 20

July 15 Bharat Kumar & Sons 10 sarees @ Rs. 300

July 20 Prem Chandra 200 m. of cloth @ Rs. 70

July 31 Bihari Brothers 100 m of Cloth @ Rs. 100

Solution:

Purchase Returns Book

Date	*Particulars*	*Details Rs.*	*Amount Rs.*
July 1	Sumit Prakash 50 m of cloth @ Rs. 20		1,000.00
July 15	Bharat Kumar & Sons 10 Sarees @ Rs. 300		3,000.00
July 20	Prem Chandara 200 m of cloth @ Rs. 70		14,000.00
July 31	Bihari Brothers 100 m of cloth @ Rs. 100		10,000.00
			28,000.00

Illustration 6:

Enter the following transactions in the appropriate book.

2008

Aug. 1 Returned to us by Harish Gupta & Co. 200 bags coffee @ Rs. 100

Aug. 17 Returned by Bipin Pal & Brothers, 300 chests tea @ Rs. 70 per chest

Aug. 31 Returned by Bhagwan Das 50 tins of ghee @ Rs. 1,000 per tin.

Solution:

Returns Inwards Book

Date	*Particulars*	*Details Rs.*	*Amount Rs.*
2008			
Aug. 1	*Harish Gupta & Co.*		
	200 bags coffee @ Rs. 100		20,000
Aug. 17	*Bipin Pal & Bros.*		
	300 chests tea @ Rs. 70 per chest		21,000
Aug. 31	*Bhagwan Das*		
	50 tins of ghee @ Rs. 1,000 per tin		50,000
	Total		91,000

Illustrations 7:

Enter the following transaction in the sales book of M/s. Prem Kumar of New Delhi.

May 7 Sold to Manish Gupta, Delhi
100 bags of Rice @ Rs. 450/- per bag
10 bags of wheat @ 500/-per bag

May 9 Sold to Rajinder Singh, Patiala
80 Bags of Rice @ 500/ Rs. per bag
30 bags of Rice @ 550/- per bag
Trade discount allowed @ 10 %

May 11 Sold to Ravinder Singh, Agra
100 Bags of Wheat @ Rs. 550/- per bag
Trade discount allowed 10%

Solution:

Sales Book

Date	*Particulars*	*Details* Rs.	*Amount* Rs.
2008			
	Manish Gupta, Delhi		
May 7	100 bags of Rice @ 450/-	45,000	
	10 bags of wheat @ 500/-	5,000	50,000
	Rajinder Singh, Patiala		
May 9	80 bags of Rice @ 500/-	40,000	
	30 bags of Rice @ 550/-	16,500	
		56,500	
	Less: trade discount 10 %	5,650	50,850
	Ravinder Singh Agra		
May 11	100 bags of wheat @ 550/-	55,000	
	Less: trade discount @ 10%	5,500	49,500
	Total (credited to sales a/c)		1,50,350

Illustration 8:

Enter the following transactions in the purchase book of M/s. Vijay Chandra.

2008 Bought of Prem Das, Delhi on credit

May 7 100 copies of Principle of Accounting Part I by C.L. Khanna @ Rs. 50/-
Trade discount allowed 10 %

May 11 Bought of P. Chand and Co. Delhi on credit
200 copies of Marcantile Law by P. S. Guglani @ Rs. 60/-
Less 10% trade discount

May 13 Bought of Ravinder Kumar, Agra on credit
100 copies of History of India Part I
by Mohan Das @ Rs. 70 less 10 % discount

Solution:

Purchase Book

Date	*Particulars*	*Details* Rs.	*Amount* Rs.
2008	*Prem Das, Delhi*		
May 7	100 copies of principle of accounting		
	by C.L. Khanna @ Rs. 50/-	5,000	
	Less: 10% discount	500	4,500
	P. Chand & Co. Delhi		
May 11	200 copies of Mercantile Law		
	by P.S. Guglani @ Rs. 60	12,000	
	Less: 10% trade discount	1,200	10,800

May 13	*Ravinder Kumar, Agra* 100 copies of history of India Part I by Mohan Das @ Rs. 70/- *Less:* 10% trade discount	7,000 700	 6,300
	Total (debited to purchase a/c)		21,600

Illustration 9:

Prepare a Cash Book from the following transactions:

2008			Rs.
Jan.	1	Cash in hand	1,000
Jan.	1	Cash at bank	15,000
Jan.	3	Received from Mohan	12,850
		and allowed him Discount	150
Jan.	4	Cash Sales	20,000
Jan.	5	Paid for Rent	4,000
Jan.	6	Cash purchasing	26,000
Jan.	7	Paid to Harish by cheque	10,000
Jan.	8	Stationery purchased	2,000
Jan.	9	Goods sold for cash	25,000
Jan.	10	Paid salary	6,000
Jan.	12	Paid to Ram Prakash	20,500
		Discount allowed by him	500
Jan.	15	Cash sales	10,000
Jan.	16	Received a cheque from Prem Das and allowed discount	15,600
Jan.	22	Paid charity	1,000
Jan.	25	Paid to travelling expenses	3,000
Jan.	29	Paid into Bank	5,000

Solution:

Cash Book

Date 2008	*Particulars*	*L.F.*	*Discount (Rs.)*	*Cash (Rs.)*	*Bank (Rs.)*	*Date* 2008	*Particulars*	*L.F.*	*Discount (Rs.)*	*Cash (Rs.)*	*Bank (Rs.)*
Jan. 1	To Bal. b/d	—	—	1,000	15,000	Jan. 5	By Rent	—	—	4,000	
Jan. 3	To Mohan	—	150	12,850	—	Jan. 6	By Purchase	—	—	26,000	
Jan. 4	To Sales	—	—	20,000	—	Jan. 7	By Harish	—	—	—	10,000
Jan. 9	To Sales	—	—	25,000	—	Jan. 8	By Stationery	—		2,000	—
Jan. 15	To Sales	—	—	10,000	—	Jan. 10	By Salary	—	—	6,000	—
Jan. 16	To Prem Dass	—	400	—	15,600	Jan. 12	By Ram Prakash	—	500	20,500	
Jan. 29	To Cash	C	—	—	5,000	Jan. 22	By Charity	—	—	1,000	
						Jan. 25	By Travelling	—	—	3,000	
						Jan. 29	By Bank	C	—	5,000	
						Jan. 31	By Balance c/d	—	—	1,350	25,600
	Total		550	68,850	35,600		Total		500	68,850	35,600
Feb. 1	To Balance b/d			1,350	25,600						

Illustration 10:

Enter the following in the purchase journal of M/s. Modern Furniture Suppliers, Pune:

Apr. 1 Bought on credit from M/s Prakash and Company at a Trade Discount of 10 %
12 Doz. Easy chairs at the rate of Rs. 1,150 per dozn.
6 doz. Folding chairs at the rate of 1,250 per doz.
10 dining Tables at the rate of Rs. 1,450 each.

Apr. 15 Purchases from Shetten and Company, Hubli:
20 Steel cupboards at the rate of Rs. 1,450 each at a Trade Discount of 10 % plus Transport charges Rs. 900.

Solution:

In the Books of M/s. Modern Furniture Suppliers

Purchases Book

Date	*Particulars*	*L.F.*	*Details*	*Amount*
April 1	M/s Prakash and Company			
	12 doz. Easy Chairs @ Rs. 1,150 per doz.		13,800	
	6 doz. Folding Chairs @ Rs. 1,250 per doz.		7,500	
	10 tables @ Rs. 1,450 each		14,500	
			35,800	
	Less: 10% discount		3,580	32,220
April 15	Shettan and Company, Hubli:			
	20 Steel cupboards @ Rs. 1,450 each		29,000	
	Less: 10% trade discount		2,900	
			26,100	
	Transport Charges		900	27,000
	Total			59,220

Illustration 11:

Compile a cash book with cash and Bank columns from the following transactions:

		Rs.
June 1	Cash Balance	50,000
	Bank Balance	1,75,000
June 5	Cash received from sale of Shares	5,50,000
June 6	Paid into Bank	5,00,000
June 7	Paid S. Bose by cheque	1,25,000
June 20	Received from A. Mukherji by a cheque for Rs. 60,000 and deposited the same in bank.	

Solution:

Cash Book

Dr.	*Receipts*							*Payments*			*Cr.*
Date	*Particulars*	*L.F.*	*Dis. (Rs.)*	*Cash (Rs.)*	*Bank (Rs.)*	*Date*	*Particulars*	*L.F.*	*Dis. (Rs.)*	*Cash (Rs.)*	*Bank (Rs.)*
June 1	To Balance b/d		50,000	1,75,000		June 6	By Bank A/c			5,00,000	
June 5	To Sale of Share A/c		5,50,000			June 7	By S. Bose				1,25,000
June 6	To Cash A/c			5,00,000							
June 20	To A. Mukherji			60,000		June 30	By Balance c/d			1,00,000	6,10,000
			6,00,000	7,35,000		June 30					
July 1	To balance b/d		1,00,000	6,10,000						6,00,000	7,35,000

Illustration 12:

Write out an analytical petty cash book from the following transactions:

2008

Aug. 1 Issued a cheque of Rs. 10,000 to the petty cashier
2 Paid electricity charges Rs. 325
4 Paid telephone charges Rs. 250
8 Paid for printing Rs. 375
15 Paid for stationery Rs. 600
20 Purchased post cards Rs. 300

Solution:

Petty Cash Book

(Amt. in Rs.)

Receipts	*Date*	*Voucher*	*Particulars*	*Total*	*Elect.*	*Telp.*	*Printing*	*Stat.*	*Post cards*
10,000	Aug 1		To Cash						
	Aug. 2		By Electricity charges	325	325				
	Aug. 4		By Telephone charges	250		250			
	Aug 8		By Printing	375			375		
	Aug 15		By Stationery	600				600	
	Aug. 20		By Post cards	300					300
				1,850	325	250	375	600	300
			By Balance c/d	8,150					
10,000				10,000					
8,150			By Balance b/d						
1,850			To Cash						

THEORY QUESTIONS

1. What are the books of original entry?
2. List the various subsidiary books. What is the purpose of each subsidiary book. Give specimen of purchase book and sales book and enter four imaginary transactions therein.
3. What is a cash book? What are different types of cash book. How is it balanced?
4. What is contra entry? How are contra entries recognised?

5. What is imprest system of petty cash? What are its advantages?
6. "The cash book generally shows a debit balance." Comment
7. What do you understand by 'Subsidiary books.' What are the objects of preparing such books.
8. Explain the following subsidiary books. Give their specimen also:
   (*i*) Sales Book
   (*ii*) Purchase Book
   (*iii*) Purchase Returns book
9. What do you understand by special purpose subsidiary books?
10. What is a petty cash book? How will you maintain the petty Cash Book on imprest system?
11. What do you mean by 'balancing of account? What are the two types of balances?
12. What is Journal Proper?

EXERCISES AND PROBLEMS

1. From the following transactions prepare a single column Cash Book:

2008			*Rs.*
Mar.	1	Commenced business with cash	20,00,000
	2	Bought goods for cash	5,00,000
	5	Sold goods for cash	4,00,000
	10	Goods purchased from Ravi on credit	10,00,000
	13	Paid to Ravi	7,00,000
	15	Cash Sales	8,00,000
	18	Purchased furniture for office	6,00,000
	20	Paid wages	38,000
	24	Paid Rent	40,000
	26	Received Commission	60,000
	28	Withdrew for personal expenses	1,00,000
	31	Paid Salary	90,000

(*Ans.:* Cash Balance Rs. 1,92,000)

2. Gopi commenced business on 1st April, 2008 with Rs. 4,00,000 as capital. He had the following cash transactions:

   Prepare double-column cash book:

2008			
April	1	Purchased furniture and paid cash	50,000
	1	Purchased goods	60,000
	4	Sold goods for cash	30,000
	5	Purchased goods	40,000
	5	Paid cash to Ram Mohan	1,12,000
	5	He allowed discount	2,000
	6	Received cash from Krishna and Co.	1,20,000
		Allowed discount	4,000
	7	Paid for petty expenses	3,000
	8	Cash Purchase	30,000
	9	Cash Sales	40,000
	11	Received from Mohan Bros.	1,20,000
	13	Paid for typewriter	1,60,000
	15	Paid for telephone	40,000
	15	Paid Ali and Sons	80,000
		They allowed discount	1,600

(*Ans.:* Cash Balance Rs. 1,35,000)

3. Enter the following transactions in the Cash Book with discount columns:

2008			
April	1	Balance from the last month	3,758
	2	Received cash from S.K. Agarwal	6,800
	4	Purchased a radioset for private use	2,000
	5	Purchased goods for cash	3,000
	6	Cash Sales	3,720
		Paid Salaries	300
	8	Received from Mukesh	2,000
	9	Paid Naresh chand in full settlement of his account of Rs. 500	450
	12	Paid for V.V.P. for goods from Chandigarh	487
	13	Sent money order to Satish	300
		Money order commission	5
	14	Krishan paid cash to us	2,472
		Discount allowed	27
	18	Cash Purchases	580
	21	Paid for General Expenses	29
	24	Received from Anand Prakash	561
	28	Paid for stationery	50
	30	Paid water rate bill	21
	31	Paid for charity	10
		Purchased a transistor for his son	400

4. Record the following transactions in Three-Column Cash Book:

2008			
June	1	Cash in hand	3,151.20
		Cash at bank	91,401.10
	2	Received a cheque from Ramesh and paid into bank	990.00
	5	Bought goods for Rs. 2,000 and paid by cheque, discount allowed 1 %	
	15	Paid trade expenses	120.00
	16	Paid taxes	400.00
	17	Paid insurance charges	100.00
	25	Sold goods for Rs. 12,500, received cheque and allowed discount 1%	
	27	Cheque received on 25th deposited into bank	
	28	Received cheque from John and Co.	6,000.00
	30	Purchased 100 National Plan Certificates for Rs. 100 each @ Rs. 95 each and paid for them by cheque.	

(*Ans.:* Cash Balance Rs. 2531.20
Bank Balance Rs. 93,286.10)

5. Prepare a three-column Cash Book:

2008			
June	1	Cash Balance	1,00,000
		Bank Balance	3,50,000
	5	Cash received from sale of shares	11,00,000
	6	Paid into Bank	10,00,000
	7	Paid Jyoti by cheque	2,50,000
	9	Paid wages in cash	60,000
	20	Received from Tareen by a cheque and sent to bank	1,20,000
	21	Drawn from bank	1,00,000
	29	Paid office salaries in cash	80,000
	30	Sold goods for cash and banked the same	1,60,000
		Paid rent by cheque	20,000
		Paid into Bank	150,000

(*Ans.:* Cash Balance Rs. 10,000; Bank Balance Rs. 14,10,000)

6. Enter the following transactions m Three-Column Cash Book:

2008			
Jan.	1	Started business with cash	10,00,000
	2	Opened current account with the Mysore Bank	4,00,000
	3	Purchased goods from Ajay by cheque	7,500
	4	Received cheque from Shyam	10,000
		Allowed him discount	500
	5	Sold goods for cash	2,000
	7	Paid into Bank	
		Cash Rs. 1,500	
		Bank Rs. 10,000	11,500
	8	Paid Vijay by cheque	17,250
		Discount received	250
		Paid carriage by cheque	9,000
	10	Drew from Bank cash for office	10,000
	30	Paid wages by cheque	3,000

(*Ans.:* Cash Balance Rs. 6,10,500; Bank Balance Rs. 3,64,750)

7. Prepare Three-column Cash Book from the following:

2008			
June	1	Cash in hand	1,60,000
		Bank Overdraft	11,40,000
	7	Received a cheque from Bina	6,50,000
	9	Deposited the above cheque into bank	
	12	Paid to Bhuwan by cheque	4,85,000
	15	Bina's cheque returned dishonoured	
	20	Withdrew from Bank for office use	50,000
	25	Cheque received from Puru	2,40,000
	28	Puru's cheque was endorsed in favour of Rohit	
	30	Income Tax paid by cheque	30,000
	30	Bank charges	5,000

(*Ans.:* Cash Balance 2,10,000
Bank Balance (Cr) Rs. 17,10,000)

8. Prepare three column Cash Book:

2008			
April	1	Cash in hand Rs. 80,000 and at Bank Rs. 5,00,000	
	4	Discounted a bill for Rs. 5,00,000 at 1% through bank	
	5	Bought goods by cheque	4,00,000
	8	Bought goods by cash	10,000
	10	Paid by cheque for a bill drawn upon us	3,00,000
	12	Paid trade expenses	5,000
	17	Paid into bank	50,000
	18	Jai who owed us Rs. 10,000 became bankrupt and paid us 50 p. in a rupees	
	20	Received Rs. 5,000 from Rajan and allowed him discount Rs. 100	
	21	Paid Rs. 12,500 to Ashu and he allowed us discount Rs. 250	
	22	Received a bill of exchange from Ram and deposited the same into Bank	1,20,000
	24	Withdrew from Bank	10,000
	25	Withdrew from Bank for private expenses	5,000
	26	Sold goods for cash	5,000
	27	Received a cheque for goods sold	4,50,000
	28	Received payment of a loan of Rs. 1,50,000 and deposited out of it Rs. 1;25,000 in the bank	

(*Ans.:* Cash Balance Rs. 52,500; Bank Balance Rs. 10,25,000)

9. Enter the following transactions in Cash Book :

2008

June 1 Balance of Cash in hand Rs. 24,000, overdraft at Bank Rs. 3,000.
2 Deposited into Bank Rs. 20,000.
Sold goods for Cash Rs. 56,000 and paid half the proceeds into Bank.
5 Received a money order from Sanjay Rs. 1,000.
8 Received Rs. 5,600 from Anuj. Paid Rs. 2,000 into Bank.
10 Received a cheque for Rs. 14,000 from Dhruv and Cash Rs. 1,800 in full settlement of Rs. 16,000 due from him.
12 Paid Rs. 13,200 to Manoj and Co., half cash and half by cheque.
13 Cheque received from Dhruv deposited into Bank.
15 Paid for purchase of Machinery Rs. 40,000.
16 Paid wages for erection of above Machinery Rs. 2,000.
17 Cheque issued for Rs. 12,000 in favour of Saini and Co. for purchase of furniture.
20 Purchased goods from Kamal Garments for Rs. 20,000 on credit.
Received a Bank Draft for Rs. 9,600 from Danu and Co. in full settlement of Rs. 10,000 due from them. Sent the draft to bank.
24 Bank issued a draft for Rs. 20,000 in favour of Kamal Garments on our request. Bank charged Rs. 50 for issuing the draft.
26 Drew from bank for petty Cash Rs. 200.
28 Paid salary by cheque Rs. 12,000.
30 Bank charges Rs. 100 and interest Rs. 3,240 charged by bank.
Deposited into bank the entire balance after retaining Rs. 8,000 at office.

(*Ans.:* Cash Balance Rs. 8,000; Bank Balance Rs. 18,210)

10. From the following transactions prepare three column Cash Book:

2008			*Rs.*
May	1	Cash in hand	4,80,000
	2	Bank Overdraft	30,40,000
	2	Fresh Capital introduced	20,00,000
	3	Deposited into Bank	15,00,000
	5	An amount of Rs. 4,20,000 due from Asha written off as bad debts in the previous year, now recovered.	
	6	Withdrew from bank for the payment of life Insurance premium	3,00,000
	8	Received a cheque from Manu for Rs. 6,00,000 and deposited the same into bank.	
	10	Sold goods to Vijay on credit	30,00,000
	12	Received a cheque for Rs. 28,00,000 from Vijay in full settlement.	
	15	Cheque received from Vijay sent to Bank.	
	18	Vijay's cheque returned by Bank dishonoured. Bank charged Rs. 2,500 on this cheque.	
	19	Received a cheque of Rs. 6,80,000 from Vipin which was endorsed to Amarpal on the same day.	
	25	Withdrew cash from Bank Rs. 5,00,000 for paying gift to his daughter on her birthday.	
	26	Bought goods from Garg General Store for Rs. 10,00,000 on credit and they allowed us trade discount of 25%.	
	28	Paid to Garg General Stores in cash in full settlement	7,00,000
	28	Sale of old machinery, payment received in cash Rs. 7,70,000	
	30	Paid Salary by cheque Rs. 1,50,000. Paid Rent in cash Rs. 2,20,000.	
	31	Paid into Current Account the entire balance after retaining Rs. 5,00,000 at office.	

(*Ans.:* Cash Balance (Dr.) Rs. 5,00,000; Bank Overdraft Rs. 11,42,500.)

Petty Cash Book

11. Prepare the columnar Petty Cash Book of Sanjay Ltd., for the month of January 2008 under the imprest system. The petty cash limit fixed was Rs. 2,500 and the cashier draws money under imprest petty cash system as and when the balance available with him is below Rs. 500.

Petty cash transactions for the month of January 2008 given below:

Jan. 1	Opening balance	2,500
2	Paid towards conveyance charges	420
3	Purchase of stationery	830
5	Wages to Sweeper	210
7	Paid towards conveyance charges	620
8	Postage stamps purchased	1,100
11	Wages to Sweeper	420
14	Telegram charges paid	95
16	Conveyance charges paid	225
20	Wages to Sweeper	490
20	Postage stamps purchased	810
23	Telegram charges	140
26	Entertainment expenses	313
26	Wages to Sweeper	630
27	Taxi charges paid	276
28	Postage stamps purchased	360
31	Entertainment expenses	270
31	Wages to Sweeper	420

12. Prepare Petty Cash Book from the following:

June 1	Received from Cashiers Rs. 1,500 as petty Cash.	
2	Postages	Rs. 90
3	Travelling	60
4	Cleaning	75
7	Petrol for Van	110
8	Travelling	125
9	Stationery	85
11	Cleaning	90
14	Postage	25
15	Travelling	40
18	Stationery	45
18	Cleaning	115
20	Postage	65
24	Delivery van service	220
26	Petrol	90
27	Cleaning	105
29	Postage	25
30	Petrol	140

13. Prepare a Purchase Book from the following transactions:

2008

June 5 Bought of Kishan and Co. Agra:
20 quintal Sugar @ Rs. 1,200 per quintal.
40 bags Rice each containing one quintal @ Rs. 1,500 per quintal Trade Discount 15%

June 10 Purchased from Chadha and Sons, Mathura:
Desi Ghee 20 tins, each containing 16 kg., @ Rs. 120 per kg.
Kerosene Oil, 1,000 litre @ Rs. 6 per litre.
Trade Discount 10%.

June 14 Purchased from Sunil Kumar, Delhi:
Wheat 30 quintals @ Rs. 500 per quintal; Gram 20 quintals
@ Rs. 1,200 per Quintal, Rice 10 quintals @ Rs. 1,400
per quintal Cartage and other expenses paid in cash Rs. 700.

June 20 Purchased for cash from Roop Chand, Delhi:
50 Bales of Cotton @ Rs. 1,500 per bale

June 25 Bought Furniture for office use from Furniture House, Meerut on Credit:
20 Godrej Chairs @ Rs. 300 per chair.
2 Godrej Tables @ Rs. 1,600 per Table.

(*Ans.:* Total of purchases Book Rs. 1,64,360).

14. Enter the following transactions in Sales Book of M/s Mira Lal and Sons, Kolkata:

2008

May 5 Sold to Sudesh Stationery House, Kolkata;
100 Dozen Pencils @ Rs. 20 per dozen.
40 dozen Pens @ Rs. 5 per pen.
Trade Discount 10 %

May 8 Sold to Kapur Stationery Shop, Indore;
20 Dozen Note Books @ Rs. 60 per dozen.
30 Gross Rubbers @ Rs. 10 per dozen.

May 20 Sold old newspapers for Rs. 300

May 24 Sold to Jain Stationery House, Lucknow for Cash;
50 dozen Pencils @ Rs. 22 per dozen.

May 28 Sold to Ghulam Ali and Sons, Agra:
20 Reams of Paper @ Rs. 80 per Ream, discount 15 %

May 31 Sold old furniture to Kamal Nath and Co. Alipur on credit Rs. 2,200

(*Ans.:* Total of Sales Book Rs. 10,120).

15. Prepare Purchases and Sales Book in the books of Deep Book Depot from the following transactions:

Jan. 1 Bought of Sunil, Mumbai on credit
200 copies Physics by Resnick Holidey @ Rs. 75
200 copies Mathematics without Fears by N. Arora @ Rs. 50

Jan. 2 Sold to Shri Ram
48 copies Physics @ Rs. 75
50 copies Mathematics without Fears @ Rs. 50

Jan. 8 Bought of Sultan Chand, Delhi
80 copies Economics by K.K. Dewet @ Rs. 100
Less: 15 % Trade Discount

Jan. 12 Sold to Saxena Bros.
40 copies Economics @ Rs. 100

Jan. 18 Sold to Kalicharan
40 copies Physics @ Rs. 75

Jan. 22 Bought of Rahul
200 copies Arithmetic @ Rs.40
Less: Trade Discount 20 %

Jan. 25 Bought of Hari Ram, Delhi on Credit
100 copies History of England @ Rs. 50
Less: 15 % Trade Discount

Jan. 31 Sold to Arun
50 copies Arithmetic @ Rs. 40

16. Prepare Returns Inward and Returns Outward Books from the following:

2008

Jan. 3 Returned to Lakhani
50 pairs of chappals being not up to the approved sample @ Rs. 42 per pair.
Less: Trade Discount 20 %

Jan. 10 Murari and Co., Fatehpuri, returned to us:
10 pairs of shoes for being defective @ Rs. 120 per pair
Less: Trade Discount 10%

Jan. 15 Returned to Baljja Shoe Co.
20 pairs of ladies chappals @ Rs. 36 per pair
Less: 15%

Jan. 22 Pratik and Sons, Roop Nagar, returned to us:
50 pairs of Shoes @ Rs. 150 per pair

Jan. 27 Manas Shoe Co. Model Town, returned to us:
20 pairs of sandals @ Rs. 85 per pair

Jan. 31 Returned to Bata Shoe Co. Defective shoes worth Rs. 1,200.

(***Ans.:*** Returns Outward Book Rs. 3,492
Returned Inward Book Rs. 10,280)

Accounting Mechanics-II: Ledger Posting and Trial Balance

LEDGER

An accounting system typically contains a large number of accounts. Collectively these individual accounts are contained in a record known as the ledger. A ledger is simply the grouping of the accounts that are used to prepare financial statements for a business. A ledger account is a summary device and it is shaped like the letter T and called a T account. Ledger is a principal book of an enterprise though it is not an independent record. It contains all the accounts in which all the business transactions pertaining to a business enterprise are recorded. The main function of the ledger is to classify and summarise all the items appearing in journal and other books of original entry under appropriate accounts so that at the end of the accounting period, each account contains the entire information of all transactions relating to it.

Relationship between Journal and Ledger

Journal and ledger are the most important books maintained in an enterprise. They are closely interrelated. Business transactions are recorded first in Journal and other books of original entry and then from these books they are transferred to Ledger. Journal records transactions in a chronological order while the ledger records the transactions in a classified form. Journal, being the book of original entry is more reliable as compared to ledger.

A journal is not useful in answering a question such as, what is the balance of cash at a certain date? This question is answered by referring to the ledger, which summarises the cumulative effect of recorded transactions in separate accounts. This is accomplished by transferring or posting information from the journal into appropriate accounts in the ledger.

POSTING

Posting is a process of transferring debits and credits from the Journal and other books of original entry to other respective accounts in the ledger. The aim of posting is to make a classified and summarised record of business transactions in appropriate accounts.

Rules Regarding Posting

The following rules are observed while posting/transferring the transactions in the ledger:.

1. Separate accounts should be opened in the ledger for posting the different transactions recorded in the book of original entry.
2. All the transactions pertaining to one account should be posted in the same account.
3. Two aspects of the business transaction, namely — debit aspect and credit aspect — should be posted on the debit side and credit side of the account respectively.

POSTING OF DIFFERENT ACCOUNT BOOKS

Cash Book

Rules regarding posting of cash book are given below:

(*i*) Transactions recorded on the debit side of Cash Book are posted on the credit side of accounts opened in the ledger.

(*ii*) Transactions recorded on the credit side of the cash book are posted on the debit side of different accounts in the ledger.

(*iii*) Contra entries appearing in the cash book are not posted.

(*iv*) Totals of discount columns of the cash book are posted in the discount account opened in the ledger. Debit side total is posted on the debit side and credit side total is posted on the credit side of the discount account.

(*v*) Balance in the cash column and bank column of the cash book is not posted anywhere. It is shown on the asset side of the Balance Sheet.

Petty Cash Book

Transaction recorded in the Petty Cash book are posted on the debit side of the accounts opened for the purpose. Balance of Petty Cash Book is not posted anywhere. It is shown on the asset side of Balance Sheet.

Purchase Book

In Purchases Book, credit purchases of goods in which the enterprises deals are recorded. Accounts of all those persons who have supplied goods are to be opened and credited with the amount of purchases made from them. Total of purchases book is to be posted on the debit side of purchases account. This is illustrated below:

Harish Jain, Delhi

Dr.	Rs.			Rs. Cr.
		20.5.2008	By purchases a/c	10,000

Summant Prasad

Dr.				Cr.
		31.5.2008	By purchases a/c	20,000

Purchase A/c

Dr.					Cr.
1.6.2008	To Sundries a/c	30,000			

Purchases Return Book

Purchases Return Book, also called Returns Outward Book, records returns of purchase made to suppliers. Personal accounts of all those persons to whom goods have been returned are debited and total of purchase returns book is credited to purchases returns account as illustrated below.

Harish Jain, Delhi

Dr.					Cr.
15.7.2008	To Purchase returns A/c	1000	1-7-2008	By Purchases A/c	10,000

Summant Prasad

Dr.					Cr.
20.6.2008	To Purchase return A/c	3,000	31.5.2008	By Purchases	20,000

Purchases Returns A/c

Dr.					Cr.
			31.7.2008	By Sundries	4,000

Sales Book

Sales Book records all credit sales. While posting Sales Book to ledger, personal accounts of the customers are opened and debited by the amount of sales made to them. Total of Sales Book is credited to Sales account. This is illustrated below.

Ram Prasad

Dr.					Cr.
2.7.2008	To Sales a/c	15,000			

Devi Prasad

Dr.					Cr.
25.6.2008	To Sales a/c	20,000			

Sales A/c

Dr.					Cr.
			15.7.2008	By sundries	35,000

Sales Returns Book/Returns Inward Book

When goods are returned by customers, they are recorded in sales returns book/returns inward book. While posting Sales Returns book to Ledger, personal accounts of the customers are credited and total of Sales Returns Book is debited to Sales Returns a/c. This is illustrated below:

Ram Prasad

Dr.					Cr.
2.7.2008	To Sales A/c	15,000	14.7.2008	By Sales returns A/c	4,000

Devi Prasad

Dr.					Cr.
25.6.2008	To Sales A/c	20,000	10.7.2008	By Sales return A/c	4,000

Sales Return a/c

Dr.					Cr.
15.7.2008	To Sundries	8,000			

Bills Receivable Book

In bills receivable book, bills received by the enterprise are recorded. While posting Bills receivable book, personal accounts of the persons giving the bills are credited. Total of Bills Receivable book is debited to Bills Receivable a/c

Sunder Kumar

Dr.					Cr.
			2008 July 10	By B/R A/c	10,000

Suresh Chander

Dr.					Cr.
			2008 July 7	By B/R A/c	15,000

Bills Receivable A/c

Dr.					Cr.
15.7.2008	To Sundries	25.000			

Bills Payable Book

The enterprise may accept so many bills in the business. Acceptances given are recorded in Bills Payable book. While posting Bills Payable Book acceptances given are debited to the personal accounts of the persons to whom they have been given and total of Bills Payable book is posted to the credit side of Bills Payable a/c. This is illustrated below :

Ram Prasad

Dr.					Cr.
2.7.2008	To B/P A/c	8,000			

Chandra Mohan

Dr.					Cr.
10.7.2008	To B/P A/c	7,000			

Bills Payable A/c

Dr.					Cr.
			15.7.2008	By sundries	15,000

POSTING OF JOURNAL

When we journalise a transaction we write out in the journal as to which account is to be debited and which account is to be credited. The same information is transferred to Ledger in the two concerned accounts. This is illustrated below:

Furniture a/c Dr. To Jain & Co. (Being furniture bought from Jain & Co. on credit)		70,000	70,000
Depreciation a/c Dr. To Furniture a/c (Being depreciation on furniture)		7,000	7,000

Furniture a/c

Dr.			Cr.
To Jain & Co.	70,000	By depreciation a/c	7,000

Dr.			Cr.
To Furniture a/c	7,000		

Jain & Co.

Dr.			Cr.
		By Furniture a/c	70,000

BALANCING OF AN ACCOUNT

Balancing of an account implies a process of ascertaining the net balance of an account after considering and comparing the total of both sides. viz., debit side and credit side. The Balance is put on the side which is smaller and the two totals — debit side and credit side are made equal. Against the balance a reference is put that it has been carried forward (c/f) or carried down (c/d). The balance of an account will be termed as debit balance if the total of debit side is greater than the total of credit side. On the other hand, if total of credit side is greater than total of debit side, balance will be a credit balance. This is illustrated below:

Mohan

	Rs.		*Rs.*
5.5.2008 To B/R a/c	7,000	1.5.2008 By purchase a/c	15,000
6.5.2008 To purchases	2,000	16.5.2008 By purchases a/c	25,000
17.5.2008 To Bank a/c	15,000		
31.5.2008 To Balance c/d	16,000		
	40,000		40,000
		1.6.2008 By balance b/d	16,000

Furniture A/c

	Rs.		*Rs.*
1.5.2008 To Bank a/c	16,000	31.5.2008 By balance c/d	16,000
	16,000		16,000
1.6.2008 To balance b/d	16,000		

TRIAL BALANCE

When all accounts of the ledger are in balance, a Trial Balance is prepared. A Trial Balance is a listing of all the accounts and their respective balances. Trial Balance is a statement of debit balances and credit balanced extracted from ledger accounts on a particular date. A Trial Balance, is, thus, a summary of all the Ledger Balances outstanding as on a particular date.

Proforma of a Trial Balance is as follows:

Trial Balance as at

Ledger Accounts	Debit Balance	Credit Balance

It must be stated here that total of debit balance column must be equal to total of credit balances column. This is so because under double entry system, for each item of debit there is a corresponding credit and secondly all the transactions recorded in the books of original entry are transferred to ledger.

Objectives of Preparing a Trial Balance

The following are the objectives of preparing a Trial Balance:

1. To check the arithmetical accuracy of accounting entries posted in the ledger. When the trial balance tallies, it is an indication of the fact that ledger accounts are arithmetically accurate. It also indicates that: (*i*) For each transactions, the debits and credits were recorded in equal amounts. (*ii*) The balance (debit balances and credit balances) for each account was calculated correctly. (*iii*) The balances of the various debit and credit accounts have been correctly added together to arrive at the total equality of the debit and credits. Of course there may be certain errors in the books of accounts in spite of the agreement of Trial Balance. These have been discussed later in a subsequent chapter.
2. To Provide a Basis for Financial statements — Trial Balance is a first step towards preparation of financial statements of an organisation. If trial balance is not prepared, it will be impossible to prepare the financial statement.
3. Trial Balance serves as a summary of all the ledger accounts and provides a complete picture of each account in the ledger.

Illustration 1:

During January 2008, Anil Kumar transacted the following business. You are required to make journal entries for the transactions and prepare cash book and other necessary ledger accounts based on the journal entries.

January 2008		*(Rs.)*
1	Commenced business with cash	20,000
2	Purchased goods on credit from Shyam	15,000
3	Purchased goods for cash	500
4	Paid Gopal an advance/for goods ordered	1,000
5	Received cash from Murthy as advance for goods ordered by him	1,500
6	Purchased furniture for office use for cash	1,000
7	Paid wages	250
8	Received commission (in cash)	300
9	Goods returned to Shyam	100
10	Goods sold to Kamal	5,000
11	Paid for postage and telegrams	100
12	Goods returned by Kamal	250
15	Paid for Stationery	100
18	Paid into bank	250

20 Goods sold for cash	375
22 Bought goods for cash	500
25 Paid salaries	350
28 Paid rent	250
31 Drew cash for personal use	500

Journal Entries

Date	Particulars		L.F.	Debit (Rs.)	Credit (Rs.)
2008					
Jan. 1	Cash account To capital account (Being the cash brought into business as capital)	Dr.		20,000	20,000
Jan. 2	Purchases account To Shyam's account (Being the goods purchased on credit)	Dr.		15,000	15,000
Jan. 3	Purchase account To cash account (Being the goods purchased for cash)	Dr.		500	500
Jan. 4	Gopal account To cash account (Being the amount paid to Gopal)	Dr.		1,000	1,000
Jan. 5	Cash account To Murthy Account (Being the cash received from Murthy)	Dr.		1,500	1,500
Jan. 6	Furniture account To cash account (Being the furniture purchased for office use for cash)	Dr.		1,000	1,000
Jan. 7	Wages account To cash account (Being the wages paid)	Dr.		250	250
Jan. 8	Cash account To commission received a/c (Being the commission received)	Dr.		3,000	3,000
Jan. 9	Shyam account To purchase returns account (Being goods returned to Shyam)	Dr.		100	100
Jan. 10	Kamal account To sales account (Being goods sold to Kamal on credit)	Dr.		5,000	5,000
Jan. 11	Postage and telegrams account To cash account (Being the amount paid for postage and telegram)	Dr.		100	100
Jan. 12	Sales returns account To Kamal account (Being the goods returned by Kamal)	Dr.		250	250

Jan. 15	Stationery account Dr. To cash account (Being the amount paid for stationery)			100	100
Jan. 18	Bank account Dr. To cash account (Being the amount deposited into the bank)			250	250
Jan. 20	Cash account Dr. To sales account (Being the goods sold for cash)			375	375
Jan. 22	Purchases account Dr. To cash account (Being the goods purchased for cash)			500	500
Jan. 25	Salaries account Dr. To cash account (Being the amount paid as salaries)			350	350
Jan. 28	Rent account Dr. To cash account (Being the rent paid)			250	250
Jan. 31	Drawings account Dr. To cash account (Being the cash drawn for personal use)			500	500

LEDGER ACCOUNTS

Cash Book

Dr. *Cr.*

Date	*Receipts*	*L.F.*	*Cash (Rs.)*	*Bank (Rs.)*	*Date*	*Payments*	*L.F.*	*Cash (Rs.)*	*Bank (Rs.)*
2008					2008				
Jan. 1	To capital a/c		20,000		Jan. 3	By purchase a/c		500	
Jan. 5	To Murthy a/c		1,500		Jan. 4	By Gopal a/c		1,000	
Jan. 8	To commission a/c		300		Jan. 6	By furniture a/c		1,000	
Jan. 18	To cash a/c	C		250	Jan. 7	By wages a/c		250	
Jan. 20	To sales a/c		375		Jan. 12	By postage & telegrams		100	
					Jan. 15	By stationery a/c		100	
					Jan 18	By bank a/c	C	250	
					Jan. 22	By purchase a/c		500	
					Jan. 25	By salaries a/c		350	
					Jan. 28	By rent a/c		250	
					Jan. 31	By drawings a/c		500	
					Jan. 31	By balance c/d		17,375	250
			22,175	250				22,175	250

Note: The letter 'C' in the Ledger Folio column denotes a contra entry. This is an entry for which the debit and credit aspects are found in the cash book itself.

Purchase Book

Dr.				Cr.
Date	*Name of Supplier*	*Ledger Folio*	*Inward Invoice No.*	*Amount (Rs.)*
2008	Shyam			15,000
Jan. 2			Total	15,000

Purchase Returns Book

Dr.				Cr.
Date	*Name of Supplier*	*Ledger Folio*	*Debit Note No.*	*Amount (Rs.)*
2008				
Jan. 9	Shyam			100
			Total	100

Sales Book

Date	*Customer*	*Invoice No.*	*Amount (Rs.)*
2008			
Jan. 10	Kamal		5,000
		Total	5,000

Sales Return Book

Dr.				Cr.
Date	*Name of Customer*	*Ledger Folio*	*Outward Invoice No.*	*Amount (Rs.)*
2008				
Jan. 12	Kamal			250
			Total	250

GENERAL LEDGER

Capital Account

2008		(Rs.)	2008		(Rs.)
Jan. 31	To balance c/d	20,000	Jan. 1	By cash a/c	20,000
		20,000			20,000
			Feb. 1	By balance b/d	20,000

Shyam's Account

2008		(Rs.)	2008		(Rs.)
Jan. 9	To Purchase returns	100	Jan. 2	By purchase a/c	15,000
Jan. 31	To balance c/d	14,900			
		15,000			15,000
			Feb. 1	By balance b/d	14,900

Purchases Account

Dr. Cr.

2008		(Rs.)	2008		(Rs.)
Jan. 2	To Shyam a/c	15,000	Jan. 31	By balance c/d	16,000
Jan. 3	To cash	500			
Jan. 22	To cash	500			
		16,000			16,000
Feb. 1	By balance b/d	16,000			16,000

Sales Account

Dr. Cr.

2008		(Rs.)	2008		(Rs.)
Jan. 31	To balance c/d	5,375	Jan. 10	By Kamal a/c	5,000
			Jan. 20	By cash	375
		5,375			5,375
			Feb. 1	By balance b/d	5,375

Purchase Returns Accounts

Dr. Cr.

2008		(Rs.)	2008		(Rs.)
Jan. 31	To balance c/d	100	Jan. 9	By Shyam a/c	100
		100			100
			Feb. 1	By balance b/d	100

Sales Returns Account

Dr. Cr.

2008		(Rs.)	2008	(Rs.)	
Jan. 12	To Kamal a/c	250	Jan. 31	By balance c/d	250
		250			250
Feb. 1	To balance b/d	250			250

Gopal's Accounts

Dr. Cr.

2008		(Rs.)	2008		(Rs.)
Jan. 4	To cash a/c	1,000	Jan. 31	By balance c/d	1,000
		1,000			1,000
Feb. 1	To balance b/d	1,000			

Wages Account

Dr. Cr.

2008		(Rs.)	2008		(Rs.)
Jan. 7	To cash a/c	250	Jan. 31	By balance c/d	250
		250			250
Feb. 1	To balance b/d	250			

Commission Received Account

Dr.					Cr.
2008		(Rs.)	2008		(Rs.)
Jan. 31	To balance c/d	300	Jan. 8	By cash a/c	300
		300			300
			Feb. 1	By balance b/d	300

Kamal's Account

Dr.					Cr.
2008		(Rs.)	2008		(Rs.)
Jan. 10	To sales a/c	5,000	Jan. 12	By sales returns a/c	250
		5,000	Jan. 31	By balance c/d	4,750
Feb 1	To balance b/d	4,750			5,000

Postage and Telegrams Account

Dr.					Cr.
2008		(Rs.)	2008		(Rs.)
Jan. 11	To cash a/c	100	Jan. 31	By balance c/d	100
		100			100
Feb. 1	To balance b/d	100			

Stationery Account

Dr.					Cr.
2008		(Rs.)	2008		(Rs.)
Jan. 15	To cash a/c	100	Jan. 31	By balance c/d	100
		100			100
Feb. 1	To balance b/d	100			

Salaries Account

Dr.					Cr.
2008		(Rs.)	2008		(Rs.)
Jan. 25	To cash a/c	350	Jan. 31	By balance c/d	350
		350			350
Feb. 1	To balance b/d	350			

Rent Account

Dr.					Cr.
2008		(Rs.)	2008		(Rs.)
Jan. 28	To cash a/c	250	Jan. 31	By balance c/d	250
		250			250
Feb. 1	To balance b/d	250			

Drawing Account

Dr. *Cr.*

2008		*(Rs.)*	2008		*(Rs.)*
Jan. 31	To cash a/c	500	Jan. 31	By balance c/d	500
		500			500
Feb. 1	To balance b/d	500			

Murthy's Account

Dr. *Cr.*

2008		*(Rs.)*	2008		*(Rs.)*
Jan. 31	To balance c/d	1,500	Jan. 5	By cash a/c	1,500
		1,500			1,500
			Feb. 1	To balance b/d	1,500

Furniture Account

Dr. *Cr.*

2008		*(Rs.)*	2008		*(Rs.)*
Jan. 6	To cash a/c	1,000	Jan. 3	By balance c/d	1,000
		1,000			1,000
Feb. 1	To balance b/d	1,000			

Illustration 2:

Enter the following into sales book and show the ledger postings:

25.6.2008 Sold to Ladies Corner, 5 bales of Laxmi sari @ Rs. 200 per sari *less* trade discount of 20%. Each bale contained 100 pieces of sari measuring 6 meters each. Excise duty of 10%, sales tax 5%, octroi 15 paise per meter.

30.6.2008 Sold to Mahila Mahal, 3,000 piece of blouse @ Rs. 36 per dozen. Blouses were sent in packets, each containing 10 units. Extra charge was levied for packing Rs. 5 per packet.

2.7.2008 Sold to Lahana Dress Co., 50 ladies coats @ Rs. 150 each less trade discount of 15%. Other charges levied Rs. 200.

Solution:

Sales Book

Date	*Particulars*	*L.F.*	*Details (Rs.)*	*Amount (Rs.)*
2008				
June 25	Ladies Corner			
	5 Bales of Laxmi sari @ 200 per sari; each bale			
	contains 100 saries measuring 6 m. each		1,00,000	
	Less discount 20%		20,000	
			80,000	
	Add excise duty 10% (10% of Rs. 1,00,000)		10,000	
	Sales tax 5% (5% of Rs. 80,000)		4,000	
	Octroi 15 paise per m.		450	94,450

June 30	Mahila Mahal 300 pieces of blouse @ Rs. 360 per dozen *Add:* Packing charges		90,000 1,500	91,500
July 2	Lahana Dress 50 Ladies coats @ R. 150 each *Less* Trade discount		7,500 1,125	
			6,375	
	Add: other charges		200	6,575
	Total			1,92,525

LEDGER

Ladies Corner

Dr. *Cr.*

Date	*Particulars*	*Amount*	*Date*	*Particulars*	*Amount*
2008 June 25	To sales a/c	Rs. 94,450			

Mahila Mahal

2008 Jun 30	To sales a/c	Rs. 91,500			

Lahana Dress

2008 July 2	To sales a/c	Rs. 6,575			

Sales A/c

			2008 July 2	By sundries	Rs. 1,92,525

Illustration 3:

Record the following transactions in the purchase day book and show the ledger postings:

(*a*) 16.10.2008 Purchased 480 kg butter from M/s. Dairy Product Co. @ Rs. 78 per kg less 15%.

(*b*) 20.12.2008 Purchased 56 kg ghee from Bharat Vegetable Products @ Rs. 120 per kg less 17.5%.

(*c*) 22.10.2008 Purchased 46 kg butter from Bazaar Milk Cooperative @ Rs. 72.5 a kg less 12.5%.

Solutions:

Purchases Book

Date	*Particulars*	*L.F.*	*Dr. Amt. (Rs.)*	*Cr. Amt. (Rs.)*
2008 Oct. 16	M/s. Dairy Products Co. 480 kg. Butter @ 78 per kg. *Less:* discount 15%		37,440 5,616	31,824
Oct. 20	Bharat Vegetable Products 56 kg. ghee @ Rs. 120 *Less:* discount 17.5%		6,720 1,176	5,544

Oct. 22	Bazar Milk Coop. Ltd. 46 kg. butter @ Rs. 72.5 per kg. *Less:* discount 12.5%	3,335 416.9	2,918
	Total		40,286

LEDGER

M/s. Dairy Products Co.

Date	Particulars	Amount	Date	Particulars	Amount
			2008 Oct. 16	*Dairy Products Co.* By purchases a/c	31,824
				M/s. Bharat Vegetable Products	
			2008 Oct. 20	By purchases a/c	5,544
				Bowbazaar Milk Co-op. Ltd.	
			2008 Oct. 22	By purchases a/c	2,918

Purchase A/c

Date	Particulars	Amount	Date	Particulars	Amount
2008 Oct. 31	To Sundries	40,286			

Illustration 4:

From the following, prepare return books, and show the ledger:

March 2008

5 Returned 10 shirts to Kundu Bros @ Rs. 50 each, less 10% trade discount

8 Kamal & Co. returned goods worth Rs. 1,500

9 Returned goods to A Roy, Rs. 750

12 Returned 60 packing boxes, Rs. 50 each, to J. Roy

14 S. Das returned 20 baba suits @ Rs. 120 each

15 Received return of blouse 30 piece @ Rs. 70 each from Silk House.

Solution:

Returns Inward Book

Date	Particulars	L.F.	Details	Total (Rs.)
2008 Mar. 8	Kamal & Co. Goods returned			1,500.00
Mar. 14	S. Das 20 baba suits @ 120			2,400.00
Mar. 15	Silk House 30 Blouse piece @ Rs. 70			2,100.00
	Total			6,000.00

Returns Outward Book

Date	Particulars	L.F.	Details	Total (Rs.)
Mar. 5	*Kundu Brothers*			
	10 shirt @ Rs. 50			500.00
	Less 10% trade discount			50.00
				450.00
Mar. 9	*A. Roy*			
	Goods returned			750.00
	J. Roy			
Mar. 12	60 packing boxes @ R. 50 each			3,000.00

LEDGER

Date	Particulars	L.F.	Amount	Date	Particulars	L.F.	Amount
				2008	Kamal & Co.		
				Mar. 8	By returns inward a/c		1,500
				2008	S. Das & Co.		
				Mar. 14	By returns inward a/c		2,400
				2008	Silk House		
				Mar. 15	By returns inwards a/c		2,100

Returns Inward A/c

2008							
Mar. 31	To Sundries		6,000				

Kundu Bros.

Date	Particulars	L.F.	Amount	Date	Particulars	L.F.	Amount
Mar. 5	To returns outwards		450.00				

A. Roy

Mar. 9	To returns outwards a/c		750.00				

J. Roy

Mar. 12	To returns outward a/c		3,000.00				

Returns Outward a/c

				2008			
				Mar. 31	By Sundries		4,200

Illustration 5:

From the following information, prepare a suitable Cash Book

April 2008		(Rs.)
1	Cash at hand	2,200
2	Cash at bank	8,700

3	Bought goods from Rahim	7,300
4	Cash sales banked	5,500
8	Sold goods to Das	8,200
9	Received cheque in full settlement of Das's a/c	8,000
10	Paid to settle Rahim's a/c	7,000
12	Purchased office furniture by cheque	3,500
13	Bought goods from P.K. Ghosh	10,400
15	Paid carriages	200
18	Bank collected dividend	500
20	Withdrawn from bank	2,000
25	Paid wages	1,500
2	Paid to P.K. Ghosh by cheque	1,000

Show also the Ledger accounts that will be prepared from the cash book.

Solution:

Cash Book

Date	*Particulars*	*L.F.*	*Dis. (Rs.)*	*Cash (Rs.)*	*Bank (Rs.)*	*Date*	*Particulars*	*L.F.*	*Dis. (Rs.)*	*Cash (Rs.)*	*Bank (Rs.)*
2008						2008					
Apr. 1	To balance b/d			2,200	8,700	Apr. 10	By Rahim a/c		300	—	7,000
Apr. 4	To Sales a/c				5,500	Apr. 12	By furniture a/c				3,500
Apr. 6	To Das		200		8,000	Apr. 15	By carriage a/c			200	
Apr. 8	To dividend a/c				500	Apr. 20	By cash a/c	C			2,000
Apr. 20	To bank a/c	C		2,000		Apr. 25	By wages a/c			1,500	
						Apr. 27	By P.K. Ghosh				1,000
						Apr. 30	By balance c/d			2,500	9,200
			200	4,200	22,700				300	4,200	22,700
May 1	To balance b/d			2,500	9,200						

LEDGER

Sales A/c

Date	*Particulars*	*L.F.*	*Amount*	*Date*	*Particulars*	*L.F.*	*Amount*
				2008			
				April 4	By bank a/c		5,500

Das A/c

April 8	To sales a/c		8,200	April 9	By bank a/c		8,000
				April 9	By discount a/c		200
			8,200				8,200

Rahim's A/c

April 10	To bank a/c		7,000	April 2	By purchase a/c		7,300
	To discount a/c		300				
			7,300				7,300

Furniture A/c

April 12	To bank a/c	3,500			

Carriage A/c

April 15	To cash a/c	200			

Wages A/c

April 25	To cash a/c	1,500			

P.K. Ghosh

April 27	To bank a/c	1,000			

Dividend A/c

			April 18	By bank a/c	Rs. 500

Discount Allowed a/c

	To Das	Rs. 200			

Discount Received A/c

				By Rahim	Rs. 1,300

Note: 1. Contra entries are not posted to ledger.
2. Purchases from Rahim and Sales to Das will be posted from purchases book and sales book, respectively.

PREPARATION OF TRIAL BALANCE

Illustration 6:

The following were the transactions of a firm dealing in furniture:

2008

1	Started business with cash	2,00,000
	Bank	8,00,000
	Furniture (goods)	5,00,000
3	Bought furniture from Ratan Bros.	2,00,000
4	Bought furniture for the office	1,00,000
6	Sold furniture to J. Mitra	2,00,000
8	Bought furniture	1,80,000
10	Returned furniture to Ratan Bros.	5,000
12	J. Mitra returned furniture	20,000
14	Paid taxi fare	1,000
15	Sold to J. Kabiraj furniture for Rs. 50,000 *Less* trade discount @ 10%	
17	Received commission from J. Das	1,500
18	Paid to Ratan Bros. by cheque	1,00,000
19	Sent to bank	20,000
17	Received a cheque of Rs. 42,500 from L. Kabiraj in full settlement of his account	
22	Received a cheque of Rs. 50,000 from J. Mitra and deposited the same into bank.	

23	Loan to Naren	15,000
24	J. Mitra's cheque dishonoured	
25	Furniture taken away for personal use	40,000
26	Received interest	1,000
27	Received dividend	2,500
29	Paid for postage stamps	500
30	Paid house rent by cheque	10,000
31	Cash withdrawn from bank	2,00,000
31	Paid salary	30,000
31	Paid for taxes	15,000

Journalise the above transaction in the books of the firm and show the ledger postings. Also prepare a trial balance as on March 31, 2008.

Solution:

JOURNAL

Date	*Particulars*		*L.F.*	*Dr.* (Rs.)	*Cr.* (Rs.)
Mar. 1	Cash a/c	Dr.		2,00,000	
	Bank a/c	Dr.		8,00,000	
	Stock a/c	Dr.		5,00,000	
	To capital a/c				15,00,000
	(Brought into the business as capital)				
Mar. 3	Purchases a/c	Dr.		2,00,000	
	To Ratan Bros.				2,00,000
	[Being the purchase of goods (furniture)]				
Mar. 4	Furniture a/c	Dr.		1,00,000	
	To Bank a/c				1,00,000
	(Being the purchase of furniture for office)				
Mar. 6	J. Mitra	Dr.		2,00,000	
	To Sales a/c				2,00,000
	(Being the sale of goods (furniture) to J. Mitra)				
Mar. 8	Purchase a/c	Dr.		1,80,000	
	To Bank a/c				1,80,000
	(Being the purchase of goods)				
Mar. 10	Ratan Bros.			5,000	
	To returns outward a/c				5,000
	(Being goods (furniture) returned to Ratan Bros.)				
Mar. 12	Returns inwards a/c	Dr.		20,000	
	To J. Mitra				20,000
	(Goods returned to J. Mitra)				
Mar. 14	Conveyance a/c	Dr.		1,000	
	To Cash a/c				1,000
	(Being the payment of Taxi Fare)				
Mar. 15	J. Kabiraj	Dr.		45,000	
	To Sales A/c				45,000
	(Being the sale of goods worth Rs. 50,000 to J. Kabiraj, trade discount being 10%)				

Date	Particulars		L.F.	Dr. Amount	Cr. Amount
Mar. 17	Bank a/c To commission (Received Commission from J. Das)	Dr.		1,500	1,500
Mar. 18	Ratan Bros. To Bank a/c (Being payment made to Ratan Bros.)	Dr.		1,00,000	1,00,000
Mar. 19	Bank a/c To cash a/c (Being money sent to Bank)	Dr.		20,000	20,000
Mar. 20	Bank a/c Discount a/c To J. Kaviraj (Being a cheque for Rs. 42,500 received from J. Kabiraj in full settlement of his account)	Dr. Dr.		42,500 2,500	45,000
Mar. 22	Bank a/c To J. Mitra (Being cheque received from J Mitra)	Dr.		50,000	50,000
Mar. 23	Loan to Naren a/c To bank a/c (Money given to Naren)	Dr.		15,000	15,000
Mar. 24	J. Mitra To bank a/c (Being the cheque of J. Mitra dishonoured)	Dr.		50,000	50,000
Mar. 25	Drawing a/c To stock (Being goods (furniture) taken for personal use)	Dr.		40,000	40,000
Mar. 26	Bank a/c To interest a/c (Being the interest received)	Dr.		1,000	1,000
Mar. 27.	Bank a/c To dividend a/c (Being the amount of dividend received)	Dr.		2,500	2,500
Mar. 29	Postage a/c To cash a/c (Payment for postage stamps)	Dr.		500	500
Mar. 30	Rent a/c To bank a/c (Being the payment of house rent)	Dr.		10,000	10,000
Mar. 31	Cash a/c To Bank a/c (Cash withdrawn from bank)	Dr.		2,00,000	2,00,000
Mar. 31	Salary a/c Tax a/c To Cash a/c (Being the payment for salary and taxes)	Dr. Dr.		30,000 15,000	45,000

LEDGER

Cash A/c

Date	Particulars	L.F.	Amount (Rs.)	Date	Particulars	L.F.	Amount (Rs.)
2008				2008			
Mar. 1	To capital a/c		2,00,000	Mar. 14	By Conveyance a/c		1,000
Mar. 31	To bank a/c		2,00,000	Mar. 19	By bank		20,000
				Mar. 29	By postage		500
				Mar. 31	By salary a/c		30,000
				Mar. 31	By taxes a/c		15,000
				Mar. 31	By balance c/d		3,33,500
			4,00,000				4,00,000
April 1	To balance b/d		3,33,500				

Bank A/c

Date	Particulars	L.F.	Amount (Rs.)	Date	Particulars	L.F.	Amount (Rs.)
Mar. 1	To capital a/c		8,00,000	Mar. 5	By furniture		1,00,000
Mar. 17	To commission a/c		1,500	Mar. 8	By purchase		1,80,000
Mar. 19	To cash a/c		20,000	Mar. 18	By Ratan Bros.		1,00,000
Mar. 20	To J Kabiraj		42,500	Mar. 23	By loan to Naren		15,000
Mar. 22	To J Mitra		50,000	Mar. 24	By J Mitra		50,000
Mar. 26	To interest a/c		1,000	Mar. 30	By rent a/c		10,000
Mar. 27	To dividend		2,500	Mar. 31	By cash a/c		2,00,000
				Mar. 31	By balance c/d		2,62,500
			9,17,500				9,17,500
April 1	To balance b/d		2,62,500				

Capital A/c

2008			2008		
Mar. 31	To balance c/d	15,00,000	Mar. 1	By cash	2,00,000
				By bank	8,00,000
				By stock	5,00,000
		15,00,000	April 1	By balance b/d	15,00,000

Stock A/c

Mar. 1	To capital a/c	5,00,000	Mar. 25	By drawings a/c	40,000
			Mar. 31	By balancing c/d	4,60,000
		5,00,000			5,00,000
April 1	To balance b/d	4,60,000			

Purchases A/c

Mar. 3	To Ratan Bros.	2,00,000	Mar. 31	By balance c/d	3,80,000
Mar. 8	To bank a/c	1,80,000			
		3,80,000			3,80,000
April 1	To balance b/d	3,80,000			

Ratan A/c

Date	Particulars	Amount	Date	Particulars	Amount
Mar. 10	To returns outward a/c	5,000	Mar. 3	By purchase a/c	2,00,000
Mar. 10	To bank a/c	1,00,000			
Mar. 31	To balance c/d	95,000			
		2,00,000			2,00,000
			April 1	By balance b/d	95,000

Furniture A/c

Date	Particulars	Amount	Date	Particulars	Amount
Mar. 5	To bank	1,00,000	Mar. 31	By balance c/d	1,00,000
April 1	To balance b/c	1,00,000			1,00,000

J. Mitra

Date	Particulars	Amount	Date	Particulars	Amount
Mar. 6	To sales a/c	2,00,000	Mar. 12	By returns inward a/c	20,000
Mar. 24	To bank a/c	50,000	Mar. 22	By bank a/c	50,000
			Mar. 31	By balance c/d	1,80,000
		2,50,000			2,50,000
April 1	To balance b/d	1,80,000			

Sales A/c

Date	Particulars	Amount	Date	Particulars	Amount
Mar. 31	To balance c/d	2,45,000	Mar. 6	By Mitra	2,00,000
			Mar. 15	By J. Kabiraj	45,000
		2,45,000			2,45,000
			April 1	By balance b/d	2,45,000

Returns Outward A/c

Date	Particulars	Amount	Date	Particulars	Amount
Mar. 31	To balance c/d	5,000	Mar. 10	By Ratan Bros.	5,000
			April 1	By balance b/d	5,000

Returns Inward A/c

Date	Particulars	Amount	Date	Particulars	Amount
Mar. 12	To J. Mitra	20,000	Mar. 31	By balance c/d	20,000
April 1	To balance b/d	20,000			

Conveyance A/c

Date	Particulars	Amount	Date	Particulars	Amount
Mar. 10	To cash a/c	1,000	Mar. 31	By balance c/d	1,000
April 1	To balance b/d	1,000			

J. Kabiraj

Date	Particulars	Amount	Date	Particulars	Amount
Mar. 15	To sales a/c	45,000	Mar. 20	By bank a/c	42,500
			Mar. 20	By discount a/c	2,500
		45,000			45,000

Commission A/c

Date	Particulars	Amount	Date	Particulars	Amount
Mar. 31	To balance c/d	1,500	Mar. 17	By bank a/c	1,500
			April 1	By balance b/d	1,500

Discount Allowed A/c

Mar. 20	To J. Kabiraj	2,500	Mar. 31	By balance c/d	2,500
April 1	To balance b/d	2,500			

Loan to Naren A/c

Mar. 23	To cash a/c	15,000	Mar. 31	By balance c/d	15,000
April 1	To balance b/d	15,000			

Drawings A/c

Mar. 25	To stock a/c	40,000	Mar. 31	By balance c/d	40,000
April 1	To balance b/d	40,000			

Interest A/c

Mar. 31	To balance c/d	1,000	Mar. 26	By bank	1,000
			April 1	By balance b/d	1,000

Dividend A/c

Mar. 31	To balance c/d	2,500	Mar. 27	By bank a/c	2,500
			April 1	By balance b/d	2,500

Postage A/c

Mar. 29	To cash a/c	500	Mar. 31	By balance c/d	500
Mar. 31	To balance b/d	500			

Rent A/c

Mar. 30	To bank a/c	10,000	Mar. 31	By balance c/d	10,000
April 1	To balance b/d	10,000			

Salary A/c

Mar. 31	To cash a/c	30,000	Mar. 31	By balance c/d	30,000
April 1	To balance b/d	30,000			

Taxes A/c

Mar. 31	To cash a/c	15,000	Mar. 31	By balance c/d	15,000
April 1	To balance b/d	15,000			

Trial Balance as on March 31, 2008

Particulars	*Dr. Balance (Rs.)*	*Cr. Balance (Rs.)*
Cash a/c	3,33,500	
Bank a/c	2,62,500	
Capital a/c		15,00,000
Stock a/c	4,60,000	
Purchase a/c	3,80,000	
Ratan Bros.		95,000
Furniture a/c	1,00,000	
J. Mitra	1,80,000	

Salary a/c	30,000	
Sales a/c		2,45,000
Returns outward a/c		5,000
Returns inward a/c	20,000	
Conveyance a/c	1,000	
Commission a/c		1,500
Discount a/c	2,500	
Loan to Naren a/c	15,000	
Drawings a/c	40,000	
Interest a/c		1,000
Dividend a/c		2,500
Postage a/c	500	
Rent a/c	10,000	
Taxes a/c	15,000	
Total	18,50,000	18,50,000

Illustration 7:

Journalise the following transactions, post them into the ledger and prepare a trial balance:

01.09.2008	Started business by bringing in cash worth Rs. 2,00,000 out of which paid into bank — Rs. 80,000
02.09.2008	Bought furniture for Rs. 20,000 and machinery Rs. 40,000.
03.09.2008	Purchased goods for Rs. 56,000.
06.09.2008	Sold goods for Rs. 32,000.
08.09.2008	Purchased goods from Jain & Co. on credit for Rs. 44,000.
10.09.2008	Paid telephone rent for the year by cheque Rs. 2,000.
11.09.2008	Bought one typewriter for Rs. 8,400 from Standard Typewriter Co. on credit.
15.09.2008	Sold goods to Shiva worth Rs. 48,000.
17.09.2008	Sold goods to Kumar for cash at Rs. 8,000.
19.09.2008	Amount withdrawn from bank for business use Rs. 6,000.
20.09.2008	Withdrew from bank for business use Rs. 14,000.
21.09.2008	Received cash from Shiva Rs. 47,600 and discount allowed Rs. 400.
22.09.2008	Paid into bank Rs. 23,200.
23.09.2008	Bought 100 shares in PQ & Co. Ltd. at Rs. 120 and brokerage paid Rs. 80.
25.09.2008	Goods worth Rs. 4,000 which were defective were returned to Jain & Co. and the balance amount due to them was settled by issuing a cheque in their favour.
28.09.2008	Bought goods worth Rs. 8,400 from Peter and supplied them to Paul for Rs. 12,000
28.09.2008	Sold 40 shares of PQ & Co. Ltd. at Rs. 130 per share and brokerage paid Rs. 80.
30.09.2008	Paul returned goods worth Rs. 400.
	Goods worth Rs. 280 returned to Peter.
	Issued a cheque for Rs. 4,000 in favour of the landlord towards rent.
30.09.2008	Paid salaries to staff Rs. 6,000.
	Received from travelling salesman Rs. 8,000 for goods sold by him after deducting his travelling expenses Rs. 400.
30.09.1999	Paid for donations Rs. 402.
	Stationery Rs. 1,800.
	Postage Rs. 996.

Journal Entries

Date	Particulars		L.F.	Dr. (Rs.)	Cr. (Rs.)
1.9.2008	Cash a/c	Dr.		2,00,000	
	To capital a/c				2,00,000
	(Being cash brought in as capital)				
1.9.2008	Bank account	Dr.		80,000	
	To cash a/c				80,000
	(Being cash deposited in bank)				
2.9.2008	Furniture account	Dr.		20,000	
	Machinery account	Dr.		40,000	
	To Cash amount				60,000
	(Being furniture & machinery purchased)				
3.9.2008	Purchases account	Dr.		56,000	
	To cash account				56,000
	(Goods purchased for cash)				
6.9.2008	Cash account	Dr.		32,000	
	To sales account				32,000
	(Goods purchased for cash)				
8.9.2008	Purchases account	Dr.		44,000	
	To Jain & Co. a/c				44,000
	(Goods purchased on credit)				
10.9.2008	Telphone rent account	Dr.		2,000	
	To bank account				2,000
	(Telephone rent paid by cheque)				
11.9.2008	Office equipment account	Dr.		8,400	
	To Standard Typewriter Co. account				8,400
	(Typewriter purchased on credit)				
15.9.2008	Shiva's account	Dr.		48,000	
	To sales account				48,000
	(Goods sold on credit)				
17.9.2008	Cash account	Dr.		8,000	
	To sales account				8,000
	(Goods sold for cash)				
19.9.2008	Drawing account	Dr.		6,000	
	To bank account				6,000
	(Amounts withdrawn from bank for personal use)				
20.9.2008	Cash account	Dr.		14,000	
	To bank account				14,000
	(Cash withdrawn for business use)				
21.9.2008	Cash account	Dr.		47,600	
	Discount	Dr.		400	
	To Shiva's account				48,000
	(Amount received from Shiva and discount allowed)				
22.9.2008	Bank account	Dr.		23,200	
	To cash account				23,200
	(Cash paid into bank)				

Date	Particulars		Dr.	Cr.
23.9.2008	Investment account To Cash a/c (Purchase of 100 shares in PQ & Co, Ltd. at Rs. 120 and brokerage paid Rs. 80, *i.e.,* Rs. 120.80 per share as cost of investment)	Dr.	12,080	12,080
25.9.2008	Jain & Co. account To purchase returns account To bank account (Defective goods worth Rs. 4,000 returned to Jain & Co. and balance due settled by cheque)	Dr.	44,000	4,000 40,000
28.9.2008	Cash account To investment account To profit on sale of investment account (Sale of 40 shares at Rs. 130 per share and brokage paid Rs. 80)	Dr.	5,120	4,832 288
28.9.2008	Purchase account To Peter's account (Goods purchased from Peter on credit)	Dr.	8,400	8,400
28.9.2008	Paul's account To sales account (Goods sold on credit to Paul)	Dr.	12,000	12,000
30.9.2008	Sales returns account To Paul's account (Defective goods returned by Paul)	Dr.	400	400
30.9.2008	Peter's account To purchase returns account (Defective goods returned to Peter)	Dr.	280	280
30.9.2008	Rent account To bank a/c (Issued a cheque to the landlord towards rent)	Dr.	4,000	4,000
30.9.2008	Salaries a/c To cash a/c (Being salaries paid to staff)	Dr.	6,000	6,000
30.9.2008	Cash a/c Travelling expenses a/c To sales a/c (Cash received from salesman for goods sold by him less travelling expenses)	Dr. Dr.	8,000 400	8,400
30.9.2008	Donation a/c Stationery a/c Postage a/c To cash a/c (Amounts paid towards donation, stationery and postage)	Dr. Dr. Dr.	402 800 996	2,198

Note: Sold 40 shares of PQ & Co. Ltd. at Rs. 130 per share and brokerage paid Rs. 80.

(*i*) Cash a/c Dr. = (Rs. 130 × 40 shares) – Rs. 80
= Rs. 5,120

(*ii*) Profit on sale of investment

Total profit on sale of investment	= Rs. 400
Less: Brokerage paid at the time of sale	= – 80
	320
Less: Brokerage paid at the time of purchase and added to cost of investments (40 shares × Rs. 0.80)	– 32
	Rs. 288

(*iii*) Investments a/c

(40 shares × Rs. 120.80) = Rs. 4,832

Cost of investment = Rs. 120 + Brokerage paid per share

= Rs. 120 + 80 = Rs. 120.80 per share

LEDGER ACCOUNT

Cash A/c

Date	*Particulars*	*Amount (Rs.)*	*Date*	*Particulars*	*Amount (Rs.)*
01.9.2008	To capital a/c	2,00,000	01.9.2008	By bank a/c	80,000
06.9.2008	To sales a/c	32,000	02.9.2008	By furniture a/c	20,000
17.9.2008	To sales a/c	8,000	02.9.2008	By machinery a/c	40,000
20.9.2008	To bank a/c	14,000	03.9.2008	By purchase a/c	56,000
21.9.2008	To Shiva's a/c	47,600	22.9.2008	By bank a/c	23,200
28.9.2008	To investment a/c	4,832	23.9.2008	By investment a/c	12,080
28.9.2008	To profit on sales of investment a/c	288	30.9.2008	By salaries a/c	6,000
			30.9.2008	By donation a/c	402
30.9.2008	To sales a/c	8,000	30.9.2008	By stationery a/c	1,800
			30.9.2008	By postage a/c	996
			30.9.2008	By balance c/d	74,242
		3,14,720			3,14,720

Purchase Returns A/c

30.9.2008	To balance c/d	4,280	25.9.2008	By Jain & Co. a/c	4,000
			30.9.2008	By Peter's a/c	280
		4,280			4,280

SUNDRY DEBTORS A/c

Shiva's A/c

15.9.2008	To sales a/c	48,000	21.9.2008	By sales return a/c	47,600
			21.9.2008	By discount a/c	400
		48,000			48,000

Paul's A/c

28.9.2008	To sales a/c	12,000	30.9.2008	By sales return a/c	400
				By balance c/d	11,600
		12,000			12,000

Jain & Co. A/c

25.9.2008	To purchase return a/c	4,000	8.9.2008	By purchase a/c	44,000
25.9.2008	To bank a/c	40,000			
		44,000			44,000

Peter's A/c

30.9.2008	To purchase return a/c	280	28.9.2008	By purchase a/c	8,400
	To balance c/d	8,120			
		8,400			8,400

Purchases A/c

3.9.2008	To cash book	56,000	30.9.2008	By balance c/d	1.08.400
8.9.2008	To Jain & Co.	44,000			
28.9.2008	To Peter's a/c	8,400			
		1,08,400			1,08,400
1.10.2008	To balance b/d	1,08,400			

Standard Typewriter

	To balance c/d	8,400	11.9.2008	By office equipment	8,400
		8,400			8,400
				By balance b/d	8,400

Drawing A/c

		Rs.			*Rs.*
19.9.2008	To bank a/c	6,000	30.9.2008	By balance c/d	6,000
	Total	6,000			6,000

Discount A/c

		Rs.			*Rs.*
19.9.2008	To Shiva's a/c	400	30.9.2008	By balance c/d	400
	Total	400			400

Investment A/c

		Rs.			*Rs.*
23.9.2008	To cash a/c	12,080	28.9.2008	By cash a/c	4,832
			30.9.2008	By balance c/d	7,248
	Total	12,080			12,080

Profit on Investment A/c

		Rs.			*Rs.*
30.9.2008	To balance c/d	288	28.9.2008	By cash a/c	288
	Total	288			288

Rent A/c

		Rs.			*Rs.*
30.9.2008	To bank a/c	4,000	30.9.2008	By balance c/d	4,000
	Total	4,000			4,000

Travelling Expenses A/c

		Rs.			*Rs.*
30.9.2008	To sales a/c	400	30.9.2008	By balance c/d	400
	Total	400			400

Donation A/c

		Rs.			*Rs.*
30.9.2008	To cash a/c	402	30.9.2008	By balance c/d	402
	Total	402			402

Stationery A/c

		Rs.			*Rs.*
30.9.2008	To cash a/c	1,800	30.9.2008	By balance c/d	1,800
	Total	1,800			1,800

Postage A/c

		Rs.			*Rs.*
30.9.2008	To cash a/c	996	30.9.2008	By balance c/d	996
	Total	996			996

Salaries A/c

		Rs.			*Rs.*
30.9.2008	To cash a/c	6,000		By balance c/d	6,000
	Total	6,000			6,000
	To Balance b/d	6,000			

Sales A/c

		Rs.			*Rs.*
30.9.2008	To balance c/d	1,08,400	6.9.2008	By Cash a/c	32,000
			15.9.2008	By Shiva's a/c	48,000
			17.9.2008	By Cash a/c	8,000
			28.9.2008	By Paul's a/c	12,000
			30.9.2008	By Cash a/c	8,000
			30.9.2008	By Travelling expenses a/c	400
	Total	1,08,400			1,08,400

Sales Return A/c

		Rs.			Rs.
30.9.2008	To Paul's a/c	400	30.9.2008	By balance c/d	400
	Total	400			400

Furniture A/c

		Rs.			Rs.
2.9.2008	To cash a/c	20,000	30.9.2008	By balance c/d	20,000
	Total	20,000			20,000

Machinery A/c

		Rs.			Rs.
2.9.2008	To cash a/c	40,000	30.9.2008	By balance c/d	40,000
	Total	40,000			40,000

Capital A/c

		Rs.			Rs.
30.9.2008	To balance c/d	2,00,000	1.9.2008	By cash a/c	2,00,000
	Total	2,00,000			2,00,000

Telephone Rent A/c

		Rs.			Rs.
10.9.2008	To bank a/c	2,000	30.9.2008	By balance c/d	2,000
	Total	2,000			2,000

Office Equipment A/c

		Rs.			Rs.
11.9.2008	To Standard Typewriter Co. a/c	8,400	20.9.2008	By balance c/d	8,400
	Total	8,400			8,400

Bank A/c

		Rs.			Rs.
1.9.2008	To cash a/c	80,000	10.9.2008	By telephone rent a/c	2,000
22.9.2008	To cash a/c	23,200	19.9.2008	By drawings	6,000
			20.9.2008	By cash a/c	14,000
			25.9.2008	By Jain & Co.	40,000
			30.9.2008	By rent	4,000
			30.9.2008	By balance c/d	37,200
		1,03,200			1,03,200

Trial Balance as on 30.09.2008

Particulars	*Debit Amount (Rs.)*	*Credit Amount (Rs.)*
Cash	74,242	
Capital		2,00,000
Bank	37,200	
Furniture	20,000	
Machinery	40,000	
Telephone rent	2,000	
Office Equipment	8,400	
Standard Typewriter		8,400
Discount	400	
Drawings	6,000	
Investments	7,248	
Profit on investments		288
Peter		8,120
Paul	11,600	
Rent	4,000	
Salaries	6,000	
Travelling expenses	400	
Donations	402	
Stationery	1,800	
Postage	996	
Purchase	1,08,400	
Purchase returns		4,280
Sales		1,08,400
Sales returns	400	
Total	3,29,488	3,29,488

Illustration 8:

The balance sheet of a company as on March 31, 2008 is given below:

	Rs.	*Rs.*
Cash	21,000	
Accounts receivable	45,000	
Inventory	5,000	
Prepaid rent	1,000	
Accounts payable		12,500
Share capital		50,000
Profit and loss account		9,500
Total	72,000	72,000

Following is the summary of transactions that occurred during April:

(*a*) Collections of accounts receivable Rs. 44,000

(*b*) Payments of accounts payable Rs. 12,000

(*c*) Acquisition of inventory on credit Rs. 40,000

(*d*) Inventory costing Rs. 35,000 was sold on credit for Rs. 42,500

(*e*) Recognition of rent expense for April Rs. 500

(*f*) Wages paid in cash for April Rs. 4.000

(*g*) Dividends declared and disbursed to shareholders in April Rs. 9,000

Prepare all ledger accounts after including the opening balances as on March 31

LEDGER ACCOUNTS

Cash A/c

Dr. *Cr.*

Date	*Particulars*	*Rs.*	*Date*	*Particulars*	*Rs.*
1.4.2008	To balance b/d	21,000	April	By a/c's payable	12,000
	To a/c's receivable	44,000		By wages	4,000
				By dividends	9,000
				By Balance c/d	40,000
	Total	65,000			65,000

Inventory A/c

Date	*Particulars*	*Rs.*	*Date*	*Particulars*	*Rs.*
1.4.2008	To balance b/d	5,000	April	By customer's a/c	35,000
	To supplier	40,000		By balance c/d	10,000
	Total	45,000			45,000

Account Payable A/c

Date	*Particulars*	*Rs.*	*Date*	*Particulars*	*Rs.*
April	To cash	12,000	1.4.2008	Balance b/d	12,500
	Balance c/d	40,500	April	By inventory	40,000
	Total	52,500			52,500

Profit and Loss A/c

Date	*Particulars*	*Rs.*	*Date*	*Particulars*	*Rs.*
	To rent expenses	500	1.4.2008	By balance b/d	9,500
	To wages expense	4,000		By customer's a/c	7,500
	To dividends	9,000		(Profit on sale of inventory)	
	To balance c/d	3,500			
	Total	17,000			17,000

Accounts Receivable Accounts

Date	*Particulars*	*Rs.*	*Date*	*Particulars*	*Rs.*
1.4.2008	To balance b/d	45,000	April	By cash	44,000
	To inventory a/c	35,000		By balance c/d	43.500
	To P & L a/c	7,500			
	(Profit on sale of inventory)				
	Total	87,500			87,500

Wages Accounts

Date	*Particulars*	*Rs.*	*Date*	*Particulars*	*Rs.*
April	To cash	4,000	1.4.2008	By P & L a/c	4,000
	Total	4,000			4,000

Prepaid Rent A/c

Date	Particulars	Rs.	Date	Particulars	Rs.
1.3.2008	To balance b/d	1,000	30.4.2008	By rent a/c	500
				Balance c/d	500
	Total	1,000			1,000

Share Capital A/c

Date	Particulars	Rs.	Date	Particulars	Rs.
	To balance c/d	50,000	1.4.2008	By balance b/d	50,000
	Total	50,000			50,000

Rent Expenses A/c

Date	Particulars	Rs.	Date	Particulars	Rs.
	To Prepaid a/c	500		By P & L a/c	500
	Total	500			500

Dividend A/c

Date	Particulars	Rs.	Date	Particulars	Rs.
April 1	To cash a/c	9,000		By P & L A/c	9,000
		9,000			9,000

Trial Balance as on April 30, 2008

Particulars	Amount Rs.	Amount Rs.
Cash	40,000	
Accounts receivable	43,500	
Inventory	10,000	
Prepaid rent	500	
Accounts payable		40,500
Share capital		50,000
Profit & Loss account		3,500
	94,000	94,000

Illustration 9:

From the following list of balances, prepare a trial balance as on 30.6.2008:

Particulars	(Rs.)
1. Opening stock	3,600
2. Wages	2,000
3. Sales	24,000
4. Bank loan	880
5. Coal and Coke	600
6. Purchase	15,000
7. Repairs	400
8. Carriage	300

9. Income-tax	300
10. Debtors	4,000
11. Leasehold premises	1,200
12. Cash in hand	40
13. Plant & Machinery	1,500
14. Loose tools	360
15. Lighting	460
16. Creditors	1,600
17. Capital	8,000
18. Miscellaneous receipts	120
19. Office salaries	500
20. Office furniture	120
21. Patents	200
22. Goodwill	3,000
23. Cash at bank	1,020

Solution:

Trial Balance as on 30.6.2008

S. No.	*Head of Accounts*	*L.F.*	*Debit Balance Rs.*	*Credit Balance Rs.*
1.	Opening stock		3,600	
2.	Wages		2,000	
3.	Sales			24,000
4.	Bank loan			880
5.	Coal and coke		600	
6.	Purchases		15,000	
7.	Repairs		400	
8.	Carriage		300	
9.	Income tax		300	
10.	Debtors		4,000	
11.	Leasehold premises		1,200	
12.	Cash in hand		40	
13.	Plant & Machinery		1,500	
14.	Loose tools		360	
15.	Lighting		460	
16.	Creditors			1,600
17.	Capital			8,000
18.	Miscellaneous receipts			120
19.	Office salaries		500	
20.	Office furniture		120	
21.	Patents		200	
22.	Goodwill		3,000	
23.	Cash at bank		1,020	
	Total		34,600	34,600

Illustration 10:

From the following ledger accounts balances prepare a trial balance as on 31.12.2008

Particulars	*(Rs.)*
1. Opening stock	7,800
2. Freehold premises	15,000
3. Plant and Machinery	4,500
4. Wages	1,000
5. Sundry debtors	6,000
6. Carriage inwards	90
7. Factory expenses	800
8. Royalty	100
9. Purchase of raw materials	7,500
10. Carriage outward	100
11. Factory rent	700
12. Capital	8,000
13. Discount allowed	400
14. Discount received	360
15. Sundry creditors	2,000
16. Insurance	200
17. Bad debt reserve	150
18. Commission received	1,500
19. Commission paid	500
20. Bad debts	150
21. Office expenses	750
22. Salaries	1,000
23. Travelling expenses	100
24. Legal expenses	100
25. Cash at bank	420
26. Cash in hand	400
27. Loan taken	3,000
28. Office taken	3,000
29. Sales (net)	33,000

Solution:

Trial Balance as on 31.12.2008

S. No.	*Head of Accounts*	*L.F.*	*Debit Balance Rs.*	*Credit Balance Rs.*
1.	Opening stock		7,800	
2.	Freehold premises		15,000	
3.	Plant and machinery		4,500	
4.	Wages		1,000	
5.	Sundry debtors		6,000	
6.	Carriage inwards		90	
7.	Carriage outwards		100	
8.	Factory expenses		800	
9.	Royalty		100	

10.	Purchase of raw materials		7,500	
11.	Factory rent		700	
12.	Capital			8,000
13.	Discount		400	
14.	Discount			360
15.	Sundry creditors			2,000
16.	Insurance		200	
17.	Bad debt reserve			150
18.	Commission		500	1,500
19.	Bad debts		150	
20.	Office expenses		750	
21.	Salaries		1,000	
22.	Travelling expenses		100	
23.	Legal expenses		100	
24.	Cash at bank		420	
25.	Cash in hand		400	
26.	Loan taken			3,000
27.	Office rent		400	
28.	Sales			33,000
	Total		48,010	48,010

Illustration 11:

The accountant of a business firm wrongly prepared the following trial balance. You are required to draw-up a trial balance correctly stating reasons in brief.

S. No.	*Head of Accounts*	*L.F.*	*Debit Balance Rs.*	*Credit Balance Rs.*
1.	Capital			60,000
2.	Stock at commencement		5,000	
3.	Discount allowed			500
4.	Commission received			700
5.	Fixed assets			60,000
6.	Sales		85,000	
7.	Purchase			45,000
8.	Return outwards			1,000
9.	Returns inwards		2,000	
10.	Carriage inwards			600
11.	Carriage outwards			700
12.	Wages and salary		25,000	
13.	Bills receivable		7,000	
14.	Debtors		9,000	
15.	Bills payable			7,000
16.	Rent		3,000	
17.	Interest paid			2,000
18.	Cash		800	
19.	Creditors		6,900	
20.	Stock at the end		33,800	
	Total		1,77,500	1,77,500

Solution:

Trial Balance as on ...

S. No.	*Head of Accounts*	*L.F.*	*Debit Balance* Rs.	*Credit Balance* Rs.
1.	Capital			60,000
2.	Stock at commencement		5,000	
3.	Discount allowed		500	
4.	Commission received			700
5.	Fixed assets		60,000	
6.	Sales			85,000
7.	Purchase		45,000	
8.	Returns outwards			1,000
9.	Returns inwards		2,000	
10.	Carriage inwards		600	
11.	Carriage outwards		700	
12.	Wages and salary		25,000	
13.	Bills receivable		7,000	
14.	Debtors		9,000	
15.	Bills payable			7,000
16.	Rent		3,000	
17.	Interest paid		2,000	
18.	Cash		800	
19.	Creditors			6,900
	Total		1,60,600	1,60,600

Reasons:

1. Discount allowed is an expense and therefore it has a debit balance.
2. Fixed assets always reflect debit balance, because assets coming in are debited.
3. Sales has credit balance.
4. Purchases has a debit balance.
5. Carriage inwards is an expense and has a debit balance.
6. Carriage outwards is an expense and has a debit balance.
7. Interest paid is an expense and has a debit balance.
8. Creditor is a liability and has a credit balance.
9. Closing stock is not an account; so it cannot have any balance, and consequently, it does not find a place in the trial balance. Only when closing stock is adjusted against purchases, it appears in the trial balance.

Illustration 12:

The trial balance of a business firm was as follows as on March 31, 2008

Particulars	*Debit Balance Rs.*	*Credit Balance Rs.*
Salary	1,600	
Rent	14,500	
Sundry debtors	21,500	
Loans from Mrs. Ravi Kumar		30,000
Cash	2,000	
Sundry creditors		13,500
Interest paid in part on loan	600	
Mr. Ravi Kumar's capital		16,250
Sales		37,900
Furniture and fixture	10,000	
Purchases	46,250	
Insurance premium	1,200	
Total	97,650	97,650

The following additional information has been given in addition to trial balance.

1. Salary due to assistants on Mar. 31 is Rs. 400.
2. Rent includes a deposit of Rs. 12,500 refundable by the landlord when the premises are vacated.
3. Sundry debtors represent the amounts invoiced but not yet collected, except for a sum of Rs. 1,100 shown as due from Mr. Anil in respect of goods sent to him on approval basis. Mr. Anil has to exercise his option by January 5, 2008, cost of the goods is Rs. 900.
4. Loan taken on January 5, 2008 carries simple interest at the rate of 12 per cent per year. The first instalment of Rs. 7,500 including interest falls for payment on May, 1 2008.
5. Inventory of goods on March 31, 2008 is Rs. 7,500 (cost.)
6. All items of furniture were bought on January 1, 2008. They are expected to be useful for 20 years at the end of which they are to be scrapped.
7. Insurance premium for the period December 1, 2007 to November 30, 2008, has been paid.

Required:

(*a*) Post the entries to ledger accounts

(*b*) Prepare adjusted trial balance as on March 31, 2008

(*c*) Ledger Accounts

Salary A/c

Date	*Particulars*	*Rs.*	*Date*	*Particular*	*Rs.*
	To balance b/d	1,600		By balance c/d	2,000
	To outstanding salaries a/c	400			
	Total	2,000			2,000

Rent Account

Date	Particulars	Rs.	Date	Particular	Rs.
	To balance b/d	14,500		By rent deposit	12,500
				By balance c/d	2,000
	Total	14,500			14,500

Sundry Debtor's Account

Date	Particulars	Rs.	Date	Particular	Rs.
	To balance b/d	21,500		By sales a/c	1,100
				By balance c/d	20,400
	Total	21,500			21,500

Loan Account

Date	Particulars	Rs.	Date	Particular	Rs.
	To balance c/d	30,000		By balance b/d	30,000
	Total	30,000			30,000

Interest A/c

Date	Particulars	Rs.	Date	Particular	Rs.
	To balance b/d	600		By balance c/d	900
	To outstanding	300			
	Total	900			900

Creditors Account

Date	Particulars	Rs.	Date	Particular	Rs.
	To balance c/d	13,500		By balance b/d	13.500
	Total	13,500			13,500

Capital Account

Date	Particulars	Rs.	Date	Particular	Rs.
	To balance c/d	16,250		By balance b/d	16,250
	Total	16,250			16,250

Furniture & Fixture Account

Date	Particulars	Rs.	Date	Particular	Rs.
	To balance b/d	10,000		By dep. a/c	125
				By balance c/d	9,875
	Total	10,000			10,000

Sales Account

Date	Particulars	Rs.	Date	Particular	Rs.
	To Sundry debtors a/c	1,100		By balance b/d	37,900
	To balance c/d	36,800			
	Total	37,900			37,900

Insurance Premium Account

Date	Particulars	Rs.	Date	Particular	Rs.
	To balance b/d	1,200		By insurance premium advance a/c	800
				By balance c/d	400
	Total	1,200			1,200

Cash Account

Date	Particulars	Rs.	Date	Particular	Rs.
	To balance b/d	2,000		By balance c/d	2,000
		2,000			2,000
	To balance b/d	2,000			

Purchase Account

Date	Particulars	Rs.	Date	Particular	Rs.
	To balance b/d	46,250		By closing stock a/c	18,400
				By balance c/d	27,850
	Total	46,250			46,250

Rent Deposit Account

Date	Particulars	Rs.	Date	Particular	Rs.
	To rent a/c	12,500		By balance c/d	12,500
	Total	12,500			12,500

Outstanding Salary Account

Date	Particulars	Rs.	Date	Particular	Rs.
	To balance c/d	400		By salary a/c	400
	Total	400			400

Outstanding Interest Account

Date	Particulars	Rs.	Date	Particular	Rs.
	To balance c/d	300		By interest	300
	Total	300			300

Depreciation Account

Date	Particulars	Rs.	Date	Particular	Rs.
	To furniture & fixtures a/c	125		By balance c/d	125
	Total	125			125

Closing Stock Account

Date	Particulars	Rs.	Date	Particular	Rs.
	To purchase a/c	18,400		By balance c/d	18,400

Insurance Premium Paid in Advance Account

Date	Particulars	Rs.	Date	Particular	Rs.
	To insurance Premium a/c	800		By balance c/d	800
		800			800

(b) Adjusted Trial Balane as on March 31, 2008

S. No.	Head of Accounts	L.F.	Debit Balance Rs.	Credit Balance Rs.
1.	Salary account		2,000	
2.	Rent account		2,000	
3.	Sundry debtors account		20,400	
4.	Loan account			30,000
5.	Cash account		2,000	
6.	Sundry creditors account			13,500
7.	Interest account		900	
8.	capital account			16,250
9.	Furniture & fixtures a/c		9,875	
10.	Sales account			36,800
11.	Insurance premium a/c		400	
12.	Purchase account		27,850	
13.	Rent deposit account		12,500	
14.	Outstanding Salary a/c			400
15.	Outstanding interest a/c			300
16.	Depreciation account		125	
17.	Insurance premium paid in advance account		800	
18.	Closing stock account		18,400	
			97,250	97,250

Note: 1. Goods sent on approval should not be treated as sales. The cost of goods with the customers should be treated as stock and is to be added with the closing stock. The sales of such goods should be deducted from sales and sundry debtors.

THEORY QUESTIONS

1. What is the objective of posting?
2. Distinguish between a journal and a ledger. Explain their functions.
3. Explain the terms ledger and trial balance. What are the reasons for preparing a trial balance?
4. What is trial balance? What are the objectives of preparing a trial balance?
5. "A trial balance is a list showing all account titles in the ledger and the total of debits and credits in each account." Do you agree with this statement? Why or why not?
6. What type of errors could cause a trial balance not to balance?
7. A trial balance may be in balance but the accounts may be incorrect. How is this possible?
8. "If a trial balance tallies it can be concluded that there are no errors in the books of accounts." Coment.
9. What do you understand by posting of a transaction?

10. How would you post cash book and petty cash book?
11. How would you post the transactions recorded in the following books:
    (*i*) Purchases books
    (*ii*) Sales book
    (*iii*) Journal
    (*iv*) Bills receivable books
    (*v*) Bills payable book
12. A number of events common to the accounting function of a business entity are presented below. Prepare a list of these events as they would occur in their logical order.
    (*a*) Determining ledger account balances
    (*b*) Analysing the transaction
    (*c*) Preparing a balance sheet
    (*d*) Preparing a trial balance
    (*e*) Occurrence of a business transaction
    (*f*) Posting from the journal to the ledger
    (*g*) Preparing profit and loss account
    (*h*) Journalising transactions.

Bank Reconciliation Statement

The Bank Reconciliation Statement is an aid used to ensure the accuracy of transactions appearing in the bank column of the Cash Book. Such transactions can be verified through an external record, namely, the bank statement received periodically from the banker. While the business keeps a record of its transactions through the bank columns in the cash book, the banker in turn maintains the bank's transactions with the business in his ledger. An extract from this ledger showing details of the transactions during a specified period is sent at frequent intervals by the bank to the business and this extract is referred to as a bank statement.

Reasons for difference between bank balances as per Cash Book and Pass Book

The relationship between the customer and the banker is that of a creditor and a debtor. So, if the bank columns of the cash book show a debit balance as on a specified date, the bank statement should show an equal amount of credit balance as on that date and vice versa. However, the balances shown by the two independent records may not always agree due to the following:

(*i*) Cheques issued by the business to its suppliers or other parties may not have been presented for payment.

(*ii*) Cheques received from customers and deposited into the bank may not have been collected by the banker.

(*iii*) Deposits may have been directly made by the customers into the bank account of the enterprise.

(*iv*) Collection charges, service charges and interest on overdraft charged by the banker. The business can ascertain the exact amount of charges and record them in the cash book only after the receipt of the bank statement.

(*v*) Interest credited by bank for the balance maintained with it and any other income such as interest on securities, dividend etc. collected by the bank on behalf of the business can be ascertained only from the bank statement.

(*vi*) Wrong entries made by the business in the Cash Book or errors committed by the bank in its ledger.

(*vii*) Omission of entries in the two sets of books.

(*viii*) Dishonour of customers' cheques deposited in the bank account.

RECONCILIATION STATEMENT

On receipt of the bank statement, a comparison of the entries in the Cash Book with those appearing in the bank statement will help in identifying the items causing the difference in the two balances. While the difference due to (*i*) and (*ii*) above will be eliminated in the near future (that is, creditors will soon present their cheques for payment and customer cheques will be collected by the bank in due course), the difference due to items (*iii*) to (*v*) can be eliminated only if such items are recorded in the Cash Book. In addition, business must rectify any errors in the Cash Book, include any transactions omitted and record the dishonour, if any, of customers' cheques. After these adjustments have been recorded, a statement will be prepared to reconcile the balance as shown by the Cash Book with that shown by the Pass Book. This statement is referred to as Bank Reconciliation Statement. It must be understood that this reconciliation statement will contain only details of:

(*a*) Cheques issued and not presented

(*b*) Cheques deposited and remaining uncollected

(*c*) Errors in the bank statement and

(*d*) Omission of entries in the bank statement

The Bank Reconciliation statement is thus an additional tool available to check the accuracy of the bank columns of the cash book.

Illustration 1:

On 31st March, 2008 the Cash Book of Rohit Kumar showed a total bank balance of Rs. 48,000 (debit). However his Pass Book showed a credit balance of Rs. 45,000 as on the same date. A detailed comparison of entries revealed the following:

(*a*) Customers cheques amounting to Rs. 9,500 had not been collected and credited by the bank as on 31.3.2008.

(*b*) Certain cheques amounting to Rs. 6,000 had not been presented for payment as on 31.3.2008.

(*c*) Bank charges of Rs. 500 and interest on investments of Rs. 3,000 collected by the Bank appear in Pass Book only.

(*d*) A customer had paid into bank directly a sum of Rs. 6,000 on March 30, 2008. This was not recorded in the Cash Book.

(*e*) A cheque for Rs. 8,000 received from a customer and deposited with bank had been dishonoured. Entry for dishonour had not been recorded in the Cash Book.

Solution:

Bank Reconciliation Statement as at 31st March, 2008

Particulars	*(+) Items*	*(–) Items*
Balance as per cash book	48,000	
Less cheques deposited but not yet credited		9,500
Add cheques issued but not presented for payment	6,000	

Less bank charges debited in pass book		500
Add Interest on Investment Credited in Pass Book	3,000	
Add direct payment made in bank a/c and not recorded in cash book	6,000	
Less cheque dishonoured and debited in Pass Book		8,000
Total	63,000	18,000
Balance as per pass book	45,000	

Illustration 2:

On 31st October 2008 the Cash Book of a trader showed a favourable balance of Rs. 3,600 but the pass bok showed a favourable balance of Rs. 3,850. The difference was due to the following reasons:

(*a*) Interest on Investment of Rs. 75 was credited in pass book but no entry was passed in cash book.

(*b*) Debit of Rs. 12.50 for bank charges appeared twice in pass book but no entry was made in cash book.

(*c*) Mr. Govindan deposited a cheque of Rs. 250 directly into Trader's Bank Account, for which there is no entry in Cash Book.

(*d*) A cheque for Rs. 50 received from Mr. Gopalan and deposited into Bank was returned dishonoured by Bank on 31st October which the Trader returned on 2nd November, 2008 Reconcile the Balance.

Solution:

Bank Reconciliation Statement as on 31st October, 2008

Particulars	*Plus amount*	*Minus amount*
Balance as per Cash book	3,600	
Interest on investment entered in pass book	75	
Bank charges entered twice in pass book		25
Cheque directly received by the bank	250	
Cheque dishonoured		50
Balance as per pass book		3,850
	3,925	3,925

Illustration 3:

Find out the balance as per pass book from the following particulars:

(*i*) Bank Overdraft as per cash book on 30th April, 2008 Rs. 2,000.

(*ii*) Cheques issued but not presented for payment Rs. 1,350.

(*iii*) Cheques deposited but not yet collected by the banker Rs. 560.

(iv) Bank charges Rs. 80 made by the bank not yet entered in the cash book.

(v) Interest on Investments collected by the bankers and credited in the pass book amounted to Rs. 905.

Solution:

Bank Reconciliation Statement As on 30th April 2008

Particulars	*Plus amount*	*Minus amount*
Overdraft as per cash book		2,000
Cheques issued but not yet presented for payment	1,350	
Cheques deposited but not yet collected		560
Bank charges		80
Interest on Investment collected by the bank	905	
Overdraft as per pass book	1,385	
	2,640	2,640

Illustration 4:

On 31st March, 2008 the pass book showed a credit balance of Rs. 10,500. The following information is also available:

1. Cheques amounting to Rs. 2,750 were deposited in the bank but cheques of Rs. 750 had not been cleared up to 31st March.
2. Cheques amounting to Rs. 3,500 were issued, but cheque for Rs. 1,200 had not been presented for payment in the bank up to 31st March.
3. Bank had given a debit of Rs. 35 for Sundry charges.
4. Bank had received directly from customers Rs. 800 and dividend of Rs. 130 up to 31st March.

Find out the balance as per the cash book.

Solution:

Bank Reconciliation Statement as on 31st March, 2008

Particulars	*Plus amount*	*Minus amount*
Balance as per pass book	10,500	
Cheques paid into bank but not yet cleared	750	
Cheques issued but not presented for payment		1,200
Bank charges	35	
Bank received directly from customers		800
Dividend received directly by bank		130
Balance as per cash books		9,155
	11,285	11,285

Illustration 5:

On 31st December 2008 there was credit balance of Rs. 12,000 in the pass book of Mr. Ram Prakash. He issued cheques of Rs. 3,000/- on 26-12-2008 out of which a cheque of Rs. 1,800/- was presented for payment on 31st Dec. 2008. Bank debited Rs. 20/- for expenses and credited Rs. 170 for interest for which no record has been made in the cash book. Ram Prakash received a cheque of Rs. 320/- from a customer but he forget to send it to bank though it was entered in the bank column of cash book.

Prepare Bank Reconciliation Statement.

Solution:

Bank Reconciliation Statement As on 31st December 2008

Particulars	*Plus amount*	*Minus amount*
Balance as per pass book	12,000	
Cheques issued but not yet presented for payment (3,000 – 1,800)		1,200
Bank charges	20	
Interest directly credited by bank		170
Cheque received but not yet sent for collection	320	
Balance as per cash book		10,970
	12,340	12,340

Illustration 6:

On 31-3-2008 the balance at the bank as shown by the pass book was Rs. 10,500. The balance did not agree with the Cash Book. The following points were discovered:

(*a*) On 28th March 2008, three cheques of Rs. 500, Rs. 600 and Rs. 1,200 were deposited but these cheques were not credited by the bank during the period.

(*b*) On 27th March 2008, cheques issued Rs. 750 and Rs. 350 to the creditors were not presented to the bank for payment.

(*c*) Interest amounting to Rs. 150 was credited in the Pass Book but was not entered in the cash book.

Ascertain the balance as per cash book.

Solution:

Bank Reconciliation Statement as on 31st March 2008

Particulars	*Plus amount*	*Minus amount*
Balance as per pass book	10,500	
Cheques paid into bank but not yet cleared (500 + 600 + 1,200)	2,300	
Cheques issued but not yet presented for payment (750 + 350)		1,100
Interest credited by bank		150
Balance as per cash book		11,550
	12,800	12,800

Illustration 7:

On January 31, 2008 Martin's cash book showed a bank overdraft of Rs. 98,700. On comparison he finds the following:

(*a*) Out of total cheques of Rs. 8,900 issued on January 27, one cheque of Rs. 7,400 was presented for payment on February 4, and another cheque of Rs. 1,500 handed over to the customer, was returned by him, and in lieu of that, a new cheque of the same amount was issued to him on February I. No entry for the return was made.

(*b*) Of the total cash and cheques worth Rs. 6,800 deposited in the bank on January 24, one cheque of Rs. 2,600 was cleared on February 1, and another of Rs. 500 was returned by the bankers on February 2.

(*c*) Bank charges Rs. 35 and bank interest Rs. 2,860 appearing in the pass book are not yet recorded in the cash book.

(*d*) Cheque deposited in his account no. 2 Rs. 1,550 wrongly credited to this account by the bank.

(*e*) A cheque of Rs. 800 drawn on this account was wrongly debited in account no. 2 by the bank

(*f*) A cheque of Rs. 160 issued for this account was recorded by mistake in each book in bank column for no. 2 account, was presented for payment on February 2.

Solution:

Bank Reconciliation Statement As on January 31, 2008

	Particulars	*Plus amount*	*Minus amount*
	Overdraft as per cash book		Rs. 98,700
Less:	cheques issued but not presented for payment (Rs. 7,400 + Rs. 1,500)	8,900	
	Cheque deposited in account no. 2 wrongly credited to this account	1,550	
	Cheque drawn on this account wrongly debited to account No. 2	800	
Add:	Cheque deposited but not credited to date (Rs. 2,600 + Rs. 500)		3,100
	Bank charges and Interest appearing in the pass book (Rs. 35 + Rs. 2,860)		2,895
		11,250	1,04,695
	Debit balance as per pass book (Overdraft)	93,445	
		1,04,695	1,04,695

Illustration 8:

Mr. Jones is having two accounts (A and B) with the Central Bank of India. On 31.12.2008 his ledger shows a balance of Rs. 5,000 in account A and an overdraft of Rs. 2,250 in account B. On verifying the ledger entries with the respective bank statements, the following mistakes were noticed:

1. A deposit of Rs. 1,500 made into A on 20-12-2008 has been entered in the ledger in account B.
2. A withdrawal of Rs. 500 from account A on 2-1-2008 has been entered in the ledger in account B.
3. Two cheques of Rs. 500 and Rs. 750 deposited in A account on 1-12-2008 (and entered in the books in B account) have been dishonoured by the bankers. The entries for the dishonour of these cheques have been entered in the books in B account.
4. In the account A and B, Mr. Jones has issued on 29-12-2008 cheques for Rs. 10,000 and 1,000, respectively, and these have not been cashed till 31-12-2008.
5. Incidental charges of Rs. 10 and 25 charged in the account A and B, respectively, have not been entered in the book.
6. The deposits of Rs. 5,000 and Rs. 3,500 made into the account A and B both on 30.12.2008 have not been credited by the bank till 31.12. 2008.
7. The bank has credited an interest of Rs. 50 for account A and has charged interest of Rs. 275 for account 'B' which have not been recorded in the books.

Draw the bank reconciliation statements for the above two accounts.

Solution:

Bank Reconciliation Statement of Mr. Jones as on December 31, 2008

	A		*B*	
	Dr.	*Cr.*	*Dr.*	*Cr.*
Balance as per ledger	5,000	—	—	2,250
(1) *Add* amount wrongly entered to the debit of account B in the ledger	1,500	—	—	1,500
(2) *Less* withdrawal wrongly entered in account B in the ledger	—	500	500	—
(3) No effect				
(4) *Add* cheques issued but not encashed	10,000		1,000	
(5) *Less* incidental charges		10		25
(6) *Less* deposits not given effect to overdraft as per passbook (in B)		5,000		3,500
(7) *Add* interest on accounts	50			275
Balance (good) as per pass book (in A)		11,040	6,050	—
	16,550	16,550	7,550	7,550

Note: An item entered wrongly in the cash book does not affect the balance in bank passbook. Hence no adjustment is needed.

Illustration 9:

The following is a summary of a cash book as presented to you for December 2008

	Rs.		*Rs.*
Receipts	1,469	Balance brought forward	761
Balance carried forward	554	Payments	1262
	2,023		2,023

All receipts are banked and payments made by cheque. On investigation you discover:

1. Bank charges of Rs. 136 entered on the bank statement had not been entered in cash book.
2. Cheques drawn amounting to Rs. 267 had been presented to the bank for payment.
3. Cheques received totalling Rs. 762 had been entered in the cash book and paid in to the bank, but had not been credited by the bank until January 2008.
4. A cheque for Rs. 22 had been entered as a receipt in the cash book instead of as a payment.
5. A cheque for Rs. 25 had been debited by the bank in error.
6. A cheque received for Rs. 80 had been returned by the bank and marked 'No funds available.' No adjustment had been made in the cash book.
7. All dividends receivable are credited directly to the bank account. During December, amounts totalling Rs. 62, were credited by the bank and no entries made in the cash book.
8. A cheque drawn for Rs. 6 had been incorrectly entered in the cash book as Rs. 66.
9. The balance brought forward should have been Rs. 71.
10. The bank statement as on December 31, 2008 showed an overdraft of Rs. 1,162.

You are required to:

(*a*) Show the adjustments required in the cash book.

(*b*) Prepare a bank reconciliation statement as on December 31, 2008.

Solution:

(a) **Cash Book**

		Rs.			Rs.
Dividends received during December	(7)	62	Balance brought forward		554
Adjustment cheque drawn for Rs. 6 entered as Rs. 66	(8)	60	Bank charges	(1)	136
Adjustment of balance brought forward on December 1, 2008	(9)	50	Adjustment repaid cheque entered as receipt	(4)	44
Balance carried forward		642	Adjustment regarding Cheque returned	(6)	80
		814			814

(b) **Bank Reconciliation Statement (On December 31, 2008)**

			(*in Rs.*)	
Balance as per bank statement on December 31, 2008			1,162	(overdrawn)
Add cheque issued but not yet presented	(2)		267	
			1,429	
Less deposits not yet credited	(3)	762		
Cheque debited in error	(5)	25	787	
Balance as per cash book on December 31, 2008			642	(overdrawn)

Illustration 10:

When Transit Co. Ltd, received its bank statement showing favourable balance of Rs. 7,392 for the period ended June 30, 2008, this did not agree with the balance shown in the cash book.

An examination of the cash book and bank statement disclosed the following:

1. A deposit of Rs. 492 paid in on June 29, 2008 had not been credited by the bank until July 1, 2008.
2. Bank charges amounting to Rs. 17 had not been entered in the cash book.
3. A debit of Rs. 42 appeared on the bank statement for an unpaid cheque, which had been returned marked 'out of date.' The cheque had been re-dated by the customer of Transit Co. Ltd. and paid into the bank again on July 3, 2008.
4. A standing order for payment of an annual subscription amounting to Rs. 10 had not been entered in the cash book.
5. On June 25, the managing director had given the cashier a cheque for Rs. 100 to pay into his personal account at the bank. The cashier had paid it into the company's account by mistake.
6. On June 27, two customers of Transit Co. Ltd. had paid direct to the company's bank account Rs. 499 and Rs. 157, respectively, for goods supplied. The advices were not received by the company until July 1, and were entered in the cash book after that date.

7. On March 30, 2008, the company had entered into a hire-purchase agreement to pay by banker's order a sum of Rs. 26, on the tenth day of each month commencing April. No entries had been made in the cash book.
8. Rs. 364 paid into the bank had been entered twice in the cash book.
9. Cheques issued amount to Rs. 4,672 had not been presented to the bank for payment until after June 30, 2008.
10. A customer of the company, who received a cash discount of 2.5% on his account of Rs. 200, paid the company a cheque on June 10. The cashier, in error, entered the gross amount in the bank column of the cash book.

After making the adjustments you are required:

(*a*) to show the necessary adjustments in the cash book of Transit Co. Ltd. bringing down the correct balance on June 30, 2008.

(*b*) to prepare a bank reconciliation statement.

Solution:

Transit Co. Ltd. Cash Book

	(Rs.)		*(Rs.)*
Balance brought forward	2,972	Bank charges	17
Sundry debtors (Rs. 499 + 157)	656	Annual subscription	10
Managing director's cheque	100	Refund of amount incorrectly banked	100
		Hire-purchase vendor	78
		Adjustment regarding cheques entered twice	364
		Discount allowed	5
		Balance carried forward	3,154
	3,728		3,728

Bank Reconciliation Statement as on June 30, 2008

	Rs.	*Rs.*
Balance as per cash book on June 30, 2008		3,154
Add: cheques issued but not yet presented	4,672 + 100	4,772
		7,926
Less: Deposit not yet credited	492	
Cheque re-presented	42	534
Balance as per pass book		7,392

Illustration 11:

On March 31, 2008 Krishna Kumar's cash book showed a bank balance (debit) of Rs. 24,250. However, the bank statement showed a credit balance of Rs. 26,950 as on the same date. A detailed comparison of entries revealed the following:

(*a*) Customers' cheque amounting to Rs. 4,225 had not been collected by the bank as on 31.3.2008.

(*b*) Certain cheques amounting Rs. 4,425 had not been presented for payment as on 31.3.2008.

(*c*) Bank charges of Rs. 500 and interest of Rs. 6,250 collected by the banker appear only in the bank statement.

(*d*) A wrong credit of Rs. 1,250 in the bank statement.

(*e*) Ramji Ltd., a customer had paid into bank directly a sum of Rs. 1,500 on March 29, 2008. This had not been recorded in the cash book.

(*f*) A cheque for Rs. 1,000 received from Bharat Ltd. a customer and deposited, had been returned unpaid. The dishonour of this cheque has not been entered in the cash book.

Prepare a bank reconciliation statement and also show cash book (with bank columns only).

Solution:

Cash Book of Krishna Kumar
Bank Columns only

	Receipts	*Bank (Rs.)*		*Payment*	*Bank (Rs.)*
2008			2008		
Mar. 31	To balance b/d	24,250	Mar. 31	By bank charges	500
Mar. 31	To interest received	1,250	Mar. 31	By Bharat Ltd.	1,000
Mar. 31	To Ramji Ltd.	1,500	Mar. 31	By balance c/d	25,500
		27,000			27,000

Bank Reconciliation Statement as on March 31, 2008

	(Rs.)	*(Rs.)*
Bank balance as per cash book		25,500
Add: Cheques issued and not presented	4,425	
Wrong credit in the bank statement	1,250	5,675
		31,175
Less: Cheques deposited and remaining uncollected		4,225
Bank balance as per bank statement		26,950

Illustration 12:

Raj Mohan maintains two accounts, known as account no. I and account no. 2 with the bank of Baroda.

On December 31, 2007 the overdraft as per passbook for account no. 1 is Rs. 43,276. But the overdraft as per cash book is not the same and on comparing the pass book and cash book, he finds the following:

(*i*) Out of the total cheques of Rs. 3,700 deposited on December 27, 2007, one cheque amounting Rs. 1,325 was collected on January 4, 2008.

(*ii*) Out of the total cheques of Rs. 6,284, issued on December 22, 2007, two cheques of Rs. 750 each were not presented until December 31, 2007.

(*iii*) A cheque amounting Rs. 1,130 was sent to the supplier, through post on December 29, 2007 and it is expected to reach him only after January 3, 2008.

(*iv*) Bank charges amounting to Rs. 31.50 and interest charges amounting to Rs. 131 not yet recorded in the cash book.

(*v*) Mr. Raj Mohan has deposited a cheque in his account No. 2, for Rs. 500 on December 2, 2007, it was wrongly credited to account no. 1 by the bank.

(*vi*) A cheque deposited on December 15, 2007, for Rs. 250 was returned dishonoured by bankers on January 2, 2008.

(*vii*) A cheque of Rs. 100 issued for account no. I by mistake was recorded in bank column of the cash book for account no. 2, and this cheque was presented for payment on January 4, 2008.

From the above particulars prepare a bank reconciliation to find out the bank overdraft as per cash book.

Bank Reconciliation Statement as on December 31, 2007

	(*Rs.*)	(*Rs.*)
Bank overdraft as per pass book		43,276
Add: Cheques issued but not presented for payment	1,500	
Add: Cheque sent to the supplier through post, but which did not reach him, hence not presented for payment	1,130	
Add: Cheque wrongly credited to account to 1 by bank instead of account no. 2	500	3,130
		46,406
Less: Cheques deposited but not yet collected by the bank	1,325	
Less: Bank charges and interest not recorded in cash book (31.50 + 131)	162.50	
Less: Cheque deposited on December 15, 2007 but not cleared by the bank until December 31, 2007	250	1,737.50
		44,668.50

Note: Item no. (vii) will not make impact as on Dec. 31 2007 as it was presented for payment only on January 4, 2008.

Illustration 13:

Prepare a bank reconciliation statement as on September 30, 2008 from the following entries in the bank column of the cash book and the corresponding pass book.

Cash Book Bank Column Only

		Rs.			*Rs.*
Sep. 1	To Balance	4,000	Sep. 4	By Drawings	350
Sep. 3	To Kamlesh	1,100	Sep. 8	By Suresh	1,650
Sep. 9	To Prabhu	750	Sep. 12	By Salary	1,400
Sep. 16	To Pawan	1,700	Sep. 16	By Manish	350
Sep. 23	To Satish	1,300	Sep. 23	By Shyam	2,100
Sep. 27	To Mohan	50	Sep. 27	By Kapil	1,000
Sep. 30	To Kapoor	175	Sep. 30	By Seeta	550
			Sep. 26	By Commission	50
			Sep. 30	By Balance carried over	1,125
		9,075			9,075

Bank Pass Book

Date	Particulars	Debit (Rs.)	Credit (Rs.)	Balance (Rs.)
2008				
Sep. 1	By Balance b/d			Cr. 4,000.00
Sep. 4	To Cheque — Drawing	350		Cr. 3,650.00
Sep. 5	By Cheque — Kamlesh		1,100	Cr. 4,750.00
Sep. 9	To Cheque — Suresh	1,650		Cr. 3,100.00
Sep. 11	By Cheque — Prabhu		750	Cr. 3,850.00
Sep. 12	To Cheque — Salary	1,400		Cr. 2,450.00
Sep. 17	To Cheque — Manish	850		Cr. 1,600.00
Sep. 20	By Cheque — Satish		1,300	Cr. 2,900.00
Sep. 30	By Dividend received		450	Cr. 3,350.00
	To Bank charges	7.50		Cr. 3,342.50
	To Electricity bill	30		Cr. 3,312.50
	To Cheque-commission	50		Cr. 3,262.50

Solution:

Bank Reconciliation Statement as on 30.09.08

			(Rs.)
Add:	Balance as per bank column of cash book		1,125.00
	Cheque issued but not presented		
	Shyam	— 2,100	
	Kapil	— 1,000	
	Seeta	— 550	3,650
			4,775
Less:	Cheques deposited but not cleared		
	Pawan	— 1,700	
	Mohan	— 50	
	Kapoor	— 175	1,925
			2,850
Add:	Amount credited in pass book only: dividend received		450
			3,300
Less:	Amounts debited in pass book only		
	Bank charges	7.50	
	Electricity bill	30	37.50
	Balance as per pass book		3,262.50

Illustration 14:

Prepare bank reconciliation statement as on November 30, 2007 from the following information:

(*a*) Balance as per passbook on 30-11-2007 – overdrawn Rs. 40,000.

(*b*) On 5-10-2007 Mr. Ram deposited a cheque for collection of Rs. 2,000 and made entry in cash book which appears in the passbook on 6-12-2007 at Rs. 1,980.

(*c*) Cheques issued to parties but not presented for payment till 30-11-2007 are of Rs. 1,050, Rs. 1,670 and Rs. 1,800.

(*d*) Cheques deposited for collection but not collected by bankers till 30-11-07 Rs. 17,520 and Rs. 820.

(*e*) Interest on investment collected by bankers on 30-11-2007 Rs. 1,910 entered in cash book on 4-12-2007 on receipt of bank intimation.

(*f*) Bank charges Rs. 180 (dated 27-11-2007) not entered in cash book.

(*g*) Cheque deposited for collection on 30-11-2007 but returned dishonoured on 6-12-2007 Rs. 1,890.

(*h*) Bankers have made a mistake in balancing by showing overdrawn balance in excess by Rs. 2,000 on 30-11-2007 which was rectified in bank passbook on 7-12-2007 when notified.

Bank Reconciliation Statement as on 30.11.2007

			Rs.	*Rs.*
(*a*) Overdraft bank balance as per pass book				40,000
Add: (*c*) Cheques issued but not presented for Payment till 30-11-2007	1,050			
	1,670			
	1,800		4.520	
(*e*) Interest on investment collected by bankers entered in cash book after 30-11-2007			1.910	6.430
Less: (*b*) Cheque deposited but collected by bankers after 30-11-2007 and appears in the passbook at Rs. 1980			2,000	
(*d*) Cheques deposited but not collected by bankers till 30-11-2007	17,520			
	820		18.340	
(*e*) Bank charges not recorded in the cash book			180	
(*g*) Cheque deposited but dishonoured			1,890	
(*h*) Bank's mistake in balancing by showing overdrawn balance in excess			2,000	24,410
Overdraft bank balance as per cash book				22,020

Illustration 15:

Prepare bank reconciliation statement from the following data as on 30-10-2007.

(*a*) Balance as per passbook on 30-10-07 overdrawn Rs. 18,408.

(*b*) Cheques drawn on 30-10-2007 but not cleared till November 2007, Rs. 6,450, Rs. 1490, and Rs. 1,852.

(*c*) Bank overdraft interest charged on 28-10-2007 not entered in cash book – Rs. 3,220.

(*d*) Cheque received on 29-10-2007 entered in cash book but not deposited to bank till November 3, 2007, Rs. 22,644 and Rs. 3,460.

(*e*) Cheque received amounting to Rs. 70 entered in cash book twice.

(*f*) Bills receivable due on 29-10-2007 sent to bank for collection on 28.10.2007 and entered in cash book forthwith but the proceeds were not credited in bank passbook till November 3, 2007 Rs. 5,960.

(*g*) A periodic payment by bank of Rs. 160 under standing instructions not entered in cash book.

(*h*) Cheque deposited on October 30, 2007 dishonoured but the entry thereof was not made in the cash book — Rs. 3,780.

Bank Reconciliation Statement as on 30.10.2007

			Rs.	Rs.
	(a)	Overdrawn bank balance as per pass book (Dr.)		18,408
Add:	(b)	Cheques drawn but not cleared till Nov. 2007	6,450	
			1,490	
			1,852	9,792
				28,200
Less:	(c)	Bank overdraft interest not entered in the cashbook	3,220	
	(d)	Cheque received and entered in the cash book but not banked (22,644 + 3,460)	26,104	
	(e)	Cheque received and entered twice in the cash book	70	
	(f)	Bills receivable sent to bank by collection but not credited by bank	5,960	
	(g)	Periodic payment by bank not entered in the cash book	160	
	(h)	Cheque deposited and dishonoured but not entered in the cash book	3,780	39,294
		Bank balance as per cash book (Dr.)		11,094

Illustration 16:

A cash book shows an overdrawn position of Rs. 1,815 on March 31, 2008 although the bank statement shows only Rs. 1,689 overdrawn. Detailed examination of the two records revealed the following:

(*a*) A cheque for Rs. 780 in favour of Narayanan had been omitted by the bank from its statement, the cheque having been debited to another customer's a/c.

(*b*) The debit side of own book had been undercast by Rs. 150.

(*c*) A cheque for Rs. 91 drawn in payment of stationery account had been entered in the cash book as Rs. 64 and was shown correctly in bank statement.

(*d*) A cheque for Rs. 105 from Dinesh, having been paid into the bank was dishonoured and shown as such on bank statement, although no entry relating to dishonour had been made in the cash book.

(*e*) The bank had debited a cheque for Rs. 63 in error. It should have been debited to Suresh's a/c.

(*f*) A dividend of Rs. 45 on equity shares had been directly collected by bank, but no entry has been made in Cash book.

(*g*) A deposit of Rs. 540 on 31-3-2008 had not been credited by the bank.

(*h*) Interest of Rs. 114 had been directly debited by bank but not recorded in cash book.

You are required to prepare a bank reconciliation statement after necessary amendment in cash book as on March 31, 2008.

Solution:

Cash Book

(Bank column only)

Date	*Receipts*	*Amount Rs.*	*Date*	*Payment*	*Amount Rs.*
31-3-2008	To dividends	45	31-3-2007	By balance b/f (incorrect balance)	1,815

31-3-2008	To error in casting	150	31-3-2008	Stationery charges — cheque drawn for Rs. 91 wrongly recorded as Rs. 64 (91 – 64)	27
31-3-2008	Balance c/d	1,866	31-3-2008	By Satish (cheque dishonoured)	105
			31-3-2008	By bank interest — interest on overdraft	114
		2,061			2,061
			1-4-2008	By balance b/d (correct balance)	1,866

Bank Reconciliation Statement as on 31.3.2008

	Particulars	Amount (Rs.)	Amount (Rs.)
	Overdraft bank balance as per cash book (as amended) (Cr.)		1,866
Add:	A cheque for Rs. 63 wrongly debited by bank	63	
	A deposit not credited by bank	540	603
			2,469
Less:	A cheque in favour of Narayanan Associates not debited by bank		780
	Overdraft bank balance as per pass book (Dr.)		1,689

THEORY QUESTIONS

1. What is Bank Reconciliation Statement ? What is the purpose of preparing it ?
2. What are the reasons of difference between bank balances as per pass book and cash book.
3. What is Bank Reconciliation Statement ?
4. Explain the reasons for difference in Cash Book and pass book balances.

EXERCISES AND PROBLEMS

1. From the following particulars, prepare a Bank Reconciliation Statement showing the balance as per Bank Pass Book on 31st March, 2008. The following cheques were paid into the firm's current account in March, 2008 but were credited by the bank in April 2008.

   Ashok Rs. 2,500, Mukesh Rs. 3,000, Sudesh Rs. 2,400.

   The following cheques were issued by the firm in March 2008 and were cashed in April 2008.

   Kumud Rs. 3,000, Kamana Rs. 5,000, Ayesha Rs. 3,000.

   A cheque for Rs. 1,000 which was received from a customer was entered in the bank column of the Cash Book in March, 2008, but the same was paid into bank in April, 2008.

   The Pass Book shows a credit of Rs. 2,500 for interest and a debit of Rs. 500 for bank charges.

   The balance as per Cash Book was Rs. 1,80,000 on 31st March 2008.

(*Ans.:* Balance as per Pass Book Rs. 1,84,100)

2. On 31st December, 2008 the Pass Book of a merchant shows the credit balance of Rs. 6,714.

   The cheques and drafts sent to the bank but not collected and credited amounted Rs. 1,580 and three cheques drawn for Rs. 600, Rs. 300 and Rs. 400 respectively were not presented for payment till 31st January next year.

Bank has paid a bill payable amounting to Rs. 2,000 but it has not been entered in the Cash Book and a bill receivable of Rs. 1,000 which was discounted with the bank was dishonoured by the drawer on due date.

The bank has charged Rs. 26 as its commission for collecting outstation cheques and has allowed interest Rs. 20 on the trader's balance.

Prepare a Bank Reconciliation Statement and show the balance as shown in the Cash Book.

(***Ans.:*** Balance as per Cash Book Rs. 5,000)

3. On 30th June, 2008, the bank column of Sunil's Cash Book showed a debit balance of Rs. 16,500. On examination of the Cash Book and bank statement you find that:

(*a*) Out of total cheques amounting to Rs. 16,000 issued, cheques amounting to Rs. 11,600 have been presented for payment upto 30th June, 2008, cheques for Rs. 1,600 were presented in July, 2008 and the rest have not been presented at all.

(*b*) Out of total cheques amounting to Rs. 12,000 sent to bank for collection, cheques of Rs. 8,200 were credited in Pass Book upto 30th June, 2008, cheques amounting to Rs. 2,400 were credited in July 2008 and the rest have not been collected so far.

(*c*) On 28th June a customer deposited Rs. 7,000 direct in the bank account but it was entered only in the Pass Book.

(*d*) Debit side of Sunil's Cash Book (Bank Column) has been overcast by Rs. 200.

(*e*) No entry has been made in the Cash Book for the Rent of Rs. 1600 paid by bankers according to Sunil's standing instructions.

(*f*) The Pass Book showed a credit of Rs. 640 for interest and a debit of Rs. 80 for bank charges, but these have not been entered in the Cash Book.

Prepare a Bank Reconciliation Statement as on 30th June, 2008

(***Ans.:*** Balance as per Pass Book Rs. 22,860)

4. From the following particulars prepare a Bank Reconciliation statement showing the balance as per Cash Book on 31.12.2007.

The following cheques were paid into bank in Dec., 2007 but were credited by bank in January 2008.

Sarika	Rs. 3,500
Bhawana	Rs. 2,500
Pooja	Rs. 2,000

The following cheques were issued by the firm in Dec., 2007 but were presented in January 2008.

Asha	Rs. 4,000
Usha	Rs. 4,500

A cheque for Rs. 1,000 which was received from a customer was entered in the bank column of the cash book in December 2007 but was omitted to be banked in Dec. 2007. The pass book shows a debit balance of Rs. 100 for bank charges and a credit balance of Rs. 2,000 for interest.

Interest on investment Rs. 2,000 collected by bank appeared in the Pass Book. The bank balance as per Pass Book was Rs. 62,000 on 31st Dec. 2007.

(***Ans.:*** Balance as per Cash Book Rs. 59,000)

5. On 30th June 2008, the Cash Book of M/s. Radhey and Sons showed a balance of Rs. 2,000 at Bank. They had sent cheques amounting to Rs. 10,000 to the bank before 30th June, but it appears from the Pass Book that cheques worth only Rs. 4,000 had been credited before that date. Similarly out of cheques of Rs, 5,000 issued during the month of June, cheques for Rs. 250 were presented and paid in July.

The Pass Book also showed the following payments:

(1) Rs. 320 as premium on the life policy according to standing instructions; and

(2) Rs. 2,000 against a pro-note, as per instructions.

The Pass Book showed that the bank had collected Rs. 600 as interest on Government Securities. The bank had charged interest Rs. 50 and bank charges Rs. 20. There was no entry in cash book for the payments, interest etc.

Prepare the Bank Reconciliation Statement as on 30th June 2008.

(***Ans.:*** Balance as Pass Book (Dr.) Rs. 11,080)

6. On checking Rajan's Cash Book with the Bank Statement of his overdraft current account for the month of November, 2007 you find the following:
   (*a*) Cash Book showed an overdraft of Rs. 4,500.
   (*b*) The payment side of the Cash Book had been undercast by Rs. 150.
   (*c*) A cheque of Rs. 750 drawn on his saving account has been shown as drawn on current account.
   (*d*) Cheques amounting to Rs. 7,000 drawn and entered in the Cash Book had not yet been presented.
   (*e*) Cheques amounting to Rs. 6,000 sent to the bank for collection, though entered in the Cash Book, had not been credited by the bank.
   (*f*) Bank charges of Rs. 75 as per Bank Statement had not been taken into Cash Book.
   (*g*) Dividends of the amount of Rs. 2,500 had been paid direct into the bank and not entered in the Cash Book.

   You are required to prepare a Bank Reconciliation Statement on 30th Nov., 2007.

(***Ans.:*** Overdraft as per Pass Book Rs. 475)

7. A Bank Pass Book for Account No. 1 shows an overdraft of Rs. 6,500 on 31st March, 2008. This does not agree with the Cash Book balance. From the following particulars ascertain the Cash Book balance:

   Cheques amounting to Rs. 15,000 were paid into bank in March out of which, it appears, only cheques amounting to Rs. 4,500 were credited by bank. Cheques issued during March amounted in all to Rs. 11,000. Out of these, cheques for Rs. 3,000 were unpaid on 31st March 2008. The bank has wrongly debited Account No. 1 with Rs. 500 in respect of a cheque drawn on Account No. 2. The account stands debited with Rs. 150 for interest and with Rs. 30 for Bank charges. The bank has paid the annual subscription of Rs. 100 to a club according to the instructions. The entries for interest charges and subscription have not been made in the Cash Book.

(***Ans.:*** Dr. Balance as per Cash Book Rs. 1,780)

8. The bank pass book of Ravi showed an overdraft of Rs. 17,000 in his account, on 31st March 2008. On going through the pass book, the accountant found the following:
   (*a*) A cheque of Rs. 550 credited in the pass book on 28th March, being dishonoured, is debited again in the pass book on 1 April 2008. There was no entry in cash book about the dishonour of the cheque until 15 April.
   (*b*) Out of Rs. 10,500 paid in by Ravi in cash and by cheques on 31 March, cheques amounting to Rs. 4,000 were collected on 7 April.
   (*c*) Bankers had credited his account with Rs, 1500 for interest by them on his behalf but the same had not been entered in his cash book.
   (*d*) Out of cheques amounting to Rs. 3,900 drawn by him on 27 March a cheque for Rs. 1,250 was encashed on 3 April.

(c) Bankers seem to have given him wrong credit for Rs. 300 paid in by him in Account No. 2 and wrong debit.

Prepare Bank Reconciliation Statement on 31st March, 2008.

(*Ans.:* Overdraft Balance as per Cash Book Rs. 15,580)

9. On 31st December 2007 the Cash Book showed an overdraft of Rs. 5,670.

From the following particulars make out a Bank Reconciliation Statement and ascertain the balance as per Bank Pass Book:

(a) Cheques drawn but not cashed before 31st Dec. 2007 amounted to Rs. 3,946.

(b) Cheques paid into the Bank but not collected and credited before 31st Dec. 2007 amounted to Rs. 4,891.

(c) A bill receivable for Rs. 520 previously discounted with the Bank had been dishonoured and debited in the Pass Book.

(d) Debit is also made in the Pass Book for Rs. 120 on account of interest on overdraft and Rs. 55 on account of charges for collecting bills and cheques.

(e) The bank has collected interest on investment and credited Rs. 760 in the Pass Book.

(*Ans.:* Overdraft as per Pass Book Rs. 6,550)

10. On 31st January, 2008 Cash Book showed a Bank overdraft of Rs. 12,500. On comparing it with the Pass Book, the following differences were noted:

(a) Cash and cheques amounting to Rs. 1,340 were sent to Bank on 27th January but cheques worth Rs. 230 were credited on 2nd February and one cheque for Rs. 45 was returned by them as dishonoured on 4th February.

(b) During the month of January, cheques issued to creditors amounted Rs. 1,670. Out of these, cheques worth Rs. 1,370 were presented for payment on 5th February.

(c) According to the standing orders, the Bankers have paid during the month of January the following:

(a) Life Insurance Premium Rs. 170

(b) Television Licence Fee Rs. 120

(c) Driving Licence Fee Rs. 22

(d) Bankers have collected Rs. 150 as dividend on the shares.

(e) Bankers have given a wrong credit for Rs. 150.

(f) Interest charged by the bank Rs. 125.

Prepare a Bank Reconciliation Statement as on 31st January 2008.

(*Ans.:* Overdraft Balance as per Pass Book Rs. 11,542).

Errors and Their Rectification

The trial balance is prepared to ensure the arithmetical accuracy of the ledger of a business and also to ensure that for every debit entry a credit of an equal amount has been recorded. Thus, a trial balance in which the total of the debits does not equal the total of credits can be taken as an evidence for the existence of some errors in the records. On the other hand, a trial balance in which the total of the debits equals the total of credits is not a conclusive proof of the accuracy of the records. Certain errors may not effect the agreement of a trial balance as the erroneous entries may not violate the dual aspect concept. It means that even if the Trial Balance agrees, steps should be taken to ensure that the records are free from errors.

To understand the nature of errors and their rectification we may classify them into: (*i*) errors disclosed by a Trial Balance and (*ii*) errors not disclosed by a Trial Balance.

ERRORS DISCLOSED BY A TRIAL BALANCE

The errors which cause a mismatch in the trial balance totals are frequently referred to as errors disclosed in a Trial Balance. However, the mismatch does not automatically point to the actual errors. It is only the diligence and ingenuity of the person preparing the accounts which would help in the location of the errors.

The various errors which would cause a mismatch in the trial balance totals are as follows:

(*i*) Wrong totalling in a subsidiary book: For example, if the total of the purchase for a month is stuck as Rs. 26,150 instead of Rs. 26,250 then the debit in the purchases account would be Rs. 26,150 (as the total from the subsidiary book will be posted to the debit of the purchase account). The total of the credits posted in the individual suppliers a/c would be Rs. 26,250 and in the Trial Balance the total credits will exceed total debits by Rs. 100.

(*ii*) Wrong calculation of balances in a ledger account: For example, if the debit balance in the furniture a/c has been taken as Rs. 5,650 instead of Rs. 5,850 then the Trial Balance will show the total credits exceeding the total debits by Rs. 200.

(*iii*) Partial omission of an entry: If the debit or credit aspect of a transaction has been omitted to be recorded, the Trial Balance will disagree. For example, if a cash sales of Rs. 800 is omitted to be recorded in the Sales a/c then the total debits will exceed the total credits by Rs. 800.

(*iv*) Posting an aspect of a transaction more than once: For example, if an amount of Rs. 2,000 paid to XY Limited has been posted to the debit of XY Limited a/c twice, then the debits will exceed the credits by Rs. 2,000.

(*v*) Debit entries wrongly recorded as credit entries or vice-versa: for example, if an amount of Rs. 3,500 received from Z is posted to the credits of Z's a/c then the debits will exceed the credits by Rs. 7,000.

(*vi*) Errors in totalling the debit column or the credit column of the Trial Balance: Obviously, if a total mistake occurs while casting either the debit side or credit side of the Trial Balance, it will not tally.

(*vii*) Balance of ledger accounts are wrongly transferred to the trial balance: For example, the balance of Rs. 46,945 in the Plant and Machinery a/c is transferred to the trial balance as Rs. 46,495. This will cause the credits to exceed the debit by Rs. 450.

(*viii*) Omitting to include an account's balance in the trial balance: When an account which is outstanding in the ledger account is omitted to be included in the trial balance, it will not tally.

SUSPENSE ACCOUNT

When a combination of the various errors mentioned above have been committed, the mismatch in the totals of the Trial Balance will be totally different for the amounts of the individual transactions and only through scrutiny and checking of the books of accounts will help in detecting the errors. Sometimes, when the Trial Balance disagrees and sufficient time is not available to scrutinize the books, the accountant will include 'Suspense A/c' in the Trial Balance to make it agree and proceed with the preparation of 'Profit and Loss A/c' and Balance Sheet. For instance, if the totals of the credits in a Trial Balance exceeds the debits by Rs. 2,550 then a suspense a/c with a debit balance of 2,550 will be included in the Trial Balance. At a later date, the books may be scrutinised to detect the errors and the rectification entries passed to clear the balance in the Suspense A/c.

ERRORS NOT DISCLOSED BY TRIAL BALANCE

Even though a trial balance may be in agreement, certain errors might have been committed while recording the transactions. Such errors are referred to as errors not disclosed by Trial Balance.

The errors which will not cause a mismatch in the totals of a Trial Balance are as follows:

(*a*) *Omission of the recording of a transaction from the books of accounts:* If the withdrawal of goods worth Rs. 1,200 by the proprietor is omitted to be recorded in the books, the Trial Balance will still agree as both the debit and credit aspects have been omitted to be recorded.

(*b*) *Recording a transaction at an amount which is totally different from the actual amount:* If the purchases of goods worth Rs. 7,500 is recorded in the Purchase book as Rs. 5,700 the error will not cause the trial balance to disagree.

(*c*) *Compensating errors:* These are quite difficult to detect. If a cash discount of Rs. 215 allowed to a customer has been posted to the credit of his account as Rs. 251 and a cash sale of Rs. 2,851 has been posted to sales account as Rs. 2,815, then the excess credit caused by the first error would be exactly compensated by the lower credit recorded by the second error and the trial balance will be in agreement.

(*d*) *Posting of an aspect of a transaction on the correct side of wrong account:* If the amount of Rs. 800 received from MN Ltd. a debtor, is posted to the credit of NM Ltd. a/c, also a debtor, the Trial Balance totals will still agree, because both are debit accounts and the total effect is the same.

(*e*) *Recording both aspects of a transaction more than once in the books of accounts:* If a sales of Rs. 3,500 made to PQR Ltd. is entered in the Sales Book twice, the error will not cause a mismatch in the totals of Trial Balance.

(*f*) *Errors of principle:* If the machinery a/c is debited for an amount of repair charges incurred for the machinery, the error will not be disclosed by the Trial Balance. This is because that both machinery a/c and repairs a/c are debit a/cs and it is a question of principle that repairs charges should not be debited to the machinery a/c. Hence, the total effect will be the same and therefore the Trial Balance will tally.

Illustration 1:

Rectify the following errors and prepare suspense account:

(*i*) Goods purchased from Mani of Rs. 300 passed through Sales Book.

(*ii*) Received one bill from Arun Rs. 500 passed through bills payable book.

(*iii*) An item of Rs. 150 relating to prepaid rent account has omitted to be brought forward.

(*iv*) An item of Rs. 40 in respect of purchase returns instead of being debited to the personal account from returns outward book had been wrongly entered in the purchase book and posted therefrom wrongly to the debit of personal account.

(*v*) Rs. 500 paid to Mehta Bros. against our acceptance were debited to Malhotra Bros. A/c.

(*vi*) Received final dividend of Rs. 20 from Ajit whose account had already been written off as bad debts, now credited to a newly opened account and was included in the list of creditors.

(*vii*) Bills received from Das for repairs done to radio Rs. 150 and radio supplied Rs. 950 was entered in the invoice book as Rs. 1,000.

Solution:

Sl. No.	*Particulars*		*L.F.*	*Dr. Amount (Rs.)*	*Cr. Amount (Rs.)*
(*i*)	Sales a/c	Dr.		300	
	Purchase a/c	Dr.		300	
	To Mani				600
	(Being the goods purchased wrongly passed through sales book)				
(*ii*)	Bills receivable a/c	Dr.		500	
	Bills payable a/c	Dr.		500	
	To Arun				1,000
	(Being the rectification of Bills Receivable from Arun passed through Bills payable book)				

(iii)	Prepaid rent a/c To suspense (Being the omission of prepaid account in the books, now rectified by passing an entry)	Dr.	150	150
(iv)	Suspense a/c To Purchase returns a/c To Purchase a/c (Being the error in respect of purchase returns wrongly entered in purchases book now rectified)	Dr.	80	40 40
(v)	Bills Payable a/c To Malhotra Bros. (Being the acceptance from Mehta Bros. Wrongly debited to Malhotra Bros.)	Dr.	500	500
(vi)	Ajit To Bad debts recovered a/c (Being the bad debts recovered from Ajit wrongly included in the list of creditors)	Dr.	20	20
(vii)	Repairs a/c Furniture and fitting a/c To Purchase a/c To Das (Being the bill received from Das for repairs done, has been wrongly entered in the purchases book with wrong amount)	Dr. Dr.	150 950	1,000 100

Suspense A/c

	Rs.		*Rs.*
To Balance (difference in trial balance)	70	By Prepaid rent	150
To Purchase returns	40		
To Purchases	40		
Total	150		150

Illustration 2:

Pass the rectification entries and show the suspense Account for the following errors, detected after the preparation of the Trial Balance:

(*a*) A Cheque for Rs. 220 received from a tenant for rent has been entered in the cash book, but the double entry has not been completed.

(*b*) The account of Rama Rao, a debtor for Rs. 160 had been written off as bad, but the entry has been made only in the personal account.

(*c*) The discount column on the debit side of the cash book Rs. 200 had been posted to the credit of Discount Received Account.

(*d*) The Sales Day Book is undercast by Rs. 3,150.

(*e*) Rs. 95 received for commission is not posted to commission A/c.

(*f*) Goods returned Rs. 27 to R.K. and Company, though entered in the Returns Book, is left unposted.

Solution:

Sl. No.	*Particulars*	*L.F.*	*Dr. Amount (Rs.)*	*Cr. Amount (Rs.)*
(*a*)	Cash a/c Dr.		220	
	To Rent a/c			220
	(Being the rent received from a tenant has not been entered in the books)			
(*b*)	Bad debts a/c Dr.		160	
	To suspense a/c			160
	(Being the entry for Bad debts not posted in the ledger)			
(*c*)	Discount received a/c Dr.		200	
	Discount allowed a/c Dr.		200	
	To Suspense a/c			400
	(Being the discount allowed wrongly posted to discount received a/c, no entry being made in discount allowed a/c)			
(*d*)	Suspense a/c Dr.		3,150	
	To Sales a/c			3,150
	(Being the rectification of undercasting of sales book)			
(*e*)	Suspense a/c Dr.		95	
	To Commission a/c			95
	(Being the commission received omitted to be posted in commission)			
(*f*)	R.K. Company Dr.		27	
	To Purchases returns			27
	(Being the returns outward omitted to be posted in books)			

Suspense A/c

	Rs.		*Rs.*
To Sales	3,150	By Balance	2,685
To Commission	95	By Bad debts	160
		By Discount received a/c	200
		By Discount allowed a/c	200
Total	3,245		3,245

Illustration 3:

An accountant who finds his Trial balance not agreeing opens a Suspense Account and rectifies the following errors:

(*i*) A cheque of Rs. 750 received for loss of stock by fire had been deposited in the proprietor's private Bank Account.

(*ii*) An item of purchase of Rs. 151 was entered in the purchase book as Rs. 15 and posted to the supplier's account Rs. 51.

(*iii*) A sales return of Rs. 500 was not entered in the financial accounts though it was duly taken in the stock book.

(*iv*) An amount of Rs. 300 was received in full settlement from a customer after he was allowed a discount of Rs. 50 but while writing the books, the amount received was entered in the discount column and discount allowed in the amount column.

(*v*) Bills receivable from Mr. A of Rs. 1,000 was posted to the credit of bills payable account and also credited to the account of Mr. A.

Show the suspense account and find out the opening balance.

Solution:

Suspense A/c

Sl. No.	*Particulars*		*L.F.*	*Dr. Amount (Rs.)*	*Cr. Amount (Rs.)*
(*i*)	Drawings a/c	Dr.		750	
	To Loss of stock a/c				750
	(Being the rectification of a cheque wrongly passed to proprietor's private bank a/c)				
(*ii*)	Purchase a/c	Dr.		136	
	To Supplier's personal a/c				100
	To Suspense a/c				36
	(Being the rectification of undercasting of purchases amount in purchases book and supplier's a/c)				
(*iii*)	Sales return a/c	Dr.		500	
	To customer's a/c				500
	(Being the sales return transaction omitted to be recorded in books)				
(*iv*)	Bank a/c	Dr.		250	
	To Discount allowed a/c				250
	(Being the amount received from a Customer wrongly entered in discount allowed column)				
(*v*)	Bills Payable a/c	Dr.		1,000	
	Bills Receivable a/c	Dr.		1,000	
	To suspense a/c				2,000
	(Being bill received from Mr. A wrongly posted to Bills payable a/c and on credit side of Mr. A's a/c)				

Suspense A/c

	Rs.		*Rs.*
To Balance	2,036	By Purchases	36
(Difference transferred to trial balance)		By Bills payable	1,000
		By Bills receivable	1,000
Total	2,036		2,036

Illustration 4:

The credit column of a Trial balance as on 31st March, 2008 is short by Rs. 3,800. On 1.4.2008 the following errors were discovered:

(*i*) A credit item of Rs. 9,300 has been debited to the personal account of Raman as Rs. 3,900.

(*ii*) Rs. 7,500 written off as depreciation on plant and machinery account has not been debited depreciation account.

(*iii*) A discount of Rs. 4,500 allowed to Nataraj and Sons has been credited to them as Rs. 5,400.

(*iv*) The total of Sales Returns Book has been undercast by Rs. 1000.

Pass the rectification entries. Assuming that the difference in Trial Balance is taken to a suspense account. You need not show the suspense account.

Solution:

Sl. No.	Particulars		L.F.	Dr. Amount Rs.	Cr. Amount Rs.
(i)	Suspense a/c To Raman's a/c (Being the rectification of a credit item of Rs. 93 wrongly debited as Rs. 39)	Dr.		13,200	13,200
(ii)	Depreciation a/c To Suspense a/c (Being the rectification of omission of posting to depreciation a/c)	Dr.		7,500	7,500
(iii)	Natraj & Sons a/c To Suspense a/c (Being the rectification of discount allowed of Rs. 45 credited as Rs. 54)	Dr.		900	900
(iv)	Sales returns a/c To Suspense a/c (Being the rectification of understanding of the sales returns book)	Dr.		1,000	1,000

Illustration 5:

Pass the rectifying entries for the following:

(*a*) Rs. 3,000 spent on erection of factory plant were charged to repairs a/c.

(*b*) A cheque for Rs. 2,500 from Ramarao was dishonoured, its amount was posted to allowance A/c.

(*c*) A customer cheque of Rs. 1,500 received through Sitaram was credited to Sitaram's Account.

Solution:

Sl. No.	Particulars		L.F.	Dr. Amount Rs.	Cr. Amount Rs.
(a)	Plant a/c To Repairs a/c (Being the rectification of plant wrongly posted to repairs a/c)	Dr.		3,000	3,000
(b)	Ramarao To Allowance a/c (Being the cheque of Ramarao dishonoured Previously posted to Allowance a/c)	Dr.		2,500	2,500
(c)	Sitaram To Customer a/c (Being the cheque received from a customer wrongly posted to Sitaram's a/c)	Dr.		1,500	1,500

Illustration 6:

Write out the journal entries to rectify the following errors using suspense account:

(*a*) Goods of the value of Rs. 100 returned by Mr. Sharma were entered in the Sales Day Book and posted therefrom to the credit of his account.

(*b*) An amount of Rs. 150 entered in the Sales Returns Book has been posted to the Debit of Mr. Philip, who returned the goods.

(*c*) A sale of Rs. 200 made to Mr. Gupta was correctly entered in the Sales Day Book but wrongly posted to the debit of Mr. Gupta's account for Rs. 20.

Solution:

Sl. No.	*Particulars*		*L.F.*	*Dr. Amount (Rs.)*	*Cr. Amount (Rs.)*
(*a*)	Sales a/c	Dr.		100	
	Sales Returns a/c	Dr.		100	
	To Suspense a/c				200
	(Being the goods returned by Mr. Sharma wrongly entered in Sales Day Book)				
(*b*)	Suspense a/c	Dr.		300	
	To Mr. Philip				300
	(Being the goods returned by Mr. Philip wrongly posted to the debit of his account)				
(*c*)	Mr. Gupta	Dr.		180	
	To Suspense a/c				180
	(Being the goods sold to Mr. Gupta posted to his account with wrong amount)				

Illustration 7:

Give the journal entries necessary to rectify the following errors detected in the books.

(*i*) A payment of Rs. 2,500 for purchase of a typewriter for office use has been debited to purchase account from the cash book.

(*ii*) A credit sale of Rs. 1,270 to Sri Chandra Bose has been posted to the debit of Sri Chandra Guha's account from the sales day book.

(*iii*) A payment of Rs. 960 for whitewashing the office room has been charged to building account.

Solution:

Sl. No.	*Particulars*		*L.F.*	*Dr. Amount (Rs.)*	*Cr. Amount (Rs.)*
1.	Typewriter a/c			2,500	
	To Purchase a/c				2,500
	(Being the payment of Rs. 250 for purchase of typewriter debited to purchase a/c now rectified)				
2.	Sri Chandra Bose	Dr.		1,270	
	To Sri Chandra Guha				1,270
	(Being the wrong posting of credit sale to the debit of Sri Chandra Guha now rectified)				

3.	Whitewashing charges a/c Dr. To Building a/c (Being the white washing charges wrongly debited to building a/c now rectified)		940	940

Illustration 8:

Give the correct journal entries for the following:

(*a*) Cost of repairing one machine, i.e., Rs. 100 has been charged to machinery account.
(*b*) Rs. 50 paid to S. Roy in settlement of his account has been posted to the debit of purchase account.
(*c*) Goods sold on credit of Rs. 200 to B. Bose has been posted to the debit of general charges account.
(*d*) Rs. 250 received from B.K. Ghose has been credited to account of K.B. Ghose.
(*e*) Wages account includes Rs. 1,500 being wages paid to workmen engaged in construction work of the Firm's new buildings.

Solution:

Sl. No.	*Particulars*	*L.F.*	*Dr. Amount Rs.*	*Cr. Amount Rs.*
(*a*)	Repairs A/c Dr. To Machinery a/c (Being the amount for repairs wrongly charged to machinery a/c now rectified)		100	100
(*b*)	S. Roy Dr. To Purchase a/c (Being the payment to S. Roy wrongly debited to purchases a/c rectified)		50	50
(*c*)	B. Bose Dr. To General charges a/c (Being the credit sale to B. Bose wrongly debited to general charges, now rectified)		200	200
(*d*)	K. B. Ghosh Dr. To B.K. Ghosh (Being Rs. 250 received from B.K. Ghosh wrongly credited to K.B. Ghosh now rectified)		250	250
(*e*)	Building a/c Dr. To Wages a/c (Being the payment of wages for construction building debited to wages a/c, now rectified)		1,500	1,500

Illustration 9:

Give the correct journal entries with respect to the undermentioned transactions in the books of a trader:

(*i*) The discount a/c was credited by Rs. 175, the amount representing the total of the discount column on debit side of the cash book.
(*ii*) The sales day book was undercast by Rs. 1,100.
(*iii*) The sales proceeds of old furniture amounting to Rs. 1,500 were credited to the sales account.

(*iv*) Bills receivable for Rs. 350 was posted as Rs. 503 on credit of the acceptor's account.

(*v*) Repairs worth Rs. 750 to motor car account were debited to the motor car a/c.

State how the above errors will effect the agreement of the trial balance.

Solution:

JOURNAL

Sl. No.	*Particulars*		*L.F.*	*Dr. Amount Rs.*	*Cr. Amount Rs.*
(1)	Discount a/c To Suspenses a/c (Being the total of discount on the debit side of cash book wrongly credited to discount a/c, now rectified)	Dr.		350	350
(2)	Suspense a/c To Sales a/c (Being the undercasting of sales book, now rectified)	Dr.		1,100	1,100
(3)	Sales a/c To Furniture a/c (Being the sale proceeds of old furniture wrongly credited to sales a.c, now rectified)	Dr.		1,500	1,500
(4)	Acceptors a/c To Suspenses a/c (Being a bill receivable of Rs. 350 wrongly posted as 503 to the credit of acceptor's a/c now rectified)	Dr.		153	153
(5)	Repairs a/c To Motor car a/c (Being the repair of car debited to motor car a/c, now rectified)	Dr.		750	750

Suspense A/c

	Rs.		*Rs.*
To Sales A/c	1,100	By Balance b/d By Discount By Acceptors	597 350 153
	1,100		1,100

Note: The total of debit side of trial balance exceeds total of credit side by Rs. 597.

Illustration 10:

Rectify the following errors:

1. Wages paid to the workers (Rs. 250) for repairing the building have been debited to wages a/c.
2. A sum of Rs. 65 spent for repairing office furniture has been debited to furniture a/c.
3. Purchase of typewriter for Rs 800 has been passed through the day book.
4. Rupees 75 paid as the examination fees of the proprietor's son has been posted to general expenses a/c.
5. Stock of goods valued at Rs. 950 donated to ND fund has been posted to general expenses a/c.

6. Rupees 5,400 received from M. Mehta were posted to the debit side of his account.
7. Rupees 1,000 being purchases return were posted to the purchase a/c.
8. Discount of Rs. 2,000 received was posted to the debit of discount a/c.
9. Rupees 3,740 paid for repairs to motor car were debited to motor car a/c as Rs. 1,740.

Solution:

JOURNAL

Sl. No.	*Particulars*		*L.F.*	*Dr. Amount Rs.*	*Cr. Amount Rs.*
(1)	Repairs a/c To Wages a/c (Being the amount of wages paid for repairs wrongly debited to wages a/c now rectified)	Dr.		250	250
(2)	Repairs a/c To Furniture a/c (Being the sum spent for repairs of office furniture wrongly debited to furniture a/c, now rectified)	Dr.		65	65
(3)	Typewriter a/c To Purchase a/c (Being the purchase of typewriter wrongly passed through day book, now rectified)	Dr.		800	800
(4)	Drawing a/c To General expenses a/c (Being the payment of examination fees of the proprietor's son wrongly debited to general expenses, now rectified)	Dr.		75	75
(5)	Donations a/c To General expenses a/c (Being the stock of goods donated to ND Funds wrongly debited to general expenses, now rectified)	Dr.		950	950
(6)	Suspenses a/c To M. Mehta a/c (Being the receipt of Rs. 5,400 from M. Mehta wrongly debited to his account, now rectified)	Dr.		10,800	10,800
(7)	Suspense a/c To Purchase return a/c To Purchase a/c (Being the amount of purchase returns wrongly debited to purchase now rectified)	Dr.		2,000	1,000 1,000
(8)	Suspense a/c To Discount a/c (Being the discount of Rs. 2,000 was debited to discount a/c, now rectified)	Dr.		4,000	4,000
(9)	Repairs a/c To Motor car a/c To Suspense a/c (Being the payment of Rs. 3,740 for repairs to motor car wrongly debited to motor car as Rs. 1,740, now rectified)	Dr.		3,740	1,740 2,000

Illustration 11:

The trial balance of M/s Ltd., as on March 31, 2008 did not balance. The difference amount of Rs. 76 was transferred to the credit of suspense account, and the accountant proceeded with the preparation of final accounts. After completion of final accounts, the following errors were discovered:

(*a*) Total of sales figure was taken as Rs. 58,726 instead of Rs. 58,762.

(*b*) A discount of Rs. 52 allowed to Mr. X was not recorded in the discount allowed account.

(*c*) The total of purchase returns book was undercast by Rs. 43.

(*d*) Sale of old furniture for Rs. 130 was wrongly entered in machinery a/c.

(*e*) A credit purchase for Rs. 49 made from Mr. Y was recorded in purchase book, but was omitted in Y's account.

(*f*) Rupees 320 received from P was posted to the credit of Mr. R.

(*g*) A credit sale made to Mr. S for Rs. 250 was recorded twice in his account.

(*h*) Depreciation on plant and machinery was wrongly recorded as Rs. 750 instead of Rs. 950.

(*i*) Rupees 50 of wages paid on March 30, 2008, are not debited to wages account.

Give Journal entries to rectify the above errors, and prepare suspense account.

Solution:

Rectification of Errors

Sl. No.	*Particulars*		*L.F.*	*Dr. Amount Rs.*	*Cr. Amount Rs.*
(*a*)	Suspense a/c To Sales a/c (Being the sales figure undercast by Rs. 36)	Dr.		36	36
(*b*)	Discount a/c To Suspense a/c (Being the discount allowed not recorded earlier)	Dr.		52	52
(*c*)	Suspense a/c To Purchase return a/c (Being the total purchase returns undercast by Rs. 43)	Dr.		43	43
(*d*)	Machinery a/c To Furniture a/c (Being the sale of furniture wrongly credited to machinery a/c earlier)	Dr.		130	130
(*e*)	Suspense a/c To Y's a/c (or creditor a/c) (Being the credit purchase made from Y not recorded in his account)	Dr.		49	49
(*f*)	R a/c To P a/c (Being the entry to rectify the wrong credit given to R instead of P)	Dr.		320	320
(*g*)	Suspense a/c To S a/c (Being the entry to rectify the error of debiting S twice)	Dr.		250	250

(h)	Depreciation To Suspense a/c (Being the entry to record depreciation figure correctly)	Dr.		200	200
(i)	Wages a/c To Suspense a/c (Being the entry to record the wages, which was not recorded earlier)	Dr.		50	50

Suspense A/c

	Rs.		Rs.
To Sales a/c	36	By Balance b/d	76
To Purchase return	43	By Discount allowed a/c	52
To Y's a/c	49	By Depreciation a/c	200
To S's a/c	250	By Wages a/c	50
Total	378		378

Illustration 12:

You are presented with a trial balance showing a difference which has been carried to suspense account, and the following errors are revealed:

(*a*) Rupees 850 paid in cash for a typewriter was charged to office expenses account.

(*b*) A cash sale of Rs. 2,500 to Ram correctly entered in the cash book, was posted to the credit of Ram's account in the sale ledger.

(*c*) Goods amounting to Rs. 400 returned by Mohan were entered in the sales book and posted there from to the credit of Mohan's account.

(*d*) Bills receivable from Ravi for Rs. 1,500 posted to the credit of bills payable account and credited to Ravi's account.

(*e*) Goods amounting to Rs. 5,000 sold to Arun were correctly entered in the Sales book but posted to Arun's account for Rs. 9,000.

(*f*) Sales returns book was overcast by Rs. 50.

Journalise the necessary corrections and prepare the suspense account.

Solution:

Journal Entries

Sl. No.	*Particulars*		*L.F.*	*Dr. Amount Rs.*	*Cr. Amount Rs.*
(*a*)	Office equipment a/c To Office expenses a/c (Purchase of a typewriter wrongly charged to office expenses, now rectified)	Dr.		850	850
(*b*)	Ram a/c To Sales a/c (Cash sale wrongly credited to customer's a/c, now rectified)	Dr.		2,500	2,500
(*c*)	Sales a/c Sales return a/c To Suspense a/c (Goods returned by Mohan wrongly entered in the sales day book)	Dr. Dr.		400 400	800

(*d*)	Bills payable a/c Bills receivable a/c To Suspense a/c (Bills receivable from Ravi credited to bills payable a/c though correctly credited to Ravi, now rectified)	Dr. Dr.	1,500 1,500	 3,000
(*e*)	Suspense a/c To Arun's a/c (Goods sold to Arun Rs. 5,000 wrongly posted to his account as Rs. 9,000, now rectified)	Dr.	4,000	 4,000
(*f*)	Suspense a/c To Sales return a/c (Error caused by overcasting the sales return book, now rectified)	Dr.	50	 50

Suspense Account

Date	*Particulars*	*Rs.*	*Date*	*Particulars*	*Rs.*
	To Sales return a/c	50		By Difference in Trial Balance) (Balancing fig.	250
	To Arun a/c	4,000		Sales a/c	400
				Sales return a/c	400
				Bills payable a/c	1,500
				Bills receivable a/c	1,500
	Total	4,050			4,050

Illustration 13:

Mr. Rajan closes his books on March 31 every year. In August 2008, he found that his books for the year 2007-08 contained some errors in spite of an agreed trial balance. The errors were:

(*a*) Rs. 1,600 paid for purchase of office furniture was posted to the purchase account.

(*b*) The sales book was overcast by Rs. 500.

(*c*) Rs. 550 paid for freight on machinery was debited to freight account for Rs. 1,050.

(*d*) Opening stock was overstated by Rs. 6,000 by a wrong casting in the inventory.

(*e*) An amount of Rs. 1,400 was received in full settlement from a customer after he was allowed a discount of Rs. 140 but while writing the books the amount received was entered in the discount column and the discount allowed was entered in the amount column.

(*f*) A Cheque of Rs. 14,660 received from Mr. Sunil, after allowing him discount of Rs. 140 was endorsed to Mr. Anil in full settlement for Rs. 15,000. The cheque was finally dishonoured but no entries for dishonour were passed in the books.

Give journal entries to rectify the above errors using the P & L adjustment account, where necessary.

Solution:

Journal Entries

Sl. No.	Particulars	L.F.	Dr. Amount Rs.	Cr. Amount Rs.
(a)	Office furniture a/c Dr. To P & L adjustment a/c		1,600	1,600
(b)	P&L adjustment a/c Dr. To Suspense a/c		500	500
(c)	Machinery a/c Dr. Suspense a/c Dr. To P&L Adjustment a/c		550 500	1,050
(d)	P & L Adjustment a/c Dr. To opening stock		6,000	6,000
(e)	Cash a/c Dr. To P & L adjustment		1,260	1,260
(f)	Sunil's a/c Dr. P & Ł adjustment a/c To Anil's a/c		14,800 200	15,000

The P/L adjustment a/c is used because the profits for 2007-08 are already arrived at in the balance sheet. Adjustment a/c can be adjusted against the balance in the P/L a/c.

Illustration 14:

The account of a business firm prepared the trial balance and the total of debits equalled the total of credits. However, some of the errors subsequently discovered were as follows:

(*i*) The sales day book was overcast by Rs. 2,500.
(*ii*) Machinery maintenance expenditure of Rs. 17,500 had been debited to machinery a/c.
(*iii*) A Purchase return of Rs. 2,000 had been posted to the credit of the supplier account.
(*iv*) An amount of Rs. 10,000 received from a customer had been omitted to be posted to the customer's account.
(*v*) The purchases day book was undercast by Rs. 500.

After correcting the above errors the suspense account would have a balance of:

(*a*) Rs. 2,050 (Debit).
(*b*) Rs. 3,000 (Credit).
(*c*) Nil.
(*d*) Rs. 3,000 (Debit).
(*e*) None of the above.

Solution:

Suspense A/c

	Rs.		Rs.
To Customer a/c	10,000	By Sales a/c	2,500
		By Supplier a/c	4,000
		By Purchase a/c	500
		By Bal. c/d	3,000
Total	10,000		10,000

Option (*d*) is correct.

Illustration 15:

This trial balance of M/s. P.M. Kashyap as on 31st March 2008 did not tally. The difference of Rs. 15,100 was transferred to the credit of suspense a/c. After the completion of final accounts, the following errors were discovered.

(*a*) Total of Sales figure was taken as Rs. 56,000 instead of 65,000.

(*b*) The total of purchases Returns book was undercast by Rs. 100.

(*c*) Sale of old furniture for Rs. 900 was wrongly entered in machinery a/c.

(*d*) A credit purchase of Rs. 5,000 made from Mr. Y was recorded in purchases book but was not posted in Y's account.

(*e*) Rs. 1,000 received from A was posted to the credit of B.

(*f*) A credit sale of Rs. 2,000/- made to Mr. S was recorded twice in his account.

(*g*) Wages amounting to Rs. 1000 were paid on 20th March, 2008. They were recorded in Cash Book but were not recorded in the wages a/c.

Give journal entries to record the above transactions and prepare the suspense a/c.

Solution:

Date	*Particulars*		*L.F.*	*Dr. Amount Rs.*	*Cr. Amount Rs.*
(*a*)	Suspense a/c	Dr.		9,000	
	To Sales a/c				9,000
	(Being the sales figure undercast by Rs. 9,000)				
(*b*)	Suspense a/c	Dr.		100	
	To Purchase returns a/c				100
	(Being the total of purchases returns undercast by Rs. 100)				
(*c*)	Machinery a/c	Dr.		900	
	To Furniture				900
	(Being the sale of old furniture wrongly entered in Machinery a/c)				
(*d*)	Suspense a/c	Dr.		5,000	
	To Y				5,000
	(Being the credit purchase of Rs. 5,000 made from Y not recorded in his account earlier)				
(*e*)	B	Dr.		1,000	
	To A				1,000
	(Being the wrong credit given to B now rectified)				
(*f*)	Suspense a/c	Dr.		2,000	
	To S				2,000
	(Being the entry for rectifying the error of debiting S twice)				
(*g*)	Wages a/c	Dr.		1,000	
	To Suspense a/c				1,000
	(Being the amount of wages not recorded earlier)				

Suspense A/c

	Rs.		Rs.
To Sales a/c	9,000	By Balance b/d	15,100
To Purchase returns a/c	100	By Wages a/c	1,000
To Y	5,000		
To S	2,000		
Total	16,100		16,100

THEORY QUESTIONS

1. Explain the errors which affect the agreement of trial balance.
2. Explain the errors which are not disclosed despite the agreement of a trial balance.

EXERCISES AND PROBLEMS

1. Rectify the following errors:
   (*a*) A purchase of Rs. 200 from Ram was omitted to be entered in the Purchase book.
   (*b*) A credit sale of Rs. 527 to John was recorded as Rs. 725.
   (*c*) A purchase of office furniture for Rs. 1,000 from Salwan Furniture was entered through Purchase Book.
   (*d*) Rent paid to landlord Rs. 600 was debited to his personal account.
   (*e*) Purchases Book was undercast by Rs. 200.
2. Give Journal Entries to rectify the following errors:
   (*i*) An account of Rs. 4,000 spent for the extension of machinery has been debited to wages A/c.
   (*ii*) Rs. 150 paid as cartage for the newly purchased furniture posted to cartage A/c.
   (*iii*) A builder's bill for Rs. 6,000 for erection of a small cycle shed was debited to repairs A/c.
   (*iv*) A cheque of Rs. 2,000 received from Ashok was dishonoured and had been posted to the debit side of 'Allowance A/c.'
   (*v*) Rs. 1,000 paid for the newly purchased 'cooler' posted to 'purchase account.'
3. Make the necessary correcting entries and show the Suspense Account.
   (*i*) The Purchases Book was undercast by Rs. 1,000.
   (*ii*) The Sales Book was overcast by Rs. 50.
   (*iii*) Rs. 20 received from Kiran were posted to the debit of his A/c.
   (*iv*) The total of the credit of Ajay's A/c has been over added by Rs. 500.
   (*v*) A discount of Rs. 18 allowed to a customer has been credited to his account as Rs. 81.
   (*vi*) Goods for Rs. 1,000 returned to Sharma, though entered in the Return Book has been posted to his account.
4. There was a difference of Rs. 725 in a Trial Balance. It has been transferred to credit side of suspense A/c. Later on following errors were discovered. Pass the rectifying entries and prepare suspense A/c:
   (*a*) An amount of Rs. 375 has been posted in the debit side of commission account instead of Rs. 275.
   (*b*) Goods of Rs. 200 purchased from Deepak have been posted to his account as Rs. 250.
   (*c*) Total of Sales Returns Book was overcast by Rs. 475.

(*d*) A credit amount of Rs. 50 was posted as Rs. 150 to the debit side of a personal account.

(*e*) Goods of Rs. 300 were sold to Nitin, but it was recorded in Purchase Book.

5. Pass rectification entries for the following transaction:

(*i*) A bill of exchange (received from Preeti) for Rs. 3,000 had been returned by the bank with whom, it had been discounted, as dishonoured and had been credited to Bank A/c and debited to Bill Receivable A/c.

(*ii*) A purchase of goods from Anku amounting to Rs. 300 has been wrongly passed through the Sales Book.

(*iii*) On 31st Dec. 2008 goods of the value of Rs. 200 were returned by Gopi Chand and were taken into stock on the same date, but no entry was passed in the books.

(*iv*) An amount of Rs. 2,000 due from Deepak, which has been written off as a Bad debt in a previous year, was unexpectedly recovered and has been posted to the personal account of Deepak.

(*v*) A cheque for Rs. 500 received from Manish was dishonoured and had been posted to the debit side of Sales Returns Account.

(*vi*) A Bill Receivable of Rs. 400 received from Ram was passed through the Bills Payable Book.

(*vii*) Rs. 480 paid for wages to workmen for making showcases had been charged to wages A/c.

(*vii*) Rs. 5,000 paid for the purchase of a Motor cycle for the proprietor had been charged to miscellaneous expenses A/c.

(*ix*) X was paid cash Rs. 5,600 but Y was debited by Rs. 5,000.

(*x*) Purchases Returns Book was carried forward as Rs. 132 instead of 123.

6. An Accountant, while balancing his books found that there was a difference of Rs. 17,190 in the Trial Balance. Being required to prepare the final accounts, he placed this difference to a newly opened Suspense Account which was carried forward to the next year, when the following errors were discovered:

(*a*) Goods bought from a merchant for Rs. 1,100 had been posted to the credit of his account as Rs. 110.

(*b*) An item of Rs. 2,124 entered in the Sales Return Book had been posted to the debit of the customer who returned the goods.

(*c*) Sundry items of plant sold for Rs. 52,000 had been entered in the Sales Book, the total of which book had been posted to Sales Account.

(*d*) Rs. 12,000 owing by a customer had been omitted from the schedule of Sundry Debtors.

(*e*) Rs. 462 discount received from a creditor had been duly entered in his account but not posted to Discount Account.

Give Journal entries necessary to correct these errors and prepare the Suspense account.

7. The books of a private firm have been posted upto 31st December. 2008, how would you correct the following errors which were subsequently found therein:

(*i*) An amount of Rs. 1,000 received from Motilal on 1st January, 2003 had been entered in the Cash Book as having been received on 31st December, 2008.

(*ii*) Rs. 750 paid for the purchase of a consumable durable for one of the partners has been charged to General Expenses A/c.

(*iii*) An addition in the returns inward book has been cast Rs. 100 short.

(*iv*) A cheque of Rs. 200 drawn for petty cash Account in the Ledger.

(*v*) Rs. 15 appearing in the discount column on the credit side of the cash book, had not been posted to a personal account.

Journalise the necessary corrections.

8. The book-keeper of a firm, having been unable to agree the Trial balance, raised a Suspense Account in which he entered the amount by which it was out of balance. The following errors were discovered:
   (*a*) Goods bought from a supplier amounting to Rs. 77 had been noted to the credit of his account as Rs. 770.
   (*b*) A dishonoured Bill of Exchange receivable for Rs. 800 returned to the firm's bank had been credited to the Bank A/c and debited to Bills Receivable Account. A cheque was received later from the customer for Rs. 800 and duly paid.
   (*c*) An item of Rs. 80 entered in the Sales Return Book had been posted to the debit of the customer who returned the goods.
   (*d*) An amount of Rs. 800 owing by a customer had been duly entered in his account, but not posted to the Discount Account.
   (*e*) Bills Receivable from W Rs. 1,600 posted to the credit of Bills Payable Account and credited to W.
9. The accountant of a firm finds that the trial balance as on 31st December, 2008 is out by an excess debit of Rs. 566. He placed the amount in the Suspense Account. In the first week of January, 2009, he discovered the following errors. Pass journal entries necessary to rectify these errors and show the Suspense Account as it would appear at the end of the week. Do you have any comment to make?
   (*a*) Cash paid to Amar Nath, Rs. 150, was posted on the credit of Amar Singh's Account as Rs. 114.
   (*b*) Discount allowed by Jones Rs. 10, was not entered in the Cash book, but Jones stands debited correctly.
   (*c*) No entry was made for goods worth Rs. 80 taken away by proprietor for personal use.
   (*d*) Rs. 1,000 received from Jhaveri Bros. for interest on loan advanced to them were recorded in the cash book. But the entry was not posted in the ledger.
   (*e*) The total of Returns Outward Book was short by Rs. 200.

(***Hint:*** At the end of the week, the Suspense Account will indicate a debit balance of Rs. 380. It means that there are still some errors left undetected, due to which trial balance will not tally).

10. An accountant, while balancing his books found that there was a difference of Rs. 135 in the trial balance. Being required to prepare the final accounts he placed the difference to a newly opened Suspense Account, which was carried forward to the next year when the following errors were discovered:
   (*a*) Salary for the month of March was posted twice, Rs. 77.50.
   (*b*) Interest on investments collected by the bankers, were posted directly in concerned accounts through the pass book, but no entry was made in the bank column of the cash book Rs. 37.50.
   (*c*) Goods worth Rs. 350 were distributed as free samples but this fact has not been taken into Books.
   (*d*) Rent of Rs. 175 received from Ashok credited both to Rent Account and Ashok Account.
   (*e*) A purchase of a chair from Mohan Furniture Mart for Rs. 32.50 has been entered in the purchase book as Rs. 28.
   (*f*) Old machinery sold to the proprietor Kamal for Rs. 200 was entered in Sales Book as sale to Kishore.
   (*g*) Cash purchases from Ajay Rs. 94.50 were recorded in Cash Book as well as in Purchases Book and Posted from both.
   (*h*) Closing stock has been undervalued by Rs. 150.

Preparation of Financial Statements: Profit and Loss Account and Balance Sheet

Trial Balance is first step towards preparation of financial statements — namely, Trading and Profit and Loss Account and Balance Sheet. Trading and Profit and Loss Account are prepared in order to determine the income earned or loss incurred during the accounting period. Balance Sheet indicates the financial position of the enterprise. However, before preparing trading account, profit and loss account and balance sheet, certain adjustment entries are required.

Adjustment Entries

As stated earlier, financial accounting uses accrual basis of accounting which is supported by Generally Accepted Accounting Principles (GAAP). Under accrual basis of accounting:

1. Revenue are recognised when earned, without regard to the timing of cash receipts.
2. Expenses are recognised either (*a*) in the period in which related revenues are recognised or (*b*) when incurred, without regard to the timing of cash disbursements.

Another basis of accounting, which is not supported by GAAP is the cash basis. Unlike the accrual basis, the cash basis of accounting links revenues and expenses of an accounting period to the timing of cash flows. Specifically, revenue is recognised in the period in which cash is received and expenses is recognised at the time cash is paid. The cash basis of accounting is objective and relatively easy to use and is employed by individuals, individual professionals such as lawyers, accountants, teachers, small businesses. However, it is opposed to accrual basis of accounting as a basis of preparing financial statements of a business enterprise.

When the accrual basis of accounting is used, adjusting entries are required at the end of the period to record any previously unrecognised changes in assets, liabilities, revenues, or expenses. Adjusting entries are made to modify certain account balances at the end of the accounting period so that they will reflect fairly the situation as of the end of the period. Adjusting entries can be referred to as internal transactions, distinct from external transactions which are between a business entity and the parties external to the entity. It should be noted that the external (exchange) transactions are already found recorded in the accounting records and different ledger accounts.

The following are a few examples of situations where adjusting entries are needed and the accountant has to process these additional information before preparing the financial statements on the basis of trial balance:

(*a*) The accountant may know (or be instructed by the Accounts Manager) that the depreciation on building is to be charged at the rate of 10%.

(*b*) The accountant would ascertain that the salary of some workers for January is unpaid at the end of the month.

(*c*) The accountant is informed by the store-keeper that the goods lying unsold in the store (representing closing stock) is worth Rs. 17,000 at cost.

(*d*) The accountant knows or is informed that the loan of Rs. 2,00,000 was taken at an interest of 12% per annum. He also knows that the interest accrued for January is unpaid as on January 31, since there is no ledger account for any interest paid.

(*e*) The accountant knows that the insurance premium was paid for the whole year whereas the accounts are being prepared for one month.

(*f*) The accountant is informed that Rs. 50,000 may not be collected from PQR Company owing to some technical dispute.

Thus, if profit and loss account is to report a realistic net profit (or net loss) based on accrual accounting, all revenues earned during the period and all expenses incurred must be shown. Therefore, revenues and costs must be properly matched or aligned for the reporting period in question, popularly known as matching concept in the accounting literature.

Generally, four general types of adjustment (adjusting entries) are needed at the end of the accounting period prior to the preparation of financial statements:

1. Unrecorded revenue earned during the accounting period.
2. Unrecorded expenses incurred during the accounting period.
3. Aligning recorded costs with the appropriate accounting periods, i.e., considering expenditures benefiting more than one accounting period.
4. Aligning recorded revenue with the appropriate accounting periods, i.e. considering revenues received in advance.

Adjustment in the first two categories — unrecorded revenues and unrecorded expenses — are referred to as accruals such as salaries and wages incurred but not paid, interest earned but not received. Adjustments in the last two categories — reflecting recorded costs and revenues with the appropriate periods — are referred to as deferrals such as prepaid expenses, unearned revenue and depreciation.

Adjusting entries have following features:

1. Every adjusting entry affects both the profit and loss account and the balance sheet.
2. Adjusting entries do not directly affect the cash account.
3. They are generally recorded at the end of the accounting period.
4. A profit and loss account balance (revenue or expense) is changed.
5. A balance sheet account balance (asset or liability) is changed.

TYPES OF ADJUSTING ENTRIES

The different items or situations which are subject to adjusting entries before preparing financial statements are explained below:

Closing Inventory

Under the periodic verification method, the closing inventory of every item is arrived at by physically counting the inventory available and assigning a value to the same. In concerns adopting the periodic verification method, the value of closing inventory will be brought into the books of accounts through the following journal entry:

Closing inventory A/c Dr.
To Trading A/c

While the closing inventory appears on the credit side of the trading account to reduce the cost of goods sold, it also appears as an asset in the Balance Sheet.

Outstanding or Accrued Expense

The nominal accounts record the actual expense paid during the accounting period. However, prior to the preparation of the financial statements, it must be ensured that all expenses which have fallen due to be paid but which have not been paid during the accounting period are also brought into the books to help in the proper matching of revenues and expenses. For example, ABC Trading Company had the practice of paying the salaries of the employees on 4th of the subsequent month. During the financial year ending 31st March, 2008 the salaries account shows a debit balance of Rs. 55,000. The salaries of Rs. 6,000 pertaining to March 2008 were paid on 4th April, 2008. While preparing the financial statements for the year ending 31st March, 2008, the salaries of Rs. 6,000 of March must also be included. This is done with the following adjusting journal entry:

Salaries A/c Dr. 6,000
To Outstanding Salaries A/c 6,000

The above journal entry increase the salaries to the correct amount of Rs. 61,000 and the outstanding salaries of Rs. 6,000 will be shown as a liability in the Balance Sheet.

The adjusting journal entry to record any outstanding accrued expense is

Expense A/c Dr.
To Outstanding Expense A/c

While the amount of expense taken from the Trial Balance will be increased by the amount outstanding and shown in the Trading and Profit and Loss Account, the actual amount outstanding will be shown as a liability in the Balance Sheet.

In the subsequent accounting period, the outstanding expense liability will be transferred to the expense or nominal account and will be setoff by the entry of actual payments when it is made.

Prepaid Expense

Certain expenses paid may relate to more than one accounting period. In such cases, it is necessary to identify that portion of the expenditure for which the benefit is yet to be received by the concern and treat that part of the expenditure as prepaid.

ABC Trading Company took an insurance cover for all assets against fire on 1st October 2007 and paid the annual premium of Rs. 2,400 on the same day. Since the benefit of the entire expenditure will expire only on 30th September, 2008 it is necessary to recognise this aspect while preparing the financial statements as on 31st March, 2008.

The amount of expense prepaid on 1st October, 2007 = (1/2 × 2,400 = Rs. 1,200)

The adjusting entry to record the prepaid insurance is

Prepaid Insurance A/c	Dr.	1,200	
To Insurance A/c			1,200

This ensures that the insurance expense is reported at the correct figure of Rs. 1,200 in the profit and loss account and the prepaid amount is shown as an asset in the balance sheet.

The journal entry to record any prepaid expense is,

Prepaid Expense A/c Dr.
To Expense A/c

In the subsequent accounting period, the balance in the prepaid expense account will be transferred back to the expense account.

Outstanding or Accrued Income

An income appearing in the ledger account may not represent the income that must have been received during the year. If a portion of an income has not yet been received or outstanding as at the end of the accounting period then the outstanding amount must be brought into books.

ABC Trading Company would have received the interest of Rs. 350 [5,000 × (14/100) × 1/2] during the accounting period ending 31st March 2008, the interest of Rs. 350 for the next six months will be received only in the subsequent accounting period. However, while preparing the financial statements, the total interest revenue to be recognised is the amount of Rs. 350 actually received plus the interest of Rs. 175 pertaining to the period 1st January, 2008 to 31st March, 2008.

The following adjusting entry will bring into books the amount of outstanding interest:

Outstanding Interest A/c	Dr.	175	
To Interest Received A/c			175

While the interest received will be increased to Rs. 525 and shown in the profit and loss account, the outstanding interest account will be listed as an asset in the Balance Sheet.

In the subsequent accounting period, the amount in the outstanding interest A/c will be transferred to interest received A/c and the actual receipt of the interest will offset the former transfer entry.

To record any outstanding income in the books of accounts, the journal entry is:

Outstanding Income A/c Dr.
To Income A/c

Income Received in Advance

While preparing the financial statements, adjustments may be necessary in respect of any income received in advance.

India Today publications has received subscriptions amounting to Rs. 50,000 during the financial year ending 31st December, 2007, out of this Rs. 2,500 represent subscriptions relating to the next financial year.

The entry to adjust for the income received in advance will be,

Subscriptions A/c Dr. 2,500
To Subscriptions Received in Advance 2,500

With the posting of the above journal entry, the subscriptions account will be shown in the profit and loss account at the credit figure of Rs. 47,500 and in the balance sheet, the subscriptions received in advance as liability. Any income received in advance is a liability as benefits are yet to be conferred to the person from whom the amount has been received. The journal entry to record the adjustment of any income received in advance is

Income A/c Dr.
To Income Received in Advance A/c

Depreciation

Depreciation is the acquisition cost of an asset (less the expected salvage value) spread over the economic life of that asset. The purpose of charging depreciation over the economic life of the asset is to match the cost of the asset over the period for which revenue is earned by using the asset.

There are two methods of recording depreciation. Under the first method, the asset account is directly credited for the depreciation and the written down value is readily ascertained. The journal entry to record depreciation under the method is

Depreciation A/c Dr.
To Asset A/c

Under the second method, the depreciation charged is credited to a depreciation provision a/c and the written down value of the asset is shown in the balance sheet by deducting the provision from the original cost of the asset. The journal entry recorded under this method is

Depreciation A/c Dr.
To Depreciation Provision A/c

Balance in Depreciation is transferred to Profit and Loss A/c. The accounting entry is as under:

Profit and Loss A/c Dr.
To Depreciation A/c

Depreciation provision account, if opened, will be shown by way of deduction from the relevant asset a/c in the balance sheet.

PROVISION FOR BAD DEBITS, CASH DISCOUNTS PAYABLE AND CASH DISCOUNTS RECEIVABLE

Bad Debts

The sales revenue recorded in the books of accounts of an organisation represent the amount realised or to be realised from the sale of goods. When goods are sold on credit it may sometimes happen that even though customers bought them with every intention of paying for them, due to certain subsequent change in circumstances, they may not be able to fulfil their obligations. For instance, if a customer, subsequent to the date of credit sales, is adjusted an insolvent and his estate cannot pay anything towards satisfaction of the amount due from him, then logically, the entry passed at the time of sale should be removed by reversing it, as the situation is similar to the sale not having taken place. In practice, however, instead of reversing the previous entry, the amount which cannot be recovered is considered as a loss called 'Bad debts.'

Example:

ABC Ltd., had debtors outstanding to the extent of Rs. 75,000/- as on 31st March 2007. Mr. X, who owed Rs. 1,500/- to the company has been adjudged insolvent and his estate is unable to pay anything.

The journal entry to record the above loss would be —

Bad debts A/c	Dr.	1,500/-	
To X A/c		Cr.	1,500/-

Note that the sales account remains unchanged. However, in the income statement, while sales revenue will appear at the full figure, the bad debts will appear as a loss and thus the reduction in the amount realised will be accounted for. The Accounts Receivable account will also appear in the Balance Sheet at the realisable value of Rs. 73,500/-.

The journal entry for recording bad debts is —

Bad Debts A/c Dr.
To Accounts Receivable A/c

Provision for Bad and Doubtful Debts

We have already seen that according to the realisation concept, the amount to be recognised as revenue is the amount that is reasonably certain to be realised. When there is a possibility that all the sales revenue may not be realised in the future due to occurrence of bad debts, the sales revenue, then, in the income statement should reflect this position. However, in practice, the sales revenue is shown as the gross figure and any possible loss due to bad debts is shown as an expense.

When bad debts are expected to occur in the future, (*a*) the exact amount of loss may not be known and (*b*) a particular debtor's account cannot be identified to write off the expected loss or even if the debtor's account can be identified, a reduction in claim can be given effect to only when it becomes certain. To circumvent these problems, usually a provision is made for the expected bad debts loss out of profits of the current year. This reduces the profit and hence the income statement conforms to the realisation principle and also prevents an estimated portion of profits from being distributed to the proprietors. The provision in this context means any amount retained by providing for any known decline in value of assets of which the amount cannot be determined with substantial accuracy. For creating the provision for bad and doubtful debts, the journal entry is,

Profit and Loss A/c Dr.
To Provision for Bad Debts A/c.

Example:

The Accounts Receivable of PQR Ltd. was Rs. 1,50,000/- as on 31st March, 2008. It was estimated that Rs. 5,000/- of the amount due may turn out to be uncollectable during the forthcoming year.

For creation of the provision the journal entry will be,

Profit and Loss A/c Dr. 5.000/-
To Provision for Bad Debts A/c 5,000/-

While the amount of the possible loss will appear on the debit side of the profit and loss account, the provision created, though a liability will be shown as a deduction from Accounts Receivable on the asset side of balance sheet. This would ensure that the current asset is shown at the realizable value.

Balance Sheet of PQR Ltd., as on 31.03.2008

Liabilities	*Assets*	*Rs.*	*Rs.*
	Accounts Receivables	1,50,000.00	
	Less Provision for bad debts	5,000.00	1,45,000.00

Estimating Bad and Doubtful Debts

Any one of the following methods may be used to estimate the amount of possible bad debts.

1. Bad debts may be estimated as a percentage of total sales during the year. This method can be used only when there are no cash sales or such sales are negligible.
2. Bad debts may be estimated as a percentage of credit sales.
3. Estimate bad debts as a percentage of receivable outstanding at the end of the accounting period.

The percentage used will be based on the judgement of the management and the past experience with regard to bad debts. Another logical way to estimate bad debts would be to draw up an aging schedule for the outstanding debtors and apply different percentages for amounts outstanding for various lengths of time.

Treatment of Bad Debts when a Provision for Bad Debts Exists

Let us extend the example of PQR Ltd., to the financial year ending 31st March, 2008.

The following details are available:

Bad debts during the year	Rs.	3,500
Accounts Receivable as on 31.3.2008	Rs.	1,70,000

PQR Ltd., would like to maintain the provision at 5% of Sundry Debtors.

The Accounts Receivables of Rs. 1,70,000/- as on 31/3/2008 is after accounting for the bad debts of Rs. 3,500/-. When bad debts occurred, the following entry would have been passed.

Bad Debts A/c Dr. 3,500/-
To Sundry Debtors A/c 3,500/-

Since provision for bad debts to the extent of Rs. 5,000/- already exists, the actual bad debts of Rs. 3,500/- will be transferred at the end of the year to this provision account and not to the profit and loss account.

The entry for the transfer will be:

Provision for the Bad Debts A/c Dr. Rs. 3,500/-
To Bad Debts A/c Rs. 3,500/-

At this point the Provision A/c will appear as under:

Provision for Bad Debts A/c

31.03.2008	*Rs.*	*1.4.2007*	*Rs.*
To Bad Debts A/c	3,500.00	By balance b/d	5,000.00

Since the provision has been utilised to the extent of Rs. 3,500/-, only Rs. 1,500/- is left for setting off any bad debts in the following year. However, PQR Ltd., wishes to maintain the provision at 5% on debtors. So, the balance required in the provision account as on 31.3.2008 is,

$$1{,}70{,}000 \times \frac{5}{100} = \text{Rs. } 8{,}500$$

To bring up the provision to the required balance, a further appropriation of Rs. 7,000/- (8,500/- – 1,500/-) will have to be made from the profits and loss account. Entry will be,

Profit and Loss A/c	Dr.	7,000.00	
To Provision for Bad Debts A/c			7,000.00

The provision account after posting this entry will appear as follows:

Provision for Bad Debts A/c

Dr. *Cr.*

		Rs.			*Rs.*
31.03.2008	To Bad Debts	3,500.00	01.04.2007	By Balance	5,000.00
31.03.2008	To Balance c/d	8,500.00	31.03.2008	By Profit and Loss A/c	7,000.00
		12,000.00			12,000.00

The balance sheet will again show the Accounts Receivable at their realisable value.

Balance Sheet of PQR Ltd., as on 31.3.2008

Liabilities	*Assets*	*Rs.*	*Rs.*
	Accounts Receivables	1,70,000.00	
	Less: Provision for Bad Debts	8,500.00	1,61,500.00

We will extend the above example to yet another financial year.

The following details are available for the year ending 31.3.2009

Bad Debts during the year	1,000.00
Sundry Debtors as on 31.3.2003	1,10,000

PQR Ltd., would like to maintain the provision for bad debts as 5% of debtors.

As in the previous year, the total bad debts will be transferred to the provision for bad debts.

Provision for Bad Debts A/c	Dr.	1,000.00	
To Bad Debts A/c			1,000.00

The provision account after the above transfer will appear as follows:

Provision for Bads Debts A/c

Dr.					*Cr.*
31.3.2009	To Bad debts	1,000.00	01.04.2008	By Balance b/d	8,500.00

The provision required on the closing debtors will be,

(5 ÷ 100) × 1,10,000 = Rs. 5,500/-

The opening provision of Rs. 8,500/- has been utilised only to the extent of Rs. 1.000/- and therefore, Rs. 7,500/- is the amount available for further appropriation. Since the balance to be carried forward to the next accounting year is only Rs. 5,500/- a sum of Rs. 2,000/- (7,500/- less 5,500/-) can be transferred back to Profit and Loss A/c as excess provision which is not required to be carried forward. So, to retain a balance of Rs. 5,500/- in the provision account, the journal entry will be,

Provision for Bad Debts A/c	Dr.	2,000.00	
To Profit & Loss A/c			2,000.00

Provision for Bad Debts A/c

Dr.				*Cr.*
31.3.2009	To Bad Debts A/c	1,000	1.4.2008 By Balance b/d	8,500
31.3.209	To Profit & Loss A/c	2,000		
31.3.2009	To Balance c/d	5,500		
		8,500		8,500

The balance sheet will show the realisable value of sundry debtors.

Balance Sheet of PQR Ltd., as on 31.3.2009

Liabilities	*Assets*	*Rs.*	*Rs.*
	Accounts Receivables *Less:* Provision for Bad Debts	1,10,000.00 5,500.00	1,04,500.00

Recovery for Bad Debts Written Off

Sometimes, an amount written off as bad debts may be subsequently recovered. Any such recovery must be treated as a windfall and transferred to the Profit and Loss A/c as a gain.

The journal entries will be,

At the time of receipt of the amount

Bank a/c or Cash A/c Dr.

To Bad Debts Recovered A/c

At the end of the financial year,

Bad Debts Recovered A/c. Dr.

To Profit and Loss A/c.

Provision for Discounts on Accounts Receivables

The organisations which allow the facility of making payments before the due date,and enable their debtors to avail of cash discount, must take into account the possible amount of discounts that may be allowed on closing debtors in the forthcoming year. This is necessary to show the closing debtors at their realisable value.

The principles for creation and maintenance of the provisions for discounts on debtors are the same as those discussed in the section on provision for bad debts. The only additional point to be noted is that discounts will be estimated on debts considered goods, *i.e.*, closing sundry debtors minus provision for bad debts.

The illustration given here explains the methods of maintaining a provision for discounts on debtors. The following details are available for M Limited.

	Year Ending		
	31.3.2006 *Rs.*	*31.3.2007* *Rs.*	*31.3.2008* *Rs.*
Accounts Receivables	5,00,000	4,50,000	6,00,000
Discounts Allowed		1,000	8,000

While the company maintains 5% provision for bad debts, it would like to maintain 3% provision for discounts beginning from 31.3.2006.

The entries in the provision for discounts on receivables and the relevant extracts from the balance sheets are given below:

Provision for Discounts on Accounts Receivables A/c

Dr.	*Rs.*		*Cr.* *Rs.*
31.3.2006		31.3.2006	
To Balance c/d	14,250/-	By Profit & Loss A/c	14,250/-
	14,250/-		14,250/-
31.3.2007		1.4.2006	
To Discounts Allowed	1,000/-	By Balance b/d	14,250/-
To Profit and Loss a/c	425/-		
To Balance c/d	12,825/-		
	14,250/-		14,250/-
31.3.2008		1.4.2007	
To Discounts allowed	8,000/-	By Balance b/d	12,825/-
To Balance c/d	17,100/-	By Profit and Loss A/c	12,275/-
Total	25,100/-		25,100/-

Working Notes:

31.3.2006

Accounts Receivables		5,00,000.00
Less: Provision for bad debts at 5%		25,000.00
Debts considered goods		4,75,000.00
Provision for discounts on Accounts Receivable	(3/100) × 4,75,000/-	= 14,250.00

31.3.2007)

Accounts Receivables	4,50,000.00
Less: Provision for Bad debts at 5%	22,500.00
Debts considered good	4,27,500.00

Provision for discount on Accounts Receivable =	
(3/100) × 4,27,500/- =	12,825.00
Opening Balance of Provision	14,250.00
Less: Discounts allowed during the year	1,000.00
	13,250.00

Since provision to be carried forward is only Rs. 12,825/- an amount of Rs. 425/- would be transferred to Profit and Loss A/c as excess provision.

31.3.2008	
Accounts Receivables	6,00,000.00
Less: Provision for Debts at 5%	30,000.00
Debts considered good	5,70,000.00
Provision for discounts on Receivables (3/100) × 5,70,000 =	17,100.00
Opening Balance of Provision	12,825.00
Less: Discounts allowed	8,000.00
	4,825.00

Additional amount to be transferred from Profit and Loss A/c (17,100 – 4,825) = 12,275/-

Balance Sheet of M. Ltd. as on 31.3.2006

Liabilities	*Assets*	*Rs.*	*Rs.*
	Accounts Receivable	5,00,000.00	
	Less: Provision for Bad Debts	25,000.00	
		4,75,000.00	
	Less: Provision for discounts	14,250.00	4,60,750.00

Balance Sheet of M. Ltd. as on 31.3.2007

Liabilities	*Assets*	*Rs.*	*Rs.*
	Accounts Receivable	4,50,000.00	
	Less: Provision for Bad Debts	22,500.00	
		4,27,500.00	
	Less: Provision for discounts	12,825.00	4,14,675.00

Balance Sheet of M. Ltd. as on 31.3.2008

Liabilities	*Assets*	*Rs.*	*Rs.*
	Accounts Receivable	6,00,000.00	
	Less: Provision for Bad Debts	30,000.00	
		5,70,000.00	
	Less: Provision for discounts	17,100.00	5,52,900.00

Reserve for discounts on Accounts Payable

Organisations may like to show the sundry creditors in the balance sheet at the net payable value by estimating in advance the amount of cash discounts that may be received at the time of settlement amounts due. This is usually done by creating a reserve for discounts on creditors and then transferring the discounts received to such reserve. Since, income in respect of discounts receivable is recognised in advance, the journal entry for creating the reserve will be:

Reserve for Discount on Accounts Payable A/c Dr.
To Profit and Loss A/c

The following illustration explains the mechanics of maintaining the reserve for discount on creditors.

The following details are available from the books of R. Limited.

	Year Ending		
	31.3.2006 *Rs.*	*31.3.2007* *Rs.*	*31.3.2008* *Rs.*
Accounts Payable	2,20,000.00	3,25,000.00	2,75,000.00
Discounts Received		3200.00	900.00

R. Limited would like to maintain a reserve for discount on Accounts Payable at 2% beginning from 31.3.2006.

The reserve account and the relevant extracts from the balance sheet are shown below:

Reserve for Discounts on Accounts Payable A/c

Dr.			*Cr.*
	Rs.		*Rs.*
31.3.2006 To Profit and Loss A/c	4,400	31.3.2006 By Balance c/d	4,400
	4,400		4,400
1.4.2006 To Balance b/d	4,400	31.3.2007 By Discounts received A/c	3,200
31.3.2007 To Profit and Loss A/c	5,300	By Balance c/d	6,500
	9,700		9,700
1.4.2008 To Balance b/d	6,500	31.3.2008 By Discounts received a/c	900
		By Profit and Loss A/c	100
		By Balance c/d	5,500
	6,500		6,500

Working Notes:

31.3.2006	
Accounts Payable	2,20,000/-
Reserve for discounts on Accounts Payable at 2%	4,400/-
31.3.2007	
Accounts Payable	3,25,000/-
Reserve for discounts at 2%	6,500/-
Opening Balance of Reserve	4,400/-
Less: Discounts received (4,400 + 3,200 – 6,500)	3,200/-
	1200/-
Additional reserve required = 6,500 – 1,200 =	5,300/-
31.3.2008	
Accounts Payable	2,75,000/-
Reserve for Discounts at 2%	5,500/-

Opening balance of reserve	6,500/-
Less: Discounts received	900/-
	5,600/-

Since the available reserve exceeds the amount to be carried forward, the amount of excess Rs. 100 will be transferred to the profit and loss account to off-set the income taken in excess in the previous year.

Balance Sheet of R. Limited as on 31.3.2006

Liabilities	*Rs.*	*Assets*	*Rs.*
Accounts Payable	2,20,000.00		
Less: Reserve for discounts	4,400.00		
	2,15,600.00		

Balance Sheet of R. Limited as on 31.3.2007

Liabilities	*Rs.*	*Assets*	*Rs.*
Accounts Payable	3,25,000.00		
Less: Reserve for discounts	6,500.00		
	3,18,500.00		

Balance Sheet of R. Limited as on 31.3.2008

Liabilities	*Rs.*	*Assets*	*Rs.*
Accounts Payable	2,75,000.00		
Less: Reserve for discounts	5,500.00		
	2,69,500.00		

CLOSING ENTRIES

The accounting treatment of the adjustments to be given effect to the various accounts for the preparation of financial statements have been discussed above. The next stage in the preparation of financial statements is the recording of the closing journal entries for the drawing up of the trading and profit and loss accounts. While the balance sheet is a mere listing of the assets and liabilities, the trading and profit and loss accounts are prepared in the form of ledger accounts and postings can be made into such accounts only if they have been entered in the book of prime entry of Journal. The trading and profit and loss accounts are nominal accounts and all expenses and incomes are transferred to this account. While expenses are shown on the debit side, the incomes are posted on the credit side.

Entries for the Preparation of Trading Account

(*i*) The purchases and sales returns must be transferred to the purchases and sales accounts respectively so that the net purchases and net sales can be determined. The entries for the transfer of returns are,

Purchases Returns A/c Dr.
  To Purchases A/c
Sales A/c Dr.
  To Sales Returns A/c

(*ii*) For the transfer of opening stock, purchases and other direct expenses such as carriage inwards, wages etc., the entry is

Trading A/c Dr.
To Opening Stock A/c
To Purchase A/c
To Direct Expenses A/c

(*iii*) For the transfer of net sales to trading account, the entry is,

Sales A/c Dr.
To Trading A/c

(*iv*) The balance in the trading account is found and the gross profit / loss is determined. For transferring the gross profit or gross loss to profit and loss account, the entry is:

(*a*) In case of gross profit

Trading A/c Dr.
To Profit and Loss A/c

(*b*) In case of gross loss

Profit and Loss A/c Dr.
To Trading A/c

Entries for Preparation of Profit and Loss Account:

(*i*) For transfer of all expenses, other than direct expenses, to profit and loss account the entry is,

Profit and Loss A/c Dr.
To Expenses A/c

(*ii*) For transfer of all income, other than sales and related income, to profit and loss account, the entry is,

Income A/c Dr.
To Profit and Loss A/c

(*iii*) The credit balance in the profit and loss account represents the net profit earned and belongs to the proprietors. The entry for the transfer of net profit is,

Profit and Loss A/c Dr.
To Capital A/c

The debit balance in profit and loss account represent the net loss. The entry for the transfer of net loss is

Capital A/c Dr.
To Profit & Loss A/c

Adjustments in the Capital Account

The capital account of the proprietor as shown in the balance sheet should reveal the net amount owning to him by the business as on the closing date. The opening balance of the capital account must be adjusted for:

(*i*) Drawings
(*ii*) Net Profit earned during the year/Net loss occurred during the year
(*iii*) Salary, if any, due to the proprietor
(*iv*) Interest on capital, if any, due to the proprietor
(*v*) Interest on drawings, if any, due from the proprietor

We have already seen the entry needed to transfer the net profit/ net loss to the capital account. The entries for the other adjustments will be as under:

For Transfer of drawings,

Capital A/c Dr.
To Drawings A/c

For providing for salary payable to proprietor

Proprietor's Salary A/c Dr.
To Capital A/c

The Proprietor's salary will be shown as an expense in the profit and loss account.

For interest on capital

Interest on Capital A/c. Dr.
To Capital A/c

The interest on capital will be shown as an expense in the profit and loss account.

For interest on drawings,

Capital A/c Dr.
To Interest on Drawings A/c

The interest on drawings will be shown as an income in the profit and loss account.

While the entries for the adjustement of drawings and net profit/net loss in the capital account are in the nature of closing entries, all other items will be entered in the capital account only with the help of adjusting entries.

With the completion of the positing of adjusting and closing entries in the general ledger, balances will exist only for the assets, liabilities and capital account. These balances will be carried forward to the next accounting period. At the beginning of the subsequent accounting period, when a new general ledger is brought into use, the opening assets and liabilities will be brought into the ledger through an opening journal entry.

The opening journal entry is,

Assets A/c Dr.
To Liabilities A/c
To Capital A/c

Capital and Revenue Receipts and Expenditures

After explaining the adjusting and closing entries, it would be appropriate to discuss separately the different types of receipts and expenditures whose understanding are useful while preparing the financial statement of a business enterprises.

Expenditure

Expenditure can be classified in to three categories:

1. Capital Expenditure:

It means an expenditure which has been incurred for the purpose of acquiring an asset to be held in business on long-term basis which results in increasing the earning capacity of the business. Some examples of capital expenditure are:

(*a*) Expenditure incurred on the purchase of furniture, plant, copyright, patents, goodwill etc.

(*b*) Expenditure incurred in increasing the capacity or efficiency of a fixed asset.

(*c*) Expenditure incurred on purchase of shares and debentures of other companies for a long duration.

2. Revenue Expenditure:

Expenditure incurred in running the business is termed as revenue expenditure. Examples of revenue expenditure are (*i*) rent, salaries, office expenses, cost of manufacturing and selling the product, repairs, depreciation etc.

3. Deferred Revenue Expenditure:

It is that revenue expenditure which is incurred in one accounting period but the benefit of which is available in future periods, e.g., Development costs in mines and plantations, discount on debentures in limited companies, market research, cost of experiments. Deferred revenue expenditure is written off over a number of years.

Receipts:

Receipts are of two types: Capital Receipts and Revenue Receipts.

1. Capital Receipts

Capital receipts consist of payments made to the enterprises either by shareholders, or by proprietors of business, receipts from sale of fixed assets of a business or loan raised.

It may be noted here that capital receipt is different from capital profit. For example, if the price of machinery costing Rs. 20.000/- is sold for Rs. 21,000/-, there is a capital receipt of Rs. 21,000/- but capital profit is only Rs. 1,000/-. Suppose the same machinery is sold for Rs. 15,000/- then there is a capital receipt of Rs. 15,000/- but there is a capital loss of Rs. 5,000/-.

2. Revenue Receipts

Any receipt which is not a capital receipt is termed as revenue receipt. Examples of revenue receipts are (*i*) Amount from sale of goods (*ii*) Amount received from rendering services to other parties, for example, Interest received, commission received.

Capital receipts and Capital expenditure is not shown in Trading and Profit and Loss a/c. It is only revenue receipts and revenue expenditure of the current year which are shown in trading and profit and loss a/c. It may also be noted that capital profit is transferred to Capital Reserve whereas capital loss is charged to profit and loss a/c of the same year or over a few years in case it occurs in the course of purchase and sale of goods and services and are included in the profit and loss a/c in the year in which they occur.

PREPARING PROFIT AND LOSS ACCOUNT

From the given Trial Balance we can prepare a Profit and Loss account to determine the profit and loss made by a business organisation during a particular period. At the time of preparation of profit and loss account, the following points may be kept in mind:

All expenses are debited to Profit and Loss Account

All incomes are credited to Profit and Loss Account

Balance, if any would be the profit/loss.

Further we may have to give special treatment to adjustment entries also (discussed in detail earlier in the chapter).

The profit is credited to Reserves account. If there is net loss, it is debited to Reserves account in the Balance Sheet, in the case of companies and in the case of sole trader and partnership, the net profit is credited to capital account and net loss is debited to capital account.

Sometimes, it is possible to first determine the gross profit (arising out of trading operations) and then deduct all administrative and selling expenses from gross profit to determine the net profit. Whether or not a separate Trading Account is prepared to determine gross profit or loss, the Net Profit/Net Loss remains the same.

It is necessary to emphasise here that Profit and Loss account (including Trading account) is usually prepared on 'Accrual Basis.' In other words all expenses incurred and due are debited to Profit and Loss account whether they are actually paid for or not. Similarly all incomes earned and due are credited to profit and loss account whether they are actually received or not.

A simple Example: Trading Account

The following is a simple example of a Trading Account.

Trading Account for the period ending

	Rs.	*Rs.*		*Rs.*	*Rs.*
To Opening Inventory:			By Sales	7,90,000	
Raw Materials	90,000		*Less:* Returns	10,000	7,80,000
Work-in-progress	70,000				
Finished goods	2,40,000	4,00,000	By Closing inventory:		
Purchases	5,00,000		Raw materials	40,000	
Less Returns	15,000	4,85,000	Work-in-progress	80,000	
Carriage inwards		10,000	Finished goods	3,00,000	4,20,000
Wages		40,000			
Factory expenses		20,000			
Fuel and Power		5,000			
Trading Expenses		15,000			
Gross Profit Transferred to P & L A/c		2,25,000			
		12,00,000			12,00,000

Important Points

Opening inventory is debited to Trading Account. Closing inventory is credited to Trading Account. (The information relating to opening inventory is usually provided in trial balance. The Closing stock figures is indicated in the 'Adjustments' outside the Trial Balance).

Purchases (Less Returns) are debited to Trading Account. Sales (less returns) are credited to Trading Account.

All expenses relating to trading and manufacturing activities are debited to Trading Account.

The Gross Profit (or Loss) is then transferred to Profit and Loss account.

Note that there is no hard and fast rule about segregation of expenses between Trading Account and Profit and Loss account. What is indicated above is based in Generally Accepted Accounting Principles. However, in specific circumstances it may become necessary to adopt a flexible approach. The question of segregation of expenses does not arise where only the Profit and Loss account is prepared without a separate Trading Account.

A Simple Example: Profit and Loss Account

Given below is a simple example of a Profit and Loss Account. You may notice that it starts with gross profit (on credit side). If there is no separate Trading Account prepared, all the debits and credits of trading account appear individually in the Profit and Loss account. Where a separate Trading Account is prepared, only the figure of gross profit (or loss as the case may be) appears in the Profit and Loss account as a starting point.

The Profit and Loss account shown below is not an exhaustive list of expenses and incomes. It is a simplified version of a typical Profit and Loss account without taking any "adjustments" to be made into account.

Profit and Loss Account for the period ending 31.3.2008

Dr.	*Rs.*		*Cr.* *Rs.*
To Salaries	30,000	By Gross Profit	2,25,000
To Printing & Stationery	15,000	By`Rent received	2,000
To Postage and Telephone	2,500	By other income	10,000
To Audit Fee	4,000		
To Office Rent	5,000		
To Insurance	10,000		
To Repair & Maintenance	5,000		
To General Expenses	4,000		
To Interest on Loans	8,000		
To Net Profit transferred to Reserves or Capital	1,53,500		
	2,37,000		2,37,000

Profit and loss account may be prepared in the 'T' form (as shown above) or in the vertical form. If the profit and loss is prepared in the vertical form, the revenue are shown first and all expenses are shown as a deduction from the total revenues. A sample of vertical format is shown below:

Profit and Loss Account of ... for the year ended

Revenue

Sales
Other (Dividends, Interest etc.)

Expenses

Raw Materials Cost
Employee's remuneration and benefits
Other Expenses
Depreciation

Profit before Interest

Interest
Previous year's adjustment

Profit before Taxation

Income Tax
Net Profit available for appropriation

Appropriation

Interim dividend
Proposed final dividend
Transfer to General Reserve

WHAT IS A BALANCE SHEET?

A balance sheet, also commonly referred to as a statement of financial position, is a statement of assets and liabilities of business enterprises at a particular date. The balance sheet summarises and reveals the financial position of an enterprises on a particular date, by showing what it owns and what it owes. Because the balance sheet is a snap shot as of an instant in time, it is a status report rather than flow report.

The balance sheet is a fundamental or first accounting statement in the sense that every accounting transaction can be analysed in terms of its dual impact on the balance sheet. Moreover, most often, revenues and expenses are defined in terms of changes in assets and liabilities. Thus, a thorough understanding of the nature and measurement of assets and liabilities is needed to understand net income and its components. A Balance Sheet has no debit and credit side. It is prepared on a particular date and as such, it shows the assets and liabilities of a business enterprises on that date. Even a single transaction will cause a change in the assets and liabilities of the enterprises as shown in the Balance Sheet. Therefore, it is true only for the date on which it has been prepared. It is called Balance Sheet because it is actually a sheet containing balances of ledger accounts which have not been closed by transfer to trading and profit and loss a/c.

The balance sheet is also called a statement of sources of funds (i.e., liabilities or obligations) and utilisation of funds (i.e., assets or resources). The financial position of an enterprise includes its economic resources (assets), economic obligations (liabilities), owner's equity and their relationship to each other on a particular date. The balance sheet reveals an enterprise's resource structure (major classes and amounts of assets) and its financial structure (major classes and amounts of liabilities and equity). As stated in chapter 3, the balance sheet is a detailed summary of the basic accounting equation (which must always remain in balance):

Assets = Liabilities + Owner's Equity

The balance sheet is prepared in terms of certain accounting concepts such as: (*i*) Money measurement, i.e., amounts are expressed in money and reflect only those matters that can be measured in monetary terms, (*ii*) entity — i.e., the balance sheet is prepared from the point of view of the business as a separate entity, distinguished from its owners and individuals associated with it, (*iii*) going concern, i.e., the balance sheet assumes that the enterprise is a going concern (*iv*) cost concept — i.e., amounts stated in a balance sheet are regulated by the historical cost concept (*v*) dual-aspect — i.e., assets listed on a balance sheet are equal in total to the liabilities and shareholders equity.

The proper heading of a balance sheet consists of (*a*) the name of organisation (*b*) the title of the statement, and (*c*) the date for which the statement is prepared.

It should be understood that the balance sheet does not aim to show the value of an enterprise. Together with other financial statements and other information, however, it provides information that is useful to external users who desire to make their own estimates of a company's value. More specifically, the balance sheet helps in assessing the solvency (liquidity), financial structure, and operating capability of a business enterprise.

To sum up, while preparing Profit and Loss Account and Balance Sheet, the following important points should be noted:

(*i*) Start with a tallied trial balance. It provides the arithmetical accuracy of entries made in the books, namely, cash book, journal and ledger. However, there are certain errors which are not disclosed by a trial balance.

(*ii*) On account of certain errors if the trial balance is not tallied, the Suspense Account is opened with the difference of two sides and the same is inserted on the side having difference. If suspense account shows:

(*a*) Debit balance, record on the asset side of Balance Sheet.

(*b*) Credit balance, record on the liabilities side of Balance Sheet.

The Suspense Account is closed after rectifying the errors. Real and Personal Accounts items alone are taken to Balance Sheet.

(*iii*) Adjustments given at the end of a trial balance should be given double-entry effect, otherwise accounts will not be complete. The balance sheet will not tally.

(*i*) The treatment of adjustments for expenses and incomes in balance sheet is:

(*a*) Outstanding liabilities for expenses shown on liabilities side;

(*b*) Prepaid expenses shown on assets side;

(*c*) Income received in advance shown on liabilities side;

(*d*) Income earned but not received, and income accrued but not due, shown on assets side;

(*e*) Fixed assets are recorded at cost minus depreciation;

(*f*) Closing stock recorded at cost price or Net realisable value price whichever is less.

Profit and Loss Account may be divided into three components.

Trading Account	To reflect gross profit or loss arising out of trading and manufacturing operations.
Profit and Loss Account	To reflect the net profit or loss of the entire business after duly accounting for all administrative and selling expenses.
Profit and Loss Appropriation A/c	To reflect the various appropriations made out of disposable profits like dividends, transfer to reserves etc.

It is not always necessary to prepare a separate trading account. Balance sheet is just a statement of assets and liabilities. It is not an account like profit and loss account. Hence Debit (Dr.) or Credit (Cr.) do not figure in a balance sheet.

Profit and loss account is prepared for an accounting period. On the other hand, a balance sheet is prepared as on a particular day (usually the last day of the accounting period).

ARRANGEMENT OF ASSETS AND LIABILITIES ITEMS ON THE BALANCE SHEET

In the case of a company, The Companies Act 1956 provides that balance sheet should be prepared as per schedule VI given therein and assets and liabilities should be written in the sequence (or order) shown in the Schedule. However, in the case of sole proprietorship, and partnership, no rule is provided for recording assets and liabilities on the balance sheet.

Generally, assets and liabilities on a balance sheet may be written on

(*a*) liquidity basis, and

(*b*) fixity basis.

Liquidity basis is that basis where assets and liabilities are arranged according to their realisability and payment preference. Fixity basis is the basis when assets and liabilities are arranged in the order of permanence. Proformas of balance sheet on liquidity basis and fixity basis are given below:

Proforma of a Balance Sheet (in order of Liquidity/Liquidity Basis)

Balance Sheet as at ...

Liabilities	*Rs.*	*Assets*	*Rs.*
Current Liabilities:		**Current Assets:**	
Bank Overdraft	—	Cash in Hand	—
Outstanding Expenses	—	Cash at Bank	—
Bills Payable	—	Prepaid Expenses	—
Sundry Creditors	—	Sundry Debtors	—
Income Received in Advance	—	Accrued Income	—
		Bills Receivables	—
		Stock (closing)	—
Fixed Non-Current Liabilities		**Non-Current Assets (Fixed Assets):**	
Loan	—	Investments	—
Capital:	—	Furniture and Fixture	—
		Loose Tools	—
Opening Balance	—	Plant and Machinery	—
Add Net Profit (less loss)	—	Building	—
Less Drawing	—	Land	—
		Goodwill	—

Proforma of Balance Sheet
(In order of Permanence/Fixity Basis)

Balance Sheet as at...

Liabilities	*Rs.*	*Assets*	*Rs.*
Capital:		**Non-Current Assets/Fixed Asset:**	
Opening Balance	—	Goodwill	—
Add Net Profit (Less Loss)	—	Land	—
Less Drawings	—	Building	—
		Plant and Machinery	—
Non-Current/Fixed Liabilities:		Loose Tools	—
		Furniture & Fixture	—
Loan	—	Investments	—
Current Liabilities:		*Current Assets:*	
Income Received in Advance	—	Stock (Closing)	—
Sundry Creditors	—	Accrued Income	—
Bills Payable	—	Sundry Debtors	—
Outstanding expenses	—	Prepaid expenses	—
Bank Overdraft	—	Bills Receivable	—
		Cash at Bank	—
		Cash in Hand	—

MEANING OF BALANCE SHEET ITEMS

The data shown in Balance Sheet and Profit and Loss account are not only the balances of individual accounts but sometimes they are grouped balance of many accounts and they lack uniformity and homogeneity. For the purpose of making comparisons and interpretation these items of data is to be split or broken up into many components. This process is known as financial analysis. Financial analysis involves the division of facts on the basis of some definite plans, classifying them into classes on the basis of certain objectives and presenting them in most convenient, simple and understandable form, *i.e.*, its classification and arrangement of data.

A clear and current understanding of the basic dimensions of the balance sheet and the meanings which they signify and the amount which they represent is very essential for the proper analysis and interpretation of financial statements. The various items of the balance sheet may be grouped as under:

Current Assets

All assets which are acquired for reselling during the course of business are to be treated as current assets. These are acquired through cash and are easily convertible into cash. Examples are Cash and Bank balances. Inventory, Accounts Receivable etc.

Deferred Expenditure

It is shown at a point of time as assets in Balance Sheet. For example, research and development expenses of Rs. 1,00,000 resulting in a new product may be written off over 5 years. At the end of the first year, an amount of Rs. 80,000 (being Rs. 1,00,000 – Rs. 20,000) will be shown in the Balance Sheet as deferred expenditure.

Other Assets

The assets possess a tangible form but are not directly used in the operations of business.

Current Liabilities

All short-term obligations generally due and payable within one year are current liabilities, e.g., Bills payable, Accounts payable etc.

Non-Current Liabilities

All such liabilities payable over a longer period of time generally, after one year, are non-current liabilities, e.g., Debentures, Long-term loans etc.

Net Worth

Net worth is the amount of funds invested at the risk of the owners of the business concern. It is arrived after deducting all outside liabilities both current and non-current from total assets of the concern. Hence net worth equals the capital and Reserve of the concern.

Financial Analysts analyse the balance sheets and profit and loss accounts in great detail to assess the financial position of the companies by comparing the performance over a period time and also by comparing performance of one company with others in similar business. Such comparisons with similar other companies are called inter-firm comparisons.

Financial Analysts use several financial ratios calculated from the data available in balance sheet and profit and loss account to assess the solvency, liquidity and profitability of an organisation.

The American terms of various assets and liabilities and some other items and their equivalent Indian terms are given below:

American Terminology	*Indian Terminology*
Accounts Receivable	Sundry Debtors/Debtors
Accounts Payable	Sundry Creditors/Creditors
Notes Receivable	Bills Receivable
Notes Payable	Bills Payable
Marketable Securities	Investments

Inventory	Inventory/Stock
Stock	Share
Stockholder	Shareholders
Common Stock	Equity Share or Equity Share Capital (As per the context)
Paid in Capital	Paid up Capital
Property, Plant and Machinery	Fixed Assets
Deferred Revenues	Incomes Received in Advance/Pre-received Income
Deferred Charges	Deferred Expenses/Deferred Revenue Expenditure
Gross Margin	Gross Profit
Sales Discount	Cash Discount Allowed
Retained Earnings	Credit Balance of P & L Account

Note:

(*i*) The term 'deferred revenues' should not be confused with the term, 'deferred revenue expenditure.' In Indian terminology, deferred revenue expenditure means expenditure in respect of which benefits may be received over a period of time longer than a year.

(*ii*) In India, cash discounts allowed are usually shown as an expenditure in the Profit and Loss account and not netted out from sales.

ADJUSTING ITEMS

Treatment of various types of items that require adjustments for the preparation of a balance sheet are given as under:

Adjustment	*Adjusting Entry*	*Treatment in Balance Sheet*
1. Outstanding expenses	Expenses a/c Dr. To Outstanding Exp. a/c	Shown on the Liabilities side
2. Prepaid Expenses	Prepaid Expenses a/c Dr. To Expenses a/c	Shown on the Asset side
3. Closing Stock	Closing Stock Dr. To Trading a/c	Shown on the Asset side
4. Accrued Income	Accrued income Dr. To Income a/c	Shown on the Asset side
5. Depreciation	(*a*) Depreciation a/c Dr. To Assets a/c (*b*) Depreciation a/c Dr. To provision for depreciation	Shown by way of deduction from the value of the Asset on the Asset side
6. Income Received in Advance	Income a/c Dr. To Income received in Advance a/c	Shown on the Liabilities side
7. Provision for Bad Debts	Profit & Loss a/c Dr. To Provision for Bad Debts	Deducted from Sundry debtors on the Asset side
8. Provision for Discount	Profit & Loss a/c Dr. To Provision for discount on Debtors	Deducted from Sundry debtors on the Asset side
9. Reserve for Discount on Creditors	Reserve for Discount on Creditors Dr. To Profit and Loss a/c	Shown by way of Deduction from Sundry Creditors

LIMITATIONS OF BALANCE SHEET

A balance sheet contains useful information about liquidity, operating capability and financial flexibility of an enterprise and this is very useful to external users and others in making sound investment decisions. However, in spite of being a useful financial statement, it has some limitations.

Balance Sheet is considered to be a static document and it reflects the position of the concern at a given date. The real position of the concern may be changing day-to-day, and the same is not depicted in Balance Sheet.

Balance Sheet is not a valuation statement. The values shown in it are not real values of assets. Thus exact position of the business cannot be gauged from balance sheet.

A balance sheet is prepared based on certain accounting policies. Such policies relate to inventory valuation (*i.e.*, closing stock), depreciation etc. Inventory may be valued using several methods like First-in-First Out (FIFO), Last-in-First-Out (LIFO), weighted average cost etc. Similarly, depreciation may be provided using straight line method or written down value method. The management may select accounting policies which may not reflect real financial position.

Similarly, accounting policies may differ from company to company in respect of accounting for prepaid expenses, prior period adjustment, classification between revenue and capital expenditure, writing-off preliminary expenses etc. However, it is suggested that the same accounting policies are consistently used by management from year to year. Whenever there is a change in accounting policy, the effect of such a change is indicated in the notes to balance sheet.

Management may follow accounting procedures and treatments which may result into window-dressing of balance sheets with a view to forecast a better picture to shareholders, bankers and financial institutions. It is a rosier picture that what it actually is. Window-dressing is accomplished in general ways, say by not making adequate provisions (though prudence would require them) for expenses and potential losses, by taking into account income even before its actual accrual, by suppressing vital information by playing around with inter-corporate adjustments etc.

Illustration 1:

From the following particulars prepare provision for doubtful debts account and bad debts account.

2007 Jan. 1	Provision for Doubtful Debts	Rs. 2,500
Dec. 31	Bad Debts	Rs. 1,870
	Debtors	Rs. 20,000

Make provision for bad debts at 5% on debtors.

Solution:

Provision for Doubtful Debts A/c

Date	*Particulars*	*Amount Rs.*	*Date*	*Particulars*	*Amount Rs.*
2007	To Bad Debts A/c	1,870	2007	By Balance b/d	2,500
Dec. 31	To Balance c/d	1,000		By Profit & Loss A/c	370
		2,870			2,870

Bad Debts A/c

Date	Particulars	Amount Rs.	Date	Particulars	Amount Rs.
	To Balance (given)	1,870		By Provision for Bad Debts (Transfer)	1,870
		1,870			1,870

Illustration 2:

From the following figures, you are required to show:

(*a*) Provision for doubtful debts account
(*b*) Bad Debts account
(*c*) Profit and Loss account

Provision for Doubtful Debts 1-4-2006 Rs. 1,000
Provision for Doubtful Debts 31-3-2007 Rs. 2,000
Debts Written off in 2006-2007 Rs. 1,200

Solution:

Provision for Doubtful A/c

Date	Particulars	Amount Rs.	Date	Particulars	Amount Rs.
2007			2006		
Mar. 31	To Bad debts written off	1,200	Mar. 31	By Balance (given)	1,000
Mar. 31	To Balance (Closing)	2,000		By Profit & Loss A/c (Bal. Fig.)	2,200
		3,200			3,200

Bad Debts A/c

Date	Particulars	Amount Rs.	Date	Particulars	Amount Rs.
2007 Mar. 31	To Balance (Given)	1,200	2007	By Provision for Bad Debts (transfer)	1,200
		1,200			1,200

Profit and Loss A/c

Date	Particulars	Amount Rs.	Date	Particulars	Amount Rs.
2008					
Mar. 31	To Provision for Doubtful Debts	2,200			
		2,200			

Illustration 3:

On 1st January, 2006 the reserve for Doubtful Debts account showed a balance of Rs. 10,000. During the year the bad debts written off amounted to Rs. 10,000/- and the Sundry Debtors at the end stood at Rs. 2,40,000/- on which the provision for doubtful debts was to be 5%.

During 2007 the bad debts written off amounted to Rs. 4,000/- and the closing balance of debtors was Rs. 1,40,000/-. The concern continued to provide for doubtful debts at 5% on closing balance of debtors.

Show the provision for doubtful debts account for 2006 and 2007. All bad debts written off are adjusted through the Provision Account.

Solution:

Provision for Doubtful Debts A/c

Date	*Particulars*	*Amount Rs.*	*Date*	*Particulars*	*Amount Rs.*
2006			2006		
Dec. 31	To Bad debts written off	10,000	Jan. 1	By Balance (given)	10,000
Dec. 31	To Balance (Closing) (5/100 × 2,40,000)	12,000	Dec. 31	By Profit & Loss a/c (Bal. Fig.)	12,000
		22,000			22,000
2007			2007		
Dec. 31	To Bad Debts	4,000	Jan. 1	By balance b/d	12,000
Dec. 31	To Balance (Closing) (5/100 × 1,40,000)	7,000			
Dec. 31	To P & L A/c (Bal. Fig.)	1,000			
		12,000			12,000

Illustration 4:

There were Rs. 2,500 bad debts during the year ended 31st March, 2008. An amount of Rs. 3,000/- for provision of bad debts is brought forward from last year. During the year ended at 31st March, 2008 provision of Rs. 1,750/- was made for bad and doubtful debts. Prepare bad debts account and provision for bad & doubtful debts account.

Solution:

Bad Debt A/c

Date	*Particulars*	*Amount Rs.*	*Date*	*Particulars*	*Amount Rs.*
2008			2008		
Mar. 31	To Balance (Given)	2,500	Mar. 31	By Provision for Bad Debts	2,500
		2,500			2,500

Provision for Bad & Doubtful Debts A/c

Date	*Particulars*	*Amount Rs.*	*Date*	*Particulars*	*Amount Rs.*
2008					
Mar. 31	To Bad Debts	2,500	2007	By Balance b/d	3,000
Mar. 31	To Balance (Closing)	1,750	2008	By Profit & Loss A/c	1,250
			Mar. 31	(Bal. Fig.)	
		4,250			4,250

Illustration 5:

The following figures appear in the books of a firm:

Provision for doubtful debts on 1-1-2007 Rs. 6,500
Bad debts written off during the year Rs. 4,000

Sundry debtors on 31.12.2007 Rs. 75,000. Of the sundry debtors Rs. 2,000 was bad and the provision for doubtful debts was to be maintained at 5% on sundry debtors. Pass Journal entries.

Solution:

Journal Entries

Sl. No.	*Particulars*		*L.F.*	*Amount Dr. (Rs.)*	*Amount Cr. (Rs.)*
1.	Bad Debts A/c	Dr.		4,000	
	To Sundry Debtors A/c				4,000
	(Being bad debts provided on debtors)				
2.	Provision for Bad & Doubtful Debts A/c	Dr.		4,000	
	To Bad Debt A/c				4,000
	(Being bad debts transferred)				
3.	Profit & Loss A/c	Dr.		3,650	
	To Provision for doubtful debts A/c				3,650
	(Being provision on debtors transferred to P & L A/c)				
4.	Provision for Bad & Doubtful Debts A/c	Dr.		1,150	
	To Profit & Loss A/c				1,150
	(Being provision on debtors transferred to P & L A/c and Provision for doubtful debts)				

Illustration 6:

The following balances appear in the trial balance of Joshi & Co. relating to the accounts for the year ending December 31, 2007.

Wages a/c	Rs. 30,000
Salaries a/c	Rs. 40,000
Rent a/c	Rs. 5,000
Advertising a/c	Rs. 17,000

It is found that following adjustments have not been made in the books:

1. Wages due but not paid	Rs. 3,000
2. Salaries paid in advance	Rs. 2,000

3. Unpaid Rent Rs. 1,000
4. Advertising expenses not recorded in the books Rs. 2,000

You are required to pass necessary journal entries to adjust these items. Also show how these items would appear in trading and profit and loss accounts and balance sheet.

Solution:

Journal Entries

Sl. No.	*Particulars*		*Amount Dr. (Rs.)*	*Amount Cr. (Rs.)*
1.	Wages a/c To Outstanding wage a/c (Being the amount of outstanding wages)	Dr.	3,000	3,000
2.	Prepaid salaries a/c To Salaries a/c (Being the salaries paid in advance)	Dr.	2,000	2,000
3.	Rent a/c To Outstanding rent a/c (Being the amount of rent outstanding)	Dr.	1,000	1,000
4.	Advertising a/c To Outstanding advertising a/c (Being the amount of advertising outstanding)	Dr.	2,000	2,000

Profit and Loss A/c
for the year ended Dec. 31, 2007

		Amount (Rs.)		*Amount (Rs.)*
Wages	30,000			
Add: Outstanding	3,000	33,000		
Salaries	40,000			
Less: paid in advance	2,000	38,000		
Rent	5,000			
Add: unpaid	1,000	6,000		
Advertising	17,000			
Add: Unpaid	2,000	19,000		

Balance Sheet
as on 31st Dec. 2007

Liabilities	*Rs.*	*Assets*	*Rs.*
Outstanding expenses:		Prepaid expenses:	
Wages	3,000	Salaries	2,000
Rent	1,000		
Advertising	2,000		

Illustration 7:

A company has a bad debts provision of Rs. 20,000. The amount of debtors at the end of the year amounted to Rs. 3,20,000 out of these Rs. 2,60,000 are good debtors and Rs. 60,000 is doubtful on which a provision of 40 per cent is to be made. Show as these items will appear in the books.

Solution:

Provision for Bad and Doubtful Debts A/c

(Amt. in Rs.)

To Balance c/d (60,000 × 40%)	24,000	By Balance b/d By Profit & Loss a/c	20,000 4,000
	24,000		24,000
		By Balance b/d	24,000

Profit and Loss A/c

To Provision for Bad Debts *Less:* Old Provision	24,000 20,000	4,000		

Illustration 8:

The following balances appeared in the trial balance of X on December 31, 2007.

Debtors	Rs. 1,00,000
Bad Debts	Rs. 5,000
Provision for bad debts (1.1.2007)	Rs. 6,000

It was found that bad debts worth Rs. 3,000 were not recorded in the books till Dec. 31, 2007. It was decided that a provision for bad debts equal to 8 per cent on the closing debtors will be adequate. You are required to prepare bad debts accounts and provision for bad debts account. Also show how these items would appear in profit and loss account and balance sheet.

Solution:

Bad Debts

(Amt. in Rs.)

		Rs.			*Rs.*
31-12-2007 31-12-2007	To Balance b/d To Debtors a/c	5,000 3,000	31-12-2007	By Provision for Bad Debts	8,000
		8,000			8,000

Provision for Bad Debts a/c

	To Bad debts To Balance c/d (New Provision)	8,000 7,760		By balance b/d By Profit and Loss a/c	6,000 9,760
		15,760			15,760

Profit & Loss A/c

To Bad debts *Add:* Bad debts	5,000 3,000		
	8,000		
Add: New Provision	7,760		
	15,760		
Less: Old provision	6,000		
	9,760		

Balance Sheet

Debtors		1,00,000	
Less Bad Debts (not recorded)		3,000	
		97,000	
Less: Provision		7,760	89,240
Note: Debtors on 31.12.2007		1,00,000	
Less: Bad debts not recorded		3,000	
		97,000	

New Provision for Bad Debts = 97,000 × 8/100 = 7,760

Illustration 9:

A firm had the following balances on April 1, 2006:

Provision for doubtful debts	Rs. 6,500
Provision for discount on debtors	Rs. 3,200
Reserve for discount on creditors	Rs. 4,800

During the year ended March 31, 2007, bad debts amounted to Rs. 4,500, discounts allowed were Rs. 15,800 and discount received were Rs. 9,700. During the year 2007-08, bad debts amounting to Rs. 2,300 were written off while discount allowed and received were Rs. 12,500 and Rs. 8,900 respectively. Sundry debtors were Rs. 1,50,000 on 31-3-2007 and Rs. 90,000 on 31-3-2008. Sundry creditors were Rs. 1,05,000 and Rs. 1,26,000 on 31-3-2007 and 31-3-2008 respectively. It is the firm's policy to maintain a provision of 5 percent against bad and doubtful debts and 3 percent for discount on debtors and reserve of 2 percent on creditors. Show the necessary accounts for the year 2006-2007 and 2007-2008.

Solution:

Bad Debts A/c

(Amt. in Rs.)

2007 Mar. 31	To Sundry debtors	4,500	2007	By Provision for Bad and doubtful debt	4,500
2008 Mar. 31	To Sundry debtors	2,300	2008 Mar. 31	By Provision for Bad and doubtful debts	2,300

Provision for Bad and Doubtful Debts

2006				2006		
Mar. 31	To Bad debts transfer (a/c)		4,500		By Balance b/d	6,500
				2007		
Mar. 31	To balance c/d		7,500	Mar. 31	By P & L A/c	5,500
			12,000			12,000
2008						
Mar. 31	To Bad debts	2,300		Apr. 1	By balance b/d	7,500
	To P & L	700				
	To balance c/d	4,500	7,500			

Discount on Debtors A/c

2007			2007		
Mar. 31	To Sundry debtors	15,800		By Provision for Discount on debtors	15,800
2008			2008		
Mar. 31	To Sundry debtors	12,500	Mar. 31	By Provision for discount on debtors	12,500

Provision for Discount on Debtors

2007			2007		
Mar. 31	To Discount a/c	15,800	Apr. 1	By balance c/d	3,200
Mar. 31	To Balance c/d	4,275	2001		
			Mar. 31	By P & L A/c	16,875
		20,075			20,075
2008			2007		
Mar. 31	To discount a/c	12,500	Apr. 1	By balance c/d	4,275
Mar. 31	To balance c/d	2,565	2008		
			Mar. 31	By P & L a/c	10,790
		15,065			15,065
			Apr. 1	By balance b/d	2,565

Discount on Sundry Creditors

2007			2007		
Mar. 31	To Reserve for Discount on Sundry creditors	9,700	Apr. 1	By Sundry Creditors	9,700
2008			2008		
Mar. 31	To Reserve for Discount on Sundry Creditors	8,900	Mar. 31	By Sundry creditors	8,900

Reserve for Discount on Sundry Creditors

2006		*Rs.*	2007		*Rs.*
Apr. 1	To Balance b/d	4,800	Mar. 31	By discount on sundry creditors	9,700
2007					
Mar. 31	To P & L a/c	7,000	Mar. 31	By balance c/d	2,100
		11,800			11,800

Date	Particulars	Amount	Date	Particulars	Amount
2007 Apr. 1	To Balance b/d	2,100	2008 Mar. 31	By Discount on sundry creditors	8,900
2008 Mar. 31	To P & L A/c	9,320	Mar. 31	By Balance c/d	2,520
		11,420			11,420
2008 Apr. 1	To Balance b/d	2,520			

Illustration 10:

A company maintains its Reserve for bad debts @ 5% and reserve for discount on Debtors @2%. You are given the following details:

	2006 (Rs.)	2007 (Rs.)
Bad Debts	1,600	3,000
Discount allowed	2,400	1,000
Recovery of Bad Debts written off in earlier years	1,000	600

Sundry Debtors (before writing off bad debts and discount) amounted to Rs. 1,20,000 on December 31, 2006 and Rs. 90,000 on December, 31, 2007.

On January 1, 2006 reserve for bad debts and reserve for discount on debtors had balances of Rs. 900 and Rs. 1,600, respectively. Show the reserve for bad debts account and reserve for discount on debtors Account for 2006 and 2007.

Solution:

Reserve for Bad Debts Accounts

(*Amt. in Rs.*)

Dr. Cr.

Date	Particulars	Amount	Date	Particulars	Amount
31-12-2006	To Bad debts	1,600	1-1-2006	By Balance b/d	9,100
31-12-2006	To Profit and Loss a/c	1,700			
31-12-2006	To Balance c/d (a)	5,800			
		9,100			9,100
31-12-2007	To Bad debts	3,000	1-1-2007	By Balance b/d	5,800
31-12-2007	To Balance c/d (c)	4,000	31-12-2007	By Profit and Loss a/c	1,200
		7,000			7,000
			1-1-2008	By Balance b/d	4,000

Reserve for Discount on Debtors Account

Dr. Cr.

Date	Particulars	Amount	Date	Particulars	Amount
31-12-2006	To Discount Allowed	2,400	1-1-2006	By Balance b/d	1,600
31-12-2006	To Balance c/d (b)	2,204	31-12-2006	By Profit and Loss a/c	3,004
		4,604			4,604
31-12-2007	To Discount allowed	1,000	1-1-2007	By Balance b/d	2,204
31-12-2007	To Balance c/d	1,520	31-12-2007	By Profit and Loss a/c	296
		2,520			2,520
			1-1-2008	By Balance b/d	1,520

Notes:

(*a*) Actual Balance of Sundry Debtors as on 31-12-2007		= 1,20,000
Less: Bad Debts =	Rs. 1,600	
Discount Allowed =	Rs. 2,400	= 4,000
		1,16,000
Reserve for Bad Debts to be created @ 5% on Rs. 1,16,000 =		5,800
(*b*) Reserve for discount to be created @ 2% on Rs. (Rs. 1,16,000 – 5,800)		= 2,204
(*c*) Actual Balance of Sundry Debtors as on 31-12-2007		= 84,000
Less: Bad Debts =	Rs. 3,000	
Discount Allowed =	Rs. 1,000	= 4,000
Reserve for Bad Debts to be created @5% on Rs. 80,000		80,000
(*d*) Reserve for discount to be created @2% on Rs. (80,000 – 4,000)		= 1,520

Recovery of bad debts written off in earlier years to be transferred to bad debts recovery a/c or bad debts dividend a/c where from it would be transferred directly to profit and loss a/c since it is a clear profit.

Illustration 11:

A machinery item was bought on 16-2-2008 and was sold on 15-10-2007. The following relevant information is available:

1. Cost of purchase of the machinery Rs. 4,00,000
2. Transportation and installation costs Rs. 20,000
3. Estimated useful life at the time of acquisition is 20 years.
4. Estimated scrap value at the time of disposal Rs. 1,000
5. The firm closes its books of account on March 31, every year
6. Depreciation was provided on the straight-line method; in the year of acquisition/disposal it is the policy of the firm to provide one-half of a year's depreciation.
7. Amount realised from sale of machine Rs. 1,50,000.

The accounting treatment for purchase and sale would be:

(*a*) Record Rs. 4,00,000 in machinery account as cost on acquisition and charge Rs. 1,44,300 as loss on sale.

(*b*) Record Rs. 4,20,000 in machinery account as cost on acquisition and charge Rs. 1,44,300 as loss on sale.

(*c*) Record Rs. 4,19,000 in machinery account as cost on acquisition and charge Rs. 1,44.300 as loss on sale.

(*d*) Debit Rs. 4,00,000 to machinery account on acquisition and credit Rs. 1,50,000 to the same account on sale.

(*e*) None of the above.

Required: Among the above choices, which one is correct?

Solution:

Capitalisation of Machinery = Rs. (4,00,000 + 20,000)
= Rs. 4,20,000

Depreciation per year on straight line basis = Rs. (4,20,000 – 1,000) / 20
= Rs. 20,950

Total Depreciation provided:			(Rs.)
Year ended	31-03-2002	(1/2 × 20,950)	10,475/-
Year ended	31-03-2003		20,950/-
Year ended	31-03-2004		20,950/-
Year ended	31-03-2005		20,950/-
Year ended	31-03-2006		20,950/-
Year ended	31-03-2007		20,950/-
Year ended	31-03-2008	(1/2 × 20,000)	10,475/-
			1,25,700

Book value as on date of sale = Rs. (4,20,000 – 1,25,700) = Rs. 2,94,300

Loss on Sale = Rs. 2,94,300 –1,50,000 = Rs. 1,44,300

Choice B is correct.

Illustration 12:

A company had sales of Rs. 1,50,000 during 2007, receivable account has opening balance of Rs. 17,500 and provision for doubtful debts Rs. 2,500. Data for 2007: Collections on account receivable Rs. 1,35,000. Bad Debts expenses was estimated at 2% on credit sales. Write-offs of bad debts during 2007 were Rs. 3,500. The balance on 31.12.2007 in the accounts receivable account and provision for doubtful debts account respectively were:

(*a*) Rs. 3,25,000 (debit) and Rs. 89,000 (credit)

(b) Rs. 3,54,000 (debit) and Rs. 94,000 (credit)

(*c*) Rs. 29,000 (debit) and Rs. 2,000 (credit)

(*d*) Rs. 29,000 (debit) and Rs. 3,000 (credit)

(*e*) None of the above

Solution:

The closing balances of the receivable accounts and provision for doubtful debts accounts can be ascertained by preparing these ledger accounts.

Receivable Accounts

(Amt. in Rs.)

Dr.					*Cr.*
01-01-2007	To Balance b/d	17,500	31-12-2007	By Bank a/c (collection)	1,35,000
	To Sales c/d	1,50,000		By Bad debts a/c	3,500
				By Balance c/d	29,000
		1,67,500			1,67,500

Provision for Bad Debts Account

Dr.					Cr.
31.12.2007	To Bad Debts a/c	3,500	01.01.2008	By Balance b/d	2,500
	To Balance c/d	2,000	31.12.2008	By profit &loss a/c	3,000
		5,500			5,500

Choice (*c*) is correct.

Illustration 13:

The closing balance on the debtor's account amounted to Rs. 50,000. Net sales for the year totalled Rs. 6,00,000. The irrecoverable debts are found to be Rs. 5,700. Past trends suggest that 5 per cent of debts eventually have to be written off as irrecoverable. The existing provision of doubtful debts amount to Rs. 1,500. The appropriate accounting procedure in these circumstances will be:

(*a*) To provide a sum of Rs. 5,700 towards provision for doubtful debts required in respect of the year.
(*b*) To provide Rs. 6,400 as the additional provision for doubtful debts.
(*c*) To transfer Rs. 1,500 to the profit and loss account.
(*d*) To write off Rs. 6,415 as bad debts.
(*e*) None of the above.

Solution:

	Year end balance on the debtors' account	=	50,000
Less:	Irrecoverable debts	=	5,700
			44,300
	Provision for doubtful debts @ 5% of Rs. 44,300	=	2,215
Add:	Irrecoverable debts	=	5,700
			7,915
Less:	Existing provision for doubtful debts	=	1,500
	Additional provision for doubtful debts to be made	=	6,415

Choice (b) is correct.

Illustration 14:

In a firm a shortage of stock has arisen during the year ended September 30, 2007. The firm gathers the following information:

Opening Stock	=	Rs. 87,500
Purchases	=	Rs. 2,87,500
Closing Stock (on physical verification)	=	Rs. 50,000

The goods are sold at a uniform markup of 20 per cent on selling price. The following details regarding Sundry Debtors are available:

Balance as on 01-10-2007	10,000
Balance as on 30-09-2008	27,500
Cash and cheques received from customers in the year	3,90,000
Sales returns	12,500

The shortage of stock is

(*a*) Rs. 80,000
(*b*) Rs. 55,000
(*c*) Rs. 5,000
(*d*) Rs. 25,500
(*e*) None of the above.

Solution:

Sundry Debtors A/c

(Amt. in Rs.)

Dr. Cr.

Particulars	*Rs.*	*Particulars*	*Rs.*
To Balance b/d	30,000	By Sales Returns	12,500
To Sales (balancing figure)	4,00,000	By Cash & Bank	3,90,000
		By Balance c/d	27,500
	4,30,000		4,30,000

Memorandum Trading Account

Particulars	*Rs.*	*Particulars*	*Rs.*
To Opening stock	87,500	By sales	4,00,000
To Purchase	2,87,500	By Closing stocks	55,000
To Gross Profit @20% of Rs. 4,00,000	80,000		
	4,55,000		4,55,000
Closing stock	55,000		
Less: Physical Stock	50,000		
Shortage of Stock	5,000		

Illustration 15:

The stocks held by a firm at their godown were completely damaged by fire on February 1, 2008.

The books of accounts, show the following information:

	(Rs.)
Sales — year ended December 31, 2007	2,00,000
Sales — January 2008	50,000
Purchases — year ended December, 2007	1,25,000
Purchases — January 2008	20,000
Stocks — 1-1-2007	37,500
Stocks — 31-12-2007	25,000

Taking the gross profit ratio to be constant from 2007 to January, 2008, insurance claim for inventory should be lodged for —

(*a*) Rs. 20,000
(*b*) Rs. 10,625
(*c*) Rs. 27,500
(*d*) Rs. 37,500
(*c*) None of the above.

Solution:

Workings:

Gross Profit for the year ended
December 31, 2007 = Rs. 2,00,000 + 25,000 – (1,25,000 + 37,500) = Rs. 62,500

$$\text{Gross Profit margin (ratio)} = \frac{62{,}500 \times 100}{2{,}00{,}000} = 31.25\%$$

Gross Profit earned during Jan. 2008 = Rs. 50,000 × 31.25% = Rs. 15,625
Value of Closing Stock as on Jan. 31, 2008 = Rs. (25,000 + 20,000 + 15,625 – 50,000)
= Rs. 10,625

Choice (b) is correct.

Illustration 16:

The sundry debtors account and sundry creditors account of a company are given below which are incomplete:

Sundry Debtors' Account

To Balance c/d	17,500	By Sales returns	7,500
To Cash & cheque received	2,40,000	By Discount allowed	1,000
To Bad debts	2,500		
To Balance c/d	20,000		

Sundry Creditors' Account

To Purchase Returns	1,500	By Balance c/d	7,500
To Discount Received	400	By Cash & cheque paid	1,15,000
To Reserve for Discount	250		
To Balance c/d	12,500		

The following further information is made available:

(*i*) While the opening stock was Rs. 9,000, the closing stock has been ascertained at Rs. 12,500

(*ii*) Expenses during the year:
Carriage inwards, Rs. 1,000
Salaries, Rs. 6,000
Depreciation, Rs. 1,77,500

(*iii*) You may take the opinion that closing balances of the sundry debtors and sundry creditors accounts given above as correct.

The Gross Profit for the year — ended March 31, 2008 would be:

(*a*) Rs. 1,04,600
(*b*) Rs. 1,28,100
(*c*) Rs. 1,34,100
(*d*) Rs. 1,29,000
(*e*) None of the above.

Solution:

Sundry Debtors Account

	Rs.		*Rs.*
To Balance b/d	17,500	By Cash & cheque received	2,40,000
To Sales (Balancing figure)	2,53,000	By Sales returns	7,500
		By Discount allowed	1,000
		By Bad debts	2,500
		By Balance c/d	20,000
	2,71,000		2,71,000

Sundry Creditors' Account

	Rs.		Rs.
To Cash & cheque paid	1,15,000	By Balance b/d	7,500
To Purchase returns	1,500	By Purchases (Bal. figure)	1,21,900
To Discounts received	400		
To Balance c/d	12,500		
	1,29,400		1,29,400

Trading Account for the year ended March 31, 2008

		Rs.			Rs.
To Opening stock		9,000	By Sales	2,53,500	
To Purchases	1,21,900		*Less:* Returns	7,500	2,46,000
Less: Returns	1,500	1,20,400	By Closing stock		12,500
To Carriage inward		1,000			
To Gross profit		1,28,100			
		2,58,500			2,58,500

Choice (*b*) is correct.

Illustration 17:

On 31.12.2007 the following Trial Balance was prepared from the books of Raju:

	Dr. (Rs.)	Cr. (Rs.)
Sundry Debtors	50,600	—
Sundry Creditors	—	10,000
Bills Receivable	5,000	—
Plant & machinery	75,000	—
Purchases	90,000	—
Capital	—	70,000
Freehold Premises	50,000	—
Salaries	11,000	—
Wages	14,400	—
Postage and Stationery	750	—
Carriage In	750	—
Carriage Out	1,000	—
Bad Debts	950	—
Bad Debts Provisions	—	350
General Charges	1,500	—
Cash at Bank	5,300	—
Cash in Hand	800	—
Bills Payable	—	5,000
Reserve	—	20,000
Sales	—	2,31,700
Closing Stock	30,000	—
Total	3,37,050	3,37,050

The following adjustments are required:

(1) Raju gets a salary of Rs. 9,000 p.a.

(2) Allow 5% interest on capital.

(3) Bad debts provision to be adjusted to 2½% on sundry debtors.

(4) 2½% of the net profit to be credited to Reserve.

(5) It was discovered in January 2007 that stock sheets as on 31.12.2006 were overcast by Rs. 1,000.

You are required to prepare Trading and Profit and Loss account for the year ended 31st December, 2007 and a Balance Sheet as at that date.

Solution:

Trading and Profit and Loss A/c for the year ending 31st December, 2007

		Rs.		Rs.
To Purchases	90,000		By Sales	2,31,700
Less: Overcast stock	1,000	89,000		
To Wages		14,400		
To Carriage inward		750		
To Gross profit		1,27,550		
		2,31,700		2,31,700
To Salaries	11,000		By Gross profit	1,27,550
Add: O/S	9,000	20,000		
To Post. & Stationery		750		
To Carriage out		1,000		
To Bad debts	950			
Add: New provision	1,265			
	2,215			
Less: Old provision	350	1,865		
To General Charges		1,500		
To Interest on Capital		3,500		
To Net profit transferred to Capital Account		98,935		
		1,27,550		1,27,550

Balance Sheet as at 31st December, 2007

Liabilities		Rs.	*Assets*		Rs.
Capital	70,000.00		Plant & Machinery		75,000.00
Add: Interest on Capital	3,500.00		Freehold Premises		50,000.00
	73,500.00		Sundry Debtors	50,600.00	
Add: Net Profit	96,461.60	1,69,961.60	*Less:* Provision	1,265.00	49,335.00
Sundry Creditors		10,000.00	Bills Receivable		5,000.00
Bills Payable		5,000.00	Closing stock		30,000.00
Reserve	20,000.00		Overstated		1,000.00
			Stock '90		
Add: 2½% of Net P.	2,473.40	22,473.40	Cash at Bank		5,300.00
O/S Salaries		9,000.00	Cash in Hand		800.00
		2,16,435.00			2,16,435.00

Illustration 18:

From the following Trial Balance prepare Trading and Profit and Loss Account for the year ended 31st December, 2007 and Balance Sheet as on that date:

	Dr. (Rs.)	Cr. (Rs.)
Drawings	10,000	—
Stock on 1-1-2007	46,000	—
Purchases and Purchases Returns	1,50,200	600
Cash in Hand	3,400	—
Bank Balance	22,660	—
Freehold Premises	38,600	—
Trade Expenses	840	—
Printing, Stationery and Advertising	1,640	—
Professional Charges	280	
Commission Received	—	3,300
Investments as on 1st Jan. @ 10%	4,000	
Interest on above	—	200
Sundry Debtors and Creditors	36,000	29,000
Wages	25,000	—
Salaries	14,000	
Capital	—	1,14,000
Income Tax	1,600	
Discount allowed and received	6,300	4,600
Sales Returns and Sales	550	2,08,950
Bills Receivable/Bills Payable	3,200	10,000
Office furniture	3,050	—
Rent, Rates and Insurance	4,000	—
Bad Debts Provision	—	670
Total	3,71,320	3,71,320

Adjustments:

(*a*) Provide for wages Rs. 5,000.

(*b*) Write Off 5% depreciation on freehold premises and 10% on office furniture.

(*c*) Insurance to the extent of Rs. 200 relates to 2008.

(*d*) Stock on 31-12-2007 is Rs. 5,20,000.

(*e*) Charge interest on capital 5% and on drawings Rs. 300.

(*f*) Further bad debts are Rs. 1,000.

(*g*) Provide for doubtful debts @ 5% on sundry debtors.

(*h*) Make provision for discount on debtors and reserve for discount on creditors @ 2%.

Solution:

Trading A/c for the year ending 31st December, 2007

		Rs.			Rs.
To opening Stock		46,000	By Sales	2,08,950	
To Purchases	1,50,200		*Less:* Returns	550	2,08,400
Less: Return	600	1,49,600	By Closing Stock		52,000
To wages	25,000				
Add: O/S	5,000	30,000			
To Gross Profit transferred to Profit & Loss A/c		34,800			
		2,60,400			2,60,400

Profit and Loss Account for the year ending 31st December, 2007

		Rs.			Rs.
To Trade Expenses		840	By Gross Profit		34,800
To Printing, Stationery and Advt.		1,640	By Commission		3,300
To Professional Fee		280	By Investments	200	
To Discount		6,300	*Add:* Accrued	200	400
To Salaries		14,000			
To Income Tax		1,600	By Discount		4,600
To Rent, Rates and Insurance	4,000		By Interest on drawings		300
Less: Prepaid	200	3,800			
To Depreciation on freehold premises		1,930	By Reserve for discount on Creditor		580
To Depreciation on Office furniture		305			
To Interest on Capital		5,700			
To Bad Debts	1,000				
Add: New Provision	1,750				
	2,750				
Less: Old Provision	670	2,080			
To Provision for discount on debtors		665			
To Net Profit		4,840			
		43,980			43,980

Balance Sheet as at 31st December, 2007

Liabilities		Rs.	*Assets*		Rs.
Capital	1,14,000		Freehold premises	38,600	
Add: Interest on Capital	5,700		*Less:* Depreciation	1,930	36,670
	1,19,700		Office Furniture	3,050	
Less: Drawings	10,000		*Less:* Depreciation	305	2,745
	1,09,700		Investments	4,000	
Less: Interest on drawings	300		*Add:* Accrued interest	200	4,200
	1,09,400		Sundry Debtors	36,000	
Add: Net Profit	4,840	1,14,240	*Less:* Bad Debts	1,000	
Sundry Creditors	29,000			35,000	
Less: Provision for discount	(580)	28,420	*Less:* New Provision	(1,750)	
Bills Payable		10,000		33,250	
O/S. Wages		5,000	*Less:* provision for discount	(665)	32,585
			Bills receivable		3,200
			Prepaid Insurance		200
			Closing Stock		52,000
			Cash in Hand		3,400
			Cash at Bank		22,600
		1,57,660			1,57,660

Illustration 19:

From the following Trial Balance of Shri Chandershekar, prepare Trading and Profit and Loss Account for the year 31st March, 2008 and Balance Sheet as on that date after taking into account the adjustments given at the bottom of the trial balance.

Debit Balance	*Dr. (Rs.)*	*Credit Balance*	*Cr. (Rs.)*
Chandershekar's Drawings	4,500	Chandershekar's Capital	24,000
Purchases	20,000	Sales	30,500
Returns Inwards	1,500	Discount	1,900
Stock (1-4-2007)	8,000	Sundry Creditors	10,000
Salary	4,200	Bills Payable	2,500
Wages	1,200		
Rent	350		
Bad Debts	400		
Discounts	700		
Sundry Debtors	14,000		
Cash in Hand	260		
Cash at Bank	5,940		
Insurance	400		
Trade Expenses	300		
Printing	150		
Furniture	2,000		
Machinery	5,000		
	68,900		68,900

Adjustments:

(*a*) Closing stock was valued at Rs. 7,000.

(*b*) Insurance was prepaid to the extent of Rs. 60.

(*c*) Outstanding liabilities were: Salary Rs. 200, wages Rs. 200.

(*d*) Make provision for doubtful debts at 5% on sundry debtors.

(*e*) Calculate Interest on Capital 5% p.a.

(*f*) Depreciate machinery at 5% and Furniture at 10%.

(*g*) Provide for discount on creditors at 1%.

Solution:

Trading A/c for the year ending 31st March, 2008

Liabilities		*Rs.*	*Assets*		*Rs.*
To Opening Stock		8,000	By Sales	30,500	
To Purchases		20,000	*Less:* Returns	1,500	29,000
To Wages	1,200		By Closing Stock		7,000
Add: O/S	200	1,400			
To Gross Profit transferred to Profit & Loss A/c		6,600			
		36,000			36,000

Profit and Loss Account for the year ending 31st March, 2008

Liabilities		*Rs.*	*Assets*	*Rs.*
To Salary	4,200		By Gross Profit	6,600
Less: O/S	200	4,400	By Discounts	1,900
To Rent		350	By Discount on Creditors	100
To Bad Debts	400		By Net Loss	
Add: New Provision	700	1,100	transferred to capital a/c	390
To Discount		700		
To Insurance	400			
Less: Prepaid	60	340		
To Trade Expenses		300		
To Printing		150		
To Interest on capital		1,200		
To Depreciation on Machinery		250		
To Depreciation on Furniture		200		
		8,990		8,990

Balance Sheet as at 31st March, 2008

Liabilities		*Rs.*	*Assets*		*Rs.*
Capital	24,000		Machinery	5,000	
Add: Interest	1,200		*Less:*Depreciation	250	4,750
	25,200		Furniture	2,000	
Less: Net loss	390		*Less:*Depreciation	200	1,800
	24,810		Sundry Debtors	14,000	
*Less:*Drawings	4,500	20,310	*Less:* New provision	700	13,300
Sundry Creditors	10,000		Closing Stock		7,000
Less: Discount	100	9,900	Prepaid Insurance		60
Bills Payable		2,500	Cash In Hand		260
O/S Salary		200	Cash at Bank		5,940
O/S Wages		200			
		33,110			33,110

Illustration 20:

The following Trial Balance was extracted from the books of Mr. X as on 31st December, 2007.

Debit Balance	*Dr. (Rs.)*	*Credit Balance*	*Cr. (Rs.)*
Plant and machinery	20,000	Opening Stock	34,200
Manufacturing Wages	34,500	Motor Car	12,000
Salaries	15,850	Sales Return	3,100
Furniture	10,000	Purchases	1,02,000
Freight on Purchases	1,860	Bad Debts	1,400
Building	24,000	Interest and Bank Charges	400
Freight on Sales	2,140	Cash at Bank	4,200
Manufacturing Expenses	9,500	Cash in hand	1,120
Insurance and Tax	4,250	*Credit Balances*	
Goodwill	25,000	Capital Account	80,000
General Expenses	8,200	Sundry Creditors	44,560

Factory Fuel and Power	1,280	Bank Loan	15,000
Sundry Debtors	78,200	Purchases returns	1,740
Factory Lighting	950	Sales	2,50,850
		Reserve for Bad debts	2,000

Prepare Trading and Profit and Loss Account for the year ended 31st December, 2007 and the balance Sheet as on that date taking into consideration the following information:

(*a*) Stock in hand on 31st December, 2007 was valued at Rs. 30,500.

(*b*) Depreciate Plant and Machinery by 10% Furniture by 5% and Motor car by Rs. 1,000.

(*c*) Bring provision for Bad debts to 5% on Sundry Debtors.

(*d*) A commission of 1% on the gross profit is to be provided for Works Manager.

(*e*) A commission of 2% (two percent) on net profit (after charging the Works Manager's Commission but before charging General Manager's Commission) is to be paid to the General Manager.

Solution:

Trading A/c for the year ending 31st December, 2007

		Rs.			*Rs.*
To Opening Stock		34,200	By Sales	2,50,850	
To Purchases	1,02,000		*Less:* Returns	3,100	2,47,750
Less: Return	1,740	1,00,260	By Closing Stock		30,500
To Freight on Purchases		1,860			
To Manufacturing Wages		34,500			
To Manufacturing expenses		9,500			
To Factory, fuel & Power		1,280			
To Factory Lighting		950			
To Gross Profit transferred to Profit and Loss A/c		95,700			
		2,78,250			2,78,250

Profit and Loss Account for the year ending 31st December, 2007

		Rs.		*Rs.*
To Salaries		15,850	By Gross Profit	95,700
To Freight on Sales		2,140		
To Insurance & Tax		4,250		
To General Expenses		8,200		
To Bad Debts	1,400			
Add: New Provision	3,910			
	5,310			
Less: Old Provision	2,000	3,310		
To Intt./Bank Charge		400		
To Dep. On P&M		2,000		
To Dep. On Furniture		500		
To Dep. On Motor car		1,000		
To Work Manager Commission		957		
To GM Commission		1,142		
To Net Profit		55,951		
		95,700		95,700

Balance Sheet as at 31st December, 2007

Liabilities		*Rs.*	*Assets*		*Rs.*
Capital	80,000		Plant & machinery	20,000	
Add: Net Profit	55,951	1,35,951	*Less:* Depreciation	(2,000)	18,000
Sundry Creditors		44,560	Furniture	10,000	
Bank Loan		15,000	*Less:* Depreciation	(500)	9,500
Work Manager Commission		957	Building		24,000
G.M. Commission		1,142	Motor Car	12,000	
			Less: Depreciation	1,000	11,000
			Goodwill		25,000
			Closing Stock		30,500
			Debtors	78,200	
			Less: New Provision	3,910	74,290
			Cash in Hand		4,200
			Cash at Bank		1,120
		1,97,610			1,97,610

Illustration 21:

From the under-mentioned details extracted from the books of Mr. Venkatramana prepare Trading and Profit and Loss Account and Balance Sheet as on 31st March, 2008.

	Amount (Rs.)
Plant and Machinery	28,800
Stock on 1-4-2007	89,680
Sundry Creditors	59,630
Sundry Debtors (including Bharat's dishonoured bill of Rs. 1,000)	62,000
Cash in Hand	3,030
Cash at Bank	18,970
Fixture & Fittings	8,970
Provision for doubtful debts	2,500
Bills receivable	9,500
Travelling Expenses	1,880
Repair & renewals	3,370
Bad Debts	3,620
Returns Inward	2,780
Sales	3,65,430
Manufacturing Wages	40,970
Purchases	2,56,590
Salaries	11,000
Rent & Taxes	5,620
Interest & Discount (Dr.)	5,870
Commission Received	5,640
Insurance (Including premium of Rs. 300 p.a. paid upto 30.9.2008)	400
6% Loan Account (Cr.)	20,000
Venkataramana's Capital A/c	1,10,400
Venkataramana's Drawings A/c	10,550

Depreciate plant and machinery by 10% and fixture and fitting 5% p.a. Commission earned but not received amounts to Rs. 600/-. Manufacturing wages include Rs. 1,200 for erection of new machinery purchased last year. Charge interest on capital @ 6%. Interest on loan for the last two months is not paid.

Stock in hand on 31st March, 2008 was Rs. 1,28,960. Write off half of Bharat's dishonoured bill. Create a provision of 5% on Sundry Debtors.

Solution:

Trading A/c for the year ending 31st March, 2008

		Rs.			*Rs.*
To Opening Stock		89,680	By Sales	3,65,430	
To Purchases		2,56,590	*Less:* Returns	2,780	3,62,650
To Manufacturing Wages	40,970		By Closing Stock		1,28,960
Less: Wages paid for installation of machine	1,200	39,770			
To Gross Profit transferred to Profit & Loss A/c		1,05,570			
		4,91,610			4,91,610

Profit and Loss Account for the year ending 31st March, 2008

		Rs.			*Rs.*
To Travelling Expenses		1,880.00	By Gross Profit		1,05,570.00
To Repair & Renewals		3,370.00	By Commission	5,640	
To Bad Debts	3,620		*Add:* Due but not received	600	6,240.00
Less: Old Provision	2,500				
	1,120				
Add: Dishonoured Bill	500				
	1,620				
Add: New Provision	3,050	4,670.00			
To Salaries		11,000.00			
To Rent & Taxes		5,620.00			
To Intt, & Discount	5,870				
Add: O/S Interest	200	6,070.00			
To Insurance	400				
Less: Prepaid	(150)	250.00			
To Depreciation on P & M (10%) 2,880+1,200)		3,000.00			
To Dep. On Furniture		448.50			
To Interest on Capital		6,624.00			
To Net Profit		68,877.50			
		1,11,810.00			1,11,810.00

Balance Sheet as at 31st March, 2008

Liabilities		*Rs.*	*Assets*		*Rs.*
Capital	1,10,400		Plant & Machinery	30,000	
Add: Interest	6,624		*Less:* Depreciation	(3,000)	27,000.00
	1,17,024		Furniture	8,970	
Less: Drawings	10,550		*Less:* Depreciation	(448.5)	8,521.50
	1,06,474		Debtors	61,500	
Add: New Profit	68,877.5	1,75,351.50	*Less:* New Provision	3,050	58,450.00

6% Loan	20,000		Bills receivable	9,500.00
Add: O/S Interest	200	20,200.00	Insurance Premium paid in advance	150.00
Creditors		59,630.00	Commission due	600.00
			Closing Stock	1,28,960.00
			Cash In Hand	3,030.00
			Cash at Bank	18,970.00
		2,55,181.50		2,55,181.50

Illustration 22:

The Trial Balance of Mr. Chakravarty as on 31.12.2007 was as follows:

Debit Balance	*Dr. (Rs.)*	*Credit Balance*	*Cr. (Rs.)*
Purchases	1,62,505	Sales	2,52,600
Debtors	50,200	Reserve for doubtful debts	5,200
Opening Stock	26,725	Creditors	30,326
Wages	23,137	Bills Payable	3,950
Salaries	5,575	Outstanding Wages	2,000
Furniture	7,250	Trade expenses accrued but not paid	700
Postage	4,226	Capital	10,000
Power & Fuel	1,350		
Trade Expenses	5,831		
Bad Debts	525		
Loan at 10% to Amar 1.9.2007	3,000		
Cash in hand and at Bank	10,000		
Drawings	4,452		

Prepare Trading and Profit and Loss Account for the year ended 31st December, 2007 and the Balance Sheet as on that date taking into account the following information:

(*a*) Depreciation on furniture is to be charged at 10% p.a.

(*b*) Debtors include an item of Rs. 500 due from the customer who has become insolvent (nothing shall be received from his estate).

(*c*) Reserve for doubtful debts is to be maintained at 5% on debtors.

(*d*) Goods valued at Rs. 1,500 have been destroyed by fire and the insurance company has admitted the claim for Rs. 1,000.

(*e*) Stocks as at 31.12.2007 was Rs. 12,250.

Solution:

Trading A/c for the year ending 31st December, 2007

	Rs.		*Rs.*
To Opening Stock	26,725	By Sales	2,52,600
To Purchases	1,62,505	By loss by fire	1,500
To Wages	23,137	By Closing Stock	12,250
To Power & Fuel	1,350		
To Gross Profit transferred to Profit and Loss A/c.	52,633		
	2,66,350		2,66,350

Profit and Loss Account for the year ending 31st December, 2007

		Rs.			Rs.
To Salaries		5,575	By Gross Profit		52,633
To Postage		4,226	By Reserve b/d	5,200	
To Trade Expenses		5,831	*Less:* New Provision	2,485	2,715
To Bad Debts	525		By Interest		100
Add: Dishonoured	500	1,025			
To Loss due to fire	1,500				
Less: Insurance claim	1,000	500			
To Dep. On Furniture		725			
To Net Profit		37,566			
		55,448			55,448

Balance Sheet as at 31st December, 2007

Liabilities		Rs.	*Assets*		Rs.
Capital	10,000		Furniture	7,250	
Add: Net Profit	37,566		*Less:* Depreciation	725	6,525
	47,566		Debtors	49,700	
Less: Drawings	4,452	43,114	*Less:* Provision	(2,485)	47,215
Creditors		30,326	Loan to Amar	3,000	
Bills Payable		3,950	*Add:* Interest	100	3,100
Outstanding wages		2,000	Insurance Claim		1,000
Trade Expenses			Closing stock		12,250
Accrued but not paid		700	Cash in Hand & Bank		10,000
		80,090			80,090

Illustration 23:

From the following Trial Balance of Sun Shine and Company prepare Trading, Profit and Loss account and Balance Sheet. The following Trial Balance was extracted from the books of Mr. X as on 31st December, 2007.

	Dr. (Rs.)	*Cr. (Rs.)*
Capital		25,000
Loans		5,000
Sales		35,000
Accounts Payable		4,000
Bills Payable		5,000
Purchase Returns		2,000
Dividends Received		3,000
Plant and Machinery	13,000	
Buildings	17,000	
Receivable	9,650	
Purchases	18,000	
Discount Allowed	1,200	
Wages	7,000	
Salaries	3,000	
Travelling Expenses	750	
Freight	200	

Insurance	300	
Commission Paid	100	
Cash in Hand	100	
Bank	1,600	
Repairs	500	
Interest on Loans	600	
Opening Inventory	6,000	
	79,000	79,000

Additional data:

(*a*) Closing Inventory Rs. 8,000.

(*b*) Depreciation on Plant and Machinery at 15% and 10% on Building.

(*c*) Provision for doubtful receivable Rs. 500.

(*d*) Insurance prepaid Rs. 50.

(*e*) Outstanding rent Rs. 100.

Solution:

Trading & Profit and Loss A/c for the year ending 31st December, 2007

Liabilities		*Rs.*	*Assets*	*Rs.*
To Op. Inventory		6,000	By Sales	35,000
To Purchases	18,000		By Closing Stocks	8,000
Less: Return	2,000	16,000		
To Wages		7,000		
To Gross Profit transferred to Profit and Loss A/c.		14,000		
		43,000		43,000
To Discount allowed		1,200	By Gross Profit b/d	14,000
To Salaries		3,000	By Dividends received	3,000
To Travelling Expenses		750		
To Freight		200		
To Insurance	300			
Less: Prepaid	(50)	250		
To Commission		100		
To Repair		500		
To Interest on Loan		600		
To Rent outstanding		100		
To Provision for doubtful receivable		500		
To Depreciation:				
Plant and machinery		1,950		
Building		1,700		
To Net Profit		6,150		
		17,000		17,000

Balance Sheet as at 31st December, 2007

Liabilities		*Rs.*	*Assets*		*Rs.*
Capital	25,000		Plant & machinery	13,000	
Add: Net Profit	6,150	31,150	*Less:* Depreciation	(1,950)	11,050
Loan		5,000	Building	17,000	
Account payable		4,000	*Less:* Depreciation	(1,700)	15,300
Bills payable		5,000	Cash in Hand		100
Outstanding Rent		100	Cash at Bank		1,600
			Account receivable	9,650	
			Less: provision for doubtful debts	500	9,150
			Closing inventory		8,000
			Insurance		50
		45,250			45,250

Illustration 24:

Prepare Trading and Profit and Loss Account and Balance Sheet from the following data of Premier and Company:

Trial Balance as on 31. 12. 2007

Particulars	*Debit (Rs.)*	*Credit (Rs.)*
Sales		3,00,000
Plant and Machinery	1,20,000	
Rent, Rates & Taxes	20,000	
Sales Returns	30,000	
Freight	4,000	
Accounts Receivable	70,000	
Opening Inventory	1,20,000	
Purchase	2,30,000	
Discount paid	5,000	
Interest on Bank Loan	5,000	
Salaries	70,000	
Cash in Hand	5,000	
Purchase Returns		10,000
Bank Loan		1,50,000
Capital		1,81,500
Accounts Payable		40,000
Bills Payable		26,000
Legal Charges	500	
General Expenses	8,000	
Cash at Bank	20,000	
Total	7,07,500	7,07,500

Adjustments:

1. Provision for bad and doubtful receivable @ 5% on Accounts Receivable.
2. Interest on Bank Loan outstanding Rs. 7,000.
3. Closing inventory as on 31.12.2007 Rs. 1,20,000.

Solution:

Premier and Company

Trading and Profit and Loss Account for the year ending 31.12.2007

Dr.	*Rs.*	*Rs.*		*Rs.*	*Rs.* *Cr.*
To opening inventory		1,20,000	By Sales	3,00,000	
To Purchases	2,30,000		*Less:* Returns	30,000	2,70,000
Less: Return	10,000	2,20,000	By Closing inventory		1,20,000
To Gross Profit c/d		50,000			
		3,90,000			3,90,000
To Rent, Rates & Taxes		20,000	By Gross Profit		50,000
To Freight		4,000	By Net Loss c/d		73,000
To Discount		5,000			
To Int. on Bank Loan	5,000				
Add: O/S	7,000	12,000			
To Salaries		70,000			
To Legal expenses		500			
To General charges		8,000			
To Provision for bad and doubtful		3,500			
		1,23,000			1,23,000

Balance Sheet as on 31.12.2007

Dr. *Liabilities*	*Rs.*	*Rs.*	*Assets*	*Rs.*	*Rs.* *Cr.*
To Capital	1,81,000		Plant & Machinery		1,20,000
Less: Net Loss	73,000	1,08,500	Debtors	70,000	
Bank Loan		1,50,000	*Less:* Provision for Bad and Doubtful receivable	(3,500)	66,500
Accounts Payable		40,000	Cash in hand		5,000
Bills Payable		26,000	Cash at bank		20,000
Outstanding Interest		7,000	Closing inventory		1,20,000
		3,31,500			3,31,500

Illustration 25:

The following is the Trial Balance of Raman Traders as on 31st December, 2007

Dr.	*Rs.*	*Cr.*	*Rs.*
Cash in Hand	1,500	Sales	2,50,000
Cash at Bank	3,000	Returns outwards	2,000
Purchases	1,10,000	Capital	56,000
Returns Inwards	1,500	Accounts payable	30,000
Wages	20,000		
Power and Fuel	8,000		
Carriage Outwards	6,000		
Carriage Inwards	5,000		
Opening inventory	6,000		
Land	10,000		
Building	80,000		

Machinery	30,000	
Patents	15,000	
Salaries	12,000	
Sundry Expenses	6,000	
Insurance	1,000	
Drawings	8,000	
Accounts Receivable	15,000	
Total	3,38,000	3,38,000

You are required to prepare Trading and Profit and Loss Account for the year ended 31.12.2007 and Balance Sheet as at 31.12.2007. Adjustments to be made are given below:

1. Closing Inventory as at 31.12.2007, Rs. 20,000.
2. Provision for bad and doubtful receivable at 5% on debtors.
3. Outstanding Salary Rs. 5,000 outstanding wages Rs. 3,000.
4. Depreciation 10% on all assets.

Solution:

Raman Traders

Trading and Profit and Loss Account for the year ending 31. 12. 2007

Dr. Cr.

	Rs.	*Rs.*		*Rs.*	*Rs.*
To Opening Inventory		6,000	By Sales	2,50,000	
To Purchases	1,10,000		*Less:* Returns	1,500	2,48,500
Less: Return	2,000	1,08,000	By Closing Inventory		20,000
To Wages	20,000				
Add: Outstanding	3,000	23,000			
To Fuel and Power		8,000			
To Carriage Inwards		5,000			
To Gross Profit c/d		1,18,500			
		2,68,500			2,68,500
To Carriage Outwards		6,000	By Gross Profit b/d		1,18,500
To Salaries	12,000				
Add: Outstanding	5,000	17,000			
To Sundry Expenses		6,000			
To Provision for Bad and Doubtful Debts		750			
To Depreciation on Building		8,000			
To Depreciation on Machinery		3,000			
To Insurance		1,000			
To Depreciation on Patents		1,500			
To Net Profit c/d		75,250			
		1,18,500			1,18,500

Balance Sheet as on 31.12.2007

Dr. *Cr.*

Liabilities	*Rs.*	*Rs.*	*Assets*	*Rs.*	*Rs.*
To Capital	56,000		Land & Building		10,000
Add: Net loss	75,250		Building	80,000	
	1,31,250		*Less:* Depreciation	(8,000)	72,000
Less: Drawings	(8,000)	1,23,250	Machinery	30,000	
Accounts Payable		30,000	*Less:* Depreciation	(3,000)	27,000
Outstanding Salaries		5,000	Patents	15,000	
Outstanding Wages		3,000	*Less:* Depreciation	1,500	13,500
			Accounts Receivable	15,000	
			Less: Provision for Bad and Doubtful Debts	(750)	14,250
			Cash in Hand		1,500
			Cash at Bank		3,000
			Closing Stock		20,000
		1,61,250			1,61,250

Illustration 26:

The following is the trial balance of Y on December 31, 2007

	Rs.	*Rs.*
Bills Payable		7,000
Land and Building	40,000	
Stocks 1.1.2007	40,000	
Capital A/c		1,50,000
Plant and Machinery	66,000	
Bills Receivable	15,000	
Purchases	1,30,000	
Sales		2,20,000
Wages	35,000	
Salaries	5,700	
Rent and Taxes	2,000	
General Office Expenses	5,000	
Interest on Capital	8,000	
Furniture and Fixture	3,000	
Cash at Bank	2,300	
Discount	5,000	
Creditors		10,000
Debtors	30,000	
	3,87,000	3,87,000

You are required to prepare trading account, profit and loss account and a balance sheet after taking into account the following: (*i*) Write off 7.5% depreciation on plant and machinery and 5 per cent depreciation on land and building; (*ii*) Create a provision of 5% on debtors for bad debts.

Solution:

Trading and Profit and Loss A/c for the year ending 31st December, 2007

	Rs.		Rs.
To Opening Stock	40,000	By Sales	2,20,000
To Purchases	1,30,000		
To Wages	35,000		
To Gross Profit c/d	15,000		
	2,20,000		2,20,000
To Salaries	5,700	By Gross Profit b/d	15,000
To Rent and Taxes	2,000	By Net Loss	19,150
To General Office Expenses	5,000		
To Interest on Capital	8,000		
To Discount	5,000		
To Depreciation on:			
Plant & Machinery	4,950		
Land & Building	2,000		
To Provision for Bad Debt	1,500		
	34,150		34,150

Balance Sheet as on December 31. 2007

		Rs.			Rs.
Bills payable		7,000	Cash at Bank		2,300
S. Creditors		10,000	Bills receivable		15,000
Capital	1,50,000		Debtors	30,000	
Less: Net loss	19,150	1,30,850	*Less:* Provision	1,500	28,500
			Furniture & fixture		3,000
			Plant and Machinery	66,000	
			Less: Depreciation	4,950	61,050
			Land & building	40,000	
			Less: Depreciation	2,000	38,000
		1,47,850			1,47,850

Illustration 27:

On March 31,2008 the following trial balance was prepared from the books of White Brothers:

	Rs.	Rs.
Sundry Debtors	31,000	
Sundry Creditors		10,000
Bills Receivable	5,000	
Plant and Machinery	75,000	
Purchases	2,00,000	
Capital A/c		1,00,000
Freehold Premises	1,00,000	
Salaries	21,000	
Wages	24,000	
Postage & Stationery	2,000	
Carriage Inwards	1,750	
Carriage Outwards	750	

Bad Debts	950	
Bad debts Provision		350
Office Expenses	1,500	
Cash at Bank	6,000	
Cash in Hand	1,100	
Bills Payable		8,000
Reserve		40,000
Sales		3,41,700
Closing Stock	30,000	
	5,00,050	5,00,050

The following adjustments are required:

1. White gets a salary of Rs. 10,000 p.a.
2. Allow 10% interest
3. Bad debts provision to be adjusted to 2.5 percent on sundry debtors.
4. Depreciate plant and machinery @ 10% p.a. and freehold premises @ 5%.

Solution:

Trading and Profit and Loss A/c for the year ending 31st March, 2008

		Rs.		*Rs.*
To Purchases		2,00,000	By sales	3,41,700
To Wages		24,000		
To Carriage Inward		1,750		
To Gross Profit c/d		1,15,950		
		3,41,700		3,41,700
To Salaries		21,000	By Gross profit b/d	1,15,950
To Postage & Stationery		2,000		
To Carriage Outward		750		
To Office Expenses		1,500		
To Bad Debts	950			
Add: New Provision	775			
	1,725			
Less: Provision	350	1,375		
To Depreciation on Plant & Machinery		7,500		
To Depreciation on Freehold Premises		5,000		
To Interest on Capital		10,000		
To Salary to White		10,000		
To Net Profit		56,825		
		1,15,950		1,15,950

Balance Sheet as on March 31, 2008

		Rs.			*Rs.*
Bills Payable		8,000	Cash at Bank		6,000
S. Creditors		10,000	Cash in Hand		1,100
Reserve Capital	1,00,000		Bills Receivable		5,000
Add: Int. on Capital	10,000		Stock Debtors	31,000	
Add: Salary	10,000		*Less:* Provision	775	30,225
Add: Net Profit	56,825	1,76,825	Closing Stock		30,000
Reserve		40,000	Pland and Machinery	75,000	
			Less: Depreciation	7,500	67,500
			Freehold Premises	1,00,000	
			Less: Depreciation	5,000	95,000
		2,34,825			2,34,825

Illustration 28:

The following balance sheet of Shri Jhivan Lal as on 31st December, 2007 was prepared by a novice on the basis of net Figures:

	Rs.		*Rs.*
Sundry Creditors	15,000	Land and Buildings	15,700
Bills Payable	2,500	Plant and Machinery	4,500
Capital	30,000	Furniture & Fixtures	950
		Sundry Debtors	7,600
		Investments	5,000
		Stock in Trade	8,000
		Cash in Hand	1,250
		Cash at Bank	4,500
	47,500		47,500

You are required to revise it, if necessary, and draw it up in the proper descriptive manner after taking the following into consideration:

(*i*) Profit for the year ending on above date amounts to Rs. 5,000 without, however, taking into consideration the following adjustments:

(*a*) Fire Insurance for Building, plant and machinery for I year from July 1, 2007 — Rs. 200 was charged entirely to the revenue account of the year.

(*b*) Interest on investment including an addition @ 6% per annum accrued for the last quarter (October to December 2007, received in January 2008 was not taken into account:

(*c*) Staff salary for December 2007 — Rs. 500 was paid in January 2008 without provision in the Revenue Account.

(*d*) Interest on capital @ 5% was not provided.

(*ii*) You are required to make necessary revision in the profit estimate of the year after giving effect to the above adjustments:

(*a*) Depreciation has been charged on (*i*) Land and Building @ 2%, nothing charged or to be charged, however, on the extension made during the year amounting to Rs. 1,000; (*ii*) on plant and machinery @ 10%; and (*iii*) on furniture and fixture @5% per annum;

(*b*) Bad debts reserve @ 5% has been raised on sundry debtors;

(*c*) There has been an addition to investment during the year for Rs. 500;

(*d*) Drawings by Jivan Lal during the year amounted to Rs. 3,000;

(*e*) Included in creditors is a provision for contingency amounting to Rs. 500 and for expenses Rs. 750;

(*f*) Stock has been valued at market rate being lower than cost.

Solution:

Statement Showing Profit for the year ended December 31, 2007

		Rs.	*Rs.*
Profit as originally determined			5,000
Add: (*a*)	Fire insurance on building, plants and machinery for the period 1.1.2008 to 30.6.2008 wrongly charged		100
(*b*)	Interest accrued on investments for the period from 1.10.2007 to 31.12.2007 not credited		75
			5,175
Less: (a)	Staff salary for December, 2007 not provided	500	
(*b*)	Interest on Capital not charged	1,400	1,900
	Profit for the year		3,275

Note: (*a*) Interest on capital is computed as under:

		Rs.
	Capital as per original balance sheet	30,000
Add:	Drawings for the year charged there against	3,000
		33,000
Less:	Profit for the year credited thereto	5,000
	Capital before adjustment for drawings and interest	28,000
	Interest @ 5% thereon	1,400

(*b*) Balance on 1.1.2007 of fixed assets is determined as under:

			Land and Building	*Plant and Machinery*	*Furniture and Fixture*
	Balances as per Balance Sheet		15,700	4,500	950
Less:	Additions during the year		1,000	—	—
			14,700	4,500	950
	Depreciation:	2/98 × 14,700	300	—	—
		10/90 × 4,500	—	500	—
		5/95 × 950	—	—	50
			15,000	5,000	1,000

Shri Jivan Lal

Balance Sheet as on December 31, 2007

		Rs.			*Rs.*
Capital as at 1.1.2007	28,000		Land & building as on 1.1.2007	15,000	
Add: Profit	3,275		Addition during the year	1,000	
Add: Interest	1,400			16,000	
	32,675		*Less:* Depreciation	(300)	15,700

Liabilities		Rs.	Assets		Rs.
Less: Drawings	(3,000)	29,675	Plant & Machinery as at 1-1-2007	5,000	
Bills Payable		2,500	*Less*: Depreciation	500	4,500
Sundry creditors		13,750	Furniture & Fixtures as at 1-1-2007	1,000	
Provision for exp.		1,250	*Less:* Depreciation	50	950
Provision for contingencies		500	Investment as at 1-1-2007	4,500	
			Add: Additions	500	5,000
			Stock in trade at market price		8,000
			Sundry debtors	8,000	
			Less: Reserve for Bad Debts	400	7,600
			Interest Accrued on investments		75
			Prepaid Expenses		100
			Cash at Bank		4,500
			Cash in Hand		1,250
		47,675			47,675

Illustration 29:

Prepare Trading and Profit and Loss Account and Balance Sheet as on 31st March, 2007 from the following balance:

	Rs.
M. Mirza's capital account	1,19,400
M. Mirza's Drawings account	10,550
Sundry Creditors	59,630
15% Loan a/c (Cr.)	20,000
Cash in Hand	3,030
Cash at Bank	18,970
Sundry Debtors (including Badri Das for dishonoured bill of Rs. 1,000)	62,000
Bills Receivable	9,500
Provision for Doubtful Debts	2,500
Fixtures and Fittings	8,970
Plant and Machinery	28,800
Stocks, April 1, 2006	89,680
Purchases	2,56,590
Manufacturing wages	40,970
Sales	3,56,430
Returns Inwards	2,780
Salaries	11,000
Rent & Taxes	5,620
Interest and Discount (Debit)	5,870
Travelling Expenses	1,880
Repairs and Renewals	3,370
Insurance (including premium of Rs. 300 p.a. paid upto Sept. 30, 2007)	400
Bad debts	3,620
Commission Received	5,640

Stocks in hand on March 31, 2007 was Rs. 1,28,960. Write off half of Badri Das's dishonoured bill. Create a provision of 5% on Sundry Debtors. Charge 10% interest on Capital. Manufacturing Wages include Rs. 1,200 for erection of new machinery purchased last year. Depreciate Plant and Machinery by 15% and Fixtures and Fittings by 10% per annum. Commission earned but not received amount to Rs. 600. Interest on loan for the last two months is not paid.

Solution:

Trading and Profit & Loss Account of Mr. M. Mirza
for the year ended March 31, 2007

		Rs.			Rs.
To Opening Stock		89,680	By Sales	3,56,430	
To Purchases		2,56,590	*Less:* Returns	2,780	3,53,650
To Mfg. Wages	40,970		By Closing stock		1,28,960
Less: Charged to P&M	1,200	39,770			
To Gross Profit c/d		96,570			
Total		4,82,610	Total		4,82,610
To Salaries		11,000	By Gross profit		96,570
To Rent & Taxes		5,620	By Commission	5,640	
To Interest & Discount	5,870		*Add:* Accrued	600	6,240
Add: Interest O/S	500	6,370			
To Travelling Expenses		1,880			
To Repair & Renewals		3,370			
To Insurance	400				
Less: Ins. Prepaid	150	250			
To Bad Debts	3,620				
Add: 1/2 of Badri Dass's dishonoured bill	500				
	4,120				
Add: Provision for Bad & Doubtful Debts (5% on Rs. 61,000)	3,050				
	7,170				
Less: Existing Provision for Bad & Doubtful Debts to commission	2,500	4,670			
To Depreciation on:					
Plants & Machinery 15%		4,500			
Fixtures & Fittings		897			
To Interest on Capital		11,940			
To Net Profit c/d		52,313			
		1,02,810			1,02,810

Balance Sheet of Mr. M. Mirza as on 31st March 2007

Liabilities		Rs.	*Assets*		Rs.
Sundry Creditors		59,630	Plant & Machinery	28,800	
15% loan account	20,000		*Add:* Wages for Erection of the New Machine	1,200	
Add: Interest O/s	500	20,500		30,000	
Capital a/c	1,19,400		*Less:* Depreciation	(4,500)	25,500
Less: Drawing	(10,550)		Fixture & Fittings	8,970	
	1,08,850		*Less:* Depreciation	897	8,073

Add: Interest on capital for the year	11,940		Cash at Bank		18,970
Add: Net profit	52,313	1,73,103	Cash in Hand		3,030
			Bills Receivable		9,500
			Sundry Debtors	62,000	
			Less: Bad Debts	500	
				61,500	
			Less: Provision for bad & doubtful debts	(3,050)	58,450
			Stocks		1,28,960
			Insurance prepaid		150
			Commission accrued		600
		2,53,233			2,53,233

THEORY QUESTIONS

1. What basis of accounting is required by Generally Accepted Accounting Principles on the profit and loss account and balance sheet?
2. Explain the basic difference between accrual basis accounting and cash basis accounting. Which of the two is required by Generally Accepted Accounting Principles?
3. What are adjusting entries. Why are they needed for preparing financial statements?
4. List different types of adjusting entries.
5. What are prepaid expenses and unearned revenues?
6. What are accrued expenses and accrued revenues. Give an example of an adjustment to record each of these items.
7. At the end of an accounting period, certain accounts are adjusted. Why?
8. Explain the difference between deferrals and accruals as classification of adjusting entries.
9. "The net income of a business entity is determined by measuring the amount of revenue generated and subtracting expenses incurred, appropriately measured. As a consequence the resulting difference, net profit, is a precise measure of operating performance for the period under consideration." Comment.
10. If a company fails to accrue salaries at the end of a month, what will be the effect of this omission on the financial statements?
11. Distinguish between: (*a*) capital and revenue expenditures, (*b*) capital and revenue receipts.
12. What is a trading account? What are its purposes?
13. What are the objectives of preparing profit and loss account?
14. Give a specimen of trading, profit and loss account, using imaginary figures.
15. What is a balance sheet? What are its characteristics?
16. Explain the rationale behind preparing a balance sheet. What are its limitation?
17. Explain the linkage between trial balance, profit and loss account and balance sheet.
18. A company balance sheet is a major financial statement. What information does it contain?
19. What are the purposes behind a balance sheet?
20. List the major sections (and the components of each section) of a balance sheet.
21. Following is a list of major classifications and subclassifications on the balance sheet.

    Number them in the order in which they normally appear on a balance sheet.

    Current liabilities
    Liabilities

Owners' equity
Long-term liabilities
Long-term investments and funds
Intangible assets
Operational assets (property, plant, and equipment)
Current assets
Retained earnings
Contributed capital
Assets
Other assets
Deferred charges

EXERCISES AND PROBLEMS

I. From the following Trial Balance of Shri Ram, prepare Trading and Profit and Loss Account for the year ended 31st December, 2007 and a Balance Sheet as on that date:

Dr. *Balances*	*Rs.*	*Cr.* *Balances*	*Rs.*
Opening Stock	20,000	Sales	2,70,000
Purchases	80,000	Purchase Returns	4,000
Sales Return	6,000	Discount	5,200
carriage Inwards	3,600	Sundry Creditors	25,000
Carriage Outwards	800	Bills Payable	1,800
Wages	42,000	Capital	75,000
Salaries	27,500		
Plant & Machinery	90,000		
Furniture	8,000		
Sundry Debtors	52,000		
Bills Receivable	2,500		
Cash in Hand	6,300		
Travelling Expenses	3,700		
Lighting (Factory)	1,400		
Rent & Taxes	7,200		
General Expenses	10,500		
Insurance	1,500		
Drawings	18,000		
Total	3,81,000	Total	3,81,000

Adjustments:

(*a*) Stock on 31st December, 2007 was valued at Rs. 24,000 (Market value Rs. 30,000).

(*b*) Wages outstanding for December, 2007 amounting to Rs. 3,000.

(*c*) Salaries outstanding for December, 2007 amounted to Rs. 2,500.

(*d*) Prepaid insurance amounted to Rs. 300.

(*e*) Provide depreciation on plant and machinery at 5% and on furniture at 20%.

(***Ans.:*** Gross Profit Rs. 1,42,000, Net Profit Rs. 87,700, Balance Sheet Rs. 1,77,000)

2. Following is the trial balance of Mr. A as at 31st December, 2007:

Dr. *Balances*	*Rs.*	*Cr.* *Balances*	*Rs.*
Mr. A's building	1,500	Capital Account	12,500
Purchase	4,000	Sales	28,020
Furniture	1,320	Returns outwards	800
Scooter	2,000		
Returns inward	1,150		
Stock on 1st January, 2007	16,900		
Bad debts	150		
Carriage inward	350		
General expenses	600		
Bad debts provision			350
Bank loan			2,500
Interest on bank loan	150		
Commission			450
Insurance & Taxes	1,000		
Scooter expenses	1,300		
Salaries	2,200		
Cash in hand	1,000		
Debtors and creditors	1,500		4,000
	48,620		48,620

Prepare the final accounts for the year ending 31st December, 2007 taking into accounts the following adjustments:

(*a*) Closing stock 31-12-2007 was valued at Rs. 2,170.

(*b*) Commission include Rs. 150 being commission received in advance.

(*c*) Salaries have been paid for 11 months.

(*d*) Bank Loan has been taken at 10% p.a. interest.

(*e*) Depreciate building by 5% and Scooter by 15%.

(*f*) Write off Rs. 100 as further bad debts and maintain bad debts provision at 5% on debtors.

(*g*) Scooter is used for business as well as for private purposes equally.

(***Ans.:*** Gross Profit Rs. 8,590/-, Net Profit Rs. 3,120/-, Balance Sheet Rs. 21,700/-)

3. From the following prepare Trading and Profit and Loss account for the year 2007 and Balance sheet as on 31st December, 2007:

	Dr. (Rs.)	*Cr. (Rs.)*
Building	25,000	—
Machinery	11,000	—
Furniture	5,000	—
Bank	4,500	—
Cash	5,500	—
Loan (since 1-1-2007)	—	15,000
Capital	—	26,000
Debtors/Creditors	25,000	20,000
Opening stock	6,000	—
Purchases/Returns	1,25,000	5,000
Sales/Returns	6,000	1,61,000
Rent	3,000	—
Establishment	3,000	—
P.F. deducted from salaries	—	500

Interest (10%)	1,000	—
Electricity	500	—
Phone	500	—
Commission	3,000	—
Insurance premium	500	—
Bad debts	1,000	—
Bills receivable	2,000	—
	2,27,500	2,27,500

Provide depreciation on building at 5% Machinery at 15% and furniture at 10%. Stock was not taken on 31-12-2007 but only on 7-1-2008. The transactions from 1-1-2008 to 7-1-2008 are sales Rs. 12,500, Purchase Rs. 7,500, stock on 7.1.2007 Rs. 9,000 and Gross Profit 20%. During the year machinery to the value of Rs. 5,000 was destroyed by Fire and insurance claim was settled Rs. 4,000 and credited to machinery account. Also provide for Employer's share of P. F. Rs. 500: provision for bad debts at 5%, commission to the Manager at 10% on net profit after providing the commission.

(*Ans.:* Gross Profit Rs. 40.500/-, Net Profit Rs. 15,000/-,
Balance Sheet Rs. 79,000/-, Closing Stock Rs. 23,000/-)

4. From the following trial balance prepare trading and profit and loss account and a balance sheet as on 31st December, 2007:

Dr. Balances	*Rs.*	*Cr. Balances*	*Rs.*
Purchases	90,000	Sales	1,77,000
Returns Inwards	2,250	Returns Outwards	3,100
Carriage on Purchases	1,300	Creditors	14,000
Carriage on sales	750	Interest on Investments	1,800
Stock 1.1.2007	16,100	Provision for Bad Debts	1,450
Cash	1,500	Commission Received	3,750
Building	75,000	Sales Tax Collected	3,000
Machinery	36,000	Accumulated Depreciation	10,000
Fuel and Power	4,250	A's Capital	60,000
Debtors	40,750	B's Capital	45,000
Investment	18,000		
Rent	2,000		
General expenses (including insurance premium of Rs. 1,000/- paid for one year ending 30th June 2007)	7,500		
Wages and Salaries	10,500		
Sales Tax Paid	2,200		
A's Drawings	5,000		
B's Drawings	6,000		
	3,19,100		3,19,000

Adjustments:

(*a*) Write off Rs. 750 as bad debts and create a provision for doubtful debts @ 5% on debtors.
(*b*) Provide 2% for discount on debtors and creditors.
(*c*) Depreciate building by 5% and machinery by 10%.
(*d*) Rent is payable at the rate of Rs. 200 per month.
(*e*) One-third of the commission received is in respect of work to be done next year.
(*f*) Interest on Drawings is to be provided as follows:
Interest on A's Drawings: Rs. 250/- and Interest on B's Drawings Rs. 300/-
(*g*) Closing stock was valued at Rs. 28,350/-.

(*Ans.:* Gross Profit Rs. 84,050/-, Net Profit Rs. 69,620/-, Balance Sheet Rs. 1,96.590/-)

5. A book keeper has submitted to you the following trial balance wherein the totals of debit and credit balance are not equal:

	Dr. (Rs.)	*Cr. (Rs.)*
Capital	—	15,340
Cash in Hand		60
Purchases	17,980	—
Sales	—	22,120
Cash at Bank	1,770	—
Fixtures & Fittings	450	—
Freehold Premises	3,000	—
Lighting and Heating	130	—
Bills Receivable	—	1,650
Returns Inwards	—	60
Salaries	2,150	—
Creditors	—	3,780
Debtors	11,400	—
Stocks (1-1-2007)	6,000	—
Printing	450	—
Bills Payable	3,750	—
Rates, Taxes and Insurance	380	—
Discount Received/Allowed	890	400
	48,350	43,410

You are required to:

1. Draft the Trial Balance correctly.
2. Prepare a Trading and Profit and Loss Account and a Balance Sheet after taking into account the following adjustments:
   (*a*) Stock in hand 31-12-2007 was valued at Rs. 3,600.
   (*b*) Depreciate fixtures and fittings by Rs. 50.
   (*c*) Rs. 700 was due and unpaid in respect of salaries.
   (*d*) Rates and insurance had been paid in advance to extent of Rs. 80.

(*Ans.:* Gross Profit Rs. 1,680/-. Net Profit Rs. 980/-, Balance Sheet Rs. 21,960/-)

6. From the following Trial Balance, prepare Trading and Profit and Loss Account for the year ended 31st December, 2007 and Balance Sheet as on that date:

	Dr. (Rs.)	*Cr. (Rs.)*
Purchases and Sales	2,75,000	5,20,000
Returns Inwards	15,000	—
Returns Outwards	—	9,000
Carriage	12,400	—
Wages and Salaries	58,600	—
Trade Expenses	2,200	—
Rent	—	13,000
Insurance	2,000	—
Audit Fees	1,200	—
Debtors/Creditors	1,10,000	62,100
B/R and B/P	3,300	2,200
Printing and Advertising	5,500	—
Commission	—	1,000
Opening Stock	36,000	—

Cash in Hand	12,800	—
Cash at Bank	26,800	—
Bank Loan	—	20,000
Interest on Loan	1,500	-
Capital	—	2,50,000
Drawings	15,000	—
Fixed Assets	3,00,000	—
	8,77,300	8,77,300

Adjustments:

(*i*) Stock at the end Rs. 60,000/-.

(*ii*) Depreciate fixed assets by 10%.

(*iii*) Commission earned but not received amounts to Rs. 400/-.

(*iv*) Rent received in advance Rs. 1,000/-.

(*v*) Interest on Bank Loan @ 15% p.a. is unpaid for the last six months.

(*vi*) Allow 8% interest on capital and charge Rs. 900/- as interest on Drawings.

(*Ans.:* Gross Profit Rs. 1,92,000/-. Net Profit Rs. 1,42,400/-. Balance Sheet Rs. 4,83,300/-)

7. From the following Trial Balance prepare Trading and Profit and Loss Account and Balance Sheet as on 31-12-2007:

	Dr. (Rs.)	*Cr. (Rs.)*
Capital	—	5,000
Cash in Hand	750	—
Bank Overdraft 2%		1,000
Purchases and Sales	6,000	7,500
Returns	500	1,000
Establishment Charges	1,250	—
Taxes and Insurance	250	—
Bad Debts Reserve	—	500
Bad Debts	250	—
Sundry Debtors and Creditors	2,500	925
Commission	—	250
Investments	2,000	—
Stock on 1-1-2007	1,500	—
Drawings	700	—
Furniture	300	—
Bills Receivable & Bills Payable	1,500	1,250
Collected Sales Tax	—	75
	17,500	17,500

Adjustments:

(*a*) Salary Rs. 50 and taxes Rs. 200 are outstanding but insurance Rs. 25 prepaid.

(*b*) Commission amounting to Rs. 50 has been received in advance for work to be done next year.

(*c*) Interest accured on investments Rs. 105.

(*d*) Bad Debts Reserve is to be maintained at Rs. 500.

(*e*) Depreciation on furniture is to be charged at 10%.

(*f*) Stock on 31st December, 2007 was valued at Rs. 2,250.

(*g*) A Fire occurred on 25th December, 2007 in the godown and stock of the value of Rs. 500 was destroyed. It was fully insured and insurance company admitted the claim in full.

(*Ans.:* G. P. Rs. 3,250/-, N. P. Rs. 1,500/-, B/S Rs, 9,400/-)

8. Prepare Trading and Profit and Loss Account and Balance Sheet as on 31st December, 2007 from the following:

	Rs.		*Rs.*
Capital	41,000	Trade Expenses	7,700
Life Insurance Premium	1,400	Sundry Creditors	4,500
Plant and Machinery	2,500	Sales	62,000
Stock in the Beginning	7,500	Returns Outwards	500
Purchases	43,600	Special Rebates (Dr.)	400
Returns Inwards	3,000	Special Rebates (Cr.)	600
Sundry Debtors	10,500	Rent for Premises Sublet	500
Furniture	4,550	Lighting	200
Motor Car	20,000	Motor Car Expenses	3,150
Freight and Duty	1,000	Bank Balance	7,600
Carriage in	400	Loan from Suresh @ 12% p.a.	5,000
Carriage out	150	Interest on Loan from Suresh (Dr.)	450

Adjustments:

1. Stock on 31st December, 2007 was valued at Rs. 12,500/-
2. Stock of Rs. 3,000 was burnt by fire on 25th December. It was fully insured and the Insurance company admitted the claim in full.
3. Goods worth Rs. 900 were distributed as free samples. Goods worth Rs. 750 were used for personal purposes by the Proprietor and Goods worth Rs. 250 were given away as charity.
4. Depreciate Motor Car by 15%.
5. The Motor Car is used; partly for business and partly for domestic purposes; therefore, one-third of the car expenses including car depreciation is to be in proprietor's A/c.
6. Rent for 2 months is receivable on Premises sublet.
7. Balance at Bank on 31st December, 2007 as ascertained from the pass Book is Rs. 7,540/- the difference representing Bank Charges.
8. Included in Trade Expenses is Insurance Premium of Rs. 1,200/- paid for the year ending 31st March, 2007.

(***Ans.:*** G. P. Rs. 24.400/-, N. P. Rs. 11,540/-, B/S Rs. 57,990)

9. Prepare Trading and Profit and Loss Account for the year ended 31st December, 2007 and Balance Sheet on that date:

	Rs.		*Rs.*
Capital	20,500	Purchases Returns	2,000
Creditors	15,000	Sales	1,44,800
Outstanding Expenses	3,400	Provision for Bad Debts	300
Rent Received	300	Advertisement Development	4,000
Plant and Machinery	10,000	Power	4,000
Goodwill	2,500	Depreciation of Machinery	500
Agents Şamples	1,350	Salary	17,200
Opening Stock	16,000	Discount Received	900
Debtor	7,300	General Expenses	4,100
Cash at Bank	1,000	Prepaid expenses	200
Cash in Hand	55	Salary to Agent	4,500
Drawings	2,500	Rent and Insurance	9,950
Purchases	85,500	Discount Allowed	2,500
Carriage Inward	750	Sales Return	300
Wages	11,500	Commission to Agents	1,445

Adjustments:

1. Closing Stock was valued at Rs. 15,700. Goods costing Rs. 1,000 was destroyed by fire. The insurance company admitted the claim of Rs. 790 only.
2. Write off Rs. 500 as Bad Debts and create a provision for doubtful debts on debtors at 5%.
3. Depreciate Agents samples by $33^1/_3$%.
4. Write off Advertisement Development by 25%.
5. Charge 5% Manager's Commission on Net Profits.
6. Proprietor withdrew Rs. 100 for his private use. This amount was included in General Expenses.
7. There is a contingent liability of Rs. 6,000 in respect of a court case.

(*Ans.:* G. P. Rs. 45,450/-, N. P. Rs. 4,100/-, B/S Rs. 40,605)

10. On 31st December, 2007 the following trial balance has been extracted:

Dr. Balances	*Rs.*		*Rs.*
Drawings	3,000	Establishment	8,097
Sundry Debtors	19,100	Rates, Taxes and Insurance	3,891
Interest on Loan	200	Advertisement	2,264
Cash in Loan	3,050	*Cr. Balances:*	
Stock (1.1.2007)	5,839	Capital A/c	30,000
Motor Vehicles	9,000	Sundry Creditors	8,401
Cash at Bank	4,555	Loan on Mortgage	8,500
Land and Building	12,000	Bad Debts Provision	710
Purchases	67,458	Sales	1,11,243
Sales Returns	7,821	Purchase Returns	1,346
Carriage in	3,929	Discounts	440
Carriage out	1,404	Bills Payable	2,714
General Expenses	4,489	Rent Received	250
Bills Receivable	6,882		

Adjustments:

1. Depreciate Land and Buildings at 5% and Motor Vehicle at 15%.
2. Interest on Loan is @ 5% taken on 1st January, 2007.
3. Goods costing Rs. 600 were sent to customer on sale or return for Rs. 700 on 30th December, 2007 and has been recorded in the books as actual sale.
4. Salaries amounting to Rs. 700 and Rates amounting to Rs. 400 are due.
5. There has been a fire on 1st January, 2007 destroying goods worth Rs. 200/-.
6. The Bad Debts provision is to be brought up to 5% on Sundry Debtors.
7. The stock in hand on 31st December, 2006 was valued at 6,850/-.
8. Goods costing Rs. 500 were taken away by the proprietor for his personal use, but no entry has been made in the books of accounts.
9. Prepaid Insurance amounted to Rs. 175.
10. Provide for Manager's commission at 5% on net profit after charging such commission.

(*Ans.:* G. P. Rs. 34,192/-, N. P. Rs. 10,097/-, B/S Rs. 58,042)

11. From the following Trial Balance of Mr. Axe, prepare a Trading and Profit & Loss for the year ended on 31st December, 2007 and a Balance Sheet as on that date:

Dr. Balances	*Rs.*		*Rs.*
Materials consumed	15,000	Bank charges	30
Carriage	820	Coal, gas and water	220
Wages	3,610	B/R	400

Power and Fuel	540	*Cr. Balances:*	
Trade	1,450	Axe's Capital A/c	18,000
Bad Debts	180	Sales	24,000
Returns	500	Loan from Kapil @ 12% (taken on 1.4.2007)	1,000
Fires Insurance	300	Bank	820
Rates & Taxes	520	Outstanding Wages	340
Cash in Hand	160	Trade Expenses accrued but not paid	200
Stock on 31.12.2007	4,650	Discount	60
Plant & Machinery	8,000	Creditors	1,240
Interest on Kapil's Loan	60	Apprentice Premium	450
Debtors	5,400	B/P	370
Salaries	2,000	Provision for Doubtful Debts	760

Adjustments:

1. Carry forward the following unexpired amounts:
   (*a*) Fire Insurance Rs. 50
   (*b*) Rates & Taxes Rs. 120
   (*c*) Apprentice Premium Rs. 150
2. Wages include Rs. 500 spent on installation of a new machine on 1st January, 2007.
3. Depreciation is to be charged on Plant and machinery at 10% and Furniture at 20%. Loose Tools are revalued at Rs. 1,200.
4. Make a Provision of Rs. 400 for doubtful debts on Debtors.
5. Accrued Income Rs. 230.

(***Ans.:*** G. P. Rs. 3,810/-, N. L. Rs. 1,250/-, B/S Rs. 20,900)

12. From the following ledger balances prepare Trading Account, Profit & Loss Account and a Balance Sheet as at 31st December. 2007:

Capital Account on 1-1-2007	50,000	Fire Insurance Premium A/c	900
Stock Account on 1-1-2007	8,000	Bad Debts A/c	2,100
Purchases A/c	20,000	Discount Account (Dr.)	500
Sales A/c	80,000	Apprenticeship Prem. (Cr.)	1,500
Returns Inwards A/c	1,500	Printing and Stationery A/c	250
Returns Outwards A/c	400	Rates and Taxes A/c	350
Carriage Outward A/c	2,500	Travelling Expenses A/c	150
Carriage Inward A/c	1.200	Sundry Trade Expenses A/c	200
Wages A/c	3,300	Business Premises A/c	55,000
Salaries A/c	5,500	Furniture & Fixture A/c	2,500
Rent A/c	1,100	Bills Receivable A/c	3,500
Freight and Dock Charges A/c	2,400	Bills Payable A/c	2,500
Sundry Debtors A/c	20,000	Investments A/c	3,000
Sundry Creditors A/c	15,800	Cash in Hand	250
Packing Machinery A/c	4,500	Cash at Bank	3,500
Smith's Loan A/c	5,000	Proprietor's Withdrawals	3,000

Adjustments to be made are:

1. Stock in hand at 31st December, 2007 Rs. 7,000.
2. Wages to labourers for the last month are outstanding Rs. 300/-.
3. Salaries to Clerks for the month of December, 2007 are outstanding Rs. 500.
4. Rent of godowns for the last month is outstanding Rs. 100.
5. Fire Insurance Premium are Rs. 600 paid in July, 2007, to run for one year from 1st July, 2007 to 30th June, 2008.
6. Apprenticeship Premiums are for three years paid in advance on 1st January, 2007.

7. A stationery bill for Rs. 30 remains unpaid and unrecorded.
8. Depreciate: Business Premises by 5%: furniture and fixture by 10% packing machinery by 10%.
9. Interest on Investments at 5% for the half year to 31st December, 2007 has accrued.
10. Interest on Smith's Loan for one year has accrued at 7%.
11. Interest on capital to be allowed at 5% for the year.
12. Interest on Drawings to be charged to him, as ascertained for the year Rs. 80.

(*Ans.:* G. P. Rs. 50,700/-, N. P. Rs. 31,875/-, B/S Rs. 1,01,525/-)

13. From the following Trial Balance extracted from the books of Ram Singh, prepare a Trading and Profit and Loss Account for the year ended 30st September, 2008 and a Balance Sheet as on that date:

	Rs.	*Rs.*
Capital Account	—	45,000
Drawings Account	3,240	—
Land and Buildings	12,500	—
Plant & Machinery	7,135	—
Furniture and Fixtures	625	—
Carriage (Inwards)	2,185	—
Wages	10,735	—
Salaries	2,335	—
Bad Debts Provision as on 1-10-2007	—	1,235
Sales	—	45,615
Sales Returns	880	—
Bank Charges	70	—
Coal, Gas and Water	360	—
Rates & Taxes	420	—
Discounts Accounts Balance	—	60
Purchases	21,080	—
Purchases Returns	—	4,230
Bills Receivable	635	—
Trade Expenses	995	—
Sundry Debtors	18,900	—
Sundry Creditors	—	6,085
Stock (1st October, 2007)	13,210	—
Apprentice Premium (paid by apprentice in factory)	—	250
Fire Insurance	245	—
Cash at Bank	6,500	—
Cash in Hand	425	—
	1,02,475	1,02,475

Adjustments:

1. Carry forward the following unexpired amounts:
   (*i*) Fire insurance Rs. 62.50
   (*ii*) Rates and taxes Rs. 120
   (*iii*) Apprentice premium Rs. 200
2. Transfer to building account Rs. 1,500 from purchases and Rs. 1,000 from wages, representing cost of material and labour spent on additions to building made during the year.
3. Charge depreciation on Land and Building at 2.5% and on Plant and Machinery 10%.
4. Make a provision of 5% on Sundry Debtors for bad debts.
5. Charge 5% interest on capital but not on drawings.
6. The value of stock as on 30th September, 2008 was Rs. 14,695.

(*Ans.:* G.P. Rs. 18,590/-, N.P. Rs. 11,769/-, B/S Rs. 62,064).

Depreciation Accounting

LONG-TERM ASSETS

This chapter discusses the accounting problems related to the use of long-term assets whose benefits to a firm extend over many accounting periods, specially the issue of depreciation accounting.

Before taking up depreciation, it should be understood that the costs relating to the use of long-term assets should be properly calculated and matched against the revenue earned so that periodic net income can be determined. These use costs or expenses or periodic write-offs are known by different names for different category of assets as shown here:

Types of Long-term Assets	*Term of expense for write-off or use costs*
1. Tangible assets:	
(*i*) Land	None
(*ii*) Plant, building, equipment tools, furniture, fixtures, vehicles	Depreciation
(*iii*) Natural resources such as oil timber, coal, ore, mineral deposits	Depletion
2. Intangible assets such as patent, copyrights, trade marks, goodwill	Amortisation

Among the above assets, land is a tangible asset that has an indefinite or unlimited useful life. Therefore, it is not subject to depreciation or periodic write-off to expenses.

Depletion is the name of expenses or write-off in the case of natural resources. Depletion refers to the systematic and rational allocation of the acquisition cost of natural resources to future periods in which the use of those natural resources contributes to revenue. Natural resources are exhausted or used up through mining, cutting, pumping, etc.

The term amortisation is used in case of intangible assets. Amortisation refers to the systematic and rational allocation of the acquisition cost of intangible assets to future periods in which the benefits contribute to revenue. It is the periodic write-off to expenses of the intangible asset's cost over its expected useful life.

The term depreciation refers to periodic allocation of the acquisition cost of a tangible long-term asset over its useful life. Depreciation has been discussed in detail later.

ACCOUNTING PROBLEM IN LONG-TERM ASSETS

Basically, there are two problems relating to accounting of long-term asset. First, what is the original acquisition cost of a particular long-term asset. Second, how should the amount of expense or periodic write-off be determined and allocated against yearly revenue to reflect the asset's consumption. The other related issues are how should subsequent expenditures such as repairs, maintenance and additions be treated, how should disposal of long-term assets be recorded. These accounting problems are graphically presented in Fig. 10.1.

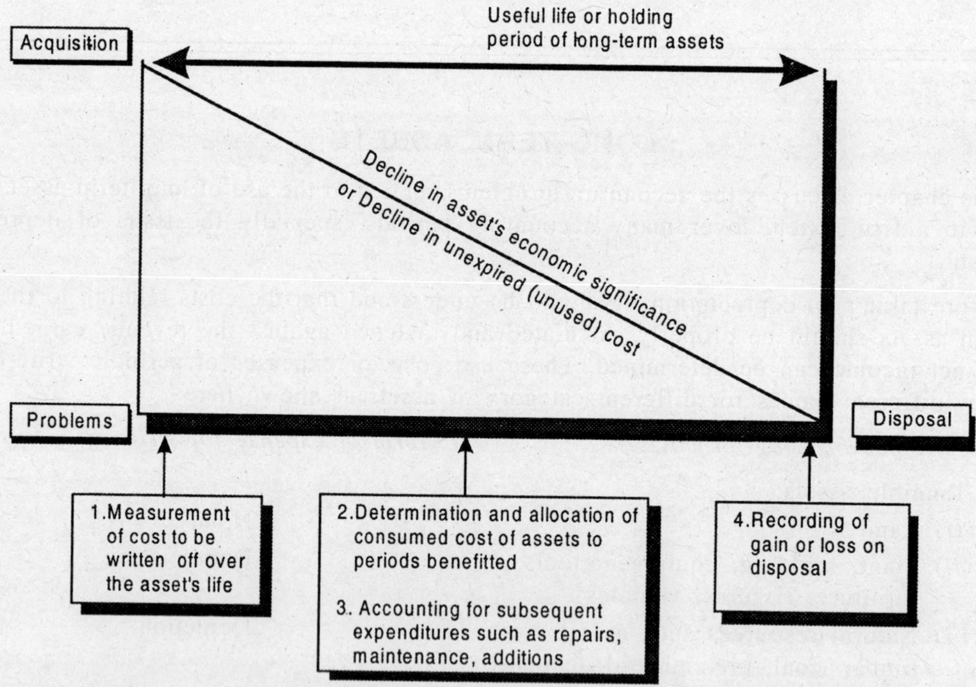

Fig. 10.1 Accounting problems of long-term assets

For accounting purposes, the acquisition cost of a long-term asset having a limited useful life indicates the prepaid cost of a bundle of future services or benefits that will help earn future revenues. Acquisition cost of long-term assets are like inventories and prepaid expenses. Acquisition cost includes all expenditures necessary to get the long-term assets in place and ready for use.

Cost of a long-term asset is easy to determine when the asset is purchased for cash. In this case, cost of asset is equal to cash paid for the asset plus expenditures for freight, insurance while in transit, sales tax, special foundations, installation and other necessary costs. When a second hand asset is purchased, the initial costs of getting it ready for use, such as expenditure for new parts, repairs and painting are added to the cost of the asset.

Some costs associated with the acquisition of an asset are not added to the cost if they are not found necessary to get the asset ready for use, and therefore, do not increase asset's usefulness. Expenditures resulting from carelessness or errors in installing the asset, from vandalism or from other unusual occurrences do not increase the usefulness of the assets and should be treated as an expense.

If a debt is incurred for the purchase of the asset, the interest charges are not the cost of the asset but are the cost of borrowing money to purchase the asset. They are, therefore, an expense for the period. But interest incurred during the construction period of an asset is treated as part of the cost of an asset.

The cost of land includes not only the negotiated price but also other expenditures such as broker's commission, title fees, surveying fees, lawyer's fees, accrued taxes paid by the purchaser, assessment for local improvements such as streets and sewage systems, cost of draining, clearing, levelling and grading. Any salvage recovered from the old building will be deducted from the cost of the land.

Improvement to land such as parking lots, private sidewalks, driveways, fences are not added to the cost of land but to a separate land improvement account. These expenditures are depreciated over the estimated lives of the improvements.

When an existing or old building or used machinery is purchased, its cost includes the purchase price plus all repair, renovation and other expenses incurred by the purchaser prior to use of the asset. Ordinary repair costs incurred after the asset is placed in use are not normal operating expenses when incurred.

When a business constructs its own buildings the cost includes all reasonable and necessary expenditures such as those for materials, labour, some related overhead and indirect costs, architects' fees, insurance during construction, interest on construction loans during the period of construction, lawyer's fees. If outside contractors are used in the construction, the net contract price plus other expenditures necessary to put the building in usable condition are included.

Sometimes, basket purchases (also known as group purchases, package purchases) of assets are made by the purchaser wherein two or more types of long-term assets are acquired in a single transaction, and for a lumpsum. In basket or package purchases, cost of each asset acquired must be measured and recorded separately. For example, assume that a purchaser has bought land and the building situated on the land for a lumpsum payments of Rs. 8,50,000. The total purchase price can be divided between these two assets on the basis of relative market or appraisal values, as shown here.

Asset	*Estimated market value (Rs.)*	*Percent of total (%)*	*Allocation of purchase price (Rs.)*	*Estimated useful life*
Land	1,00,000	10	85,000	Indefinite
Building	9,00,000	90	7,65,000	30 yrs.
	10,00,000	100	8,50,000	

When a long-term asset is purchased and a non-cash consideration is included in part or in full payment for it, the cash equivalent cost is measured as any cash paid plus current market value of the non-cash consideration given. Alternatively, if the market value of the non-cash consideration given cannot be determined, the current market value of the asset purchased is used for measurement purposes.

As a general rule, long-term assets are recorded at cost due to the basic criterion of objectivity. However, there could be some exceptions to this rule of cost basis. For example, if an asset is acquired by donation or by paying substantially less than the market value of the asset, then it is recorded at its fair market value. Similarly, if the value of land increases sharply after its acquisition due to some abnormal factors, such as discovery of mineral deposits or oil, the amount originally recorded as the cost of land may be increased to reflect current value of the land.

NATURE OF DEPRECIATION

As stated earlier, depreciation is a term applicable in case of plant, building, equipment, furniture, fixtures, vehicles, tools. These long-term or fixed assets have a limited useful life, *i.e.,* they will provide service to the entity (in the form of helping in the generation of revenue) over a limited number of future accounting periods. Depreciation implies allocating the cost of a tangible fixed or long-term asset over its useful life. Depreciation makes a part of the cost of asset chargeable as an expense in profit and loss account of the accounting periods in which the asset has helped in earning revenue.

Thus, allocating the capitalised cost of an asset into expense for different accounting periods is known as depreciation.

The Institute of Chartered Accountants of India defines depreciation as follows:

> "Depreciation is a measure of the wearing out, consumption or other loss of value of depreciable asset arising from use, effluxion of time or obsolescence through technology and market changes. Depreciation is allocated so as to charge a fair proportion of the depreciable amount in each accounting period during the expected useful life of the asset. Depreciation includes amortisation of assets whose useful life is pre-determined."

SSAP 12 of the UK also defines the depreciation in the same manner.

"Depreciation is the measure of the wearing out, consumption or other loss of value of a fixed asset whether arising from use, affluxion of time or obsolescence through technology and market changes."

International Accounting Standards Committee defines this term as follows:

> "Depreciation is the allocation of the depreciable amount of an asset over its estimated useful life. Depreciation for the accounting period is charged to income either directly or indirectly."

Depreciation accounting is based on the matching concept wherein an attempt is made to match a part of acquisition cost of an asset (shown as depreciation) with the revenue generated by the use of such asset. To determine the amount of depreciation, three items are needed: (*i*) actual acquisition cost,(*ii*) estimated net residual value, and (*iii*) estimated useful life. Of these three items, two are estimates, residual value and useful life. Due to this, it can be said that the amount of depreciation recorded in an accounting period is only an estimate. To take an example, assume an asset was purchased for Rs 1,00,000 and it has a life of 10 years. At the end of 10 years, the asset can be sold for Rs 10,000. It means that decline in value of Rs 90,000 (Rs 1,00,000 — Rs 10,000) is an expense for generating the revenue realised during the ten-year period that the asset was used. Therefore, in order to determine correct net income figure, Rs 90,000 of expense shall be allocated to these periods and matched against the revenue. Failure to do so would overstate income for these periods. Depreciation expense for each accounting year can be determined as follows:

Acquisition cost	Rs. 1,00,000
Less: Salvage or residual value	Rs. 10,000
Amount to be depreciated over useful life	Rs. 90,000
Estimated useful life	10 years

$$\text{Annual depreciation expense } \frac{\text{Rs. } 90{,}000}{10 \text{ years}} = \text{Rs. } 9{,}000$$

It should be understood that depreciation accounting becomes necessary due to the assets (except land) losing economic utility, significance or potential. Many factors cause decline in the utility of the asset for the business, such as wear and tear, passage of time, obsolescence, technological change, etc.

Causes for Depreciation

Depreciation implies a decline in the service potential of an asset and the decline in the service potential makes the asset have only a limited useful life. Unless the asset should eventually be retired from its planned use, there is no cause for depreciation. For example, services provided by land do not decrease over time, therefore, land is not depreciated and all costs are recovered when the land is sold.

There are many factors that cause decline in the service potential or economic utility of asset, and hence, become the causes of depreciation. However, the major causes are physical deterioration and obsolescence.

Physical deterioration of the asset results from use and physical factors such as normal wear and tear, chemical action such as rust, effects of wind and rain. To some extent, maintenance and repairs may partially check or offset deterioration. Therefore, while estimating the useful life and salvage value of the asset, a given level of maintenance is assumed. However, this does not eliminate the need for depreciation.

Obsolescence is another important cause for depreciation. Obsolescence is non-physical factor and means becoming out-of-date. With fast-changing technology as well as fast-changing demands, machinery and even buildings often become obsolete before they wear out. Inventions may result in new processes that reduce the unit cost of production to the point where continued operation of old equipment is not economical. Firms replace computers that work as well as when they were purchased because new, smaller computers occupy less space and compute faster.

It should also be noted that replacing the asset is not essential to the existence of depreciation. Depreciation is the expiration or disappearance of service potential from the time the plant asset is put into use until the time it is retired from service. Whether or not the asset is replaced does not effect the amount or treatment of its depreciation.

Accountants rightly do not differentiate between physical deterioration and obsolescence and are not interested in identifying the specific causes of depreciation for determining the amount of depreciation. These and other causes are only helpful in estimating an asset's useful life in which the accountants are interested because the useful life of an asset is used to measure the amount of depreciation.

FACTORS THAT EFFECT THE COMPUTATION OF DEPRECIATION

The computation of depreciation for an accounting period depends on the following factors:

1. Depreciable Assets: Depreciable assets are assets which:

(*i*) are expected to be used during more than one accounting period;

(*ii*) have a limited useful life; and

(*iii*) are held by an enterprise for use in the production or supply of goods and services, for rental to others, or for administrative purposes and not for the purpose of sale in the ordinary course of business.

2. Useful Life: Useful life is either:

(*i*) the period over which a depreciable asset is expected to be used by the enterprise; or

(*ii*) the number of production or similar units expected to be obtained from the use of the asset by the enterprise.

The useful life of a depreciable asset is shorter than its physical life and is:

(*i*) predetermined by legal or contractual limits, such as the expiry dates;

(*ii*) directly governed by extraction or consumption;

(*iii*) dependent on the extent of use and physical deterioration on account of wear and tear which again depends on operational factors, such as, the number of shifts for which the asset is to be used, repair and maintenance policy of the enterprise, etc.;

(*iv*) reduced by obsolescence arising from such factors as:

(*a*) technological changes

(*b*) improvement in production methods

(*c*) change in market demand for the product or service output of the asset

(*d*) legal or other restrictions.

Since the estimated useful life of the asset is determined at the time of acquisition it may become necessary to revise the estimate after a period of usage. According to AS 6, when the original estimated useful life is revised, the unamortised depreciable amount of the asset is charged to revenue over the revised remaining useful life. Another method to be adopted for taking into account the revised life of the asset is to recompute the aggregate depreciation charged to date on the basis of the revised useful life of the asset and to adjust the excess or short depreciation so determined in the accounting period of revision.

3. Depreciable Amount: Depreciable amount of a depreciable asset is its historic cost, or other amount substituted for historic cost in the financial statements, less the estimated residual value.

Historic cost of a depreciable asset represents its money outlay or its equivalent in connection with its acquisition, installation and commissioning as well as for additions to or improvement thereof. The historic cost of a depreciable asset may undergo subsequent changes arising as a result of increase in long-term liability on account of exchange fluctuations, price adjustments, change in duties or similar factors.

4. Residual Value: The residual value of an asset is often insignificant and can be ignored in the calculation of the depreciable amount. If the residual value is likely to be significant, it is estimated at the date of acquisition, or the date of any subsequent revaluation of the asset, on the basis of the realisable value prevailing at the date for similar assets which have reached the end of their useful lives and have operated under conditions similar to those in which the asset will be used. The gross residual value in all cases is reduced by the expected costs of disposal at the end of the useful life of the asset.

According to ICAI's AS 6 "Any addition or extension to an existing asset which is of a capital nature and which becomes an integral part of the existing asset is depreciated over the remaining useful life of that asset. As a practical measure, however, depreciation is sometimes provided on such addition or extension at the rate which is applied to an existing asset. Any addition or extension which retains a separate identity and is capable of being used after the existing asset is disposed off, is depreciated independently on the basis of an estimate of its own useful life."

NEED FOR DEPRECIATION

The need for charging a reasonable amount of depreciation over the estimated useful life of the asset arises for the following purposes:

1. To ascertain the true income: The basic need of depreciation is to ascertain the true income. If depreciation is ignored, the loss that is occurring in respect of fixed assets will be ignored. The loss will suddenly loom large when the asset becomes useless or valueless. From another angle, when goods are produced it involves use of fixed assets — the reduction in their value should be treated as an element of cost of production of goods. Therefore, depreciation should be debited to P & L A/c before profit is ascertained.

2. To show the asset at its proper value: In the absence of depreciation charge, the asset will be shown at its acquisition cost every year in the balance sheet. If depreciation is not allowed, the Balance Sheet would fail to show the true financial position. Therefore, depreciation must be accounted for in order to present the assets at their proper value.

3. To maintain the capital invested: Depreciation helps to maintain the capital invested in the asset intact in the business so that it can be reinvested in the profit earning process.

4. To retain fund for replacement: The other need for depreciation is to retain out of profit funds for replacement of assets. The amount debited in P & L A/c are retained in the business. These are available for replacement of the assets when its life is over.

5. To allocate the cost of fixed asset to product: The business firms, to find out the accurate cost of production, requires to allocate the cost of fixed asset to product.

6. To compute tax liability: In such a case the rate of depreciation is influenced by tax laws.

METHODS OF DEPRECIATION

There are different methods for allocating costs of fixed depreciable assets. Such allocation has a direct effect on the determination of net income because depreciation expense is a necessary charge and as such is deducted from the revenues in a given period.

Various methods of depreciation are generally classified as follows:

1. On the Basis of Time
   - (*i*) Straight Line Method
   - (*ii*) Decreasing Charge Depreciation
     - (*a*) Written down value method
     - (*b*) Double method
     - (*c*) Sum of year digit method
2. On the Basis of Investment
   - (*i*) Annuity Method
   - (*ii*) Sinking Fund Method
3. On the Basis of Output

1. Straight Line Method

This method assumes that depreciation is a function of time rather than use. This method is based on the assumption that each accounting period receives same benefits from using the assets. It allocates an equal amount of depreciation in each accounting periods of the service life of the assets. Therefore, it is called Straight Line Method.

The formula for calculating depreciation charge for each accounting period is

$$\text{Annual Depreciation} = \frac{\text{Acquisition cost} - \text{Estimated scrap value}}{\text{Estimated Life in Years}}$$

Advantages:

(*i*) It is simple in use.

(*ii*) It realistically matches cost and revenue and determine income of each period easily.

(*iii*) There is no change either in the rate or the amount of depreciation over the useful life of the assets. Such a procedure provides for improved comparability.

Disadvantages:

(*i*) It ignores the cost of capital.

(*ii*) It is based on the wrong assumption of equal utility of the assets during the useful life.

(*iii*) It is also wrong to consider depreciation as a function of time rather than use,

(*iv*) The maintenance of asset is generally costly in the later years with the result that deductions from the revenue would be greater in later years than in the earlier years.

The journal entry for recording depreciation is:

Depreciation A/c Dr.

To Asset A/c

Illustration 1:

A firm bought a plant for Rs. 4,00,000 on 1.1.07 and its useful life was estimated to be 10 years. Its scrap value at the end of period was Rs. 40,000. Find out amount of depreciation by straight line method.

Solution:

$$\text{Annual Depreciation} = \frac{\text{Cost} - \text{Estimated scrap value}}{\text{Estimated Life in Years}}$$

$$= \frac{\text{Rs. }4{,}00{,}000 - \text{Rs. }40{,}000}{10\text{ years}} = \text{Rs. }36{,}000$$

Illustration 2:

ABC Ltd. acquires a machine on 1st July 2006 at a cost of Rs. 2,80,000 and spent Rs. 20,000 on its installation. The firm writes off depreciation at 10% of the original cost every year. The books are closed on 31st December every year. Prepare machinery A/c for 3 years.

Solution:

Machinery A/c

		Rs.			Rs.
2006	To Bank	2,80,000	2006	By Depreciation A/c	15,000
July 1	To Bank (installation exps.)	20,000	Dec. 31	By Balance c/d	2,85,000
		3,00,000			3,00,000
2007			2007		
Jan. 1	To Balance b/d	2,85,000	Dec. 31	By Depreciation A/c	30,000
			Dec. 31	By Balance c/d	2,55,000
		2,85,000			2,85,000
2008			2008		
Jan. 1	To Balance b/d	2,55,000	Dec. 31	By Depreciation A/c	30,000
			Dec. 31	By Balance c/d	2,25,000
		2,55,000			2,55,000

Sale of Asset: If the asset is disposed of in the middle of the year, the amount realised should be credited to the asset a/c for the time it has been in use. Any balance left in the asset account will be profit or loss and should be transferred to P & L a/c.

Illustration 3:

Z Ltd. purchased machine for Rs. 200,000 on 1-1-2004. The machine is depreciated at 10% p.a. on the original cost. On 1-7-2006 the machine was sold for Rs. 1.20.000. Prepare Machinery A/c assuming the books are closed on 31st December every year.

Solution:

Machinery A/c

		Rs.			Rs.
2004			2004		
Jan. 1	To Bank	2,00,000	Dec. 31	By Depreciation A/c	20,000
			Dec. 31	By Balance c/d	1,80,000
		2,00,000			2,00,000
2005			2005		
Jan. 1	To Balance b/d	1,80,000	Dec. 31	By Depreciation a/c	20,000
			Dec. 31	By Balance c/d	1,60,000
		1,80,000			1,80,000
2006			2006		
Jan. 1	To Balance b/d	1,60,000	July 1	By Depreciation a/c	10,000
			July 1	By Bank	1,20,000
				By P & L a/c (loss)	30,000
		1,60,000			1,60,000

Illustration 4:

On July 1,2007, Gopal Ltd. purchased secondhand machine for Rs. 20,000 and spent Rs. 3,000 on reconditioning and installing. On Jan. 1,2008 the firm purchased new machine worth Rs. 12,000. On June 30, 2008 the machine purchased on January 1, 2008 was sold for Rs. 8000.

On July 1, 2009 fresh machine was purchased on installment basis, payment for this machine was to made as follows:

July 1, 2009, Rs. 5000, June 2010, Rs. 6,000, June 30, 2011, Rs. 5500

Payment in 2010, 2011 include interest Rs 1000 & Rs. 500 respectively.

The Company writes off depreciation @ 10% p.a. on original cost. The A/cs are closed every year on 31st March. Show the machine A/c for 3 years:

Solution:

Machine A/c

2007		Rs.	2008		Rs.
July 1	To Bank	20,000	Mar. 31	By Depreciation	2025
	To Bank (Exp.)	3,000	Mar. 31	(1,725 + 300)	
	To Bank	12,000		By Balance c/d	32,975
		35,000			35,000
2008			2009		
Apr. 1	To Balance b/d	32,975	Mar. 31	By Depreciation	3,500
				(2,300 + 1,200)	
				By Balance c/d	29,475
		32,975			32,975
2009			2009		
Apr. 1	To Balance b/d	29,475	June 30	By Dep. (on Second machinery for 3 months)	300
July 1	To Hire Vendor	15,000	Dec. 31	By Bank	8,000
			2010	By P & L a/c (loss)	2,200
			Mar. 31	By Depreciation (2,300 + 1,125)	3,425
				By balance c/d	30,550
		44,475			44,475

Illustration 5:

On 1st Jan. 2005, a company purchased a machine costing Rs. 5,00,000. Its estimated working life is 20 years at the end of which it will fetch Rs. 20,000. Additions are made on 1st Jan. 2006 and 1st July 2007 to the value of Rs. 80,000 (scrap value Rs. 4000) and Rs. 40,000 (scrap value Rs. 2,000) respectively.

The life of both the new machines is 20 years. Show machine a/c for first four years.

Solution:

Machine A/c

2005		Rs.	2005		Rs.
Jan. 1	To Bank	5,00,000	Dec. 31	By Depreciation	24,000
			Dec. 31	By Balance c/d	4,76,000
		5,00,000			5,00,000
2006			2006		
Jan. 1	To Balance b/d	4,76,000	Dec. 31	By Depreciation	27,800
Jan. 1	To Bank	80,000	Dec. 31	By Balance c/d	5,28,200
		5,56,000			5,56,000

2007			2007			
Jan. 1	To Balance b/d	5,28,000	Dec. 1	By Depreciaiton		
July 1	To Bank	40,000		(24,000 + 3800 + 950)		28,750
			Dec. 1	By Balance c/d		5,39,450
		5,68,200				5,68,200
2008			2008			
Jan. 1	To Bal. b/d	5,39,450	Dec. 31	By Depreciation		
				(24,000 + 3,800 + 1,900)		29,700
			Dec. 31	By Balance c/d		5,09,750
		5,39,450				5,39,450

Note: In case, no method of depreciation has been stated in an examination problem, it is appropriate to use straight line method.

Illustration 6:

Rubal Ltd. purchased a machine costing Rs. 3,00,000 on 1st April 2006 and an additional machine on 1st Oct 2006 costing Rs. 2,00,000 and on 1st July 2007 costing Rs. 1,00,000.

On 1st Jan. 2008, one-third of Machine purchased on 1st April 2006 was sold at Rs. 30,000.

Prepare machine a/c for 3 years, it is given that depreciation is charged @ 10% p.a. on straight line method.

Solution:

Machine A/c

		Rs.			*Rs.*
2006			2006		
Apr. 1	To Bank	3,00,000	Dec. 31	By Depreciation (22,500 + 5,000)	27,500
Oct. 1	To Bank	2,00,000	Dec. 31	By Balance c/d	4,72,500
		5,00,000			5,00,000
2007			2007		
Jan. 1	To Balance b/d	4,72,500	Dec. 31	By Depreciation	
July 1	To Bank a/c	1,00,000		(30,000 + 20,000 + 5,000)	55,000
			Dec. 31	By Balance c/d	5,17,500
		5,72,500			5,72,500
2008			2008		
Jan. 1	To Balance b/d	5,17,500	Jan. 1	By Bank	30,000
			Dec. 31	By P&L a/c (loss)	52,500
				By Depreciation	50,000
				By Balance c/d	3,85,000
		5,17,500			5,17,500

2. Diminishing Balance Method

Under this method, a fixed percentage is applied to book value of the assets (cost of assets). In other words, the depreciation is calculated on the reducing balance (assets cost-depreciation) and not on the original cost. The procedure is that depreciation calculated is deducted from the cost of assets and balance known as the written down value. The written down value at the end of the estimated useful life of the assets should equal the estimated salvage or scrap value.

The formula for determining the rate of depreciation in diminishing balance method is as follows:

$$\text{Rate of depreciation} = 1 - \sqrt[n]{\frac{s}{c}}$$

Advantages:

1. It is easy to use.
2. There is same weightage, in totality, on profit and loss A/c, of depreciation.
3. It facilitates replacement of fixed assets as it makes more funds available at an early stage.
4. This method is permissible under the Income Tax Act.
5. The higher depreciation is charged in the earlier years when the machine is most efficient compared to later years.

Disadvantages:

1. Under this method, value of asset can never be zero.
2. It is difficult to calculate proper rate of depreciation.
3. There is no provision of interest on capital invested in use of assets.

Illustration 7:

Y Ltd. Co. purchased a machine costing Rs. 3,00,000 on 1st Jan. 2005. The depreciation is to be charged at 20 % p.a. on Diminishing Balance method.

Write up Machinery A/c for first four years.

Solution:

Machinery A/c

2005		*Rs.*	2005		*Rs.*
Jan. 1	To Bank	3,00,000	Dec. 31	By Depreciation	60,000
			Dec. 31	By Balance c/d	2,40,000
		3,00,000			3,00,000
2006			2006		
Jan. 1	To Balance	2,40,000	Dec. 31	By Depreciation	48,000
			Dec. 31	By Balance c/d	1,92,000
		2,40,000			2,40,000
2007			2007		
Jan. 1	To Balance b/d	1,92,000	Dec. 31	By Depreciation	38,400
			Dec. 31	By Balance c/d	1,53,600
		1,92,000			1,92,000
2008			2008		
Jan. 1	To Balance b/d	1,53,600	Dec. 31	By Depreciation	30,720
			Dec. 31	By Bal. c/d	1,22,880
		1,53,600			1,53,600

Illustration 8:

X Ltd. bought a machinery for Rs. 30,000 on 1st April 2006. One more machine was purchased on Oct. 1, 2006 costing Rs. 20,000. On July 1, 2007, a new machinery for Rs. 10,000 was added to the existing machinery.

On 1st Jan. 2008, one-third of the machinery which was installed on April 1, 2006 was sold for Rs. 3,000. Show the machinery A/c in the books of X Ltd. The rate of depreciation is 10 % on reducing balance method.

Solution:

Machinery A/c

Date	Particulars	Rs.	Date	Particulars	Rs.
2006			2006		
Apr. 1	To Bank	30,000	Dec. 31	By Depreciation	2,750
Oct. 1	To Bank	20,000		By Balance c/d	47,250
		50,000			50,000
2007			2007		
Jan. 1	To Balance b/d	47,250	Dec. 31	By Depreciation	5,225
July 1	To Bank	10,000	Dec. 31	By Depreciation	52,025
		57,250			57,250
2008			2008		
Jan. 1	To Balance b/d	52,025	Jan. 1	By Depreciation	3,000
			Jan. 1	By P & L a/c (loss)	5,325
			Dec. 31	By Depreciation	4,370
			Dec. 31	By Balance c/d	39,330
		52,025			52,025

Illustration 9:

A machine is purchased for Rs. 3,00,000 and its estimated useful life is 3 years with scrap value Rs. 30,000. It is decided to depreciate the machine by diminishing balance method. Find out the rate of depreciation p.a.

Solution:

S = Rs. 30,000 C = Rs. 3,00,000 n = 3

$$r = 1 - \sqrt[n]{\frac{s}{c}} = 1 - \sqrt[3]{\frac{30,000}{3,00,000}}$$

$$= 1 - \sqrt[3]{\frac{1}{10}}$$

$$= \frac{1(1)^{1/3}}{10}$$

$$= \frac{1-1}{2.154}$$

$$= 1.0 - .464$$

$$= .536$$

$$= 53.6\ \%$$

Illustration 10:

On first April 2006, a firm purchased a machinery for Rs. 200,000. On October 1, 2006 an additional machinery costing Rs. 1,00, 000 was purchased. On 1st, October 2007 the machinery

Purchased on 1st April 2006, having become obsolete, was sold for Rs. 90,000. On first October, 2008 new machinery was purchased for Rs. 2,50,000 while the machinery purchased on 1st October 2006 was sold for Rs. 85,000 on the same day.

The firm provides depreciation on its machinery @ 10% p.a. on original cost on 31st March every year.

Show machinery A/c, Provision for Depreciation A/c and Depreciation A/c for the period of 3 years ending 31st March 2009.

Solution:

Machinery A/c

2006		*Rs.*	2006		*Rs.*
Apr. 1	To Bank	2,00,000	Mar. 31	By Balance c/d	3,00,000
Oct. 1	To Bank	1,00,000			
		3,00,000			3,00,000
2007			2007		
Apr. 1	To Balance b/d	3,00,000	Oct. 1	By Bank (Sale)	90,000
			Oct. 1	By Pro. for Dep. A/c	30,000
			Oct. 1	By P & L A/c (loss)	80,000
				By Balance c/d	10,000
		3,00,000			3,00,000
2008			2008		
Apr. 1	To Balance b/d	1,00,000	Oct. 1	By Bank (Sales)	85,000
Oct. 1	To Bank	2,50,000	Oct. 1	By Prov. for Dep. A/c	20,000
Oct. 1	To P & L A/c (Profit)	5,000	2009		
			Mar. 31	By Balance c/d	25,000
		3,55,000			3,55,000

Depreciation A/c

2007		*Rs.*	2007		*Rs.*
Mar. 31	To Prov. for Dep. a/c	25,000	Mar. 31	By P & L a/c	25,000
		25,000			25,000
2007			2007		
Oct. 1	To Prov. Dep. a/c	10,000	Mar. 31	By P & L a/c	20,000
2008					
Mar. 31	To Prov. for Dep. a/c	10,000			
		20,000			20,000
2008			2009		
Oct. 1	To Prov. for Dep. a/c	5,000	Mar. 31	By P & L a/c	17,500
2009					
Mar. 31	To Prov. for Dep. a/c	12,500			
		17,500			17,500

Provision for Depreciation A/c

2007		Rs.	2007		Rs.
Mar. 31	To Balance c/d	25,000	Mar. 31	By Dep. A/c	25,000
		25,000			25,000
2007			2007		
Oct. 1	To Machinery a/c		Apr. 1	By Balance b/d	25,000
	(20,000 + 10,000)	30,000	Oct. 1	By Dep. A/c	10,000
	To Balance c/d	15,000	2008		
			Mar. 31	By Dep. A/c	10,000
		45,000			45,000
2008			2008		
Mar. 31	To Machinery		Apr. 1	By Bal. B/d	15,000
	(5,000 + 10,000 + 5,000)	20,000	Oct. 1	By Dep. A/c	5,000
2009			2009		
Mar. 31	To Balance c/d	12,500	Mar. 31	By Dep. A/c	12,500
		32,500			32,500

Illustration 11:

ABC Ltd. purchased secondhand machinery on 1st April 2007 for Rs. 3,70,000 and installed it at a cost of Rs. 30,000. On 1st Oct. 2008 it purchased another machinery for Rs, 1,00,000 and on 1st Oct. 2009, it sold off the first machine purchased in 2007, for Rs. 2,80,000.

On the same date it purchased a machinery for Rs. 2,50,000. On 1st Oct 2010, the second machinery purchased for Rs. 1,00,000 was sold off for Rs. 20,000.

In the beginning depreciation was provided on Machinery at rate of 10% p.a. on the original cost each year on 31st March. From the year 2008-2009, however, the company changed the method of providing depreciation and adopted the written down value method, the rate of Depreciation being 15%.

Give machinery A/c for the period 2007-2011.

Solution:

Working:

(*i*) Machine sold on 1st Oct. 2008

w.d.v. on April 1, 2008	3,06,000
Less: Dep. @ 15% p.a. for 6 month	22,950
	2,83,050
Less: Sale	2,80,000
Loss	3,050

Machinery sold on 1st Oct. 2009

W.D.V. on April 1, 2009	78,625
Less: Dep @ 15% p.a. for 6 month	5,897
	72,728
Less: Sale	20,000
Loss	52,728

Machinery A/c

2007		Rs.	2007		Rs.
Apr. 1	To Bank	3,70,000	Mar. 31	By Depreciation A/c	40,000
Apr. 1	To Bank	30,000	Mar. 31	By Balance c/d	3,60,000
		4,00,000			4,00,000
2008			2008		
Apr. 1	To balance b/d	3,60,000	Mar. 1	By Depreciation A/c (54,000 + 7,500)	61,500
Oct. 1	To Bank	1,00,000	Mar. 1	By Balance c/d (3,06,000 + 92,500)	3,98,500
		4,60,000			4,60,000
2009			2009		
Apr. 1	To Balance b/d	3,98,500	Oct. 1	By Bank	2,80,000
Oct. 1	To Bank	2,50,000	Oct. 1	By Dep.	22,950
			Oct. 1	By P & L A/c (loss)	3,050
			2009		
			Mar. 31	By Depreciation A/c (13,875 + 18,750)	32,625
			Mar. 31	By Balance c/d (78,625 + 2,31,250)	3,09,875
		6,48,500			6,48,500
2009			2009		
Apr. 1	To Balance b/d	3,09,875	Oct. 1	By Bank	20,000
			Oct. 1	By Depreciation	5,897
				By P & L A/c (loss)	52,728
			2010		
			Mar. 31	By Depreciation	34,688
			Mar. 31	By Balance c/d	1,96,562
		3,09,875			3,09,875

Illustration 12:

On 1st Jan. 2006, Asha Ltd. purchased machinery for Rs. 1,20,000 and on 30 June 2007, one more machine of worth Rs. 2,00,000. On 31 March 2008, one of the original machinery which had cost Rs. 50,000 was found to have become obsolete and was sold as scrap for Rs. 7,000. It was replaced on that date by a new machine costing Rs. 80,000. Depreciation is to be provided @ 15% p.a. on W.D.V. method. Accounts are closed on 31 December every year. Show machinery A/c for 3 years.

Solution:

Machinery A/c

2006		Rs.	2006		Rs.
Jan. 1	To Bank	12,00,000	Dec. 31	By Depreciation A/c	1,80,000
			Dec. 31	By Balance c/d	10,20,000
		12,00,000			12,00,000

2007			2007		
Jan. 1	To Balance b/d	10,20,000	Dec. 31	By Depreciation	1,68,000
June 30	To Bank	2,00,000	Dec. 31	By Bal. c/d	10,52,000
		12,20,000			12,20,000
2008			2008		
Jan. 1	To balance b/d	10,52,000	Mar. 31	By Bank (sale)	7,000
Mar. 31	To Bank	80,000	Mar. 31	By Depreciation A/c	1,350
			Dec. 31	By P & L A/c (loss)	27,770
				By depreciation (1,52,380 + 9,000)	1,61,380
				By Bal. c/d	9,34,500
		11,32,000			11,32,000
2009					
Jan. 1	To Balance b/d	9,34,500			

Illustration 13:

Y Ltd. company purchased a secondhand machinery on 1st January 2007 for Rs. 3,70,000 and immediately spent Rs. 20,000 on its repairs and Rs. 10,000 for installation. On 1st July 2008, it purchased another machinery for Rs. 1,00,000.

On 1st July 2009, it sold off the first machine for Rs. 2,50,000 and bought another for Rs. 3,00,000. Depreciation was provided on the machine @ 10% on original cost annually on 31st December. With effect from 1st Jan., 2010, the company changed the method of providing Depreciation and adopted the W.D.V. method and rate of Depreciation was 15 % p.a.

Prepare Machinery A/c for 4 years.

Solution:

Machinery A/c

		Rs.			*Rs.*
2007			2007		
Jan. 1	To Bank	3,70,000	Dec. 31	By Dep. a/c	40,000
	To Bank	30,000	Dec. 31	By Balance c/d	3,60,000
		4,00,000			4,00,000
2008			2008		
Jan. 1	To Balance b/d	3,60,000	Dec. 31	By Dep. (40,000 + 5,000)	45,000
July 1	To Bank	1,00,000	Dec. 31	By Bal. c/d	4,15,000
		4,60,000			4,60,000
2009			2009		
Jan. 1	To Balance b/d	4,15,000	July 1	By Depreciation	20,000
July 1	To Bank	3,00,000	July 1	By Bank	2,50,000
			July 1	By P & L A/c (loss)	50,000
			Dec. 31	By Depreciation (20,000 + 5,000)	25,000
			Dec. 31	By Balance c/d (78,625 + 2,31,250)	3,70,000
		7,15,000			7,15,000
2010			2010		
Jan. 1	To Balance b/d	3,70,000	Dec. 31	By Depreciation	55,500
				By Balance c/d	3,14,500
		3,70,000			3,70,000

Illustration 14:

Manoj Ltd. purchased a Computer Costing Rs. 80,000 on Jan. 2000. The expected life is 5 years and scrap value Rs. 5000. Find the annual depreciation for 5 years by sum-of-years-digit methods.

Solution:

C = Rs. 80,000 S = Rs. 5,000 N = 5

$$\text{Annual Depreciation} = \frac{N(C-S)}{\text{Sum}}$$

$$\text{Where sum} = \frac{N(N+1)}{2}$$

$$\text{Sum} = \frac{5(5+1)}{2} = 15$$

Year	*Calculation*	*Depreciation*
1.	$\frac{5(75,000)}{15}$	Rs. 25,000
2.	$\frac{4(75,000)}{15}$	Rs. 20,000
3.	$\frac{3(75,000)}{15}$	Rs. 15,000
4.	$\frac{2(75,000)}{15}$	Rs. 10.000
5.	$\frac{1(75,000)}{15}$	Rs. 5,000

Illustration 15:

A bus was purchased by a Transport Company for Rs. 10,00,000 on 1st Jan. 2000. The scrap value is estimated at the end of 5 years is Rs. 1,00,000. The rate of depreciation is 20% p.a. Calculate the annual Depreciation by Double Declining method.

Solution:

The rate of Depreciation = 20 × 2 = 40 % p.a

End of Year	*Asset Cost at Beginning of year*	*Amount of Depreciation*
1	1,00,000	4,00,000
2	6,00,000	2,40,000
3	3,60,000	1,44,000
4	2,16,000	86,400
5	1,29,600	51,840

3. Unit of Production Method:

Under this method depreciation expense is allocated in proportion to the degree of asset used for production because estimation of useful life is done in terms of units of output or services hour and not a calendar time period. A machine can produce a limited number of quantity or run for a limited hours. As a result of this limitation, the depreciation is related to usage and not to time. Under this method, the following is calculated:

Depreciation Per annum = Dep. expense Per unit × No. of units produced during the year

or

Dep. expense Per hour × No. of hours used during the year

$$\text{Dep. Per unit} = \frac{\text{Cost} - \text{Scrap value}}{\text{Total estimated unit of output or service hrs.}}$$

Illustration 16:

X Ltd., bought a machine for Rs. 4,00,000 expected to run 72,000 hrs. Its salvage value is estimated at Rs. 40,000. Calculate depreciation for an accounting year in which it was used for 20,000 hrs.

Solution:

$$\text{Dep. per hour} = \frac{4,00,000 - 40,000}{72,000}$$

$$= \frac{3,60,000}{72,000} = \text{Rs. } 5$$

Dep. Amount for Accounting period = 20,000 × 5 = Rs. 1,00,000

4. Annuity Method:

The main disadvantages of the different methods of depreciation discussed earlier are that they do not consider the interest on the capital invested on fixed assets. Annuity method deals with the effect of cost of capital in depreciation calculation. It makes treatment more explicit by showing the interest payment in the P&L A/c. Under this system the capital sum is assumed to earn a certain rate of interest. The assets is, therefore, charged with interest along with actual payment; interest is calculated on the debit balance of the assets on the commencement of the year. The following journal entry is made:

Assets A/c Dr.

To Interest A/c

At the same time, fixed amount is charged as a depreciation expense so that it eliminates the asset or brings down its salvage value, as the case may be. The important point to be noted is that the amount of depreciation to be charged every year must be calculated as to reduce the assets together with interest accumulated thereon to its salvage value at the end of the useful life of the assets.

Illustration 17:

X Ltd. acquires a lease costing Rs. 2,00,000 on April 1, 2007 for a term of 4 years. You find from annuity tables that in order to write off lease on the annuity method at 6 % p.a. interest, the

amount to be written off annually works out to be Rs. 288591 for every rupee. Prepare lease A/c for 4 years. Books are closed on 31st March every year.

Solution:

Lease A/c

			Rs.			Rs.
2007				2008		
Apr.	1	To Bank	2,00,000	Mar. 31	By Dep.	57,718
		To Interest	12,000		By Bal. c/d	1,54,282
		(6% of Rs. 20,000)	2,12,000			2,12,000
2008				2009		
Apr.	1	To Bal. b/d	1,54,282	Mar. 31	By Dep.	57,718
		To Interest	9,527		By Bal. c/d	1,05,821
		(6% of Rs. 1,54,282)	1,63,529			1,63,539
2009				2010		
Apr.	1	To Bal. b/d	1,05,821	Mar. 31	By Dep.	57,718
		To Interest	6,349		By Bal. c/d	54,452
		(6% of Rs. 1,05,821)	1,12,170			1,12,170
2010				2011		
Apr.	1	To Balance b/d	54,452	Mar. 31	By Depreciation	57,718
		To Interest (balancing fig.)	3,266			
			57,718			57,718

Working:

Depreciation = Rs. 2,00,000 × .288591

= Rs. 57,718.2

5. Sinking Fund Method:

Under this method, the amount of depreciation goes on accumulating till the asset is completely worn out. This method provides necessary cash to replace the asset at end of its useful life. The amount of depreciation is fixed and remains same for every year and is charged to P&L A/c. The amount of depreciation is invested outside the business every year. The process of investing amount of depreciation and interest goes on till the time of replacement of asset. At the time of replacement all the investments are sold out and cash received, and the new asset purchased.

Journal Entries:

(*a*) At the end of first year

(*i*) For setting aside amount of Depreciation
Depreciation A/c ... Dr.
  To Sinking Fund A/c

(*ii*) For transfer of Depreciation A/c to P&L A/c
P & L A/c ... Dr.
  To Depreciation A/c

(*iii*) For Investment of Amount
Sinking Fund Investment A/c ... Dr.
  To Bank A/c

(*b*) Subsequent Year

(*i*) For receiving interest
Bank A/c Dr.
To sinking fund A/c

(*ii*) For setting aside amount of Depreciation

(*iii*) Depreciation A/c Dr.
To Sinking fund a/c

(*iv*) For transferring Depreciation A/c to P & L A/c
P & L A/c Dr.
To Depreciation A/c

(*v*) For investing amount of depreciation + interest received
Sinking fund investment A/c Dr.
To Bank A/c

(*c*) Last Year

i, ii & iii entry remain same as in (b), but amount is not invested.

(*iv*) On sale of investment
Bank A/c Dr.
Sinking Fund A/c (if loss) Dr.
To Sinking Fund Investment A/c
To Sinking fund (in profit)

(*v*) On Sale of Asset
Bank A/c Dr.
To Asset A/c

(*vi*) Sinking Fund A/c balance is transferred to asset a/c and any balance left in the asset a/c is transferred to P&L A/c.

Illustration 18:

X Ltd. bought a machinery for Rs. 2,00,000 on 1st Jan. 2000. The useful life was estimated at 3 years with a scrap value of Rs. 20,000. The Company uses Sinking Fund Investment Method, investment to carry 5 % p.a. Interest. The sinking Fund Table shows that .31720 at 5% p.a. will in 3 years accumulate to Re. I. Prepare Machinery A/c, Sinking Fund A/c & S.F. Investment.

Solution:

Machinery A/c

		Rs.			*Rs.*
2000			2000		
Jan. 1	To Bal b/d	2,00,000	Dec. 31	By Sinking Fund a/c	1,80,000
				By Cash	20,000
		2,00,000			2,00,000
2001		*Rs.*	2001		*Rs.*
Jan. 31	To Bal. c/d	57,097		By Dep. a/c	57,097
2001			2001		
Dec. 31	To Bal. c/d	1,17,053	Jan. 31	By Bal. b/d	57,097
			Dec. 31	By Dep.	57,097
			Dec. 31	By Interest	2,859
		1,17,053			1,17,053
2002		*Rs.*	2002		*Rs.*
Dec. 1	To Machinery a/c	1,80,000	Jan 31	By Bal c/d	1,17,053
			Dec. 31	By Dep.	57,097
				By Interest	5850
		1,80,000			1,80,000

Sinking Fund Investment a/c

		Rs.			Rs.
2000			2000		
Jan. 1	To Bank	57,097	Dec. 31	By Bal. c/d	57,097
2002			2002		
Jan. 1	To Balance b/d	57,097	Dec. 31	By Bank	1,17,053
Jan. 1	To Bank	59,956			
		1,17,053			1,17,053

Illustration 19:
(Insurance Policy Method)

Y Ltd. purchased a Machinery for Rs. 4,00,000 on 1st Jan. 2007 to be replaced after 4 years. An Insurance Policy is taken to ensure availability of funds at the time of replacement, the annual premium being Rs. 90,000.

Prepare Machinery A/c, Dep. Fund A/c, Dep. Fund Policy A/c.

Solution:

Machinery A/c

		Rs.			Rs.
2007			2007		
Jan. 1	To Bal. b/d	4,00,000	Dec. 31	By Dep. Fund A/c	4,00,000

Depreciation A/c

		Rs.			Rs.
2007			2007		
Dec. 31	To Bal. c/d	90,000	Dec. 31	By Dep. a/c	90,000
2008			2008		
Dec. 31	To Bal. c/d	1,80,000	Jan. 1	By Balance b/d	90,000
			Dec. 31	By Dep. A/c	90,000
		1,80,000			1,80,000
2009			2009		
Dec. 31	To Bal. c/d	2,70,000	Jan. 1	By Bal. b/d	1,80,000
			Dec. 31	By Dep. A/c	90,000
		2,70,000			2,70,000
2010			2010		
Dec. 31	To Machinery a/c	4,00,000	Dec. 31	By Bal. b/d	2,70,000
			Dec. 31	By Dep. A/c	90,000
			Dec. 1	By Dep. Fund Policy A/c	40,000
		4,00,000			4,00,000

Depreciation Fund Policy A/c

		Rs.			Rs.
2007			2007		
Jan. 1	To Bank	90,000	Dec. 31	By Bal. c/d	90,000
2008			2008		
Jan. 1	To Bal. b/d	90,000	Dec. 31	By Bal. c/d	1,80,000
	To Bank	90,000			
		1,80,000			1,80,000

2009 Jan. 1	To Bal b/d	1,80,000	2009 Dec. 31	By Bal. c/d	2,70,000
	To Bank	90,000			
		2,70,000			2,70,000
2010 Jan. 1	To Bal. b/d	2,70,000	2010 Dec. 31	By Bank	4,00,000
	To Bank A/c	90,000			
	To Depreciation Fund (Profit)	40,000			
		4,00,000			4,00,000

Illustration 20:

General Manufacturers had a debit of balance of Rs. 8,00,000 in their machinery account on 1.1.2000. The concern was charging depreciation @ 15% p.a. on diminishing balance. On 31.3.2000, a part of the machinery purchased on 1.1.1997 at a cost of Rs. 70,000 was sold for Rs. 45,000. New machinery was purchased for Rs. 80,000 on 1.7.2000 and Rs. 6,700 was spent for installation. On 31.12.2000 the concern decided to change the depreciation method from diminishing balance method to straight-line method. It was also decided to charge depreciation @ 10 % p.a. under the new method. Prepare machinery account for the year 2000.

Solution:

Machinery A/c

Dr. *Cr.*

		(Rs.)			*(Rs.)*
01.01.2000	To Balance b/d	8,00,000	31.03.2000	By Bank	45,000
31.03.2000	To Profit & Loss a/c (Profit on sale) (1)	3,623	31.12.2000	By Depreciation (3)	1,29,214
01.07.2000	To Bank	86,700	31.12.2000	By Balance	8,21,964
31.12.2000	To Profit and loss a/c (Excess depreciation charged) (2)	1,05,855			
		9,96,178			9,96,178

	Rs.
1. Calculation of Profit/Loss on sale of machinery	
Cost of machinery sold	70,000
Depreciation for 1997	10,500
	59,500
Depreciation for 1998	8,925
	50,575
Depreciation for 1999	7,586
	42,989
Depreciation for 2000 (i.e., for 3 months)	1,612
	41,377
Realisation from sale	45,000
Book value at the time of sale	41,377
Profit on sale of machinery	3,623

2. Additional/Excess depreciation due to change in the method of depreciation

	Rs.
Book value of machinery on 1.1.2000	8,00,000
Book value on 1.1.1997	
(8,00,000) × (100/85) × (100/85) × (100/85)	13,02,666
Cost of machinery	70,000
	12,32,666
Depreciation for 1997 under WDV	1,84,900
	10,47,766
Depreciation for 1998 under WDV	1,57,165
	8,90,601
Depreciation for 1999 under WDV	1,33,590
	7,57,011
Depreciation under WDV @ 15 % p.a.	
(1,84,900 + 1,57,165 + 1,33,590)	4,75,655
Depreciation under SLM @ 10 % p.a. for 3 years	3,69,800
Excess depreciation charged	1,05,855

3. Depreciation for 2000

	Rs.
Depreciation (on machinery sold) for 1997 for 3 months	1,612
Depreciation on remaining machinery purchased on 1.1.1996	1,23,267
Depreciation on newly purchased machinery for 6 months	4,335
	1,29,214

EVALUATION OF ACCELERATED METHODS

The use of accelerated methods of depreciation provide certain benefits and is useful to business enterprises in many respects. Some benefits which may occur to business entities are as follows:

1. Cash Flow: In terms of cash flow, initial depreciation serves the purpose of an interest-free loan to the tax payer with respect to the year of erection of building or installation of machinery and plant. Since it results in postponement of the tax liability of the assesses, the amount of tax saved in the initial years results in a net addition to cash flow, which is repaid through a higher tax liability during the later year.

Depreciation is an expense that does not use funds currently. In the preparation of changes in financial position, depreciation is added back to net income in calculating funds provided by operations. Because it is added back to net income, the funds from operations is often defined as net income plus depreciation. However, depreciation is not a source of fund. Funds from other operations come from revenues from customers, not by making accounting entries.

In fact, depreciation expense results from an outflow of funds in an earlier period, that is only now being recognised as an operating expense. The following example explains the fact that depreciation does not produce funds.

Assume a company has net income in 2007 of Rs. 20,000 resulting from revenues of Rs. 1,25,000, expenses other than depreciation of Rs. 95,000 and Rs. 10,000 of depreciation. Now assume that depreciation increases to Rs. 25,000 while other expenses and revenues are unchanged: net income is Rs. 5,000 (ignore income tax in both instances). The following exhibit shows that changes in depreciation do not effect funds from operations; funds from operations would be the same Rs. 30,000 in both situations.

Impact of Depreciation on Funds from Operations

	Income Statement			*Funds from Operations*	
		(i) Depreciation Rs. 10,000			
	Revenue	Rs. 1,25,000		Net Income	Rs. 20,000
Less:	Expense except Depreciation	Rs. 95,000	*Add:*	Expenses not using capital: Depreciation	Rs. 10,000
		Rs. 30,000			
	Depreciable expenses	Rs. 10,000		Total funds from operations	Rs. 30,000
	Net income	Rs. 20,000			
		(ii) Depreciation Rs. 25,000			
	Revenue	Rs. 1,25,000		Net Income	5,000
Less:	Expenses except depreciation	95,000	*Add:*	Expenses not using Capital Depreciation	25.000
		30,000		Total funds from operations	30,000
	Depreciation	25,000			
	Net income	5,000			

Depreciation does help determine cash flow, however, by its effect on the measurement of taxable income and thus tax expenses. The more rapid the rate of depreciation charges for tax purposes, the slower the rate of tax payment. For this reason, accelerating depreciation for tax purposes stimulates acquisition of depreciable assets and is viewed as significant in increasing the rate of capital formation. An increasing dependence on this source of finance would suggest lessening reliance of companies on the capital market.

2. Tax Advantage: Many companies may adopt accelerated depreciation methods for tax return purposes because of the tax advantage that they entail. Higher depreciation charges mean lower income and lower taxes. If accelerated methods are used for tax purposes they do not have to be used for financial reporting purposes. Every rupee that can be justified as a deduction saves the company about 50 per cent in tax money. Since the total tax deduction is limited to the total cost of the asset, the different depreciation methods merely shift the years in which the deduction is made. In so far as the deduction is made in earlier years rather than later, this saves interest but more than that it put the taxpayer into possession of funds at an earlier date and this increases his flexibility of financial management.

The actual tax-saving argument is sometimes short-sighted, but the saving of interest and the increased financial flexibility are actual and constitute the real pressure behind depreciation accounting. Thus, accelerated depreciation serves the purpose of an interest-free loan.

3. Benefit to Growing Company: The postponement of the liability under accelerated depreciation may be very useful for a growing firm investing more and more in fixed capital and more so for a new firm which may take some time to stabilise its business. When a company is expanding, the higher depreciation charges will help in expansion and investment which are essentially needed for the company.

4. Replacement of Assets: Accelerated depreciation may induce the tax payer to replace old machinery or equipment before the end of its useful life by new and improved models and also gain a tax advantage. But this would be just one of the considerations in deciding the proper time for replacement. Accelerated depreciation methods allow a business to recover more of the investments in a fixed asset in the first few years of the assets life. This is an important factor in any situation in which there is a high rate of technological change. It is also important when inflation is a factor and depreciation is limited to the original cost of a long-term asset.

Accelerated depreciation does provide an incentive to invest in fixed assets and it particularly helps a growing firm rather than a stationary or a declining one. As far as the form of accelerated depreciation is concerned, the diminishing balance or sum-of-the-years-digits method seems preferable to a straight-line method particularly with respect to plant and machinery. Selective use of initial depreciation and at varying rates for investment in priority sectors is likely to serve a better purpose than its general use. In case of underdeveloped economies, initial depreciation has a special role to play for encouraging investment in backward region and also in small and medium sized enterprises.

FACTORS INFLUENCING SELECTION OF DEPRECIATION METHOD

Depreciation has a significant effect in determining the financial position and result of operations of an enterprise via calculating net income as well as deduction from taxable income. The quantum of depreciation to be provided in an accounting period involves the exercise of judgement by management in the light of technical, commercial, accounting and legal requirements, and accordingly, may need periodical review.

If it is considered that the original estimate of useful life of an asset requires any revision, the unamortised depreciable amount of the asset is charged to revenue over the revised remaining useful life. Alternatively, the aggregate depreciation charged to date is recomputed on the basis of the revised useful life and the excess or short depreciation so determined is adjusted in the accounting period of revision.

There are several methods of allocating depreciation over the useful life of the asset. Those most commonly employed in industrial and commercial enterprises are the straight-line method and the reducing balance method. The management selects the most appropriate methods based on various important factors, e.g.: (*i*) type of asset, (*ii*) the nature of the use of such asset, and (*iii*) circumstances prevailing in the business. A combination of more than one method is sometimes used. In respect of depreciable assets which do not have material value, depreciation is often allocated full in the accounting period in which it is acquired.

The following factors influence the selection of a depreciation method.

1. Legal Provisions: The statute governing an enterprise may be the basis for computation of depreciation. In India, in the case of company, the Companies Act, 1956, provides that the provision of depreciation, unless permission to the contrary is obtained from the central government, should either be based on reducing balance method at the rate specified in the Income-Tax Act/ Rules or on the corresponding straight-line depreciation rates which would write off 95 per cent of the original cost over the specified period. Where the management's estimate of the useful life of an asset of the enterprise is shorter than that envisaged under the provision of the relevant statute, the depreciation provision is appropriately computed by applying a higher rate. If the management's estimate of the useful life of the asset is longer than that envisaged under the statute, depreciation rate lower than that envisaged by the statute can be applied only in accordance with the requirements of the statute.

For tax purposes, the asset should be written off as quickly as possible. Of course, a firm can deduct only the acquisition cost less salvage value, from the otherwise taxable income over the life of the asset. Earlier deductions are, however, worth more than later ones because a rupee of taxes saved today is worth more than a rupee of taxes saved tomorrow, i.e., the goal of the firm in selecting a depreciation method for tax purpose should be to maximise the present value of the reductions in tax payments from claiming depreciation. When tax rates remain constant over time and there is a flat tax rate (e.g., income is taxed at a 40 per cent rate), this goal can usually be achieved by maximising the present value of the depreciation deductions from otherwise taxable income.

2. Financial Reporting: The goal in financial reporting for long-life assets is to seek a statement of income that realistically measures the expiration of those assets. The only difficulty is that no one knows, in any satisfactory sense, just what portion of the service potential of a long-life asset expires in any one period. All that can be said is that financial statements should report depreciation charges based on reasonable estimates of assets' expiration so that the goal of fair presentation can more nearly be achieved.

3. Effect on Managerial Decision: The suitability of a depreciation method should not be argued only on the basis of correct portrayal of the objective facts but should also be decided in terms of their various managerial effects.

Depreciation and its financing effect take the less basic but still realistic approach that, regardless of any effect which depreciation may have upon the total revenue stream, the recognition of depreciation either through the cost of product or as an element in administration and marketing expenses, does cut down the showing of net income available for dividends, and thus, restricts the outflow of cash. The actual tax-saving argument is sometimes short sighted, but the saving of interest and the increased financial flexibility are actual and constitute the real pressure behind depreciation accounting.

Business managers consider these points, but they have the added responsibility of protecting management against the possible distortions of reported costs and misleading incomes which these pressures might engender.

A depreciation method which would lead to unwise dividends, distributing cash which was later needed to replace the asset, would be a poor method. A depreciation method which matches the asset costs distributed period by period against the revenues produced by the asset, thus helping management to make correct judgement regarding operating efficiency, would be a good method.

4. Inflation: Depreciation is a process to account for decline in the value of assets and for this many methods such as straight line, different accelerated methods are available. In recent years, inflation has been a major consideration in selecting a method of depreciation. To take an example, suppose one bought a car for Rs. 10,00,000 five years ago and wrote off Rs. 2,00,000 every year to account for depreciation using straight-line method, expecting that a new car can be purchased after five years. However, five years later, it is found that the same car costs Rs. 15,00,000 whereas only Rs. 10,00,000 has been saved through depreciation.

Why a new car or new asset cannot be purchased with the accumulated amount of depreciation? The difficulty has been created by the inflation. In fact, inflation has eaten into the money saved through depreciation over the five years. This means that a business enterprise (or the owner of car) eats into the asset faster than the rate of depreciation as the cost of replacing the asset is increasing.

The accelerated methods of depreciation tend to write off Rs. 10,00,000 (the price of car in the above example) over the five years. But higher amounts are written off in the beginning as depreciation, and hence, larger amounts are accumulated through depreciation which increase the 'replacement capability' of a business enterprise.

The problem created by inflation in depreciation accounting has contributed in the emergence of the concept of inflation accounting. In inflation accounting, an attempt is made to increase the depreciation amount in line with inflation so that enough money to replace the asset at its current inflated cost can be accumulated.

5. Technology: Depreciation is vital because it decides the regenerating capacity of industry and enables enterprises to set aside an amount before submitting profits to taxation, for replacing machines. Realistically, the depreciation that enterprises are eligible for and capable of accumulating should cover the purchase price of assets, when the time comes for replacement.

But the critical question is, when exactly does the time for replacement come ? Life of machine is no longer an engineering concept. Many electronic companies in the US had to write off their assets in three years because new technologies came in and old machines became scrap overnight. Commercial life of machine is decided by technological progress. The arrival of new machines is not governed by the depreciation policies of government. Therefore, the shorter the period over which the enterprise is able to recover depreciation, the better its chances to adapt to the new technology and survive. In an industry which are exposed to rapid technological progress, a fixed depreciation rate is the surest way to force it into bankruptcy.

Accumulating enough depreciation for buying new technology does not depend merely on a rate of depreciation. Business enterprises should have profit to provide for depreciation resulting into adequate money for replacement at the proper time. An industry in which profits are likely to be high in the initial years will have to provide more depreciation in those years than in the later years when the profit is likely to be low.

6. Capital Maintenance: During inflation, depreciation, if based on historic cost of assets, helps a business firm to gather an amount equivalent to the historical cost of the asset less its salvage value. This treatment of depreciation facilities in maintaining only the 'money capital' or financial capital of business enterprises. However, this results into matching between historic amount of depreciation and sales in current Rupees. The result is that reported net income is overstated and dividend is distributed from the net income which is not real but fictitious. This way of income measurement and maintaining only financial capital during inflation results into erosion of real capital of business enterprises.

However, if depreciation is provided on replacement or current value of assets, it gives matching between current cost (depreciation) and current revenues. This does not involve any hoarding income as is found when depreciation is determined on historical cost. Depreciation on current value of assets provides real operating income in the profit and loss account. This means that capital of business enterprise would be maintained in real terms. Valuation of fixed cost in terms of current cost reflects the current value of operating capability of business enterprises.

CHANGE IN DEPRECIATION METHOD

The depreciation method selected should be applied consistently from the period to period. According to ICAI's AS 6, a change from one method of providing depreciation to another should be made only if the adoption of the new method is required by statute or for compliance with an accounting standard or if it is considered that the change would result in a more appropriate preparation or presentation of the financial statements of the enterprise. When such a change in the method of depreciation is made, the unamortised depreciable amount of the asset is charged to revenue over the remaining useful life by applying the new method.

When there is change from one method of depreciation to another, the unamortised cost of the asset should be written off over the remaining useful life on the new basis commencing with the period in which the change is made. The effect should be disclosed in the year of change, if material.

Depreciable amounts are allocated to each accounting period during the useful life of the asset by a variety of systematic methods. Whichever method of depreciation is selected, its consistent use is necessary irrespective of the level of profitability of the enterprise and of taxation consideration, in order to provide comparability of the result of operations of the enterprise from period to period.

DISCLOSURE ON DEPRECIATION

According to AS-6, the following information should be disclosed in the financial statements:

(*i*) the historical cost or other amount substituted for historical cost of each class of depreciable assets,

(*ii*) total depreciation for the period for each class of assets, and

(*iii*) the related accumulated depreciation.

The Accounting Standard 6 has proposed that the following information should also be disclosed in the financial statement alongwith the disclosure of other accounting policies:

(*i*) Depreciation methods used,

(*ii*) Depreciation rates or the useful lives of the assets, if they are different from the principal rates specified in the statute governing the enterprise.

Also, in case the depreciable assets are revalued, the provision for depreciation is based on the revalued amount, on the estimate of the remaining useful life of such assets. In case the revaluation has a material effect on the amount of depreciation, the same is disclosed separately in the year in which revaluation is carried out.

Any adjustment for the excess or short depreciation made in any accounting period due to the revision in estimate of the useful lives of depreciable assets is treated as an extraordinary item and disclosed accordingly.

A change in the method of depreciation is treated as a change in an accounting policy and is disclosed accordingly.

THEORY QUESTIONS

1. List three major types of long-term (fixed) assets, present examples of each and indicates for each type the term that denotes the periodic write off to expense.
2. In what way is land different from other long-term assets.
3. In general, what amounts constitute the initial cost of fixed assets?
4. What is a basket purchase ? What measurement problem does it pose?
5. Distinguish between depreciation, depletion and amortisation.
6. In computing depreciation, what factors or values must be known or estimated. Identify and explain the nature of each.
7. Which of the following qualities are characteristic of plant assets?

   (*a*) Intangible

   (*b*) Tangible

(*c*) Capable of repeated use in the operation of the business

(*d*) Held for sale in the normal course of business

(*e*) Used continuously in the operations of the business

(*f*) Long-lived

8. Estimated useful life and residual value of a long-term asset relate to the current owner or user rather than to all potential users. Explain this statement.
9. Why is it useful to think of plant assets as a bundle of services?
10. Explain why the recognition of depreciation expenses is necessary to match revenues and expenses properly.
11. Explain the nature of depreciation.
12. Discuss the factors influencing depreciation.
13. What kind of a depreciation expenses pattern is provided under the straight-line method ? When would its use be appropriate?
14. What are accelerated methods of depreciation ? What benefits are associated with these methods?
15. "The major purpose of depreciation accounting is to provide funds for the replacement of assets as they wear out." Do you agree? Explain.
16. "Accounting for depreciation assets would be greatly simplified if accouting periods were only long enough or the life of the assets short enough." What is the point behind the quotation?
17. Explain the benefit of accelerating depreciation when the total depreciation taken is no more than if straight-line depreciation is used.
18. What is the principal argument supporting accelerated depreciation methods?
19. How is disposal of fixed assets treated in accounting?
20. What factors should be considered while selecting a depreciation method?
21. Alpha Company borrowed Rs. 5 lakh to finance the purchase of a new office building which was ready for immediate use. May Alpha add a portion of the interest on Rs. 5 lakh to the building's cost. Explain.
22. Explain why the recognition of depreciation expenses is necessary to match revenue and expenses properly.
23. A company purchased a building five years ago. The market value of the building is now greater than it was when the building was purchased. Should the company stop depreciating the building?
24. Is the purpose of depreciation to determine the value of fixed asset?
25. What is the difference between depreciation for accounting purposes and for income tax purposes?
26. Are the amounts at which plant assets are reported in the balance sheet their approximate market values as of the balance sheet date? Discuss.
27. In what sections of the income statement are gains and losses from the disposal of plant assets presented?
28. Simon is in business as a demolition contractor. Most of the equipment which he started with (valued at Rs. 4 lakh) has a probable life of eight to ten years. Until he received appropriate advice from his accountant, he had ignored depreciation. What have been the effect of continuing to do so?
29. List the factors which should be the basis for selecting a method of providing depreciation of any specific assets or group of assets.
30. Replacing the asset is not essential to the existence of depreciation. Depreciation is the expiration or disappearance of service potential from the time an asset is put into use until the time it is retired from service." Explain.
31. Discuss the disclosure guidelines given in AS 6 'Depreciation Accounting' about depreciation.
32. Why does an accountant provide for depreciation when he measures profit ?

33. Contrast straight-line depreciation with accelerated depreciation in terms of the effect of each on reported net income.
34. Explain how charging depreciation affect:
    (*a*) the income statement, and
    (*b*) the balance sheet.
35. Why may depreciation for the financial statements be different from depreciation charged for income tax purposes?
36. Under what circumstances are accelerated methods of depreciation most appropriate?
37. If a company uses accelerated depreciation for a building rather than the straight-line method, what effect does that choice have on the financial statements in the year of acquisition?
38. "An accelerated depreciation method should be used because of the large decline in the value of an asset early in its life." Evaluate this statement.
39. The manager of an electricity company stated that since its transmission lines are kept in good condition by regular repairs and maintenance and their efficiency remains constant, the lines do not depreciate. Do you agree with this statement?
40. In a year in which the cost of replacing an asset rises, should depreciation be charged on that asset? Why?
41. Distinguish between Annuity Method and Sinking Fund Method of providing depreciation.
42. Explain the following Methods of Depreciation :
    (*i*) Service Hours Method
    (*ii*) Unit of Output Method.

EXERCISES AND PROBLEMS

1. On 1st April 2008, X Ltd. purchased a machinery for Rs. 3,00,000 and incurred Rs. 30,000 towards installation charges. It is estimated that the machinery will have a scrap value of Rs. 30,000 at the end of the useful life which is four years.

   Prepare machinery A/c for first four years ending 31st March every year.

(*Ans.:* Depreciation Rs. 75,000 p.a.)

2. A Co. purchased a Machine for Rs. 40,000 on 1st April 2008. It immediately spent Rs. 10,000 for installation. After using it for 5 years it was sold at Rs. 27,000. You are required to prepare Machine A/c. The rate of depreciation is 10 % p.a. on straight line method.

(*Ans.:* Profit Rs. 2000)

3. Gautam & Co. purchased Plant & Machinery for Rs. 1,00,000 on 1st July 2000. The asset was to be depreciated at the end of each year at rate of 10 % p.a. on written down value basis. The machinery was sold on 1 Jan. 2004 for Rs. 56,500.

   Prepare Machinery A/c assuming accounting year to end on 30 June every year.

(*Ans.:* Loss Rs. 12,755)

4. X purchased a secondhand machinery on 1-2-2007 for Rs. 50,000; paid Rs. 11,000 for its overhauling and Rs. 5,000 for its installation which was completed by 31-3-2007. The company provides depreciation on its machinery at 15% p.a. on diminishing balance method from the date it was put to use and closes its books on 31st Dec. every year. On 1-10-2008 a repair work was carried out on the machine and Rs. 5,000 were paid for the same.

   The machine was sold on 31-10-2009 for a sum of Rs. 11,000 and amount of Rs. 1000 was paid as dimantling charges. Prepare Machinery A/c from 2007 to 2009.

(*Ans.:* Loss Rs. 33,566)

5. A Co. had bought machinery for Rs. 1,10,000 on 1st Jan. 2005. This machinery was for the first four years credited for depreciation on written down value method at rate of 10% p.a.. During the fifth year, the part of machine (original Cost Rs. 10,000) became useless and sold for Rs. 2,000. Prepare Machinery A/c.

(*Ans.:* Loss Rs. 4,561 Balance Rs. 53,144)

6. On 1st Jan. 2006, a company purchased a machinery costing Rs. 2,50,000, working life 20 years and scrap value Rs. 10,000. Additions are made on 1st Jan. 2007 to the value of Rs. 40,000, estimated life 20 years and scrap value Rs. 2000 and one more machine of Rs, 20,000, estimated life 20 yrs. and scrap value Rs. 1,000.

   One Machine purchased on 1st Jan. 2006 sold on 31 Dec. 2010 at Rs. 1,35,000. Accounts are closed on 31 Dec. Prepare Machinery A/c for 5 years.

(*Ans.:* Loss Rs. 45,000)

7. On 1st Jan. 2008, Y Ltd. purchased machinery for Rs. 1,20,000 and on 30 June 2009, it acquired additional machinery at a cost of Rs. 20,000. On 31st Mar. 2010 one of the original machines which had cost Rs. 5,000 was found to have become obsolete and was sold as scrap for Rs. 500. It was replaced by a new machine costing Rs. 8,000. Depreciation is provided at rate of 15% on W.D.V. method. Accounts are closed on 31st December every year. Prepare Machinery A/c for 3 years.

(*Ans.:* Loss Rs. 2,977 Bal. Rs. 93,450)

8. A transport Co. purchases 5 Trucks at Rs. 2,00,000 each on I April 2002, The company writes off depreciation @ 20% p.a. on original cost and accounts are closed on 31st December every year. On 1st Oct. 2004, one of the trucks is involved in an accident and is completely destroyed. Insurance Company pays Rs. 90,000 in full settlement of the claim. On the same day the Co. purchased an old truck for Rs. 1,00,000 and spent Rs. 20,000 on its overhauling. Prepare Truck A/c for 3 years.

(*Ans.:* Loss Rs. 10,000 Bal Rs. 4,74,000)

9. A company purchased on 1st Jan. 2004 a secondhand plant for Rs. 30,000 and immediately spent Rs. 20,000 in overhauling it. On July 1 2004 additional machinery costing Rs. 25,000 was purchased. On July 1, 2006 the plant purchased on Jan. 1, 2004 became obsolete and was sold for Rs. 10,000. On that date new machinery was purchased at a cost of Rs. 60,000. Depreciation was provided annually on 31st Dec. at the rate of 10% p.a. on original cost of the Assets. In 2007, however, the Co. changed this method of providing depreciation and adopted the method of writing off 15% on diminishing value. Prepare Machinery A/c from 2004 to 2009.

(*Ans.:* Loss Rs. 27,500 Bal. 46,520)

10. On 1-1-2000 A purchased Roasting machine for Rs. 60,000 and Grinding machine for Rs. 40,000. On 1-1-2001 he purchased one oil Expeller for Rs. 1,00,000. On 1-1-2002, the Roasting machine got out of order and a new Roaster was purchased costing Rs. 1,20,000 after surrendering the old one and paying Rs. 90,000. On 1-1-2003, Oil Expeller purchased on 1-1-2001 was destroyed by fire and the insurance Co. paid Rs. 60,000 only.

    Prepare Machinery A/c for 2000-2003. Depreciation is charged @ 10 % p.a. on W.D.V. method.

(*Ans.:* Bal. Rs. 1,23.244; Loss in exchange Rs. 18,000; Loss by Fire Rs. 21,000)

11. The valuation of a group of assets (Plant & Machinery), on 1-1-2004 was Rs. 3,20,000 and its estimated life was 8 years. The following purchases and sales took place upto 31 Dec 2006.

    Purchases: 31 Mar. 2004, Cost Rs. 1,50,000 estimated life 10 yrs.

    30 Sep. 2005, Cost Rs. 1,20,000 estimated life 6 yrs.

    30 April 2006, Cost Rs. 2,00,000 estimated life 8 yrs.

    Sales: Out of initial group of assets, a machine (whose valuation on 1 Jan. 2004 was Rs. 50,000 was sold for Rs. 47,000 on 30 June 2006.)

    Assuming a break-up value of each asset to be 10% of initial cost, prepare the Assets A/c for 3 years

(*Ans.:* Profit Rs. 11,063 Bal. Rs. 5,74,250)

12. ABC Ltd. purchased on 1-1-2000 secondhand Machine for Rs. 4,00,000 overhauling and installation charges for the same were Rs. 1,00,000. Another machine was purchased for Rs. 2,00,000 on 1-7-2000.

    On 1-7-2002, the machine installed on 1-1-2000 was sold for Rs. 2,50,000. Dismantling charges for the machine sold on 1-7-2002 were Rs. 10,000. On the same date another machine was purchased for Rs. 8000 and was commissioned on 30-9-2002. The company has adopted Calendar year as its financial year. Under the existing practice, the company provides depreciation @ 10 % p.a. on original cost. In 2003, it has been decided that depreciation will be charged on D.B.M. @ 15% p.a. The charge is not to be made with retrospective effect.

    Show Plant A/c from 2000 to 2004.

(***Ans.:*** Bal. on 31-12-2004 Rs. 6,71,925 & loss Rs. 1,35,000)

13. Beauty Ltd. purchased an asset for Rs. 84,000 with estimated life of 6 years. You are required to open the assets A/c for 6 years when Depreciation is charged by sum-of-year-digits method.

14. A lease was purchased on 1-4-2000 for five years at a Cost of Rs. 50,000. It is proposed to depreciate the lease by annuity method charging 5% interest. Show the lease A/c for 5 yrs and also the relevant entries in the P & L A/c. The reference of the annuity table shows that to depreciate Re. 1 by annuity method over 5 years by charging interest @ 5% one must write off a sum of Re. 0. .30975 every year.

(***Ans.:*** Annuity Dep. Rs. 11,549)

15. Deepak Ltd. purchased a lease for a sum of Rs. 6,00,000 for 7 years. It is proposed to depreciate it under the annuity method after charging interest @ 4% p.a. Reference to the annuity table indicated that 0.16660961 @ 4% p.a. is required to write off Re. 1 in 7 years. Prepare Lease A/c for first 4 years.

16. Z Ltd. bought one machine for Rs. 2,00,000 on 1st Jan. 2000. The useful life was estimated at 3 years with a scrap value of Rs. 20,000. Find out depreciation charged from profit and loss A/c by Sinking Fund Method. The Sinking fund Table shows that 0.317208 at 5% p.a. will in 3 years accumulate to Re. 1.

(***Ans.:*** Depreciation Rs. 57097.44)

17. A Co. purchased 3 years Lease on Jan. 1, 2007 for Rs. 25,000. It decided to provide for the replacement of the Lease at the end of 3 years by setting up a Sinking Fund. It is expected that investment will fetch interest @ 5%. Table shows that an annual payment of Re. 1 @ 5% compound interest in 3 years accumulate Rs. 3.1525. Investments are made to the nearest rupee. On 31st Dec. 2009 Investments are sold for Rs. 15,250. Show Lease A/c, Sinking Fund A/c. Sinking Fund Investment A/c.

(***Ans.:*** Rs. 7392.22 will be saved each year)

18. Mr. X takes a Lease, on 1-4-2007 for 5 years on a payment of Rs. 10,00,000. He proposes to provide for its replacement by means of an insurance policy for Rs. 10,00,000. The annual premium is Rs. 97,500. On 1st April 2012, the Lease is renewed for a further period of 5 years for the same amount. Show necessary accounts.

(***Ans.:*** Profit Rs. 5,12,500)

19. A Co. purchased a Lease for 3 years for Rs. 30,00,000. On 1st Jan. 2007 it decided to provide for its replacement by taking an insurance policy for Rs. 3,00,000. The annual premium was Rs. 95,000.

    On 1-1-2010, the Lease is renewed for a further period of 3 years for Rs. 3,00,000. Show necessary accounts.

(***Ans.:*** Profit Rs. 15,000).

Inventory Valuation

MEANING OF INVENTORY

Inventory includes tangible property that (*i*) is held for sale in the normal course of business, or (*ii*) will be used in producing goods or services for sale. Inventories are current assets and reported on the balance sheet. As current assets they can be used or converted into cash within one year or within the next operating cycle of the business, whichever is longer.

According to Accounting Standard (AS) - 2 Revised, issued by the Institute of Chartered Accountants of India, inventories are assets:

(*i*) held for sale in the ordinary course of business;

(*ii*) in the process of production for such sale; or

(*iii*) in the form of materials or supplies to be consumed in the production process or in the rendering of services.

Inventories include goods purchased and held for resale, for example, goods purchased by a retailer and held for resale, computer software held for resale or land and other property held for resale.

Inventories are kept by manufacturing firms and merchandising (retailing) firms. For merchandising firms, inventories are often the largest or most invaluable current asset. The types of inventory usually held by these two kinds of enterprise are as follows:

(A) Manufacturing Enterprises

(*i*) Finished goods inventory — goods produced, completed and kept ready for sale.

(*ii*) Work-in-progress inventory — goods in the process of being produced but not yet completed as finished goods. When completed, work-in-progress inventory becomes finished goods inventory.

(*iii*) Raw material inventory — items purchased or acquired for using in making finished goods. Such items are known as raw material inventory until used. When raw materials are used, they become the part of the work-in-progress inventory, (work-in-progress includes cost such as raw materials, direct labour and factory overhead).

(B) Merchandising Enterprises

In merchandising or retailing firms, inventory consists of goods (generally known as merchandise held for resale in the normal course of business. The goods are acquired in a finished condition and are ready for sale without further processing.

NEED FOR INVENTORIES

Inventory is one of the major problems that accountants face today. It is difficult to value in terms of cash. It is almost impossible to assess its value in terms of future profits. The basic reason for holding inventories is that it is physically impossible and economically impractical for each inventory item to arrive exactly where it is needed and exactly when it is needed. The following are the reasons for carrying inventories:

Level	*Reason*
Fundamental (Primary)	Physical impossibility of getting the right amount of stock at the exact time of need. Economical impracticability of getting the right amount of stock at exact time in need.
Secondary	Favourable return on investment. Buffer to reduce uncertainty. Decouple operations. Level or smooth production. Reduce material handling costs. Allow production of family of parts. Price changes (can be disadvantageous). Bulk purchases. Display of customers.

Inventory is not purchased as investment or to hold or to realise a gain from possession but rather to sell and realise a gain from resale. In fact, each purchase of saleable goods is in anticipation of the very next sale. Inventory should be considered as an investment and should compete for funds with other investments contemplated by the business firm.

Inventory represents a type of business insurance which assures the company that it will not have to close down due to shortages of saleable goods. Inventory is a variable cost insurance. That is the cost of this insurance will vary in the same direction as the value of sales. As the sale increases, the company will find it necessary to maintain a larger and larger inventory to meet the expanded sale volume.

It is often claimed that, for seasonal industries, it is advisable to have adequate opening inventories. If attractive quantity discounts are available, a business enterprise may prefer to buy in excess of its current sales requirements and can build up additional inventories. Many firms, especially those that sell in seasonal markets — buy in excess of their needs when supply prices are favourable. They store the goods and can then maintain sales during a period of unfavourable supply prices.

OBJECTIVES OF INVENTORY MEASUREMENT

The measurement of inventory has a significant effect on income determination and financial position of a business enterprise. The American Institute of Certified Public Accountants (US) states:

"A major objective of accounting for inventories is the proper determination of income through the process of matching appropriate costs against revenues."[1]

It is significant to observe that a direct relationship exists between cost of goods sold and closing inventory. Cost of goods sold is measured by deducting closing inventory from cost of goods available for sale. Because of these relationships, it may be said that the higher the cost of closing inventory, the lower the cost of goods sold will be and the higher the resulting net income.

On the contrary, the lower the value of closing inventory, the higher the cost of goods sold and the lower the net income. Items which are not in the closing inventory are considered as sold and become the part of cost of goods sold. In this way, measurement of closing inventory influences the income statements (through influencing cost of goods, and net income) and balance sheet because inventory appears as current assets on the balance sheet.

Also, closing inventory influences net income of not only the current period but it also influences the net income of the next accounting period because closing inventory of the current period becomes the opening inventory for the next period and thus becomes cost of goods sold.

Since closing inventory determines cost of goods sold, the most common objective of inventory measurement is the attempt to match costs with related revenues in order to compute net income within the traditional accounting structure. The relationship of inventories to the process of income measurement is similar to the common characteristics of prepaid expenses and plant and equipment. The expression, matching costs against revenues, means determining what portion of the cost of goods available for sale should be as cost of the period and deducted from the revenue of the current period and what portion should be carried (as inventory) to be matched against the revenue of the following period.

Other things remaining the same, i.e., if all other items appearing on an income statement are constant and also income-tax rates do not change, any change in the amount of closing inventory will bring similar change in the amount of reported net income. This is illustrated in the following data taken to explain this situation.

Effect of Inventory Value on Net Income

Data	*Amounts (Rs. in lakh)* *Situations*			
	A	B	C	D
Sale	50	50	50	50
Opening inventory	6	6	6	6
Purchases	40	40	40	40
Goods available for sale	46	46	46	46
Closing inventory	8	10	12	14
Cost of goods sold	36	36	34	32
Net income	12	14	16	18

In the above example, it can be noticed that in all four situations, (A, B, C, D) sale, opening inventory, purchases are identical. As the value of closing inventory changes among the four situations, net income also changes, to the extent the closing inventory increases or decreases. For instance, closing inventory increases by Rs. 2 lakh from situation A to B, from B to C, C to D, so net income also goes up by Rs. 2 lakh.

1. American Institute of Certified Public Accountants, Accounting Research Bulletin No. 43, AICPA, 1968.

A second objective of inventory measurement is to state the fair value of inventory which appears as current assets on the balance sheet. This, alongwith other assets reflect the value of assets to the firm, and in turn, the financial position of a business enterprise.

Further, the value of inventory will help permit investors and other users to predict the future cash flows of the firm. This can be accomplished from two points of view. First, the amount of inventory resources available will support the inflow of cash through their sale in the ordinary course of business. Second, the amount of inventory resources available will, under normal circumstances, have an effect on the amount of cash required during the subsequent period to acquire the merchandise that will be sold during the period.

INVENTORY COSTING METHODS

The pricing or costing of inventory is one of the most interesting and most widely debated problems in accounting. Generally, inventories are priced at their cost in conformity with the cost concept. According to AICPA (US): "The primary basis of accounting for inventory is cost, which is the price paid or consideration given to acquire an asset. As applied to inventories, cost means in principle, the sum of the applicable expenditures and charges directly or indirectly incurred in bringing an article to its existing condition and location."

The cost of inventory, as per the above definition and in practice as well includes the following costs:

(*i*) Invoice price less cash discounts.

(*ii*) Freight or transportation, insurance including insurance in transit.

(*iii*) Applicable taxes and tariffs. Other costs such as these for purchasing, receiving and storage should theoretically be included in inventory cost. In practice, however, it is so difficult to allocate these costs to specific inventory items and also sometimes these costs are often not material in amount that they are in most cases considered an expenses of the accounting period instead of an inventory cost.

According to AS-2 (Revised) issued by The Institute of Chartered Accountants of India, the cost of inventories comprises all cost of purchases, cost of conversion and other cost incurred in bringing that inventories to their present location and condition (paragraph 6).

Inventory costing is quite simple when acquisition prices remain constant. When prices of identical lot of purchases vary in the accounting period, it is difficult to say which price should be used to measure the closing inventory. Also, when identical items are bought and sold, it is often impossible to tell which items have been sold and which are still in inventory. For this reason, it is necessary to make assumption about the order in which items have been sold.

Two terms — goods flow and cost flow — are useful in considering the problems of pricing inventories under fluctuating prices. Goods flow refers to the actual physical movement of goods in the firm's operations. Cost flow is the real or assumed association of costs with goods either sold or in inventory. The assumed cost flow may or may not be the same as the actual goods flow. Though this statement or practice may appear strange, there is nothing wrong or illegal about this practice. Generally Accepted Accounting Principles (GAAP) accept the use of an assumed cost flow that does not reflect the real physical movement of goods. In fact, the assumption about the cost flow is more important to goods flow as the former helps in determining net income which is the major objective of inventory valuation.

There are four generally accepted methods of inventory pricing, each based on a different assumption of cost flow:

1. First In First Out (FIFO)
2. Last In First Out (LIFO)
3. Average Cost Method
4. Specific Identification Method

The Accounting Standard No. 2 issued by The Institute of Chartered Accountants of India has recommended the use of FIFO (First in First out) or weighted average cost method for valuation of inventory. It also permits the use of specific identification method when specific costs are attributed to identified items of inventory.

The inventory costing methods are also known as cost flow assumptions. The specific identification method allocates costs according to the physical flow of goods. The other methods assume certain cost flow patterns that may or may not reflect the physical flow of goods.

1. First In First Out (FIFO)

The FIFO assumption of cost flow is recognised intuitively as being generally consistent with the physical flow of products and goods in most merchandising operations. This method follows the principle that goods received first are sold first. After the first lot or batch of goods purchased is exhausted, the next lot is taken up for sale. It does not suggest, however, that the same lot will be sold.

Sometimes, all items are tagged with their arrival date and sold in date order specially with stocks that deteriorate. The inventory is priced at latest stock.

Arguments in Favour of FIFO: The FIFO method depends on the assumption that it is a good inventory management to sell or use the oldest goods first and maintain a current inventory representing the most recent purchases. It has the advantage that management has little or no control over the selection of units in order to influence recorded profits. It also has the advantage of not being influenced by the arbitrary choices of customers. As a result, it provides a more consistent and systematic determination of inventory and cost of goods sold. It also permits better comparison among different firms in the same industry and among several years.

Another benefit of FIFO is that it combines all elements of profit reported at the time of sale. Under FIFO, no separation can be made of gains and losses arising from price changes and income resulting from managerial decisions in the course of normal operations.

A third benefit of FIFO is the presentation of the ending inventory for balance sheet purposes in terms of the most recent costs which can be assumed to approximate replacement cost. The closeness of approximation to replacement cost depends on the stock turnover. When the stock turnover is rapid, the inventory valuation will reflect current prices unless prices change considerably after the recent purchases.

Arguments Against FIFO: With the FIFO method, the inventory is valued at costs that most closely represent the current cost. However, cost of goods sold is matched with costs that date back in time. If the prices of goods are rising rapidly, the cost of goods sold may be understated. If the sales price is fixed, then sale revenue may not produce enough income to cover the purchase of goods. The valuation of inventory in terms of current costs depend on the frequency of price changes and the stock turnover. In case stocks turn over rapidly, the inventory valuations will reflect current prices. But it is argued that the inventory valuations will hardly be identical with replacement costs under FIFO except accidently or under unusual conditions of stable prices from the date of acquisition of the ending inventory to the date of the balance sheet.

The objectives of matching current cost with current revenues is not achieved under the FIFO method. There are other limitations under the FIFO method. FIFO costing is improper if many lots of goods are purchased during the period at different prices. This method overstates profit especially with high inflation. It does not consider the cost of replacing used goods, a situation created by high inflation.

The FIFO method is suitable where (*i*) the size and cost of units are large, (*ii*) goods are easily identified as belonging to a particular purchased lot, and {iii) not more than two or three different receipts of the goods are on hand at one time.

2. Last In First Out

Under LIFO, latest stocks of goods flow into costs of goods sold and oldest stocks are included in stocks of inventories. This method is based on the assumption that cost of goods sold is charged at prices which almost correspond to the replacement cost of the goods. The main objective in LIFO is the matching of current cost against current revenues, resulting in an operating income which excludes gain and loss from the holding of inventories,

In LIFO, a distinction is often made between natural LIFO where cost flows demonstrably reflect physical flows, and artificial LIFO where cost flows demonstrably contradict physical flows. In fact, there is no necessary connection between physical flows and inventory valuation and the relation of one to the other is simply a convenient assumption. The actual flow of goods will more commonly follow the FIFO concept.

Advantages:

1. It is a cost method that prices goods sold in a systematic and realistic manner. It provides a better matching of current costs with current revenues.
2. It results in real income in time to rising prices by maintaining net income at a lower level than other costing methods.
3. In industries subject to sharp price fluctuations for goods, the method minimises unrealised inventory gains and losses and tends to stabilise reported operating profits. Income is reported only when it is available for distributions as dividends or for other purposes.
4. Probably the most important argument in favour of LIFO is its role in tax saving. It is generally considered a cheap form of tax avoidance by business firms. By valuing inventory at beginning-of-period price and calculating cost of sales at the prices of the period, the firm creates secret reserves which are not taxed. As long prices and inventory levels do not decline, this benefit remains, and in this case the tax saving will be eliminated by higher tax rates.
5. LIFO produces an income statement which shows correct profit or losses and financial position. It correlates current cost and sales and income statements show the result of operation, excluding profits or losses due to changing price levels.

Disadvantages:

1. The valuation of inventory for balance sheet purposes is out-of-date, as it reflect prices of some past period. Inventory valuations do not reflect the current prices, and therefore, are useless in the context of current conditions.
2. The argument that LIFO should be used for matching current costs with current revenue, is not sound. The recent purchase costs are matched against the revenue of the current period. However, unless both purchases and sales occur regularly in even quantities, the revenue will not be matched with the current costs at the time of sale. When purchases

are irregular and unrelated to the timing of sales, the matching is illogical and unsystematic particularly if prices and costs are changing rapidly.

3. The profit of a firm can be manipulated with the LIFO method in operation. By timing purchases, a company can cause higher or lower costs to flow into the income statement, thus increasing or decreasing reported net income at will.
4. Another limitation which also results from LIFO's lowering of the earnings figure is the effect it will have on existing bonus and profit sharing plans. Employees and managers who are interested in the growth of these plans may have difficulty in understanding a drop in benefits created wholly, or partially, by an accounting change.

During a period of rising costs, LIFO produces the desirable effect of reducing taxable income and tax liability; thereby conserving cash. On the other hand, it also effects the profit reported in the financial statements. However, each business entity considering the adoption of LIFO should weigh the advantages and disadvantages as they affect the company's circumstances and environment and its future policies.

Timing the Adoption of LIFO: The decision as to when LIFO should be adopted depend on many factors which will be different in every case. Generally, the principal factors governing the question of 'when' include:

(*i*) Rise in price, because price increases paper profits in the inventory.

(*ii*) High taxes, because a tax saving (or deferment) is the most tangible benefit from choosing LIFO.

(*iii*) Normal inventory quantities, because if there is a substantial increase in inventory quantities during years of inflated prices, the equivalent of such increased quantities may remain indefinitely in the LIFO inventory at the high prices.

(*iv*) No foreseeable conditions that could cause the liquidation of the inventory during the high price and high tax period, because such liquidation would mean that the recognition of income was only temporarily deferred and the income may actually be taxed at a higher rate.

3. Average Cost Methods

The use of average cost methods permits each purchase price to influence the inventory valuation and the cost of goods sold. The assumption is that the buying and selling operation results in the aggregation of costs and the assignment of these costs of goods sold and goods unsold on the basis of a single price. This single price is assumed to be a representative unit cost of all goods handled during a specific period. No specific flow of goods is assumed, unless it can be said that it represents a random selection of goods by customers so that any item handled during the period has an equal chance of appearing in the inventory at the end of the period. Usually, however, it is not thought to be in agreement with the physical flow of goods but in conflict with it.

Average costs do not reflect either the matching of current costs with current revenues or balance sheet valuations in terms of current costs. In this respect, they are somewhat neutral with regard to income determination and balance sheet valuation. But the extent to which they are neutral depends, in part, on how the average is computed.

Generally, simple average and weighted average price can be calculated for inventory costing under the average cost methods. Simple average price is an average of prices without having any regard to the quantities involved.

Under weighted average, total quantities and total costs are considered in computing the average price and not the total of rates divided by total number of rates as in simple average. The weighted average is calculated each time a purchase is made. The quantity bought is added to the stock in hand and the new revised balance is then divided by the new total value of the total stock.

4. Specific Identification Method

The specific identification method involves:

(*a*) Keeping track of the purchase price of each specific unit.

(*b*) Knowing which specific units are sold.

(*c*) Pricing the ending inventory at the actual prices of the specific units not sold.

The objective is to match the unit cost of the specific item sold with sales revenue. This method is based on the assumption that each unit purchased, sold or in inventory has its own identity, that it is separate and distinguishable from any other unit. Each unit sold or remaining in inventory is identified and its specific unit cost is used in calculating cost of goods sold or ending inventory cost. To take an example, assume that an art dealer purchased two seemingly identical pieces of pottery during a period.

The first piece is purchased for Rs. 3,000 and the second is purchased several months later for Rs. 3,500. Assume also that only one of these items is sold by the dealer during the period. The amounts assigned to cost of goods sold and ending inventory will depend on which specific piece of pottery is sold. If the item sold is the first piece of pottery, cost of goods sold is Rs. 3,000 and ending inventory is Rs. 3,500. On the other hand, if the second piece is sold, the numbers would be reversed; that is cost of goods sold will be Rs. 3,500 and ending inventory would be Rs. 3,000.

The specific identification method provides a highly objective procedure for matching costs with sales revenue because the costs flow pattern matches the physical flow of the goods. However, this method does not work for large volumes of identical low-cost items. This method is appropriate for companies that handle a relatively low volume of physical units, each having a high cost per unit, such as original oil paintings, antiques, diamonds, automobiles, jewellery, furs, etc. The specific identification method is not appropriate where each unit is the same in appearance but is differentiated from other units through serial numbers, such as the same model of washers, refrigerators or televisions.

To illustrate the above four inventory valuation methods an example is taken here. Assume the following data about the goods purchased and sold by a company.

Beginning inventory	60 units	@ Rs. 10 =	600
Purchase	100 units	@ Rs. 11 =	1,100
	100 units	@ Rs. 13 =	1,300
	40 units	@ Rs. 15 =	600
Total	300 Units		Rs. 3,600
Unit sold	220	?	
Units in inventory	80	?	

Under different inventory pricing methods, the cost of goods sold and inventory will be as follows. Remember, these methods will be simply dividing the cost of goods available for sale, i.e., Rs. 3,600 between cost of goods sold and ending inventory.

1. First In First Out Method

(A) Ending inventory:

Units	Cost (Rs.)	Total (Rs.)
40	@ 13	520
40	@ 15	600
80		1,120

(B) Cost of goods sold:

Goods Available

	Units	Cost (Rs.)	Total (Rs.)
Beginning inventory	60	@ 10	600
Purchases:	100	@ 11	1,100
Purchases:	100	@ 13	1,300
	40	@ 15	600
	300		3,600
Cost of goods available for sale			3,600
Less: Ending inventory			1,120
Cost of goods sold			2,480

2. Last In First Out Method

(A) Ending inventory

Units	Cost (Rs.)	Total (Rs.)
60	@ 10	600
20	@ 11	220
80		820

(B) Cost of goods sold

	Units	Cost (Rs.)	Total (Rs.)
Beginning inventory	60	@ 10	600
Purchase	100	@ 11	1,100
	100	@ 13	1,300
	40	@ 15	600
	300		3,600
Cost of goods available for sale			3,600
Less: Ending inventory			820
Cost of goods sold			2,780

3. Simple Average Method

$$\text{Average unit cost} = \frac{\text{Total of rates of goods}}{\text{No. of rates}}$$

: $\frac{49}{4}$

: Rs. 12.25

(A) Ending inventory : 80 units × Rs. 12.25

: Rs. 980

(B) Cost of goods sold:

Cost of goods available for sale	Rs. 3,600
Less: Ending inventory	Rs. 980
Cost of good sold	Rs. 2,620

4. Weighted Average Method

$$\text{Average unit cost} = \frac{\text{Cost of goods available for sale}}{\text{Total unit available for sale}}$$

$$\text{Rs. } \frac{3,600}{300} : \text{Rs. } 12$$

(A) Ending inventory : 80 units × Rs. 12
: Rs. 960

(B) Cost of goods sold

Cost of goods available for sale	Rs. 3,600
Less: Ending inventory	Rs. 960
Cost of goods sold	Rs. 2,640

5. Specific Identification Method

In order to apply this method, further assume that 80 unsold units which are in inventory, consist of 20 units from beginning inventory, 10 units from each of the first two purchase and all 40 of the last units purchased. Assuming this the costs of goods sold and cost of inventory under this method will be as follows:

(A) Ending inventory

Units	*Cost (Rs.)*	*Total (Rs.)*
20	@ 10	200
10	@ 11	110
10	@ 13	130
40	@ 15	600
80		1,040

(B) Cost of goods sold

	Units	*Goods Available Cost (Rs.)*	*Total (Rs.)*
Beginning inventory	60	@ 10	600
Purchases:	100	@ 11	1,100
	100	@ 13	1,300
	40	@ 15	600
	300		3,600

Cost of goods available for sale	Rs. 3,600
Less: Ending inventory	Rs. 1,040
Cost of goods sold	Rs. 2,560

LOWER OF COST OR MARKET (LCM)

Different methods of inventory costing such as FIFO and LIFO, determine the value of inventory in terms of historical cost. However, according to conservatism concept, inventory should be reported on the balance sheet at the lower of its cost or its market value. Generally speaking, inventory is valued in terms of cost. But there should be a departure from the cost basis of valuing inventory and it should be reduced below cost when the utility of goods has declined and its sale proceeds or value of the items will be less than their cost. The decline in the value of inventory below cost can be due to different causes such as physical deterioration, obsolescence, drops in price level, etc. In these situations, inventory is reported at market value. The difference in value (cost – market value) is recognised as a loss of the current period.

It should be understood that the market value of inventory needs to be estimated as the inventory has not, in fact, been sold. As a rule, the market value concept is used in terms of current replacement cost of inventory, that is, what it will cost currently to purchase or manufacture the item. Thus, the LCM rule recognises a holding loss in the period in which the replacement cost of an item dropped, rather than in the period in which the item is actually sold. The holding loss as stated earlier is the difference between purchases cost and the subsequent lower replacement cost. If applicable the LCM rule simply measures inventory at the lower (replacement) market figure. As a result, net income decreases by the amount that the closing inventory has been written down. When the closing inventory becomes part of the cost of goods sold in a future period when selling prices are low, the lower carrying value of closing inventory helps in maintaining normal profit margins in the period of sale.

While applying the rule of lower of 'cost or market' the following upper and lower boundaries are used with regard to market value (current replacement cost) concept:

1. Market value, should not be higher than the estimated net realisable value, i.e., the estimated selling price of the item less the costs associated with selling it.
2. Market value should not be lower than the net realisable value less a normal profit margin.

The above rules on 'lower of cost or market' is summarised as follows:

"Use historical cost if the cost price is lowest; otherwise, use the next-to-lowest of the other three possibilities."

The following example presents the application of 'lower of cost or market' in different situation. In this example, four possible situations A, B, C and D are assumed and historical cost, current replacement cost, net realisable value and net realisable value less profit margin figures of inventory are given.

The value at which inventory will be in these different situation is indicated by star*

Situation	*Historical Cost (Rs.) (Rs.)*	*Current Replacement (Rs.)*	*Net Realisable Value (Ceiling) (Rs.)*	*Net Realisable Value Less Profit Margin (floor) (Rs.)*
A	700 *	800	1,000	900
B	900	800 *	900	700
C	900	700	900	800 *
D	1,000	900	800 *	700

The above example proves that not all decreases in replacement prices are followed by proportionate reductions in selling prices (net realisable value). Therefore, the application of LCM rule is subject to the following additional guidelines:

(*i*) If selling price is not expected to drop, inventory may be priced at cost even though it exceeds replacement cost.

For example, assume that an item costing Rs. 80 is being sold for Rs. 100 during the year, yielding a gross profit of 20 per cent on sales. If the selling price remains at Rs. 100 and the replacement cost drops to Rs. 60 (a 25 per cent decline), inventory will not be written down.

However, if there is a proportionate decrease in the selling price, i.e., selling price also declines by 25 per cent and becomes Rs. 75, then inventory will be shown at Rs. 60 replacement cost.

In this case, after showing the inventory at Rs. 60, the current period's income will be less by Rs. 20 (the difference between the historical cost and replacement cost). Further, when this item valued at Rs. 60 is sold in a subsequent period for Rs. 75, a normal gross profit of 20 per cent on sales will be reported (Rs. 75 – Rs. 60 = Rs. 15 gross profit margin).

(*ii*) If selling price is expected to drop but less than proportionately to the decline in replacement cost, inventory is written down only to the extent necessary to maintain a normal gross profit in the period of sale. Taking the above example if the selling price drops from Rs. 100 to Rs. 90 and the replacement cost declines to Rs. 60, inventory will be shown at Rs. 72 (Rs. 90 – 20 per cent of Rs. 90). This amount maintains a 20 per cent gross profit margin when the item is sold for Rs. 90.

Arguments in Support of LCM Rule

Supporters of the LCM Rule argue that an exception to the historical costs basis is desirable because it (LCM) serves the useful purpose of achieving better matching of costs and revenues and contributes to usefulness of periodic income measurement. The arguments in favour of LCM rule is that no assets should appear on a business enterprise's balance sheet in an amount greater than is likely to be recovered from the use or sale of that asset in the normal course of events. Unrecoverable amounts have no value and therefore are not assets. International Accounting Standards Committee observes:

> "The historical cost of inventories may not be realisable if their selling prices have declined, if they are damaged, or if they have become wholly or partially obsolete. The practice of writing inventories below historical cost to net realisable value accords with the view that current assets should not be carried in excess of amounts expected to be realised. Declines in value are computed separately for individual items, groups or similar items, an entire class of inventory (for example, finished goods), or items relating to a class of business, or they are computed on an overall basis for all the inventories down based on a class of inventory, on a class of business, or on an overall basis results in offsetting losses incurred against unrealised gains."

Depending on the character and composition of the inventory, the rule of cost or market, whichever is lower may properly be applied either directly to each item or to the total of the inventory (or in some cases to the total of the components of each major category). The method should be that which most clearly reflects periodic income.

Criticism of LCM Rule

At the outset it may be noted that lower of cost or market is not a method of inventory costing but rather one of recognising measurable expected loss. The cost or market concept when applied to inventories is tied closely to the concept of realisation of revenue at the time of sale, but with the recognition of loss as soon as evidence of loss appears. The principal objections to the rule center around its violation of the historical cost principle. LCM rule is criticised on many grounds:

(*i*) It violates the concept of consistency because it permits a change in valuation base from one period to another and even within the inventory itself. It treats value increases and value decreases differently. If the market value of goods is greater than its cost, there is no recognition of the increased value on the balance sheet.

(*ii*) It is termed as a major cause of distortion of profit and loss.

(*iii*) Although it may be considered conservative with respect to the current period, it is unconservative with respect to the income of future period.

(*iv*) The current period may be charged with the result of inefficient purchasing and management, which should be included in the measurement of operating performance at the time of sale. However, it may also be argued that these should be recorded in the current period rather than in the period of sale.

(*v*) An increase in the market price in a subsequent period may result in an unrealised gain if the original cost is always used as the basis for comparison with the current market price (assuming of course that market in both periods is below the original cost).

(*vi*) The cost or market rule is said to permit excessive subjectivity in the accounts. This is based on the assumption that market is always more subjective than cost.

ICAI's Guidelines on Inventory Valuation

The Institute of Chartered Accountants of India has revised Accounting standard (AS)-2: Valuation of Inventories in July 1999. The revised standard supersedes AS-2 issued in June 1981, and AS-2 (Revised) comes into effect in respect of accounting period commencing on or after 1st April 1999 and it is mandatory in nature. The AS-2 (Revised) has listed the following guidelines.

1. Inventories should be valued at the lower of cost and net realisable value.
2. Net realisable value is defined as the estimated selling price in the ordinary course of business less the estimated cost of completion and estimated costs necessary to make the sale. An assessment is made of net realisable value at each balance sheet date.
3. The cost means historical cost comprising: (*i*) all costs of purchase (*ii*) cost of conversion and (*iii*) other costs incurred to bring the inventories to their present location and condition.
4. For the purpose of comparing historical cost with net realisable value each item in the inventory may be clear with separately, or similar items may be dealt with as a group.
5. The standards mentions the following formulas for determining the historical cost:
   (*a*) Specific identification of cost,
   (*b*) First in First out (FIFO) and
   (*c*) Weighted average cost.
6. The cost of inventories of items that are not ordinarily interchangeable and goods or services produced and segregated for specific projects should be assigned by specific identification of their individual costs (para 14).
7. The cost of inventories, other than those dealt with in paragraph 14, should be assigned by using First in First out, or weighted average cost formula.
8. Standard cost method or the retail method for the measurement of the cost of inventories, may be used for convenience if the results approximate the actual cost.
9. The historical cost of manufactured inventories may be arrived at on the basis of either direct costing or absorption costing. Where absorption costing has been used, the allocation of fixed assets of inventories should be based on the normal capacity of the production facilities.

10. When the costs of conversion of each product are not separately identifiable, they are allocated between the products on a rational and consistent basis.
11. Inventory of by-products should be valued at lower of cost and net realisable value. Where the by-products, by their nature, are immaterial, they are measured at net realisable value and this value is deducted from the cost of main product.
12. The financial statements should disclose:
    (a) The accounting policies adopted in measuring inventories, including the cost formula used; and
    (*b*) The total carrying amount of inventories and its classification appropriate to the enterprise.

Common classifications are raw materials, and components, work in progress, finished goods, stores and spares, and loose tools.

CONSISTENCY IN THE VALUATION OF INVENTORY

The principle of consistency is one of basic concepts underlying reliable financial statements. The principle means that once a company has adopted a particular accounting method, the company should follow that method consistently rather than switch methods from one year to the next. If a company ignores the principle of consistency in accounting for inventories, it could cause its net income for any given year to increase or decrease merely by changing its method of inventory valuation. The principle of consistency does not mean that every company in an industry must use the same accounting method; it does mean that a given company should not switch year after year from one accounting method to another.

It should be understood that a company has considerable latitude in selecting a method of inventory valuation best suited to its needs. The principle of consistency comes into a play after a given method has been selected. It is also true that change from one inventory method to another will usually cause reported income to change significantly in the year in which the change is made. Frequent switching of methods would make the income statement undependable as a means of portraying trends in operating results. Because of the principle of consistency, the user of financial statements is able to assume that the company has followed the same accounting methods it used in the preceding year. Thus, the value of financial statements is increased because they enable the user to make reliable comparison of the results achieved from year to year.

The principle of consistency does not mean that a business can never change its method of inventory valuation. However, when a change is made, the effects of the change upon reported net income should be disclosed fully in the footnotes accompanying the financial statements. Adequate disclosure of all information necessary for the proper interpretation of financial statements is another basic principle of accounting. Even when the same method of inventory valuation is being followed consistently, the financial statements should include a disclosure of the valuation method in use.

INVENTORY SYSTEMS

There are two principal ways of accounting for inventories.

Perpetual Inventory System

The perpetual inventory method requires a continuous records of addition to or reductions in materials, work-in-progress and cost of goods sold on a day-to-day basis. Such a record facilitates managerial control and preparation of interim financial statements. Physical inventory counts are usually taken at least once a year in order to check on the validity of the accounting records.

The perpetual inventory system may give such additional information as goods ordered, expected delivery date and unit costs. Usually, these records are maintained on a quantity basis but values can be included. It is an essential feature of the perpetual inventory method that items of stock are checked periodically, normally at least once or twice each year. This ensures that the stock records tally with the physical stocks, which is vital if the control procedure is to function properly.

The perpetual inventory method has the following advantages:

1. The stock-taking task which is long and costly is avoided under this method. On the other hand, the inventory of different items of materials in accordance with the stores ledger can be promptly prepared for the preparation of the income statement and balance sheet at interim periods, if required, without a physical inventory being taken.
2. Management may be informed daily of number of units and the value of each kind of material-on-hand-information which tends to eliminate delays and stoppage in production.
3. The investment in materials and supplies may be kept at the lowest point in conformity with operating requirements.
4. A system of internal check is always in operation and the activities of different departments, such as purchasing, stores and production are continuously checked against each other. This results into detailed and reliable checks on the stores also.
5. It is not necessary to stop production so as to carry out a complete physical stock-taking.
6. Perpetual inventory records provide details about material cost for individual products, jobs, processes, production orders or departments. This information is helpful to management in exercising control over costs.
7. Discrepancies and errors are promptly discovered and localised and remedial action can be taken to avoid their occurrence in the future.
8. This method has a moral effect on the staff; makes them disciplined and careful and acts as a check against dishonest actions.
9. The disadvantages of excessive stock are avoided, such as loss of interest on capital invested in stock, loss through deterioration, risk of obsolescence.

Periodic Inventory System

Under the periodic method, the entire book inventory is verified at a given date by an actual count of materials on hand. This physical inventory is usually taken near the end of the accounting period. Some firms even suspend plant operations when this is done. This method provides for the recording of purchases, purchase returns and purchase allowances on a daily basis but does not provide for a continuous inventory or for a daily computation of the goods sold.

At the end of each accounting period, a physical count is made of the quantity of goods on hand and the value of the inventory is determined by using an inventory pricing method (FIFO, LIFO or average cost) and attaching costs to units counted. The cost of goods sold is computed by deducting closing inventory from the sum of opening inventory and purchases made during the current period. It is assumed that goods not on hand at the end of accounting period have been sold. There is no system and accounting for shrinkage, losses, theft and waste throughout the accounting period and they can be discovered only after the end of the period.

Taking a physical inventory at the year-end is an important task in the periodic inventory system. It must be ensured that all items have been counted accurately. Counting procedures usually involve teams of people assigned to specific sections of the factory, and to inventory storage areas. Large items are counted individually, while small items may be weight-counted. Counted items are tagged to prevent double counting and information from the tags concerning each item's description and quantity is recorded on the inventory sheet.

THEORY QUESTIONS

1. Define inventory and identify the costs that should be included as inventory costs.
2. What is meant by goods flow and cost flow?
3. Briefly describe each of the following inventory pricing methods under a periodic inventory system:
   (*a*) First In First Out (FIFO)
   (*b*) Last In First Out (LIFO)
   (*c*) Average cost method
4. Why is inventory an important item to both internal management and external users of financial statements?
5. Explain the application of the cost principle to an item in the closing inventory.
6. When a perpetual inventory system is used, unit costs of the items sold are known at the date of each sale. In contrast, when a periodic inventory system is used, unit costs are known only at the end of the accounting period. Why are these statements correct?
7. Different inventory costing methods may be applied with either a periodic inventory system or a perpetual inventory system. Briefly explain how the methods are applied in each system.
8. Contrast the effects of LIFO versus FIFO on reported assets (i.e., closing inventory) when (*a*) prices are rising, and (*b*) prices are falling.
9. Contrast the income statement effect of LIFO versus FIFO (i.e., on reported net income) when (*a*) prices are rising, and (*b*) prices are falling.
10. The weighted average inventory costing method usually produces different results when a perpetual inventory system is used rather than a periodic inventory system. Explain why?
11. Explain the application of the LCM rule to the closing inventory and its effect on the income statement and balance sheet when market price is lower than cost.
12. When should net realisable value be used in costing an item in the closing inventory?
13. Why do relatively stable purchase prices reduce the significance of the choice of an inventory pricing method?
14. If prices have been rising, which inventory pricing method — FIFO, LIFO, weighted average, yields: (*a*) the lowest inventory amount (*b*) lowest net income (*c*) largest inventory amount (*d*) largest net income.
15. Discuss the effect on reported income of applying the lower of cost or market rule.
16. Contrast the accounting procedures for periodic and perpetual inventory system.
17. Which inventory pricing methods give the same results (closing inventory and total cost of goods sold) when applied under a perpetual inventory system and a periodic inventory system?
18. Under which method of cost flow are (*a*) the earliest costs assigned to inventory (*b*) latest costs assigned to inventory (*c*) average costs assigned to inventory.
19. What are the relative advantages and disadvantages of FIFO and LIFO from management point of view?
20. Which of the following companies would find a perpetual inventory system practical — a drug store, a grocery store, a restaurant, an automobile dealer, a wholesale autoparts? Why?
21. What methods can be used to determine lower of cost or market?
22. In the phrase 'lower of cost or market' what is meant by 'market'?

23. "Cost flow assumptions for inventory are required only because specific identification of item sold is costly. Specific identification is theoretically superior to any cost flow assumption and eliminates the possibility of income manipulation available with some cost flow assumption." Comment.
24. "LIFO provides a more meaningful income statement than FIFO, even though it provides a less meaningful balance sheet." Does it ever? Does it always?
25. Assume that the cost basis for inventory is changed from historical cost to current cost, the current costs exceed historical costs at the end of the year of change and that all year-end inventory is sold during the following year. What will be the impact of the change on net income for the year of change? On income for the following year? On total income over the two years?
26. Does the LIFO method mean that the items in the inventory are assumed to be the most recent (last) acquisitions? Explain.
27. "A departure from the cost basis of pricing the inventory is required when the utility of goods is no longer as great as it cost." In the light of this statement evaluate 'lower of cost or market' (LCM) rule.
28. Is the use of an appropriate valuation method for the inventory at the end of the year more important in producing a dependable income statement, or in producing a dependable balance sheet? Give arguments.
29. Why do some accountants consider the net income reported by business during a period of rising prices to be overstated?
30. Assume that a business uses the FIFO (First In First Out) method of inventory valuation during a prolonged period of inflation and that the business pays dividends equal to the amount of reported net income. Suggest a problem that may arise in continued successful operation of the business.
31. If costs are rising, which cost flow assumption will give the lowest net income in the current accounting period? The highest net income? The lowest ending inventory cost? The highest ending inventory cost? An ending inventory cost closest to the current replacement cost?
32. Why might the management of a company choose the LIFO cost flow assumption even though its use causes the company's net income to be lower?
33. If the ending inventory for 2008 is valued at market under the lower of cost or market rule, what is the effect on the financial statements for 2008? 2009? What is the meaning of the term market?
34. When a company changes from FIFO to LIFO, what effect does the change have on current net income and working capital?
35. Describe the calculation of cost of goods sold under the periodic inventory system.
36. The consistency principle means that the same accounting principles (or methods) used this period were also used last period. Does this mean that once a company decides to use FIFO, it can never switch to LIFO or weighted average?
37. Would there be any difference between using LIFO or FIFO if unit costs of inventory purchased remained constant over time? Explain.

EXERCISES AND PROBLEMS

1. You are presented with the following information by Sphix Engineering Co. relating to the first week of September, 2008:

Materials — The transactions in connection with the materials are as follows:

Days	*Receipts Units*	*Rat per unit (Rs.)*	*Issues Units*
1st	40	15.00	
2nd	20	16.50	
3rd			30

4th	50	14.30	20
5th			40
6th			

Calculate the cost of materials issued under FIFO method and Weighted Average Method of issue of materials.

Ans.:

	Cost of materials issued		*Stock*	
	Units	*Amt.*	*Units*	*Amt.*
FIFO	90	1359	20	286
Weighted Average	90	1350	20	295

2. Show the stores ledger entries as they would appear when using
   (*a*) the weighted average method
   (*b*) the LIFO method of pricing issues, in connection with the following transactions:

April		*Unit*	*Value*
1	Balance in hand	300	600
2	Purchased	200	440
4	Issued	150	
6	Purchased	200	460
11	Issued	150	
19	Issued	200	
20	Purchased	200	480
27	Issued	250	

In a period of rising prices such as above what are the effects of each method?

Ans.: (*a*) 150 units Rs. 342 (*b*) 150 units Rs. 300

3. Explain the following two methods of pricing of materials issues and also the circumstances under which these methods are used — LIFO and FIFO. Draw a stores ledger card, recording the following transactions that took place in a month under the above two methods;

2008		
Jan. 1	Opening stock	200 pieces @ Rs. 2 each
Jan. 5	Purchases	100 pieces @ Rs. 2.20 each
Jan. 10	Purchases	150 pieces @ Rs. 2.40 each
Jan. 20	Purchases	180 pieces @ Rs. 2.50 each
Jan. 22	Issues	150 pieces
Jan. 25	Issues	100 pieces
Jan. 27	Issues	100 pieces
Jan. 28	Issues	200 pieces

Ans.: LIFO closing stock 80 units, Rs. 172
FIFO closing stock 80 units, Rs. 200

4. The Fair Deal Granary was not maintaining a perpetual inventory system for its stocks unit recently. Only physical inventory was taken at the end of each month. The physical inventory at the end of December 2007 showed 200 bags of fine rice at Rs 212.25 per bag. The following purchases were made in January 2008:

3rd	400 bags at Rs 218.00 per bag
10th	900 bags at Rs 223.50 per bag
15th	400 bags at Rs 220.00 per bag
28th	700 bags at Rs 213.00 per bag
30th	300 bags at Rs 224.00 per bag

On 31st January, 2008 the physical stock was 1,200 bags. You are required to calculate the value of the stock on 31st January 2008 according to First-in, First-out, Last-in, First-out and Weighed Average Cost Method.

5. Oil India is a bulk distributor of petrol. A periodic inventory of petrol on hand is taken when the books are closed at the end of each month. The following information is taken for the month of June 2008:

		Rs.
Sales		9.45,000
General administrative cost		25,000
Opening stock 1,00,000 litres @ Rs 30 per litre		
Purchase (including freight in)		
June 1	2,00,000 litres @ Rs 28.50 per litre	
June 30	1,00,000 litres @Rs 30.30 per litre	
Closing stock June 30		1.30,000 litres

Compute the following data by the first-in first-out, weighted average and last-in first-out method of inventory costing:

(*a*) Value of inventory June 30

(*b*) Amount of the cost of goods sold for June

(*c*) Profit or loss for June

Ans.:

Method	*Value of inventory*	*Cost of goods*	*Profit or loss (Rs.)*
FIFO	38,85,000	78,45,000	13,55,000
Weighted Average	39,00,000	78,30,000	13,70,000
LIFO	39,30,000	72,00,000	14,00,000

6. The purchases and issues of material X in the month of January 2007 is as follows:

January	3	Purchases 800 units @ Rs. 20 per unit
January	8	Purchases 700 units @ Rs. 18 per unit
January	9	Issue 600 units
January	11	Issue 800 units
January	17	Purchases 800 units @ Rs. 20 per unit
January	25	Purchases 500 units @ Rs. 25 per unit
January	31	Issue 1000 units

The standard price per unit of material is Rs. 20 fixed for the year 2007. Show the stores ledger account and determine the price variance for the month of January.

Ans.: Closing stock at cost 400 units Rs. 9,100
Closing stock at standard price of Rs. 20 will be Rs. 8,000
Material price variance Rs. 9,100 – 8,000 = Rs. 1,100 (Adverse)

7. On January 1, Mr. G started a small business buying and selling a special yarn. He invested his savings of Rs. 4,00,000 in the business and during the next six months, the following transactions occurred.

Date of receipt		*Yarn purchases*		*Yarn Sales*			
		Quantity	*Total cost boxes*	*Date (Rs.)*		*Quantity boxes*	*Total value (Rs.)*
January	13	200	7,200	February	10	500	25,000
February	8	400	15,200	April	20	600	27,000
March	11	600	24,000	Jun	25	400	15,200
April	12	400	14,000				
June	15	500	14,000				

The yarn is stored in premises Mr. G has rented and the closing stock of yarn counted on 30th June was 500 boxes.

Other expenses incurred and paid in cash during the six months period amounted to Rs. 2,300.

Required:

(*a*) Calculate the value of the material issues during the six month period and the value of closing stock at the end of June, using the following methods of pricing:

(*i*) FIFO

(*ii*) LIFO, and

(*iii*) Weighted average

(*b*) Calculate and discuss the effect each of the three methods of material pricing will have on the reported profit of the business, and examine the performance of the business during the six month period.

Ans.: (*a*) (*i*) FIFO — Closing stock Rs. 14,000 (500 × Rs. 28)
Cost of sales (including stock loss)
= Rs. 60,400

(*ii*) LIFO — Closing stock = Rs. 19,600
Cost of sales = Rs. 54,800

(*iii*) Weighted Average Method:
Closing stock = Rs. 16,486
Cost of sales = Rs. 57,914.

(*b*) Profit calculations:

	FIFO (Rs.)	*LIFO (Rs.)*	*Weighted Average (Rs.)*
Sales	67,200	67,200	67,200
Cost of sales & stock loss	(60,400)	(54,800)	(57,914)
Other expenses	(2,300)	(2,300)	(2,300)
	4,500	10,100	6,986

Comment: (*i*) The large purchase at the highest purchase price is in March. This purchase could have been delayed until April so as to take advantage of the lower price.

(*ii*) The stock loss has cost over Rs. 3,000. This should be investigated. A materials control procedure should be implemented.

Statement of Changes in Financial Position (SCFP)

Financial statement of a business enterprise, i.e., income statement and balance sheet are important statements to judge the results of business operation and financial position at the beginning and end of the year. The income statement sets forth the enterprise's revenues, expenses, gains and losses. The balance sheet portrays the overall financial position of a business enterprise at a specific date during the recurring cycles of investment, recovery of investment and reinvestment. The income statement, however, neither shows the effects of all the events which affected an enterprise's liquidity — its ability to meet its cash obligations on time — nor does it reflect all the flows of resources into or out of the enterprise during the period. Also, the correct appraisal of performance requires knowledge about movement of funds during a year and their impact on the financial position; this is not achieved in balance sheet as it depicts only summarised financial position on a particular date. To overcome these deficiencies, a second performance related statement needs to be prepared which is popularly known as Statement of Changes in Financial Position, or Funds Statement.

CONCEPT OF STATEMENT OF CHANGES IN FINANCIAL POSITION (SCFP)

A statement of changes in financial position (funds statement) helps us to understand how and why a business enterprise has acquired its resources and what those resources were used for. The objectives of funds statement are (1) to summarise the financing and investing activities of the entity, including the extent to which the enterprise has generated funds from operations during the period and (2) to complete the disclosure of changes of financial position during the period.

Concept of Funds

A statement of changes in financial position can be prepared using different concepts of funds as a basis. For instance, statement of changes in financial position may focus on changes in working capital, cash, or total financial resources of a business enterprise. This chapter discusses the preparation of statement of changes in financial position on working capital basis. Cash Flow Statement has been discussed in the next chapter.

Funds defined as Working Capital

In common usage, the term funds means cash. However, accountants and financial executives think of 'funds' in a broader sense. They view the funds available to a business enterprise as its working capital. Working capital is defined as current assets minus current liabilities and thus, is a broader definition of funds than is cash.

Since funds have been defined as the difference between current assets and current liabilities, it is necessary to know which accounts are covered and which are not covered by this definition.

(1) Current Assets: The term current assets is used to mean cash and other assets or resources generally identified as those which are reasonably expected to be realised in cash or sold or consumed during the normal operating cycle of the business. These include: (*i*) cash and bank balances; (*ii*) temporary investments, bills receivables, debtors, and stock in trade; (*iii*) prepayments like salary paid in advance, unexpired insurance, prepaid rent, prepaid interest which can be consumed during the normal operating cycle of business.

(2) Current Liabilities: The term "current liabilities' is used to denote obligations such as (*i*) ones which are payable within one year, and (*ii*) which are paid out of current assets or by clearing current liabilities. These include amounts payable to (*a*) creditors, (*b*) bills payable, (*c*) bank overdraft, and (*d*) outstanding bills on account of wages, salary, commission, rent, royalties etc.

(3) Non-Current Accounts: For the purpose of preparing funds flow statement all accounts which are not current accounts are treated as non-current accounts. Examples of such accounts are included in the following list:

Non-current accounts on the liabilities side of the balance sheet	*Non-current accounts on the assets side of the balance sheet*
1. Equity share capital 2. Preference share capital 3. Redeemable preference share capital 4. Long-term loans 5. Debentures 6. Security premium account 7. Share forfeited account 8. Profit and loss account (credit balance) 9. Appropriation to profit, e.g., transfer to general reserve, dividend equalisation fund, insurance fund, compensation fund, debentures sinking fund, capital redemption reserve account. 10. Provision like provision for tax, provision for depreciation on fixed assets, proposed dividend. 11. Capital reserve.	1. Goodwill 2. Land 3. Building 4. Machinery 5. Furniture 6. Long-term investments 7. Patent right 8. Trade mark 9. Profit and loss account (debit balance) 10. Discount on issue of shares and debentures 11. Preliminary expenses 12. Other deferred expenditure like advertisement cost.

The basic objective of the statement of changes in financial position, working capital oasis, is to explain the changes in the working capital for a specified period of time. In the process of achieving this objective, the statement should enable the user to identify the changes as they relate to three basic causes.

(*a*) Amount of changes in working capital associated with the operating activities of the firm.

(*b*) Long-term financing or other sources that cause an increase in the working capital.

(*c*) Long-term investment activities or other uses that cause a reduction in the working capital.

If the amount of working capital increased during a given fiscal period, this means that more working capital was generated than was used for various business purposes; if a decrease in working capital occurred, the reverse is true. One of the key purposes of statement of changes in financial position is to explain fully the increase or decrease in working capital during an accounting period.

Sources and Uses of Working Capital

Any transaction that increases the amount of working capital is a source of working capital. For example, the sale of merchandise at a price greater than its cost is a source of working capital, because the increase in cash or receivable from the sale is greater than the decrease in inventory. Any transaction that decreases working capital is a use of working capital. For example, either incurring current liability to acquire a non-current asset or using cash to pay expenses represents a decrease in working capital.

The principal sources and uses of working capital are listed below:

Sources of Working Capital

The following are the sources of working capital:

1. Funds from Business Operations

If the inflow of funds from sales exceeds the outflow of funds to cover the cost of merchandise purchases and expenses of doing business, current operations will provide a net source of funds. If the inflow of funds from sales is less than these outflows, operation will result in a net use of funds. Working capital provided by operations is the net increase or decrees in working capital resulting from the normal business activities of earning revenue and paying expenses. However, not all the expenses require the use of funds in the current period; therefore the amount of funds provided by operations is not the same as the amount of net income earned during the period.

The following points explain this situation:

(*i*) Some expenses do not reduce working capital. Some expenses, such as depreciation and amortisation of intangible assets reduce net income but have no immediate effect on the amount of working capital provided by operations, i.e., these items do not reduce working capital. The net income figure therefore understates the amount of working capital provided by operations by amount of depreciation expense recorded during the period. Thus funds provided by operations would be computed in the following manner:

Funds from Operations:	
Net income	—
Add: Depreciation expense	—
Funds provided by operations	—

The addition of depreciation expense to the net income figure has led some people to believe that depreciation expenses is a source of funds. However, it is important for the users of financial statement to understand that depreciation is neither a source nor a use of working capital (funds). No funds flow into business as a result of recording depreciation expense. It is shown in the statement of changes in financial position merely to explain one of the differences between the concept of net income and the concept of working capital provided by operations.

(*ii*) Some items increase income but do not increase working capital — some items in the income statement increase net income without increasing working capital; such items must be deducted from net income in arriving at working capital provided by operations.

(*iii*) Non-operating gains and losses — non-operating gains and losses, if material in amount, should be eliminated from net income in order to show the working capital provided by 'normal' operations. For example, assume that plant costing Rs. 1,00,000 is sold at Rs. 1,20,000, at a net gain of Rs. 20,000. In the statement of changes in financial position, the entire Rs. 1,20,000 as proceeds from sale will be reported as funds provided by the sale of plant. The Rs. 20,000 non-operating gain, however, is included in the net income for the period. In determining the amount of working capital provided by operations, this Rs. 20.000 non-operating gain must be deducted from the net income figure because the entire proceeds from sale of the plant arc reported elsewhere in the statement of changes in financial position.

As a separate example, assume that the same plant is sold for Rs. 90,000; then the non-operating loss of Rs. 10,000 should be added back to net income to arrive at working capital provided by operations and the working capital provided through sale of plant should be reported at Rs. 90,000.

Briefly, the procedure of computing funds provided by operations can be summarised as follows:

Funds from Operations

Net profit (or loss) as per the profit and loss account

Add: (*i*) Depreciation expense.

(*ii*) Amortisation of goodwill, patents and other intangible assets.

(*iii*) Amortisation of extraordinary losses occurred in previous periods.

(*iv*) Amortisation of discount on debentures.

(*v*) Loss on sale of non-current assets such as plant, equipment etc.

Less: (*i*) Gain on sale of non-current assets such as plant, equipment etc.

(*ii*) Profit or revaluation surplus of non-current assets.

(*iii*) Dividends and interest on investments (earned but not received)

(*iv*) Amortisation of premium received on debentures

= Fund from Business Operations

2. Sales of Non-current Assets

A business may obtain working capital by selling non-current assets, such as plant and equipment or long-term investments, in exchange for current asset. As long as current assets are received, the sale is a source of funds regardless of whether the non-current assets are sold at a gain or loss. For example, assume that a business firm sells for Rs. 2,50,000 a plant which cost Rs. 3,00,000. Although the plant was sold at a loss, the firm has increased its current assets by Rs. 2,50,000 by selling the plant. Thus, the transaction is a source of working capital.

3. Long-term Borrowing

Long-term borrowing, such as issue of debentures and bonds result in an increase in current assets, thereby increasing working capital. Short-term borrowing, however, does not increase working capital. When a company borrows cash on short-term credit or by signing a short-term note payable, working capital is unchanged because the increase in current assets is offset by an increase in current liabilities of the same amount.

4. Issue of Additional Equity Capital

The issue of additional equity shares results in an inflow of current assets, thereby increasing working capital. In a similar manner, additional investments of current assets by owners represent source of funds in single proprietorship and partnership.

Uses of Working Capital

The following are the uses of working capital:

1. Declaration of Cash Dividend

The declaration of a cash dividend results in a current liability (dividend payable) and is therefore a use of funds. It should be understood that it is the declaration of dividend, rather than the payment of the dividend which is the use of funds. Actual payment of the dividend reduces current assets and current liabilities by the same amount and thus has no effect upon the amount of working capital. Issue of shares in lieu of dividend does not involve any distribution of assets and, therefore, are not a use of funds.

2. Purchase of Non-current Assets

Purchases of non-current assets, such as plant and equipment, reduce current assets or increase current liabilities. In either case, working capital is reduced.

3. Repayment of Long-term Debt

Working capital is decreased when current assets are used to repay long-term debt. However, repayment of short-term debt is not a use of funds, since current assets and current liabilities decrease by the same amount.

EFFECT OF TRANSACTIONS ON WORKING CAPITAL

In preparing a statement of changes in financial position, on working capital basis or funds flow statements, it is convenient to classify business transactions into three categories:

(*a*) Both debit and credit aspects of the transaction affecting current accounts only. (*b*) Both debit and credit aspects of the transaction affecting non-current accounts only. (*c*) One aspect of the transaction affecting current account and another aspect affecting a non-current account (non-current asset or non-current liability).

The effect of above-mentioned categories of transactions on the funds flow statement can be analysed with the help of following examples:

1. Transactions affecting current accounts only — do not result in flow of fund

These transactions produce changes in working capital accounts but do not change the amount of working capital. Few examples of such transactions are given below:

S. No.	*Transaction*	*Journal entry*	*Effect on current asset/ current liability*	*Net effect on working capital*
1.	Bills receivable collected	Bank a/c Dr. To Bills receivable	Increase in C.A. Decrease in C.A.	Nil
2.	Goods purchased for cash	Purchase a/c Dr. To Cash	Increase in C.A. Decrease in C.A.	Nil
3.	Goods purchased on credit	Purchases a/c Dr. To Creditors	Increase in C.A. Increase in C.L.	Nil
4.	Bills payable paid	Bills payable a/c Dr. To Cash	Decrease in C.L. Decrease in C.A.	Nil

Hence, such transaction would not be reflected as a source or use in a working capital basis statement of changes in financial position.

2. Transactions affecting non-current accounts only — do not result in flow of fund

These transactions have no direct effect on the amount of working capital. The entry to record depreciation is an example of such a transaction. Such transactions may not be considered in preparing a statement of changes in financial position on working capital basis. Few more examples of such transactions are:

S. No.	*Transaction*	*Journal entry*	*Effect on current asset/ current liability*	*Net effect on working capital*
1.	Building purchased and shares issued in satisfaction of purchase price	Building a/c Dr. To Share capital	Nil	Nil
2.	Preliminary expenses written off	Profit & Loss a/c Dr. To Preliminary expenses	Nil	Nil
3.	General reserve created	Profit & Loss Appr. a/c Dr. To General reserve	Nil	Nil
4.	Goodwill written off	Profit & Loss a/c Dr. To Goodwill a/c	Nil	Nil

3. Transactions affecting non-current account and current account — resulting either as a source of fund or application of fund

These transactions bring about either an increase or a decrease in the amount of working capital.

If changes in non-working capital accounts are analysed, these events are brought to light, and their effect on working capital will be reported in the statement of changes in financial position.

Few examples of such transactions and their effects on working capital are shown below:

S. No.	*Transaction*	*Journal entry*	*Effect on current asset/ current liability*	*Net effect on working capital*
1.	Building sold for cash	Bank a/c Dr. To Building	Increase in current asset Non-current asset	Increase in working capital
2.	Redeemable preference shares redeemed	Redeemable preference shares a/c Dr. To Bank	Non-current liability Decrease in current asset	Decrease in working capital
3.	Loan repaid	Loan a/c Dr. To Bank	Non-current liability Decrease in current asset	Decrease in working capital
4.	Issue of share capital (for cash)	Bank a/c Dr. To Share capital	Increase in current asset non-current a/c	Increase in working capital
5.	Debentures redeemed	Debentures a/c Dr. To Bank	Non-current liability Decrease in current asset	Decrease in working capital

MAIN STEPS IN PREPARING THE STATEMENT

In order to prepare a statement of changes in financial position on a working capital basis, it is necessary to have balance sheets at two points in time and an income statement covering that span of time. The steps involved in preparing the statement are as follows:

1. Determine the change (increase or decrease) in working capital.
2. Determine the adjustments account to be made to net income.
3. For each non-current account on the balance sheet, establish the increase or decrease in that account. Analyse the change to decide whether it is a source (increase) or use (decrease) of working capital.
4. Be sure the total of all sources including those from operations minus the total of all uses equals the change found in working capital in step 1.

General Rules for Preparing Funds Flow Statement

The following general rules should be observed while preparing funds flow statement:

(1) Increase in a current asset means increase (plus) in working capital.
(2) Decrease in a current asset means decrease (minus) in working capital.
(3) Increase in a current liability means decrease (minus) in working capital.
(4) Decrease in a current lability means increase (plus) in working capital.
(5) Increase in current asset and increase in current liability does not affect working capital.
(6) Decrease in current asset and decrease in current liability does not affect working capital.
(7) Changes in fixed (non-current) assets and fixed non-current liabilities affects working capital.

Schedule of Changes in Working Capital

Many business enterprises prefer to prepare another statement, known as schedule of changes in working capital, while preparing a funds flow statement, on a working capital basis. This schedule of changes in working capital provides information concerning the changes in each individual current assets and current liabilities accounts (items). This schedule is a part of the funds flow statement and increase (decrease) in working capital indicated by the schedule of changes in working capital will be equal to the amount of changes in working capital as found by funds flow statement. The schedule of changes in working capital can be prepared by comparing the current assets and current liabilities at two periods. The format of schedule of changes in working capital is as follows:

Schedule of Changes in Working Capital

Items	*As on*	*As on*	*Changes*	
			Increase	*Decrease*
A. Current Assets:				
Cash balance				
Bank balance				
Accounts receivable (Debtors)				
Marketable Securities				
Stock				
Prepaid expenses				
B. Current liabilities:				
Bank overdraft				
Accounts payables (creditors)				
Outstanding expenses				
Total				
Net increase/decrease in working capital				

Format of Funds Flow Statement

A funds flow statement can be prepared in statement form or 'T' form. Both the formats are being given below:

Funds Flow Statement (Statement Form)

A. Sources of Funds:

(*i*) Funds from business operations
(*ii*) Sale of fixed asset
(*iii*) Issue of shares
(*iv*) Issue of debentures
(*v*) Long-term borrowings
Total Sources

B. Application of Funds:

(*i*) Loss from business operation
(*ii*) Payment of dividend
(*iii*) Payment of tax
(*iv*) Purchase of fixed asset

(*v*) Payment of long-term loans
(*vi*) Redemption of debentures
(*vii*) Redemption of preference shares
Total uses
Net increase/decrease in Working capital
(Total sources minus Total uses)

Funds Flow Statement ('T' Form)

Sources of Funds	*Rs.*	*Application of Funds*	*Rs.*
(i) Funds from business operations		(i) Loss from business operations	
(ii) Sale of fixed assets		(ii) Payment of dividend	
(iii) Issue of shares		(iii) Payment of tax	
(iv) Issue of debentures		(iv) Purchase of fixed assets	
(v) Long-term borrowings		(v) Payment of long-term loans	
(vi) Decrease in working capital (if application amount is more than the sources amount)		(vi) Redemption of debentures	
		(vii) Redemption of preference shares	
		(viii) Increase in working capital (if sources are more than the application amount)	
Total		Total	

TREATMENT OF PROVISION FOR TAXATION AND PROPOSED DIVIDENDS

Provision for Taxation

There are two possible treatment about the provision for taxation:

(1) Provision for taxation can be treated as a current liability and it will decrease the working capital in the schedule of changes in working capital. However, payment of tax does not affect working capital because it involves both current asset and current liability account, *i.e.,* payment decreases cash or bank balance on the one hand and decreases the current liability (tax provision) by the equivalent amount on the other hand.

(2) Provision for taxation may be considered as non-current item. Such a treatment does not change working capital position. Provisions made for taxation during the current year is transferred to adjusted profit and loss account. The amount paid as tax is shown as an application of fund.

Proposed Dividends

There are also two treatments about the proposed dividend.

(1) Proposed dividends can be considered as current liability and hence will decrease working capital in the schedule of changes in working capital. However, when dividends are paid, it is not treated as uses of funds.

(2) Proposed dividend can be treated as non-current item. In this case, proposed dividend for current year is added back to retained profit in order to find out funds from operations. Then, payment of dividend, will be shown as application of funds. Generally, it is treated as non-current item.

Example: Compute funds from Operations from the following income statement:

Income Statement

	Rs.		*Rs.*
To Salaries	10,000	By G/P b/d	2,000
To Rent	4,000	By Rent	10,000
To Depreciation	2,000	By Interest amount	8,000
To Preliminary expenses	4,000	By Net loss	10,000
To Loss on sale of furniture	10,000		
	30,000		30,000

Solution:

Funds from Operations

Net loss as per Income statement		(10,000)
Add: Items which do not decrease funds :		
Depreciation	Rs. 2,000	
Preliminary expenses	Rs. 4,000	
Loss on sale of furniture	Rs. 10,000	16,000
Funds from operations		6,000

Notes: Rent and interest on investment, alternatively can be considered as non-operating income and in such case, they will have to be excluded (deducted) while calculating funds from operations. Also, then, these items will he shown under 'non-operating income' in the funds flow statement.

Example:

From the following balance sheets for the years 2004 and 2005; find out funds from operations.

	2004 *(Rs.)*	2005 *(Rs.)*
General reserve	10,000	12,500
Goodwill	5,000	2,500
Provision for depreciation on plant	5,000	6,000
Preliminary expenses	3,000	2,000
Profit and loss appropriation A/c	15,000	20,000

Solution:

Funds from Operations

	Rs.
Profit and loss appropriation account as on December 31, 2005	20,000
Add: Items not decreasing funds :	
Transfer to general reserve	2,500
Goodwill written off	2,500
Provision for depreciation on Plant	1,000
Preliminary expenses written off	1,000
	27,000
Less: Profit and loss appropriation account balance as on December 31, 2004	15,000
Funds from operations	12,000

The funds from operations can also be found by preparing adjusted profit and loss account as given below:

Adjusted Profit and Loss Account

	Rs.		*Rs.*
To Transfer to general reserve	2,500	By Balance b/d	15,000
To Goodwill written off	2,500	By Funds from operations (balancing figure)	12,000
To Preliminary expenses written off	1,000		
To Provision for depreciation	1,000		
To Balance c/d	20,000		
	27,000		27,000

Illustration 1:

The following are the balance sheet of a company for the years 2004 and 2005 and income statement for the year 2005:

Balance Sheets as on December 31, 2004 and December 31, 2005

	Dec. 31, 2005 *Rs.*	*Dec. 31, 2004* *Rs.*	*Increase (decrease)* *Rs.*
Assets:			
Current assets:			
Cash	19,000	17,400	1,600
Debtors	24,600	24,000	600
Inventory	33,000	34,000	(1,000)
Prepaid insurance	4,000	3,600	400
Long-term assets:			
Machinery	3,60,000	3,50,000	10,000
Less: Accumulated depreciation	(1,68,000)	(1,66,000)	(2,800)
Total assets	2,71,800	2,63,000	8,800
Liabilities and Equity			
Current liabilities:			
Creditors	33,600	32,400	1,200
Salaries payable	600	1,000	(400)
Income-taxes payable	4,400	3,400	1,000
Long-term loan	46,000	40,000	6,000
Equity Capital	1,00,000	1,00,000	—
Retained earnings	87,200	86,200	1,000
Total liabilities	2,71,800	2,63,000	8,800

Income Statements for the year ending 2005

	Rs.
Sales	63,800
Expenses:	
Cost of goods sold	45,600
Salaries	8,400
Rent	1,200
Depreciation	2,800

Insurance	600
Interest	400
Income-tax	1,000
Total expenses	60,000
Net Income	3,800

Statement of Retained Earnings

Retained earnings for the year 2004	86,200
Add: Net income for the year 2005	3,800
	90,000
Less: Dividends	2,800
	87,200

You are required to prepare a Funds Flow Statement on a working capital basis.

Solution:

Funds Flow Statement
(Working Capital Basis)

	Rs.	*Rs.*	*Rs.*
(A) Sources of Funds:			
(*i*) Funds from operations:			
Net income	3,800		
Add: Non-cash charges:			
Depreciation	2,800		
Funds provided by operations		6,600	
(*iii*) Other sources			
Long-term borrowings		6,000	12,600
(B) Uses of Funds:			
(*i*) Purchase of machinery		10,000	
(*ii*) Dividends		2,800	
Total uses			12,800
Changes in Working capital			(200)

The above statement presentation is a two parts statement; the sources are first detailed and then totalled, followed by the detail information and total for uses. The difference between the sources and uses must equal the change in working capital.

It can be noticed that sources of funds (working capital) is sub-divided into two parts; the first part is concerned with sources from operations, and the second part deals with other sources.

Uses of working capital in the above statement do not include any uses for operations, such as salaries and rent, because these have been included automatically by starting the funds flow statement with the net income rather than with revenue. Generally, the most common uses of funds shown are for the firm's investment activities such as the purchase of the new equipment, declaration of dividends, or payment of long-term liabilities.

Using the figures given in the Illustration 1, the Schedule of Changes in Working capital can be prepared as follows:

Schedule of Changes In Working Capital
(Changes in Current Assets and Current Liabilities)

	December 31, 2005	*December 31, 2004*	*Increase (Decrease)*
Current assets:	*Rs.*	*Rs.*	*Rs.*
Cash	19,000	17,400	1,600
Accounts receivable	24,600	24,000	600
Inventory	33,000	34,000	(1,000)
Prepaid insurance	4,000	3,600	400
Total current assets	80,600	79,000	1,600
Current liabilities:			
Accounts payable	33,600	32,400	1,200
Salaries payable	600	1,000	(400)
Income-taxes payable	4,400	3,400	1,000
Total current liabilities	38,600	36,800	1,800
Working capital	42,000	42,200	(200)

Illustration 2:

Following are the summarised Balance Sheets of A. Co. Ltd. as on 31st December, 2004 and 2005:

Liabilities	*2004 Rs.*	*2005 Rs.*	*Assets*	*2004 Rs.*	*2005 Rs.*
Share Capital	2,00,000	2,50,000	Land & Buildings	2,00,000	1,90,000
General Reserve	50,000	60,000	Machinery & Plant	1,50,000	1,69,000
Profit & Loss A/c	30,500	30,600	Stock	1,00,000	74,000
Bank loan	70,000	—	Sundry debtors	80,000	64,200
Sundry creditors	1,50,000	1,35,200	Cash	500	600
Provision for taxation	30,000	35,000	Bank	—	8,000
			Goodwill	—	5,000
	5,30,500	5,10,800		5,30,500	5,10,800

Additional information supplied:

During the year ended 31st December 2005:

(*a*) Dividend of Rs. 23,000 was paid:

(*b*) Assets of another company were purchased for a consideration of Rs. 50,000 payable in shares. The following assets were purchased: Stock Rs. 20,000: Machinery Rs. 25,000.

(*c*) Machinery was purchased for Rs. 8,000.

(*d*) Depreciation written off: Building Rs. 10,000, Machinery Rs. 14,000.

(*e*) Income-tax paid during the year Rs. 28,000. Provision of Rs. 33,000 was charged to profit and loss A/c.

Prepare a Statement of Sources and Applications of funds for the year ended 31st December, 2005.

Solution:

Statement of Sources and Applications of Funds

Sources	*Rs.*	*Applications*	*Rs.*
Issue of shares	20,000	Dividend paid	23,000
Fund from operation	90,100	Purchase of machinery	8,000
		Income-tax paid	28,000
	1,10,100	Bank loan paid	70,000
Decrease in working capital (as per statement)	18,900		
	1,29,000		1,29,000

Statement of Changes in Working Capital

	2004 *Rs.*	*2005* *Rs.*	*Increase* *Rs.*	*Decrease* *Rs.*
Current Assets:				
Stock	1,00,000	74,000		26,000
Sundry debtors	80,000	64,200		15,800
Cash	500	600	100	
Bank	—	8,000	8,000	
Total (A)	1,80,500	1,46,800		
Current Liabilities:				
Sundry Creditors	1,50,000	1,35,200	14,800	
Total (B)	1,50,000	1,35,200		
Working Capital (A–B)	—	18,900	18,900	
	30,500	30,500	41,800	41,800

Adjusted Profit & Loss A/c

	Rs.		*Rs.*
To Depreciation:		By Balance b/d	30,500
Land & Building	10,000	By Funds from operation	90,100
Machinery	14,000	(balancing figure)	
To General reserve	10,000		
To Dividend	23,000		
To Provision for tax	33,000		
To Balance c/d	30,600		
	1,20,600		1,20,600

Share Capital A/c

	Rs.		*Rs.*
To Balance c/d	2,50,000	By Balance b/d	2,00,000
		By Machinery purchase	25,000
		By Stock	20,000
		By Goodwill (balancing figure)	5,000
	2,50,000		2,50,000

Machinery A/c

	Rs.		Rs.
To Balance b/d	1,50,000	By Depreciation	14,000
To Share capital (purchase)	25,000	By Balance c/d	1,69,000
To Cash (purchase)	8,000		
	1,83,000		1,83,000

Provision for Income-tax

	Rs.		Rs.
To Cash (tax paid)	28,000	By Balance b/d	30,000
To Balance c/d	35,000	By P & L a/c	33,000
	63,000		63,000

Illustration 3:

From the following balance sheets of A Ltd. make out the statement of sources and uses of funds:

Liabilities	*2004* Rs.	*2005* Rs.	*Assets*	*2004* Rs.	*2005* Rs.
Equity share capital	3,00,000	4,00,000	Goodwill	1,15,000	90,000
8% Redeemable			Land and Bldg.	2,00,000	1,70,000
Preference shares	1,50,000	1,00,000	Plant	80,000	20,000
General Reserve	40,000	70,000	Debtors	1,60,000	2,00,000
Profit & Loss A/c	30,000	48,000	Stock	77,000	1,09,000
Proposed dividend	42,000	50,000	Bills receivable	20,000	30,000
Creditors	55,000	83,000	Cash in hand	15,000	10,000
Bills payable	20,000	16,000	Cash at bank	10,000	8,000
Provision for taxation	40,000	50,000			
	6,77,000	8,17,000		6,77,000	8,17,000

Additional information: (*i*) Depreciation of Rs. 10,000 and Rs. 20,000 have been charged on plant account and land and buildings account respectively in 2005; (*ii*) An interim dividend of Rs. 20,000 has been paid in 2005 (*iii*) Income-tax Rs. 35,000 was paid during the year 2005.

Solution:

Statement of Sources and Applications of Funds for the year ended 31st December, 2005

Sources	*Rs.*	*Applications*	*Rs.*
Issue of equity share capital	1,00,000	Redemption of preference share capital	50,000
Sale of land	10,000	Purchase of plant	1,30,000
Funds from operation	2,18,000	Dividend paid (42,000 + 20,000)	62,000
		Income-tax	35,000
		Increase in working capital	51,000
	3,28,000		3,28,000

Schedule of Changes in Working Capital

	2004 Rs.	2005 Rs.	Increase Rs.Rs.	Decrease
Current Assets:				
Cash in hand	15,000	10,000	—	5,000
Cash in bank	10,000	8,000	—	2,000
Bills receivable	20,000	30,000	10,000	—
Stock	77,000	1,09,000	32,000	—
Debtors	1,60,000	2,00,000	40,000	—
Total (A)	2,82,000	3,57,000	82,000	7,000
Current Liabilities:				
Creditors	55,000	83,000	—	28,000
Bills payable	20,000	16,000	4,000	—
Total (B)	75,000	99,000		
Working Capital (A – B)	2,07,000	2,58,000		
Increase in working capital	51,000	—	—	51,000
	2,58,000	2,58,000	86,000	86,000

Adjusted Profit and Loss Account

	Rs.		Rs.
To Goodwill	25,000	By Balance b/d	30,000
To Depreciation:		By Funds from operation	2,18,000
Land & Building	20,000		
Plant	10,000		
To General Reserve	30,000		
To Proposed dividend	50,000		
To Interim dividend	20,000		
To Provision for Taxation	45,000		
To Balance c/d	48,000		
	2,48,000		2,48,000

Goodwill

	Rs.		Rs.
To Balance b/d	1,15,000	By Adjusted P & L A/c	25,000
		By Balance c/d	90,000
	1,15,000		1,15,000

Land and Buildings

	Rs.		Rs.
To Balance b/d	2,00,000	By Adjusted P & L A/c (Depreciation)	20,000
		By Bank	10,000
		By Balance c/d	1,70,000
	2,00,000		2,00,000

Plant A/c

	Rs.		Rs.
To Balance b/d	80,000	By Adjusted P & L A/c	10,000
To Bank (balancing figure)	1,30,000	By Balance c/d	2,00,000
	2,10,000		2,10,000

General Reserve

	Rs.		Rs.
To Balance c/d	70,000	By Balance c/d	40,000
		By Adjusted P & L A/c	30,000
	70,000		70,000

Proposed Dividend

	Rs.		Rs.
To Dividend paid	42,000	By Balance b/d	42,000
To Balance c/d	50,000	By Adjusted P & L A/c	50,000
	92,000		92,000

Provision for Taxation

	Rs.		Rs.
To Income-tax	35,000	By Balance b/d	40,000
To Balance c/d	50,000	By Adjusted P & L A/c	45,000
	85,000		85,000

SIGNIFICANCE OF STATEMENT OF CHANGES IN FINANCIAL POSITION — WORKING CAPITAL BASIS

A better understanding and analysis of the affairs of a business enterprise requires the knowledge about the movements in assets, liabilities and capital which have taken place during the year and their consequent effect on its financial position. This information is not specifically disclosed by a profit and loss account and balance sheet but can be made available in working capital based funds flow statement.

The funds flow statement is in no way a replacement for the profit and loss account and balance sheet although the information which it contains is a selection, reclassification and summarisation of information contained in these two statements. The balance sheet gives a "snapshot" view at a point in time of the sources from which a firm has acquired its funds and the uses which the firm has made of these funds. The equities side of the balance sheet delineates these sources, and the asset side shows the uses. The income statement is a flow statement; it explains changes that occurred in the retained earnings account by summarizing the increases (revenues) and decreases (expenses) in retained earnings during the accounting period. A funds flow statement explains the changes that took place in a balance sheet account or group of accounts during the period between dates of two balance sheets "snapshots." It shows the manner in which the operations of an enterprise have been financed and in which its financial resources have been used. It also distinguishes the use of funds for the long-term from the short-term. For example, it distinguishes the use of funds for the purchase of new fixed assets from funds used in increasing the working capital of the company. Thus, it provides a meaningful link between the balance sheets at the beginning and at the end of a period and profit and loss account for that period. It should be understood, however, that a funds statement does not purport to indicate the requirements of a business for capital.

The concept of working capital is in conformity with normal accrual accounting procedures. Hence, a funds flow statement based on the concept of net working capital fits well with other statements. Above all, working capital is also a measure of the short-term liquidity of the firm. Therefore, an analysis of factors bringing about a change in the amount of net working capital is useful for decision-making by shareholders, creditors, lenders and management.

Limitations of Statement of Changes in Financial Position — Working Capital Basis

The working capital concept of funds enlarges the problem of valuation because it includes inventory and prepaid items. Thus, the measurement of working capital flows is less precise than for cash. A fund statement based on the working capital concept is usually a brief presentation, and many significant inter-firm transactions are not disclosed. For example, significant addition to inventories financed by short-term credits would not be shown because the two items are offset in the computation of the net change in working capital. Furthermore, transactions not affecting working capital, such as the acquisition of plant and equipment by the issuance of equity capital, would not be included in the statement. Therefore, the funds statement in this presentation would not disclose structural changes in the financial relationships in the firm or major changes in policy regarding investments in current assets and short-term financing.

Relationship between Working Capital Basis Statement of Changes in Financial Position and Income Statement

The income statement is based on the accrual principle: Cash significant events are reported, whether or not they coincide with actual cashflows. The accrual principle necessarily involves the use of estimates and artificial allocations in seeking to predict future cash effects of current events, and attempting to measure the current consequences of the past cash flows.

Working Capital provided by operations is derived from the income statement by omitting certain items that do not affect working capital. For this reason, working capital provided by operations depends on many of the same estimates and conventions that enter into the measurement of net income. Over time, cumulative amounts of income, working capital, and cash should coincide — the only difference should be the timing of the reported flows. Because most financial decisions must be based on annual data, and timing differences between the reported annual flows can be substantial, these differences have a significant impact on the actions taken by decision makers.

THEORY QUESTIONS

1. Explain why an adequate amount of working capital is essential to the successful operation of a business enterprise.
2. What are the primary ways in which an enterprise generates working capital and the primary ways in which a firm uses working capital.
3. Explain the different concepts of funds used in the preparation of statement of changes in financial position.
4. How does a funds flow differ from a balance sheet and income statement?
5. What information/statements are required to prepare a statement of sources and application of funds?

6. Define the following, giving suitable examples:
   (*i*) Current Assets (*ii*) Current Liabilities (*iii*) Non-current Accounts.
7. Discuss the different sources and uses of working capital.
8. Explain effect of different transactions on working capital.
9. List the different steps in preparing funds flow statements.
10. How are taxes and proposed dividends treated in preparing working capital basis funds flow statement?
11. Explain the importance of statement of changes in financial position, working capital basis.

EXERCISES AND PROBLEMS

1. From the following particulars of M/s. Tushar Ltd. prepare Funds Flow Statements and Schedule of Changes in Working Capital:

Liabilities:	2007	2006
	Rs.	*Rs.*
Equity share capital	2,10,000	1,50,000
Profit and Loss A/c	1,62,000	66,000
14% Debentures	1,80,000	21,0,000
Creditors	60,000	30,000
Proposed Dividend	15,000	6,000
Provision for Tax	12,000	6,000
Provision for Doubtful Debt	9,000	6,000
	6,48,000	4,74,000

Assets:	2007	2006
	Rs.	*Rs.*
Fixed Assets	3,72,000	3,06,000
Investments	48,000	18,000
Debtors (all good)	45,000	24,000
Other Current Assets	1,80,000	1,20,000
Discount on Issue of Debentures	3,000	6,000
	6,48,000	4,74,000

Additional Information:

(*a*) The provision for depreciation stood at Rs. 90,000 on 31-12-2006 and at Rs. 1,14,000 on 31-12-2007. A fixed asset costing Rs. 42,000 (Book value Rs. 24,000) was disposed of for Rs. 15,000.

(*b*) An Interim dividend @ 15% was paid on equity shares. New equity shares were issued on 31-12-2007.

(*c*) Tax provided during the year Rs. 9,000.

(*d*) Some Investments were sold for Rs. 30,000 at a profit of 25% on cost.

(*Ans.:* Net increase in working capital Rs. 51,000; Funds from operations Rs. 1,93,500; Purchase of fixed assets for cash Rs. 1,32,000; Tax paid during the year Rs. 3,000; Profit on sale of investments Rs. 6,000, Loss on sale of fixed assets Rs. 9,000.)

2. From the following particulars, prepare Funds Flow Statement:

	March 31, 2007	*March 31, 2008*
	Rs.	*Rs.*
Current Assets	64,000	64,000
Fixed Assets:		
Land	20,000	30,000
Buildings	50,000	55,000
Machinery	80,000	86,000
	2,14,000	2,35,000

Current Liabilities	36,000	41,000
Bank Loan	30,000	45,000
Capital	1,48,000	1,49,000
	2,14,000	2,35,000

During the year, drawings by the proprietor for personal use amounted to Rs. 25,000. Rs. 9,000 was charged as depreciation on Machinery during the year ending March 31, 2008.

(*Ans.:* Net decrease in working capital Rs. 5,000; Funds from operations Rs. 26,000 + 9,000 = Rs. 35,000; Machinery purchased for cash Rs. 15,000.

3. From the following Summarised Balance Sheets of M/s G. Ltd., prepare the Funds Flow Statement for the year ended on 31st March, 2007:

	Year ending 31st March 2006 *Rs.*	2007 *Rs.*
Liabilities:		
Share Capital	10,00,000	10,50,000
Capital Reserve	50,000	50,000
Loans	5,00,000	6,50,000
Sundry Creditors	6,00,000	7,85,000
	21,50,000	25,35,000

	Year ending 31st March 2006 *Rs.*	2007 *Rs.*
Assets:		
Fixed Assets :		
Cost Less Depreciation	12,30,000	13,75,000
Stock in Trade	4,10,000	5,60,000
Sundry Debtors	3,40,000	2,10,000
Cash at Bank .	20,000	5,000
Discount on Issue of Shares	—	5,000
Profit &. Loss A/c	1,50,000	3,50,000
	21,50,000	25,35,000

The company issued share capital to a firm against the following assets purchased: Fixed Assets: Rs. 25,000, Stock in Trade: Rs. 20,000, During 2006-07, Depreciation was provided on Fixed Assets as Rs. 1,15,000.

(*Ans.:* Decrease in working capital Rs. 1.80,000: Total sources Rs. 1,70 000; Total uses Rs. 3,50,000; Loss from business operations Rs. 1,15,000)

4. Following are the Balance Sheets of M/s X Co. Ltd. for the two years:

	31.3.02 *Rs.*	*31.3.03* *Rs.*	*Assets*	*31.3.02* *Rs.*	*31.3.03* *Rs.*
Share capital	5,00,000	7,00,000	Plant and Machinery	5,00,000	8,00,000
P & L A/c	1,00,000	1,60,000	Land and Buildings	80,000	1,20,000
Gen. Reserve	50,000	70,000	Stock	1,00,000	75,000
S. Creditors	1,03,000	1,20,000	S. Debtors	1,50,000	1,60,000
Bills Payable	20,000	25,000	Cash in hand	20,000	20,000
Outstanding Exp.	7,000	5,000			
Provision for Taxation	20,000	25,000			
Proposed Dividend	50,000	70,000			
	8,50,000	11,75,000		8,50,000	11,75,000

Additional Information:

(*i*) An interim dividend of Rs. 20,000 was paid during the year.

(*ii*) Income-tax Rs. 15,000 was paid on 2002-03.

(*iii*) During the year Rs. 50,000 was charged as depreciation on Plant and Machinery.

(*iv*) One machine costing Rs. 12,000 (on which Rs. 7,000 has been written off as depreciation) was sold for Rs. 8,000 during the year.

Prepare the Schedule of Changes in Working Capital and the Funds Flow Statement. Also show the detailed workings clearly.

(*Ans.:* Net decrease in working capital Rs. 35,000; Funds from operation Rs. 2,37,000)

5. From the following information, prepare a statement of Sources and Applications of Funds for the year ended December 31, 2008.

(*i*) Increase in working capital Rs. 4,000.

(*ii*) Net profit Rs. 10,750 before writing off goodwill.

(*iii*) Depreciation provided on fixed assets Rs. 1,750.

(*iv*) Dividend paid Rs. 3,500.

(*v*) Goodwill Rs, 5,000 written off out of profits.

(*vi*) Rs. 5,000 share capital was issued for cash.

(*vii*) Machinery was purchased for Rs. 10,000.

(*Ans.:* Funds from operations Rs. 12,500, Total sources Rs. 17,500, Total applications Rs. 13,500)

6. Following are the Balance Sheets of X Co. Ltd. as on 31st March, 2005 and 2006:

Liabilities	2005 *Rs.*	2006 *Rs.*	*Assets*	2005 *Rs.*	2006 *Rs.*
Pref. Share capital	—	2,00,000	Goodwill	20,000	30,000
Eq. share capital	4,20,000	5,20,000	Buildings	6,00,000	5,80,000
General Reserve	1,00,000	1,10,000	Machinery	3,00,000	3,38,000
Creditors	4,40,000	2,68,000	Stock	2,00,000	1,48,000
Profit and Loss a/c	61,000	71,200	Debtors	1,40,400	1,08,000
14% Debentures	2,00,000	—	Cash/Bank	20,600	37,200
Unclaimed dividend	—	2,000			
Provision for tax	60,000	70,000			
	12,81,000	12,41,200		12,81,000	12,41,200

Information:

(*i*) Dividend paid in cash Rs. 50,000 during the year.

(*ii*) Assets acquired for Rs. 1,00,000 payable in equity shares; stock Rs. 50,000, Machine Rs. 40,000 and goodwill.

(*iii*) Machine purchased for cash Rs. 12,000.

(*iv*) Provision for tax during the year Rs. 66.000.

(*v*) Debenture-holders accept preference shares in settlement of their claims.

(*vi*) Depreciation on building Rs. 20,000.

Prepare Funds Flow Statement and Schedule of Changes in Working Capital.

(*Ans.:* Net increase in working capital Rs. 92,200; Funds from operations Rs. 1,06,200; Depreciation on machinery Rs. 14,000]

(*Hint:* Dividend proposed during the year Rs. 52,000 (paid Rs. 50,000 + Unclaimed Rs. 2,000)

7. From the particulars of X Co., Ltd., prepare funds flow statement and schedule of changes in working capital:

Liabilities	*31-3-09* *Rs.*	*31-3-08* *Rs.*	*Assets*	*31-3-09* *Rs.*	*31-3-08* *Rs.*
Equity share Capital	7,00,000	5,00,000	Fixed Assets	12,40,000	10,20,000
14% Debentures	6,00,000	7,00,000	Investments	1,60,000	60,000
Profit and Loss a/c	5,40,000	2,20,000	Debtors (All good)	1,50,000	80,000
Creditors	2,00,000	1,00,000	Other Current Assets	6,00,000	4,00,000
Proposed dividend	50,000	20,000	Discount on Issue of Debentures	10,000	20,000
Provision for Tax	40,000	20,000			
Provision for Doubtful Debts	30,000	20,000			
	21,60,000	15,80,000		21,60,000	15,80,000

The following additional information is given:

(*i*) Tax provided during the year, Rs. 30,000.

(*ii*) Some investments were sold for Rs. 1,00,000 at a profit of 25% on cost.

(*iii*) An interim dividend @ 15% was paid on equity shares. New equity shares were issued on 31st March, 2009.

(*iv*) Provision for depreciation stood at Rs. 3,00,000 on 1st April, 2008 and at Rs. 3,80,000 on 31st March, 2009. A fixed asset costing Rs. 1.40,000 (Book value, Rs. 80,000) was sold for Rs. 50,000.

(**Ans.:** Increase in Working Capital Rs. 1,70,000; Total Sources Rs. 9,95,000; Total uses Rs. 8,25,000).

8. Following are the summarised balance sheets of a Limited Co. as at March 31, 2006 and March 31, 2007

Liabilities	*On March 31*		*Assets*	*On March 31*	
	2006 *Rs.*	*2007* *Rs.*		*2006* *Rs.*	*2007* *Rs.*
Sundry Creditors	39,010	41,135	Cash at Bank	3,000	2,700
Bills Payable	33,780	11,525	Sundry Debtors	85,175	72,625
Bank Overdraft	60,000	Nil	Sundry Advances	2,315	735
Provision for Income Tax	40,000	49,000	Stock	1,09,040	97,370
Reserves	48,000	50,000	Land & Buildings	1,48,000	1,54,250
Profit & Loss A/c	39,690	41,220	Plant & Machinery	1,12,950	1,16,200
Share Capital	2,00,000	2,60,000	Goodwill	Nil	9,000
	4,60,480	4,52,880		4,60,480	4,52,880

Additional Information is as under:

(*i*) An interim dividend of Rs. 26,000 and a final dividend of Rs. 54,000 were paid during 2006-07.

(*ii*) The assets of another company were purchased for Rs. 60,000 payable in fully paid shares of the company. The assets purchased comprised of Stock Rs. 22,000 and Machinery: Rs. 29,000.

(*iii*) Additional plant purchased worth Rs. 6,000.

(*iv*) Depreciation provided during the current year.
Land & Buildings — Rs. 3,750; Plant & Machinery — Rs. 12,000.

(*v*) Income Tax paid during the year Rs. 30,000.

You are required to prepare the Funds Flow Statement and a statement of Changes in Working Capital for the year ending on March 31, 2007.

(***Ans.:*** Funds from operations Rs. 1,38,280; increase in working capital 54,030)

9. Following are summarised Balance Sheets of X Ltd. as on 31st December, 2004 and 2005.

Liabilities	*2004*	*2005*	*Assets*	*2004*	*2005*
Equity share capital	2,00,000	2,50,000	Bank	35,000	16,000
12% Debentures	1,00,000	80,000	Stock	40,000	75,000
10% Pref. share capital	50,000	80,000	B/R	20,000	50,000
Public deposits	20,000	30,000	Debtors	70,000	1,00,000
Loans	50,000	80,000	Machinery	75,000	60,000
Reserves	20,000	25,000	Furniture	10,000	8,000
P&L A/c	50,000	60,000	Land	1,70,000	2,80,000
Provision for Dep. on Machinery	10,000	15,000	Buildings	1,40,000	99,000
Dividend Proposed	20,000	25,000	Goodwill	30,000	25,000
Creditors	40,000	50,000			
B/P	30,000	18,000			
	5,90,000	7,13,000		5,90,000	7,13,000

Additional Information:

(*i*) Depreciation charged during 2005 was Rs. 4,000 on Furniture, Rs. 12,000 on Machinery and Rs. 20,000 on Buildings.

(*ii*) Redemption of debentures was made at 10% premium.

(*iii*) Part of machinery was sold for Rs. 15,000 at a loss of Rs. 4,000.

(*iv*) During 2005, interim dividend was paid Rs. 10,000 and income tax was paid Rs. 5.000.

You are required to prepare Fund Flow Statement and Schedule of Changes in Working Capital from the above particulars. Working notes are also required.

(***Ans.:*** Increase in working capital Rs. 78,000
Funds from operations Rs. 1,02,000
Total sources Rs. 2,58,000
Total uses Rs. 1,80,000)

10. From the following Balance sheets of A Ltd., prepare Funds Flow Statement and a schedule of changes in working capital:

Liabilities	*As on 31-12-2000* *Rs.*	*As on 31-12-2001* *Rs.*
Equity Share Capital	2,00,000	2,80,000
Profit and Loss A/c	88,000	2,16,000
14% Debentures	2,80,000	2,40,000
Creditors	40,000	80,000
Proposed Dividend	8,000	20,000
Provision for Tax	8,000	16,000
Provision for Doubtful Debts	8,000	12,000
	6,32,000	8,64,000

Assets	*As on 31-12-2000* *Rs.*	*As on 31-12-2001* *Rs.*
Fixed Assets	4,08,000	4,96,000
Investments	24,000	64,000
Debtors (all good)	32,000	60,000
Other Current Assets	1,60,000	2,40,000
Discount on issue of debentures	8,000	4,000
	6,32,000	8,64,000

Additional information:

(*a*) The provision for depreciation stood at Rs. 1,20,000 on 31-12-2000 and at Rs. 1,52,000 on 31-12-2001. A fixed asset costing Rs. 56,000 (book value Rs. 32,000) was sold for Rs. 20,000.

(*b*) An interim dividend @15% was paid on equity shares.
New equity shares were issued on 31-12-2001.

(*c*) Tax provided during the year Rs. 12,000.

(*d*) Some of the investments were sold for Rs. 20,000 at a profit of 2½% on cost.

(***Ans.:*** Funds from operations Rs. 2,62,000; Increase in working capital Rs. 68,000)

Cash Flow Statement

CONCEPT

A cash flow statement discloses net increase (or decrease) in cash during an accounting period. As per AS 3 (Revised) the objective of cash flow statement is to provide information about cash flows of an enterprise which is useful in providing the users of financial statements with a basis to assess the ability of a enterprise to generate cash and cash equivalents to utilise those cash flows. The statement deals with the provisions of information about changes in cash and cash equivalents during the accounting year. It classifies cash flows into operating, investing and financing activities.

DEFINITION IN AS 3

The following terms are used in this Statement with the meanings specified:

Cash comprises cash on hand and demand deposits with banks.

Cash equivalents are short-term, highly liquid investments that are readily convertible into known amounts of cash and which are subject to an insignificant risk of changes in value.

Cash flows are inflows and outflows of cash and cash equivalents.

Operating activities are the principal revenue-producing activities of the enterprise and other activities that are not investing or financing activities.

Investing activities are the acquisition and disposal of long-term assets and other investments not included in cash equivalents.

Financing activities are activities that result in changes in the size and composition of the owners' capital (including preference share capital in the case of a company) and borrowings of the enterprise.

Cash and Cash Equivalents

1. Cash equivalents are held for the purpose of meeting short-term cash commitments rather than for investment or other purposes. For an investment to qualify as a cash equivalent, it must be readily convertible to a known amount of cash and be subject to an insignificant risk of changes in value. Therefore, an investment normally qualifies as a cash equivalent only when it has a short maturity of, say, three months or less from the date of acquisition. Investments in shares are excluded from cash equivalents unless they are, in substance, cash equivalents; for example, preference shares of a company acquired shortly before their specified redemption date (provided there is only an insignificant risk of failure of the company to repay the amount at maturity),
2. Cash flows exclude movements between items that constitute cash or cash equivalents because these components are part of the cash management of an enterprise rather than part of its operating, investing and financing activities. Cash management includes the investment of excess cash in cash equivalents.

CLASSIFICATION OF CASH INFLOWS AND OUTFLOWS

A cash flow statement focuses on various activities and items which bring about changes in the cash balance between two balance sheet dates. This statement covers all items which increase or decrease the cash of a business enterprise. For example, this statement includes items like receipts from debtors and payments to creditors. On the contrary, this statement will not cover items which have no immediate effect on cash increase or decrease. For instance, goods purchased on credit and goods sold on credit will not be included in this statement as these transactions have no effect on inflow and outflow of cash.

A cash flow statement aims to determine the effects on cash of different types of cash inflows and outflows. In this process, all cash flows, i.e., activities resulting into cash flows are classified into different categories. The ICAI's AS3 'Cash Flow Statement' has classified cash flows into three categories:

(1) Operating Activities (or Flows)
(2) Investing Activities (or Flows)
(3) Financing Activities (or Flows)

Figure 13.1 displays the classification of cash inflows and cash outflows relating to operating activities, investing activities and financing activities.

(1) Operating Activities: Operating activities are those transactions which are considered in the determination of net income. Examples of cash inflows in this category are cash received from debtors for goods and services, interest and dividend received on loans and investment. Examples of cash outflows in this category are cash payments for goods and services; merchandise; wages; interest; taxes; supplies and others.

AS 3 Cash Flow Statement states:

(*i*) The amount of cash flows arising from operating activities is a key indicator of the extent to which the operations of the enterprise have generated sufficient cash flows to maintain the operating capability of the enterprise, pay dividends, repay loans and make new investments without recourse to external sources of financing. Information about the specific components of historical operating cash flows is useful, in conjunction with other information, in forecasting future operating cash flows.

Classification of Cash Inflows and Cash Outflows

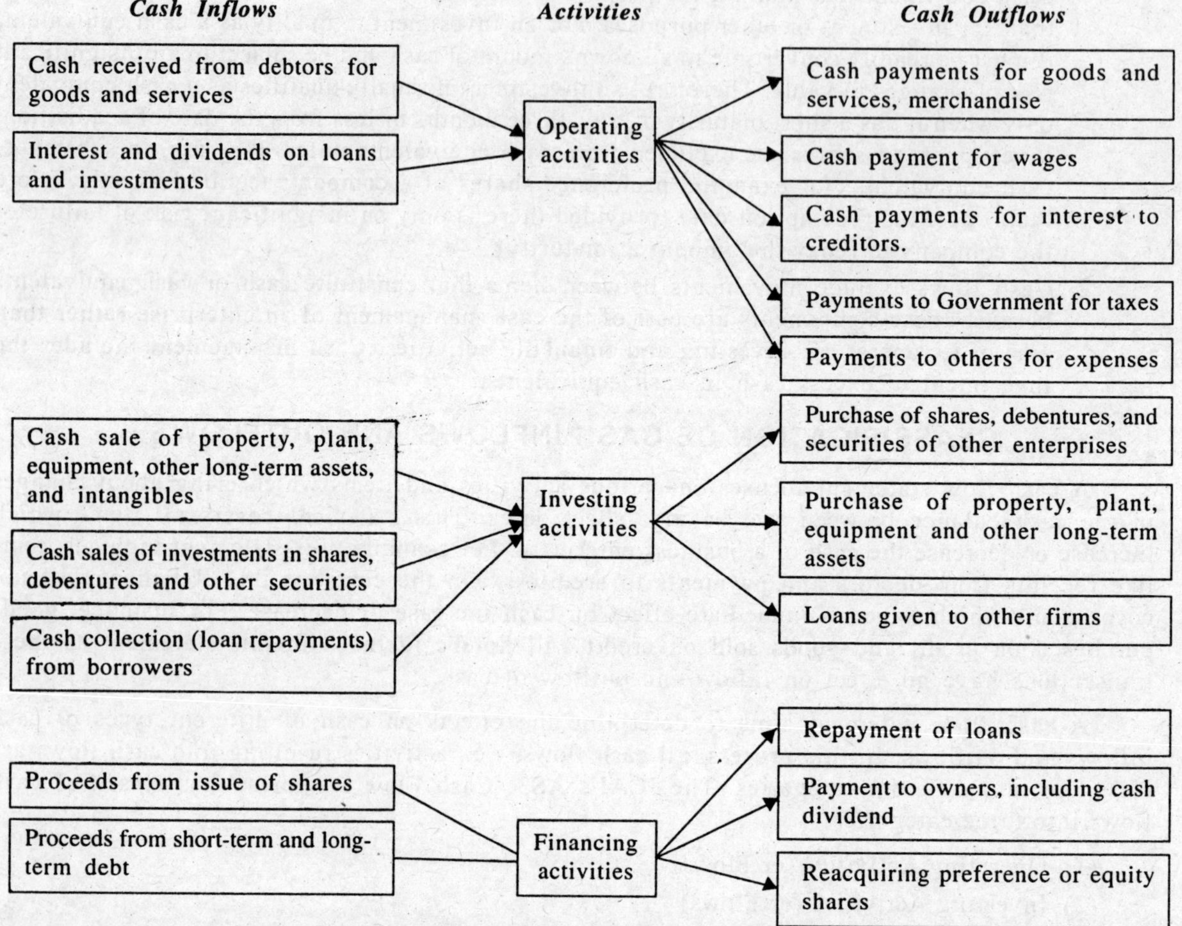

Fig. 13.1 Classification of Cash Inflows and Outflows relating to Operating Activities, Investing Activities and Financing Activities

(*ii*) Cash flows from operating activities are primarily derived from the principal revenue-producing activities of the enterprise. Therefore, they generally result from the transactions and other events that enter into the determination of net profit or loss. Examples of cash flows from operating activities are:

(*a*) cash receipts from the sale of goods and the rendering of services;

(*b*) cash receipts from royalties, fees, commissions and other revenue;

(*c*) cash payments to suppliers for goods and services;

(*d*) cash payments to and on behalf of employees;

(*e*) cash receipts and cash payments of an insurance enterprise for premiums and claims, annuities and other policy benefits;

(*f*) cash payments or refunds of income-taxes unless they can be specifically identified with financing and investing activities; and (*g*) cash receipts and payments relating to future contracts, forward contracts, option contracts and swap contracts when the contracts are held for dealing or trading purposes.

(*iii*) Some transactions, such as the sale of an item of plant, may give rise to a gain or loss which is included in the determination of net profit or loss. However the cash flows relating to such transactions are cash flows from investing activities.

(*iv*) Cash flows from operating activities are determined according to the activities relating to the business in which the enterprise deals, e.g., interest and dividend received by financial institutions will be treated as operating cash flow. Similarly, an enterprise may hold securities and loans for dealing or trading purposes, in which case they are similar to inventory acquired specifically for resale. Therefore, cash flows arising from the purchase and sale of dealing or trading securities are classified as operating activities. In the same manner, cash advances and loans made by financial enterprises are usually classified as operating activities since they relate to the main revenue-producing activity of that enterprise.

(2) Investing Activities: Investing activities include acquisition of long-term or fixed assets; disposal of long-term or fixed assets; acquisition and disposal of intangible assets; purchase and sale of shares, debentures and other securities; lending of money and its subsequent collection. Cash inflows from investing activities generally include cash sales of property, plant, equipment and intangible assets, cash sales of investments in shares, debentures and other securities, cash collection (loans repayments) from borrowers. Cash outflows are purchase of shares, debentures and securities of other enterprises, purchase of property, plant, equipment and other long-term assets, loan given to other firms.

According to AS 3 Cash Flow Statement:

(*i*) The separate disclosure of cash flows arising from investing activities is important because the cash flows represent the extent to which expenditures have been made for resources intended to generate future income and cash flows. Examples of cash flows arising from investing activities are:

(*a*) Cash payments to acquire fixed assets (including intangibles). These payments include those relating to capitalised research and development costs and self constructed fixed assets;

(*b*) cash receipts from disposal of fixed assets (including intangibles);

(*c*) cash payments to acquire shares, warrants or debt instruments of other enterprises and interests in joint ventures (other than payments for those instruments considered to be cash equivalents and those held for dealing or trading purposes);

(*d*) cash receipts from disposal of shares warrants or debt instruments of other enterprises and interests in joint ventures (other than receipts from those instruments considered to be cash equivalent and those held for dealing or trading purposes);

(*e*) cash advances and loans made to third parties (other than advances and loans made by a financial enterprise);

(*f*) cash receipts from the repayment of advances and loans made to third parties (other than advances and loans of a financial enterprise);

(*g*) cash receipts from future contracts, forward contracts, option contracts and swap contracts except when the contracts are held for dealing or trading purposes, or the payments are classified as financing activities; and

(*h*) cash receipts from future contracts, forward contracts, option contracts and swap contracts except when the contracts are held for dealing or trading purposes, or the receipts are classified as financing.

(*i*) When a contract is accounted for as a hedge of an identifiable position, the cash flows of the contract are classified in the same manner as the cash flow of the position being hedged.

(3) Financing Activities: Financing activities relate to long-term liability and equity capital. A firm engages in financing activities when it obtains resources from owners, returns resources to owners, borrows resources from creditors and repays amounts borrowed. Cash inflows include proceeds from issue of shares and short-term and long-term borrowings. Cash outflows include repayment of loans and payments to owners, including cash dividends. Repayment of accounts payable or accrued liabilities are not considered repayment of loans under financing activities but are classified as cash outflows under operating activities. AS 3 Cash Flow Statement observes:

The separate disclosure of cash flows arising from financing activities is important because it is useful in predicting claims on future cash flows by providers of funds (both capital and borrowings) to the enterprise. Examples of cash flows arising from financing activities are:

(*a*) cash proceeds from issuing shares or other similar instruments;

(*b*) cash proceeds from issuing debentures, loans, notes, bonds and other short or lone-term borrowings: and

(*c*) cash repayments of amounts borrowed.

CASH FLOW STATEMENT AND CASH RECEIPTS AND DISBURSEMENTS

A cash flow statement differs from the summary of cash receipts and disbursements. A cash flow statement is prepared by a rearrangement of items on the income statement and balance sheet, rather than from entries made to the cash account. Cash flow statement may also highlight the amount of cash generated by the firm's operations. This is not reported in statement of cash receipts and disbursements.

CASH FLOW AND INCOME STATEMENT

Cash flow statement apparently differs from income statement. An income statement includes adjustments in respect of expenses accrued in the calculation of periodic income, whereas cash flow statement excludes such adjustments. The largest item of difference between them is the allocation of fixed assets costs as depreciation. Also, the procedures adopted in the two statements are reflected in changes in balance sheet items. These would include changes in balances of trade debtors and trade creditors.

CASH PROFIT (CASH NET INCOME)

Accrual-based profit and loss account reveals accrual net income. By adjusting the items on the profit and loss account, one can arrive at cash profit or cash net income. It should be noted that cash profit relates to operating activities in the same way as profit and loss account focuses on net income determination from operating activities. But profit and loss account does not show cash inflow and outflow relating to operating activities because profit and loss account is prepared on accrual basis.

Cash profit and cash flow is not the same thing. Cash profit is confined to indicating cash flow relating to operating activities. But cash flow is a total concept indicating total inflows and outflows. For example, issue of equity shares is a source of cash inflow but will not be used for determining cash profit. Similarly, plant purchased will be cash outflow for its full value, but will not be used for determining cash profit.

PRESENTATION OF CASH FLOW STATEMENT

A cash flow statement can be presented in either the direct or indirect format. The investing and financing sections will be the same under either format. However, the operating section will be different.

Direct Method

Direct method is that method whereby major classes of gross cash receipts and gross cash payments are disclosed. Enterprises that utilise the direct method should report separately the following classes of operating cash receipts and payments:

1. Cash collected from customers, including lessees, licensee, and other similar items.
2. Interest and dividends received.
3. Other operating cash receipts, if any.
4. Cash paid to employees and other suppliers of goods or services, including suppliers of insurance, advertising, and other similar expenses.
5. Interest paid
6. Income-taxes paid
7. Other operating cash payments, if any.

Companies that use the direct method must provide a reconciliation of net income to net cash flow from operating activities in a separate schedule in the financial statements.

According to AS 3 Cash Flow Statement:

The direct method provides information which may be useful in estimating future cash flows and which is not available under the indirect method and is therefore, considered more appropriate than the indirect method. Under the direct method, information about major classes of gross cash receipts and gross cash payments may be obtained either:

(*a*) from the accounting records of the enterprise; or

(*b*) by adjusting sales, cost of sales (interest and similar income, and interest expense and similar charges for a financial enterprise) and other items in the statement of profit and loss for:

(*i*) changes during the period in inventories and operating receivables and payables;

(*ii*) other non-cash items; and

(*iii*) other items for which the cash effects are investing or financing cash flows.

Illustration 1:

From the following Profit and Loss Account of ABC Ltd. for the year ended 31st March 2007, calculate cash generated from "Operating Activities" by Direct Method.

Profit and Loss Account
for the year ended 31st March, 2007

		Rs.		*Rs.*
To Opening stock		1,60,000	By Sale (cash)	42,50,000
To Purchases (cash)		31,00,000	By Commission accrued	40,000
To Wages	4,40,000		By Dividend received	60,000
Add: Outstanding	60,000	5,00,000	By Profit on sale of Plant	2,40,000

To Salaries	2,20,000		(Sale proceeds 22,40,000	
Add: Outstanding	20,000		– Book value Rs. 20,00,000)	
	2,40,000		By Closing stock	2,20,000
Less: Prepaid	10,000	2,30,000		
To Office expenses		80,000		
To Selling expenses		1,20,000		
To Depreciation		1,10,000		
To Income tax paid		20,000		
To Goodwill written off		44,000		
To Preliminary expenses written off		20,000		
To Net profit		4,26,000		
		48,10,000		48,10,000

Solution: Cash Flow from Operations

(A) Cash Receipt from Operating Activities:		
Cash sales	Rs. 42,50,000	
Less:		
(B) Cash payments due to operating activities:		
Purchases	31,00,000	
Wages	4,40,000	
Salaries	2,20,000	
Office expenses	80,000	
Selling expenses	1,20,000	39,60,000
Cash flow from operations before tax		2,90,000
Less: Income tax paid		20,000
Net cash inflow from operations		2,70,000

Notes:

(1) Non-cash charges such as depreciation, Goodwill written off, Preliminary expenses written off have been ignored as these do not involve any outflow of cash.

(2) Dividend received and profit on sale of plant are to be treated under cash flow from 'investing activities.'

(3) Commission accrued does not involve any cash inflow, hence ignored.

(4) Changes in current assets and current liabilities are ignored.

Illustration 2:

From the following Profit and Loss A/c and additional information of M/s. Anurag Enterprises, Compute cash flow from operations.

Profit and Loss Account

for the year ended 31st March, 2007

		Rs.		*Rs.*
To Opening stock		1,60,000	By Sales:	
To Purchases			Cash	6,00,000
Cash	2,00,000		Credit	10,00,000
Credit	6,00,000	8,00,000	By Closing stock	2,08,000
To Wages		48,000	By Commission	1,12,000
To Office expenses		1,76,000	By Royalties	80,000
To Selling expenses		96,000	By Discount received	40,000
To Bad debts		16,000		
To Discount allowed		32,000		

To Depreciation	1,20,000		
To Provision for tax	2,40,000		
To Net profit	3,52,000		
	20,40,000		20,40,000

Additional Information:

	March 31 2006	March 31 2007
Debtors	1,20,000	1,44,000
Creditors	1,12,000	80,000
O/s Selling expenses	24,000	32,000
Prepaid office expenses	16,000	24,000
Accrued royalties	96,000	88,000
Advance commission	72,000	64,000
Provision for tax	3,20,000	4,80,000

Solution:

		Rs.
Cash flow from Operations		
(A) Receipts from operations:		
Cash sales		6,00,000
Cash received from debtors*1		9,76,000
Cash from royalties*2		88,000
Cash from commission*3		1,04,000
		17,68,000
Less:		Rs.
(B) Operating cash payments		
Cash purchases	2,00,000	
Cash paid to creditor*4	6,32,000	
Cash selling expenses	88,000	
Cash office expenses	1,92,000	11,12,000
Cash inflow from operations before tax		6,56,000
Less: Income tax paid (on operating incomes)		80,000
Net cash flow from operations		5,76,000

****1 Cash received from debtors → prepare debtors a/c***

Debtors A/c

	Rs.		Rs.
To Bal. b/d	1,20,000	By Cash received (Bal. fig.)	9,76,000
To Sales (credit)	10,00,000	By Bal. c/d	1,44,000
	11,20,000		11,20,000

****2 Cash from Royalties***

Opening bal. + Royalties as per P & L A/c – Closing Bal. = Cash from Royalties
96,000 + 80,000 – 88,000 = Rs. 88,000

****3 Cash from commission***

Closing bal. of advance + Commission as per P & L A/c – Opening bal = Cash from commission
64,000 + 1,12,000 – 72,000 = 1,04,000

4 Cash paid to creditors

Op. Bal. + purchases – Cl. Bal. = Cash paid to creditors
80,000 + 6,00,000 –1,12,000 = Rs. 6,32,000

Indirect Method

Under the indirect method, the net cash flow from operating activities is determined by adjusting net profit or loss for the effects of:

(*a*) changes during the period in inventories and operating receivables and payables;

(*b*) non-cash items such as depreciation, provisions, deferred taxes, and unrealised foreign exchange gains and losses; and

(*c*) all other items for which the cash effects are investing or financing cash flows.

Alternatively, the net cash flow from operating activities may be presented under the indirect method by showing the operating revenues and expenses excluding non-cash items disclosed in the statement of profit and loss and the changes during the period in inventories and operating receivables and payables.

The indirect method starts with net income and reconciles it to net cash flow from operating activities. The cash flow from operating activities is found by adjusting net income for (*i*) changes in current assets and current liabilities and (ii) depreciation expense. Depreciation expense is not a cash flow. Because it decreases net income, it is added back to net income in order to arrive at the operating cash flow. The following summarizes the process:

Change	*Adjustment to Net Income*
Decrease in a current asset	Add
Increase in a current asset	Subtract
Decrease in a current liability	Subtract
Increase in a current liability	Add

The indirect method is more widely used, since it shows the relationship between the income statement and the balance sheet and therefore aids in the analysis of these statements.

Reporting Cash Flows from Investing and Financing Activities

An enterprise should report separately major classes of gross cash receipts and gross cash payments arising from investing and financing activities.

Both the approaches, direct and indirect, result in the same amount for cash flow from operations after making necessary adjustments. However, both the approaches have the arguments, pros and cons.

The arguments in favour of direct approach are that it identifies the major categories of cash receipts and cash payments arising from operating activities; it provides a more useful basis for estimating future cash flows; and it provides information that is not otherwise available in the balance sheet and profit and loss account. The direct method is a better indicator of company solvency, has a sounder conceptual framework and reflects accepted business practice. It permits an evaluation of cash flow relating to specific line items of income statement such as sales and cost of goods sold. The empirical evidence indicates that the direct method is superior over the indirect method in predicting future operating cash flows and future net operating cash flows.

On the other hand, followers of the indirect approach argue that indirect method is less costly and more convenient to use by firms. It is said that the direct approach would require information that is hard to collect and sensitive. One difficulty with the direct approach is that some of the cash flows may have characteristics of more than one category of cash flow.

However, the indirect method has also been criticised on two grounds. First, it contains unnecessary detail and may confuse the users. Another limitation of the indirect method is that the adding of expenses such as depreciation suggests that expenses are a source of cash. The conceptual and practical problems which underlie the indirect method are as follows:

(*i*) Ambiguity in the definition of "operations."

(*ii*) Diversity in reporting practices.

(*iii*) Impact of changes in the reporting entity on the non-cash current accounts.

(*iv*) Use of absorption costing in accounting for manufactured inventory,

(*v*) Measurement of current portion of long-term leases.

(*vi*) Reclassifications between current and non-current accounts.

Figures 13.2 and 13.3 show respectively direct and indirect method of preparing cash flow statement.

ABC Company

For the year Ended December 31, 2008

	Rs.	*Rs.*
(A) Cash Flow From Operating Activities:		
Cash Receipts from:		
Sales		
Interest Received		
Cash Payments for:		
Purchases		
Operating Expenses		
Interest Payments		
Income Taxes		
Net Cash Flow from Operating Activities		
(B) Cash Flows from Investing Activities		
Sale of Plant Assets		
Sale of Investments		
Purchase of Plant Assets		
Purchase of Investments		
Net Cash Flows Used by Investing Activities		
(C) Cash Flows from Financing Activities		
Repayment of Bonds and Debentures		
Issue of Common shares		
Dividends Paid		
Net Cash Flows from Financing Activities		
Net Increase (Decrease) in Cash		

Fig. 13.2 Cash Flow Statement (Direct Method)

ABC Company

For the Year Ended December 31, 2008

	Rs.	Rs.
(A) Cash Flows from Operating Activities		
Net Income		
Adjustments to Reconcile Net Income to Net Cash provided by Operating Activities		
Depreciation		
Gain on Sale of Investments		
Loss on Sale of Plant Asset		
Decrease in Accounts Receivable		
Increase in Inventory		
Decrease in Prepaid Expenses		
Increase in Accounts Payable		
Increase in Accrued Liabilities		
Decrease in Income Taxes Payable		
Net Cash Flows from Operating Activities		
(B) Cash Flows from Investing Activities		
Sale of Plant Assets		
Sale of Investments		
Purchase of Plant Assets		
Purchase of Investments		
Net Cash Flows Used by Investing Activities		
(C) Cash Flows from Financing Activities		
Repayment of Bonds and debentures		
Issue of common shares		
Dividends Paid		
Net Cash flows from Financing Activities		
Net Increase (Decrease) in cash		

Fig. 13.3 Cash Flow Statement (Indirect Method)

PREPARING CASH FLOW STATEMENT

Before preparing cash flow statement, first of all, the following three steps have to be completed:

(1) Determining cash flows from operations or operating activities.

(2) Determining cash flows from investing activities.

(3) Determining cash flows from financing activities.

After obtaining information regarding the above, a cash flow statement can be prepared. The three steps have been discussed below:

Cash Flow from Operations

The profit and loss account focuses on net income determination from operating activities. However, it does not show cash inflow and outflow relating to operating activities because the profit and loss account is prepared on accrual basis. In preparing profit and loss account, revenues are recorded even though cash for them has not been received. Similarly, expenses are recorded even though they may not have been paid. Therefore, to find cash flows from operations, one need to convert accrual basis income statement figures to cash basis by making adjustments. By way of adjustments, earned revenues will be converted into cash received from sales or customers and incurred expenses will be converted into cash expended, i.e., expenses actually paid in cash.

The conversion of accrual basis income statement to cash basis income statement along with required adjustment has been shown in Figure 13.4.

The conversion process displayed in Figure 13.4 can be described as follows, using a short-cut calculation:

Accrual-Basis Net Income

Deduct Increase in Accounts Receivable (or Add Decrease in Accounts Receivable)
Deduct Increase in Merchandise Inventory (or Add Decrease in Merchandise Inventory)
Deduct Increase in Prepaid Expenses (or Add Decrease in Prepaid Expenses)
Add Increase in Accounts Payable (Or Deduct Decrease in Accounts Payable)
Add Increase in Accrued Expenses (or Deduct Decrease in Accrued Expenses)
Add Depreciation and Amortization Expenses for the year

↓

Cash-Basis Net Income

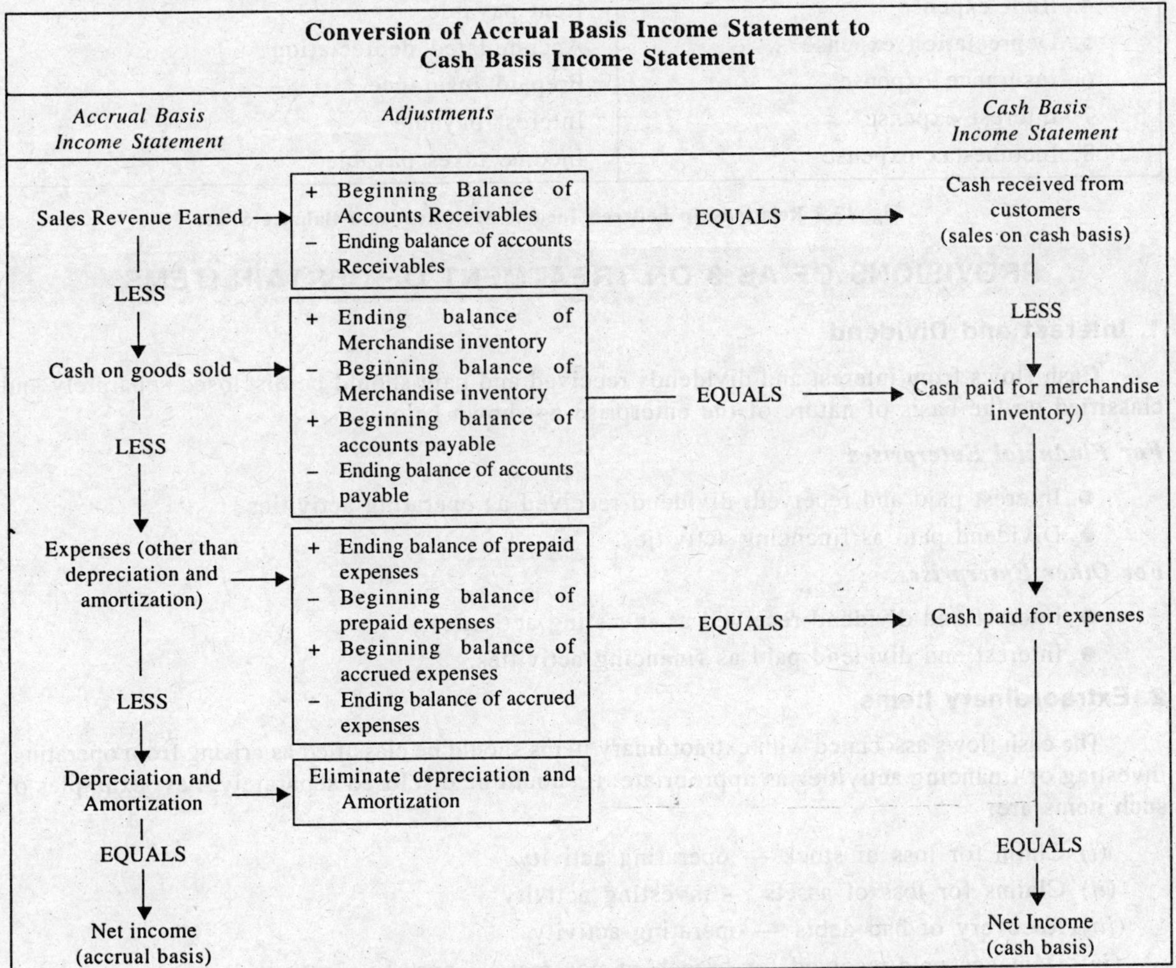

Fig. 13.4 Relationship of Accrual Basis and Cash Basis of Accounting

While making conversion, one should know the relationship between income statement accounts and balance sheet changes. Each individual item on the income statement should be viewed as it relates to a balance sheet account. On the accrual basis of accounting, the explanation for the difference between the amount of sales revenue and the receipts from those sales is found in the changes in accounts receivable and debtors account. Similarly, the difference between the amount of an expense and the amount of payments for that expense is found in the changes of its associated asset or liability, such as prepaid rent or rent payable. If there is no associated balance sheet account for an item on the income statement, it is presumed that the amount shown on the income statement resulted in a cash flow exactly equal to that revenue or expense. Figure 13.5 shows relationship between some income statement accounts and balance sheet accounts.

Financial Statement Relationship

Income Statement Accounts	*Related to Balance Sheet Accounts*
1. Sales	Debtors
2. Cost of goods sold	(Inventory) (Creditors)
3. Salaries expenses	Salaries payable
4. Rent expense	Rent payable
5. Depreciation expense	Accumulated depreciation
6. Insurance expense	Prepaid insurance
7. Interest expense	Interest payable
8. Income-tax expense	Income taxes payable

Fig. 13.5 Relationship between Income Statement and Balance Sheet

PROVISIONS OF AS 3 ON TREATMENT OF CERTAIN ITEMS

1. Interest and Dividend

Cash flows from interest and dividends received and paid should be disclosed separately and classified on the basis of nature of the enterprise as shown below:

For Financial Enterprises

- Interest paid and received, dividend received as operating activities
- Dividend paid as financing activities.

For Other Enterprises

- Interest and dividend received as investing activities
- Interest and dividend paid as financing activities.

2. Extraordinary Items

The cash flows associated with extraordinary items should be classified as arising from operating, investing or financing activities as appropriate. It should be disclosed separately. Few examples of such items are:

(*i*) Claim for loss of stock — operating activity
(*ii*) Claims for loss of assets — investing activity
(*iii*) Recovery of bad debts — operating activity
(*iv*) Damages paid/received for breach of contract — operating activity

(*v*) Winnings from lotteries — investing activity

(*vi*) Cost of legal action to protect property title — investing activity

3. Taxes on Income

Cash flows arising from taxes on income should be separately disclosed and should be classified as cash flows from operating activities unless they can be specifically identified with financing and investing activities.

For instance:

(*i*) Provision for taxation for the current year — non-cash change under operating activity

(*ii*) Tax paid — operating cash outflow

(*iii*) Income tax refund — cash inflow from operating activity

(*iv*) Capital gains tax — cash outflow from investing activity

(*v*) Corporate dividend tax — cash outflow from financing activity.

4. Foreign Currency Cashflows

Foreign currency cashflows should be converted at the exchange rate of the date of cash flow. Exchange gain/loss on cash and cash equivalents held in foreign currency will be reported as part of reconciliation of change in cash and cash equivalents for the period and, hence, not reported in cash flow statement.

5. Non-cash Transactions

Investing and financing transactions that do not require the use of cash or cash equivalents are not shown in the cash flow statement. Examples of such non-cash transactions are:

(*i*) Issue of shares or debentures for a consideration other than cash, i.e., against building, machinery etc.

(*ii*) Conversion of debentures into equity shares.

(*iii*) Purchase of business by issue of shares.

AS 3 (Revised) recommends that such transactions may be disclosed under footnote to cash-flow statement.

6. Investments in Subsidiaries, Associates and Joint Ventures

Acquisition of interest in any subsidiary, associates or in any joint venture is treated as "Investing Activity." Similarly, sale or disposal of such interest and receipt of interest or dividends on such investments is treated as "Investing Activity."

Illustration 3: (Classification of Cashflows)

Giving reason, classify the following into cashflows from:

1. Operating Activities,
2. Investing Activities, and
3. Financing Activities;

(*i*) Cash sales of goods-in-trade;

(*ii*) Cash paid to suppliers of raw materials;

(*iii*) Cash payments of salaries and wages to employees;

(*iv*) Cash payments to acquire a fixed asset, say, machinery;

(*v*) Cash proceeds from issuing shares at a premium;
(*vi*) Payment of dividends;
(*vii*) Interest received on investment;
(*viii*) Interest paid on debentures;
(*ix*) Payment of income tax; and
(*x*) Cash repayment of a long-term loan.

Solution:

1. Cash Flows from Operating Activities

(*i*) Cash sales of goods-in-trade: Normal business activity of selling inventories or goods-in-trade (cash inflow).

(*ii*) Cash paid to suppliers of raw materials: Routine payments for purchasing the goods (cash outflow).

(*iii*) Cash payments of salaries and wages: Cash payments to staff for their services in the office (cash outflow).

(*ix*) Payment of income tax: Payment of tax on business income (cash outflow).

2. Cash Flows from Investing Activities

(*iv*) Cash payment to acquire a fixed asset, say, machinery: Purchase of long-term asset (cash outflow).

(*vii*) Interest received on investment: It is an income on investments (cash inflow).

3. Financing Activities

(*v*) Cash proceeds from issuing shares at premium: Issue of share capital along with the premium (cash inflow).

(*vi*) Payment of dividends: It is related to issue of share capital, a financing activity (cash outflow).

(*viii*) Interest paid on debenture: Payment associated with loan (or borrowed) capital (cash outflow).

(*x*) Cash repayment of a long-term loan : Redemption of loan or borrowed capital (cash outflow).

Illustration 4: (Cash Flows from Operating Activities)

The net income reported on the income statement for the year was Rs. 1,10,000 and depreciation of fixed assets for the year was Rs. 44,000. The balances of the current asset and current liability accounts at the beginning and end of the year are as follows:

	End of the Year (Rs.)	*Beginning of the Year (Rs.)*
Cash	1,30,000	1,40,000
Debtors	2,00,000	1,80,000
Inventories	2,90,000	3,00,000
Prepaid Expenses	15,000	16,000
Accounts payable	1,02,000	1,16,000
Calculate cash from operating activities		

Solution:

Cash Flow from Operating Activities

		Rs.
Net income		1,10,000
Add: Depreciation		44,000
Operating profit before working capital changes		1,54,000
Add: Decrease in Inventories	10,000	
Decrease in prepaid expenses	1,000	11,000
		1,65,000
Deduct: Increase in Debtors	20,000	
Decrease is Accounts Payable	14,000	34,000
Net cash flow from operating activities		1,31,000

Illustration 5: (Cash flow from operation-indirect Method

From the following, calculate cash from operation by Indirect Method:

Profit and Loss Account

For the year ended 31st March, 2008

		Rs.		Rs.
To Opening stock		2,00,000	By Sales	45,00,000
To Purchases		36,40,000	By Closing stock	2,40,000
To Wages	2,25,000			
Add: Outstanding	25,000	2,50,000		
To Manufacturing expenses		75,000		
To Gross profit c/d		5,75,000		
		47,40,000		47,40,000
To Salaries	1,37,500		By Gross profit b/d	5,75,000
Add: Outstanding	62,500	2,00,000	By Rent received	37,500
To Insurance	30,000		By Commission accrued	17,500
Less: Prepaid	7,500	22,500	By Net loss	55,000
To Office expenses		1,17,500		
To Selling expenses		1,45,000		
To Depreciation		1,25,000		
To Share issue expenses w/o		75,000		
		6,85,000		6,85,000

Solution:

Calculation of Cash from Operating Activities

"Indirect Method"

		Rs.
Net loss as per Profit and Loss A/c (before tax and extraordinary item)		(55,000)
Adjustments for Non-cash charges and Non-operating items		
Add: Depreciation	1,25,000	
Add: Share issue expenses w/o	75,000	2,00,000
		1,45,000

Less: Rent received (Non-operating)		(37,500)
Operating profit before Working Capital Changes		1,07,500
Adjustment for current assets/liabilities:		
Add: Increase in Current liabilities:		
Wages o/s	25,000	
Salaries	62,500	87,500
		1,95,000
Less: Increase in Current Assets:		
Stock	40,000	
Prepaid insurance	7,500	
Accrued commission	17,500	(65,000)
Net cash from operating activities		1,30,000

Illustration 6: (Cashflows from Operating Activities)

X Ltd. has the following balances on 01-01-2007

	Rs.	*Rs.*
Fixed assets	15,00,000	
Less: Depreciation	(5,00,000)	10,00,000
Bank		87,500
Other current assets		6,25,500
Current liabilities		2,50,000

Next year's estimate are:

(*i*) The company will acquire fixed assets costing Rs. 2,50,000 after selling one machine for Rs. 70,000, costing Rs. 1,50,000 on which depreciation provided will amount to Rs. 90,000.

(*ii*) The net profits will be Rs. 1,75,000 after providing for a depreciation of Rs. 1,50,000.

(*iii*) Current assets and current liabilities (other than bank balance) at 31-12-2007 are estimated to be Rs. 7,50,000 and Rs. 4,00,000 respectively.

At the end of the accounting year, the company deposits all the cash into the bank. Calculate the cash flows from operations and investing activities for the year 2007.

Solution:

Cashflows from Operating Activities

	Rs.	*Rs.*
Net profit after depreciation	1,75,000	
Add: Depreciation provided	1,50,000	
Less: Profit on sale of machinery	(10,000)	
Operating profit before working capital changes	3,15,000	
Less: Increase in assets	(1,25,000)	
Add: Increase in current liabilities	1,50,000	
Net cash from operating activities		3,40,000

Cashflows from Investing Activities

Sale of machine	70,000	
Purchase of machine	(2,50,000)	
Net cash used in investing activities		(1,80,000)

Working Note:

Calculation of profit on sale of machinery: 70,000 – (1,50,000 – 90,000) = Rs. 10,000.

Illustration 7: (Cash from operation and extraordinary activities)

From the following information calculate cash from operations:

Profit and Loss Account
for the year ended 31st March 2008

	Rs.		*Rs.*
To Opening stock	1,50,000	By Sales	32,75,000
To Purchases	14,50,000	By Closing stock	3,25,000
To Wages	70,000		
To Gross profit c/d	19,30,000		
	36,00,000		36,00,000
To Operating expenses	11,10,000	By Gross profit b/d	19,30,000
To Interest on debentures	18,000	By Interest on investments	15,000
To Depreciation	1,20,000	By Dividend received	18,000
To Loss on sale of plant	40,000	By Profit on sale of land	20,000
To Discount on issue of shares	10,000	By Rent received	12,000
To Goodwill w/o	15,000	By Refunds of tax	8,000
To Provision for tax	30,000	By Insurance claims for loss of stock	1,25,000
To General Reserve	25,000		
To Proposed dividend	1,80,000		
To Interim dividend	70,000		
To Net profit	5,10,000		
	21,28,000		21,28,000

Additional Information:

	31-03-07 *Rs.*	31-03-08 *Rs.*
Stock	1,40,000	1,00,000
Debtors	25,000	1,00,000
Creditors	15,000	50,000
Provision for Tax	50,000	60,000
Prepaid expenses	18,000	20,000
Outstanding salaries	20,000	25,000
Accrued commission	15,000	30,000

Solution:

Cash Flow from Operating Activities

		Rs.	*Rs.*
	Net Profit before Tax and Extraordinary items (1)		6,82,000
	Adjustment for: Non-cash Charges and Non-operating items		
Add:	Depreciation	1,20,000	
	Goodwill	15,000	
	Discount on issue of shares	10,000	
	Loss on sale of plant	40,000	
	Interest on Debentures (2)	18,000	2,03,000
			8,85,000

Profit on Sale of Land (3)	20,000	
Interest Received (3)	15,000	
Dividend Received (3)	18,000	(53,000)
Operating profit before working Capital Changes		8,32,000
Adjustment for Working Capital:		
Add: Decrease in Current Assets and Increase in current liabilities:		
Stock	40,000	
Debtors	35,000	
O/s Salaries	5,000	(80,000)
		9,12,000
Less: Increase in current assets and decrease in current liabilities:		
Debtors	75,000	
Accrued Commission	15,000	
Prepaid Expenses	2,000	(92,000)
		8,20,000
Less: Tax Paid		(12,000)
Cash flow before Extraordinary items		8,08,000
Add: Cash from Extra ordinary items (Insurance claims for loss of Stock (4))		1,25,000
Net Cash Flow from Operations		9,33,000

Working Notes:

		Rs.
(1) Net Profit as per P and L A/c		5,10,000
Add: Tax and Appropriations:		
Provision for Tax	30,000	
Proposed Dividend	1,80,000	
Interim Dividend	70,000	
General Reserve	25,000	3,05,000
		8,15,000
Less: Tax Refund and Extraordinary Receipts (8,000 + 1,25,000)		1,33,000
		6,82,000

(2) Interest on Debentures to be adjusted against Financing Activities.

(3) Interest Received, Dividend Received. Profit on sale of Fixed Assets are covered by Investing Activities.

(4) Insurance claims for loss of Stock is treated under Operating Activities while loss of assets under "Investing Activities."

Illustration 8: (Indirect Method)

The following data are provided for Zia Ltd.:

Income Statement Data for 2007

	Rs.
Revenues	84,000
Cost of goods sold	(48,000)
Depreciation expense	(4,000)
Interest expense	(6,000)
Other expenses	(22,000)
Net income	4,000

Comparative Balance Sheets Data

	2007 Rs.	2006 Rs.
Current Assets:		
Cash	20,000	16,000
Debtors (net)	12,000	7,000
Stock in hand	16,000	14,000
Non-current Assets:		
Plant and Machinery	24,000	20,000
Less: Accumulated depreciation	(8,000)	(4,000)
Total assets	64,000	53,000
Liabilities:		
Creditor	12,000	14,000
Non-current note payable	20,000	20,000
Less: Discount on note	(1,600)	(2,000)
	30,400	32,000
Owner's Equity:		
Equity Share capital	24,000	14,000
Retained earnings	9,600	7,000
	33,600	21,000

Required: Prepare statement of cashflows using the indirect method. [AS 3 (Revised)]

Solution:

Zia Ltd.
Cashflow Statement for the year ended 31st December 2007
[AS 3 (Revised) (Indirect Method)

	Rs.	Rs.
(A) Cashflows from operating activities		
Net income before tax	4,000	
Adjustments for:		
Depreciation	4,000	
Aamortization of discount on note payable	400	
Interest expense	6,000	
Operating profit before working capital changes	14,400	
Increase in Debtors	(5,000)	
Increase in Inventories	(2,000)	
Decrease in Creditors	(2,000)	
Net cash provided by operating activities		5,400
(B) Cashflows from investing activities		
Purchase of Plant and machinery	(4,000)	
Net cash used in investing activities		(4,000)
(C) Cashflows from Financing activities		
Issue of share capital	10,000	
Interest paid	(6,000)	
Dividends paid	(1,400)	
Net cash from financing activities		2,600
Net cash from financing activities		
Net increase in cash and cash equivalents (A + B + C)		4,000
Cash and cash equivalents at the beginning of the period		16,000
Cash and cash equivalents at the end of the period		20,000

Note:

Dividends paid have been calculated as under:

	Rs.
Retained earnings at the beginning	7,000
Add: Net income	4,000
	11,000
Less: Retained earnings at the end	9,600
Dividend paid	1,400

Illustration 9: (Direct and Indirect Methods)

From the following particulars, prepare Cash Flow Statement for the year ended 31st March, 2005 using.

(a) Direct Method
(b) Indirect Method

(a) Income Statement of M/s Ali Pvt. Ltd.

For the year ended 31st March 2005

		Rs.
Turnover		12,80,000
Less Cost of Goods Sold		8,00,000
		4,80,000
Add Other Receipts:		
Insurance Claims for loss of Stock due to fire		20,000
		5,00,000
Less Operating Expenses	3,16,000	
Interest on Debentures	6,000	
Depreciation	84,000	
Discount on Debentures w/o	400	4,06,400
Profit before Tax		93,600
Less Provision for Tax		36,800
Profit after Tax		56,800

(b) The Assets and Liabilities as on 31.3.2004 and 31st March 2005 were as under:

	31-03-2004 *Rs.*	31-03-2005 *Rs.*
Stock	72,000	88,000
Debtors	16,000	15,200
Bills Receivable	12,000	22,000
Cash and Bank balance	44,800	99,200
Creditors	31,200	38,000
Bills Payable	8,000	6,000
O/s Expenses	12,400	17,600

(c) Additional Information:

(*i*) Fully paid Equity shares of the face value of Rs. 80,000 were allotted at a premium of @20%.

(*ii*) Fixed assets were acquired for Rs. 60,000 and the payment was made in 6% convertible debentures at par.

(*iii*) Income Tax paid during the year amounted to Rs. 38,000.

(*iv*) Company paid a dividend and corporate dividend tax thereon for the year ended 31st March 2004 amounting to Rs. 44,000.

(v) 9% Debentures for Rs. 1,20,000 were redeemed at a premium of 2%.

Solution: (a) Cashflow Statement (Direct Method)

	Rs.	*Rs.*
Cashflow from Operating Activities		
(*a*) Operating cash receipts:		
Cash from customers (1)	12,70,800	
(*b*) Operating cash payments (2)	11,22,000	
Cash Flow from operations (a– b)	1,48,800	
Income tax paid	(38,000)	
	1,10,800	
Cashflow from Extraordinary items:		
Add: Claims received	20,000	
Net cashflow from operating activities:		1,30,800
Cashflow from Financing Activities:		
Issue of shares at premium (3)	96,000	
● Redemption of debentures	(1,22,400)	
● Interest on debentures	(6,000)	
● Dividend and corporate dividend tax	(44,000)	
Net cash used in financing activities		(76,400)
Net increase in cash and cash equivalents		54,400
Cash and cash equivalents in the beginning		44,800
Cash and cash equivalents at the end		99,200

> Financing and investing activities not affecting Cashflow — Issue of debentures against acquisition of land Rs. 60,000

Working Notes:

(1) Receivables A/c (Debtors + Bills receivables)

	Rs.		*Rs.*
To Balance b/d	28,000	By Cash received (B.F.)	12,70,800
To Sales (credit)	12,80,000	By Balance c/d	37,200
	13,08,000		13,08,000

(2) Payables A/c (Creditors + Bills Payable)

	Rs.		*Rs.*
To Cash paid	8,11,200	By Balance b/d	39,200
To Balance c/d	44,000	By Purchases*	8,16,000
	8,55,200		8,55,200

Operating Expenses A/c

	Rs.		*Rs.*
To Cash paid (Bal. figure)	3,10,800	By Balance b/d	12,400
To Balance c/d	17,600	By Profit and Loss a/c (Income statement)	3,16,000
	3,28,400		3,28,400

*Purchases = Closing Stock + Cost of Goods sold – Opening stock
Purchases = 88,000 + 8,00,000 – 72,000 = 8,16,000

Thus operating cash payment =	8,11,200	(To creditors)
and operating Expenses paid	3,10,800	
	11,22,000	

	Rs.
Face Value of Shares issued	80,000
Add Premium @ 20%	16,000
	96,000

(3) Cashflow Statement as per AS 3 (Revised)

(Indirect Method)

	Rs.	Rs.
I. Cashflow from Operating Activities:		
Net Profit before Tax and Extraordinary Item	73,600	
Adjustment for Non-cash and Non-operating items		
Depreciation	84,000	
Discount on Issue of Debentures	400	
Interest on Debentures	6,000	
Operating profit before Working Capital Changes	1,64,000	
Adjustment for current items		
– Increase in Stock	(16,000)	
– Increase in Bills Receivable	(10,000)	
– Decrease in Bills Payable	(2,000)	
+ Decrease in Debtors	800	
+ Increase in creditors	6,800	
+ Increase in o/s Expenses	5,200	
Cash generated from operation	1,48,800	
Less: Income Tax paid	38,000	
Cash flow from operation before Extraordinary, item	1,10,800	
Add: Insurance Claim for loss of stock	20,000	
Net Cash generated from operation		1,30,800
II. Cashflow from Investing Activities	—	—
III. Cashflow from Financing Activities		
Issue of shares at premium	96,000	
Redemption of Debentures	(1,22,400)	
Interest on Debentures	(6,000)	
Dividend and corporate dividend Tax	(44,000)	
Net cash used in Financing Activities		(76,400)
Net Increase in Cash and Cash Equivalents		54,400
Cash and Cash Equivalents in the beginning		44,800
Cash and Cash Equivalents at the end		99,200

Illustration 10: (Cashflow Statement)

From the following details relating to the Accounts of Grow More Ltd. prepare Cashflow Statement:

	31-03-2007 (Rs.)	31-03-2006 Rs.)
Liabilities		
Share Capital	10,00,000	8,00,000
Reserve	2,00,000	1,50,000
Profit and Loss Account	1,00,000	60,000
Debentures	2,00,000	—
Provision for taxation	1,00,000	70,000
Proposed dividend	2,00,000	1,00,000
Sundry Creditors	7,00,000	8,20,000
	25,00,000	20,00,000
Assets		
Plant and Machinery	7,00,000	5,00,000
Land and Building	6,00,000	4,00,000
Investments	1,00,000	—
Sundry Debtors	5,00,000	7,00,000
Stock	4,00,000	2,00,000
Cash on hand/bank	2,00,000	2,00,000
	25,00,000	20,00,000

(*i*) Depreciation @ 25% was charged on the opening value of Plant and Machinery.

(*ii*) During the year one old machine costing 50,000 (WDV 20,000) was sold for Rs. 35,000.

(*iii*) Rs. 50,000 was paid towards income tax during the year.

(*iv*) Building under construction was not subject to any depreciation.

Prepare Cashflow Statement.

Solution:

Grow More Ltd.

Cashflow Statement

For The Year Ended 31 March, 2007

	Rs.	*Rs.*
(A) Cashflows from Operating Activities		
Net Profit before Tax and Extraordinary items*	3,20,000	
Adjustment for:		
Transfer to General Reserve	50,000	
Depreciation	1,25,000	
Profit on sale of Plant and Machinery	(15,000)	
Operating Profit before Working Capital changes	4,80,000	
Increase in Stock	(2,00,000)	
Decrease in debtors	2,00,000	
Decrease in creditors	(1,20,000)	
Cash generated from operations	3,60,000	
Income tax paid	(50,000)	
Net cash provided by operating activities		3,10,000
(B) Cashflows from Investing Activities		
Purchase of fixed assets	(3,45,000)	
Expenses on building	(2,00,000)	
Increase in investments	(1,00,000)	
Sale of old machine	35,000	
Net cash used in investing activities		(6,10,000)

(C) Cashflows from Financing Activities		
Proceeds from issue of shares	2,00,000	
Proceeds from issue of debentures	2,00,000	
Dividend paid	(1,00,000)	
Net cash provided by financing activities		3,00,000
Net increase in cash and cash equivalents (A+B+C)		Nil
Cash and Cash equivalents at the beginning of the year		2,00,000
Cash and Cash equivalents at the end of the year		2,00,000

Working Notes:

Provision for Taxation Account

	Rs.		*Rs.*
Bank (Paid)	50,000	Balance b/d	70,000
Balance c/d	1,00,000	Profit and Loss Account (Balancing figure)	80,000
	1,50,000		1,50,000

* Rs. 40,000 + Rs. 2,00,000 (Provision for dividend) + Rs. 80,000 (Provision for Tax)

Plant and Machinery Account

	Rs.		*Rs.*
Balance b/d	5,00,000	Depreciation	1,25,000
Bank (Balancing figure)	3,45,000	Bank (Sale)	20,000
		Balance c/d	7,00,000
	8,45,000		8,45,000

Illustration 11: (Loss on Machinery discarded)

Following are the Balance Sheets of Suhani Ltd. as on 31st March 2004 and 2005:

	31-03-05 *Rs.*	31-03-04 *Rs.*
Liabiliies		
Share Capital	4,00,000	3,00,000
General Reserve	1,00,000	80,000
Profit & Loss A/c	50,000	30,000
Debentures	1,00,000	1,50,000
Provision for Taxation	40,000	50,000
Proposed Dividend	40,000	30,000
Trade Creditors	70,000	90,000
	8,00,000	7,30,000
Assets		
Goodwill	90,000	1,00,000
Plant and Machinery	4,29,250	2,98,000
Investments	60,000	1,00,000
S. Debtors	1,10,000	1,60,000
Stock	80,000	50,000
Prepaid Expenses	5,750	4,000
Cash and Bank balance	20,000	10,000
Discount on Debentures	5,000	8,000
	8,00,000	7,30,000

Additional Information:

(*i*) Depreciation on Plant and Machinery has been charted @ 15%

(*ii*) A machine costing Rs. 10,000 (W.D.V. Rs. 3,000) has been discarded. An old machine costing Rs. 50,000 (W.D.V. Rs. 20,000) has been sold for Rs. 35,000.

(*iii*) A profit of Rs. 10.000 has been earned by sale of investments.

(*iv*) Debentures have been redeemed at 5% premium.

(*v*) Rs. 45,000 income tax has been paid and adjusted against provision for taxation.

Prepare Statement of Changes in Financial Position — cash basis.

Solution:

Statement of Changes in Financial Position (Cash Basis)

For The Year Ended 31st March 2005

	Rs.	*Rs.*
Cashflow from operating Activities		
Net Profit before tax and extraordinary items:	1,75,000	
Adjustment for Non-cash and Non-operating items:		
Depreciation	75,750	
Goodwill w/o	10,000	
Loss on machine discarded	3,000	
Profit on sale of Investment	(10,000)	
Profit on sale of Machine	(15,000)	
Loss (premium) on Redemption of Debentures	2,500	
Discount on Issue of Debentures	3,000	
Cash generated from operation before Tax	1,84,250	
Less: Tax paid	45,000	
Cash generated from Operating activities before Working Capital changes	1,39,250	
Adjustments for Working Capital		
Decrease in Debtors	50,000	
Increase in Stock	(30,000)	
Increase in Prepaid Expenses	(1.750)	
Decrease in Trade creditors	(20.000)	
Net cashflow from Operating Activities		1,37,500
II Cashflow from Investing Activities:		
Sale of Investments	50,000	
Sale of Machinery	35,000	
Purchase of Machinery	(2,30,000)	
Net cash used in Investing Activities		(1,45,000)
III Cashflow from Financing Activities:		
Issue of Shares	1,00,000	
Redemption of Debentures	(52,500)	
Payment of Dividend	(30,000)	
Net Cash generated from Financing Activities		17,500
Net Increase in Cash and Cash Equivalents		10,000
Cash and Cash equivalents at the beginning		10,000
Cash and Cash equivalents at the end		20,000

Working Notes:

(1) Profit and Loss A/c (Adjusted)

	Rs.		Rs.
To Provision for tax	35,000	By Balance b/d	30,000
To General Reserve	20,000	By Net Profit before tax and	1,15,000
To Proposed dividend	40,000	Extraordinary items	
To Balance c/d	50,000		
	1,45,000		1,45,000

(2) Plant and Machinery A/c

	Rs.		Rs.
To Balance b/d	2,98,000	By Depreciation*	75,750
To Profit on sale (Tr. to P and L A/c)	15,000	By Bank (sale)	35,000
To Bank (Purchased)	2,30,000	By Loss on sale (Tr. to P and L A/c)	3,000
(Bal. figure)		By Balance c/d	4.29,250
	5,43,000		5,43,000

		Rs.
	*W.D.V. as on 1.4.2004	2,98,000
Less:	W.D.V. of machine sold (20,000 + 3.000)	23,000
		2,75,000
	* Depreciation @ 15%	41,250
	W.D.V. after Depreciation	2,33,750
	Cost of Machinery acquired	2,30,000**
	*Depreciation on Machinery Purchased	34,500
	W.D.V.	1,95,500
	*Thus total Depreciation charged Rs. (41.250 + 34.500)	75,750

** Rs. (4,29.250 – 2.33750) = $\left(1{,}95{,}500 \times \frac{100}{85}\right)$ = Rs. 2,30,000

(3) Provision for Tax A/c

	Rs.		Rs.
To Bank	45,000	By Balance b/d	50,000
To Balance c/d	40,000	By P and L A/c (B.F.)	35,000
	85,000		85,000

Illustration 12 (Cashflow Statement — Indirect Method)

Presented below is the comparative balance sheets for Jyoti Ltd. at 31 March:

	2006 Rs.	2005 Rs.
Cash	40,000	57,000
Accounts receivable	77,000	64,000
Inventory	1,32,000	1,40,000
Prepaid expenses	12,140	16,540
Land	1,25,000	1,50,000
Equipment	2,00,000	1,75,000

Accumulated Depreciation-Equipment	(60,000)	(42,000)
Building	2,50,000	2,50,000
Accumulated depreciation — Building	(75,000)	(50,000)
	7,01,140	7,60,540
Accounts payable	33,000	45,000
Bonds payable	2,35,000	2,65,000
Equity share capital (Rs. 10 shares)	2,80,000	2,50,000
Retained earnings	1,53,140	2,00,540
	7,01,140	7,60,540

Additional information:

(*i*) Operating expenses include depreciation expense of Rs. 70,000 and amortization of prepaid expenses of Rs. 4,400.

(*ii*) Land was sold for cash at book value.

(*iii*) Cash dividends of Rs. 74,290 were paid.

(*iv*) Net income for 2006 was Rs. 26,890.

(*v*) Equipment was purchased for Rs. 65,000 cash. In addition equipment costing Rs. 40,000 with a book value of Rs. 13,000 was sold for Rs. 15,000 cash.

(*vi*) Bonds were redeemed at face value by issuing 3,000 equity shares of Rs. 10 at par.

Instructions:

Prepare a statement of cashflows for 2006 using the indirect method [AS 3 (Revised)]

Solution:

Jyoti Ltd.
Cashflows Statement for the Year Ended 31 December 2006
[AS 3 (Revised)] (Indirect Method)

	Rs.	*Rs.*
(A) Cashflows from Operating Activities		
Net Income	26,890	
Adjustments for:		
Depreciation	70,000	
Amortization of prepaid expenses	4,400	
Gain on sale of equipment	(2,000)	
Operating profit before working capital changes	99,290	
Increase in Accounts Receivable	(13,000)	
Decrease in Inventories	8,000	
Decrease in Accounts Payable	(12,000)	
Net cash from operating activities		82,290
(B) Cashflows from Investing Activities		
Sale of Land	25,000	
Sale of Equipment	15,000	
Purchase of Equipment	(65,000)	
Net cash used in investing activities		(25,000)
(C) Cashflows from Financing Activities		
Dividends Paid	(74,290)	
Net cash used in financing activities		(74,290)
Net decrease in cash and cash equivalents (A + B + C)		(17,000)
Cash and cash equivalents at the beginning of the period		57,000
Cash and cash equivalents at the end of the period		40,000

Significant Non-cash Transaction
Redemption of Bonds in exchange for Equity Share Capital Rs. 30,000

Working Note:

Equity Share Capital Account

	Rs.		*Rs.*
Balance c/d	2,80,000	Balance b/d	2,50,000
		Bonds payable account	30,000
	2,80,000		2,80,000

Bonds Payable Accounts

	Rs.		*Rs.*
Equity Share Capital Account	2,35,000	Balance b/d	2,65,000
Balance c/d	30,000		
	2,65,000		2,65,000

SIGNIFICANCE OF CASHFLOW STATEMENT

Cash basis funds flow statements are important for a number of reasons:

(1) First, by focusing on cashflows, it explains the nature of the financial events which have affected the cash position. This statement explains the reason for the difference between opening and closing cash balance.

(2) The statement is important for financial planning purposes. For example, budgeted cash statements are a crucial element in the process of budget plans. These surpluses and shortfalls are expressed sequentially over the planning period and require management to deal with the forecasted cash surplus or deficit, the former involving a short-term investment of surplus cash, the latter a, short-term borrowing arrangement.

(3) This statement brings into sharp focus the enterprise's earning capacity with its spending and operating activity. Accounting principles restrict the income statement to matching periodic revenues with the cost of earning those revenues. Statement of changes in cash is not restricted in this way; hence, it provides an extended view of the financial inflows and outflows by including both capital and revenue flows.

(4) Cash flow statement provides an insight into the critical areas of financial management by identifying two important classes of cashflows, namely, operating cashflows and financing cashflows. This distinction draws attention to the net cashflows from operations and the net financing cashflows. The net operating cashflows classify the capability of the firm to support dividend payments to shareholders. It is these net cashflows which are of critical importance to investors and shareholders in predicting the amount of cash likely to be distributed in the future in the form of liquidation distributions or repayment of principal and in the evaluation of risk.

(5) The significance of cash flow statement lies in the increased complexity of business activity. This complexity results in a greater disparity between the time when income and expense items are reported and the time when the related cash flows occur. It may also result in a greater variability of cashflows.

ICAI's AS 3 Cashflow Statement contains the following explanations on the utility of cashflow statement:

1. Information about the cashflows of an enterprise is useful in providing users of financial statements with a basis to assess the ability of the enterprise to generate cash and cash equivalents and the needs of the enterprise to utilise those cashflows. The economic

decisions that are taken by users require an evaluation of the ability of an enterprise to generate cash and cash equivalents and the timing and certainty of their generation.

2. Users of an enterprise's financial statements are interested in how the enterprise generates and uses cash and cash equivalents. This is the case regardless of the nature of the enterprise's activities and irrespective of whether cash can be viewed as the product of the enterprise, as may be the case with a financial enterprise. Enterprises need cash for essentially the same reasons, however different their principal revenue-producing activities might be. They need cash to conduct their operations, to pay their obligations, and to provide returns to their investors.
3. A cash flow statement, when used in conjunction with the other financial statements, provides information that enables users to evaluate the changes in net assets of an enterprise, its financial structure (including its liquidity and solvency) and its ability to affect the amounts and timing of cash flows in order to adapt to changing circumstances and opportunities. Cashflow information is useful in assessing the ability of the enterprise to generate cash and cash equivalents and enables users to develop models to assess and compare the present value of the future cashflows of different enterprises. It also enhances the comparability of the reporting of operating performance by different enterprises because it eliminates the effects of using different accounting treatments for the same transactions and events.
4. Historical cashflow information is often used as an indicator of the amount, timing and certainty of future cashflows. It is also useful in checking the accuracy of past assessments of future cashflows and in examining the relationship between profitability and net cash flow and the impact of changing prices.

Limitations of Cashflow Statement

Cash flow can be more precisely measured than can other concepts of funds because the valuation problem of cash are not as great as for other financial resources. However, movement of cash may be easily influenced. For example, payment of liabilities, may be temporarily delayed or marketable securities may be sold, increasing cashflow for a given period. This statement, since it does not cover non-cash items, is not useful in analysing changes in financial position of an enterprise. Cash and changes in cash are not adequate to measure change in financial position. For instance, an enterprise may possess very satisfactory financial (cash) position during a particular month. But if the firm has to pay creditors next month, or make payments for the plant purchased in the near future the cash position of the firm will be adversely affected. In this way statement of changes in financial position measured through cash only has drawbacks and does not indicate accurately the changes in financial position. The statement has utility for making short-term financial planning but for long-term planning this statement would not be useful. Because of the limited usefulness of statement of changes in cash, the preparation of statement of changes in working capital (popularly known as funds flow statement) has been suggested.

STATEMENT OF CHANGES IN TOTAL FINANCIAL RESOURCES

One of the limitations of working capital concept of funds is that it omits a few major financial and investment transactions. Important information regarding changes in the resources of the firm and in the financial structure of the firm are omitted. Such items do not, of course, affect net working capital, but if included, would certainly provide quantitative and analytical information for decision-making. For example, issuing equity shares, or debentures for purchase of buildings or plant and machinery has no effect on working capital, but is a significant financial transactions that should be disclosed.

Under the total financial resources concept of funds, the statement is not limited to transactions affecting working capital but would also be extended to cover all significant financial transactions that would otherwise be omitted under the other concepts of funds. That is, the total financial resources concept requires that all material financial transactions be disclosed in the statement of changes in financial position. Transactions that technically do not increase or decrease funds (regardless of the concept of funds employed) but that represent significant financing and investing activities entered into by an entity must also be disclosed within the statement. Disclosure of a significant transaction that does not increase or decrease funds is made by showing one side of the transaction as a source of funds and the other side of the transaction as a corresponding use of funds. Transactions that affect financial position but do not increase or decrease funds include the following:

(*a*) Purchase of non-current assets, e.g., property and equipment by issuing share capital or debenture or long-term debt.

(*b*) Reduction of a long-term liability by the issuance of share capital or the incurrence of another long-term liability or a reduction in a non-current asset.

The above statement would be more useful in summarising the resources from which the funds have been obtained and the uses to which they have been put. The statement can analyse sources and uses in two categories of items (*i*) those which affect working capital (*ii*) those which do not affect working capital. Such a statement is, certainly, more informative and, therefore, potentially more useful in disclosing the firm's financing and investing activities during the two balance sheet dates. The fact that items which do not affect working capital are separately dealt with implies that it retains all the advantages of the working capital concept and, in addition, has the additional advantage of providing a complete picture of the total financial and investment activities of the firm.

As stated earlier, this statement includes significant transactions involving flows of non-cash resources even if cash itself is not affected. To recognize changes in all resources, these transactions are reported as both sources and uses of cash.

The following illustration explains it:

1. Purchased a Rs. 5,00,000 building for Rs. 1,00,000 cash and Rs. 4,00,000 mortgage note.

   Source of Cash:

Issuing Mortgage note	Rs. 4,00,000

   Use of Cash:

Purchase of Building	Rs. 5,00,000

2. Issued a promissory note to acquire land at a cost of Rs. 50,000

   Source of Cash:

Issuing promissory note	Rs. 50,000

   Use of Cash:

Purchase of land	Rs. 50,000

3. Issued 10,000 shares in exchange for 1,000 convertible debentures with Rs. 10,000 book value and Rs. 1,00,000 face value.

   Source of Cash

   Issue of Shares Rs. 1,00,000

Use of Cash
Retirement of debentures Rs. 1,00,000

It can be noticed that each side of the transaction has a significant impact on the company's financial position. By applying the total resources concept, the statement of changes in financial position reflect more fully these significant events.

Limitations of Statement of Changes in Financial Position on Total Resources Basis

The statement of changes in financial position, on total resources basis, has the following limitations:

Firstly, the concept of financial resources is vague and illdefined. The separate items included in the classification of sources and applications of funds do not necessarily represent increases and decreases of resources. Therefore, there is no direct disclosure of the extent to which the total resources of the firm have changed during the period.

Secondly, acquisitions of property in exchange for shares cannot be measured with the same degree of reliability as assets acquired for cash. Therefore, the summation of gross additions to plant and equipment for example, may result in misleading interpretations of the amount of resources acquired.

THEORY QUESTIONS

1. Why is cashflow statement a useful statement?
2. Identify the three major types of activities classified on a cash flow statement and give examples of cash inflow and cash outflow in each classification.
3. What limitations of funds flow statement are overcome by a cashflow statement.
4. What are the purposes of cashflow statement?
5. Discuss the procedures in preparing a cashflow statement.
6. What are the two methods of determining cashflows from operations? Generally which of these methods is preferable?
7. "A cash flow statement is required to explain changes in cash account balances between balance sheet dates." Explain this statement.
8. List the common sources and uses of cash in each activity area — operating, investing and financing.
9. Discuss the guidelines as contained in AS 3 on cash flow statement.
10. Discuss the main features of AS 3. What changes have been made in this standard?
11. Distinguish between 'Cash' and 'Cash equivalent.'
12. Distinguish among cashflows from operating, investing and financing activities. Provide examples of each type of activity as per AS 3. Show a proforma statement of cashflows.
13. Discuss the Direct Method and Indirect Method of preparing cashflow statement.

EXERCISES AND PROBLEMS

1. The following is the financial position of Aruna Limited:

	2004 Rs.	2005 Rs.
Liabilities:		
Equity Share Capital	4,50,000	5,00,000
General Reserve	40,000	70,000
Profit & Loss Account	30,000	48,000
Proposed dividend	42,000	50,000
Creditors	55,000	83,000
Bills payable	20,000	16,000
Provision for Taxation	40,000	50,000
	6,77,000	8,17,000
Assets:		
Goodwill	1,15,000	90,000
Land and Building	2,00,000	1,70,000
Plant	80,000	2,00,000
Debtors	1,60,000	2,00,000
Stock	77,000	1,09,000
Bills receivable	20,000	30,000
Cash	25,000	18,000
	6,77,000	8,17,000

Additional Information:

(*i*) Depreciation of Rs. 15,000 and Rs. 25,000 have been charged on Plant, and Land and Building respectively.

(*ii*) An interim dividend of Rs. 20,000 has been paid in 2005.

(*iii*) An income-tax of Rs. 35,000 was paid during 2005.

Calculate cash from operating activities as per AS 3 (Revised).

(***Ans.:*** Rs. 1,35,000)

2. From the following particulars, calculate cash from operating activities by applying:

(*a*) Direct Method

(*b*) Indirect Method

Profit and Loss A/c

for the year ended 31st March, 2005

	Rs.		Rs.
To Opening stock	60,000	By Sales	6,00,000
To Purchases	3,00,000	By Stock (Closing)	85,000
To Wages	75,000		
To Gross Profit c/d	2,50,000		
	6,85,000		6,85,000
To Salaries	50,000	By Gross profit b/d	2,50,000
To General expenses	15,000		
To Insurance	10,000		
To Depreciation	75,000		
To Provision for tax	30,000		
To Net profit	70,000		
	2,50,000		2,50,000

Additional Information:

	31-3-04	31-03-05
	Rs.	*Rs.*
Salaries o/s	5,000	7,500
Prepaid insurance	5,000	5,000
Debtors	50,000	70,000
Bills receivable	25,000	15,000
Creditors	35,000	25,000

Income tax paid during the year amounted to Rs. 25,000.

(*Ans.:* Rs. 97,500)

3. (Investing and Financing activities not affecting cash)

The Following are the Balance Sheets of Huda Ltd. as on 31st March, 2004 and 31st March, 2005.

Liabilities	31-03-04	31-03-05
	Rs.	*Rs.*
Share Capital	4,00,000	5,20,000
General Reserve	1,00,000	1,00,000
Profit & Loss Account	79,380	82,440
S. Creditors	79,000	82,270
Bills Payable	67,560	23,050
Bank Overdraft	1,19,020	—
Provision for Tax	80,000	1,00,000
	9,24,960	9,07,760
Assets		
Goodwill	—	40,000
Land & Building	2,97,000	2,88,500
Plant and Machinery	2,25,900	2,32,400
Stock	2,22,080	1,94,740
Advances	4,630	1,470
Debtors	1,70,350	1,45,250
Cash at Bank	5,000	5,400
	9,24,960	9,07,760

Additional Information:

(*i*) During the year ended 31st March, 2005, an additional dividend of Rs. 52,000 was paid.

(*ii*) The assets of another company were purchased for Rs. 1,20,000 payable in fully paid shares of the company. The assets consisted of Stock Rs. 43,280, Machinery Rs. 36,720 and Goodwill Rs. 40,000. In addition plant was purchased amounting to Rs. 11,300.

(*iii*) Income tax paid during the year was Rs. 50,000.

(*iv*) The net-profit for the year before tax amounted to Rs. 1,25,060.

Prepare Cashflow Statement as per AS 3 (Revised)

(*Ans.:* Cash from operating activities: Rs. 1,82,720
Cash from investing activities: (Rs. 11,300)
(use)
Net increase in cash and cash equivalents Rs. 400

4. From the following Profit and Loss A/c Calculate Cash from operating activities.

To Salaries	1,80,000	By Gross Profit b/d	5,40,000
To Rent	90,000	By Profit on Sale of Land	28,000
To Office Expenses	30,000	By Dividend Received	20,000
To Depreciation	24,000	By Income Tax Refund	8,000
To Loss on Sale of Plant	12,000	By Rent Received	40,000
To Goodwill w/o	30,000		
To Discount on Issue of Debentures w/o	10,000		

To Preliminary Expenses w/o	8,000	
To Proposed Dividend	60,000	
To Provision for Tax	60,000	
To Net Profit c/d	1,32,000	
	6,36,000	6,36,000

Income Tax paid during the year amounted to Rs. 50,000.

(**Ans.:** Cash generated from operating activities Rs. 1,98,000.)

5. From the following information compute:
   (1) Cash flow from Operating activities
   (2) Cash flow from Investing activities
   (3) Cash flow from Financing activities.

(*i*) Sales made during the year	
Cash —	2,00,000
Credit —	3,50,000
Purchases Cash —	Nil
Credit —	3,00,000
(*ii*) Salaries incurred during the year	62,500
(*iii*) Depreciation	1,50,000
(*iv*) Goodwill w/o	12,500

(*v*) Issue of 1,00,000 equity shares of Rs. 10 each at premium of 20%.

(*vi*) Issue of equity shares of Rs. 25,00,000 as purchase consideration of Building of Rs. 30,00,000

(*vii*) Purchase of Machinery for cash — 4,20,000

(*viii*) Dividend of last year amounting to Rs. 1,00,000 was paid. Dividend of Rs. 2,50,000 was declared but not yet paid.

(*ix*) An equipment (Book value Rs. 50,000) sold for Rs. 60,000

(*x*) Closing Balances — Debtors — Rs. 85,000

Creditors — Rs. 1,00,000, Salaries o/s Rs. 12,500

(***Ans.:*** Cash from Operating activities — Rs. 2,15,000

Cash used in Investing activities — Rs. (3,60,000)

Cashflow from financing activities — Rs. 11,00,000

6. Following are the Balance Sheets of Vrinda Ltd. as on 31st March, 2004 and 2005

Liabilities	31-03-04 *Rs.*	31-03-05 *Rs.*
Equity Share Capital	12,00,000	12,75,000
Profit and Loss Appropriation A/c	2,17,500	3,67,500
Mortgaged Loans	—	75,000
S. Creditors	1,35,000	75,000
	15,52,500	17,92,500
Fixed Assets	11,10,000	12,60,000
Stock	1,35,000	1,05,000
Debtors	2,47,500	2,92,500
Cash and Bank Balance	60,000	1,35,000
	15,52,500	17,92,500

Prepare Cashflow Statement as per AS 3 (Rev.)

(*Ans.:* Cash From Operating Activities — Rs. 75,000
Cash used in Investing Activities — Rs. (1,50,000)
Cashflow from Financing Activities — Rs. 1,50,000
Increase in Cash and Cash Equivalents Rs. 75,000

7. (From Trial Balance : Indirect Method)

Usha Ltd. had the following condensed Trial Balance at the end of 31 March 2006:

	Rs.		*Rs.*
Cash	7,500	Current liabilities	15,000
Accounts receivable	30,000	Long-term notes payable	25,500
Investments	20,000	Bonds payable	25,000
Plant assets	67,500	Capital stock	75,000
Land	40,000	Retained earnings	24,500
	1,65,000		1,65,000

During 2006-07 the followings occurred:

(*i*) A tract of land was purchased for Rs. 7,750 cash.

(*ii*) Bonds payable in the amount of Rs. 6,000 were retired for cash at face and book value.

(*iii*) An additional Rs, 20,000 equity shares were issued at par for cash.

(*iv*) Dividends totalling Rs. 9,375 were paid.

(*v*) Net income for 2006-07 was Rs. 28,450 after allowing for depreciation of Rs. 9,500.

(*vi*) Land was purchased through the issuance of Rs. 22,500 in bonds.

(*vii*) Usha Ltd. sold part of its investments portfolio for Rs. 12,875 cash. This transaction resulted in a gain of Rs. 1,375 for the firm.

(*viii*) Current liabilities increased to Rs. 18,000 at 31.03.2007.

(*ix*) Accounts receivable at 31st March 2007 total Rs. 38,000.

(*x*) The cash balance at 31st March 2007 is Rs. 48.825.

Instructions:

Prepare a statement of cash flows for 2006-07 with the indirect method [AS 3 (Revised)]

(*Ans.:* Net cash from operating activities Rs. 31,575
Net cash from investing activities Rs. 5,125
Net increase in cash and cash equivalent Rs. 41,325

8. From the following Balance Sheets of Twenty First Century Ltd. and additional information prepare a Cashflow Statement as per AS 3 (Revised)

Liabilities	31-3-2004	31-3-2005
	Rs.	*Rs.*
Equity Share Capital	12,00,000	15,00,000
General Reserve	3,00,000	3,50,000
Profit and Loss A/c	1,00,000	1,50,000
9% Debentures	6,00,000	4,00,000
Creditors	4,90,000	5,60,000
Proposed Dividends	1,20,000	1,80,000
Provision for Taxation	1,00,000	1,30,000
	29,10,000	32,70,000

Assets		
Building	8,00,000	7,60,000
Machinery	5,00,000	7,20,000
Short-Term Investments	3,00,000	4,50,000
Inventories	4,00,000	4,70,000
Debtors	6,70,000	5,30,000
Cash at Bank	2,20,000	3,30,000
Prepaid Expenses	20,000	10,000
	29,10,000	32,70,000

Additional Information:

(*i*) Debentures were redeemed at a premium of 10% on 1st April, 2004.

(*ii*) Income tax paid during the year amounted to Rs. 1,40,000.

(*iii*) A machine which appeared at a W.D.V. of Rs. 80,000 was sold for Rs. 1,30,000 and a new machine costing Rs. 3,60,000 was acquired during the year.

(*Ans.:* Net cash flow from operating activities: Rs. 5,66,000
Net cash used in investing activities: Rs. (3,80,000)
Net increase in cash and cash equivalents: Rs. 1,10,000

9. From the summary cash account of N. Ltd. prepare cashflow statement for the year ended 31st March 2008 in accordance with AS 3 (Revised) using the direct method and indirect method. The company does not have any equivalents.

Summary Cash Account
for the year ended 31-03-2008

(*Rs. '000*)

	Rs.		*Rs.*
Balance on 1-4-2007	50	Payment to suppliers	2,000
Issue of equity shares	300	Purchase of fixed assets	200
Receipts from customers	2,800	Overhead expenses	200
Sale of fixed assets	100	Wages and salaries	100
		Taxation	250
		Dividend	50
		Repayment of bank loan	300
		Balance on 31-03-2008	150
	3,250		3,250

(**Ans.:** Net cash from operating activities in Rs. (000) Rs. 250
Net cash used in investing activities Rs. (100)
Net increase in cash: Rs. 100

10. From the following Balance Sheet of Ahmed Ltd. prepare a Cashflow Statement

Liabilities	31-03-04	31-03-05
	Rs.	*Rs.*
12% Preference Share Capital	—	90,000
Equity Share Capital	7,20,000	8,10,000
General Reserve	36,000	45,000
Profit and Loss Account	18,000	21,600
15% Debentures .	1,08,000	1,17,000
S. Creditors	2,16,000	1,98,000
Bank overdraft	2,25,000	1,22,400
Provision for Taxation	54,000	75,600
Proposed Dividend	90,000	1,04,400
	14,67,000	15,84,000

Assets		
Fixed Assets	7,38,000	7,20,000
Less: Provision for Depreciation	(1,98,000)	(2,70,000)
	5,40,000	4,50,000
Stock	5,40,000	6,30,000
Debtors	3,60,000	4,32,000
Prepaid Expenses	5,400	9,000
Cash and Bank	21,600	63,000
	14,67,000	15,84,000

Interest paid on debentures — Rs. 16,200

Prepare Cashflow Statement

(*Ans.:* Cash from Operating activities — Rs. 43,200
Cash from Investing Activities —Rs. 18,000
Cash used in Financing Activities — Rs. 82,800
Net Increase in Cash and Cash equivalent — Rs. 1,44,000

11. From the following condensed comparative Balance Sheet of Bangalore Mills Ltd. and additional information, prepare a Cashflow Statement for the year 2006.

Liabilities	2005 *Rs.*	2006 *Rs.*	*Assets*	2005 *Rs.*	2006 *Rs.*
Share capital	70,000	80,000	Plant & machinery	62,000	66,000
Security Premium	9,000	11,000	Accumulated		
Retained earnings	23,820	30,820	Depreciation on		
7% Mortgage loan	—	20,000	plant and machinery	(37,000)	(26,200)
Creditors	6,900	6,000	Building	95,000	1,16,000
Outstanding salaries	2,000	1,400	Accumulated		
Provision for taxation	1,000	1,400	depreciation on building	(43,000)	(45,000)
			Land	10,000	12,000
			Stock	10,220	9,620
			Debtors	8,600	7,600
			Prepaid expenses	720	800
			Cash	6,180	9,800
	1,12,720	1,50,620		1,12,720	1,50,620

Additional information:

1. Plant costing Rs. 16,000 (accumulated depreciation Rs. 14,800) was sold during the year for Rs. 1.200.
2. Building was acquired during the year at a cost of Rs. 21,000. In addition to cash payment of Rs. 1,000, a 7% mortgage loan was raised for the balance.
3. Dividend of Rs. 8.000 was paid during the year.
4. A sum of Rs. 13,900 was transferred to provision for taxation account in 2006.

(*Ans.:* Net cash generated from operations: Rs. 21,420
Net cash used in investing activities: Rs. (71,800)
Net cash from financing activities Rs. 4,000
Net increase in cash : Rs. 3,600

12. Balance sheets of M/s. Ram and Shyam as on January 1, 2006, were as follows:

Liabilities	*January 1, 2006 Rs.*	*December 31, 2006 Rs.*	*Assets*	*January 1, 2006 Rs.*	*December 31, 2006 Rs.*
Creditors	40,000	44,000	Cash	10,000	7,000
Mrs. Ram's loan	25,000	—	Debtors	30,000	50,000
Loan from bank	40,000	50,000	Stock	35,000	25,000
Capital	1,25,000	1,53,000	Machinery	80,000	55,000
			Land	40,000	50,000
			Building	35,000	60,000
	2,30,000	2,47,000		2,30,000	2,47,000

During the year a machine costing Rs. 10,000 (accumulated depreciation. Rs. 3,000) was sold for Rs. 5,000. The balance of provision for depreciation against machinery as on 1st January 2006 was Rs. 25,000 and on 31st December 2006 Rs. 40,000. Net profit for the year amounted to Rs. 45,000.

Required: Prepare a Cashflow Statement [AS 3 (Revised)]

(*Ans.:* Net cash generated from operations: Rs. 59,000
Net cash used in investing activities: Rs. (30,000)
Net cash used in financing activities Rs. (32,000)
Net decrease in cash: Rs. (3,000).

Financial Statement Analysis

MEANING OF FINANCIAL STATEMENT ANALYSIS

Financial Statement Analysis is an analysis which highlights important relationships in the financial statements. Financial Statement analysis embraces the methods used in assessing and interpreting the results of past performance and current financial position as they relate to particular factors of interest in investment decisions. It is an important means of assessing past performance and in forecasting and planning future performance. According to Lev:[1]

"Financial Statement Analysis is an information processing system designed to provide data for decision making models, such as the portfolio selection model, bank lending decision models, and corporate financial management models."

OBJECTIVES OF FINANCIAL STATEMENT ANALYSIS

The major objectives of financial statement analysis is to provide decision makers information about a business enterprise for use in decision-making. Users of financial statement information are the decision makers concerned with evaluating the economic situation of the firm and predicting its future course. Financial statement analysis can be used by the different users and decision makers to achieve the following objectives:

1. Assessment of Past Performance and Current Position

Past performance is often a good indicator of future performance. Therefore, an investor or creditor is interested in the trend of past sales, expenses, net income, cash flow and return on investment. These trends offer a means for judging management's past performance and are possible indicator of future performance. Similarly, the analysis of current position indicates where the business stands today. For instance, the current position analysis will show the types of assets owned by a business enterprise and the different liabilities due against the enterprise.

1. Baruch Lev, *Financial Statement Analysis, A New Approach,* Prentic Hall, 1974, p. 5.

It will tell what the cash position is, how much debt the company has in relation to equity and how reasonable the inventories and receivables are.

2. Prediction of Net Income and Growth Prospects

The financial statement analysis helps in predicting the earning prospects and growth rates in the earnings which are used by investors while comparing investment alternatives and other users interested in judging the earning potential of business enterprises. Investors also consider the risk or uncertainty associated with the expected return. The decision makers are futuristic and are always concerned with the future. Financial statements which contain information on past performances are analysed and interpreted as a basis for forecasting future rates of return and for assessing risk.

3. Prediction of Bankruptcy and Failure

Financial statement analysis is a significant tool in predicting the bankruptcy and failure probability of business enterprises. After being aware about probable failure, both managers and investors can take preventive measures to avoid/minimise losses. Corporate managements can effect changes in operating policy, reorganise financial structure or even go for voluntary liquidation to shorten the length of time losses.

In accounting and finance area, empirical studies conducted have suggested a set of financial ratios which can give early signal of corporate failure. Such a prediction model based on financial statement analysis is useful to managers, investors and creditors. Managers may use the ratios prediction model to assess the solvency position of their firms and thus can take appropriate corrective actions. Investors and shareholders can use the model to make the optimum portfolio selection and to bring changes in the investment strategy in accordance with their investment goals. Similarly, creditors can apply the prediction model while evaluating the creditworthiness of business enterprises.

4. Loan Decision by Financial Institutions and Banks

Financial statement analysis is used by financial institutions, loaning agencies, banks and others to make sound loan or credit decision. In this way, they can make proper allocation of credit among the different borrowers. All lenders are primarily concerned with repayment of loan and payment of interest on the due dates. This require comprehensive investigation and analysis of the financial statements submitted by the borrowers. Financial statement analysis helps in determining credit risk, deciding terms and conditions of loan if sanctioned, interest rate, maturity date etc.

TECHNIQUES OF FINANCIAL STATEMENT ANALYSIS

Various techniques are used in the analysis of financial data to emphasise the comparative and relative importance of data presented and to evaluate the position of the firm. These techniques of financial analysis are intended to show relationships and changes. Among the more widely used of these techniques are the following:

(1) Horizontal Analysis
(2) Vertical Analysis
(3) Trend Analysis
(4) Ratio Analysis

1. Horizontal Analysis

The percentage analysis of increases and decreases in corresponding items in comparative financial statements is called horizontal analysis. Horizontal analysis involves the computation of amount changes and percentage changes from the previous to the current year. The amount of each item on the most recent statement is compared with the corresponding item on one more earlier statements. The increase or decrease in the amount of the item is then listed, together with the per cent of increase or decrease. When the comparison is made between two statements, the earlier statement is used as the base. If the horizontal analysis includes three or more statements, there are two alternatives in the selection of the base. First, the earliest date or period may be used as the basis for comparing all later dates or periods; or second, each statement may be compared with the immediately preceding statement.

Figures 14.1 and Fig. 14.2 present the comparative balance sheet and profit and loss account respectively of a company with the amount of increase or decrease and percentae changes shown. The per cent change is computed as follows:

$$\text{Percentage Change} = \frac{\text{Amount of change}}{\text{Previous year amount}} \times 100$$

COMPARATIVE BALANCE SHEET WITH HORIZONTAL ANALYSIS

ABC Company Ltd., Balance Sheet

December 31, 2008 and December 31, 2007

(Rs. in '000)

			Increase	*(Decrease)*
	2008	*2007*	*Amount*	*Percentage*
	(Rs.)	*(Rs.)*	*(Rs.)*	*(Rs.)*
Assets:				
Current Assets:				
Cash	161	192	(31)	(61.10)
Marketable securities	652	819	(167)	(20.4)
Receivables	2,346	2,050	296	14.4
Inventories	1,940	1,758	182	10.4
Prepaid expense and deferred charges	578	312	266	85.3
Total Current Assets	5,677	5,131	546	10.6
Properties:				
Land, buildings, machinery and equipment less accumulated depreciation of Rs. 5,386 and Rs. 4,801	5,977	5,389	588	10.9
Long-term receivables and other non-current assets	488	258	230	89.1
	12,142	10,778	1,364	12.7
Liabilities:				
Current Liabilities:				
Payables	2,989	1,828	1,161	63.5
Taxes payable	156	268	(112)	(41.8)
Dividends payable	180	210	(30)	(14.3)
Total current liabilities	3,325	2,306	1,019	44.2

Long-term Liabilities:				
Long-term debentures	988	409	579	141.6
Other long-term liabilities	219	203	16	7.9
Deferred income tax liabilities	1,048	723	325	45.0
Total Liabilities	5,580	3,641	1,939	53.3
Ownership:				
Equity capital	621	414	207	50.0
Preference capital	312	520	(208)	(40.0)
Treasury stock at cost	(1,081)	(728)	(353)	48.5
Total ownership	6,562	7,137	(575)	8.1
Total Liabilities and Ownership	12,142	10,778	1,364	12.7

Fig. 14.1 Comparative Balance Sheet with Horizontal Analysis

Comparative Profit and Loss Account with Horizontal Analysis
ABC Company Ltd.
Income Statement for years Ended
December 31, 2008, and December 31, 2009

	(Rs. in '000)		*Increase (Decrease)*	
	2009	*2008*	*Amount*	*Percentage*
Sales	10,631	10,600	31	0.3
Costs and Expenses:				
Cost of goods sold	7,129	6,887	242	3.5
Selling and administration expenses	2,378	2,166	212	9.8
Total costs and expenses	9,507	9,053	454	5.0
Earnings from Operations	1,124	1547	(423)	(27.3)
Unusual charges	(563)	—	(563)	NA
Other income and expenses including interest expenses of Rs. 183 and Rs. 114	(31)	77	(108)	(140.3)
Earnings Before Income Taxes	530	1,624	(1,094)	(67.4)
Provision for income taxes	198	701	(503)	(71.8)
Net Earnings	332	923	(591)	(64.0)

Fig. 14.2 Comparative Income Statement with Horizontal Analysis

2. Vertical Analysis

Vertical Analysis uses percentages to show the relationship of the different parts to the total in a single statement. Vertical analysis sets a total figure in the statement equal to 100 per cent and computes the percentage of each component of that figure. The figure to be used as 100 per cent will be total assets or total liabilities and equity capital in the case of balance sheet and revenue or sales in the case of the profit and loss account.

3. Trend Analysis

Using the previous year's data of a business enterprise, trend analysis can be done to observe percentage changes over time in selected data. In trend analysis, percentage changes are calculated for several successive years instead of between two years. Trend analysis is important because, with its long-run view, it may point to basic changes in the nature of the business. By looking at a trend in a particular ratio, one may find whether that ratio is falling, rising or remaining relatively constant. From this observation, a problem is detected or the sign of good management is found.

Trend analysis uses an index number over a period of time. For index numbers, one year, the base year is equal to 100 per cent. Other years are measured in relation to that amount. For example, an analyst may be interested in sales and earnings trends for the past five years. For this purpose, sales and earnings data of a company are given to prepare further the trend analysis or percentages.

ABC Company

Annual Performance *(Rs. '000)*

	Year 1	*Year 2*	*Year 3*	*Year 4*	*Year 5*
Sales	202.0	215.0	243.0	320.0	415.0
Net Earnings	10.9	11.7	13.5	15.4	18.8

The above data show a fairly healthy growth pattern but the pattern of change from year to year can be determined more precisely by calculating trend percentage. To do this, a base year is selected and then the data are divided for each of the other years by the base year data. The resultant figures are actually indexes of the changes occurring throughout the period. If year 1 is chosen as the base year, all data for year 2 through 5 will be related to year 1, which is represented as 100%.

To create the following table, each year sales is divided from year 2 through years 5 — by Rs. 202, the year 1 sales in thousands of Rupees. Similarly, the net earnings for years 2 through 5 were divided by Rs. 10.9, the year 1 net earnings.

Annual Performance (Percentage of Base Year)

Sales	*Year 1*	*Year 2*	*Year 3*	*Year 4*	*Year 5*
Sales	100	106	120	158	205
Net Earnings	100	107	124	141	172

The trend percentages reveal that the growth in earnings outstripped the growth in sales for years 2 and 3, then fell below the sales growth in the last two years. It is clear in this analysis of comparative statements that a disproportionate increase in operating expenses emerged in year 5. One may analyse the year 4 data to determine if net income was affected for the same reason or if the reduced growth was caused by other factors.

4. Ratio Analysis

Ratio analysis is an important means of expressing the relationship between two numbers. A ratio can be computed from any pair of numbers. To be useful, a ratio must represent a meaningful relationship, but use of ratios cannot take the place of studying the underlying data.

Ratios are guides or shortcuts that are useful in evaluating the financial position and operations of a company and in comparing them to previous years or to other companies. The primary purpose of ratios is to point out areas for further investigation. They should be used in connection with a general understanding of the company and its environment.

Comparison of income statement and balance sheet numbers, in the form of ratios, can create difficulties due to the timing of the financial statements. Specifically, the profit and loss account covers the entire fiscal period, whereas the balance sheet is for a single point in time, the end of the period. Ideally then, to compare an income statement figure such as sales to a balance sheet figure such as receivable, we usually need a reasonable measure of average receivables for the year that the sales figure cover. However, these data are not available to the external analyst. In some cases, the analyst should take the next best approach, by using an average of beginning and ending balance sheet figures. This approach smooths out changes from beginning to end, but it does not eliminate problem due to seasonal and cyclical changes. It also does not reflect changes that occur unevenly throughout the year..

COMMON SIZE STATEMENTS

Common size statements involve expressing comparison in percentages. Common size statements may be prepared in order to compare percentages of a current period with past periods, to compare individual business, or to compare one business with industry percentages published by trade associations and financial information services.

Common size financial statements contain the percentage of a key figure alone, without the corresponding amount figures. The use of percentages is usually preferable to the use of absolute figures. An illustration will make this clear. If company A earns Rs. 10,000 and Company B earns Rs. 1,000, which is more profitable? The answer is likely to be company A. However, the total shareholders' equity of company A is Rs. 10,00,000 and company B is Rs. 10,000 the return on equity will be as follows:

$$\text{Return on Equity} = \frac{\text{Earnings}}{\text{Equity}}$$

$$\text{Company A} = \frac{\text{Rs. } 10{,}000}{\text{Rs. } 10{,}00{,}000} = 1\%$$

$$\text{Company B} = \frac{\text{Rs. } 1{,}000}{\text{Rs. } 10{,}000} = 10\%$$

Comparing the return on equity, it can be clearly said that company B is more profitable than company A.

The use of common size statements can make comparisons of business enterprises of different sizes much more meaningful since the numbers are brought to common base, *i.e.,* per cent. Such statement allow an analyst to compare the operating and financing characteristics of two companies of different sizes in the same industry.

Care must be exercised in the use of common size statements when the absolute figures are small, because a small absolute change can result in a very substantial percentage change. For example, if net profits last year amounted to Rs. 1,000 and increased this year to Rs. 5,000, this would be an increase of only Rs. 4,000 in net profits, but it represents a substantial increase in percentage terms.

Common size statements can be prepared in vertical analysis and horizontal analysis formats. In vertical analysis format, a figure from a year is compared with a base selected from the same year. For example, if advertising expenses were Rs. 10,000 in 2008 and sales were Rs. 10,00,000, the advertising expenses will be 1% of sales. In horizontal analysis format, the amount of an item (an account) is expressed in terms of that same account figure for a selected base year. For example, if sales were Rs. 8,00,000 in 2008 and Rs. 12,00,000 in 2009, then sales increased to 150% of the 2008 level in 2009, an increase of 50%.

FOCUS OF FINANCIAL STATEMENT ANALYSIS

Financial Statement Analysis involves evaluating different aspects of a business enterprise which are of great importance to different users such as management, investors, creditors, bankers, analysts, investment advisers etc. Generally, the following analyses are made while making financial statement analysis:

I. Liquidity or Short-Term Solvency Analysis
II. Analysis for Measuring the Movement of Current Assets
III. Profitability Analysis
IV. Capital Structure or Gearing Analysis
V Market Strength or Investor Analysis
VI. Growth and Stability Analysis.

I. Liquidity or Short-Term Solvency Analysis (or Ratios)

Liquidity or short-term solvency analysis aims to determine the ability of a business to meet its financial obligations during the short-term and to maintain its short-term debt-paying ability. The aim of liquidity analysis is for a company to have adequate funds on hand to pay bills when they are due and to meet unexpected needs for cash. If a business enterprise cannot maintain its short-term debt paying ability, obviously it cannot maintain a long-term debt-paying ability or long-term solvency. Shareholders also will not be satisfied with such a state of affairs of the company. Even a business enterprise on a very profitable course will find itself bankrupt if it fails to meet its obligations to short-term creditors.

Liquidity analysis mainly focuses on balance sheet relationships that indicate the ability of a business to liquidate current and non-current liabilities. The ratios that evaluate liquidity relate to working capital or some part of it, because it is out of working capital that debts are paid as they mature. The comparisons and ratios related to evaluating liquidity or short-term solvency are as follows:

1. Working Capital Position

The working capital of a business is the excess of current assets over current liabilities. This is computed by subtracting current liabilities from the current assets. The resulting working capital figure is taken as one of the primary indicators of the short-term solvency of the business. The working capital formula is as follows:

$$\text{Working Capital} = \text{Current assets} - \text{Current liabilities}$$

The current working capital amount should be compared with past amounts to determine if working capital is reasonable. Caution must be exercised, because the relative size of the firm may be expanding or contracting. Further, the absolute amounts of working capital are difficult to use in comparing companies of different sizes or in comparing such amounts with industry figures.

2. Current Ratio

Current ratio is sometimes referred to as working capital ratio or banker's ratio. Current ratio expresses the relationship of current assets to current liabilities. It is widely used as a broad indicator of a company's liquidity and short-term debt-paying ability. The current ratio is computed by dividing the total current assets by the total current liabilities. The current ratio formula is as follows:

$$\text{Current ratio} = \frac{\text{Current assets}}{\text{Current liabilities}}$$

Current ratio is a more dependable indication of solvency than is working capital. For many years the guideline for the minimum current ratio has been 2 : 1. The assumption is even if the value of current assets declines by 50%, the firm can still pay its current liabilities. But nowadays there has been a decline in the liquidity of many firms. It can be said that in some industries, a current ratio substantially below 2 is adequate, while some other industries may require a ratio much larger than 2. In general, the shorter the operating cycle, the lower the normal current ratio. The longer the operating cycle, the higher the normal current ratio. A higher current ratio enables a firm to pay off current obligations and thus provides adequate margin of safety to the creditors.

A company's current ratio can be compared with the company's past current ratios and with industry averages as well. Such comparisons can help in determining if the current ratio is high or low at this period in time. However, these comparisons do not indicate why the current ratio is high or low. Possible reasons for unsatisfactory current ratio can be found from an analysis of the individual accounts and items which make up the current asset and current liability.

Example: The following are the current assets and current liabilities in respect of two companies, Company A and Company B.

	Company A	*Company B*
Current assets	Rs. 4,50,000	Rs. 1,60,000
Current liabilities	Rs. 1,50,000	Rs. 80,000

The current ratio will be as follows:

$$\text{Current ratio} = \frac{\text{Current assets}}{\text{Current liabilities}}$$

$$\text{Company A} = \frac{\text{Rs. 4,50,000}}{\text{Rs. 1,50,000}} = 3 : 1$$

$$\text{Company B} = \frac{\text{Rs. 1,60,000}}{\text{Rs. 80,000}} = 2 : 1$$

3. Acid Test Ratio or Quick Ratio

The current ratio is generally used to evaluate an enterprise's overall short-term solvency or liquidity position. At many times, it is desirable to know more immediate position or instant-debt-paying ability of a firm than that indicated by the current ratio. Further, the current ratio does not take into account the make-up or composition of current assets. For example, a rupee of cash or debtor is considered more readily available to meet obligations than a rupee of inventory. The quick ratio is designed to overcome this problem by relating the most liquid assets to current liabilities. Cash, marketable securities or short-term investments, receivables and prepaids are included within the meaning of most liquid assets ; inventory is excluded. The acid test ratio is as follows:

$$\text{Acid Test} = \frac{\text{Current Assets} - \text{Inventory}}{\text{Current Liabilities}}$$

It may be preferable to have a better view of liquidity by excluding some other items in current assets that may not represent relatively current cash flow. Examples of items to be excluded are prepaids and miscellaneous items such as assets held for sale. This is considered a more conservative manner of computing the acid test ratio and the formula of acid test ratio in this situation will be as follows:

$$\text{Acid Test} = \frac{\text{Cash} + \text{Marketable Securities} + \text{Net Receivable and Debtors}}{\text{Current Liabilities}}$$

Inventory should be removed from current assets when computing the acid test ratio. Some of the reasons for this are that inventory may be slow moving or possibly obsolete and parts of the inventory may have been pledged to specific creditors. For example, a winery has inventory that requires considerable time for aging and therefore a considerable time before sale. To include the wine inventory in the test computation would overstate the liquidity. There is also a valuation problem with inventory, because it is stated at a cost figure that is likely to be materially different from a fair current valuation. In summary, inventory should be left out of the computation because of possible misleading liquidity indications.[2]

The usually guideline for the acid test ratio is 1.00. However, some industries may find that a ratio less than 1.00 is adequate, while others need a ratio greater than 1.00. For example, a typical grocery store sells only for cash and therefore does not have receivables. This type of business can have an acid test substantially below the 1.00 guideline and still have adequate liquidity.

Example: A firm has following current assets and current liabilities:

Debtors	Rs. 5,000
Inventory	Rs. 20,000
Cash	Rs. 5,000
Total current assets	Rs. 30,000

Total current liabilities Rs. 20,000

The acid test or quick ratio is as follows:

$$\text{Quick ratio} = \frac{\text{Quick assets}}{\text{Current liabilities}}$$

$$= \frac{\text{Rs. } 10{,}000}{\text{Rs. } 20{,}000}$$

$$= 0.5:1$$

4. Cash Ratio

Liquidity of a firm can be viewed from an extremely conservative point of view. This may be the case when severe liquidity problem with inventory and receivables are likely to happen or when the company has pledged its receivables and inventory. In this situation, the short-term liquidity of a company may be measured through cash ratio. The cash ratio relates cash and marketable securities to current liabilities. The cash ratio is computed as follows:

$$\text{Cash Ratio} = \frac{\text{Cash} + \text{Marketable Securities}}{\text{Current Liabilities}}$$

2. Charles H. Gibson, *Financial Statement Analysis*, South-Western Publishing Co., 1992, p. 236.

Cash ratio is not given much importance unless a firm is in deep financial trouble. It is not considered pragmatic to expect a business enterprise to have enough cash and marketable securities to cover current liabilities. However, in the case of very slow-moving inventories and receivables and highly speculative companies, cash ratio is of great importance. A high cash ratio indicates that a business enterprise is not using its resource cash to best advantage. A low cash ratio reflects an immediate problem with paying bills.

II. Analysis for Measuring the Movement of Assets-Activity Ratios

Activity ratios also known as turnover ratios indicate the efficiency with which an enterprise's resources are utilised. Liquidity or short-term analysis (current ratio and acid test ratio) will show misleading results if debtors are too high because of slow collections. Similarly, the current ratio will be misleading if inventory is not sold and thus remains at high levels. Since liquidity ratios (i.e., current ratio and acid test ratio) ignore the movement of current assets, it is necessary for short-term creditors to make an analysis of how fast the debtors and stock are turned into cash so that their claims can be met timely. Moreover, the overall profitability of the business depends upon: (1) the rate of return of capital employed; and (2) the turnover, i.e., the speed at which the capital employed in the business rotates. Hence, in order to find out which part of capital (i.e., assets) is efficiently employed and which part not, different activity or turnover ratios are calculated. Mainly activity ratios include:

(1) Capital turnover ratio

(2) Asset turnover ratio

(3) Networking capital turnover ratio

(4) Inventory turnover ratio

(5) Debtor's turnover ratio or Receivables turnover.

(1) Capital Turnover Ratio

This ratio measures the effectiveness with which a firm uses its financial resources. It indicates the number of times the capital has been rotated in the process of doing business. This ratio is computed as follows:

$$\frac{\text{Net sales (Or cost of goods sold)}}{\text{Capital employed or owners' equity}}$$

Net sales = Total sales less returns (if any)

Cost of goods sold = Opening stock + Purchases + Direct expenses – Closing stock

OR

Sales – Gross profit

Illustration 1:

A firm has opening and closing stock of Rs. 30,000 and Rs. 20,000 respectively. Its administrative and selling expenses are Rs. 10,000; Purchases Rs. 3,10,000; Sales Rs. 5,00,000; Debentures Rs. 50,000 (representing one-third of owner's equity). The capital turnover ratio is as follows:

$$\text{Capital turnover ratio} = \frac{\text{Cost of goods sold}}{\text{Owner's equity}}$$

Cost of goods sold = Opening stock + Purchases – closing stock

$$= 30,000 + 3,10,000 - 20,000$$

$$= \text{Rs. } 3,20,000$$

$$\text{Capital or owner's equity} = 3 \text{ times Debentures}$$

$$= 3 \times 50,000 = 1,50,000$$

$$\text{Capital turnover ratio} = \frac{3,20,000}{1,50,000} = 2.133 \text{ times}$$

2. Asset Turnover Ratio

This ratio reveals the number of times the net tangible assets (i.e., total assets less current liabilities less intangibles) are turned over during the year. Strictly speaking, average net tangible assets should be used in calculating this ratio. But, invariably net tangible assets at the end of the year is used.

$$\text{Asset Turnover} = \frac{\text{Turnover}}{\text{Net Tangible Assets}}$$

An improvement in asset turnover ratio as compared to the previous year indicates that the turnover of the company has improved. In cases where assets are not revalued or replaced, its magnitude will be decreasing over the years due to depreciation. Then, obviously, the ratio will be higher as the turnover figures for the future will reflect an increasing trend.

Another form of assets turnover ratio can be computed as *fixed assets turnover ratio*. This ratio indicates the extent to which the investments in fixed assets have contributed to sales. If compared with a previous period, it indicates whether investment in fixed assets has been judicious or not.

The higher this ratio, better it is because it indicates higher efficiency indicating that investment in fixed assets has resulted in higher sales. A lower ratio may point to the underutilization or non-utilization of certain assets. The ratio is calculated as follows:

$$\frac{\text{Net sales}}{\text{Fixed assets less depreciation}}$$

Illustration 2:

The following details have been given to you for M/s. ABC Ltd. for two years. You are required to find out fixed assets turnover ratio and comment on it.

	2007 *Rs.*	2008 *Rs.*
Fixed assets at written down value	15,00,000	30,00,000
Sales less returns	60,00,000	80,00,000

Solution:

$$\text{Fixed assets turnover ratio} = \frac{\text{Sales}}{\text{Fixed assets}}$$

For 2007

$= 60,00,000 \div 15,00,000$

$= 4$ times

For 2008

$= 80,00,000 \div 30,00,000$

$= 2.67$ times.

Comment: There has been decline in the Fixed Assets Turnover Ratio though absolute figures of sales have gone up. It indicates increase in the investment in fixed asset has not brought about proportionate gain. However, before concluding, results for next two to three years must also be seen.

(3) Net Working Capital Turnover Ratio

This ratio indicates whether or not working capital has been effectively utilised in making sales. This ratio is computed by dividing the net sales or cost of goods sold by net working capital. Net working capital signifies the excess of current assets over current liabilities. The ratio is calculated as follows:

$$\frac{\text{Net Sales}}{\text{Net Working Capital}}$$

A high net working capital ratio (if it is expressed in percentage) indicates efficient use of working capital and quick turnover of current assets like stock and debtors. A low ratio indicates low turnover of these assets.

(4) Inventory Turnover Ratio

Inventory turnover measure the relative size of inventory and influences the amount of cash available to pay liabilities. A smaller, faster-moving inventory means that the company has less cash tied up in inventory. On the contrary, a build up in inventory means that a recession or some other factor is preventing sales from keeping pace with purchasing and production. Ideally, inventory should be maintained at an optimum level to support production and sales. Inventory turnover ratio is calculated by using the following formula:

$$\text{Inventory turnover} = \frac{\text{Cost of goods sold}}{\text{Average Inventory}}$$

Average inventory is obtained using a simple average process by dividing the opening and closing inventory by the two. Cost of goods sold is obtained by deducting gross profit from sales.

Illustration 3:

A firm has opening and closing inventory of Rs. 56,000 and Rs. 44,000 respectively. The firm has sold goods for Rs. 5,00,000 at gross profit margin of 20%. The inventory turnover ratio is as follows:

$$\text{Inventory turnover} = \frac{\text{Cost of goods sold}}{\text{Average Inventory}}$$

$$= \frac{\text{Rs.}5{,}00{,}000 - \text{Rs.}1{,}00{,}000}{1/2\ (\text{Rs.}56{,}000 + \text{Rs. } 44{,}000)}$$

$$= \frac{\text{Rs. } 4{,}00{,}000}{\text{Rs. } 50{,}000}$$

$= 8$ times per year

(5) Receivables Turnover Ratio

The ability of a company to collect for credit sales in a timely way affects the company's liquidity. The relationship between credit sales and accounts receivables may be stated as the receivable turnover. Receivables or debtors turnover determines the liquidity of one item of current assets and finds out how faster debts are being collected. The formula for computing receivables turnover is as follows:

$$\text{Receivable Turnover} = \frac{\text{Net Credit Sales}}{\text{Average Accounts Receivables or Debtors}}$$

Receivables turnover shows how many times, on average, the receivables were turned into cash during the period. A high debtors turnover ratio indicates shorter time span between credit sales and cash collection. This ratio requires one balance sheet account and one profit and loss account item. In case, credit sales figure is not given, total sales figure can be used to compute receivables turnover.

Illustration 4:

A firm has opening and closing debtors of Rs. 40,000 and Rs. 75,000 respectively and credit sales of Rs. 3,45,000. The debtors turnover ratio is as follows:

$$\text{Debtors turnover ratio} = \frac{\text{Credit Sales}}{\text{Average Debtors}}$$

$$= \frac{\text{Rs. } 3{,}45{,}000}{\text{Rs. } 57{,}500}$$

$$= 6 \text{ times per year}$$

$$\text{Debt Collection period} = \frac{12 \text{ months}}{\text{Debtors turnover}}$$

$$= \frac{12 \text{ months}}{6 \text{ times}}$$

$$= 2 \text{ months.}$$

III. Profitability Analysis (Or Ratios)

The long-term survival of a business enterprise depends on satisfactory income earned by it. An evaluation of a company's past profits may give the investors, creditors and others a better understanding for decision-making. The profitability position also affects the liquidity position which is vital to creditors as well. Profitability ratios try to establish relationship among profit, turnover, capital employed etc. These ratios are:

1. Earnings Margin

It is the ratio of net income to turnover, expressed as a percentage.

$$\text{Earnings Margins} = \frac{\text{Net Income}}{\text{Turnover}} \times 100\%$$

Earnings margin is not the same as margin of profits. Margin of profits refers to the direct operating results only and is the amount before income tax and before non-operating income and charges. In earnings margin, only the final net profit is used.

Illustration 5:

The Profit and Loss Account of ABC Ltd. is given as follows:

ABC Pvt. Ltd.

Profit and Loss Account

Particulars	*Rs.*	*Particulars*	*Rs.*
Cost of goods sold	30,00,000	Sales	50,00,000
Interest on Debentures	1,00,000	Income from Investments	1,00,000
Provision for Taxation	10,00,000		
Net profit after tax	10,00,000		
	51,00,000		51,00,000

Calculate earnings margin.

$$\text{Earnings margin} = \frac{\text{Net profit after tax}}{\text{Sales (Turnover)}} \times 100\%$$

$$= \frac{\text{Rs. } 10,00,000}{\text{Rs. } 50,00,000} \times 100 = 20\%$$

2. Return on Capital Employed or Return on Investment (ROI)

This ratio measures profitability in relation to the total capital employed in a business enterprise. The terms invested capital, capital funds and total capital may be used interchangeably. It is a useful ratio when comparing the overall performances of companies, particularly where they have different proportions of debt in their capital structure.

This ratio would also show whether the company's borrowing policy is wise economically and whether the capital had been employed fruitfully. For example, if funds have been borrowed at 8% and return on capital is 7½%, it would be better not to borrow unless it is essential. It would also show that the firm had not been employing the funds efficiently. The business can survive only when the return on capital is more than the cost of capital.

$$\text{Return on Capital} = \frac{\text{Profit before interest and tax}}{\text{Total capital employed}}$$

According to some analysts, short-term borrowings, such as bank loans, commercial paper, and deferred tax liability, should be included under capital. Current accrued payables which are not interest bearing should be excluded because their interest component is not observable.

Illustration 6:

Given below is the Balance Sheet of ABC Co. Ltd. as on 31st March, 2008:

Liabilities	*Rs.*	*Assets*	*Rs.*
Equity share capital	20,00,000	Fixed Assets	30,00,000
Reserves	5,00,000	Current Assets	25,00,000
Surplus — Profit for the year	5,00,000	Discount on issue of debentures	1,00,000
10% Debentures	10,00,000		
Current liabilities	16,00,000		
	56,00,000		56,00,000

Find out Return on Capital Employed/ROI.

Solution:

$$\text{Return on investment} = \frac{\text{Profit before interest etc.}}{\text{Capital employed}} \times 100$$

Profit before interest = Profit (given in B/S) + interest on debentures
= 5,00,000 + 1,00,000 (10% of 10,00,000)
= Rs. 6,00,000

Capital employed = Fixed assets + Working capital
= 30,00,000 + (25,00,000 – 16,00,000)
= Rs. 39,00,000

OR

Capital employed = **Equity share capital + Reserves & Surplus + Long-term debts – Discount on issue of debentures**
= 20,000 + 5,00,000 + 5,00,000 + 10,00,000 – 1,00,000
= 39,00,000

$$\text{Return on Capital/ROI} = \frac{6,00,000}{39,00,000} \times 100 = 15.4\%$$

3. Return on Equity

Return on equity is derived by taking net income and dividing it by the shareholders' equity. This indicates the returns which the management is realising from the shareholders' equity and shows how effectively ordinary shareholder funds are being utilised by the management. As long as it is above the current interest rates, a company is doing fairly well.

$$\text{Return on Equity} = \frac{\text{Profit After Taxation} - \text{Preference Dividends}}{\text{Ordinary Shareholders' Funds}} \times 100\%$$

It is obvious that both the ratios — return on capital and return on equity — will be influenced when a company has raised new capital during the course of the year. That is, in other words, the ratios will be artificially low. Also, the ratios do not take into account the effect of financial leverage which undesirably tends to increase the variability of earnings for the ordinary shares. In fact, ordinary shareholders of a company having higher dose of borrowings expect large returns to compensate for the high levels of risk. Financial analysts, sometimes in such cases, find out the trade-off between higher earnings and increased variability of earnings to determine whether the management has chosen the optimum amount of financial leverage.

Illustration 7:

Calculate Returns on Equity (ROE) from the following information:

	Rs.
10% Preference share capital (fully paid-up)	10,00,000
1,60,000 Equity shares of Rs. 10 each fully paid	16,00,000
Reserves and surplus	64,00,000
Net profit after tax	23,75,000

Solution:

$$\text{Return on equity} = \frac{\text{Net profit} - \text{Preference dividend}}{\text{Equity shareholders' fund}}$$

Preference dividend = 10% on 10,00,000 = Rs. 1,00,000

Equity shareholders's funds:	*Rs.*
Paid-up equity share capital	16,00,000
+ Reserves & surplus	64,00,000
	80,00,000

$$\text{Return on equity} = \frac{23,75,000 - 1,00,000}{80,00,000} \times 100$$

$$= \frac{22,75,000}{80,00,000} \times 100 = 28.44\%$$

IV. Capital Structure or Gearing Analysis (Ratios)

Gearing ratio, i.e., the relationship of long-term debt to total capital is considered the most important by many investors and financial analysts. Popularly known as debt-equity ratio, this ratio has utility to many including shareholders, creditors, business managers, suppliers and other user groups. Gearing ratios are used to indicate:

(*i*) The cushion of assets/profits available to holder of fixed income capital should assets/profits decline.

(*ii*) The gearing advantage of potentially higher assets/profits attributable to ordinary shareholders and the correspondingly higher risk which is incurred.

(*iii*) The scope for raising additional fixed-income capital at reasonable costs, from the point of view of the company.

The debt-equity ratio is computed as follows:

$$\text{Debt-equity ratio} = \frac{\text{Loan Capital + Preference Share Capital}}{\text{Net Tangible Assets}}$$

Net tangible assets (or total capital) is obtained by subtracting the intangible assets and the current assets from total assets. Loan capital plus preference capital constitutes the amount of long-term debt. Alternatively, long-term debt can be derived by subtracting current liabilities from total liabilities.

Other variants of debt-equity ratio are as follows:

(1) $\frac{\text{Long-term liabilities}}{\text{Equity (or net worth)}} \times 100$

(2) $\frac{\text{External equities}}{\text{Internal equities}}$

(3) $\frac{\text{Long-term debts}}{\text{Owner's equities}}$

(4) $\frac{\text{Long-term debts}}{\text{Shareholder's funds + Long-term debt}}$

Sometimes capital gearing is calculated in terms of debt to equity ratio and not total capital. Capital gearing ratios, calculated in these two manners, provide essentially the same information.

It is desirable that the investors select a standard method and follow it consistently throughout. It is said that as a rule of thumb, one should not opt for a company whose long-term debt exceeds two-thirds of its total capitalisation. Debt equity ratio is very helpful in assessing a company — whether the company is marching steadily into or out of debt. In younger and aggressive companies, comparatively speaking the long-term debts may at times exceed the shareholders' equity which means that a company will not be able to get out of the difficult situation easily. A company depending on large amounts of debt should manage and perform well to avoid any worse contingencies. Debt equity ratios should be analysed not for one but for many years to determine a trend. If it is found that equity component is continuously increasing than the long-term debt, there may not be any cause for concern.

Illustration 8:

From the following, calculate debt-equity ratio:

	Rs.
Equity Share Capital:	
10,000 Equity Shares of Rs. 100 each	10,00,000
General Reserve	4,50,000
Accumulated Profits	3,00,000
Debentures	7,50,000
Sundry Trade Creditors	4,00,000
Outstanding Expenses	1,00,000

Solution:

(1) Debt-equity Ratio $= \dfrac{\text{External equities}}{\text{Internal equities}}$

$$= \frac{\text{Debentures + Trade creditors + Outstanding expenses}}{\text{Equity share capital + General reserve + Accumulated profits}}$$

$$= \frac{7{,}50{,}000 + 4{,}00{,}000 + 1{,}00{,}000}{10{,}00{,}000 + 4{,}50{,}000 + 3{,}00{,}000} = \frac{12{,}50{,}000}{17{,}50{,}000}$$

$= 0.71 : 1.$

(2) Debt equity Ratio $= \dfrac{\text{Long-term debts}}{\text{Owners' equity}}$

$$= \frac{\text{Debentures}}{\text{Equity share capital + General reserve + Accumulated profits}}$$

$$= \frac{7{,}50{,}000}{17{,}50{,}000} = 0.43 : 1$$

(3) Debt-equity Ratio $= \dfrac{\text{Long-term debts}}{\text{Shareholders' funds + Long-term debts}}$

$$= \frac{7{,}50{,}000}{17{,}50{,}000 + 7{,}50{,}000} = \frac{7{,}50{,}000}{25{,}00{,}000}$$

$= 0.3 : 1$

Interest Coverage Ratio

Interest coverage ratio determines the debt servicing capacity of a business enterprise keeping in view fixed interest on long-term debt. The formula for this ratio is:

$$\text{Interest Coverage Ratio} = \frac{\text{Earnings before Interest and Taxes (EBIT)}}{\text{Interest}}$$

If a business enterprise is able to earn a return on the assets higher than the rate of interest on long-term debt, the enterprise makes an overall profit. However, if the enterprise runs the risk of not earning a return on assets equal to the interest cost of the long-term loan, the enterprise makes an overall loss. The interest coverage ratio measures the degree of protection creditors have from default on the payment of interest by the company.

Illustration 9:

ABC Ltd. has earned net profit of Rs. 3,50,000 during the year 2007-2008. It has paid income tax Rs. 1,50,000 and interest on debentures as Rs. 1,25,000.

The interest coverage ratio may be calculated as follows:

$$\frac{3{,}50{,}000 + 1{,}50{,}000 + 1{,}25{,}000}{1{,}25{,}000}$$

$$= \frac{6{,}25{,}000}{1{,}25{,}000} = 5 \text{ times.}$$

V. Market Strength Analysis or Investor Analysis

The market strength analysis or investor analysis are especially important for investors while analysing information about a company. This analysis helps the investors to decide about a company as an investment opportunity at a point of time. These ratios are also known as stock market ratios, investment ratios or market test ratios. The ratios under this category are as follows:

1. Earnings Per Share

Earnings per share is derived by dividing the profit of a company by the total number of shares outstanding. Earnings here means the net profit, net income or the net earnings. This is the amount by which the total revenues exceed the total expenses for the year.

$$\text{Earnings After Tax} = \frac{\text{Earnings After Tax} - \text{Preference Dividends}}{\text{Number of Ordinary Shares}}$$

The net earnings figure is the amount which is completely free from any obligations and the company can plough it back into the company, pay to the ordinary shareholders as dividends or a combination of both. This amount is also known as the earnings available for ordinary shareholders.

Illustration 10:

Net profit before tax Rs. 1,00,000

Tax rate – 40% of net profit

10% Preference share capital (Rs. 10 each)	Rs. 1,00,000
Equity share capital (Rs. 10 shares)	Rs. 1,00,000

$$\text{Earnings per share} = \frac{\text{Net profit after tax and Pref. dividend}}{\text{Number of equity shares}}$$

$$= \frac{\text{Rs.}1{,}00{,}000 - 40{,}000\ (\text{tax}) - 10{,}000\ (\text{Pref. dividend})}{10{,}000}$$

$$= \frac{50{,}000}{10{,}000} = \text{Rs. 5 per share.}$$

Earnings per share can either be primary or diluted. Primary earnings per share is the earnings per share for the number of ordinary shares outstanding as on the beginning of the report period. Diluted earnings per share, on the other hand, is calculated after taking into account convertible debentures, bonds etc. (which have been converted into ordinary shares) during the year. It is computed in the same manner as primary earnings per share except that it assumes that all investments with the convertibility clause were converted at the beginning of the year. In case a company has bonds and debentures which are convertible into ordinary shares, it is always useful to compute fully diluted earnings per share (assuming full conversion) as well as earnings per share on a normal basis. This implies adding back the interest paid on the convertibles, recalculating the numerator and then dividing by the total number of ordinary shares on the assumption that conversion has taken place.

2. Dividend Per Share

The dividend per share can be net or gross. Net dividend per share is the dividend declared on a single ordinary share for the year, the net of basic rate tax.

$$\text{Net Dividend Per Share} = \frac{\text{Ordinary dividends paid to ordinary shareholders}}{\text{Number of ordinary shares}}$$

Gross dividend per share is net dividend per share together with the associated tax credit.

$$\text{Gross Dividend Per Share} = \frac{\text{Net dividend per share}}{1 - \text{Basic rate of tax}}$$

Alternatively,

Gross Dividend Per Share = Net Dividend Per Share + Associated Tax Credit

3. Gross Dividend Yield

The gross dividend yield is the gross dividend per share divided by the ordinary share price, expressed as a percentage.

$$\text{Gross Dividend Yield} = \frac{\text{Gross dividend per share}}{\text{Ordinary share price}} \times 100\%$$

For example, if a company declares dividend at 20% on its shares, each having a paid-up value of Rs. 8 and market price of Rs. 25, the dividend yield ratio will be calculated as follows:

$$\text{Dividend per share} = \frac{20}{100} \times 8 = \text{Rs. } 1.60$$

$$\text{Dividend yield ratio} = \frac{\text{Dividend per share}}{\text{Market price per share}} \times 100$$

$$= \frac{1.6}{25} \times 100 = 6.4\%$$

The gross dividend yield indicates the current level of income from a share. Dividend yields are normally calculated using gross dividends rather than net dividends because it helps in better analysis and comparison with other types of investments. Also, investors pay income tax at rates other than the basic rate. If the dividend yield is calculated on a net basis, the level of tax rate which has been deducted should be made clear.

Besides indicating the general level of the market, dividend yield reflects the market estimates of future dividend growth and risk. The higher the dividend growth expectations for a given share, the lower the current yield; the higher the market's estimate of risk, the greater the current yield.

4. Dividend Cover

Dividend cover denotes the number of times the dividend per share is covered by earnings per share

$$\text{Dividend Cover} = \frac{\text{Earnings per share}}{\text{Dividend per share}}$$

Dividend cover helps in assessing the prospects for dividend increases. Or, alternatively, the possibility of a dividend cut, should profits decline. For the purpose of dividend cover, full distribution earnings per share is normally taken into account. In other words, it is assumed that all profits are distributed as dividends. The gross dividend per share should be taken to ensure consistency in the resulting figure of dividend cover.

5. Payout Ratio

Payout ratio measures the proportion of earnings per share which are paid out as dividends.

$$\text{Payout Ratio} = \frac{\text{Net dividend per share}}{\text{Net earnings per share}} \times 100\%$$

The percentage of available earnings paid out as ordinary dividends has a vital influence on the market's behaviour towards those issues which are not in the growth category. For those companies which have paid dividends in the form of stock dividends and cash, only the cash dividend should be included in calculating the payout ratio. In the case of dividends paid out as stock dividends, the investor receives nothing that was not already owned and the company gives up nothing of value.

Illustration 11:

Compute the payout ratio and retained earning ratio from the following data:

	Rs.		*Rs.*
Net profit	20,000	No. of equity shares	3,000
Provision for tax	10,000	Dividend per equity share	Re. 0.80
Preference Dividend	4,000		

Solution:

$$\text{Payout Ratio} = \frac{\text{Dividend per equity share}}{\text{Earnings per equity share}} \times 100$$

$$\text{Earnings per Share} = \frac{\text{Profit available to equity shareholders}}{\text{No. of equity share}}$$

$$= \frac{20{,}000 - 10{,}000 - 4{,}000}{3{,}000} = \frac{6{,}000}{3{,}000}$$

$$= 2$$

$$\text{Dividend Payout Ratio} = \frac{\text{Re. } 0.80}{2} \times 100 = 40\%$$

$$\text{Retained Earning Ratio} = \frac{\text{Retained earnings}}{\text{Total earnings (after tax and Pref. dividend)}} \times 100$$

Retained Earnings = Profit available for equity shareholders – Dividends paid
= 6,000 – 2,400 = Rs. 3,600

$$\text{Retained Savings Ratio} = \frac{3{,}600}{6{,}000} \times 100 = 60\%$$

6. Dividends to Cashflow

'Dividends to cashflow' is a more useful ratio than the payout ratio. It helps in understanding the past trend in this regard and is greatly helpful in estimating future dividends than the conventional payout ratio.

$$\text{Dividend to Cashflow} = \frac{\text{Dividend paid on ordinary shares}}{\text{Net earnings available for ordinary share}}$$

7. Price/Earnings (P/E) Ratio

It is the market price of shares expressed as a multiple of earnings per share.

$$\text{Price/Earnings (P/E) Ratio} = \frac{\text{Price per ordinary shares}}{\text{Earnings per share}}$$

Many investors consider P/E ratio as the best indicator of the ongoing performance of a company. This ratio along with the payout ratio indicates the market estimates of future dividend growth and risk. High growth shares have high P/E ratios as investors are willing to pay a greater multiple of current earnings to achieve a higher future growth. If high risk is found in a share, it reduces its market price and hence automatically reduces its P/E ratio. Payout ratios can have a positive influence on P/E ratio. High P/Es are not always bad. If investors are willing to pay a high price for a share in relation to its earnings, then they are doing so in the belief that the company has a bright future. That it will continue to strengthen and grow in future. Buying a share with a high P/E is described as buying a security with a high multiple. It should be understood here that the common share dividends come out of the earnings per share. A drop in earnings could mean that a dividend is in trouble.

The elements which govern the P/E ratio are:

(*i*) Those factors that are fully reflected in the financial data (tangible factors) — Growth of earnings and sales in the past; Profitability or rate of returns on invested capital; Stability of past earnings; Dividend rate and record, and; Financial strength or credit standing.

(*ii*) Those factors that are reflected to an indefinite extent in the data (intangible factors) — Quality of management; Nature and prospects of the industry, and competitive position and individual prospects of the company.

8. Net Asset Value Per Share

This ratio is also known as the book value per share. Net asset value per share is the value of net tangible assets attributable to one ordinary share. Net asset value is, simply put, the shareholder's equity. Net asset value or book value has nothing to do with the market value as shares usually sell in the stock market at several times its net asset or book value.

$$\text{Net Asset Value Per Share} = \frac{\text{Ordinary share capital} + \text{Reserves} - \text{Intangibles}}{\text{Number of ordinary shares outstanding at balance sheet date}}$$

Net asset value applies to ordinary shares only. However, it does not mean that investors can get that amount if the company is liquidated. The amounts attributed to the assets are only attempts at fair and systematic evaluation, not at guessing what these assets would bring if sold in the market place. Net asset or book value can be considered only as the theoretical value of ordinary shares if the assets of the company were liquidated at the amounts attributed to them on the balance sheet. It is not unusual for a share price to be very different from the net asset value per share, even where assets in the balance sheet have recently been revalued. In general, the market price of a share will be influenced by earnings and the dividend-paying potential. Share prices will not be significantly influenced by the net asset value per share except where:

(*a*) The company is an investment vehicle for specific types of assets (e.g., investment trusts, property companies).

(*b*) It seems probable that the company will be liquidated.

(*c*) A takeover bid of the company seems likely.

The net asset value per share figure is useful while comparing shares of one company with shares of other companies operating in the same industry. If it is found that a company is selling shares at a much lower ratio of market price to book value than other companies in the same industry, it indicates a good investment opportunity. When a share can be bought for less than its net asset value, it is an indication that share will have good value in the future. In case of mutual funds, net asset value ratio is important as it is determined at or near the price at which the mutual fund will buy and sell its shares. In the stock market, it is often found that a share is selling five times, seven times (and more) its book value. The lower the multiple, the greater will be probable value of the share.

9. Cashflow Per Share

Cashflow per share is a useful indicator of a company's general ability to leverage itself, to pay dividends, to convert accounting earnings into cash and to enjoy financial flexibility.

$$\text{Cash Flow Per Share} = \frac{\text{Cash flow from operations after taxes}}{\text{Ordinary shares outstanding at balance sheet date}}$$

The amount of cash flow does not totally belong to ordinary shareholders, as the earnings belong; it is also meant to pay the expenses and claims prior to the payment of dividend.

VI. Growth and Stability Analysis or Ratios

Growth and stability ratios measure the performance and financial strength of a company apart from market valuation. Stability ratios are useful in evaluating the quality of bonds, debentures, preference shares, etc. These ratios are calculated over time and relate to sales, total returns, and earnings per share. Such ratios are:

(1) Growth in Sales $= \dfrac{\text{Sales in final period}}{\text{Sales in base period}}$

(2) Growth in Total Returns $= \dfrac{\text{Net earnings for total capital in final period}}{\text{Net earnings for total capital in base year}}$

(3) Growth in Earnings $= \dfrac{\text{Earnings per share in final period}}{\text{Earnings per share in base period}}$

(4) Maximum decline in coverage of interest charges $= \dfrac{\text{Worst year (or lowest year)}}{\text{Average of previous three years}}$

Normally interest charges may include any of the following combinations:

— Interest on short and long-term debts, including capital leases
— Interest on expenses plus an interest component for Operating leases
— Interest on expenses on short and long-term debts plus rentals on both capital and operating bases
— Total fixed charges, rentals and preferred dividends.

(5) Per cent Decline in Return on Total Capital $= \dfrac{\text{Worst year (or lowest year)}}{\text{Average of previous three years}}$

(6) Per cent Decline in Return on Ordinary Capital $= \dfrac{\text{Worst year (or lowest year)}}{\text{Average of previous three years}}$

(7) Percentage Decline in Earnings Per Share $= \dfrac{\text{Worst year (or lowest year)}}{\text{Average of previous three years}}$

LIMITATIONS OF FINANCIAL RATIOS

Financial statement analysis through ratios is useful because they highlight relationships between items in the financial statements. However, they have a number of limitations which should be kept in mind while preparing or using them.

(1) Ratios are based on accounting figures given in the financial statements. However, accounting figures are themselves subject to deficiencies, approximations, diversity in practice or even manipulation to some extent. Therefore, ratios are not very helpful in drawing reliable conclusions.

(2) Ratios have inherent problem of comparability. Companies otherwise similar may employ different accounting methods, which can cause problems in comparing certain key relationships.

For example, inventory turnover can be different for a company using FIFO than for the company using LIFO method of inventory valuation. Similarly the differences in accounting methods relating to depreciation, estimates of the life of asset, amortisation of intangibles and preliminary expenses, treatment of extraordinary items etc. can create the problem of comparability among the companies even in the same industry.

(3) Inflation may limit the utility of accounting ratios. Due to inflation, historical cost-based financial statements and accounting figures do not reflect current value figures, especially in the case of assets purchased at different dates by the different enterprises. Since financial statements are not adjusted in terms of inflation effect, accounting ratios calculated (using varying cost or prices) have distortions and become deceptive. Sometimes, gains (reflected through ratios) over time in sales, net income and other key figures disappear when the accounting data are adjusted for changes in price levels.

(4) Accounting ratios are not totally dependable and they must be used after giving due weightage to general economic conditions, industry situation, position of firms within the industry, mode of operations, size of firm, diversity of product which can make the business enterprises completely dissimilar and thus affect the computation of accounting ratios.

(5) The different methods of computation also influence the utility of accounting ratios. The different concepts used for determining numerator and denominator in a particular accounting ratio will not help in drawing reliable conclusions even in identical situations.

Illustration 12:

The working capital of ABC Ltd. has deteriorated in recent years and now stands as under:

Current Assets	*Rs.*	*Current Liabilities*	*Rs.*
Inventory	5,60,000	Creditors	4,90,000
Debtors	3,50,000	Bank loan	2,10,000
Cash	70,000		
	9,80,000		7,00,000

(*a*) Compute the current and quick ratios.

(*b*) A further bank loan of Rs. 50,000 against debtors is under negotiation. Assuming the loan is received, calculate the revised current and quick ratios.

(*c*) There is also a negotiation going on for discounting the debtors of Rs. 3,50,000 for Rs. 3,15,000 to a collection agency for immediate cash. Also obsolete stocks worth Rs. 1,25,000 are being sold for Rs. 80,000. Of the cash to be realised by the two transactions, the bank loan is proposed to be reduced to Rs. 1,00,000. Calculate the current ratio after the transactions are put through.

Solution:

(*a*) $$\text{Current Ratio} = \frac{\text{Current assets}}{\text{Current liabilities}} = \frac{9,80,000}{7,00,000} = 1.4$$

$$\text{Quick Ratio} = \frac{\text{Liquid assets}}{\text{Current liabilities}} = \frac{4,20,000}{7,00,000} = 0.6$$

(*b*) $$\text{Revised current ratio} = \frac{10,30,000}{7,50,000} = 1.37$$

$$\text{Revised quick ratio} = \frac{4,70,000}{7,50,000} = 0.63$$

(*c*) Financial position after the transactions:

	Rs.
Current Assets:	
Inventory	4,35,000
Debtors	—
Cash	3,55,000
	7,90,000
Current Liabilities:	
Creditors	4,90,000
Bank Loan	1,00,000
	5,90,000

$$\text{New current ratio} = \frac{7,90,000}{5,90,000} = 1.34$$

$$\text{New quick ratio} = \frac{3,55,000}{5,90,000} = 0.6$$

Cash balance = Rs. 70,000 + Rs. 3,15,000 + Rs. 80,000 – Rs. 1,10,000
= Rs. 3,55,000

Illustration 13:

From the following annual accounts of New Horizon Limited you are required to calculate the following ratios and comment on the results, indicating what other information you require.

(*i*) Gross profit percentage
(*ii*) Net profit percentage
(*iii*) Return on total assets
(*iv*) Quick assets ratio
(*v*) Debtors collection period
(*vi*) Stock turnover
(*vii*) Fixed assets turnover
(*viii*) Return on shareholders' funds
(*ix*) Current ratio
(*x*) Debt ratio

Balance Sheet at 31 December, 2007

	(*Rs. '000*)
Share capital	450
Retained profits	240
	690
12% Debentures	700
Trade creditors	620
Proposed dividend	45
	2,055

Fixed assets net of depreciation	875
Stocks	310
Debtors	770
Bank balance	100
	2,055

Extracts from year's Profit and Loss Account

	(Rs.)
Sales for the year	31,00,000
Gross profit	17,25,000
Expenses	8,05,000
Depreciation	2,50,000

Solution:

(*i*) Gross profit percentage $= \frac{1725}{3100} \times 100\% = 55.6\%$

(*ii*) Net profit percentage $= \frac{670}{3100} \times 100\% = 21.6\%$

(*iii*) Return on total assets $= \frac{670}{2055} \times 100\% = 32.6\%$

(*iv*) Quick ratio $= \frac{870}{665} = 1.3 : 1$

(*v*) Debtors collection period $= \frac{770}{3100} \times 365 = 91$ days

(*vi*) Stock : turnover $= \frac{3100}{310} = 10$ times

(*vii*) Fixed assets : turnover $= \frac{3100}{875} = 3.5$ times

(*vii*) Return on shareholders' funds $= \frac{586}{690} \times 100\% = 84.9\%$

(*ix*) Current ratio $= \frac{1180}{665} = 1.8:1$

(*x*) Debt ratio $= \frac{1365}{2065} \times 100\% = 66.4\%$

Very few ratios have an absolute value but they are used in a relative way in intra and inter-firm comparisons. Both gross and net margins are calculated using the profit before tax and interest to identify the trading profit, irrespective of the capital structure in force. Both these figures seem satisfactory but knowledge of the industry is necessary. Also the returns on shareholders' funds and on total assets both appear quite satisfactory.

The quick ratio exceeds the 1 : 1 norm and the current ratio is near the 2:1 norm, but this requirement varies widely. On the other hand the debt ratio seems high, as two-thirds of all assets are financed by debt.

Asset turnover ratios also need comparisons to make any judgment but the debtors collection period of 91 days would seem too long for most industries, especially if credit is granted on a net monthly basis.

Illustration 14:

XYZ Company's financial statements contain the following information:

	2002	*2003*
	Rs.	*Rs.*
Cash	2,00,000	1,60,000
Sundry debtors	3,20,000	4,00,000
Temporary investments	2,00,000	3,20,000
Stock	18,40,000	21,60,000
Prepaid expenses	28,000	12,000
Total current assets	25,88,000	30,52,000
Total assets	56,00,000	64,00,000
Current liabilities	6,40,000	8,00,000
Loans	16,00,000	16,00,000
Capital	20,00,000	20,00,000
Retained earnings	4,68,000	8,12,000

Statement of Profit for the current year

	Rs.
Sales	40,00,000
Less cost of goods sold	28,00,000
Less interest	1,60,000
Net profit	10,40,000
Less taxes @ 50%	5,20,000
Profit after taxes	5,20,000
Profit distributed	2,20,000

From the above, appraise the financial position of the company from the point of view of: (*i*) Liquidity, (*ii*) Profitability, and (*iii*) Activity.

Solution:

1. Liquidity Ratios:

(*a*) Current Ratio (2003) $= \dfrac{\text{Current assets}}{\text{Current liabilities}} = \dfrac{\text{Rs. }30,52,000}{\text{Rs. }8,00,000} = 3.81$

(*b*) Acid test Ratio (2003) $= \dfrac{\text{Liquid assets}}{\text{Current liabilities}} = \dfrac{\text{Rs. }30,52,000 - 21,72,000}{\text{Rs. }8,00,000} = 1.1$

2. Leverage Ratios:

(*a*) Debt Equity Ratio (2003) $= \dfrac{\text{Long-term debts}}{\text{Equity funds}} = \dfrac{\text{Rs. }16,00,000}{\text{Rs. }28,12,000} = .57$

(*b*) Interest Coverage Ratio (2003) $= \dfrac{\text{EBIT}}{\text{Interest Charge}} = \dfrac{\text{Rs. }12,00,000}{\text{Rs. }1,60,000} = 7.5$ times.

3. Profitability Ratios:

(*a*) Gross Profit Ratio (2003) $= \frac{\text{Gross Profit}}{\text{Sales}} \times 100 = \frac{\text{Rs. } 12,00,000}{\text{Rs. } 40,00,000} \times 100 = 30\%$

(*b*) Net Profit Ratio (2003) $= \frac{\text{Net Profit}}{\text{Sales}} \times 100 = \frac{\text{Rs. } 5,20,000}{\text{Rs. } 40,00,000} \times 100 = 13\%$

(*c*) Return on Total Assets (2003) $= \frac{\text{Profit after Tax}}{\text{Total Assets}} \times 100 = \frac{\text{Rs. } 5,20,000}{\text{Rs. } 64,00,000} \times 100$

$= 8.12\%$

(*d*) Return on Cap. Emp. (2003) $= \frac{\text{PAT} + \text{Int } (1 - \text{T})}{\text{Total Cap Emp.}} \times 100$

$= \frac{\text{Rs. } 5,20,000 + 80,000}{\text{Rs. } 44,12,000} \times 100 = 13.6\%$

(*e*) Return on Equity Funds (2003) $= \frac{\text{Profit after Tax}}{\text{Equity Funds}} \times 100 = \frac{\text{Rs. } 5,20,000}{\text{Rs. } 28,12,000} \times 100$

$= 18.5\%$

4. Activity Ratios:

(*a*) Debtors Turnover (2003) $= \frac{\text{Sales}}{\text{Average Debtors}} = \frac{\text{Rs. } 40,00,000}{\text{Rs. } 3,60,000} = 11.1 \text{ times}$

(*b*) Stock Turnover (2003) $= \frac{\text{Cost of goods sold}}{\text{Average Stock}} = \frac{\text{Rs. } 28,00,000}{\text{Rs. } 20,00,000} = 1.4 \text{ times}$

(*c*) Total Assets Turnover (2003) $= \frac{\text{Sales}}{\text{Average Assets}} = \frac{\text{Rs. } 40,00,000}{\text{Rs. } 60,00,000} = .67 \text{ times}$

On the basis of the above ratios, it can be said that the firm's position is sound from the point of view of liquidity, solvency and profitability. However, its activity ratios do not represent a satisfactory position. Better position will be reflected only if the ratios are compared with the performance of other firms in the same industry.

Illustration 15:

The balance sheet of XYZ company is given below:

(Rs. in lakhs)

Liabilities	*Amount*	*Assets*	*Amount*
Equity share capital	250	Fixed Assets	400
General Reserve	280	Investment	50
P&L A/c (current year)	30	Stock	460
Secured loans — Long-term	300	Debtors	460
Secured loans — Short-term	360	Cash in hand	10
Creditors .	150	Misc. expenditure (not written off)	20
Other liabilities	30		
	1,400		1,400

Additional Information:

(*a*) From the Profit and Loss Account Rs. 90 lakhs were transferred to General Reserve during the year.

(*b*) Interest cost amounted to Rs. 120 lakhs.

(*c*) Taxation @ 40%

You are required to calculate (*i*) Debt equity ratio (*ii*) Current ratio (*iii*) Interest coverage ratio.

Solution:

$$\text{Current Ratio} = \frac{\text{Current Assets}}{\text{Current Liabilities}} = \frac{\text{Rs. 930 lakhs}}{\text{Rs. 540 lakhs}} = 1.73$$

$$\text{Debt Equity Ratio} = \frac{\text{Debt}}{\text{Equity}} = \frac{\text{Rs. 300 lakhs}}{\text{Rs. 560 lakhs}} = 0.54$$

$$\text{Interest Coverage Ratio} = \frac{\text{EBIT}}{\text{Interest}} = \frac{\text{Rs. 320 lakhs}}{\text{Rs. 120 lakhs}} = 2.66$$

Working Notes:

Current Assets	***Rs.***	***Debt***	***Equity***	***Rs.***
Stock	460 lakhs	Term loan Rs. 300 lakhs	Capital	250 lakhs
Debtors	460 lakhs		Reserve	280 lakhs
Cash	10 lakhs		P&L A/c	30 lakhs
	930 lakhs			560 lakhs

Current liabilities	***Rs.***	***EBIT***		***Rs.***
Short-term loan	360 lakhs	Profit for the year (30 + 90)		120 lakhs
Trade Credit	150 lakhs	Interest		120 lakhs
Other liabilities	30 lakhs	Tax @ 40%	$\frac{120 \times 40}{60}$	80 lakhs
	540 lakhs			320 lakhs

Illustration 16:

Calculate the P/E ratio from the following:

	Rs.
Equity Share Capital (Rs. 20 each)	50,00,000
Reserves and Surplus	5,00,000
Secured Loans at 15%	25,00,000
Unsecured Loans at 12.5%	10,00,000
Fixed Assets	30,00,000
Investments	5,00,000
Operating Profit	25,00,000
Income-tax rate	50%
Market price/share	Rs. 50

Solution:

	Rs.	
Operating Profit		25,00,000
Less: Interest on:		
Secured loans @ 15%	3,75,000	
Unsecured Loans @ 12.5%	1,25,000	5,00,000
Profit before Tax (PBT)		20,00,000

Less: Income Tax @ 50%	10,00,000
Profit after tax (PAT)	10,00,000
No. of Equity Shares	2,50,000

$$\text{EPS} = \frac{\text{Profit after tax}}{\text{No. of equity shares}} = \frac{\text{Rs. } 10,00,000}{2,50,000} = \text{Rs. } 4$$

P/E ratio = Market price per share/EPS = Rs. 50/Rs. 4 = 12.50

Illustration 17:

ABC Distributors has the following Balance Sheet and Income Statement:

Balance Sheet

Liabilities	*Amount*	*Assets*	*Amount*
Shareholders' Equity	3,00,000	Long-term Assets	3,50,000
(50,000 shares)		Cash	25,000
Long-term debt	1,00,000	Accounts Receivables	60,000
Accounts payable	80,000	Inventory	65,000
Other current liabilities	20,000		
	5,00,000		5,00,000

Income Statement

Particulars	*Amount Rs.*
Sales	9,00,000
Cost of Goods Sold	4,00,000
General, Administrative and Selling Expenses	1,00,000
Other expenses	2,50,000
Net Income (PAT)	1,50,000

You are required to:

(*a*) Determine ABC Distributor's liquidity position by calculating the Current ratio, Working Capital, the ratio of Current Assets to Total Assets, the ratio of Current Liabilities to Total Assets and the Cash Conversion cycle.

(*b*) Calculate the current market price per share of ABC's Stock if its P/E ratio is eight.

Solution:

Various Ratios of ABC Distributors may be found as follows:

Current assets	= Cash + Accounts receivable + Inventory
	= 25,000 + 60,000 + 65,000 = 1,50,000
Current liabilities	= Accounts payable + Other current liabilities
	= 80,000 + 20,000 = 1,00,000
Current Ratio	= Current assets/Current liabilities
	= 1,50,000/1,00,000 = 1.5
Net working capital	= 1,50,000 – 1,00,000 = 50,000
Current assets/Total assets	= 1,50,000/5,00,000 = 0.30
Current liabilities/Total assets	= 1,00,000/5,00,000 = 0.20

Receivables Turnover	= Sales/Accounts receivables = 15.00
Inventory Turnover	= Cost of goods sold/Inventory = 6.15
Payable Turnover	= $\frac{\text{Cost of goods sold}}{\text{Accounts Payable}}$ = 5.00
Average collection period	= 365/Receivables turnover = 24.33 days
Inventory conversion period	= 365/Inventory turnover = 59.35 days
Payable Deferral period	= 365/Payables turnover = 73 days
Cash conversion cycle	= 10.68 days (24.33 + 59.35 − 73)

Calculation of Market price of Share of ABC Distributors

EPS =PAT/No. of shares	= 1,50,000/50,000 = 3.00
Price = (EPS) × (P/E) (3.00 × 8)	= Rs. 24.00

Illustration 18:

Following is the Balance Sheet of M/s. Bintex Co. Ltd. Bangalore, as on 31st December, 2007

Liabilities	*Rs.*	*Assets*	*Rs.*
Share capital:		Land	4,00,000
Authorised, issued and fully paid up:		Building	21,00,000
50,000 9% preference		Plant and machinery	1,19,00,000
shares of Rs. 100 each	50,00,000	Furniture and Fittings	1,50,000
5,00,000 equity shares of Rs. 10 each	50,00,000	Office cars, trucks	1,50,000
	1,00,00,000	Stock	1,50,00,000
Capital reserves	5,00,000	Accounts receivable	6,00,000
General reserves	10,00,000	Cash and bank	2,00,000
Sinking fund reserves	15,00,000		
7% Debentures	50,00,000		
Bank overdraft	85,00,000		
Notes payable	15,00,000		
Account payable	25,00,000		
	Rs. 3,05,00,000		3,05,00,000

Compute the following from the above balance sheet:

(1) Net worth
(2) Total value of equity
(3) Shareholders' reserves
(4) Total fixed assets
(5) Total current assets
(6) Working capital
(7) Long-term liabilities

(Show the workings, where necessary)

Solution:

(1) Net Worth

This represents the net assets of the company. It is also equivalent to proprietors' fund and paid up capital plus reserves. This can be obtained by calculating both ways Assets Approach and Liabilities Approach as given below:

		Rs.
(*a*) Gross assets as per balance sheet		3,05,00,000
Less: *Liabilities*	*Rs.*	
7% Debentures	50,00,000	
Bank overdraft	85,00,000	
Notes payable	15,00,000	
Accounts payable	25,00,000	
		1,75,00,000
Net worth		1,30,00,000

Alternatively

(*a*) Paid up capital		
Preference share capital	50,00,000	
Equity share capital	50,00,000	
		1,00,00,000
Reserves:		
Capital reserve	5,00,000	
General reserve	10,00,000	
Sinking fund reserve	15,00,000	30,00,000
Net worth		1,30,00,000

(2) Total value of equity

This can be obtained by adding up Equity Paid up Capital with reserves and surpluses belonging to equity shareholders. Alternatively the same can be obtained by subtracting from net worth of the company what is due to preferences shareholders:

	Rs.
Net worth as calculated under (1)	1,30,00,000
Less: Preference share capital	50,00,000
Total value of equity	80,00,000

(3) Shareholders' reserves:	
Capital reserve	5,00,000
General reserve	10,00,000
Sinking fund reserve	15,00,000
Total	30,00,000

(4) Total fixed assets	
Land	4,00,000
Building	21,00,000
Plant and machinery	1,19,00,000
Furniture and fittings	1,50,000
Office cars and trucks	1,50,000
Total	1,47,00,000

(5) Total current assets:

Stock		1,50,00,000
Account receivable		6,00,000
Cash at bank		2,00,000
Total		1,58,00,000

(6) Working capital

This represents excess of current assets over current liabilities:

	Rs.	
Current assets as calculated under (5)		1,58,00,000
Less: Current liabilities:		
Bank overdraft	85,00,000	
Notes payable	15,00,000	
Accounts payable	25,00,000	1,25,00,000
Working capital		33,00,000

(7) Long-term liabilities

7% debentures	50,00,000
	50,00,000

Illustration 19:

Calculate and comment on the rate of return on total assets from the following data of two companies:

	Go Slow Co.	*Go Fast Co.*
Sales		2,52,75,000
Total assets	42,50,000	
Net profit in sales	6%	4%
Turnover of assets	6 times	6 times
Gross margin	20,68,000	12%

Solution:

	Rs.	*Rs.*
Sales	Rs. 42,50,000 × 6 = 2,55,00,000	Rs. 2,52,75,000
Total assets	Rs. 42,50,000	Rs. 2,52,75,000 ÷ 6 = 42,12,500
Net profit in sales	6% of Rs. 2,55,00,000 = Rs. 15,30,000	4% of Rs. 2,52,75,000 = Rs. 10,11,000
Rate of return on total assets	$\frac{\text{Rs. } 15,30,000}{\text{Rs. } 42,50,000}$ = 36%	$\frac{\text{Rs. } 10,11,000}{\text{Rs. } 42,12,500}$ = 24%

The rate of return on total assets in respect of Go Fast Co. is less than that of Go Slow Co. as the total assets are same (approx.) in both the Cos. Net profit in sales in Go Fast Co. is 2/3rd of net profit of Go Slow Co. and similar is the case of rate of return on total assets.

Illustration 20:

The following are the ratios relating to the activities of National Traders Ltd.:

Debtors velocity	3 months
Stock velocity	8 months
Creditors velocity	2 months
Gross profit ratio	25%

Gross profit for the current year ended 31st December amounted to Rs. 4,00,000. Closing stock of the year is Rs. 10,000 above the opening stock. Bills Receivables amount to Rs. 25,000 and bills payable to Rs. 10,000. Find out:

(*a*) Sales
(*b*) Sundry debtors
(*c*) Closing stock
(*d*) Sundry creditors.

Solution:

(*a*) Determination of sales:

$$\text{Gross profit ratio} = \frac{\text{Gross profit}}{\text{Sales}} \times 100$$

$$25 = \frac{\text{Rs. } 4,00,000}{\text{Sales}} \times 100$$

$$\text{Sales} = \frac{\text{Rs. } 4,00,000}{25} \times 100 = \text{Rs. } 16,00,000$$

(*b*) Determination of sundry debtors:

Debtors' velocity is 3 months. In other words, debtors' collection period is 3 months, or debtors' turnover ratio is 4. Assuming all sales to be credit sales and debtors turnover ratio being calculated on the basis of the year-end figures, debtors would be determined as follows:

$$\text{Debtors' turnover ratio} = \frac{\text{Credit sales}}{\text{Closing debtors + Bills receivable}}$$

or

$$\text{Closing debtors + Bills receivables} = \frac{\text{Credit sales}}{\text{Debtors' turnover ratio}}$$

$$= \frac{\text{Rs. } 16,00,000}{4}$$

$$= \text{Rs. } 4,00,000$$

$$\text{Closing debtors} = \text{Rs. } 4,00,000 - \text{Rs. } 25,000$$

$$= \text{Rs. } 3,75,000$$

(*c*) Determination of closing stock:

Stock velocity of 8 months signifies that the turnover is 8 months. In other words, stock turnover ratio is 1.5 = (12 months ÷ 8).

$$\text{Stock turnover} = \frac{\text{Cost of goods sold (Sales − Gross Profit)}}{\text{Average stock}}$$

$$\text{Average stock} = \frac{\text{Rs. } 12,00,000}{1.5} = \text{Rs. } 8,00,000$$

Closing Stock − Opening stock = Rs. 10,000 ... (1)

$$\frac{\text{Closing stock + Opening stock}}{2} = \text{Rs. } 8{,}00{,}000 \quad \text{... (2)}$$

or

Closing Stock + Opening stock = Rs. 16,00,000 ... (3)

Subtracting equation (1) from equation (3) (i.e., Rs. 16,00,000 − 10,000)

	Rs.
Opening stock	15,90,000
Opening stock	7,95,000
Closing stock	8,05,000

(*d*) Determination of sundry creditors:

Creditors velocity of 2 months signifies that the credit payment period is 2 months. In other words, creditors turnover ratio is 6 (12 months ÷ 2). Assuming all purchases to be credit purchases and creditors turnover is based on year-end figures, we have:

$$\text{Creditors turnover ratio} = \frac{\text{Credit purchases}}{\text{Creditors + Bills payable}}$$

$$6 = \frac{\text{Rs. } 12{,}10{,}000}{\text{Creditors + Rs. } 10{,}000}$$

$$\text{Creditors + Rs. } 10{,}000 = \frac{\text{Rs. } 12{,}10{,}000}{6} = \text{Rs. } 2{,}01{,}667$$

Creditors = Rs. 2,01,667 − Rs. 10,000 = Rs. 1,91,667

Credit purchases are calculated as follows:

Cost of goods sold = Opening stock + Purchases − Closing stock

Rs. 12,00,000 = Rs. 7,95,000 + Purchases − Rs. 8,05,000

Rs. 12,00,000 + Rs. 10,000 = Purchases

Rs. 12,10,000 = Purchases (credit)

Illustration 21:

The capital of E. Co. Ltd., is as follows:

	(Rs.)
9% Preference shares of Rs. 10 each	3,00,000
Equity shares of Rs. 10 each	8,00,000
	11,00,000

The accountant has ascertained the following information:

Profit (after tax at 60%) Rs. 2,70,000: Depreciation Rs. 60,000; Equity dividend paid 20%; market price of equity shares Rs. 40. You are required to state the following, showing the necessary workings:

(*a*) Dividend yield on the equity shares.

(*b*) Cover for the preference and equity dividends.

(*c*) Earnings for equity shares.

(*d*) Price-earnings ratio.

Solution:

(*a*) Dividend yield on the equity shares:

$$= \frac{\text{Dividend per share}}{\text{Market price per share}} \times 100$$

$$= \frac{\text{Rs. } 2(20\% \text{ of Rs. } 10) \times 100}{\text{Rs. } 40} \times 100 = 5\%$$

(*b*) Dividend coverage ratio:

(*i*) Preference $= \frac{\text{Profits after taxes}}{\text{Dividend payable to preference shareholders}}$

$$= \frac{\text{Rs. } 2{,}70{,}000}{\text{Rs. } 27{,}000 \ (9\% \text{ of Rs. } 3{,}00{,}000)}$$

$$= 10 \text{ times}$$

(*ii*) Equity $= \frac{\text{Profits after taxes} - \text{Preference share dividends}}{\text{Dividend payable to equity shareholders at current rate of Rs. 2 per share}}$

$$= \frac{\text{Rs. } 2{,}70{,}000 - \text{Rs. } 27{,}000}{\text{Rs. } 1{,}60{,}000 \ (80{,}000 \text{ shares} \times \text{Rs. } 2)}$$

$$= \frac{\text{Rs. } 2{,}43{,}000}{\text{Rs. } 1{,}60{,}000} = 1.52 \text{ times}$$

(*c*) Earnings for equity shares:

$$= \frac{\text{Earnings available to equity shareholders}}{\text{Number of the equity share outstanding}}$$

$$= \frac{\text{Rs. } 2{,}43{,}000}{80{,}000} = \text{Rs. } 3.04 \text{ per share}$$

(*d*) Price-earning (P/E) ratio:

$$\text{P/E ratio} = \frac{\text{Market price per share}}{\text{Earnings per share}}$$

$$= \frac{\text{Rs. } 40.00}{\text{Rs. } 3.04} = 13.2 \text{ times}$$

Illustration 22:

With the help of the following ratios regarding Indu Films, draw the Balance Sheet of the Company for the year 2007:

Current Ratio	2.5
Liquidity Ratio	1.5
Net Working Capital	Rs. 3,00,000

Stock Turnover Ratio (cost of sales/closing stock)	6 times
Gross Profit Ratio	20 per cent
Fixed Assets Turnover Ratio (on cost of sales)	2 times
Debt Collection Period	2 months
Fixed assets to shareholders net worth	0.80
Reserve and surplus to capital	0.50

Solution:

Balance Sheet as on...

Liabilities	*Rs.*	*Assets*	*Rs.*
Share capital	5,00,000	Fixed assets	6,00,000
Reserve and surplus	2,50,000	Stock	2,00,000
Long-term borrowings (balancing figure)	1,50,000	Debtors	2,50,000
Current liabilities	2,00,000	Bank	50,000
	11,00,000		11,00,000

Working Notes:

If Current Liabilities	=	1
Current assets	=	2.5
It means the difference of working capital	=	1.5
Working Capital is 1.5	=	Rs. 3,00,000
Therefore, Current Assets	=	Rs. 5,00,000
Current Liabilities	=	Rs. 2,00,000
Liquidity ratio	=	1.5
Therefore, the liquid assets (Bank and debtors (2,00,000 × 1.5)	=	3,00,000
Stock (5,00,000 – 3,00,000, i.e., current assets – liquid assets)	=	2,00,000
Cost of sales (as stock turnover ratio is 6)	=	12,00,000
Sales as G/P ratio is 20 per cent, 12,00,000 + 20/80 × 12,00,000)	=	15,00,000
Fixed Assets are Rs. 12,00,000/2 since fixed assets turnover is ratio 2	=	6,00,000
Debtors are Rs. 15,00,000/6 since debt collection period is 2 months	=	2,50,000

Shareholders Net worth $\left(\frac{6,00,000 \times 1}{0.80}\right) = 7,50,000$

Out of Shareholders net worth, reserves and surplus = 2,50,000

Therefore, share capital = 5,00,000

THEORY QUESTIONS

1. What do you mean by financial statement analysis? What arc its purposes?
2. Discuss the importance of financial ratios.
3. Explain the financial ratios:
   (*a*) Liquidity ratio
   (*b*) Profitability ratio
   (*c*) Capital structure ratio
4. In what way market strength ratios are useful to investors?

5. Discuss the computation and significance of the following financial ratios:
   (*a*) Current ratio
   (*b*) Quick ratio
   (*c*) Inventory turnover ratio
   (*d*) Debt-equity ratio
   (*e*) Accounts receivables ratio
   (*f*) Earnings margin
   (*g*) Earning per share.
6. What are the limitations of accounting ratios?
7. What is meant by horizontal and vertical analysis of financial statement. Explain giving suitable examples.
8. What is asset turnover? What influence does a higher asset turnover tend to have on the rate of return on assets?
9. What is the key question in assessing liquidity? What ratios are used in this regard?
10. What are trend percentages and how are they calculated?
11. Distinguish between horizontal analysis and vertical analysis of financial statements.
12. What are common size percentages and how are they used?
13. Discuss the significance of equity ratio and explain how it is computed.
14. What similarities and differences exist in the objectives of investors and credit in using financial statement analysis.
15. "Net income based on historical financial statements is a useless measurement because it is influenced by so many arbitrary decisions." Examine the rationale of this statement.
16. What are the objectives associated with horizontal and trend analysis of a company's financial statements?
17. Company A and Company B both have net income of Rs. 10,00,000. Is it possible to say that these companies are equally successful? Why or why not?

EXERCISES AND PROBLEMS

1. From the following annual statement of Pioneer Ltd., calculate the following ratios: (a) Gross Profit Ratio; (b) Current ratio; (c) Liquid ratio; (d) Debt-equity ratio; and (e) Return on equity ratio.

Trading and Profit and Loss Account

for the year ended 31st December, 2007

	Rs.		*Rs.*
Materials consumed:		Sales	85,000
Opening stock	9,050	Profit on sale of investments	600
Purchases	54,525	Interest on investments	300
	63,575		
Closing stock	14,000		
	49,575		
Carriage inwards	1,425		
Office expenses	15,000		
Sales expenses	3,000		
Financial expenses	1,500		
Loss on sale of assets	400		
Net profit	15,000		
	85,900		85,900

Balance Sheet as on 31st December, 2007

		Rs.			Rs.
Share Capital:			Fixed Assets:		
2,000 Equity Shares of			Buildings	15,000	
Rs. 10 each		20,000	Plant	8,000	
Reserves		9,000			23,000
Profit and Loss account		6,000	Current Assets:		
Bank overdraft		3,000	Stock in trade	14,000	
Sundry creditors:			Debtors	7,000	
for expenses	2,000		Bills receivable	1,000	
for others	8,000	10,000	Bank	3,000	25,000
		48,000			48,000

(*Ans.:* (*a*) Gross Profit Ratio 40%; (*b*) Current Ratio 1.92 : 1; (*c*) Liquid Ratio 1.1 : 1 Bank overdraft has not been taken as a current liability (*d*) Debt-Equity Ratio:

(*i*) $\frac{\text{All debts}}{\text{Equity}} = 0.371 : 1$

(*ii*) $\frac{\text{All debts}}{\text{All Debts + Equity}} = 0.271 : 1$

(*iii*) Return on Investment Ratio $= \frac{\text{Net profit}}{\text{Capital employed}}$

$= \frac{15,000}{35,000} = 42.85$

2. Following is the Profit and Loss Account and balance sheet of A Limited for the year ended 31st December, 2007 and balance sheet as on that date. Calculate the different ratios and comment on the financial position of the company.

Profit and Loss Account for the year ended 31 December, 2007

		(Rs.)
Net sales		3,00,000
Less: Cost of Goods sold		2,58,000
Gross profit		42,000
Operating Expenses:		
Selling	2,200	
General and administration	4,000	
Rent of Office	2,800	
		9,000
		33,000
Gross Operating profit		33,000
Depreciation		10,000
		23,000
Other Income:		
Interest on Government Securities		1,500
Gross Income		24,500
Other expenses:		
Interest on bank overdraft	300	
Interest on debentures	4,200	
		4,500
Net Income before Tax		20,000
Tax @ 50 per cent on Net Income		10,000
Net Income after tax		10,000

Balance Sheet as on 31st December, 2007

Liabilities	*Rs.*	*Assets*		*Rs.*
Sundry Creditors	6,000	Cash		5,000
Bills payable	10,000	Investments (Govt. securities)		15,000
Outstanding expenses	1,000	Sundry Debtors		20,000
Provision for taxation	13,000	Stock		30,000
Total current liabilities	30,000	Total Current Assets		70,000
6 per cent mortgage debentures	70,000	Fixed Assets	1,80,000	
7 per cent preference shares	10,000	*Less:* Provision for dep.	50,000	1,30,000
Equity shares	50,000			
Reserve and surplus	40,000			
Total claim on assets	2,00,000			2,00,000

(***Ans.:*** Gross Profit Ratio 14 per cent. Net Profit Ratio (after considering interest on bank overdraft); 7.56 per cent ROI 13.53 per cent, stock turnover Ratio 8.6. Debt Collection Period 24 days. Fixed Assets Turnover 2.3, Fixed Assets Ratio 7.6, Debt-equity ratio 70/100 = .7, Current ratio 2.3).

3. Following is the balance sheet of C Ltd. as on 31st December, 2007

Liabilities		*Rs.*	*Assets*	*Rs.*
Equity share capital		20,000	Goodwill	12,000
Capital reserve		4,000	Fixed assets	28,000
8% loan on mortgage		16,000	Stocks	6,000
Trade creditors		8,000	Debtors	6,000
Bank overdraft		2,000	Investments	2,000
Taxation: Current		2,000	Bank	6,000
Future		2,000		
Profit and loss A/c:				
Profit for 2007 after taxation and interest on fixed deposits	12,000			
Less: Transfer to Reserve	4,000			
Dividend	2,000	6,000		
		60,000		60,000

Sales amounted to Rs. 1,20,000

Calculate ratio for:

(*i*) Testing liquidity

(*ii*) Testing solvency

(*iii*) Testing profitability

(*iv*) Testing capital gearing and

(*v*) Comment on the significant thereof.

4. From the following particulars extracted from the financial statements of Sun and Co. Ltd. Compute: (*a*) Current Ratio (*b*) Acid Test Ratio (*c*) Stock Turnover Ratio (*d*) Debtors' Turnover Ratio and (*e*) Creditors' Turnover Ratio for the two years 2007 and 2008 independently and comment on the liquidity position of the company:

	2007 Rs.	2008 Rs.
Opening stock	47,000	53,000
Closing stock	53,000	67,000
Sales less returns	2,52,000	3,65,000
Provision for bad debts	2,000	3,000
Sundry creditors	32,000	35,000
Purchases	1,80,000	1,90,000
Sundry debtors	42,000	63,000
Cash	10,000	15,000
Bank	8,000	10,000
Bills Receivable	15,000	20,000
Bills Payable	29,000	30,000
Marketable Securities	8,000	8,000

5. A. Ltd. and B. Ltd. produce and sell the same product but under different brand names. Their profit and loss statements and Balance Sheets are given below for the year ending 2008.

Profit and Loss Statement

(Figures in Rs. lakhs)

	A Ltd.	B. Ltd.
Sales	25.00	30.00
Less: Costs: Materials	4.00	2.00
Labour	2.00	7.00
Overheads: Fixed	9.00	2.00
Variable	2.00	9.00
Total cost	17.00	20.00
Gross margin	8.00	10.00
Interest	2.00	4.00
Profit before taxes	6.00	6.00
Taxes	3.00	3.00
Profit after taxes	3.00	3.00
Dividends declared	2.00	2.00
Retained earnings	1.00	1.00

Balance Sheet

(Fig. in Rs. lakhs)

	A Ltd.	B Ltd.
A. Capital Liabilities:		
1. Equity capital	10.00	20.00
2. Debenture capital	8.00	20.00
3. Creditors	5.00	15.00
4. Reserves	17.00	5.00
	40.00	60.00

B. Assets:		
1. Plant and machinery	8.00	34.00
2. Buildings	6.00	16.00
3. Inventories	18.00	2.00
4. Debtors	7.00	1.00
5. Cash	1.00	7.00
	40.00	60.00

Required: Evaluate the performance of two organisations for the current year and assess the expected problem by using the relevant ratios.

6. A condensed balance sheet and other financial data for Alpha Company appear below:

Alpha Company
Balance Sheet
December 31, 2007

Assets	*(Rs.)*
Current Assets	1,00,000
Plant Assets	1,40,000
Total Assets	2,50,000
Liabilities and Equity	
Current Liabilities	1,00,000
Long-term Liabilities	75,000
Total Liabilities	1,75,000
Common Equity	75,000
Total Liabilities and Equity	2,50,000
Income Statement Data	
Net Sales	3,75,000
Interest Expense	4,000
Net Income	22,500

The following account balances existed at December 31, 2006. Total Assets, Rs. 2,00,000; Equity, Rs. 65,000. The tax rate is 35 per cent.

Industry norms as of December 31, 2007 were:

Debt-equity ratio	1.75
Profit margin	0.12
Return on total assets	0.15
Return on stockholders' equity	0.30
Total asset turnover	1.71

Calculate and evaluate the following ratios for Alpha Company as of December 31, 2007:

(*a*) Debt-equity ratio
(*b*) Profit margin
(*c*) Return on total assets
(*d*) Return on stockholders' equity
(*c*) Total asset turnover

7. Here are the income statements and balance sheets of A Company and B Company, taken from their annual reports for the year ended December 31, 2007.

Income Statement

For the year 2007

	A Company Rs.	*B Company Rs.*
Sales	80,00,000	70,00,000
Cost of goods sold	60,00,000	47,00,000
Selling, general, and administrative expenses	12,00,000	19,00,000
Interest on debt:	—	70,000
Income before taxes	8,00,000	3,30,000
Income taxes	3,90,000	1,60,000
Net income	4,10,000	1,70,000
Dividends declared	1,00,000	70,000

Condensed Balance Sheets

As of December 31, 2007

	A Company	*B Company*
Assets	*Rs.*	*Rs.*
Cash	3,00,000	3,00,000
Accounts receivable	8,00,000	6,50,000
Inventory	13,00,000	8,50,000
Net plant and equipment	21,00,000	15,00,000
Total assets	45,00,000	33,00,000
Liabilities and Equity		
Accounts payable	7,10,000	4,00,000
Taxes payable	3,90,000	1,60,000
Long-term debt	—	14,00,000
Common equity	22,00,000	8,00,000
Retained earnings	12,00,000	5,40,000
Total liabilities and equity	45,00,000	33,00,000

On the basis of the available information, which do you consider to be (*i*) more liquid, (*ii*) more solvent, (*iii*) more profitable? Explain your conclusions.

Part Two

Cost and Management Accounting

Nature of Cost Accounting

The Chapter 1 titled 'Financial and Management Accounting: An Overview' has presented discussion on different aspects of financial accounting and management accounting.

The present chapter discusses nature, scope and importance of cost accounting.

Modern business needs relevant and timely information about business activities to plan accurately for the future, to control business results, and to make a proper appraisal of the performances of persons working in an organisation. The fulfilment of these goals requires details about the costs incurred and benefits (revenues) obtained which are provided by what is known as "cost accounting." In comparison, financial accounting does not provide management with detailed cost and revenue information relevant to its needs.

COST ACCOUNTING

Cost accounting, as a tool of management, provides management with detailed records of the costs relating to products, operations or functions. Cost accounting refers to the process of determining and acumulating the cost of some particular product or activity. It also covers classification, analysis and interpretation of costs. The costs so determined and accumulated may be the estimated future costs for planning purposes, or actual (historical) costs for evaluating performance.

COST ACCOUNTANCY

Cost accounting has been differentiated from cost accountancy. The Institute of Cost and Management Accountants, London has defined cost accountancy as the "application of costing and cost accounting principles, methods and techniques to the science, art and practice of cost control and ascertainment of profitability as well as presentation of information for the purpose of managerial decision-making." According to this definition the term "cost accountancy" includes costing, cost accounting, budgetary control, cost control and cost audit. Although literature in the U.K. and Europe in the area of cost accounting tends to differentiate between cost accounting and cost accountancy, U.S. literature does not appear to point out any basic difference between these two terms.

COSTING

Cost Accounting and Costing have distinctly different meanings. The Institute of Cost and Management Accountants (ICMA), London has defined costing as the ascertainment of costs. Costing includes the 'techniques' and 'processes' of ascertaining costs. The 'technique" refers to principles and rules which are applied for ascertaining costs of products manufactured and services rendered. There are mainly two methods of costing known as job costing and process costing. The 'process' includes the day-to-day routine of determining costs within the method of costing (either job or process) adopted by a business enterprise. Within such a process, there could be historical costing, marginal costing, absorption costing, standard costing etc.

In practice, the three terms cost accounting, cost accountancy, and costing are most often used interchangeably although they are defined differently.

COST ACCOUNTING AND MANAGEMENT

Management requires adequate, systematic and useful cost data and reports to manage a business enterprise and to achieve business objectives. The useful information provided by cost records and reports in cost accounting assists management in performing the following important tasks:

1. Cost accounting helps in determination and analysis of cost of departments, processes, jobs, products, sales territories, sales order etc. This advantage is not available to manufacturing companies alone. In fact, the analysis of cost and income can be made in almost all types of organisations — profit or non-profit.

The example given below points out how cost accounting by products, may reveal facts and data which cannot be developed in financial accounting. Cost statements produced at regular, short intervals, which are not prepared in financial accounting, would have enabled the firm to take prompt action to overcome the problems of producing and selling Product C.

The analysis (based on cost statements) points out that the contribution of firm products to total net profit (15%) vary significantly among products. Product C does not cover its prime costs, and causes a net loss to the firm of Rs 8,000 in the year; its selling and distribution costs are also particularly more compared to the other products.

The firm may decide to discontinue product C, but before deciding this, an enquiry may be made of the cost structure to find out whether or not more efficient manufacturing, selling and distribution is possible. At the same time attention must be paid to pricing policy. It should be investigated as to whether the selling price of this product can be increased to a profitable level.

Cost Statements

Particulars	*A*	*B*	*C*	*D*	*Total*
Sales	Rs. 60,000	Rs. 60,000	Rs. 40,000	Rs. 40,000	Rs. 2,00,000
Materials	30,000	22,000	26,000	24,000	1,02,000
Wages	12,000	8,000	12,000	8,000	40,000
Direct Exp.	2,000	2,000	3,000	1,000	8,000
Prime Cost	44,000	32,000	41,000	33,000	1,50,000

Work Exp.	1,600	2,000	500	200	
Selling Exp.	400	1,600	2,000	400	
Distribution Exp.	1,000	400	3,500	200	
General Adm. Exp.	1,000	4,000	1,000	200	
Overhead costs	4,000	8,000	7,000	1,000	20,000
Total cost	48,000	40,000	48,000	34,000	1,70,000
Profit	12,000	20,000	–(8,000)	6,000	30,000
Percentage Profit/Loss	20%	$33^1/_3$%	(–)20%	15%	15%

2. Cost accounting helps management in controlling cost which is probably the most important objective of every business firm. Cost accounting facilitates this task through accumulation and utilisation of cost data regarding different products, activities or functions. Each cost should be examined in the light of service or benefit obtained so that management can keep the cost at the lowest possible point.
3. One of the important uses (perhaps the most important) of cost information is in helping to make revenue and profitability decisions. These decisions can be divided into the following three categories:
   (*i*) Pricing — Cost data are vital in pricing new products, and to make a decision as to whether to lower or raise a price.
   (*ii*) Product mix — Management generally has to make short-term and long-term product mix decisions. For short-term cost data are used to determine which product to push in the market. Similarly, in the long run the questions of increasing and decreasing capacity can be solved with the help of relevant cost information.
   (*iii*) Profit-volume decisions — The profit is mainly the result of a combination of three factors, *viz.*, cost, volume, selling price. Decisions like reducing price and having additional sales, maintaining status quo and accepting a lower income, increasing quality of the product and having extra volume of sales, increasing selling price and improving the turnover, are significant.

   Cost data assists managements in making sound decisions in all these important areas.
4. Cost accounting helps in making special cost studies and investigations which are vital to management in formulating policies and plans directed towards profitable operations. Such special studies include pricing of a new product or new services, elimination of seasonal conditions, expansion or contraction programmes, replacement of machinery and equipment, dropping a product, changes in methods of distributing products, changes in production methods.
5. Cost accounting assists and participates in the formulation and execution of budgets and standards. Cost information for managerial decision making and planning is the most important justification of a sound cost accounting system.

OBJECTIVES OF COST ACCOUNTING

There is a direct relationship among information needs of management, cost accounting objectives, and techniques and tools used for analyses in cost accounting. Cost accounting has the following three important objectives:

1. To determine product costs.
2. To facilitate planning and control of regular business activities.
3. To supply information for short- and long-run decisions.

Product Costing

The objective of determining the cost of products is of prime importance in cost accounting. The total product cost and cost per unit of product are important in making inventory valuation, deciding price of the product, and managerial decision-making. Product costing covers the entire cycle of accumulating manufacturing and other costs and subsequently assigning them to work-in-progress and finished goods.

Planning and Control

Another important objective of cost accounting is the creation of useful cost data and information for the purposes of planning and control by management. The different alternative plans are evaluated in terms of respective cost and associated benefits.

The management control over business operations aims to establish balance between actual and budgeted performances. A properly designed cost accounting system includes the following steps in the control process:

1. Comparing actual business performances with budgets and standards.
2. Analysing the variance between budget and standards and actuals by causes, and management responsibility so that corrective action may be taken.
3. Providing managers with data and reports about their individual performances and performance of subordinates.

Information for Decisions

An important purpose of the cost accounting system is to provide data and special analyses for short and long-run decisions of a non-recurring nature. Appropriate cost information must be accumulated to make a wide variety of short- and long-run decisions.

COST ACCOUNTING AND MANAGEMENT ACCOUNTING

Although over the years, the subject matter of cost accounting has broadened, it is concerned mainly with the techniques of product costing and deals with only cost and price data. It is limited to product costing procedures and related information processing. It helps management in planning and controlling costs relating to both production and distribution activities.

Management accounting may be defined as the application of accounting techniques for providing information designed to help all levels of management in planning and controlling the activities of a business enterprise and in decision making. Management accounting is not confined to the area of product costing, cost and price data. In management accounting, the objective is to have a data pool which will include any and all information that management may need. For example, if management decides to depend on long-term debt for expansion of business, it may be investigated as to what effect this decision will have upon the earnings per share? Should debt in the capital structure be too large or small? Similarly, management may be interested in knowing the adequacy of cashflow receipts to pay current obligations or the effect of inflation on business decisions and performances. Thus, management accounting helps management in the total situation.

In spite of the differing parameters of cost accounting and management accounting, cost accounting is generally indistinguishable from what is known as management or managerial accounting. Both these accounting systems are closely linked as they use common basic data and reports to a significant degree. Much of the information used to prepare accounting statements and reports in cost accounting is also used in management accounting reports. Management accounting utilises the same (and also additional) data to prepare budgets, performance reports, control reports, data analyses for decision-making, planning and control purposes.

ADVANTAGES OF COST ACCOUNTING

Business enterprises can derive many advantages from the cost accounting system. Some advantages are listed below:

1. The cost accounting system provides data about profitable and unprofitable products and activities. After investigating the causes of low profitability and unprofitability, management can take suitable corrective measures which may lead to higher profit.
2. All items of costs can be analysed to minimise the losses and wastage emerging from the manufacturing process and reduce the costs associated with different activities.
3. Production/manufacturing methods may be improved or changed so that costs can be controlled and profit increased.
4. Cost data can be obtained and compared with standard cost within the firm or industry.
5. Cost accounting helps management in avoiding losses arising due to many factors, such as low demand, competitive conditions, change in technology, seasonal demand for the product and the like.
6. Cost accounting also provides cost data and information to determine the price of the product. The cost of the product is perhaps the most important determinant of product pricing.
7. Negotiations with government and labour unions can easily, be made with the information provided by the cost accounting system.
8. Cost accounting helps management in knowing the costs of different alternatives and selecting the most advantageous course of action. Decisions like make or buy, continue or drop a product, buy or lease, sell or process further, operate or shut down and other short-term decisions are easily solved with the help of cost accounting data.
9. More accurate and reliable financial accounts can be prepared promptly for use of management.
10. An adequate cost accounting system ensures maximum utilisation of physical and human resources, checks fraud and manipulations, and helps employees as well as the employer in their basic goals of getting higher earnings and maximising the profit of the concern.

METHODS OF COSTING

As stated earlier, the term "costing" refers to the techniques and processes of determining costs of a product manufactured or a service rendered. Different methods are applied in business enterprises to ascertain costs depending upon the nature of the product, production method and specific business conditions. For example, in a textile or steel company, raw material passes through different stages (processes) and production is done continuously. In some other industries, production is done at different customers' specific orders and each job is obviously different from the other job. In service industries like transport, hospital, banks etc., all activities and costs incurred relate mainly to performing certain services (or activities). There are two methods of costing:

(A) Job Costing
(B) Process Costing

All other methods of costing are only variants of the above two methods of costing. All possible variations of job and process costing are as follows:

(A) Job Costing	**(B) Process Costing**
(*i*) Batch Costing	(*i*) Unit or Single Output Costing
(*ii*) Contract or Terminal Costing	(*ii*) Operating (Service) Costing
(*iii*) Multiple or Composite Costing	(*iii*) Operation Costing

Job Costing

Job costing is used in those business concerns where production is carried out as per specific order and customers' specifications. Each job (or product) is separate and distinct from the other jobs or products. The method is popular in enterprises engaged in house-building, ship-building, machinery production and repair. Job costing has the following variants:

(i) Batch Costing

Batch costing is based on the concept of contract costing. This method is used to determine the cost of a group of identical or similar products. The batch consisting of similar products is the unit and not the single item within the batch. This method can be usefully applied for the production of nuts and bolts, medicines, components and other items which are manufactured in distinct batches.

(ii) Contract or Terminal Costing

This method of costing, based on the principle of job costing is used by house builders and civil contractors. The contract becomes the cost unit for which relevant costs are accumulated.

(iii) Multiple or Composite Costing

This costing method is used in those industries where the nature of the product is complex, such as motor cars, aeroplanes, etc. In such cases costs are accumulated for different components making the final product and then totalled to ascertain the total cost of the product.

Process Costing

This costing method is used in those industries where production is done continuously, such as chemicals, oil, gas, paper, etc. It is difficult to trace the costs to specific units and the total cost is averaged for the number of units manufactured. Sometimes, total cost and per unit cost is calculated at each stage of production for control purposes. Process costing has the following variants:

(i) Unit or Single Output Costing

This method is used where a single item is produced and the final production is composed of homogeneous units. The per unit cost is obtained by dividing the total cost by the total number of units manufactured.

(ii) Operating (Service) Costing

Operating costing method is used by those organisations which render services and do not manufacture any physical item, such as transport, power house, hospital. The cost units differ among these service organisations depending upon the nature of service being rendered. But usually the units are passenger-mile, tonne-mile, a bed in hospital, per student in a college.

(iii) Operation Costing

This costing method aims at ascertaining the costs of each operation in place of each process. In this method the assumption is that output is achieved through a number of different operations.

Besides the above variants of job costing and process costing, the different techniques or types of costing (discussed below) can be found in these two methods of costing and can be used to determine costs therein.

TECHNIQUES (TYPES) OF COSTING

The terms 'techniques' or 'types' refer to the manner of ascertaining costs of a product, job or activity. But these terms (techniques or types) also necessarily indicate what types of costs are being ascertained such as historical cost, standard cost, absorption (full) cost, marginal cost etc. It is clear that the term 'Methods of Costing' itself signifies only the method(s), job costing or process costing, that is being used to determine costs without indicating the types of costs (historical, standard, full or marginal) which are ascertained under the two methods of costing (Job or Process Costing), The following are generally the techniques of costing.

(1) Historical Costing

Historical costing is a system of costing under which costs are determined after they have been incurred.

(2) Standard Costing

Under standard costing, standard costs are determined and used, and then compared with the actual costs to determine the extent of variances so that remedial action can be taken. Standard costs are the predetermined costs in conformity with the most efficient operation and use of the resources within the film.

(3) Absorption or Full Costing

Under this costing method, all manufacturing costs, fixed and variable, are charged to products, jobs, processes, etc. and are included in total cost.

(4) Variable or Marginal Costing

Variable costing method charges only variable production costs to products or jobs, and thus the cost of the products or jobs consists of only variable production and not fixed production costs. The fixed production, administration, selling and distribution costs are written off against profits in the periods which they arise.

(5) Uniform Costing

Truly speaking, uniform costing is not a technique of costing, but is an attempt by several undertakings and organisations to use similar costing principles and/or practices.

COSTING SYSTEM

The term 'costing system' refers to an accounting system followed to accumulate costs, to ascertain costs of products or jobs, to prepare cost information using some procedures and principles for recording of cost data. Since there are two basic methods of costing — Job Costing and Process Costing, to ascertain costs, the costing system followed by business enterprises are also divided into two categories:

1. Job Order Costing System
2. Process Costing System

It should be understood that within these two costing systems, further, business enterprises may follow different techniques of costing such as historical cost, standard cost, full cost, marginal cost etc., which have been discussed earlier.

INSTALLATION OF A COST ACCOUNTING SYSTEM

A cost accounting system is a system that accumulates costs, assigns them to cost objects, *i.e.*, products, jobs, processes, etc. and reports cost information. In addition to this, a proper cost accounting system assists management in the planning and control of business operations, in analysing product profitability, and in accomplishing business objectives through optimum utilisation of available resources. The underlying principles, procedures and objects of all costing system are the same, but the application of these principles and methods may vary with the circumstances.

The installation of costing system in organisations is not an easy task. There are many difficulties, as listed below, which are faced by organisations while setting up costing system.

(1) Opposition from the Existing Staff

The existing staff is likely to oppose the introduction of costing system, may resent the additional work and may not provide cooperation which is necessary for the success of cost accounting system.

(2) Shortage of Trained Manpower

Installation of cost accounting system requires trained staff to operate the system effectively which organisations may not have, thus affecting adversely the better application of the system.

(3) Error in Measuring Requirements

The organisations, big and small, have varying requirements as to the costing system. Organisations may not know their specific requirements accurately. Consequently, the installation of costing system will either not meet their requirements or will provide unnecessary sophistication and dose of accounting procedures.

(4) Non-cooperation from Management

Resistance is noticed not only from the lower and middle staff but also from the members of top management. Managers may not support the Managing Director in his efforts to minimise costs and control activities as these might be looked upon as an interference in their managerial authorities.

ARGUMENTS AGAINST COST ACCOUNTING

Cost accounting undoubtedly helps managements in managing the affairs of business efficiently and in accomplishing business goals. However, some organisations do not look with favour the installation of cost accounting system. Some arguments which are advanced against adopting cost accounting are as follows:

(1) The system of cost accounting may prove costly and small organisations may not find it profitable. The collection, analysis, allocation and maintenance of cost data is a time-consuming and difficult task which requires efficient manpower.

(2) All business organisations are required to prepare financial accounts to determine profit and financial position. Installation of cost accounting system along with financial accounting system increases work load.

(3) Cost accounting system itself is not an end but only a means to achieve certain objectives. The system itself will not improve efficiency, control costs and avoid wastage. Sometimes management personnel become inactive with the mere installation of the cost accounting system.

However, all the above arguments are not valid. Keeping in view the advantages and contributions of cost accounting to management, as explained earlier, it can be rightly said that cost accounting is necessity for all business organisations. For manufacturing firms, cost accounting is vital necessity to reduce cost, to avoid waste, to improve efficiency and to provide cost data to management for planning, control and decision making.

COST CENTRES

The Institute of Cost and Management Accountants, London defines cost centres as "a location, person, or item of equipment (or a group of these) for which costs may be ascertained and used for the purposes of cost control." A cost centre is an organisational segment or area of activity considered to accumulate costs. The following are the types of cost centres usually found in a manufacturing company.

Impersonal Cost Centre

A cost centre which consists of a location or item of equipment (or a group of these).

Personal Cost Centre

A cost centre which consists of a person or group of persons.

Operation Cost Centre

A cost centre which consists of the machines and/or persons carrying out similar operations.

Process Cost Centre

A cost centre which consists of a specific process or a continuous sequence of operations.

COST UNITS

The Institute of Cost and Management Accountants, London has defined a cost unit as follows: "A unit of quantity of product, service or time (or a combination of these), in relation to which cost may be ascertained or expressed."

In the job costing method, cost unit is a single specific order; in batch costing it consists of a group of similar articles; and in contract costing, it consists of a single product (contract). The cost units used in different industries cannot be uniform. The cost units and centres should be those which suit the business and which are readily understood and accepted by all concerned.

The following Table gives examples of cost units (i.e., unit of cost activity) and method of costing used in different industries.

Cost Unit and Method of Costing

Industry/Enterprise	*Cost Unit*	*Method of Costing*
1. Building	House or square foot of area	Job Costing
2. Chemical	Tonne, pound or kilogram	Process Costing
3. Cement	Tonne	Process Costing
4. Automobile	Number	Process Costing
5. Steel	Tonne	Process Costing
6. Transport	Tonne kilometre, Passenger kilometre	Operating Costing
7. Cable	Metre	Process Costing
8. Gas	Cubic foot or cubic metre	Process Costing

9. Nuts and bolts	Gross or some measure of standard weight	Job Costing
10. Power	Kilowatt hour	Process Costing
11. Paper	Ream	Process Costing
12. Timber	Cubic foot	Process Costing
13. Brewery	Per dozen bottles or per gallon of draught brew	Process Costing
14. Biscuits	Per (WT)	Process Costing
15. Hospital	Per bed occupied/out-patient visit	Operating Costing
16. Case-making	Per case	Job Costing
17. Road Contractor	Per mile	Job Costing
18. Ice cream	Per gallon	Process Costing
19. Knitted textiles	Per pound/kg of fabric	Process Costing
20. Canned fruit	Per dozen cans or per gross cans	Process Costing
21. Soft drinks	Cases of 24 bottles each	Process Costing
22. Oil extraction, petrochemicals	Gallons, litres, tonnes	Process Costing
23. Pharmaceuticals	1000 nos. tablets, ampulses	Process Costing
24. Machine building	Numbers	Job Costing
25. Readymade garments	Numbers	Batch Costing
26. Aircraft	Numbers	Job Costing
27. Sugar	Tonnes, kilograms	Process Costing
28. Furnishing	Each article by numbers	Job Costing
29. Confectionary	Per kg	Process Costing
30. Clothing (automatic process)	Per dozen articles	Process Costing
31. Bicycle manufacturing	Number	Multiple Costing
32. Textiles	Metres, yards	Process Costing
33. Flour	Tonnes	Process Costing
34. Parts manufacturing	Nos. of articles in tens, hundreds, thousands	Job Costing

THEORY QUESTIONS

1. What is cost accounting? What are its objectives? How do cost accounting records help in the planning and control of operations of a business enterprise?
2. What is meant by cost accounting? In what essential respects does cost accounting differ from financial accounting?
3. Explain fully the concept of cost. How does cost accounting contribute to the effective and efficient management of an industrial establishment?
4. A cost keeping system that simply records costs for the purpose of fixing sale prices has accomplished only a small part of its mission." What are other functions of costing?
5. "Cost accounting is an unnecessary luxury for business establishments." Do you agree with the statement? Discuss.
6. Explain the important objectives of cost accounting.
7. What is cost accounting? Discuss briefly its important functions in a business firm.
8. "Cost accounting has come to be an essential tool of the management." Comment.
9. "Cost accounting is a system of foresight and not a postmortem examination, it turns losses into profits, speeds up activities and eliminates waste." Discuss.
10. What is a cost centre and how does it differ from a department of a factory?

11. How far is cost information helpful for the following purposes:
    (*a*) Fixation of selling prices
    (*b*) Control of costs
    (*c*) Management decisions.
12. List *A* gives you different methods of costing which can be used in one or more industries or organisations given in List *B*. Mention the correct costing method of the industries in List *B*.

    List A Process, operating, single output, job, contract, multiple

    List B (*i*) Chemical works
    (*ii*) Road transport company
    (*iii*) Coal
    (*iv*) Nursing home
    (*v*) Paint
    (*vi*) Construction industries
    (*vii*) Cement manufacturing
    (*viii*) Soap manufacturing
    (*ix*) Railways
    (*x*) Ship builders
    (*xi*) Bicycle manufacturing
    (*xii*) Readymade garments
    (*xiii*) Telephone
    (*xiv*) Cotton textiles
    (*xv*) Aluminium
    (*xvi*) Paper mill
    (*xvii*) Furniture manufacturing
    (*xviii*) Meat packing
    (*xix*) Sugar
    (*xx*) Steel
    (*xxi*) Paper boxes
    (*xxii*) Air conditioners
    (*xxiii*) Locomotive
    (*xxiv*) Tyres and tubes
    (*xxv*) Leather
    (*xxvi*) Pianos
    (*xxvii*) Toys and novelties
    (*xxviii*) Oil refinery
    (*xxix*) Baby food
    (*xxx*) Radio receivers

(***Ans.:*** (*i*) Process; (*ii*) Operating; (*iii*) Single; (*iv*) Operating; (*v*) Process; (*vi*) Contract; (*vii*) Process; (*viii*) Process; (*ix*) Operating; (*x*) Contract; (*xi*) Multiple; (*xii*) Batch; (*xiii*) Operating; (*xiv*) Process; (*xv*) Process; (*xvi*) Process; (*xvii*) Job; (*xviii*) Process; (*xix*) Process; (*xx*) Process; (*xxi*) Process; (*xxii*) Multiple; (*xxiii*) Multiple; (*xxiv*) Process; (*xxv*) Process; (*xxvi*) Batch; (*xxvii*) Batch; (*xxviii*) Process; (*xxix*) Batch; (*xxx*) Multiple.

Cost : Concepts and Classifications

The three important areas in cost accounting are cost ascertainment, cost analysis and cost control. For cost accounting to be useful in these areas, costs must be accumulated, classified and grouped in such a manner that (*i*) total costs and unit costs can be determined: (*ii*) trends in costs behaviour can be observed; (*iii*) cost can be controlled; and (*iv*) useful analysis can be made based on past as well as future costs for planning, control and decision-making. These requirements call for an understanding of the concept of cost and of its appropriate classifications. The purpose of this chapter is to explain the concept of cost and of different cost classifications.

COST

Cost is the amount of expenditure, actual (incurred) or notional (attributable), relating to a specific thing or activity. The specific thing or activity may be product, job, service, process or any other activity.

Cost is the amount of resources given up in exchange for some goods or services. The resources given up are generally in terms of money or, if not in terms of money, they are always expressed in monetary terms. The term 'cost' itself is without any significant meaning and, therefore, it is always advisable to use it with an adjective or phrase that will convey the meaning intended, such as prime, direct, indirect, fixed, variable, controllable, opportunity, imputed, sunk, differential, marginal, replacement and the like. Each such adjective or description implies a certain attribute or characteristic which is important in computing, measuring and analyzing the cost.

Basically, when a cost is incurred, it could be in the form of deferred cost (asset) or expired cost (expense). Deferred costs are unexpired costs, capitalised costs, which provide benefits in the future periods and known as assets and hence appear on the balance sheet. Examples of deferred or unexpired costs are plant, equipment, building, inventory, prepaid rent and insurance. When these deferred costs (assets) are used up, to the extent used, they become expenses and appear on the income statement and are deducted from revenues. Expired costs are costs which have been used up totally in generating revenue. They are not capitalised but only shown as expenses on income statement.

EXPENSES

Expenses are expired costs, incurred and totally used up in generation of revenue. Examples of expired costs are costs of goods sold expense, selling and administrative expenses. Expenses need not necessarily have to be paid in cash immediately, even a promise to pay could be made for the benefits obtained. The manufacturing costs are capitalised in the form of finished goods inventory and when a sale is made, they expire (becoming expenses). The cost of unsold inventory which was an asset earlier, now becomes expenses (costs of goods sold) as it has contributed to the generation of revenue.

Factory (or manufacturing) overhead is treated as cost (an asset) because this is included in the cost of finished goods inventory which is an asset unless sale is made. Selling and administrative expenses, when not included in the cost of finished goods inventory, are treated only as expenses and not cost (asset). Factory overheads are assets because they are supposed to add utility to the goods manufactured. For example, depreciation of a factory machine increases the utility of the goods manufactured which are therefore included in work-in-progress and finished goods inventory. But selling and distribution overheads do not add to the utility of goods manufactured and are treated merely as expenses and are deducted from revenues whenever incurred. Similarly, depreciation of a factory building is a cost, but depreciation of an office building is an expense.

LOSS

Loss is lost cost. The term 'loss' is used to describe mainly two accounting events. In traditional financial accounting it is used to denote a situation where expenses exceed revenues for an accounting period, that is, the opposite of net income (earnings) for the accounting period. Secondly, a loss arises due to the cost of an asset being more than the sale proceeds when the asset is sold. This unfavourable event does not arise from a normal business activity but from non-operating transactions or events. This definition of loss is used to identify the opposite of gain. That is, if no benefit is received from the cost incurred or it becomes definite that no benefit will accrue, the cost becomes a lost cost, *i.e.,* loss.

Loss is unrelated to revenue generation and is only offset against revenue of the period in which the loss occurred. Examples of loss are, loss on sale of fixed asset, loss of a stock due to fire.

CLASSIFICATION OF COSTS

The achievement of the objectives of cost accounting requires that cost should be ascertained, classified and grouped. Cost classification may be defined as the process of grouping costs according to their common characteristics. There are many objectives of cost classifications depending on the requirements of management. However, the following objectives are considered very useful and significant.

(*i*) Determining product costs for stock valuation and profit measurement

(*ii*) Planning

(*iii*) Decision Making

(*iv*) Control

The different cost classifications are as follows:

1. Natural classifications of costs
   (*i*) Direct material
   (*ii*) Direct labour
   (*iii*) Direct expenses
   (*iv*) Factory overhead
   (*v*) Selling and distribution and administrative overheads
2. Cost behaviour (In relation to changes in output, activity or volume)
   (*i*) Fixed cost
   (*ii*) Variable cost
   (*iii*) Mixed cost (Semi-variable and Semi-fixed cost)
3. Degree of Traceability to the Product
   (*i*) Direct cost
   (*ii*) Indirect cost
4. Degree of Association with the Product
   (*i*) Product cost
   (*ii*) Period cost
5. Functional Classification of Costs
   (*i*) Manufacturing cost
   (*ii*) Selling and distribution cost
   (*iii*) Administrative cost
6. Relationship with the Accounting Period
   (*i*) Capital cost
   (*ii*) Revenue cost
7. Costs for Decision Making and Planning
   (*i*) Opportunity cost
   (*ii*) Sunk cost
   (*iii*) Relevant cost
   (*iv*) Differential cost
   (*v*) Imputed cost
   (*vi*) Out-of-pocket cost
   (*vii*) Fixed, variable and mixed cost
   (*viii*) Shutdown cost
8. Costs for Control
   (*i*) Controllable and uncontrollable cost
   (*ii*) Standard cost
   (*iii*) Fixed, variable and mixed cost
9. Other Costs
   (*i*) Joint cost
   (*ii*) Common cost

NATURAL CLASSIFICATION OF COSTS

The term "natural classification" refers to the basic physical characteristics of the cost. In a manufacturing concern, generally, the following costs are incurred:

1. Direct materials: Direct materials refers to the cost of materials which are conveniently and economically traceable to specific units of output. The term "direct materials" is denoted by certain other names also, such as process material, prime cost material, production material, stores material, construction materials. Some examples of direct materials are: raw cotton in textiles, crude oil to make diesel, steel to make automobile bodies. The following group of materials fall within the definition of direct materials:

(*a*) All materials specially purchased for a particular job, order, process or product.

(*b*) All materials (including primary materials and raw materials) acquired and subsequently requisitioned from the stores for production.

(*c*) Components or parts purchased or produced and requisitioned from the storeroom.

(*d*) Material passing from one process to another process.

(*e*) Primary packing materials, e.g., wrappings, cardboard boxes, etc.

Items, such as import duties, dock charges, transport cost of materials, storing of materials, cost of purchasing and receiving materials are properly added to their invoiced price and thus, the materials are charged out at this increased cost.

2. Direct labour: Direct labour is defined as the labour of those workers who are engaged in the production process. It is the labour expended directly upon the materials comprising the finished product. Other terms for the direct labour are: process labour, productive labour, operating labour. Examples are the labour of machine operators and assemblers. However, a worker may be performing direct labour for a certain number of hours but be an indirect worker for the balance of the day. For example, manufacturing concerns frequently have workers who may be working on an assembly line or operating a machine as direct workers for three or four hours but later in the day may help in repairing machinery or in doing other work as indirect workers.

3. Direct expenses (Chargeable expenses): These include any expenditure other than direct material and direct labour directly incurred on a specific product or job. Such special necessary expenses can be identified with product or job and are charged directly to the product as part of the prime cost. Examples of direct expenses are:

(*a*) Cost of hiring special machinery or plant.

(*b*) Cost of special moulds, designs and patterns.

(*c*) Experimental costs and expenditure on model and pilot schemes.

(*d*) Fees paid to architects, surveyors and other consultants.

(*e*) Cost of transport and conveyance to the site of job or operations.

(*f*) Inward carriage and freight charges on special materials.

(*g*) Cost of patents and royalties.

(*h*) Cost of defective work, e.g., where several trials are necessary before an appropriate one is obtained. The cost of such trials is taken as direct expense.

(*i*) Licence fees.

(*j*) Hire charges for plants and equipments for a specific product or job.

(*k*) Components and parts processed for a special job.

(*l*) Insurance charges on special materials chargeable to a job.

Other things remaining the same, the term 'direct expenses' (chargeable expenses), whenever used in costing, refers to a specific product or job. That is, whether some expenses are direct or not, is decided in terms of specific job or product as product or job is considered the cost unit. However, some expenses which cannot be directly identified with product or job (and hence are not direct expenses), can sometimes be identified with a department, function, territory, customer, division etc. For example, salary of branch office manager, depreciation of plant, rent and rates, heating and lighting, insurance expenses etc. are direct in relation to some department or activity but become indirect with regard to a product or job because these expenses are incurred for more than one product or job.

The total of the above three elements of costs (*i*) direct materials, (*ii*) direct labour and (*iii*) direct expenses, are prime cost. According to Official Terminology of Chartered Institute of Management Accountants (London), prime cost is the total cost of direct material and direct labour. Thus, direct expenses is not included in prime cost as per CIMA Terminology. The CIMA defines direct cost which can be economically indentified with a specific saleable cost unit.

4. Factory overhead: Factory overhead, also called manufacturing overhead or factory burden, may be defined as the cost of indirect materials, indirect labour and indirect expenses. The term "indirect materials" refers to materials that are needed for the completion of the product but whose consumption with regard to the product is either so small or so complex that it would not be appropriate to treat it as direct materials item. They are production supplies and other materials that cannot conveniently or economically be charged to a specific unit of output. Examples of such items are lubricants, cotton waste, handtools, works stationery etc.

The term "indirect labour" is the labour cost of production-related activities that cannot be associated with or conveniently and economically traced to specific products via physical observation. Some examples of indirect labour are: foremen, shop clerks, general helpers, cleaners, material handlers, plant guards, employees engaged in maintenance work or other service work.

The term "indirect expenses" covers all indirect expenditure incurred by the manufacturing enterprise from the time production has started to its completion and its transfer to the finished goods store. Any expenses not classified as direct expenses are known as indirect expenses. The Institute of Cost and Management Accountants (UK) defines indirect expenses as the "expenses which cannot be allocated but which can be apportioned to or absorbed by cost centres or cost units." They are incurred for the benefit of more than one product, job or activity and must be apportioned by appropriate bases to the various functions. Expenses of this type include items such as heat, light, maintenance, factory manager's salary etc.

The total of (*i*) prime cost, and (*ii*) factory overheads is known as 'Factory cost.' Direct labour and factory overhead together are known as Conversion Costs because they are the costs of converting raw materials into finished products.

5. Selling, distribution and administrative overheads: Selling and distribution overheads usually begin when the factory costs end. Such expenses are generally incurred when the product is in saleable condition. It covers the cost of making sales and delivering/despatching products. These costs include advertising, salesmen's salaries and commissions, packing, storage, transportation, and sales administrative costs.

Administrative overhead includes costs of planning and controlling the general policies and operations of a business enterprise. Usually, all costs which cannot be charged either to the production or sales division are considered as administrative costs. Typical of such items are fees of the board of directors, the chairman's salary, the rent for general offices and costs of the general accounting and other departments. Sometimes, some such expenses such as manager's salary are often allocated to manufacturing and included in factory overhead.

The sum of (*i*) Prime cost, (*ii*) Factory overhead and (*iii*) Selling and distribution and administrative Overhead is the total cost, *i.e.*, the cost "to make and sell."

Figure 16.1 presents the natural classification of costs as discussed above.

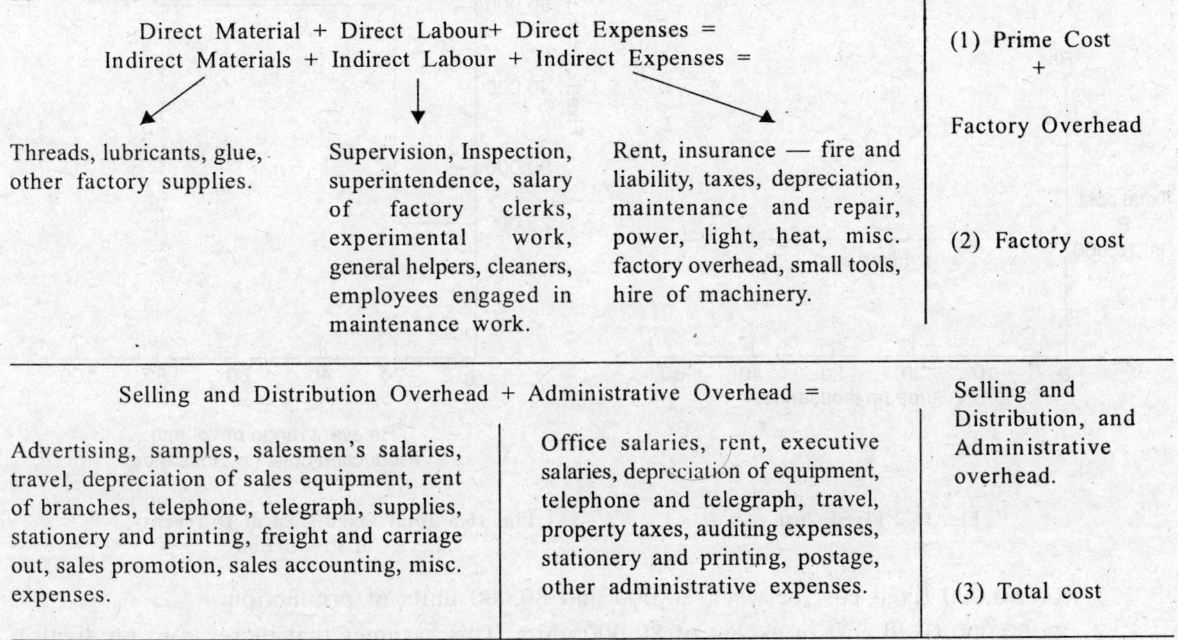

Fig. 16.1 Natural Classification of Costs in a Manufacturing Concern

COST BEHAVIOUR (IN RELATION TO CHANGES IN OUTPUT OR ACTIVITY OR VOLUME)

Costs can be classified into (*i*) fixed, (*ii*) variable and (*iii*) mixed costs, in terms of their variability or changes in cost behaviour in relation to change in output, or activity or volume. Activity may be indicated in any forms such as units of output, hours worked, sales, etc.

Fixed Cost

Fixed cost is a cost which does not change in total for a given time period despite wide fluctuations in output or volume of activity. These costs are also known as standby costs, capacity costs or period costs. Examples of fixed costs are rent, property taxes, supervising salaries, depreciation on office facilities, advertising, insurance, etc. They accrue or are incurred with the passage of time and not with the production of the product or the job. Any fixed cost can be represented by a constant (See Fig. 16.2).

However, it should be improper to say that fixed costs never change in amount. The basic concept is that the term "fixed" refers to fixity (non-variability) related to specific volume (or relevant range); the term does not imply that there will be no changes in fixed cost. This characteristic of fixed cost has been shown in Fig. 16.3. According to Fig. 16.3, the following are the fixed costs at different levels of production:

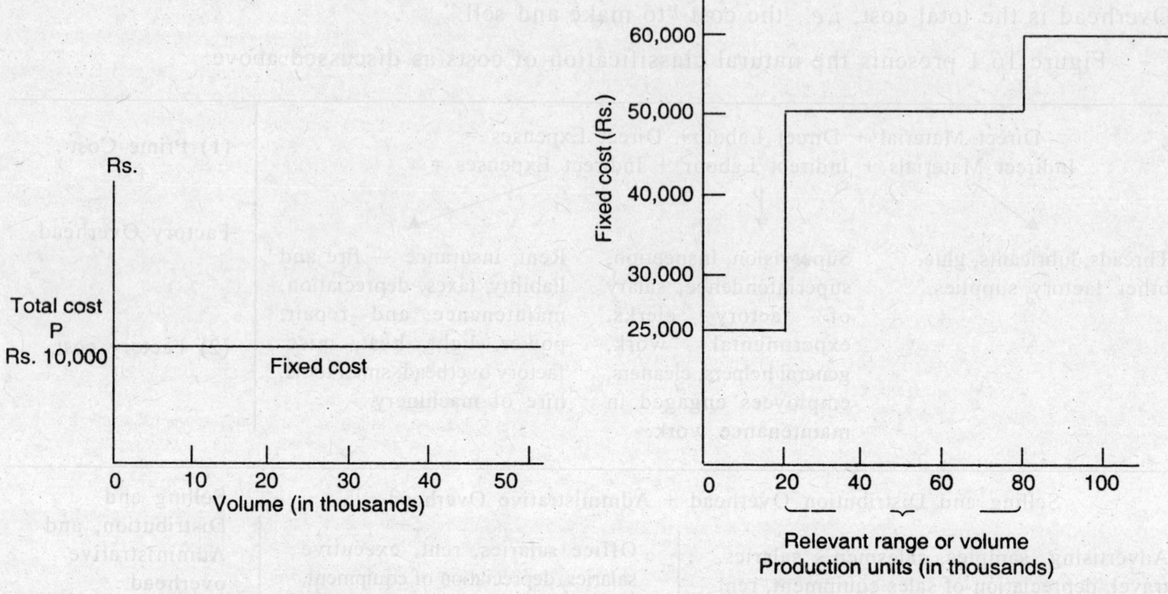

Fig. 16.2 Fixed Cost

Fig. 16.3 Total Fixed Cost at Different Levels of Production

1. Rs. 50,000 fixed cost between 20,000 and 80,000 units of production.
2. Rs 60,000 fixed cost in excess of 80,000 units. This assumes that increase in production after a certain level (80,000 units) requires increase in fixed expenses which have been fixed earlier, *e.g.*, additional supervision, increase in quality control costs.
3. Rs. 25,000 fixed cost from zero units (shut down) to 20,000 units. This explains that if the level of activity comes to less than 20,000 units, some fixed costs may not be incurred. For example, if the plant is shut down or production is reduced, many of the fixed costs, such as costs on accounting functions, supplies, staff, will not be incurred.

However, if laying off of staff and personnel, etc. is not possible, then the fixed cost will remain **Rs. 50,000.**

Variable Cost

Variable costs are those costs that vary directly and proportionately with the output. There is a constant ratio between the change in the cost and change in the level of output. Direct materials cost and direct labour cost are the costs which are generally variable costs. For example, if direct material cost is Rs. 50 per unit, then for producing each additional unit, a direct material cost of Rs. 50 per unit will be incurred. That is, the total direct material cost increases in direct proportion to increase in units manufactured. However, it should be noted that it is only the total variable costs that change as more units are produced; the per unit variable cost remains constant.

Variable cost is depicted in Fig. 16.4. Figure 16.4 shows graphically the behaviour pattern of direct material cost. For every increase in the units produced there is a proportionate increase in the cost. When production increases to 3,000 units from a level of 2,000 units, the cost of direct materials increases in direct proportion at the constant rate of Rs 50 per unit. The variable cost line is shown as linear rather than curvilinear. That is, on a graph paper a variable cost line appears as an unbroken straight line in place of a curve.

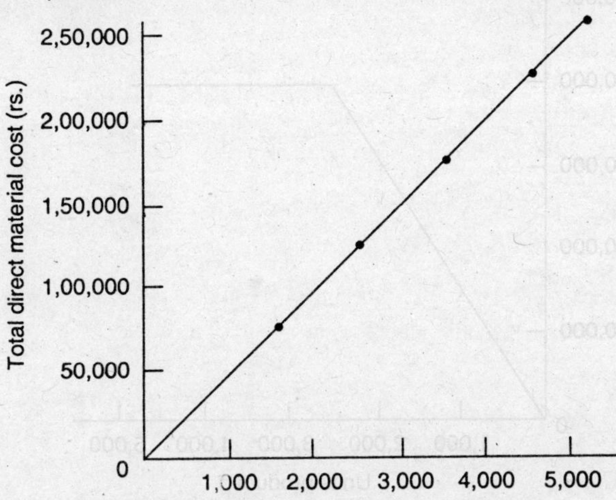

Fig. 16.4 Behaviour of Variable Costs

Mixed Cost

Mixed costs are costs made up of fixed and variable elements. They are a combination of semi-variable costs and semi-fixed costs. Because of the variable component, they fluctuate with volume; because of the fixed component, they do not change in direct proportion to output. Semi-fixed costs are those costs which remain constant upto a certain level of output after which they become variable as shown in Fig. 16.5. Semi-variable cost is the cost which is basically variable but whose slope may change abruptly when a certain output level is reached as shown in Fig. 16.6.

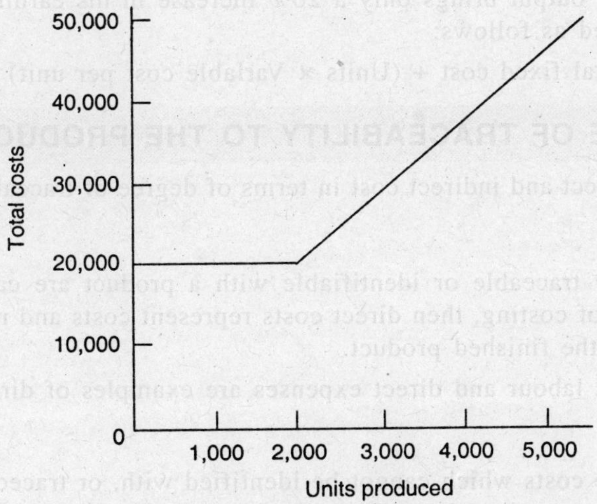

Fig. 16.5 Semi-fixed Cost

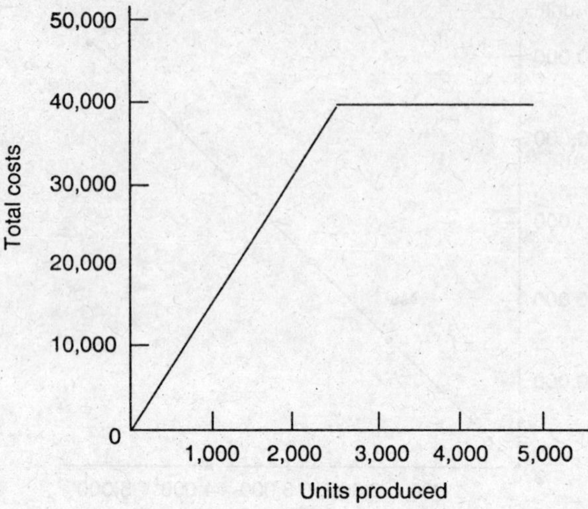

Fig. 16.6 Semi-variable Cost

An example of mixed cost is the earnings of a worker who is paid a salary of Rs. 1,500 per week (Fixed) plus a bonus of Re. 1 for each unit completed (variable). If he increases his weekly output from 1,000 units to 1,500 units, his earnings increase from Rs. 2,500 to Rs. 3,000.

Earnings	*Units produced*	
	1,000	1,500
Fixed component (Rs.)	1,500	1,500
Variable component (Rs.)	1,000	1,500
Total (Rs.)	2,500	3,000

An increase of 50% in output brings only a 20% increase in his earnings. Mathematically, mixed costs can be expressed as follows:

Total mixed cost = Total fixed cost + (Units × Variable cost per unit)

DEGREE OF TRACEABILITY TO THE PRODUCT

Cost is divided into direct and indirect cost in terms of degree of traceability to the product.

Direct Cost

Costs which are easily traceable or identifiable with a product are called direct costs. If output units are the objects of costing, then direct costs represent costs and resources that can be traced to or identified with the finished product.

Direct materials, direct labour and direct expenses are examples of direct costs.

Indirect Cost

Indirect costs are those costs which cannot be identified with, or traced to a single product because they are incurred for several products. The examples of indirect costs are: indirect materials (lubricants and scrap materials), salary of factor supervisors (indirect labour), rent, rates and depreciation (indirect expenses). Indirect costs, often referred to as overheads, have to be apportioned to different products.

Costs also may be direct or indirect with respect to particular company segments or divisions. That is some costs which are indirect for a product, may be traced to a segment or department and thus, will be direct costs for that department. A segment may mean any one of a number of things, viz., department division, specific activity, sales territory and the like.

Before dividing the cost into direct and indirect, it is necessary to know whether it is being associated with a product, sales area, department or some other activity. For example, if a salesman simultaneously handles several products, his salary is an indirect cost for each product, but a direct cost to his sales area or department.

ASSOCIATION WITH THE PRODUCT

Cost is classified into product costs and period costs in terms of association with the product.

Product Cost

Product costs are those costs which are identified with the product and included in inventory values. In other words, the costs that are included in the cost of manufacturing a product are called product costs. In a manufacturing concern, it is composed of four elements: (*i*) direct materials, (*ii*) direct labour, (*iii*) direct expenses and (*iv*) manufacturing overhead. That is, product cost is a full factory cost. Prior to sale, product costs are deferred as inventories and until the goods are sold, are shown on the balance sheet as assets. As finished inventory goods is sold, product costs are transferred from the inventory accounts to the cost of goods sold account, thus becoming expenses and part of the period costs at the time revenue is realised.

Period Cost

Period costs are the costs which are not identified with product or job and are deducted as expenses during the period in which they are incurred. They are not carried forward as a part of value of inventory to the next accounting period.

These costs are necessary to generate revenues but they cannot be directly associated with units of product. Difference of opinion exists regarding whether certain costs should be considered as product or period costs. It is generally accepted that selling and administrative expenses should be treated as period costs for the following reasons:

(*i*) It is difficult to select equitable bases to apportion these costs to products. On the other hand, product costs can be assigned to specific products through objective and direct measurements and some by allocation.

(*ii*) The majority of these expenses are fixed regardless of the change in production or activity.

(*iii*) It is difficult, if not impossible, to determine the relationship between the incurrence of these costs and the production of individual units of output.

(*iv*) It is difficult to get evidence as to any future benefits that would be obtained from these expenses at the end of the accounting period. Such is the case with clerical salaries, used postage, office supplies, rent, advertising, sales promotion, consulting fees which may be expected to provide future benefits, but they are usually expensed when incurred. Even if it is argued that there will be future benefits, it is difficult to make accurate measurements of such benefits.

Effect of Product Costs and Period Costs

The net income of a business enterprise is influenced by the amount of product costs and period costs. Therefore, the manner in which some costs are divided as product or period will have a bearing on the reported net income of a business firm. Product costs, in the first instance, influence the value of inventory. Therefore, such costs should be included in the cost of product. Product costs affect net income in the period in which products representing the product costs have been sold. This event of influencing net income may take place in the current accounting period or subsequent accounting period. In other words, products costs do not reach the income statement and will not influence net income of a business enterprise until the product is sold. However, period costs appear directly on the income statement in the month or the period in which they are incurred.

FUNCTIONAL CLASSIFICATION OF COSTS

Functional classification of costs refers to how the cost was used (manufacturing, administration or selling). A functional classification implies that the business performs many functions for which costs are incurred. In measuring net income, expenses are usually classified by function and grouped under the headings of manufacture, selling and administrative costs. Manufacturing costs are all production costs incurred to manufacture the products and to bring them to a saleable condition, including direct material, direct labour and indirect manufacturing (or factory overhead) costs. Selling and administrative charges may be treated as expenses when incurred or charged to prepaid expense accounts such as prepaid insurance. Functional classification is also important because it provides an opportunity to the management to evaluate the efficiency of departments performing different functions in the organisation.

RELATIONSHIP WITH ACCOUNTING PERIOD

Capital Cost and Revenue Cost

Costs can also be divided into two broad classes on the basis of the accounting period to which they relate: (*i*) capital expenditures and (*ii*) revenue expenditures. A capital expenditure provides benefit to future periods and is classified as an asset; a revenue expenditure is assumed to benefit the current period and is classified as an expense. A capital expenditure will flow into the cost stream as an expense when the asset is used up or written off.

The distinction between capital and revenue expenditures is viral to the proper matching of costs and revenue and to the accurate measurement of periodic net income.

COSTS FOR DECISION MAKING AND PLANNING

Opportunity Cost

Opportunity cost is the cost of opportunity lost. Opportunity cost is the cost of selecting one course of action in terms of the opportunities which are given up to carry out that course of action. Opportunity cost is the benefit lost by rejecting the best competing alternative to the one chosen. The benefit lost is usually the net earnings or profits that might have been earned from the rejected alternative. For example, assume that a manufacturer can sell a semi-finished product to a customer for Rs 5,00,000. He decides, however, to keep it and finish it. The opportunity cost of the semi-finished product is Rs. 5,00,000 because this is the amount of economic resources foregone by the manufacturer to complete the product. Similarly, capital which is invested in plant and inventories cannot now be invested in shares and debentures that will earn interest and dividends. The loss of interest and dividend that would be earned is the opportunity cost. Other examples of opportunity cost are when the owner of a business foregoes the opportunity to employ himself elsewhere; or a machine used to make Product A is said to have an opportunity cost if the machine can be sold or if it can also make Product B.

Opportunity costs are important in decision-making and evaluating alternatives. Decision making is selecting the best alternative which is facilitated by the help of opportunity costs. But opportunity cost are not recorded in an accounting system as they relate to opportunities lost.

Sunk Cost

A sunk cost is the cost that has already been incurred. Generally known as unavoidable cost, it refers to all past costs since these amounts cannot be changed once the cost is incurred. They are the costs which have been created by a decision in the past and cannot be changed or avoided by any decision that is made in the future. Examples of sunk costs are the book values of existing assets, such as plant and equipment, inventory, investment in securities, etc. Except the possible gains or losses on sales of any of such assets, the book value is not relevant for decisions regarding whether to use them or dispose thereof.

Some argue that the total cost of a fixed asset is not the sunk cost, but sunk cost is the difference between the purchase price of a fixed asset and the net amount that could be realised from its sale. For example, if a plant has a book value of Rs 10,00,000 and a scrap value of Rs. 50,000 then the sunk cost is Rs. 9,50,000 (Rs. 10,00,000 – 50,000) and not Rs. 10,00,000. That is, the sunk cost is the difference between book value and scrap value.

Relevant Cost

Relevant costs are those future costs which differ between alternatives. Relevant costs may also be defined as the cost which are affected and changed by a decision. On the contrary, irrelevant costs are those costs which remain the same and not affected by the decision whatever alternative is chosen.

Relevant costs have the following two features:

(*i*) Relevant costs are only future costs, *i.e.,* those costs which are expected to be incurred in future. Relevant costs therefore, are not historic (sunk) costs which have already been incurred and cannot be changed by a decision.

(*ii*) Relevant costs are only incremental (additional) or avoidable costs. Incremental costs refer to as increase in cost between two alternatives. Avoidable costs are those which are not incurred from one alternative to another.

To take an example, assume a business firm purchased a plant for Rs. 10,00,000 and has now a book value of Rs. 1,00,000. The plant had become obsolete and cannot be sold in its present condition. However, the plant can be sold for Rs. 1,50,000 if some modification is done on it which will cost Rs. 60,000. In this example, Rs. 60,000 (modification cost) and Rs. 1,50,000 (sales value) both are relevant as they reflect future incremental costs and future revenues respectively. The firm will have incremental benefit of Rs. 90,000 (Rs 1,50,000 – Rs 60,000) on sale of the plant.

Rs. 10,00,000 has already been incurred and being a sunk cost is not relevant to the decision, *i.e.,* whether modification should be done. Similarly, the book value of Rs. 1,00,000 which has to be written off, whatever alternative future action is chosen is also not relevant because it cannot be changed by any future decision.

Differential Cost

Differential cost is the difference in total costs between any two alternatives. Differential costs are equal to the additional variable expenses incurred in respect of the additional output, plus the increase in fixed costs, if any. This cost may be calculated by taking the total cost of production without the additional contemplated output and comparing it with the total costs incurred if the extra output is undertaken.

Differential costs are also known as incremental costs, although technically an incremental cost should refer only to an increase in cost from one alternative to another; decrease in cost should be referred to as decremental cost. Differential cost is a broader term, encompassing both cost increases (incremental costs) and cost decreases (decremental costs) between alternatives.

For example, assume that a company has normal capacity to manufacture 50,000 units of a product; production beyond that point would require the installation of additional plant and equipment that would increase the amount of fixed costs. Normal utilisation of available capacity ranges between 40,000 and 50,000 units. Fixed costs for the range of output and expanded capacity have been estimated as follows:

	Normal capacity	*Expanded capacity*
Number of units	40,000 to 50,000	50,000 to 60,000
Fixed costs	Rs. 2,00,000	Rs. 2,50,000

Now assume that the variable cost is Rs. 4 per unit. A statement comparing manufacturing costs at three different production levels would be as follows:

	Number of Units		
	40,000	50.000	60000
Variable costs	Rs. 1,60,000	Rs. 2,00,000	Rs. 2,40,000
Fixed costs	Rs. 2,00,000	2,00,000	2,50,000
Total manufacturing cost	3,60,000	4,00,000	4,90,000
Average per unit	Rs. 9.0	Rs. 8	Rs. 8.17
Incremental costs	—	40,000	90,000
Additional output (units)	—	10,000	10,000
Incremental cost per unit	—	Rs. 4.00	Rs. 9.00

The additional capacity which would be required to expand operations to 60,000 units would increase the fixed costs by Rs. 50,000. The incremental cost of an additional 10,000 units would total Rs. 90,000 or Rs. 9.00 per unit. The average cost of the 60,000 units would be Rs. 8.17 per unit.

The concept of differential costing is vital in planning and decision making. It is an important tool in evaluating the profitability of alternative choice decisions and helping management in choosing the best alternative. The differential cost analysis can assist management in knowing the additional profit that would be earned if idle or unused capacity is used for extra production or if some additional investment are made by the firm.

Imputed Cost

Imputed costs are costs not actually incurred in some transaction but which are relevant to the decision as they pertain to a particular situation. These costs do not enter into traditional accounting system. Interests on internally generated funds, rental value of company-owned property and salaries of owners of a single proprietorship or partnership are some examples of imputed costs. Costs paid or incurred are not imputed costs. For example, if Rs. 5,00,000 is paid for purchase of raw materials, it is an outlay cost but not an imputed cost, because it would enter into ordinary accounting systems. When a company uses internally generated funds, no actual interest payment is required. But if the internally generated funds are invested in some projects, interest would have been earned. The revenue foregone (loss of interest) represents an opportunity cost, and thus, imputed costs are opportunity costs.

Out-of-Pocket Cost

While imputed costs do not involve cash outlays, out-of-pocket costs signify the cash cost incurred on an activity. Non-cash costs such as depreciation are not included in out-of-pocket costs. This cost concept is significant for management in deciding whether or not a particular project will at least return the cash expenditures associated with the project selected by management. Similarly acceptance of a special order for production may necessitate the consideration of out-of-pocket costs that need not be incurred if the special order proposal is not accepted. Depreciation on plant and equipment is not relevant in decision-making because no cash goes outside the business.

Fixed, Variable and Mixed Costs

Fixed, variable and mixed costs have been explained in the preceding sections.

Shut Down Cost

Shut down costs are those costs which have to be incurred under all situations in the case of stopping manufacture of a product or closing down a department or a division. Shutdown costs are always fixed costs. If the manufacture of a product is stopped, variable costs like direct materials, direct labour, direct expenses, variable factory overhead will not be incurred. However, a part of fixed costs (if not total fixed costs) associated with the product will be incurred such as rent, watchman's salary, property taxes, etc. Such fixed costs are unavoidable. Some Fixed costs associated with the product become avoidable and need not be incurred in case production is stopped such as supervisor's salary, factory manager's salary, lighting, etc. Shutdown costs, thus refer to minimum fixed costs which are incurred in the case of closure of a department or division.

COSTS FOR CONTROL

Controllable and Uncontrollable Cost

The concept of controllable cost is very important in cost accounting and contributes to the achievement of the objectives of cost control and responsibility accounting. The ICMA (UK) defines controllable costs as "a cost which can be influenced by the action of a specified member of an undertaking" and a non-controllable cost as "a cost which cannot be influenced by the action of a specified member of an undertaking." Basically, a controllable cost is the cost over which a manager has direct and complete decision authority. That is, controllable costs can be controlled (reduced) by a manager at a given organisational level. Some examples of controllable costs are indirect labour, lubricants, cutting tools and power costs incurred in the machining department.

Controllable costs do not imply that they are 100% controllable. Some costs are partly controllable by a responsibility centre manager. For example, the cost of raw materials is controlled by the production managers as well as purchase managers. The production manager controls at quantity level, and the purchase manager at the price level. Such costs are reported to both of them, but one responsible manager should be held accountable for those costs which he can control.

The term "controllable cost" should not be confused with the terms "variable cost", "direct cost." These terms are not synonymous. Variable costs vary with the output but are not necessarily controllable. For example, factory supplies used for servicing plant and equipment may vary with the output in the production department, but the production manager cannot control them.

It is contended that two factors: (*i*) the time period factor, and (*ii*) the decision-making authority, can make a cost controllable or uncontrollable. If the time period is long enough, all costs can be controllable and curtailed. Similarly, the decision-making authority influences the cost. If a responsibility center manager has been delegated the authority to spend the cost, he can control it. But all costs can be said to be controllable by somebody in the organisation. The managing director of a company is responsible for all costs. But practically, the responsibility and authority of controlling costs is delegated to different levels in the organisation.

Standard Cost

Standard costs are those costs which are planned or predetermined cost estimates for a unit of output in order to provide a basis for comparison with actual costs. Standard costs are used to prepare budgets. Standard cost is a unit concept and indicates standard cost per unit of output, per labour hour etc. On the contrary, the term "Budgeted Cost" is a total concept and indicates total budgeted cost of an item at some activity level or output level such as budgeted cost of material is Rs. 8,00,000 if 8000 units are manufactured.

Fixed, Variable and Mixed Costs

Fixed, variable and mixed costs have been discussed earlier in this chapter.

OTHER COSTS

Joint Cost

Joint costs arise where the processing of a single raw material or production resources results in two or more different products simultaneously. Joint costs relate to two or more products produced from a common production process or element — material, labour, or overhead or any combination thereof, or so locked together that one cannot be produced without producing the other(s).

Thus, joint cost is the cost of two or more products that are not identifiable as individual types of products until a certain stage of production known as the split-off point (point of separation) is reached, For example, kerosene, fuel oil, gasoline and other oil products are derived from crude oil. Joint costs are total costs incurred upto the point of separation. Joint costs can be apportioned to different products only by means of some suitable bases of apportionment.

Common Cost

Common costs are those which are incurred for more than one product, job, territory or any other specific costing object. Common costs are not easily identifiable with individual products and, therefore, are generally apportioned.

Common costs are not only common to products, but they may be common to processes, functions, responsibilities, customers, sales territories, periods of time and similar costing units. For example, the salary of a manager of a production department which is manufacturing three products is an example of common cost with respect to the products. But his salary is direct cost to the departments located in the factory. The basic point is that a particular (common) cost may be direct to one object and common as far as other objects are concerned.

Although both the terms, "common costs" and "joint costs' are sometime used interchangeably, they differ from each other. Joint costs emerge when multiple products are manufactured in a common process and when common inputs are used. The multiple products have a definite quantitative relationship to each other and the production of one product influences the output of the other product, though in a lesser proportion. Common costs are not the result of any manufacturing compulsion or the use of any single raw material. Besides common costs can be apportioned to costing objects like products, job, department, etc. without much difficulty. But the apportionment of joint cost involves many difficulties in cost accounting.

COST CONTROL

Cost control can be defined as the comparative analysis of actual costs with appropriate standards or budgets to facilitate performance evaluation and formulation of corrective measures. It aims at accomplishing conformity between actual result and standards or budgets. Cost control is keeping expenditures within prescribed limits. Cost control has the following features:

1. Creation of responsibility centres with defined authority and responsibility for cost incurrence.
2. Formulation of standards and budgets that incorporate objectives and goals to be achieved.
3. Timely cost control reports (responsibility reporting) describing the variances between budgets and standards and actual performance.
4. Formulation of corrective measures to eliminate and reduce unfavourable variances.
5. A systematic and fair plan of motivation to encourage workers to accomplish budgetary goals.
6. Follow-up to ensure that corrective measures are being effectively applied.

Cost control does not necessarily mean reducing the cost but its aim is to have the maximum utility of the cost incurred. In other words, the objective of cost control is the performance of the same job at a lower cost or a better performance for the same cost.

COST REDUCTION

Meaning

Cost reduction may be defined as an attempt to bring costs down. Cost reduction implies real and permanent reduction in the unit cost of goods manufactured or services rendered without impairing their (product or goods) suitability for the use intended. The goal of cost reduction is achieved in two ways: (i) by reducing the cost per unit and (ii) by increasing productivity. The steps for cost reduction include elimination of waste, improving operations, increasing productivity, search for cheaper materials, improved standards of quality, finding other means to reduce unit costs.

Difference between Cost Control and Cost Reduction

Cost reduction is a much wider concept than cost control. As stated earlier, cost control aims at controlling costs within prescribed limits with the help of budgets and standards. The following are the differences between the two:

Cost Control	*Cost Reduction*
1. Cost control process involves (*a*) setting targets and standards (*b*) ascertaining actual performance (*c*) comparing actual performance with targets (d) investigating the variances and (*e*) taking corrective action.	1. Cost reduction is not concerned with setting targets and standards and maintaining performance according to standards. Cost reduction is the final result in the cost control process.
2. Cost control aims at achieving standards, *i.e.*, cost targets. It assumes existence of standards.	2. Cost reduction aims at improving the standards. It challenges standards and assumes existence of concealed potential savings in the standards.
3. It follows a conservative procedure and lacks dynamic approach.	3. It is continuous, dynamic and innovative in nature, looking always for measures and alternative to reduce costs.
4. It is a preventive function.	4. It is a corrective function.
5. In cost control, costs are optimised before they are incurred.	5. In cost reduction, there is always assumed a scope for reducing the incurred costs under controlled conditions.
6. It is generally applicable to items which have standards.	6. This is applicable to every activity of the business.
7. It contains guidelines and directive of management as to how to do a thing.	7. It adds thinking and analysis to action at all levels of management.

Tools and Techniques of Cost Reduction

Generally speaking, the following tools and techniques are used for the purpose of cost reduction:

1. Value analysis or value engineering
2. Work study
3. Job evaluation and merit rating
4. Production planning and control
5. Organisation and method study
6. Operations and method study
7. Rationalisation
8. Quality control
9. Economic order quantity
10. Use of better technology
11. Mechanisation and automation
12. Standardisation
13. Simplification
14. Classification and codification
15. Variety reduction
16. Improvement in the design of a product
17. Market research
18. Inventory management and control.

Illustration 1:

A company manufactures and retails clothing. You are required to group the costs which are listed below and numbered 1 to 20 into the following classification: (Each cost is intended to belong to only one classification).

(*a*) Direct Materials
(*b*) Direct Labour
(*c*) Direct Expenses
(*d*) Indirect Production Overhead
(*e*) Selling and Distribution Costs
(*f*) Research and Development Costs
(*g*) Finance Cost
(*h*) Administration Costs

1. Telephone rental plus metered calls
2. Wages of security guards for factory
3. Parcels sent to customers
4. Wages of operatives in cutting department
5. Developing a new product in the laboratory
6. Wage of fork lift truck drivers who handle raw materials
7. Wages of storekeepers in materials store
8. Chief accountant's salary
9. Cost of painting advertising slogans in delivery vans
10. Auditor's fee
11. Cost of advertising on television
12. Lubricants for sewing machines
13. Floppy disks for general office computer
14. Maintenance contract for office photo copying machine
15. Interest on bank overdraft
16. Market research undertaken prior to new product launch
17. Carriage on purchase of raw materials
18. Royalty paid on number of units of a particular product produced
19. Road licences for delivery vehicles
20. Amount payable to a company for broadcasting music throughout the factory.

Solution:

Cost element	*Number*
Direct materials	17
Direct labour	4
Direct expenses	18
Finance cost	15
Research and development expenses	5
Selling and distribution cost	3, 9, 11, 16, 19
Administration cost	1, 8, 10, 13, 14
Indirect production costs	2, 6, 7, 12, 20

COST STATEMENT OR COST SHEET

Cost Statement is a statement which is prepared usually to present the detailed costs of total production during the period in question. It provides information relating to cost per unit at different stages of the total cost of production or at different stages of completion of the product. Sometimes standard cost data are also provided to facilitate comparison with the actual cost incurred. The preparation of the cost sheet requires understanding of the treatment of the following items:

1. *Stock of raw materials:* The cost statement requires the determination of the value of raw materials consumed for the output produced. If the opening stock of raw materials, purchase of raw materials during the period and closing stock of raw materials are given, then the value of raw materials consumed is computed as follows:

	Rs.
Opening stock of raw materials	—
Add: Purchase of raw materials	—
Total	
Less: Closing stock of raw materials	
Value of raw materials consumed	

2. *Stock of work-in-progress:* Work-in-progress represents the accumulated costs on goods that have not yet been completed. As such these goods are not yet available for sale. The degree of completion of work-in-progress is usually expressed as a fraction or as a percentage, such as 2/5 complete for materials or 50% complete for labour.

Work-in-progress is valued on a prime cost or factory cost basis. In case it is to be valued on a factory cost basis, the following procedure would be followed:

	Rs.
Prime Cost	
Add: Factory overhead	—
Add: Work-in-progress (beginning)	—
Total	—
Less: Work-in-progress (closing)	—
Factory Cost	—

3. *Stock of finished goods:* Finished goods inventory covers the products on which all factory work been completed. It carries the cost of completed production. Nothing more is to be done to finished goods at the factory and no further costs are added to finished goods. If opening and closing stock of finished goods are given, then they would be adjusted as under:

	Rs.
Cost of production	—
Add: Finished goods (beginning)	—
Total	
Less: Finished goods (closing)	—
Cost of goods sold	—

As stated earlier, cost sheet gives details about the cost of manufacturing a product or completing an activity. A cost sheet discloses:

(1) Prime Cost
(2) Factory Cost (also known as Works Cost)
(3) Cost of Production
(4) Total Cost (or Cost of Sales)

A cost sheet shows total cost and cost per unit. Cost per unit is obtained by dividing total cost by the number of units produced. A cost sheet will have separate columns for the total and the unit cost of each element of cost. Cost sheet can be prepared on weekly, monthly or other time period basis as desired by management. Specimen of a cost sheet is given below:

Specimen of Cost Sheet

Cost Sheet for the Period ______________

Production ______________ Units

	Total cost (Rs.)	*Cost per unit (Rs.)*
Direct Materials		
Opening stock...		
Purchases...		
Carriage inwards...		
Less: Closing stock...		
Less: Scrap		
I. *Direct materials consumed*		
Direct wages		
Direct expenses		
II. *Prime Cost*		
Add: Factory Overheads:		
Indirect materials		
Loose tools		
Indirect wages		
Rent and rates (factory)		
Lighting and heating (factory)		
Power and fuel		
Repairs and maintenance		
Cleaning		
Drawing office expenses		
Cost of research and experiments		
Depreciation of factory plant		
Works stationery		
Welfare service expenses		
Insurance— Fixed assets etc.		
— Stock and finished goods		
Works manager's salaries		
III. *Factory or Works Cost*		
Add: Office and Administrative Overheads:		
Rent and rates (office)		
Salaries (office)		
Lighting and heating		
Insurance of office building and equipments etc.		
Telephone and postages		
Printing and stationery		
Depreciation of furniture and office equipments and building		

	Total cost (Rs.)	Cost per unit (Rs.)
Legal expenses		
Audit fees		
Bank charges		
IV. *Cost of Production*		
Add: Selling and Distribution Overheads:		
Showroom rent and rates		
Lighting and heating		
Salesmen's salaries		
Commissions		
Travelling expenses of salesmen		
Sales printing and stationery		
Advertising		
Bad debts		
Postage		
Depreciation and expenses of delivery van		
Debt collection expenses		
Carriage freight outwards		
Samples and other free gifts		
V. *Cost of Sales*		
Net profit (or loss)		
Sales		

Note: Items of expenses which are an appropriation of profit should not form a part of the costs of a product. Examples of such expenses are: (*i*) Income Tax; (*ii*) Dividends to shareholders; (*iii*) Commission (out of profit) to Managing Directors or Partners; (*iv*) Capital loss, *i.e.*, loss arising out of sale of assets, (*v*) Interest on loan; (*vi*) Donations: (*vii*) Capital expenditure: (*viii*) Discount on shares and debentures; (*ix*) Underwriting commission; (*x*) Writing off goodwill.

Illustration 2:

From the following particulars, prepare a cost sheet for the year ended 31-12-2008:

	Rs.
Stock of finished good (1-1-2008)	6,000
Stock of raw materials (1-1-2008)	40,000
Work-in-progress (1-1-2008)	15,000
Purchase of raw materials	4,75,000
Carriage inwards	12,500
Factory rent, taxes	7,250
Other production expenses	43,000
Stock of goods (31-12-2008)	15,000
Wages	1,75,000
Work manager's salary	30,000
Factory employees salary	60,000
Power expenses	9,500
General expenses	32,500
Sales for the year	8,60,000
Stock of raw materials	50,000
Work-in-progress (31-12-2008)	10,000

Solution:

Cost Sheet for the Year Ending 31-12-2008

	Rs.	Rs.
Stock of raw materials on 1-1-2008	40,000	
Add: Purchase during the year	4,75,000	
	5,15,000	
Less: Stock of materials on 31-12-2008	50,000	
Cost of materials consumed		4,65,000
Wages		1,75,000
Carriage inwards		12,500
Prime Cost		6,52,500
Add: Factory overheads:		
Works manager's salary	30,000	
Factory employees salary	60,000	
Factory rent, taxes and insurance	7,250	
Power expenses	9,500	
Other production expenses	43,000	
	1,49,750	
Add: Work-in-progress (1-1-2008)	15,000	
	1,64,750	
Less: Works-in-progress (31-12-2008)	10,000	
		1,54,750
Factory Cost		8,07,250
Add: Office overheads:		
General expenses		32,500
Total Cost		8,39,750
Add: Stock of finished goods (1-1-2008)		6,000
		8,45,750
Less: Stock of finished goods (31-12-2008)		15,000
Cost of Sales		8,30,750
Profit		29,250
Total Sales		8,60,000

Illustration 3:

A manufacturing company has shown Rs. 3,23,80,000 as "Establishment Expenses" which include the following expenses:

	('000) Rs.
1. Warehouse wages	3,600
2. Office salaries	2,260
3. Office lighting	140
4. Directors' remuneration	2,800
5. Rent, rates and insurance of warehouses	620
6. Warehouse lighting	540
7. Trade magazine	140
8. Bank charges	200
9. Bad debts	340

10. Agents' commission	11,500
11. Warehouse repair	1,020
12. Travelling expenses	1,520
13. Rent, rates and insurance of office	460
14. Printing and stationery	3,000
15. Donation	300
16. Discount allowed	3,940

From the above information, find out the total of (*i*) selling expenses (*ii*) distribution expenses (iii) administration expenses and (*iv*) expenses which will not be considered in determining total costs.

Solution:

	('000) Rs.	('000) Rs.
(*i*) *Selling Expenses:*		
Bad debts	340	
Agents' commission	11,500	
Travelling expense	1,520	13,360
(*ii*) *Distribution Expenses:*		
Warehouse wages	3,600	
Rent, rates and insurance of warehouse	620	
Warehouse lighting	540	
Warehouse repair	1,020	5,780
(*iii*) *Administrative Expenses:*		
Office salaries	2,260	
Office lighting	140	
Directors' remuneration	2,800	
Trade magazine	140	
Bank charges	200	
Rent, rates and insurance of office	460	
Printing and stationery	3,000	9,000
(*iv*) *Expenses Not to be Used in Estimating Costs:*		
Donation	300	
Discount allowed	3,940	4,240
		32,380

Note: Discount allowed has been assumed to be cash discount. Cash discount is a financial item and, therefore not considered in cost accounts.

Illustration 4:

Vijay Industries manufactures a product X. On 1st January 2008, there were 5000 units of finished product in stock. Other stocks on 1st January 2008 were as follows:

Works-in-progress	Rs. 57,400
Raw materials	Rs. 1,16,200

The information available from cost records for the year ended 31st December 2008 was as follows:

	Rs.
Direct materials	9,06,900
Direct labour	3,26,400
Freight on raw materials purchased	55,700
Indirect labour	1,21,600
Other factory overheads	3,17,300

Stock of raw materials on 31-12-2008	96,400
Work in progress on 31-12-2008	78,200
Sales (150000 units)	30,00,000
Indirect materials	2,13,900

There are 15000 units of finished stock in hand on 31st December 2008. You are required to prepare:

A statement of cost and profit assuming that opening stock of finished goods is to be valued at the same cost per unit as the Finished stock at the end of the period.

Solution:

Statement of Cost and Profit of Product X

Particulars	*Amount (Rs.)*	*Amount (Rs.)*
Opening Stock of Raw Materials	1,16,200	
Add: Direct materials	9,06,900	
Add: Freight on raw materials purchased	55,700	
	10,78,800	
Less: Closing stock of raw materials	96,400	
Value of Raw Materials Consumed		9,82,400
Add: Direct wages		3,26,400
Prime Cost		13,08,800
Add: Factory overheads:		
Indirect materials	2,13,900	
Indirect labour	1,21,600	
Other factory overheads	3,17,300	
	6,52,800	
Add: Opening work-in-progress	57,400	
	7,10,200	
Less: Closing work-in-progress	78,200	6,32,000
Works Cost of Goods Manufactured		19,40,800
Add: Opening stock of Finished goods 5000 units @ Rs. 12.13		60,650
		20,01,450
Less: Closing stock of Finished goods 15000 units @ Rs 12.13		1,81,950
Cost of Goods Sold		18,19,500
Profit		11,80,500
Sales		30,00,000

Working Notes:

Units produced during the year are not given and therefore have been computed as follows:

Sales = Opening stock + Units produced – Closing stock

1,50,000 = 50004 + X – 15,000

– X = 5000 – 15,000 – 1,50,000

Hence X = 1,60,000 units

$$\text{Value of closing stock} = \frac{\text{Total cost}}{\text{Units produced}} = \frac{\text{Rs. }19,40,800}{1,60,000} = \text{Rs. } 12.13 \text{ per unit}$$

= 15000 units × Rs. 12.13 = Rs. 1,81,950

Value of opening stock of 5000 units × Rs 12.13 = Rs. 60,650

Illustration 5:

The books of Adarsh Manufacturing Company present the following data for the month of April 2008.

Direct labour cost Rs. 17,500 being 175% of works overheads
Cost of goods sold excluding administrative expenses Rs. 56,000.
Inventory accounts showed the following opening and closing balances:

	April 1	*April 30*
Raw materials	Rs. 8,000	Rs. 10,600
Work-in-progress	10,500	14,500
Finished goods	17,600	19,000

Other data are:

Selling expenses	Rs. 3,500
General and administrative expenses	2,500
Sales for the month	75,000

You are required to:

(*i*) Compute the value of materials purchased

(*ii*) Prepare a cost statement showing the various elements of cost and also the profit earned.

Solution:

(i) Computation of Value of Materials Purchased

	Rs.
Cost of goods sold	56,000
Add: Closing stock of finished goods	19,000
	75,000
Less: Opening stock of finished goods	17,600
Cost of goods manufactured	57,400
Add: Opening stock of work-in-progress	14,500
	71,900
Less: Opening stock of work-in-progress	10,500
Works cost	61,400
Less: Factory overheads (100/175 of direct labour cost)	10,000
Prime cost	51,400
Less: Direct labour	17,500
Raw materials consumed	33,900
Add: Closing stock of raw materials	10,600
Raw materials available	44,500
Less: Opening stock of raw materials	8,000
Value of materials purchased	36,500

(ii) Cost Statement

Raw materials consumed (as calculated above)	33,900
Add: Direct labour cost	17,500
Prime cost	51,400
Add: Factory overheads	10,000
Works cost	61,400

Add: Opening work-in-progress	10,500
	71,900
Less: Closing work-in-progress	14,500
Cost of goods manufactured	57,400
Add: Opening stock of finished goods	17,600
	75,000
Less: Closing stock of finished goods	19,000
Cost of production of goods sold	56,000
Add: General and administrative expenses	2,500
Add: Selling expenses	3,500
Cost of sales	62,000
Profit (balancing figure Rs. 75,000 – Rs. 62,000)	13,000
Sales	75,000

Illustration 6:

The following particulars relating to the year 2007 have been taken from the books of a company manufacturing and selling a chemical mixture:

	kg.	*Rs.*
Stock on January 1, 2007		
Raw materials	2,000	2,000
Finished mixture	500	1,750
Factory stores		7,250
Purchases:		
Raw materials	1,60,000	1,80,000
Factory Stores		24,250
Sales:		
Finished mixture	1,53,050	9,18,000
Factory scrap		8,170
Factory wages		1,78,650
Power		30,400
Depreciation of machinery		18,000
Salaries:		
Factory		72,220
Office		37,220
Selling		41,500
Expenses:		
Direct		18,500
Office		18,200
Selling		18,000
Stock on December 31, 2007		
Raw materials	1,200	
Finished mixture	450	
Factory stores		5,550

The stock of finished mixture at the end of 2007 is to be valued at the factory cost of the mixture for that year. The purchase of raw materials remained unchanged throughout 2007.

Prepare a statement giving the maximum possible information about cost and its break-up for the year 2007.

Solution:

Statement of Cost for the Year 2007

		Quantity (kg.)	*Amount (Rs.)*
Raw materials consumed:			
Opening stock		2,000	2,000
Add: Purchases		1,60,000	1,80,000
		1,62,000	1,82,000
Less: Closing stock of raw materials at current prices		1,200	1,350
Cost of raw materials consumed		1,60,800	1,80,650
Factory wages			1,78,650
Direct expenses			18,500
Prime Cost		1,60,800	3,77,800
Add: Factory overheads (Factory stores)			
Opening stock	7,250		
Add: Purchases	24,250		
	31,500		
Less: Closing stock	5,550		
Factory stores consumed	25,950		
Power	30,400		
Depreciation	18,000		
Salaries	72,220		1,46,570
			5,24,370
Less: Sale of scrap		7,800	8,170
Factory cost		1,53,000	5,16,200
Add: Opening stock of finished mixture		500	1,750
		1,53,500	5,17,950
Less: Closing stock of finished mixture (valued at factory cost for current year production)		450	1,518
		1,53,050	5,16,432
Add: Office overheads:			
Salaries	37,220		
Expenses	18,200		55,420
Cost of production of finished mixture sold			5,71,852
Add: Selling and distribution overhead:			
Salaries	41,500		
Expenses	18,000		59,500
Cost of goods sold or cost of sales:			6,31,352
Profit			2,86,648
Sales		1,53,050 kg	9,18,000

Working Notes:

1. Value of closing stock of raw materials $\left(\frac{\text{Rs. } 1,80,000}{\text{Rs. } 1,60,000} \times 1,200 \text{ kg}\right)$ = Rs. 1,350

2. Value of factory scrap given in the question is Rs. 8,170. Hence quantity of factory scrap will be

		(kg.)
	Sales	1.53,050
Add:	Closing stock	450
		1,53,500
Less:	Opening stock	500
	Produced during the year	1,53,000
	Inputs introduced	1,60,800
	Scrap	7,800

Illustration 7:

The following figures are extracting from the trial balance of Gogetter Co. on 30th September, 2008.

	Rs.	*Rs.*
Inventories:		
Finished Stock	80,000	
Raw Materials	1,40,000	
Work-in-Process	2,00,000	
Office appliances	17,400	
Plant and machinery	4,60,500	
Buildings	2,00,000	
Sales		7,68,000
Scales return and rebates	14,000	
Materials purchases	3,20,000	
Freight incurred on materials	16,000	
Purchases returns		4,800
Direct labour	1,60,000	
Indirect labour	18,000	
Factory supervision	10,000	
Repairs and upkeep factory	14,000	
Heat, light and power	65,000	
Rates and taxes	6,300	
Miscellaneous factory expenses	18,700	
Sales commission	33,600	
Sales travelling	11.000	
Sales promotion	22,500	
Distribution dept. sales and expenses	18,000	
Office salaries and expenses	8,600	
Interest on borrowed funds	2,000	

Further details are available as follows:

(*i*) Closing Inventories:	
Finished goods	1,15,000
Raw materials	1,80,000
Work-in-progress	1,92,000
(*ii*) Accrued Expenses on:	
Direct labour	8,000
Indirect labour	1,200
Interest on borrowed funds	2,000
(*iii*) Depreciation to be provided on:	
Office appliance	5%
Plan and machinery	10%
Buildings	4%

(*iv*) Distribution of the following costs:
Heat, light and power to factory, office and selling in the ratio 8 : 1 : 1.
Rates and taxes two-thirds to factory and one-third to office. Depreciation on buildings to factory, office and selling in the ratio 8 : 1 : 1.
With the help of the above information, you are required to prepare a condensed profit and loss statement of Gogetter Co. for the year ended 30th September, 2008 along with supporting schedules:
(*a*) Cost of sales.
(*b*) Selling and distribution expenses.
(*c*) Administration expense.

Solution:

Gogetter Company

Profit and Loss Statement

For the Year Ended 30th September, 2008

	Rs.	*Rs.*
Gross Sales	7,68,000	
Less: Returns	14,000	7,54,000
Less: Cost of sales (Schedule 1)		7,14,020
Net operating profit		39,980
Less: Interest on borrowed funds		4,000
Net profit		35,980

(i) Schedule 1: Cost of Sales

	Rs.	*Rs.*
Raw Material:		
Opening Balance		1,40,000
Add: Material purchased	3,20,000	
Add: Freight on material	16,000	
Less: Purchased returns	(4,800)	3,31,200
Cost of materials available		4,71,200
Less: Closing stock		1,80,000
Raw materials consumed		2,91,200
Direct labour		1,68,000
Prime Cost		4,59,200
Factory Overheads:		
Indirect labour	19,200	
Factory supervision	10,000	
Repairs and factory upkeep	14,000	
Heat, light and power	52,000	
Rates and taxes	4,200	
Miscellaneous factory expenses	18,700	
Depreciation of plant	46,050	
Depreciation of buildings	6,400	1,70,550
Gross Works Cost		6,29,750
Add: Opening work-in-process		2,00,000
		8,29,750

Less: Closing work-in-process	1,92,000
Works Cost	6,37,750
Add: Administration expenses (Schedule 3)	18,870
Cost of production	6,56,620
Add: Opening stock of finished goods	80,000
	7,36,,620
Less: Closing stock of finished goods	1,15,000
Cost of Production of Goods Sold	6,21,620
Add: Selling and distribution overheads (Schedule 2)	92,400
Cost of sales	7,14,020

(ii) Schedule 2: Selling and Distribution Overheads (Expenses)

Sales commission	33,600
Sales travelling	11,000
Sales promotion	22,500
Distribution deptt: Salaries and expenses	18,000
Heat, light and power	6,500
Depreciation of buildings	800
	92,400

Schedule 3: Administrative Overheads (Expenses)

Office salaries and expenses	8,600
Depreciation on office appliances	870
Depreciation of buildings	800
Heat, light and power	6,500
Rates and taxes	2,100
	18,870

Illustration 8:

The following inventory data relates to XYZ Ltd.

	Inventories	
	Beginning	*Ending*
Finished goods	Rs. 1,10,000	95,000
Work-in-progress	Rs. 70,000	80,000
Raw materials	Rs. 90,000	95,000

Additional information:

Cost of goods available for sale	Rs. 6,84,000
Total goods processed during the period	Rs. 6,54,000
Factory overheads	Rs. 1,67,000
Direct materials used	Rs. 1,93,000

Requirements:

(*i*) Determine raw materials purchases

(*ii*) Determine the direct labour cost incurred

(*iii*) Determine the cost of goods sold

Solution:

		Rs.
(i)	*Raw Materials purchases*	
	Direct Materials used	1,93,000
Add:	Closing Stock	95,000
		2,88,000
Less:	Opening Stock	90,000
		1,98,000
(ii)	*Direct Labour cost incurred*	
	Goods processed during the period	6,54,000
Add:	Closing Work-in-process	80,000
		7,34,000
Less:	Opening Work-in-process	70,000
	Cost of goods introduced during the period for processing	6,64,000
Less:	Factory overheads	1,67,000
	Prime Cost	4,97,000
Less:	Direct Materials used	1,93,000
	Direct Labour cost incurred	3,04,000
(iii)	*Cost of goods sold*	*Rs.*
	Cost of goods available for sale	6,84,000
Add:	Opening Stock of Finished Goods	1,10,000
		7,94,000
Less:	Closing stock of finished goods	95,000
	Cost of goods sold	6,99,000

Illustration 9:

X Ltd. manufactures four brands of toys — A, B, C and D. If the company limits the manufacture to just one brand, the monthly production will be —

A - 50000 units
B - 100000 units
C - 150000 units
D - 300000 units

You are given the following set of information from which you are requested to find out the profit or loss made on each brand showing clearly the following elements —

(*a*) Direct Cost
(*b*) Works Cost
(*c*) Total Cost

	A	*B*	*C*	*D*
Actual production (units)	6,750	18000	40500	94500
Direct wages (Rs.)	15,000	27,500	37,500	1,05,000
Direct materials cost (Rs.)	50,000	92,500	1,27,500	3,80,000
Selling pence per unit (Rs.)	20	15	10	8

Factory overhead expenditure for the month was Rs 1,62,000. Selling and distribution cost should be assumed @20% of works cost. Factory overbear expenses should be allocated to each brand on the basis of units which could have been produced in a month when single brand production was in operation.

Solution:

The relative ratios of each brand of products are as follows:

1 unit of A = 2 units of B = 3 units of C = 6 units of D. Therefore, the overhead ratio in the inverse order should be 1 : 2 : 3 : 6. In case of D, the overhead expense rate will be:

$$\frac{\text{Rs. }1,62,000}{6750 \times 6 + 18000 \times 3 + 40500 \times 2 + 94500}$$

$$= \frac{\text{Rs. }1,62,000}{\text{Rs. }2,70,000}$$

$= \text{Re. } 0.60$

The overhead expense rate for the various brands are:

A — Rs. 6 × 0.60 = Rs. 3.60

B — Rs. 3 × 0.60 = Rs. 1.80

C — Rs. 2 × 0.60 = Rs. 1.20

D — Re. 1 × 0.60= Rs. 0.60

This follows the logic that the rate should be highest in case of brand which will be produced in least number when single brand production is in operation.

Statement of Profitability of Brands

	A *Rs.*	*B* *Rs.*	*C* *Rs.*	*D* *Rs.*	*Total* *Rs.*
Direct materials	50,000	92,500	1,27,500	3,80,000	6,50,000
Direct wages	15,000	27,500	37,500	1,05,000	1,85,000
Prime cost	65,000	1,20,000	1,65,000	4,85,000	8,35,000
Factory overhead	24,300	32,400	48,600	56,700	1,62,000
Works cost	89,300	1,52,400	2,13,600	5,41,700	9,97,000
Selling and distribution cost (20% of works cost)	17,860	30,480	42,720	1,08,340	1,99,400
Total cost	1,07,160	1,82,880	2,56,320	6,50,040	11,96,400
Sales	1,35,000	2,70,000	4,05,000	7,56,000	15,66,000
Profit	27,840	87,120	1,48,680	1,05,960	3,69,600

Illustration 10:

On June 30, 2008, a flash flood damaged the warehouse and factory of ABC Corporation completely destroying the work-in-progress inventory. There was no damage to either the raw materials or finished goods inventories. A physical verification taken after the flood revealed the following valuations:

Raw Materials	Rs. 62,000
Work-in-progress	0
Finished goods	Rs. 1,19,000

The inventory on Jan. 1, 2008, consisted of the following:

Raw materials	Rs. 30,000
Work-in-progress	Rs. 1,00,000
Finished Goods	Rs. 1,40,000
	2,70,000

A review of the books and records disclosed that the gross profit margin historically approximated 25% of sales. The sales for the first six months of 2008 were Rs. 3,40,000. Raw Material purchases were Rs. 1,15,000, Direct Labour costs for this period were Rs. 80,000 and manufacturing overhead has historically been 50% of direct labour. Compute the cost of work-in-progress inventory lost at June 30, 1996 by preparing a statement of cost and profit.

Solution:

Computation of Work-in-Progress Inventory Lost on June 30, 2008

		Rs.
Sales		3,40,000
Less: Gross Profit @ 25%		85,000
Cost of Goods sold		2,55,000
Add: Closing Stock of Finished Goods		1,19,000
		3,74,000
Less: Opening Stock of Finished Goods		1,40,000
Cost of Finished Goods Produced (1)		2,34,000
Less: Raw Materials Consumed:		
Purchases	1,15,000	
Add: Opening Stock	30,000	
	1,45,000	
Less: Closing stock	62,000	
	83,000	
Add: Wages	80,000	
Manufacturing Overhead	40,000	
Opening Stock of Work-in-progress	1,00,000	
		3,03,000
Closing stock of work-in-progress		69,000
This can be verified as follows:		*Rs.*
Raw Materials Consumed		83,000
Direct Wages		80,000
Manufacturing Overhead		40,000
Work-in-progress		1,00,000
		3,03,000
Less: Closing stock of work-in-progress		69,000
Work Costs		2,34,000
Add: Opening stock of Finished Goods		1,40,000
		3,74,000
Less: Closing stock of finished goods		1,19,000
Cost of goods sold		2,55,000
Add: Gross profit @ 25%		85,000
Sales		3,40,000

THEORY QUESTIONS

1. Define the term 'cost.' How is it different from expense?
2. What is meant by 'differential cost'?
3. What is the meaning of the term incremental cost? Does incremental cost mean the same thing as variable cost?
4. Explain the nature of product and period cost. How do they affect net income of a business enterprise?
5. "Product cost is a general term that denotes different costs allocated to products for different purposes." Describe three purposes. Explain the composition of 'product cost' for the purpose of external financial reporting along with its rationale.
6. Distinguish between
   (*a*) Expired cost and unexpired cost
   (*b*) Direct and indirect costs.
7. (*a*) Distinguish between fixed cost and variable costs.
   (*b*) Explain the significance of 'decision-making cost.'
   (*c*) Elucidate the meaning and formulation of 'Product cost' for the purpose of income measurement and determination of financial position.
8. Distinguish between:
   (*a*) Prime cost and conversion cost.
   (*b*) Controllable and uncontrollable cost.
9. Bring out clearly the significance of the following costs for management:
   (*a*) Opportunity cost
   (*b*) Sunk cost
   (*c*) Imputed costs
   (*d*) Out-of-pocket costs
10. Discuss the various costs used in decision-making and explain their characteristics.
11. Distinguish between period costs and product costs. Why is this distinction considered important?
12. Distinguish between the following:
    (*i*) Controllable cost and Non-controllable cost, and
    (*ii*) Direct material and indirect material.
13. (*a*) Distinguish between out-of-pocket cost and opportunity cost.
    (*b*) Explain and illustrate the distinction between 'direct cost' and 'indirect cost' specially from the point of view of decision making.
14. Explain whether you agree with each of the following statements:
    (*a*) "All direct costs are variable."
    (*b*) "Variable costs are controllable and fixed costs are not."
    (*c*) "Sunk costs are irrelevant when providing decision-making information."
15. Lists two costs which are used in decision making but not entered in the accounting system under the designation.
16. Name a cost which is reflected in the accounting system but not used in decision making.
17. Distinguish between:
    (*i*) Cost Control and Cost Reduction
    (*ii*) Cost allocation and cost absorption
    (*iii*) Controllable cost and uncontrollable cost
    (*iv*) Direct and indirect labour cost.

EXERCISES AND PROBLEMS

1. The following data arc related lo the manufacture of a standard product during the month of December, 2008.

	Rs.
Raw materials consumed	15,000
Direct wages	9,000
Machine hours worked	900
Machine hours rate	5
Administrative overheads	20% on works cost
Selling overheads	Re. 0.50 per unit
Units produced	17,100
Units sold	16,000 (at Rs. 4 per unit)

You are required to prepare a cost sheet from the above showing:

(*a*) The cost per unit

(*b*) The profit per unit sold and profit for the period.

(***Ans.:*** Cost per unit Rs. 2. Profit per unit sold Rs 1.50; and Profit Rs. 24,000)

2. A factory produces a standard product. The Following information is given to you from which you are required to prepare a cost sheet for January, 2009.

	Rs.
Raw materials consumed	91,000
Direct wages	29,000
Other direct expenses	11,000

Factory overheads 80% of direct wages

Office overheads 10% of works cost

Selling and distribution expenses Rs. 2 per unit sold.

Units produced and sold during the month 10,000.

Also find the selling price per unit on the basis that profit mark up is uniformly made to yield a profit of 20% of the selling price. There was no stock or work-in-progress either at the beginning or at the end of the period.

(***Ans.:*** Cost of sales Rs. 1,89,620; profit Rs. 47,405.)

3. From the following particulars of a manufacturing firm, prepare a statement showing:

(*a*) Cost of materials consumed.

(*b*) Works cost.

(*c*) Cost of production.

(*d*) Percentage of works overhead to productive wages.

(*e*) Percentage of general overhead to works cost.

	Rs.
Stock of materials on January 1, 2009	40,000
Purchase of raw materials in January 2009	11,00,000
Stock of finished goods on 1-1-2009	50,000
Productive wages	5,00,000
Finished goods sold	24,00,000
Works overhead charges	1,50,000
Office and general expenses	1,00,000
Stock of materials on 31-1-2009	1,40,000
Stock of finished goods on 31-1-2009	60,000

(***Ans.:*** (*a*) Rs 10,00,000; (*b*) 16,50,000;
(*c*) Rs 17,50,000; (*d*) 30% and
(*e*) 6.6%.

4. The following data have been extracted from the books of M/s. Moonshine Industries for the calendar year 2009.

	(Rs. '000)
Opening stock of raw materials	25,000
Purchase of raw materials	85,000
Closing stock of raw materials	40,000
Carriage inward	5,000
Wages — Direct	75,000
Indirect	10,000
Other direct charges	15,000
Rent and rates — Factory	5,000
Office	500
Indirect consumption material	500
Depreciation — Plant etc.	1,500
Office furniture	100
Salary — Office	2,500
Salesman	2,000
Other factory — expenses	5,700
Other office expenses	900
Managing Director's remuneration	12,000
Other selling expenses	1,000
Travelling expenses of salesmen	1,100
Carriage and freight outward	1,000
Sales	2,50,000
Advance income tax paid	15,000
Advertisement	2,000

The Managing Director's remuneration is to be allocated as Rs. 40,00,000 to the factory, Rs. 20,00,000 to the office and Rs 60,00,000 to the selling departments. From the above information prepare (*a*) Prime cost (*b*) Works cost (*c*) Cost of production (*d*) Cost of sales and (*e*) Net profit.

(***Ans.:*** Prime cost Rs 16,50,00,000. Factory cost Rs. 19,77,00,000, Cost of production Rs. 19,77,00,000. Cost of sales Rs. 21,08,00,000 Profit Rs. 3,92,00,000. Income tax is not included in costs.)

5. The following particulars relate to a company for a period of three months:

Raw materials 1-1-2009	55,000
Raw materials 31-3-2009	35,000
Factory wages	80,000
Materials purchased	60,000
Sales	1,54,000
Indirect expenses	10,000
Stock of finished goods (1-1-2009)	Nil
Stock of finished goods (31-3-2009)	30,000
No. of units produced during the period was	2,000

Prepare a statement of cost for the period and compute the price to be quoted for 500 units in order to realize the same % of profit as for the period under review, assuming no alteration in wages and cost of materials.

(***Ans.:*** Price to be quoted Rs. 46,750).

Materials Control

MATERIALS

The term "materials", generally used in manufacturing concerns, refers to raw materials used for production, sub-assemblies and fabricated parts. The terms "materials" and "stores" are sometimes used interchangeably. However, both the terms differ. "Stores" is wider in meaning and comprises many other items besides raw materials, such as tools, equipments, maintenance and repair items, factory supplies, components, jigs, fixtures. Sometimes, finished goods and partly finished goods are also included within the scope of this term.

CONCEPT AND OBJECTIVES OF MATERIALS CONTROL

Materials cost constitute a prime part of the total cost of production of manufacturing firms. Materials control basically aims at efficient purchasing of materials, their efficient storing and efficient use of consumption.

Materials control consists of controls at two levels: (*i*) quantity controls, and (*ii*) financial controls. For instance, the production department in a manufacturing company aims at quantity controls, *i.e.*, lesser and lesser units should be used in the production department. Although lesser units would result in lower investments on purchase of materials, yet the user (production) department normally does not think in terms of expenditure. In contrast, the finance manager is interested in keeping the investments on materials at the lowest point. In materials control an equilibrium has to be maintained between two opposing needs, *i.e.*, (*i*) maintenance of sufficient inventory for efficient production and (*ii*) maintenance of investment in inventory at the lowest level. The following are the objectives in a good system of materials control:

1. Material of the desired quality will be available when needed for efficient and uninterrupted production.
2. Material will be purchased only when need exists and in economic quantities.

3. The investment in materials will be maintained at the lowest level consistent with operating requirements.
4. Purchase of materials will be made at the most favourable prices under the best possible terms.
5. Materials are protected against loss by fire, theft; handing with the help of proper physical controls.
6. Materials should be stored in such a way that they can provide minimum of handing time and cost.
7. Vouchers will be approved for payment only if the material has been received and is available for issue.
8. Issues of material are properly authorised and properly accounted for.
9. Materials are, at all times, charged as the responsibility of some individual.

CREATING A PURCHASE DEPARTMENT

It is useful to set up a separate purchase department to perform purchasing activities relating to purchase of materials and other stores. The organisation of the purchase department depends on the size of the organisation and the quantum of purchases it is likely to make. A purchase department generally performs the following functions:

(*i*) Purchasing materials and stores after receiving requisitions from the stores department for regular or routine items or from the departmental head, works manager or planning department for the purchase of special items, if any.

(*ii*) Purchasing materials of right quality.

(*iii*) Determining the quantity, quality, items, price, time to buy and the supplier from whom purchases are to be made.

(*iv*) Possessing knowledge about possible sources of supply, prices of materials and supplies prevailing in the market, terms and conditions relating to purchases, market trends, usual lead time taken by the suppliers.

(*v*) Having expertise in drafting of purchase agreements and contracts.

(*vi*) Avoiding the purchase of obsolete, deteriorated and surplus materials.

(*vii*) Purchasing at the most favourable terms and conditions, at the lowest rates and from the best market and the most reliable suppliers.

(*viii*) Ensuring timely delivery of purchased items.

(*ix*) Comparing the invoice received from the suppliers with the purchase order to ensure that materials received are of right quality, in right quantity and at right prices.

(*x*) Knowing the defaulter suppliers.

(*xi*) Having information about consumption and usage pattern of materials of production and other departments and stock levels maintained by them and the stores department.

(*xii*) Preparing a latest list of approved suppliers along with brief particulars about their dealing terms.

(*xiii*) Possessing details about materials and stores received, on order, and outstanding.

Qualities of Purchase Manager

A purchase manager or a purchaser should possess the following qualities:

(*i*) Having information and knowledge about all aspects of materials to be purchased such as quantity, specifications, quality, price, purchasing procedures etc.

(*ii*) Having knowledge about the sources of supply, market conditions, terms of delivery, qualities and dealings of different suppliers.

(*iii*) Knowing the policy of management, funds position, requirements of manufacturing units and stores departments.

(*iv*) Having good information base such as price lists, business journals and periodicals, catalogues, industrial directories to enable him to find the best market for the purchase of materials.

(*v*) Having knowledge about government policies, taxes on purchase of such materials, import and export restrictions thereon.

(*vi*) Having fair knowledge about the legal provisions and rules relating to making of agreement and contract.

(*vii*) Having expertise and skill to organise and manage his department efficiently and in coordination and cooperation with other departments of the organisation.

ISSUES IN MATERIALS PROCUREMENT

It is generally accepted that quantities be bought in economic size so that there may not be over-stocking. If a company purchases in large quantities, the cost of carrying the inventory would be high because of the high investment involved. Working capital which could have been used for other productive purposes has to be diverted. Over-stocking requires more storage space which, in turn, means increases in insurance expenses, storage costs and deterioration in quality and depreciation in quantity. In contrast, if purchases are made in small quantities (under-stocking), frequent orders would have to be placed for the purchase of materials. There will be danger of "stock outs" also. Because of under-stocking, production is likely to suffer; materials have to be purchased immediately at high prices; low output would increase cost and decrease profit; the other department's work may be adversely affected.

Economic Order Quantity (EOQ) (Reorder Quantity)

The *EOQ* is the optimum or the most favourable quantity which should be purchased each time the purchases are to be made. The *EOQ* is one where the costs of carrying inventory is equal or almost equal to the cost of not carrying inventory (Cost of placing order). Also at *EQQ* level, the total of these two costs is minimum.

The cost of carrying the inventory is the real out-of-pocket cost associated with having inventory on hand, such as warehouse charges, insurance, heat, light, and losses due to spoilage, breakage, pilferage. Another opportunity cost, which is not out-of-pocket cost, is important and should be considered, *i.e.*, cost incurred (capital used) in purchasing the inventory. If funds have been borrowed to finance the inventory purchase, interest payments on borrowed funds will be the direct cost. Carrying or holding costs of inventory are explicit as well as implicit. That is, some costs are readily ascertained from accounting records while others require extensive study to estimate them because they are not expressly stated. Insurance on inventory is an explicit cost while the cost of funds invested in inventory are implicit costs. Generally, inventory carrying costs are considered to be proportional to the value of inventory carried.

The costs of not carrying adequate inventory arise because of frequent placing of order at short intervals. This includes costs, such as extra purchasing, handling and transportation costs, higher price due to small order quantities, frequent stock-outs resulting in disruption of production schedules, overtime and extra set up time, loss of sales and customer goodwill, etc.

The costs of carrying the inventory, and ordering costs change in the reverse order. The costs of placing the order decrease as the size of the order increase since with a bigger size of order, the number of the order will be lower. However, simultaneously the costs of carrying the inventory will go up because purchases have been made in large quantities. It may be possible to have a point which provides the lowest total cost and this point (ideal size) is known as the *EQQ*. This equilibrium can be determined mathematically as follows:

$$EOQ = \sqrt{\frac{2 \times U \times O}{IC}}$$

where U = Annual usage in units
O = Cost of placing an order
I = Per cent cost of carrying inventory
C = Cost per unit of material

Assume

Annual usage units = 6,000
Cost of placing an order = Rs. 30
Carrying cost as a percent of inventory = 20%
Cost per unit of material = Rs. 5

Then,

$$EOQ = \sqrt{\frac{2 \times 6{,}000 \times 30}{5 \times 20\%}}$$

$$= \sqrt{3{,}60{,}000}$$

$$= 600 \text{ units}$$

In the above example, the *EOQ* is 600 units. That is, ten orders per year are needed. At the level of 600 units, the ordering costs and the carrying costs are equal and also the total cost is at minimum as it is clear from Table 17.1.

Table 17.1 Showing Economic Order Quantity

Annual usage	*Orders per year*	*Units per order*	*Average inventory (units)*	*Value per order (Rs.)*	*Average inventory amount (Rs.)*	*Order cost*	*Carrying cost (20%)*	*Total cost (Rs.)*
6,000 units	1	6,000	3,000	30,000	15,000	30	3,000	3,030
	2	3,000	1,500	15,000	7,500	60	1,500	1,560
	3	2,000	1,000	10,000	5,000	90	1,000	1,090
	4	1,500	750	7,500	3,750	120	750	870
	5	1,200	600	6,000	3,000	150	600	750
	6	1,000	500	5,000	2,500	180	500	680
	7	857	429	4,285	2,142	210	428	638
	8	750	375	3,750	1,875	240	376	616
	9	667	334	3,335	1,668	270	334	604
	10	600	300	3,000	1,500	300	300	600
	11	545	273	2,725	1,363	330	272	602
	12	500	250	2,500	1,250	360	250	610

Table 17.1 shows that quantities of other orders resulting in more or less than ten orders per year are not economical as they involve higher total costs.

The *EOQ* formula is sometimes expressed in the following manner which is not in any way different from the formula explained earlier.

$$EOQ = \sqrt{\frac{2U \times P}{S}}$$

where U = Annual demand or consumption or purchased quantity (in units)
P = Cost of placing an order
S = Annual cost of carrying inventory per unit (Storage and interest)

When to Order (Reorder Level)

The *EOQ* determines how much to buy at a particular time. But the question "when to buy" is equally important for business firms. This question is easy to answer only if we know the lead time — the time interval between placing an order and receiving delivery — and know the *EOQ*, and are certain of the consumption pattern during lead time. The order point or re-order level is a point or quantity level at which if materials in stores reach, the order for supply of materials must be placed. This point automatically initiates a new order. The order point is calculated from three factors:

1. The expected usage.
2. The time interval between initiating an order and its receipt, referred to as the lead time.
3. The minimum inventory, or safety stock.

For example, if daily usage is 400 units of material which have a lead time of 20 days and the safety (minimum) stock is 500 units, the order point will be calculated as follows:

Daily consumption × lead time	= 400 × 20 =	8,000
Add safety stock	=	500
Order point units	=	8,500

The order point is determined after considering the worst possible expected conditions. This only ensures that the minimum stock will always remain in the inventory and will not be used atleast in the short run. However, situations may arise where there will be stock-out and thus, the order point may not be an absolutely accurate forecasting.

Determinations of Safety or Minimum Stock Levels

It is advisable to carry a reserve or safety stock to prevent stock-out. The safety should be used only in abnormal circumstances, and the working stock in ideal or normal conditions. Therefore, for normal working conditions, the stock should not be allowed to fall below the safety limit, kept only for emergencies. If the usage pattern is known with certainty, and the lead time is also known accurately, then no safety stock would be needed. However, if either usage or lead time is subject to variation then it is necessary for a business firm to maintain safety stock levels equal to the difference between the expected usage over lead time and the maximum usage over lead time that the firm feels is necessary for cost minimisation. The safety stock level can be computed by using the following formula:

Safety stock level = (Maximum rate or consumption – Average rate of consumption) × Lead time

That is, $= (425 - 400) \times 20$ days

$= 500$ units

Maximum Stock Level

The maximum level ensures that the stocks will not exceed this limit although there may be low demand for materials or quick delivery from the suppliers. Maximum stock level can be computed as follows:

Maximum stock level = Re-order level + *EOQ* – (Minimum consumption × Minimum re-order period)

Danger Level

Generally the danger level of stock is indicated below the safety or minimum stock level. Sometimes, depending on the practices of the firm and circumstances prevailing, the danger level is determined between re-order level and minimum level. In the second case (danger level being between re-order level and minimum level), the firm can only take steps to ensure that materials ordered will arrive in time.

Average Stock Level

Average stock level is computed in the following manner:

$$= \frac{\text{Minimum stock} + \text{Maximum stock}}{2}$$

Or

$$= \frac{\text{Minimum level} + \text{Re} - \text{order quantity}}{2}$$

The following example further illustrates the different stock levels.

Maximum usage (units)	650 per day
Minimum usage (units)	300 per day
Normal usage (units)	500 per day
Economic order quantity (units)	75,000
Re-order period — lead time	25 to 30 days
Minimum level (units)	5,000

(10 days at normal usage)

The different stock levels will be as follows:

Re-order level = Normal usage × Normal lead time + Minimum level

$= (500 \times 30) + 5{,}000$

$= 20000$ units

Maximum level = Re-order level + *EOQ* – Minimum quantity used in re-order period

$= 20{,}000 + 75{,}000 - (300 \times 25)$

$= 87{,}000$ units

$$\text{Average level} = \frac{\text{Maximum} + \text{Minimum}}{2}$$

$$= \frac{87{,}500 + 5{,}000}{2}$$

$= 46{,}250$ units

Illustration 1:

From the details given below, calculate:

(*i*) Re-ordering Level
(*ii*) Maximum Level
(*iii*) Minimum Level
(*iv*) Danger Level

Cost of placing a purchase order is Rs. 20.

Number of units to be purchased during the year is 5,000.

Purchase price per unit inclusive of transportation cost is Rs. 50.

Annual cost of storage per unit is Rs. 5

Details of lead time: Average 10 days, Maximum 15 days. Minimum 6 days. For emergency purchases 4 days.

Rate of Consumption Average : 15 units per day, Maximum: 20 units.

Solution:

(*i*) Re-ordering Level (ROL) = Maximum Usage per day × Maximum Re-order period
= 20 units per day × 15 days
= 300 units

(*ii*) Maximum Level (WN 1 and 2) = ROL + ROQ – (Min. Rate of Consumption × Min. Re-order Period)
= 300 units + 200 units – (10 units per day × 6 days)
= 440 units.

(*iii*) Minimum Level = ROL – (Average rate of consumption × Average re-order period)
= 300 units – (15 units per day × 10 days)
= 150 units.

(*iv*) Danger Level = Average consumption × Lead time for emergency purchases
= 15 units per day × 4 days
= 60 units.

Working Notes:

1. *ROQ* $= \sqrt{\frac{2U \times P}{S}} = \sqrt{\frac{2 \times 5000 \text{ units} \times \text{Rs. } 20}{\text{Rs. } 5}}$
= 200 units

Where: *ROQ* = Reorder Quantity
U = Annual Consumption
P = Cost per order
S = Storage Cost per unit

2. Average Rate of Consumption

$$= \frac{\text{Minimum Rate of Consumption } (x) + \text{Maximum Rate of Consumption}}{2}$$

$$15 \text{ units per day} = \frac{x + 20 \text{ units per day}}{2}$$

or $x = 10$ units per day.

Illustration 2:

G. Ltd. produces a product which has a monthly demand of 4,000 units. The product requires a component X which is purchased at Rs. 20. For every finished product, one unit of component is required. The ordering cost is Rs. 120 per order and the holding cost is 10% p.a.

You are required to calculate

(*i*) Economic order quantity.

(*ii*) If the minimum lot size to be supplied is 4,000 units, what is the extra cost, the company has to incur?

(*iii*) What is the minimum carrying cost, the company has to incur?

Solution:

(*i*) *Computation of Economic Ordering Quantity*

$$EOQ = \sqrt{\frac{2U \times P}{S}}$$

Where U = Annual Consumption

P = Cost of Placing an Order

S = Storage Cost per unit per annum

$$= \sqrt{\frac{2 \times 48{,}000 \text{ units} \times \text{Rs. } 120}{10\% \times \text{Rs. } 20}} = \sqrt{5{,}76{,}000}$$

= 2,400 units.

(*ii*) *Extra Cost Incurred by the Company*

Total cost when order size is 4000 units

= Total Ordering Cost + Total Carrying Cost

= 12 orders × 120 + 4,000 × 1/2 × 20 × 10/100

= Rs. 1,440 + Rs. 4,000 = Rs. 5,440

Total cost when order size is 2400 units

Total Cost = 20 orders × Rs. 120 + 2,400 × 1/2 × 20 × 10/100

= Rs. 2,400 + Rs. 2,400 = Rs. 4,800

Extra Cost incurred by the company = Rs. 5,440 – Rs. 4,800 = Rs. 640

(*iii*) *Minimum Carrying Cost*

The carrying or storage cost depends upon the size of the order. It will be minimum when the order size is least.

In the question the two order sizes are 2,400 units and 4,000 units. Hence, 2,400 units is the least of the two order sizes. At this order size carrying cost will be minimum.

The minimum carrying cost in this case will be as under:

Minimum Carrying Cost = 1/2 × 2,400 units × 10/100 × Rs. 20 = Rs. 2,400

Illustration 3:

ZEE is product manufactured out of three raw materials M, N and Q. Each unit of ZEE requires 10 kgs, 8 kgs, and 6 kgs of M, N and Q respectively. The re-order levels of M and N are 15,000 kgs and 10,000 kg respectively while the minimum-level of Q is 2,500 kg. The weekly production of ZEE varies from 300 to 500 units, while the weekly average production is 400 units. You are required to compute:

(*i*) the minimum stock level of M.

(*ii*) the maximum stock level of N and

(*iii*) the re-order level of Q.

The following additional data are given:

	M	*N*	*Q*
Re-order Quantity (in kgs)	*20,000*	*15,000*	*20,000*
Delivery (in weeks)			
Minimum	2	4	3
Average	3	5	4
Maximum	4	6	5

Solution:

(*i*) Minimum Stock Level of M

= Re-order Level – (Average Usage × Average Delivery Time)

= 15,000 kgs – (400 units of Zee × 10 kgs per unit × 3 weeks)

= 15,000 – 12,000 = 3,000 kgs.

(*ii*) Maximum Stock Level of N

= Re-order Level + Re-order Quantity – (Minimum Usage × Minimum Re-order Period)

= 10,000 kgs. + 15,000 kgs. – (300 × 8 × 4) kgs.

= 15,400 kgs.

(*iii*) Re-order Level of Q

= Maximum Re-order period × Maximum Usage

= 5 × 500 × 6

= 15,000 kgs.

Illustration 4:

M/s. Tubes Ltd. are the manufacturers of picture tubes for T.V. The following are the details of their operation during 2008:

Average monthly market demand	2,000 Tubes
Ordering cost	Rs. 100 per order
Inventory carrying cost	20% per annum
Cost of tubes	Rs. 500 per tube
Normal usage	100 tubes per week
Minimum usage	50 tubes per week
Maximum usage	200 tubes per week
Lead time to supply	6-8 weeks

Compute from the above:

1. Economic Order Quantity. If the supplier is willing to supply quarterly 1,500 units at a discount of 5%, is it worth accepting?
2. Maximum level of stock.
3. Minimum level of stock.
4. Reorder level.

Solution:

1. $EOQ = \sqrt{\frac{2UP}{S}}$

Where U = Annual usage of tubes

= Normal usage per week × 52 weeks

= 100 tubes × 52 weeks = 5,200 tubes

P = Ordering cost per order = Rs. 100 per order

S = Inventory carrying cost per unit per annum

20% × Rs. 500 = Rs. 100 per unit per annum

$$EOQ = \sqrt{\frac{2 \times 5,200 \text{ units} \times \text{Rs. } 100}{\text{Rs. } 100}} = 102 \text{ tubes (approx.)}$$

Evaluation of offer: If the supplier is willing to supply 1,500 units at a discount of 5%.

(*i*) Total Cost when order size is 1500 units

= Cost of 5,200 Units + Ordering Cost + Carrying Cost

$$= 5,200 \text{ units} \times \text{Rs. } 475 + \frac{5,200 \text{ units}}{1,500 \text{ units}} \times \text{Rs. } 100 + \frac{1}{2} \times 1,500 \text{ units} \times 20\% \times \text{Rs. } 475$$

= Rs. 24,70,000 + Rs. 346.67 + Rs. 71,250

= Rs. 25,41,596.67

(*ii*) Total Cost (when order size is 102 units):

$$= 5,200 \text{ units} \times \text{Rs. } 500 + \frac{5,200 \text{ units}}{102 \text{ units}} \times \text{Rs. } 100 + 102 \text{ units} \times 20\% \times \text{Rs. } 500$$

= Rs. 26,00,000 + Rs. 5,098.03 + Rs. 5,100

= Rs. 26,10,198.03

The above calculation shows the total cost under quarterly supply of 1,500 units with 5% discount is lower than that when order size is 102 units. Therefore, the offer should be accepted. However, while accepting this offer consideration of capital blocked on order size of 1,500 units per quarter has been ignored.

2. *Maximum Level of Stock*

= Re-order level + Re-order quantity – (Min. usage × Min. Re-order period)

= 1,600 units + 102 units – 50 units × 6 weeks

= 1,402 units.

3. *Minimum Level of Stock*

= Re-order level – (Normal usage × Average Re-order period)
= 1,600 units – 100 units × 7 weeks = 900 units.

4. *Reorder Level*

= Maximum Consumption × Maximum Re-order Period
= 200 units × 8 weeks
= 1,600 units.

Illustration 5:

Material *X* and *Y* are used as follows:

Level

Minimum usage – 50 units each per week.
Maximum usage – 150 units each per week.
Normal usage – 100 units each per week.
Ordering quantities *X* = 600 units

Y = 1000 units

Delivery period *X* = 4 to 6 weeks

Y = 2 to 4 weeks

Calculate for each material: (*a*) Minimum level; (*b*) Maximum level; and (*c*) Order level.

Solution:

Material X

Ordering level = Maximum usage × Maximum delivery period
= 150 × 6
= 900 units

Minimum level = Ordering level – (Normal usage × Normal delivery period)
= 900 – (100 × 5)
= 900 – 500
= 400 units

Maximum level = (Ordering level + Ordering quantity) – (Minimum usage × Minimum delivery period)
= 900 + 600 – (50 × 4)
= 1,500 – 200
= 1,300 units

Material Y

Ordering level = Maximum usage × Minimum delivery period
= 150 × 4
= 600 units

Minimum level = Ordering level – (Normal usage × Normal delivery period)
= 600 – (100 × 3)
= 600 – 300
= 300 units

Maximum level = (Ordering level + Ordering quantity) – (Minimum usage × Minimum delivery period)
= 600 + 1,000 – (50 × 2)
= 1,600 – 100
= 1500 units

Notes: Normal period of delivery has been computed as follows:

$$\text{Material X} = \frac{(4+6)}{2} = 5 \text{ weeks}$$

$$\text{Material Y} = \frac{(2+4)}{2} = 3 \text{ weeks}$$

Illustration 6:

From the following data, calculate the economic order quantity and the re-order point for Part Z:

Working days in a year	200
Safety stock	400 units
Lead time	10 days
Order costs	Rs. 300 per order
Holding costs	15% of cost
Annual consumption	10,000 units
Cost per unit	Rs. 10

Solution:

$$EOQ = \sqrt{\frac{2U \times P}{S}}$$

$$= \sqrt{\frac{2 \times 10{,}000 \times \text{Rs. } 300}{15\% \times 10}} = \sqrt{\frac{6{,}00{,}000}{1.5}} = 2{,}000 \text{ units}$$

Trial and error calculation to arrive at the above answer:

Times ordered	4	5	6
Order size (Units)	2,500	2,000	1,666
Average stock (Units)	1,250	1,000	833
Holding costs (Rs.)	1,875	1,500	1,250
Order costs (Rs.)	1,200	1,500	1,800
	Rs. 3,075	Rs. 3,000	Rs. 3,050

Economic order quantity: 2,000 units, order 5 times per annum.

Re-order point:

Daily consumption X lead time (10,000 ÷ 200) × 10 =	500
Add safety stock	400
Re-order point	900 Units

Holding cost has been calculated as follows:

Average stock units × cost per unit × 15%

Illustration 7:

The Purchase Department of your organisation has received an offer of quantity discounts on its orders of materials as under:

Price per kg.	*Kgs.*
1,200	Less than 500
1,180	500 and less than 1,000
1,160	1,000 and less than 2,000
1,140	2,000 and less than 3,000
1,120	3,000 and above.

The annual requirement for the material is 5,000 kgs. The ordering cost per order is Rs. 1,200 and the carrying cost is estimated at 20% per annum.

You are required to compute the most economic order quantity presenting the information in a tabular form.

Solution:

Ordering quantity (kg.) EOQ	*Price per kg. (Rs.)*	*Purchasing cost of 5,000 kg. (Rs.)* 5,000 × Per order delivery cost	*Ordering cost (Rs.)* $\frac{5000 \times 1200}{\text{Ordering quantity}}$	*Inventory carrying (Rs.)* $\frac{EOQ}{2} \times$ Price per kg. × 20%	*Total cost (Rs.)*
400	1,200	60,00,000	15,000	48,000	60,63,000
500	1,180	59,00,000	12,000	59,000	59,71,000
1,000	1,160	58,00,000	6,000	1,16,000	59,22,000
2,000	1,140	57,00,000	3,000	2,28,000	59,31,000
3,000	1,120	56,00,000	2,000	3,36,000	59,38,000

The above table shows that most economical purchase level is at a level where the ordering quantity is 1,000 kgs., since at this level the total cost (*i.e.*, inventory carrying cost and ordering cost) is the minimum.

Illustration 8:

Shriram Enterprises manufactures a special product "ZED." The following particular were collected for the year 2008:

(*a*) Monthly demand of ZED 1,000 units.
(*b*) Cost of placing an order Rs. 100.
(*c*) Annual carrying cost per unit Rs. 15.
(*d*) Normal usage 50 units per week.
(*e*) Minimum usage 25 units per week.
(*f*) Maximum usage 75 units per week.
(*g*) Re-order period 4 to 6 weeks.

Compute from the above

1. Re-order quantity
2. Re-order level
3. Minimum level
4. Maximum level
5. Average stock level

Solution:

1. Re-order quantity (of units used)

$$= \sqrt{\frac{2U \times P}{S}}$$

where U = Annual demand of input units
P = Cost of placing an order
S = Annual carrying cost per unit

$$= \sqrt{\frac{2 \times 2,600 \times \text{Rs.}\,100}{\text{Rs.}\,15}} = \sqrt{34667}$$

= 186 units (approx.)

2. Re-order level = Maximum re-order period × Maximum usage
= 6 weeks × 75 units
= 450

3. Minimum level = Re-order level – (Normal usage × Average re-order period)
= 450 units – (50 units × 5 weeks)
= 450 units – 250 units = 200 units

4. Maximum level = Re-order level + Re-order quantity – (Minimum usage × Minimum order period)
= 450 units + 186 units – (25 units × 4 weeks)
= 536 units

5. Average stock level = 1/2 (Minimum stock level + Maximum stock level)
= 1/2 (200 units + 536 units)
= 368 units

Working Notes:

U = Annual demand of input units for 12,000 units of 'ZED'
= 53 weeks × Normal usage of input units per week
= 52 weeks × 50 units of input per week
= 2,600 units

Illustration 9:

XYZ Company buys in lots of 500 boxes which is a 3 months' supply. The cost per box is Rs. 125 and the ordering cost is Rs. 150. The inventory carrying cost is estimated at 20% of unit value. What is the total annual cost of the existing inventory policy? How much could be saved by employing the economic order quantity?

Solution:

	Rs.
(*i*) Ordering Cost	
4 orders in a year @ Rs. 150 each order	600
Carrying cost of average inventory	
$\frac{500}{2}$ = 250 units × 20% × 125 =	6,250
Total annual cost of existing inventory policy	6,850

(*ii*) Economic Order Quantity {EOQ)

$$= \sqrt{\frac{2U \times P}{S}}$$

$$= \sqrt{\frac{2 \times 2000 \times 150}{20\% \text{ of Rs.} 125}}$$

$$= \sqrt{\frac{6,00,000}{25}}$$

= 155 units

(*iii*) Ordering Cost

$$= \frac{2000}{155} = 12.90 \text{ or } 13 \text{ orders approx.}$$

13 orders are to be placed at Rs. 150 each	1,950.00
carrying cost of average inventory	
$= \frac{155}{2} \times \frac{20}{100} \times 125$	1,937.50
Total annual cost	3,887.50

Saving in annual cost if EOQ is adopted

Rs. 6,850 – Rs. 3,887.50 = Rs. 2,962.50

Illustration 10:

The following information in an inventory problem is available:

Annual demand	2400 units
Unit price (Rs.)	2.40
Ordering cost (Rs.)	4.00
Storage cost (Rs.)	2% per year
Interest rate	10% p.a.
Lead time	1/2 month.

Calculate EOQ, Re-order level and total annual inventory cost. How much does the total inventory cost vary if the unit price is changed to Rs. 5?

Solution:

Inventory carrying cost = 10% + 2% = 12% p.a.

Carrying cost per unit p.a. = 12% of Rs. 2.40 – Rs. 0.288

$$EOQ = \sqrt{\frac{2U \times P}{S}} = \sqrt{\frac{2 \times 2400 \times 4}{0.288}} = \sqrt{66667} = 258 \text{ units}$$

ROL = 1/2 month × 2400/12 = 100 units

Total Annual Inventory Cost:	Rs.
Cost of 2,400 units at Rs. 2.40	5,760.00
Ordering cost 2,400/258 = 9.3 orders Approximately 10 orders at Rs. 4	40.00
Carrying cost of average inventory of 258 units $= \frac{258}{2} = 129$ units *i.e.,* 129 units × Rs. 0.288	37.15
Total Annual Inventory Cost	5,837.15

Unit Price Rs. 5

$$EOQ = \sqrt{\frac{2 \times 2400 \times 4}{12\% \text{ of } 5.00}} = \sqrt{32000} = 179 \text{ units}$$

Total Annual Inventory Cost:	Rs.
Cost of 2400 units at Rs. 5 each	12,000
Ordering cost 24000/179 = 13.4 orders Or 14 orders at Rs. 4 each	56.00
Carrying cost 179.2 × 0.60	53.70
Total annual inventory cost	12,109.70

Difference = Rs. 12,109.70 – 5,837.15
= Rs. 6,272.55

Illustration 11:

A Ltd. is committed to supply 24,000 bearings per annum to B Ltd. on a steady basis. It is estimated that it costs 10 paise as inventory holding cost per bearing per month and that the set-up cost per run of bearing manufacture is Rs. 324.

(*i*) What should be the optimum run size for bearing manufacture?

(*ii*) What would be the interval between two consecutive optimum runs?

(*iii*) Find out the minimum inventory cost per annum.

Solution:

(*i*) Optimum run size for bearing manufacture

$$= \sqrt{\frac{2 \times \text{Annual supply of bearings} \times \text{Set-up cost per production run}}{\text{Annual holding cost per bearing}}}$$

$$= \sqrt{\frac{2 \times 24{,}000 \text{ bearings} \times \text{Rs. } 324}{12 \text{ months} \times 0.10\text{P.}}} = \sqrt{12960000}$$

= 3600 bearings

(*ii*) Interval between two consecutive optimum runs

$$= \frac{12 \text{ months}}{\text{Number of production runs per annum}} = \frac{12 \text{ months}}{\left(\dfrac{\text{Annual production}}{\text{Optimum run size}}\right)}$$

$$= \frac{12 \text{ months}}{\left(\dfrac{24,000 \text{ bearings}}{3,600 \text{ bearings}}\right)} = \frac{12 \text{ months}}{6.66}$$

= 1.8 months or 55 days approximately.

(*iii*) Minimum inventory cost per annum

= Total production run cost + Total carrying cost per annum

$$= \frac{24,000 \text{ bearings}}{3,600 \text{ bearings}} \times \text{Rs. } 324 + (1/2)\ 3,600 \text{ bearings} \times 0.10 \text{ P} \times 12 \text{ months}$$

= Rs. 2,160 + Rs. 2,160

= Rs. 4,320

INVENTORY SHORTAGES (LOSSES) AND AVERAGES

Under the perpetual inventory system, inventory accounts are maintained up-to-date in a stores ledger. It is, however, necessary to make physical counts of the materials at regular intervals to compare with the stores ledger records. It is possible that physical counting of materials may not agree with the stores ledger. The difference may be because of the following reasons:

A. *Unavoidable*

1. Evaporation
2. Absorption, moisture
3. Temperature changes affecting the volume of stock
4. Shrinkage
5. Deterioration of quality in stores, e.g., through rust
6. Loss due to breaking bulk or cutting up.

B. *Avoidable*

1. Pilferage
2. Unsuitable storage
3. Careless handling
4. Under and over issues
5. Materials unused but not returned to stores

INVENTORY CONTROL

Nature of Inventory

Inventory is stores of goods and stocks. The Council of the Institute of Chartered Accountants of India (Accounting Standards 2) defines inventories as:

"Tangible property held (*i*) for the sale in the ordinary course of business, or (*ii*) in the process of production for such sale, or (*iii*) for consumption in the production of goods or service for sale, including maintenance supplies and consumables other than machinery spares."

In other words, in manufacturing organisations, inventories include (*a*) raw-materials, (*b*) work-in progress, (*c*) finished product goods, and (*d*) manufacturing supplies. In trading concerns, inventories consists of (*a*) merchandise held for sale, and (*b*) office, packing and other supplies.

Meaning of Inventory Control

Inventory control is the technique of maintaining inventory items (raw materials, work-in-progress, finished products, factory supplies) at desired levels. Manufacturing firms face several inventory control problems as compared to service-oriented organisations. In manufacturing organisations, production is of some tangible physical product. Therefore, emphasis is given to control of all inventory items. In service organisations, the focus is on service, and therefore there is very little emphasis on inventory control. In such service firms, services are used (consumed) as they are generated and not stocked for future consumption. However, there are some service organisations, such as hospitals, military organisations, educational institutions which have to maintain inventories of items related to their nature of work.

Importance of Inventory Control

Inventory control is of great significance in almost all types of business enterprises. If inventories pile up due to over-production or slow demand, capital is tied up which cannot be used for other productive purposes. Alternatively, production is likely to suffer because of inadequate inventory on hand. As stated earlier in this chapter, the basic objective of inventory control is identical to materials control, i.e., maintaining inventory of adequate size for uninterrupted production and lowest investment on the inventory in conformity with production requirements.

Inventory control is also necessary because of the following significant factors:

1. *Demand fluctuations:* There are likely to be fluctuations in demand pattern. To cope with the changing consumers' demand, it is necessary that adequate inventory should be maintained.
2. *Uncertainty about lead time:* Sometimes the supplier may take more time in supplying the raw materials than expected. During this additional time, inventory has to be maintained so that the production does not suffer.
3. *Avoiding over-stocking and under-stocking:* Over-stocking and under-stocking both are undesirable and should he avoided.

The ABC Method

In a large manufacturing company where stocks of direct materials and component parts consist of many thousands of different items, companies find it useful to divide materials, parts, supplies and finished goods into sub-classifications for purposes of inventory control. Many business firms introduce a system of analysing stocks by value categories known as "ABC Analysis." Under this method, inventory items are ranked according to investments in each item in the inventory. The large value items are grouped together into one class for inventory control purposes. The lowest value items are grouped into another class and those items which are of intermediate value are grouped into a "middle" classification. High value items are labelled "Class A", middle value items, "Class B" and low value items, "Class C." All items in stock are listed in order of descending values showing quantity held and the corresponding value of the materials (see Table 17.2).

The percentage given in Table 17.2 are only guidelines and are subject to change according to prevailing circumstances and choice of management. Table 3.3 shows that only 20% of the items represent 72% of the total costs.

Table 17.2
Stock Analysis under ABC

Class	*Items*		*Investment*	
	No. of items	*Per cent of total items*	*Total cost (Rs.)*	*Per cent of total*
A	20,000	20%	2,88,000	72%
B	30,000	30%	76,000	19%
C	50,000	50%	36,000	9%
	100,000	100%	4,00,000	100%

The items under Class A are subject to greater continuous control and planning than are the items under other categories. The Class A items account for high annual consumption costs and correspondingly high investment in inventories. Because of high investments in Class A items, there would be frequent ordering and low safety stocks. This also assumes that the cost of placing and following up orders is relatively low in comparison with the costs of carrying excess inventories. A number of things can be done to reduce inventory of 'A' items. For example, A items can generally be ordered for specific runs, the economic order quantity could be applied; local suppliers could be asked to stock supplies so that delivery time can be shortened. On the other hand, where the total annual purchase cost is relatively low as in the case of Class C items, there will be less frequent ordering and higher safety stocks. Items in Class C receive the least amount of control and should be under simple physical controls such as the two-bin system with safety stocks.

A graph can be prepared to show quantity and amount of items in different categories in descending order of value (Fig. 17.1).

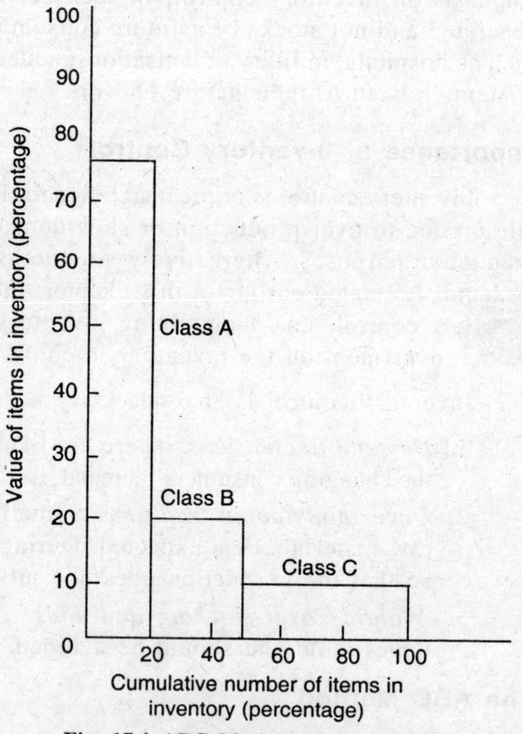

Fig. 17.1 ABC Method of Inventory Classifications

Just-In-Time Method

Just-In-Time (JIT) is a purchasing and inventory control method in which materials are obtained just in time for production to provide finished goods just in time for sale. A just-in-time manufacturing system requires making goods or services only when the customer, internal or external, requires it. JIT requires better coordination with suppliers so that materials arrive immediately prior to their use. JIT reduces or eliminates inventory and the costs associated with carrying the inventory. JIT emphasizes that workers immediately correct the system making defective units because they have no inventory. With no inventory to draw from for delivery to customers, just-in-time relies on high quality materials and production. It is required that the companies that use just-in-time manufacturing must eliminate all the sources of failure in the system. Production people must be better trained so that they can carry out their works without errors. Suppliers must be able to produce and deliver defect free materials or components just when they are required, and equipment must be maintained so that machine failures are eliminated.

JIT applies to raw materials inventory as well as to work-in-process inventory. The goals are that both raw materials and work in process inventory are held to absolute minimums. JIT is used to complement other materials planning and control tools, such as EOQ and safety stock levels. In JIT system, production of an item does not commence until the organization receives an order. When an order is received for a finished product, production people give orders for raw materials. As soon as production is complete to fill the order, production ends. In theory, in JIT, there is no need for inventories because no production takes place until the organization knows that it will sell them. In practice, however, companies using just in time inventory generally have a backlog of orders or stable demand for their products to assure continued production.

The fundamental objective of JIT is to produce and deliver what is needed, when it is needed at all stages of the production process — just in time to be fabricated, sub-assembled, assembled, and despatched to the customer. Although in practice there are no such perfect plans, JIT is an ideal and therefore a worthy goal. The benefits are low inventory, high manufacturing cycle rates, high output per employee, minimum floor space requirements, minimum indirect labour, and perfect in-process control. An associated requirement of a successful JIT operation is the pursuit of perfect quality in order to reduce, to an absolute minimum, delays caused by defective product units.[1]

INVENTORY TURNOVER

Business enterprises can analyse the turnover of different items of stock to find out which stocks are slow moving. Inventory turnover ratio enables the management to avoid capital being locked up in undesirable stocks. This ratio indicates the efficiency or inefficiency with which inventories are maintained. Inventory turnover ratio is calculated as follows:

$$\frac{\text{Cost of materials consumed}}{\text{Cost of average stock held during the period}}$$

The cost of average stock here is taken as the average of opening and closing stock.

The stock turnover can also be calculated in days as below:

$$\frac{\text{Days during the period}}{\text{Inventory turnover ratio}}$$

Detection of Slow-moving and Non-moving or Obsolete Materials

It is essential for a business firm to detect slow-moving and non-moving or obsolete materials. Obsolete materials become useless or obsolete due to change in product, process, design or method of production. Obsolete materials are different from slow-moving materials. Slow-moving stocks move at a slow rate. In case of slow and non-moving materials, capital remains locked unnecessarily and also cost of storing continue to be incurred if these materials are stored in excess of the requirements. Management should make proper investigation into slow-moving and obsolete materials and take steps to minimise losses arising therefrom. Management should prepare regular reports to examine the situations relating to these stocks so that useless stocks could be disposed of or used in some profitable work and effective steps could be taken to increase the movement of slow moving stocks.

1. Milton F. Usry and Lawrence H. Hammer, *Cost Accounting, Planning and Control,* Cincinnati: South Western Publishing Co., 1999, p. 257.

Illustration 12:

Compute the materials turnover ratio for materials A and B and comment upon the results.

	Materials A (Rs.)	*Materials B (Rs.)*
Opening stock	10,000	35,000
Purchase during the year	76,000	50,000
Closing stock	6,000	25,000

Solution:

Cost of materials consumed	*Materials A (Rs.)*	*Materials B (Rs.)*
Opening stock	10,000	35,000
Add: Purchases	76,000	50,000
	86,000	85,000
Less: Closing stock	6,000	25,000
Cost of materials consumed	80,000	60,000
Average stock held:	*Materials A*	*Materials B*
Opening stock	10,000	35,000
Closing stock	6,000	25,000
	16,000	60,000
	16,000 ÷ 2	60,000 ÷ 2
Average stock	8,000	30,000

$$\text{Material turnover ratio} = \frac{\text{Cost of materials consumed}}{\text{Cost of stock held}}$$

$$\text{Materials } A = \frac{80,000}{8,000} = 10 : 1 \text{ or } 10$$

$$\text{Materials } B = \frac{60,000}{30,000} = 2 : 1 \text{ or } 2$$

$$\text{Materials turnover in days} = \frac{\text{Days during the year}}{\text{Materials turnover ratio}}$$

$$\text{Materials } A = \frac{365}{10} = 36.5 \text{ days}$$

$$\text{Materials } B = \frac{365}{2} = 182.2 \text{ days}$$

From the above results, it can be said that materials *A* are very fast moving materials, while materials *B* are very slow moving when compared with materials *A*. Since, the normal standard inventory turnover ratio should be 2 : 1, the materials *B* turnover ratio can be said to be normal. Materials *A* turnover ratio is 36.5 days which shows that an average stock is being kept for 36.5 days. In contrast, materials *B* average stock is being kept for 182.5 days. Therefore, materials *B* are slow-moving materials.

Illustration 13:

A factory uses 4,000 varieties of inventory. In terms of inventory holding and inventory usage, the following information is compiled:

No. of varieties of inventory	*%*	*% value of inventory holding (average)*	*% of inventory usage (in end-product)*
3,875	96.875	20	5
110	2.750	30	10
15	0.375	50	85
4,000	100.000	100	100

Classify the items of inventory as per ABC analysis with reasons:

Solution:

Classification of the Items of Inventory as per ABC Analysis

Category A: 15 number of varieties of inventory items, should be classified as those of A category because of the following reasons:

(*i*) They constitute 0.375% of total number of varieties of inventory items handled by stores of factory. This is the minimum as per the given classification in the table.

(*ii*) The total usage of these items is 50% of total use value of inventory holding (average) which is maximum according to the given table.

(*iii*) The consumption of these items is about 85% of usage in end product.

Category B: 110 number of inventory items, should be classified as those of *B* category because of the following reasons:

(*i*) They constitute 2.750% of total number of varieties of inventory items handled by the stores of the factory.

(*ii*) They require moderate investment of about 30% of total use value of inventory holding (average).

(*iii*) Their consumption is moderate about 10% of inventory usage in the end-product.

Category C: 3,875 number of varieties of inventory items, should be classified as those of category *C* because of the following reasons:

(*i*) They constitute 96.875% of total varieties of inventory items handled by stores of factory.

(*ii*) They require investment of 20% of total use value of average inventory holding.

(*iii*) Their consumption is minimum, i.e., just 5% of inventory usage in end product.

THEORY QUESTIONS

1. Describe the meaning objectives, and basic principles of materials control system.
2. What are the important requirements of a materials control system?
3. Explain ABC system of inventory control.
4. Explain Just-In-Time purchases.
5. What do you understand by 'inventory control'? State its objects.
6. What is ABC analysis? Discuss its role in a sound system of materials control.
7. What are the objectives in a good system of material control.
8. What are the functions of a purchase department.
9. Write a note on qualities of purchase manager.
10. Explain EOQ. List the possible costs of carrying and not carrying the inventory.

11. Discuss the following:
    (*i*) When to order
    (*ii*) Minimum stock level
    (*iii*) Maximum stock level.
12. Define inventory control. What is its importance?
13. Discuss ABC method of Inventory Control.
14. What is Inventory Turnover? How does it help in detecting slow-moving and non-moving materials?

EXERCISES AND PROBLEMS

1. A manufacturer buys certain equipment from an outside supplier at Rs. 30 per unit. Total annual needs are 800 units. Further the following data are available.

Annual return on investment	10%
Rent, taxes, insurance per unit per year Re. 1	
Cost of placing an order	Rs. 100

Determine the economic order quantity

(*Ans.:* 200 units.)

2. Two components, A and B are used as follows:
Normal usage per week each 50 units
Minimum usage 25 units per week each
Maximum usage 75 units per week each
Re-order quantity A-300 units, B-500 units
Re-order period A, 4 to 6 weeks, B, 2 to 4 weeks
Calculate the each component:
(*a*) Re-order level (*b*) Minimum level (*c*) Maximum level.

(*Ans.:* Re-order level A = 450 units, B = 300 units
Minimum level A = 200 units, B = 150 units
Maximum level A = 650 units, B = 750 units
Average stock level A = 425 units, B = 450 units.

3. Calculate EOQ from the following information. Also state the number of orders to be placed in a year. Consumption of materials per annum 10,000 kg.

Ordering costs per order	Rs. 50
Cost per kg. of raw materials	Rs. 2
Storage costs	8% on average inventory

(*Ans.:* EOQ 2500 kg., No. of order in a year 4.)

4. A firm is able to obtain quantity discounts on its orders of materials as follows:

Price per Kg. (Rs.)	*Kgs.*
6.00	Less than 250
5.90	250 and less than 800
5.80	800 and less than 2000
5.70	2000 and less than 4000
5.60	4000 and over

The annual demand for the material is 4000 Kgs. Stock holding costs are 20% of material cost per annum.
The delivery cost per order is Rs. 6.00.
You are required to calculate the best quantity to order.

(*Ans.:* 800 kgs.)

5. About 50 items are required every day for a machine. A fixed cost of Rs. 50 per order is incurred for placing an order. The inventory carrying cost per item amount to Re. 0.02 per day. The lead Period is 32 days. Compute: (*i*) Economic Order Quantity, (*ii*) Re-order Level.

6. From the following information calculate Economic Order Quantity, and the number of orders to be placed in one quarter of the year:

(*i*) Quarterly consumption of materials	2,000 kg.
(*ii*) Cost of placing one order	Rs. 50
(*iii*) Cost Per unit	Rs. 40
(*iv*) Storage and carrying Cost	8% on average inventory

(***Ans.:*** EOQ 500 kg., No. of orders per quarter 4)

7. If the minimum stock level and average stock level of raw-material *A* are 4,000 and 9,000 units respectively, find out its 'Re-order quantity.'

(***Ans.:*** Re-order quantity 10,000 units.)

8. Calculate the material turnover ratio from the following information:

	Material X (*Rs.*)	*Material Y* (*Rs.*)
Opening Stock	25,000	87,500
Closing Stock	15,000	62,500
Purchases	1,90,000	1,25,000

Determine the fast moving material

(***Ans.:*** Turnover ratio)

Material X-10

Material Y-2

Material X is the fast moving material.

9. The following information is available about a company.

	Opening stock	*Purchases*	*Closing stock*
Material A	700 kg	11,500 kg	200 kg
Material B	200 litres	11,000 litres	1,200 litres
Material C	1,000 kg	1,800 kg	1,200 kg

The inventory is valued @ Re. 1 per kg or litre.

Calculate the material turnover ratio for each of the above materials and express in number of days the average inventory held. What conclusions can be drawn?

(***Ans.:*** Turnover ratio		No. of days inventory held
Material A	26.67	14 days approx.
Material B	14.29	26 days approx.
Material C	1.46	250 days

Material A has the highest inventory turnover ratio, while material C has the lower turnover ratio. Therefore, purchase of material C should be controlled.

Labour Costs Accounting and Control

Proper control and accounting for labour costs is one of the most important objectives of all business firms. Cost accounting for labour has three primary objectives:

1. Determining labour costs in the cost of product or service.
2. Reporting labour costs for planning and control.
3. Reporting labour costs for decision-making.

For a manufacturing business firm engaged in producing a specific product, labour costs are accumulated and charged to the product as they are produced. Similarly, in a service (not-for-profit) organisation, total cost as well as the cost of different functions (services) are to be determined. This helps the organisation to know what it costs them to provide a service or perform some activities.

The second objective is to provide management with labour cost information for effective planning of the labour force in the organisation and for adequate control of labour costs. The control process of labour cost involves a comparison of actual labour costs with standard labour cost. The differences between the two are then analysed and possible reasons are determined so that management can take suitable action to control the labour cost expenditure in future periods.

Labour cost information is used for decision-making purposes also. Many managerial decisions, such as pricing decision, expansion of business, dropping a product line, replacement of plant and equipment, entering into a new market, etc. require information about current actual labour costs and emerging trends therein.

ORGANISATION FOR LABOUR CONTROL

The significant portion of labour costs in the total cost of production points out its importance and need for effective control over labour and labour-related costs. The following departments/functions contribute to the efficient utilisation of labour and adequate control over labour costs.

1. Personnel Department
2. Engineering Department
3. Time-keeping Department
4. Payroll Department
5. Cost Accounting Department

WAGE SYSTEMS

An important aspect of labour cost control is a wage system designed primarily for exercising management control over labour. The following objectives should be considered in the selection of a wage system:

1. Acceptance by employees to avert slowdowns and work stoppages.
2. Provision for flexibility.
3. Provision for economy in administration.
4. Supplying of labour statistics for use in industrial relations and for trade associations, government agencies, and competitors.
5. Stabilisation of labour turnover.
6. Minimising of absenteeism.
7. Provision for incentive plans.

Basically there are two wage systems to pay for labour: (*i*) straight time which is by hour, day, or week, and (*ii*) piece work, which is by the unit of product.

Straight Time

Under the time basis, the worker is paid at an hourly, daily or weekly rate and his remuneration depends upon the time for which he is employed and not upon his production. If a worker works for an overtime, the wage agreement usually provides that all hours worked in excess of an agreed number are paid for at a higher rate. The time basis wage system for direct labour is found in those industries where:

1. The speed of production cannot be influenced by the energy or dexterity of the worker.
2. The quality of work is of paramount importance.
3. It is difficult to measure the work done by the employee.

From the point of view of the worker, the straight time method has both advantages and disadvantages. Workers have feelings of security and certainty which appeal to them. They can depend upon a definite wage or salary regardless of the amount of work completed or the efficiency of their work, provided it is above the minimum requirements. However, this wage system does not give proper recognition or reward to efficient workers whose productivity is above the average of the other workers. There is little incentive to achieve better or superior performance.

From the employer's view-point, time wage systems are easy to compute and understand and provide economy in time-keeping and payroll recording. But on the other hand, constant supervision is required, otherwise considerable wasted time may be paid for. Among the workers, the inefficient workers receive the same wages as the efficient workers, thus tending to cause dissatisfaction and frustration among the workers and increasing the labour cost per unit produced.

The time basis is still the most popular wage system for workers, such as clerks, accountants, stenographers, factory helpers, members of the supervisory staff and officers whose work cannot be standardised and measured satisfactorily. This is preferred by skilled and efficient workers with whom the quality of work is a more important factor than volume of production.

Piece Work

Under this method, a fixed rate is paid for each unit produced, job performed or number of operations completed, and the worker's wages thus depend upon his output and not upon the time he spends in the factory.

Piece-rates are of advantage to management in the following respects:

1. Managerial supervision is not much needed for production, since each worker assumes responsibility for his own time and output.
2. Higher production reduces overhead costs per unit of output.
3. Labour costs can be computed in advance of production with the aid of fixed rate per unit or job.
4. Labour control becomes easier by isolating workers whose work is inefficient and below the minimum standard requirements.

Piece work has some limitations too. It attaches more premium to quantity than the quality of work. It has the tendency of increasing imperfections, spoiled work, and defectives and higher depreciation costs result because of considerable wear and tear of plant and machinery. Also, this system does not maintain a regular wage for the employee.

To avoid the limitations of straight or simple piece work system, a guarantee is normally provided in the system that the employee's wages shall not fall below a certain minimum figure. This is known as "piece rates with guaranteed day rate." Under this method the worker receives a straight piece-rate for the number of pieces produced, provided that his total wage is greater than his earnings on a time rate basis. When the piece-rate earnings fall below this level, the time rate earnings are paid instead. An alternative form of the methods is the guaranteed time rate (per hour, day or week), plus a piece-rate payment for output above a stated minimum. Labour cost per piece decreases with increasing production until piece-rate earnings exceed the guarantee, thereafter, the labour cost per piece remains constant.

INCENTIVE WAGE PLANS

The basic purpose of an incentive wage is to induce a worker to produce more so that he can earn a higher wage and, at the same time, unit costs can be reduced. Incentive wage plans aim to ensure greater output, to help control over labour costs by minimisation of total cost for a given volume of production and to have a basis for reward from hours served to work accomplished.

Incentive wage scheme has the following objectives:

1. Uninterrupted and higher production without any dispute between the labour and management.
2. Stability in labour turnover.
3. Reducing labour absenteeism.
4. Developing cooperation, mutual trust, attitude of team work among workers and between workers and supervisory staff.

5. Control of labour cost and reduction in labour cost per unit of output.
6. Improving administrative efficiency.
7. Accurate budgeting through reliable labour cost information.
8. Generating workers' satisfaction by avoiding work stoppage, slow down, and by providing incentive scheme.

The following are the essentials (desirable characteristics) of a successful incentive wage plan:

1. A wage incentive system should be based upon standards of performance — time and motion studies, job evaluation, and merit rating.
2. The incentive plan should be understood by all employees before installation (or hiring).
3. All direct labour tasks should be on an incentive basis.
4. Only standard or acceptable quality production should be considered while determining the bonus.
5. Once the standard is set, it should not be changed unless the method changes.
6. The incentive programme must be fairly and intelligently administered.
7. It is highly desirable that indirect personnel share in the incentive plan.
8. A high reward should be paid for performance above standard.
9. Individual incentives should be used wherever it is possible to do so.
10. Minimum wage should be guaranteed to every worker.
11. The views of both employers and employees should be considered while designing incentive schemes.
12. The cost of establishing and operating the incentive plans should be reasonable.
13. The incentive plans should help in standard cost and budgetary control programmes.

Incentive wage plans involve wage rates based upon various combinations of output and time and are known as "different piece-rates" and "bonus-plans' as well. Generally, the following types of incentive plans are used:

1. Taylor Differential Piece-rate System
2. Merrick Differential Piece-rate System
3. Gantt Task Bonus Plan
4. Premium Bonus Plans (Halsey, Halsey-Weir, Rowan, Bedaux, Emersion, etc.)

Taylor Differential Piece-rate System

Under this system there are two wage rates, a low one for output below standard and a higher one for above standard performance. The system aims to discourage below average workers by providing no guaranteed hourly wage and by setting low piece-rates for low level production, and a high rate resulting in high earnings if an efficient level of production is attained. For example, in a factory, workers earn Rs. 240 per eight hour day and that production averages 12 units per hour per worker or Rs. 2.50 paise per unit. The Taylor system might suggest a pay of Rs. 2 per unit if the worker averaged 14 units or less per hour, but Rs. 3 per unit to workers averaging 15 units or more per hour. The main advantages of the Taylor system are that it provides a strong incentive to the efficient worker, and is simple to understand and operate. But the incentive level may be set so high that it cannot attract most workers.

Merrick Differential Piece-rate System

This is an improvement over the Taylor system and depends on using three rates instead of two as in the Taylor system. Normal piece-rates are paid on output, when it does not exceed 83% of the standard output. 110% of normal piece-rate are paid when the output is between 83% and 100%, and 120% of the normal piece-rate is paid if the output is above 100%.

The Merrick system is useful to highly efficient workers`as it provides incentives for higher production. Similarly, it takes into account the less efficient worker who can at least achieve 83% of the standard output. This minimum output is probably achievable by all workers.

Gantt Task and Bonus Plan

This system combines a guaranteed time-rate with a bonus and piece rate plan using the differential piece-rate principle. Remuneration under the plan is computed as follows:

Output	*Payment*
1. Output below standard (high task)	Time-rate (guaranteed)
2. Output is standard	Bonus @ 20% on the time-rate
3. Output above standard	High piece-rate on worker's whole output

This plan provides incentives and opportunities to those who reach high level production. At the same time it provides security and encouragement to less skilled workers. It is simple to understand and workers are also satisfied in that they receive the total reward for their efforts. A limitation of the plan is the tendency on the part of trade unions to demand a high fixed guaranteed time-rate. But the incentive element of the plan would be lost in case too high a rate is fixed.

Premium Bonus Plans

Under the time-rates basis, any additional production above normal levels benefits the employer, whereas with the piece-rates system the benefit goes to the employees (apart from indirect benefits to the employer). Bonus plans have been developed to produce a compromise, in that any savings are shared between employer and employee. The following are the principal schemes under premium bonus plans.

1. Halsey Premium Plan

The principle of the Halsey scheme is that the worker receives a fixed proportion of any time which he can save by completing the job in less than the allowed time. The most common fixed proportion is 50% but this can be varied. This plan ensures that the employee receives time wages until he produces in less than standard time. For above standard production, savings are shared with the employer with the result that the rate of increase happen to be lower for the employee. The cost per unit decreases when production exceeds standard.

2. Halsey-Weir Plan

This plan is also known as the Weir Premium Scheme and is based on a $33\frac{1}{3} : 66\frac{2}{3}$ sharing plan. Under this scheme the total enrolments of a worker are the aggregate of guaranteed hourly wages for actual time worked, plus the amount of bonus at the rates of $33\frac{1}{3}\%$ of the time saved. Bonus is allowed at the same hourly rate at which he shall be paid for actual time worked.

3. *Rowan Plan*

This scheme is similar to the Halsey Plan in that a standard time is fixed for the completion of a job and the bonus is paid in respect of the item saved. But a ceiling is applied to the size of the bonus. The bonus hours are calculated as a proportion of the time taken which the time saved bears to the time allowed, and is paid for at time-work rates. The bonus may be computed as follows:

$$\text{Bonus} = \frac{\text{Time taken}}{\text{Time allowed}} \times \text{Time saved} \times \text{Time rate}$$

4. *Bedaux Point Plan*

Under the Bedaux point plan a guaranteed hourly rate is paid until standard production is attained, and a premium or additional wage is paid for units in excess of standard. Instead of being paid as piece-rate, an hour's work is converted to points by dividing a standard hour's production in units into 60 minutes. In other words, if 10 units are standard, then each unit is 6 points and if 15 units are standard then each unit is 4 points. At standard performance the worker produces a point per minute and for the first 60 points produced in an hour, the worker receives the hourly rate. For excess production, it is common practice to pay the worker 75% of the rate, and the foremen, supervisors and the other indirect labour personnel receive 25% of the rate.

5. *Emerson Efficiency Plan*

Under the Emerson plan a minimum daily wage is guaranteed and a standard time is determined for each job or operation. During each payroll period a record is kept of the hours worked and the units produced, and the efficiency of each employee is then determined by dividing actual hours into the standard time for the units produced. For example, if the standard is 10 units per hour and a worker produces 320 units in an 80-hour week, the standard time for his output is 32 hours and he has worked at 80% efficiency. Below 67% efficiency, the worker is paid his hourly rate, and from 67% upto 100% efficiency, step bonus rates apply. Above 100% efficiency, an additional bonus of 1% of the hourly rate is paid for each 1% increase in efficiency.

6. *Groups Bonus Schemes*

Where a group of workers is collectively responsible for manufacturing a product, it may not be possible to adopt individual incentive schemes. The production of the workers as a whole is measured, and the total bonus determined by one of the individual incentive schemes capable of group application. The computed bonus can then be shared equally, or between workers of different skills in differing specified proportions. A group bonus scheme has the following objectives:

1. Developing collective interest and team spirit among all workers and employees.
2. Developing interest among foremen and supervisors to improve performance.
3. Reducing spoilage in materials consumption.
4. Reducing idle time.
5. Achieving maximum production at minimum cost.
6. Motivating workers to produce more to get bonus on the basis of team performance.

Group bonus schemes may be employed:

1. where individual output cannot be measured, but that of a group of worker can, e.g., on a production line;

2. where output depends less upon the efforts of particular individuals, and more upon the combined efforts of a group department, or even of the whole undertaking; or
3. where the management wishes to encourage a team spirit.

The following types of group bonus schemes are in common use:

(i) Budgeted Expenditure Bonus

In this scheme the value of bonus depends upon savings in actual expenditure as compared with the budget. This scheme can be applied to indirect workers and staff besides direct workers.

(ii) Cost Efficiency Bonus

This bonus is allowed for savings in specific costs, e.g., labour cost or materials cost.

(iii) Priestman System

This is a system used in foundries in which a production standard is fixed every month for the entire work. Where production exceeds the standard, workers receive during the following month additional pay equal to the percentage in output over standard. Where production does not exceed standard, no bonus is paid though time rates are guaranteed.

(iv) Towne Gain-sharing System

This method introduced by H. R. Towne in the USA is based on the principle that bonus consists of half reduction in labour cost below standard. The bonus is divided between foremen and operatives, but it is generally paid half-yearly. It tends to be ineffectual as an incentive to individual effort. The payment to foremen and supervisory staff, however, encourages them to reduce labour costs.

In India, payment of bonus under the Payment of Bonus Act 1965 is compulsory, although the amount of bonus may vary from company to company. A minimum bonus of 8.33% is payable whether a company has earned profit or not. The amount of minimum bonus is generally treated as an item of direct labour cost. However, the amount exceeding the minimum bonus is an appropriation of profit. Bonus linked with productivity is treated as an item of overhead cost.

PROFIT SHARING AND CO-PARTNERSHIP

Profit sharing schemes are schemes in which there is an agreement between the employer and his workers whereby he pays them in addition to wages, a predetermined share of the profits of undertakings. Co-partnership or co-ownership confers upon employees the opportunity to share in the capital of the business and to receive that part of the profits that accrue to their share of ownership. Both profit sharing and co-partnership schemes recognise the contribution of employees in the profit of the business firm.

These schemes, however, suffer from the following limitations:

1. Lazy and inefficient workers share equally with hard-working and efficient workers.
2. When the share is paid to the workers in cash they tend to regard it merely as a bonus and not as a share of the result achieved jointly by themselves and their employers.
3. It is difficult to determine the share of profits to be given to each worker and there may be a certain amount of distrust about declared profits also.
4. The additional earnings under these plans are relatively small and may appear to the workers totally insignificant.
5. The share of profits to be paid to workers may be reduced by bad management.

6. Distribution of the benefit under schemes is done normally once in a year. Therefore, employees do not have much interest in it.
7. Sometimes, this scheme is restricted to employees who have a specified number of years of service in the factory. Thus, this creates dissatisfaction among the newer and younger employees who also have contributed to the profits of the year.
8. The workers share in the good years, but do not bear their share of losses incurred in other years.

WORK STUDY

The successful operation of incentive wage schemes depends on making a proper work study. Work study is the study of job, methods and equipment to ensure that the best way to do the job has been followed by a worker. Work study consists of two complementary techniques or methods: (*i*) methods study, and (*ii*) work measurement.

Method Study

Method study is done to improve methods of production and to achieve the most effective use of materials, manpower and plant. The following stages are involved in methods study:

1. First of all, work for the purpose of methods study should be selected. Generally, methods study is done in jobs which involve complexity and costly operations.
2. After selecting a particular job or work, details about the work should be gathered, such as purpose, location, sequence, relationship with the other work, methods of working, operators and, facilities, etc.
3. After studying the relevant details of a work, an improved method should be developed for effectiveness, efficiency and operational simplicity. Unnecessary operations, activities should be avoided. An improved method might change the location and sequence of work, production methods, layout.
4. The method so developed should be used for the job or work for which it has been designed.
5. Follow-up is necessary to enquire as to whether the improved method is being implemented in practice and to find out deviations, if any.

Methods study ensures efficient and maximum use of resources like material, labour, plant facilities; it improves the production methods by reducing/eliminating the work content and unnecessary methods; and it attains the maximum production which is good for the firm as well as the workers.

Work Measurement

Work measurement aims at determining the effective time required to perform the work. The ineffective, wasteful or avoidable time is separated from effective required time to complete the work. The effective time so established in work measurement can be used for the following purposes:

1. Incentive wage schemes which require time taken for completing a work.
2. Improving utilisation of men, machines and materials.
3. Assisting in production control.
4. Setting labour standards.
5. Achieving the objectives of cost control and cost reduction.

The following stages are involved in work measurement:

1. Selection of the work.
2. Measuring the actual time taken in the work done.
3. The total time so established for a job should be adjusted for fatigue, time taken in setting the tools, idleness involved in the work itself, etc.

The standard time is further considered to know the time saved under incentive schemes and to determine the wage rate at the incentive level. This is explained with the help of the following example:

	Minutes per job
Time before incentive schemes	50
Allowances 10%	5
Basic or standard time	55
Time saved under incentive conditions (20%)	11
Time under incentive conditions	44

JOB EVALUATION AND MERIT RATING

Job Evaluation

Job evaluation is the technique of analysis and assessment of jobs to determine their relative value within the firm so that a fair wage and salary structure can be established for the various job positions. In other words, job evaluation aims at providing a rational and equitable basis for differential salaries and wages for different classes of workers. Following are the objectives (or benefits) of job evaluation:

1. It aims at developing a systematic and rational wage structure as well as job structure.
2. It aims at establishing consistency between the wage and salary structure adopted within the firm and that of other firms within the industry or geographical area.
3. Controversies and disputes relating to salary between the employers and employees can be settled by designing job evaluation techniques within the firm which can satisfy both employers and employees.
4. Wage and salary structure established on the basis of job evaluation will be fair, reliable and satisfying to the employees. Employees' skills, efforts, competence are properly considered in determining wage rates.
5. Stability and fairness in the wage and salary structure are very useful for the administration which can formulate business policies and plans as workers' cooperation is fully ensured.
6. Job evaluation discloses characteristics and conditions relating to different jobs and these job requirements are very helpful at the time of recruiting the workers. The employment department can appoint only those workers who are found suitable in terms of such job requirements.

Methods of Job Evaluation

Methods of job evaluation can be listed as follows:

Point Ranking Method

Under this method each job is analysed in terms of job factors. Job factors may consist of elements like skill, effort, working conditions, hazards, responsibility. However, different job factors may emerge in different jobs. After specifying job factors, each of them is assigned weightage or points depending on its value for the job. For example, in a particular job, education may be given the higher point as compared to supervision, if the job requires a high degree of education. Finally, the jobs are ranked in the order of points or weights secured by them. Grades are further developed for these different weightages so that wage rates or wage structure can be suitability designed for them. For example, the following wage scales can be worked out depending on the weight's grade.

Weights or Points	*Grade*	*Salary Scale (Rs.)*
50-100	I	10000-15000
151-200	II	15000-20000
201-250	III	20000-30000
251-300	IV	30000-40000
301-350	V	40000-50000
351-400	VI	50000-60000
401-450	VII	60000-80000
451-500	VIII	80000-100000

This method is theoretically sound and objective, but it is difficult to operate. The relative weights and points of different job factors need to be developed very carefully and in an objective manner.

Ranking Method

The ranking method only requires that different jobs in an organisation should be rearranged in an order which can be done either from the lowest to the highest or in the reverse. Before doing ordering of jobs, all jobs should be properly studied in terms of job requirements, worker's qualification, responsibilities, working conditions, etc. Finally, wage scales are determined in terms of ranks.

This method is very simple to operate, less costly and easy to understand. However, this method may be useful for small organisations only, where jobs are few and well defined. But in a large organisation where jobs are complex and highly involved, this method cannot be beneficial.

Grading Method

This method is an improvement over the ranking method. Under this method, a hypothetical scale or standard of job values is determined and each job after being analysed in terms of a predetermined grade, is given a grade or class. Predetermined grades or yardsticks are formulated after examining existing jobs in the enterprise. The grades or the class should be established after making an investigation of job factors, such as complexity in the job, supervision, responsibility, education, etc.

This method is simple, less costly and administratively feasible. It attempts at applying a rational basis for grading jobs.

MERIT RATING

Merit rating is the comparative evaluation and analysis of the individual merits of the employees. It analyses the differences in performance between employees who are working on similar jobs and would therefore earn the same wages. In this task, merit rating accomplishes more than job evaluation. Merit rating has the following objectives:

1. To evaluate the merit of an employee for the purpose of promotion, increment, reward and other benefits.

2. To establish and develop a wage system and incentive scheme.
3. To determine the suitability of an employee for a particular job.
4. To analyse the merits (or demerits) of a worker and help him in developing his capability and competence for the job.

The characteristics and factors that are considered in merit appraisal of the workers are the following:

1. Cooperation
2. Quality of work done
3. Attendance and regularity
4. Education, skill, experience
5. Character and integrity
6. Initiative

Merit rating is beneficial to the business enterprise and the workers. It increases the output, improves labour-management relations and encourages workers to have fair competition among themselves. However, merit rating has the following drawbacks:

1. The rating of employees may be subjective and this creates dissatisfaction among them.
2. Evaluators or raters tend to give much premium to past ratings of an employee who might have improved himself in the course of time.
3. Rates may be influenced by raters' own attitudes and self-made rating factors which are not consistent with the merit rating process. Incentives schemes may not be introduced advantageously if merit rating is inaccurate, unreliable and subjective.

Differences between Job Evaluation and Merit Rating

Job evaluation and merit rating differ on the following counts:

1. Job evaluation is the assessment of the relative worth of jobs within a business enterprise and merit rating is the assessment of the relative worth of an employee with respect to a job. In other words, job evaluation rates the jobs, but merit rating rates employees on their jobs.
2. Job evaluation helps in establishing a rational wage and salary structure. But merit rating helps in fixing fair wages for each worker in terms of this competence and performance.
3. Job evaluation brings uniformity in wage and salary rates. But merit rating aims at providing a fair rate of pay for different workers on the basis of their performances.

TIME AND MOTION STUDY

Time study determines the time spent on each element of a job. The total time taken by all elements (stages) of a job is called the standard time. This standard time is the time which should be taken by an average employee to complete a job under standard (normal) working conditions.

Motion study implies dividing the work into fundamental elements or basic operations of a job or a process for the purpose of eliminating unnecessary (defective) elements or operations in a job. After investigating all movements in a job, process, or operation, it finds out the most scientific and systematic method of performing the operation or completing the job. Thus, time study fixes the standard time for a job or process, and motion study eliminates wasteful motions or the movement of a worker on the job. Both are complementary to each other.

Objectives

Following are the objectives of time and motion study:

1. Eliminating unnecessary motions, fatigue and improving human efforts.
2. Improving method, procedure, techniques, process relating to a job.
3. Utilising effectively materials, machines, human resources and other facilities.
4. Improving working environment, layout and design of plant and equipment.

Benefits

Time and motion study is quite beneficial to the management in the following respects:

1. Proper and fuller utilisations of materials, plant, labour and other resources.
2. Help in assessment of labour requirements.
3. Setting of labour cost standards and control of the labour cost.
4. Determination of fair wage rates and effective wage incentive schemes.
5. Preparation of labour budgets.
6. Standardising jobs, equipments, methods by determining the best method of operating in the time set.
7. Improvement in work methods by comparing the time taken to complete the same type of work under different possible methods.
8. Proper planning and effective cost control.

LABOUR TURNOVER

Labour turnover is the rate at which employees leave employment at a factory and is normally measured as the ratio of the number of persons leaving in a period to the average number on the payroll. For example, if 100 persons leave a company in a year and the average number on the payroll is 500, labour turnover is expressed as 20% p.a. In this calculation all persons who leave must be included, whether they leave voluntarily or are dismissed and irrespective of whether they are replaced. There are three methods of measurement of labour turnover.

1. $$\frac{\text{All employees leaving}}{\text{Average number employed}} \times 100$$

2. $$\frac{\text{Number of replacement in a period}}{\text{Average number employed}} \times 100$$

3. $$\frac{\text{All employees leaving plus new employees}}{\text{Average number employed}} \times 100$$

Among the three methods, the first method is to be preferred, as it is more appropriately a long-term indicator. This formula is more satisfactory as management is primarily concerned with the loss of labour, after money has been spent on training. The effects of a high or low turnover rate should then be analysed, *e.g.*, on training costs, on production efficiency and employee morale.

Causes of Labour Turnover

Labour turnover is caused by many factors which may be listed as follows:

Avoidable Causes

These causes may be eliminated by taking suitable measures by the business firm. Avoidable causes are the following:

1. Low wages and earnings.
2. Unsatisfactory working conditions.
3. Bad relations among workers and between workers and supervisor.
4. Existence of rival trade unions in the organisation.
5. Unsuitability of job.
6. Lack of conveyance, accommodation, medical, educational facilities, recreational amenities, etc.

Unavoidable Causes

Sometimes, workers have to leave the organisation because of management requirements and actions. These are known as unavoidable causes and may be described as follows:

1. Termination of service due to misbehaviour, indiscipline, etc.
2. Retrenchment or lay off due to shortage of resources, low demand, seasonal nature of business.

Personal Causes

Sometimes workers leave the organisation at their own will and management can do nothing in this regard. These are known as personal factors which are the following:

1. Change for better job
2. Death
3. Retirement due to old age and ill health
4. Family troubles and constraints
5. Change for a better place, environment.

Cost of Labour Turnover

The cost of labour turnover consists of two elements:

1. Preventive costs
2. Replacement costs

Preventive Costs

Preventive costs include all those costs which are incurred to prevent workers from leaving the organisation and keeping them satisfied. Preventive costs may broadly be of following types:

1. *Personal administration.* A part of personal administration may be incurred to establish a good relationship between the management and the employees and to remove workers' grievances. These costs are known as preventive costs.

2. *Medical and health care.* The costs incurred for providing medical benefits to the workers and their families are included in the labour turnover costs.

3. *Welfare measures.* Welfare measures include facilities like sports, educational facilities, transport, housing, cooperative stores, canteens. The availability of these facilities prevent workers from leaving the organisation and keep them satisfied.

4. *Wage and retirement benefits.* These include facilities like pension, provident fund, gratuity, bonus, incentive schemes. If an organisation has provided these benefits, the rate of labour turnover will be appreciably reduced.

Replacement Costs

Replacement costs include the costs which are incurred for the recruitment and training of new workers. Also, they cover costs which arise as a result of wastage, losses, lower production because of less competent and inexperienced new employees. Broadly, they include the following items:

1. *Personnel department expenses:* The personnel department has to recruit new workers in case of high labour turnover and therefore the costs of the personnel department goes up.

2. *Cost of training of new workers:* New workers are first to be given necessary training before they are given regular jobs. Also, production time is lost during the training of the workers.

3. *Inefficiency of new workers:* New employees are comparatively less efficient and therefore, production is adversely effected.

4. *Delay in getting new workers:* It takes time to find new workers who will be suitable for the jobs. In the meantime, existing employees may be given overtime which is again a burden on the organisation.

5. *Cost of breakages of tools and equipments:* New workers, being inexperienced break more tools than the old experienced workers. Sometimes, machine break-down may occur and hamper production.

6. *Costs of spoilage and defectives:* More spoilage and defectives are likely to occur due to mishandling and carelessness of the new workers. The greater the spoilage and defectives, the larger will be the cost of production.

TREATMENT OF LABOUR COST-RELATED ITEMS

Overtime

Overtime is the time put in by employees and work done by them beyond normal hours of work. According to the Factories Act 1948, every worker is to be paid overtime at a higher rate, generally at double the normal wage rate, if he is required to work for more than 8 hours a day. In case the Factories Act is not applicable in some situations, it is the practice to pay to workers for overtime work at higher rate. The excess over normal wage rate is called overtime premium. In cost accounting, the overtime premium is separated from regular earnings and consideration must be given to the reasons for the overtime payment to decide as to how they should be treated in cost accounts.

Treatment of Overtime Premium

The treatment of overtime premium is decided in terms of factors and reasons which has caused overtime work. They are explained as follows:

1. Accepting rush orders which cannot be finished in regular working hours and therefore, overtime work becomes necessary. In this case, since the overtime work is due to one particular order, the overtime premium should be charged to that particular order or job. Also, payment for such overtime work should be recovered from the customer who has given such an order. That is, the contract price for the job would include the overtime premium factors.
2. Scheduling more production than can be completed in normal working hours. For example, a company with a normal capacity of 8000 units to be completed in 800 labour hours decides to produce 10,000 units which requires 1000 labour hours, 200 overtime hours are

necessary. Such overtime work may be caused due to temporary higher demand, higher seasonal demand or due to company's own decision for additional production. In this case, the overtime premium will be charged to each of 10000 units completed during the period. Overtime premium cannot be charged to only 2000 units that have to be completed after regular working hours.

3. Overtime work may become necessary because of abnormal circumstances, *i.e.,* factors which are beyond the control of management, such as fire, flood etc. In this case, the overtime premium is transferred to Costing Profit and Loss A/c and is not charged to the units or jobs completed.
4. Overtime work may be caused due to fault, delay of another department in the organisation. In this case, the overtime premium is charged to the department which is at fault or is responsible for the delay.

Overtime payments made to workers engaged in direct labour are treated as direct labour cost and charged to the jobs or units completed. Overtime payments made to indirect labour are the part of factory overheads, overtime payments made to the staff of administrative departments are treated as administrative overheads and overtime payments made to the staff of selling and distribution departments are treated as selling and distribution overheads.

Idle Time

Where workers are remunerated on a time basis, some difference between the time for which they are paid and that which is actually spent upon production is bound to arise. This difference is known as idle time, and represents the time for which the employer must pay but from which he obtains no direct advantage. Idle time does not include holidays, leave etc. Idle time may be normal or abnormal.

Normal Idle Time

Normal idle time is that idle time which is unavoidable, is of normal nature and is inherent in a production or work environment. Normal idle time is caused by factors such as:

1. Time lost in moving from one job to another.
2. Time lost in waiting for materials or instructions.
3. Time taken in getting from the gate of the factory to the department in which the worker is engaged and the reverse journey at the end of the day.
4. Temporary absences from duty because of minor accidents, personal needs, tea-breaks, etc.

The wastage of time due to the above factors cannot be avoided and therefore idle time must be accepted as implied in production. Under the above situations idle time will be of normal variety and constitute a legitimate charge to factory overhead. Thus, payment made for idle time is part of the cost of a product or job.

Abnormal Idle Time

Abnormal idle time is that time which is not caused by or connected with the usual routine of manufacture. The time wasted may represent abnormal idle time. The loss (or expenses) incurred and caused by abnormal conditions, cannot be regarded as part of the cost of the product and should be transferred to the costing profit and loss account. Examples of abnormal idle time would be:

1. Time lost through the breakdown of machinery due to the inefficiency of the works engineers or to the failure of the power supply.

2. Time lost through lack of materials occasioned by the slackness of the store-keeper in notifying the buying department of his requirement.
3. Bottlenecks in production, resulting in a temporary absence of parts for further processing.
4. Strike, lock-outs, fire, wind, water damage etc.

Fringe Benefits

An employee's salary or wage normally consists of basic wages, dearness allowance, house rent allowance, city compensatory allowance, etc. Besides the salary, workers are provided some indirect cash or fringe benefits, such as vacation and holiday pay, workmen's compensation insurance, pension costs, hospitalisation benefits, group insurance, sick pay, overtime and night shift premium, profit sharing bonus. These indirect benefits constitute fringe benefits. They tend to improve employee morale, loyalty and stability. The cost of these benefits are treated as a direct charge to production by using a supplemental wage rate. Alternatively, they are treated as factory overhead.

Shift Premium

Payment of higher hourly rates for evening and night shifts is a common feature. Treatment of shift premium follows the same reasoning as overtime premium. Where shift premium is needed to meet the requirements of a particular order or job, the additional cost should be charged to the job concerned and is accordingly excluded from production overhead. When shift premium is incurred in order to increase the output as a whole, the premium element should be separated from direct wages and treated as production overhead. In this case similar operations should carry the same cost, regardless of when they were performed and should be spread over all units manufactured.

Holiday and Vacation Pay

Most employees are entitled to statutory holiday or compulsory holidays such as Independence day, Republic day, etc. Payments which are made to an employee while he is absent on vacation and holidays, are accrued monthly and spread out over the year's production. The total amount is charged to the full year's overhead expense. In this way no single period is forced to carry the whole burden. This should not be treated otherwise because the number of holidays vary from month to month. If the expenses are apportioned monthly on the month's production, the cost of production in a particular month would be too heavy as compared with the costs in other months, when there are no holidays.

Alternatively, an inflated rate of direct wages can be used to absorb both the normal weekly wages and the appropriate part of holidays.

Learners' or Apprentices' Wages

In many plants new workers receive some preliminary training before they can become economically productive. Apprentices generally take more than skilled workers to perform a given task and they are likely to cause more scrap. On the other hand, they are paid a lower rate per hour. The wage of workers under training who cannot normally make any real contribution to production, should be treated as production overhead and should be charged to the annual output through inclusion in the factory overhead rates.

In case of unusual training programmes due to the opening of a new plant or the activities of a second or third shift, a case can be made for treating the training cost as development or starting load cost and deferring a portion of the cost over a considerable period of time or over the life of the contract.

Attendance Bonuses

Sometimes workers who perform the full number of shifts in a working week, or who lose no time over a stated period, are entitled to an attendance bonus. Such bonuses are part of wages and sometimes are treated as direct wages and charged by means of an inflated direct wages rate. Alternatively, they may be treated as a production overhead. In process or contracting industries, they may properly be charged direct to the process concerned.

Leave with Pay

In a factory, workers are entitled to annual leave with full pay for some days in a year. Besides, medical leave, casual leave, earned leave, special leave, etc. are also available. It is not generally treated as a direct charge to a product or job but as factory overhead and recovered through departmental overhead rates. Alternatively, an inflated rate of direct wages cost can be applied to absorb both normal wages and an appropriate portion of leave with pay.

Employer's Contribution to Insurance

The employer's share of insurance for the employees engaged in manufacturing is treated as production overhead. When a contractor's employees tend to remain on one job for many weeks at a time, it is possible to treat the contribution as a direct charge to the contract concerned. In the case of process workers too, it is frequently possible to charge insurance contribution direct to the process. Also, an inflated direct labour rate can be employed so as to absorb the contributions, but this practice is rarely followed.

Casual Workers

Casual workers should be issued clock cards to show the number of hours worked. If casual workers are engaged on specific production or jobs, they should be treated as direct charge to the specific production. If these workers are performing indirect work, it should be treated as overhead expense. Due care should be exercised by the wage department in making payment to casual workers. The clock cards should be properly signed by the foreman and forwarded to the wages department for payment.

Out-Workers

In some trades, for example, in knit wear and in manufacturing lampshades certain work is performed by workers in their own homes. In such cases there is no need to maintain time records as the workers are paid according to the work they complete. However, control should be exercised over out-workers in the following respects:

1. Issue of materials to out-workers and its comparison with the finished output.
2. Inspection of the output and rejection of the defective work.
3. Return of the output within the agreed time so as to fulfil customer's orders and contracts.

Outside Workers

Outside workers are employees working outside the factory on building sites or moving from place to place on small installations or repair work. If these employees report to the factory first for instructions, their arrival times can be recorded. But if they go direct to the site, it may be necessary for them to complete their own time sheets with some supervision or check on times. For example, a foreman may travel from site to site or the customer may be asked to sign the time sheet which will form the basis of a charge to him. Where a large number of workers are engaged upon a site for a long period, e.g., on a civil engineering contract, it is usual for time recording clocks to be installed at the site. When casual workers are engaged for outside work, a head office clerk should attend to pay these workers. Alternatively, the foreman may be issued a petty cash fund from which to make the payments.

Illustration 1:

XYZ Ltd. employs its workers for a single shift of 8 hours for 25 days in a month. The company has recently fixed the standard output for a mass production item and introduced an incentive scheme to boost output. Details of wages payable to the workers are as follows:

(*i*) Basic wages/piece work wages @ Rs. 2 per unit subject to a guaranteed minimum wages of Rs. 60 per day.

(*ii*) Dearness allowance at Rs. 40 per day.

(*iii*) Incentive bonus:

Standard output per day per worker: 40 units;

Incentive bonus for efficiency above 80%; Rs. 50 for every 1% increase above 80%.

The details of performance of four workers for the month of April 2008 are as follows:

Worker	*No. of days worked*	*Output (units)*
A	25	820
B	18	500
C	25	910
D	24	780

Calculate the total earnings of each of the workers.

Solution:

Statement of Total Earnings of Each Worker

Worker	*Days Worked*	*Output*	*Basic Wages Rs.*	*Dearness Allowance Rs.*	*Incentive Rs.*	*Total Earnings Rs.*
A	25	820 unit	1,640	1,000	100	2,740
B	18	500 units	1,080	720	—	1,800
C	25	910 units	1,820	1,000	550	3,370
D	24	780 units	1,560	960	50	2,570

Working Notes:

(1) The worker B has been allowed of guaranteed minimum wages @ Rs. 60 per day for 18 days, since piece work wage is only Rs. 1,000 (i.e., 500 × Rs. 2)

(2) Incentive has been computed as follows:

Workers	*Efficiency*	*Incentive @ Rs. 50 for each 1% increase in efficiency above 80%*
A	$\frac{820}{25 \times 40} = 82\%$	100
B	$\frac{500}{18 \times 40} = 69\%$	—
C	$\frac{910}{25 \times 40} = 91\%$	550
D	$\frac{780}{24 \times 40} = 81\%$	50

Illustration 2:

A worker produced 200 units in a week's time. The guaranteed weekly wage payment for 45 hours is Rs. 81. The expected time to produce one unit is 15 minutes which is raised further by 20% under the incentive scheme. What will be the earnings per hour of that worker under Halsey (50% sharing) and Rowan bonus schemes?

Solution:

Earning per hour under Halsey (50% sharing) Bonus Scheme

Time allowed for actual weekly production = 200 units × 18 minutes = $\frac{3600 \text{ minutes}}{60 \text{ minutes}}$

(Refer WN 1) = 60 hours

Time Saved = Time Allowed – Actual Time taken

= 60 hours – 45 hours = 15 hours

Total earnings = (Hours worked × Rate per hour) + 1/2 × (Time saved × Rate per hour)

(Refer WN 2) = 45 hours × Rs. 1.80 + 1/2 × 15 hours × Rs. 1.80

= Rs. 81 + Rs. 13.50 = Rs. 94.50

Earning per Hour = $\frac{\text{Rs. } 94.50}{45 \text{ hours}}$ = Rs. 2.10 hour

Earnings per hour under Rowan Bonus Scheme

$$\text{Total earnings} = \text{Hours worked} \times \text{Rate per hour} + \left(\frac{\text{Time saved}}{\text{Time allowed}} \times \text{Time taken} \times \text{Rate per hour}\right)$$

$$= 45 \text{ hours} \times \text{Rs. } 1.80 + \left(\frac{15 \text{ hours}}{60 \text{ hours}} \times 45 \text{ hours} \times \text{Rs. } 1.80\right)$$

= Rs. 81 + Re. 20.25 = Rs. 101.25

Earnings per hour = $\frac{\text{Rs. }101.25}{45\text{ hours}}$ = Rs. 2.25 per hour.

Working Notes:

1. Expected time to produce one unit under incentive scheme = 15 × 3 minutes (20%)
   = 18 minutes
   = Rs. 1.80
2. Wage rate per hour (Rs. 81/45 hours) = Rs. 1.80

Illustration 3:

From the following particulars, you are required to work out the earnings of a worker for a week under:

(*i*) straight piece rate,
(*ii*) differential piece rate,
(*iii*) Halsey Premium scheme (50% sharing), and
(*iv*) Rowan Premium scheme:

Weekly working hours	48
Hourly wage rate (Rs.)	7.50
Piece rate per unit (Rs.)	3.00
Normal time taken per piece	24 minutes
Normal output per week	120 pieces
Actual output for the week	150 pieces
Differential piece rate	80% of piece rate when output is below normal and 120% of piece rate when output is above normal.

Solution:

Computation of Workers' weekly earning under Different Wage Plans:

(*i*) Straight Piece Rate = Weekly Output × Piece Rate per unit
Earnings = 150 units × Rs. 3 = Rs. 450

(*ii*) *Differential Piece Rate*

Efficiency level achieved = $\frac{150\text{ pieces}}{120\text{ pieces}}$ × 100 = 125%

(*i*) *Straight Piece Rate*

= Weekly Output × Piece Rate per unit

Earnings = 150 units × Rs. 3 = Rs. 450

(*ii*) *Differential Piece Rate*

Efficiency level achieved = $\frac{150\text{ pieces}}{120\text{pieces}}$ × 100 = 125%

The efficiency level achieved is more than 80%. Hence, a high differential piece rate (*i.e.*, at 120%) is applicable, i.e., (Rs. 3 × 120%) = Rs. 3.60 per piece

Earnings = 150 pieces × Rs. 3.60 = Rs. 540

(*iii*) *Halsey Premium Scheme (50% sharing)*

Standard Hours for Actual Production = (48/120) × 150 = 60 hours

Time Saved = 60 hours – 48 hours = 12 hours

Earnings = Hours Worked × Rate per hour + 1/2 of time saved × Rate per hr.

= 48 × Rs. 7.50 + 1/2 × 12 × 7.50 = Rs. 360 + Rs. 45

= Rs. 405

(*iv*) *Rowan Premium Scheme*

$$\text{Earnings} = \text{Hours Worked} \times \text{Rate per hour} + \frac{\text{Time saved}}{\text{Time Allowed}} \times \text{Time taken} \times \text{Rate per hr.}$$

= 48 × Rs. 7.50 + 12/60 × 48 × 7.50

= Rs. 360 + 72 = Rs. 432

Illustration 4:

A job can be executed either through workman *A* or *B*. *A* takes 32 hours to complete the job while *B* finishes it in 30 hours. The standard time to finish the job is 40 hours.

The hourly wage rate is same for both the workers. In addition workman is entitled to receive bonus according to Halsey plan (50% sharing) while *B* is paid bonus as per Rowan plan. The works overheads are absorbed on the job at Rs. 7.50 per labour hour worked. The factory cost of the job comes to Rs. 2,600 irrespective of the workman engaged.

Find out the hourly wage rate and cost of raw materials input. Also show cost against each element of cost included in factory cost.

Solution:

Basic Calculations

1. *Computation of Time saved and Wages*

Workman	*A*	*B*
Standard Time (Hrs.)	40	40
Actual Time (Hrs.)	32	30
Time Saved (Hrs.)	08	10
Wages paid @ Rs. *x* per Hr. (Rs.)	32*x*	30*x*

2. *Computation of Bonus*

	Halsey Plan	Rowan Plan
Time saves (Hrs.)	8	10
Bonus (Rs.)	$\frac{8 \text{ Hrs.} \times \text{Rs. } x}{2} = 4x$	$\frac{10 \text{ Hrs.}}{40 \text{ Hrs.}} \times 30 \text{ Hrs.} \times \text{Rs. } x = 7.5x$

3. *Computation of Total Wages*

Workman A: 32*x* + 4*x* = Rs. 36*x*

Workman B: 30*x* + 7.5*x* = Rs. 37.5*x*

4. *Computation of Factory Cost of the Job*

Workman	*A*	*B*
	Rs.	*Rs.*
Material	*y*	*y*
Wages (as per above)	36*x*	37.5*x*
Works Overhead	240	225
Factory Cost	2,600	2,600

From the above, the following simultaneous equation can be made out:

$$36x + y + 240 = 2{,}600 \quad \ldots (i)$$
$$37.5x + y + 225 = 2{,}600 \quad \ldots (ii)$$

On subtracting (*i*) from (*ii*) we get the following results:

$$1.5x - 15 = 0$$
or $$1.5x = 15$$
or $$x = \text{Rs. } 10 \text{ per hour.}$$

On substituting the value of x in equation (i)

$$36 \times 10 + y + 240 = 2{,}600$$
or $$y = 2{,}600 - 360 - 240$$
or $$y = \text{Rs. } 2{,}000$$

The wage rate per hour is Rs. 10 and the cost of raw material input is Rs. 2.000 for the job.

Illustration 5:

In a factory Ram and Sham produce the same product using the same input of same material and at the same normal wage rate.

Bonus is paid to both of them in the form of normal time wage rate adjusted by the proportion which time saved bears to the standard time for the completion of the product. The time allotted to the product is fifty hours. Ram takes thirty hours and Sham takes forty hours to produce the product. The Factory Cost of the product for Ram is Rs. 3,100 and for Sham Rs. 3,280. The Factory Overhead Rate is Rs. 12 per man hour.

Calculate: (*i*) Normal Wage Rate; (*ii*) Cost of material used for the product; and (*iii*) the input of material if the unit material cost is Rs. 16.

Solution:

Let x be the cost of material and y be the normal rate of wages per hour

Factory Cost of Workman Ram

	Rs.
Materials	x
Wages	$30y$
Bonus (30y × 20/50)	$12y$
Overheads	360
Factory Cost	$x + 42y$ + Rs. 360

Factory Cost of Workman Sham

Material	x
Wages	$40y$
Bonus (40y × 10/50)	$8y$
Overheads	480
	$x + 48y + 480$

The following two equations can be made

$$x + 42y + 360 = \text{Rs. } 3{,}100 \quad \ldots (i)$$
$$x + 48y + 480 = \text{Rs. } 3{,}280 \quad \ldots (ii)$$

On subtracting equation (i) from equation (ii)

$$6y + 120 = 180$$
or $$6y = 180 - 120$$
$$y = 60/6 = 10$$

On substituting the value of x in equation (i)

$$x + 420 + 360 = 3{,}100$$

or $$x = 3{,}100 - 780$$

or $$x = 2{,}320$$

Thus:

(*i*) Normal Wage Rate is Rs. 10 per hour

(*ii*) Cost of material used for the product is Rs. 2,320

(*iii*) Input of material is 2.320/16 = 145 units.

Illustration 6:

A company has its factories at two locations. Rowan plan is in use at location *A* and Halsey plan at location *B*. Standard time and basic rate of wages are same for a job which is similar and is carried out on similar machinery. Time allowed is 60 hours.

Job at location '*A*' is completed in 36 hours while at *B*, it has taken 48 hours. Conversion costs at respective places are Rs. 1,224 and Rs. 1.500. Overheads account for Rs. 20 per hour.

Required:

(*a*) To Find out the normal wage rate, and

(*b*) To compare respective conversion costs.

Solution:

Let Rs. x per hour be the normal wage rate:

∴ Wages at location *A* will be Rs. $36x$ and Rs. $48x$ for location B.

Time allowed is 60 hours.

Hence, for tune saved, bonus will be payable as under:

Location A

$$\text{Bonus under Rowan Scheme} = \frac{\text{Time saved}}{\text{Time allowed}} \times \text{Hrs. worked} \times \text{Rate}$$

$$= \frac{24}{60} \times 36 \times x = \text{Rs. } 14.4x$$

Total wages Rs. $36x$ + Rs. $14.4x$ – Rs. $50.4x$

Overheads @ Rs. 20 per hour worked Rs. 720.

Hence, total Conversion Cost is $50.4x + 720$ = Rs. 1,224 (given)

OR $x = 10$

Location B

Bonus under Halsey plan = 50% of Time saved × Rate per hour

= 50% of 12 × x = Rs. $6x$

Total Wages = $48x$ + Rs. $6x$ = Rs. $54x$

Overheads Rs. 20 per hour = Rs. 960

Total Conversion Cost is $54x + 960$ = Rs. 1,500

OR x = Rs. 10

Comparative Conversion Cost

Particulars	*A (Rowan)*	*B (Halsey)*
Wages @ Rs. 10 per hour	Rs. 360	Rs. 480
Bonus	Rs. 144	Rs. 60
Overheads	Rs. 720	Rs. 960
	Rs. 1,224	Rs. 1,500

Illustration 7:

The standard hours of job X is 100 hours. The job has been completed by Amar in 60 hours. Akbar in 70 hours and Anthony in 95 hours. The bonus system applicable to the job is as follows:

Percentage of time saved to time allowed	*Bonus*
Saving upto 10%	10% of time saved
From 11% to 20%	15% of time saved
From 21 % to 40%	20% of time saved
From 41% to 100%	25% of time saved

The rate of pay is Rs. 10 per hour. Calculate the total earnings of each worker and also the rate of earnings per hour.

Solution:

Statement of Total Earnings and Rate of Earnings per Hour

Particulars	*Workers*		
	Amar	*Akbar*	*Anthony*
Standard hours of Job	100 hours	100 hours	100 hours
Time taken on the Job (i)	60 hours	70 hours	95 hours
Time saved	40 hours	30 hours	5 hours
Percentage of time saved to time allowed	40%	30%	5%
Bonus (as percentage of time saved)	20%	20%	10%
Bonus hours (W/N 1) (ii)	8	6	0.50
Total hours to be paid (i) + (ii)	68	76	95.5
Total earning @ Rs, 10 per hour	Rs. 680	Rs. 760	Rs. 955
Rate of earning per hour	Rs. 11.33	Rs. 10.857	Rs. 10.052

Working Notes:

1. Computation of Bonus hours as percentage of time saved:

Amar	40 hours × 20%	= 8 hours
Akbar	30 hours × 20%	= 6 hours
Anthony	5 hours × 10%	= 0.5 hours

2. Computation of Rate of Earning per hour:

$$= \frac{\text{Total earnings}}{\text{Total time taken on the job}}$$

$$\text{Amar} = \frac{680}{60 \text{ hours}} = 11.33$$

$$\text{Akbar} = \frac{\text{Rs. } 760}{70 \text{ hours}} = \text{Rs. } 10.857$$

$$\text{Anthony} = \frac{\text{Rs. } 955}{95 \text{ hours}} = \text{Rs. } 10.052$$

Illustration 8:

The Cost Accountant of Tirupati Electronics Ltd. has computed labour turnover rates for the quarter ending 31st March, 2009 as 10%, 5% and 3% respectively under 'Flux Method', 'Replacement Method' and 'Separation Method.' If the number of workers replaced during that quarter is 30, find out the number of (*a*) workers recruited and joined and (*b*) workers left and discharged.

Solution:

Computation of Labour Turnover Rate

1. Replacement Method $= \dfrac{\text{Number of replacements}}{\text{Average number of workers}}$

= Putting the values in formula

$$\frac{5}{100} = \frac{30}{\text{Av. No. of workers}}$$

Hence, average number of workers $= \dfrac{30 \times 100}{5} = 600$

2. Separation Method $= \dfrac{\text{No. of Separations}}{\text{Average Number of workers}}$

or $= \dfrac{3}{100} = \dfrac{X}{600}$

$X = 18$

3. Flux Method $= \dfrac{\text{Number of Separations + Number of Additions}}{\text{Average number of workers}}$

$$= \frac{10}{100} = \frac{18 + \text{No. of Additions}}{600}$$

$$= \text{No. of Additions} = \frac{600 - 1800}{100} = \frac{4,200}{100}$$

$= 42$

Hence, the number of Additions $= 42$

From the above, the following information as desired by the question can be computed.

(*a*) Workers recruited and joined = 42

(*b*) Workers left and discharged = 18

Illustration 9:

The management of Sunshine Ltd. wants to have an idea of the profit lost/foregone as a result of labour turnover last year.

Last year sales amounted to Rs. 66.00,000 and the PV Ratio was 20%. The total number of actual hours worked by the direct labour force was 3.45 lakhs. As a result of the delays by the Personal Department in filling vacancies due to labour turnover, 75,000 potentially productive hours were lost. The actual direct labour hours included 30,000 hours attributable to training new recruits, out of which half of the hours were unproductive. The costs incurred consequent on labour turnover revealed on analysis the following:

	Rs.
Settlement cost due lo leaving	27,420
Recruitment costs	18,725
Selection costs	12,750
Training costs	16,105

Assuming that the potential production lost due to labour turnover could have been sold at prevailing prices, ascertain the profit foregone last year on account of labour turnover.

Solution:

Basic Calculations

(*i*) Actual Productive Hours = Actual Hrs. Worked – Unproductive Training Hrs.
= 3,45,000 hrs. – 15,000 Hrs. = 3,30,000

(*ii*) Sales per Productive Hour = Total Sales/Actual Productive Hrs.
= Rs. 66,00,000/3,30,000 hrs. = Rs. 20

(*iii*) Potential Productive Hours Lost = 75,000 hrs.

(*iv*) Sales Foregone = 75,000 hrs. × Rs. 20 = Rs. 15,00,000

(*v*) Contribution Foregone = Sales Foregone × *P/V Ratio*
= Rs. 15,00,000 × 20% = Rs. 3,00,000

M/s. Sunshine Ltd.

Statement of Profit Foregone as a Result of Labour Turnover

		Rs.
Contribution Foregone (See note (v) above)		3,00,000
Add: Settlement Cost due to leaving	27,420	
Recruitment Costs	18,725	
Selection Costs	12,750	
Training Costs	16,105	75,000
Total Profit Foregone		3,75,000

Illustration 10:

From the following information calculate Labour turnover rate:

No. of workers as on 01-01-2008= 7,600

No. of workers as on 31-12-2008 = 8,400

During the year, 80 workers left while 320 workers were discharged. 1,500 workers were recruited during the year of these, 300 workers were recruited because of exits and the rest were recruited in accordance with expansion plans.

Solution:

Labour turnover rate:

It comprises of computation of labour turnover by using following methods:

(*i*) *Separation Method:*

$$= \frac{\text{No. of workers left + No. of workers discharged}}{\text{Average number of workers}} \times 100$$

$$= \frac{(80+320)}{(7{,}600+8{,}400)\div 2} \times 100$$

$$= \frac{400}{8{,}000} \times 100 = 5\%$$

(*ii*) *Replacement Method:*

$$= \frac{\text{No. of workers replaced}}{\text{Average number of workers}} \times 100$$

$$= \frac{300}{8{,}000} \times 100 = 3.75\%$$

(*iii*) *New Recruitment:*

$$= \frac{\text{No. of workers newly recruited}}{\text{Average number of workers}} \times 100$$

$$= \frac{1{,}200}{8{,}000} \times 100 = 15\%$$

Flux Method:

$$= \frac{\text{No. of separations + No. of workers recruited}}{\text{Average number of workers}} \times 100$$

$$= \frac{(400+1{,}500)}{(7{,}600+8{,}400)\div 2} \times 100$$

$$= \frac{1{,}900}{8{,}000} \times 100 = 23.75\%.$$

THEORY QUESTIONS

1. What are the merits and demerits of time rate and piece-rate systems of wage payment? State the situations in which each system is effective and useful.
2. What are the reasons for booking workers on idle time in a factory? How is idle time controlled and treated in cost accounts?
3. List the characteristics desirable in any Incentive Wages Plan.
4. Distinguish between systems of wage payments known as Taylor's Differential Piece-Rate and Emerson's Efficiency system.
5. What is labour turnover? How will you measure it. What are its causes and effects on labour costs?
6. What is idle time? Indicate the different categories into which idle time can be classified and state which of them can be effectively controlled and how?
7. (*a*) Describe the treatment of payments to labour for overtime work and in respect of holiday with pay in cost accounts.

   (*b*) Distinguish between Taylor's differential piece-rate and the Emerson Efficiency Plan system of incentive wage payments.
8. Write a short essay on "Time and Motion Study," stating the benefits to be derived by management from such study.

9. How are payments to workers in respect of overtime work and set-up time treated in cost accounts?
10. What is idle time? Explain the causes leading to idle time and its treatment in cost accounts.
11. Explain the nature and significance of 'Labour Turnover.'
12. What are the effects of labour turnover on cost of production.
13. Enumerate the causes of labour turnover. What is the impact of high labour turnover on the cost of production.
14. What do you understand by overtime premium? What is the effect of overtime payment on productivity and cost? Discuss the treatment of overtime premium in cost accounts and suggest a procedure for control of overtime.
15. What do you understand by time and motion study? Explain how standard time is set under time study. State how time and motion study is useful to management.
16. Define job evaluation and distinguish it from merit rating. Explain the method and objectives of job evaluation.
17. What do you understand by 'idle time'? Distinguish between 'Normal' and 'Abnormal idle time.' How would you deal with each one of them in cost accounts? Give a suitable example to clarify your answer.

EXERCISES AND PROBLEMS

1. There are two piece-workers, Rakhal and Upendra, who are paid Rs. 5 for each piece work executed, which costs Rs. 15 per piece in materials.

   In a working day of 8 hours, Rakhal can complete 4 pieces and Upendra only 3. If the overhead charges be Rs. 1.50 per hour show which of the two piece workers is more useful to the factory.

(Ans.: Rakhal's cost of production is Rs. 23 per unit. Upendra's cost of production is Rs. 24 per unit. Rakhal's employment will be useful as his cost is lesser than that of Upendra's cost)

2. From the following data, prepare a statement showing the cost per day of 8 hours of engaging a particular type of labour:
   (*a*) Monthly salary (basic + dearness allowance) Rs. 2,000
   (*b*) Leave salary payable lo the workman 5% of salary
   (*c*) Employer's contribution to P.F. 8% of salary (items a and b)
   (*d*) Employer's contribution to State insurance 2½% of salary (item a + b)
   (*e*) Prorata to labour expenditure on amenities Rs. 179.5 per head per month.
   (*f*) No. of working hours a month 200.

(Ans.: Rs. 100)

3. An employee working under a bonus scheme saves in a job for which the standard time is 60 hours. Calculate the rate per hour worked and wages payable to a worker if incentive bonus of 10% on the hourly rate is payable when standard time (namely, 100% efficiency) is achieved, and a further incentive bonus of 1% on hourly rate for each 1% in excess of that 100% efficiency is payable.

   Assume that the normal rate payment is Rs. 5 per hour.

(Ans.: Hourly Rate Rs. 6.50, total wages payable Rs. 325.)

4. Calculate the standard labour hour rate for workman of Grade III from the following data:

Basic Pay	Rs. 2,000 p.m.
D.A.	Rs. 1,500 p.m.
Fringe benefits	Rs. 1,000 p.m.
Number of working days per hour	300

Leave Rules

30 days C.L. with full pay

20 days S.L. with half pay. Usually, sick leave is fully availed of. What should be the labour cost per hour, if no sick leave is availed of during the year?

(*Ans.:* Standard labour hour rate:

(*i*) When sick leave is availed Rs. 26.25

(*ii*) When sick leave is not availed Rs 25.00.)

5. In a factory bonus system, bonus hours are credited to the employee in the proportion of time taken, which time saved bears to time allowed. Jobs are carried forward from one week to another. No overtime is worked and payment is made in full for all units worked on including those subsequently rejected.

From the following information you are required lo calculate for each employee:

(*a*) bonus hours and amount of bonus earned.

(*b*) total wages cost.

(*c*) wages cost of each good unit produced.

	A (*Rs.*)	*B* (*Rs.*)	*C* (*Rs.*)
Basic wage rate per hour	25	40	30
Units produced	2,500	2,200	3,600
Time allowed per 100 units	2 hrs. 36 min.	3 hrs.	1 hr. 30 min.
Time taken	52 hrs.	75 hrs.	48 hrs.
Rejects	100 units	40 units	400 unit.

(*Ans.:*

	A	*B*	*C*
Bonus hours	13	—	6
Bonus earned	Rs. 260	—	Rs. 160
Total wages cost	Rs. 1,560	Rs. 3,000	Rs. 1,600

Wages cost per unit Re. 0.65, Rs. 1.39, Re. 0.50 of good output.)

6. Ever-ready Tools Ltd. has two factories, Factory No. 1 employs 130 and Factory No. 2 employs 150 direct workers. Both the factories work 40 hours per week and 50 weeks in a year. Overhead rates are as under:

Factory No. 1	Rs. 25 per hour
Factory No. 2	Rs. 20 per hour

Current expenses are as under:

Factory No. 1	Rs. 70,000
Factory No. 2	Rs. 50,000

Analyse these figures and state probable causes of discrepancy.

(*Ans.:* Factory 1 under recovery Rs. 5,00,000

Factory 2 over recovery Rs. 10,00,000

7. A company's basic wage rate is Rs. 3 per hour and its overtime rates are:

Evenings: Time and one-third.

Weekends: Double time

During the previous year the following hours were worked:

	Hours
Normal time	2,20,000
Time plus one-third	20,000
Double time	10,000

The following time has been worked on three jobs

	Job X	*Job Y*	*Job Z*
	hr.	*hr.*	*hr.*
Normal time	3,000	5,000	4,000
Evening overtime	300	600	1,050
Weekend overtime	100	50	300

You are required to calculate the labour cost chargeable to each job in each of the following circumstances:

(*a*) Where overtime is worked regularly throughout the year as company policy due to labour shortage.

(*b*) Where overtime is worked irregularly to meet the spasmodic production requirements.

(*c*) Where overtime is worked specifically at the customer's request to expedite delivery.

(*Ans.*:

	Job X (Rs.)	*Job Y (Rs.)*	*Job Z (Rs.)*
Situation (*a*)	10,880	18,080	17,120
Situation (*b*)	10,200	16,950	16,050
Situation (*c*)	10,800	17,700	18,000)

Overheads: Distribution

CONCEPT

Factory overhead costs are operating costs of a business enterprise which cannot be traced directly to a particular unit of output, *i.e.*, product or jobs. Factory overhead is the aggregate of indirect materials, indirect wages and indirect expenses. The term "overhead" is used interchangeably with such terms as "burden", "supplementary costs", "indirect expense", "factory expense."

FACTORY OVERHEADS — ACCOUNTING AND DISTRIBUTION

Factory Overheads by nature cannot be identified or associated directly with specific products or jobs. However, they should be included in total cost of products or jobs. The following steps are important in distribution of overhead costs among products or jobs.

1. Collection and codification
2. Allocation and apportionment
3. Absorption

COLLECTION AND CODIFICATION OF FACTORY OVERHEADS

The first step in distribution of factory overhead costs is their collection and codification under proper headings. Similar overhead cost items should be grouped together. The grouping of overhead costs is done through a technique known as "codification." Codification is a method of identifying and describing various overhead expenses in numbers or letters or in a combination of both so that cost data can easily be collected. Codification of the entire items is done through a proper coding system. Following are briefly the objectives of codification:

1. To collect overhead items of similar nature.
2. To help in the allocation and apportionment of overhead costs to different departments or cost centres.
3. To make an analysis of overhead cost items for planning and control purposes.

4. To help in adopting a mechanised system of accounting.
5. To maintain a reasonable number of accounts which could be economical and useful.

Methods of Codification

Generally, the codification follows Standing Order Number or Cost Accounting Number. Standing Order Number covers production overhead items and Cost Accounting Number includes administration, selling and distribution overhead items. However, both follow the same principle of accumulating overhead cost items. Some important methods of codification are the following:

Serial Numbering System

Under this method each item is allotted a fixed number in serial order, *e.g.*,

01 Factory supplies
02 Indirect labour
03 Insurance
04 Factory rent

Number Blocks

Under this method, a block number is assigned to cover items of expenditure, *e.g.*, 0.10 for maintenance expenses, 11-20 for supervision expenses, etc.

Combination of Alphabets and Numbers

Under this method a code is used which combines the number as well as the alphabets, *e.g.*,

M_1 = Maintenance of plant
M_2 = Maintenance of tools
M_3 = Maintenance of factory building
M_4 = Maintenance of office building

In the above example, M stands for maintenance and different numbers for different types of maintenance expenses.

Numerical Codes

Under this system, a code number usually consisting of nine digits is used. The first two digits signify whether the cost is fixed or variable, the next three indicate head of expense, the next two the analysis of expense for further subdivision, and the last two digits indicate the cost centre which incurs the expenditure, e.g.,

10/121/05/08 Fixed/salary/officers/production.

Mnemonic Method

Under this method, the letters, alphabets are used to indicate an item such as D.P.T. for depreciation on plant and tools.

Among the above methods, the numerical code method is more suitable than the others for a large organisation. This method is easy to operate where a mechanical system of accounting is used. A large number of items could be covered under this method.

Sources of Overhead Collection

Different sources are available in an organisation to collect overhead expenses such as:

1. Store requisitions for items like indirect materials.
2. Financial accounts — A large number of items may be taken from the financial accounts of the business enterprise.

3. Wages book — Most indirect wages and labour-related costs.
4. Cash book — for indirect expenses.
5. Registers and reports — Plant and machinery register for depreciation, scrap, waste, spoilage can be discovered through investigation.

ALLOCATION AND APPORTIONMENT OF FACTORY OVERHEADS

Departmentalisation of Overhead

Departmentalisation of factory overhead means dividing the company into segments called departments or cost centres where expenses are incurred. In a manufacturing concern, there are mainly two types of cost centres — producing departments and service departments. A production department represents a subunit of the company where manufacturing activity takes place. Some typical examples of producing departments include assembly, finishing, blending, painting and grinding departments. Service departments represent cost centres which provide support for the producing departments. Materials handling, personnel, plant maintenance, inspection, storage, purchasing, receiving, shipping, medical and other similar activities which are not directly involved in production are considered to be service activities.

Primary Distribution

Some factory overheads can be directly identified with a particular department or cost centre as having been incurred for that cost centre. Examples of such factory overheads are repairs and maintenance expenses incurred in specific departments, supervision, indirect labour, overtime, indirect materials and factory supplies, equipment depreciation.

Expenses such as power, light, rent, depreciation of factory building, expenses shared by all departments, cannot be charged directly to a department, be it producing or service. These expenses do not originate in any specific department. They are incurred for all and must, therefore, be apportioned or prorated to any or all departments using such items. Cost apportionment is the process of charging expenses in an equitable proportion to the various cost centres or departments. The Institute of Cost and Management Accountant (U.K.) defines cost apportionment, "as the allotment of proportions of items of cost to cost centres or cost units." The apportionment should be done on some rational and equitable bases. In cost accounting this is known as primary distribution or factory overhead.

It would be difficult to give a comprehensive list of the bases of apportionment, but the following bases are in common use:

1. Floor area occupied — overheads such as lighting and heating, rent and rates, depreciation on building, building repairs, caretaking, watching and patrolling.
2. Capital values — Depreciation on plant and machinery, insurance on building, and plant and machinery, maintenance of plant and machinery.
3. Direct labour hours and/or machine hours — Insurance on jigs, tools and fixtures, power, works management remuneration, repairs and maintenance cost.
4. Number of workers employed — canteen, accident insurance, medical, dental and first aid, pensions, personnel department expenses, profit sharing payments, recreation, supervision, time office, wages department.
5. Technical estimate — fire prevention, oil and grease, steam, water without meter.

Illustration 1:

The Modern Company has four departments. A, B and C are the production departments and D is a servicing department. The actual cost for a period are as follows:

		Rs. ('000)
Indirect materials		
Production department	A	950
	B	1,200
	C	200
Servicing department		1,500
Indirect wages		
Production department	A	900
	B	1,100
	C	300
Servicing department		1,000
Rent		2,000
Repair		1,200
Depreciation		900
Light		200
Supervision		3,000
Insurance		1,000
Employee's insurance (employer's liability)		300
Power		1,800

The following data are also available in respect of four departments:

	Departments			
	A	*B*	*C*	*D*
Area (sq. ft.)	150	110	90	50
No. of workers	24	16	12	8
Total wages ('000)	Rs. 8,000	Rs. 6,000	Rs. 4,000	Rs. 2,000
Value of plant ('000)	Rs. 24,000	Rs. 18,000	Rs. 12,000	Rs. 6,000
Value of stock ('000)	Rs. 15,000	Rs. 9,000	Rs. 6,000	

Apportion the above costs to the various departments on the most equitable method.

Solution:

Departmental Distribution Summary

Rs. ('000)

Items	*Basis*	*Total*	*Production Departments* *A*	*B*	*C*	*Servicing Department* *D*
Indirect material	Allocation	3,850	950	1,200	200	1,500
Indirect wages	Allocation	3,300	900	1,100	300	1,000
Rent	Area	2,000	750	550	450	250
Repairs	Plant value	1,200	480	360	240	120
Depreciation	Plant value	900	360	270	180	90
Light	Area	200	75	55	45	25
Supervision	No. of workers	3,000	1,200	800	600	400
Insurance	Value of stock	1,000	500	300	200	—
Employees Insurance	Wages	300	120	90	60	30
Power	Plant value	1,800	720	540	360	180
	Total	17,550	6,055	5,265	2,635	3,595

Notes: (*i*) it has been assumed that insurance has been taken for stock.

(*ii*) Power expenses have been apportioned on the basis of value of plant because no other information has been given.

Illustration 2:

Selfhelp Ltd. has gensets and produces its own power. Data for power costs are as follows:

Horse Power Hours .	*Production deptts.*		*Service deptts.*	
	A	*B*	*X*	*Y*
Needed capacity production	10,000	20,000	12,000	8,000
Used during the month of May	8,000	13,000	7,000	6,000

During the month of May. costs for generating power amounted to Rs. 9,30.000; of this Rs. 2,50,000 was considered to be fixed cost. Service Deptt. X renders service to A, B and Y in the ratio 13 : 6 : 1, while Y renders service to A and B in the ratio 31 : 3. Given that the direct labour hours in Deptts. A and B are 1,650 hours and 2,175 hours respectively, find the power cost per labour hour in each of these two Deptts.

Solution:

Selfhelp Ltd.

Overheads Distribution Summary

Particulars	*Basis of charge*	*Total Rs.*	*Production deptts.*		*Service deptts.*	
			A *Rs.*	*B* *Rs.*	*X* *Rs.*	*Y* *Rs.*
(1)	(2)	(3)	(4)	(5)	(6)	(7)
Fixed cost	H.P. Hours needed at capacity production (5 : 10 : 6 : 4)	2,50,000	50,000	1,00,000	60,000	40,000
Variable Cost	H.P. Hours used (8 : 13 : 7 : 6)	6,80,000	1,60,000	2,60,000	1,40,000	1,20,000
Total overheads		9,30,000	2,10,000	3,60,000	2,00,000	1,60,000
Service Deptt. X overheads apportioned to A, B and Y (13 : 6 : 1)			1,30,000	60,000	−2,00,000	10,000
Service Deptt. Y overheads apportioned to A and B (31 : 3)			1,55,000	15,000		−1,70,000
Total overheads of production deptts.			4,95,000	4,35,000	—	—
Labour hours worked			1,650	2,175		
Power cost per labour hour			300	200		

APPORTIONMENT OF SERVICE DEPARTMENTS OVERHEADS TO PRODUCING DEPARTMENTS

Secondary Distribution

The primary distribution of factory overhead apportions all overhead costs to the different departments or cost centres — both production and service departments. However, it is necessary that overhead costs of service departments (accumulated through direct allocation or primary distribution) should be further assigned to producing departments. This is due to the reason that service departments do not themselves manufacture anything and it is the production departments or cost centres which are involved in manufacturing activities. The reassignment or reapportionment of service departments overhead to producing departments or centres is termed as secondary distribution.

Secondary distribution is useful in the following manner:

1. It helps in determining the cost of products or jobs sold and value of inventory.
2. It helps in determining the effect of various managerial decisions and actions on the total cost of the business firm. For example, decisions as to add or to drop a product line require information about its cost effect, which can be estimated after secondary distribution has been made.
3. It helps subsequently in determining the price of the product or job. In case of contracts based cost in place of market price, secondary distribution helps in fixing a selling price which is advantageous to the parties concerned.
4. It promotes motivation among employees of the producing departments to take up service department activities.

Bases for Secondary Distribution

It is difficult to suggest a sample list of service departments and equitable bases of distribution of overhead costs. The general basis for apportioning service departments' overheads to producing departments are the following:

1. *Services rendered (benefits obtained):* This is perhaps the most popular method of apportioning service department costs. The services rendered to different departments, *i.e.*, benefits obtained by them can be a suitable basis.
2. *Ability to pay:* This method suggests that a large share of servicing departments overhead costs should be assigned to those producing departments whose product contributes the most to the income of a business enterprise.
3. *Survey or analysis:* This method is applied where a suitable base is difficult to find or it would be too costly to select a method which is considered suitable. For example, the postage cost could be apportioned on a survey of postage used during a year.
4. *Efficiency or incentives:* This method uses standards and budgets and apportions the overhead costs on the basis of a present budget or standard. Sometimes, this method is used along with the bases of services rendered or ability to pay method.

In selecting a suitable base for apportioning service department overheads, considerations should be given to practicability, simplicity, economy, theoretical soundness and assistance in accurate costing and cost control.

The following list gives a few service departments and bases commonly used to apportion the respective overhead costs:

Service Department	*Apportionment Base*
Personnel	Number of employees, labour hours, labour cost.
Purchasing	Number of orders, cost of materials.
Receiving	Cost materials, number of units, number of orders.
Stores	Cost of materials number of requisitions filled, number of units handled.
Factory Office	Number of employees, labour hours, labour cost.
Machine Maintenance and Repair	Machine hours, labour hours, labour cost, services rendered.

Engineering	Machine hours, labour hours, services rendered.
Payroll or Time-keeping Department	Total labour or machine hours of number of employees in each department.
Welfare, Canteen, Recreation, Medical	Number of employees in each department.
Building Service Department	Relative area of each department.
Internal Transport Service	Weight, value, graded products, weight and distance.

Inter-departmental Services

While apportioning service departments overheads, one may notice two situations: (*i*) The entire amount of a servicing department is to be distributed to only the producing departments. This does not involve any practical difficulty and provides the simplest and quickest method for apportioning costs of the servicing department. (*ii*) Services provided by some servicing departments are used partly by other servicing departments. That is, many service departments serve each other. For example, the payroll department in a firm prepares payroll for the entire organisation, but it depends on the building maintenance department for repair and maintenance services. Similarly, the building maintenance department provides services for all departments using the building, but it gets service from departments like stores, factory office, and personnel. This second situation is known as interdepartmental services.

Methods

There are mainly two methods of dealing with interdepartmental service:

A. Continuous apportionment: In this method, the process of apportioning service departments overhead is continued until the figures become immaterial or totally exhausted. The following steps are involved in this method:

(*a*) Use the given percentages to apportion the original total of the first service department. This closes the account of the first service department and transfers prorated amounts to other departments.

(*b*) Use the given percentages of second service department whose total is made up of original amount plus prorated amount of service department first. This closes the account of second service department and assigns prorated amounts to the other departments including service department first also.

(*c*) Follow the same procedure to all other service departments.

(*d*) Repeat a second cycle of apportionment starting with the service department first, whose total consists, at present, only of amounts prorated from other service departments. In this way, the service department totals become less and less with each cycle of apportionment because each time a substantial amount is apportioned to the producing departments.

(*e*) Stop the above cycle at any point where it is found that the remaining figure (to be apportioned) are too small to be of any consequence or when the Figures are totally exhausted.

Illustration 3:

The overhead of a manufacturing company has been analysed to the point of primary distribution.

		Rs.
Production departments:	Machine	10,00,000
	Assembly	4,00,000
Service departments:	Canteen	2,00,000
	Powerhouse	3,00,000

The canteen is to be apportioned on the basis of employees:

	Employees	%
Machine	240	60
Assembly	140	35
Powerhouse	20	5
	400	100

The powerhouse is to be apportioned on the basis of electricity used:

	Thousand kilowatts	%
Machine	270	75
Assembly	36	10
Canteen	54	15
	360	100

Solution:

The apportionment would be done in the following manner:

		Machine	*Assembly*	*Canteen*	*Powerhouse*
Primary apportionment		10,00,000	4,00,000	2,00,000	3,00,000
Apportion:	Canteen	1,20,000	70,000	– 2,00,000	10,000
	Powerhouse	2,32,500	31,000	46,500	– 3,10,000
	Canteen	27,900	16,300	– 46,500	2,300
	Powerhouse	1,800	200	300	– 2,300
	Canteen	200	100	– 300	
Total Service Deptts.		3,82,400	1,17,600		
Total Production Overhead		13,82,400	5,17,600		

B. Algebraic method or simultaneous equation: This method helps in finding out the amount of overhead of each servicing department by solving simultaneous equations. The total expenses of service departments can be directly transferred to production departments.

Illustration 4:

A company has three production departments: A, B and C and two service departments, P and Q. The following figures are available as per departmental distribution summary:

		Rs.
Production departments	A	3,150
	B	3,700
	C	1,400
Service departments	P	2,250
	Q	1,000

The expenses of the service departments are to be apportioned on a percentage basis as follows:

	A	*B*	*C*	*P*	*Q*
Service deptt. P	40%	30%	20%	—	10%
Service deptt. Q	30%	30%	20%	20%	—

Solution:

Let X = total overhead of deptt. P

Y = total overhead of deptt. Q

Therefore $X = 2{,}250 + \frac{20}{100}Y$ ... (1)

$Y = 1{,}000 + \frac{10}{100}X$ ... (2)

$10X = 22{,}500 + 2Y$ ... (3)

$10Y = 10{,}000 + 1X$ ... (4)

Mulilplying equation (3) by 5

$50X - 10Y = 1{,}12{,}500$ ... (5)

$-X + 10Y = 10{,}000$ ... (6)

Adding $49X = 1{,}22{,}500$

$X = 2{,}500$

and $Y = 1{,}250$

Secondary Distribution Summary

	Total	*Production Department*			*Servicing Dept.*	
	Rs.	*A Rs.*	*B Rs.*	*C Rs.*	*P Rs.*	*Q Rs.*
As per summary	11,500	3,150	3,700	1,400	2,250	1,000
Service Deptt. P		1,000	750	500	–2,250	250
	11,500	4,150	4,450	1,900		1,250
Service Deptt. Q		375	375	250	250	– 1,250
	11,500	4,525	4,825	2,150	—	—

Service departments' overheads represent the sum of the service department cost plus the costs apportioned from other service departments. After obtaining total overhead cost of servicing departments the total of each service department is apportioned to producing departments on the basis of percentage or proportion (for the services rendered) of the specific producing departments.

Illustration 5:

A factory is having three production departments: A, B and C and two service departments — Boiler-House and Pump-Room. The boiler-house has to depend upon the pump-room for supply of water and pump-room in its turn is dependent on the boiler-house for supply of driving the pump. The expenses incurred by the production departments during a period are: A, Rs. 8,00,000; B, Rs. 7,00.000: and C, Rs. 5,00,000. The expenses for boiler-house are Rs. 2,34,000 and the pumproom are Rs. 3,00,000.

The expenses of the boiler-house and pump room are apportioned to the production departments on the following basis:

	A	*B*	*C*	*B.H.*	*P.R.*
Expenses of boiler-house	30%	40%	30%	—	10%
Expenses of pump-room	40%	20%	20%	20%	—

Show clearly as to how the expenses of boiler-house and pump-room would be apportioned to A, B and C departments. Use algebraical equation.

Solution:

Let X be the overhead of boiler-house and Y be the total overhead of pump-room

$$X = 2{,}34{,}000 - 2Y$$
$$Y = 3{,}00{,}000 + 1X$$
$$10X - 2Y = 23{,}40{,}000 \quad \ldots (i)$$
$$-X - 10Y = 30{,}00{,}000 \quad \ldots (ii)$$

On multiplying Equation (*i*) by 5 and adding it to Equation (*ii*)

$$50X - 10Y = 1{,}17{,}00{,}000$$
$$-X + 10Y = 30{,}00{,}000$$
$$49X = 1{,}47{,}00{,}000$$
$$X = 3{,}00{,}000$$

On substituting this value in Equation (*ii*)

$$-3{,}00{,}000 + 10Y = 30{,}00{,}000$$
$$10Y = 33{,}00{,}000$$
$$Y = 3{,}30{,}000$$

Distribution of Overheads

	Total	*Departments*		
		A	*B*	*C*
	Rs.	*Rs.*	*Rs.*	*Rs.*
Amount for the Departments	20,00,000	8,00,000	7,00,000	5,00,000
Boiler-house	2,70,000 *	60,000	1,20,000	90,000
Pump-room	2,64,000 **	1,32,000	66,000	66,000
	25,34,000	9,92,000	8,86,000	6,56,000

* Rs. 3,00,000 less 1/10 for the Pumproom
** Rs. 3,30,000 less 1/5 for the Boilerhouse.

ABSORPTION OF FACTORY OVERHEADS

Meaning of Absorption

After all service departments overheads have been apportioned to producing departments, the next step is to spread factory overhead to different products or jobs produced. This is termed as "overhead absorption" in cost accounting. The Institute of Cost and Management Accountants (U.K.) defines overhead absorption as "the allotment of overhead to cost units." Known by different names, such as recovery overhead application, overhead costing, levy, burden rate, etc. the term "absorption" implies that expenses pertaining to a producing department or cost centre are, finally charged to or absorbed in the cost of products, jobs, etc. passing through it. As a result of absorption, the cost of each unit of product of the producing departments includes an equitable share of the total overhead of that department.

Methods of Absorption

Some methods of overhead absorption have to be applied to absorb factory overhead to individual products or jobs, etc. on some equitable basis. The rate which is used to charge overhead cost to the products or jobs is known as absorption rate. The following are the generally recognised methods of absorption or absorption rates:

Percentage on Direct Materials

An absorption rate based on materials cost is obtained by dividing total estimated factory overhead by total direct materials cost expected to be used in the manufacturing process. If factory overhead is Rs. 3,00,000 and materials cost is Rs. 2,50,000, the absorption rate will be:

$$\frac{\text{Rs. }3,00,000}{\text{Rs. }2,50,000} \times 100 = 120\%$$

Each job or product would be charged on the basis of 120% absorption rate. For example, if the materials cost of product is Rs. 50,000, the factory overhead to be charged for their product would be Rs. 60,000 (50,000 × 120%).

Advantages: The "percentage on direct material cost" method is simple and easy to understand and apply. This method will give correct overhead cost figure where the prices of raw materials do not differ significantly, where quantity and cost of materials in each product are uniform, and where processing for the different products is also uniform. It is useful in very simple types of small business firms.

Disadvantages: This method has the following disadvantages:

1. There is no logical relationship between material cost of a product and factory overhead used in production.
2. Materials prices are subject to fluctuations quite often and this phenomenon leads to high or low overhead costs, even though overhead figures remain unchanged.
3. Most of the overhead expenses vary with time. For example, a product or job using cheap materials but a longer period of processing should bear more for overhead as compared to a job or product which uses expensive materials but a shorter period of processing. But the use of direct material cost totally ignores the time factor which is an important factor in allocation/apportionment of overhead costs.
4. This method is not proper where part of the materials passes through all processes, and part through only some processes.
5. The mere fact that a job consumes material of a very expensive nature does not imply that the overhead incurred on that job will also be heavier. If the materials cost basis is used to charge overhead, the product using expensive materials will, in this case, be charged with more than its share of overhead.

Percentage on Direct Wages

Percentage on Direct Wages is computed in the following manner:

$$\frac{\text{Factory overhead}}{\text{Direct labour cost}} \times 100$$

If factory overhead is Rs. 2,00,000 and the direct labour cost is also Rs. 2.00,000 then absorption rate based on direct wages will be 100%.

A job or a product with a direct labour cost of Rs 30,000 would be charged with Rs. 30,000 for factory overhead.

Advantages: This method has the following advantages:

1. It is simple to operate and understand.
2. It considers the time factor, as labour cost is computed by multiplying number of hours spent on work by an hourly labour rate. The more hours worked, the higher the labour-cost and the greater the use and therefore the charge for factory overhead.
3. Labour rates fluctuate, but less frequently than that of prices of materials.

Disadvantages: The disadvantages are:

1. It depends on cost of direct labour which may not reflect accurately the contribution of factory overhead in the cost of product. Many expenses such as taxes, property insurance, depreciation are functions of time.
2. It does not take into account variations, if any, in the rates of remuneration for different types of labour and therefore, the wages incurred on different jobs are not necessarily in the same ratio as the hours spent. This fact would be clear where workers are paid on a piece-rate basis as in this system wages depend on output and not upon time. This limitation is clear from the following example:

	Job A (16 hr.)	*Job B (20 hr.)*
Direct materials	600	600
Direct labour	400	400
Prime cost	1,000	1,000
Factory overhead (75% on direct wages)	300	300
Factory cost	1,300	1,300

3. As job B has taken 25% extra time to complete work than A, the job carried out by B must have occupied the factory for a longer period than A's, but as is clear from the above statement, the charge for factory overhead is the same in each case.
4. Total direct labour cost represents the sum of high and low-wage production workers. By applying overhead on the basis of direct labour cost, a job or product is charged with more overhead when a high rate operator performs work instead of a low-rate worker leading to incorrect distribution of factory overhead.

Prime Cost Percentage

The prime cost basis combines the total of direct materials cost and direct labour cost and uses this total as a basis for charging overhead. The formula used in determining the rate is:

$$\frac{\text{Factory overhead}}{\text{Prime cost}} \times 100$$

If in a case the factory overhead is Rs. 4,56,000 and prime cost is Rs. 6,00,000, then prime cost percentage rate will be

$$\frac{4,56,000}{6,00,000} \times 100 = 76\% \text{ of prime cost}$$

Advantages: This method is simple to operate. It considers both materials and labour in charging overhead to each job or product. The prime cost data is easily available without any additional problem of accumulation.

Disadvantages: The disadvantages are:

1. Two items, *i.e.,* materials and labour both of which possess many disadvantages influence the charging of factory-overhead to jobs and products.
2. Where the cost of materials is a larger part of the prime cost, the time factor (direct labour costs) will be ignored which is more related to the factory overhead.
3. It ignores time factor in absorbing factory overhead.
4. It can be useful to only a few departments where the type of labour and value of materials used are constant.

The following example illustrates the demerits of this method:

	Job A	*Job B*
Direct materials	Rs. 30,000	Rs. 4,000
Direct wages (Job A 50 hours @ Rs. 4 per hour and Job B 200 hours @ Rs. 4 per hour)	200	800
Prime cost	Rs. 30,200	Rs. 4,800
Factory overhead (50% on prime cost)	15,100	2,400
Factory cost	45,300	7,200

The above example indicates that the labour expended on job B is four times that of job A. But this fact is not reflected in the factory overhead charged to these two jobs.

Unit of Production Basis

The unit of production method is the simplest and most direct method of charging factory overhead. The unit might be a kilo, foot, a machine, a hundred pieces or whatever unit of measure is used for the product. As a formula, the computation is as follows:

$$\frac{\text{Factory overhead}}{\text{Units of production}}$$

If factory overhead is Rs. 3,00,000 and the company intends to produce 2,50,000 units during the next period, each unit completed would be charged with Rs. 1.20 (3,00,000 ÷ 2,50,000 units) as its share of factory overhead. Thus, an order with 1,000 completed units would be charged Rs. 1,200 (1,000 units × Rs. 1.20) for factory overhead.

The usefulness of this method is limited normally to those situations where only one product is produced. It is used most satisfactorily in small manufacturing concerns having relatively simple manufacturing processes or in large concerns manufacturing few articles in large quantities. If several products manufactured are alike or closely related, absorption of factory overhead can be made on a weight or a point basis, such as in the following example:

Points value of Product A	5 points
Points value of Product B	7 points
Production units A 4,000, B 5,000.	

Overhead to be absorbed Rs. 5,50,000

$$\text{Rate per unit} = \frac{5{,}50{,}000}{(4{,}000 \times 5) + (5{,}000 \times 7)} = \text{Rs. } 10$$

Rate per unit of A = 5 × Rs. 10 = Rs. 50

Rate per unit of B = 7 × Rs. 10 = Rs. 70

Labour Hour/Production Hour Rate

One of the most widely used methods for overhead application is the labour hour basis. Since many companies require direct labour workers to record their time spent on each job, or in each department of a process cost factory, the data for absorption of overhead on this basis is readily available. The equation for determining the overhead rate under this method is:

$$\frac{\text{Factory overhead}}{\text{Direct labour hours}}$$

If factory overhead is Rs. 4,00,000 and direct labour hours are 2,00,000, then overhead rate based on direct labour hours would be Rs. 2 per hour of direct labour (Rs. 4,00,000 ÷ 2,00,000 hours). A product that requires 5,000 direct labour hours would be charged with Rs. 10,000 (5,000 hours × Rs. 2) for factory overhead.

Advantages: The following are the advantages:

1. As long as direct labour is the chief factor in manufacturing processes, the direct labour hours method is useful as the most equitable basis for charging overhead.
2. This method uses the lime factor and production taking the same time is charged with the same amount of overhead, though the direct labourer may be getting different wage rates.

Disadvantages: The disadvantages are:

1. The method requires accumulation of direct labour hours by job, product or department. Time-keeping should be adequate to provide this information.
2. This method cannot be used where machines are used extensively for production.

Machine Hours Rate

The machine hour rate is used where the work is performed primarily on machines. The formula used in computing the rate is:

$$\frac{\text{Factory overhead}}{\text{Machine hours}}$$

If factory overhead is Rs. 3,00,000 and total machine hours are 1,50,000, the machine hour rate is Rs. 2 per machine hour (Rs. 3,00,000 ÷ 1.50,000 hours).

Advantages: This method can be used advantageously where the machine is the major factor in production. In capital-intensive industries, plants and machines are used in large quantities and one "operator may attend to several machines or several operators may attend to a single machine. By making the machine the basis, overhead costs can be equitably absorbed among different products.

Disadvantages: The disadvantages are:

1. Machine hour data has to be collected and therefore it requires additional clerical work. The cost of collection and accounting activities goes up and therefore, is not workable for small business firms.

2. The method cannot be used universally by all business concerns. It can be used where production is mainly through machines.

Types of Machine Hour Rate

Two types of machine hour rate may be calculated such as:

1. *Ordinary machine hour rate* — This rate takes into account only those overhead expenses which are directly attributed to the running of a machine. Such expenses are power, fuel, repair, maintenance and depreciation. The total of all these expenses is divided by the total machine hours.
2. *Composite machine hour rate* — This method takes into account not only expenses directly connected with the machine as mentioned above, but also other expenses which are known as standing or fixed charges. Such expenses are rent and rates, supervisory, labour, lighting and heating, etc. These expenses being fixed in nature are determined for a particular period and then apportioned among different departments on some equitable bases. The overhead expenses thus apportioned to each department are further apportioned among the machines (machine cost centres) in that department, on an equitable basis. Generally composite machine hour rate is calculated.

The following are bases used for the apportionment of expenses for computing machine hour rate.

Overhead Expenses	*Basis*
1. Standing Charges	
(*i*) Supervision	Estimated time devoted to each machine
(*ii*) Rent and rates	Floor area occupied by each machine
(*iii*) Heating and lighting	Number of points or floor occupied by each machine
(*iv*) Lubricating oil and consumable stores	Capital values, machine hours or past experience
(*v*) Insurance	Insured value of each machine
(*vi*) Miscellaneous expenses	Equitable basis depending on facts
2. Machine or Variable Expenses	
(*i*) Depreciation	Machine hours
(*ii*) Repairs	Machine hours or capital values or cost of repairs spread over the working life of machine
(*iii*) Power	Horse power of machines or machine hours or meter readings

SELECTING AN ABSORPTION RATE

The above absorption rates have their own merits and demerits. The method to be used depends on the factors and circumstances prevailing in a manufacturing firm. Whatever method is selected by a firm, it must achieve the following objectives:

1. The basic objective is to select an absorption rate which helps in determining the accurate amount of factory overhead to be charged to individual products, jobs, processes, etc.
2. A secondary objective in selecting a method of absorption is to minimise clerical effort and cost. When two or more absorption rates tend to charge the same amount of overhead, the simplest base could be used.
3. The selection of an absorption rate is also influenced by other factors, such as type of industry, legal requirements, if any, policy of management, etc. in addition to the suitability of a method under specific circumstances.

Illustration 6:

The production department of a factory furnishes the following information for the month of October:

Materials used	Rs. 54,000
Direct wages	Rs. 45,000
Overhead	Rs. 36,000
Labour hours worked	36,000
Hours of machine operation	30,000

For an order executed by the department during the period, the relevant information was as under:

Materials used	Rs. 6,00,000
Direct wages	Rs. 3,20,000
Labour hours worked	3,200
Hours of machine operation	2,400

Calculate the overhead charges chargeable to the job by the following methods: (*i*) Direct materials cost percentage rate, (*ii*) Labour hour rate, and (*iii*) Machine hours rate.

Solution:

(i) Direct materials cost percentage rate:

$$\frac{\text{Overhead}}{\text{Direct materials}} \times 100 = \frac{36,000}{54,000} \times 100 = 66.67\%$$

Materials used on the order Rs. 6,00,000

Overhead @ 66.67% = Rs. 4,00,000

(*ii*) Labour hours rate:

$$\frac{\text{Overhead}}{\text{Labour hours}} = \frac{36,000}{36,000} = \text{Re, } 1$$

Overhead @ Re. 1 for 3,200 hours = Rs. 3,200.

(*iii*) Machine hours rate:

$$\frac{\text{Overhead}}{\text{Machine hours}} = \frac{36,000}{30,000} = \text{Rs. } 1.20$$

Overheads @ Rs. 1.20 for 2,400 hours = Rs. 2,880.

Illustration 7:

Atlas Engineering Ltd. accepts a variety of jobs which require both manual and machine operations. The budgeted Profit and Loss Account for the period 2008-09 is as follows:

		(in lakhs of rupees)
Sales		75
Less: Cost of Sales		
Direct Materials	10	
Direct Labour	5	
Prime Cost	15	
Production Overhead	30	
Production Cost	45	
Administrative, Selling and Distribution Overhead	15	60
Profit		15

Other Budgeted Data

Labour hours for the period	2,500
Machine hours for the period	1,500
No. of jobs for the period	300

An enquiry has been received recently from a customer and the production department has prepared the following estimate of the prime cost required for the job:

	Rs.
Direct material	2,500
Direct labour	2,000
Prime Cost	4,500
Labour hours required	= 80
Machine hours required	= 50

You are required to:

(*a*) Calculate by different methods, six overhead absorption rates for absorption of production overhead and comment on the suitability of each.

(*b*) Calculate the production overhead cost of the order based on each of the above rates.

(*c*) Give your recommendation to the company.

Solution:

(a) Atlas Engineering Ltd.

Computation of Overhead Absorption Rates for Absorption of Production Overheads

Sl. No.	*Methods of Absorption*	*Formula*	*Overhead Absorption Rate*
1.	Direct Labour Hour Rate	$\frac{\text{Production Overheads}}{\text{Direct Labour Hrs.}} = \frac{\text{Rs. }30,00,000}{2,500 \text{ hrs.}}$	= Rs. 120
2.	Machine Hour Rate	$\frac{\text{Production Overheads}}{\text{Machine Hours}} = \frac{\text{Rs. }30,00,000}{1,500 \text{ hrs.}}$	= Rs. 200
3.	Percentage of Direct Material Cost	$\frac{\text{Production Overheads}}{\text{Direct Material Cost}} = \frac{\text{Rs. }30,00,000}{\text{Rs. }10,00,000} \times 100$	= 300%
4.	Percentage of Direct Wages Cost	$\frac{\text{Production Overheads}}{\text{Direct Labour Cost}} = \frac{\text{Rs. }30,00,000}{\text{Rs. }5,00,000} \times 100$	= 600%
5.	Percentage of Prime cost	$\frac{\text{Production Overheads}}{\text{Prime Cost}} = \frac{\text{Rs. }30,00,000}{\text{Rs. }15,00,000} \times 100$	= 200%
6.	Job Rate	$\frac{\text{Production Overheads}}{\text{No. of Jobs}} = \frac{\text{Rs. }30,00,000}{300}$	= Rs. 10,000

(b) Statement of Production Overhead Cost for the Job

(Under Different Methods)

Methods	*Production Overhead Cost for the job Rs.*
1. Direct Labour Hour Rate	80 hrs. × 120 = 9,600
2. Machine Hour Rate	50 hrs. × 200 = 10,000
3. Percentage of Direct Material Cost	300% of Rs. 2,500 = 7,500
4. Percentage of Direct Labour Cost	600% of Rs. 2,000 = 12,000
5. Percentage of Prime Cost	200% of Rs. 4,500 = 9,000
6. Job Rate	1 × Rs. 10,000 = 10,000

Comments

(*a*) Labour Hour Rate and Machine Hour Rate both are based on time. They are generally preferred since most overheads vary with time.

(*b*) Direct Material Cost Percentage Method is suitable only if all the jobs use the same materials and labour, and machine time does not vary significantly.

(*c*) Direct Labour Cost Percentage method may be used if the labour rates for different jobs do not vary much.

(*d*) Percentage of Prime Cost is simple but has the disadvantages of both Percentage of Direct Material Cost and Percentage of Direct Labour Cost.

(*e*) Job Rate Method is very simple and acceptable if all the jobs are of the same type. If they art different, this method is not appropriate for charging overheads.

(c) Recommendation to the Company

It will be appropriate to have separate overhead rates based on labour hours and machine hours for absorption of labour related overhead and machine related overhead respectively. However, if the degree of mechanisation is very high in the factory and a single rate is desired for simplicity, the machine hour rate may be used for absorption of production overhead?

Illustration 8:

The following information is made available from the costing records of a factory:

(*i*) The original cost of the machine	Rs. 1,00.000
Estimated life	10 years
Residual value	Rs. 5,000

Factory operates for 48 hours per week — 52 weeks in a year. Allow 15% towards machine maintenance downtime. 5% may be allowed as setting up time.

(*ii*) Electricity used by the machine is 10 units per hour at a cost of 50 paise per unit.

(*iii*) Repairs and maintenance cost is Rs. 500 per month.

(*iv*) Two operators attend the machine during operation along with two other machines. Their total wages, including fringe benefits, amount to Rs. 5,000 per month.

(*v*) Other overheads attributable to the machine are Rs. 10,431 per year.

Using the above data, calculate machine hour rate.

Solution:

			Rs.
Calculation of Machine Hour rate			
Annual Working Hours 48 × 52	=		2,496
Less: Machine maintenance and setting up time. (15% + 5%) = 20%	=		499
Normal working Hours per annum	=		1,997
Standing Charges per annum:		Rs.	Rs.
Two operators wages along with two other machines = $\frac{5,000 \times 12 \times 1}{3}$		20,000	
Other overheads		10,431	
Total Standing Charges		30,431	
Hourly Rate of Standing Charges Rs. 30431/1997			15,238
Variable expenses per hour:			
Depreciation: $\frac{1,00,000 - 5,000}{10 \times 1997}$			4.757
Repairs and Maintenance = $\frac{500 \times 12}{1997}$			3.004
Power 10 unit × 50 paisa			5.000
Machine hour rate			27.999

Illustration 9:

A machine was purchased on 1st January 2008 for Rs. 5 lakhs. The total cost of all machinery inclusive of the new machine was Rs. 75 lakhs. The following further particulars are available:

Expected life of the machine 10 years.

Scrap value at the end of 10 years Rs. 5,000.

Repairs and Maintenance for the machine during the year Rs. 2.000.

Expected number of working hours of the machine per year 4,000 hours.

Insurance premium annually for all machines Rs. 4,500.

Power consumption for the machine per hour @ 75 paise per unit — 25 units.

Area occupied by the machine 100 sq. ft.

Area occupied by other machines 1,500 sq. ft.

Rent per month of the department Rs. 800.

Lighting charges for 20 points for the whole department out of which three points are for the new machine — Rs. 120 per month.

Compute the machine hour rate for the new machine.

Solution:

Computation of Machine Hour Rate

Standing Charges	*Rs. per annum*	*Re. per hour*
Insurance (WN 2)	300	
Repairs & Maintenance	2,000	
Rent (WN 3)	600	
Light Charges	216	
	3,116	
Hrly. Rate of Standing Charges	3,116/4,000 hrs.	0.779
Machine Expenses:		
Depreciation (WN 1)*		12.375
Electricity Consumption: 25 units per hour @ Re. 0.75 per unit		18.750
Machine Hour Rate		31.904

* Depreciation may also be taken as a standing charge.

Working Notes:

1. *Depreciation of Machine*

	Rs.
Cost of New Machine	5,00,000
Less: Scrap Value	5,000
Net Cost of the Machine	4,95,000
Life of the Machine	10 years

Depreciation per hour: $\frac{4,95,000}{10 \text{ years} \times 4,000}$ = Rs. 12.375

2. *Insurance for the Machine*

Total cost of all Machines Rs. 75,00,000

Total insurance premium paid for all machines Rs. 4,500

Total annual insurance premium of the new machine: $\frac{4,500 \times 5,00,000}{75,00,000}$ = Rs. 300

3. *Rent for the Machine*

Rent paid per annum Rs. 9,600

Total area occupied 1,600 sq. ft.

Rent for the area occupied by the machine (100 sq. ft.) $\frac{9,600 \times 100}{1,600}$ = Rs. 600

4. *Lighting Charges for the Machine*

Total annual lighting charges of 20 points for the whole department Rs. 1,440

Lighting charges of the machine p.a. $\frac{\text{Rs.} 1,440 \times 3 \text{ points}}{20 \text{ points}}$ = Rs. 216.

OVERHEAD RATES: ACTUAL VS. PREDETERMINED (STANDARD)

The basic purpose of overhead absorption rates is to absorb total factory overhead in products or jobs manufactured. This objective can be achieved through actual overhead rate or predetermined overhead rate.

Actual Overhead Rate

When the absorption is based on actual overhead, it is known as actual absorption rate. This can be calculated only after the end of the accounting period when all cost and production figures have been collected. This method has the following disadvantages:

1. Product cost cannot be determined until some considerable time after the end of the accounting period. This may not help in controlling cost and in fixing selling prices.
2. There are likely to be variations in the overhead incurred because of the seasonal nature of some overhead costs, change in the volume of production and efficiency of the factory for different periods.
3. Some overhead costs are of fixed nature, such as depreciation, supervision, property taxes, etc. These overhead costs being constant give a different per unit cost when divided by differing production volumes. Also, some overheads like fire insurance premium are paid in advance but this should be charged to all work done/products manufactured during the year. How should the absorption be done? It creates an inequitable situation.

Predetermined Overhead Rate or Standard Rate

Because of the limitations of the actual overhead rate stated above, a predetermined or standard overhead rate is generally used by companies. This is a rate calculated in advance of the period in which it is to be used by dividing the estimated period overhead to be absorbed by the estimated period production. Production may be measured in any of the absorption bases, such as prime cost, labour hours, etc.

The primary objective of predetermined overhead rate is to provide a reasonably constant unit cost and to avoid unit cost fluctuations caused by seasonal overhead cost fluctuations changes in volume, or accounting methods.

Secondly, predetermined overhead rates also make possible the immediate costing of job or product completed during the month. When a job is finished, the absorption rate is multiplied by the absorption base to find out the total amount to be charged to the product or job. Under a process costing system predetermined overhead rate is used to charge overhead to the output of the process in question.

Thirdly, predetermined rates contribute effectively to standard costing and budgetary control programmes as these programmes use estimated costs and standard cost to measure production activities.

Under- or Over-absorption of Overhead

The use of a predetermined or standard rate may, therefore, result in under-absorption or over-absorption. When the amount absorbed is less than the actual overhead, there is under-absorption. Over-absorption arises when the amount absorbed is more than the actual overhead. Since actual overheads are not recorded in cost accounts, under-absorption and over-absorption can be treated in any one of following ways:

1. In a seasonal business firm, the balance (due to under or over-absorption) may be carried forward to the subsequent period with the expectation that it will be counterbalanced at the end of accounting period. This is clear from the following example:

Months	Production units	Overhead absorbed Rs. 2 per unit	Actual overhead	Under or over-absorption
July	1,000	2,000	3,000	– 1,000
August	1,500	3,000	4,200	– 1,200
September	3,000	6,000	3,800	+ 2,200

2. A supplementary rate can be used to adjust the amount of under or over-absorption. The supplementary rate is determined by dividing the amount of under or over-absorption by the actual absorption base. Under-absorption is adjusted by using a plus supplementary rate while a minus supplementary rate is used to correct over-absorption. For instance, in the above example, a plus supplementary rate of Re. 1 per unit (Rs. 1,000/1,000 units) can be used to increase the recorded overhead by Rs. 1,000 for the month of July. Similarly, a minus supplementary rate of Re. 0.733 $\left(\frac{2,200}{3,000}\right)$ can be used to decrease the recorded overhead by Rs. 2,200.

Illustration 10:

The Cost Account of Novo Chemicals Ltd. determined the overhead recovery rate for the year (based on direct labour hours) with the following estimates:

	Rs.
Indirect labour	1,15,000
Inspection	70,000
Factory supervision	50,000
Depreciation and maintenance	1,25,000
Total factory overhead	3,60,000
Direct labour hours	75,000
Hourly wage rate	Rs. 15

The actual results for the year are as follows:

	Rs.
Indirect labour	99,000
Inspection	73,000
Factory supervision	51,000
Depreciation and maintenance	1,15,000
Total actual factory overhead	3,38.000
Direct labour hours	67,600
Hourly wage rate	Rs. 16

Calculate the pre-determined overhead recovery rate and find out the amount of over/under-absorption if any.

How will you treat the over/under-absorption amount in Cost Accounts?

Solution:

Predetermined overhead recovery rate = Estimated Overheads/Estimated direct labour hours
= 3,60,000/75,000
= Rs. 4.80 per hour

Overheads recovered = 67,600 × 4.8
= Rs. 3,24,480

Under-recovery of overheads	= Rs. 3,38,000 – Rs. 3,24,480
	= Rs. 13,520
Supplementary rate (Positive)	= 13,520/67,600
	= Re. 0.20 per hour

The under-recovery of Rs. 67,600 may be charged from production on the basis of supplementary overhead rate amounting to Re. 0.20 per direct labour hour.

Illustration 11:

The actual total expenditure of a light engineering factory was Rs. 6,75,912. Overheads were recorded at the rate of Rs. 2 per hour at normal capacity of the factory. Out of 10,000 units produced, only 8,000 units were sold. 500 units were in work in progress. Actual hours worked were 2,84,756. Sixty per cent of the difference between the actual and applied overheads was due to fluctuations in material prices and labour rates. There was a fire in the factory during this accounting period and the company lost Rs. 50,000 of which the buildings accounted for Rs. 30,000 and the balance represented loss of materials stored in the godown. A sum of Rs. 10,000 was paid as wages to workmen during the strike period. The balance amount represented the difference between the actual and applied overheads due to operational efficiency or inefficiency.

Calculate the under/over absorption of production overheads for the period and state the appropriate treatment in cost accounts.

Solution:

Unabsorbed Overhead:

Overheads recovered from production 2,84,756 × 2 =	5,69,512
Actual Overheads	6,75,912
Under Recovery	1,06,400

Out of the total amount of unabsorbed overheads Rs. 1,06,400, 60% was due to fluctuations in the price of material and labour rates. The amount of Rs. 63,840 (*i.e.,* 60% of Rs. 1,06,400) should therefore be charged to units produced by means of supplementary rate.

$$\text{Supplementary Rate} = \frac{63,840}{10,500} = \text{Rs. } 6.08$$

Apportionment of Overheads

The amount of Rs. 63,840 will be apportioned between Cost of Sales, Finished Goods and Work-in-progress as follows:

			Rs.
Cost of Sales A/c	(8,000 × 6.08)	=	48,640
Finished Goods A/c	(2,000 × 6.08)	=	12,160
Work-in-progress A/c	(500 × 6.08)	=	3,040
			63,840

The balance of Rs. 42,560 (40% of Rs. 1,06,400) which represents unabsorbed overheads on account of abnormal factors such as strike, operational inefficiency etc. should be charged to Costing Profit & Loss Account.

Illustration 12:

Sweet Dreams Ltd. uses a historical cost system and absorbs overhead on the basis of predetermined rate. The following data are available for the year ended 31st March, 2009:

	Rs.
Manufacturing overheads —	
Amount actually spent	1,70,000
Amount absorbed	1,50,000
Cost of goods sold	3,36,000
Stock of Finished goods	96,000
Works-in-progress	48,000

Using two methods of disposal of under-absorbed overheads show the implication on the profits of the company under each method.

Solution:

The following are the two methods for disposal of under-absorbed overheads:

The total unabsorbed overhead of Rs. 20,000 can be written off in Costing Profit and Loss Account. In case of this method, the profits of the concern will get reduced by Rs. 20,000 for the period.

Supplementary: A supplementary rate may be used to adjust the overhead cost of each cost unit. The total under-absorbed amount may, at the end of accounting period, be apportioned on proportionate basis over cost of goods sold; stock of finished goods and work-in-progress. This can be done as shown below:

Apportionment of Under-Absorbed Overhead

	Rs.	*Rs.*	*Rs.*
Cost of goods sold (WN 1)	3,36,000	14,000	3,50,000
Stock of finished goods (WN 2)	96,000	4,000	1,00,000
Work-in-progress (WN 3)	48,000	2,000	50,000
	4,80,000	20,000	5,00,000

Working Notes:

(1) Under-absorbed overheads absorbed by cost of goods sold

$$= \frac{\text{Rs. } 3,36,000}{\text{Rs. } 4,80,000} \times \text{Rs. } 20,000 = \text{Rs. } 14,000$$

(2) Under-absorbed overheads absorbed by stock of finished goods

$$= \frac{\text{Rs. } 96,000}{\text{Rs. } 4,80,000} \times \text{Rs. } 20,000 = \text{Rs. } 4,000$$

(3) Under-absorbed overhead absorbed by WIP

$$= \frac{\text{Rs. } 48,000}{\text{Rs. } 4,80,000} \times \text{Rs. } 20,000 = \text{Rs. } 2,000$$

ADMINISTRATIVE OVERHEADS

Administrative overheads are those expenses which are incurred for formulating the policy, directing the organisation and controlling the operations of an undertaking. In other words, administrative overheads are incurred for general management and control of the organisation. Administrative overheads include the following items of overheads:

A. Indirect material:

1. Printing and stationery used in the office.
2. Cost of brushes, dusters and other office supplies.

B. Indirect labour:

1. Salaries, allowances, fees of board of directors, managing director, chairman, board staff, cost accountant, accounts manager and his staff, secretary and his staff, treasurer and his staff.
2. Salaries, allowances, fees of legal adviser and his staff, public relations officer and his staff, remuneration of internal auditors and statutory auditors.

C. Indirect expenses:

1. Office rent, rates and insurance
2. Office lighting, heating and cleaning
3. Depreciation and repairs of office buildings, furniture and fittings
4. Legal charges
5. Bank charges
6. Trade subscriptions and donations
7. Miscellaneous office expenses

There is lesser fluctuations in the amounts of administrative overheads as compared to factory overheads which may change largely in relation to changes in output.

Distribution of Administrative Overheads

The method of distributing administrative overheads is more or less the same as in the case of factory overheads. All items of administrative overheads are collected and grouped under proper classification heads. The overheads are then apportioned among the various administrative departments (cost centres). Some examples of administrative departments are office department, accounts department, personnel department, secretarial department, law department. Those administrative overheads which can be identified with specific departments are directly allocated to them. The remaining administrative overheads are apportioned among those administrative departments for which they have been incurred on an equitable basis.

A single rate for the total administrative overheads may be obtained without going into details of these overheads incurred for various departments. The Administrative Overhead Rate may be computed using any one of the following bases:

(1) As a percentage of Factory Cost: $\frac{\text{Total Administrative Overhead}}{\text{Total Factory Cost}} \times 100$

(2) As a percentage of factory Overheads: $\frac{\text{Total Administrative Overhead}}{\text{Total Factory Overhead}} \times 100$

(3) As a percentage of Sales: $\frac{\text{Total Administrative Overhead}}{\text{Total Sales}} \times 100$

(4) As a percentage of Gross Profit: $\frac{\text{Total Administrative Overhead}}{\text{Gross Profit}} \times 100$

(5) As a percentage of Conversion Costs: $\frac{\text{Total Administrative Overhead}}{\text{Total Conversion Costs}} \times 100$

Conversion cost include the cost of direct labour, direct expenses and factory overheads.

The above treatment, i.e., calculating an administrative overhead rate for charging administrative overheads, is based on the assumption that administrative overheads are an additional and separate element of cost of a product or job.

Besides the above treatment, the following two procedures are also suggested to deal with the administrative overheads:

1. *Apportionment between production and selling divisions:* Under this method administrative overheads are divided between production and selling divisions on some suitable basis. After such distribution, administrative overheads lose their identity. This method follows the logic that an organisation has only two functions to perform, namely, production and selling.
2. *Transfer to costing profit and loss account:* Under this method, administrative overheads are transferred to Costing Profit and Loss Account. This method is based on the assumption that administrative overheads are not directly concerned with the production function of the organisation and therefore should not be included in the cost of production. This method reduces the cost of product or job.

SELLING AND DISTRIBUTION OVERHEADS

Selling overheads include the costs incurred in promoting sales and retaining customers. Distribution overheads include the costs of the process which begins with making the packed product available for despatch and ends with making the reconditioned returned empty packages available for reuse. Distribution overheads strictly begin when an order has been obtained and generally ends when goods are despatched.

Broadly, selling overheads include the following items:

(*a*) *Indirect materials:* They include cost of printing and stationery, mailing literature, catalogue, price lists etc.

(*b*) *Indirect labour:* This includes salaries, commission, allowances etc. of salesman, representative, sales manager, marketing manager etc.

(*c*) *Indirect expenses:* Advertising, bad debts, rent of showroom, insurance of showroom, collection charges, travelling and entertainment expenses, expenses of branch establishment, sales office expenses, fees of directors who devote time to sales function, are some examples of indirect expenses.

Broadly, distribution overheads include the following items:

(*a*) *Indirect materials:* Cost of packing cases; oil, grease, spare parts used in maintenance of delivery vehicles.

(*b*) *Indirect labour:* Wages of packers, van drivers, despatch clerks, etc.

(*c*) *Indirect expenses:* Godown expenses including rent, insurance, freight, carriage outwards and other transport charges, depreciation and running expenses of delivery vans.

Apportionment of Selling and Distribution Overheads

Although, selling and distribution overheads differ in nature with each other, for the purpose of apportionment and absorption, both the overheads can be taken together. Selling and distribution overheads should be classified into two groups in order to charge them finally to products.

(*a*) *Direct overheads:* Direct overheads are the overheads which can be directly indentified with a particular product or products. For example, sales promotion expenses or transport charges incurred for a product should be charged directly to that product only.

(*b*) *Indirect overheads:* These are such selling and distribution overheads which cannot be identified with particular product or products. Such indirect overheads are apportioned using the following steps:

(1) *Collection and classification of overheads:* All selling and distribution overheads should be collected and classified according to their nature into certain groups such as advertising, exhibition, bad debts, depreciation of vehicles used for sale, discount, freight, heating, insurance, lighting, packing, postage, commission, rent, repairs, etc.

(2) *Apportionment of overheads:* After collecting and classifying overheads, they should be further allocated to one or more cost centres or departments or functions to which they relate. If any item (items) of overheads cannot be totally transferred to a particular department or functions it should be apportioned among the departments or functions on an equitable basis for which they have been incurred. Some examples of apportionment of overheads in terms of functions (or departments) are the following:

(*i*) *Direct selling:* This includes overheads such as expenses incurred on sales executive, sales staff, sales office expenses, etc.

(*ii*) *Advertisement and sales promotion:* This includes expenses incurred on exhibition, posters, cinema slides, distribution of samples, etc.

(*iii*) *Credit and collection:* This includes costs incurred on debt collection, bad debts, legal costs.

(*iv*) *Transportation:* Costs such as insurance for goods in transit, demurrage, maintenance staff, depreciation of transport vehicles are included in this group.

(*v*) *Warehousing and storage costs:* This includes expenses incurred on secondary packing for storage, warehouse rent, internal transport, insurance, etc.

(*vi*) *General administration:* This includes costs such as royalty on sales, sales invoicing maintenance of accounts, cost of investment in stocks.

The above costs which belong to different cost centres are subsequently apportioned to various areas or territories or zones on an equitable basis as shown in Fig. 19.2.

	Function	*Basis of Apportionment*	*Total Rs.*	*Territories*			
				I East zone	*II West zone*	*III North zone*	*IV South zone*
1.	Direct selling	Allocation					
2.	Advertising and sales promotion	Sales value					
3.	Credit & Collection	No. of orders or Cash collected					
4.	Transportation	Sales value					
5.	Warehousing	Sales value					
6.	General administration	No. of orders or No. of invoices or Sales value					

Fig. 19.2

(3) *Absorption of overheads:* After apportionment of overheads, selling and distribution overheads of each territory, or zone or area are charged to different products sold in that area or territory on a suitable basis. This may be done by one or more of the following methods:

(i) *Rule per article* — If this method is adopted, the overhead costs are divided by number of products sold in that territory during a certain period.

(ii) *A percentage of sales* — This is suitable for apportionment of direct selling costs, general administration, finance costs, etc. If selling overhead of a sales zone is Rs. 50,000 and the sales of that zone are Rs. 2,00,000, an addition should be made to the cost of products by 25% of the selling price of that product.

(iii) *A percentage of works cost* — Where selling overheads are small, this method can be adopted, even though various articles are produced, as little advantage would be gained by using a more complicated system.

(iv) *A percentage of cash collected* — This method may be used for apportionment of credit and collection costs such as bad debts, legal expenses, etc.

Illustration 13:

Following data is available relating to a company for a certain month:

	Territory		
	I	*II*	*III*
Selling expenses	Rs. 7,600	Rs. 4,200	Rs. 6,240
Distribution costs	Rs. 4,000	Rs. 1,800	Rs. 2,000
No. of units sold	Rs. 16,000	Rs. 6,000	Rs. 10,000
Sales	Rs. 76,000	Rs. 28,000	Rs. 52,000

The company adopts sales basis and quantity basis for application of selling and distribution costs, respectively. Compute (*a*) The territory-wise overhead recovery rates separately for selling and distribution costs, and (*b*) The amounts of selling and distribution costs chargeable to a consignment of 2,000 units of a product, sold in each territory at Rs. 4.50 per unit.

Solution:

(*a*) Computation of Overhead Recovery Rates

1. Selling Cost Recovery Rate = $\frac{\text{Selling Expenses}}{\text{Sales}} \times 100$

2. Distribution Cost Recovery Rate = $\frac{\text{Distribution Costs}}{\text{No. of Units Sold}}$

Territory	*Selling Cost Recovery Rate*	*Distribution Cost Recovery Rate*
I	$\frac{\text{Rs. } 7,600}{\text{Rs. } 76,000} \times 100 = 10\%$ on sales	$\frac{\text{Rs. } 4,000}{\text{Rs. } 16,000} = 25$ paise per unit
II	$\frac{\text{Rs. } 4,200}{\text{Rs. } 28,000} \times 100 = 15\%$ on sales	$\frac{\text{Rs. } 1,800}{\text{Rs. } 6,000} = 30$ paise per unit
III	$\frac{\text{Rs. } 6,200}{\text{Rs. } 52,000} \times 100 = 12\%$ on sales	$\frac{\text{Rs. } 2,000}{\text{Rs. } 10,000} = 20$ paise per unit

(*b*) Computation of Selling and Distribution Costs Chargeable to Consignment

Territory	*I*	*II*	*III*
No. of units sold	2,000	2,000	2,000
Sales at Rs. 4.50 per unit	9,000	Rs. 9,000	Rs. 9,000
Selling cost chargeable	900.00	Rs. 1,350.00	Rs. 1,080.00
Distribution cost chargeable	500.00	Rs. 600.00	Rs. 400.00
Total	Rs. 1,400.00	Rs. 1,950.00	Rs. 1,480.00

Illustration 14:

XYZ Ltd. a manufacturing company, having an extensive marketing network throughout the country, sells its products throughout four zonal sales offices, viz., A, B, C, and D. The budgeted expenditure for January 2008 are given below:

			Rs.
Sales Manager's salary			1,20,000
Expenses relating to Sales Manager's office			80,000
Travelling salesman's salaries			3,20,000
Travelling expenses			36,000
Advertisements			30,000
Godown Rent Zone	'A'	15,000	
	'B'	25,200	
	'C'	9,800	
	'D'	18,000	68,000
Insurance on inventories			20,000
Commission on sales @ 5% on Sales			6,00,000

The following further particulars are also available:

Zone	*Sales in Rs. lakh*	*No. of salesmen*	*Total mileage covered*	*Allocation of advertisement*	*Average stock in Rs. lakhs*
A	36	5	6,000	30%	6
B	48	6	14,000	30%	8
C	16	2	4,500	20%	4
D	20	3	5,500	20%	2

Based on the above details, compute zonewise selling overheads, as a percentage to sales.

Solution:

Books of XYZ Ltd.

Computation of Zonewise Selling Overhead Rates

Items of expense	*Basis of charge*	*Total Rs.*	*Zones*			
			A *Rs.*	*B* *Rs.*	*C* *Rs.*	*D* *Rs.*
Sales manager's salary	Sales	1,20,000	36,000	48,000	16,000	20,000
Sales manager's office exp.	Sales	80,000	24,000	32,000	10,667	13,333
Salesmen's salaries	No. of Salesmen	3,20,000	1,00,000	1,20,000	40,000	60,000
Travelling expenses	Mileage covered	36,000	7,200	16,800	5,400	6,600
Advertisement	Budgeted ratio	30,000	9,000	9,000	6,000	6,000
Godown rent	Actuals	68,000	15,000	25,200	9,800	18,000
Insurance	Average inventory	20,000	6,000	8,000	4,000	2,000

Commission on sales	Sales	6,00,000	1,80,000	2,40,000	80,000	1,00,000
Total overheads		12,74,400	3,77,200	4,99,000	1,71,867	2,25,933
Amount of sales		1,20,00,000	36,00,000	48,00,000	16,00,000	20,00,000

Overheads as a percentage of sales = $\frac{\text{Overhead}}{\text{Sales}} \times 100$

	10.62%	10.48%	10.40%	10.74%	11.30%

Illustration 15:

A company manufacturing a sole product sells it through three salesmen, A, B and C stationed in three regions. Besides, sales are also effected through a sales depot situated at the company's headquarters. The following information is obtained from the books of the company for December 2009.

Sales	Rs. 4 lakhs
Cost of sales	2.50 lakhs
Gross profit	1.50 lakhs, 37.5% of sales
Selling expenses:	
Salesmen's salaries	Rs. 3,500
Commission	22,000
Travelling expenses	9,000
Advertisement expenses	60,000
Other selling expenses	35,500
	Rs. 1,30,000
Net profit	Rs. 20,000, 5% of sales

The management is not satisfied with the net profit and asks you to investigate. You find that salesman B and C are paid salaries at Rs. 1,500 and Rs. 2,000 per month respectively besides a commission of 5% on sales. The salesman, A, however, receives a commission of 10% on sales but no salary. Travelling expenses paid were Rs. 2,000, Rs. 4,000 and Rs. 3,000 respectively for A, B and C. Advertising expenses were apportioned equally to A, B and C, after deducting a sum of Rs 3,000 spent in headquarters. Other selling expenses for headquarters amounted to Rs. 17,500, the rest being apportioned to A, B and C, on the basis of sales. The break-up of the sales was as follows:

Headquarters		Rs. 40,000
Salesman	A	80,000
	B	1,20,000
	C	1,60,000

Prepare a statement showing the individual profit or loss from each salesman. Comment on the results indicating your suggestions for improving the position.

Solution:

Statement of Profit and Loss

Items	*Total*	*Headquarters*	*Salesman*		
			A	*B*	*C*
Sales	Rs. 4,00,000	Rs. 40,000	Rs. 80,000	Rs. 1,20,000	Rs. 1,60,000
Less: Cost of sales (62.5% of sales)	2,50,000	25,000	50,000	75,000	1,00,000
Gross Profit	1,50,000	15,000	30,000	45,000	60,000
Salaries	3,500	—	—	1,500	2,000
Commission	22,000	—	8,000	6,000	8,000
Travelling	9,000	–	2,000	4,000	3,000
Advertising	60,000	3,000	19,000	19,000	19,000
Other selling expenses	35,500	17,500	4,000	6,000	8,000
	1,30,000	20,500	33,000	36,500	40,000
Net profit	20,000	– 5,500	– 3,000	8,500	20,000

According to the statement, the headquarters and the salesman A are showing a net loss of Rs. 5,500 and Rs. 3,000 respectively. In the case of headquarters, for a gross profit of Rs. 15,000 the selling expenses are Rs. 20,500, besides the sales being only Rs. 40,000. In spite of Rs. 19.000 being .spent on advertisement, the sales of the salesman A are only Rs. 80,000. The existing state of affairs at the headquarters may be corrected by cutting down selling costs or stop it from selling anything at all. In the case of the salesman A, attempt should be made to push up or change the salesman himself. If possible, the sales territory in charge of A may be closed down and attempts may be made to push up the sales of the other two territories.

TREATMENT OF SOME ITEMS OF EXPENSES

Interest on Capital

There is a difference of opinion as to whether interest on capital employed in manufacture should be treated as an item of cost.

The following arguments are advanced to support treating interest as an item of costs:

1. Interest is the reward of capital just as wages are the reward of labour. Profit, in the true sense, cannot be computed without considering interest.
2. The comparison of operations, different processes, etc. without due consideration of the interest factor may lead to unreliable conclusions.
3. Interest considers time factors as it is computed on the basis of time and time is regarded as an important factor in production.
4. The inclusion of interest is of particular importance where articles of different values are produced and the capital invested in each product line differs considerably.
5. The cost of carrying inventory cannot be determined without giving due recognition to the interest on capital employed in it.

The following arguments are against including interest in the cost accounts:

1. Cost accounting considers only actual expenditures and can include only interest paid.
2. The interest factor is in no way connected with cost of manufacture. Whatever may be the method of raising finances — owned capital, loans, debentures, etc. does not affect manufacturing cost. It only affects the profits of the period.

3. Inclusion of interest in product costing will inflate the values of inventory and work-in-progress and therefore will tend to increase the profit unreasonably.
4. Interest is calculated on capital and the term "capital" has many concepts such as total capital employed in business, both equity capital and borrowed capital.
5. A reliable and correct rate of interest is difficult to determine and is likely to be influenced by naked fluctuations.
6. The cost accounting and product costing systems get complicated unnecessarily by inclusive of interest on capital and financial statements also become misleading.

There is one point upon which opinion is not divided. If interest is to be considered at all, it must not be confined merely to such interest as may actually have been paid by the business. In other words, interest should be ignored entirely or else included in respect of the whole capital employed, whether such capital requires the payment of interest or not. Therefore, if it is decided to exclude interest from the cost accounts, interest which has been paid, must also be ignored.

Of late, cost accountants in India tend to agree that interest on capital or funds borrowed from outside and paid or to be paid in cash should be included in product cost. This has been supported on the grounds that it implies cash outflow and affects the operating results of a business firm. The Bureau of Industrial Costs and Prices in India includes actual interest on borrowed funds as an element of cost in cost price studies. However, the Bureau does not consider the notional type of interest (interest on owned capital) as an element of cost.

Depreciation

Depreciation is the diminution in the value of Fixed assets due to use and/or the lapse of time. The following are the methods of depreciation.

1. *Straight line method:* This method provides for depreciation by means of equal periodic charges over the life of the asset. For example, suppose the cost of a plant is Rs. 1,00,000 and its life is 10 years. Then the charge of depreciation per annum will be Rs. 10,000.
2. *Diminishing balance method:* This method tends to write-off higher amounts in the beginning and comparatively lower amounts in subsequent parts of the life of an asset. The amount of depreciation is calculated at a constant rate at the balance of the value of the asset after deducting the amounts of depreciation previously provided. For example, taking the above illustration, the amounts of depreciation at the rate of 10% p.a. would be Rs. 10,000 for the first year, Rs. 9,000 for the second year, Rs. 8,100 for the third year, and so on.
3. *Production unit method:* This method charges the amount of depreciation by means of fixed rate per unit of production calculated by dividing the value of the asset by the estimated number of units to be produced during its life. The formula for calculating depreciation under this method is as follows:

$$\text{Depreciation (per unit)} = \frac{\text{Original cost-residual value}}{\text{Estimated output during its life}}$$

4. *Annuity method:* This method assumes that the capital used in the purchase of plant should have earned interest if invested somewhere else. The amount of depreciation in this method is calculated by dividing the aggregate of the cost of the asset depreciated and interest at a given rate, at a constant rate, on the written down value of the asset.
5. *Sinking fund method:* Under the annuity method, expected interest on the investment (equivalent to the cost of the asset) is assumed. However, no actual investment is made.

But under the sinking fund method, the amount of depreciation written off every year is invested in some securities, which would accumulate at compound interest to provide, at the end of the life of the asset, a sum equal to its cost. This method provides for depreciation of fixed periodic charges.

6. *Endowment policy method:* This method is similar to the sinking fund method. It provides for depreciation by means of fixed periodic charges equivalent to the premium on an endowment policy for the amount required to provide, at the end of the life of the asset, a sum equal to its cost. The amount of depreciation is equivalent to the premium payable on the policy.
7. *Production hour method:* This method provides for depreciation by means of a fixed rate hour of production by using the following formula:

$$\text{Depreciation (per unit)} = \frac{\text{Cost of the asset}}{\text{Estimated number of working hours of its life}}$$

8. *Sum-of-the year digits method:* This method provides for depreciation by means of different periodic rates computed according to the following formula. If n is the estimated life of the asset, the rate is calculated for each period as a fraction in which the denominator is always the sum of the series 1, 2, 3,... n and the numerator for the first period is n, for the second period is n–1 and so on.

Rent

The rent payable by a manufacturer or businessman who does not have his own building is undoubtedly an expense which must be charged to production. In many cases, however, the premises are owned by the business and no rent is paid. In such circumstances, a charge in lieu of rent should be made in the cost accounts in order that the true cost of production may be ascertained.

Capacity

The term "capacity" signifies volume capacity of a business enterprise. It can be measured in the following manner.

1. *Maximum theoretical capacity:* It is that capacity of a plant or department which will be achieved under 100% operating time. It assumes round-the-clock operation of all plants with no allowance for machine downtime, waits and delays or holidays. It cannot be achieved in reality.
2. *Practical capacity:* The practical capacity of a plant is the theoretical maximum capacity less normal and unavoidable operating interruption, such as repairs, wait, breaks, machine failure, etc.
3. *Normal activity or capacity:* Normal capacity involves consideration of both the ability to produce and the ability to sell. For this, a sales budget is prepared which determines normal activity. This is a long-term measure that represents the practical plant capacity less the estimated idle capacity.
4. *Expected activity or capacity:* This capacity indicates the activity budgeted for the current year. It can be more or less than the normal activity level, but will never be more than the practical capacity. It is similar to normal capacity but for a short period of time.

The normal capacity concept is generally the most suitable for product cost determination which further help in determining selling prices and valuation of inventories for purposes of financial statements. Expected capacity level tends to increase product unit costs when lower output than normal capacity output is achieved.

Idle Capacity

Idle capacity denotes that plant, machinery and equipments are available for manufacturing or other purposes, but are not being used totally. The Institute of Cost and Management Accountants (U.K.) defines idle capacity cost as "the cost of abnormal idleness of fixed assets or available services." Idle capacity is the difference between the normal capacity and capacity utilised based on expected sales. For example, if the normal capacity of a plant is to produce 50,000 units a month, but the plant is being used to manufacture only 40,000 units per month due to some reason (say, a low market demand of the product), then, in such a situation 10,000 units will be treated as the idle capacity of the plant. The idle capacity may arise due to lack of product demand, non-availability of raw materials, shortage of skilled labour, absenteeism, shortage of power, fuel or supplies, seasonal nature of the product, etc.

Idle capacity costs are mostly fixed in nature and are to be incurred because of unused capacity. Such costs consist of depreciation, maintenance, insurance premium, rent, property taxes, certain utilities, management and supervisory salaries and similar annual expenses. These costs remain unabsorbed or unrecovered due to underutilisation of plant capacity. Idle capacity cost can be computed in the following manner:

$$\text{Idle capacity cost} = \text{Idle capacity} \times \frac{\text{Total overhead related to a plant}}{\text{Normal plant capacity}}$$

Idle capacity cost can be divided into normal and abnormal idle capacity cost. Under normal circumstances such as servicing of a machine, intermittent use of plant during the processing might cause idle capacity, such costs are treated as an overhead expense. If the idle capacity costs have occurred due to abnormal circumstances such as lack of work or jobs, such costs would be transferred to the costing profit and loss account and hence would not be included in the factory overheads. If the idle capacity cost is due to seasonal normal factors, then the cost would be charged to units produced by inflating overhead rates.

Idle Facilities

In a firm, idle facilities may be caused due to not using the facilities provided by fixed assets (such as plant, equipment, building, space etc.) and service functions (such as personnel services, productions services, material services etc.). The term idle facility is therefore broader and includes many factors causing idle facility besides including the factors responsible for idle capacity. The term 'idle facility' is considered different from 'idle capacity' in the sense that the idle capacity generally refers to underutilisation of production or plant capacity and idle capacity costs are mostly fixed in nature and cannot be absorbed or recovered due to underutilisation of plant capacity. If a part of total facilities is not being utilised due to any reason such as lack of power, lack of demand, non-availability of raw material, fuel etc., it is known as idle facilities. Idle facilities is different from idle time and in an organisation idle time may not be found although there exists idle facilities. The treatment of cost of idle facilities is similar to that of idle capacity cost.

Set-up Time

Often, machinery and support equipment must be adjusted before a particular operation or job can be started. The time involved in getting the equipment ready for production is usually traceable to a specific operation or job and therefore, would be regarded as part of the direct cost of the job. Alternatively, setting up cost can be normally treated as a factory overhead and charged to all products, jobs, etc.

Packing Expenses

In almost all business firms manufacturing some product, expenses are incurred on packing materials which are known as packing expenses. Packing materials usually include items such as wrapping paper bags, boxes, wood, twine, hoops, iron, cartons, glue, etc.

Packing expenses are treated in cost accounts in the following manner:

1. Prime packing materials, i.e., materials which are necessary for the product are charged to the cost of the product as an element of prime cost, e.g., paper required for wrapping in the manufacture of cigarettes.
2. Secondary packing materials are needed while delivering/transporting the products and such expenses are treated as distribution overhead.
3. Special packing material expenses if required by the customer, are charged directly to the job or product.
4. Fancy packing expenses to attract customers are selling overhead.
5. The overhead costs of the packing department should be apportioned to different products on some suitable basis such as labour cost, sale value of the product, if they cannot be charged directly to the product.

Research and Development

The cost of research specifically undertaken for a job or product may be regarded as a direct cost of that job and charged thereto. If costs on research and development are incurred for the general advantage, they may be charged to production overhead. Research directed towards the improvement of methods and current products may be treated as production overhead and should be charged to production generally. But costs incurred for the search of new products, discovery or development of new methods, products or processes are not connected with current production and should be charged directly to profit and loss account.

Bad Debts

From past experience, the average bad debts incurred may be determined. This figure should be expressed as a percentage of the credit sales of the business and the resulting figure included in the distribution overhead.

Catalogues and Price Lists

The production of catalogues is often costly and takes place at intervals of several years. For costing purposes the expenditure incurred including the cost of staff engaged in collecting the necessary information, is charged to a suspense account and a proportion of the costs is allocated to selling and distribution every year. In such a way, the full cost of the publication is recovered from sales by the time a new edition is brought out. In financial accounts the cost of catalogues is unusually written off in the year in which it is incurred.

Tools

In most manufacturing concerns, tools are used in the manufacture of articles. Tools include drills, reamers, plugs and dies, go and no-go gauges and general cutting tools for lathes, milling machines, shapers and the like. The accounting treatment of tools is as follows:

1. Tools are treated as indirect materials if they are used for more than one product. The cost associated with such tools would be equitably apportioned among different products.

2. Sometimes tools are requisitioned and acquired for a specific job or product to ensure better quality and lowest cost for the product. When the expenditures can be measured and traced to the product which will receive the exclusive benefit from the use of tool, they are charged directly to the product. In such a case tools are treated as direct expense.
3. Tools received with machines and equipment are capitalised as capital expenditure but tools purchased subsequently are only revenue expenditures.
4. In computing the machine hour rate (for absorption of overhead) the cost of tools, depreciation, repair and maintenance are taken into account.

Patterns

Patterns are used in foundry work, where molten metal, usually cast iron, is poured into moulds. Patterns are generally permanent. Basically, there are two possibilities. First, a foundry may design its own product which may be useful to buyers. Second, the foundry (often) makes castings to a particular design of requirement of its customers. In both the cases, the cost of the patterns is treated as direct expenses like special tools.

Designs

In a company engaged in the manufacture of some complete articles, the design function includes the following functions:

1. Originating and developing new products.
2. Improving and developing the current product lines according to changes in technology and customer's habits.
3. Specifying and communicating the standards of quality.
4. Interpreting the product in the form of product specifications and/or materials and parts lists.
5. Preparing drawings and plans to define and interpret each component for manufacture.

The cost of a design may be charged totally to a specific order from a customer or alternatively, the cost of design may be apportioned over a number of years as part of research and development expenses. In this way it can be treated as a deferred revenue expenditure.

Blue Prints

A drawing office in a manufacturing company prepares drawings and blue prints with respect to products or customer's orders. Blue prints are copies of drawings prepared for immediate use. The following accounting treatments are in practice:

1. The cost of blue prints for immediate use is charged direct to the specific product or customer's order.
2. The cost of drawings for specific products or jobs is charged directly to the specific products or jobs.
3. The cost of drawings for standard and regular products is depreciated over the period of their life and therefore only depreciated value is considered for the year ending.

Advertising

Normal advertising in trade journals, periodicals and newspapers, by posters, radio or television and the cost of publicity literature and samples are treated as selling and distribution overhead at the time they are incurred and apportioned over the various products. Expenditure on advertising of a more permanent nature without regard to any specific product or article such as extensive campaigning required to launch a new product must be considered as a whole and apportioned in a more or less arbitrary manner. Alternatively, such advertising costs can be capitalised and written off over a short period of years in the profit and loss account. In such a case advertising depends upon policy and not upon output.

Royalties

Royalties of general nature may be treated as part of selling overhead but those paid for the use of patents or the right to market particular products are normally charged direct.

THEORY QUESTIONS

1. What are the requisites of a good method of absorption of factory overhead?
2. Explain how would you treat under/over-absorption of overheads in cost accounts.
3. Discuss the secondary distribution of overheads.
4. Describe the different bases on which factory expenses can be apportioned. Describe the merits and suitability of each of them.
5. Write a detailed critical note on the direct labour cost method of absorption of factory overheads.
6. What information is necessary to calculate a machine hour rate for overhead absorption? State the conditions in which the method is most effective.
7. Discuss the importance of machine hours as a basis for the absorption of factory overheads.
8. Explain the concept of absorption of factory overheads.
9. What do you understand by classification, allocation and apportionment in relation to overhead expenses?
10. Briefly describe two ways of dealing with apportioning service department costs among departments which, in addition to doing work for the main operation departments, also serve one another.
11. State in short the reasons for the use of predetermined rates for factory overhead absorption.
12. Describe the "prime cost" method of absorption of factory overheads. Explain fully and illustrate the basic conditions necessary for its application.
13. Distinguish between cost allocation, cost apportionment and cost absorption.
14. Why do you consider departmentalisation of overheads necessary?
15. Explain the different methods for apportionment of Service Department's cost over Production Departments.
16. Explain why predetermined overhead absorption rates are preferred to overhead absorption rates calculated from factual information after the end of a financial period.
17. What are the causes of under/over absorption of factory overheads? How will you deal with these in cost accounts?
18. Explain the nature of administrative overheads. How are they apportioned to products?
19. Discuss the methods of absorption of selling and distribution overheads.
20. What problems are faced in applying administrative costs partly to the manufacturing and partly to the selling departments of a concern? How will you control administrative overhead of a concern?
21. Set out the main arguments in favour of inclusion of interest on capital in cost accounts.
22. How do you deal with the following in cost accounts:
    (*a*) Advertising.
    (*b*) Research and development cost
    (*c*) Bad debts.
    (*d*) Rent of factory buildings.
23. "Interest is a factor which cannot be disregarded by management." Comment on this statement.

24. The level of production activity fluctuates widely in your company from month to month. Because of this the incidence of depreciation on unit cost varies considerably. The management decides that you find out a suitable method to correct this.

25. In a manufacturing company where costing is done with a view to fix prices, state whether and, if so, to what extent the following items are included in cost:
   (*i*) Interest on borrowings
   (*ii*) Bonus and gratuity
   (*iii*) Depreciation on plant and machinery

26. Discuss the treatment of the following items in cost accounts:
   (*i*) Capacity cost
   (*ii*) Set-up time
   (*iii*) Packing expenses
   (*iv*) Blue print and design.

EXERCISES AND PROBLEMS

1. A manufacturing company has 2 Production Departments — X and Y and 3 Service Departments — Time keeping. Stores and Maintenance. The departmental summary showed the following expenses for October 2009.

	Rs.	*Rs.*
Production Departments:		
X	16,000	
Y	10,000	26,000
Service Departments:		
Time-keeping	4,000	
Stores	5,000	
Maintenance	3,000	12,000
		38,000

The other information are:

Particulars	*Production Departments*		*Service Departments*		
	X	*Y*	*Time-keeping*	*Stores*	*Maintenance*
No. of employees	40	30	20	16	10
No. of stores requisitions	24	20	—	—	6
Machine-hours	2,400	1,600	—	—	—

You are required to make departmental allocation of expenses.

(*Ans.:* Total overhead costs
Deptt. X Rs. 22,845
Deptt. Y Rs. 15,155)

2. Deccan Manufacturing Ltd. have three departments which are regarded as production departments. Service department's costs are distributed to these production departments using the "Step Ladder Method" of distribution. Estimates of factory overhead costs to be incurred by each department in the forthcoming year are as follows. Data required for distribution is also shown against each department:

Department	*Factory overhead Rs.*	*Direct labour hours*	*No. of employees*	*Area in sq. m.*
Production:				
X	1,93,000	4,000	100	3,000
Y	64,000	3,000	125	1,500
Z	83,000	4,000	85	1,500
Service				
P	45,000	1,000	10	500
Q	75,000	5,000	50	1,500
R	1,05,000	6,000	40	1,000
S	30,000	3,000	50	1,000

The overhead costs of the four service departments are distributed in the same order, viz., P, Q, R and S respectively on the following basis:

Department	*Basis*
P	Number of Employees
Q	Direct Labour Hours
R	Area in Square Metres
S	Direct Labour Hours

You are required to:

(*a*) Prepare a schedule showing the distribution of overhead costs of the four service departments to the three production departments; and

(*b*) Calculate the overhead recovery rate per direct labour hour for each of three production departments.

(*Ans.:* (*a*) Total overheads: Production Departments X Rs. 3,00,000, Y Rs. 1,35,000, Z Rs. 1,60,000
(*b*) Recovery rate: X Rs. 75, Y Rs. 45, Z Rs. 40.)

3. Modern Manufacturers Ltd. has three Production Departments P_1, P_2, P_3 and two Service Departments S_1 and S_2, the details pertaining to which are as under:

	P_1	P_2	P_3	S_1	S_2
Direct wages (Rs.)	3,000	2,000	3,000	1,500	195
Working hours	3,070	4,475	2,419	—	—
Value of machines (Rs.)	60,000	80,000	1,00,000	5,000	5,000
H.P. of machines	60	30	50	10	—
Light points	10	15	20	10	5
Floor space (Sq. ft.)	2,000	2,500	3,000	2,000	500

The following figures extracted from accounting records are relevant:

Rent and rates	Rs. 5,000
General lighting	600
Indirect wages	1,939
Power	1,500
Depreciation on machines	10,000
Sundries	9,695

The expenses of the Services Departments are allocated as under:

	P_1	P_2	P_3	S_1	S_2
S_1	20%	30%	40%	—	10%
S_2	40%	20%	30%	10%	—

Find out the total cost of Product X which is processed for manufacture in Departments P_1, P_2 and P_3 for 4, 5 and 3 hours respectively, given that its Direct Material Cost is Rs. 50 and Direct Labour Cost Rs. 30.

(*Ans.:* Total Cost of Product X Rs. 117.25.

4. You are supplied with the following information and required to work out the production hour rate of recovery of overheads in departments, A, B and C.

Particulars	*Total*	*Production Departments*			*Service Deptt.*	
		A	*B*	*C*	*P*	*Q*
Rent	12,000	2,400	4,800	2,000	2,000	800
Electricity	4,000	800	2,000	500	400	300
Indirect labour	6,000	1,200	2,000	1,000	800	1,000
Depreciation of machinery	5,000	2,500	1,600	200	500	200
Sundries	4,500	910	2,143	847	300	300
Working hour	—	1,000	2,500	1,400	—	—

Expenses of Service Department P and W are apportioned as under:

	A	*B*	*C*	*P*	*Q*
P	30%	40%	20%	—	10%
Q	10%	20%	50%	20%	—

(*Ans.:* Deptts. A Rs. 9.50, B Rs. 6; C Rs. 5)

5. From the following information relating to the machine "skylack" installed in a factory, work out the machine hour rate.

Purchase price of the machine with scrap value of zero — Rs. 90,000

Installation and incidental charges incurred on the machine — Rs. 10,000

Life of machine is 10 years of 2,000 working hours each year.

Repair charges 50% of depreciation. Machine consumes 10 units of electric power per hour @10 paise per unit; oil expenses @ Rs. 2 per day of eight hours; consumable stores @ Rs. 10 per day of eight hours. Two workers are engaged on the machine @ Rs. 4 per day of eight hours.

6. An engineering company, engaged in the manufacture of various heavy engineering products, has installed one Pegard Numerical Control Horizontal Borer for specialised manufacturing operations. Calculate machine hour rate on the basis of the following particulars:

(*i*) F.O.B. cost of machine, Rs. 24 lakhs, (*ii*) Customs duty, insurance, freight, etc. Rs. 11 lakhs, (*iii*) Installation expense: Rs. 3 lakhs, (*iv*) Cost of tools adequate for 2 years only Rs. 4 lakhs, (*v*) Cost of machine room Rs. 3 lakhs, (*vi*) Cost of air-conditioning for machine room Rs. 2 lakhs, (*vii*) Rate of interest on term loan to finance the above capital expenditure 12% per annum, (*viii*) Salaries, etc. for operators and supervisory staff Rs. 2 lakhs per year, (*ix*) Cost of electricity Rs. 11 per hour, (*x*) Consumption of stores Rs. 5,000 per month, (*xi*) Other expenses Rs. 5 lakhs per annum, (*xiii*) Assume rate of depreciation as 10% per annum on fixed assets, (*xiii*) Total working hour in the machine room is 200 hours in a month, (*xiv*) Loading and unloading time is 10% of machine time, (*xv*) You can make suitable assumptions, if necessary, for purpose of your computation.

(*Ans.:* Rs. 915.20)

7. A cost centre in a factory furnishes the following conditions:

Normal working hours per week	40 hours
Number of machines	15
Normal weekly loss of hours on maintenance, etc.	4 hours per machine
Estimated annual overhead	Rs. 1,55,520
Estimated direct wages rate	Rs. 3 per hour
Number of weeks worked per year	48

Actual results in respect of a 4-week period are:

Overhead incurred	Rs. 15,000
Wages incurred	Rs. 7,000
Machine hours produced	2,200

You are required to: (*a*) calculate the overhead rate per machine hour; and (*b*) the amount of under/over-absorption of both wages and overhead.

(***Ans.:*** (*a*) Rs. 6, (*b*) overhead under-absorbed Rs. 1,800; and wages over-absorbed Rs. 200.)

8. Compute the machine hour rate from the following data:

(*i*)	Total machine cost to be depreciated	Rs. 2,30,000
(*ii*)	Life 10 years	
(*iii*)	Depreciation on straight line	
(*iv*)	Departmental overheads (annual)	
	Rent	Rs. 50,000
	Heat and lighting	Rs. 20,000
	Supervision	Rs. 1,30,000
(*v*)	Department area	70,000 sq. ft.
	Machine area	2,500 sq. ft.
(*vi*)	26 machines in the department	
(*vii*)	Annual cost of reserve equipment for the machines	1,500
(*viii*)	Hours run on production	1,800
(*ix*)	Hours for setting and adjusting	200
(*x*)	Power cost Re. 0.50 per hour of running time	
(*xi*)	Labour (*a*) when setting and adjusting, full time attention; (*b*) when machine is producing; one man can look after 3 machines.	
(*xii*)	Labour rate Rs. 6 per hour	

(***Ans.:*** Machine hour rate Rs. 20.14)

9. (*a*) From the following data for the month of March 2008, compute the machine hour rate to be charged in respect of a job carried out during the month on a printing machine in a job printing press:

(*i*)	Cost of the printing machine	Rs. 77,000
(*ii*)	Estimate life of machine	10 years
(*iii*)	Anticipated scrap value at the end of 10 years	Rs. 5,000
(*iv*)	Normal working hours per month	600
(*v*)	Hours run on trial runs and job setting	20
(*vi*)	Hours lost due to repairs (normal)	50
(*vii*)	Hours lost due to power failure (abnormal)	80
(*viii*)	Cost of maintenance	3,300
(*ix*)	Supervisors' salary	800
(*x*)	Cost of printing ink, etc.	2,400
(*xi*)	Electricity charges	720
(*xii*)	Other fixed charges	3,000
(*xiii*)	Overtime hours worked to complete job on time	100
(*xiv*)	Rate of wages per nour (normal)	8
(*xv*)	Rate of wages per hour (overtime)	12
(*xvi*)	Rate of wages per hour (during power failure)	4

(*b*) If you were to quote for a job to be executed in July 2008 requiring 300 machine hours, to what extent, if any, would be guided by the machine hour rate of March 2008. Give reason for your answer.

(*Ans.:* (*a*) Machine hour rate Rs. 16.55

(*b*) Since there are equal number of days in March and July, the machine hour rate of March can be used for quoting the price of a job in the month of July 2008. However, adjustment may have to be made if there is any change in the variable costs such as ink, electricity charges, etc.

10. Sankalp Industries absorbs factory overhead costs at Rs. 2.50 per direct labour hour. Both opening and closing balance of work-in progress and finished goods inventories are zero.

The following data are available for the year 2009 and the fact that all goods produced have been sold:

Direct labour hours used	50,000
Direct labour cost	Rs. 1,00,000
Indirect labour cost	25,000
Indirect materials cost	10,000
Depreciation of plant and equipment	50,000
Miscellaneous factory overheads	50,000

Assuming that all goods produced have been sold —

(i) Calculate factory overheads incurred and factory overheads absorbed; and

(ii) Pass a journal entry for disposing of overhead or under-absorbed factory overheads.

(*Ans.:* Factory overhead incurred Rs. 1,35,000

Factory overhead absorbed Rs. 1,25,000

Plus supplementary overhead rate Rs. $\frac{10,000}{50,000 \text{ hrs.}}$ = Re. 0.20 per hour)

Job, Contract and Batch Costing

NATURE OF JOB COSTING

Job costing is a costing method applied to determine the cost of specific jobs or lots of production generally manufactured according to customers' specifications. The main feature of the job order costing system is that no two orders are necessarily alike and all orders do not pass through the same manufacturing process. Generally, the job order system is used by manufacturing concerns where an order is produced to a customer's specifications, such as building, contracting, machine tool manufacturing, furniture, foundries, job printing and general engineering. A job may be a product, unit, batch, sales order project, contract, service, specific programme or any other cost objective that is clearly distinguishable and unique in terms of materials and other services used.

Advantages

Job costing has the following advantages:

1. More accurate costing is possible because all costs are compiled and specifically identified with a specific order or product.
2. It is simple as the recording of direct materials and direct labour hours is done by product or job.
3. Job cost sheets can be used to control efficiency and estimate future work.
4. It provides a basis for comparing one job cost to another or for comparing a job cost sheet to a cost estimate.

Disadvantages

Job costing has the following disadvantages:

1. It requires detailed record-keeping for different jobs.
2. The record-keeping for different jobs may prove complicated.
3. A job may be charged for inefficiencies (downtime) although it has not caused it.

JOB COST SHEET AND JOB LEDGER

The focal point of a job order cost system is the cost sheet on which charges for direct materials, direct labour, and indirect manufacturing costs can be accumulated as work on a job order progresses. It is in summary form and records the job number and other specifications and descriptive information as given in the production order. The design of the cost sheet and the number of columns to be used must be determined in terms of departmental and manufacturing characteristics of the business operations. Basically, the recorded costs are grouped under three major headings: material costs, labour costs and applied manufacturing overhead costs. Figure 20.1 presents a specimen of a job cost sheet. When a product order is started in process, a cost sheet identified by a job number is set up in the accounting department.

ABC Company
Job Order Cost Sheet

Customer Name............................	Date..................	Job Order No..	
		Product Description..	
		Selling Price......................Total Cost..............	
		Cost Per Unit..	
	Department 1	*Department 2*	*Department 3*
Materials: Date(s) Requisition no. Amount			
Labour: Date(s) Job time card no. Amount			
Overhead: Rate/Basis Amount absorbed			

Cost Summary	Dept. 1	Dept. 2	Dept. 3	Total
Material	....	....	....	....
Labour	....	....	....	....
Overhead	....	....	....	....
Total	....	....	....	....
Units completed	....	....	Date Completed	....

Fig. 20.1 Specimen of a Job Cost Sheet

When the job order is finished/completed, the cost summary at the bottom of the form is completed and a unit cost for the job order is computed.

RECORDING COSTS ON JOBS

Materials Costs

Materials used in manufacturing and/or completing jobs are known as *direct materials* which become part of the finished product. Direct materials are directly charged to the job on which they are used and indirect materials or factory supplies are part of manufacturing overhead and are apportioned to the various jobs.

Labour Costs

Direct labour costs can be identified with specific jobs with the help of job time tickets. When a worker begins work on an order, the starting time is noted on the ticket; when the job order is finished, the stopping time is written in and the time spent on a job is noted. Earnings (wages) are then computed using the employee's hourly rate.

Direct Expenses

Generally speaking, direct expenses are directly charged to individual jobs for which they are incurred. The invoices (of direct expenses) as documentary evidence can be marked with the number of the jobs to which the cost is to be allocated.

Overhead

Overhead costs are usually charged to work-in-progress by means of a predetermined absorption rate calculated in advance of production. This is derived on the basis of budgeted figures.

RECORDING COMPLETED JOBS

When a job is finished, its cost is determined by totalling price costs and absorbed overhead. The cost sheet is then marked "completed" and removed from the job ledger. An entry is made to the proper account in the finished goods ledger.

When no unit on a Job order is completed, the total cost incurred on the job order so far becomes work-in-progress. Under job costing, the value of closing work-in-progress is obtained from the work-in-progress account. The work-in-progress at the end of an accounting period is carried forward to the subsequent accounting period as opening stock. The expenditure incurred on the job in this subsequent period is added to the opening stock.

Illustration 1:

The following information for the year ended 31st December, 2008 is obtained from the books and records of a factory:

	Completed Job *Rs.*	*W.I.P.* *Rs.*
Raw material supplied from stores	88,000	32,000
Wages	1,00,000	40,000
Chargeable expenses	10,000	4,000
Materials returned to stores	1,000	

Factory overheads are 80% of wages. Office overheads are 25% of factory cost and selling distribution overheads are 10% of cost of production.

The complete jobs realised Rs. 4,10,000. Write up:

(*i*) Work-in-progress Ledger Control Account

(*ii*) Completed Job Ledger Control Account; and

(*iii*) Cost of Sales Account.

Solution:

Consolidated Work-in-Progress A/c

Dr.			*Cr.*
	Rs.		*Rs.*
To Raw material consumed	32,000	By balance c/d	1,35,000
To Wages	40,000		
To Chargeable expenses	4,000		
To Factory overheads (80% of wages)	32,000		
Factory cost	1,08,000		
To Administrative overheads (25% of Rs. 1,08,000)	27,000		
	1,35,000		1,35,000

Note: Selling and distribution overhead has not been charged in Work-in-progress A/c.

Consolidated Completed Job A/c

Dr.				*Cr.*
		Rs.		*Rs.*
To Raw material consumed	88,000	87,000	By Customer's A/c (Amount of Jobs completed & Realised)	4,10,000
Less: Returned to store	(–) 1,000			
To Wages		1,00,000		
To Chargeable Expense		10,000		
To Factory overheads (80% of Rs. 1,00,000 of wages)		80,000		
Factory Cost		2,77,000		
To Admn. overheads (25% of Rs. 2,77,000)		69,250		
Cost of production		3,46,250		
To Selling and distribution overhead		34,625		
To N.P. transferred to P and L A/c		29,125		
		4,10,000		4,10,000

Cost of Sales Account

Dr.			*Cr.*
	Rs.		*Rs.*
To Material	87,000	By Balance c/d	3,80,875
To Wages	1,00,000		
To Direct Charges	10,000		
To Factory overhead (80% of wages)	80,000		
Factory cost	2,77,000		

To Admn. overheads (25% of Rs. 2,77,000)	69,250		
	3,46,250		
To Selling and distribution (10% of Rs. 3,46,250)	34,625		
Cost of sales	3,80,875		3,80,875

CONTRACT COSTING

Contract costing, sometimes known as terminal costing, follows the same principles as job costing and is used by such concerns as firms of builders and public works contractors who undertake work on a contract basis.

Following are the special features of contract costing:

1. The contractor begins work on a small number or large contracts in the course of a year.
2. The contracts are completed away from the contractor's premises.
3. The contracts may continue over more than one accounting period.
4. Materials are purchased and delivered direct to the contract site and/or are drawn from the central stores.
5. The payroll is prepared at either the site or at a central administrative office.
6. Sub-contractors may be employed, e.g., ventilation engineers, lift manufacturers, flooring specialists, etc.
7. Plant and equipment may be purchased, or hired for the duration of the contract from another business or from a central plant department.
8. Payment by the customer for various stages of the contract is made only on receipt of architect's certificate for the completed stage. A reduction called retention money is withheld by the customer until a specific period of time, agreed in the original contract, has passed.
9. The contract price is normally estimated in advance of the work. Additional work found necessary may be charged on a cost-plus basis. In addition, clauses may be inserted to allow the contractor to pass on to the customer additional costs incurred as a result of increase in material, labour and other costs.

RECORDING COSTS ON CONTRACT

Under contract costing, a contract is basically the cost unit and for the purpose of control, it can be regarded as a cost centre. Under contract costing only allocation is required directly to the contract. Overhead costs are normally incurred at the head office and are sometimes known only as storage costs. Such overhead costs tend to be of a small figure and are often absorbed on some arbitrary basis such as a percentage on prime cost.

A separate account, the contract account, is opened for each individual contract for the purpose of determining the profit or loss on each contract. In the contract account the following costs are recorded:

Materials

Materials required for a specific contract are debited to the contract account. Materials returned under the materials returned note are credited with the contract.

Materials transferred from one contract to another are recorded in material transfer notes; the contract receiving the material is debited and the contract giving the material is credited. Materials not required for current use are sometimes sold at the site, and the amount received from sale of materials is credited to the contract account, and any profit or loss, being the difference between the cost and sale value, is transferred to the profit and loss account. This also applies not only to materials, but also to sale of plant, machinery, tools, etc. At the end of the accounting period the value of materials remaining unutilised on site is carried forward as a charge against the next period. In the accounting year, the amount will be debited to the materials or stores at site account and credited to the contract account. Materials stolen or destroyed by fire are transferred to the profit and loss account and also shown on the credit side of the contract account.

The customer or contractee may supply certain materials from own stock to be utilised in construction work. Such materials should not be debited (charged) to the contract account: a separate memorandum record outside the account will be sufficient. Such materials do not affect the contract price.

Wages

Wages of all workers engaged on a particular contract are allocated direct to that contract, regardless of work they perform. Where workers move from one contract to another, time-sheets must be maintained and wages may be distributed on the basis of time spent under each contract. The wages of the head office and central stores are considered as overhead and are charged to contracts on an equitable basis. Wages accrued or outstanding at the end of the period should appear on the debit side of contract.

Expenses

All expenses other than material and wages are charged to individual contracts as and when they are incurred. Examples of such expenses are hire charge of plants obtained from outside, architects' and consultants' fees, electricity, insurance, etc.

Plant and Machinery

For use of plant and machinery in a particular contract, the depreciation may be charged in any one of the following ways:

1. When the plant has been specially purchased for a particular contract and will be exhausted at site, the total cost of the plant is debited to the contract in which it is used. When the contract is completed or the plant is no longer required, it may be sold at site and contract is credited with the sale proceeds. If it is not sold, the contract is credited with the depreciated (revalued amount) value. Thus the contract account stands debited with the amount of depreciation. This method has the drawback that the debit side is unnecessarily inflated with the plant value, and the cost of contract at first sight appears to be very high. In order to overcome this problem, the difference between the original cost at commencement and the depreciated value at the end of the period is obtained and charged to the contract account concerned as plant depreciation.
2. When the plant is sent to the contract site only for a short period, it is usual to charge the contract for the use on a daily or hourly basis. Depreciation is charged at an hourly rate for the hours the plant has worked. If the plant is taken on hire, only the hire charges are debited to the contract and not depreciation.

Sub-Contract

When a sub-contractor is engaged for a special work connected with the main contract, the work performed by the sub-contractor forms a direct charge to the main contract. The payments made to sub-contractors are charged in totals to the concerned contract account as direct expense and no detailed record, or break-up of the sub-contract amount is necessary for cost purposes.

Materials issued to the sub-contractor, free of charge, should be charged to the contract account. Heavy tools and equipment may be supplied to sub-contractor on a rental basis. The depreciation on these equipments should be charged to the contract account and the rental received is credited to it or shown as a deduction from the sub-contractor's bill.

VALUE AND PROFIT OF CONTRACT

As the contract work proceeds, the surveyor appointed by the contractee issues certificates to the effect that so much portion has been completed. The contractor will get money according to this certificate and a certain portion thereof shall be retained by the contractee. The money so retained is called retention money. For example, if a certificate has been issued for Rs. 2,00,000 and 70% has been paid. The following entries will be made:

First Method

1.	Contractee's account Dr.	2,00,000	
	To contract A/c		2,00,000
	(Being value of the work certified)		
2.	Bank A/c Dr.	1,40,000	
	To contractee's A/c		1,40,000
	(Being amount of cash received)		

Second Method

The amount of work certified will be debited to the work-in-progress account and credited to the contract account. The work-in-progress account is shown as an asset in the balance sheet after deducting the amount received from the contractee. Until the contract is completed, the amount received from the contractee is advance payment and is deducted from work-in-progress in the balance sheet. When the contract is completed, the contractee account is debited with the contract price. In the next year, the work-in-progress account is transferred to the debit side of the contract account. On completion of the contract, the contractee's personal account is debited and the contract account credited. Taking the above example, the journal entries will be as follows:

1.	Work-in-progress A/c	Dr.	Rs. 2,00,000	
	To Contract A/c			Rs. 2,00,000
	(Being amount received)			
2.	BankA/c	Dr.	Rs. 1,40,000	
	To Contractee's A/c			Rs. 1,40,000
	(Being amount received)			

Balance Sheet

Asset Side	*(Rs.)*	
Work-in-progress	2,00,000	
Less: Amount received	1,40,000	60,000

Such work which has not been so far approved by the contractee's architect or surveyor is termed as "work uncertified." It is valued at cost and credited to the contract account and debited to the work-in-progress account, which will be transferred in the next year to the debit side of the contract account.

Work certified and work uncertified can be found in the following manner:

Cost of Work Certified:
Cost of work to date
Less: Cost of work uncertified
Materials on hand
Plant at site
Cost of work certified

Cost of Work Uncertified:
Total cost to date
Less: Cost of work certified
Materials in hand
Plant at site
Cost of work uncertified

WORK-IN-PROGRESS

Work-in-progress includes the amount of work certified (valued at contract price) and the amount of work uncertified. The work-in-progress account will appear on the asset side of the balance sheet. The amount of cash received from the contractee and reserve for contingencies (as discussed in the case of incomplete contracts) will be deducted out of this amount. The work-in-progress account appears as follows in the balance sheet:

1. When work certified has been treated according to the first method:

Balance Sheet as on ________

Work-in-progress:
Balance in the contractee's A/c
Add: Work uncertified
Less: Reserve for unrealised profit

2. When work certified has been treated according to the second method:

Balance Sheet as on ________

Work-in-progress:
Value of work certified ________
Cost of work uncertified ________
Less: Reserve for unrealised profit ________
Less: Amount received from contractee ________

In contract accounts the value of work-in-progress consists of: (*i*) the cost of work completed both certified and uncertified, (*ii*) the cost of work not yet complete; and (*ii*) the amount of profit taken as credit. Taking these into account, the work-in-progress in the balance sheet can be shown as follows:

Balance Sheet as on ________

Work-in-progress:
Cost of work certified
Cost of work uncertified
Less: Amount received from contractee
Add: Profit taken as credit to profit and loss A/c

PROFIT ON INCOMPLETE CONTRACTS

Many contracts take more than one financial accounting year to be completed. A problem arises whether profit on such a contract should be worked out only on its completion or whether some profits may be computed every year. The conservative method is to value work-in-progress only at cost and no credit is taken for profit till it is actually earned. This method, however, results in wide fluctuations in the net profit of the enterprise from year to year. If several contracts are completed in a year, the profit will be high while in extreme cases in some years, when not a single contract is fully completed, the profit will be nil. It becomes necessary, therefore, to compute profit on partly completed contracts and take credit for a part of it in the accounts at the year end.

The manner of computation of profit is largely dependent upon how for the contract has advanced, *i.e.*, the stage of completion it has reached.

1. Profit should be considered in respect of work certified only, work uncertified should always be valued at cost.
2. For contracts which have been completed less than one-fourth of the contract, no profit should be computed and credited to the profit and loss account.
3. In case of contracts which are complete by more than 25% but less than 50%, one-third of notional profit, reduced in the ratio of cash received to work certified, is transferred to profit and loss A/c. The balance in the notional profit is carried forward in the same contract as profit in suspense as a provision against future losses, increase in costs and other contingencies. The following formula is used to determine the amount or profit to be transferred to profit and loss A/c:

$$\frac{1}{3} \times \text{Notional Profit} \times \frac{\text{Cash Received}}{\text{Work Certified}}$$

   Normal profit is the difference between the value of work certified and cost of work certified. It is determined in the following manner:

   Notional profit = Value of work certified – (cost of work to date – cost of work not yet certified)
4. In case contracts are complete between 50% and 90%, two-third of notional profit, reduced by the proportion of cash received to work certified, is transferred to profit and loss A/ c. The formula to be used for this purpose is:

$$\frac{2}{3} \times \text{Notional Profit} \times \frac{\text{Cash Received}}{\text{Work Certified}}$$

5. In case contracts are complete by 90% or more than 90%, the contract is considered almost complete. In such contracts, the estimated total profit is first determined by deducting the total costs to date and additional expenditure necessary to complete the contract from the contract price. A portion of this estimated total profit is credited to profit and loss A/c, which can be determined by using any one of the following formulae:

   (*i*) $\text{Estimated Profit} \times \frac{\text{Work Certified}}{\text{Contract Price}}$

$$(ii)\ \text{Estimated Profit} \times \frac{\text{Work Certified}}{\text{Contract Price}} \times \frac{\text{Cash Received}}{\text{Work Certified}}$$

or

$$\text{Estimated Profit} \times \frac{\text{Cash Received}}{\text{Work Certified}}$$

The second formula is preferable to first formula. In case estimated profit cannot be determined due to some reason, *e.g.*, if additional expenditure is not mentioned, then the amount of profit to be transferred to profit and loss A/c is determined using the following formula:

$$\text{Notional Profit} \times \frac{\text{Work Certified}}{\text{Contract Price}}$$

6. The total of loss, if any, should be transferred to the profit and loss account by crediting the contract account.

In contract accounting, the profit earned on contracts is reduced proportionately by the amount of cash received, otherwise the unrealised profit may stand for distribution as dividends. Also, the sound principle of conservatism requires that all future contingencies and possible losses should he accounted for before determining the profit on contract.

COST-PLUS CONTRACT

A cost-plus contract is a contract in which the value of the contract is determined by adding a fixed margin of profit to the total cost of the contract. The contractee agrees to pay this inflated value of contract which includes a profit margin as per the agreement. Both the parties determine in advance the possible costs that would be included in the cost of contract. The profit to be added to the cost of contract may be agreed as a percentage on cost or the capital employed. Cost-plus contracts are generally needed when the costs of contracts cannot be accurately determined due to unstable and fluctuating conditions of materials, labour and service, etc. The price of materials, labour and services usually tend to fluctuate over a long period.

Cost-plus contracts are useful to both the parties, contractor (manufacturer), contractee (Customer). The contractor is suitably protected against any fluctuations in the prices of materials, labour, and over-head which will be used in production or completion of the job. A cost-plus contract is beneficial to the contractee (customer) also. The contractee is protected against an uncertain market which may push up the cost of the contract. The price agreed to be paid by the contractee is based on actual cost. In this way, the contract price is not determined arbitrarily.

Sometimes a contract may contain an "escalator clause" which provides for change in the price of the contract due to change in the prices of the raw materials, labour and overhead services. The contractor presents evidential proof of increased costs to the contractee to claim reimbursements. Under the escalator clause the contract price is increased for a given increase in the prices of inputs. For instance, it may be agreed that if the prices of raw materials go up by 15%, the contract price will be increased by 2%.

Illustration 2:

Compute a conservative estimate of profit on a contract (which is 80% complete) from the following particulars. Illustrate at least four methods of computing the profit:

		Rs.
(i)	Total expenditure to date	1,02,000
(ii)	Estimated further expenditure to complete the contract (including contingencies)	20,400
(iii)	Contract price	1,83,600
(iv)	Work certified	1,20,000
(v)	Work uncertified	10,200
(vi)	Cash received	97,920

Solution:

Profit on incomplete contracts may be calculated according to any of the following four methods:

		Rs.
Total Contract Price		1,83,600
Less: Expenditure to date	1,02,000	
Estimated further expenditure	20,400	1,22,400
Estimated Profit		61,200

Profit to be taken to P&L Account:

Ist Method:

$$\frac{61{,}200}{1{,}83{,}600} \times 1{,}20{,}000 = \text{Rs. } 40{,}000$$

IInd Method:

$$\text{Estimated profit} \times \frac{\text{Work certified}}{\text{Contract price}} \times \frac{\text{Cash received}}{\text{Work certified}}$$

$$61{,}200 \times \frac{1{,}20{,}000}{1{,}83{,}600} \times \frac{97{,}920}{1{,}20{,}000} = \text{Rs. } 32{,}640$$

IIIrd Method:

$$\text{Estimated profit} \times \frac{\text{Cost of work to date}}{\text{Estimated total cost}}$$

$$61{,}200 \times \frac{1{,}02{,}000}{1{,}22{,}400} = \text{Rs. } 51{,}000$$

IVth Method:

$$\text{Estimated profit} \times \frac{\text{Cost of work to date}}{\text{Estimated total cost}} \times \frac{\text{Cash received}}{\text{Work certified}}$$

$$61{,}200 \times \frac{1{,}02{,}000}{1{,}22{,}400} \times \frac{97{,}920}{1{,}20{,}000} = \text{Rs. } 41{,}616$$

Alternatively, notional profit can be used to determine amount to be transferred to P & L a/c.

Notional profit = Work Certified + Work uncertified – Total expenditure

= Rs. 1,20,000 + 10,200 – 1,02,000

= Rs. 28,200

Since more than half the work is complete, the profit to be taken in P & L Account may be reduced to 2/3 as shown below:

Rs. 28,200 × 2/3 =Rs. 18,800

The profit calculated as above (Rs. 18,800) may further be reduced on cash basis;

$$\text{Rs. } 18{,}800 \times \frac{97{,}920}{1{,}20{,}000} = \text{Rs. } 15{,}340$$

Illustration 3:

An expenditure of Rs. 1,94,000 has been incurred on a contract to the end of 31st March, 2008. The value of work certified is Rs. 2,20,000. The cost of work done but not yet certified is Rs. 6,000. It is estimated that the contract will be completed by 30th June, 2008 and an additional expenditure of Rs. 40,000 will have to be incurred to complete the contract. The total estimated expenditure on the contract is to include a provision of 2½ % for contingencies. The contract price is Rs. 2,80,000 and Rs. 2,00,000 has been realised in cash upto 31st March, 2008.

Calculate the proportion of Profit to be taken to the Profit and Loss Account as on 31st March. 2008 under different methods.

Solution:

	Rs.
(i) Total Profit	
Total Expenditure upto 31st March, 2008	1,94,000
Less: Cost of work uncertified	6,000
Cost of work certified	1,88,000
Value of work certified	2,20,000
Total profit =	32,000

		Rs.
(ii) Estimated Profit:		
Expenditure upto 31-3-2008		1,94,000
Estimated additional expenditure		40,000
		2,34,000
Add: 2½% of contingencies	$\frac{2{,}34{,}000 \times 5}{100 \times 2}$	5,850
Estimated Total Cost		2,39,850
Contract Price		2,80,000
Estimated Profit =		40,150

(iii) Profit taken to the credit of P & L A/c

(a) Estimated Profit × $\frac{\text{Certified work}}{\text{Contract price}}$

$$= 40{,}150 \times \frac{2{,}20{,}000}{2{,}80{,}000} = \text{Rs. } 31{,}546.42$$

(*b*) By Applying conservative method:

$$\text{Estimated Profit} \times \frac{\text{Cash Received}}{\text{Contract Price}}$$

$$40{,}150 \times \frac{2{,}00{,}000}{2{,}80{,}000} = \text{Rs. } 28{,}678.57$$

Illustration 4:

Paramount Engineers are engaged in construction and erection of a bridge under a long-term contract. The cost incurred unto 31-03-2009 was as under:

Fabrication	*Rs. in lakhs*
Direct Materials	280
Direct Labour	100
Overheads	60
	440
Erection costs to date	110
	550

The contract price is Rs. 11 crores and the cash received on account till 31-03-2009 was Rs. 6 crores.

A technical estimate of the contrast indicates the following degree of completion of work.

Fabrication — Direct Material — 70%, Direct Labour and Overheads 60%, Erection — 40%. You are required to estimate the profit that could be taken to Profit and Loss Account against this partly completed contract as at 31-03-2009.

Solution:

Estimation of Profit to be taken to Profit and Loss Account against partly completed contract as at 31-3-2009.

$$\text{Profit to be taken to P/L Account} = \frac{2}{3} \times \text{Notional profit} \times \frac{\text{Cash received}}{\text{Work certified}}$$

(Refer to working notes 1, 2, 3 & 4)

$$= \frac{2}{3} \times \text{Rs. } 92.48 \text{ lakhs} \times \frac{\text{Rs. } 600 \text{ lakhs}}{\text{Rs. } 642.48 \text{ lakhs}}$$

$$= \text{Rs. } 57.576 \text{ lakhs}$$

Working Notes:

1. Statement showing estimated profit to date and future profit on the completion of contract

(Rs. in lakhs)

Particulars	*Cost to date*		*Further costs*		*Total*
	% completion to date	*Amount Rs. (a)*	*% completion to be done*	*Amount Rs. (b)*	*Cost Rs. (a) + (b)*
Fabrication costs:					
Direct material	70	280.00	30	120.00	400.00
Direct labour	60	100.00	40	66.67	166.67
Overheads	60	60.00	40	40.00	100.00
Total fabrication costs (A)		440.00		226.67	666.67
Erection cost (B)	40	110.00	60	165.00	275.00
Total estimated cost (A + B)		550.00		391.67	941.67
Profit *(Refer to working note 2)*		92.48		65.85	158.33
		642.48		457.52	1,100.00

2. Profit to date (Notional Profit) and future profit are calculated as below:

$$\text{Profit to date (Notional Profit)} = \frac{\text{Estimated profit on whole contract} \times \text{Cost to date}}{\text{Total cost}}$$

$$= \frac{\text{Rs.}\,158.33 \times \text{Rs.}\,550}{\text{Rs.}\,941.67}$$

$$= \text{Rs. } 92.48 \text{ (lakhs)}$$

$$\text{Future profit} = \text{Rs. } 158.33 - \text{Rs. } 92.48$$

$$= \text{Rs. } 65.85$$

3. Work certified:

= Cost of the contract to date + Profit to date

= Rs. 550 + Rs. 92.48 = Rs. 642.48 lakhs

4. Degree of Completion of Contract to date:

$$= \frac{\text{Cost of the contract to date}}{\text{Contract pice}} \times 100$$

$$= \frac{\text{Rs. } 642.48 \text{ lakhs}}{\text{Rs. } 1{,}100 \text{ lakhs}}$$

$$= 58.40\%.$$

Illustration 5:

Pioneer Construction Company Ltd. obtained a contract for the erection of a multi-storey building. Building operations started in July 2007. The contract price was Rs. 9,00,000. On 30th June 2008, the end of the financial year, the cash received on account was Rs. 3,60,000, being 80% of the amount on the surveyor's certificate.

The following additional information is given:

	Rs.
Materials issued to contract	1,80,000
Materials on hand at site as on 30th June 2008	7,500
Wages	2,46,600
Plant purchased specially for contract and to be depreciated at 10% per annum	30,000
Direct expenses incurred	12,900
General overhead allocated to contract	7,600
Work finished but not yet certified, cost	15,000

You are required to prepare the contract account and statement showing the profit on the contract to 30th June 2008 indicating what proportion of the profit the company would be justified in taking to the credit of the profit and loss account, and to show what entries in respect of the contract would appear in the balance sheet.

Solution:

Pioneer Construction Co. Ltd.

2008		*Rs.*	*2008*		*Rs.*
June 30	To Materials	1,80,000	June 30	By Plant at site	27,000
	To Plant	30,000		By Materials in hand	7,500
	To Wages	2,46,600		By Cost of contract c/d	4,42,600
	To Direct expenses	12,900			
	To General overheads	7,600			
		4,77,100			4,77,100
	To Cost of contract b/d	4,42,600		By Work-in-progress:	
	To Profit and loss A/c	11,946		Work certified	4,50,000
	To Work-in-progress (Reserve)	10,454		Work uncertified	15,000
		4,65,000			4,65,000

Statement Showing Computation of Profit Taken to Profit and Loss Account

Profit made to date	Rs. 22,400
Profit taken to profit and loss account	
$22{,}400 \times \frac{2}{3} \times \frac{80}{100}$	11,946
(since half the contract is complete 2/3rd profit as reduced on cash basis may safely be taken to the profit and loss A/c)	
Profit taken back to W.I.P. being reserve carried forward	10,454

Extract from the Balance Sheet as on 30th June, 2008

		Rs.	
	Assets:		
	Plant at site: cost	30,000	
Less:	Depreciation provided	3,000	Rs. 27,000
	Current assets:		
	Work-in-progress. Work certified	4,50,000	
	Work uncertified	15,000	
		4,65,000	

Less: Balance of profit not taken to profit and loss	10,454	
	4,54,546	
Less: Cash received from contractee	3,60,000	
	94,546	
Add: Materials at site	7,500	1,02,046

Illustration 6:

	2007	*2008*
	Rs.	*Rs.*
Materials issued	3,00,000	84,000
Direct wages	2,30,000	1,05,000
Direct expenses	22,000	10,000
Indirect expenses	6,000	1,400
Work certified	7,50,000	10,00,000
Work uncertified	8,000	—
Materials at site	5,000	7,000
Plant issued	14,000	2,000
Cash received from contractor	6,00,000	10,00,000

The value of plant at the end of 2007 and 2008 was Rs. 7,000 and Rs. 5,000 respectively.

Prepare: (*i*) the contract account and (*ii*) contractee account for two years 2007 and 2008 taking into consideration such profit for transfer to the profit and loss account as you think proper.

Solution:

Contract Account for 2007

	Rs.			*Rs.*
To Materials issued	3,00,000	By Materials at site		5,000
To Direct wages	2,30,000	By Plant at site		7,000
To Direct expenses	22,000	By Work-in-progress:		
To Indirect expenses	6,000	Work certified	7,50,000	
To Plant issued	14,000	Work uncertified	8,000	
To Profit c/d	1,98,000			7,58,000
	7,70,000			7,70,000
To Profit and loss A/c	1,05,600	By Profit b/d		1,98,000
To Work-in-progress	92,400			
	1,98,000			1,98,000

Profit taken to profit and loss account: $\text{Total Profit} \times \frac{2}{3} \times \frac{\text{Cash received}}{\text{Work certified}}$

$$= \text{Rs. } 1{,}98{,}000 \times \frac{2}{3} \times \frac{5{,}00{,}000}{7{,}50{,}000}$$

Contract Account for 2008

	Rs.		Rs.
To Materials at site b/d	5,000	By Materials at site	7,000
To Plant at site b/d	7,000	By Plant at site	5,000
To Work-in-progress b/d	6,65,600	By Contractee A/c	10,00,000
To Materials issued	84,000		
To Direct wages	1,05,000		
To Direct expenses	10,000		
To Indirect expenses	1,400		
To Plant issued	2,000		
To Profit and loss A/c	1,32,000		
	10,12,000		10,12,000

Contractee's Account for 2007 and 2008

2007	Rs.	2007	Rs.
To Balance c/d	6,00,000	By Bank	6,00,000
	6,00,000		6,00,000
2008	**Rs.**	**2008**	**Rs.**
To Contract A/c	10,00,000	By Balance b/d	6,00,000
		By Bank	4,00,000
	10,00,000		10,00,000

Illustration 7:

Alcon Construction Company Ltd. commenced its business of construction on 1-1-2007. The Trial Balance as on 31-12-2007 showed the following balances:

	Dr. (Rs.)	Cr. (Rs.)
Paid-up share capital		1,00,000
Cash received on account of contract (80% of work certified)		1,20,000
Land and buildings	30,000	
Machinery at cost (75% at site)	40,000	
Bank	4,000	
Materials at site	40,000	
Direct labour	55,000	
Expenses at site	2,000	
Lorries and vehicles	30,000	
Furniture	1,000	
Office equipment	10,000	
Postage and telegrams	500	
Office expenses	2,000	
Rates and taxes	3,000	
Fuel and power	2,500	
	2,20,000	2,20,000

The contract price is Rs. 3,00,000 and work certified is Rs. 1,50,000. The work completed 'since certification' is estimated at Rs. 1,000 (at cost). Machinery costing Rs. 2,000 was returned to stores at the end of the year. Stock of materials at site on 31-12-2007 was of the value of Rs. 5,000. Wages outstanding were Rs. 200. Depreciation on machinery at 10%.

You are required to calculate the profit from the contract and show how the work-in-progress will appear in the balance sheet as on 31-12-2007.

Solution:

Alcon Construction Company Ltd.

Contract Account

Dr.				*Cr.*
	Rs.			*Rs.*
To Materials	40,000	By Work certified		1,50,000
To Direct labour	55,000	By Work uncertified		1,000
To Expenses	2,000	By Materials at site		5,000
To Wages outstanding	200	By Machinery		
To Fuel & power	2,500	At site	25,200	
To Machinery at site	30,000	Returned to stores	1,800	
				27,000
To Balance c/d	53,300			
	1,83,000			1,83,000
To Profit & Loss a/c	28,427	By Balance b/d		53,300
To Work-in-progress (Reserve)	24,873			
	53,300			53,000

1. Profit taken to P&L A/c

$$\text{Profit} = \text{Notional profit} \times \frac{\text{Cash certified}}{\text{Work certified}} \times \frac{2}{3}$$

$$= 53{,}300 \times \frac{80 \times 2}{100 \times 3} = \text{Rs. } 28{,}427$$

$$= 53{,}300 - \text{Rs. } 28{,}427 = \text{Rs. } 24{,}873$$

Balance Sheet as on 31st Dec. 2007

	Rs.
Assets:	
Work-in-progress:	
Work certified	1,50,000
Cost of work Uncertified	1,000
	1,51,000
Less: Reserve	24,873
	1,26,127
Less: cash received from contractee	1,20,000
	6,127

Illustration 8:

The following is the trial balance of Cosmos Construction Limited, engaged in the execution of Contract No. 303, for the year ended 31st December, 2007.

	Rs.	*Rs.*
Contractee's Account: 75% of work certified		3,60,000
Accumulated depreciation account		50,000
Creditors		12,000
Buildings	2,00,000	
Bank balance	45,000	
Share capital		5,00,000

Materials	2,00,000	
Wages	1,80,000	
Expenses	47,000	
Plant	2,50,000	
	9,22,000	9,22,000

The work on Contract No. 303 was commenced on 1st January, 2007.

Materials costing Rs. 1,70,000 were sent to the site of the contract but those costing Rs. 6,000 were destroyed in an accident. Plant costing Rs. 50,000 was used on the contract all through the year. Plant with a cost of Rs. 2 lakhs was used from 1st January to 30th September. 2007 and was then returned to the stores.

The contract was for Rs. 6,00,000 and the contractee pays 75% of the work certified. The cost of work uncertified was estimated to be Rs. 15,000 on 31st December, 2007, on which date materials costing Rs. 4,000 were at the site of the contract.

Expenses are charged to the contract at 25% of wages. Plant is to be depreciated at 10% according to the straight line method for the entire year.

Prepare Contract No. 303 Account for the year 2007 and make out the Balance Sheet of Cosmos Construction Limited as on 31st December, 2007.

Solution:

Cosmos Construction Co.

Contract No. 303 A/c

Particulars		*Rs.*	*Particulars*		*Rs.*
To Materials issued		1,70,000	By Work-in-progress		
To Wages		1,80,000	Certified	4,80,000	
To Expenses (25% of wages)		45,000	Uncertified	15,000	4,95,000
To Depreciation of plant			By Materials at site		4,000
10% on Rs. 50,000 =	5,000		By Materials destroyed		6,000
10% on Rs. 2,00,000 = (for 9 months)	15,000	20,000			
To Balance c/d		90,000			
		5,05,000			5,05,000
To Profit & Loss A/c		45,000	By Balance b/d	90,000	
To Reserve		45,000			
		90,000			90,000

Transfer to Profit and Loss A/c is calculated as under = Rs. $90,000 \times \frac{75}{100} \times \frac{2}{3}$ = Rs. 45,000

Work certified: Contractee pays 75% of the work certified. Hence work certified will be Rs. $4,80,000\left(3,60,000 \times \frac{100}{75}\right)$. Rs. 3,60,000 has been paid to the contractor:

Profit and Loss A/c

	Rs.		Rs.
To Materials destroyed	6,000	By Contract A/c	45,000
To Depreciation A/c (Not charged to contract)	5,000		
To Unabsorbed expenses	2,000		
To Balance c/d	32,000		
	45,000		45,000

Balance Sheet as on 31st December 2007

	Rs.			Rs.
Capital	5,00,000	Bank balance		45,000
Profit & Loss A/c	32,000	Building		2,00,000
Creditors	12,000	Materials		30,000
		Materials at site		4,000
		Work-in-progress:		
		Work certified	4,80,000	
		Uncertified	15,000	
			4,95,000	
		Less: Reserve	45,000	
			4,50,000	
		Less: Cash received	3,60,000	90,000
		Plant	2,50,000	
		Less: Depreciation (50,000 + 20,000 + 5,000)	75,000	1,75,000
	5,44,000			5,44,000

Illustration 9:

Surya Construction Ltd. with a paid-up share capital of Rs. 50 lakhs undertook a contract to construct MIG apartments. The work commenced on the contract on 1st April 2006. The contract price was Rs. 60 lakh. Cash received on account of the contract upto 31st March, 2007 was Rs. 18 lakh (being 90% of the work certified). Work completed but not certified was estimated at Rs. 1,00,000. As on 31st March 2007 material at site was estimated at Rs. 30,000, machinery at site costing Rs. 2,00,000 was returned to stores and wages outstanding were Rs. 5,000. Plant and machinery at site is to be depreciated at 5%.

The following were the ledger balance (Dr.) as per trial balance as on 31st March 2007:

	Rs.
Land and Building	23,00,000
Plans and Machinery (60% at site)	25,00,000
Furniture	60,000
Materials	14,00,000
Fuel and Power	1,25,000
Site expenses	5,000
Office expenses	12,000
Rates and taxes	15,000
Cash at Bank	1,33,000
Wages	2,50,000

Prepare the Contract Account and Balance Sheet.

Solution:

Contract Account

Dr.					*Cr.*
		Rs.			*Rs.*
To Materials	14,00,000		By Work certified		
Less: Material at site	(–) 30,000	13,70,000	$\frac{18,00,000 \times 100}{90} =$	20,00,000	
To Wages	2,50,000		By Work uncertified	1,00,000	21,00,000
Add: O/s	+ 5,000	2,55,000			
To Fuel & Power		1,25,000			
To Site expenses		5,000			
To Office expenses		12,000			
To Rates & Taxes		15,000			
To Depreciation on Machine at site $\left(\frac{25,00,000 \times 60 \times 5}{100 \times 100}\right)$		75,000			
To Balance c/d		2,43,000			
		21,00,000			21,00,000
To Profit and loss A/c $2,43,000 \times \frac{1}{3} \times \frac{90}{100}$		72,900	By Balance b/d		2,43,000
To Reserve transferred to W/P		1,70,100			
		2,43,000			2,43,000

Working Notes: (1) Work Certified

	Rs.
$\frac{18,00,000 \times 100}{90} =$	20,00,000
Less: Cash Received =	18,00,000
	2,00,000
Less: Profit transferred to WIP	1,70,100
	29,900
Add: Work uncertified	1,00,000
Work-in-progress	1,29,000

(2) No depreciation has been charged on Land and Building and as the same have not been shown at site.

(3) Machinery returned to stores Rs. 2,00,000 – 5% of Rs. 2,00,000
= Rs. 2,00,000 – 10,000
= Rs. 1,90,000

Balance Sheet
as on 31st March 2007

Liabilities	*Amt.(Rs.)*	*Assets*		*Amt (Rs.).*
Authorised and subscribed capital	—	Work in progress		1,29,900
Issued and paid-up capital	50,00,000	Land and Building		23,00,000
O/s Wages	5,000	Machinery		
Profit and loss a/c	72,900	At site	15,00,000	
		(–) Depreciation	(–) 75,000	
			14,25,000	
		(–) Returned	(–) 1,90,000	12,35,000
		Machinery at office	10,00,000	
		(+) Returned from site	+ 1,90,000	11,90,000
		Furniture		60,000
		Bank		1,33,000
		Materials at site		30,000
	50,77,900			50,77,900

Illustration 10:

A contractor, who prepares his account on 31st December each year, commenced a contract on 1st April, 2007. The costing records concerning the said contract reveal the following information on 31st December 2007.

Materials charged to site	Rs. 2,58,100
Labour engaged	5,60,500
Foremen's salary	79,300

Plants costing Rs. 2,60,000 had been on site for 146 days. Their working life is estimated at 7 years and their final scrap value at Rs. 15,000. A supervisor, who is paid Rs. 4,000 p.m., has devoted approximately three-fourths of his time to this contract. The administrative and other expenses amounts to Rs. 1,40,000. Materials in hand at site on 31st December, 2007 cost Rs. 25,400. Some of the material costing Rs. 4,500 was found unsuitable and was sold for Rs. 4,000 and a part of the plant costing Rs. 5,500 (on 31-12-2007) unsuited to the contract was sold at a profit of Rs. 1,000.

The contract price was Rs. 22,00,000 but it was accepted by the contractor for Rs. 20,00,000. On 31st December, 2007 two-thirds of the contract was completed. Architect's certificate had been issued covering 50% of the contract price and Rs. 7,50,000 has so far been paid on account. Prepare contract account and state how much profit or loss should be included in the financial accounts to 31st December, 2007. Workings should be clearly given. Depreciation is charged on time basis.

Solution:

Contract Account
(From April 1, Dec. 31 2007)

Particulars	*Rs.*	*Particulars*	*Rs.*
To Materials	2,58,100	By Materials at site	25,400
To Labour engaged	5,60,500	By Materials sold	4,000
To Foreman's salary	79,300	By Profit and loss A/c	500
To Supervisor's salary (WN: 1)	27,000	(Loss on sale of materials)	

To Depreciation of Plant (WN: 2)	14,000	By Cost of work done c/d	10,49,000
To Administrative and other expenses	1,40,000		
	10,78,900		10,78,900
To Cost of work done b/d	10,49,000	By Work-in-progress:	
To Profit c/d	2,13,250	Work certified (WN: 3)	10,00,000
		Work uncertified (WN: 3)	2,62,250
	12,62,250		12,62,250
To Profit and Loss A/c (2,13,250 × 2/3 × 7,50,000/10,00,000)	1,06,625	By Profit b/d	2,13,250
To Work-in-progress A/c (Reserve)	1,06,625		
	2,13,250		2,13,250

Contractee's Account

To Balance c/d	Rs. 7,50,000	By Bank	Rs. 7,50,000

Extracts from Balance Sheet as on 31st December, 2007

Liabilities	*Rs.*	*Assets*		*Rs.*
Profits and Loss A/c	1,07,125	Work-in-progress:		
		Work certified	10,00,000	
		Work uncertified	2,62,250	
			12,62,250	
		Less: Reserve	1,06,625	
			11,55,625	
		Less: Cash received	7,50,00	4,05,625
		Material at site		25,400
		Plant at site		2,40,500

Working Notes:

1. Supervisor's Salary: 3/4 (9 months × Rs. 4,000) = Rs. 27,000
2. Depreciation of Plant: (Rs. 2,60,000 – Rs. 15,000)/7 years × 146/365 = Rs. 14,000
3. Cost of Work Uncertified:

   Cost of 2/3rd of the contract is Rs. 10,49,000

   The estimated cost of the total contract will amount to to Rs. 10,49,000 × 3/2 = Rs. 15,73,500

   Cost of 50% of the contract, as certified by the architect would be Rs. 15,73,500/2 = Rs. 7,86,750.

   Cost of Work done but uncertified would, therefore be, Rs. 10,49,000 – Rs. 7,86,750 = Rs. 2,62,250

4. Profit and Loss Account

To Contract A/c (Loss on sale of materials)	Rs. 500	By Contract A/c (Profit transferred)	Rs. 1,06,625
To Balance c/d	1,07,125	By Profit on sale of plant	1,000
	1,07,625		1,07,625

5. Plant Account

To Balance b/d	Rs. 2,60,000	By Contract A/c (Depreciation)	14,000
To Profit and loss a/c (Profit on sale of plant)	1,000	By Bank (Sale)	6,500
		By Balance c/d	2,40,500
	2,61,000		2,61,000

BATCH COSTING

As stated earlier, a job order can be for an item or a number of items. In the case of the latter, the order is strictly a batch and the batch cost must be divided by the quantity to give the cost per item. While job costing is concerned with the costing of jobs that are made to a customer's particular requirements, batch costing is used where articles are manufactured in definite batches and held in stock for sale to customers generally. When each order is finished/completed, the cost sheet is totalled and the total cost divided by the quantity produced to show the cost per article or per dozen, etc.

ECONOMIC BATCH QUANTITY

What should be the optimum size of a batch, is an important question. If the size is higher, the unit costs may tend to decline, but the units in inventory will go up. The size of the batch influences the clerical and other machine set-up costs also. Therefore an economic batch quantity should be determined. Generally, the following formula is used which is similar in nature to economic order quantity.

$$E = \sqrt{\frac{2US}{C\left(1-\frac{U}{R}\right)}}$$

Where E = Economic order quantity
U = Annual usage in units
S = Set-up and order processing costs
R = Annual rate of production
C = Cost of carrying one unit in inventory for one year

If the production of the batch is done over a short period, $\frac{U}{R}$ loses its significance and only then the following formula is applied:

$$E = \sqrt{\frac{2US}{C}}$$

Illustration 11:

A jobbing factory has undertaken to supply 200 pieces of a component per month for ensuing six months. Every month a batch order is opened against which materials and labour hours are booked at actuals. Overheads are levied at a rate per labour hour. The selling price contracted for is Rs. 8 per piece. From the following data, present the cost and profit per piece of each batch order and overall position of the order for 1,200 pieces.

Month	*Batch output (Rs.)*	*Material cost (Rs.)*	*Direct wages (Rs.)*	*Direct labour (hr.)*
Jan.	210	650	120	240
Feb.	200	640	140	280
March	220	680	150	280
April	180	630	140	270
May	200	700	150	300
June	220	720	160	320

The other details are:

Month	Chargeable expenses (Rs.)	Direct labour (hr.)
Jan.	12,000	4,800
Feb.	10,560	4,400
March	12,000	5,000
April	10,580	4,600
May	13,000	5,000
June	12,000	4,800

Solution:

Cost Sheet for Six Months Ending 30th June

(Output 1230 units)

Month	*Jan.*	*Feb.*	*March*	*April*	*May*	*June*	*Total*
Batch output (in units)	210	200	220	180	200	220	1,230
Sales value (in Rs.)	1,680	1,600	1,760	1,440	1,600	1,760	9,840
Cost of materials (in Rs.)	650	640	680	630	700	720	4,020
Direct wages (in Rs.)	120	140	150	140	150	160	860
Chargeable expenses (in Rs.)	600	672	672	621	780	800	4,145
Total cost (in Rs.)	1,370	1,452	1,502	1,391	1,630	1,680	9,025
Total cost per unit (in Rs.)	6.52	7.26	6.83	7.73	8.15	7.64	7.34
Profit per batch (in Rs.)	310	148	258	49	–30	80	815
Profit per unit (in Rs.)	1.48	0.74	1.17	0.27	–0.15	0.36	0.66

Overall position of the order for 1,200 units:

Sales value of 1,200 units @ Rs. 8 per unit	Rs. 9,600
Total cost for 1,200 units @ Rs. 7.34 per unit	Rs. 8,808
Profit	Rs. 792

Note: Chargeable expenses have been charged to different batches on the basis of direct labour hours for different months, e.g.,

For January $\frac{\text{Rs. } 12,000}{4,800} \times 240 = 600.$

THEORY QUESTIONS

1. (*i*) What is the nature of job costing? How are the costs recorded on job orders?
   (*ii*) Explain the meaning of contract costing and batch costing.
2. Indicate how you would deal with the following items:
   (*a*) Plant and machinery purchased and used on contract work.
   (*b*) Amounts received from contractee.
   (*c*) Materials lying unused at site.
3. (*i*) Discuss the implications of cost-plus contracts from the viewpoint of:
   (*a*) Manufacturer
   (*b*) Customer
   (*ii*) What is the relevance of the escalation clause provided in a contract?

EXERCISES AND PROBLEMS

Job Costing

1. The following information for the year ending December 31, 2007 is obtained from the books and records of a factory:

	Completed jobs	*Work-in-progress*
	Rs.	*Rs.*
Raw materials supplied from stores	90,000	30,000
Wages	1,00,000	40,000
Chargeable expenses	10,000	4,000
Materials transferred to work-in-progress	2,000	2,000
Materials returned to stores	1,000	

Factory overheads is 80% of wages and office overhead is 25% of factory cost.

The value of executed contracts during 2008 was Rs. 4,10,000. Prepare the:

(*i*) consolidated completed jobs account, and (*ii*) consolidated work-in-progress account.

2. A factory uses a job costing system. The following data are available from the books at the year ending 31st March 2008:

	Rs.
Direct material	9,00,000
Direct wages	7,50,000
Profit	6,09,000
Selling and distribution overhead	5,25,000
Administrative overhead	5,20,000
Factory overhead	4,50,000

Required:

(*a*) Prepare a cost sheet indicating the prime cost, works cost, production cost, cost of sales and value.

(*b*) In 2008-09, the factory has received an order for a number of jobs. It is estimated that the direct materials would be Rs. 12,00,000 and direct labour would cost Rs. 7,50,000. What would be the price for these jobs if the factory intends to earn the same rate of profit on sales, assuming that the selling and distribution overhead has gone up by 15%. The factory recovers factory overhead as a percentage of direct wages and administrative and selling and distribution overhead as a percentage of works cost, based on the cost rates prevalent in the previous year.

(***Ans.:*** (*a*) Prime cost Rs. 16,50,000, Works cost Rs. 21,00,000, Production cost Rs. 25,20,000. Cost of sales Rs. 30,45,000, Sales value Rs. 36,54,000.

(*b*) Sales value Rs. 42.84,000. Profit Rs. 7,14,000.

3. Mayur Engineering, engaged in job work, has completed all jobs in hand on 30th December, 2007 except Job No. 447. The cost sheet on 30th December showed direct materials and direct labour costs of Rs. 40,000 and Rs. 30,000 respectively as having been incurred on job No 447.

The costs incurred by the business on 31st December, 2007, the last day of the accounting year, were as follows:

Direct materials (Job 447)	Rs. 2,000
Direct labour (Job 447)	Rs. 8,000
Indirect labour	Rs. 2,000
Miscellaneous factory overhead	Rs. 3,000

It is the practice of business to make the jobs absorb factory overheads on the basis of 120 per cent of direct labour cost.

Calculate the value of work-in-progress of Job No. 447 on 31st December, 2007.

(***Ans.:*** Works cost Rs. 1,25,600.)

Contract Costing

4. A contractor commenced work on a particular contract on 1st April 2007. He closes the books of accounts for the year on 31st December of each year. The following information is revealed from his costing records on 31st December. 2007.

Materials sent to site	Rs. 43,000
Foreman	12,620
Labour	1,00,220

A machine costing Rs. 30,000 remained in use on site for 1/5th of the year. Its working life was estimated at 5 year and scrap value at Rs. 2,000.

A supervisor is paid Rs. 2,000 per month and had devoted half of his time on contract.

All other expenses were Rs. 14,000. The materials on site were Rs. 2,500. The contract price was Rs. 4,00,000.

On 31st December, 2007, 2/3rd of the contract was completed. However, the architect gave certificate only for Rs. 2,00,000 on which 80% was paid. Prepare contract account.

(*Ans.:* Profit transferred to P&L A/c Rs. 35,683)
Profit transferred to Reserve Rs. 31,222.

Hint:

(*i*) Depreciation on plant = $\frac{\text{Rs. } 30{,}000 - \text{Rs. } 2{,}000}{5 \times 5}$ = Rs. 1,120

(*ii*) Cost of work uncertified: expenditure incurred to date Rs. 1,79,960
Less: Materials at site 2,500
1,77,460

Rs. 1,77,460 represents the cost of completing 2/3 of the total contract. Thus the estimated cost of the total contract will amount to Rs. 2,66,190 $\left(\text{i.e., } 1{,}77460 \times \frac{3}{2}\right)$

The architect's certificate represents 1/2 of the contract price. It therefore covers an expenditure of Rs. 1,33,095 (i.e., 2,66,190 × 1/2)

The cost of work uncertified is, therefore, Rs. 44,365 (i.e., Rs. 1,77,460 – Rs. 1,33, 095)

(*iii*) Profit taken to profit and loss account.

$= 66{,}905 \times \frac{2}{3} \times \frac{80}{100}$

= Rs. 35,683 (approx.)

5. From the information given below relating to an unfinished contract, ascertain:
(*a*) Profit on work certified.
(*b*) Cost of work-in-progress at the end of year.

	Rs.
Materials sent to site	86,000
Labour engaged on site	65,000
Plant issued	80,000
Direct expenses	8,000
Establishment charges	4,000
Materials returned to stores	600
Work certified	1,90,000
Uncertified work	7,700
Materials in hand	2,000

Wages accrued	300
Cash received	1,61,500
Depreciation of plant	7,000

(*Ans.:* Profit Rs. 20,000)

6. Thekedar accepted a contract for the construction of a building for Rs. 10,00,000, the contractee agreeing to pay 90% of work certified as complete by the aechitect. During the first year, the amounts spent were:

	Rs.
Materials	1,20,000
Labour	1,50,000
Machinery	30,000
Other Expenses	90,000

At the end of the year, the machinery was considered to be of a value Rs. 20,000, and materials at site were of the value of Rs 5,000. Work certified during the year totalled Rs. 4,00,000. In addition, work-in-progress, but not certified at the end of the year, had cost Rs. 15,000.

Prepare the contract account in the books of Thekedar. Also show the various Figures of profit that can be transferred reasonably to the profit and loss account.

(*Ans.:* Profit Rs. 15,000, Profit in reserve Rs. 35,000.

7. Ms. Raju and Mohan Contractors Ltd. were engaged on one contract during the year 2007. The contract price was Rs. 4,00,000. The Trial Balance extracted from their books on 31st December. 2007 stood as follows:

Share Capital		Rs. 80,000
Sundry Creditors		8,000
Land & Buildings	Rs. 34,000	
Bank	9,000	
Contract Account:		
Materials	75,000	
Plant	20,000	
Wages	1,05,000	
Expenses	5,000	
Cash received being 80% of work certified		1,60,000
	2.48,000	2,48,000

Of the Plant and Materials charged to the contract, Plant costing Rs. 3,000 and materials costing Rs. 2,400 were destroyed by an accident.

On 31st December, 2007, Plant which cost Rs. 4,000 was returned to the store, the value of materials on site was Rs. 3,000 and the cost of work done but not certified was Rs. 2,000.

Charge 10% depreciation on plant. Prepare Contract Account for the year 2007 and balance sheet as on 31st December 2007.

(*Ans.:* Profit transferred to P & L A/c Rs. 11,040
Profit transferred to Reserve Rs. 9,660
B/S total Rs. 93,640
It has been presumed that plant and materials have been lost on account of accident in the beginning of the year.

8. Anand Company of builders took to a multi-storeyed structure for Rs. 40,00,000, estimating the cost to be Rs. 36,80,000. At the end of the year the company had received Rs. 14,00,000 being 90% of the work certified: work done but not certified was Rs. 40,000.

Following expenditure was incurred:

Materials	Rs. 4,00,000
Labour	10,00,000
Plant	80,000

Materials costing Rs. 20,000 were damaged. Plant is considered as having depreciated at 25%. Prepare contract account and show all the possible figures, that can reasonably be credited to Profit and Loss Account.

(*Ans.:* 2/3 of Rs. 2,40,000 notional profit on cash basis Rs. 1,44,000. Notional profit × cash received , contract price of Rs. 86,000, Notional profit X cost of work done / estimated total cost Rs. 91,304; Notional profit X work certified / Contract price Rs. 96,000.

9. SV construction Ltd. has obtained a contract for construction of a bridge. The value of the contract is Rs. 12 lakh and the work commenced on 1st October, 2007. The following details are shown in their books for the year ending 30th September 2008.

	Rs.
Plant purchased	60,000
Wages paid	3,40,000
Material issued to site	3,36,000
Direct expenses	8,000
General overheads apportioned	32,000
Wages accrued as on 30-9-2008	2,800
Materials at site as on 30-9-2008	4,000
Direct expenses accrued as on 30-9-2008	1,200
Work not certified at cost	14,000
Cash received being 80% of work certified	6,00,000

Life of plant purchased is 5 years and scrap value is nil.

1. Prepare the contract account for the year ending 30th September, 2008.
2. Show the amount of profit which you consider might be fairly taken on the contract and how you have calculated it.

(*Ans.:* Profit taken to Profit and Loss A/c Rs. 19,200.)

10. Kapoor Engineering Company undertakes a long-term contract which involves the fabrication of prestressed concrete blocks and the erection of the same on consumer's site.

The following is supplied regarding the contract which is incomplete on 31st March, 2007.

Cost incurred:

Fabrication costs to date:	*Rs.*
Direct materials	2,80,000
Direct labour	90,000
Overheads	75,000
	4,45,000
Erection costs to date	15,000
Total	4,60,000
Contract price	8,19,000
Cash received on account	6,00,000

Technical estimate of work completed to date:

Fabrication:

Direct materials 80%

Direct labour and overheads 75%

Erection 25%

You are required to prepare a statement for submission to the management indicating:

(*a*) the estimated profit on the completion of the contract, and

(*b*) the estimated profit to date on the contract.

(*Ans.:* Estimated profit Rs. 1,38,000 on contract.)

Process Costing

NATURE OF PROCESS COSTING

Process costing is that form of operations costing which is used where standardised goods are produced in large volume with continuous production flow. This costing method is used in industries like chemicals, petroleum, textiles, steel, rubber, cement, plastic, shoes, sugar and coal. Those concerns which produce items such as screws, bolts and small electrical parts can also use this costing method. Process costing is also used in the assembly type industry which manufactures items, such as typewriters, automobiles, aeroplanes and household electrical appliances such as washing machines, refrigerators, electrical irons, radios, television sets, etc. For example, an electronics manufacturing company may have the following process or cost centres: materials set-up, wiring, and soldering. Service industries, such as gas, water, electric power and heat may also follow process cost accounting.

Characteristics

A process costing method has the following distinctive characteristics:

1. *Cost collection:* Manufacturing costs are accumulated for each production department or process.
2. *Time period assumption:* Manufacturing costs are accumulated by department or process for specific time periods, say a month, and the process costing is designed to measure units produced during this period.
3. *Averaging process:* The most important point is that product costing under process costing is an averaging process. The unit cost is obtained by accumulating all manufacturing costs and dividing it by units produced or some measure of production.
4. *Separate ledger:* Each process or department has its own account and records the processing costs incurred by the department.

5. *Homogeneous product:* Under processing industries, the production is continuous and emphasis is on uniform or standardised product. It is difficult to identify a specific unit of output with the time of production.
6. *Transfer to finished goods:* Completed units and their associated costs are transferred to next process if something is still to be done on those units. Completed units are transferred to finished goods if nothing is to be done.
7. *Cost of spoiled units:* Cost of lost or spoiled units is added to the cost of good units completed, thus increasing the average cost per unit.

Process Costing and Job Costing

Process costing and job costing differ on the following counts:

1. *Applicability:* Job costing is applicable in situations where the objective is to identify costs with specific products or jobs. Process costing, on the other hand, is used in case of mass production of similar units that continuously pass through different departments or processes.
2. *Cost collection:* In job costing, manufacturing costs are accumulated for particular jobs or batches of product using job cost sheets. In process costing, manufacturing costs are accumulated for entire departments or processes and the cost of particular jobs or batches or products is not determinable.
3. *Time period assumption:* In job costing, costs are accumulated for a specific product or job without taking into account the production time which may be more than one accounting period. In process costing, costs are accumulated for specific departments/processes for a given time period (say a month). That is, production is measured for specific time periods in process costing.
4. *Purpose:* In job costing production is generally dependent on customers' orders and specifications. Under process costing, production is done for storing stock of goods and for future sale.
5. *Computation of unit costs:* In job costing unit cost is obtained by dividing the cost of the job order by units produced in the job order. Under process costing, unit costs are obtained by dividing departmental/process costs by process production.
6. *Work-in-progress:* In job costing, one work-in-progress account is maintained. But in process costing, individual work-in-progress accounts are prepared for each production/ process department to ascertain manufacturing costs by process.

COSTING PROCEDURES UNDER PROCESS COSTING

In process costing, an account is maintained for each process to which all costs of material, labour, direct expenses and overhead are debited.

Materials

In process costing all the materials required for production are issued to the first process, where after processing, they are passed on to the next process and so on; each process merely performs the same operation on the material which has been passed on from the first process. Alternatively, materials may pass from the first process to the second process, where extra or new raw materials are added, then more materials are added in the next process; this may continue until completion.

Labour

Labour costs incurred in a particular process are posted to the debit of the process account concerned. However, where workers are engaged in more than one process, the gross wages are distributed to each process on the basis of time spent on each process.

Direct Expenses

Items of expenditure which can be directly attributed to a process are debited to the relative process account. Examples of such expenses are cost of electricity, depreciation and hire charges of equipment.

Factory Overhead

Expenses which are not charged direct are apportioned on the basis of absorption rates. Also, overhead may be recovered at a predetermined rate based on direct wages, prime cost, etc.

PREPARATION OF PROCESS COST ACCOUNTS

As stated earlier, for each process an individual process account is prepared. The method of preparing process accounts is discussed herewith on the basis of the following situations which may be found in a production situation:

1. Process costing having no process loss and no opening and closing work-in-progress.
2. Process costing having process losses or gains (normal loss, abnormal loss, abnormal gain).
3. Process costing having opening and closing work-in-progress at various stages of completion. Besides, there may be process losses or gains.

Process Costing Having No Process Loss and No Opening and Closing Work-in-Progress

The preparation of process accounts is very easy, if no loss or gain has arisen during the processing operation of the product. All costs of material, labour, direct expense, and apportioned overhead are debited to the process account. The total (accumulated) costs of the process are transferred to the second process as raw materials (input) for that process.

Illustration 1:

Prepare process cost accounts from the following data:

Items	*Total*	*Process*		
		I	*II*	*III*
Direct material	4,40,000	3,60,000	60,000	20,000
Direct wages	80,000	20,000	40,000	20,000
Direct expenses	1,00,000	60,000	—	40,000

Production overhead incurred is Rs. 1,60,000 and is recovered on 200% of direct wages. Production during the period was 20,000 units. There was no opening or closing work-in-progress.

Process I Account

	Cost per unit	Amount		Cost per unit	Amount
To Direct material	18.00	3,60,000	By Output transferred		
To Direct wages	1.00	20,000	Process II	24.00	4,80,000
To Direct expenses	3.00	60,000			
To Production overhead	2.00	40,000			
	24.00	4,80,000		24.00	4,80,000

Process II Account

To Output from Process I	24.00	4,80,000	By Output transferred to		
To Direct material	3.00	60,000	Process III	33.00	6,60,000
To Direct wages	2.00	40,000			
To Production overhead	4.00	80,000			
	33.00	6,60,000		33.00	6,60,000

Process III Account

To Output from Process II	33.00	6,60,000	By Output transferred to		
To Direct materials	1.00	20,000	finished stock	39.00	7,80,000
To Direct wages	1.00	20,000			
To Direct expenses	2.00	40,000			
To Production overhead	2.00	40,000			
	39.00	7,80,000		39.00	7,80,000

Illustration 2:

From the following figures show the cost of three processes of manufacture. The production of each process is passed on to the next process immediately on completion.

	Process A	*Process B*	*Process C*
Wages and materials	Rs. 30,400	Rs. 12,000	Rs. 29,250
Works overheads	5,600	5,250	6,000
Production in units	36,000	37,500	48,000
Stock (Units from preceding process — 1st July. 2008)		4,000	16,500
Stock (Units from preceding process — 31st July, 2008)		1,000	5,500

Solution:

Process A Account

To Wages and materials	Rs. 30,400	By Transfer to process B	
To Works overheads	5,600	@ Re. 1 per unit	Rs. 36,000
	36,000		36,000

Process B Account

To Stock: unit from preceding process @ Re. 1 per unit	Rs. 4,000	By Stock: units from preceding process @ Re. 1 per unit	Rs. 1,000
To Transfer from Process A	36,000	By Transfer to Process C	
To Wages and material	12,000	@ Rs. 1.50 per unit	56,250
To Works overheads	5,250		
	57,250		57,250

Process C Account

To Stock: units from preceding process @ Rs. 1.50 per unit	Rs. 24,750	By Stock: units from preceding process @ Rs. 1.50 per unit	Rs. 8,250
To Transfer from Process B	56,250	By Transfer to finished goods account @ Rs. 2 per unit	Rs. 1,08,000
To Wages and materials	29,250		
To Works overheads	6,000		
	1,16,250		1,16,250

Illustration 3:

The Neodrug manufacturers process a product 'plant food' through three distinct processes, the product of one process being transferred to the next process and so on to finished product intact.

Raw materials, labour and direct expenses incurred on each of the processes are given below:

Particulars	*Process A*	*Process B*	*Process C*
Raw materials	Rs. 1,00,000	Rs. 80,000	Rs. 20,000
Labour	50,000	60,000	70,000
Direct expenses	15,000	25,000	50,000

The overhead expenses for the period amounted to Rs. 3,60,000 and is to be distributed to the processes on the basis of labour wages.

There were no stocks in any of the processes at the beginning or at the close of the period. Ignore wastages.

(*a*) Assuming that the output was 1,00,000 kilos, show the process accounts of A, B and C indicating also the unit cost per kilo under each element of cost and the output in each process.

(*b*) If 10% of the output is estimated to be lost in the course of sale and sampling, what should be the selling price per unit (correct to two decimal place) so as to provide for gross profit of 33½ on selling price.

Solution:

Process A

	Per kg.	*Total*		*Per kg.*	*Total*
To Raw materials	1.00	1,00,000	By Transfer to process B	2.65	2,65,000
To Labour	0.50	50,000			
To Direct expenses	0.15	15,000			
To Overheads	1.00	1,00,000			
	2.65	2,65,000		2.65	2,65,000

Process B

	Rs.	*Rs.*		*Rs.*	*Rs.*
To Transfer from Process A	2.65	2,65,000	By Transfer to Process C	5.50	5,50,000
To Raw materials	0.80	80,000			
To Labour	0.60	60,000			
To Direct expenses	0.25	25,000			
To Overheads	1.20	1,20,000			
	5.50	5,50,000		5.50	5,50,000

Process C

	Rs.	Rs.		Rs.	Rs.
To Transfer from Process B	5.50	5,50,000	By Transfer to finished goods A/c	8.30	8,30,000
To Raw materials	0.20	20,000			
To Labour	0.70	70,000			
To Direct expenses	0.50	50,000			
To Overheads	1.40	1,40,000			
	8.30	8,30,000		8.30	8,30,000

(*b*) Cost of finished goods Rs. 8,30,000

Profit ($33^1/_3$% on selling prices) 4,15,000

Sales 12,45,000

Gross output 1,00,000 kg.

Less: Wastage 10% 10,000

90,000 kg.

Selling price per kg. $= \dfrac{12{,}45{,}000}{90{,}000 \text{ kg.}}$ = Rs. 13.83 per kg.

Process Costing Having Process Losses and/or Gains

All materials put into process are not likely to be good saleable products. Some loss, scrap and wastage is inevitable in process industries. Process loss can be divided into two categories: (*i*) Normal loss, (*ii*) Abnormal loss. Normal loss is the loss which is unavoidable, uncontrollable and expected in normal conditions. It may be inherent in the manufacturing process. Abnormal process loss is controllable and avoidable and generally caused by abnormal or unexpected conditions, such as bad designing, poor materials, accident and negligence, etc.

The treatment of normal and abnormal losses differ in process accounts. Normal losses are absorbed by good production. Assume, for example, that 25,000 units of a mixture were put into process and that during processing 5,000 units were lost through evaporation. This in an unavoidable loss. If the total cost recorded was Rs. 25,00,000 the remaining 20,000 units would be assigned a unit cost of Rs. 125.

$$\frac{\text{Cost of production}}{\text{Number of units completed}} = \frac{\text{Rs. } 25{,}00{,}000}{20{,}000} = \text{Rs. } 125$$

Abnormal losses are valued as good units. The unit cost which is used to value good units is also applied for valuation or abnormal loss units. The cost of abnormal loss units computed in this manner is transferred to a separate abnormal loss account and credited to relevant process account. Subsequently, this loss is transferred to the costing profit and loss account and the abnormal loss account is thus closed.

Waste

Waste is without any value. If waste is part of the normal process loss, the cost is absorbed by the good production. Alternatively, if waste represents abnormal process loss, the waste (abnormal loss) is valued like good units and treated as abnormal process loss.

Scrap

Scrap means discarded material emerging from certain manufacturing operations. It has some but minor value. Where the normal loss is in the form of scrap and has some realisable value, the process account is credited with the amount which could be realised from sale of normal scrap. The abnormal loss, if represented by scrap may have a similar realisable value. The amount realised from sale of scrap representing abnormal loss is credited to the abnormal loss account and the balance in the abnormal loss account is transferred to the costing profit and loss account. The question of crediting the amount realised from sale of scrap representing abnormal loss in the relevant process account does not arise. The relevant process account is credited and the abnormal loss account is debited with the cost of abnormal loss valued as finished output. In case there are normal loss, abnormal loss, scrap, the following procedure will help in the preparation of process accounts:

1. Normal loss should be computed on the basis of information given in the question.
2. The cost per unit of production after taking into account normal loss units should be determined assuming that abnormal loss does not exist. The cost per unit is calculated on the basis of the following information:
   (*a*) Normal production, *i.e.*, inputs (units) minus normal loss units.
   (*b*) Normal cost of production, *i.e.*, all costs incurred (appearing on the debit side of a process account) minus proceeds (if any) realised from the sale of normal loss units.

   Normal cost of production divided by normal production will give the cost per unit of output.
3. The cost per unit determined as above is used to value abnormal loss units and that would be the cost of abnormal loss.
4. The abnormal loss account is debited and the relevant process account credited with the amount and quantity of abnormal loss as calculated in (3) above.
5. The cost per unit as obtained in (3) will also be used to determine the cost of good production units produced by the process.
6. The proceeds realised from the sale of normal loss representing scrap is transferred to the relevant process account.
7. The proceeds realised from the sale of abnormal loss representing scrap is transferred to a separate abnormal loss account and not to the relevant process account.
8. The abnormal loss account is closed by transferring the total cost of abnormal loss units to the costing profit and loss account if there is no scrap. In case abnormal loss represents scrap, only the net amount (total cost of abnormal loss units minus scrap) will be transferred to the costing profit and loss account.

Abnormal Gain (Effectives)

Abnormal gain arises when the actual loss is less than the normal loss expected. The abnormal gain is valued in the same manner as abnormal loss and is credited to a separate account known as the abnormal gain account. The abnormal gain account appears on the debit side of the relevant process account. The amount of scrap which would otherwise have been realised, had there been normal loss and no abnormal gain, is debited to the abnormal gain account and the balance is credited to the costing profit and loss account. Cost per unit of output computed (as mentioned above) is used to value the output transferred to the next process.

Illustration 4:

The following data are available pertaining to a product after passing through two processes A and B.

Output transferred to process C from process B, 9120 units for Rs. 49,263.

Expenses incurred in Process C:

Sundry materials	Rs. 1,480
Direct labour	Rs. 6,500
Direct expenses	Rs. 1,605

The wastage of process C is sold at Re. 1.00 per unit. The overhead charges were 168% of direct labour. The final product was sold at Rs. 10.00 per unit fetching a profit of 20% on sales.

Find the percentage of wastage in process C and prepare Process C Account.

Solution:

Let the total finished output be x units

Total Sales Rs. $10x$

Wastage in units $(9,120 - x)$

Sales Value $1 \times (9,120 - x)$ or Rs. $9,120 - x$

Profit Rs. $2x$.

$$\text{Total Sales} = \text{Total Cost} + \text{Profit}$$

$$10x = 69,768 - (9,120 - x) + 2x$$

$$7x = 69,768 - 9,120$$

$$x = 60,648/7 = 8,664 \text{ units}$$

$$\text{Wastage} = 9,120 - 8,664 = 456 \text{ units}$$

$$\text{Percentage to input} = \frac{456}{9,120} \times 100 = 5\%$$

Process X Account

Particulars	*Units*	*Rs.*	*Particulars*	*Units*	*Rs.*
To Tr. from Process B	9,120	49,263	By Wastage	456	456
To Sundry materials		1,480	By Tr. to finished		
To Direct labour		6,500	Goods stock a/c	8,664	69,312
To Direct expenses		1,605	(@ Rs. 8 per unit)		
To Overhead		10,920			
	9,120	69,768		9,120	69,768

Illustration 5:

In a certain process, material is mixed and cooked in batches of 1,000 lbs each. Cooking results in 10 per cent loss of weight of the mixture. Since the cooking requires considerable skill and constant watching, there is generally a further loss for spoilage which is not discovered until processing has been completed. Also, past experience shows that normally two batches out of every *ten* started in the process are spoiled in this way.

In a given month, the production records show:

(*i*) Production started in the process — 50 batches of 1,000 lbs each.

(*ii*) Production completed and transferred to finished goods is 34,200 lbs.

(*iii*) There is no inventory of work-in-process at the beginning or end of the month.

Costs recorded during the month amounted to Rs. 45,000. Prepare the Process Account for the month and determine the cost per pound of finished product.

Solution:

Dr. Cr.

Process Account

Particulars	*Quantity lbs*	*Amount Rs.*	*Particulars*	*Quantity lbs.*	*Amount Rs.*
To Inputs	50,000	45,000	By Normal loss in weight $\frac{50{,}000 \times 10}{100}$	5,000	—
			By Spoilage $\frac{50 \times 2 \times 1{,}000}{10}$	10,000	—
			By Abnormal loss	800	1,029
			By Finished stock A/c	34,200	43,971
	50,000	45,000		50,000	45,000

Working Notes:

Calculation of cost of abnormal loss

Net cost = Rs. 45,000

Net Output (lbs 50,000 – lbs 15,000) = lbs. 35,000

Actual Output = lbs 34,200

Abnormal Loss = (lbs. 35,000 – lbs. 34,200) = lbs 800

$$\text{Cost of Abnormal Loss} = \frac{45{,}000 \times 800}{35{,}000} = \text{Rs. } 1{,}029$$

Illustration 6:

The finished product of a manufacturing company passes through three processes, viz., I, II and III. The normal wastage in each process is 5%, 7% and 10% for the processes I, II and III respectively (calculated with reference to the number of units fed into each process). The scrap generated out of wastage has a sale value of 70 paise per unit, 80 paise per unit and Rupee I per unit in the process I, II and III respectively. The output of each process is transferred to the next process and the finished output emerges from the process III and transferred to stock. There was no stock of work-in-progress in any process in a particular month. The details of cost data for the month are given below:

Particulars	Processes I	II	III
Materials used (Rs.)	1,20,000	40,000	40,000
Direct labour cost (Rs.)	80,000	60,000	60,000
Production expenses (Rs.)	40,000	40,000	28,000
Output in Units (actuals)	38,000	34,600	32,000

Process I was fed with 40,000 units of raw input at cost of Rs. 3,20,000.

Prepare the Process Accounts.

Solution:

Process I Account

Particulars	*Units (Nos.)*	*Amount Rs.*	*Particulars*	*Units (Nos.)*	*Amount Rs.*
To Units introduced	40,000	3,20,000	By Normal loss		
To Materials used	–	1,20,000	(5% @ 70 p. per unit)	2,000	1,400
To Direct Labour	—	80,000	By Transfer to Process II		
To Production expenses	—	40,000	@ Rs. 14.70 per unit	38,000	5,58,000
	40,000	5,60,000		40,000	5,60,000

Process II Account

Particulars	*Units (Nos.)*	*Amount Rs.*	*Particulars*	*Units (Nos.)*	*Amount Rs.*
To Transfer from Process I A/c	38,000	5,58,000	By Normal loss		
To Materials used	—	40,000	(7% @ 80 paise per unit)	2,660	2,128
To Direct labour	—	60,000	By Abnormal loss (WN I)	740	14,584
To Production expenses	—	40,000	By Transfer to Process III		
			@ 19.7078	34,600	6,81,888
	38,000	6,98,600		38,000	6,98,600

Process III Account

Particulars	*Units (Nos.)*	*Amount Rs.*	*Particulars*	*Units (Nos.)*	*Amount Rs.*
To Transfer from			By Normal loss @ 10%		
Process II Account	34,600	6,81,888	at Re. 1 per unit	3,460	3,460
To Materials used	—	40,000	By Transfer to finished		
To Direct labour	—	60,000	stock A/c @ 25,896	32,000	8,28,700
To Production expenses	—	28,000			
To Abnormal effectives A/c	860	22,272			
(@ Rs. 25.8968 (WN 2)					
	35,460	8,32,160		35,460	8,32,160

Working Notes:

1. Amount of Abnormal Loss in Process II

$$= \frac{\text{Normal cost}}{\text{Normal output}} \times \text{Abnormal cost in units}$$

$$= \frac{6{,}98{,}600 - 2{,}128}{3{,}88{,}000 - 2{,}660} \times 740 = \text{Rs. } 14{,}584.$$

2. Amount of abnormal effectives in Process III

$$= \frac{8{,}09{,}888 - 3{,}460}{34{,}600 - 3{,}460} \times 860 = \text{Rs. } 22{,}272$$

Illustration 7:

A product passes through three processes — P, Q, and R. The details of expenses incurred on the three processes during the year 2008 were as under:

Particulars	*P*	*Q*	*R*
Units issued	10,000		
Cost per unit	100		
Sundry materials	Rs. 10,000	15,000	5,000
Labour	Rs. 30,000	80,000	65,000
Direct expenses	Rs. 6,000	18,150	27,200
Sale Price of output per unit	Rs. 120	165	250

Management expenses during the year amounted to Rs. 80,000 and selling expenses were Rs. 50,000. Both these are not allocable to the processes.

Actual output of the three processes was as under:

Process P — 9,300 units; Process Q — 5,400 units; Process R — 2,100 units.

Two-thirds of the output of process P and one-half of the output of process Q was passed on to the next process and the balance was sold. The entire output of process R was sold.

The normal wastage of the three processes calculated on the input of every process was:

Process P — 5 per cent; Process Q — 15 per cent; Process R — 20 per cent.

The wastage of Process P was sold at Rs. 2 per unit, that of Process Q at Rs. 5 per unit and that of Process R at Rs. 10 per unit.

Prepare the three Process Accounts and a Statement of Income for 2008, showing fully the accounting treatment of Process Wastage.

Solution:

Process P Account

Particulars	*Unit*	*Rs.*	*Particulars*	*Units*	*Rs.*
To Input	10,000	10,000,000	By Normal wastage	500	1,000
To Sundry Materials		10,000	By Abnormal wastage (WN 1)	200	22,000
To Labour		30,000	By Process P Stock A/c	9,300	10,23,000
To Direct expenses		6,000	(@ Rs. 110 per unit)		
	10,000	10,46,000		10,000	10,46,000

Process P Stock Account

Particulars	Unit	Rs.	Particulars	Units	Rs.
To Process P A/c	9,300	10,23,000	By Sales (@ Rs. 120)	3,100	3,72,000
To Profit		31,000	By Process Q	6,200	6,82,000
			(@ Rs. 110 per unit)		
	9,300	10,54,000		9,300	10,54,000

Process Q Account

Particulars	Unit	Rs.	Particulars	Units	Rs.
To Process P Stock A/c	6,200	6,82,000	By Normal Wastage	930	4,650
To Materials		15,000	By Process Q Stock A/c	5,400	8,10,000
To Labour		80,000	(@ Rs. 150 per unit)		
To Direct expenses		18,150			
To Abnormal effective A/c	130	19,500			
(WN 2)					
	6,330	8,14,650		6,330	8,14,650

Process Q Stock Account

Particulars	Unit	Rs.	Particulars	Units	Rs.
To Process Q A/c	5,400	8,10,000	By Sales	2,700	4,45,500
To Profit		40,500	(@ Rs. 165 per unit)		
			By Process R	2,700	4,05,000
			(@ Rs. 150 per unit)		
	5,400	8,50,500		5,400	8,50,500

Process R Account

Particulars	Unit	Rs.	Particulars	Units	Rs.
To Process Q Stock A/c	2,700	4,05,000	By Normal wastage	540	5,400
To Sundry materials		5,000	By Abnormal wastage (WN 3)	60	13,800
To Labour		65,000	By Finished goods A/c	2,100	4,83,000
To Direct expenses		27,200	(@ Rs. 230 per unit)		
	2,700	5,02,200		2,700	5,02,200

Finished Goods Stock Account

Particulars	Unit	Rs.	Particulars	Units	Rs.
To Process R A/c	2,100	4,83,000	By Sales (@ Rs. 250) per unit	2,100	5,25,000
To Profit		42,000			
	2,100	5,25,000		2,100	5,25,000

Income Statement

		Rs.	Rs.
Profit from:			
Process P Stock A/c		31,000	
Process Q Stock A/c		40,500	
Finished Goods Stock A/c		42,000	1,13,500
Profit from Abnormal Effectives of Process Q			
Cost value		19,500	
Less: Sale value of 130 units @ Rs. 5 per unit actually realised		650	18,850
			1,32,350
Less: Loss on account of Abnormal wastage process P cost	22,000		
Less: Sale value of 200 units @ Rs. 10 per unit	400	21,600	
Process R cost	13,800		
Less: Sale value of 60 units @ Rs. 10 unit	600	13,200	34,800
Gross profit			97,550
Less: Management expenses		80,000	
Selling expenses		50,000	1,30,000
Net loss			32,450

Working Notes:

1. Cost of Abnormal Wastage $= \frac{\text{Normal cost}}{\text{Normal output}} \times$ Abnormal Wastage in units

$$= \frac{10,46,000 - 1,000}{950} \times 200 = \text{Rs. } 22,000$$

2. Cost of Abnormal Effectives $= \frac{\text{Normal cost}}{\text{Normal output}} \times$ Ab. Effective in units

$$= \frac{7,95,150 - 4,650}{5,270} \times 130$$

$= $ Rs. 19,500

3. Cost of Abnormal Wastage $= \frac{\text{Normal cost}}{\text{Normal output}} =$ Ab. Wastage in units

$$= \frac{5,02,200 - 5,400}{2,700 - 540} \times 60 = \text{Rs. } 13,800$$

Illustration 8:

The product rnanufactured by the Standard Chemicals Ltd. passes through three processes I, II and III. The following costs have been incurred for the month of September 2008.

Details	*Process I (Rs.)*	*Process II (Rs.)*	*Process III (Rs.)*
1. Material consumed	40,000	7,500	5,000
2. Direct wages	22,500	10,000	10,000
3. Direct expenses	20,500	2,250	2,505
Total (Rs.)	83,000	19,750	17,505

	(units)	(units)	(units)
4. Output	3,900	3,850	3,200
5. Furnished process stock:			
(*i*) 01-9-2008	600	550	800
(*ii*) 30-9-2008	500	800	Nil
6. Stock valuation on 01-9-2008 (Rs. per unit)	24.50	31.00	37.00
7. Percentage of wastage	2	5	10
8. Net realisable value of wastage per unit (Rs.)	13.50	16.25	21.00

Four thousand units or raw materials were introduced in Process No. I at a cost of Rs. 20,000.

Stocks are valued and transferred to subsequent processes at weighted average cost. The percentage of wastage is commuted on the number of units entering the process concerned.

Prepare (*i*) Process Accounts; (*ii*) Process Stock Accounts; (*iii*) Normal Wastage Accounts, (iv) Abnormal Wastage Effectives Account.

(i) & (ii)

Process I Account

Particulars	*Units*	*Rs.*	*Particulars*	*Units*	*Rs.*
To Input	4,000	20,000	By Normal wastage	80	1,080
To Materials		40,000	By Abnormal wastage	20	520
To Direct Wages		22,500	By Process I Stock A/c	3,900	1,01,400
To Direct Expenses		20,500			
	4,000	1,03,000		4,000	1,03,000

Process I Stock Account

Particulars	*Units*	*Rs.*	*Particulars*	*Units*	*Rs.*
To Balance b/d	600	14,700	By Process II A/c	4,000	1,03,200
(@ Rs. 24.5 per unit)			By Balance c/d	500	12,900
To Process I A/c	3,900	1,01,400	(@ Rs. 25.8 per unit)		
	4,500	1,16,100		4,500	1,16,100

Process I Account

Particulars	*Units*	*Rs.*	*Particulars*	*Units*	*Rs.*
To Process I Stock A/c	4,000	1,03,200	By Normal wastage	200	3,250
(@ Rs. 25.8 per unit)			By Process Stock A/c	3,850	1,21,275
To Direct material		7,500			
To Direct wages		10,000			
To Direct expenses		2,250			
To Abnormal effectives A/c	50	1,575			
	4,050	1,24,525		4,050	1,2+,525

Process II Stock Account

Particulars	*Units*	*Rs.*	*Particulars*	*Units*	*Rs.*
To Balance b/d	550	17,050	By Process III A/c	3,600	1,13,175
(@ Rs. 31 per unit)			By Balance c/d	800	25,150
To Process II A/c	3,850	1,21,275	(@ Rs. 31.44 per unit)		
	4,400	1,38,325		4,400	1,38,325

Process III Account

Particulars	*Units*	*Rs.*	*Particulars*	*Units*	*Rs.*
To Process II Stock A/c	3,600	1,13,175	By Normal Wastage A/c	360	7,560
To Materials		5,000	By Abnormal Wastage A/c	40	1,520
To Direct Wages		10,000	By Process III Stock A/c	3,200	1,21,600
To Direct Expenses		2,505			
	3,600	1,30,680		3,600	1,30,680

Process III Stock Account

Particulars	*Units*	*Rs.*	*Particulars*	*Units*	*Rs.*
To Balance b/d	800	29,600	By Finished goods stock A/c	4,000	1,51,200
(@ Rs. 37 per unit)			(@ Rs. 37.8 per unit)		
To Process III A/c	3,200	1,21,600			
	4,000	1,51,200		4,000	1,51,200

(iii) Normal Wastage Account

Particulars	*Units*	*Rs.*	*Particulars*	*Units*	*Rs.*
To Process I A/c	800	1,080	By Sale proceeds:		
To Process II A/c	200	3,250	Process I	800	1,080
			Process II	150	2,438
			By Abnormal Effectives A/c	50	812
	1,000	4,330		1,000	4,330

(iv) Abnormal Wastage Account

Particulars	*Unit*	*Rs.*	*Particulars*	*Units*	*Rs.*
To Process I A/c	20	20	By Sales Proceeds:		
To Process III A/c	40	1,520	Process I	20	270
			Process III	40	840
			By Costing P/L A/c		930
	60	2,040		60	2,040

Abnormal Effectives Account

Particulars	*Unit*	*Rs.*	*Particulars*	*Units*	*Rs.*
To Normal wastage A/c	50	812	By Process II A/c	50	1,575
To Costing P/L A/c		763			
	50	1,575		59	1,575

Working Notes:

1. Cost of Abnormal Wastage in Process I $= \dfrac{\text{Normal Cost}}{\text{Normal Output}} \times$ Ab. Wastage in Units

$$= \frac{1{,}03{,}000 - 1{,}080}{3{,}920} \times 20$$

$$= \frac{1{,}01{,}920}{3{,}920} \times 20 = \text{Rs. } 520$$

2. Cost of Abnormal Effectives in Process II $= \dfrac{\text{Normal Cost}}{\text{Normal Output}} \times$ Ab. Effectiveness in Units

$$= \frac{1{,}22{,}950 - 3{,}250}{3{,}800} \times 50$$

$$= \frac{1{,}19{,}700}{3{,}800} \times 50 = \text{Rs. } 1{,}311$$

3. Cost of Abnormal Wastage in Process III $= \dfrac{\text{Normal Cost}}{\text{Normal Output}} \times$ Ab. Wastage in Units

$$= \frac{1{,}30{,}680 - 7{,}560}{3{,}600 - 360} \times 40$$

$$= \frac{1{,}23{,}120}{3{,}240} \times 40 = \text{Rs. } 1{,}520$$

Process Costing having Work-in-Progress at Different Stages of Completion

When a process consists of opening and closing stock fully completed, the cost unit is obtained by dividing the total cost including the cost of opening stock by the number of units completed. This unit cost is used to price the output transferred to the next process and to value the units which remain in inventory. The following example illustrates this situation:

Process I

	Units	*Rs.*		*Units*	*Rs.*
To Stock (opening)	2,000	3,500	By Transfer to second process	9,000	27,000
To Materials	10,000	20,050	By Stock	3,000	9,000
To Wages		9,450			
To Overhead		3,000			
	12,000	36,000		12,000	36,000

$$\text{Unit cost} = \frac{\text{Rs. } 36{,}000}{12{,}000 \text{ units}} = \text{Rs. 3 per unit}$$

The unit cost, Rs. 3 per unit, has been used to price the goods transferred to the second process as well as to the stock.

Closing Work-in-Progress

In most situations, process may consist of partially completed closing units at the end of an accounting period. It is apparent that a partially completed unit must carry a cost that is lower than a finished unit. It follows that where there are inventories of closing work-in-progress, units costs cannot be computed by simply dividing the total cost by the number of units processed. Units in work-in-process must be converted to a base that can be equated with finished production. This analysis is known as Equivalent Production Analysis.

Equivalent units are defined in I.C.M.A. Terminology of Management and Financial Accountancy as follows:

"Equivalent units are a notional quantity of completed units substituted for an actual quantity of incomplete physical units in progress, when the aggregate work content of the incomplete units is deemed to be equivalent to that of the substituted quantity. The principle applies when operations costs are being apportioned between work-in-progress and completed output."

Equivalent Production Analysis

Before unit costs can be computed, closing inventories of work-in-progress must be converted into finished equivalents (also called equivalent production). This is done by multiplying the actual number of units in process by their stage of completion measured in terms of cost. Thus 2,000 units in an inventory estimated to be 50% complete are equal in cost to 1,000 units that have been completed:

Actual number of units × Stage of completion = Finished equivalent

2.000 × 50% = 1.000

The following four possibilities may exist with regard to work-in-progress or the question of equivalent production:

1. Closing work-in-progress without any process loss or gain.
2. Closing work-in-progress with process loss or gain.
3. Opening and closing work-in-progress with no process loss or gain.
4. Opening and closing work-in-progress along with process loss or gain.

Situation I (Only Closing Work-in-Progress)

In this case equivalent production is determined in the case of closing work-in-progress by applying percentages of completion for each element of cost. After computing equivalent production, the cost per unit of equivalent production is found and this cost per unit is used to value the finished output transferred to the second process and also closing work-in-progress units. It should be noted that the cost per unit (for each element of cost) is applied to equivalent production of work-in-progress units and not to work-in-progress units directly.

Illustration 9:

Prepare statement of equivalent production, statement of cost and process account from the following information:

Units introduced	7,600
Output (units)	6,000

Process cost (Rs.):

Material	14,560
Labour	21,360
Overhead	14,240

Degree of completion for closing work-in-progress

Material	80%
Labour	70%
Overhead	70%

Solution:

Statement of Equivalent Production

Input	*Output items*	*Units*	*Equivalent Production* *Materials units*	*%*	*Labour units*	*%*	*Overhead units*	*%*
Units introduced	1. Units completed and transferred	6,000	6,000	100	6,000	100	6,000	100
7,600	2. Work-in-progress	1,600	1,280	80	1,120	70	1,120	70
7,600		7,600	7,280		7,120		7,120	

Statement of Cost

Element cost	*Cost (Rs.)*	*Equivalent production*	*Cost per completed unit (Rs.)*
Material	14,560	7,280	2
Labour	21,360	7,120	3
Overhead	14,240	7,120	2
	50,160		7

Statement of Apportionment of Cost

Output transferred		6,000 × Rs. 7 = 42,000
Work-in-progress:		
Material	1,280 × 2 = 2,560	
Labour	1,120 × 3 = 3,360	
Overhead	1,120 × 2 = 2,240	= 8,160
		50,160

Process Account

	Units	*Amount*		*Units*	*Amount*
To Materials	7,600	14,560	By Output transferred	6,000	42,000
To Labour		21,360	By Closing work-in-progress	1,600	8,160
To Overhead		14,240			
	7,600	50,160		7,600	50,160

Illustration 10:

A manufacturing concern, engaged in mass production produces standardised electric motor in one of its departments. From the following particulars of a job of 50 motors, you are required to value the work-in-progress and finished goods.

(*a*) Costs incurred as per job card:

Direct material	Rs. 75,000	Overheads	Rs. 60,000
Direct labour	Rs. 20,000		

(*b*) Selling price per motor: Rs. 4,500

(*c*) Soiling and distribution expenses are at 30% of sales value.

(*d*) 25 motors are completed and transferred to finished goods.

(*e*) Completion stage of work-in-progress:

Direct Material 100% Direct Labour and Overhead 60%

Solution:

Statement of Equivalent Production and Cost

	Direct Material		*Labour & Overhead*		
Particulars	*%*	*Qty.*	*%*	*Qty.*	*Total*
Transferred to finished goods	100	25	100	25	
Work-in-progress	100	25	60	15	
Equivalent units		50		40	
Total cost (Rs.)		75,000		80,000	1,55,000
Cost per equivalent unit (Rs.)		1,500		2,000	3,500

Actual Cost of Production per Unit of Finished Goods

Direct material	Rs. 1,500
Labour & Overhead	Rs. 2,000
Total	Rs. 3,500

Market Value per Unit of Finished Goods

Selling price	Rs. 4,500
Less: Selling and distribution overheads @ 30% of Rs. 4,500	Rs. 1,350
	Rs. 3,150

Stocks should be at the lower of the cost (i.e., Rs. 3,500) or market value (i.e., Rs. 3,150). Hence, basis of valuation will be market value in this case.

Value of Work-in-Progress

Direct Material: Rs. 1,500 × 25 units	= Rs. 37,500
Labour & Overhead: Rs. (3,150 – 1,500) × 15 units	= Rs. 24,750
	Rs. 62,250

Value of Finished Goods Stock

25 units × Rs 3,150	= Rs. 78,750
Total Value of Inventory = Rs. 78,750 + Rs. 62,250	= Rs. 1,41,000

Situation 2 (Closing Work-in-Progress and Process Loss or Gain)

Process loss may occur (*i*) early in a process or during a process; or (*ii*) at the final stages of a process. The point of occurrence of normal losses (spoiled units) has an important bearing on deciding which of the following two approaches should be used in process accounting:

1. *First Approach:* Cost of normal loss units should be spread over the entire production, i.e., cost of normal loss units should be included in the cost of all units computed as equivalent production.

2. *Second Approach:* Cost of normal loss units should be included in the cost of all good units which have been completed and thus cost of normal loss units will not be charged to closing work-in-progress.

The first approach is followed when normal loss occurs at the beginning of or during a process. Since the normal loss occurs early in processing it applies to both completed production and units that are left in process; all work (production) done in that period should be charged with the normal loss. This is achieved by using a value of zero as the finished equivalent of the units lost, thus forcing the good unit that remains to absorb the cost of the bad units. The normal loss units are completely ignored, the cost per unit is increased. Costs for the period are divided by a smaller number of equivalent units, thereby increasing the cost per unit. Cost apportionment to units completed and units still in process is computed using the higher unit cost. Thus, normal spoilage costs are automatically spread over all the equivalent good units (units completed and units in process).

The second approach is followed when normal process loss occurs at the end of a process (e.g., loss discovered after final inspection). In this case, as mentioned above, cost of normal loss units is included in the cost of only completed units and not in closing work-in-progress units. If the lost units occur at the end of a process, they are usually regarded as belonging to the completed units and hence costs are charged to those units which have been finished. Since none of the units lost or spoiled (normal loss units) come from closing work-in-progress, no part of the cost of spoiled units should be charged to the units still in process; the cost of spoiled units must be absorbed by the good units completed. This is done by first treating the normal loss units as completed and charging them with the same cost that applies to good completed units. The cost charged to normal loss units is then added to the cost of the good completed units, thus excluding any of the cost of the normal loss units in cost of work-in-progress units.

In absence of specific information regarding occurrence of normal loss, it should be preferably assumed that normal loss has taken place during a process and not at the end of a process. Hence, in such a case, the first approach (as mentioned above) should be followed.

Illustration 11: (Normal Loss at Beginning of or during a Process)

AB Ltd. is engaged in the process engineering industry. During the month of April 2008, 2000 units were introduced in Process X. The normal loss was estimated at 5% of input. At the end of the month, 1,400 units had been produced and transferred to process Y, 460 units were incomplete units and 140 units during the process had to be scrapped. The incomplete units had reached the following stage of completion:

Material	75% Completed
Labour	50% "
Overhead	50% "

Following is further information in Process X:

	Rs.
Cost of the 2,000 units	58,000
Additional direct material	14,400
Direct labour	33,400
Direct overhead	16,700

Units scrapped realised Rs. 10 each.

Prepare a statement of equivalent production, statement of cost, statement of evaluation and the Process X account.

Solution:

Statement of Equivalent Production

Units output	*Units*	*Equivalent Production*					
		Materials		*Labour*		*Overhead*	
		Qty.	*% of completion*	*Qty.*	*% of completion*	*Qty.*	*% of completion*
Normal loss	100	—	—	—	—	—	—
Abnormal loss	40	40	100	40	100	40	100
Completed and transferred to Process Y	1,400	1,400	100	1,400	100	1,400	100
Work-in-progress	460	345	75	230	50	230	50
	2,000	1,785		1,670		1,670	

Statement of Cost

Element of cost	*Cost (Rs.)*	*Equivalent*	*Cost per unit (Rs.)*
Materials: Unit introduced	58,000		
Direct	14,400		
	72,400		
Less: Scrap realisation	1,000		
	71,400	1,785	40
Direct labour	33,400	1,670	20
Overheads	16,700	1,670	10
Total	1,21,500		70

Statement of Apportionment of Cost

Production	*Element of cost*	*Equivalent production*	*Cost per unit (Rs.)*	*Cost (Rs.)*	*Total cost (Rs.)*
Abnormal loss	Material	40	40	1,600	
	Labour	40	20	800	
	Overhead	40	10	400	2,800
Finished production	Material	1,400	40	56,000	
	Labour	1,400	20	28,000	
	Overhead	1,400	10	14,000	98,000

Work-in-progress	Material	345	40	13,800	
	Labour	230	20	4,600	
	Overhead	230	10	2,300	20,700
					1,21,500

Process X Account

	Units	*Rs.*		*Units*	*Rs.*
Units introduced	2,000	58,000	Normal loss	100	1,000
Material		14,400	Abnormal loss	40	2,800
Labour		33,400	Transfer to Process Y	1,400	98,000
Overheads		16,700	Balance c/d	460	20,700
	2,000	1,22,500		2,000	1,22,500

Illustration 12: (Normal Loss at the End of a Process)

The finished products of a factory pass through two processes, the entire material being placed in process at the beginning of the first process. From the following production and cost data relating to the first process, prepare a statement of equivalent production, statement of cost, and process account of spoilage of 1,000 kg occur at the end of the first process.

Process costs	*Rs.*
Materials	60,000
Labour	33,600
Overhead	22,400
Units put into Process I	12,000
Transferred to Process II	10,000
Closing inventory (20% complete)	1,000

Solution:

Statement of Equivalent Production

Inputs	*Outputs*	*Units*	*Equivalent Production*					
			Materials Units	*%*	*Labour Units*	*%*	*Overhead Units*	*%*
Units Introduced	1. Normal loss	1,000	1,000	100	1,000	100	1,000	100
	2. Units completed & transferred	10,000	10,000	100	10,000	100	10,000	100
12,000	3. Closing work-in-progress	1,000	1,000	100	200	20	200	20
12,000		12,000	12,000		11,200		11,200	

Statement of Cost

Element of cost	*Cost Rs.*	*Equivalent production units*	*Cost per unit Rs.*
Material	60,000	12,000	5.00
Labour	33,600	11,200	3.00
Overheads	22,400	11,200	2.00
	1,16,000		10.00

Statement of Cost Apportionment

		Rs.
(*i*) Completed units transferred to Process II	10,000 × 10 =	1,00,000
Add: Cost of normal loss units	1,000 × 10 =	10,000
		1,10,000
(*ii*) Work-in-progress		
Material	1,000 × 5 =	5,000
Labour	200 × 3 =	600
Overheads	200 × 2 =	400
		6,000

Illustration 13: (Normal Loss during a Process)

R.P. Ltd. furnishes you the following information relating to Process B for the month of October 2007.

(*i*) Opening work-in-progress — NIL
(*ii*) Units introduced — 10,000 units @ Rs. 3 per unit.
(*iii*) Expenses debited to the process:

Direct materials	Rs. 14,650
Labour	Rs. 21,148
Overheads	Rs. 42,000

(*iv*) Normal loss m process — One per cent of input
(*v*) Closing work-in-progress — 350 units —

Degree of completion	
Material	100%
Labour and overheads	50%

(*vi*) Finished output 9,500 units
(*vii*) Degree of completion of abnormal loss:

Material	100%
Labour and overheads	80%

(*viii*) Units scrapped as normal loss were sold at Re. 1 per unit.
(*ix*) All the units of abnormal loss were sold at Rs. 2.50 per unit.

Prepare:

1. Statement of Equivalent production;
2. Statement of cost of finished goods. Abnormal loss and Closing work-in-progress.

Solution:

1. Statement of Equivalent Production (Process B)

	Total units	Equivalent Production: Material units	Completion %	Labour units	Completion %	Over-heads	Completion %
Finished output	9,500	9,500	100	9,500	100	9,500	100
Normal loss 1% of input of 10,000	100	—	—	—	—	—	—
Abnormal loss (balancing fig.)	50	50	100	40	80	40	80
Closing work-in-progress	350	350	100	175	50	175	50
	10,000	9,900		9,715		9,715	

Statement of Cost per Equivalent Unit

	Material	Labour	Overhead
Units introduced 10,000 × 3	30,000	—	—
Add: Direct material	14,650		
	44,650		
Less: Sale of normal scrap 100 × 1	100		
	44,550	21,148	42,000
Cost per equivalent unit of production	Rs. 44,550 / 9,900	Rs. 21,148 / 9,715	Rs. 42,000 / 9,715
	= Rs. 4.50	= Rs. 2.18	= Rs. 4.32

Total cost per unit of production = (4.50 + 2.18 + 4.32) = Rs. 11.00

2. Statement of Cost

Finished goods	= 9,500 × 11			1,04,500
Abnormal loss:				
Material	= 50 × 4.50	=	225.0	
Labour	= 40 × 2.18	=	87.2	
Overheads	= 40 × 4.32	=	172.8	485
Closing WIP:				
Material	= 350 × 4.50	=	1,575	
Labour	= 175 × 2.18	=	383	
Overhead	= 175 × 4.32	=	756	2,713
		Total		1,07,698

3. Process B Account

	Units	Amount (Rs.)		Units	Amount (Rs.)
To Opening WIP	Nil	Nil	By Normal loss	100	100
To Units introduced	10,000	30,000	By Abnormal loss	50	485
To Direct materials		14,650	By Finished output (Rs. 11 per unit)	9,500	1,04,500
			By Closing WIP c/d	350	2,713

To Labour		21,148			
To Overheads		42,000			
	10,000	1,07,798		10,000	1,07,798
To Material	12,000	60,000	By Spoilage	1,000	—
			By Output transferred	10,000	1,10,000
To Labour		33,600	By Closing work-in-progress	1,000	6,000
To Overhead		22,400			
	12,000	1,16,000		12,000	1,16,000

Note: As entire material is placed in the process at the beginning of the first process, it has been assumed that closing work-in-progress is complete 100% with regard to materials. Therefore, percentage of completion of 20% has been applied only in case of labour and overhead.

Situation 3 (Opening and Closing Work-in-Progress without Process Loss or Gains)

A process account may have opening work-in-progress as well as closing work-in-progress. The treatment of closing work-in-progress is the same with regard to equivalent production and determining its cost. In case of opening work-in-progress, the production or finished units completed during the period will comprise two lots: (*i*) the first lot will be opening work-in-progress which is partially incomplete and which will be completed during the period; (*ii*) the second lot of production will be of those units which are introduced into the process during the current period and have been completed during the period.

Since costs tend to vary from period to period, each lot may carry different units costs. The procedure of calculating equivalent production for opening work-in-progress units depends on which method of costing (cost flow assumption) has been used. If standard costing is not used, a method of costing can be selected from the following widely used methods:

1. First-in-First-out (FIFO)
2. Weighted Average Costing
3. Last-in-First-out (LIFO)

FIFO: The FIFO method of costing is based on the assumption that opening work-in-progress units are the first to be completed, the first cost incurred in the period should be attached lo units in opening work-in-progress. After opening work-in-progress units have been completed, new units are taken up during the current period. Equivalent production of opening work-in-progress can be calculated as follows:

Equivalent production = Units in opening W.I.P. × Percentage of work needed to finish the units.

Cost associated with the opening inventory in process are separated from costs of units started and completed during the period, and the costs of the two periods are not combined before final transfer of completed units out of process. No unit of opening work-in-progress is automatically found in closing work-in-progress.

Weighted Average Costing: Under average costing, opening work-in-progress units and costs both are combined with new production started in current period (both unit and cost) and weighted average cost per unit is determined by dividing the total cost (opening work-in-progress cost + current cost) by equivalent production. Costs attached with the opening inventory lose their identity because of this merger. The opening inventory cost is treated as if it were current period cost. No distinction is made between completed units from opening inventory and completed units from the new production. In fact, all units finished during the current accounting period are treated as if they were started and finished during that period. Therefore, equivalent, production (of opening work-in-progress) will be all units of opening work-in-progress. There is only one final unit cost for all completed units — a weighted average unit cost.

FIFO and average costing, although based on different costing concepts, do not necessarily produce significantly different unit costs. The differences in unit costs between the two costing methods may exist only under the following conditions:

1. Opening work-in-progress units are large, relative to the number of units started during the current period. The lesser number of units in opening inventory will have little influence on the average cost.
2. The stage of completion of the opening work-in-progress units is quite advanced. In absence of this, previous period costs of opening inventory will not have any impact on the average cost.
3. Previous period costs are substantially different from current period costs.

Average costing under normal conditions (if the above conditions do not exist) is the most appropriate, accurate and simple. However, if the above conditions prevail, the average cost may not be helpful in efficiency measurement and cost control.

LIFO: In LIFO method the assumption is that the units entering into the process in the last are the first to be completed. This method influences differently the costs of complete units and the closing work-in-progress. The cost of opening work-in-progress is charged to the closing work-in-progress and thus the closing work-in-progress appears at the cost of opening work-in-progress. The completed units appear at their current costs.

Illustration 14:

The accountant of a chemical company provides you the following data:

	Units	*Amount (Rs.)*
Work-in-process, beginning of period	2,000	
Direct materials		4,200
Direct labour and manufacturing overhead		1,950
Addition to work-in-process in April	4,000	
Direct materials		9,000
Direct labour and manufacturing overhead		7,500
Total		22,650
Work-in-process end of period	1,500	

Further, work-in-process at the beginning of the period is complete to the extent: materials 100% and labour and manufacturing overhead 75%. Work-in-process at the end of the period is complete to the extent: materials 100% and direct labour and manufacturing overhead only 50%.

You are required to:

(*i*) Calculate the number of units of product transferred to finished-goods stock during the period. Assume no units are lost in process.

(*ii*) Calculate the number of equivalent whole units of work completed during the period.

(*iii*) Calculate the unit cost for materials during the month of April using First-in, First-out method of inventory issue.

(i) Number of Units of Product Transferred to Finished Goods Stock

	Units
Opening work-in-progress	2,000
Add: Units introduced in April	4,000
	6,000
Less: Closing work-in-progress	1,500
Number of units transferred	4,500

(ii) Statement of Equivalent Production (FIFO Method)

	Units	*Materials*		*Labour & Overheads*	
		Degree of completion	*Equivalent units*	*Degree of completion*	*Equivalent units*
Opening work-in-progress (completed now)	2,000	—	—	25	500
Units introduced & completed	2,500	100	2,500	100	2,500
Units introduced but incomplete	1,500	100	1,500	50	750
	6,000		4,000		3,750

(iii) Statement of Unit Cost of Materials

Cost of materials incurred during the period	Rs. 9,000
Equivalent production	4,000 units
Cost per unit Rs. 9,000 / 4,000	Rs. 2.25

Illustration 15:

Prepare a statement of equivalent production, statement of cost, process account from the following information using the average method:

Opening Stock	2,000 units
Material	Rs. 10,000
Labour	Rs. 4,000
Overhead	Rs. 5,000
Units introduced	Rs. 80,000 units
Material	Rs. 40,000
Wages	Rs. 31,000
Overhead	Rs. 30,000

During the period 60,000 units were completed and transferred to Process II.

Closing stock 40,000 units, degree of completion.

Material	100%
Wages and overhead	25%

Solution:

Statement of Equivalent Production

Inputs	*Output*	*Equivalent Production*			
		Material		*Labour & Overhead*	
		Units	*%*	*Units*	*%*
Opening (20,000 units) Introduced (80,000 units)	1. Opening W.I.P. (20,000 units)	20,000	100	20,000	1000
	2. Units completed (40,000 units)	40,000	100	40,000	100
	3. Closing W.I.P. (40,000 units)	40,000	100	10,000	25
1,00,000	1,00,000	1,00,000		70,000	

Statement of Cost

Elements	*Opening cost (Rs.)*	*Current cost (Rs.)*	*Total cost Rs.*	*Equivalent production*	*Cost per unit*
Material	10,000	40,000	50,000	1,00,000	0.50
Labour	4,000	31,000	35,000	70,000	0.50
Overhead	5,000	30,000	35,000	70,000	0.50
	19,000	1,01,000	1,20,000		1.50

Statement of Apportionment of Cost

(i) Units competed and transferred 60,000 × 1.50 = Rs. 90,000

(ii) Closing work-in-progress:

Material	40,000 × 0.50 = 20,000	
Labour	10,000 × 0.50 = 5,000	
Overhead	10,000 × 0.50 = 5,000	30,000
Total cost		1,20,000

Process Account

	Units	Amount		Units	Amount
To Opening stock	20,000	19,000	By Units completed and transferred	60,000	90,000
To Materials	80,000	40,000	By Closing W.I.P.	40,000	30,000
To Labour		31,000			
To Overhead		30,000			
	1,00,000	1,20,000		1,00,000	1,20,000

Illustration 16:

From the following information prepare: (*a*) Statement of equivalent production (*b*) Statement of cost for each element (*c*) Statement of apportionment of cost and (*d*) Process account for Process A using the LIFO method of inventory costing for the month of December 2007.

Units in process. Dec. 2007 (All material used, 50% completed regarding labour and overhead)	10,000
New units introduced	20,000
Total units	30,000

Production report reveals the following information:

Units completed	15,000
Units in process on December 31, 2007	
(All material used, 50% complete regarding labour and overhead)	15,000
Loss in process	Nil

Cost Record

Work-in-process as on December 1, 2007

	Rs.
Material	3,600
Labour	3,900
Overhead	3,900
Cost for December, 2007	
Material	14,400
Labour	31,150
Overhead	31,150
Total cost	88,100

Solution:

Process A (LIFO Method)

Statement of Equivalent Production

Input		*Output*		*Equivalent Production*					
Particulars	*Units*	*Particulars*	*Units*	*Material*		*Labour*		*Overhead*	
				Units	*%*	*Units*	*%*	*Units*	*%*
Opening stock	10,000	Unit completed	15,000	15,000	100	15,000	100	15,000	100
New units introduced	20,000	Closing inventory							
		(*a*) work on O/WIP	10,000*	—		—		—	
		(*b*) New units	5,000	5,000	100	2,500	50	2,500	50
	30,000		30,000	20,000		17,500		17,500	

* No work has been done on units which represented opening work-in-process.

Statement of Cost of Each Element

Elements of cost	*Cost in process* *Rs.*	*Equivalent production* *Units*	*Cost per unit* *Rs.*
Material	14,400	20,000	0.72
Labour	31,150	17,500	1.78
Overhead	31,150	17,500	1.78
	76,700		

Statement of Apportionment of Cost

Item	*Elements*	*Equivalent production*	*Cost per unit*	*Cost*	*Total*
		Units	*Rs.*	*Rs.*	*Rs.*
Units completed	Material	15,000	0.72	10,800	
	Labour	15,000	1.78	26,700	
	Overhead	15,000	1.78	26,700	64,200

Closing inventory					
Opening WIP	Material	—	0.72		
	Labour	—	1.78		
	Overhead	—	1.78		
New units	Material	5,000	0.72	3,600	
	Labour	2,500	1.78	4,450	
	Overhead	2,500	1.78	4,450	12,500
					76,700

Process A Account

Particulars	*Units*	*Amount Rs.*	*Particulars*	*Units*	*Amount Rs.*
To Opening WIP	10,000	11,400	By Units completed	15,000	64,200
Units introduced	20,000		By Closing stock	15,000	23,900
Material		14,400			
Labour		31,150			
Overhead		31,150			
	30,000	88,100		30,000	88,100

Note: Process A/c has been credited with an amount of Rs. 23,900 being the cost of closing stock, determined as follows:

Costs of opening WIP:	*Rs.*
Material	3,600
Labour	3,900
Overhead	3,900
	11,400
Add: Cost of work done on opening WIP	Nil
Add: Costs of newly introduced units	12,500
	23,900

Illustration 17: (Average Costing)

Following information is available regarding process A for the month of February, 2008:

Production Record	
Units in process as on 1.2.2008	4,000
(All materials used, 25% complete for labour and overhead)	
New units introduced	16,000
Units completed	14,000
Units in process as on 28.2.2008	6,000
(All materials used, $33\frac{1}{3}$% complete for labour and overhead)	

Cost Records	*Rs.*
Work-in-process as on 1.2.2008	
Materials	6,000
Labour	1,000
Overhead	1,000
	8,000
Cost during the month	
Materials	25,600
Labour	15,000
Overhead	15,000
	55,600

Presuming that average method of inventory is used, prepare:

(*i*) Statement of equivalent production.

(*ii*) Statement showing cost for each element.

(*iii*) Statement of apportionment of cost.

(*iv*) Process cost account for process A.

Solution:

(i) Statement of Equivalent Production

(Average Cost Method)

Particulars			*Materials*		*Labour*		*Overhead*	
Input	*Output*	*Units*	*% completion*	*Equivalent units*	*% c completion*	*Equivalent units*	*% completion*	*Equivalent units*
20,000	Completed WIP	14,000 6,000	100 100	14,000 6,000	100 $33^1/_3$	14,000 2,000	100 $33^1/_3$	14,000 2,000
20,000		20,000		20,000		16,000		16,000

(ii) Statement of Cost

Particulars	*Materials*	*Labour*	*Overhead*	*Total*
Cost of Opening Work-in-progress (Rs.)	6,000	1,000	1,000	8,000
Cost incurred during the month (Rs.)	25,600	15,000	15,000	55,600
Total Cost (Rs.) (*i*)	31,600	16,000	16,000	63,600
Equivalent units: (*ii*)	20,000	16,000	16,000	
Cost per equivalent unit (Rs.) (*iii*) = (*i*)/(*ii*)	1.58	1	1	3.58

(iii) Statement of Cost Apportionment

			Rs.	*Rs.*
Cost of output transferred: (*i*)	14,000 units @	Rs. 3.58		50,120
Cost of closing work-in-progress (*ii*)				
Materials	6,000 units @	Rs. 1.58	9,480	
Labour	2,000 units @	Re. 1	2,000	
Overhead	2,000 units @	Re. 1	2,000	13,480
Total cost: (*i*) + (*ii*)				63,600

(iv) Process A Account

Dr. Cr.

Particulars	*Units*	*Rs.*	*Materials*	*Units*	*Rs.*
To Opening WIP	4,000	8,000	By Completed units	14,000	50,120
To Materials	16,000	25,600	By Closing WIP	6,000	13,480
To Labour		15,000			
To Overhead		15,000			
	20,000	63,600		20,000	63,600

Situation 4 (Opening and Closing Work-in-Progress with Process Losses or Gains)

In this situation, due adjustments are made for normal loss, abnormal loss, and abnormal gain in calculation of equivalent production. However, there is no change in the treatment of normal loss, abnormal loss and abnormal gain. Normal spoilage cost is borne by the good units produced; proceeds realised from the sale of normal loss scrap are credited to the relevant process account. These proceeds (sale of scrap) are also taken into account while calculating cost per unit of equivalent production. Abnormal loss units are valued like good units.

Illustration 18:

The in process inventory in Process No. 2 at the beginning of a period was valued at Rs. 2,950 made up of Rs 1,400 towards materials, Rs. 1,000 towards labour and Rs. 550 towards overheads for 100 units. The value added during the period was Rs. 53,600 towards an introduction of 4,100 units from the previous process besides Rs. 40,800 towards labour and Rs. 19,400 towards overheads. Out of 3,600 units completed, 3.300 units were transferred to the next process leaving the balance in stock. 400 units were held back in process with half completion towards labour and overheads while 200 units were loss in processing considered normal and hence should be borne by the entire inventory. Prepare a cost of production statement using average cost basis.

Solution:

Statement of Equivalent Production

	Total units	*Materials*	*Labour*	*Overheads*
Completed units (including 300 held in stock)	3,600	3,600	3,600	3,600
Closing WIP	400	400	200	200
Normal loss	200	—	—	—
	4,200	4,000	3,800	3,800

Statement of Cost Per Equivalent Unit

	Materials *Rs.*	*Labour* *Rs.*	*Overheads* *Rs.*
Opening WIP	1,400	1,000	550
Cost of units introduced	53,600	40,800	19,400
	55,000	41,800	19,950
Output (units)	4,000	3,800	3,800
Cost per unit (Rs.)	13.75	11.00	5.25

Cost of Production Statement

			Rs.
Cost of unit transferred:			
3,300 × (13.75 + 11 + 5.25)			99,000
Cost of units held in stock:			
300 × (13.75 + 11 + 5.25)			9,000
Cost of WIP:			
Material	400 × 13.75	= 5,500	
Labour	200 × 11.0	= 2,200	
Overheads	200 × 5.25	= 1,050	8,750
			1,16,750

Illustration 19:

The following data relate to Process Q:

(*i*) Opening work-in-process 4,000 units
Degree of completion:

Materials	100%	Rs. 24,000
Labour	60%	Rs. 14,400
Overheads	60%	Rs. 7,200

(*ii*) Received during the month of April 2008 from Process P 40,000 units — Rs. 1,71,000

(*iii*) Expenses incurred in Process Q during the month

Materials	Rs. 79,000
Labour	Rs. 1,38,230
Overheads	Rs. 69,120

(*iv*) Closing work-in-process: 3,000 units
Degree of completion:

Materials	100%
Labour & Overheads	50%

(*v*) Units scrapped
Degree of completion:

Materials	100%
Labour and Overheads	80%

(*vi*) Normal loss: 5% of current input
(*vii*) Spoiled goods realised Rs. 1.50 each on sale.
(*viii*) Completed units are transferred to warehouse.

Required: Prepare:

(*i*) Equivalent units statement.
(*ii*) Statement of cost per equivalent unit and total costs.
(*iii*) Process Q Account.
(*iv*) Any other account necessary.

Solution:

(i) Statement of Equivalent Production

Input Units	*Particulars*	*Output Units*	*Equivalent Production*					
			Materials		*Labour*		*Overheads*	
			% Completion	*Units*	*% Completion*	*Units*	*% Completion*	*Units*
4,000	Opening work-in-progress (units, completed and transferred to warehouse)	4,000	—	—	40	1,600	40	1,600
40,000	Units completed and transferred to warehouse	33,000	100	33,000	100	33,000	100	33,000
	Closing work-in-progress	3,000	100	3,000	50	1,500	50	1,500
	Normal Loss	2,000	—	—	—	—	—	—
	Abnormal Loss	2,000	100	2,000	80	1,600	80	1,600
				38,000		37,700		37,700

(ii) Statement of Cost Per Equivalent Unit and Total Cost

Particulars	*Material I* (*Process P*)	*Material II* (*Process Q*)	*Labour & Overhead* (*Process Q*)
Cost (Rs.)	1,71,000	79,000	2,07,350
Less: Recovery from sale of scraped 2,000 units at Rs. 1.50 per unit being normal loss	—	3,000	—
	1,71,000	76,000	2,07,350
Equivalent Production	38,000	38,000	37,700
Cost per unit	Rs. 4.5	Rs. 2	Rs. 5.50
Cost of Completed Units:			
Opening stock 4,000 units			45,600
Cost incurred to complete opening stock into finished products (1,600 × 5.50)			8,800
			54,400
Cost of 33,000 completed units (33,000 units × Rs. 12)			3,96,000
Total cost of 37,000 completed units			4,50,400
Cost of closing WIP 3,000 units (3,000 units × Rs. 6,50) + (1,500 units × Rs. 5.50)			27,750
Cost of 2,000 Abnormal Loss units (2,000 units × Rs. 6.50) + (1,600 units × Rs. 5.50)			21,800
			4,99,950

(iii) Process Q Account

Particulars	*Units*	*Rs.*	*Particulars*	*Units*	*Rs.*
To Opening work-in-progress	4,000	45,600	By Normal Loss	2,000	3,000
To Units received	40,000	1,71,000	By Completed Units (Transferred to Warehouse)	37,000	4,50,400
To Costs incurred:					
Materials		79,000	By Closing Work in Progress	3,000	27,750
Labour		1,38,230	By Abnormal Loss	2,000	21,800
Overheads		69,120			
	44,000	5,02,950		44,000	5,02,950

(iv) Abnormal Loss Account

Particulars	*Units*	*Rs.*	*Particulars*	*Units*	*Rs.*
To Process Q Account	2,000	21,800	By Sale Proceeds	2,000	3,000
			By Profit & Loss a/c (loss)		18,800
		21,800			21,800

Illustration 20:

The following data pertains to process I for March 2007 of Beta Ltd.:

Opening work-in-progress 1,500 units at Rs. 15,000

Degree of completion:

Material 100%: Labour and Overheads $33^1/_4$%

Input of material: 18,500 units at Rs. 52,000
Direct labour Rs. 14,000
Overheads Rs. 28,000
Closing in work-in-progress 5,000 units
Degree of completion: Material 90% and Labour and Overhead 30%

Normal Process Loss is 10% of total input
(Opening work-in-progress units + Units put in)
Scrap value Rs. 2.00 per unit.
Units transferred to the next process: 15,000 units.

You are required to:

(*a*) Compute equivalent units of production
(*b*) Compute cost per equivalent unit for each cost element, i.e., materials, labour and overheads.
(*c*) Compute the cost of finished output and closing work-in-progress.
(*d*) Prepare the process and other accounts.

Assume: (*i*) FIFO Method is used by the Company.
(*ii*) The cost of opening work-in-progress is fully transferred to the next process.

Solution:

(a) Statement of Equivalent Units of Production

Input	*Units*	*Output*	*Units*	*Equivalent Production*			
				Material		*Labour & Overhead*	
				%	*Units*	*%*	*Units*
Op. WIP	1,500	Work on opening WIP	1,500	—	—	66	1,000
Introduced	18,500	Introduced and completed in the period	13,500	100	13,500	100	13,500
Normal Loss			2,000				
Closing WIP			5,000	90	4,500	30	1,500
			22,000		18,000		16,000
		Less: Abnormal gain	2,000	100	2,000	100	2,000
	20,000		20,000		16,000		14,000

(b) Statement of Cost per Equivalent Unit for each Cost Element

		Cost Rs.	*Equivalent unit* Rs.	*Cost per equivalent unit*
Material Rs.	52,000			
Less: Scrap value	4,000	48,000	16,000	3
Labour		14,000	14,000	1
Overheads		28,000	14,000	2

(c) Statement of Cost of Finished Output and Closing Work-in-Progress

Particulars	*Elements*	*Equivalent unit*	*Cost per unit* Rs.	*Cost of equivalent units* Rs.	*Total* Rs.
Opening WIP (1,500 units)	—	—	—		15,000
Opening WIP	Material	Nil	—	—	—
—	Labour	1,000	1	1,000	
—	Overhead	1,000	2	2,000	3,000
Cost of Opening WIP completed during the period					
Units introduced and completed during the period	Material	13,500	3	40,500	
—	Labour	13,500	1	13,500	
—	Overhead	13,500	2	27,000	81,000
Total cost of 15,000 Units of finished output					99,000
Closing WIP (5,000 Units)	Material	4,500	3	13,500	
	Labour	1,500	1	1,500	
	Overhead	1,500	2	3,000	
Total cost of closing WIP (5,000 units)					18,000

(d) Process Account I

	Units	*Rs.*		*Units*	*Rs.*
To Balance b/d	1,500	15,000	By Normal loss	2,000	4,000
To Units introduced (Direct material)	18,500	52,000	By Transfer to Process I	15,000	99,000
To Direct labour	—	10,000	By Balance c/d	5,000	18,000
To Overhead	—	28,000			
To Abnormal gain (2,000 × 6)	2,000	12,000			
	22,000	1,21,000		22,000	1,21,000

Abnormal Gain Account

		Rs.			*Rs.*
To Process I A/c	2,000	4,000	By Process I	2,000	12,000
To Profit & Loss A/c		8,000			
		12,000			12,000

JOINT PRODUCT AND BY-PRODUCT

Joint Product

Joint products may be defined as distinctly different major products that are inevitably produced simultaneously from common inputs or by common processing. The quantity and sales value of each joint product are such that none of them may be designated as minor products; all joint products are major products.

Many industries, such as chemicals, oil refining, mining, meat packing and similar industries are involved in such joint production processes and manufacture two or more products from the same raw material. In oil refining, for example, fuel, oil, gasoline, kerosene, lubricating oils are but a few of the many products that emerge.

An increase in the output of one product will bring about an increase in the quantity of others, or vice versa, but not necessarily in the same proportion. At the same phase of production, two or more separately identifiable products will result from the joint production process. This phase or point is referred to as the split-off point.

Joint Products have the following Characteristics:

I. Joint products are the primary objectives of manufacturing operations.
2. The sales value of each of the joint products are relatively high and none of the joint products are significantly greater in value than other joint products.
3. The joint products may require further processing or may be sold directly after the split-off point.
4. Joint products require simultaneous common processing.
5. The manufacturer has little or no control over the relative quantities of the various products that will result.

By-product

The term "by-product" is often used synonymously with the term "minor products." It refers to those multiple products that have insignificant sales values relative to those of major products. Otherwise, by-products are the same as joint products. By-products are those products that result incidentally from the manufacture of the main product or products. Processing is not aimed in their direction.

ACCOUNTING FOR JOINT PRODUCT COST

When two or more products are classified as joint products, each individual product must be charged with a proportionate share of the total cost of the joint products. Prior to the point of split off, products are not subject to identification and costs are joint; after separation, product identification is possible and costs become separable. Thus, joint cost is a cost incurred prior to the point at which separately identifiable products emerge from the same process.

Accounting for joint product costs achieve the following objectives:

1. Allocating joint product costs incurred prior to the split-off point.
2. Identifying the production costs incurred after the split-off point to process joint products.

If a product is sold immediately after split-off, its unit costs consist totally of allocated joint costs. If a joint product is processed further after split-off, its unit cost will contain allocated joint costs plus the material, labour and overhead costs of additional processing. The following are apportionment bases usually found in practice for apportionment of joint costs:

1. Physical quantity method.
2. Relative marker or sales value method.
3. Average unit cost method.
4. Weighted average cost method.

Physical Quantity Method

Under the quantity method, cost allocation is a simple apportionment of cost in proportion to volume. These physical measures may be units, pounds, kilograms, tonnes, gallons, etc.

The following example illustrates this method:

Product	*kg.*	*Proportion to total*	*Cost allocated (Rs.)*	*Cost per kg. (Rs.)*
A	30,000	1/2	1,80,000	6
B	20,000	1/3	1,20,000	6
C	10,000	1/6	60,000	6
	60,000		3,60,000	6

Relative Market or Sales Value Method

The relative sales value method is often used to apportion joint product costs at the split-off point. The result is a percentage of cost to sales value for the output of the joint process. The sales value of each of the joint products is then multiplied by this percentage to arrive at the apportioned cost for that joint product.

The data given in the above example is being used herewith to explain the sales value method.

Product	*Quantity produced*	*Unit sales price*	*Sales value of production*		*Cost apportioned*	
		Rs.	*Rs.*	*%*	*Total*	*per unit*
A	30,000	4	1,20,000	20	72,000	2.4
B	20,000	9	1,80,000	30	1,08,000	5.4
C	10,000	30	3,00,000	50	1,80,000	18.0
	60,000		6,00,000	100	3,60,000	

Cost can be allocated in the following two ways:

1. Ratio of cost to sales value = $\frac{\text{Rs. } 3,60,000}{\text{Rs. } 6,00,000} = 60\%$

Product A	60% of Rs. 1,20,000	=	Rs. 72,000
Product B	60% of Rs. 1,80,000	=	Rs. 1,08,000
Product C	60% of Rs. 3,00,000	=	Rs. 1,80,000

2. Ratio of sales value of product to total sales value applied to total cost

Product A	20% of Rs. 3.60,000	=	Rs. 72.000
Product B	30% of Rs. 3,60,000	=	Rs. 1,08,000
Product C	50% of Rs. 3,60,000	=	Rs. 1,80,000

Profits under the Sales Value Method Move as the Sales Price

Product	Cost (Rs.)	Selling price (Rs.)	Profit	
			Amount (Rs.)	%
A	72,000	1,20,000	48,000	40%
B	1,08,000	1,80,000	72,000	40%
C	1,80,000	3,00,000	1,20,000	40%

Average Unit Cost Method

This method apportions total manufacturing costs to the various products by using an average unit cost obtained by dividing the total number of units produced into the total manufacturing cost. If all units produced are measured in terms of the same unit and do not differ greatly, this method can be used without much disadvantage. But when the units manufactured are not measured in similar terms, this method cannot be applied.

The average cost is computed by using the following formula:

$$\frac{\text{Total manufacturing cost}}{\text{Total number of units produced}}$$

Weighted Average Cost Method

Under this method, weight factors are often assigned to each unit based upon size of the unit, difficulty of manufacture, time used in making the units, difference in type of labour employed, amount of material used, etc. Finished production of every kind is multiplied by weight factors to apportion total costs to individual units. This method is also known as the survey method.

ACCOUNTING FOR BY-PRODUCTS

By-products can be classified into two categories according to their marketable condition at the spilt-off point: (*i*) those sold in their original form without need for any further processing: (*ii*) those which require further processing in order to be saleable. Because of wide variations in the nature of by-products, different accounting treatments are found in practice, such as the following:

1. *Sales of by-product as other income:* If the value of the by-product is comparatively small, many manufacturers treat the by-product like scrap material, and sell it. The sale proceeds of by-product are treated as other income.
2. *Sales of by-products as a reduction in the cost of joint products:* This method can be followed by reducing the cost of the main product by the total estimated income from the by-product less the selling expense incurred in effecting the sale of the by-product. By-products which are not sold, are kept in stock at nil value.
3. *Treating by-products having no cost at the time of separation but charging them with all costs after separation:* In such a case, costs incurred after separation should be deducted from the saleable value of the by-product and the balance should be credited to the profit and loss account or the relevant process account.
4. *Recording costs of by-products:* This method is applied when the by-products are of relatively high value and also require additional processing after separation from the main product. This requires apportionment of joint costs of the product upto the split-off point.

The cost of further processing the by-product is debited to the by-product account. This by-product account is credited with the sale proceeds of the by-product and any profit or loss is transferred to the costing profit and loss account.

5. *Replacement cost method:* The replacement cost method is used in those industries where by-products resulting from the manufacturing process are used within the company. The cost assigned to the by-product is the purchase or replacement cost existing in the market.
6. *Market value (reversal cost) method:* This method reduces the manufacturing cost of the main product, not by the actual revenue received, but by an estimated market value of the by-product prevailing at the time the by-product is recovered or sold.

Illustration 21:

B Ltd. manufacturers Product A which yield two by-products B and C. The actual joint expenses of manufacture for a period were Rs. 8,00,000.

It was estimated that the profits on each product as a percentage of sales would be 30%, 25% and 15% respectively. Subsequent expenses were:

	A	*B*	*C*
Materials	Rs. 10,000	Rs. 7,500	Rs. 2,500
Direct wages	20,000	12,500	5,000
Overheads	15,000	12,500	7,500
	45,000	32,500	15,000
Sales were	Rs. 6,00,000	Rs. 4,00,000	Rs. 2,50,000

Prepare a statement showing the apportionment of the joint expenses of manufacture over the different products.

Solution:

Statement Showing Apportionment of Joint Costs

	Products		
	A	*B*	*C*
Sales	Rs. 6,00,000	Rs. 4,00,000	Rs. 2,50,000
Less: Profit	1,80,000	1,00,000	37,500
Total cost	4,20,000	3,00,000	2,12,500
Less: Selling expenses (presumed to be as a percentage of sales)	19,200	12,800	8,000
Cost of manufacturing	4,00,800	2,87,200	2,04,500
Less: Subsequent costs	45,000	32,500	15,000
Share of joint costs	3,55,800	2,54,700	1,89,500

Working Notes:

	Total costs of all products (Rs. 4,20,000 + Rs. 3,00,000 + Rs. 2,12,500)	9,32,500
Less:	Total manufacturing costs (Rs. 8,00,000 + 92,500)	8,92,500
	Balance being selling expenses	40,000

Illustration 22:

Two products P and Q are obtained in a crude form and require further processing at a cost of Rs. 5 for P and Rs. 4 for Q per unit before sale. Assuming a net margin of 25 per cent on cost, their sale prices are fixed at Rs. 13.75 and Rs. 8.75 per unit respectively. During the period, the joint cost was Rs. 88,000 and the outputs were:

P 8,000 units

Q 6,000 units

Ascertain the joint cost per unit.

Solution:

Statement Ascertaining Joint Cost per unit

Output (Units) *Products*	*8,000* *P*	*6,000* *Q*
	Rs.	*Rs.*
Selling Price per unit	13.75	8.75
Less: Margin @ 25% on cost or 20% on sales	2.75	1.75
Cost of Sales	11.00	7.00
Less: Post split off cost	5.00	4.00
Joint cost per unit	6.00	3.00
Share in joint cost of units P and Q can be obtained by apportioning it in the ratio of 8 : 3 (W/N)	64,000	24,000
Ascertained joint Cost per unit	8.00	4.00
	(Rs. 64,000/8,000 units)	(Rs. 24,000/6,000 units)

Working Note:

Output (Units)	8,000		6,000
Total Pre-split off Cost (Rs.) (8.000 × 6)	48,000	(6,000 × 3)	18,000
Total Joint Cost Ratio between two products	8		3

Illustration 23:

In the course of manufacture of the main product 'P', by-products 'A' and 'B' also emerge. The joint expenses of manufacture amount to Rs. 1,19,550. All the products are processed further after separation and sold as per details given below:

	Main Product	*By-product*	
	P	*A*	*B*
	(Rs.)	*(Rs.)*	*(Rs.)*
Sales	90,000	60,000	40,000
Cost beyond split-off stage	6,000	5,000	4,000
Profit as percentage of sales	25%	20%	15%

Selling and administration overheads are absorbed as percentage of cost of sales. Prepare a statement showing the apportionment of joint cost to the main product and by-products. Also prepare main product 'P' account.

Solution:

Statement showing the Apportionment of Joint Costs

	Main product	By-product		Total
	P	A	B	
	Rs.	*Rs.*	*Rs.*	*Rs.*
Sales	90,000	60,000	40,000	1,90,000
Less: Profit (i.e., 25%, 20% and 15% respectively from P, A and B)	22,500	12,000	6,000	40,500
Cost of sales	67,500	48,000	34,000	1,49,500
Less: Selling expenses (675 : 480 : 340) Rs. 1,49,500 – Rs. 1,19,550 – 14,000 = Rs. 14,950	6,750	4,800	3,400	14,950
Cost of Production	60,750	43,200	30,600	1,34,550
Less: Cost after separation	6,000	5,000	4,000	15,000
Value at split-off point	54,750	38,200	26,600	1,19,550

P (Main Product) Account

	Rs.		*Rs.*
To Joint expenses of Manufacture	1,19,550	By Transfer of share in joint expenses:	
To Separate expenses	6,000	By-product A	38,200
		By-product B	26,600
		By Cost of Product of P	60,750
	1,25,550		1,25,550
To Cost of Product of P	60,750	By Sales	90,000
To Selling and Admn. Exp.	6,750		
To Profit	22,500		
	90,000		90,000

Illustration 24:

A factory is engaged in the production of a chemical BOMEX and in the course of its manufacture a by-product BRUCIL is produced, which after further processing has a commercial value. For the month of April, 2007, the following are the summarised cost data:

	Joint Expenses	Separate Expenses	
		BOMEX	BRUCIL
	Rs.	*Rs.*	*Rs.*
Materials	1,00,000	6,000	4,000
Labour	50,000	20,000	18,000
Overheads	30,000	10,000	6,000
Selling price per unit		98	34
Estimated profit per unit on sale of BRUCIL			4
		Units	Units
No. of units produced		2,000	2,000

The factory uses reverse cost method of accounting for by-products whereby the sales value of by-products after deduction of the estimated profit, post separation costs and selling and distribution expenses relating to the by-products is credited to the joint process cost account.

You are required to prepare statement showing:

(i) the Joint Cost allocable to BOMEX.

(ii) the product-wise and overall profitability of the factory for April, 2007.

Solution:

(1) Statement of Joint Cost Allocable to BOMEX

Total joint expenses	*Rs.*	*Rs.*
Materials	1,00,000	
Labour	50,000	
Overheads	30,000	
		1,80,000
Less: Joint Cost allocable to the production of 2,000 units of BRUCIL at the split-off point (See Working Note)		32,000
Cost of production of 2,000 units of BOMEX		1,48,000

(ii) Productwise and Overall Profitability Statement for the Month of April 2007

Particulars		*Products* BOMEX		BRUCIL	*Total* Rs.
Sales (Units)		2,000		2,000	
Selling price per unit (Rs.)		98		34	
Total sales (Rs.)		1,96,000		68,000	
Less: Cost of production at the split off point	1,48,000		32,000		
Post Separation Cost	36,000		28,000		
		1,84,000		60,000	
Profit (Rs.)		12,000		8,000	20,000

Working Note:

Computation of the joint Expenses Chargeable to the By-product BRUCIL

Units produced	2,000
Selling price unit (Rs.)	34
Total Sales: (2,000 × Rs. 34) (Rs.)	68,000
Less: Profit (2,000 × Rs. 4)	8,000
Cost of Sales	60,000
Less: Selling and distribution expenses	Nil
Less: Expenses after separation (Rs. 4,000 + Rs. 18,000 + Rs. 6,000)	28,000
Cost of Production at the split-off point	32,000

THEORY QUESTIONS

1. Discuss the distinguishing features of a process cost system.
2. Compare the cost accumulation and summarising procedures of a job order cost system and a process cost system.
3. What is equivalent production? What is its effect on computed unit cost?

4. Discuss the possible effects on a department's unit costs when materials are added to work-in-progress.
5. How is opening work-in-progress handled in average costing.
6. What are some of the disadvantages of the FIFO costing method?
7. What is the meaning of the term "split-off"? What is its significance in product costing?
8. What are joint costs? What problems are created by joint costs?
9. Explain the difference between a main product and a by-product.
10. How can the income from the sale of by-products be shown on the income statement?
11. Does the showing of income from by-products on the income statement influence the unit cost of the product?
12. What is the difference between physical quantity method and sales value method?
13. Define and explain the term "joint products and by-products." Enumerate the method which may be employed in costing "joint product."
14. Define joint products and by-products. Explain the various bases available for apportionment of joint costs to joint products.
15. Explain with an example the concept of 'equivalent production' for valuation of work-in-progress.
16. (*i*) What are the three most common methods of allocating joint product cost? Write a brief explanatory note on each.
    (*ii*) Explain the procedure of accounting for by-products.

EXERCISES AND PROBLEMS

1. From the following figures, prepare process accounts indicating the cost of process and the total cost. The production was 480 articles per week.

	Process I	*Process II*	*Process III*
Materials	Rs. 3,000	Rs. 1,000	Rs. 400
Labour	1,600	4,000	1,200
Factory Overheads	520	1,440	500

Office overheads amounting to Rs. 1,700 should be apportioned on the basis of wages. Ignore stock in hand and work-in-progress at the beginning and end of the week.

(*Ans.:* Process I — Transfer to Process 1. Rs. 5,520
Process II — Transfer to Process II, Rs. 12,960
Process III — Transfer to Finished stock Rs. 15,360

2. Prepare process cost accounts from the following details:

	Process A	*Process B*
Materials	Rs. 30,000	Rs. 3,000
Labour	10,000	12,000
Overheads	7,000	8,600
Input (Units)	20,000	17,500
Normal loss	10%	4%
Sale value wastage per unit	Re. 1 per unit	Rs. 2 per unit

There was no opening or closing stock of any type. The Final output from Process B was 17,000 units. Prepare process cost accounts showing the calculations of abnormal loss or gain

(*Ans.:* Process A abnormal loss @. Rs. 2.50 per unit: Process B abnormal gain @ Rs. 3.925 per unit.)

3. A product is obtained after passing it through three processes. The following information is collected for March 2008:

	Process I	Process II	Process III
Direct materials	Rs. 5,200	Rs. 3,960	Rs. 5,924
Direct wages	Rs. 4,000	Rs. 6,000	Rs. 8,000
Output in units during the month	950	840	750
Normal Loss (%)	5	10	15
Value of scrap (per unit)	Rs. 4	Rs. 8	Rs. 10

Additional information:

1,000 units at Rs. 6 each was introduced in Process I. There was no stock of materials or work-in-process at the beginning or at the end of that month. The production overheads were Rs. 18,000 for that month. Prepare Process Accounts indicating normal loss, abnormal loss and abnormal gain.

(***Ans.:*** No. 1: Normal loss 50 units; No II: abnormal loss 15 units; No. III: abnormal gain 36 units @ Rs. 76 per unit. Production overhead apportioned in the ratio of wages.)

4. In a process engineering factory, a product has to pass through three distinct processes before it is ready for sale. From the information appended below, work out the selling price of the product if the management decides to have a mark-up of 25% over its works cost.

	I	II	III
1. Stages of production			
2. Input of raw materials at Rs. 4 per kg	1,00,000		
3. Normal loss on input of each stage	5%	5%	5%
4. Delivered to next process (kg.)	90,000	80,000	—
5. Total direct labour cost (Rs.)	14,000	15,000	30,000
6. Variable overheads % on direct labour	150%	120%	100%
7. Fixed overheads % on direct labour	250%	140%	200%
8. Finished stocks held back at the stage	4,000	4,000	—

For the purpose of this exercise, abnormal loss, if any, may be charged to the respective stages since output of each stage can also be diverted to other processes for manufacture of other chemicals.

(***Ans.:***

	Process I	Process II	Process III
Closing stock	20	24	600
Normal loss	5 kg.	4.5 kg.	4 kg.
Abnormal loss	1 kg.	1.5 kg.	-

5. Product Z is obtained after it passes through three distinct processes. The following information is obtained from the accounts for the month ending December 31, 2008:

Items	*Total* *Rs.*	*Process* *Rs.*	*Rs.*	*Rs.*
Direct material	7,542	2,600	1,980	2,962
Direct wages	9,000	2,000	3,000	4,000
Production overhead	9,000			

1,000 units at Rs. 3 each were introduced to Process I. There was no stock, material or work-in-progress at the beginning or end of the period. The output of each process passes direct to the next process and finally to finished stores. Production overhead is recovered at 100% of direct wages. The following additional data are obtained:

Process	*Output during the month*	*Percentage of normal loss to input*	*Value of scrap per unit*
Process I	950	5%	Rs. 2
Process II	840	10%	4
Process III	750	15%	5

Prepare the process cost accounts and abnormal gain or loss accounts.

(*Ans.:* Process I 950 units Rs. 9,500
II 840 units Rs. 16,800
III 750 units Rs. 28,500
Abnormal loss Process II - 15 units Rs. 300 units
Abnormal gain process III - 36 units. Rs. 1,368

6. Product X is obtained after it is processed through three distinct processes. The following cost information is available for this operation.

	Total	*Process*		
		I	*II*	*III*
	Rs.	*Rs.*	*Rs.*	*Rs.*
Materials	5,625	2,600	2,000	1,025
Direct wages	7,330	2.250	3,680	1,400
Production overheads	7,330	—	—	—

500 units @ Rs. 4 per unit were introduced in process I. Production overheads are absorbed as a percentage of direct wages.

The actual output and normal loss of the respective processes are:

	Output unit	*Normal loss on input*	*Value of scrap per unit Rs.*
Process I	450	10%	2
Process II	340	20%	4
Process III	270	25%	5

There is no stock or work-in-progress in any process.

Show:

(*i*) the three process accounts.

(*ii*) the abnormal loss and abnormal gain accounts.

(*Ans.:* Process I — Transfer to process II 450 units Rs. 9,000
Process II — Abnormal loss 20 units Rs. 1,000. Transfer to process III 340 units Rs. 17,000.
Process III — Abnormal gain 15 units Rs. 1,200. Transfer to finished stock 270 units Rs. 21,600.

7. The finished product of a factory has to pass through three processes A, B and C. The normal wastage of each process is 2% in A. 5% in B and 10% in C, The percentage of waste is computed on the number of units entering each process.

The scrap value of wastage of process A. B and C are Rs. 10, Rs. 40, Rs. 20 per 100 units respectively. The output of each process is transferred to the next process and the finished products are transferred from Process C into stock. The following further information is obtained:

	Processes		
	A	*B*	*C*
	Rs.	*Rs.*	*Rs.*
Materials consumed	12,000	4,000	4,000
Direct labour	8,000	6,000	6,000
Manufacturing expenses	2,000	4,000	2,000

2,000 units were put into process A at a cost of Rs. 16,000. The output of each process has been A: 19,600 units. B: 18,400 units and C: 16,700 units.

There was no stock of work-in-progress in any process:

Prepare the process accounts.

(*Ans.:* Process A, units 19,600 Rs. 37,960, Rs. 609
Process B, units 18,400 Rs. 50,959, Abnormal loss (Process B) 220 units, Rs. 609
Process C, finished goods units 16,700, Rs. 63,120, Abnormal gain Process C 140 units Rs. 529.

8. A Product passes through three processes. Figure relating to production for the 6 months of 2008 are as follows:

	Process I	*Process II*	*Process III*
Raw materials used	1,000 kg.		
Cost per kg.	Rs. 200		
Manufacturing wages and expenses	Rs. 72,500	Rs. 40,800	Rs. 10,710
Weight lost	5%	10%	20%
Scrap sold at Rs. 50 per kg.	50 kg.	30 kg.	51 kg.
Sales price per kg.	Rs. 350	Rs. 500	Rs. 800

Management expenses were Rs. 17,500, selling expenses Rs. 10,000 and interest on borrowed capital Rs. 4,000.

Two-thirds of Process I and one-half of Process II are passed on to the next process and the balances are sold.

You are required to prepare process cost accounts in a form suitable for presentation to the directors at their next board meeting when the production policy of the company will be discussed.

9. X Ltd. produces a chemical, which requires processing in 3 departments, in the second department materials are added doubling the number of units. The following information relate to the operations of Department No. 2 for the month of September:

Units received from department No. 1	10,000
Units transferred to department No. 3	16,000

The balance of the units were still in process, 100% complete as to material and 50% complete as to labour and overhead.

Cost transferred from department No. 1	1,20,000
Cost added by the department:	
Materials	35,200
Labours	36,000
Factory overhead	28,800

Prepare a cost of production statement for department No 2 for September.

(***Ans.:*** Cost of Production for Dept. 2 Units 16,000 Rs. 1,81,760, cost of work-in-progress Rs. 38,240. Units in W.I.P. 4,000.)

10.

Units put into process	2,500
Units completed	2,000
Work-in-progress at close	500
Process costs:	
Materials	Rs. 22,500
Labour	6,750
Overhead	2,250

Work-in-progress is completed 40% as to materials, labour and overhead. Find out the,

(*i*) Equivalent production

(*ii*) Cost per unit of equivalent production, and

(*iii*) Process account

(***Ans.:*** Equivalent unit: Materials, labour and overhead 2,200 units each: Cost per unit Materials Rs. 10.227, labour Rs. 3.068, overhead Rs. 1.022.)

11. From the following details prepare statement of equivalent production, statement of cost and find the value of:

(*a*) Output transferred, and

(*b*) Closing work-in-progress applying average method of valuation of process stock.

Opening work-in-progress	2,000 units
Materials (100% complete)	Rs. 7,500
Labour (60% complete)	3,000
Overheads (60% complete)	1,500
Units introduced into this process	8,000

There are 2,000 units in process and the state of completion is estimated to be:

Materials	100%
Labour	50%
Overheads	50%

8,000 units are transferred to next process.

The process costs for the period are:

Materials	Rs. 1,00,000
Labour	78,000
Overhead	39,000

(*Ans.:* Equivalent units: Materials 10,000, labour and overheads 90,000 each: (*a*) Rs. 1,99,784, (*b*) Rs.35,723.

12. The following figures relate to a single industrial process:

Quantity of work-in-process at commencement 8,000 units.

Costs of work-in-process at commencement:

Material	Rs. 29,600
Wages	6,600
Overhead	5,800

During the period under review, a further 32,000 units were introduced and the additional costs were: Material Rs. 1,12,400, Wages Rs. 33,400, Overhead Rs. 30,200. At the end of the period 28,000 units were fully processed and 12,000 units remained in process. This closing stock was complete as regards material cost and one-third complete as regards wages and overhead.

Using the average method of valuation, tabulate these production and cost figures to give quantities, unit values, and total values for completed output and for each of the three elements comprising the closing work-in-process.

(*Ans.:* Equivalent units: Materials 40,000, labour and overhead 32,000 units each. Cost per unit: materials Rs. 3.55, labour Rs. 1.25, overhead Rs. 1.125: Cost of completed output Rs. 1,65,900, cost of work-in-process Rs. 52,100.

13. GH and Co. manufactures a product in one process. Process costing is followed and work-in-process stocks at the end of each month are valued on a FIFO basis.

At the beginning of the month June 2008, the inventory of work-in-process showed 400 units, 40% complete, valued as follows:

	Rs.
Materials	3,600
Labour	3,400
Overhead	1,000
Total	8,000

In the month of June, materials were purchased for Rs. 75,000. Wages and overhead in the month amounted to Rs. 79,800 and Rs. 21,280 respectively. Actual issue of materials to production was Rs. 68,500. Finished stock in the month was 2,500 units. There was no loss in process.

At the end of the month the work-in-process inventory was 500 units, 60% complete as to labour and overheads and 80% complete as to materials.

Prepare a statement of equivalent production, statement of cost and process account.

(*Ans.:* Value of finished stock Rs. 1,56,095
Value of work-in-process Rs. 21,485).

14. The following details relate to an intermediary process in a factory:

	% Degree of completion	No. of Units	Cost Rs.
Opening work-in-progress:		300	12,300
(a) Materials	50%		
(b) Labour	80%		
(c) Overheads	80%		
Transfer from previous process	100%	3,800	1,36,800
Process material added			7,900
Direct wages			37,400
Overheads			14,960
Transfer to next progress (finished)	100%	3,500	
Closing work-in-progress:		600	
(a) Material	100%		
(b) Labour	80%		
(c) Overheads	80%		

Prepare:

(a) Process cost accounts for the intermediary process.
(b) Statement of equivalent units (on FIFO basis).
(c) Statement of distribution of cost on the basis of equivalent units.

(*Ans.:* Transfer to next process 3,500 units Rs. 1,79,840
Closing stock 600 units Rs. 29,520).

15. From the following details prepare a statement of equivalent production, statement of cost and find the value of:

(a) Output transferred, and
(b) Closing work-in-progress.

Opening work-in-process: 2,000 units

The cost are:

	Rs.
Materials (100% complete)	7,500
Labour (60% complete)	3,000
Overhead (60% complete)	1,500
Units introduced into this process	8,000

There are 2,000 units in process and the stage of completion is estimated to be:

Material	100%
Labour	50%
Overheads	50%

8,000 units are transferred io the next process

The process costs for the period are:

	Rs.
Material	1,00,000
Labour	78,000
Overhead	39,000

(*Ans.:* Cost of output transferred Rs. 1,89,000 cost of closing W.I.P. Rs. 40,000.)

Joint Products and By-products

16. Hyderabad Chemical Company Ltd. manufactures a particular brand of phenyl. The phenyl passes through three important processes. During the month of January, 2007, 600 gross of bottles were produced. The cost books shrw the following information:

	Process A	Process B	Process C
Materials	Rs. 8,000	4,000	3,000
Labour	6,000	5,000	5,000

Direct expenses	1,200	400	1,000
Cost of bottles	—	4,060	—
Cost of corks	—	—	650

The indirect expenses for this period were Rs. 3,200. The by-products of Process B were sold for Rs. 480 and the residue of Process C was sold for Rs. 250. Prepare the process accounts, find out the cost of production in each process and the cost of finished product per gross of bottles.

(*Ans.:* Finished goods stock Rs. 40,780.
Indirect expenses should be apportioned as a percentage of labour cost.

17. Calculate the estimated cost of production of by-products X and Y at the point of separation from the main product.

	By-product X	*By-product Y*
Selling price per unit	Rs. 12	Rs. 24
Cost per unit after separation from the main product	Rs. 3	Rs. 5
Units produced	500	200

Selling expenses amount to 25% of total works cost, i.e., including both pre-separation and post-separation work cost.

Selling prices are arrived at by adding 20% of total cost, i.e., the sum of works cost and selling expenses.

(*Ans.:* Total cost By-product X Rs. 2,500, By-product Y Rs. 2,200
Cost per unit *X* Rs. 5, *Y* Rs. 11.)

18. From the following information, find the profit made by each product apportioning joint costs on sales-value basis.

Joint costs:

Direct material	Rs. 1,26,000
Power	25,000
Petrol, oil lubricants	5,000
Labour	7,500
Other charges	4,100

	Product X	*Product Y*
Selling costs	Rs. 20,000	Rs. 80,000
Sales	1,52,000	1,68,000

(*Ans.:*

	Product X	*Product Y*
Total costs (Rs.)	9,91,000	1,67,990
Profit (Rs.)	52,390	10)

19. From the following particulars, find out the cost of joint products A, B and C under Average Unit Cost Method:

(*a*) Pre-separation joint costs: Rs. 30,000

(*b*) Other production data:

Product	*Units produced*	*Raw materials used (Units)*
A	1,000	4,000
B	400	8,000
C	600	8,000
Total	2,000	20,000

(*Ans.:* Total costs (Rs.)

Product A	15,000
Product B	6,000
Product C	9,000)

Service Costing

CONCEPT

Service costing, also known as *operating costing*, is especially used where services are rendered and articles are not produced. According to Institute of Cost and Management Accountants (UK) operating costing is "that form of operation costing which applies where standardised services are provided either by an undertaking or by a service cost centre within an undertaking." Service costings are particularly suitable for the costing of road and rail transport services, electricity undertakings and hospitals, etc. The following cost units are usually applied in different service undertaking:

Nature of Business	*Cost Unit*
Public carriers, trucks, goods trains	Per tonne km. or per km
Electricity supply	Per kilowatt hour
Passenger buses and trains	Per km
Hospitals	Per patient day
	Per bed, per operation
Road maintenance	Per km of road
Hotels	Per room
Road lighting	Per lamp
Canteen	Per meal

NATURE OF SERVICING COSTS

Servicing costs are usually collected under the following headings:

1. Fixed or standing charges.
2. Semi-fixed or maintenance charges.
3. Variable or running charges.

An important feature of service costing is that mostly such costs are fixed in nature. For example, the costs of operating a theatre are usually not influenced by the size of the audience.

TRANSPORT COSTING

In transport undertakings, the cost unit is normally the tonne-mile or passenger-mile but the organisation of transport undertakings varies according to the nature of the undertakings. For example, rail transport is more complicated than road transport as provision has to be made not only for the vehicles but also for the maintenance of the permanent way, the station, signalling facilities, yards, engines, wagons etc. For the railway, separate cost centres need to be established.

COMPOSITION OF COSTS

In transport operating costing, the total costs consist of: (*i*) standing charges, (*ii*) running (variable) charges, and (*iii*) maintenance charges.

Standing Charges

In motor transport costings, the following are commonly the standing charges:

1. Licence duty and insurance
2. Garage costs and administrative expenses
3. Drivers' wages
4. Depreciation and
5. Tax

Running (Variable) Costs

The following variable costs are found in motor transport costings:

1. Petrol
2. Oil and
3. Grease

Maintenance Charges

1. Repairs and maintenance
2. Tyres
3. Garage charges

Cost Units

In transport costing, passenger-kilometre or tonne-kilometre is generally the cost unit. After collecting total cost, the cost per unit (the passenger km or tonne-km) is determined. The cost per unit is calculated as follows:

No. of vehicles × Capacity × Distance travelled × Days × Passenger/Weight actually carried.

ASCERTAINMENT OF COSTS

Accumulation and control of costs in transport costing are achieved through a daily log sheet and operating cost sheet. A daily log report is a document which contains information regarding each journey, *e.g.*, passenger or weight carried, starting and returning time, distance covered, oil or petrol used. Figure 22.1 gives a proforma of a Daily Log Sheet.

DAILY LOG SHEET

Vehicle No. ______________________ Date ______________________

Driver's Name ______________________ Starting time ______________________

Licence No. ______________________ Returning time ______________________

Particulars of Journey

Trip No.	*Starting*		*Arriving*		*Goods Carried*
Place	*Time*	*Place*	*Time*	*Out collected en route*	*Distance*

Petrol consumption:	Time lost:	Worker's time
At start ______	Loading ______	Driver ______
Recd./purchased	Unloading ______	
during the journey ______	Traffic ______	Mechanic ______
At finish ______		
Total consumption ______	Accident ______	Cleaner ______
Oil ______		
Grease ______		

Fig. 22.1 Daily Log Sheet

The operating cost sheet or cost statement is also known as the performance statement for each vehicle. Such cost sheets (Fig. 22.2) accumulate relevant costs regarding a vehicle from different sources, such as daily log sheet, wage book, purchase register or summary, repairs details, etc. Operating costs on a cost sheet are usually divided into three headings:

1. Running (variable) charges.
2. Standing (fixed) charges.
3. Maintenance charges.

The operating cost sheet acts as a cost control device. The total and per unit cost calculated can be compared with past figures and performance can be evaluated.

POWER HOUSE COSTING

Power house costing is applied in those undertakings which are engaged in the production of steam and generation of electricity. In large firms, a power house (boiler house) is generally a service department assisting the production department. Operating cost statement in this case can be prepared after collecting data about the costs of producing the steam and costs of generating the electricity. The unit of cost for production of steam may be 'per lb' and for generation of electricity 'per kilowatt.' A composite unit of cost may be used, i.e., the kilo watt-hour. A proforma of a power house operating cost sheet is given in Fig. 22.3. This operating cost sheet also shows different elements of cost of steam production and generation of electricity.

(ABC Transport Company)

Cost Sheet (Monthly)

Vehicle No. ____________ Month ____________

Registration No. ____________ Days operated ____________

Charges	Amount Rs.	P.
(A) Running Charges:		
Petrol		
Oil		
Grease		
Total		
(B) Standing Charges:		
Depreciation		
Insurance		
Interest		
Tax		
Licence fees		
Driver's salary		
Total		
(C) Maintenance Charges:		
Repairs		
Tyres		
Spares		
Garage charges		
Total		
Total charges Rs. ____________		
Total tonne-km/passenger km ____________		
Cost per tonne-km/passenger km ____________		

Fig. 22.2 Cost Sheet

CANTEEN COSTING

In most organisations, canteen facilities are provided at subsidy so that food and other items can be provided at minimum price. The costs are accumulated on a cost sheet which gives the total cost incurred. From the total cost the subsidy is deducted to arrive at the net cost of operating the canteen. After comparing the net cost with the sales proceeds, profit/loss is calculated. A specimen of canteen cost sheet is given in Fig. 22.4.

Illustration 1:

A Truck starts with a load of 10 tonnes of goods from station *P*. It unloads 4 tonnes at station *Q* and rest of the goods at station *R*. It reaches back directly to station *P* after getting reloaded with 8 tonnes goods at station *R*. The distances between *P* to *Q*, *Q* to *R* and then from *R* to *P* are 40 km, 60 km and 80 km respectively. Compute Absolute tonne-km and commercial tonne-km.

POWER HOUSE COST SHEET

Month____________ Total steam consumption____________

Total steam produced____________ Electricity generated____________

Items	*Cost per unit (Cost per 1,000 lb)*	*Total cost*
(A) Fixed Overheads:		
Rent, rates, etc.		
Depreciation of plant		
Depreciation of building		
Insurance		
(B) Maintenance Charges:		
Meters		
Furnace		
Service Materials		
Tools and accessories		
(C) Labour Charges:		
Cost handlers		
Ash removers		
(D) Fuel:		
Fuel		
Power		
(E) Water Charges:		
Water purchased		
Water softening		
(F) Supervision and Other Charges:		
Foremen		
Engineers		
General labourer		
Cleaners		
Total		

Fig. 22.3 Power House Cost Sheet

Solution:

While computing the absolute tonne-km., the travel between any two stations is considered individually. However, while computing commercial tonne-km, the trip is considered as a whole. On this basis the tonne-km have been computed as follows:

$$\text{Distance } P \xrightarrow[40\text{ km}]{} Q \xrightarrow[60\text{ km}]{} R \xrightarrow[80\text{ km}]{} P$$

$$\begin{aligned}
\text{Absolute tonne-km} &= 10 \text{ tonne} \times 40 \text{ km} + 6 \text{ tonne} \times 60 \text{ km} + 8 \text{ tonne} \times 80 \text{ km} \\
&= 1{,}400 \text{ tonne-km.} \\
\text{Commercial tonne-km} &= \text{Average Load} \times \text{Total Kilometres Travelled} \\
&= \left(\frac{10+6+8}{3}\right) \text{tonne} \times 180 \text{ km.} \\
&= 8 \text{ tonne} \times 180 \text{ km.} \\
&= 1{,}440 \text{ tonne-km}
\end{aligned}$$

CANTEEN COST SHEET

Month ________

Items	Total costs		Cost per meal
	Current month (Rs. P)	Previous month (Rs P)	
(A) Provisions:			
Bread			
Biscuits			
Cakes			
Eggs			
Meat			
Fish			
Vegetables			
Milk			
Fruit			
Others			
(B) Labour and supervision:			
Supervisor			
Cooks			
Helpers			
Counter clerks			
Cleaners			
Sweepers			
(C) Maintenance:			
Crockery			
Glassware			
Towels			
Rent			
Light			
Gas			
Insurance			
Consumable stores			
Total cost			
Less: Subsidy			
Net cost			
Sales			
Profit/Loss			

Fig. 22.4 Canteen Cost Sheet

Illustration 2:

A transport company maintains a fleet of lorries for carrying goods from Delhi to Panipat, 100 kms off. Each lorry, which operates 25 days on an average in a month, starts every day from Delhi with a load of 4 tonnes and returns from Panipat with a load of 2 tonnes. Calculate the total commercial tonne-kms and cost per commercial tonne-km when the total monthly charges for a lorry, are Rs 27,000. What rate per tonne should the company charge if it plans to earn a gross profit of 20% on the freightage?

Solution:

Commercial tonne-kms = Load × Distance × No. of days × Capacity Utilised
= 4 × 100 × 25 + 2 × 100 × 25
= 10,000 + 5,000
= 15,000 tonnes-kms.

Cost per commercial tonne-km

$$= \frac{\text{Total monthly charges}}{\text{Total commercial tonne-kms.}}$$

$$= \frac{\text{Rs. } 27{,}000}{15{,}000}$$

= Rs. 1.80

	Rs.
Rate to be charged	
Cost per commercial tonne-km =	1.80
Add: Profit 1/5 of Sales of Freightage	
or 1/4 of cost $\frac{180\times1}{4}$ =	.45
Rate per tonne-kin =	2.25

Illustration 3:

Saitravels owns a bus and operates a tourist service on daily basis. The bus starts from Newcity to Restvillage and returns back to Newcity the same day. Distance between Newcity and Restvillage is 250 kms. This trip operates for 10 days in a month. The bus also plies for another 10 days between Newcity and Shivapur and returns back to Newcity the same day; distance between these two places is 200 kms. The bus makes local sightseeing trips for 5 days in a month, covering a total distance of 60 kms per day.

The following data are given:

Cost of Bus Rs. 3,50,0000
Depreciation 25%
Driver's salary Rs. 1,200 p.m.
Conductor's salary Rs. 1,000 p.m.
Part-time clerk's salary Rs. 400 p.m.
Insurance Rs. 1,800 p.a.
Diesel consumption 4 kms per litre @ Rs. 8 per litre.
Token tax Rs. 2,400 p.a.
Permit fee Rs. 1,000 p.m.
Lubricant oil Rs. 100 for every 200 kms.
Repairs and maintenance Rs. 1,500 p.m.
(Normal capacity 50 persons).

While plying to and from Restvillage the bus occupies 90% of the capacity and 80% when it piles between Newcity to Shivapur (both ways), in the city the bus runs full capacity. Passenger Tax is 20% of net takings of the travels' Firm. Calculate the rate to be charged to Restvillage and Shivapur from Newcity per passenger, if the profit required to be earned is 33% of net takings of the Firm.

Solution:

Basic Calculations

	Kms.
(i) *Total kms covered per month*	
Restvillage and Back 2 × 250 × 10 days	5,000
Shivapur and back 2 × 200 × 10 days	4,000
Local Trips @ 60 km for 5 days	300
	9,300
(ii) *Fuel Cost*	
(a) Diesel required $\frac{9,300}{4} \times 8$	= 18,600
(b) Oil required $\frac{9,300}{200} \times 100$	= 4,650
	23,250
(iii) *Total Effective Passenger-km per month*	
Restvillage 2 × 250 × 50 × 10 × 90/100	= 2,25,000
Shivapur 2 × 200 × 50 × 10 × 80/100	= 1,60,000
Local trips 5 × 60 × 50	= 15,000
	4,00,000

(iv) *Computation of Operating Cost*

Operating Cost Statement for the Month

	Rs.	Rs.
Fixed Charges:		
Driver's salary	1,200	
Conductor's salary	1,000	
Clerk's salary	400	
Insurance 1,800/12	150	
Token tax 2,400/12	200	
Permit fee	1,000	= 3,950
Running charges:		
Depreciation		
$3{,}50{,}000 \times \frac{24}{100 \times 12}$	7,292	
Repairs and Maintenance	1,500	
Fuel cost	23,250	= 32,042
Total cost		= 35,992

Computation of Charges Per Passenger km.

Total Cost (as per (4) above)	Rs. 35,992
Profit on Takings (WN 1)	Rs. 53,719
Add: 20% for Passenger Tax (WN 2)	Rs. 10,744
Total Fare	Rs. 64,463

$$\text{Rate per Passenger km} = \frac{\text{Total fare}}{\text{Effective passenger km. per month}}$$

$$= \frac{\text{Rs. } 64{,}463}{4{,}00{,}000} = \text{Re. } 0.161$$

Charges per passenger

(*a*) From Newcity to Restvillage: 250 × 0.161 = Rs. 40.25

(*b*) From Newcity to Shivapur: 200 × 0.161 = Rs 32.20

Working Notes:

1. *Computation of Net Takings*

Let total takings be x

Profit is 33% of Net Takings (i.e., before passenger tax) = $.33x$

$x = 35,992 + .33x$

or $.67x = 35,992$

or x = Rs. 53,719

2. *Computation of Passenger Tax* (20% of Net Takings)

53,719 × 20/100 = Rs. 10,744

Illustration 4:

A lodging home is being run in a small hill station with 50 single rooms. The home offers concessional rates during six off-season months in a year. During this period, half of the full-room rent is charged. The management's profit margin is targeted at 20% of the room rent. The following are the cost estimates and other details for the year ending 31st March, 2009 (assume a month to be of 30 days):

(*a*) Occupancy during the season is 80%, while in the off season is 40% only:

(*b*) Expenses:

	Rs.
(*i*) Staff Salary (excluding room attendants)	2,75,000
(*ii*) Repairs to Buildings	1,30,500
(*iii*) Laundry and Linen	40,000
(*iv*) Interior and Tapestry	87,500
(*v*) Sundry Expenses	95,400

(*c*) Annual depreciation is to be provided for buildings at 5% and on furniture and equipments at 15% on straight line basis:

(*d*) Room attendants are paid Rs. 5 per room day on the basis of occupancy of the rooms in a month;

(*e*) Monthly lighting charges are Rs. 120 per room, except in four months of winter when it is Rs. 30 per room and this cost is on the basis of full occupancy for a month; and

(*f*) Total investments in the home is Rs. 100 lakhs of which Rs. 80 lakhs relate to buildings and balance for furniture and equipments.

You are required to work out the room rent chargeable per day both during the season and the off season months, on the basis of the foregoing information.

Solution:

Basic Calculations

(i) Computation of Estimated Costs for the year ending 31-3-2009

	Rs.
Salary	2,75,000
Repairs	1,30,500
Laundry and Linen	40,000
Interior Decoration	87,500

Depreciation:		
5% on 80 lakhs	4,00,000	
15% on 20 lakhs	3,00,000	7,00,000
Miscellaneous Expenses		95,400
Total costs		13,28,100

(*ii*) Number of Room Days in a year:

Season's Occupancy for 6 months @ 80% (50 × 0.8 × 6 × 30) = 7,200 room days

Off-season's occupancy for 6 months @ 40% (50 × 0.4 × 6 × 30) = 3,600 room days

Total Room Days during the year 10,800

(*iii*) Attendants' Salary

For Rs. 10,800 Room Days @ Rs. 5 per day = Rs. 54,000

(*iv*) Light Charges for 8 months at Rs. 120 per month or 120/30 = Rs. 4 per room day

Light Charges for 4 months of winter at Rs. 30 per month or 30/30 = Re. 1 per room day

Total lighting charges:	*Rs.*
— during season @ Rs. 4 for 7,200 days	28,800
— during 2 months of off-season @ Rs. 4 for 1,200 days (2/6 × 3,600)	4,800
— during 4 months of winter at Re. 1 for 2,400 days (4/6 × 3,600)	2,400
Total	36,000

Statement of Total Estimated Cost

	Rs.
1. Expenses as per (*i*) above	13,28,400
2. Attendants salary as per (*iii*) above	54,000
3. Lighting Charges as per (*iv*) above	36,000
Total cost	14,18,400
Computation of Total Full Room Days	
During Season	7,200
During off-season (equivalent to 50% rate of 3,600 days)	1,800
Total Full Room Days	9,000
Computation of Room Rent	
Cost per Room Day (i.e., 14,18,400/9,000)	Rs. 157.60
Add: Profit Margin at 20% of rent or 25% of cost	39.40
Room Rent	197.00

Thus, during season, room rent of Rs. 197 is to be charged.
During off-season, room rent of Rs. 98.50 is to be charged.

Illustration 5:

Mr. Harry is a travelling inspector for the Environment Production Agency. He uses his own car and the agency reimburses him at Rs. 180 per kilometre. Mr. Harry claims he needs Rs.. 2.20 per kilometer just to break-even. A scrutiny of his expenses by the agency reveals the following:

	Rs.
Oil charge every 4,800 km.	120
Maintenance (other than oil) every 9,600 km.	1,800
Yearly insurance (comprehensive with accident benefits)	4,000
Cost of car, with an average residual value of Rs. 60,000 and with a useful life of 3 years.	1,08,000

Petrol is Rs. 5 a litre and Harry gets 8 kms per litre for his car. When Harry is on the road, he averages 192 kilometres a day. He works 5 days a week, has 10 days' vacation in a year besides 6 holidays and spends 15 working days a month in the office.

You are required to determine:

(*a*) An equitable rate of reimbursement on the basis of the schedule he presently follows and (*b*) the number of kilometres a year he would have to travel, to break-even at the current rate of reimbursement.

Solution:

Total days in a year	365 days
Less: Non-working days = 2 × 52	104 days
Number of working days in a year = 5 × 52 = 260 + 1	261 days
Less: Vacation	10 days
Holidays	6 days
Office work 15 × 12 =	180 days
	196 days
Net 65 days ×	192 kms.
	= 12,480 kms. in a year

Statement of Operational Cost Per Kilometre

Particulars	Basic of apportionment		Amount Rs.	Per km. Rs.
A. Fixed Charges:				
Depreciation	$\frac{1,08,000 - 60,000}{3}$ =	16,000		
Yearly insurance		4,000		
Total		20,000		
Fixed charges per km	$\left(\frac{20,000}{12,480}\right)$			1.626
B. Variable cost:				
Oil, charge = $\frac{120}{4,800}$ × 12,480			312.00	0.0250
Maintenance = $\frac{1,800}{9,600}$ × 12,180			2,340.00	0.1875
Petrol $\frac{5}{8}$ × 12,480			7,800	0.6250
Total			10,452.00	0.8375
Total Cost (A + B)			30,452.00	2.4401

(*a*) Equitable rate of reimbursement = 2.44

(*b*) Current reimbursement rate = 1.8 per km

Less: Variable cost = 0.8375 per km

Contribution 0.9625 per km

$$\text{B.E.P. (km)} = \frac{\text{Fixed cost}}{\text{Contribution per kilometre}} = \frac{20{,}000}{0.9625} = 20{,}780 \text{ kms.}$$

He has to travel 20,780 kms in a year in order to break-even at the current rate of reimbursement, i.e., 320 km average daily instead of present average of 192 km a day.

THEORY QUESTIONS

1. What do you understand by operating costing? In what industries is this costing applied?
2. Write notes an (*i*) Transport-costing (*ii*) Power house costing and (*iii*) Canteen costing.

EXERCISES AND PROBLEMS

1. Mr. Ahuja runs a tempo service in the town and has two vehicles. He furnishes you the following data and wants you to compute the cost per running mile.

	Vehicle A	*Vehicle B*
	Rs.	*Rs.*
Cost of vehicle	25,000	15,000
Road licence fee per year	750	750
Supervision and salary (Yearly)	1,800	1,200
Driver's wage per hour	4	4
Cost of fuel per litre	1.50	1.50
Repairs and maintenance per mile	1.50	2.00
Tyre cost per mile	1.00	0.80
Garage rent per year	1,600	550
Insurance premium yearly	850	500
Miles run per litre	6	5
Mileage run during the year	15,000	6,000
Estimated life of vehicles	1,00,000 miles	75,000 miles

Charge interest at 10% p.a. on the cost of vehicle. The vehicles run 20 miles per hour on an average.

(***Ans:*** Operating cost per mile vehicle A Rs. 3.70, B Rs. 4.25.)

2. Mr. X owns a bus which runs according to the following schedule:

(*i*) Delhi to Chandigarh and back the same day:

Distance covered	150 km. one way
Day's run	10
Seating capacity occupied	90%

(*ii*) Delhi to Agra and back the same day:

Distance covered	120 km one way
Day's run	10
Seating capacity occupied	80%

(*iii*) Delhi local:

Distance covered per day	40 km
Day's run	4
Seating capacity occupied	100%

(*iv*) Following are other details:

	(*Rs.*)
Cost of the bus	Rs. 60,000
Depreciation @ 20% p.a.	
Salary of driver	350 p.m.
Salary of conductor	350 p.m.
Salary to part-time accountant	160 p.m.
Insurance	5% p.a.
Diesel consumption 4 km litre @ Rs 1 per litre	
Road tax	600 p.a.
Lubricant oil	10 per 100 km
Repairs and maintenance	500 per month
Permit fee	284 per month

The bus has a capacity of 50 persons. Passenger tax is 20% of the total takings. Calculate the bus fare to be charged from each passenger to earn a profit of $33^1/_3\%$ on total takings.

(***Ans.:*** Total takings Rs. 10,243)

3. From the following data calculate the cost per mile of a vehicle:

	Rs.
Value of vehicle	15,000
Road licence for the year	500
Insurance charges per year	100
Garage rent per year	600
Driver's wage per month	200
Cost of petrol per litre	0.80
Miles per litre	8
Proportional charge for tyre and maintenance per mile	0.20
Estimated life	1,50,000 miles
Estimated annual mileage	6,000 miles
Ignore interest on capital	

(***Ans.:*** Running cost per mile Re. 1.00)

Marginal (Variable) Costing

CONCEPT OF MARGINAL COST, MARGINAL COSTING

Marginal cost, in cost accounting, means variable production costs, i.e., the costs which tend to vary in direct proportion to the changes in the production level. If an extra unit of output is produced, the costs which could be incurred for producing this extra unit, will only be marginal (variable) costs since fixed costs remain constant.

Marginal costing is a costing technique in which only variable manufacturing costs are considered and used while valuing inventories and determining cost of goods sold. That is, only variable manufacturing costs are considered product costs and are allocated to products manufactured. These costs include direct materials, direct labour and variable factory overhead. Fixed factory (manufacturing) overheads are not considered product costs and are not used to value inventories and determine the cost of goods sold and are excluded from the cost of product. Fixed manufacturing costs are treated as period costs in marginal costing, *i.e.,* costs which are a function of a time rather than of production. In marginal costing, fixed manufacturing overheads are written off to the profit and loss account in the period in which they are incurred.

ABSORPTION COSTING

Absorption costing, also known as full costing, is a costing technique in which all manufacturing costs, variable and fixed, are considered as costs of production and are used in determining the cost of goods manufactured and inventories. All manufacturing costs are fully absorbed into finished goods.

DIFFERENCE BETWEEN MARGINAL COSTING AND ABSORPTION COSTING

Marginal costing and absorption costing differ from each other in the following, respects:

1. *Cost element in product cost:* Marginal costing, and absorption costing differ only in the treatment of fixed factory (manufacturing) overheads in the accounting records and financial statement. In both the costing techniques it is agreed that selling and administrative expenses, whether variable or fixed, are period costs and these costs are not treated as product costs with the result that selling and administrative expenses are not included in the costs of inventories, and costs of goods sold. Similarly, it is also agreed that variable manufacturing costs are product costs, *i.e.,* costs to be charged to the product. The disagreement between the two, is only in regard to the treatment of fixed manufacturing costs.
2. *Inventory values:* Marginal costing and absorption costing do influence inventory values differently. The value of inventories under marginal costing is relatively at a lower figure as inventories are determined in terms of only variable production costs. In absorption costing value of inventories is comparatively at a higher figure because it considers fixed factory overhead also besides the variable production costs.
3. *Difference in net income:* The treatment of fixed factory overhead brings differences in the net income figures in the two costing techniques. The magnitude of any difference in net income is a function of fixed manufacturing costs per unit and the change in inventory levels.

The question of difference in net income has been further explained in the following pages while discussing income statement under absorption costing and marginal costing.

INCOME STATEMENTS UNDER ABSORPTION COSTING AND MARGINAL COSTING

Income Statement under Absorption Costing

Under absorption costing all costs are divided into three categories: manufacturing, selling and administrative costs. In the income statement, all manufacturing costs (variable and fixed) are subtracted from the sales revenue to get a gross margin/gross profit on sales and selling and administrative expenses (fixed and variable) are deducted from gross margin to arrive at the net income.

It should be clearly understood that fixed manufacturing overhead are charged to units produced on the basis of per unit fixed manufacturing overhead rate obtained by dividing the standard fixed manufacturing overhead by nominal output level as follows:

$$\frac{\text{Standard fixed manufacturing overhead}}{\text{Normal output (Capacity)}}$$

If production is above or being the normal or standard output, adjustments are made for volume (capacity) variances, if the volume (capacity) variance is favourable, i.e., over-absorption (actual production being higher than normal capacity production), the amount of over-absorption is deducted from the total cost of goods manufactured and sold. If the volume (capacity) variance is unfavourable, *i.e.,* under-absorption (actual production being lesser than normal capacity production), the amount of under-absorption is added to the cost of goods manufactured and sold. A proforma of income statement prepared under absorption costing is given in Fig. 23.1.

Income Statement under Marginal Costing

Under marginal costing, only variable costs of production (direct material, direct labour and variable manufacturing) are subtracted from sales revenue to determine a balance which is known by different names, such as marginal contribution, marginal income (profit), marginal revenue, marginal balance, profit pick-up, etc. All fixed costs, and variable selling, distribution and administrative costs are deducted from this balance to arrive at the net income. Since fixed manufacturing costs are not charged to products under marginal costing, there can be no volume (capacity) variance. Marginal contribution/marginal income under marginal costing is greater than the gross profit/gross margin under absorption costing. Figure 23.2 depicts a proforma of income statement prepared under marginal costing.

INCOME STATEMENt (Absorption Costing)

	Amount *Rs.*
Sales	....
Less: Manufacturing costs:	
(1) Variable production costs:	
Direct material cost	....
Direct labour cost	....
Variable manufacturing overhead	....
	....
(2) Fixed factory (manufacturing) overhead	....
Cost of goods manufactured	....
Add: Beginning inventory	....
Cost of goods available for sale	....
Less: Closing inventory	....
Cost of goods sold	....
Over- or under-applied factory (manufacturing) overhead (Over-absorption to be deducted and under-absorption to be added)	....
Cost of goods sold at actual	....
Gross profit on sales	....
Less: Fixed selling and administrative expenses	....
Variable selling and administrative expenses	....
Net Income	....

Fig. 23.1 Income Statement Proforma (Absorption Costing)

Under marginal costing, fixed manufacturing overhead are excluded and therefore inventory values are lower than inventory value computed under absorption costing. Income may be higher or lower depending upon whether inventories are built up or liquidated. That is the income statement under absorption costing may reflect higher profit if the production is more than the normal capacity production and also lower sales has been made. This happens because above normal capacity production has over-absorbed its actual fixed manufacturing overhead.

Absorption/full costing and marginal costing influence differently gross profit, net profit, and inventory values of different month/periods. The following data and income statement prepared under both costing techniques explain this situation.

Income Statement of Marginal Costing

	Amount (Rs.)
Sales	....
Less: Variable production costs:	
Direct material costs	....
Direct labour cost	....
Variable manufacturing (factory) overhead	....
Cost of goods manufactured	....
Add: Beginning inventory	....
Cost of goods available for sale	....
Less: Closing inventory	....
Cost of goods sold	....
Marginal contribution	....
Less: Fixed manufacturing overhead	....
Variable selling and administrative expenses	....
Fixed selling and administrative expenses	....
Net income	....

Fig. 23.2 Income Statement Proforma (Marginal Costing)

Data:

Normal capacity 20,000 units per month
Variable costs (direct materials, direct labour, variable factory overhead) per unit Rs. 6.
Fixed factory overhead Rs. 25,000 per month or Rs. 1.25 per unit at normal capacity.
Fixed selling and administrative expenses are Rs. 5,000 p.m.
Variable selling and administrative expenses are Re. 1.00 per unit sold.
Sales price per unit is Rs. 10.
Actual production, sales and inventories in units are:

	First month	*Second month*	*Third month*	*Fourth month*
Unit in beginning inventory	—	—	3,000	1,000
Units produced	17,500	21,000	19,000	20,000
Units sold	17,500	18,000	21,000	16,500
Units in closing inventory	—	3,000	1,000	4,500

Solution:

Income Statement (Absorption Costing)

	First month	*Second month*	*Third month*	*Fourth month*
Sales (Rs.)	1,75,000	1,80,000	2,10,000	1,65,000
Variable cost per unit Rs. 6	1,05,000	1,26,000	1,14,000	1,20,000
Fixed factory overhead @ Rs. 1.25	21,875	26,250	23,750	25,000
Cost of goods manufactured	1,26,875	1,52,250	1,37,750	1,45,000
Add: Beginning inventory	—	—	21,750	7,250
Cost of goods available for sales	1,26,875	1,52,250	1,59,500	1,52,250
Less: Ending inventory	—	21,750	7,250	32,625
Cost of goods sold	1,26,875	1,30,500	1,52,250	1,19,625
Over- or under-applied factory overhead	3,125	(1,250)	1,250	—
Cost of goods sold at actual	130,000	1,29,250	1,53,500	1,19,625
Gross profit on sales	45,000	50,750	56,500	45,375
Selling and administrative expenses (fixed and variable)	22,500	23,000	26,000	21,500
Net income for the month	22,500	27,750	30,500	23,875

Note: In absorption costing income statement. Fixed factory expenses are included in the unit cost and also in the inventory values.

(*i*) Ending inventory: Second month $\frac{3,000}{21,000} \times 1,52,250 = \text{Rs. } 21,750$

Third month $\frac{1,000}{22,000} \times 1,50,500 = \text{Rs. } 7,250$

Fourth month $\frac{4,500}{21,000} \times 1,52,250 = \text{Rs. } 32,625$

(*ii*) In First month, Rs. 3,125 is under-absorbed factory overhead due to production less than normal capacity and should be added to the cost of goods sold.

(*iii*) In the second month, Rs. 1,250 is over-absorbed due to higher production and has, therefore been subtracted.

(*iv*) In the third month, Rs. 1,250 is under-absorbed and has been added back to cost of goods sold.

(*v*) In the fourth month, production is at normal capacity and there is no under- or over-absorption.

Income Statement (Marginal Costing)

	First month	*Second month*	*Third month*	*Fourth month*
Sales (Rs.)	1,75,000	1,80,000	2,10,000	1,65,000
Variable production cost:				
Variable manufacturing costs Rs. 6 per unit	1,05,000	1,26,000	1,14,000	1,20,000
Cost of goods manufactured	1,05,000	1,26,000	1,14,000	1,20,000
Add: Beginning inventory	—	—	18,000	6,000

Cost of goods available for sale	1,05,000	1,26,000	1,32,000	1,26,000
Less: Closing inventory	—	18,000	6,000	27,000
Cost of goods sold	1,05,000	1,08,000	1,26,000	99,000
Contribution	70,000	72,000	84,000	66,000
Less: Fixed factory overhead	25,000	25,000	25,000	25,000
Fixed selling and administrative expenses	5,000	5,000	5,000	5,000
Variable selling and administrative expenses	17,500	18,000	21,000	16,500
Total fixed costs and non-manufacturing variable costs	47,500	48,000	51,000	46,500
Net income for the month	22,500	24,000	33,000	19,500

Note: Under marginal costing, Fixed factory (manufacturing) overhead costs are not included in the product costs and costs of inventories.

(*i*) Valuation of closing inventory

Second month = 3,000 × Rs. 6 = Rs. 18,000

Third month = 1,000 × Rs. 6 = Rs. 6,000

Fourth month = 4,500 × Rs. 6 = Rs. 27,000

(*ii*) The question of under- or over-absorption of factory overhead does not arise under marginal costing.

A comparison of the income statements leads to the following conclusions:

1. Under variable costing, the closing inventory is costed at a smaller figure because only variable costs are charged to the product.
2. Both costing methods report the same amount of profit in periods in which production and sales are equal and there is no inventory change (first month). This is because the amount of fixed factory overhead costs charged to the period was the same in each case. Under marginal costing Rs. 25,000 was deducted from sales as period costs. Under absorption costing Rs. 25,000 was charged to the sales in two parts: (a) Rs. 21,875 as part of the cost of sales (17,500 units × Rs. 1.25); and (b) Rs. 3,125 as unfavourable volume (capacity) variance.
3. When inventory of manufactured goods fluctuates from period to period, net income will differ somewhat under the two methods because absorption costing requires that part of the period costs be included in inventory, whereas marginal costing excludes period costs. Therefore:

   (*i*) When production exceeds sales (the inventory is increased), the net income reported under absorption costing is higher than imported under variable costing. This follows because under absorption costing, a portion of the fixed costs budgeted for the period is shifted to the following period in the closing inventories whereas under marginal costing the total fixed costs are charged against income. This is clear from comparing the net income of the second and fourth month.

   (*ii*) When sale exceeds production (the inventories are decreased), marginal costing shows a higher profit because only current period costs are being charged against current revenues, whereas under absorption costing the period costs previously included in inventory are now being charged against current revenues. This situation is illustrated by the income of the third month.
4. Under marginal costing profits always move in the same direction as sales volume. They cannot, of course, increase or decrease in direct proportion because unit fixed costs do

not remain constant. Profit reported under absorption costing behave irregularly and sometimes in the opposite direction from sales. For example, sales of the fourth month are lower than the sales of the first month, yet the net income reported for the fourth month is higher than the net income for the first month.

5. The above income statements are prepared on the assumption that selling prices remained constant and that there were no changes in either the manufacturing costs or the selling and administrative expenses. Further, it has been assumed that overheads costs are absorbed at predetermined rates based on normal capacity.
6. The aggregate net income (of different months or periods taken together) will be the same under both costing methods provided production and sales, in total, are equal. In the above example, total production are 77,500 units and total sales are 73,000 units. Since production and sales are unequal, the combined net income is not the same.

Reconciliation of Net Income

The differences in the net income between absorption costing and marginal costing are due to: (*i*) amount of fixed factory overhead charged to inventory, (*ii*) Over or under-absorbed fixed factory overhead having been deferred in absorption costing. The entire difference in net income can be explained by the amount of fixed factory overhead that is included in the beginning and closing inventories.

Reconciliation of Differences between Absorption and Marginal Costing Income

	Second month (Rs.)	*Third month (Rs.)*	*Fourth month (Rs.)*
Marginal costing income	24,000	33,000	19,500
Absorption costing income	27,750	30,500	23,875
Difference to be explained	(3,750)	2,500	(4,375)
1. Differences in the value of opening and closing inventories:			
(*a*) Second month:			
Opening	0	—	—
Closing 18,000 – 21,750	(3,750)		
(*b*) Third month:			
Opening 18,000 – 21,750	—	3,750	
Closing 6,000 – 7,250	—	(1,250)	—
(*c*) Fourth month:			
Opening 6,000 – 7,250	—	—	(1,250)
Closing 27,000 – 32,625	—	—	(5,625)
	(3,750)	2,500	(4,375)

Inventory Values

Differences between the net incomes reported under absorption costing and marginal costing are also reflected in inventory values. As stated earlier, inventories under absorption costing absorb a part of the fixed manufacturing costs of a period, whereas inventories under marginal costing include only the variable manufacturing costs. Closing inventories calculated from the data given above would be as follows:

Closing Inventories

	First month	Second month	Third month	Fourth month
Absorption costing @ Rs. 7.25 per unit	—	21,750	7,250	32,625
Margin costing @ Rs. 6.00 per unit	—	18,000	6,000	27,000

The following summarises the differences between marginal costing and absorption costing with regard to effect on net income:

1. If production = sales; absorption profit = marginal costing profit.
2. If production > sales; absorption profit > marginal costing profit.
3. If production < sales; absorption profit < marginal costing profit.
4. If production fluctuates and sales are constant; absorption profit fluctuates and marginal costing profit is constant.
5. If production is constant and sales fluctuates: both profits vary in the direction of sales.

ADVANTAGES OF MARGINAL COSTING

The marginal costing has great potentialities for management in different managerial tasks and decision-making processes. Marginal costing is particularly useful to management in (*i*) profit planning, (*ii*) product pricing decisions, (*iii*) cost control, (*iv*) managerial decision-making, and (*v*) the impact of fixed costs.

Profit Planning

Profit planning, generally known as budget or plan of operations, may be defined as the planning of future operations to attain a defined profit goal. Under marginal costing, the cost data needed for profit planning and decision-making are readily available from the accounting records and statements. It facilitates the analysis of cost-volume-profit relationships by separating fixed and variable costs on the income statement. Marginal costing helps management in planning and evaluating the profit resulting from a change in volume, in the sales-mix, in make or buy situations, in the selection of the most profitable products, customers, territories, and other segments of the entire business.

Product Pricing Decisions

Marginal costing provides more useful information to management for pricing than absorption costing. Marginal costing serves as the basis of product pricing in many cases. Under marginal costing, management has the data to determine when it is advisable to accept orders if other than normal conditions exist. In some cases, a sales order can be accepted even if it contributes partly to fixed costs. However, the full cost and not only the variable cost should be the basis of product pricing in the long-run. The full cost is the cost which includes variable manufacturing cost and fixed manufacturing cost incurred in the production process.

Cost Control

Marginal costing provides continuing opportunities to review period costs in relation to the level of sales and net income. Separation of variable and period costs supports the use of standards, budgets, and responsibility reporting to aid management in controlling costs. Marginal costing helps in preparing reports for all departments or responsibility centres based on standard costs, flexible budgets, and a division of all costs into their fixed and variable components. All managers can examine and interpret their reports with respect to the cost variances originating in their respective areas of responsibility. Reports prepared on the marginal costing basis and accompanied by additional information become valuable planning and control tools.

Impact of Fixed Costs

Marginal costing evaluates the impact of fixed costs on profits because the total amount of fixed costs for the period appears in the income statement. It is argued that managerial decisions can be easily made if fixed expenses are separated and are not mixed in controlling operating costs.

Managerial Decision Making

The identification and classification of costs as either fixed or variable provide a framework for the accumulation and analysis of costs. This also provides a basis for the study of contemplated changes in production levels of proposed actions concerning new markets, plant expansion or contraction, or special promotional activities. The marginal income figure is useful figure to management because it can be readily projected to measure increments in net income which accompany increments in sales.

LIMITATIONS OF MARGINAL COSTING

The limitations of marginal costing are listed below:

1. The marginal costing method requires that all costs should be divided into fixed and variable components. It cannot be true under all circumstances. Examples of factors that might affect this assumption include quantity discounts on materials and labour efficiency variances.
2. Complete product cost does not depend only on variable costs. Fixed costs should be considered in determining the product cost and for long-range pricing and other long-run policy decisions.
3. Income figure obtained under marginal costing have to be used carefully if management decides to expand business or drop a product line. Management has to consider other factors also before deciding to drop a product line such as customer goodwill.

COST-VOLUME PROFIT (CVP) ANALYSIS

Profits of business firms are the result of many factors such as: (*i*) selling prices, (*ii*) volume of sales (*iii*) unit variable costs (*iv*) total fixed costs, (*v*) combinations in which the various product lines are sold, etc. To do an affective job in planning, management must have analyses which allow reasonably correct predictions of how profits will be affected by a change in any one of these factors. A cost volume profit (CVP) analysis is useful to management in knowing how profit is influenced by sales volume, sales price, variable expenses and fixed expenses.

Broadly, CVP analysis uses the techniques of (*i*) Break-even analysis and (*ii*) Profit-volume (P/V) analysis.

Break-even Analysis

A break-even analysis indicates at what level cost and revenue are in equilibrium. It is a simple and easily understandable method of presenting to management the effect of changes in volume on profits. Detailed analysis of break-even data will reveal to management the effect of alternative decisions which reduce or increase costs and which increase sales volume and income. It is a device which portrays the effects of any type of future planning by evaluating alternative courses of action.

Break-even Point

The break-even point can be defined as the point or sales level at which profits are zero and there is no loss. That is, break-even point is that point at which total costs are equal to total sales revenue. At the break-even point profit being zero, contribution (sales-variable cost) is equal to the fixed cost. If the actual volume of sales is higher than the break-even volume, there will be a profit. Beyond the break-even point, all the marginal contribution represents income.

Assume that a company manufactures and sells a single product as follows:

Selling price per unit = Rs. 20
Variable cost per unit = Rs. 10
Total fixed cost = Rs. 1,00,000

The break-even sales to cover fixed costs will be 10,000 units,

Selling price per unit = Rs. 20
Variable cost per unit = Rs. 10
Contribution = Rs. 10

$$\text{Break-even volume} = \frac{\text{Rs. 1,00,000 fixed cost}}{\text{Rs. 10 contribution margin}}$$

= 10,000 units.

If the company can sell more than 10,000 units, it will earn profits because fixed costs remain constant. If less than 10,000 units are sold, a loss will be incurred. The profits will be equal to the number of units sold in excess of 10,000 units multiplied by the unit contribution margin. For example, if 25,000 units are sold the company will be operating at 15,000 units above its break-even point and will earn a profit of Rs. 1,50,000 (15,000 units × Rs. 10 contribution margin).

Break-even Formula

The break-even point can be obtained directly by a mathematical formula. The basic formula to find out the break-even point is:

$$\text{Break-even sales (units)} = \frac{\text{Fixed cost}}{\text{Contribution margin per unit}}$$

$$\text{Break-even sales (volume)} = \frac{\text{Fixed cost}}{\text{C/S ratio (also known as P/V ratio*)}}$$

$$\text{Break-even sales volume)} = \frac{\text{Total fixed expenses}}{1 - \text{Total variable expenses/Total sales volume}}$$

$$\text{Cash break-even point (units)} = \frac{\text{Cash fixed cost}}{\text{Cash contribution per unit}}$$

* C/S ratio is popularly known as P/V ratio because after fixed costs are fully recovered, i.e., after break-even point all contributions (sales-variable costs) become profit. However, before break-even point all contributions will not become profit since fixed costs are yet to be recovered.

Break-even Chart

Total revenues and total costs at different sales volume can be estimated and plotted on a break-even chart. This chart is constructed as follows:

1. A horizontal base line, the x-axis, is drawn and spaced into equal distances representing either plant capacity, sales volume or number of units.
2. A vertical line, the y-axis, is drawn on the left side of the chart and also spaced into equal parts. This line indicates sales revenue and also costs.
3. A line parallel to the horizontal line (x-axis) is drawn for fixed costs.
4. A total cost line is drawn starting at the y-axis fixed cost point and moving to the right. This total cost line represents the total of all items of cost, fixed and variable.
5. The sales line is drawn starting at the zero point on the vertical axis and ending at the top on the right side.
6. The total cost line intersects the sales line at a point which is known as the break-even point.
7. The area to the left of the break-even point between the total cost line and the sales line is the loss area; the profit area lies to the right of the break-even point above the total cost line.

The data from the previous example are presented on the break-even chart (see Fig. 23.3).

From Fig. 23.3, it can be observed that the break-even point occurs when sales are 10,000 units at Rs. 2,00,000.

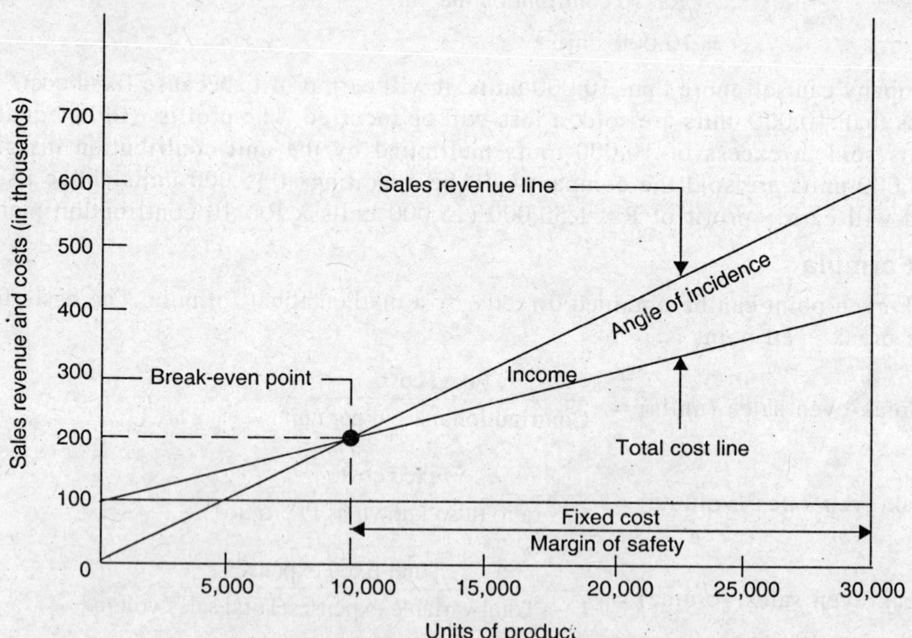

Fig. 23.3 Break-even Chart

Cash Break-Even Point

If a firm has a minimum of available cash, management may want to know the volume of sales that will cover all cash expenses, during a period. This is known as the cash break-even point.

Not all fixed operating costs involve cash payments. For example, depreciation expense is a non-cash charge. To Find the cash break-even point, the non-cash charges must be subtracted from total fixed operating costs. Therefore, the cash break-even position is lower than the usual break-even point. The formula is:

$$\text{BEP} = \frac{\text{FC} - \text{d}}{\text{P} - \text{V}}$$

where P = selling price per unit
V = unit variable cost
FC = fixed operating costs
d = depreciation expenses

Thus, cash break-even point indicates break-even sales to cover only the fixed costs involving cash payments and to break-even.

Margin of Safety

This is the difference between sales and the break-even point. If the distance is relatively short, it indicates that a small drop in production or sales will reduce profits considerably. If the distance is long, it means that the business can still make profits even after a serious drop in production. It is important that there should be a reasonable margin of safety, otherwise a reduced level of production may prove dangerous. The margin of safety can be found by using the following formula:

$$\text{Margin of safety} = \text{Profit} \div \text{P/V ratio}$$

$$\text{or Margin of safety} = \frac{\text{Profit} \times \text{Sales}}{\text{Sales} - \text{Variable cost}}$$

Angle of Incidence

This is the angle at which the sales line cuts the total cost line. Management's aim will be to have as large an angle of incidence as possible because a large angle of incidence shows a high rate of profit. A narrow angle would show that even fixed overheads are absorbed and profit accrues at a relatively low rate of return, indicating that variable costs form a large part of cost of sales.

Sales Formula

Often, it is necessary to know what level of sales is required to achieve a desired level of profit. The desired sales can be expressed in various ways:

Sales = Fixed cost + Variable cost + Profit

or

Sales = (Profit + Fixed cost)/P/V ratio

Basic Assumptions in Break-even Analysis

Break-even analysis is based on several assumptions, listed as follows:

1. Selling prices and pricing policy will remain constant at all sales levels. If this is not true, sales revenue cannot be plotted as a straight line.
2. All costs and expenses can be separated into fixed and variable components.

3. The total of the fixed costs is constant at all sales levels; the unit variable costs remain the same. If this is not true, straight lines cannot be drawn.
4. Production and sales quantities are equal.
5. Managerial policies, technological methods, and efficiency of men and machines will not change and cost control will neither be strengthened nor weakened.
6. Volume is assumed to be the only important factor affecting cost behaviour. Other influencing factors such as unit prices, sales-mix, labour strikes, and production methodology remain constant.
7. In case of multiple products being manufactured by the enterprise, the sales-mix should remain unchanged. That is, the calculation of the break-even point in the case of multiple products predetermines the number of units to be sold in respect of each product. This multiproduct sales-mix should remain unchanged.

Profit/Volume (P/V) Analysis

A P/V graph is sometimes used in place of or along with a break-even chart. Profits and losses are given on a vertical scale; and units of products, sales revenue or percentage of activity are given on a horizontal line. The horizontal line is drawn on the graph to separate profits from losses. The profits and losses at various sales levels are plotted and connected by the profit line. The break-even point is measured at the point where the profit line intersects the horizontal line. The P/V graph may be preferred to the break-even chart because profit and losses at any point can be read directly from the vertical scale; but a the P/V graph does not clearly show how costs vary with activity.

Data used earlier to prepare the break-even chart are also used in preparing the P/V graph (see Fig. 23.4)

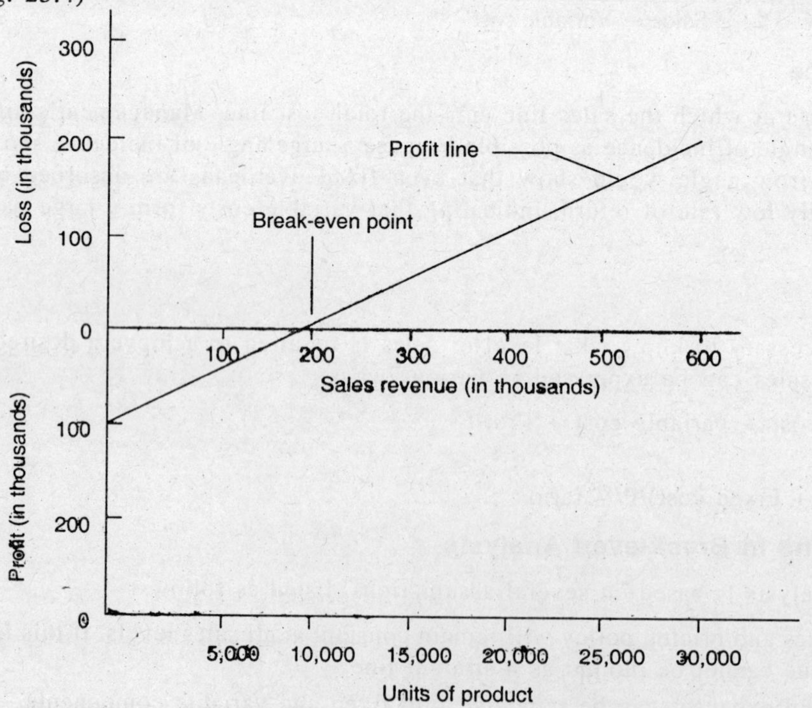

Fig. 23.4 Profit Volume (P/V) Graph

Role of CVP Analysis

A cost-volume profit analysis can be used to measure the effect of factor changes and management decision alternatives on profits. These factors include possible changes in selling prices, changes in variable or fixed cost, expansion or contraction of sales volume, or other changes in operating methods or policies. Cost-volume profit analysis is also useful for problems of product pricing, sales-mix, adding or deleting product lines, and accepting special orders.

(1) Changes in Selling Prices

The CVP graph is frequently used to illustrate the potential profit effects of contemplated price changes. Effects on the profit pattern are as follows:

(i) *Increase in selling price:* If the selling price is increased, it increases the P/V ratio, and the rate of fixed costs recovery is increased. The break-even point (break-even volume) declines, profit beyond the break-even point increases, losses below the break-even point decreases.

(ii) *Decrease in selling price:* If the selling price decreases, it decreases the P/V ratio and the rate of fixed cost recovery declines. The break-even point increases.

Assume, for example, that a company produces a product with a selling price of Rs. 10 per unit and a variable cost of Rs. 4 per unit. Fixed costs are Rs. 36,000 per year. The effect of a 20% increase and 20% decrease in the present selling price is given below:

	Selling price		
	Present	*20% Increase*	*20% Decrease*
Selling price per unit	Rs. 10.00	Rs. 12.00	Rs. 8.00
Variable cost per unit	4.00	4.00	4.00
Marginal contribution per unit	6.00	8.00	4.00
P/V ratio	60%	$66^2/_3$%	50%
Fixed costs	36,000	36,000	36,000
Break-even point in units	6,000	4,500	9,000
In volume	60,000	54,000	72,000
Changes in break-even point	—	—	—
In units	0%	– 25%	+50%
In sales volume	0%	– 10%	+20%

(2) Changes in Variable Costs

The CVP graph is used to evaluate the impact of increases and decreases in variable costs per unit.

(i) *Increase in variable costs:* An increase in variable costs has the same effect as a decrease in the selling price. It decreases the P/V ratio and the rate of fixed cost recovery is slower. The break-even point moves to higher level; profits after the break-even point decreases; losses before the break-even point increases.

(ii) *Decrease in variable costs:* A decrease in variable costs has the same effect as an increase in the selling price. A higher P/V ratio is achieved and the rate of fixed costs recovery is increased. The break-even point declines, profits beyond the break-even point are higher; losses before the break-even point are lower.

To illustrate the effect of change in variable costs, assume a company is selling a product for Rs. 40 a unit and has a variable cost of Rs. 20 per unit. Fixed costs total Rs. 48,000 per year. The effects of a 20% increase and a 20% decrease in variable cost are given in the following table:

	Present variable cost (Rs.)	*20% Increase (Rs.)*	*20% Decrease (Rs.)*
Unit selling price	40.00	40.00	40.00
Variable cost per unit	20.00	24.00	16.00
Marginal contribution	20	16.00	24.00
P/V ratio	50%	40%	60%
Fixed costs	48,000	48,000	48,000
Break-even point:			
Sales volume	96,000	1,20,000	80,000
Units	2,400	3,000	2,000

(3) Changes in Fixed Cost

Increases and decreases in the fixed cost do not have any impact on the P/V ratio but they change the break-even point. With the same P/V ratio, the rate of the fixed costs recovery remains the same.

(i) *Increase in fixed costs:* If fixed costs are increased, the break-even point (break-even-volume) is higher. Profits above the break-even point are lower by the amount of the increase in fixed costs; below the break-even point losses increase by the amount of increase.

(ii) *Decrease in fixed costs:* If fixed costs are decreased, it lowers the break-even point. The profits are greater by the amount of the decrease, and losses are smaller by the amount of the decrease in fixed costs.

Assume that a company has a P/V ratio of 40% and present fixed costs of Rs. 50,000. The effects of change in the fixed costs by Rs. 10,000 are as follows:

	Present fixed cost	*Increase by*	*Decrease by*
		Rs. 10,000	Rs. 10,000
Fixed costs	Rs. 50,000	Rs. 60,000	Rs. 40,000
P/V ratio	40%	40%	40%
Break-even point (Rs.)	1,25,000	1,50,000	1,00,000
Decrease	0	+ 25,000	– 25,000

From the above example, it is clear that the P/V ratio is the same in each situation and break-even point can be determined by dividing the amount of the change by the P/V ratio:

$$= \frac{\text{Change in fixed costs}}{\text{P/V ratio}}$$

$$= \frac{\text{Rs. } 10{,}000}{40\%} = \text{Rs. } 25{,}000$$

DESIRED OR TARGET PROFIT

Sometimes, management faces two decisions: (*i*) to increase sales volume through reduction in selling prices, and (*ii*) to increase selling prices in case the P/V ratio is low, with the expectation that a higher profit will be earned. These decisions should be taken carefully after studying the profit pattern and other factors, otherwise the results can be harmful particularly for those companies whose P/V ratios are already low. Also, if reduction in selling prices does not increase the sales volume, the price reduction will result only in lower profits.

The increase in sales volume required to overcome the effect of a price reduction is relatively greater when the rate of the contribution margin per unit is relatively greater as compared to when the rate of the contribution margin per unit is relatively low. If a product makes only a small contribution, then a reduction in selling price makes it all the more difficult to recover the fixed costs and to earn profits.

Similarly, a business firm may think of increasing the selling price if the P/V ratio is low. However, increase in selling price may reduce the sales volume.

MULTI-PRODUCT SITUATIONS

When there are multiple products with different contribution margins, the mix of the product has a direct effect on the fixed costs recovery and total profits of the firm. Different products have different P/V ratios because of different selling prices and variable costs. The total profits depend to some extent upon the proportions in which the products are sold.

For example, assume that a company with fixed costs of Rs. 25,000 per month manufactures two products A and B with P/V ratios as follows:

	Product A	*Product B*
Unit selling price	Rs. 10	Rs. 20
Variable, costs	4	16
Marginal contribution	6	4
P/V ratio	60%	20%

With comparatively low variable costs product A has a relatively high P/V ratio; each unit of product A sold contributes Rs. 6 to fixed costs recovery and profit. Product B, with comparatively high variable costs, has a low P/V ratio; each unit sold contributes only Rs. 4 to fixed costs recovery and profit. Other things being equal, the sale of product A is more profitable than that of product B, despite the fact that the selling price of product B is twice that of product A. It is correct to say that profits will decline as the sales mix shifts from product A to product B. This also implies, however, that new analyses of profit volume relationship must be made as the product-mix changes.

LIMITATIONS OF CVP ANALYSIS

CVP analysis is a useful planning and control device, usually in the form of a chart, showing how revenue, costs, and profit fluctuate with volume. The CPV technique is useful to management in areas of budgeting, cost control and decision making. In spite of CVP being a useful technique, it suffers from some limitations.

Firstly, because of the many assumptions, CVP is only an approximation at best. If prices, unit costs, sales-mix, operating efficiency, or other relevant factors change, then the overall CVP analysis and relationships also must be modified. Because of these assumptions, cost data are of limited significance.

In a multi-product situation, different products typically yield different contribution margins and are produced in various volumes with differing costs. As a result neither the revenue curve nor the cost curve is necessarily straight and the break-even point is difficult to find.

Therefore, while preparing or interpreting cost-volume profit analysis, all assumptions and limitations should be carefully considered. A series of CVP analysis based on different sets of assumptions and circumstances may be prepared to reflect situations prevailing in different business enterprises. When circumstances change, CVP analysis should also be revised to reflect the changing situations. It is also necessary to have up-to-date analysis so that it can act as a useful device in profit forecast, budgeting, cost control and managerial decision-making.

Illustration 1:

Prepare Income Statements under Absorption costing and under Marginal costing from the information relating to the year 2007-08.

Opening Stock = 1,000 units valued at Rs. 70,000 including variable cost of Rs. 50 per unit.
Fixed Cost = Rs. 1,20,000
Variable Cost = Rs. 60 per unit
Production = 10,000 units
Sales = 7,000 units @ Rs. 100 per unit.

Stock is valued on the basis of FIFO.

Solution:

Income Statement
(Absorption Costing)

	(Rs.)	(Rs.)
Sales		70,00,000
Less: Cost of goods sold:		
Opening stock (1,000 units × Rs. 70)	70,000	
Variable cost (10,000 units × Rs. 60)	6,00,000	
Fixed cost	1,20,000	
Cost of goods available for sales	7,90,000	
Less: Closing stock (4,000 units) 4,000 units × Rs. 72 =	2,88,000	
		5,02,000
Net Income		1,98,000

Income Statement (Marginal Costing)

	Rs.	Rs.
Sales		7,00,000
Less: Cost of goods sold:		
Opening stock (1,000 units × Rs. 50)	50,000	
Variable cost (10,000 units × Rs. 60)	6,00,000	
	6,50,000	
Less: Closing stock (4,000 units × Rs. 60)	2,40,000	4,10,000
Contribution margin		2,90,000
Less: Fixed Cost		1,20,000
Net Income		1,70,000

Difference in Net income = Rs. 1,98,000 – 1,70,000
= Rs. 28,000

This difference in net income is due to difference in inventory values:

	Absorption Costing (Rs.)	*Marginal Costing (Rs.)*
Opening stock	Rs. 70,000	Rs. 50,000
Closing stock	Rs. 2,88,000	2,40,000
Difference	2,18,000	1,90,000

Net difference = 2,18,000 – 1,90,000
= Rs. 28,000

Note: 1. It has been assumed that fixed cost is fixed production cost.
2. It has been assumed that variable cost (Rs. 60 per unit) is variable production cost.

Illustration 2:

Your company has a production capacity of 12,500 units and normal capacity utilisation is 80%. Opening inventory of finished goods on 1-1-2008 was 1,000 units. During the year ending 31-12-2008 it produced 11,000 units while it sold only 10,000 units.

Standard variable cost per unit is Rs. 6.50 and standard fixed factory cost per unit Rs. 1.50. Total fixed selling and administration overhead amounted to Rs. 10,000. The company sells its product at Rs. 10 per unit.

Prepare income Statements under Absorption Costing and Marginal Costing. Explain the reasons for difference in profit, if any.

Solution:

Income Statement for the year ended 31st Dec., 2008 (Under Absorption Costing Method)

	Rs.	*Rs.*
Sales: 10,000 units @ Rs. 10 per unit		1,00,000
Less: Cost of goods sold:		
Variable Production Costs:		
11,000 units @ Rs. 6.50 per unit	71,500	
Fixed factory cost @ Rs. 1.50 per unit		
11,000 × 1.50 =	16,500	
	88,000	
Add: Opening stock: 1,000 units		
@ Rs. 8 per unit (i.e., Rs. 6.50 + Rs. 1.50)	8,000	
Costs of goods available for sales	96,000	
Less: Closing stock: 2000 units valued at current cost.		
$\frac{96,000 \times 2,000}{12,000}$	16,000	80,000
Gross Profit		20,000
Less: Fixed selling and administrative overhead		10,000
Net Profit		10,000

Income Statement for the year ended 31st December, 2008 (Under Marginal Costing Method)

	Rs.	*Rs.*
Sales: 10,000 Units @ Rs. 10 per unit		1,00,000
Less: Marginal Cost:		
Variable production cost:		
11,000 units @ Rs. 6.50 per unit	71,500	
Variable cost of opening stock of finished stock		
(1,000 units @ Rs. 6.50 per unit)	6,500	
Cost of goods available for sales	78,000	

Less: Closing stock of finished stock: 2000 units @ Rs. 6.50 per unit	13,000	
	65,000	65,000
Contribution		35,000
Less: Fixed selling and administrative overhead	10,000	
Fixed factory cost @ Rs. 1.50 per unit	16,500	26,500
Net Profit		8,500

Reason for difference: The difference in profits, Rs. 1,500 (*i.e.*, Rs. 10,000 – Rs. 8,500), as arrived at under absorption and marginal costing methods is due to the element of fixed cost included in the valuation of opening and closing stock under the absorption costing method.

Illustration 3:

'LMN' limited sells its product at Rs. 3 per unit. The company uses a First-in, First-out actual costing system. A new fixed manufacturing overhead allocation rate is computed each year by dividing the actual fixed manufacturing overhead cost by the actual production costs. The following simplified data are related to its first two years of operation:

	Year I	*Year II*
Unit Data		
Sales	1,000	1,200
Production	1,400	1,000
Cost		
	Rs.	*Rs.*
Variable manufacturing	700	500
Fixed manufacturing	700	700
Variable marketing and administration	1,000	1,200
Fixed marketing and administration	400	400

Required:

(*i*) Prepare income statements based on:

(*a*) absorption costing and (*b*) variable costing for each year.

(*ii*) Give reasons for the differences in the answer.

Solution:

(i) Income Statement

(Absorption Costing)

	Year I (*Rs.*)	*Year II* (*Rs.*)
Sales	3,000	3,600
Less: Cost of goods sold:		
Opening stock	Nil	400
Variable manufacturing	700	500
Fixed manufacturing	700	700
Cost of goods available for sales	1,400	1,600
Less: Closing inventory $\frac{400}{1,400}$ × Rs. 1,400 (Year I)	400	240*
Cost of goods sold	1,000	1,360

Gross Profit	2000	2,240
Less: Variable Marketing and Administration	(1,000)	(1,200)
Fixed Marketing and Administration	(400)	(400)
Net Income	600	640

Note: In year II, FIFO method of inventory valuation is used. That is, closing inventory of 200 units belong to current production lot. Therefore, value of 200 units will be

$$\frac{200}{1,000} \times \text{Rs. } 1,200 = \text{Rs. } 240$$

Income Statement
(Marginal Costing)

	Year I	*Year II*
Sales	3,000	3,600
Less: Cost of goods sold:		
Opening stock	Nil	200
Variable manufacturing	700	500
Cost of goods available for sales	700	700
Less: Closing stock @ Rs. 0.50 (400 units, 200 units)	200	100
Cost of goods sold	500	600
Contribution margin	2,500	3,000
Less: Fixed manufacturing	(700)	(700)
Variable Marketing and Administration	(1,000)	(1,200)
Fixed Marketing and Administration	(400)	(400)
Net Income	400	700

(*ii*) The difference in profit figures between absorption costing and variable costing is due to the factory cost attached to inventory. Difference in Net Income is due to difference in inventory values. This is explained as below:

		Year I (Rs.)	*Year II (Rs.)*
Absorption costing net income		600 ↑	640
Marginal costing net income		400	700 ↓
		200	60
Absorption costing inventory:	Opening	Nil	400
	Closing	400	240
	Difference	400	160
Marginal costing inventory:	Opening	Nil	200
	Closing	200	100
Difference		200	100
Net difference		200	60

Illustration 4:

Hind General Corporation produces only one product which had the following costs:

Variable manufacturing costs Rs. 4 per unit

Fixed Manufacturing costs Rs. 2,00,000 per year

The normal capacity is set at 2,00,000 units. There are no work-in-progress inventories.

In 2008, the company produced 2,00,000 units and sold 90 per cent of them at a price of Rs. 7 per unit. In 2009, the company produced 2,10,000 units and sold 2,15,000 units at the same price.

You are required to prepare income statements for 2008 and 2009 based on absorption costing and marginal costing.

Solution:

Hind General Corporation

Income Statement (Marginal Costing Basis)

Particulars	*2008* *Rs.*	*2009* *Rs.*
Sales at Rs. 7	12,60,000	15,05,000
Inventory-opening at Rs. 4	Nil	80,000
Variable manufacturing costs at Rs. 4	8,00,000	8,40,000
Standard variable cost of goods	8,00,000	9,20,000
Inventory-closing at Rs. 4	80,000	60,000
Standard variable cost of sales	7,20,000	8,60,000
Contribution margin	5,40,000	6,45,000
Fixed manufacturing costs	2,00,000	2,00,000
Net Income	3,40,000	4,45,000

Income Statement

(Absorption Costing Basis)

Particulars	*2008* *Rs.*	*2009* *Rs.*
Sales at Rs. 7	12,60,000	15,05,000
Inventory-opening at Rs. 5	Nil	1,00,000
Variable manufacturing costs at Rs. 4	8,00,000	8,40,000
Fixed manufacturing costs at Re. 1	2,00,000	2,10,000
Total goods at standard cost	10,00,000	11,50,000
Inventory closing at Rs. 5	1,00,000	75,000
Standard cost of sales	9,00,000	10,75,000
Under (over) absorbed fixed costs	Nil	(10,000)
Actual cost of sales	9,00,000	10,65,000
Net Income	3,60,000	4,40,000

Illustration 5:

The following cost information relates to factory X for two years.

	2008	*2009*
Installed capacity (units)	10,000	10,000
Opening stock (units)	Nil	1,000
Closing stock (units)	1,000	Nil
Output (units)	10,000	9,000
Selling price per unit	14	14
Fixed costs for the year	85,000	85,000
Variable cost per unit	2.90	2.90

Work out the profit under absorption costing and marginal costing for the two years. Also state any abnormality in the results disclosed by absorption costing. Assume FIFO basis.

Solution:

Income Statement
(Absorption Costing)

	2008 (Rs.)	2009 (Rs.)
Sales	1,26,000	1,40,000
Less: Cost of goods sold:		
Opening stock	Nil	11,400
Variable production cost	29,000	26,100
Fixed cost	85,000	85,000
Cost of goods available for sales	1,14,000	1,22,500
Less: Closing stock	11,400	Nil
Cost of goods sold	1,02,600	1,22,500
Net profit	23,400	17,500
Net profit as percentage of sales	18.6%	12.5%

Note: It has been assumed that variable cost and fixed cost are production cost.

Income Statement
(Marginal Costing)

	2008 (Rs.)	2009 (Rs.)
Sales	1,26,000	1,40,000
Less: Cost of goods sold:		
Opening stock	Nil	2,900
Variable production cost	29,000	26,100
Cost of goods available for sales	29,000	29,000
Less: Closing stock	2,900	Nil
Cost of goods sold	26,100	29,000
Contribution margin	99,900	1,11,000
Less: Fixed Cost	85,000	85,000
Profit	14,900	26,000
Percentage of sales	11.8%	18.6%

Illustration 6:

Using the information below prepare profit statements for the months of June and July using (*i*) marginal costing (*ii*) full absorption costing. Also, explain why the two methods disclose different amounts of profit for June and July.

Data per unit:	Rs.
Selling price	50
Direct material cost	18
Direct labour cost	4
Variable production overheads	3

Monthly costs:	
Fixed production overheads	99,000
Fixed selling expenses	15,000
Fixed administration expenses	25,000

Variable selling costs are 10% of sales revenue and normal production capacity is 11,000 units per month.

	Sales (units)	*Production (units)*
June	10,000	12,000
July	12,000	10,000

Solution:

Profit Statement — Marginal Costing

	June	*July*
Sales units	10,000	12,000
Production units	12,000	10,000
Sales at Rs. 50	5,00,000	6,00,000
Less: Cost of goods sold:		
Variable production costs at Rs. 25	3,00,000	2,50,000
Add: Opening stock	—	50,000
Cost of goods available for sales	3,00,000	3,00,000
Less: Closing stock	50,000	—
Cost of goods sold	2,50,000	3,00,000
Contribution	2,50,000	3,00,000
Less: Fixed costs.		
Production overheads	(99,000)	(99,000)
Selling expenses	(15,000)	(15,000)
Variable selling expenses	(50,000)	(60,000)
Administrative expenses	(25,000)	(25,000)
Net profit	61,000	1,01,000

Working Note:

Variable production costs:	
Direct material cost	18
Direct wages	4
Variable production overheads	3
	Rs. 25

Profit Statement — Absorption Costing

	June	*July*
Sales units	10,000	12,000
Production units	12,000	10,000
Sales at Rs. 50	5,00,000	6,00,000
Less: Cost of goods sold:		
Production costs absorbed at Rs. 34	4,08,000	3,40,000
Add: Opening stock	—	68,000
Cost of goods available for sales	4,08,000	4,08,000

Less: Closing stock	68,000	—
Cost of goods sold	3,40,000	4,08,000
(over) under-absorbed fixed Production overheads at Rs. 9	(9,000)	9,000
Adjusted cost of goods sold	3,31,000	4,17,000
Gross profit	1,69,000	1,83,000
Less: Variable selling expenses	(50,000)	(60,000)
Fixed selling expenses	(15,000)	(15,000)
Fixed administration expenses	(25,000)	(25,000)
Net profit	Rs. 79,000	Rs. 83,000

Working Note:

Production costs:	*Rs.*	
Direct material cost	18	
Direct wages	4	
Variable production overheads	3	
Fixed production overheads	9	(Rs. 99,000 ÷ 11,000 units)
	Rs. 34	

Taken together, the two costing techniques disclose the same total profit for the two months.

In June marginal costing discloses Rs. 18,000 less profit than full absorption costing. This difference is caused by 2,000 units being in stock. Under absorption costing the fixed production overhead absorbed by these units cost Rs. 18,000 (2000 × Rs. 9), and this amount is carried forward in the cost of stock rather than being written off against profit in June as with the marginal costing.

In July, sales exceed production by 2000 units, and the Rs. 18,000 of fixed production overheads is charged against revenue, as the stocks created in June have been sold.

Illustration 7:

ABC Motors assembles and sells motor vehicles. It uses an actual costing system, in which unit costs are calculated on a monthly basis. Data relating to March and April, 2009 are:

	March	*April*
Unit data:		
Beginning Inventory	0	150
Production	500	400
Sales	350	520
Variable-cost data:		
Manufacturing Costs per unit produced	Rs. 10,000	Rs. 10,000
Distribution costs per unit sold	3,000	3,000
Fixed-cost data:		
Manufacturing Costs	Rs. 20,00,000	Rs. 20,00,000
Marketing Costs	6,00,000	6,00,000

The selling price per motor vehicle is Rs. 24,000.

Required:

(*i*) Present income statements for ABC Motors in March and April of 2009 under (*a*) variable costing, and (*b*) absorption costing.

(*ii*) Explain the differences between (*a*) and (*b*) for March and April.

Solution:

(i) Income Statement (Variable Costing)

	March (Rs.)	April (Rs.)
Sales	84,00,000	1,24,80,000
Less: Variable cost of goods sold:		
Opening stock	Nil	15,00,000
Variable manufacturing cost	50,00,000	40,00,000
Cost of goods available for sales	50,00,000	55,00,000
Less: Closing stock	15,00,000	3,00,000
Cost of goods sold	35,00,000	52,00,000
Contribution Margin	49,00,000	72,80,000
Less: Other costs:		
Fixed manufacturing	(20,00,000)	(20,00,000)
Fixed marketing	(6,00,000)	(6,00,000)
Variable distribution	(10,50,000)	(15,60,000)
Net Income	12,50,000	31,20,000

Income Statement

(Absorption Costing)

	March (Rs.)	April (Rs.)
Sales	84,00,000	1,24,80,000
Less: Cost of goods sold:		
Opening stock	Nil	21,00,000
Variable manufacturing cost	50,00,000	40,00,000
Fixed manufacturing cost	20,00,000	20,00,000
Cost of goods available for sales	70,00,000	81,00,000
Less: Closing stock	21,00,000	4,50,000
Cost of goods sold	49,00,000	76,50,000
Gross profit	35,00,000	48,30,000
Less: Distribution Cost	(10,50,000)	(15,60,000)
Fixed marketing	(6,00,000)	(6,00,000)
Net income	18,50,000	(26,70,000)

Note: The company follows actual costing system and calculates unit costs on monthly basis. Therefore, for April month, inventory of 30 units has been valued as follows:

Variable manufacturing cost 30 × Rs. 10,000	=	30,00,000
Fixed manufacturing cost @ Rs. 5000 × 30	=	15,00,000
(*i e.,* 20,00,000 ÷ Current Production 400 units)		
That is, inventory at Rs. 15,000 per unit	=	45,00,000

For March month, inventory of 150 units has been calculated as follows:

Variable manufacturing Rs. 10.000 × 150	=	Rs. 15,00,000
Fixed manufacturing Rs. 4000 × 150	=	Rs. 6,00,000
That is, inventory at Rs. 14,000 per unit	=	Rs. 21,00,000

(ii) Difference in Profit

	March	April
Absorption Costing profit	Rs. 18,50,000	Rs. 26,70,000
Variable costing profit	↑12,50,000	↓31,20,000
	6,00,000	4,50,000

Difference in profit is due to difference in inventory values in the two costing techniques

	March (Rs.)	April Rs.)
Absorption costing:		
Opening stock	Nil	21,00,000
Closing stock	21,00,000	4,50,000
Difference	21,00,000	16,50,000
Variable costing:		
Opening stock	Nil	15,00,000
Closing stock	15,00,000	3,00,000
Difference	15,00,000	12,00,000
Net difference (effect)	6,00,000	4,50,000

Illustration 8:

The ratio of variable cost to sales is 70%. The break-even point occurs at 60% of the capacity sales. Find the capacity sales when fixed costs are Rs. 90,000. Also compute profit at 75% of the capacity sales.

Solution:

Basic Calculations

$$\frac{\text{Variable cost}}{\text{Sales}} = 70\%$$

$$\text{Hence } \frac{\text{Contribution}}{\text{Sales}} = 30\% \text{ or P/V Ratio} = 30\%$$

Computation of Capacity Sales

$$\text{Break-even Point} = \frac{\text{Fixed cost}}{\text{P/V ratio}} = \frac{\text{Rs. 90,000}}{30\%} = \text{Rs. 3,00,000} \quad \ldots (i)$$

$$\text{Break-even Point (as given)} = 60\% \text{ of capacity sales}$$

$$\text{Hence Capacity Sales} = \frac{\text{Rs. 3,00,000}}{60\%} = \text{Rs. 5,00,000}$$

Computation of Profit at 75% of the Capacity Sales

	Rs.
75% of Capacity sales (75% × Rs. 5,00,000)	3,75,000
Less: Variable Cost (70% × Rs. 3,75,000)	2,62,500
Contribution	1,12,500
Less: Fixed Cost	90,000
Profit	22,500

Illustration 9:

Profit/Volume Ratio of a company is 50%, while its margin of safety is 40%. If sales volume of the company is Rs. 50 lakhs, find out its break-even point and net profit.

Solution:

$$\text{Margin of safety} = \frac{\text{Excess sales over break-even sales}}{\text{Actual sales}}$$

$$40\% = \frac{x}{50 \text{ lakhs}}$$

or x = 20 lakhs

Hence (i) Break-even Sales = 50 lakhs – 20 lakhs = 30 lakhs

Variable Cost of Break-even Sales = Rs. 15 lakhs.

Hence Fixed Costs = Rs. 15 lakhs.

(ii) Net Profit = Contribution – Fixed Cost

= 50 lakhs × 50/100 – 15 lakhs

= 25 lakhs – 15 lakhs = Rs. 10 lakhs

Illustration 10:

X Ltd. has earned contribution of Rs. 2,00,000 and net profit of Rs. 1,50,000 on sales Rs. 8,00,000. What is its margin of safety?

Solution:

$$\text{P/V Ratio} = \frac{\text{Contribution}}{\text{Sales}} \times 100$$

$$= \frac{\text{Rs.}2,00,000}{\text{Rs.}8,00,000} \times 100 = 25\%$$

$$\text{Margin of safety} = \frac{\text{Profit}}{\text{PV ratio}} = \frac{\text{Rs.}1,50,000}{25\%}$$

= Rs. 6,00,000

Illustration 11:

If margin of safety is Rs. 2,40,000 (40% of sales) and P/V ratio is 30% of AB Ltd. Calculate its (1) Break-even sales and (2) Amount of profit on sales of Rs. 9,00,000.

Solution:

Basic Calculation

$$(i)\ \text{Margin of Safety or Profit} = \frac{\text{Profit}}{\text{P/V Ratio}}$$

= Margin of safety × P/V ratio

= Rs. 2,40,000 × 30% = Rs. 72,000

(*ii*) Total Sales $= \dfrac{\text{Margin of safety}}{40\%}$

$= \dfrac{\text{Rs. } 2{,}40{,}000}{40\%} = \text{Rs. } 6{,}00{,}000$

(*iii*) Contribution = Sales × P/V Ratio

= Rs. 6,00,000 × 30% = Rs. 1,80,000

(*iv*) Fixed Cost = Contribution– Profit

= Rs. 1,80,000 – Rs. 72,000

= Rs. 1,08,000

Computation of Break-even Sales

$$\frac{\text{Fixed cost}}{\text{P/V ratio}} = \frac{\text{Rs. } 1{,}08{,}000}{30\%} = \text{Rs. } 3{,}60{,}000$$

Computation of Profit on Sales of Rs. 9,00,000

= Sales × PN Ratio – Fixed Cost

= Rs. 9,00,000 × 30% – Rs. 1,08,000

= Rs. 2,70,000 – Rs. 1,08,000 = Rs. 1,62.000

Illustration 12:

(*i*) Ascertain profit, when sales = Rs. 2,00,000
Fixed Cost = Rs. 40,000
BEP = Rs. 1,60,000

(*ii*) Ascertain sales, when fixed cost = Rs. 20,000
Profit = Rs. 10,000
BEP = Rs. 40,000

Solution:

(*i*) P/V ratio $= \dfrac{\text{Fixed cost} \times 100}{\text{B.E.P.}} = \dfrac{\text{Rs. } 40{,}000 \times 100}{\text{Rs. } 1{,}60{,}000} = 25\%$

Contribution = Sales × P/V Ratio = F.C. + Profit

= Rs. 2,00,000 × 25% = Rs. 50,000

or Rs. 50,000 = Rs. 40,000 + Profit

or Profit = Rs. 10,000

(*ii*) Contribution = F.C. + Profit = Rs. 20,000 + Rs. 10,000

= Rs. 30,000

P.V. Ratio $= \dfrac{\text{Rs. } 20{,}000}{\text{Rs. } 40{,}000} \times 100 = 50\%$

Also, P/V ratio $= \dfrac{\text{Contribution}}{\text{Sales}} \times 100$

or Sales $= \dfrac{C}{\text{P/V ratio}} \times 100 = \dfrac{\text{Rs. } 30{,}000}{50\%} = \text{Rs. } 60{,}000$

Illustration 13:

The profit volume ratio of X Ltd. is 50% and the margin of safety is 40%. You are required to calculate the net profit if the sales volume is Rs. 1,00,000.

Solution:

$$\text{Margin of Safety} = \frac{\text{Excess sales over break-even sales}}{\text{Actual sales}}$$

40/100 = X/1,00,000

or 100X = 40,00,000

or X = Rs. 40,000

Break-even Sales = Rs. 1,00,000 – Rs. 40,000 = Rs. 60,000

Profit Volume Ratio = 50%

Variable Cost = 50%

Hence, Variable Cost is Rs. 60,000 – 60,000 × 50/100 = Rs. 30,000

Fixed Cost = Rs. 60,000 – Rs. 30,000 = Rs. 30,000

Contribution on Sales of Rs. 1,00,000 = Rs. 50,000

Less: Fixed Cost = Rs. 30,000

Profit = Rs. 20,000

Illustration 14:

Company sells its product at Rs. 15 per unit. In a period, if it produces and sells 8,000 units, it incurs a loss of Rs. 5 per unit. If the volume is raised to 20,000 units, it earns a profit of Rs. 4 per unit.

Calculate break-even point in terms of rupees as well as in units.

Solution:

I.	Sales = 8000 Units × Rs. 15 per Unit =	Rs. 1,20,000
	Loss = 8000 Units × Rs. 5 per Unit =	Rs. 40,000
II.	Sales = 20,000 Units × Rs. 15 per Unit =	Rs. 3,00,000
	Profit = 20,000 Unit × Rs. 4 per Unit ==	Rs. 80,000
I.	Sales	Profit/Loss
	1,20,000	(–) 40,000
II.	3,00,000	(+) 80,000

$$\text{P/V Ratio} = \frac{\text{Change in Profit}}{\text{Change in Sales}} = \frac{1,20,000}{1,80,000} = \frac{2}{3} \text{ or } 66\frac{2}{3}\%$$

Sales at Break-even point (in Rs.)

Fixed Cost = S × PV Ratio – Profit

(On the basis raised volume II)

$$\text{Fixed Cost} = \text{Rs. } 3,00,000 \times \frac{2}{3} - 80,000$$

Fixed Cost = Rs. 2,00,000 – Rs. 80,000 = Rs. 1,20,000

$$\text{B.E.P.} = \frac{F}{P/V \text{ Ratio}} = \frac{1,20,000 \times 3}{2} = \text{Rs. } 1,80,000$$

$$\text{Sales at Break-even point (in units)} = \frac{\text{Sales in Rs.}}{\text{Selling price per unit}}$$

$$= \frac{\text{Rs. } 1,80,000}{15} = 12,000$$

Note: (1) Rs. 5 per unit loss is given in the question, in the indirect way it is a variable cost per unit.
(2) Change in Profit is computed by adding loss of Rs. 40,000 in the profit of Rs. 80,000 because loss of Rs. 40,000 has also been covered in the second period of time or in the second option if the volume is raised to 20,000 units.

Illustration 15:

A company has earned a contribution of Rs. 2,00,000 and net profit of Rs. 8,00,000. What is the margin of safety?

Solution:

Given Contribution = Rs. 2,00,000
Net profit = Rs. 1,50,000
Sales = Rs. 8,00,000

$$\text{P/V ratio} = \frac{\text{Contribution}}{\text{Sales}} \times 100$$

$$= \frac{2,00,000}{8,00,000} \times 100 = 25\%$$

$$\text{Margin of safety} = \frac{\text{Profit}}{\text{P/V ratio}} = \frac{1,50,000}{25\%} \times 100$$

$$= \text{Rs. } 6,00,000$$

Margin of safety = Rs. 6,00,000

Or
We know

$$S - V = F + P$$

or $$S - V = C$$

$\therefore$ $$C = F + P$$

Putting the values = 2,00,000 = F + 1,50,000
F = 2,00,000 – 1,50,000
= Rs. 50,000

$$\text{Break-even point} = \frac{\text{Fixed cost}}{\text{P/V ratio}}$$

$$= \frac{\text{Rs. } 50,000}{25\%} \times 100 = \text{Rs. } 2,00,000$$

Margin of safety = Actual sales – Break-even sales = Rs. 8,00,000 – Rs. 2,00,000
= Rs. 6,00,000

Illustration 16:

B & Co. has recorded the following data in the two most recent periods

Total cost of production	*Volume of production (units)*
14,600	800
19,400	1,200

What is the best estimate of the firm's fixed costs per period?

Solution:

	Period 1	*Period 2*	*Difference*
Total Cost of Production (Rs.)	14,600	19,400	4,800
Volume of Production (Units)	800	1,200	400

$$\text{Variable Cost per units} = \frac{\text{Difference in Total Cost of Production}}{\text{Difference in Volume of Production}}$$

$$= \frac{\text{Rs. } 4{,}800}{400 \text{ units}} = \text{Rs. } 12$$

Fixed Cost = Total Cost of Production of a period – Total Variable Cost
= 14,600 – 800 units × Rs. 12
= Rs. 14,600 – Rs. 9,600 = Rs. 5,000

Illustration 17:

A Ltd. maintains a margin of safety of 37.5% with an overall contribution to sales ratio of 40%. Its fixed costs amount to Rs. 5 lakhs. Calculate the following:

(*i*) Break-even Sales:
(*ii*) Total Sales;
(*iii*) Total Variable Costs:
(*iv*) Current Profit;
(*v*) New "Margin of Safety" if the sales volume is increased by 7½%.

Solution:

(*i*) Break-even Sales $= \dfrac{\text{Fixed Cost}}{\text{P/V Ratio}}$

$$= \frac{5 \text{ lakhs}}{40\%} = \text{Rs. } 12.50 \text{ lakhs}$$

(*ii*) Total sales = Break-even Sales – Margin of Safety
Margin of Safety = Actual sales – Break-even Sales
Let Actual Sales be Rs. 100
Margin of Safety is Rs. 37.5
Hence, Break-even Sales will be Rs. 62.5
In case Break-even Sales are 62.5; Actual Sales are Rs. 100
Hence, if Break-even Sales are Rs. 12.5 lakhs

Actual sales will be $= \frac{100}{62.5} \times 12.5$

= Rs. 20 lakhs

(*iii*) Contribution = Sales – Variable Costs

Hence, Total Variable Costs = 60% of Rs. 20 lakhs

= Rs. 12 lakhs

(*iv*) Current Profit = Sales – (Variable Costs + Fixed Costs)

= Rs. 20 lakhs – (Rs. 12 lakhs + Rs. 5 lakhs)

= Rs. 20 lakhs – Rs. 17 lakhs

= Rs. 3 lakhs

(*v*) New Margin of Safety if sales volume is increased by 7.5%

New Sales Value = Rs. 20 lakhs + 7.5% of 20 lakhs = Rs. 21.50 lakhs

Hence, New Margin of Safety = 21.50 lakhs – B.E. Sales of Rs. 12.50 lakhs = Rs. 9 lakhs.

Illustration 18:

A company has annual fixed costs of Rs. 14,00,000. In 2008 sales amounted to Rs. 60,00,000 as compared with Rs. 45,00,000 in 2007 and profit in 2008 was Rs. 4,20,000 higher than in 2007.

(*i*) At what level of sales does the company break-even?

(*ii*) Determine profit or loss on a forecast sales volume of Rs. 80,00,000.

(*iii*) If there is a reduction in selling price in 2009 by 10% and the company desires to earn the same profit as in 2008, what would be the required sales volume?

Solution:

$$\text{PV Ratio} = \frac{\text{Increase in profit}}{\text{Increase in sales}} \times 100$$

$$= \frac{4,20,000}{15,00,000} \times 100 = 28\%$$

(*i*) Break-even Sales $= \frac{\text{Fixed cost}}{\text{PV ratio}}$

$$= \frac{14,00,000}{28\%}$$

= 50,00,000

(*ii*) Profit on sales of Rs. 80,00,000

Total Contribution 80,00,000 × 28/100	= 22,40,000
Less: Fixed Cost 1	4,00,000
Profit	8,40,000

(*iii*) If Present Selling Price is	Rs. 100
Variable Cost is (100 – 28)	Rs. 72
New Selling Price (100 – 10)	Rs. 90
New Contribution	Rs. 18

New PV Ratio $\frac{18}{90} \times 100 =$ 20%

Profit in 2008:

Contribution 60,00,000 × 28/100 =	16,80,000
Less: Fixed Cost	14,00,000
Profit	2,80,000

Sales for Desired Profit of Rs. 2,80,000 = $\frac{\text{Fixed cost + Desired profit}}{\text{New PV ratio}}$

$= \frac{14,00,000 + 2,,80,000}{20\%}$

$= \frac{16,80,000}{20\%}$ = Rs. 84,00,000

Illustration 19:

A Company manufactures radios, which are sold at Rs. 1,600 per unit. The total cost is composed of 30% for direct materials, 40% for direct wages and 30% for overheads. An increase in material price by 30% and in wage rates by 10% is expected in the forthcoming year, as a result of which the profit at current selling price may decrease by 40% of the present profit per unit. You are required to prepare a statement showing current and future profit at present Selling Price.

How much Selling Price should be increased to maintain the present rate of profit?

Solution:

Let X be the cost, Y be the profit and Rs. 1,600 selling price per unit of radio manufactured by a company.

Hence

$X + Y =$ Rs. 1,600 ... (*i*)

Statement of Present and Future Cost of a Radio

Particulars	*Present cost (Rs.)*	*Increase in cost (Rs.)*	*Anticipated future (Rs.)*
	(*a*)	(*b*)	(*c*) = (*a*) + (*b*)
Direct material	0.3X	0.09X	0.39X
Direct labour	0.4X	0.04X	0.44X
Overheads	0.3X		0.30X
Total	X	0.13X	1.13X

An increase in material price and wage rates resulted into a decrease in current profit by 40 per cent at present selling price; therefore we have:

1.13 X + 0.6 Y = 1,600 ...(*ii*)

On solving (*i*) and (*ii*) we get:

X = Rs. 1,207.55

Y = Rs. 392.45

Current profit Rs. 392.45 or 32.5% of cost

Future profit Rs. 235.47

Statement of revised selling price to maintain the present rate of profit

	Rs.
Direct material cost 0.39 × Rs. 1,207.55	470.94
Direct labour cost (0.44 × Rs. 1,207.55)	531.32
Overheads 0.30 × Rs. 1,207.55	362.27
Total cost	1,364.53
Profit (32.5% of total cost)	443.47
Revised selling price	1,808.00

Illustration 20

XYZ Ltd. furnishes you the following income information:

Particulars	*Year 2009*	
	First-half (Rs.)	*Second half (Rs.)*
Sales	8,10,000	10,26,000
Profit earned	21,600	64,800

From the above, you are required to compute the following assuming that the fixed cost remains the same in both the periods:

(*i*) P/V Ratio

(*ii*) Fixed Costs

(*iii*) The amount of profit or loss where sales are Rs. 6,48,000.

(*iv*) The amount of sales required to earn a profit of Rs. 5,08,000.

Solution:

(*i*) *Computation of PV Ratio*

$$(i)\ \text{PV Ratio} = \frac{\text{Change in profit}}{\text{Change in sales}} \times 100$$

$$= \frac{43{,}200}{2{,}16{,}000} \times 100 = 20\%$$

(*ii*) *Computation of Fixed Cost*

Fixed Cost (For 1st half) = Contribution – Profit
= 8,10,000 × 20% – 21,600
= 1,62,000 – 21,600
= Rs. 1,40,400

(*iii*) Contribution = 20% × Rs. 6,48,000 = Rs. 1,29,600

Loss = Rs. 1,29,600 – 1,40,400 = Rs. 10,800

(*iv*) Computation of sales to earn a profit of Rs. 1,08,000.

$$\frac{\text{Fixed cost + Desired profit}}{\text{PV ratio}}$$

$$= \frac{1,40,400 + \text{Rs. } 1,08,000}{20\%} = \text{Rs. } 12,42,000$$

Illustration 21:

The following costs and sales of a manufacturing company for the first half and second half of 2008-09 are given:

	First-half *Rs.*	*Second-half* *Rs.*
Sales	24,00,000	30,00,000
Total Costs	21,80,000	26,00,000

You are asked to determine:

(*i*) Contribution/sales ratio of the firm.

(*ii*) Annual Fixed Costs.

(*iii*) Break-even Point.

(*iv*) Margin of Safety as Percentage of Sales:

Solution:

(a) Computation of Contributions/Sales Ratio

Particulars	*First-Half (Rs.)*	*Second Half (Rs.)*	*Change (Rs.)*
Sales	24,00,000	30,00,000	6,00,000
Total cost	21,80,000	26,00,000	4,20,000
Profit	2,20,000	4,00,000	1,80,000

$$\text{Contribution/Sales Ratio} = \frac{\text{Change in Profit}}{\text{Change in Sales}}$$

$$= \frac{1,80,000}{6,00,000}$$

$$= 0.3 \text{ or } 30\%$$

(*b*) *Computation of Fixed Cost for 2008-09*

Total Sales for the year = Rs. 54,00,000

Total Costs = Rs. 47,80,000

PV Ratio is = 30%

Total Variable Costs = 70% of Rs. 54,00,000

= 37,80,000

Fixed Costs = Total Costs – Variable Costs

= Rs. Rs. 47,80,000 – Rs. 37,80,000

= Rs. 10,00,000

(*c*) Break-even Point $= \frac{\text{Fixed Costs}}{\text{PV ratio}}$

$= \frac{\text{Rs. } 10,00,000}{30\%}$

= Rs. 33,33,333

(*d*) Marginal of safety as a percentage of sales

Margin of Safety (MS) = Sales – Break-even sales

= Rs. 54,00,000 – Rs. 33,33,333

= Rs. 20,66,667

Margin of safety as % of sales $= \frac{20,66,667}{54,00,000} \times 100 = 38.3\%$

Illustration 22:

Raj Ltd. manufactures three products X, Y and Z. The unit selling prices of these products are Rs. 100, Rs. 160 and Rs. 75 respectively. The corresponding unit variable costs are Rs. 50, Rs. 80 and Rs. 30. The proportions (quantity-wise) in which these products are manufactured and sold are 20%, 30% and 50% respectively. The total fixed costs are Rs. 14,80,000.

Calculate overall break-even quantity and the product-wise break up of such quantity.

Solution:

Overall Break-Even Quantity

Products	*X*	*Y*	*Z*
Selling price per unit (Rs.)	100	160	75
Less: Variable cost per unit (Rs.)	50	80	30
Contribution per unit (Rs.)	50	80	45
Share in Total sales	20%	30%	50%
Proportionate contributions per unit	10	24	22.50

Composite contribution per unit = 56.5

Composite Break-even Point $= \frac{\text{Total Fixed Cost}}{\text{Composite Contribution per unit}}$

$= \frac{\text{Rs. } 14,80,000}{\text{Rs. } 56.5} = 26,195 \text{ units}$

Product-wise break-up of overall break-even quantity:

Product X: 26,195 units × 20/100 = 5,239 units

Product Y: 26,195 units × 30/100 = 7,858 units

Product Z: 26,195 units × 50/100 = 13,098 units

Illustration 23:

A single product company sells its products at Rs. 60 per unit. In 1996, the company operated at a margin of safety of 40%. The fixed costs amounted to Rs. 3,60,000 and the variable cost ratio to sales was 80%.

In 1997, it is estimated that the variable cost will go up by 10% and the fixed costs will increase by 5%.

Find the selling price required to be fixed in 1997 to earn the same P/V ratio as in 1996.

Assuming the same selling price of Rs. 60 per unit in 1997, find the number of units required to be produced and sold to earn the same profit as in 1996.

Solution:

Basic Calculations:

1. P/V Ratio in 1996

P/V Ratio $= \dfrac{\text{Selling Price per unit} - \text{Variable Cost per unit}}{\text{Selling Price per unit}} \times 100$

$= \dfrac{\text{Rs. } 60 - \text{Rs. } 48}{\text{Rs. } 60} \times 100 = \dfrac{\text{Rs.} 12}{\text{Rs.} 60} \times 100 = 20\%$

2. Number of units sold (in 1996)

Break-even Point $= \dfrac{\text{Fixed cost}}{\text{Contribution per unit}} = \dfrac{\text{Rs.} 3,60,000}{\text{Rs.} 12} = 30,000$ units

The margin of safety is 40%. Hence break-even point is at 60% of units sold.

or No. of units sold $= \dfrac{\text{Break-even point}}{60\%} = \dfrac{30,000}{60} \times 100 = 50,000$ units

3. Profit earned in 1996

Profit = Units sold in 1996 × Contribution per unit – Fixed costs
= 50,000 units × Rs. 12 – Rs. 3,60,000
= Rs. 6,00,000 – Rs. 3,60,000 = Rs. 2,40,000

Fixation of Selling Price in 1997

Variable Cost per unit in 1997 = Rs. 48 + Rs. 4.80 = Rs. 52.80
Fixed cost in 1997 = Rs. 3,60,000 + Rs. 18,000 – Rs. 3,78,000
P/V Ratio in 1996 = 20%
Since P/V ratio is 20%. Hence, Variable cost is 80%

Hence, the required selling price $= \dfrac{\text{Rs.} 52.80}{80\%} = \text{Rs. } 66$

Number of units to be produced and sold in 1997 to earn the same profit as in 1996

Profit in 1996 = Rs. 2,40,000
Fixed cost in 1997 = Rs. 3,78,000
Desired contribution in 1997
(Rs. 2,40,000 + Rs. 3,78,000) = Rs. 6,18,000
Contribution per unit in 1997 = Selling price per unit – Variable cost per unit
= Rs. 60 – Rs. 52.80 = Rs. 7.20

Number of units to be produced and sold in 1997 $= \dfrac{\text{Fixed cost in 1997}}{\text{Contribution per unit in 1997}}$

$$= \frac{\text{Rs. } 6{,}18{,}000}{\text{Rs. } 7.20} = 85.833 \text{ units}$$

Illustration 24:

A company producing a single product sells it at Rs. 50 per unit. Unit variable cost is Rs. 35 and fixed cost amounts to Rs. 12 lakhs per annum. With this data you are required to calculate the following, treating each independent of the other:

(*a*) P/V Ratio and Break-even Sales.

(*b*) New Break-even Sales if variable cost increases by Rs. 3 per unit, without increase in selling price.

(*c*) Increase in sales required if profits are to be increased by Rs. 24 lakhs.

(*d*) Percentage increase/decrease in sales volume units to

(*i*) an increase of Rs. 3 in the variable cost per unit.

(*ii*) a 10% increase in selling price without affecting existing profits quantum.

(*e*) Quantum of advertisement expenditure permissible to increase sales by Rs. 1.2 lakhs, without affecting existing profits quantum.

Solution:

(*a*) PV Ratio $= \dfrac{\text{Contribution per unit}}{\text{Selling price per unit}}$

$$= \frac{50 - 35}{50} = 30\%$$

Break-even Sales $= \dfrac{\text{Fixed cost}}{\text{P.V. Ratio}}$

$$= \frac{12.00}{30\%} = \text{Rs. } 40 \text{ lakhs}$$

(*b*) Revised PV Ratio $= \dfrac{\text{Existing contribution per unit}}{\text{Selling price per unit}}$

$$= \frac{15 - 3}{50} = \frac{12}{50} = 24\%$$

Revised Break-even Sales $= \dfrac{12}{24\%} = \text{Rs. } 50 \text{ lakhs}$

(*c*) Increase in Sales Required $= \dfrac{\text{Increase in contribution}}{\text{P/V ratio}}$

$= \dfrac{24}{30\%} = \text{Rs. 8 lakhs}$

(*d*) (*i*) Percentage in Sales Volume (units) $= \dfrac{\text{Reduction in contribution}}{\text{New contribution per unit}}$

$= \dfrac{3}{12} \times 100$

$= 25\%$

(*ii*) Percentage Decrease in Sales Volume (units)

$= \dfrac{\text{Increase in contribution per unit}}{\text{New contribution per unit}}$

$= \dfrac{5 (\textit{i.e.}, 10\% \text{ of Rs. } 50)}{20, \textit{i.e.}, (55 - 35)}$

$= 25\%$

(*e*) The contribution by sales arising out of advertisement expenses should be equal to amount of Rs. 1.2 lakhs the sale increase to avoid profit or loss. Hence, 30% of 1.2 lakhs or Rs. 36,000 should be the maximum permissible advertisement expenditure for being incurred to get an increase of sale of Rs. 1.2 lakhs without affecting existing profits.

Illustration 25:

A company wants to buy a new machine to replace one which is having frequent breakdown. It received offers for two models M1 and M2. Further details regarding these models are given below:

	M1	*M2*
Installed capacity (units)	10,000	10,000
Fixed overhead per annum (Rs.)	2,40,000	1,00,000
Estimated profit at the above capacity (Rs.)	1,60,000	1,00,000

The product manufactured using this type of machine (M1 or M2) is sold at Rs. 100 per unit. You are required to determine:

(*a*) Break-even level of sales for each model.

(*b*) The level of sales at which both the models will earn the same profit.

(*c*) The model suitable for different levels of demand for the product.

Solution:

(a) Basic Calculations

Statement showing Comparative Parameters of two Machines

Type of Machines	*Model M1*	*Model M2*
1. Installed capacity (units)	10,000	10,000
2. Fixed overhead per annum (Rs.)	2,40,000	1,00,000
3. Selling price of the product (Rs.)	100	100
4. Estimated profit at the above capacity (Rs.)	1,60,000	1,00,000
5. Total sales value (Rs.)	10,00,000	10,00,000
6. Total contribution (Rs.) (2) + (4)	4,00,000	2,00,000
7. Variable cost	6,00,000	8,00,000
8. Variable cost per unit	Rs. 60	Rs. 80
9. P/V ratio = Contribution/Sales	0.40	0.20

Computation of Break-even Sales

	Model M1	*Model M2*
Break-even Sales	$\frac{\text{Fixed cost}}{\text{P/V ratio}}$	$\frac{\text{Fixed cost}}{\text{P/V ratio}}$
	$= \frac{\text{Rs. } 2,40,000}{.40}$	$= \frac{\text{Rs. } 1,00,000}{.20}$
	= Rs. 6,00,000	Rs. 5,00,000
BEP in units	= 6,000 units	5,000 units

(*b*) Sales at which both models will earn the same profit.

Let the units sold be taken as x

Total Cost for Model 1 = $60x$ = 2,40,000

Total Cost for Model 2 = $80x$ = 1,00,000

On putting these figures in the form of a simultaneous equation:

$$60x + 2,40,000 = 80x + 1,00,000$$

or $$20x = 1,40,000$$

or $$x = 7,000 \text{ units}$$

Thus, at 7,000 units of output, the total costs under both the machines will be the same and hence earn the same profit.

(c) Model Suitable for different levels of Demand: In view of the above stated comparative parameters Model M2 is suitable for low demand since it has a lower Break-even Point and Lower Fixed Cost and makes higher profit between 5,000 units and 7,000 units than Model MI. In case the level of demand for the product exceeds 7,000 units, Model M1 is better since it makes higher profit.

This can be substantiated by profitability of two models of Machines at different levels (6,000 units and 8,000 units) as being depicted below:

Levels of Demand	6,000 units		8,000 units	
Types of Machines	*M1*	*M2*	*M1*	*M2*
Total Contribution (Rs.)	2,40,000	1,20,000	3,20,000	1,60,000
Less: Fixed cost (Rs.)	2,40,000	1,00,000	2,40,000	1,00,000
Profit	—	20,000	80,000	60,000

Illustration 26:

The variable cost structure of a product manufactured by a company during the current year is as under:

	Rs. per unit
Material	120
Labour	30
Overheads	12

The selling price per unit is Rs. 270 and the fixed cost and sales during the current year are Rs. 14 lakhs and Rs. 40.5 lakhs respectively.

During the forthcoming year, the direct workers will be entitled to a wage increase of 10% from the beginning of the year and the material cost, variable overhead and fixed overhead are expected to increase by 7.5%, 5% and 3% respectively.

The following are required to be computed:

(*a*) New sale price in the forthcoming year if the current P/V ratio is to be maintained.

(*b*) Number of units that would require to be sold during the forthcoming year so as to yield the same amount of profit in the current year, assuming that selling price per unit will not be increased.

Solution:

Current Year's Statement of Profitability

Units sold 15,000

Particulars		*Rs.*	*Total*
Selling price per unit (Rs.)		270	
Less: Variable cost per unit:			
Material	120		
Labour	30		
Overheads	12		
		162	
Contribution per unit		108	
Total contribution (15,000 units × Rs. 108)			16,20,000
Less: Fixed cost			14,00,000
Profit			2,20,000
P/V Ratio (108/270)			40%

(a) Statement Showing New Seeing Price for the Forthcoming Year
(Retaining Current Year's P/V Ratio)

Particulars	*Rs.*	*Rs.*
(1) Variable cost per unit:		
Material	129.00	
Labour	33.00	
Overhead	12.60	
		174.60
(2) Selling price (174.60 × 100/60)		291.00
(3) Contribution (2) – (1)		116.40
(4) P.V. Ratio		40%

(b) Computation of Number of Units to be Sold during Forthcoming Year
(Maintaining the Current Year's Profit)

Particulars	*Rs.*	*Rs.*
(*i*) Current Year Profit	2,20,000	
(*ii*) Revised Fixed Cost	14,42,000	16,62,000
(*iii*) Required Contribution (Rs. 270 – Rs. 174.60)		95.40
(*iv*) Number of Units to be sold (16,62,000/95.40)		17,422 units

Working Note:

Computation of Variable Cost per Unit

	Current year	*Forthcoming year*	
	Rs.	*Increase %*	*Total (Rs.)*
Material	120.00	7.5 (120 × 1.075)	129.00
Labour	30.00	10 (30 × 1.10)	33.00
Overhead	12.00	5(12 × 1.05)	12.60
	162.00		174.60
Fixed cost	Rs. 14,00,000	3(14,00,000 × 1.03)	14,42,000

Illustration 27:

ABC Ltd. which produces three products furnishes the following data for the year 2009:

	Products		
	Alfa	*Beta*	*Gamut*
Selling Price per unit	Rs. 100	75	50
Profit/Volume Ratio	10%	20%	40%
Maximum Sales Potential (units)	40,000	25,000	10,000
Raw Material as % of Variable Cost	50%	50%	50%

The company uses the same raw material for all the three products. Raw material is in short supply and the company has a quota for supply of raw material of the value of Rs. 18,00,000 for the year 2009 for manufacture of its products to meet its sales. Total fixed cost is Rs. 6,80,000.

You are required to:

(*a*) Determine a sales mix which will give the maximum overall profit keeping in view the short supply of raw material.

(*b*) Compute the maximum profit.

Solution:

Particulars		*Products*		
		Alfa	*Beta*	*Gama*
Selling Price per unit	Rs.	100	75	50
Profit volume ratio		10%	20%	40%
Contribution per unit	Rs.	10	15	20
Variable cost per unit	Rs.	90	60	30
Raw material per unit	Rs.	45	30	15
Contribution per rupee of raw material	=	10/45	15/30	20/15
	=	2/9	1/2	4/3
Ranking		3	2	1

(a) Computation of Sales Mix

Product	*Units* Rs.	*Sales* Rs.	*Raw material used*
Gama	10,000	5,00,000	1,50,000
Beta	25,000	18,75,000	7,50,000
Alfa	20,000	20,00,000	9,00,000
Balance	55,000	43,75,000	18,00,000

(b) Computation of Profit

Product	*Sales* Rs.	*P/V Ratio*	*Contribution*
Gama	5,00,000	40	2,00,000
Beta	18,75,000	20	3,75,000
Alfa	20,00,000	10	2,00,000
			7,75,000
	Less: Fixed cost		6,80,000
	Net Profit		95,000

Illustration 28:

A company has two Plants at Locations I and II, operating at 100% and 75% of their capacities respectively. The company is considering a proposal to merge the two plants at one location to optimise available capacity. The following details are available in respect of the two plants, regarding their press performance/operations:

Particulars	*Location I*	*Location II*
Sales (Rs. in lakhs)	200	75
Variable cost (Rs. in lakhs)	140	54
Fixed cost (Rs. in lakhs)	30	14

For decision-making purposes you are required to work out the following information:

(*a*) The capacity at which the merged plant will break-even.

(*b*) The profit of the merged plant working at 80% capacity.

(*c*) Sales required if the merged plant is required to earn an overall profit of Rs. 22 lakhs.

Solution:

Comparative Performance of Plant at 100% Capacity

(Rs. in lakhs)

Plants	*Plant Location-I*	*Plant Location-II*	*Merged Plant*
Capacity levels	100%	100%	100%
Sales	200	100	300
Less: Variable cost	140	72	212
Contribution	60	28	88
Less: Fixed cost	30	14	44
Profit/(Loss)	30	14	44
P/V ratio (%): (Contribution/Sales)	30%	28%	29.33
Break-even sales (Fixed cost/P/V Ratio)	44/29.33%		150

(*a*) Capacity at BEP (%): $\frac{150}{300} \times 100 = 50\%$

(*b*) Computation of Profitability of the Merged Plant at 80% Capacity

(Rs. in lakhs)

Particulars	*Rs.*
Sales (80% of 300)	240.00
Less: Variable cost	169.60
Contribution	70.40
Less: Fixed cost	44.00
Profit	26.40

(c) Computation of sales required to earn desired profit of Rs. 22 lakhs:

Contribution required (Rs. in lakhs):

Fixed cost	44.00	
Desired profit	22.00	66.00
P/V Ratio (%)		29.33%
Desired sales level (Rs. in lakhs)	$\frac{66 \times 100}{29.33}$	= 225.00

Illustration 29:

An automobile manufacturing company produces different models of cars. The budget in respect of model 118 for the month of September, 2008 as under:

Budgeted output		*40,000 units*
	(Rs. in lakhs)	*(Rs. in lakhs)*
Net Realisation		700
Variable costs:		
Materials	264	
Labour	52	
Direct expenses	124	
		440
Specific fixed costs	90	
Allocated fixed costs	112.50	202.50
Total costs		642.50
Profit		57.50
Sales		700.00

Calculate:

(*i*) Profit with 10 per cent increase in selling price with a 10 per cent reduction in sales volume.

(*ii*) Volume to be achieved to maintain the original profit after a 10 per cent rise in material costs, at the originally budgeted selling price per unit

Solution:

(i) Statement of Profit

(with 10 per cent increase in selling price with a 10 per cent reduction in sales-volume)

	(Rs. in lakhs)
Sales Revenue: (A) (WN 1)	693
Variable Costs: (B) (WN 2)	396
Contribution [(A) – (B)}	297
Less: Total Fixed Costs	202.5
Profit	94.5

Working Notes:

1. Selling Price (per unit) $= \frac{\text{Rs. } 7{,}00{,}00{,}000}{40{,}000 \text{ units}}$ = Rs. 1,750

   New Selling Price (per unit) = Rs. 1,750 + Rs. 175 = Rs. 1,925

   Reduced Sales volume = 36,000 units

   Total sales revenue = Rs. 1,925 × 36,000 = Rs. 693 lakhs.

2. (*i*) *Variable Costs per Unit*

	Rs.
Materials Cost	= 660
Labour cost	= 130
Direct expenses	= 310
Total variable cost	= 1,100

(ii) Volume to be achieved to maintain original profit

	Rs.	*Rs.*
Selling Price (per unit) (as per Working Note)		1,750
Less: Variable Cost:		
Material Cost (Rs. 660 + Rs. 66)	726	
Labour Cost	130	
Direct expenses	310	1,166
Contribution per unit		584

Desired contribution = Fixed Cost + Original Profit
= Rs. 202.50 + Rs. 57.50
= Rs. 260 lakhs

No. of cars to be sold to maintain original profit at original sales price = $\frac{\text{Rs. 260 lakhs}}{\text{Rs. 584}}$

= 44,520.547 or say 44,521 cars.

Illustration 30:

Two Firms A & Co. and B & Co. sell the same type of product in the same market. Their budgeted Profit & loss Account for the year ending 31st March, 2008 are as follows:

Particulars	*A & Co.*		*B & Co.*	
	Rs.	*Rs.*	*Rs.*	*Rs.*
Sales		5,00,000		6,00,000
Variable Costs	4,00,000		4,00,000	
Fixed Costs	30,000	4,30000	70,000	4,70,000
Net profit		70,000		1,30,000

Required;

1. Calculate at which sales volume both the firms will earn equal profit.
2. State which firm is likely to earn greater profits in condition of
   (*i*) heavy demand for the product, and
   (*ii*) low demand for the product

Give reasons.

Solution:

1. Computation of Sales Volume for Equal Profits

Particulars	*A & Co.*	*B & Co.*
Sales (Rs.)	5,00,000	6,00,000
Less: Variable costs (Rs.)	4,00,000	4,00,000
Contribution (Rs.)	1,00,000	2,00,000
P/V Ratio (C/S × 100)	20%	33.33%

Sales Volume = $\frac{\text{Difference in Fixed Cost}}{\text{Difference in P/V Ratio}}$

(for both the firms to earn equal profit) = $\frac{\text{Rs. 40,000}}{13.33\%}$

= Rs. 3,00,000

2. The PV ratio of B & Co. at 33.33% is higher than that of A & Co. at 20% and therefore B & Co. will earn higher profit if the sales volume exceeds the level of Rs. 3,00,000.

As a matter of fact for each additional unit of product's sale above Rs. 3,00,000 the profit of B & Co. will rise by Rs. 33.33 which exceeds by Rs. 13.33, the profit of A & Co. under similar circumstances. However, below that level, profit for A & Co. will be greater. Hence, it can generally be concluded that B & Co. is likely to earn higher profits under conditions of heavy demand for the product above Rs. 3,00,000. On the other hand A & Co. is expected to make higher profits under conditions of low demand for the product below sales volume of Rs. 3,00,000.

Illustration 31:

Indian Plastics make plastic buckets. An analysis of their accounting reveals:

Variable cost per bucket	Rs. 20
Fixed cost	Rs. 50,000 for the year
Capacity	2,000 buckets per year
Selling price per bucket	Rs. 70

Required:

(*i*) Find the break-even point.

(*ii*) Find the number of buckets to be sold to get a profit of Rs. 30,000.

(*iii*) If the company can manufacture 600 buckets more per year with an additional fixed cost of Rs. 2,000, what should be the selling price to maintain the profit per bucket as at (*ii*) above?

Solution:

(*i*) BEP = Fixed cost/contribution per unit
= 50,000/50 = 1,000 buckets.

(*ii*) Buckets to be sold for desired profit of Rs. 30.000

$$\text{Sales for Desired Profit} = \frac{\text{Fixed cost + Desired profit}}{\text{Contribution per unit}}$$

$$= \frac{50,000 + 30,000}{50}$$

= 80,000/50
= 1,600 buckets

(*iii*) Computation of new selling price:

	Rs.
Profit per bucket at sales of 1,600 buckets:	
Sales (1.600 × 70)	1,12,000
Less: Variable cost 1,600 × 20	32,000
Contribution	80,000
Less: Fixed costs	50,000
Profit	30,000
Profit per bucket 30,000/1,600 =	18.75
Total sales 1,600 + 600 = 2,200 buckets.	
Total profit desired = 2,200 × 18.75 =	Rs. 41,250

Let selling price be '*x*'

The following equation can be made:

Total sales	= Total cost + Profit
2,200x	= 20(2,200) + 52,000 + 41,250
2,200x	= 1,37,250
or x	= Rs. 62.39 per bucket

Note: It has been assumed that 600 more buckets to be manufactured are in addition to 1,600 buckets as computed under (*ii*) above.

Illustration 32:

Cadbury Schweppes Limited, a British chocolate and soft drink company, is planning to establish a subsidiary company in India to produce, Schweppes Mineral Water.

Based on the estimated annual sales of 40,000 bottles of the mineral water, cost studies produced the following estimates for the Indian subsidiary:

	Total annual costs	*Per cent of total annual cost that is variable*
Material	Rs. 1,93,600	100%
Labour	90,000	70%
Overhead	80,000	64%
Administration	30,000	30%

The Indian production will be sold by manufacturer's representatives who will receive a commission of 8 per cent of the sale price. No portion of the British office expenses is to be allocated to the Indian subsidiary.

It is required to:

(*i*) compute the sale price per bottle to enable management to realise an estimated 10 per cent profit on sale proceeds in India, and

(*ii*) calculate the break-even point in rupee sales for the Indian subsidiary on the assumption that the sale price is Rs. 11 per bottle.

Solution:

(*i*) Computation of Selling Price per Unit

Let the selling price per unit be x

Total sales	40,000x
Total Commission	3,200x
Total profit	4,000x

Total sales = Total cost + Profit

40,000x = 1,93,600 + 90,000 + 80,000 + 30,000 + 3,200x + 4,000x

or 40,000x = 3,93,600 + 7,200x

or 32,800x = 3,93,600

or x = Rs. 12

(ii) Computation of Break-even Point

Sales (40,000 × 11)		Rs. 4,40,000
Less: Marginal cost:		
Material	Rs. 1,93,600	
Labour 90,000 × 70/100	63,000	
Overhead 80,000 × 64/100	51,200	

Administration $30{,}000 \times \frac{30}{100}$	9,000	
Sales commission 4,40,000 × 8/100	35,200	3,52,000
Total contribution		88,000

$$\text{Break-even sales} = \frac{\text{Fixed cost} \times \text{Total sales}}{\text{Total contribution}}$$

$$= \frac{27{,}000 + 28{,}800 + 21{,}000 \times 4{,}40{,}000}{88{,}000}$$

$$= \frac{76{,}800}{88{,}000} \times 4{,}40{,}000 = \text{Rs. } 3{,}84{,}000$$

Illustration 33:

A factory engaged in manufacturing plastic buckets is working to 40% capacity and produces 10,000 buckets per annum.

The present cost break-up for one bucket is as under:

Material	Rs. 10
Labour cost	3
Overheads	5 (60% fixed)

The selling price Rs. 20 per bucket.

If it is decided to work the factory at 50% capacity the selling price falls by 3%. At 90% capacity, the selling price falls by 5% accompanied by a similar fall in the prices of material.

You are required to calculate the profit at 50% and 90% capacities and also calculate break-even points for the same capacity productions.

Solution:

Statement Showing Profit and Break-even Point at Different Capacity Levels

Capacity levels *Production (units)*	*50%* *12,500*		*90%* *22,500*	
	Per unit	*Total*	*Per unit*	*Total*
(*i*) Sales	Rs. 19.40	Rs. 2,42,500	Rs. 19.00	Rs. 4,27,500
Variable cost:				
Materials	10.00	1,25,000	9.50	2,13,750
Wages	3.00	37,500	3.00	67,500
Variable overheads	2.00	25,000	2.00	45,000
(*ii*) Total variable cost	15.00	1,87,500	14.50	3,26,250
(*iii*) Contribution (i-ii)	4.40	55,000	4.50	1,01,250
(*iv*) Fixed costs		30,000		30,000
(*v*) Net profit (iii-iv)		25,000		71,250

Break-even point:	at 50% capacity	at 90% capacity
	$\dfrac{\text{Fixed cost}}{\text{Contribution per unit}}$	$\dfrac{\text{Fixed cost}}{\text{Contribution per unit}}$
Units	$\dfrac{30{,}000}{4.40}$ = 6.818 units	$\dfrac{30{,}000}{4.50}$ = 6,667 units
Sales value	Rs. 1,32,270	Rs. 1,26,673

Illustration 34:

The Chief Cost Accountant of Vikas Limited found to his surprise that the actual profit for the period ending 30th June 2009 was the same as budgeted in spite of realising 10% more than the budgeted selling prices. The following were the results:

Particulars	*Budget Rs.*	*Actuals Rs.*
Sales	5,00,000	8,25,000
Variable costs of sales	3,00,000	5,75,000
Fixed costs	1,00,000	1,50,000
Profit	1,00,000	1,00,000

You are required to assist the Chief Cost Accountant in preparing the necessary explanations as to why the profit remained the same despite an increase in sales.

Solution:

In order to assist the Chief Accountant of Vikas Ltd., in preparing the necessary explanations, for the profit remaining the same, in spite of an increase in sale revenue, the following factors may be considered:

Factors contributing to the increase in profit:	*Rs.*
(*i*) Increase in sales revenue due to increased selling price (Working Note 1)	75,000
(*ii*) Increase in contribution on account of increased sales volume (Working Note 4)	1,00,000
	1,75,000
Factors contributing to the increase in cost:	
(*i*) Increase in variable costs (Working Note 5)	1,25,000
(*ii*) Increase in fixed cost	50,000
	1,75,000

Working Notes:

1. Increase in sales revenue due to price increase (10% more than the budgeted)

$$= \frac{\text{Rs. } 8{,}25{,}000 \times 100}{110} = \text{Rs. } 75{,}000$$

2. Increase in sales volume = (Actual sales – Sales revenue due to increased selling price – Budgeted sales)

= Rs. 8,25,000 – Rs. 75,000 – 5,00,000

= Rs. 2,50,000

3. Budgeted P/V Ratio $= \dfrac{\text{Budgeted contribution} \times 100}{\text{Budgeted sales}}$

$$= \frac{\text{Rs. } 5{,}00{,}000 - \text{Rs. } 3{,}00{,}000 \times 100}{\text{Rs. } 5{,}00{,}000}$$

= 40%

4. Increase in contribution due to higher sales volume = Rs. 2,50,000 × 40% = Rs. 1,00,000
5. Budgeted proportion of variable cost (on the sale of Rs. 7,50,000)

$$= \frac{\text{Budgeted cost}}{\text{Budgeted sales}} \times \text{Actual sales volume}$$

$$= \frac{\text{Rs. } 3{,}00{,}000}{\text{Rs. } 5{,}00{,}000} \times \text{Rs. } 7{,}50{,}000$$

= Rs. 4,50,000

Increase in variable cost

= (Actual variable cost of sales – Budgeted proportion of variable cost)
= Rs. 5,75,000 – Rs. 4,50,000 = Rs. 1,25,000

A perusal of the above-mentioned factors clearly shows that the profit of M/s. Vikas Ltd., has increased by Rs. 1,75,000 due to increase in selling price (Rs. 75,000) and contribution on increased volume (Rs. 1,00,000). At the same time the cost of the firm has also increased to the tune of Rs. 1,75,000 (increase in variable cost Rs. 1,25,000 and increase in fixed cost Rs. 50,000). Since the increase in profit equals to the increase in cost, therefore, the profit of the firm has remained the same as shown in the budget.

Illustration 35:

Taurus Ltd. produces three products — A, B and C, from the same manufacturing facilities. The cost and other details of the three products are as follows:

	A	*B*	*C*
Selling price/unit (Rs.)	200	160	100
Variable cost/unit (Rs.)	120	120	40
Fixed expenses/month (Rs.) 2,76,000			
Maximum production per month (units)	5,000	8,000	6,000
Total hours available for the month 200 hours			
Maximum demand per month (units)	2,000	4,000	2,400

The processing hours cannot be increased beyond 200 hours per month.

You are required to:

(*a*) Compute the most profitable product-mix:

(*b*) Compute, the overall break-even sales of the company for the month based on the mix calculated in (*a*) above.

Solution:

M/s. Taurus Limited

(*a*) Computation of Most Profitable Product Mix:

Products	*Number of units to be produced (Note 1)*	*Contribution per unit*	*Total contribution*
		Rs.	*Rs.*
A	2,000	80	1,60,000
B	1,600	40	64,000
C	2,400	60	1,44,000
		Total contribution:	3,68,000
		Less: Fixed expenses:	2,76,000
		Profit:	92,000

(*b*) Computation of Overall Break-even Sales

$$\text{Break-even sales} = \frac{\text{Fixed costs}}{\text{Total contribution}} \times \text{Total sales}$$

$$= \frac{\text{Rs. } 2,76,000}{\text{Rs. } 3,68,000} \times \text{Rs. } 8,96,000$$

$$= \text{Rs. } 6,72,000$$

Working Notes:

(1) Statement showing units to be produced

	Products	A	B	C
(*i*)	Selling price per unit (Rs.)	200	160	100
(*ii*)	Variable cost per unit (Rs.)	120	120	40
(*iii*)	Contribution per unit (*i*) – (*ii*)	80	40	60
(*iv*)	Maximum production per hour (units)	5,000 / 200 = 25	8,000 / 200 = 40	6,000 / 200 = 30
(*v*)	Contribution per hour (Rs.) (Maximum production per hour × Contribution per unit)	Rs. 80 × 25 2,000	Rs. 40 × 40 1,600	Rs. 60 × 30 1,800
(*vi*)	Ranking	I	III	II
(*vii*)	Units to he produced	2,000	1,600	2,400
(*viii*)	Time required for the units to be produced (hrs.)	80	40	80

(2) Statement of Contribution

Products (*i*)	*Units* (*ii*)	*Selling price per unit* (*iii*) (*Rs.*)	*Variable cost per unit* (*iv*) (*Rs.*)	*Sales revenue* (*v*) (*Rs.*)	*Variable cost* (*vi*) (*Rs.*)	*Contribution* (*vii*) (*Rs.*)
A	2,000	200	120	4,00,000	2,40,000	1,60,000
B	1,600	160	120	2,56,000	1,92,000	64,000
C	2,400	100	40	2,40,000	96,000	1,44,000
Total				8,96,000	5,28,000	3,68,000

Illustration 36:

The budgeted income statement by product lines of Multiproducts Ltd. for 2007 is as follows:

	Product A *Rs.*	*Product B* *Rs.*	*Product* *Rs.*
Sales	8,00,000	5,00,000	3,00,000
Variable Expenses:			
Cost of goods sold	90,000	2,70,000	1,50,000
Selling	30,000	90,000	45,000
Fixed Expenses:			
Overhead	36,000	90,000	54,000
Administrative	16,000	40,000	24,000
Income before tax	28,000	10,000	27,000
Income tax @ 40%	11,200	4,000	10,800
Net income	16,800	6,000	16,200

All products are manufactured in the same facilities under common administrative control. Fixed expenses are allocated among the products in proportion of their budgeted sales volume:

(*a*) Compute the budgeted break-even point of the company as a whole, from the data provided.

(*b*) What would be the effect on Budgeted Income, if half of the budgeted sales volume of product B were shifted to product A and C in equal rupee amounts, so that the total budgeted sales in rupees remain the same.

(*c*) What would be the effect of the shift in the product mix suggested in (*b*) above on the budgeted break-even point of the whole company?

Solution:

(*a*) Budgeted BEP for the company as a whole

Composite PV ratio $= \dfrac{\text{Total contribution}}{\text{Total sales}} \times 100$

$= \dfrac{80{,}000 + 1{,}40{,}000 + 1{,}05{,}000}{10{,}00{,}000} \times 100$

$= \dfrac{3{,}25{,}000}{10{,}00{,}000} \times 100 = 32.5\%$

BEP for the company $= \dfrac{\text{Total fixed costs}}{\text{Composite PV ratio}}$

$= \dfrac{52{,}000 + 1{,}30{,}000 + 78{,}000}{32.5\%}$

$= \dfrac{2{,}60{,}000}{32.5} \times 100 = \text{Rs. } 8{,}00{,}000$

(*b*) Effect on Budgeted Income if half the sales of Product B are shifted equally to Products A and C.

	Product A	*Product B*	*Product C*
Sales (i)	3,25,000	2,50,000	4,25,000
Variable expenses			
Cost of goods sold	1,46,250	1,35,000	2,12,500
Selling	48,750	45,000	63,750
Fixed expenses (apportioned according to sales):			
Overhead	58,500	45,000	76,500
Administrative	26,000	20,000	34,000
Total cost (ii)	2,79,500	2,45,000	3,86,750
Income before tax (i) – (ii)	45,500	5,000	38,250
Income tax @ 40%	18,200	2,000	15,300
Net Income	27,300	3,000	22,950
Total Net Income			Rs. 53,250

The original budgeted income is Rs. 39,000. Hence, the income would increase by Rs. 14,250 as a result of the proposed change.

(*c*) Break-even after shift in the product mix

$$\text{Composite PV Ratio} = \frac{\text{Total contribution}}{\text{Total sales}} \times 100$$

$$= \frac{1{,}30{,}000 + 70{,}000 + 1{,}48{,}750}{10{,}00{,}000} \times 100$$

$$= \frac{3{,}48{,}750}{10{,}00{,}000} \times 100 = 34.875\%$$

Break-even point of the company as a whole

$$= \frac{\text{Total fixed expenses}}{\text{Composite PV ratio}}$$

$$= \frac{2{,}60{,}000}{34.475\%}$$

$$= \text{Rs. } 7.45{,}520$$

Thus, the break-even point will stand reduced to sales of Rs. 7,45,520 from Rs. 8,00,000 as a result of shift in the total production-mix.

THEORY QUESTIONS

1. What do you mean by marginal costing? Discuss its usefulness and limitations.
2. Write a lucid note on marginal costing indicating its effect on profit computations.
3. What are the most important areas of management decisions opened up by the application of the marginal (direct) costing method? Answer briefly and to the point.

4. Marginal costs reveal the lowest price at which a product can be sold during a trade depression, but they also reveal to management the most profitable lines during the period of intense trade activity. Explain with examples, the second part of this statement.
5. Discuss the following terms in relation to marginal costing:
   (*a*) Key factor (*b*) P/V ratio, and (*c*) Margin of safety.
6. (*a*)What do you understand by the term "margin of safety" with reference to volume of production?
   (*b*) How do the following reflect on a break-even volume and on a P/V ratio: (*i*) increase in total fixed cost; (*ii*) increase in total physical sales; (*iii*) decrease in variable costs per unit.
7. What do you understand by the term "break-even analysis"? Enumerate its uses.
8. How do income statements prepared under the absorption costing and marginal costing concepts differ?
9. Compared with absorption costing when will variable costing report lower profits, higher profits, the same profits?
10. In what ways is variable costing better adapted to managerial use in profit planning, decision-making and control?
11. Why do the supporters of marginal costing state that fixed costs are not to be included in inventories?
12. Discuss the uses of CVP analysis and its significance to management.
13. "In classifying a particular cost as fixed or variable, the volume or activity level is extremely important." Discuss and illustrate this statement.
14. "The contribution approach is the foundation of CVP logic and related techniques." Discuss.
15. Discuss the role of contribution in marginal costing in decisions relating to fixation of selling price.
16. State with reasons whether the following propositions are correct:
    (*a*) In an undertaking with a high fixed cost, break-even point can be attained at a lower level of activity.
    (b) Profit is represented by the product of the margin of safety and the P/V ratio.
    (c) In relation to normal sales, a low margin of safety along with a high P/V ratio is generally an indication of high fixed costs.
17. Distinguish between "marginal costing" and "absorption costing."
18. "The effect of a price reduction is always to reduce the P/V ratio, to raise the break-even point, and to shorten the margin of safety. Explain with a suitable illustration.
19. Define break-even point. How can the break-even point be computed?
20. How is a break-even chart prepared? What information does the break-even chart give?
21. What are the basic assumptions in cost-volume-profit analysis?
22. Describe how a P/V chart is drawn. How does the P/V chart differ from a break-even chart?
23. For product-mix decisions, what criteria can be used to select products that will maximise net income?
24. Break-even analysis assumes that variable costs and revenues are linear and that fixed costs are fixed. Briefly explain why these assumptions may not be realistic.
25. Can there be two break-even points. Show with the help of a graph.
26. Distinguish between contribution and profit.

EXERCISES AND PROBLEMS

1. The following data has been taken from the records of a company. You are required to find out net profit using the technique of marginal costing..

		Rs.
Sales		75,000
Variable costs:		
Direct materials	Rs. 22,500	
Direct wages	12,500	
Factory overheads	5,250	
Administration, selling and distribution overheads	8,000	
	48,250	
Fixed costs:		
Factory overheads	2,000	
Administrative and other overheads	3,350	
	5,350	
Total cost		53,600
Profit		21,400

2. Using the information given below, calculate the net income for the months of October, November and December and the value of finished goods on hand at the end of period using absorption costing and marginal costing. Also, comment on the differences in profits under these two methods.

	October	November	December
Production	45,000	36,000	45,000
Sales	36,000	42,000	48,000
Opening stock	—	9,000	3,000
Closing stock	9,000	3,000	
Additional information:			
Selling price per unit		Rs. 50	
Variable cost per unit		Rs. 30	
Fixed cost per unit		Rs. 10	
Total Fixed costs per month		Rs. 3,90,000	
Normal output per month		39,000 months	

(*Ans.:* Profit under absorption costing. October Rs. 4,20,000, November Rs. 3,90,000, December Rs. 5,40,000. Profit under marginal costing, October Rs. 3,30,000. November Rs. 4,50,000, December Rs. 5,70,000. Difference in profits of different months is due to differences in values of closing stocks which are determined differently under both the methods.)

3. The following data were taken from the cost and production records of a company at the end of an accounting period:

		Rs.
Sales revenue		1,28,000
Cost of goods manufactured:		
Fixed	32,000	
Variable	48,000	80,000
Selling and administrative expenses:		
Fixed	20,000	
Variable	0	20,000
Opening inventory of finished goods		Nil
Normal and actual production		10,000 units

Closing inventory of finished goods 2,000 units

Calculate the net income for the period and the value of the finished goods on hand at the end of the period using (*a*) absorption costing, and (*b*) marginal costing.

(***Ans.:*** Net profit, Absorption costing Rs. 44,000, Variable costing Rs. 37,600, Closing stock absorption costing Rs. 16,000, Variable costing Rs. 9,600.)

4. A company produces a single product that sells for Rs. 150 per unit. Standard capacity is 1,00,000 units per year. On Jan. 1, 2009, there was no inventory of finished goods, production and sales for the year were as follows:

	Number of units	
Quarter	*Produced*	*Sold*
First	2,00,000	1,00,000
Second	3,00,000	2,50,000
Third	2,00,000	2,50,000
Fourth	3,00,000	4,00,000
	10,00,000	10,00,000

Manufacturing costs and selling and administrative expenses were as follows:

	Fixed	*Variable (per unit)*
Raw material	—	27
Direct labour	—	25
Indirect manufacturing cost	Rs. 2,00,000	18
Selling and administrative expenses	80,000	20
	Rs. 2,80,000	Re. 90

Prepare: (*a*) Quarterly income statements under absorption costing and variable costing; (*b*) account for the difference between the net incomes reported under each concept.

5. The directors of a company have been studying the following condensed profit reports for the years 2007 and 2008.

	2007	*2008*
Sales (Rs.)	3,00,000	4,50,000
Profit (or loss) (Rs.)	55,000	35,000

The directors are perturbed over the trend, for a 50% increase in sales resulted in a decrease in profit in 2008. The chief cost accountant explains that unabsorbed overhead was charged to 2008 operations. His statement was based on the following data:

Data	*2007*	*2008*
Sales (units)	20,000	30,000
Production (units)	30,000	20,000
Sales price per unit	Rs. 15	15
Variable cost per unit (Rs.)	5	5
Fixed factory overhead (Rs.)	1,80,000	1,80,000
Fixed factory overhead per unit (standard)	6	6
Fixed selling and administrative expenses	25,000	25,000

Prepare: (*a*) income statement by the conventional method to which the chief cost accountant referred; (*b*) income statements by variable costing method.

(***Ans.:*** Net profit, Absorption costing 2007, Rs. 55,000; 2008, Rs. 35,000. Variable costing 2007, Rs. 5,000 loss, 2008, Rs. 95,000.)

6. From the following data calculate:
   (*i*) P/V ratio
   (*ii*) Profit when sales were Rs. 20,000
   (*iii*) New break-even point if selling price is reduced by 20%

Fixed expenses	Rs. 4,000
Break-even point	Rs. 10,000

(***Ans.:*** P/V ratio 40%; Profit Rs. 4,000; BEP Rs. 16,000)

7. The following Figures arc available from the records of Venus Electricals as at 31st March:

	2007	*2008*
	Rs. lakhs	*Rs. lakhs*
Sales	150	200
Profit	30	50

Calculate:
   (*a*) The P/V ratio and total fixed expenses;
   (*b*) The break-even level of sales;
   (*c*) Sales required to earn a profit of Rs. 90 lakhs:
   (*d*) Profit or loss that would arise if the sales were Rs. 280 lakhs.

(***Ans.:*** (*a*) 40%, 130 lakhs (*b*) Rs. 75 lakhs
(*c*) Rs. 300 lakhs (*d*) Rs. 82 lakhs)

8. Two manufacturing companies which have the following operating details decide to merge.

	Company No. 1	*Company No. 2*
Capacity utilization %	90	60
Sales (Rs. lakhs)	540	300
Variable cost (Rs. lakhs)	396	325
Fixed costs (Rs. lakhs)	80	50

Assuming that the proposal is implemented, calculate:
   (*i*) Break-even sales of merged plant and the capacity utilization at that stage.
   (*ii*) Profitability of the merged plant at 80% capacity utilization.
   (*iii*) Sales turnover of the merged plant to earn a profit of Rs. 75 lakhs.
   (*iv*) When the merged plant is working capacity to earn a profit of Rs. 75 lakhs what percentage increase in selling price is required to sustain an increase of 5% of fixed overheads.

(***Ans.:*** (*i*) 25.909% P/V ratio, Rs. 501.67 lakhs, 45.6% (*ii*) Rs. 98 lakhs (*iii*) Rs. 791.23 lakhs (*iv*) 0.8215%.)

9. Company A and Company B, both under the same management, make and sell the same type of product. Their budgeted profit and loss accounts for January-June 2008 are as under:

	Company A		*Company B*	
	Rs.	*Rs.*	*Rs.*	*Rs.*
Sales		3,00,000		3,00,000
Less: Variable cost	2,40,000		2,00,000	
Fixed costs	30,000	2,70,000	70,000	2,70,000
		30,000		30,000

You are required to:
   (*i*) Calculatc the break-even point for each company.
   (*ii*) Calculate the sales volume in which each of the two companies will make a profit of Rs. 10,000.
   (*iii*) Assess how their profitability will change with decrease or increase in volume.

(***Ans.:*** (*i*) A Rs. 1,50,000; B Rs. 2,10,000; (*ii*) A Rs. 2,00,000; B Rs. 2,40,000.)

10. The following figures relate to a company manufacturing a varied range of product.

	Total cost	*Total sales*
Year ending 31st Dec. 2007	19,83,600	22,23,000
Year ending 31st Dec. 2008	21,43,200	24,51,000

Assuming stability in prices, with variable costs carefully controlled to reflect predetermined relationships, and an unvarying figure for fixed costs, calculate:

(*a*) The profit/volume ratio, to reflect the rates of growth for profit and sales

(*b*) Fixed cost

(*c*) Fixed cost % to sales

(*d*) Break-even point

(*e*) Margin of safety for the year 2007 and the year 2008.

(***Ans.:*** (*a*) 30% (*b*) Rs. 4,27,500

(*c*) 2007, 19.23%, 2008, 17.44% (*d*) Rs. 14,25,000

(*e*) 2007, Rs. 7,98,000, 2008 Rs. 10,26,000

11. A company has a P/V ratio of 40 per cent. By what percentage must sales be increased to offset —

(*i*) 10 per cent reduction in selling price, and

(*ii*) 20 per cent reduction in selling price?

(***Ans.:*** Hint.)

Let the present units sold be 100 @ Re. 1/- per unit	*Rs.*
Present total sales	100
Present variable cost	60
Present contributions	40

(P/V ratio 40%)

(*i*) If selling price is reduced by 10%

Selling price per unit	0.90
Variable cost per unit	0.60
Contribution per unit	0.30

In order to maintain the same contribution, viz., Rs. 40 the volume of sales should be:

$$\frac{\text{Present total contribution}}{\text{New contribution per unit}} \times \text{New selling price per unit}$$

$$\frac{40}{30} \times 90 = 120 \text{ or } \frac{1200}{.90} \text{ units or } 133\frac{1}{3} \text{ units.}$$

Thus, the volume of sales will have to be increased by 33% from the existing level if the selling price is reduced by 10%.

(*ii*) If the selling price is reduced by 20%

	Rs.
Selling price per unit	0.80
Variable cost per unit	0.60
Contribution per unit	0.20

For maintaining the same contribution the volume of sales should be:

$$\frac{40}{0.20} \times 0.80 = \text{Rs. } 160 \text{ or } \frac{1604}{.80} = 200 \text{ units}$$

Thus, the volume of sales will have to be increased by 100% over the existing, if the selling price is reduced 20%.

12. Two competing companies ABC Ltd. and XYZ Ltd. produce and sell in the same type of product in the same market. For the year ending March 2009, their forecasted profit and loss accounts are as follows:

		ABC Ltd.		XYZ Ltd.
Sales		Rs. 2,50,000		Rs. 2,50,000
Less: Variable costs of sales	Rs. 2,00,000		1,50,000	
Fixed costs	25,000	2,25,000	75,000	2,25,000
Forecasted net profit before tax		25,000		25,000

You are required to compute:

1. P/V ratio
2. Break-even sales volume

You are also required to state which company is likely to earn greater profits in conditions of:

(*a*) low demand, and

(*b*) high demand.

(*Ans.:* P/V Ratio ABC Ltd. 20%, XYZ Ltd. 40%; Break-even sales volume ABC Ltd. Rs. 1,25,000. XYZ Ltd. Rs. 1,87,500. In case of low demand, profit situation for ABC Ltd. will be better as it has a larger safety margin and lower amount of fixed costs. In case of high demand, XYZ will do better since additional sales will give profit at 40% (P/V ratio) whereas in case of ABC Ltd. additional sales will give profit at 20% (P/V ratios).

13. The budgeted sales of three products of a company are as follows:

	Product		
	X	Y	Z
Budgeted sales in units	10,000	15,000	20,000
Budgeted selling price per unit	4	4	4
Budgeted variable cost per unit	2.5	3	3.5
Budgeted fixed expenses total	12,000	9,000	7,500

From the information you are required to compute the following for each product:

(*a*) The budgeted profit

(*b*) The budgeted break-even sales

(*c*) The budgeted margin of safety in terms of sales value.

(*Ans.:*

	X	Y	Z
Profit	3,000	6,000	2,500
Break-even sales	Rs. 32,000	36,000	60,000
Margin of safety	Rs. 8,000	24,000	20,000)

14. Tractors Ltd. have an installed capacity of 5000 tractors per annum. They are presently operating at about 35% of installed capacity. For the coming year, they have budgeted as follows:

Production/Sales	4,000 units
Costs	*Rs. (Crores)*
Direct materials	8.00
Direct wages	0.60
Factory expenses	0.80
Administrative expenses	0.20
Selling expenses	0.20
Profit	1.00

Factory expenses as well as selling expenses are variable to the extent of 20%.

Calculate the break-even capacity utilisation percentage.

(*Ans.:* 40%).

15. From the following data, calculate break-even point expressed m terms of units and also the new B.E.P., if selling price is reduced by 10%.

Fixed expenses:	
Depreciation	Rs. 1,00,000
Salaries	Rs. 1,00,000
Variable expenses:	
Materials	Rs. 3 per unit
Labour	Rs. 2 per unit
Selling price	Rs. 10 per unit

(***Ans.:*** (*i*) 40,000 units (*ii*) 50,000 units)

16. From the following information relating to Quick Standards Ltd., you are required to find out: (a) Contribution, (*b*) Break-even point in units, (*c*) Margin of safety, (*d*) Profit.

Total fixed costs	Rs. 4,500
Total variable costs	7,500
Total sales	15,000
Units sold	5,000 (Units)

Also calculate the volume of sales to earn profit of Rs. 6,000.

(***Ans.:*** (*a*) Rs. 75,000 (*b*) 3,000 units
(*c*) Rs. 6,000, 40% (*d*) Rs. 3,000

17. S. Ltd. furnishes you the following information relation to the half year ended 30th June. 2007.

Fixed expenses	Rs. 45,000
Sales value	1,50,000
Profit	30,000

During the second half of the year, the company has projected a loss of Rs. 10,000.

Calculate:

(*i*) The break-even point and margin of safety for six months ending 30th June. 2007

(*ii*) Expected sales volume for second half of the year assuming that the P/V ratio and fixed expenses remain constant in the second half year also.

(*iii*) The break-even point and margin of safety for the whole year 2007.

(***Ans.:*** (*i*) BEP Rs. 90,000, margin of safety Rs. 60,000.
(*ii*) Sales Rs. 70,000
(*iii*) BEP Rs. 1,80,000
Margin of safety Rs. 40,000)

18. Delhi equipments Ltd., manufactures four components, the cost particulars of which are given below:

	Components			
	A	*B*	*C*	*D*
Elements of·cost:				
Direct material	Rs. 80	100	100	120
Direct labour	20	25	25	30
Variable overhead	10	12	15	10
Fixed overhead	15	23	20	20
	125	160	160	180
Output per machine hour (units)	4	2	3	3

The key factor is shortage of machine capacity.

You are required to advise management as to whether they should continue to produce all or some of these components (which are used in its main product) or they should buy them from a supplier who has quoted the following prices:

A = Rs. 115; B = Rs. 175; C = Rs. 135; D = Rs. 185.

(***Ans.:*** Hint.)

Statement of Profitability

	Components			
	A	*B*	*C*	*D*
Direct material	Rs. 80	Rs. 100	Rs. 100	Rs. 120
Direct labour	20	25	25	30
Variable overhead	10	12	15	10
Marginal cost per unit	110	137	140	160
Purchase price per unit	115	175	135	185
Excess of purchase price over marginal cost	5	38	—	25
Excess of marginal cost over purchase price	—	—	5	—
Decline in profitability per machine hour if purchase is made from outside	5 × 4 = 20	38 × 2 = 76	—	25 × 3 = 75
Increase in profitability per machine hour if purchase is made from outside			– 5 × 3 = 15	

The above analysis shows:

(*i*) Component C should be purchased from outside whether there is a key factor or not since its marginal cost is more than its purchase price. Purchasing from outside will push up the profitability by Rs. 15 per machine hour.

(*ii*) Continue the production of components A, B and D in case shortage of machine capacity is not the key factor.

(*iii*) In case shortage of machine capacity is the key factor as given in the question, the management must decide about the ranking of the three components. The above analysis shows that ranking should be in the order of A, D and B.

This is because in case of A, if it is purchased from outside, the loss of profitability will be only Rs. 20 per machine hour, while in case of D and B it will be Rs. 75 and Rs. 76 per machine hour respectively.

19. From the following data, which product would you recommend for manufacture in the factory?

Per unit of	*Product A*	*Product B*
Standard manufacturing time	2 hours	3 hours
Direct materials	50	30
Direct labour @ Rs. 10 per hour	20	30
Variable overhead @ Rs. 6 per hour	12	18
Selling price	200	240

Total machine hours available in the factory are 60,000.

20. Calculate the effect on profit of a proposed change in "Sales Mix" from the following data:

Existing sales mix	*M*	*N*	*O*	*P*	*Total*
Sales (in Rs.)	80,000	1,00,000	40,000	20,000	2,40,000
Variable cost (in Rs.)	48,000	68,000	32,000	8,000	1,56,000
Fixed cost (in Rs.)					58,800
Proposed sales mix	Rs. 60,000	88,000	80,000	12,000	2,40,000

21.(*a*) The following particulars are extracted from the records of a company:

	Product A	*Product B*
Sales (per unit)	Rs. 100	Rs. 120
Consumption of material	2 kg.	3 kg.
Material cost	Rs. 10	Rs. 15
Direct wages cost	15	10
Direct expenses	5	6
Machine hours used	3	2

Overhead expenses:		
Fixed	5	10
Variable	15	20

Direct wage per hour is Rs. 5. Comment on the profitability of each product (both use the same raw material) when (*i*) Total sales potential in units is limited; (*ii*) Total sales potential in value is limited; (*iii*) Raw material is in short supply: and (*iv*) Production capacity (in terms of machine hours) is the limiting factor.

(*b*) Assuming raw material as the key factor, availability of which is 10,000 kg. and maximum sales potential of each product being 3,500 units, find out the product mix which will yield the maximum profit.

(*Ans.:* Hint).

	Per unit of	
	A	*B*
Sales	Rs, 100	Rs. 120
Direct material	10	15
Direct wages	15	10
Direct expenses	5	6
Variable overhead	15	20
Marginal cost	45	51
Contribution per unit	55	69
P/V ratio	55%	57.5%
Contribution per kg of material	27.5	23
Contribution per machine hour	18.3	34.5

(*i*) In case total sales potential in units is a limiting factor, B is more profitable as it is making a larger contribution per unit as compared to A.

(*ii*) In case total sales potential in value is a limiting factor, still B is more profitable since its P/V ratio is higher than that of A.

(*iii*) In case raw material is in short supply, A is more profitable as its contribution per kg. of material is higher than that of Product B.

(*iv*) In case production capacity is limited, B is more profitable since it gives higher contribution per machine hour than A.

Note: Best situation is obtained when contribution per unit of key factor is the maximum.

(*b*) In case raw material is the key factor, A is more profitable to produce as its contribution per kg of material is higher than that of B. If 3,500 units of A are manufactured, total material consumption will be 7,000 kg (i.e., 3,500 × 2 kg.). The balance of 3,000 kg. of material can be used to manufacture 1,000 units (3,000 ÷ 3) of B. The total profit by this product mix will be as follows:

Contribution:

Product A 3,500 units @ Rs. 55 each		Rs. 1,92,500
Product B 1,000 units @ Rs. 69 each		69,000
Total contribution:		2,61,500
Total fixed costs:		
Product A 5 × 3,500	= Rs. 17,500	
Product B 10 × 3,500	= 35,000	52,500
Total profit		2,09,000

22. A, B and C are three similar plants under the same management who want them to merge for better operation. The details are as under:

Plant	*A*	*B*	*C*
Capacity operated	100%	70%	50%
	Rs. (in lakhs)	Rs. (in lakhs)	Rs. (in lakhs)
Turnover	300	280	150
Variable cost	200	210	75
Fixed cost	70	50	62

Find out:

(*i*) The capacity of the merged plant for break-even.

(*ii*) The profit at 75% capacity of the merged plant.

(*iii*) The turnover, from the merged plant to give a profit of Rs. 28 lakhs.

(***Ans.:*** (*i*) 52%; (*ii*) Profit Rs. 80.5 (lakhs); (*iii*) Rs. 600 lakhs.

23. Sunita Manufacturing Company produces chairs. An analysis of their accounting reveals:

Fixed cost	Rs. 50,000 for the year
Variable cost	Rs. 20 per chair
Capacity	2,000 chairs per year
Selling price	Rs. 70 per chair

(*i*) Find the break-even point.

(*ii*) Find the number of chairs to be sold to get a profit of Rs. 30,000.

(*iii*) What will be the answer for (*i*) and (*ii*) if selling price changes to Rs. 60 per chair?

(*iv*) If the company can manufacture 600 chairs more per year with an additional Fixed cost of Rs. 2,000, what should be the selling price to maintain the profit per chair as at (*ii*) above?

24. SV Ltd., a multi-product company furnishes you the following data relating to the year 2008.

	First half of the year *Rs.*	*Second half of the year* *Rs.*
Sales	45,000	50,000
Total Cost	40,0C0	43,000

Assuming that there is no change in prices and variable cost and that the fixed expenses are incurred equally in the two half year periods, calculate for the year 2008.

(*i*) The P/V ratio

(*ii*) Fixed expenses

(*iii*) Break-even sales

(*iv*) Percentage of margin of safety

[***Ans.:*** (*i*) 40%; (*ii*) 26,000; (*iii*) 65,000 (*iv*) 31.58%.]

Alternative Choices Decisions

DECISION MAKING

Decision making is the process of evaluating two or more alternatives leading to a final choice, popularly known as Alternative Choices Decisions. Decision making is closely associated with planning for the future and is directed towards a specific objective or goal.

DIFFERENTIAL ANALYSIS

Differential analysis may be defined as the use of relevant costs and relevant revenues in making decisions. Relevant costs and benefits are very important in evaluating alternatives, in ascertaining the effect of various alternatives on profit and selecting the alternative with the greatest benefit. The relevant costs and revenues are the differences between the alternatives under consideration. The amount of such differences are called differentials and the accounting analysis concerned with the effect of alternatives on revenues and costs is called differential analysis. Relevant revenues and relevant costs are also known as differential revenues and differential costs. Differential revenue is the amount of increase or decrease in revenue expected from a particular course of action as compared with an alternative. Differential analysis provides a decision rule to managers in decision making which is: the alternative that gives the greatest incremental profit should be selected. Incremental profit is the difference between the relevant revenues and relevant costs of each alternative.

In case, decision affects both revenue and costs, management must estimate the changes in each to estimate the change in profit. In many decisions, only costs will change. In this case, the most beneficial (profitable) decision will be the one with the lowest cost because the lowest cost alternative will give the highest profit, provided all other factors and situations remain constant.

TYPES OF CHOICES DECISIONS

Most management decisions may be referred to as alternative choice decisions. Alternative choice decisions cover situations with two or more alternative courses of action from which the manager (decision-maker) must select the best alternative. A decision involving more than two alternatives is called a multiple alternative choice decision. Some examples of alternative choice decisions are: make or buy, own or lease, retain or replace, repair or renovate, now or later, change versus status quo, slower or faster, export versus local sales, shutdown or continue, expand or contract, change the product-mix, take or refuse orders, place special orders, select sales territories, replace present equipment with new machinery, sell at split-up point or process further, etc.

Some of the above alternative choices decisions and the information relevant to the decisions are discussed below.

Make or Buy

Make or buy decisions arise when a company with unused production capacity consider the following alternatives:

(*a*) To buy certain raw materials or subassemblies from outside suppliers.

(*b*) To use available capacity to produce the items within the company.

A make or buy decision is basically one of determining which alternative is economically most desirable and most effectively utilises the firm's resources. These decisions can effect the firm's production methods and capacities, available working capital, cost of borrowing funds, and competitive position. Costs that will be incurred under both alternatives are not relevant to the analysis. The firm should make an analysis of the cost, quality and quantity considerations of the individual make or buy decision. Differential cost analysis is especially useful if the company has idle capacity and idle workers that can be used to make the tools or parts. Other potential use of available capacity should also be considered and qualitative factors must be evaluated in the decision process. These considerations include price stability from suppliers, reliability of delivery and quality of the material or component involved. Qualitative factors are not included in differential cost analyses, but they should be used to test the reasonableness of any decision based purely on quantitative cost studies.

For example, assume that a company can make a part that it has been purchasing at a unit cost of Rs. 30. The company has been operating at 75% of normal capacities and in the foreseeable future no use for the excess capacity is contemplated except for the possible production of the part. Fixed manufacturing cost amounts to Rs. 17,00,000 a year whether the plant operates at 75% or 100% of capacity. The cost to manufacture 50,000 units of the part that will be needed has been estimated as follows:

	Units cost	*Total cost*
Direct materials	12.5	6,25,000
Direct labour	8.0	4,00,000
Variable manufacturing overhead	5.0	2,50,000
Total incremental cost	25.5	12,75,000
Cost to purchase part	30.0	15,00,000
Net advantage in parts production	4.5	2,25,000

In the above analysis the fixed manufacturing overhead has not been considered because it has to be incurred under both alternatives. Logically, the costs that will be increased or decreased as a result of making the part should be considered. In some cases, both the variable and fixed costs will be affected.

Add or Drop Products

The decision to eliminate an unprofitable product is a special case of product profitability evaluation. To evaluate the financial consequences of eliminating a product, it is necessary to concentrate on the differential or incremental profit effect of the decision. An important factor in the decision to add or drop a product is whether it will increase or decrease the future income of the business. Appropriate cost and profit measures must be developed for each alternative.

Assume a company is considering dropping product B from its line because accounting statements show that product B is being sold at a loss.

Income Statement

	Product A	*Product B*	*Product C*	*Total*
Sales revenue	50,000	7,500	12,500	70,000
Cost of sales:				
Direct material	7,500	1,000	1,500	10,000
Direct labour	15,000	2,000	2,500	19,500
Indirect manufacturing cost (50% of direct labour)	7,500	1,000	1,250	9,750
	30,000	4,000	5,250	39,250
Gross margin on sales	20,000	3,500	7,250	30,750
Selling and administrative expenses (allocation on arbitrary basis)	12,500	4,500	4,000	21,000
Net income (loss)	7,500	(1,000)	3,250	9,750

Additional Information:

(*i*) Factory overhead costs are made up of fixed costs of Rs. 5,850 and variable costs of Rs. 3,900. Variable costs by products are: product A Rs. 3,000, product B, Rs. 400, and product C Rs. 500.

(*ii*) Fixed costs and expenses will not be changed if product B is eliminated.

(*iii*) Variable selling and administrative expenses to the extent of Rs. 11,000 can be traced to the product as follows: A, Rs. 7,500; B, Rs. 1,500; C, Rs. 2,000.

(*iv*) Fixed selling and administrative expenses are Rs. 10,000.

The decision to drop product B cannot be reasonably made from the above data prepared under a conventional income statement. This information together with the following statement may be helpful to management.

	Product A *Rs.*	*Product B* *Rs.*	*Product C* *Rs.*	*Total* *Rs.*
Sales revenue	50,000	7,500	12,500	70,000
Less: Variable product Costs:				
Direct material	7,500	1,000	1,500	10,000
Direct labour	15,000	2,000	2,500	19,500

	Factory overhead	3,000	400	500	3,900
	Selling and administrative expenses	7,500	1,500	2,000	11,000
		33,000	4,900	6,500	44,400
	Contribution margin	17,000	2,600	6,000	25,600
Less:	Fixed costs:				
	Factory overhead				5,850
	Selling and administrative expenses				10,000
Total fixed costs					15,850
Net income					9,750

This statement shows that product B exceeds its variable costs by Rs. 2,600. If the sale of product B were discontinued, this marginal contribution would be lost and the net income of the firm would be reduced by Rs. 2.600. That is, net income will be Rs. 7,150 (Rs. 9,750 – Rs. 2,600). In this illustration it has been assumed that sales of products A and C will not be increased after product B is dropped. Further, it has been assumed that dropping product B will not change the fixed costs and expense. If these assumptions are not true, new analysis must be made. Assume, for example, that after dropping product B, the sales of product A increase by 10%. The total profit of the firm will not increase by this sales increase. Product A makes only a marginal contribution of 34%.

Sales revenue	Rs. 50,000	100%
Variable costs	33000	66%
Marginal contribution	17,000	34%

On additional sales of Rs 5,000, the marginal contribution would be Rs. 1,700

Sales revenue	Rs. 5,000
Variable costs (66%)	3,300
Marginal contribution (34%)	1,700

This contribution is less than Rs. 2,600 now being realised on the sales of product B. It would take additional sales of product A of approximately Rs. 7,647 to equal the marginal contribution of Rs. 2,600 now being made by product B:

$$\frac{\text{Marginal contribution of product B}}{\text{Marginal contribution of product A}} = \frac{2,600}{34\%} = \text{Rs. } 7,647$$

It is possible that dropping product B may result in reduction in some of the fixed costs. Product B now contribute Rs. 2,600 towards recovery of fixed costs and expenses. Only if the fixed costs and expenses can be reduced by more than this amount, it will be advisable to drop product B.

Sell or Process Further

The decision whether a product should be sold at the split-of point or processed further is faced by many manufacturers. The choice between selling a product at split-off or processing it further is a short-run operating decision. Additional processing adds value to a product and increases its selling price above the amount for which it could be sold at split-off. The decision to process further depends upon whether the increase in total revenues exceeds the additional costs incurred for processing beyond split-off. Generally speaking, there are two general conditions under which a sell or process further decision could occur.

1. The company is evaluating the possibility of processing beyond split-off and must incur certain equipment costs and other fixed costs if additional processing is to occur.
2. The company already processes a product beyond split-off and has invested in the equipment and required personnel.

The first situation is really a capital budgeting problem and here it is not sufficient to determine whether incremental revenues exceed incremental costs. Since new investments in machinery and building are involved, the rate of return on this investment must also be considered.

In the second situation, the relevant costs are only those costs which relate to the additional processing of each product beyond the split-off point. The joint costs are relevant to the further processing decisions. Certain fixed costs such as supervisory salaries are related to additional processing. If these costs are eliminated by selling products at split-off, they are incremental and should be included in the decision analysis. If salaried personnel are assigned other duties in the company when additional processing is discontinued, the salary costs are not incremental since they are incurred under either decision alternative. If the equipment used for additional processing sits idle or can be used in other processes, it should be ignored in the decision analysis. Depreciation expense is never relevant in short-run operating decisions, since depreciation is an allocation of costs incurred in a past period.

In deciding upon which course of action to follow, the company compares the contribution margin from the sale of the partially processed product with the contribution margin from the sale of the completely processed product. The revenue to be derived from the sale of the partially processed product is the opportunity cost attached to the decision of further processing. Assume, for example, a partially processed product can be sold for Rs. 90 per unit which is manufactured at a cost of Rs. 60. Further processing can be done at an additional cost of Rs. 30 per unit and the final product can be sold at Rs. 150 per unit. The firm can produce 10,000 units. The analysis is shown below:

	Sell	*Process and Sell*
Sales revenue (10,000 units)	Rs. 9,00,000	Rs. 15,00,000
Less: Manufacturing costs	6,00,000	9,00,000
	3,00,000	6,00,000

Net advantage in further processing Rs. 6,00,000 – 3,00,000 = Rs. 3,00,000

Thus, there is a net advantage of Rs. 3,00,000 in processing the product further. The market value of the partially processed product (Rs. 9,00,000) is considered to be the opportunity cost of further processing.

The figure of net advantage of Rs. 3,00,000 can be arrived at in the following manner also:

Revenue from sale of final product (10,000 × 150)		Rs. 15,00,000
Less: Additional processing cost (10,000 × 30)	3,00,000	
Revenue from sale of intermediate product	9,00,000	12,00,000
Net advantage in further processing		3,00,000

Operate or Shutdown

Differential cost analysis is also used when a business is confronted with the possibility of a temporary shutdown. This type of analysis has to determine whether in the short-run a firm is better off operating than not operating. As long as the products sold recover their variable costs and make a contribution towards the recovery of fixed costs, it may be preferable to operate and not to shutdown. Also management should consider the investment in the training of its employees which would be lost in the event of a temporary shutdown. Recruiting and training new workers would add to present costs. Another factor is the loss of established markets. Also, a temporary shutdown does not eliminate all costs. Depreciation, taxes, interest, and insurance costs are incurred during shutdown also. The other points (benefits) which should be considered are the following, avoiding operations losses, savings in maintenance and repair costs, savings in indirect labour costs, savings in fixed costs.

A company operating below 50% of its capacity expects that the volume of sales will drop below the present level of 10,000 units per month. Management is concerned that a further drop in sales volume will create a loss and has under consideration a recommendation that operations be suspended, until better market conditions prevail and also a better selling price. The present operating income statement is as follows:

Sales revenue (10.,000 units @ Rs. 3.00)		Rs. 30,000
Less: Variable costs @ Rs. 2,00 per unit	20,000	
Fixed costs	10,000	30,000
Net Income		0

The following income statements have been prepared for sales at different capacities:

	Units Produced					
	Shutdown	2,000	4,000	6,000	8,000	10,000
Sales revenue @ Rs. 3	0	6,000	12,000	18,000	24,000	30,000
Variable costs @Rs. 2	0	4,000	8,000	12,000	16,000	20,000
Contribution	0	2,000	4,000	6,000	8,000	10,000
Fixed costs	4,000	10,000	10,000	10,000	10,000	10,000
Loss	4,000	8,000	6,000	4,000	2,000	0

It would appear that shutdown is desirable when the sales volume drops below 6,000 units per month, the point at which operating losses exceed the shutdown cost. This volume of 6,000 units could be arrived at without an income statement as follows:

Fixed costs if plant operates	Rs. 10,000
Fixed costs if plant shutsdown	4,000
Additional cost to be recovered when operating	6,000

Each unit of product sold contributes Re. 1.00 to fixed costs recovery:

Selling price per unit	Rs. 3.00
Variable cost per unit	Rs. 2.00
Contribution	Rs. 1.00

Sale of 6,000 units is necessary to recover Rs. 6,000 of fixed costs.

$$\frac{\text{Rs. } 6{,}000}{\text{Re. } 1.00} = 6{,}000 \text{ units}$$

If the selling price is cut to Rs. 2.80, the contribution margin will be Re. 0.80 per unit.

Required sale to recover an additional Rs. 6,000 of fixed costs.

$$\frac{\text{Rs. } 6{,}000}{\text{Re. } 0.80} = 7{,}500 \text{ units}$$

That is, sales of 7,500 units would be necessary to recover an additional Rs. 6,000 of fixed costs.

Special Orders

The question of special orders or one time orders arises when a company has excess or idle production capacity and management considers the possibility of selling additional products at less than normal selling prices, provided that such a special order will not affect the regular sales of the same product.

The basic problem is to determine an acceptable, price for the special order units. Cost analysis using the contribution approach is a useful technique to determine the short-run profit effects of special order transactions. In deciding the pricing of special orders where normal operations are not disturbed and where unused production capacity exists, it is not advisable to attach fixed costs to products. Price determination should take into account the recovery of incremental (variable) costs caused by accepting the special order. If the normal fixed costs are included in the price of the special order, the price may be too high and the business firm could lose the entire order and the contribution margin to be earned on the special order. Only the relevant (variable) costs should be used in the decision analysis to arrive at an appropriate price. Fixed costs are relevant only if incurred to facilitate the special order.

The following example illustrates the special order decisions.

A manufacturing company produces 20,000 units by operating at 60% of the capacity and sells at a price of Rs. 30 per unit. The budgeted figures for the year 2008 are as follows:

	Production (20,000 units)
Raw material @ Rs. 4.25	Rs. 85,000
Direct labour @ Rs. 5.75	1,15,000
Variable factory overhead @ Rs. 7.75	1,55,000
Fixed factory overhead	1,25,000
Variable selling costs 2.75% of selling price	
Fixed selling and administrative costs	72,500

The company receives a special order for 10,000 units from a firm. The company desires to earn a profit of Re. 1.00 per unit and no selling expenses are to be incurred for the special order. The minimum price on the special order and income statements are as follows:

Pricing of Special Order

	(10,000 units) *(Rs.)*
Variable costs to be incurred:	
Raw materials	4.25
Direct labour	5.75
Variable overhead	7.75
Variable cost per unit	17.75
Desired profit	1.00
Minimum price	18.75

Increase in sales = 10,000 units × Rs. 18.75 – Rs. 1,87,500

Income Statement

	Without special order (Rs.)	Special order (Rs.)	With special order (Rs.)
Sales	6,00,000	1,87,500	7,87,500
Less: Variable costs:			
Raw materials	85,000	42,500	1,27,500
Direct labour	1,15,000	57,500	1,72,500
Variable factory overhead	1,55,000	77,500	2,32,500
Variable selling costs (2.75% of selling price)	16,500	—	16,500
Total variable costs	3,71,500	1,77,500	5,49,000
Less: Fixed costs:			
Fixed factory overhead	1,25,000	—	1,25,000
Fixed selling and administrative cost	72,500	—	72,500
Total fixed costs	1,97,500		1,97,500
Total costs	5,69,000	1,77,500	7,46,500
Net income before taxes	31,000	10,000	41,000

From the above analysis it is clear that the acceptance of the social order will increase the profit by Rs. 10,000. Also the bid price (Rs. 18.75) is significantly less than the normal price of Rs. 30. However, before arriving at a proper decision, management should consider some qualitative factors other than just the immediate impact on income. An important point is the effect on regular customers. If regular customers are paying more for the products, they may demand price reduction or quit buying from the firm and seek another source of supply. Another consideration is the possibility of special order customers being the regular customers.

Replace or Retain

The decision to replace or retain plant and equipment is also an important decision and should be taken very carefully. The differential costs which are important in retain or replace decisions are the following: change in fixed overhead costs, loss on sale of old equipment, capital investment and related costs such as rate of return and interest. Management should also consider differential benefits likely to be derived such as higher production and increased sales, realisable value of old machine, savings in operating costs, tax advantages, if any. Suppose a company has purchased a plant for Rs. 1,00,000 five years ago which has a life of 10 years with no salvage value. The present book value is Rs. 50,000. Management is considering the replacement of this plant with a new plant costing Rs. 80,000 having a life of five years with no scrap value at the end of its life. The costs of operating present plant and the proposed plant are as follows:

	Present plant (Rs.)	Proposed plant (Rs.)
Variable costs:		
Labour, supplies, power, etc.	80,000	48,000
Fixed costs: Insurance, taxes, etc.	10,000	12,000
Depreciation		16,000
	90,000	76,000

It appears that the proposed plant would result into cost savings of Rs. 24,000 (Rs. 1,00,000 – 76,000). However, the book value of the present equipment is a sunk cost and not relevant in the decision. The following table helps in making a better analysis of the data:

	Present plant *Rs.*	*Proposed plant* *Rs.*
Variable costs:		
Labour, supplies, power, etc.	80,000	48,000
Fixed costs: insurance, taxes, etc.	10,000	12,000
Depreciation	0	16,000
	90,000	76,000

The purchase of the new plant results in a saving of Rs. 14,000 (Rs. 90,000 - 76,000). Management has to consider whether this benefit is enough to justify the investment of Rs 80,000 in new machinery.

LIMITATIONS OF DIFFERENTIAL ANALYSIS

Differential analysis helps in evaluating decision alternatives. Relevant costs and revenues are the factors that differ between alternatives. The primary objective is to select the least costly alternative. However, cost computations and profit estimates are one means of tackling such problems. Many projects and proposals are rejected simply because the costs involved are too high or relative income potential was lower than that of an alternative. Yet, the project may have been beneficial to the company in that it would have allowed the company to balance its risk, or to offer a complete product line which would have attracted new customers to all the company's products. Perhaps this is the very reason why the cost accountant needs to be extremely careful in the translation of the data with which he works.

Managers must study carefully the data to be used in decision-making. Other qualitative factors besides cost should be given proper attention. The pressure of competition, the maintenance of sources of supply and of certain marketing outlets, and the maintenance of the existing personnel organisation and morale may often be the real determinants of business decisions. The quantitative information alone does not provide a solution to all business problems. Sometimes, other factors are more important than cost factors.

Illustration 1:

P Ltd., is at present operating at 80% capacity level, the production being 15,000 units per annum. The company operates a flexible budgetary control system. The following relevant cost data are obtained from the company's budget at different capacity utilisation levels:

Capacity utilisation level

	80%	*100%*
Sales	Rs. 20,00,000	Rs. 25,00,000
Variable overheads	Rs. 2,25,000	Rs. 2,50,000
Semi-variable overheads	Rs. 1,05,000	Rs. 1,11,000
Fixed overheads	Rs. 4,00,000	Rs. 4,70,000
Output (in units)	15,000	18,750

Material and labour cost per unit are constant under present conditions. The management expects a profit margin of 10% on sales.

You are required to compute the differential cost of producing the additional 3,750 units by increasing the capacity utilization level to 100 per cent and the minimum price per unit at 10% profit on cost.

Solution:

	Rs.	*Rs.*
Sales at 80% capacity		20,00,000
Less: Profit 10% $\left(\frac{20,00,000 \times 10}{100}\right)$		2,00,000
Cost of goods sold:		18,00,000
Less: Expenses	Rs.	
Variable overheads	2,25,000	
Semi-variable overheads	1,05,000	
Fixed overheads	4,00,000	7,30,000
Cost of material and labour at 80% capacity		10,70,000

Therefore, material and labour cost at 100% capacity

$$\frac{10,70,000 \times 100}{80} = \textbf{Rs.}\ 13,37,500$$

Differential cost analysis is as follows:

	80% capacity 15,000 units Rs.	*100% capacity 18,750 units Rs.*	*Differential cost Rs.*
Material and labour	10,70,000	13,37,500	2,67,500
Variable expenses	2,25,000	2,50,000	25,000
Semi-variable expenses	1,05,000	1,11,000	6,000
Fixed expenses	4,00,000	4,70,000	70,000
Total cost	18,00,000	21,68,500	3,68,500

(*a*) Differential Cost for 3750 Units = Rs. 3,68,500

(*b*) Minimum Price = $\frac{\text{Rs.}3,68,500}{3,750 \text{ units}}$ Rs. 98.266

Add: 10% Profit on cost 9.826

108.092

Illustration 2:

A company has an installed production capacity of 1,00,000 units and presently it is working at 70% capacity utilisation. As production capacity utilisation increases, cost per unit decreases as follows:

Capacity utilisation	*Cost per unit*
70%	Rs. 97
80%	Rs. 92
90%	Rs. 87
100%	Rs. 82

The company has received three export orders from different sources as under:

Source A: 5,000 units at Rs. 55 per unit

Source B: 10,000 units at Rs. 52 per unit

Source C: 10,000 units at Rs. 51 per unit

Advise the company whether any or all the export orders should be accepted or not

Solution:

Statement showing Differential Costs at Different Capacity Utilisation Level (Installed Capacity 1,00,000 units)

Capacity Utilisation	*Production at different levels capacity utilisation*		*Unit cost Rs.*	*Total cost Rs.*	*Differential cost Rs.*	*Differential cost per unit*
Per cent	*Units*					
70	70,000	$\left(1{,}00{,}000 \times \frac{70}{100}\right)$	97	67,90,000	—	—
80	80,000	$\left(1{,}00{,}000 \times \frac{80}{100}\right)$	82	73,60,000	5,70,000	57 $\left[\frac{5{,}70{,}000}{10{,}000}\right]$
90	90,000	$\left(1{,}00{,}000 \times \frac{90}{100}\right)$	87	78,30,000	4,70,000	47 $\left[\frac{4{,}70{,}000}{10{,}000}\right]$
100	1,00,000		82	82,00,000	3,70,000	37 $\left[\frac{3{,}70{,}000}{10{,}000}\right]$

Statement showing Profit or Loss Accepting the Various Export Orders

Export order source	*Export order*	*Capacity utilisation*	*Differential costs*			*Price per unit*	*Sales revenue from the export order*	*Profit or (loss)*
			Per unit		*Total*			
	Unit	*Per cent*	*Rs.*		*Rs.*	*Rs.*	*Rs.*	*Rs.*
A	5,000	75	57		2,85,000	55	2,75,000	(10,000)
B	10,000	85	First 5,000 units being upto 80% @ Rs. 57 Next 5,000 units Rs. @ Rs. 47		5,20,000	52	5,20,000	Nil
C	10,000	95	First 5,000 units being upto 90 % @ Rs. 47 Next 5,000 units @ Rs. 7		4,20,000	51	5,10,000	90,000
Total	25,000	95%			12,25,000		13,05,000	80,000

It is clear from the above statement that it is advantageous for the company only when it accepts all the export orders. If the company accepts export orders only from one or two of three sources, it will suffer a loss. Therefore, the company should accept export orders from all the three sources to earn additional profits.

Illustration 3:

A Company has the option to procure a particular material from two sources:

Source I assures that defectives will not be more than 2% of supplied quantity.

Source II does not give any assurance, but on the basis of past experience of supplies received from it, it is observed that defective percentage is 2.8%.

The material is supplied in lots of 1,000 units. Source II supplies the lot at a price, which is lower by Rs. 100 as compared to Source 1. The defective units of material can be rectified for use at a cost of Rs. 5 per unit.

You are required lo find out which of the two sources is more economical.

Solution:

Comparative Statement of Procuring Material from Two Sources

	Material source I	*Material source II*
Defectives (in %)	2 *(Future estimate)*	2.8 *(Past experience)*
Units supplied (in one lot)	1,000	1,000
Total defective units in a lot	20 *(1,000 units × 2%)*	28 *(1,000 units × 2.8%)*
Additional price paid per lot (Rs.) (A)	100	—
Rectification cost of defect (Rs.) (B)	100 *(20 units × Rs. 5)*	140 *(28 units × Rs. 5)*
Total additional cost per lot (Rs.): {(A) + (B)}	200	140

Decision: On comparing the total additional cost incurred per lot of 1,000 units, we observe that it is more economical, if the required material units are procured from material Source II.

Illustration 4:

The accounts of a company are expected to reveal a profit of Rs. 14,00,000 after charging fixed costs Rs. 10,00.000 fur the year ended 31st March. 2008. The selling price of the product is Rs. 50 per unit and variable cost per unit is Rs. 20.

Market investigations suggest the following responses to the price changes:

Alternatives	*Selling Price reduced by*	*Quantity Sold increased by*
I	5%	10%
II	7%	20%
III	10%	25%

Evaluate these alternatives and state which of the alternatives, on profitability consideration, should be adopted for the forthcoming year.

Solution:

Statement for evaluating three alternatives on profitability consideration

	Alternatives I	II	III
Selling price per unit (Rs.)	47.50 (Rs. 50 – 5% of Rs. 50)	46.50 (Rs. 50 – 7% of Rs. 50)	45.00 (Rs. 50 – 10% of Rs. 50)
Less: Variable cost per unit (Rs.)	20.00	20.00	20.00
Contribution per unit (Rs.)	27.50	26.50	25.00
Revised quantity of units to be sold (Refer to Working Note 3)	88,000	96,000	1,00,000
Total contribution (Rs.)	24,20,000 (88,000 units × Rs. 27.50)	25,44,000 (96,000 units × Rs. 26.50)	25,00,000 (1,00,000 units × Rs. 25)

Recommendation: An evaluation of the above three alternatives on profitability consideration clearly shows that alternative II is the best as it gives maximum contribution and hence profitability. Therefore, this alternative should be adopted.

Working Notes:

1. *Contribution per unit*

= Rs. Selling price per unit – Variable cost per unit
= Rs. 50 – Rs. 20 = Rs. 30

2. *Expected quantity of units to be sold*

	(Rs.)
Profit	14,00,000
Add: Fixed costs	10,00,000
Total contribution	24,00,000

$$\text{Quantity of units sold} = \frac{\text{Total contribution}}{\text{Contribution per unit}} = \frac{\text{Rs. } 24{,}00{,}000}{\text{Rs. } 30} = 80{,}000 \text{ units.}$$

(Refer to working note 1)

3. Revised quantity of units to be sold

Alternatives	*Units to be sold*
I	80,000 units + 10% of 80,000 units = 88,000 units
II	80,000 units + 20% of 80,000 units = 96,000 units
III	80,000 units + 25% of 80,000 units = 1,00,000 units

Illustration 5:

The costs per unit of three products X, Y and Z are given below:

Products	*X*	*Y*	*Z*
Direct Material (Rs.)	20	16	18
Direct Labour (Rs.)	12	14	12
Variable Overheads (Rs.)	8	10	6
Fixed Expenses (Rs.)	6	6	4
	Rs. 46	46	40
Profit	18	14	12
Selling Price (Rs.)	64	60	52
No. of units produced	10,000	5,000	8,000

Production arrangements are such that if one product is given up the production of the others can be raised by 50%. The directors propose that product *Z* should be given up because the contribution from the product is the lowest. Present suitable analysis of the data indicating whether the proposal should be accepted.

Solution:

1. *Computation of present profit*

	Rs.
Product *X* (10,000 × 18)	1,80,000
Product *Y* (5,000 × 14)	70,000
Product *Z* (8,000 × 12)	96,000
	3.46,000

2. *Computation of Fixed Cost*

	Rs.
Product *X* (10,000 × 6)	60,000
Product *Y* (5,000 × 6)	30,000
Product *Z* (8,000 × 4)	32,000
	1,22,000

3. Computation of Profit Under Proposed Situation (*Product Z discontinued*)

Product *X* (15,000 × 40)	Rs. 6,00,000
Product *Y* (7,500 × 40)	3,00,000
	9,00,000
Add: Total Fixed Cost [as per calculation above]	1,22,000
Total Cost (1)	10,22,000
Sales:	
Product *X* (15,000 × 64)	9,60,000
Product *Y* (7,500 × 60)	4,50,000
Total Sales (2)	14,10,000
Profit = (2) – (1) = (3)	3,88,000

Thus, the profit under the proposed situation will increase by Rs. 42,000 (*i.e.*, 3,88,000 – 3,46,000). Hence, the proposal for discontinuance or product *Z* should be accepted.

Note: It has been assumed that fixed costs of Rs. 1,22,000 are for the business as a whole. They have been simply apportioned to Product *X*, *Y*, and *Z* and they will continue to be same even after the Product *Z* is discontinued.

Illustration 6:

Quality Product Limited has drawn up the following budget for the year 2007.

	Rs.
Raw Materials	20,00,000
Labour, stores, power and other variable costs	6,00,000
Fixed Manufacturing Overheads	7,00,000
Packing and variable distribution cost	4,00,000
Fixed general overheads including selling	3,00,000
	40,00,000
Sales Revenue @ Rs. 50 per unit	50,00,000
Budgeted Profit	Rs. 10,00,000

The General Manager suggests to reduce selling prices by 5% and expects to achieve an additional volume of 5%. The more intensive manufacturing programme will involve additional costs of Rs. 15,000 for production planning. It will also be necessary to open an additional sales office at the cost of Rs. 1,00,000 per annum.

The Sales Manager, on the other hand, suggests to increase selling price by 10% which it is estimated will reduce sales volume by 10%, At the same time a saving in manufacturing overheads and general overheads of Rs. 50,000 and Rs. 1,00,000 per annum respectively is expected on this reduced volume.

Which of these two proposals would you accept and why? Show complete working.

Solution:

Computation of Profit as per Proposal of General Manager

1. New Sales Volume (Units 100,000 + 5%)		1,05,000
		Rs.
2. Sales Value (1,05,00 × 4,750)		49,87,500
3. Cost of Sales:		
Variable costs = $\frac{30,00,000}{1,00,000} \times 1,05,000$		31,50,000
Fixed Cost:		
Present = 7,00,000 + 3,00,000		10,00,000
Additional Fixed Cost		1,15,000
Total costs		42,65,000
Profit (2) – (3) = (4)		7,22,500

Computation of Profit as per Proposal of Sales Manager

1. Sales Volume (1,00,000 – 1,000)		9,00,000
		Rs.
2. Sales Value (90,000 × 55)		49,50,000
3. Cost of Sales		
Variable Cost = $\frac{30,00,000}{1,00,000} \times 90,000$		27,00,000
Fixed cost:		
Present	10,00,000	
Less: Saving in Fixed Cost	1,50,000	8,50,000
Total Cost		35,50,000
Profit = (2) – (3)		14,00,000

The profit as per the proposal of Sales Manager is much higher as compared to the proposal of the General manager. Hence, the proposal of the Sales Manager should be accepted.

Illustration 7:

The following particulars are taken from the records of a company engaged in manufacturing two Products, A and B, from a certain material:

Particulars	*Product A (per unit) Rs.*	*Product B (per unit) Rs.*
Sales	2,500	5,000
Material cost (Rs. 50 per kg.)	500	1,250
Direct labour (Rs. 30 per hour)	750	1,500
Variable overhead	250	500
Total fixed overheads: Rs. 10,00,000		

Comment on the profitability of each product when:

(*i*) Total sales in value is limited.

(*ii*) Raw materials is in short supply.

(*iii*) Production capacity is the limiting factor.

(*iv*) Total availability of raw materials is 20,000 kg and maximum sales potential of each product is 1,000 units.

Find the product mix to yield maximum profits.

Solution:

Basic Calculations

Statement of Evaluation of Products A and B

Particulars	*Product A* *Rs.*	*Rs.*	*Product B* *Rs.*	*Rs.*
Sales		2,500		5,000
Less: Variable costs:				
Material cost	500		1,250	
Direct labour	750		1,500	
Variable overhead	250		500	
		1,500		3,250
1. Contribution per unit		1,000		1,750
2. P/V Ratio	$= \frac{1,000}{2,500} \times 100$		$\frac{1,750}{5,000} \times 100$	
	= 40%		35%	
3. Material in kg. per unit	$= \frac{\text{Rs. } 500}{\text{Rs. } 50}$		$\frac{\text{Rs. } 1,250}{\text{Rs. } 50}$	
	= 10 kg.		25 kg.	
4. Contribution per kg. of Material	= Rs. 100		Rs. 70	
5. Labour hour per unit	$= \frac{\text{Rs.} 750}{30}$		$\frac{1,500}{30}$	
6. Contribution per Labour Hour	= Rs. 40		Rs. 35	

(*i*) *Comment on the Profitability of each product when total sales in value is limited.*

Product A has a higher P/V ratio than Product B and hence Product A is more profitable.

(ii) *Comment on the Profitability of each product when raw materials is in short supply*
Product A has a higher contribution per kg of raw material than Product B. Hence, Product A is more profitable.

(iii) *Comment on the Profitability of each product when production capacity is the limiting factor.*
Product A has a higher contribution per labour hour than Product B. Hence, Product A is more profitable.

(iv) *When raw material and sales quantity both are limiting factors:*

Statement of Product Mix to Yield Maximum Profits

(When total availability of raw material is 20,000 kg)

Products	*Units to be made*	*Raw material consumed (kg.)*	*Contribution per unit (Rs.)*	*Total contribution (Rs.)*	*Fixed cost (Rs.)*	*Profit (Rs.)*
(I)	*(II)*	*(III)*	*(IV)*	*(V)*	*(VI)*	*(VII)=(V)–(VI)*
A	1,000	10,000 (1,000 units × 10 kg.)	1,000	10,00,000		
B	400	10,000 (400 units × 25 kg.)	1,750	7,00,000		
		20,000		17,00,000	10,00,000	7,00,000

Illustration 8:

Due to industrial depression, a plant is running, at present, at 50% of its capacity. The following details are available:

	Cost of production per unit
Direct material	Rs. 2
Direct labour	1
Variable overhead	3
Fixed overhead	2
	8
Production per month	20,000 units
Total cost of production	Rs. 1,60,000
Sale price	1,40,000
Loss	20,000

An exporter offers to buy 5,000 units per month at the rate of Rs. 6.50 per unit and the company hesitates to accept the offer for fear of increasing its already large operating losses.

Advise whether the company should accept or decline this offer.

Solution:

Statement of Profit

	Existing situation	*Proposed situation*		
				Total
	20,000 Units	20,000 Units	5,000 Units	25,000 Units
A. Sales Rs.	1,40,000	1,40,000	32,500	1,72,500

B. Variable costs: (Rs.)				
Direct material	40,000	40,000	10,000	50,000
Direct labour	20,000	20,000	5,000	25,000
Variable overheads	60,000	60,000	15,000	75,000
Total variable cost	1,20,000	1,20,000	30,000	1,50,000
C. Contribution (A) – (B) (Rs.)	20,000	20,000	2,500	22,500
D. Fixed costs (Rs.)	40,000	40,000	—	40,000
Profit (loss) Rs.	(20,000)	(20,000)	2,500	(17,500)

The company should accept the offer since the amount of loss will stand reduced from 20,000 to Rs. 17,500.

Illustratiion 9:

Auto Parts Ltd. has an annual production of 90,000 units for a motor component. The component's cost structure is as below:

	Rs.
Materials	270 per unit
Labour (25% fixed)	180 per unit
Expenses:	
Variable	90 per unit
Fixed	135 per unit
Total	675 per unit

(*a*) The purchase manager has an offer from a supplier who is willing to supply the component at Rs. 540. Should the component be purchased and production stopped?

(*b*) Assume the resources now used for this component's manufacture are to be used to produce another new product for which the selling price is 485.

In the latter case the material price will be Rs. 200 per unit, 90,000 units of this product can be produced on the same cost basis as above for labour and expenses. Discuss whether it would be advisable to divert the resources to manufacture the new products, on the footing that the component presently being produced would, instead of being produced, be purchased from the market.

Solution:

(a) Statement showing the Variable Cost and Purchase Cost of Component ... Used by Auto Parts Ltd.

Variable cost	*Per unit* Rs.	*Total for 90,000 units* Rs.
Materials	270	2,43,00,000
Labour	135	1,21,50,000
Expenses	90	81,00,000
Total variable cost (when component is produced)	495	4,45,50,000
Cost of purchase (when component is purchased)	540	4,86,00,000
Difference, excess of purchase price over variable cost	45	40,50,000

Fixed expenses not being affected, it is evident from the above statement that if the component is purchased from the outside supplier, the company will have to spend Rs. 45 per unit more and on 90,000 units the company will have to spend Rs. 40,50,000 more. Therefore, the company should not stop the production of the component.

(b) The following statement shows the cost implications of the proposal to divert the available facilities for a new product:

Statement showing the Contribution per Unit if the Existing Resources are Used for the Production of Another New Product

	Rs.	*Rs.*
Selling price of the new product per unit		485
Less: Materials cost	200	
Labour (variable)	135	
Expenses (variable)	90	425
Contribution per unit		60
Loss per unit if the present component is purchased:		
Purchase price of the existing product		540
Less: Total variable cost of producing the existing component		495
Excess cost		45

Thus, if the company diverts its resources for the production of another new product, it will benefit by Rs. 15, *i.e.,* Rs. 60-45 per unit. On 90,000 units the company will save Rs. 13,50,000. Therefore, it is advisable to divert the resources to manufacture. The new product and the component present produced should be purchased from the market. This is also brought out by the following figures:

	Rs.
Total cost producing the component (90,000 × 675) (A)	6,07,50,000
Cost of purchasing the component (90,000 × 540)	4,86,00,000
Fixed expenses, not having been saved (90,000 × 180, *i.e.,* 675 – 495)	1,62,00,000
	6,48,00,000
Less: Contribution from the new product (90,000 × 60)	54,00,000
Total cost if component is purchased and new product is made (B)	5,94,00,000
Savings (A – B)	13,50,000

Illustration 10:

Nubo Manufacturing Company is presently operating at 50% of practical capacity producing about 50,000 units annually of a patented electronic component. Nubo recently received an offer from an overseas market to sell 30,000 components at Rs. 6.00 per units FOB Nubo's Plant. Nubo has not previously sold components in the market. Budgeted production costs for 50,000 and 80,000 units of output are as follows:

Units	50,000	80,000
Costs:	*Rs.*	*Rs.*
Direct material	75,000	1,20,000
Direct labour	75,000	1,20,000
Factory overheads	2,00,000	2,60,000
	3,50,000	5,00,000
Cost per unit	Rs. 7.00	Rs. 6.25

The sales manager thinks the order should be accepted, even if it results in a loss of Re. 1.00 per unit because he feels the sales may build up future markets. The production manager does not wish to have the order accepted primarily because the order would show a loss of Re. 0.25 per unit when computed on the new average unit cost. The cost accountant has made a quick computation indicating that accepting the order will actually increase profit.

You are required to:

(a) Explain what apparently caused the drop in cost from Rs. 7.00 per unit to Rs. 6.25 per unit when budgeted production increased from 50,000 to 80.000 units. Show supporting computations.

(b) Should the order be accepted?

Solution:

From the given data at two levels of production, the costs per unit at 50,000 and 80,000 units are ascertained as under:

Units of production	*Total cost (Rs.)*	*50,000 C.P.U. (Rs.)*	*Total cost (Rs.)*	*80,000 C.P.U. (Rs.)*
Direct material	75,000	1.50	1,20,000	1.50
Direct labour	75,000	1.50	1,20,000	1.50
Factory overhead	2,00,000	4.25	2,60,000	3.25
	3,50,000	7.25	5,00,00	6.25

(a) The reason for the difference in average units cost of factory overhead was caused by some of the overheads being fixed within the total overhead under different levels of output. The fixed portion may be ascertained first as follows:

Change in cost (overhead) at two levels = Rs. 60,000

Change in output at two levels = 30,000 units

Thus, variable cost P.U. $= \frac{\text{Rs. } 60{,}000}{30{,}000} = \text{Rs. } 2$

Therefore, amount of variable cost at 50,000 units = 50,000 × 2 = Rs. 1,00,000 variable cost

Fixed overhead (Rs. 2,00,000 – Rs. 1,00,000) = Rs. 1,00,000 fixed cost

So at 50,000 units, the cost P.U. of fixed portion of overhead = Rs. 2 (Rs. 1,00,000 ÷ 50,000) and at 80,000 units the cost P.U. of fixed portion of overhead = Rs. 1.25 = (Rs. 1,00,000 ÷ 80,000). Thus, there is a decrease in unit cost to the tune of Re. 0.75. Hence there is a drop in cost from Rs. 7 to Rs. 6.25 due to the incidence of fixed overhead being spread over to increased number of production.

(*b*) So when the variable cost P.U. remains constant, the total variable cost will vary in direct proportion with the volume of production; but since the total amount of fixed overhead is the same at different levels of production; the impact of fixed overhead on the cost of production of more number of units is favourable, as C.P.U. comes down with the increase in production volume. Hence, the order for the overseas market is acceptable.

Illustration 11:

The present output details of a manufacturing department are as follows:

Average output per week 48,000 units from 160 employees

Saleable value of output	Rs. 6,00,000
Contribution made by output towards fixed expenses and profit	Rs. 2,40,000

The Board of Directors plans to introduce more mechanisation into the department at a capital cost of Rs. 1,60,000. The effect of this will be to reduce the number of employees to 120, and increasing the output per individual employee by 60%. To provide the necessary incentive to achieve the increased output, the Board intends to offer a 1% increase on the piece work rate of Re. 1 per unit for every 2% increase in average individual output achieved.

To sell the increased output, it will be necessary to decrease the selling price by 4%.

Calculate the extra weekly contribution resulting from the proposed change and evaluate for the Board's information, the desirability of introducing the change.

Solution:

Working Notes:

1. ***Present average output per employee and total future expected output per week***

$$\text{Present average output per employee per week} = \frac{\text{Total present output}}{\text{Total number of present employees}}$$

$$= \frac{48{,}000 \text{ units}}{160 \text{ employees}}$$

$$= 300 \text{ unit}$$

$$\text{Total future expected output per week} = \text{Total number of future employees} \left(\text{Present output} + \text{60\% of present output per employee}\right)$$

$$= 120 \text{ employees } (300 \text{ units} + 60\% \times 300 \text{ units})$$

$$= 57{,}600 \text{ units}$$

2. ***Present and proposed piece work rate***

Present piece work rate = Re. 1.00 per unit

Proposed piece work rate + Present piece work rate + 30% × Re. 1

= Re. 1.00 + 0.30P

= Rs. 1.30 per unit

3. ***Present and proposed sale price per unit***

Present sale price per unit (Rs. 6,00,000/48,000 units) Rs. 12.50

Proposed sale price per unit (Rs. 12.50 – 4% × Rs. 12.50) = Rs. 12

4. ***Present marginal cost (excluding wages) per unit:***

$$= \frac{\text{Present sales value} - \text{Fixed expenses and profit} - \text{Contribution towards present wages}}{\text{Present ouput (units)}}$$

$$= \frac{\text{Rs. } 6{,}00{,}000 - \text{Rs. } 2{,}40{,}000 - \text{Rs. } 48{,}000}{48{,}000 \text{ units}} = \text{Rs. } 6.50 \text{ unit}$$

Statement of extra weekly contribution
(information resulting from the proposed change of mechanisation meant for Board's evaluation)

Expected sales units		57,600
(Refer to Working Note 1)	Rs.	Rs.
Sales value: (A)		6,91,200
(57,600 units × Rs. 12)		
(Refer to Working Note 3)		
Marginal costs (excluding wages): (B)	3,74,400	
(57,600 units × Rs. 6.50)		
(Refer to Working Note 4)		
Wages: (C)	74,880	
(57,600 units × Rs. 1.30)		
(Refer to Working Note 2)		
Total marginal cost: (D) = [(B) + (C)]		4,49,280
Marginal contribution: [(A) – (D)]		2,41,920
Less: Present contribution		2,40,000
Increase in contribution (per week)		1,920

Evaluation: Since the mechanisation has resulted in the increase of contribution to the extent of Rs. 1,920 per week, therefore the proposed change should be accepted.

Illustration 12:

A company produces three products. The cost data are as under:

		A	*B*	*C*
Direct Materials	Rs.	64	152	117
Direct Labour:				
Deptt.	Rate per hour	Hrs.	Hrs.	Hrs.
1	5	18	10	20
2	6	5	4	7
3	4	10	5	20
Variable overheads		Rs. 16	9	21
Fixed overheads	Rs. 4,00,000 per annum.			

The budget was prepared at a time, when the market was sluggish. The budgeted quantities and selling prices are as under:

Product	*Budgeted Qty.*	*Selling price (Rs.)/Unit*
A	9,750	270
B	7,800	280
C	7,800	400

Later the market improved and the sales quantities could be increased by 20% for product A and 25% each for products B and C. The sales manager confirmed that the increased quantities could be achieved at the prices originally budgeted. The production manager stated that the output cannot be increased beyond the budgeted level due to limitation of direct labour hours in Department 2.

Required:

(*i*) Present a statement of budgeted profitability.

(*ii*) Set optimal product mix and calculate the optimal profit.

Solution:

Statement of Budgeted Profitability

Products		*A*	*B*	*C*	*Total*
Budgeted Quantity (Units)	(1)	9,750	7,800	7,800	
	(2)	Rs.	Rs.	Rs.	
Selling Price per unit		270	280	400	
Variable Cost per unit:					
Direct Materials		64	152	117	
Direct Labour		160	94	222	
Variable Overheads		16	9	21	
Total Variable Cost per unit	(3)	240	255	360	
Contribution per unit	(4) = [(2) − (3)]	30	25	40	
Total Contribution	(1) × (4)	2,92,500	1,95,000	3,12,000	7,99,500
Less: Fixed cost					4,00,000
Profit					3,99,500

(2) Statement of Optimal Product Mix and Profit

Products		*A*	*B*	*C*	*Total*
Contribution per unit	(1)	30	25	40	
Direct labour hours in Department 2	(2)	5	4	7	
Contribution per direct labour hour (1)/(2)	(Rs.)	6	6.25	5.71	
Ranking		II	I	III	
Optimal Product Mix Units	(3)	11,700 (58,500 hrs.)	9,750 (39,000 hrs.)	5,292 (37,044 hrs.)	
Total contribution (Rs.) (1) × (3)		3,51,000	2,43,750	2,11,680	8,06,430
Less: Fixed cost (Rs.)					4,00,000
Optimal Profit					4,06,430

Working Notes:

1. Total hours available in Department 2

Products *(a)*	*Units* *(b)*	*Hrs. per unit* *(c)*	*Total Hrs.* *(d) = (b) × (c)*
A	9,750	5	48,750
B	7,800	4	31,200
C	7,800	7	54,600
Total			1,34,550

2. Maximum Sales Quantities of Products (under improved market conditions)

Products	*Units*	*Increase in percentage*	*Total number of units*
A	9,750	20	11,700
B	7,800	25	9,750
C	7,800	25	9,750

Illustration 13:

M/s. Mars Ltd. are manufacturing three products. The cost details are as follows:

Particulars	*Products*					
	A		B		C	
	Units	*Rs.*	*Units*	*Rs.*	*Units*	*Rs.*
Direct materials	4	12	5	15	6	18
Direct labour		5		6		6
Direct expenses		8		9		11
		25		30		35
Selling price		35		40		50
		10		10		15
No. of units sold	20,000		40,000		20,000	
		2,00,000		4,00,000		3,00,000
Total contribution				Rs. 9,00,000		
Less: Fixed costs				Rs. 7,50,000		
				Rs. 2,50,000		

The direct materials were all imported. Due to foreign exchange restrictions, henceforth, the company can import only 3,00,000 units of raw materials. The company can produce in all 1,00,000 units maximum (all products). However, they can market only 20,000 units of product A & C each. There is a local substitute material which is available at a price of Rs. 3.75 per unit. Besides, the company has to spend Rs. 50,000 on intermediaries and consumables, if local substitute material is used in the production process. There was also a third party who was willing to take a part of the plant on lease upto 50,000 units capacity of B and willing to pay lease charges of Rs. 2,75,000.

You are required to advise the management:

(*i*) What should be the quantum of production/sales mix of products with existing import restrictions?

(*ii*) Whether the company can optimise production of 1,00,000 units with local substitute materials?

(iii) Whether the company can enhance profits by leasing out a part of the plant to the third party and restricting its own production?

Solution:

(i) Statement of Quantum of Productions/Sales Mix of Products
(with existing import restrictions)

Products	*A*	*B*	*C*	*Total*
Selling price per unit (Rs.)	35	40	50	
Less: Variable cost per unit	25	30	35	
Contribution per unit of product (Rs.) (1)	10	10	15	
Units of Materials (2)	4	5	6	
Contribution per unit of material (Rs.) (3) = (1) ÷ (2)	2.50	2	2.50	
Ranking	I	II	I	
Units made (4)	20,000	20,000	20,000	
(Materials consumed)	(80,000 units)	(1,00,000 units)	(1,20,000 units)	

Total contribution (Rs.) (5) = (1) × (4)	2,00,000	2,00,000	3,00,000	Rs. 7,00,000
Less: Fixed costs (Rs.)				Rs. 7,50,000
Profit (Loss)				Rs. (50,000)

(ii) Use of Local substitute of Material

	(Output 1,00,000 units) Rs.	Rs.
Contribution per unit of product B on using local Substitute material (Rs. 10 – Rs. 3.75)	6.25	
Total Contribution on 40,000 units of product B (40,000 units × Rs. 6.25)		2,50,000
Less: Intermediaries Expenses		50,000
Net additional Contribution		2,00,000
Loss on Present Output of 60,000 units [as per (1)]		50,000
Net Profit		1,50,000

Thus, the company can have optimum production of 1,00,000 units by using local substitute of material.

(*iii*) Evaluation of Leasing Out a part of the Plant Total contribution on sale of 20,000 units of Products A and C and 10,000 units of Product B by using imported material (20,000 units × Rs. 10 + 10,000 units × Rs. 10 + 20,000 units × Rs. 15)	6,00,000
Less: Fixed Assets	7,50,000
Profit (Loss)	(1,50,000)
Add: Lease Rent received	2,75,000
Net Profit	1,25,000

Conclusion: The net profit is Rs. 1,50,000 in case the company uses local substitute of material and the plant capacity fully for producing 1.00,000 units, whereas by leasing out the plant capacity upto 50,000 units of Product B for a rent of Rs 2,75,000, the company makes a profit of Rs. 1,25,000/-. A comparative study of the two alternatives suggests that it will be better for the company to have optimum production of 1,00,000 units by using local substitute of material.

Illustration 14:

A manufacturing company produces and sells three products P, Q and R. It has an available machine hour capacity of one lakh hours, interchangeable among the three products. Presently, the company produces and sells 20,000 units of P and 15,000 units each of Q and R. The unit selling price of the three products are Rs. 25, Rs. 32 and Rs. 42 for P, Q and R respectively. With this price structure and the aforesaid sales-mix the company is incurring loss. The total expenditure, exclusive of fixed charges presently Rs. 5 per unit, is Rs. 13.75 Lakhs. The unit cost ratio among the products P, Q and R is 4: 6:7. Since the company desires to improve its profitability without changing its cost and price structures, it has been considering the following three mixes so as to be within its total available capacity:

Products	*Mix I (in units)*	*Mix II (in units)*	*Mix III (in units)*
P	25,000	20,000	30,000
Q	15,000	12,000	5,000
R	10,000	18,000	35,000

You are required to compute the quantum of loss now incurred and advise the most profitable mix which could be considered, by the company.

Solution: Basic Calculation

1. Computation of Equivalent Production

Products	*Present Production*	*Cost Ratio*	*Equivalent Units*
P	20,000	4	80,000
Q	15,000	6	90,000
R	15,000	7	1,05,000
	50,000		2,75,000

2. Computation of Variable Cost Per Unit

Total Variable Cost: Rs. 13,75,000

Hence, Variable Cost per equivalent unit Rs. 5 (i.e., Rs. 13,75,000/2,75,000)

Variable Cost of product P is Rs. 20 per unit

Variable Cost of product Q is Rs. 30 per unit

Variable Cost of product R is Rs. 35 per unit

3. Computation of Present Profit (Loss)

Contribution from Products:			*Rs.*
P	20,000 × (25 – 20)	=	1,00,000
Q	15,000 × (32 – 30)	=	30,000
R	15,000 × (42 – 35)	=	1,05,000
Total contribution			2,35,000
Less: Fixed @ Rs. 5 per unit for 50,000 units			2,50,000
	Loss		(15,000)

Statement of Comparative Contribution for Different Mixes

Products	*Contribution* *Mix I* *Rs.*	*Mix II* *Rs.*	*Mix III* *Rs.*
P	1,25,000	1,00,000	1,50,000
Q	30,000	24,000	10,000
R	70,000	1,26,000	1,05,000
Total	2,25,000	2,50,000	2,65,000

Fixed cost of Rs. 2,50,000 is constant at all levels of activity. Mix III is giving the highest contribution of the three and hence is the best and, therefore, recommended.

Note: It has been stated that the machine capacity is interchangeable and the company has selected the three mixes "so as to be within its total available capacity." No capacity constraint has been considered.

Illustration 15:

A company produces a single product which is sold by it presently in the domestic market at Rs. 75 per unit. The present production and sale is 40,000 units per month representing 50% of the capacity available. The cost data of the product are as under:

Variable costs per unit Rs. 50

Fixed costs per unit month Rs. 10 lakhs.

To improve the profitability, the management has 3 proposals on hand as under:

(*a*) to accept an export supply order for 30,000 units per month at a reduced price of Rs. 60 per unit, incurring addition variable costs of Rs. 5 per unit towards export packing, duties, etc.;

(*b*) to increase the domestic market sales by selling to a domestic chain stores 30,000 units at Rs. 55 per unit, retaining the existing sales at the existing price;

(*c*) to reduce the selling price for the increased domestic sales as advised by the sales department as under:

Reduce selling price per unit by Rs.	*Increased in sales expected (in units)*
5	10,000
8	30,000
11	35,000

Prepare a table to present the results of the above proposals and give your comments and advice on the proposals.

Solution:

The three proposals can be studied by differential cost analysis. The present capacity utilisation is only 50% and as such there is a scope to increase the sales up to another 4,000 units. The comparison of proposals will depend on contribution generated since the fixed cost is not affected upto full utilisation and as such not relevant for decision-making.

Statement showing Contribution at Various Price Levels

Particulars	*Proposal (a)*		*Proposal (b)*	*Proposal (c)*		
	Present Level	*Export Order*	*Domestic Order*	*Price*	*Reduction*	
Selling price per unit Rs.	75	60	55	70	67	64
Variable cost per unit Rs.	50	55	50	50	50	50
Contribution per unit Rs.	25	05	05	20	17	14
Quantities in units	40,000	30,000 (addl.)	30,000 (addl.)	50,000 (total)	70,000 (total)	75,000 (total)
Existing contribution (Rs. in lakh)	10	—	—	—	—	—
Additional contribution (Rs. in lakh)		1.5	1.5			
Total contribution for revised quantity (Rs. in lakhs)				10.0	11.9	10.5
Total contribution Rs. in lakhs	10.00	11.5	11.5	10.0	11.9	10.5
Proposal		(a)	(b)	c(i)	c(ii)	c(iii)

Comments and Advice:

(1) In case only cost considerations are considered, proposal to reduce selling price by Rs. 8 to get a gross sales of 7,000 units is most profitable since it yields a total contribution of Rs 11.9 lakhs.

(2) In between export order as per proposal (a) and increased domestic order as per proposal (b) there is no change in additional profitability since both yield same results.

(3) However keeping in mind the impact on other domestic sale, if a part of production alone is sold at a drastically reduced price of Rs. 55 per unit, it is desirable to go for export order. This will also enable gaining valuable foreign exchange. Besides with exchange rate fluctuations it may result in higher profits, in case the selling price is quoted in foreign currency.

(4) Reduction in selling price against possible increased sales is full of doubt and has only a marginal effect of Rs. 40,000 as additional profit.

Thus, on the whole it is better to go for export order.

Illustration 16:

Sum Toys (P) Ltd. manufactures and sells children's toys of high quality over an extensive market, utilising the services of skilled artists who are paid at an average rate of Rs. 15 per hour. The total no. of skilled labour hours available in a year is only 14,000. The details of planned production for 2009-10, estimated cost and unit selling prices are given below:

Toy	*Production Planned (unit)*	*Cost of Production per Unit*			*Selling price per unit*
		Direct Materials Rs.	*Direct Labour Rs.*	*Fixed Overheads Rs.*	*Rs.*
A	3,000	20	10	15	70
B	4,000	24	12	18	92
C	4,000	32	12	18	95
D	3,000	40	16	24	110
E	2,400	60	20	30	180

Variable overhead costs amount to 50% of the direct labour cost.

The company has estimated the following maximum and minimum demands for each product:

	A	*B*	*C*	*D*	*E*
Maximum (units)	5,000	6,000	6,000	4,000	4,000
Minimum (units)	1,000	1,000	1,000	500	500

Solution: Basic Calculations

Statement of Priority of Production Taking Labour Time as Key Factor

Product	*Selling Price per Unit*	*Total Variable Cost*				*Contribution*		*Production Priority*
		Direct Materials	*Direct Labour*	*Variable Overheads*	*Total*	*Per Units*	*Per Labour Hour*	
	Rs.	Rs.	Rs.	Rs.	Rs.	Rs.	Rs.	
A	70	20	10	5	35	35	52.50	IV
B	92	24	12	6	42	50	62.50	II
C	95	32	12	6	50	45	56.25	III
D	110	40	16	8	64	46	43.13	V
E	180	60	20	10	90	90	67.50	I

Contribution per labour hour has been derived as follows:

$$\frac{\text{Product per unit contribution} \times \text{Rs. 15 average labour rate}}{\text{Product direct labour cost}}$$

$$\text{Product } A = \frac{\text{Rs. } 35 \times 15}{10} = 52.5$$

$$B = \frac{50 \times 15}{12} = 62.5$$

$$C = \frac{45 \times 15}{12} = 56.25$$

$$D = \frac{46 \times 15}{16} = 43.13$$

$$E = \frac{90 \times 15}{20} = 67.50$$

(a) Statement of Estimated Profit for 2009-10

(As per Company's Production Plan)

Product	*Vol. of Sales (units)*	*Contribution per unit (Rs.)*	*Total Contribution (Rs.)*	*Total Fixed cost (Rs.)*	*Profit (Rs.)*
A	3,000	35	1,05,000	45,000	60,000
B	4,000	50	2,00,000	72,000	1,28,000
C	4,000	45	1,80,000	72,000	1,08,000
D	3,000	46	1,38,000	72,000	66,000
E	2,400	90	2,16,000	72,000	1,44,000
			8,39,000	3,33,000	5,06,000

(b) Production Plan for Maximum Profits

Product	*Volume of Sales (units)*	*Hours required*	*Contribution per unit (Rs.)*	*Total Contri- bution (Rs.)*	*Priority*
E	4,000 (Max.)	5,334	90	3,60,000	I
B	6,000 (Max.)	4,800	50	3,00,000	II
C	3,331 (Balance)	2,665 (Bal. hrs.)	45	1,49,895	III
A	1,000 (Minimum)	667	35	35,000	IV
D	500 (Minimum)	534	46	23,000	V
		14,000		8,67,895	

(*c*) The maximum profit under plan (*b*) suggested would amount to Rs. 8,67,895 – Rs.3,33,000 = Rs. 5,34,895.

Illustration 17:

A company producing products 'PIE' and 'SIGMA' using a single production process, has the following cost data:

	PIE	SIGMA
Selling price per unit (Rs.)	20	30
Variable cost per unit (Rs.)	11	16
Machine hours required per unit production (hrs.)	1	2
Market limitation (units)	1 lakh	2.5 lakhs

Total machine hours available — 4 lakhs
Fixed cost per annum — Rs. 26 lakhs

Considering the limiting factors of machine hours and market limitations, you are required to:

(*a*) indicate the best combination of products to give optimum contribution;
(*b*) show the additional machinery requirement to be augmented on rental basis at an annual rent of Rs. 1.5 lakhs per machine to provide additional capacity of 30,000 hours per machine;
(*c*) change in number of machines to be rented if the annual rental charges reduce to Rs. 1,25,000 per machine.

Solution:

Evaluation Parameters for Optimum Product Mix

Particulars		*Products*		*Total*
		Pie	*Sigma*	
Total Machine hours available				4 lakhs
Market Limitation (units)		1 lakh	2.5 lakhs	
Machine hours required per unit of production		1	2	
Fixed cost per annum	(Rs. in lakhs)			4.00
Selling price per unit	(Rs.)	20	30	
Variable cost per unit	(Rs.)	11	16	
Contribution per unit	(Rs.)	9	14	
Contribution per machine hour	(Rs.)	9	7	
Ranking		1	2	

(a) Statement showing Best Combination of Product Mix Towards Optimum Contribution

	Pie	*Sigma*	*Total*
Production for market demand (units)	1,00,000	1,50,000	2,50,000
Total Hours required	1,00,000	3,00,000	4,00,000
Total Contribution (Rs.) (Total Production × Contribution Per unit)	9,00,000	21,00,000	30,00,000

(b) Computation of Requirement of Additional Machines on Rental Basis

Particulars		
Annual rent per machine having capacity of 30,000 hours		Rs. 1,50,000
No. of additional units of SIGMA to be produced to meet the market demand (additional)		1,00,000 units
Requirement of machine hours for production (1,00,000 × 2)		2,00,000 hrs.
Number of Machines required (2,00,000 ÷ 30,000) = 6.67 (*i.e.*, 6 + 1)		7 machines
1. In case 6 machines are hired:		
Total Net Contribution from 6 rented machines with full capacity utilisation (Rs.)	3,60,000	
2. In case 7 machines are hired:		
(*i*) Net Contribution from 6 machines on full utilisation = (30,000 hrs. × Rs. 7 – Rent Rs. 1,50,000) × 6 = 2,10,000 – 1,50,000 = 60,000 × 6 =		3,60,000
(*ii*) Net Contribution from 7th machine = 20,000 hrs. × Rs. 7 – Rs. 1,50,000 = (10,000)		3,50,000

Thus, the net contribution will stand reduced by Rs. 10,000 in case seven machines are hired, It is, therefore, better to hire only six machines.

(*c*) In case the annual rental charges are reduced to Rs. 1,25,000, the position with be as under:

Net Contribution from 7th Machine: 20,000 hrs × Rs. 7 – Rs. 1,25,000
= Rs. 15,000

Thus, the seventh machine will also give additional contribution of Rs 15,000.

Hence, in all seven machines may be taken on rent.

THEORY QUESTIONS

1. What is meant by the term "differential costing"? Does differential cost mean the same thing as variable cost?
2. What is incremental cost? Does incremental cost mean the same thing as variable cost?
3. Give examples of how incremental costs are used in decision-making.
4. A departmental store is thinking of eliminating one of its departments because the accountant using the total cost basis to profitability analysis, says the department is operating at a loss. What should be investigated before the final decision is made?
5. Explain the meaning and features of relevant costs. Give suitable examples to support your explanation.
6. Ventilators Ltd. warns to stabilise its production through the year. The approaches recommended are:
   (*a*) Maintain production at an even pace throughout the year, and get the off-season production stored on the premises.
   (*b*) Maintain production at an even pace but offer dealers a special discount for off-season purchases.
   (*c*) Extend special terms to dealers, but maintain prices at a level that will enable regular movement of goods throughout the year.

   Discuss the relative merits and disadvantages of the above proposals.

7. Cost-benefit analysis is needed (or resolving many managerial problems. List the various items of cost and benefits that you will quantify in respect of managerial decisions:
   (*a*) change versus status quo;
   (*b*) retain or replace;
   (*c*) shutdown or continue
8. Explain the basic, characteristics of costs involved in decision-making
9. State the costing data required for (*i*) determining the priority of products, and (*ii*) make or buy decisions
10. How would you go about determining the point at which a manufacturing company that is facing a period of operating losses should shut assuming that profitability of operations is the only point to be considered
11. Why is the contribution that a product makes towards the recovery of non-escapable costs a better measure of its profitability than the profit or loss reported on its sale after it has been charged with its fair share of all costs

EXERCISES AND PROBLEMS

1. A factory is currently working at 50% capacity and produces 10,000 units of product P, the unit cost of which is Rs. 180 comprised as follows:

	Rs.
Direct materials	100
Direct labour	30
Factory overhead 30	(40% fixed)
Administration overhead	20 (50% fixed)

   The selling price per unit is Rs. 200

   If the capacity is increased to 60%, the new material cost will increase by 2% and selling price falls by 2%. At 80% capacity, raw material cost increases by 5% and selling price falls by 5%.

   You are required to work out the total costs and profit for the three capacity levels and prepare a brief note for the management on the profitability at these levels of performance with your recommendation.

(*Ans.:* Profit at 50% Rs. 2,00,000, at 60%, Rs. 2,12,000, at 80%, Rs. 2,12,000. It is advisable to run the factory at 60% capacity level. The total amount of profit at 60% and 80% capacity is the same. In fact it will be preferable to use the surplus capacity over 60% for some other purpose.

2. A firm is selling X product, whose variable cost per unit is Rs. 10 and fixed cost is Rs. 6,000. It has sold 1,000 articles during one month at Rs. 20 per unit. Market research shows that there is a great demand for the product if the price can be reduced. If the price can be reduced to Rs. 12.50 per unit it is expected that 5,000 articles can be sold in the expanded market. The firm has to take a decision whether to produce and sell 1,000 units at the rate of Rs. 20 or to produce and sell for the growing demand of 5.000 units at the rate of Rs. 12.50. Give your advice to the management in taking a decision.

(*Ans.:* Profit (*a*) 1000 units, Rs. 4,000; (*b*) 5000 units, Rs. 6,500
Proposal to manufacture and sell 5000 units is preferable.

3. A manufacturer of a certain product has been selling exclusively in the Indian market up to now. He has just received his first export enquiry and wants to quote as competitively as the circumstances will allow. His latest Indian cost sheet is:

Raw materials	Rs. 34 per unit
Direct labour	13
Services	6

Works overhead	7
Office overhead	2
	62
Profit earned in India	6
Indian selling price	68

Management is thinking of quoting a selling price somewhere between Rs. 62 and Rs. 68 per unit for this export order. One of the directors suggests quoting an even lower price based on the principles of marginal costing. As the firm's accountant, you are requested to compute the lowest price the management could quote on these principles. State clearly any assumptions that you may make on the above facts, and also on any other costs or facts.

(*Ans.:* Marginal cost of product Rs. 51. Any price above this amount can be quoted by the company.

4. On the basis of the following information in respect of an engineering company, what is the product-mix which will give the highest profit attainable? Do you recommend overtime working up to a maximum of 15,000 hours at twice the normal wages (overheads are ignored for the purpose of this question)?

Products	*A*	*B*	*C*
Raw materials per unit (kg)	10	6	15
Labour hours per unit @ Re. 1 per hour	15	25	20
Sales price per unit (Rs.)	125	100	200
Maximum production possible (Units)	6,000	4,000	3,000

1,00,000 kg. raw materials are available @ Rs. 10 per kg. Maximum production hours are 1,84,000 with facility for a further 15,000 hours on overtime basis at twice the normal wage rate.

5. A company manufactures three products A, B and C. There are no common processes and the sale of a product does not affect price or volume of sales of any other.

The company's budgeted profit/loss for 2009 has been abstracted as follows:

	Total	*A*	*B*	*C*
Sales	Rs. 3,00,000	Rs. 45,000	Rs. 2,25,000	Rs. 30,000
Production cost: Variable	1,80,000	24,000	1,44,000	12,000
Fixed	60,000	3,000	48,000	9,000
Factory cost	2,40,000	27,000	1,92,000	21,000
Selling and administration costs: Variable	24,000	8,100	8,100	7,800
Fixed	6,000	2,100	1,800	2,100
Total cost	2,70,000	37,200	2,01,900	30,900
Profit	30,000	7,800	23,100	(–) 900

On the basis of the above, the Board had almost decided to eliminate product C, on which a loss was budgeted. Meanwhile, they have sought your opinion. As the company's Cost Accountant what would you advice? Give reasons for your answer.

(*Ans.:* P/V ratio, A 28.7&, B 32.4%, C 34%

It is found that product C, though has the highest P/V Ratio, seems to be non-profitable because it has to bear a higher percentage of fixed cost as compared to its total cost. The percentage comes to about 36 $\left(\text{i.e., } \frac{11,100}{30,900} \times 100\right)$ which in case of other products is too less. Since the surplus capacity generated by one product cannot be used for other products, there seems to be no justification for discontinuing product C till some new product is developed which will have a higher P/V ratio than product C. In the present circumstances, since C has a higher P/V ratio, and if the sales continue to rise. C may start giving profit too.

6. A factory produces 24,000 units. The cost sheet gives the following information:

Direct material	Rs. 1,20,000
Direct wages	84,000
Variable overheads	48,000
Semi-variable overheads	28,000
Fixed overheads	80,000
Total Cost	3,60,000

The product is sold at Rs. 20 per unit. The management proposed to increase the production by 3,000 units for sales in the foreign market. It is estimated that semi-variable overheads will increase by Rs. 1,000. But the product will be sold at Rs. 14 per unit in the foreign market. However, no additional capital expenditure will be incurred. The management seeks your advice as cost accountant. What will you advise them?

(***Ans.:*** Sales of additional units 3000 in the foreign market will give a profit of Rs. 9,500. Hence the proposal should be accepted.

7. The budgeted results for X Co. include the following:

		Rs. in lakhs	*Variable cost as % of sales value*
Sales:	Product A	60	50%
	Product B	50	60%
	Product C	80	65%
	Product D	40	80%
	Product E	30	70%
		260	

Fixed overheads for the period Rs. 100.00 lakhs.

You are required to (*a*) Prepare a statement showing the amount of loss expected, (*b*) assuming that the sale of only one product can be increased at a time. You are asked to recommend a change in the sales volume of each product which will eliminate the expected loss.

(***Ans.:*** (*a*) Total loss Rs. 5,00,000.

(*b*) Additional sales required to break-even, assuming sales of only one product is increased at a time, to give the additional contribution of Rs. 5,00,000, is calculated as follows:

$$\text{Sales required} = \frac{\text{Under-recovery of fixed overheads}}{\text{P/V ratio of the product}}$$

Product	*Rs.*	*Rs.*
A	$\frac{5,00,000}{50\%}$	10,00,000
B	$\frac{5,00,000}{40\%}$	12,50,000
C	$\frac{5,00,000}{45\%}$	14,28,571
D	$\frac{5,00,000}{20\%}$	25,00,000
E	$\frac{5,00,000}{30\%}$	16,66,667

The company should utilise the spare capacity available for Product 'A' to achieve maximum profitability as its P/V ratio is highest. Fixed costs remaining the same at every level of production, this combination will lead to maximum profitability.

8. Quality Products Ltd. manufactures and markets a single products. The following data are available:

	Per unit		Per unit
Materials	Rs. 16	Dealer's margin	Rs. 4
Conversion costs (Variable)	12	Selling price	40

Fixed cost: Rs. 5 lakhs
Present sales: 90,000 units
Capacity utilisation: 60 per cent

There is acute competition. Extra efforts are necessary to sell. Suggestions have been made for increasing sales:

(*a*) By reducing sales price by 5 per cent.

(*b*) By increasing dealer's margin by 25 per cent over the existing rate.

Which of these two suggestions you would recommend, if the company desires to maintain the present profit? (Give reasons)

(*Ans.:* Present profit Rs. 2,20,000

(*a*) Units required to maintain the same profit 1,16,111 units

(*b*) Units required to maintain the same profit 102,857 units. Second proposal is recommended.

9. A company follows the flexible budgeting system, and the position at 70% level of production, is as follows:

Production	400 units
Direct wages	Rs. 60,000
Direct materials	80,000
Overhead:	
Fixed	84,000
Variable	42,000
	2,66,000

The selling price per unit is Rs. 865.

In the present market conditions there is hardly any chance for selling more locally. A special export order for 80 units @ Rs. 650 per unit is received, (*a*) Would it be prudent for the company to accept the order at this price? (*b*) What is the price beyond which it would be profitable to accept this order?

10. A company is at present working at 90 per cent of its capacity and producing 13,500 units per annum. It operates a Flexible Budgetary Control System. The following figures are obtained from its budget:

	90%	100%
	Rs.	*Rs.*
Sales	15,00,000	16,00,000
Fixed expenses	3,00,500	3,00,600
Semi-fixed expenses	97,300	1,00,500
Variable overhead expense	1,45,000	1,49,500
Units made	13,500	15,000

Labour and material cost per unit are constant under present conditions. Profit margin is 10 per cent.

(*a*) You are required to determine the differential cost of producing 1,500 units by increasing capacity to 100 per cent.

(*b*) What would you recommend for an export price for these 1,500 units taking into account that overseas prices are much lower than indigenous prices?

11. A toy manufacturer earns an average net profit of Rs. 3 per piece in a selling price of Rs. 15 by producing and selling 60,000 pieces at 60% of the potential capacity. Composition of his cost of sales is:

Direct material	: Rs. 4
Direct wages	: Re. 1
Works overhead	: Rs. 6 (50% fixed)
Sales	: Re. 1 (25% variable)

During the current year, he intends to produce the same number but anticipates that:

(*a*) his fixed charges will go up by 10%

(*b*) rates of direct labour will increase by 20%

(*c*) rates of direct material will increase by 5%

(*d*) selling price cannot be increased.

Under these circumstances, he obtains an order for a further 20% of his capacity. What minimum price will you recommend for accepting the order to ensure the manufacturer an overall profit of Rs. 1,80,000?

12. An umbrella manufacturer makes an average profit of Rs. 2.50 per unit on a selling price of Rs. 14.30 by producing and selling 60,000 units at 60 per cent of potential capacity.

His cost of sales per unit is as follows:

Direct Materials	Rs. 3.50
Direct Wages	Rs. 1.25
Factory-Overhead	Rs. 6.25 (50% fixed)
Sales Overhead	Re. 0.80 (25% variable)

During the current year, he intends to produce the same number but estimates that his fixed costs would go up by 10 per cent while the rates of direct wages and direct materials will increase by 8% and 6% respectively. However, the selling price cannot be changed.

Under this situation, he obtains an offer for a future 20% of his potential capacity.

What minimum price would you recommend for acceptance of the offer to ensure the manufacturer an overall profit of Rs. 1,67,300.

(*Ans.:* Selling price per unit Rs. 11.30.)

13. A multi product company has the following costs and output data for the last year:

	Product		
	X	*Y*	*Z*
	40%	35%	25%
	Rs.	*Rs.*	*Rs.*
Selling price	20	25	30
Variable cost per unit	10	15	18
Total fixed cost			1,50,000
Total sales			5,00,000

The company proposes to replace product Z by product S. Estimated cost and output data are:

Sales mix	50%	30%	20%
Selling price	20	25	28
Variable cost per unit	10	15	14
Total fixed costs			1,50,000
Total sales			5,00,000

Analyse the proposed change and suggest what decision the company should take.

(*Ans.:* Profit would increase by Rs. 15,000 and break-even point will reduce by Rs. 21,760 if product Z is replaced. Therefore, the change is beneficial and product Z may be dropped.

Standard Costing

Control of cost is one of the most important objectives of cost and management accounting and cannot be achieved without some standard against which actual can be compared. This chapter introduces the concepts and basic procedures of standard costing and also explains the techniques used in standard cost variance analysis.

DEFINITION OF STANDARD COST, STANDARD COSTING

A standard cost is a planned cost for a unit of product or service rendered. Standard costs represent excellent target costs that should be obtained. The Institute of Cost and Management Accounts (UK) defines standard cost as "a predetermined cost which is calculated from management's standards of efficient operation and the relevant necessary expenditure. It may be used as a basis for price fixing and for cost control through variance analysis." Standard cost expresses what costs should be under attainable good performance.

Standard costing is the setting of predetermined cost estimates in order to provide a basis for comparison with actual costs. The Institute of Cost and Management Accountants (UK) defines standard costing as "the preparation and use of standard costs, their comparison with actual costs, and the analysis of variances to their causes and points of incidence."

STANDARD COSTS AND ESTIMATED COSTS

The term "standard costs" should not be confused with "estimated costs." Standard cost and estimated costs differ in the following respects:

First, estimated costs are frequently less accurately determined. Estimated costs are developed from projections using averages of past data regarding performance. Standard costs are predetermined realistically and much more scientifically through the use of time and motion studies, engineering estimates and specifications, selected measures of plant capacity, cost behaviour patterns.

Second, estimated costs are not helpful to management in accomplishing managerial functions as they are not scientifically predetermined costs. But standard costs involve more sophistication, operation analysis and evaluation and comprehensive review of internal and external factors and provide reliable measures for product costing, product pricing, planning, coordination and cost control purposes.

Third, estimated cost emphasises on actual cost with which it is compared at the end of the accounting period. If the estimated costs are found higher or lower than actual costs they are revised for use in the next accounting period. In standard costing, the emphasis is on standard costs, *i.e.*, what costs of material, labour and overhead should be incurred if the factory is to be operated as a highly efficient unit with each manager, foreman, worker, plant and machine functioning as an efficient part of the production process. Under standard costing, actual costs are ascertained only to facilitate their comparison with standard costs.

ADVANTAGES OF STANDARD COSTING

Among the many advantages generally attributed to standard costing, the most important may be listed as follows:

1. *Managerial Planning:* Planning is a process of using all resources in such a manner that maximises business profits. Standard costs are more convenient than actual costs for budget preparation because the standard costs at different production levels and for different product-mixes are readily built up into total costs as called for by the budget. On the other hand, using actual costs requires a great deal of analysis and adjustment when extensive changes in product volume or product-mixes take place.
2. *Coordination:* The establishment of standards coordinates all functions — manufacturing, marketing, engineering, research, and accounting towards the achievement of a common goal. Setting standards involves defining and communicating targets so that they can work towards the attainment of the goal.
3. *Cost Control:* Cost control and cost reduction are probably the most important aims of any costing system; and standard costing gives due recognition to this fact. Cost control has the objective of production of the required quality at the lowest cost attainable under existing conditions. Standards enable management to make periodic comparison of actual costs with standard costs in order to measure performance and to take action to maintain control over costs.
4. *Economical means of costing and record-keeping:* The use of standard costs can reduce clerical labour and expense by avoiding the detailed record-keeping which is necessary when actual costs alone are used.
5. *Formulating price and production policies:* Standard costs as compared to actual costs can be used for estimating selling prices. When standard unit costs are available, expected costs and sales prices can be computed on the basis of standard costs. Standards already established can easily be modified to reflect current conditions and changes in material prices or labour rates and the price of the product can be determined on a realistic basis. Actual costs, on the other hand, may reflect excessive usage of material, abnormal labour times or an inequitable charge for overhead. Actual overhead cost per unit at any given time may be so influenced by temporary fluctuations in production levels as to make actual cost entirely unusable for pricing.
6. *Standards as incentives to employees:* If standards are reasonable and attainable they act as incentives to employees to improve their performances and to maintain the quality of the product. Standards motivate workers, supervisors and foremen to work more efficiently in the accomplishment of their respective standards.

DEVELOPING OR SETTING STANDARD

All factors related with standards-setting should be considered in the establishment of standards. Whatever method is used, standards must be established for a definite period of time so that they can be effective in performance evaluation, control and analysis of costs. Standards are usually set for a six-or-twelve-month period. Sometimes a longer period is used but rarely a shorter period. Standards are developed for:

1. Materials.
2. Labour, and
3. Overhead.

Materials Standards

Two standards must be developed for materials:

1. Materials quantity (usage) standard
2. Materials price standard

Labour Standards

As in the case of direct materials, labour standards are also established for both cost and quantity (efficiency). For standard cost purposes, direct labour is treated separately from indirect labour, which is included in the factory overhead. Two standards are usually developed for labour costs:

1. Labour usage (or efficiency) standard
2. Labour cost (or rate) standard

Factory Overhead Cost Standards

Setting Overhead Standards

Setting standard overhead cost requires the determination of: (1) standard capacity and (2) standard overhead costs for this capacity. The standard overhead costs can be computed using normal capacity. The normal or expected actual capacity aims at a production level according to an existing set of conditions. This capacity does not require complete utilisation of all available facilities but is based on the efficient utilisation of resources and operations.

After standard capacity is determined, overhead — variable and fixed — to be incurred at that capacity is prepared. The standard overhead rate is found by dividing the standard or budgeted overhead at standard capacity by the volume selected to represent standard capacity. Volume may be measured in units of product, standard capacity by the volume selected to represent standard capacity. Volume may be measured in units of product, standard productive hour (labour or machine) or some standard cost, such as direct labour.

$$\text{Standard overhead rate} = \frac{\text{Standard overhead}}{\text{Standard production}}$$

REVISION OF STANDARDS

Standard costs require continuous review and, at times, frequent change. Changing prices, technological advances, new personnel, new machinery, changing quality of materials and new labour negotiations all influence standards and make them obsolete resulting in unrealistic budgets, poor cost control, and unreasonable unit cost for inventory valuation and income determination.

A company should establish a programme to revise standards whenever required so that standards can be set at a currently attainable level. Labour rate standards should be revised for any change in labour rates; material quantity standards for any change in type, quality of material or method of production. If a new machine is purchased to replace an old machine, labour time standards and material quantity standards should be updated. In addition to these obvious revisions, in every business firm there should be a system for revising standards for adequacy and suitability at least once a year. A periodic review of standards is desirable to accomplish the objectives of standard costing.

VARIANCE ANALYSIS

The function of standards in cost accounting is to indicate variances between standard costs which are allowed and actual costs which have been recorded. The Institute of Cost and Management Accountants (UK) defines variance as the difference between a standard cost and the comparable actual cost incurred during a period. Variance analysis can be defined as the process of computing the amount of, and isolating the cause of variances between actual costs and standard costs. Variance analysis involves two phases:

1. Computation of individual variances, and
2. Determination of the cause(s) of each variance

First, we concentrate on the computation of material, labour and factory overhead variances. Analysis of causes, reporting variances to managers, and accounting disposition of variances conclude the study of standard costing in this chapter.

MATERIALS VARIANCE

The following variances constitute materials variances:

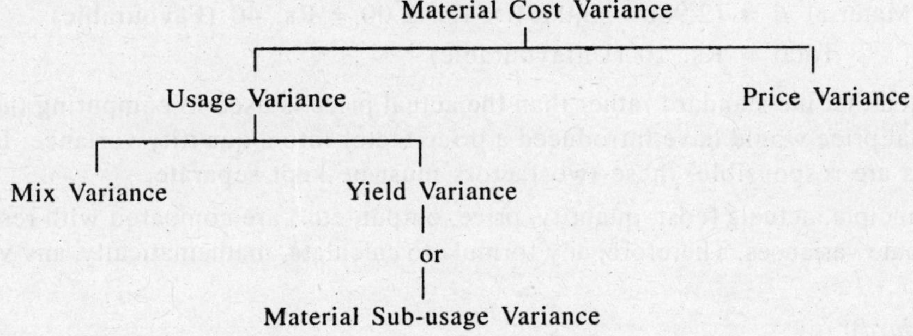

Material Cost Variance

Material cost variance is the difference between the actual cost of direct materials used and standard cost of direct materials specified for the output achieved. This variance results from differences between quantities consumed and quantities of materials allowed for production and from differences between prices paid and prices predetermined. This can be computed by using the following formula:

Material cost variance = $(AQ \times AP) - (SQ \times SP)$

where AQ = Actual quantity
AP = Actual price
SQ = Standard quantity for the actual output
SP = Standard price

Materials Usage Variance

The material quantity or usage variance results when actual quantities of raw materials used in production differ from standard quantities that should have been used to produce the output achieved. It is that portion of the direct materials cost variance which is due to the difference between the actual quantity used and standard quantity specified. As a formula this variance is shown as:

Materials quantity variance = (Actual quantity – Standard quantity) × Standard price

A material usage variance is favourable when the total actual quantity of direct materials used is less than the total standard quantity allowed for the actual output.

Illustration 1:

Compute the materials usage variance from the following information:

Standard material cost per unit		Materials issued
Material A 2 pieces @ Re. 1.00 =	2.00	Material A 2,050 pieces
Material A 3 pieces @ Re 2.00 =	6.00	Material B 2,980 pieces
	Rs. 8.00	
Units completed 1,000		

Solution:

Materials usage variance = (Actual quantity – Standard quantity) × Standard price

Material *A* = (2,050 – 2,000) × Re. 1.00 = Rs. 50 (Adverse or Unfavourable)

Material *B* = (2,980 – 3,000) × Rs. 2.00 = Rs. 40 (Favourable)

Total = Rs. 10 (Unfavourable)

It should be noted that the standard rather than the actual price is used in computing the usage variance. Use of actual price would have introduced a price factor into a quantity variance. Because different departments are responsible, these two factors must be kept separate.

As a general principle, actuals (cost, quantity, price, output, etc.) are compared with respective standard data to compute variances. Therefore, any formula to calculate, mathematically, any variance will be as follows:

(Actual – Standard)

However, one may use variance formula as Standard – Actual as it does not influence in any way variance figure calculated by using the formula 'Actual – Standard."

Materials Price Variance

A materials price variance occurs when raw materials are purchased at a price different from standard price. It is that portion of the direct materials which is due to the difference between actual price paid and standard price specified and cost variance multiplied by the actual quantity. Expressed as a formula:

Materials price variance (Actual price – Standard price) × Actual quantity

Materials price variance is unfavourable when the actual price paid exceeds the predetermined standard price. It is advisable that materials price variance should be calculated at the time of materials purchase rather than when materials are used. Purchase of materials is an earlier event than the use of materials. Therefore, a variance based on quantity purchased is basically an earlier report than a variance based on quantity actually used. This is quite beneficial from the viewpoint of performance measurement and corrective action.

Illustration 2:

Assuming in illustration 1 that material A was purchased at the rate of Re. 1.00 and material B was purchased at the rate of Rs. 2.10 the material price variance will be as follows:

Materials price variance = (Actual price – Standard price) × Actual quantity
Material A = (1.00 – 1.00) × 2,050 = Zero
Material B = (2.10 – 2.00) × 2,980 = Rs. 298 (Unfavourable)

The total of materials usage variance and price variance is equal to materials cost variance.

Materials Mix Variance

The materials usage or quantity variance can be separated into mix variance and yield variance.

A mix variance will result when materials are not actually placed into production in the same ratio as the standard formula. For instance, if a product is produced by adding 100 kg. of raw material A and 200 kg. of raw material B, the standard material mix ratio is 1 : 2. Actual raw materials used must be in this 1 : 2 ratio, otherwise a materials mix variance will be found.

Materials mix variance is that portion of the materials quantity variance which is due to the difference between the actual composition of a mixture and the standard mixture. It can be computed by using the following formula:

Materials mix variance = (Standard cost of actual quantity of the actual mixture – Standard cost of actual quantity of the standard mixture)

or

Materials mix variance = (Actual mix – Revised standard of actual input) × Standard price

Revised standard proportion is calculated as follows:

$$\frac{\text{Standard mix of a particular material}}{\text{Total standard quantity}} \times \text{Actual input}$$

Illustration 3:

A product is made from two raw materials, materials A and materials B. One unit of finished product requires 10 kg of material. The following is standard mix:

Material A	20%	2 kg @	Rs. 2.00 =	Rs. 4.00
Material B	80%	8 kg @	Rs. 1.00 =	Rs. 8.00
	100%	10 kg.	Rs. 3.00	Rs. 12.00

During a period one unit of product was produced at the following costs:

Material A	8 kg. @	Rs. 2.00	= Rs. 16.00
Material B	4 kg. @	Rs. 1.25	= Rs. 5.00
	12 kg.	Rs. 3.25	Rs. 21.00

Compute the materials mix variance.

Solution:

Materials mix variance – (Actual proportion – Revised standard proportion of actual input) × Standard price;

Revised standard proportion:

$$\frac{\text{Standard proportion of a particular mix}}{\text{Total standard quantity}} \times \text{Actual input}$$

Revised standard proportion:

$$\text{Material A} = \frac{2}{10} \times 12 = 2.40 \text{ kg}$$

$$\text{Material B} = \frac{8}{10} \times 12 = 9.60 \text{ kg}$$

Materials mix variance:

Material A = (8 kg – 2.40 kg) × 2.00
= 5.60 × 2.00 = Rs. 11.20 (Unfavourable)

Material B = (4 kg. – 9.60) × 1.00
= 5.60 × 1.00 = Rs. 5.60 (Favourable)

Total mix variance = Rs. 5.60 (Unfavourable)

Materials Yield Variance

Materials yield variance explains the remaining portion of the total materials quantity variance. It is portion of materials usage variance which is due to the difference between the actual yield obtained and standard yield specified (in terms of actual inputs). In other words, yield variance occurs when the output of the final product does not correspond with the output that could have been obtained by using the actual inputs.

The total of materials mix variance and materials yield variance equals materials quantity or usage variance. When there is no materials mix variance, the materials yield variance equals the total materials quantity variance.

The formula for computing yield variance is as follows:

Yield variance = (Actual yield – Standard yield specified) × Standard cost per unit

or

Yield variance = (Actual loss – Standard loss on actual input) × Standard cost per unit,

Illustration 4:

Standard input = 100 kgs, standard yield = 90 kgs, standard cost per kg of output = Rs. 20. Actual input 200 kgs, actual yield 182 kgs. Compute the yield variance.

Solution:

$$\text{Standard yield for the actual input} = \frac{90}{100} \times 200 = 180 \text{ kgs.}$$

Yield variance = (Actual yield – Standard yield for the actual input) × Standard cost per unit.
= (182 – 180) × Rs. 20
= 2 × 20 = 40 (Favourable)

The above yield variance can be computed by using another formula also, e.g.,

Yield variance = (Actual loss – Standard loss on actual input) × Standard cost per unit
= (18 kgs – 20 kgs) × Rs. 20
= Rs. 40 (Favourable)

In this example there is no mix variance and therefore, the materials usage variance will be equal to the materials yield variance.

The above formula uses output or loss as the basis of computing the yield variance. Yield variance can also be computed on the basis of input factors only. The fact is that loss in inputs equals loss in output. A lower yield simply means that a higher quantity of inputs have been used and the anticipated or standard output (based on actual inputs) has not been achieved. Yield, in such a case, is known as sub-usage variance (or Revised usage variance) which can be computed by using the following formula:

Sub-usage or revised usage variance = (Revised standard proportion of actual input – Standard quantity) × Standard cost per unit of input

Illustration 5:

Standard material and standard price for manufacturing one unit of a product is given below:

	Standard Material	*Standard price*
Material A	5 kg.	@ Rs. 4
Material B	3 kg.	@ Rs. 6

The actual production of the product is 400 units.

The actual material A 2,500 kg.@ Rs. 3.90
B 1,000 kg. @ Rs. 6.25

Calculate the materials sub-usage variance.

Solution:

Revised standard production of actual input:

Material A = $\frac{5}{8}$ × 3,500 = 2187.5 kg.

Material B = $\frac{3}{8}$ × 3,500 = 1312.5 kg.

Material sub-usage variance:

(Revised standard proportion of actual input – Standard quantity) × St. cost per unit of Material A

= (2,187.5 × 2,000) × 4
= 187.5 × 4 – Rs. 750 (Unfavourable)

Material B = (1,312.5 – 1200) × 6
= 112.5 × 6 = Rs. 675 (Unfavourable)

Total materials subusage variance = Rs. 1,425 (Unfavourable)

or

$$(3.500 - 3,200) \times \text{Rs. } \frac{15,200}{3,200}$$

$$= 300 \times \frac{15,200}{3,200} = \text{Rs. } 1,425 \text{ (Unfavourable)}$$

Materials yield variance always equals subusage variance. The difference lies only in terms of calculation. The former considers the output or loss in output and the latter considers standard inputs and actual input used for the actual output.

Illustration 6:

From the following particulars compute: (*a*) materials cost variance; (*b*) materials price variance; (c) materials usage variance:

Quantity of materials purchased	3,000 units
Value of materials purchased	Rs. 9,000
Standard quantity of materials required per kg of output	30 units
Standard rate of material	Rs. 2.50 per unit
Opening stock of materials	Nil
Closing stock of materials	500 units
Output during the period	80 kgs

Solution:

Materials consumed = 3,000 – 500 = 2,500 units

Actual rate of material = $\text{Rs. } \frac{9,000}{3,000}$ = Rs. 3 per unit

Standard quantity of actual output = 30 × 80 = 2,400 units

Materials cost variance = Actual cost – Standard cost
= (Actual price × Actual quantity) – (SP × Standard quantity)
= Rs. 3 × 2,500 – Rs. 2.50 × 2,400
= 7,500 – 6,000
= Rs. 1,500 Adverse

Materials price variance = Actual quantity (Actual price – Standard price)
= 2500 × (Rs. 3 – Rs. 2.50) – Rs. 1,250 (Adverse)

Materials usage variance = Standard price × (Actual quantity – Standard quantity)
= Rs. 2.50 (2,500 – 2,400)
= Rs. 250 (Adverse)

Illustration 7:

The standard materials cost to produce a tonne of chemical X is:

300 kg of material A @ Rs. 10 per kg.

400 kg of material B @ Rs. 5 per kg.

500 kg of material C @ Rs. 6 per kg.

During a period, 100 tonnes of mixture X was produced from the usage of:

35 tonnes of material A at a cost of Rs. 9,000 per tonne

42 tonnes of material B at a cost of Rs. 6,000 per tonne

53 tonnes of material C at a cost of Rs. 7,000 per tonne

Calculate the price, usage and mix variances.

Solution:

Material	*Standard*			*Actual*		
	Qty. (Rs.)	*Rate (Rs.)*	*Amount (Rs.)*	*Qty. (Rs.)*	*Rate (Rs.)*	*Amount (Rs.)*
A	30,000	10	3,00,000	35,000	9	3,15,000
B	40,000	5	2,00,000	42,000	6	2,52,000
C	50,000	6	3,00,000	53,000	7	3,71,000
	1,20,000		8,00,000	1,30,000		9,38,000

Materials cost variance = Actual cost – Standard cost for actual output
= Rs. 9,38,000 – Rs. 8,00,000
= Rs. 1,38,000 (Adverse)

Materials price variance = Actual quantity × (Actual price – Standard price)

A = 35,000 × (9– 10) = Rs. 35,000 (F)
B = 42,000 × (6 – 5) = Rs. 42,000 (A)
C = 53,000 × (7 – 6) = Rs. 53,000 (A)
Total Rs. 60,000 (A)

Materials usage variance = Standard price × (Actual quantity – Standard quantity for actual output)

A = 10 × (35,000 – 30,000) = Rs. 50,000 (A)
B = 5 × (42,000 – 40,000) = Rs. 10,000 (A)
C = 6 × (53,000 – 50,000) = Rs. 18,000 (A)
Total Rs. 78,000 (A)

Materials mix variance = Standard price × (Actual quantity – Revised standard quantity)

A = Rs. 10 × (35,000 – 32,500)
= 10 × 2,500 = Rs. 25,000 (A)

$$B = 5 \times \left(42,000 - \frac{1,30,000}{3}\right)$$

$$= 5 \times \frac{4,000}{3} = \text{Rs. } 6,667 \text{ (F)}$$

$$C = 6 \times \left(53,000 - \frac{1,62,500}{3}\right)$$

$$= 6 \times \frac{3,500}{3} = 7,000 \text{ (F)}$$

Total = 11,333 (A)

Working notes:

1. Revised standard quantity = $\frac{\text{Standard quantity of a mix} \times \text{Total actual quantity}}{\text{Total standard quantity of mixture}}$

$$A = \frac{30,000}{1,20,000} \times 1,30,000 = 32,500 \text{ kg.}$$

$$B = \frac{40,000}{1,20,000} \times 1,30,000 = \frac{1,30,000}{3}$$

$$C = \frac{50,000}{1,20,000} \times 1,30,000 = \frac{1,62,500}{3}$$

2. Standard cost per unit of output = $\frac{\text{Total standard cost}}{\text{Total standard output}}$

$$= \frac{\text{Rs. } 8,00,000}{100} = \text{Rs. } 8,000 \text{ per tonne}$$

3. Standard output for actual mix = $\frac{\text{Standard output}}{\text{Standard mix}} \times$ Actual mix

$$= \frac{100}{1,20,000} \times 1,30,000$$

$$= \frac{1,300}{12} \text{ tonnes.}$$

Materials yield variance (although not asked for in the question) would be calculated as follows:

Materials yield variance = (Actual output – Standard output for actual mixture) × Standard cost per unit of output

$$= \left(100 - \frac{1300}{12}\right) \times \text{Rs. } 8,000$$

$$= \frac{100}{12} \times \text{Rs. } 8,000$$

$$= \text{Rs. } 66,667 \text{ (Adverse)}$$

Illustration 8:

The standard cost card for product 'SIMCO' reveals:

	Rs.
Standard materials	
2 kg of A Rs. 2 per kg	4.00
1 kg of B Rs. 6 per kg	6.00
Direct labour (3 hours @ Rs. 6 per hour)	18.00
Variable overheads (3 hours @ Rs. 4 per direct labour hours)	12.00
Total standard cost per unit	40.00

It is proposed to produce 10,000 units of SIMCO in the month of March and budgeted cost based on the information contained in the standard cost card are as follows:

Direct materials

A 20,000 kg @ Rs. 2 per kg.	40,000
B 10,000 kg @ Rs. 6 per kg.	60,000
Direct labour (30,000 hours @ Rs. 6 per hour)	1,80,000
Variable overhead (30,000 hours @ Rs. 4 per direct labour)	1,20,000
	4,00,000

The actual results are:

Direct materials:	*Rs.*
A 19,000 kg @ Rs. 2.20 per kg.	41,800
B 10,000 kg @ Rs. 5.60 per kg.	56,560
Direct Labour (28,500 hours @ Rs. 6.40 per hour)	1,82,400
Variable Overheads	1,04,000
Actual production was 9,000 units	3,84,760

From the above, calculate the following variances:

(*a*) Materials: Price and usage
(*b*) Labour: Wages rate and labour efficiency
(*c*) Variable overhead total and overhead expenditure variable

Solution:

Materials price variance = Actual quantity × (Actual rate – Standard rate)

A = 19,000 × (2.20 – 2) Rs. 3,800 (A)
B = 10,100 × (5.60 – 6) Rs. 4,040 (F)
Rs. 240 (F)

Materials usage variance = Standard rate × (Actual quantity – Standard quantity for actual output)

A = 2 × (19,000 – 18,000) = Rs. 2,000 (A)
B = 6 × (10,100 – 9,000) = Rs. 6,600 (A)
Rs. 8,600 (A)

Labour rate variance = Actual time × (Actual rate – Standard rate)
= 28,500 × (6.40 – 6) = Rs. 11,400 (A)

Labour efficiency variance = Standard rate × (Actual time – Standard time for actual output)
= 6 × (28,500 – 27.000) = Rs. 9.000 (A)

Total variable overhead variance = Actual variable overheads – Recorded variable overheads
= 1,04,000 – 9,000 × 12
= 1,04,000 – 1,08,000 = Rs. 4,000 (F)

Overhead (Variable) expenditure variance
= Actual variable overheads – Standard variable overheads
= 1,04,000 – 28,500 × Rs. 4
= 1,04,000 – 1,14,000 = Rs. 10,000 (F)

Illustration 9:

A company manufacturing 'distempers' operates a costing system. The standard cost of one of the products of the company shows the following standards:

Materials	*Quantity*	*Standard price per kg. (Rs.)*	*Total Rs.*
A	40 kg.	75	3,000
B	10 kg.	50	50
C	50 kg.	20	1,000
Material cost per unit (Total)			4,500

The standard input mix is 100 kg. and the standard output of the finished product is 90 kg. The actual results for period are:

Materials used

A = 2,40,000 kg @ Rs. 80/kg.

B = 40,000 kg. @ Rs. 52/kg.

C = 2,20,000 kg. @ Rs. 21/kg.

Actual output of the finished product = 4,20,000 kg.

You are required to calculate the material price, mix and yield variances.

Solution:

Materials	*Standard*			*Actual*		
	Qty. (Rs.)	*Rate (Rs.)*	*Amount (Rs.)*	*Qty. (Rs.)*	*Rate (Rs.)*	*Amount (Rs.)*
A	2,00,000	75	1,50,00,000	2,40,000	80	1,92,00,000
B	50,000	50	25,00,000	40,000	52	20,80,000
C	2,50,000	20	50,00,000	2,20,000	21	46,20,000
	5,00,000		2,25,00,000	5,00,000		2,59,00,000

Standard output = 4,50,000 kg.

Actual output = 4,20,000 kg.

Materials cost variance = (Actual cost – Standard cost of actual output)

= 2,59,000 – 4,20,000 × 50

= 2,59,00,000 – 2,10,00,000

= Rs. 49,00,000 (A)

Materials price variance = Actual quantity × (Actual rate – Standard rate)

A = 2,40,000 × (80 – 75) = 12,00,000 (A)

B = 40,000 × (52 – 50) = 80,000 (A)

C = 2,20,000 × (21 – 20) = 2,20,000 (A)

Rs. 15,00,000

Materials usage variance = Standard rate × (Actual quantity – Standard quantity for actual output)

A = 75 × (2,40,000 – 2,00,000 × 42/45) = 40,00,000 (A)

B = 50 × (40,000 – 50,000 × 42/45) = 3,33,333 (F)
C = 20 × (2,20,000 – 2,50,000 × 42/45) = 2,66,667 (F)

Rs. 34,00,000 (A)

Material mix variance = Standard rate × (Actual quantity – Revised standard quantity)

A = 75 (2,40,000 – 2,00,000) = 30,00,000 (A)
B = 50 (40,000 – 50,000) = 5,00,000 (F)
C = 20 (2,20,000 – 2,50,000) = 6,00,000 (F)

Rs. 19,00,000

Materials yield variance = Standard cost per unit × (Actual output – Standard output for actual mix)
= 50 (4,20,000 – 4,50,000)
= Rs. 15,00,000 (A)

Illustration 10:

S.V. Ltd. manufacturers a single product, the standard mix of which is:

Material A 60% at Rs. 20 per kg.
Material B 40 % at Rs. 10 per kg.

Normal loss in production is 20% of input. Due to shortage of Material A, the standard mix was changed. Actual results for March 2009 were:

Material A	105 kg. at Rs. 20 per kg.
Material B	95 kg. at Rs. 9 per kg.
Input	200 kg.
Loss	35 kg.
Output	165 kg.

Calculate:

(*i*) Material Price Variance (*ii*) Material Usage Variance
(*iii*) Material Mix Variance (*iv*) Material Yield variance

Solution:

Workings:

1. Standard quantity for actual production —

$$\text{Material A} = \frac{60 \times 165}{80} = \frac{495}{4} \text{ kg.}$$

$$\text{Material B} = \frac{40 \times 165}{80} = \frac{165}{2} \text{ kg.}$$

2. Calculation of revised standard quantity

$$\text{Material A} = 200 \times \frac{3}{5} = 120 \text{ kg.}$$

$$\text{Material B} = 200 \times \frac{2}{5} = 80 \text{ kg.}$$

3. Calculation of standard quantity —

Material A = $\frac{120 \times 165}{160} = \frac{495}{4}$

Material B = $\frac{80}{160} \times 165 = \frac{165}{2}$

4. Calculation of standard cost per unit of output —

Material A = 60 × 20 = Rs. 1,200

Material B = $\frac{40}{100} \times 10 = \frac{\text{Rs. } 400}{1{,}600}$

Less: Loss 20% = 100 – 20 = 80

Cost per unit = $\frac{\text{Rs. } 1{,}600}{80}$ = Rs. 20

(*i*) Calculation of variances:

Material price variance = (AP – SP) × AQ

Material A = (Rs. 20 – 20) × 105 = Nil

Material B = (Rs. 9 – 10) × 95 = Rs. 95 (F)

Total Rs. 95 (F)

(*ii*) Material usage variance = (AQ – SQ) × SP

Material A = $\left(105 - \frac{495}{4}\right)$ × Rs. 20 = Rs. 375 (F)

Material B = $\left(95 - \frac{165}{2}\right)$ × Rs. 10 = Rs. 125 (A)

Total Rs. 250(F)

(*iii*) Material mix variances = (AQ – RSQ) × SP

Material A = (105 – 120) × Rs. 20 = Rs. 300 (F)

Material B = (95 – 80) × Rs. 10 = Rs. 150 (A)

Total Rs. 150(F)

(*iv*) Material yield variance = (Actual output – Std. output) × Std. cost per unit of outputs = (165 – 160) × Rs. 20 = Rs. 100(F)

Illustration 11:

The standard cost of a certain chemical mixture is:

35% Material A at Rs. 25 per kg.

65% Material B at Rs. 36 per kg.

A standard loss of 5% is expected in production

During a period there is used:

125 kg. of Material A at Rs. 27 per kg. and

275 kg. of Material B at Rs. 34 per kg.

The actual output = 365 kg

Calculate:

(*a*) Material Cost Variance
(*b*) Material Price Variance
(*c*) Material Mix Variance
(*d*) Material Yield Variance

Solution:

Material	*Standard*			*Actual*		
	kg.	*Rate*	*Amt.*	*kg.*	*Rate*	*Amt.*
A	140	25	3,500	125	27	3,375
B	260	36	9,360	275	34	9,350
	400		12,860	400		12,725

Standard output = 400 – 20 = 380 kg.
Actual output = 365 kg.
Standard cost per kg = Rs. 12,860/380 = Rs. 33.84

The various variances can now be calculated as follows:

(*a*) Material cost variance = (Actual cost – Standard cost for actual output)
= 12,725 – 365 × 33.84
= 12,725 – 12,352 = Rs. 373 (Adverse)

(*b*) Material price variance = Actual quantity × (AR – SR)
A = 125 × (27 – 25) = 250 (A)
B = 275 × (34 – 36) = 550 (F)
= Rs. 300 (Favourable)

(*c*) Material mix variance = Standard rate × (AQ – Revised standard quantity)
Material A = 25 × (125 – 140) = 375 (F)
Material B = 36 × (275 – 260) = 540 (A)
165 (Adverse)

(*d*) Material yield variance = Standard cost × (Actual output for actual mix – Standard output)
= 33.84 × (365 – 380)
= Rs. 508 (Adverse)

Working Notes:

1. Standard quantity for actual mix
Material A: 400 × 35/100 = 140 kg.
Material B: 400 × 65/100 = 260 kg.
2. Since Standard mix and Actual mix are the same, the Revised standard quantity and Standard quantity will also be the same.

Illustration 12:

Pragati Company manufactures a product P by mixing three raw materials. For every 100 kg. of output 125 kg. of raw material input are used. In April 2009, there was an output of 5,600 kg. of P. The standard and actual particulars of April, 2009 are as follows:

Raw material	Standard Mix	Standard Price per kg.	Actual Mix	Actual Price per kg.
I	50%	Rs. 40	60%	Rs. 42
II	30%	Rs. 20	20%	Rs. 16
III	20%	Rs. 10	20%	Rs. 12

Calculate all material variances. The actual quantity of material used was 7,000 kg.

Solution:

Raw material	Standard for output of 5,600 kg. Qty. kg.	Rate Rs.	Amt. Rs.	Actual for output of 5,600 kg. Qty. kg.	Rate Rs.	Amt. Rs.
I	3,500	40	1,40,000	4,200	42	1,76,400
II	2,100	20	42,000	1,400	16	22,400
III	1,400	10	14,000	1,400	12	16,800
Total	7,000 *		1,96,000	7,000		2,15,600

$\frac{*5,600}{100} \times 125$

DMCV = Std. Cost for Actual Output – Actual Cost
= 1,96,000 – 2,15,600 = Rs. 19,600 (A)

DMPV = Actual Qty. × (SR – AR)

I = 4,200 × (40 – 42) = 8,400 (A)
II = 1,400 × (20 – 16) = 5,600 (F)
III = 1.400 × (10 – 12) = 2,800 (A)

5,600 (A)

DMUV = SR × (Std. qty. for actual output – Actual quantity)

I = 40 × (3,500 – 4,200) = 28,000 (A)
II = 20 × (2,100 – 1,400) = 14,000 (F)
III = 10 × (1,400 – 1,400) = NIL

14,000 (A)

DMMV = SR × (SRQ – AQ)

Since total Std. Mix and Actual Mix are the same, the RSQ will be the same as Std. qty.

I = 40 × (3,500 – 4,200) = 28,000 (A)
II = 20 × (2,100 – 1,400) = 14,000 (F)
III = 10 × (1,400 – 1,400) Nil

14,000 (A)

The DMYV will be Nil.

Illustration 13:

Vinak Ltd. produces an article by blending two raw materials. It operates a standard costing system and the following standards have been set for raw materials:

Material	*Standard mix*	*Standard price per kg.*
A	40%	Rs. 4.00
B	60%	Rs. 3.00

The standard loss in processing is 15%.

During April 2009 the company produced 1.700 kg. of finished output. The position of stocks and purchases for the month of April 2009 is as under:

Material	*Stock on April 1, 2009 (kg.)*	*Stock on April 30, 2009 (kg.)*	*Purchasing during April 2009*	
			(kg.)	*Cost (Rs.)*
A	35	5	800	3,400
B	40	50	1,200	3,000

Calculate the following variances:

(*i*) Materials price variance
(*ii*) Materials usage variance
(*iii*) Materials yield variance
(*iv*) Materials mix variance
(*v*) Total materials cost variance.

Solution:

Standard cost of standard mix:

Type of material	*Standard quantity of material required Rs.*	*Standard price per kg. Rs.*	*Standard cost*
A	800	4	3,200
B	1,200	3	3,600
Total	2,000		6,800

Note: 1. The loss being 15% to produce 85 kg. of an article, the standard quantity of material required is 100 kg. Therefore, to produce 1,700 kg. of the article the standard quantity of material required is $\frac{100}{85} \times 1{,}700$ kg. or 2,000 kg.

2. Out of 2,000 kg of material used, 40% is type A and 60% is type B, i.e., 800 kg. of A and 1,200 kg of B are the standard quantities.

Actual Costs

Type of material	*Actual quantity of material used kg.*	*Actual price per kg. Rs.*	*Actual quantity X actual price Rs.*
A	830	4.25	3,518.75
B	1,190	2.50	2,995.00
Total	2,020		6,513.75

* Actual quantity of material A is 830 kg. out of this 35 kg. is available at the standard price of Rs. 4 per kg. and remaining 795 kg. at Rs. 4.25 per kg.
Actual quantity of material B used is 1,190 kg; out of this 40 kg is available at the standard price Rs. 3 per kg. and the remaining 1,150 kg. at Rs. 2.50.

(*i*) Materials price variance = Actual quantity × (Actual price – Standard price)

A. Standard price of 830 units @ 4		3,320.00
Actual price of 35 units @ Rs. 4	140.00	
795 units @ Rs. 4.25	3,378.75	3,518.75
		198.75 (A)
B. Standard price of 1,190 units		Rs. 3,570.00
Actual price of 40 units @ Rs. 3	120,00	
1,150 units @Rs. 2.50	2,875.00	2.995.00
		575.00 (F)
Total		376.75 (F)

(*ii*) Materials (total) usage variance = Standard price × (Actual quantity – Standard quantity)

	Rs.
A : 4 × (830 – 800)	120.00 (A)
B : 3 × (1,190 – 1,200)	30.00 (F)
	90.00 (A)

(*iii*) Materials yield variance = Standard rate × (Actual yield – Standard yield)

$$\text{Standard rate} = \frac{\text{Total standard cost}}{\text{Standard yield}} = \text{Rs.}\frac{6,800}{1,700} = \text{Rs. 4 per kg.}$$

Yield variance = 4 (1,700 – 1,717*) or Rs. 68(A).)

*By using 2,000 kg. of material, standard yield is 1,700 kg.. Therefore, the standard yield by using 2,020 kg. of material will be (1,700/2,000 × 2,020 or 1.71 kg.)

(*iv*) Material mix variance = Actual quantity × (Per unit standard cost of standard mix – per unit standard cost of actual mix)

$$= 2,020\left(\frac{6,800}{2,000} - \frac{6,890}{2,020}\right)$$

= 2,020 (3.4 – 3.410) or Rs. 22(A)

(*v*) Materials cost variance = (Actual cost – Standard cost)

= Rs. 6,513.75 – 6,800

= Rs. 286.25 (F)

Illustration 14:

JS Limited used a full standard cost system with raw material inventory carried at standard. The following data were taken from the records of the company for the year ended 31-12-2009:

	Rs.
Opening raw material inventory	300
Closing raw material inventory	250
Net purchases	410
Material price variance	10 A
Material usage variance	20 A
Direct labour cost (Actuals)	900
Direct labour cost (Standard)	840
Actual overhead cost incurred	875

Overhead cost variance	45 F
Opening work-in-progress inventory	120
Closing work-in-progress inventory	140
Opening finished goods inventory	360
Cost of goods sold reported	2,240

Note: F denotes favourable and A denotes adverse

You are required to compute:

1. Raw Material purchases at standard
2. Raw Material consumed at actuals
3. Raw Material consumed at standard
4. Labour cost variance
5. Standard overhead costs
6. Total manufacturing cost at standard cost
7. Cost of goods manufactured
8. Cost of produces sold to customers
9. Closing finished goods inventory

Solution:

	Rs.
1. Raw material purchases at standard	
Net purchases at actual	410
Less: Material price variance (A)	10
	400
2. Raw materials consumed at Actual	
Raw materials consumed at Standard (as per 3 below)	450
Add: Materials usage variance (A)	20
	470
3. Raw materials consumed at standard	
Opening stock at standard	300
Add: Purchase at standard (as per 1)	400
	700
4. Labour cost variance	
Direct labour cost at standard	840
Less: Actual direct labour cost	900
	60 (A)
5. Standard overhead cost:	
Actual overheads	875
Add: Overhead cost variance	45 (F)
	920

6. Total (or Gross) manufacturing Cost at standard	
Standard raw material cost	450
Standard direct labour cost	840
Standard overhead cost	920
	2,210
7. Cost of goods manufactured (at standard)	
Opening WIP (at standard)	120
Add: Total or Gross cost goods manufactured	2,210
	2,330
Less: Closing WIP (at standard)	140
	2,190
8. Cost of products sold to customers	
Cost of goods sold reported	2,240
Less: Adverse Variance:	
Material cost variance – Price variance	10 (A)
Usage variance	20 (A)
	30 (A)
Direct labour cost variance	60 (A)
	90 (A)
	2,150
Add: Overhead cost variance	45 (F)
	2,195
9. Closing stock of finished goods inventory at standard:	
Opening finished goods inventory at standard	360
Add: Cost of goods manufactured at standard	2,190
	2,550
Less: Cost of products sold to customers at standard	2,195
	355

LABOUR VARIANCES

Direct labour variances arise when actual labour costs are different from standard labour costs. Labour variances constitute the following:

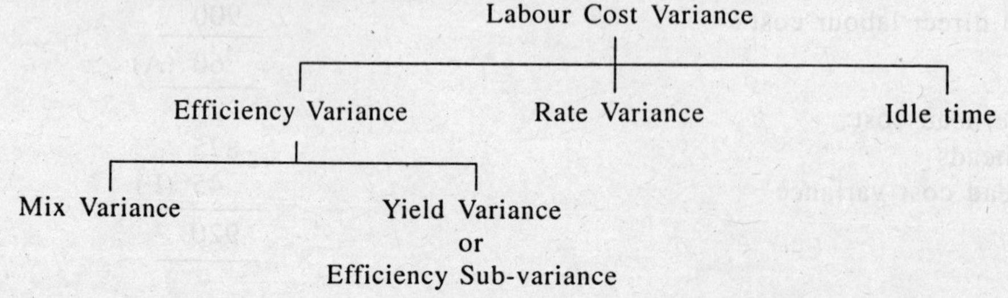

Labour Cost Variance

Labour cost variance denotes the difference between the actual direct wages paid and the standard direct wages specified for the output achieved. This variance is calculated by using the following formula:

Labour cost variance = (AH × AR – SH × SR)

where AH = Actual hours
AR = Actual rate
SH = Standard hours
SR = Standard rate

Labour Efficiency Variance

The calculation of labour efficiency or usage variance follows the same pattern as the computation of materials usage variance. If actual direct labour hours required to complete a job differ from the number of standard hours specified, a labour efficiency variance results; it is the difference between actual hours expended and standard labour hours specified multiplied by the standard labour rate per hour. The formula is:

Labour efficiency variance = (Actual hours – Standard hours for the actual output) × Std. rate per hour.

It may be noted that the standard labour hour rate and not the actual rate is used in computing labour efficiency variance. If quantity variances are calculated, changes in prices/rates are excluded, and when price variances are calculated, standard quantities are ignored.

Labour Rate Variance

Labour rate variance is computed in the same manner as materials price variance. When actual direct labour hour rates differ from standard rates, the result is a labour rate variance. It is that portion of the direct wages variance which is due to the difference between the actual rate paid and standard rate of pay specified. The formula for its calculation is:

Labour rate variance = (Actual rate – Standard rate) × Actual hours

Favourable rate variance arise whenever actual rates are less than standard rates: unfavourable is variances occur when actual rates exceed standard rates.

Labour Mix Variance

Labour mix variance is computed in the same manner as materials mix variance. Manufacturing or completing a job requires different types or grades of workers and production will be completed if labour is mixed according to standard proportions. Standard labour mix may not be adhered to under some circumstances and substitution will have to be made. There may be changes in the wage rates of some workers; there may be a need to use more skilled or expensive types of labour, *e.g.*, employment of men instead of women; sometimes workers and operators may be absent. These lead to the emergence of a labour mix variance which is calculated by using the following formula:

Labour mix variance = (Actual labour mix – Revised standard labour mix in terms of actual total hours) × Standard rate per hour.

To take an example, suppose the following were the standard cost data per unit in a factory:

Class	*Proportion* %		*Cost* *Rs.*	
A	50	3 hours @	Rs. 4.00	12
B	50	3 hours @	Rs. 2.00	6
	100	6 hours	Rs. 3.00	18

In a period, many class B workers were absent and it was necessary to substitute class B workers. Since the class A workers were less experienced with the job, more labour hours were used. The recorded costs of a unit were:

Class	*Proportions* %		*Cost* *Rs.*	
A	75	6 hours @	Rs. 4.00	24.00
B	25	2 hours @	Rs. 2.00	4.00
	100	8 hours	Rs. 3.50	28.00

Labour mix variance will be calculated as follows:

Labour mix variance = (Actual proportion – Revised standard proportion of actual total hours) × Standard rate per hour

Revised standard proportion:

Class A = $\frac{3}{6}$ × 8 = 4 hours

Class B = $\frac{3}{6}$ × 8 = 4 hours

Applying the formula:

Class A = (6 – 4) × Rs. 4 = Rs. 8 (Unfavourable)

Class B = (2 – 4) × Rs. 2 = Rs. 4 (Favourable)

Total labour mix variance = Rs. 4 (Unfavourable)

Labour Yield Variance

The final product cost contains not only material cost but also labour cost. Therefore, higher or lower output than the standard output should take into account labour yield variance also. A lower output simply means that final output does not correspond with the production units that should have been produced from the hours expended on the inputs. It can be computed by applying the following formula:

Labour yield variance = (Actual output – Standard output based on actual hours) × Average standard labour rate per unit of output

or

Labour yield variance = (Actual loss – Standard loss on actual hours) × Average standard labour rate per unit of output

Labour yield variance is also known as labour efficiency sub-variance which is computed in terms of inputs, *i.e.*, standard labour hours and revised labour hours mix (in terms of actual hours). Labour efficiency sub-variance is computed by using the following formula:

Labour efficiency sub-variance = (Revised standard mix – Standard mix) × Standard labour rate

Substitution Variance: This type or variance arises in the case of labour, due to the substitution of labour, that is when one grade of labour is substituted by another. This variance in fact represent the difference between the actual hours at standard rate of standard worker and the actual hours at standard rate of actual worker.

The formula for computation is:

Substitution variance = (Standard hours × Standard rate for standard worker) – (Standard hours × Standard rate of actual worker)

Idle Time Variance

Idle time variance occurs when workers are not able to do the work due to some reason during the hours for which they are paid. Idle time can be divided according to causes responsible for creating idle time, e.g., idle time due to breakdown, lack of materials or power failures. Idle time variance will be equivalent to the standard labour cost of the hours during which no work has been done, but for which workers have been paid for unproductive time. Suppose, in a factory 200 workers were idle because of a power failure. As a result of this a loss of production of 4,000 units of product A and 8,000 units of product B occurred. Each employee was paid his normal wage (a rate of Rs. 20 per hour). A single standard hour is needed to manufacture four units of product A and eight units of product B. Idle time variance will be computed in the following manner:

Standard hours lost:

Product A $= \frac{4{,}000}{4} = 1{,}000$ hr.

Product B $= \frac{8{,}000}{8} = 1{,}000$ hr.

Total hours lost = 2,000 hr.

Idle Time Variance (power failure)

2,000 hours @ Rs. 20 per hour = Rs. 40,000 (Adverse)

Illustration 15:

Standard hours for manufacturing two products M and N are 15 hours per unit and 20 hours per unit respectively. Both products require identical kind of labour and the standard wages rates per hour is Rs. 5. In the year 2007, 10,000 units of M and 15.000 units of N were manufactured. The total of labour hours actually worked were 4,50,000 and the actual wage bill came to Rs. 23,00,000. This include 12.000 hours paid for @ Rs. 7 per hour and 9,400 hours paid for @ Rs. 7.50 per hour, the balance having been paid at Rs. 5 per hour. You are required to compute the labour variances.

Solution:

Labour cost variance = (Actual labour cost – Standard labour cost for actual output)

Standard cost:

For Product M	= 10,000 × 15 × 5 =	7,50,000
For Product N	= 15,000 × 20 × 5 =	15.00.000
Total standard cost	=	Rs. 22,50,000

Total actual labour cost = Rs. 23,00,000

Labour cost variance = Rs. 23,00,000 – 22,50,000

= Rs. 50,000 (Adverse)

Labour rate variance = Actual hours × (Actual rate – Standard rate)

= 12,000 × (Rs. 7 – Rs. 5) = 24,000 (A)

= 9,400 × (Rs. 7.50 – Rs. 5) = 23,500 (A)

= 4,29,100 × (Rs. 5 – Rs. 5) =

Total 47,500 (A)

Labour efficiency variance = Standard rate × (Actual time – Standard time)

= Rs. 5 × (4,50,500 – 4,50,000)

= Rs. 2,500 (Adverse)

Illustration 16:

The Standard cost card for a product shows:

Material cost 2 kg. @ Rs. 2.50 each Rs. 5.00 per unit

Wages 2 hours @ Rs. 10 each Rs. 20 per unit

The actuals which have emerged from business operations are as follows:

Production 8,000 units

Material consumed 16,500 kg @ Rs. 2.40 each Rs. 39,600

Wages paid 18.000 hours @ Rs. 8 each Rs. 1,44.000

Calculate the appropriate material and labour variances.

Solution:

Materials cost variance = (Actual cost – Standard cost)

= 16,500 × 2.40 – 16,000 × 2.50)

= Rs. 39,600 – Rs. 40,000

= 400 (Favourable)

Material price variance = Actual quantity × (Actual price – Standard price)

= 16,500 × (2.40 – 2.50)

= Rs. 1,650 (Favourable)

Materials usage variance = Standard price × (Actual quantity – Standard quantity)

= 2.50 × (16,500 – 16,000)

= Rs. 1,250 (Adverse)

Labour cost variance = (Actual labour cost – Standard labour cost)

= (Rs. 1,44,000 – Rs. 1,60,000)

= Rs. 16.000 (Favourable)

Labour rate variance = Actual hours × (Actual rate – Standard rate)

= 18,000 × (Rs. 8 – Rs. 10)

= Rs. 36,000 (Favourable)

Labour efficiency variance = (Actual hours – Standard hours for actual production) × SR

= (18,000 – 16,000) × Rs 10

= Rs. 20,000 (Adverse)

Illustration 17:

The standard output of production 'EXE' is 25 units per hour in manufacturing department of a company employing 100 workers. The standard wage rate per labour hour is Rs. 6.

In a 42 hour week, the department produced 1,040 units of 'EXE' despite 5% of the time paid was lost due to an abnormal reason. The hourly wage rate actually paid were Rs. 6.20, Rs. 6 and Rs. 5.70 respectively to 10, 30 and 60 of the workers.

Compute relevant variances.

Solution:

Basic Calculations

1. *Standard man hours per unit:*
   25 units is the standard output when 100 workers work for I hour. Hence, standard man hours per unit are 100/25 = 4.
2.

Standard output: 1,040 units			*Actual Output: 1,040 units*				
Man hours for actual output	*Rate per hr.*	*Amount*	*Actual hours paid*	*Idle time hrs. for*	*Prod. hrs.*	*Rate per hour*	*Amount paid for production*
	Rs.	*Rs.*	*Rs.*	*Rs.*		*Rs.*	*Rs.*
4,160	6	24,960	420	21	399	6.20	2,604
(1,040 units × 4 hrs.)			1,260	63	1,197	6.00	7,560
			2,520	126	2,394	5,70	14,364
		24,960	4,200	210	3,990		24,528

Computations of Variances

Labour Cost Variance:

= Standard Labour Cost – Actual Labour Cost
= Rs. 24,960 – Rs. 24,528 = Rs. 432 (F)

Labour Rate Variance:

= Actual Time paid for × (Standard Rate – Actual Rate)

(*i*) 420 × (6 – 6.20) = 84 (A)
(*ii*) 1,260 × (6 – 6) = —
(*iii*) 2,520 × (6 – 5.70) = 756 (F)
672 (F)

Labour Efficiency Variance (after segregating Idle Time Variance):

= Standard Rate × (Standard Time for actual output – Actual time worked)
= Rs. 6 × (4,160 hrs. – 3,990 hrs.) = Rs. 1,020 (F)

Labour Idle Time Variance:

= Idle Time hrs. × Standard Rate
= 210 hrs. × Rs. 6 = Rs 1,260 (A)

Illustration 18:

From the following records of Apollo Bolt Nut Manufacturing Company, you are required to compute material and labour variances:

An input of 100 kg of material yields to standard output of 10,000 units.
Standard price per kg of material = Rs. 20
Actual quantity of material issued and used by production department 10,000 kg.
Actual price per kg of material = Rs. 21 per kg.
Actual output = 9,00,000 units
Number of employees = 200
Standard wage rate per employee per day = Rs. 40
Standard daily output per employee = 100 units
Total number of days worked = 50 days
(Idle time paid for and included in the above half day for each employee)
Actual wage rate per day = Rs. 45

Solution:

Direct Material Variances

DMCV = Standard Cost for Actual output – Actual Cost
= 9,000 × 20 – 10,000 × 21
= 1,80,000 – 2,10,000
= Rs. 30,000 (A)

Direct Material Cost Variance (DMCV) can be segregated into Direct Material Price Variance (DMPV) and Direct Material Usage Variance (DMUV) as shown below:

DMCV = Actual Quantity × (Standard Rate – Actual Rate)
= 10,000 kg. × (20 – 21)
= Rs. 10,000 (A)

DMUV = Standard Rate × (Standard Quantity for Actual Output – Actual Quantity)
= 20 × (9,000 – 10,000)
= Rs. 20,000 (A)

Verification:

DMCV = DMPV + DMUV
30,000 (A) = 10.000 (A) + 20,000 (A)

Direct Labour Variances

DMCV = Standard Labour Cost for Actual output – Actual Labour Cost
= 9,00,000 × .40 – 50 × 200 × 45
= 3,60,000 – 4,50,000
= Rs. 90,000 (A)

Direct Labour Cost Variance (DLCV) may be segregated into Direct Labour Rate Variance (DLRV),

Direct Labour Idle Time Variance (DLITV) and Direct Labour Revised Efficiency Variance (DLREV).

DLRV = Actual Time paid for × (SR – AR)
= 50 × 200 × (40 – 45)
= Rs. 50,000 (A)

DLITV = Idle Hours × Std. Rate
= 25 × 200 × 40
= Rs. 2,00,000 (A)

DLREV = Standard Rate × (Std. Time for Actual Output – Actual Time Worked)
= 40 × (9,000 – 5.000)
= 40 × 4,000 = Rs. 1,60,000 (F)

Verification

DLCV = DLRV + ITV + DLREV

Rs. 90,000 (A) = Rs. 50,000 (A) + Rs. 2,00,000 (A) + Rs. 1,60,000 (F)

Illustration 19:

The following standards have been set to manufacture a product:

Direct materials:

2 units of A at Rs. 4 per unit	8.00
3 units of B at Rs. 3 per unit	9.00
15 units of C at Rs. I per unit	15.00
	32.00
Direct labour 3 hrs @ Rs. 8 per hour	24.00
Total standard prime cost	56.00

The company manufactured and sold 6,000 units, of the product during the year. Direct material cost were as follows:

12,500 units of A at Rs. 4.40 per unit.
18,000 units of B at Rs. 2.80 per unit.
88,500 units of C at Rs. 1.20 per unit.

The company worked 17,500 direct labour hours during the year. For 2,500 of these hours the company paid at Rs. 12 per hour while for the remaining the wages were paid at the standard rate. Calculate materials price and usage variances and labour rate and efficiency variances.

Solution:

Output 6,000 units

	Standard			Actual		
	Qty. units	*Rate Rs.*	*Amount Rs.*	*Qty. units*	*Rate Rs.*	*Amount Rs.*
A	12,000	4.00	48,000	12,500	4.40	55,000
B	18,000	3.00	54,000	18,000	2.80	50,400
C	90,000	1.00	90,000	88,500	1.20	1,06,200
Total	1,20,000		1,92,000	1,19,000		2,11,600

Material price variance = Actual quantity × (Actual rate – Standard rate)

A = 12,500 × (4.40 – 4) = 5,000 (A)
B = 11,000 × (2.80 – 3) = 3,600 (F)
C = 88,500 × (1.20 – 1) = 17,700 (A)

Total 19,100 (Adverse)

Material usage variance = Standard rate × (Actual quantity – Standard quantity for actual output

A = 4 × (12,500 – 12,000) = 2,000 (A)
B = 3 × (18,000 – 18,000) = Nil
C = 1 × (88,500 – 90,000) = 1,500 (F)
Total Rs. 500 (Adverse)

Labour rate variance = Actual hrs. × (Actual rate – Standard rate)

(*i*) = 2,500 × (12 – 8) = 10,000 (A)
(*ii*) = 15,000 × (8 – 8) = Nil
Total = Rs. 10,000 (Adverse)

Labour efficiency variance = Standard rate × (Actual time – Standard time for actual output)
= 8 × (17,500 – 6,000 × 3)
= Rs. 4,000 (Favourable)

Illustration 20:

From the following data of A and Co. Ltd. relating to budgeted and actual performance for the month of March 2008, compute the Direct Material and Direct Labour Cost Variances.

Budgeted data for March:

Units to be manufactured	1,50,000
Units of direct material required (based on standard rates)	4,95,000
Planned purchase of raw materials (Units)	5,40,000
Average unit cost of direct material	Rs. 8
Direct labour hours per unit of finished goods	3/4 hr.
Direct labour cost (Total)	Rs. 29,92,500

Actual data at the end of March:

Units actually manufactured	1,60,000
Direct material cost (Purchase cost based on units actually issued)	Rs. 43,41,900
Direct material cost (Purchase cost based on units actually purchased)	Rs. 45,10,000
Average units cost of direct material	Rs. 8.20
Total direct labour hours for March	1,25,000
Total direct labour cost for March	Rs. 33,75,000

Solution:

Direct Material Variances

MCV = Actual material cost – Standard material cost of actual output
= 43,41,900 – 1,60,000 × 3.3 × 8
= 43,41,900 – 42,24,000
= 1,17,900 (Adverse)

MPV = Actual quantity × (Actual rate – Standard rate)
= 5,29,500 × (8.20 – 8)
= Rs. 1,05,900 (Adverse)

MUV = Standard rate × (Actual quantity – Standard quantity for actual output
= 8 × (5,29,500 – 1,60,000 × 3.30)
= 8 × (5,29,500 – 5,28,000)
= Rs. 12,000 (Adverse)

Direct Labour Variances

LCV = Actual labour cost – Standard labour cost for actual Output
= 33,75,000 – 1,60,000 × 3/4 × 26.60
= 33,75,000 – 31,92,000
= Rs. 1,83,000 (Adverse)

LRV = Actual time × (Actual rate – Standard rate)
= 1,25,000 × (27 – 26.60)
= Rs. 50,000 (Adverse)

LEV = Standard rate × (Actual time – Standard time for actual output)
= 26.60 × (1,25,000 – 1,60,000 × 3/4)
= 26.60 × (1.25,000 – 1,20,000)
= Rs. 1,33,000 (Adverse)

Working Notes:

(*i*) Standard units of direct material required per unit of output:

$$= \frac{4,95,000}{1,50,000} = 3.30 \text{ units}$$

(*ii*) Total actual quantity of direct materials used

$$= \frac{43,41,900}{8.20} = 5,29,500 \text{ units}$$

(*iii*) Standard direct labour cost per hour

$$= \frac{29,92,500}{1,50,000 \times 3/4} = \frac{29,92,500}{1,12,500} = \text{Rs. } 26.50$$

(*iv*) Actual direct labour cost per hour

$$= \frac{33,75,000}{1,25,000} = \text{Rs. } 27$$

OVERHEAD VARIANCES

The analysis of factory overhead variances is more complex than variance analysis for direct materials and direct labour. Generally, overhead variances constitute the following variances:

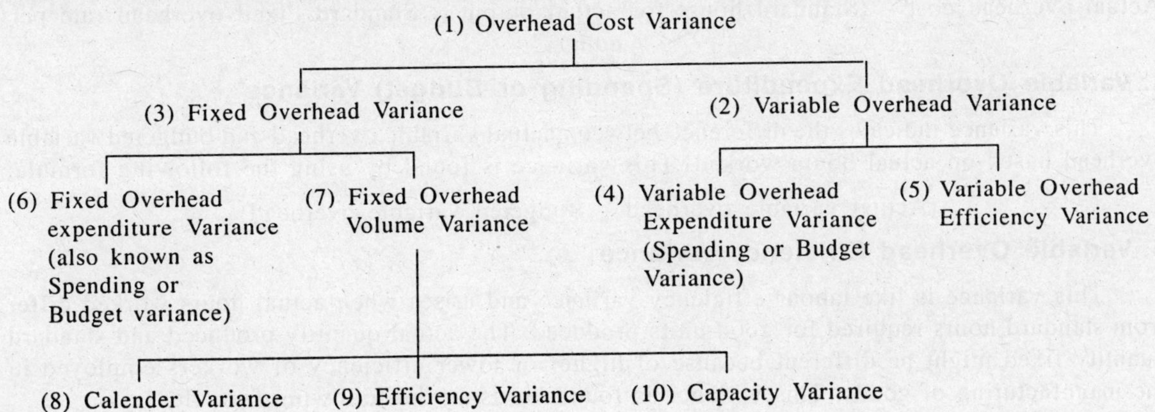

1. Total Overhead Cost Variance

This overall overhead variance is the difference between the actual overhead cost incurred and the standard cost of overhead for the output achieved. This can be computed by applying the following formula:

(Actual overhead incurred – Standard hours for the actual output × Standard overhead rate per hour)

or

Actual overhead incurred – (Actual output × Standard overhead rate per unit)

To illustrate the overall overhead variance, assume that the actual overhead for a department amounts to Rs. 10,00,000 and standard (or allowed) hours for work performed total 4,500 hours, while actual hours used are 5,000. If overhead rate is Rs. 200 per hour, the overall overhead variance will be the following:

Actual department overhead	Rs. 10,00,000
Overhead charged to production (4,500 hr. × Rs. 200)	Rs. 9,00,000
Overall or net overhead variance (Unfavourable)	Rs. 1,00,000

2. Variable Overhead Variance

It is the difference between actual variable overhead cost and standard variable overhead allowed for the actual output achieved. The formula for computing this variance is as follows:

Actual overhead cost – (Actual output × Variable overhead rate per unit):

or

Actual overhead cost – (Standard hours for actual output × Standard variable overhead rate per hour)

3. Fixed Overhead Variance

This variance indicates the difference between the actual fixed overhead cost and standard fixed overhead cost allowed for the actual output. This variance is found by using the following formula.

Fixed overhead variance = Actual overhead cost – Fixed overhead absorbed

or

Actual overhead cost – (Standard hours for actual output × Standard Fixed overhead rate per hour).

4. Variable Overhead Expenditure (Spending or Budget) Variance

This variance indicates the difference between actual variable overhead and budgeted variable overhead based on actual hours worked. This variance is found by using the following formula:

(Actual variable overhead – Budgeted variable overhead)

5. Variable Overhead Efficiency Variance

This variance is like labour efficiency variance and arises when actual hours worked differ from standard hours required for good units produced. The actual quantity produced and standard quantity fixed might be different because of higher or lower efficiency of workers employed in the manufacturing of goods. This variance is found by using the following formula:

(Actual hours – Standard hours for actual output) × Standard variable overhead rate per hour

6. Fixed Overhead Expenditure (Spending or Budget) Variance

This variance indicates the difference between actual fixed overhead and budgeted fixed overhead. The formula for computing this variance is as follows:

(Actual fixed overhead – Budgeted fixed overhead)

If actual fixed overhead costs are greater than budgeted fixed costs, an unfavourable variance results because actual costs exceed the budget. Actual overhead costs seldom equal budgeted costs because property tax rates may change, insurance premiums may increase or equipment charges may affect depreciation rates. As an illustration, assume that a company completed 36,000 units (equal to 18,000 standard productive hours) in 18,500 hours at the recorded fixed cost of Rs 75,100. The standard fixed cost rate per hour is Rs. 4. Therefore,

Expenditure variance = Actual overhead costs – Budgeted overhead costs)

That is = (75,100 – 18,500 × 4)
= (75,100 – 74,000)
= Rs. 1,100 (unfavourable)

The expenditure or budget variance provides management with information which helps in controlling costs. The budget variance is usually prepared on a departmental basis and the factors that cause the budget variance are, therefore, controllable by departmental managers.

7. Fixed Overhead Volume Variance

Volume variance relates to only fixed overhead. This variance arises due to the difference between the standard fixed overhead cost allowed (absorbed) for the actual output and the budgeted fixed overhead based on standard hours allowed for actual output achieved during the period. The variance shows the over-or-under-absorption of fixed overheads during a particular period. If the actual output is more than the standard output, there is over-absorption and variance is favourable. If actual output is less than the standard output, the volume variance is unfavourable. The formula for computing this variance is as follows:

(Budgeted overhead applied to actual output – Budgeted fixed overhead based on standard hours allowed for actual output)

or

(Actual production – Budgeted production) × Standard fixed overhead rate per unit

Volume variance is further sub-divided into three variances.

8. Fixed Overhead Calendar Variance

It is that portion of volume variance which is due to the difference between the number of actual working days in the period to which the budget is applicable and budgeted number of days in the budget period.

If actual working days is more than the budgeted working days, the variance is favourable as work has been done on days more than budgeted or allowed and vice-versa. The formula is as follows:

(No. of actual working days – No. of budgeted working days) × Standard Fixed overhead rate per day. Calender variance can be computed based on hours or output. Then the formulae are:

Hours Basis:

Calendar variance = (Revised budget capacity hours – Budgeted hours) × Standard fixed overhead rate per hour.

If revised budgeted capacity hours are more than the budgeted hours, the variance will be favourable. In the reverse situation, the variance will be unfavourable.

Output Basis

Calendar variance = (Revised budget quantity in terms of actual number of days worked – Budgeted quantity) × Standard fixed overhead rate per unit.

If revised budgeted quantity is more than the budgeted quantity the variance is favourable; if revised budgeted quantity is less, the variance will be unfavourable.

9. Fixed Overhead Efficiency Variances

It is that portion of volume variance which arises when actual hours of production used for actual output differ from the standard hours specified for that output. If actual hours worked are less than the standard hours, the variance is favourable and when actual hours are more than the standard hours, the variance is unfavourable. The formula is:

Fixed overhead efficiency variance = (Actual hours – Standard hours for actual production) × Standard fixed overhead rate per hour

or

Fixed overhead efficiency variance = (Actual production – Standard production as per actual time available) × Standard fixed overhead rate per unit

10. Fixed Overhead Capacity Variance

It is that part of fixed overhead volume variance which is due to the difference between the actual capacity (in hours) worked during a given period and the budgeted capacity (expressed in hours). The formula is:

Capacity variance (Actual capacity hours – Budgeted capacity hours) × Standard fixed overhead rate per hour.

This variance represents idle time also. If actual capacity hours are more than the budgeted capacity hours, the variance is favourable and if factual capacity hours less than the budgeted capacity hours, the variance will be unfavourable.

In case actual number of days and budgeted number of days are also given, then budgeted capacity hours will be calculated in terms of actual number of days and it will be known as revised budgeted capacity hours, *i.e.,* budgeted hours for actual days worked. In this situation, the formula for calculating capacity variance will be as follows:

Capacity variance = (Actual capacity hours – Revised budgeted capacity hours) × Standard fixed overhead rate per hour

In the above formula, the variance will be favourable if actual capacity hours are more than the revised budgeted hours. However, if actual capacity hours are lesser than the revised budgeted hours, the variance will be adverse as lesser hours means that lesser actual hours have been worked taking the actual days utilised into account.

Two-way, Three-way and Four-way Variance Analysis

The above overhead variances are also classified as Two-way, Three-way and Four-way variance. The different variances under these categories are listed below. The formulae for computing these variances are similar to as explained in the preceding section.

A. Two-way Variance Analysis

1. Controllable variance (Budget variance)
2. Volume variance (Uncontrollable variance)

B. Three-way Variance Analysis

1. Expenditure variance (Spending variance)
2. Capacity variance
3. Efficiency variance

C. Four-way Variance Analysis

1. Expenditure variance (Spending variance)
2. Variable overhead efficiency variance
3. Fixed overhead efficiency variance
4. Capacity variance

Illustration 21:

From the following data, calculate overhead variances:

	Budget	*Actual*
Output	15,000 units	16,000 units
No. of working days	25	27
Fixed overheads	Rs. 30,000	Rs. 30,500
Variable overheads	Rs. 45,000	Rs. 47,000

There was an increase of 5% in capacity.

Solution:

1. *Total overhead cost variance:*
   (Actual overhead cost – Actual units × Standard rate)
   (Rs. 30,500 + 47,000 – 16,000 × Rs. 5)
   Rs. 77,500 – Rs. 80,000 = Rs. 2,500 (Favourable)

   $$\text{Standard rate} = \frac{\text{Standard overhead}}{\text{Standard output}}$$

2. *Variable overheads expenditure variance:*
   (Actual variable cost – Actual units × Standard rate)
   (47,000 – 16,000 × Rs. 3)
   47,000 – Rs. 48,000 = Rs. 1,000 (Favourable)
3. *Fixed overhead variance:*
   Actual fixed overhead cost – (Actual units × Standard rate of fixed overhead)
   30,500 – (16,000 × 2)
   30,500 – 32,000 = Rs. 1,500 (Favourable)

4. *Volume variance:*

Actual units × Standard rate – Budgeted fixed overheads

16,000 × Rs. 2 – Rs. 30,000 = Rs. 2,000 (Favourable)

5. *Expenditure variance:*

Actual fixed overheads – Budgeted fixed overheads

Rs. 30,500 – Rs. 30,000 = Rs. 500 (Unfavourable)

6. *Capacity variance:*

Standard rate (Revised budgeted units – Budgeted units)

Revised budgeted units = Budgeted units + Increase in capacity

$= 15\,000 + \frac{5}{10} \times 15{,}000 = 15{,}750$ units

Capacity variance = Rs. 2 (15,750 units – 15,000 units)

= Rs. 2 × 750 = Rs. 1,500 (Favourable)

7. *Calendar variance:*

Increase or decrease in production due to more or less working days × Standard rate per unit. Within 25 days, Standard production with increased capacity = 15,750 units.

Within 2 days (27 – 25), production will be increased by $= \frac{15{,}750 \times 2}{25} = 1{,}260$ units

Calendar variance = 1,260 units × Rs. 2

= Rs. 2,520 (Favourable)

8. *Efficiency variance:*

Standard rate (Actual production – Standard production)

Standard production:

Budgeted production	=	15,000 units
Production increased due to increase in capacity	=	750 units
Production increased due to 2 more working days	=	1,260 units
		17,010 units

Efficiency variance = Rs. 2 (16,000 units – 17,010 units)

= Rs. 2 (–1,010 units) – Rs. 2,020 (Unfavourable)

Illustration 22:

In a factory the standard units of production for the year were fixed at 1,20,000 units and overhead expenditures were estimated to be:

	Rs.
Fixed	12,000
Variable	6,000
Semi-variable	1,800

Actual production during April of the year was 8,000 units. Each month has 20 working days.

During the month in question there was one statutory holiday. The actual overheads amounted to:

	Rs.
Fixed overhead	1,190
Variable	480
Semi-variable	192

Semi-variable charges are considered to include 60% expenses of a fixed nature and 40% of a variable character. Find out the expenditure, volume and calendar variances.

Solution:

Total overhead cost variance = Actual overheads – Recovered overheads
= 1,862 – 1,320 = Rs. 542.00 (Adverse)

(*a*) *Expenditure variance:*

Variable overheads = Actual variable overheads – Standard variable overheads absorbed
= Rs. 556.80 – Rs. 448 = 108.80 (Adverse)

Fixed overheads = Actual fixed overheads – Budgeted fixed overheads
= 1,305.20 – 1,090 = 215.20 (A)

Total overhead expenditure variance = 324.00 (Adverse)

(*b*) Volume variance:

For fixed overheads = Recovered overheads – Budgeted overheads
= Rs. 872 – 1,090 = 218.00 (Adverse)

Total = 542.00 (Adverse)

(*c*) Calendar variance (included in the volume variance):
= Fixed overhead to be absorbed per day

$$= \text{Rs.} \frac{13,080}{240} = 54.50$$

= Loss due to one day Rs. 54.50 (Adverse)

Working Notes:

1. (A) Standard rate of absorption per unit:

Fixed overheads: $\frac{\text{Budgeted fixed overheads}}{\text{Budgeted output}}$

$\frac{12,000}{1,20,000}$ Re. 0.10

Fixed overheads element in semi-variable overheads

i.e., 60% of Rs. 1,800 $\frac{1,080}{1,20,000}$ Re. 0.009

Standard rate of absorption of fixed overheads per unit Re. 0.009

(B) Budgeted variable overheads: Rs. 6,000

Add: Variable element in semi-variable overheads 40% of Rs. 1,800 720

Total budgeted variable overheads 6,720

Standard variable cost per unit $\frac{6,720}{1,20,000}$ 0.056

Variable overheads for 8.000 units @ Re 0.056 = Rs. 448

2. Budgeted annual fixed overheads are:

   Rs. 12,000 + 60% of Rs 1,800 = 13,080

   Budgeted monthly fixed overheads are = Rs. 1,090

3. Actual fixed overheads are Rs. 1,090 + 60% of Rs. 192 = Rs. 1,305.20

4. Actual variable overheads are Rs. 480 + 40% of Rs. 192 = Rs. 556.80

Illustration 23:

The following information was obtained from the records of a manufacturing unit using Standard Costing System:

	Standard	*Actual*
Production	4,000 units	3,800 units
Working days	20	21
Fixed overhead Rs.	40,000	39,000
Variable overhead Rs.	12,000	12,000

You are required to calculate the following overhead variances:

(*a*) Variable overhead variance

(*b*) Fixed overhead variance

(*i*) Expenditure variance

(*ii*) Volume variance

(*iii*) Efficiency variance

(*iv*) Calendar variance.

Also prepare a Reconciliation Statement for the standard fixed expenses worked out at Standard fixed overhead rate and the Actual fixed overhead.

Solution:

Basic calculations	*Budgeted data*	*Actual data*
Variable overhead (Rs.)	12,000	12,000
Fixed overhead (Rs.)	40,000	39,000
Production (units)	4,000	3,800
Working (days)	21	20

Standard variable overhead rate per unit $= \frac{12{,}000}{4{,}000 \text{ units}}$ = Rs. 3

Standard production per day $= \frac{4{,}000 \text{ units}}{20 \text{ days}}$ = 200 units

Standard fixed overhead per day = 200 × Rs. 10 = Rs. 2,000

(*a*) Variable overhead cost variance = Actual variable overhead – Recovered variable overhead

= 12,000 – 3,800 × 3

= 12,000 – 11,400 = Rs. 600 (A)

(*b*) Fixed overhead variance = (Actual fixed overheads – Recovered Fixed overheads)

= 39,000 – 3,800 × 10

= 39,000 – 38,000 = Rs. 1,000 (A)

(*i*) Fixed overhead expenditure variance = Actual overheads – Budgeted overheads

= 39,000 – 40,000 = Rs. 1,000 (F)

(*ii*) Fixed overhead volume variance = Recovered overheads – Budgeted overheads

= 38,000 – 40,000 = Rs. 2,000 (A)

(*iii*) Fixed overhead efficiency variance = Standard fixed overhead rate per day × (Actual time – Standard time for actual output)

= 2,000 × (21 – 3,800/200)

= 2,000 (21 – 19) = 4,000 (A)

(*iv*) Fixed overhead calendar variance = Standard fixed overhead rate per day × (Actual days – Budgeted days)

= 2,000 × (21 – 20)

= Rs. 2,000 (F)

or

Standard fixed overhead rate per day × Extra days/Deficit worked

= 2,000 × 1 = 2,000 (F)

(*c*) Reconciliation statement

Standard fixed overheads 3800 × 100		Rs. 38.000
Less: Fixed overhead expenditure variance	1,000 (F)	
Less: Fixed overhead calendar variance	2,000 (F)	3,000 (F)
		35,000
Add: Fixed overhead efficiency variance (A)		4,000
Actual Fixed Overheads		39,000

Illustration 24:

A Company has normal capacity of 100 machines working 8 hours per day of 25 days in a month. The budgeted fixed overheads of a month are Rs. 1,50,000. The Standard time required to manufacture one unit of product is 4 hours. In a particular month, the Company worked for 24 days of 750 machine hours per day and produced 4,500 units of the product. The actual fixed overheads incurred were Rs. 1,45.000.

Compute:

(*a*) Efficiency variance,
(*b*) Capacity variance,
(*c*) Calendar variance,
(*d*) Expenditure variance,
(*e*) Volume variance, and
(*f*) Total Fixed overhead variance.

Solution:

Standard/Budgeted data		*Actual data*	
Budgeted Fixed overhead (Rs.)	1,50,000	Actual fixed overhead (Rs.)	1,45,000
Budgeted output units	5,000	Actual output units	4,500
Budgeted hours	20,000	Actual hours	18,000
Budgeted days	25	Actual days	24
Standard labour hours per unit	4		
Standard hours worked per day	800		
Standard rate per unit (Rs.)	30		
Standard rate per hour (Rs.)	7.50		
Standard Fixed overhead rate per day (Rs.)	6,000		

Computation of variances:

(*a*) *Efficiency variance:*
= Standard fixed overhead rate per unit (Actual quantity of output – Standard quantity of output)
= Rs. 30 (4,500 units – 4,500 units) = Nil

(*b*) *Capacity variance*
= Standard Fixed overhead rate per hour {Actual capacity hours – Budgeted capacity hours}
= Rs. 7.50 {18,000 hours – 24 days × 800 hours}
= Rs. 7.50 {18,000 hours – 19,200 hours}
= Rs. 9,000 (Adverse)

(*c*) *Calendar variance:*
= Standard fixed overhead rate per day {Actual days – Budgeted days}
= Rs. 6,000 (24 days – 25 days)
= Rs. 6,000 (Adverse)

(*d*) *Expenditure variance*:
= {Budgeted fixed overhead – Actual fixed overhead}
= {Rs. 1,50,000 – Rs. 1,45,000}
= Rs. 5,000 (Favourable)

(*e*) *Volume variance:*
= Standard Fixed overhead rate per unit {Actual output – Budgeted output}
= Rs. 30 (4,500 units – 5.000 units)
= Rs. 15,000 (Adverse)

(*f*) Total fixed overhead variance
{Fixed overhead recovered on actual output – Actual fixed overhead incurred}
= {4.500 units × Rs. 30 – Rs. 1,45,000}
= Rs. 10,000 (Adverse)

Verification:

Total fixed overhead variance = Expenditure variance + Volume variance
or Rs. 10,000 (Adverse) = Rs. 5,000 (Favourable) + Rs. 15.000 (Adverse)
and
Volume variance = Efficiency variance + Capacity variance + Calendar variance
Rs. 15,000 (Adverse) = Nil + Rs. 9,000 (Adverse) + Rs. 6,000 (Adverse)

Illustration 25:

The following data is given:

	Budget	*Actuals*
Production (in units)	400	360
Man-hours to produce above	8,000	7,000
Variable overheads (in rupees)	10,000	9,150

The standard time to produce one unit of the product is 20 hours.

Calculate variable overhead variances.

Solution:

Basic Calculations

1. Standard Variable Overhead per unit:
   Rs. 10,000/400 units = Rs. 25 per unit
2. Standard Variable Overhead per hour:
   Rs. 10,000/8,000 hrs = Rs. 1.25 per hour
3. Recovered Variable Overhead:
   = Actual Output × Standard Variable Overhead per hour
   = 360 units × Rs. 25 = Rs. 9,000
4. Budgeted Variable Overhead (based on actual hours worked):
   = Actual Hours Worked × Standard Variable Overhead per hour
   = 7,000 Hrs. × Rs. 1.25 – Rs. 8.750
5. Standard Hours for actual output:
   = Actual Output × Standard Hours per unit
   = 360 units × 20 Hours = 7,200 hours

Computation of Variances:

(*i*) Variable Overhead Cost Variance:
= Recovered Variable Overhead – Actual Variable Overheads
= Rs. 9,000 – Rs. 9,150 = Rs. 150 (A)

(*ii*) Variable Overhead Budget or Expenditure Variance:
= Budgeted Variable Overheads – Actual Variable Overheads
= Rs. 8.750 – Rs. 9,150 = Rs. 400 (A)

(*iii*) Variable Overhead Efficiency Variance:
= Standard Variable Overhead per hour (Standard Hours for Actual Output – Actual Hours)
= Recovered Variable Overheads – Budgeted Variable Overheads
= Rs. 9,000 – Rs. 8,750
= Rs. 250 (F)

Verification

Variable Overhead Cost Variance = Variable Overhead Budgets Variance + Variable Overhead Efficiency Variance

Rs. 150 (A) = Rs. 400 (A) + Rs. 250 (F)

Illustration 26:

The following data has been collected from the cost records of a unit for computing the various fixed overhead variances for a period:

Number of Budgeted Working Days	25
Budgeted Man-hours per day	6,000
Output (budgeted) per man hour (in units)	1
Fixed Overhead cost as budgeted	Rs. 1,50,000
Actual Number of Working days	27
Actual man-hours per day	6,300
Actual Output per man-hour (in units)	0.9
Actual Fixed Overhead Variances:	Rs. 1,56,000

Calculate Fixed Overhead Variances:

(*a*) Expenditure Variance;
(*b*) Calendar Variance;
(*c*) Capacity Variance;
(*d*) Efficiency Variance;
(*e*) Volume Variance;
(*f*) Fixed Cost Variance.

Solution:

(*a*) FOEXV = Budgeted Fixed Overheads – Actual Fixed Overheads
= Rs. 1,50,000 – Rs. 1,56,000
= Rs. 6,000 (Adverse)

(*b*) FOCALV = No. off excess Working Days × Fixed Overhead Rate per Day
= 2 × 6.000 = Rs. 12.000 (Favourable)

OR Possible Overheads – Budgeted Overheads
= 27 × 6,000 – 25 × 6,000
= Rs. 1,52,000 – 1,50,000 = Rs. 12,000 (Favourable)

(*c*) FOCAPV (Revised) = Standard Overheads – Possible Overheads
= Re. 1 × 6,300 × 27 – 1,62,000
= Rs. 1,70,100 – 1,62,000 = Rs. 8,100 (Favourable)

(*d*) FOEFFV = Recovered Overheads – Standard Overheads
= 9 × 6,300 × 27 – 1,70,100
= Rs. 1,53,090 – 1,70,100 = Rs. 17,010 (Adverse)

(e) FOCV = FOEXPV + FOVV
= FOEXPV + FOCALV + FORCAPV + FOEFFV
= Rs. 6,000 (A) + Rs. 12,000 (F) + 8,100 (F) + 17,010 (A)
= Rs. 2,910 (Adverse)

CONTROL RATIOS

Control ratios are useful to management to know whether the deviations of actuals from budgeted results are favourable or unfavourable. These control ratios are expressed in percentage. The ratio is taken as favourable if it is 100% or more. In case it is less than 100%, the ratio is considered as unfavourable. Control ratios are as follows:

1. *Activity-Ratio:* Activity ratio is used to measure the level of activity achieved over a period. It is obtained when the number of standard hours equivalent to the output produced are expressed at a percentage of the budgeted hours.

$$\text{Activity ratio} = \frac{\text{Standard hrs. for actual production}}{\text{Budgeted hours}} \times 100$$

2. *Capacity Ratio:* This ratio points out to what extent budgeted hours have been utilised. This ratio shows the relationship between actual working hours and budgeted working hours.

3. *Efficiency Ratio:* Efficiency ratio shows the degree of efficiency achieved in production. It derived when the standard hours equivalent to the output produced, are expressed as a percentage of the actual hours spent in producing the output.

$$\text{Efficiency ratio} = \frac{\text{Standard hours for actual production}}{\text{Actual hours worked}} \times 100$$

Illustration 27:

In a manufacturing shop product X requires 2.5 man-hours and product Y requires 6 man-hours. In a month of 25 working days of 8 hours a day, 2,000 units of X and 1,000 units of Y were produced. The company employs 50 workers in the shop and the budgeted man-hours are 1,08,000 for the year. You are required to work out the capacity ratio, activity ratio and efficiency ratio.

Solution:

Standard man-hours produced:

Product X: 2.000 units @	2.5 Man-hours	= 5,000 Man-hours
Product Y: 1.000 units @	6 Man-hours	= 6,000 Man-hours
	Total	= 11,000 Man-hours

Budgeted man-hours per month = 1,08,000/12
= 9,000

Actual man-hours worked = 50 workers × 25 days × 8 hours = 10,000 man-hours

Ratios:

$$\text{Capacity ratio} = \frac{\text{Actual Man-hours worked}}{\text{Budgeted Man-hours}} \times 100$$

$$= \frac{10,000}{9,000} \times 100 = 111.11\%$$

$$\text{Activity ratio} = \frac{\text{Standard man-hours produced}}{\text{Budgeted man-hours}} \times 100$$

$$= \frac{11,000}{9,000} \times 100 = 122.22\%$$

$$\text{Efficiency ratio} = \frac{\text{Standard man-hours produced}}{\text{Actual man-hours worked}} \times 100$$

$$= \frac{11,000}{10,000} \times 100 = 111.00\%$$

Illustration 28:

If the 'activity ratio' and 'capacity ratio' of a company is 104% and 96% respectively, find out its 'efficiency ratio.'

Solution:

The various ratios are calculated as under:

$$(i)\ \text{Activity Ratio} = \frac{\text{Standard hours for actual production}}{\text{Budgeted hours}} \times 100$$

(*ii*) Capacity Ratio $= \dfrac{\text{Actual hours worked}}{\text{Budgeted hours}} \times 100$

(*iii*) Efficiency Ratio $= \dfrac{\text{Standard hours for actual production}}{\text{Actual hours worked}} \times 100$

From the above, it is clear that the Efficiency Ratio can be obtained by dividing Activity Ratio by Capacity Ratio.

Hence,

Efficiency Ratio (in percentage) $= \dfrac{\text{Activity Ratio}}{\text{Capacity Ratio}} \times 100$

$= \dfrac{104\%}{96\%} \times 100 = 108.33\%$

Illustration 29:

Calculate from the following figures:

(*i*) Efficiency ratio

(*ii*) Activity Ratio and

(*iii*) Capacity Ratio

Budgeted Production	880 units
Standard Hours Per Unit	10
Actual Production	750 units
Actual Working Hours	6,000

Solution:

(*i*) Efficiency Ratio $= \dfrac{\text{Standard hours for actual production}}{\text{Actual hours worked}} \times 100$

$= \dfrac{750 \text{ units} \times 10 \text{ hours}}{6{,}000} \times 100 = 125\%$

(*ii*) Activity Ratio $= \dfrac{\text{Standard hours for actual production}}{\text{Budgeted hours}} \times 100$

$= \dfrac{750 \text{ units} \times 10 \text{ hours}}{880 \text{ units} \times 10 \text{ hours}} \times 100 = 85.23\%$

(*iii*) Capacity Ratio $= \dfrac{\text{Actual hours worked}}{\text{Budgeted hours}} \times 100$

$= \dfrac{6{,}000 \text{ hours}}{880 \text{ units} \times 10 \text{ hours}} \times 100 = 68.18\%$

DISPOSITION OF VARIANCES

Variance may be disposed off in either of the following ways:

1. Inventories and the cost of goods sold may be adjusted to reflect the actual costs.
2. Variances may be transferred to the profit and loss account.

Under the First method, all variances are allocated between the inventory accounts and cost of goods sold account. This method, in fact, converts the accounts balances from standard costs to actual historical costs.

The following arguments are given in support of this method:

1. Only actual costs should be recorded in the cost of goods sold account and inventory accounts. The supporters of this method do not favour standard costs as true costs or costs suitable for use in the profit and loss account but as merely guides in factory management.
2. Variances from the standard are costs and not losses and therefore should be reflected in the inventory valuations and cost of goods sold.
3. If the variances are large, standard costs do not represent the actual costs and therefore are not good measures to determine the costs of goods sold and inventory.

Under the second method, the variances are considered as profit or loss items in the period in which they occurred. The work-in-process, finished goods inventory, and cost of goods sold are stated at standard costs. Unfavourable cost variances are deducted from the gross profit at standard costs. Favourable cost variances are added to the gross profit calculated at standard cost. The treatment of the cost variances under this method is shown on the income statement given below.

ABC Company

Income Statement for the Year Ending December 31, 2009

	Rs.	Rs.
Sales revenue		5,00,000
Cost of sales (standard)	3,00,000	
Selling and administrative expenses (standard)	1,50,000	4,50,000
Net Income (standard)		50,000
Deduct unfavourable variance from net income:		
Material price	200	
Material usage	800	
Labour efficiency	900	
Overhead:		
Volume	2,000	
Budget	1,100	5,000
		45,000

The second method has the following arguments in its favour:

1. Standard costs help in the preparation of statements at the early date; actual cost delays the determination of inventory costs and cost of goods sold.
2. Standard costs avoid the inclusion of costs due to wastage, losses, inefficiencies, excessive overheads from low production volume. Standard cost represent normal costs and therefore inventory figures are conservative and acceptable for income determination and other purposes.
3. In a multi-product company, it may be difficult to determine accurately how much variance should be distributed to each product.

4. In taking corrective action managers may find it more useful when variance are depicted in the profit and loss account. Managerial attention is usually hampered when variances are combined with cost of goods manufactured.

It is difficult to suggest which method should be followed in accounting for variances. If the variances are large and significant, the first method, *i.e.,* distribution of variances to the respective accounts appears to be appropriate for financial reporting, tax and job and contract pricing purposes. The second method may be preferable when the variances are insignificant. Thus, the treatment of variances depends on many factors such as (*i*) size of variance, (*ii*) accuracy of standard costs, (*iii*) cause of variances such as incorrect standard costs, (*iv*) timing of variances, e.g., caused by seasonal fluctuation, (*v*) type of variance material, labour, and overhead.

MANAGERIAL USES OF VARIANCES

Determination of variances is only the first step in the process of standard cost variance analysis. Mere computation of material, labour and overhead variances is useless for cost control and performance evaluation. The final objective of variance analysis is to determine the person(s) responsible for each variance and to pinpoint the cause(s) for incurrence of these variances. That is, before management can take effective action for improving control over costs, it needs to know not only the amount of variances, but also where the variances originated, who was responsible for them, and what caused them to arise.

Analysis of Variances by Responsibilities

Variances must be identified with the manager responsible for the costs incurred who should be held responsible for that cost. The cost factors which are directly controllable by operating supervision must be separated from those cost factors for which executive management is responsible.

Specific titles of individuals who are responsible for each type of variance differ among business enterprises. Generally speaking, the following personnel are held accountable for variances noted against them:

Responsibility for Cost Variances

Variance	*Personnel Responsible*
(*i*) Materials price variance	Purchasing agent or purchasing manager.
(*ii*) Materials quantity variance	Plant superintendent, departmental supervisors, machine operators, quality control department and material handlers.
(*iii*) Labour rate standard	Personnel (employment) department manager, departmental supervisor and plant superintendent.
(*iv*) Labour efficiency variance	Plant superintendent, departmental supervisors, production scheduling department, quality control department, material handlers and machine operators.
(*v*) Overhead expenditure variance	Variable portion is the responsibility of the individual foreman or supervisor, they are expected to keep actual expenses within the budget. Fixed portion is the responsibility of top management.
(*vi*) Overhead efficiency variance	Same personnel who are responsible for labour efficiency variance.
(*vii*) Overhead volume variance	Top management and production schedulers.

Analysis of Variances by Causes

Reasons for the variance should be determined and plans for necessary corrective action made either by discussing possible causes with the supervisors or by examining underlying data and records. The analysis of variances by causes is therefore an important aspect of the use of standard costs to attain effective cost control. For any standard cost variance, there are many possible causes. The following list is not all inclusive but does indicate causes responsible for variances.

Possible Causes of Standard Cost Variances

Materials Price Variance

1. Recent changes in purchase price of materials.
2. Failure to purchase anticipated quantities when standards were established resulting in higher prices owing to non-availability of quantity purchase discounts.
3. Not taking cash discounts anticipated at the time of setting standards resulting in higher prices.
4. Substituting raw material differing from original materials specifications.
5. Freight cost changes and changes in purchasing and storekeeping costs if these arc debited to the materials cost.

Materials Quantity Variance

1. Poor materials handling.
2. Inferior workmanship by machine operator.
3. Faulty equipment.
4. Cheaper, defective raw material causing excessive scrap.
5. Inferior quantity control inspection.
6. Pilferage.
7. Wastage due to inefficient production method.

Labour Rate Variance

1. Recent labour rate changes within industry.
2. Employing a man of a grade different from the one laid down in the standard.
3. Labour strike leading to utilisation of unskilled help.
4. Labour layoff causing skilled labour to be retained at higher rates, so as to prevent resignations and job switching.
5. Employee sickness and vacation time.
6. Paying a higher overtime allowance than provided for in the standard.

Labour Efficiency Variance

1. Machine breakdown, use of defective machinery and equipment.
2. Inferior raw materials.
3. Poor supervision.
4. Lack of timely material handling.
5. Poor employee performance.
6. Inefficient production scheduling — delays in routing work, materials, tools and instructions.
7. Inferior engineering specifications

8. New inexperienced employees.
9. Insufficient training of workers.
10. Poor working conditions — inadequate or excessive heating, lighting, ventilation, etc.

Overhead Volume Variance

(Factors causing either idle time or overtime of plant and facilities)

1. Failure to utilise normal capacity
2. Lack of sales order
3. Too much idle capacity
4. Inefficient or efficient utilisation of existing capacity
5. Machine breakdown
6. Defective materials
7. Labour troubles
8. Power failures.

Overhead Efficiency Variance

These included all causes which are listed under labour efficiency variance.

Analysis of Variances by Products

Since management usually wants current true costs when decisions are to be made with respect to pricing and related questions, variances are often analysed by products in order to arrive at current product costs. Companies producing non-standard goods according to customer's specifications may also help analyse variances by job orders. The analysis of variances by causes is useful in deciding whether or not cost variances should be allocated to products in arriving at product costs for pricing. Standard product costs should be reviewed periodically and revised when it is found that the standard product costs in use are no longer useful for the purpose.

Variance Reports to Management

Variance reports basically aim to inform managers responsible for the operation when actual performance differs from the standards. To be effective, the report must be timely, accurate and clearly understood by the recipients.

Control of production and costs is a matter of timing; the effectiveness of the control is often in direct proportion to the speed with which variances are reported. Timely reporting often requires daily and weekly reporting of performance information. Therefore, it is important to focus managerial attention on off-standard conditions immediately following each shift, day or week, rather than to accumulate and summarise variances from standards each month. A month, and generally even a week, is too long a period for many off-standard conditions to remain unchecked and uncorrected, because the time interval may prevent positive identification of employees who are responsible for the unsatisfactory work.

Variance analysis reports are primarily control reports. In developing and reporting the variance, it should be remembered that the variance data must (*i*) deal with relevant distinctions (*ii*) be understandable, (*iii*) measure with reasonable accuracy what they are supposed to measure, (*iv*) be presented and explained concisely, (*v*) be timely, and (*vi*) provide the amount of details needed by different persons at each level of management.

LIMITATIONS OF STANDARD COSTING

Standard costs are not without their shortcomings. The first limitation is regarding the predetermined nature of standard costs. The accuracy of standard costs is limited by the knowledge and skill of the people who created them and they contain the prejudices of their makers. Such badly conceived standard costs do not enjoy the confidence of the users of the system.

Secondly, it is difficult to select a type of standard (ideal, currently attainable, normal etc.) which can help in cost control and achieve other managerial purposes. If standards are too low, they defeat the objective of standard costing and bring the operating efficiency down. If they are too high, they can create ill-will and encourage employees to beat the system by fair means or foul.

Thirdly, a good programme of standard costing requires that both management and operating personnel should have full confidence in it and standards should be fair and workable. Educating employees is necessary in this regard. However, lack of acceptability, education and communication is a major difficulty in operating a standard costing system.

In spite of the above limitations, standard costing has developed into an extraordinary and very useful tool and has contributed much in providing different kinds of cost data for so many different purposes.

THEORY QUESITONS

1. Define and explain the concepts of standard cost and standard costing.
2. Discuss briefly the use of standard costs in the following management activities: cost reductions, operating performance, evaluation, product pricing decisions and providing incentives.
3. Compare and contrast the usefulness of ideal standards, basic standards, and currently attainable standards.
4. "Standard costs are bases for a proper managerial control of manufacturing operation." Define standard cost and explain the above statement.
5. What is standard costing and how would you distinguish it from budgetary control?
6. What are the points of similarity and difference between budgeted and standard costs?
7. "Variance analysis is an integral part of standard cost accounting." Explain this statement.
8. By purchasing low-grade materials, a company reports favourable material price variance, but it consistently experience infavourable material quantity variances. What relationship may exist between these conditions? Is the price variance really favourable?
9. What are the shortcomings of historical costs for managerial uses?
10. What is the difference between an estimated cost and a standard cost?
11. Describe briefly how standard costs are set for (*a*) material (*b*) labour.
12. Briefly explain the meaning of each of the following variances: material prices, material usage, labour efficiency, and labour rate.
13. Discuss some of the problems that might be created by standards which are set too high and by standards which are too loose.
14. What are the advantages and limitations of standard costing?
15. Discuss briefly some of the limitations of standard costs.
16. Explain why overhead variances are gene~ally treated as period costs.
17. Discuss the information which a well designed cost report should give to management from the point of view of production and control. How should such information be given?
18. What is a "two variance analysis" of factory overheads. Give a brief description.
19. Explain the term 'variance' and distinguish between controllable and uncontrollable variances.
20. Describe briefly the managerial use of variances.

EXERCISES AND PROBLEMS

1. The standard quantity and standard price of raw material required for one unit of Product A are given as follows:

	Quantity	Selling price
Material *X*	2 kg.	Rs. 3 per kg
Material *Y*	4 kg.	Rs. 2 per kg.
	6 kg.	

The actual production and relevant data are as follows:

Material	Total quantity for 500 units	Total cost (Rs.)
X	1,100 kg.	3,410
Y	1,800 kg.	3,960

Calculate the variances

(*Ans.:* Material cost variance Rs. 370(A) usage variance Rs. 100 (F)).
Material price variance Rs. 470 (A)

2. From the data given below, calculate the materials price variance, the materials usage variance and materials mix variance. Consumption per 100 units of product:

Raw material	Standard	Actual
A	40 units @ Rs. 50 per unit	50 units @ Rs. 50 per unit
B	60 units @ Rs. 40 per unit	60 units @ Rs. 45 per unit

(*Ans.:* Material price variance Rs. 300(A); Mix variance Rs. 60(A); Usage variance Rs. 500(A)

3. XY Ltd. manufacturers of Product *P*, uses a standard cost system. Standard product and cost specifications for 1,000 kg. of Product *P* are as follows:

Ingredients	Quantity (kg.)	Price Rs. per kg.	Cost
A	800	2.50	2,000
B	200	4.00	800
C	200	1.00	200
Input	1,200		3,000 = Rs. 2.50 per kg.
Output	1,000		3,000 = Rs. 3.00 per kg.

Material records indicate:	Consumption in January
A	1,57,000 kg. @ Rs. 2.40
B	38,000 kg. @ Rs. 4.20
C	36,000 kg. @ Rs. 1.10

Actual finished production for the month of January is 2,00,000 kg. Calculate:

1. Materials price variance
2. Materials mix variance
3. Materials yield variance

[*Ans.:* Rs. 4,500(F); Rs. 3,000(A); Rs. 22,500(F)].

4. The following standard and actual data is given about a product:

	Standard			Actual		
Material	*Qty.*	*Price (Rs.)*	*Total (Rs.)*	*Qty.*	*Price (Rs.)*	*Total (Rs.)*
A	500	6	3,000	400	6	2,400
B	400	3.75	1,500	500	3.60	1,800
C	300	3.00	900	400	2.80	1,120
	1,200			1,300		
Less:			Actual loss	220		
10% loss	120					
	1,080		5,400	1,080		Rs. 5,320

Calculate: (*i*) Materials cost variance
(*ii*) Materials price variance
(*iii*) Materials mix variance
(*iv*) Materials yield variance
(*v*) Total material usage variance.

(***Ans.:*** (*i*) Rs. 80(A), (*ii*) Rs. 155(F) (*iii*) Rs. 375(F), (*iv*) Rs. 450(A) (*v*) 75 (A))

5. The standard cost of a certain chemical mixture is:

40% Material A at Rs. 200 per kg.

60% Material B at Rs. 300 per kg.

A standard loss of 10% is expected in production. During a period materials used are:

90 kg. Material A at the cost of Rs. 180 per kg.

110 kg. Material B at the cost of Rs. 340 per kg.

The weight produced is 182 kg. of good production.

Calculate and present:

(*i*) Materials price variance
(*ii*) Materials usage variance
(*iii*) Materials mix variance
(*iv*) Materials yield variance

(***Ans.:*** (*i*) Rs. 2,600 (A) (*ii*) Rs. 1,577.77(F) (*iii*) Rs. 1,000 (F) (*iv*) Rs. 577.77(F))

6. Mixers Ltd. is engaged in producing a 'standard mix' using 60 kg of chemical X and 40 kg of chemical Y. The standard loss of production is 30%. The standard price of X is Rs. 5 per kg. and Y is Rs. 10 per kg.

The actual mixture and yield were as follows:

X 80 kg. @ Rs. 4.50 per kg. and

Y 70 kg. @ Rs. 8.00 per kg.

Actual yield 115 kg. Calculate material variances

(***Ans.:*** Material cost variance Rs. 230 (F)
Material price variance Rs. 180 (F)
Material usage variance Rs. 50 (F)
Material mix variance Rs. 50 (A).

7. The standard material inputs required for 1,000 kgs. of a finished product are given below:

Material (in kg)	Quantity (in Rs.)	Standard Rate per kg (in Rs.)
P	450	20
Q	400	40
R	250	60
	1,100	
Standard Loss	100	
Standard Output	1,000	

Actual production in a period was 20,000 kgs. of the finished product for which the actual quantities of material used and the prices paid thereof are as under:

Material	Quantity used (in kgs.)	Purchased price per kg. (in Rs.)
P	10,000	19
Q	8,500	42
R	4,500	65

Calculate:

(*i*) Material Cost Variance (MCV)
(*ii*) Material Price Variance (MPV)
(*iii*) Material Usage Variance (MUV)
(*iv*) Material Mix Variance (MMV)
(*v*) Material Yield Variance (MYV)
Present a reconciliation among the variances

(*Ans.:* Material Cost Variance Rs. 39,500(A)
Material Price Variance Rs. 29,500 (A)
Material Usage Variance Rs, 10,000 (A)
Material Mix Variance Rs. 26,360 (F)
Material Yield Variance Rs. 36,360 (A)

Statement of Reconciliation of Variances

Particulars	Rs.	Rs.
(*i*) Material Price Variance		29,500 (A)
(*ii*) Material Usage Variance:		
(*a*) Material Mix Variance	26,363 (F)	
(*b*) Material Yield Variance	36,363 (A)	10,000 (A)
Material Cost Variance		39,500 (A)

8. AB Ltd. has established the following standard mix for producing gallons of product A:

		Rs.
5 gallons of material X at Rs. 7 per gallon	=	35
3 gallons of material Y at Rs. 5 per gallon	=	15
2 gallons of material Z at Rs. 2 per gallon	=	4
		Rs. 54

A standard loss of 10% of output is expected to occur. Actual input was as a under:

53,000 gallons of material X at Rs. 7 per gallon.

28,000 gallons of material Y at Rs. 5.30 per gallon.

19.000 gallons of material Z as Rs. 2.20 per gallon.

Actual output for a period was 92,700 gallons of product A.

Compute:

(*i*) Material Mix Variance

(*ii*) Material Yield Variance

[*Ans.:* Material Mix Variance Rs. 9,000(A)
Material Yield Variance Rs. 16,200 (F)]

9. The standard cost of a certain chemical mixture is 40% material A @ Rs. 20 per kg.; 60% material B @ Rs. 3,000 per kg. A standard loss of 10% is expected in production. During a period of one month 90 kg. of material A @ Rs. 1,800 per kg. and 100 kg. of material B @ 3,400 per kg. were used to produce 182 kg. of good production. Calculate the (*a*) materials price variance (*b*) materials mix variance, and (*c*) materials yield variance.

[*Ans.:* (*a*) Rs. 2600 (A); (*b*) Rs. 10000 (F); (*c*) Rs. 578 (F)]

10. (*a*) The standard set for material consumption was 100 kg @ Rs. 2.25 per kg .

In a cost period:	Opening stocks was	100 kg @Rs. 2.25 per kg.
	Purchase made	500 kg @Rs. 2.25 per kg.
	Consumption	110 kg @

Calculate:

(*a*) Usage variance.

(*b*) Price variance: (*i*) when variance is calculated at point of purchase; (*ii*) when variance is calculated at point of issue on FIFO basis; (*iii*) when variance is calculated at point of issue on LIFO basis.

(*c*) What is the effect on closing stock valuation when materials are charged out to cost on basis (*ii*) and (*iii*) above?

(*Ans.:* (*a*) Usage variance Rs. 22.50 (A)
(*b*) (*i*) Rs. 50 (F) (*ii*) Re. 1 (F) (*iii*) Rs. 11 (F)

11. From the data given below, calculate labour variances for the two departments:

	Deptt. A	*Deptt. B*
Actual gross wages (Direct)	Rs. 2,000	Rs. 1,800
Standard hours produced	8,000	6,000
Standard rate per hour	Rs 30	Rs. 35
Actual hours worked	8,200	5,800

12. The details regarding composition and the weekly wage rates of labour force engaged on a job scheduled to be completed in 30 hours are as follows:

Category of workers	*No. of labourers*	*Standard hourly wage rate*	*Actual no. of labourers*	*Hourly wage rate*
Skilled	75	60	70	70
Semi-skilled	45	40	30	50
Unskilled	60	30	80	20

The work is actually completed in 32 hours. Calculate the various laЂour variances.

[*Ans.:* Labour cost variance, Rs. 13,000 (A), Rate variance Rs. 6,400 (A), Labour efficiency 6,600 (A), Mix variance Rs. 9,600 (F), Labour sub-efficiency Rs. 16,200 (A)]

13. A chemical company gives you the following standard and actual data of its Chemical No. 1456. You are required to calculate variances.

Standard data (*kg.*)		*Total* (*Rs.*)	*Actual data*		*Total* (*Rs.*)
450	of Material A @ 20 per kg.	9,000	450 kg. @ 19 per kg.	8,550	
360	of Material B @ 10 per kg.	3,600	360 kg @ 11 per kg.	3,960	12,510
810		12,600	810		
	2,400 skilled hours @ Rs. 20 per hour	48,000	2,400 hrs. @ 25	5,400	60,000
	1,200 unskilled hours @ Rs. 10 per hour	12,000	1,200 hrs. @ 15	1,500	18,000
		60,000			78,000
90	Normal loss		50 kg. Actual loss		
720		72,600	760 kg.		90,510

14. Vinak Ltd. has furnished you the following information for the month of August, 2009:

	Budget	*Actual*
Output (Units)	30,000	32,500
Hours	30,000	33,000
Fixed overhead	Rs. 45,000	50,000
Variable overhead	Rs. 60,000	68,000
Working days	25	26

Calculate the variances.

(***Ans.:*** Total overhead cost variance Rs. 4,250 (A)
Variable overhead cost variance Rs. 3,000 (A)
Fixed overhead cost variance Rs. 1,250 (A)
Expenditure variance Rs. 1,250 (A)
Volume variance Rs. 3,750 (F)
Efficiency variance Rs. 750 (A)
Capacity variance Rs. 4,500 (F)
Calender variance Rs. 1,800 (F)

15. The following figures are extracted from the books of a company: Budgeted overhead Rs. 10,000 (Fixed Rs. 6,000; Variable Rs. 4,000)

Budgeted hours	2,000
Actual overhead	10,400 (fixed Rs. 6,100; variable Rs. 4,300)
Actual hours Rs. 2,100	

Compute the overhead variances.

(***Ans.:*** Overhead cost Rs. 100(F), Variable overhead 100(A), Fixed overhead Rs. 200(F))

16. Narang Ltd., produces two commodities, Good and Better, in one of its departments. Each unit takes 5 hrs. and 10 hrs. as production time, respectively. 1,000 units of Good and 600 units of Better were produced during March 2008. Actual man-hours spent in this production were 10,000. Yearly budgeted hours are 96,000. Compute the various control ratios.

(***Ans.:*** Capacity ratio 1.25
Efficiency ratio 1.10
Activity ratio 1.8)

17. ABC Ltd. manufactures two products A and B. Product A takes 6 hours to make while product B takes 12 hours. In a month of 25 days of 8 hours each, 1,200 units of A and 750 units of B were produced. The firm employs 75 men in the department responsible for producing these two products. The budgeted hours are 1,86,000 per annum. You are required to calculate activity ratio, capacity ratio and efficiency ratio.

(*Ans.:* Activity ratio 104.5%
Capacity utilisation ratio 96.8%
Efficiency ratio 108%)

18. From the following data, calculate activity ratio. A factory manufactures two products A and B. Standard time to manufacture product A is 2 hours and product B 10 hours. The budgeted and actual production in December 2009 were as follows:

	Budgeted Production	*Actual Production*
Product A	125 units	100 units
Product B	30 units	24 units

Total hours worked were 660.

(*Ans.:* Activity ratio 80%.)

Budgeting

CONCEPT OF BUDGETING

One of the primary objectives of cost accounting is to provide information to business managements for planning and control. Budgeting acts as tool of both planning and control. Budgeting is a formal process of financial planning using estimated financial and accounting data. The Institute of Cost and Management Accountants (UK) defines a budget as "a financial and/or quantitative statement, prepared and approved prior to a defined period of time, of the policy to be pursued during that period for the purpose claiming a given objective. It may include income, expenditure and the employment of capital."

BUDGETING AND FORECASTING

Sometimes the terms "budgeting" and "forecasting" are used interchangeably. Both terms have some similarities, for example, both relate to future events and involve prediction of something. The basic difference between budgeting and forecasting lies in degree of sophistication involved in the predictions used by them. According to the National Association of Accountants (USA), "forecasting is a process of predicting or estimating a future happening." Forecasting is an essential part of the budgeting process. Forecasting is estimating future events and their effects on the budget. Forecasting comes to an end after mere estimating. Budgeting is a process of preparing budgets and further control aspects are involved in its procedure. Besides, forecasting can be made by a firm for purposes other than budgeting such as a forecast of general business conditions. Such forecasts are sometimes not used in budgeting.

Thus, budgeting is not merely forecasting of a particular event. It is not simply an estimation or prediction, it is a plan. In simple terms, budgeting is an attempt, at the beginning of the year (or at any other period), to plan the profit and loss account for the year and to aim for a definite balance sheet at its end, instead of relying upon chance.

CONCEPT OF BUDGETARY CONTROL

Budgetary control is a means of control in which the actual state affairs is compared with the budget so that appropriate action may be taken with regard to any deviations before it is too late. Briefly, the use of a budget to control a firm's activities is known as budgeting control. Budgetary control has the following objectives:

1. To provide an organised procedure for planning. It provides a detailed plan of action for a business over a definite period of time.
2. To coordinate all the activities of various departments of a business firm in such a manner that the maximum profit will be achieved for the minimum use of resources.
3. To provide a means of determining the responsibility for all deviations from the plan (budget), and to supply information on the basis of which necessary corrective action may be taken. Thus the budgetary control has the objective of controlling cost.

OBJECTIVES AND FUNCTIONS OF BUDGETING

An effective budgeting system is vital to the success of a business firm. Budgeting is needed in organisations to perform the following functions: (*i*) planning, (*ii*) coordination, (*iii*) communication, and (*iv*) control and performance evaluation.

Planning

Almost all business activities require some planning to ensure efficient and maximum use of scarce resources. The budget is a formal planning framework that provides specific deadlines to achieve departmental objectives and contributes towards the overall objectives of an organization. A budget incorporates expected performance and present managerial targets. These targets guide the business operations and help in overcoming problems and analysing the future. Budgeting influences the formulation of all business strategies and subsequently assists business managers in executing such strategies.

Coordination

Coordination is a managerial function under which all factors of production and all departmental activities are balanced and integrated to achieve the objective of the organisation. The budgeting process provides the basis for individuals in all parts of the organisation to exchange ideas on how best to achieve these objectives. According to Horngreen*, budgets help management to coordinate in the following ways:

1. The existence of a well-laid plan is the major step towards achieving coordination. Executives are forced to think of the relationships among individual operations, and the company as a whole.
2. Budgets help to restrain the empire-building efforts of executives. Budgets broaden individual thinking by helping to remove unconscious biases on the part of engineers, sales and production officers.
3. Budgets help to search out weaknesses in the organisational structure. The formulation and administration of budgets isolate problems of communication, of fixed responsibility, and of working relationships.

---

* Charles T. Horngreen, *Cost Accounting,* A Managerial Emphasis, Prentice-Hall of India, New Delhi, p. 123.

Communication

It is necessary in an efficient organisation that all people be informed about the objectives, policies, programmes and performances. This is made possible through their participation in the budgeting process. Budgets inform each manager of what others have agreed to do. They also inform managers of the resources available to achieve objectives and targets.

Control and Performance Evaluation

Budgeting enters into control at three points:

1. When a budget is being formulated, departments analyse their plans for the future and submit estimates as per their requirements, justifying each of their demands by demonstrating a need.
2. After budgets of different departments have been reviewed and approved they become targets that set desirable limits on spending.
3. At the end of the budget period, a comparison of actual expenditures with budget expenditure is made as a means of judging performance and fixing responsibility for deviations.

Budgets are the basis of performance evaluation in an organisation as they reflect realistic estimates of acceptable and expected performance. It is more accurate, reliable and reasonable to measure current performance against a budget rather than against a vague expectation or against results of previous year when conditions might have changed.

ADVANTAGES OF BUDGETING

Budgeting plays an important role in the effective use of resources and achieving overall organisational goals. It has the following advantages:

1. Budgeting compels and motivates management to make an early and timely study of its problems. It generates a sense of caution and care and adequate study among managers before decisions are made by them.
2. Budgeting provides a valuable means of controlling income and expenditure of a business as it is a "plan for spending."
3. Budgeting provides a tool through which managerial policies and goals are periodically evaluated, tested and established as guidelines for the entire organisation.
4. Budgeting helps in directing capital and other resources into the most profitable channels.
5. Budgeting coordinates and correlates all business activities. It enables management to decentralise responsibility without losing control of the business. It reveals weaknesses, inefficiencies, deviations in the organisation very promptly which can be checked immediately to achieve a desired goal.
6. The use of budgeting in an organisation develops an attitude of "cost consciousness," stimulates the effective use of resources, and creates an environment of profit-mindedness throughout the organisation.
7. It provides a norm, basis or yardstick for measuring performance of departments and individuals working in organisations.
8. Budgeting encourages productive competition, provides incentive to perform efficiently and gives a sense of purpose to each individual in the organisation.
9. Budgeting provides a systematic and disciplined approach to the solution of problems in the organisation. Horngreen observes: "The uppermost point is that budgets provide a discipline that brings planning to the forefront as a key managerial responsibility."

10. Budgeting, if executed in nearly every enterprise, helps the total national economy by providing stability of employment, economic use of resources and effective prevention of waste.

LIMITATIONS OF BUDGETING

While budgeting has many advantages that are vital to an organisation, it has certain limitations which require consideration.

1. Planning, budgeting or forecasting is not an exact science; it uses approximations and judgement which may not be cent per cent accurate. At best, a budget is an estimate; no one knows precisely what will happen in the future.
2. The success and utility of budgeting depends on the cooperation and participation of all members of management. Many a time budgeting has failed because executive management has paid only lip service to its execution.
3. A budget is only a tool and neither eliminates nor takes over the place of management. Executives generally feel "circled in" by a budget and its related figures. They fail to understand that budget is meant to provide detailed information, goals and targets which may help them in achieving the company objectives.
4. The establishment of a budgeting process takes lime. Also, sometimes too much is expected from a budget and in case expectations are not fulfilled, the blame is put on the budget.
5. Excessive emphasis on budgeting may result in attempts by lower level management and employees to buck the system by providing inaccurate estimates of future costs and revenues. As the end of budget period approaches and employees realize that actual expenses have not been as great as allowed by the budget, there may be a temptation to spend excessive amounts in order to "use up" the budget allowance. Such activities result in sub-optimal profits for the company,

BUDGETING PROCESS

The budgeting process or programme varies widely from one organisation to another. Differences in management style, organisation objectives, structure of competition and similar factors affect the procedures companies adopt in budget preparations. However, there are a set of guidelines (procedures) which are used in the budgeting process by a large number of organisations. These common steps can be listed as follows:

1. *Obtaining estimates of sales, production levels, expected costs, and availability of resources from each sub-unit/division/department:* The departmental heads or managers are required to provide estimates of future conditions and activities that will have an impact on the company.
2. *Coordinating estimates:* In many organisations, the budget committee evaluates the different plans submitted by various organisational units to determine the potentiality of plans in the overall interest of the company and to estimate what resources are available and can be fairly allocated among the various units of the organisation.
3. *Communicating the budget to responsible managers and the concerned departments:* After individual budget plans have been approved in the light of organisational goals and availability of resources, the budgets should be communicated to departments and responsible managers. Changes and modification incorporated in the final budget should be made known to managers to obtain their cooperation and support for the budgets.

4. *Implementing the budget plan:* The final budget is presented to the managers concerned and adopted as the plan of operation for the coming budget period.
5. *Reporting interim progress towards budgeted objectives:* As a feedback in the budgeting process, performance reports are prepared to inform departmental managers and top management about the performances achieved in terms of budgeted figures. Such an investigation may call for a need to revise the budget during the year. This feedback of information can also be used as a basis for preparing the next year's budget.

ORGANISATION FOR BUDGETING (THE BUDGET COMMITTEE)

Responsibility for budget direction and execution is usually placed in the hands of a Budget Committee which reports directly to top management. In large companies the budget committee is composed of executives incharge of major functions of the business and includes the sales manager, personnel manager, finance manager, the production manager, the chief engineer, the treasurer and the chief accounts officer.

The principal functions of the budget committee are to:

1. Decide the company's general policies and objectives.
2. Receive and review individual budget estimates concerning different departments/divisions.
3. Suggest changes, modifications in accordance with organisational objectives.
4. Approve budgets which act as an authority/target for departmental action.
5. Receive and analyse performance reports regarding the implementation of budgets.
6. Suggest corrective action to improve efficiency and achieve budgetary goals.

BUDGET MANUAL

A budget manual is a document which defines the responsibilities of persons engaged in a budgetary programme and sets out the routine, the forms and records required under budgeting. Budget manuals specify the procedures to be followed in developing the budget. Since organisations differ in terms of structure, method of production, and operating requirements, it is difficult to prepare a budget manual suitable for use in all business enterprises.

THE BUDGET PERIOD

The budget period is an import factor in developing a comprehensive budgeting programme. The length of the budget period depends on the type of business, the length of the manufacturing cycle from raw material to finished product, the ease of difficulty of forecasting future market conditions and other factors. However, a business enterprise generally prepares a Short-range budget, and a Long-range budget.

Short-range Budget

Short-range budgets may cover periods of three, six or twelve months depending upon the nature of the business. Most manufacturing firms use one year as the planning period. Wholesale and retail firms usually employ a six-month budget which is related to their selling seasons. In determining the period of the short-range budget, the following factors should be considered:

1. The budget period should be long enough to cover complete production of various products.
2. For business of a seasonal nature, the budget period should cover at least one entire seasonal cycle.

3. The budget period should be long enough to allow for the financing of production well in advance of actual needs.
4. The budget period should coincide with the financial accounting period to compare actual results with budget estimates and thus to facilitate better interpretation of the performance,

Long-range Budget

A long-range budget or planning is defined as a systematic and formalised process for directing controlling future operations towards a desired objective for periods extending beyond one year. Such budgets cover specific areas, such as future sales, future production, long-term capital expenditures, extensive research and development programmes, financial requirements, profit forecast. They evaluate the future implications associated with present decisions and help management in making present decisions and select the most profitable alternative.

There are many factors which are duly considered while preparing long-term budgets, such as market trends, economic factors, growth of population, consumption pattern, industrial production, national income, government economic and industrial policy. Quantitative sales can be budgeted for a three to five years period. After forecasting sales, a budgeted profit and loss account can be prepared relating anticipated sales to corresponding cost and thus net operating profit can be forecasted. Likewise, a balance sheet for many years can be prepared to forecast cash, inventory levels, accounts receivable, accounts payable, liabilities, etc. The forecasted profit and loss account and balance sheet for a long-range is a very useful tool in accomplishing the objectives of the organisation as a whole.

ELEMENTS OF A SUCCESSFUL BUDGETING PLAN

The success of the budgeting process in an organisation depends on the following essential elements:

1. *Accurate forecasting of business activities:* Forecasting is a prerequisite in a budgeting process. It is not only the starting point, but is also critical to the development of an accurate budget.
2. *Coordinating business activities:* Budgeting needs to coordinate all the individual budgets into an integrated plan as each budget has certain implications for the other budgets. There must be coordination between sales, production, purchasing, personnel budgets.
3. *Communicating the budgets:* The success of a comprehensive budgeting programme depends on communication of individual budgets to the different units in the organisation. Managers are not responsible for budget unless the budget is communicated clearly, concisely and in an authoritative manner to them.
4. *Acceptance and cooperation:* Successful budgeting also requires that budgets should be accepted by the people who must execute them. Budgeting should have the active cooperation of the entire organisation from the top to the bottom.
5. *Reasonable flexibility:* The budgeting programme should contain reasonable flexibility if the situation so demands. However, it should be noted that too much flexibility and too much tightness are both undesirable. Too much flexibility will weaken the cost control and the budget will become inoperative. Similarly, too much rigidity not permitting reasonable deviations will create problems and restrictions in the implementation of the budget.
6. *Providing a framework for evaluation:* Budgeting provides a basis to evaluate the performance of different departments.

BUDGET CENTRES

An organisation is usually broken down into different budget centres for administrative and control purposes. A budget centre is the lowest level in an organisation for which detailed costs are budgeted, separately from those of other budget centres. The main factor in setting up budget centres is one of the fixing responsibility for action and inaction. To ensure adequate cost control, the budget centres should fulfil the following conditions:

1. The budget of a particular budget centre should specify precisely the costs controllable by the person responsible for that centre.
2. Costs for which responsibility is joint, e.g., work carried out by a maintenance department should be kept separate from costs which can be controlled by one manager.
3. Cost that are apportioned between two or more budget centres should also be controlled and for such costs one person should be made responsible.

LIMITING OR PRINCIPAL BUDGET FACTOR

When budgets are made, there is invariably some factor which governs or sets a limit to the quantity which can be made or sold. This is known as the limiting or principal budget factor. The Institute of Cost and Management Accountant (UK) defines a principal budget factor as "the factor the extent of whose influence must first be assessed in order io ensure that the functional budgets are reasonably capable of fulfillment." In the field of sales, the limiting factor is customer demand which is influenced by many factors, such as price and quality of the product, competition, the general purchasing power of the public, advertising, etc. In the field of production, the principle budget factor may be plant capacity, the supply of labour of the right quality, or the availability of scarce materials.

BUDGETS AND STANDARD COSTS

Standard costs and budgets are both vital tools in planning, operation and control of a business enterprise. Both differ in the following respects:

1. A standard costing system can operate without any comprehensive budgeting system. But budgets in absence of standard costs will only be fair estimates and cannot provide a reasonable base against which the actual results can be compared.
2. The objectives of budgeting are different from standard costing. A budget is a profit plan reflecting anticipated financial inflows and outflows. Budgets include both income and expenditure, but standards are set usually for expenses only. Standard costs are developed only for the production and related in an manufacturing cost.
3. Budgets project the volume of business and levels of costs which should be maintained. That is, they reflect cost ceilings which should not be exceeded if the budgeted profit is to be attained. Standard costs emphasise the cost levels to which cost should be reduced. If costs reach this level, profit will be increased. Standards are minimum targets which are to be attained by actual performance at specific efficiency.
4. Budgets covering the entire business present the forecasted profit and loss account and sometimes balance sheet also. Therefore, budgets act as guides for operating the business on a definite course of action. Standards are frequently used only in labour operation and do not represent expected costs but the cost that should be in a certain assumed conditions of performance. Horngreen* observes that the term "standard" is a unit concept

* Charles T. Horngreen, *Cost Accounting, A Managerial Emphasis*, Prentice-Hall of India, New Delhi, p. 173.

and the term budgeted cost is a total concept. It may be helpful to think of a standard as a budget for the production of a single unit of output.

5. Budgets if achieved by the organisation do not usually involve much variance analysis. Under standard costing detailed variance analysis is carried out to find out deviations so that corrective action may be taken.
6. Review and revision of budgets is more frequently based on the changing circumstances than those of standard costs. Standard costs are more static and subject to less change.
7. Budgets are equally important for planning, organisation, coordination and control functions of management. Standard costs contribute relatively more to the control function than other managerial functions although standards are used for all business functions.

In spite of the above differences, there are some similarities between standard costing and budgeting. Both have in common the establishment of predetermined measures of performance and the comparison of actual and planned performance so as to disclose deviations which are used for the purpose of cost control. Both help in the preparation of reports which compare actual costs and predetermined costs for management planning and control. Standards are almost indispensable to the work of establishing and operating a budget. A study made by the National Association of Accountants (USA) concludes that standard costs are especially valuable in developing the cost side of the budget because they provide a reliable and convenient source of data for converting the budgeted production schedule into requirements for raw materials, labour and services.

FIXED AND FLEXIBLE BUDGETING

Fixed Budgeting

The Institute of Costs and Management Accounts (UK) defines a fixed budget as the budget which is designed to remain unchanged irrespective of the level of activity actually attained. It is based on a single level of activity. A fixed budget performance report compares data from actual operations with the single level of activity reflected in the budget. Fixed budgets do not change when production level changes.

However, in practice, fixed budgeting is rarely used. The main reason is that actual output is often significantly different from the budgeted output. In such a case the budget cannot be used for the purpose of cost control. The performance report may be misleading and will not contain very useful information. For example, if actual production is 12,000 units in place of the budgeted 10,000 units, the costs incurred cannot be compared with the budget which relates to different levels of activity. Since, in fixed budgeting, units are overlooked, a cost to cost comparison without considering the units may give misleading results.

The performance report prepared under fixed budgeting merely discloses whether actual costs were higher or lower than budgeted costs. Therefore, the fixed budget is unable to provide useful information when actual output differs significantly from expected or budgeted output. The fact that costs and expenses are affected by fluctuations in volume limits the use of the fixed budget. Clearly, the idea of comparing performance at one activity level with a plan that was developed at some other activity level is nonsense from the view point of judging how efficiently the manager has produced any given output.

A fixed budget can be usefully employed when budgeted output is close enough to the actual output. If output can be estimated within close limits, the fixed budget can be a good basis for performance measurement. Maximum managerial control may be exercised by making comparisons with actual operating figures.

FLEXIBLE BUDGETING

A flexible budget is a budget that is prepared for a range, *i.e.*, for more than one level of activity. It is a set of alternative budgets to different expected levels of activity. The flexible budget is also known by other names, such as variable budget, dynamic budget, sliding scale budget, step budget, expenses formula budget and expenses control budget. The underlying principle of a flexible budget is that every business is dynamic, ever-changing, and never static. Thus, a flexible budget might be developed that would apply to a "relevant range" of production, say 8,000 to 12,000 units. Under this approach, if actual production slips to 9,000 units from a projected 10,000 units, the manager has a specific tool (i.e., the flexible budget) that can be used to determine budgeted cost at 9,000 units of output. The flexible budget provides a reliable basis for comparisons because it is automatically geared to changes in production activity. A flexible budget has the following important features:

1. It covers a range of activity (output).
2. It is flexible, *i.e.*, easy to change with variation in production levels.
3. It facilitates performance measurement and evaluation.

Planning or budgeting for a range of activity rather than for a single level of activity is always preferable due to the uncertainty about the changes in activity levels. In flexible budgeting, that range of activity is selected, which is likely to occur. Most often, one activity level at each extreme of the activity range is selected, with one or more in between. Among different activity levels the most likely activity level is made the basis for planning business operations. Flexible budgeting makes it easy to adjust plans to changing production levels without any delay. The flexibility involved in this budget makes a very useful decision making tool for management.

Steps in Flexible Budgeting

The following steps (stages) are involved in developing a flexible budget:

1. Deciding the range of activity to which the budget is to be prepared.
2. Determining the cost behaviour patterns (fixed, variable, semi-variable) for each element of cost to be included in the budget.
3. Selecting the activity levels (generally in terms of production) to prepare budgets at those levels.
4. Preparing the budget at each activity level selected by associating the activity level with corresponding costs. The corresponding costs to be attached with each activity level are determined in terms of their behaviour. i.e., fixed, variable, semi-variable.

Advantages of Flexible Budgeting

Flexible budgeting is budgeting that is automatically tailored to any level of activity. Although it is most often associated with the control of overhead, a flexible budget may also include direct materials and direct labour. Welsch* has listed three specific uses of the flexible budget.

1. To facilitate development of the departmental expense budgets for inclusion in the profit plans.
2. To provide expense goals for the managers of responsibility centres during the period covered by the profit plan.
3. To provide adjusted budget allowances for comparison purposes (against actual expenses) in the monthly performance reports.

---

* Glenn A. Welsch, *Budgeting, Profit Planning and Control,* p. 22.

In general, flexible budgeting has the following important advantages:

1. *Accurate budgeting:* The use of flexible budgets may result in the preparation of more accurate budgets. Flexible budgeting techniques require that consideration is to be given to the output factor in budget preparation. Since all costs do not behave in the same manner (as some costs rise faster than others when production increases) a budget giving consideration to the volume (output) factor is bound to be more accurate than one where volume is not considered.
2. *Accurate performance measurement:* The flexible budgeting technique incorporates changes in activity level and compares actual results with the budget in terms of output achieved. This facilitates more meaningful comparison and evaluation between actual and budgeted data as comparable data are compared.
3. *Coordination:* Flexible budgeting results in coordination between all activities/departments of a business. Production is planned in relation lo expected sales, materials and labour are acquired to meet expected production requirements. Facilities are provided to achieve budgetary goals, and funds are made available for the investments necessary to have higher output.
4. *Control tool:* Flexible budgeting is an effective management control tool. Comparisons between the budgeted costs (at the actual production level) and actual costs form the basis for analysing cost variances and fixing responsibility for the same. In fact, managers themselves feel motivated in controlling costs for which they are responsible. This contributes to cost control throughout the organisation.

Illustration 1:

From the following data, prepare a flexible budget for production of 40,000 units and 75,000 units, distinctly showing variable cost and fixed cost as well as total cost. Also indicate element-wise cost per unit. Budgeted output is 1,00,000 units and budgeted cost per unit is as follows:

Direct Material	95
Direct labour	50
Production overhead (variable)	40
Production overhead (fixed)	5
Administration overhead (fixed)	5
Selling overhead (10% fixed)	10
Distribution overhead (20% fixed)	15

Solution:

Flexible Budget

	1,00,000 units		*40,000 units*		*75,000 units*	
	Per unit	*Total*	*Per unit*	*Total*	*Per unit*	*Total*
Variable cost:	*Rs.*	*Rs.*	*Rs.*	*Rs.*	*Rs.*	*Rs.*
Direct material	95	95,00,000	95	38,00,000	95	71,25,000
Direct labour	50	50,00,000	50	20,00,000	50	37,50,000
Production overhead	40	40,00,000	40	16,00,000	40	30,00,000
Selling overhead = $\frac{10 \times 90}{100}$	9	9,00,000	9	3,60,000	9	6,75,000
Distribution overhead = $\frac{15 \times 80}{100}$	12	12,00,000	12	4,80,000	12	9,00,000
Total variable cost	206	2,06,00,000	206	82,40,000	206	1,54,50,000

Fixed Cost:						
Production overhead	5	5,00,000	12.50	5,00,000	6.67	5,00,000
Administrative overhead	5	5,00,000	12.50	5,00,000	6.67	5,00,000
Selling overhead	1	1,00,000	2.50	10,00,000	1.33	1,00,000
Distribution overhead	3	3,00,000	7.50	30,00,000	3.00	3,00,000
Total fixed cost	14	14,00,000	35.00	14,00,000	17.67	14,00,000
Total cost	260	2,20,00,000	231.00	96,40,000	223.67	1,68,50,000

Illustration 2:

For production of 10,000 electrical automatic irons, the following are the budgeted expenses:

	Per unit
Direct materials	Rs. 60
Direct labour	30
Variable overheads	25
Fixed overheads (Rs. 1,50,000)	15
Variable expenses (direct)	5
Selling expenses (10% fixed)	15
Administration expenses (Rs. 50,000 rigid for all levels of production)	5
Distribution expenses (20% fixed)	5
Total cost of sale per unit	160

Prepare a budget for production of 6,000; 7,000; and 8,000 irons, showing distinctly marginal cost and total cost.

Solution:

Flexible Budget of Electrical Automatic Irons

Production	*6,000 units*		*7,000 units*		*8,000 units*	
	Total (Rs.)	*Per unit (Rs.)*	*Total (Rs.)*	*Per unit (Rs.)*	*Total (Rs.)*	*Per unit (Rs.)*
Direct material	3,60,000	60.00	42,20,000	60.00	4,80,000	60.00
Direct labour	1,80,000	30.00	2,10,000	30.00	2,40,000	30.00
Direct variable expenses	30,000	5.00	35,000	5.00	40,000	5.00
Variable overheads						
Production	1,50,000	25.00	1,75,000	25.00	2,00,000	25.00
Selling	81,000	13.50	94,500	13.50	1,08,000	13.50
Distribution	24,000	4.00	28,000	4.00	32,000	4.00
Marginal cost	8,25,000	137.50	9,62,500	137.50	11,00,000	137.50
Fixed production overheads	1,50,000	25.00	1,50,000	21.43	1,50,000	18.75
Administration overheads	50,000	8.33	50,000	7.14	50,000	6.25
Selling overheads	15,000	2.50	15,000	2.14	15,000	1.88
Distribution overheads	10,000	1.67	10,000	1.43	10,000	1.25
Fixed cost	2,25,000	37.50	2,25,000	32.14	2,25,000	28.13
Total cost (Marginal cost plus fixed cost)	10,50,000	175.00	11,87,500	169.64	13,25,000	165.63

Working Notes:

	Selling expenses	*Distribution expenses*
Total for 10,000 units	1,50,000	50,000
Variable: 90% and 80% respectively	1,35,000	40,000
Variable expenses per unit	13.50	4.00
Fixed expenses 10% and 20% of total, respectively	15,000	10,000

Illustration 3:

A department of Company X attains sale of Rs 6,00,000 at 80% of the normal capacity and its expenses are given below:

	Rs.
Office salaries	90,000
General expenses	2% of the sales
Depreciation	7,500
Rates and taxes	8,750
Selling costs:	
Salaries	8% of the sales
Travelling expenses	2% of the sales
Sales office	1% of the sales
General expenses	1% of the sales
Distribution costs:	
Wages	15,000
Rent	1% of the sales
Other expenses	4% of the sales

Draw up a flexible administration, selling and distribution costs budget, operating at 90%, 100% and 110% of normal capacity.

Solution:

Flexible Budget of Department ... of Company X

Items	*Basis*	*Level of Activity*			
		80% (Rs.)	*90% (Rs.)*	*100% (Rs.)*	*110% (Rs.)*
Sales		6,00,000	6,75,000	7,50,000	8,25,000
Administrative costs:					
Office salaries	Fixed	90,000	90,000	90,000	90,000
General expenses	2% of sales	12,000	13,500	15,000	16,500
Depreciation	Fixed	7,500	7,500	7,500	7,500
Rates and taxes	Fixed	8,750	8,750	8,750	8,750
Total administrative costs		1.18,250	1,19,750	1,21,250	1,22,750
Selling costs:					
Salaries	8% of sales	48,000	54,000	60,000	66,000
Travelling expenses	2% of sales	12,000	13,500	15,000	15,000
Sales office expenses	1% of the sales	6,000	6,750	7,500	8,250
General expenses	1% of the sales	6,000	6,750	7,500	8,250
Total selling costs		72,000	81,000	90,000	99,000
Distribution costs:					
Wages	Fixed	15,000	15,000	15,000	15,000
Rent	1% of the sales	6,000	6,750	7,500	8,250
Other expenses	4% of the sales	24,000	27,000	30,000	33,000
Total distribution costs:		45,000	48,750	52,500	56,250
Total admn., selling and dist. costs		2,35,250	2,49,500	2,63,750	2,78,000

Note: In the absence of information it has been assumed that office salaries, depreciation, rates and taxes and wages remain the same at 110% level of activity also. However, in practice some of these costs may change if present capacity is exceeded.

Illustration 4:

The budget manager of Jaypee Electricals Ltd. is preparing a flexible budget for the accounting year commencing from 1st April 2009. The company produces one product, component — Peekay. Direct material costs Rs. 7 per unit. Direct labour averages Rs. 2.50 per hour and requires 1.60 hours to produce one unit of Peekay.

Salesmen are paid a commission of Re. 1 per unit sold. Fixed selling and administration expenses amount to Rs. 85,000 per year.

Manufacturing overhead has been estimated in the following amounts under specified conditions of volume:

Volume of production (in units)	1,20,000	1,50,000
Expenses	*(Rs.)*	*(Rs.)*
Indirect material	2,64,000	3,30,000
Indirect labour	1,50,000	1,87,500
Inspection	90,000	1,12,500
Maintenance	84,000	1,02,000
Supervision	1,98,000	2,34,000
Depreciation — Plant and Equipment	90,000	90,000
Engineering services	94,000	94,000
Total manufacturing overhead	9,70,000	11,50,000

Normal capacity of production of the company is 1,25,000 units.

Prepare a budget of total cost at 1,40,000 units of output.

Solution:

Flexible Budget for the Year April 2009 to March 2010

Production Volume 1,40,000 Units

Items of cost	*Fixed costs (Rs.)*	*Variable cost (Rs.)*		*Total cost (Rs.)*
		Per unit	*Total*	
Direct materials	—	7.00	9,80,000	9,80,000
Indirect labour	—	4.00	5,60,000	5,60,000
Indirect materials	—	2.20	3,08,000	3,08,000
Indirect labour	—	1.25	1,75,000	1,75,000
Inspection	—	0.75	1,05,000	1,05,000
Maintenance	12,000	0.60	84,000	96,000
Supervision	54,000	1.20	1,68,000	2,22,000
Depreciation — Plant and Equipment	90,000	—	—	90,000
Engineering service	94,000	—	—	94,000
Sales commission	—	1.00	1,40,000	1,40,000
Fixed selling and distribution expenses	85,000	—	—	85,000
Total	3,35,000	18.00	25,20,000	28,55,000

Working Notes:

Segregation of semi-variable costs into fixed and variable components:

$$\text{Variable-cost per unit} = \frac{\text{Difference in cost}}{\text{Difference in output}}$$

Fixed cost = Total cost − Variable cost

(*i*) Maintenance – Variable cost per unit $= \dfrac{\text{Rs. } 1{,}02{,}000 - 84{,}000}{1{,}50{,}000 - 1{,}20{,}000}$

$= \dfrac{\text{Rs. } 18{,}000}{30{,}000 \text{ unit}}$

= Re. 0.60 per unit

Fixed cost = Rs. 84,000 – (1,20,000 × .60)

= 84,000 – 72,000

= 12,000

Variable cost = 14,000 × .60 = Rs. 84,000

(*ii*) Supervision

Variable cost per unit $= \dfrac{\text{Rs. } 2{,}34{,}000 - 1{,}98{,}000}{1{,}50{,}000 - 1{,}20{,}000}$

$= \dfrac{\text{Rs. } 36{,}000}{30{,}000 \text{ units}}$

= Rs. 1.20 per unit

Fixed cost = Rs. 1,98,000 – (1,20,000 × 1.20)

= 1,98,000 – 1,44,000

= 54,000

Variable cost = 1,40,000 units × Rs. 1.20

= Rs. 1,68,000

(*iii*) Indirect materials, Indirect labour, Inspection are fully variable costs. **This can be proved by taking these elements of costs and following the above method of segregation. For instance, as an** example, indirect materials is taken.

Indirect materials

Variable cost per unit $= \dfrac{\text{Rs. } 3{,}30{,}000 - 2{,}64{,}000}{1{,}50{,}000 - 1{,}20{,}000}$

$= \dfrac{\text{Rs. } 66{,}000}{30{,}000}$

= Rs. 2.20 per unit

Fixed cost = Rs. 2,64,000 (12,000 × 2.20)

= 2,64,000 – 2,64,000

= No fixed cost

Illustration 5:

The profitability statement of Gourmet Co. Ltd. has been summarized as follows:

	Rs.	*Rs.*
Sales		Rs. 15,00,000
Direct materials	4,50,000	
Direct wages	3,00,000	
Variable overheads	1,20,000	
Fixed overheads	4,40,000	13,10,000
Profit		1,90,000

The budgeted capacity of the company is Rs. 20,00,000 but the key factor is sales demand. It is proposed that in order to utilise the existing capacity the selling price of this only product manufactured by the company should be reduced by 5%.

You are required to prepare a forecast statement which should show the effect of the proposed reduction in selling price and include any changes in costs expected during the coming year. The following additional information is given:

(*i*) Sales forecast Rs. 19,00,000 (after reduction).
(*ii*) Direct material prices are expected to increase by 2%.
(*iii*) Direct wage rates are expected to increase by 5% per unit.
(*iv*) Variable overheads are expected to increase by 5% per unit.
(*v*) Fixed overheads will increase by Rs. 20,000.

Solution:

Forecast Statement of Profit

1. Sales			19,00,000
2. *Less:*	Variable costs:		
	Direct material	4,50,000	
Add:	For increase on account of sales volume (1/3 × 4,50,000)	1,50,000	
		6,00,000	
Add:	Increase in price (2% of Rs. 6,00,000)	12,000	6,12,000
	Direct wages	3,00,000	
Add:	For increase in sales volume (1/3 of Rs. 3,00,000)	1,00,000	
		4,00,000	
Add:	For increase in wage rates (5% of Rs. 4,00,000)	20,000	4,20,000
	Variable overheads	1,20,000	
Add:	For increase in sales volume (1/3 × 1,20,000)	40,000	
		1,60,000	
Add:	For increase in rates (5% of Rs. 1,60,000)	8,000	1,68,000
	Total variable costs		12,00,000
3. Contribution (1) – (2)			7,00,000
4. Fixed overheads		4,40,000	
Add:	Expected increase in fixed overheads	20,000	4,60,000
	Profit		2,40,000

Note:

Sales after price reduction = Rs. 19,00,000

Sales before price reduction 19,00,000 × 100/95 = Rs. 20,00,000

Increase in sales volume from present sales without price reduction over existing sales

$$\frac{5,00,000 \times 100}{15,00,000} = 33\frac{1}{3}\%$$

Illustration 6:

Paints Private Ltd. Company manufacturing a single product is facing severe competition in selling it at Rs. 50 per unit. The company is operating at 60% level of capacity at which level the sales are Rs. 12,00,000 and variable costs are Rs. 30 per unit. Semi-variable costs may be considered as fixed at Rs. 90,000 when output is nil and the variable elements is Rs. 250 for each additional

1% level of activity. Fixed costs are Rs. 1,50,000 at the present level of activity. But at 80% level of activity or above, these costs are expected to increase by Rs. 50,000.

To cope with the competition, the management of the company is considering a proposal to reduce the selling price by 5%. You are required to prepare a statement showing the operating profit at levels of activity of 60%, 70%, 80%, 90% assuming that:

(*a*) The selling price remains at Rs. 50

(*b*) The selling price is reduced by 5%

Solution:

Paints Private Ltd. Flexible Budget

	60% *(24,000 units)* *Rs.*	*70%* *(28,000 units)* *Rs.*	*80%* *(32,000 units)* *Rs.*	*90%* *(36,000 units)* *Rs.*
Variable cost	7,20,000	8,40,000	9,60,000	10,80,000
Semi-variable:				
Fixed cost	90,000	90,000	90,000	90,000
Variable	15,000	17,500	20,000	22,500
Fixed cost	1,50,000	1,50,000	2,00,000	2,00,000
Total cost	9,75,000	10,97,500	12,70,000	13,92,500
(*a*) Sales (selling price remaining at Rs. 50)	12,00,000	14,00,000	16,00,000	18,00,000
Profit	2,25,000	3,02,000	3,30,000	4,07,500
(*b*) Sales (Selling price is reduced to Rs. 47.50, 5% reduction)	11,40,000	13,30,000	15,20,000	17,10,000
Profit	1,65,000	2,32,500	2,50,000	3,17,500

TYPES OF BUDGETS

Budgets are the end product of the budgeting process. The numbers and types of budgets in a business enterprise depend on the size and nature of the business. However, in a manufacturing concern, the following budgets are generally prepared:

(A) Operating and functional budgets:

1. Sales budget
2. Production budget
3. Production cost budget
   (*i*) Direct materials budget
   (*ii*) Direct labour budget
   (*iii*) Factory overhead budget
4. Ending inventories budget
5. Cost of goods sold budget
6. Selling expense budget
7. Administrative expense budget
8. Budgeted income statement

(B) Financial budgets:

1. Capital expenditure budget
2. Research and development budget
3. Cash budget
4. Budgeted balance sheet
5. Budgeted statement of changes in financial position.

Sales Budget

The most important budget, which all other budgets are contingent upon, is the sales budget. All budgets, such as production budget, selling and distribution budget and others are all affected by the sales budget and are dependent upon the revenue derived from sales.

ABC Company Ltd.

Sales Budget for the year Ending December 31, 2008

Products	*Budgeted sales units*	*Budgeted sales price (Rs.)*	*Total*
A	70,000	80,000	56,00,000
B	80,000	1,20,000	96,00,000
Total	1,50,000		1,52,000

Fig. 26.1

Forecasting Sales

Developing a sales budget requires forecasting future sales levels. The three main factors that should be considered by management in forecasting sales are: (*a*) information concerning past performance, (*b*) information about present conditions within the individual company and in each sales territory, and (*c*) data concerning the industry and general business conditions.

The information about past performance is the starting point for sales forecasting. The sales record for past years, and particularly for the year just ending should be available to management in minute detail.

The second essential step in forecasting sales is the accumulation of data regarding conditions within the company and in each sales territory. The management can obtain a good picture of sales prospects through information sent to the head office by salesmen, dealers, and sales officers of different territories.

Information about general business conditions are known as "business barometers" and they should be considered in preparing a sales forecast. The following are important business indicators:

1. Gross national product, which is the total market value of output of goods and services produced in the entire economy.
2. Personal income and purchasing power of the population.
3. Unemployment conditions.
4. Government crop reports.
5. Steel, coal and oil production.
6. Wholesale price indices.
7. Business failures.
8. Industrial production index.

9. Governmental policies.
10. Cyclical phases of the country's economy.

Sales Analysis

After collecting all relevant information for a sales forecast, a sales analysis or budget is prepared. The sales budget is usually prepared on the lines of (*i*) product, (*ii*) territory, and (*iii*) customer.

Production Budget

After preparing the sales budget, the production budget is prepared. A production budget is stated in physical units, it specifies the number of units of each product that must be produced to satisfy the sales forecasts and to achieve the desired level of closing finished goods inventory. Essentially, the production budget is the sales budget adjusted for inventory changes as follows:

Units to produce = Budgeted sales + Desired closing inventory of finished goods – Beginning inventory of finished goods

A specimen production budget is given in Fig. 26.2.

ABC Company

Total Production Budget for the Month of December, 2008

	Products	
	A	*B*
Budgeted sales (units)	70,000	80,000
Add: Desired closing finished goods inventory	20,000	30,000
	90,000	1,10,000
Less: Beginning finished goods inventory	40,000	50,000
Units to be produced	50,000	60,000

Fig. 26.2 Production Budget

The production budget, like other budgets, is detailed by months or quarters along with a tentative annual budget. Further, budgets are prepared for every production centre for comparison with actual production.

Production Cost Budget

A production cost budget summarises the materials budget, labour budget, the factory overhead budget, and may be expressed and analysed by departments and/or products. A production cost budget, also known as a manufacturing budget is made up of three budgets: (*i*) materials, (*ii*) labour, and (*iii*) factory overhead.

Direct Materials Budget

This budget specifies the cost of direct materials used and the cost of the direct materials purchased.

Figure 26.3 explains the calculation of the direct materials budget. The usage part of the direct materials budget determines the cost of purchases of direct materials.

ABC Company

Direct Materials Budget for the Year Ending December, 2008

A. Usage Budget

	Products		
	A	*B*	*Total*
Budgeted production in units	50,000	60,000	
Direct materials requirements			
Product A 5 kg per unit	× 5		
Product B 8 kg per unit		× 8	
Direct materials usage (kg)	2,50,000	4,80,000	
Cost per kg	Re. 1.00	Rs. 1.50	
Cost of direct materials used	Rs. 2,50,000	Rs. 7,20,000	Rs. 9,70,000

B. Purchase Budget

	Direct material (in kg.)		
	A	*B*	*Total*
Direct materials usage	2,50,000	4,00,000	
Budgeted closing direct materials inventory	+ 50,000	+ 75,000	
Total requirements	3,00,000	5,55,000	
Beginning direct materials inventory	70,000	1,00,000	
Purchase of direct materials	2,30,000	4,55,000	
Cost per kg	× Rs. 1.00	× Rs. 1.50	
Cost of purchase	Rs. 2,30,000	Rs. 6,82,500	Rs. 9,12,500

Fig. 26.3 Direct Materials Budget

The direct materials budget is useful in the following ways:

1. It helps the purchasing department to prepare a schedule to ensure delivery of materials when needed.
2. It helps in fixing minimum and maximum levels of inventories in the stores department.
3. It helps the finance manager to determine the financial requirements to meet production targets.

The materials budget usually deals with direct materials only. Supplies and indirect materials are generally included in the factory overhead budget.

Direct Labour Budget

The labour budget estimates the labour, adequate in number and grades, to enable the production budget to be achieved. It is generally preferable to prepare a separate direct labour budget and to include indirect labour in the factory overhead budget. The labour budget prepared must disclose the following information: (*i*) the number of each type or grade of worker required in each period to achieve the budgeted output; (*ii*) budgeted cost of such labour in each period; and (*ii*) period of training necessary for different types of workers.

Figure 26.4 illustrates the preparation of a direct labour budget.

ABC Company

Direct Labour Budget for the Year Ending December 2008

	Products		
	A	*B*	*Total*
Budgeted production requirements	50,000	60,000	
Direct labour hours per unit	3	2	
Total direct labour hours	1,50,000	1,20,000	2,70,000
Direct labour cost per hour	Rs. 5.00	Rs. 5.00	Rs. 5.00
Total direct labour cost (Rs.)	Rs. 7,50,000	Rs. 6,00,000	Rs. 13,50,000

Fig. 26.4 Direct Labour Budget

Factory Overhead Budget

The factory overhead budget is prepared on the basis of the chart of accounts which reflects different expense accounts and which properly classifies expenses accounts and details the cost centres or departments. Although expenses can be classified in different manners such as natural classification, variability, the preparation of the factory overhead budget requires that expenses should be classified by departments since expenses are incurred by various departments. In this way departmental heads should be held accountable for expenses incurred by their departments.

Figure 26.5 depicts the factory overhead budget wherein overhead costs have been classified into fixed and variable components.

ABC Company

Factory Overhead Budget for the Year Ending December 2008

(Based on budgeted capacity of 2,70,000 direct labour hours)

Items	*Direct labour*	*Rate per direct hour Rs.*	*Total cost Rs.*
A. *Variable factory overhead:*			
(*i*) Supplies	2,70,000	1,00	2,70,000
(*ii*) Repairs	2,70,000	0.50	1,35,000
(*iii*) Indirect labour	2,70,000	1.00	2,70,000
(*iv*) Others	2,70,000	0.40	1,08,000
Total variable factory overhead cost			7,83,000
B. *Fixed factory overhead cost:*			
(*i*) Supervision		Rs. 4,00,000	
(*ii*) Depreciation		5,50,000	
(*iii*) Property tax		2,50,000	
(*iv*) Others		1,77,000	
Total fixed factory overhead cost			13,77,000
Total factory overheads cost			21,60,000

Predetermined overhead rate $= \text{Rs. } \dfrac{21,60,000}{2,70,000}$ hours

= Rs. 8.00 per direct hour

Fig. 26.5 Factory Overhead Budget

ABC Company
Ending Inventory Budget for the Year Ending December 2008

Direct materials inventory		*Rs.*
Product A	50,000 × Re. 1.00 per kg.	50,000
Product B	75,000 kg. × Rs. 1.50 kg.	1,12,500
		1,62,500
Finished goods inventory		
Product	A 20,000 units × Rs. 25.00	5,00,000
Product	B 30,000 units × Rs. 30.00	9,00,000
		14,00,000

Fig. 26.6 Ending Inventories Budget

Ending Inventories Budget

An inventory budget can be prepared to find out the values of direct materials and finished goods inventory as shown in Fig. 26.6.

Cost of Goods Sold Budget

After preparing direct materials, direct labour, factory overhead, and ending inventory budgets, the cost of goods sold budget can be prepared. The cost of goods sold budget summarises all the above budgets as shown in Fig. 26.7.

Selling Expenses Budget

Closely related with the sales budget is the selling and distribution cost budget which shows the budgeted costs of promoting sales for the budget period. It is also known as the marketing expense budget. The selling cost budget is made up of a number of cost items, some of which are fixed and some variable. The principal fixed expenses are salaries and depreciation: the principal variable expenses are commissions, travel, advertising and bad debts.

ABC Company
Cost of Goods Sold Budget for the Year Ending Dec. 31, 2008

Direct materials:	*Rs.*	*Rs.*
Beginning inventory	2,00,000	
Purchases	9,12,500	
	11,12,500	
Less: Closing inventory	1,62,500	
Cost of direct materials used		9,50,000
Direct labour		13,50,000
Factory overhead		21,60,000
Total factory cost		44,60,000
Beginning finished goods inventory		25,00,000
Total goods available for sale		69,60,000
Closing finished goods Inventory		14,00,000
Cost of goods sold		55,60,000

Fig. 26.7 Cost of Goods Sold Budget

Fig. 26.8 exhibits an annual selling expenses budget classified according to fixed and variable expenses. Separate budgets for each of these expenses may be prepared especially in the case of a large company.

ABC Company

Selling Expense Budget for the Year Ending December 31, 2008

Items	*Cost (Rs.)*	*Total cost (Rs.)*
(A) *Variable selling expenses:*		
(*i*) Sales commission	35,000	
(*ii*) Salary and wages	40,000	
(*iii*) Advertising	15,000	
(*iv*) Travelling	22,000	1,12,000
(B) *Fixed selling expenses:*		
(*i*) Warehousing	60,000	
(*ii*) Advertising	30,000	
(*iii*) Marketing manager's salary	60,000	
(iv) Depreciation	27,000	
		1,77,000
Total selling expenses		2,89,000

Fig. 26.8 Selling Expenses Budget

Administrative Expenses Budget

The administrative expenses budget covers the administrative costs for non-manufacturing business activities. The administrative expense budget contains expenses like directors' remuneration, legal charges, audit fees, salaries, rent, office expenses, interest, property taxes, postage, telephone, telegraph, etc. These expenses should be properly classified under different headings to determine the responsibility of cost incurrence and control. For example, these expenses can be classified into different categories such as company administration, general accounting, general office, etc. Figure 26.9 presents an administrative expense budget.

ABC Company

Administrative Expenses Budget for the Year Ending December 31, 2008

Items	*Amount Rs.*	*Amount Rs.*
(A) Variable administrative expenses:		
(*i*) Supplies	35,000	
(*ii*) Clerical wages	60,000	
Total variable administrative expenses		95,000
Fixed administrative expenses:		
(*i*) Director's remuneration	1,20,000	
(*ii*) Legal charges	20,000	
(*iii*) Depreciation	25,000	
(*iv*) Salaries	30,000	
(*v*) Rent	60,000	
(*vi*) Postage, telephone, etc.	32,000	
Total fixed administrative expenses		2,87,000
Total administrative expenses		3,82,000

Fig. 26.9 Administrative Expense Budget

Budgeted Income Statement

A budgeted income statements summarises all the individual budgets, i.e., sales budget, cost of goods sold budget, selling budget, and administrative expense budget. No new estimates are made; figures are taken from budgets previously prepared. This budget determines income before taxes. If the tax rate is available, net income after taxes can also be computed. Figure 26.10 exhibits a budgeted or projected income statement.

Capital Expenditure Budget

The budgeting of capital expenditure is one of the most important areas of managerial decisions. Capital expenditures represent long-term commitments. Also, the benefits of capital expenditure spread over a long period of time. Capital expenditure budgets are prepared for both short and long-range projects depending on the requirements of the business firm. Short-range projects are implemented during the current accounting period. Long-range projects are not executed in the current period, they are expressed only in general terms. They become budget commitments only when the time for their implementation approaches.

ABC Company

Budgeted income Statement for the Year Ending December, 2008

		Rs.
Sales		1,52,00,000
Cost of goods sold		55,60,000
Gross margin		96,40,000
Selling expenses	2,89,000	
Administrative expenses	3,82,000	6,71,000
Income before taxes		89,69,000
Income taxes (assuming 50%)		44,84,500
Net Income		44,84,500

Fig. 26.10 Budgeted Income Statement

Research and Development Budget

The research and development budget is the most important tool for planning and controlling research and development costs. It compels management to think in advance about the fairness of these expenses both in total amounts and in each field of a research programme. It helps in coordination with the company's other plans and projects. Since the research and development programmes compete with other desirable activities in allocation of funds, coordination is needed to balance financially immediate and long-term company plans. Also, this budget guides the research and development department to plan correctly the staff and equipment requirements and special facilities needed for the work.

Cash Budget

A cash budget contains detailed estimates of cash receipts (cash inflows) and disbursements (cash outflows) for the budget period or some other specific period. The preparation of a cash budget has the following objectives:

1. It indicates the effect on the cash position of seasonal requirements, large inventories, unusual receipts, and slowness in collecting receivables.

2. It indicates the cash requirements needed for a plant or equipment expansion programme.
3. It points up to the need for additional funds from sources such as bank loans or sales of securities and the time factors involved.
4. It indicates the availability of cash for taking advantage of discounts.
5. It assists in planning the financial requirements of bond redemption, income tax instalments, and payments to pensions and retirement funds.
6. It shows the availability of excess funds for short-term investments.

Period of Cash Budget

The period of time covered by a cash budget depends on the type of business, management planning needs, and cash position. A cash budget may generally be related to the following time periods:

1. *Operational cash planning:* Cash budget may be prepared monthly, weekly or even daily to meet informational requirements of management.
2. *Short-range:* Short-range cash budgeting is prepared annually and is in correspondence with the annual profit plan. It indicates cash inflows and outflows as generated by the annual profit plan.
3. *Long-range:* Long-range budgeting does not disclose detailed estimates of revenue and expenses. The effects of business expansion and long-term trends are incorporated in long-range cash budgeting. Long-range cash projection is in accord with (*i*) the timing of the capital expenditure projects, and (*ii*) the timing of the long-range profit plan (usually five years).

Preparation of a Cash Budget

A cash budget may be prepared by following either of the three generally accepted procedures:

1. The receipts and disbursements method.
2. The adjusted profit and loss or adjusted net income method.
3. Balance sheet method.

In the first method, all anticipated cash receipts are carefully forecasted such as cash sales, cash collections from debtors, dividends, interest on investments, proceeds from sale of assets, royalties, bank loans, etc. Likewise, cash disbursements for materials purchases, supplies, salaries, repayment of loans, dividends, taxes, expenses, purchases of plant or equipment are also determined. This method is useful for short-range cash projection but is not appropriate for long-term cash budgeting. This method is in accord with the annual profit plan.

The second approach is the profit and loss or adjusted net income method. The starting point in this approach is budgeted profit reflected in the income statement. Basically, projected profit is converted from an accrual basis to a cash basis. That is, the budgeted profit of a period is adjusted for non-cash transactions and expected cash-oriented changes in asset and liability accounts not affected by profit calculations. Using the budgeted profit for a period as a starting point, various non-cash transactions are added back to net profit for the period. Non-cash items are depreciation, bad and doubtful accounts, expired insurance premiums, expenses, and income tax accruals. After this, anticipated decreases in assets or increase in liabilities are further added and anticipated increases in assets or decreases in liabilities are deducted. The budgeted cash at the end of a period is the cash balance at the beginning of the period plus the net cash increase (or minus the net cash decrease) as indicated in the analysis of the adjusted profit method.

The third approach is the balance sheet method. In this approach, closing balances of all (budgeted) balance sheet items except cash and bank balances are found and put in a budgeted balance sheet. If the total of liabilities side items is more than the total of asset side items, the balancing figure will be cash/bank balance. On the contrary, if the total of assets side items is more than the total of liabilities side items, the balancing figure will be bank overdraft or shortage in cash. Budgeted figures of closing balance sheet items can be found after adjusting the opening balance sheet items with the transactions anticipated for the year.

Budgeted or Projected Balance Sheet

A projected balance sheet represents the expected financial position at a particular date. The projected balance sheet is prepared from the budgeted balance sheet at the beginning of the budget period and the expected changes in the account balances reflected in the operating budgets, capital expenditure budgets, and cash budget. The projected balance sheet also automatically determines the arithmetical accuracy of other budgets since they are used in preparing the forecasted balance sheet.

Budgeted Statement of Changes in Financial Position

The projected statement of changes in financial position is usually prepared from data in the budgeted income statement and changes between the projected balance sheet at the beginning of the budget period and projected balance sheet at the end of the budget period. The projected statement is very useful to management in the financial planning process.

Master Budget

A master budget sometimes called a comprehensive budget, is the summary or total budget package for a business firm. It is the end product of the budget-making process. It shows the budgeted profit and loss account for the budget period and the budgeted balance sheet at the end of the period. It reveals the top management's goals of revenues, expenses, net income, cash flows, and financial position. The other budgets prepared by a business firm are specific, i.e., they deal with separate distinct activities of the organisation such as sales, production, selling and distribution and administrative activities. They incorporate plans and budgetary goals for a small segment of a business enterprise. However to achieve business objectives, it is necessary to have coordination among different budgets reflecting diverse activities of a business firm. For example, there should be coordination between sales and production departments and the goals of the production department should match the goals of the sales department.

In the absence of coordination among the budgets, a business firm may have problems, such as surplus inventory, shortage of stock, non-availability of raw materials and other resources, employees dissatisfaction, etc. A master budget takes the macro (aggregate) view of the business enterprise and coordinates sales with production; raw materials, manpower, machinery and other resources with production targets, and the like. The master budget is an integrative tool that cuts across divisional boundaries in order to coordinate the firms' diverse activities. While master budgets provide plans for an entire system, operating budgets provide plans for the organisation's sub-system, that is, operating budgets constitute the building blocks used to complete the master budget.

REVISION OF BUDGETS

As stated earlier in the chapter, successful budgets should have adequate flexibility to meet changing business conditions. Since budgets are used for planning, operation, coordination and control, they should be revised if changes occur in the environment. Revision of budgets may be necessary due to the following factors some of which might have been considered earlier in the development of budgets:

1. Errors committed in preparing the budgets which may subsequently be known.
2. Emergence of unforeseen and unanticipated situations which may cause the budget to be revised.
3. Changes in internal factors, *e.g.*, production, forecast, capacity utilisation, etc.
4. Changes in external factors, *e.g.*, market trends, nature of the economy, prices of inputs and resources, consumers' tastes and fashions.

Changes in the above factors do not affect a firm's budgets if they are of minor significance. Some changes, however, considerably affect budgets and in this situation management is faced with two problems:

1. Whether only individual budgets should be changed; and
2. Whether the master budget be changed.

Regarding the first question, most business firms are in agreement and suggest that specific individual budgets should be changed. For instance, if there is likely to be a significant change in expected sales (increase or decrease), production and purchasing departments should be informed about this to avoid over-stocking or under-stocking.

A revision of the master budget is debatable and sometimes is opposed mainly on two counts: (*i*) the master budget process is highly complex and expensive; (*ii*) the evaluation process may take care of these changes if the changes take place. The second argument is more or less on middle ground. While it argues for revision when changes do occur, it focuses on actual effects rather than projected changes. It is felt that this avoids making small changes in the plan that are of little consequence. Those who support the revision of the master budget argue that the revised budget is a better and more effective basis for performance evaluation and control. By revising budget, all members of the organisation come to know of the expectations and standards for which they will be accountable.

Illustration 7: (Materials Requirement)

Bala Company expects to sell 84,000 units of finished goods over the next 3-month period. The company currently has 44,000 units of finished goods on hand and wishes to have an inventory of 48,000 units at end of the 3-month period. To produce 1 unit of finished goods requires 4 units of raw materials. The company currently has 2,00,000 units of raw materials on hand and wishes to have an inventory of 2,20,000 units of raw materials on hand at the end of the 3-month period. How many units of raw materials must the Bala Company purchase during the 3-month period?

Solution:

Material Requirements

Finished units to be produced	=	(84,000 units) to be sold	+	(48,000 units in) Ending inventory	–	(44,000 units) Beginning inventory
Units to be produced	=	88,000				
Units of raw materials to be used	=	4 units of raw materials per finished unit × 88,000 units = 3,52,000				
Units of raw materials to be purchased	=	3,52,000 units to be used	+	2,20,000 units desired in ending inventory	–	2,00,000 units in beginning inventory
	=	3,72,000 units.				

Illustration 8: (Production Budget)

Gama engineering Company Limited manufactures two products X and Y. An estimate of the number of units expected to be sold in the first seven months of 2007 is given below:

	Product X	*Product Y*
January 2007	500	1,400
February	600	1,400
March	800	1,200
April	1,000	1,000
May	1,200	800
June	1,200	800
July	1,000	900

1. There will be no work-in-progress at the end of any month; and
2. Finished units equal to half and anticipated sales for the next month will be in stock at the end of each month (including December, 2006)

The budgeted production and production costs for the year ending 31st December, 2007 are as follows:

	Product X	*Product Y*
Production (units)	11,000	12,000
Direct materials per unit (Rs.)	12	19
Direct wages per unit (Rs.)	5	7
Direct manufacturing charges apportionable to each type of product (Rs.)	33,000	48,000

You are required to prepare:

(*a*) A production budget showing the number of units to be manufactured each month.

(*b*) A summarised production cost budget for the six-month period January to June 2007.

Solution:

Gama Engineering Company Limited

(a) Production Budget (in Units) for the Six Months Ending 30th June, 2007

	Jan.	*Feb.*	*March*	*April*	*May*	*June*
Product X						
Closing stock	300	400	500	600	600	500
Sales	500	600	800	1,000	1,200	1,200
	800	1,000	1,300	1,600	1,800	1,700
Less: Opening stock	250	300	400	500	600	600
Production (in units)	550	700	900	1,100	1,200	1,100
Product Y						
Closing stock	700	600	500	400	400	450
Sales	1,400	1,400	1,200	1,000	800	800
	2,100	2,000	1,700	1,400	1,200	1,250
Less: Opening stock	700	700	600	500	400	400
Production (in units)	1,400	1,300	1,100	900	800	850

(b) Summarised Production Cost Budget for the Six Months Ending 30th June, 2007

	X		*Y*	
Production	*5,550*		*6,350*	
	Unit cost	*Total cost*	*Unit cost*	*Total cost*
Direct materials	Rs. 12	Rs. 66,600	Rs. 19	Rs. 1,20,650
Direct wages	5	27,750	7	44,450
Manufacturing charges	3	16,650	4	25,400
	20	1,11,000	30	1,90,500

Illustration 9:

Nestley Ltd. has prepared the following sales budget for the first five months of 2007:

	Sales Budget (Units)
January	10,800
February	15,600
March	12,200
April	10,400
May	9,800

Inventory of finished goods at the end of every month is to be equal to 25% of sales estimate for the next month. On 1st Jan., 2007, there were 2,700 units of product on hand. There is no work-in-progress at the end of any month.

Every unit of product requires two types of materials in the following quantities:

Material A — 4 kg

Material B — 5 kg.

Materials equal to one half of the requirement of next month's production are to be in hand at the end of every month. This requirement was met on 1st Jan., 2007.

Prepare the following budgets for the quarter ending 31st March, 2007.

(*a*) Production Budget (Quantitative)

(*b*) Material Purchase Budget (Quantitative).

Nestley Ltd.

Production Budget (In Units)

For quarter ending 31st March, 2007

Particulars	*Jan.*	*Feb.*	*March*
Sales	10,800	15,600	12,200
Add: Closing stock	3,900	3,050	2,600
	14,700	18,650	14,800
Less: Opening stock	2,700	3,900	3,050
	12,000	14,750	11,750

Materials Requirement Budget

For the quarter ending 31st March, 2007

Particulars	*Jan.*	*Feb.*	*March*
Production (units)	12,000	14,750	11,750
Material A	*kg.*	*kg.*	*kg.*
Required for Production	48,000	59,000	47,000
Add: Desired Closing stock	28,500	23,500	20,500
	76,500	82,500	67,500
Less: Opening stock	24,000	28,500	23,500
	52,500	54,000	44,000
Material B			
Required for Production	60,000	73,750	58,750
Add: Desired Closing stock	36,875	29,375	25,625
	96,875	1,03,125	84,375
Less: Opening stock	30,000	36,875	29,375
	66,875	66,250	55,000

Working Notes:

1. Production for April in units

Sales	10,400
Add: Closing stock	2,450
	12,850
Less: Opening stock	2,600
	10,250

2. Material required for Production in April
   A 10,250 × 4 = 41,000 kg.
   B 10,250 × 5 = 51,250 kg.

Illustration 10:

The following are the estimated sales of a company for eight months ending 30-11-2008.

Months		*Estimated Sales (units)*
April	2008	12,000
May	2008	13,000
June	2008	9,000
July	2008	8,000
August	2008	10,000
September	2008	12,000
October	2008	14,000
November	2008	12,000

As a matter of policy, the company maintains the closing balance of finished goods and raw materials as follows:

Stock item	Closing balance of a month
Finished goods	50% of the estimated sales for the next month
Raw materials	Estimated consumption for the next month.

Every unit of production requires 2 kg. of raw material costing Rs. 5 per kg. Prepare Production Budget (in units) and Raw Material Purchase Budget (in units and cost) of the company for the half year ending 30 September, 2008.

Solution:

Production Budget (In Units)

(for the half-year ending 30th September, 2008)

Month 2008	*Sales (in units)*	*Closing balance 50% of the estimated Sales for the next month*	*Opening balance*	*Production*
1	2	3	4	5 = (2) + (3) – (4)
April	12,000	6,500	6,000	12,500
May	13,000	4,500	6,500	11,000
June	9,000	4,000	4,500	8,500
July	8,000	5,000	4,000	9,000
August	10,000	6,000	5,000	11,000
September	12,000	7,000	6,000	13,000
	64,000			65,000

Purchase Budget (in Cost and Units)

(for the half-year ending 30th September, 2008)

Month 2008	*Production in units*	*Consumption (kg.) @ 2 kg. per unit*	*Closing Balance*	*Opening Balance*	*Purchase in kg.*	*Rate Rs.*	*Amount Rs.*
April	12,500	25,000	22,000	25,000	22,000	5	1,10,000
May	11,000	22,000	17,000	22,000	17,000	5	85,000
June	8,500	17,000	18,000	17,000	18,000	5	90,000
July	9,000	18,000	22,000	18,000	22,000	5	1,10,000
August	11,000	22,000	26,000	22,000	26,000	5	1,30,000
September	13,000	26,000	26,000	26,000	26,000	5	1,30,000
	65,000	1,30,000					6,55,000

Illustration 11: (Sales Overhead Budget)

You are requested to prepare a sales overhead budget from the estimates given below:

Advertisement	Rs. 2,500
Sales of the sales department	5,000
Expenses of sales department	1,500
Counter salesmen's salaries and dearness allowance	6,000
Commission to counter salesmen at 1% on their sales	

Travelling salesmen's commission at 10% on their sales and expenses at 5% on their sales The sales during the period were estimated as follows:

Counter sales	*Travelling salesmen*
Rs. 80,000	Rs. 10,000
1,20,000	15,000
1,40,000	20,000

Solution:

Sales Overhead Budget for the Period Ending

	Estimated sales		
	Rs. 90,000	*Rs. 1,35,000*	*Rs. 1,60,000*
Fixed overheads:			
Advertisement	2,500	2,500	2,500
Salaries of sales department	5,000	5,000	2,500
Expenses of sales department	1,500	1,500	1,500
Counter salesmen's salaries and DA	6,000	6,000	6,000
	15,000	15,000	15,000
Variable overheads:			
Counter salesmen's commission @ 1% on sales	800	1,200	1,400
Travelling salesmen's commission @ 10%	1,000	1,500	2,000
Expenses @ 5%	500	750	1,000
	2,300	3,450	4,400
Total sales overheads	17,300	18,450	19,400

Illustration 12: (Cash Receipts Budget)

A company normally collects cash from credit customers as follows: 50 per cent in the month of sale, 30 per cent in the first month after sale, 18 per cent in the second month after sale, and 2 per cent are never collected. Sales, all on credit, are expected to be as follows:

	Rs.
January	5,00,000
February	6,00,000
March	4,00,000
April	5,00,000

(*a*) Calculate the amount of cash expected to be received from customers during March.

(*b*) Calculate the amount of cash expected to be received from customers during April.

Solution:

	Rs.
(*a*) Budgeted cash collection in March:	
From January sales (.18 × 5,00,000)	90,000
From February sales (.30) × 6,00,000)	1,80,000
From March sales (.50 × 4,00,000)	2,00,000
Total Budgeted Collections in March	4,70,000
(*b*) Budgeted cash collections in April:	
From February sales (.18 × 6,00,000)	1,08,000
From March sales (.30 × 4,00,000)	1,20,000
From April sales (.50 × 5,00,000)	2,50,000
Total budgeted collections in April	4,78,000

Illustration 13: (Cash Budget)

The January 1 cash balance of the Jay Company is Rs. 5,000. Sales for the first four months of the year are expected to be as follows: January, Rs. 65,000; February, Rs. 54,000; March,

Rs. 66,000; and April, Rs. 63,000. On January 1, uncollected amounts for November and December of the previous year are Rs. 13,500 and Rs. 39,150, respectively. Collections from customers follow this pattern; 55% in the month of sale, 30% in the month following the sale, 13% in the second month following the sale, and 2% uncollectable.

Materials purchases for December were Rs. 10,000. Forecast purchases for the coming year are: Rs. 12,500; February, Rs. 16,500: March, Rs. 13,000; and April, Rs. 14,000. Purchases are usually paid by the 10th of the month following the month of purchase. Other cash expenditures of Rs. 41,000 are forecasted for each month.

Calculate:

(*i*) Expected cash collection during February

(*ii*) Expected cash balance February 1

(*iii*) Expected cash balance, February 29.

Solution:

Cash Budget of Jay Company for Months of January and February

	January (Rs.)	*February (Rs.)*
Opening Balance	5,000	27,550
Receipts — From customers	73,550	60,510
(A)	78,550	88,060
Payments:		
For purchases	10,000	12,500
Other expenditure	41,000	41,000
Total payments (B)	51,000	53,500
Closing Balance (A) – (B)	37,550	34,560

Thus,

(*i*) Expected cash collections during February = Rs. 60,510

(*ii*) Expected cash balance: February 1 = Rs. 27,550

(*iii*) Expected cash balance: February 29 = Rs. 34,560

Working Note:

Collections on account of sale:

January:

For November arrears 13,500 × 13/15 = Rs. 11,700

For December arrears $\frac{39,150}{45} \times 30$ = 26,100

For January sales 65,000 × 55/100 = 35,750

73,550

February:

For December arrears $\frac{39,150}{45} \times 13$ = Rs. 11,310

For January sales 65,000 × 30/100 Rs. 19,500

For February sales 54,000 × 55/100 = 29,700

60,510

Illustration 14: (Cash Budget)

ABC Co. wished to arrange overdraft facilities with its bankers during the period April to June 2007 when it will be manufacturing mostly for stock. Prepare a cash budget for the above period from the following data, indicating the extent of the bank facilities the company will require at the end of the each month:

(a)	*Sales* Rs.	*Purchases* Rs.	*Wages* Rs.
February	1,80,000	1,24,800	12,000
March	1,92,000	1,44,000	14,000
April	1,08,000	2,43,000	11,000
May	1,74,000	2,46,000	10,000
June	1,26,000	2,68,000	15,000

(*b*) 50 per cent of the credit sales are realised in the month following the sales and the remaining 50 per cent in the second month following. Creditors are paid in the month of purchase.

(*c*) Cash at bank on 1-4-2007 (estimated) Rs. 25,000.

Solution:

ABC Co.

Cash Budget for April to June 2007

	April Rs.	*May* Rs.	*June* Rs.
Opening balance (Overdraft)	25,000	56,000	(47,000)
Receipts:			
Collections from debtors	1,86,000	1,50,000	1,41,000
	2,11,000	2,06,000	94,000
Payments:			
Payments to creditors	1,44,000	2,43,000	2,46,000
Wages	11,000	10,000	15,000
Closing balance (Overdraft)	56,000	(47,000)	(1,67,000)
	2,11,000	2,06,000	94,000

The overdraft facilities required by ABC Co. for different months are as under:

(*i*) In May 2007 Rs. 47,000

(*ii*) In June 2007 1,67,000

Working Notes:

Collections from Debtors

April 2007	Rs.	
Sales for February	1,80,000 × 1/2	90,000
Sales for March	1,96,000 × 1/2	96,000
		1,86,000

May 2007		
Sales for March	1,92,000 × 1/2	96,000
Sales for April	1,08,000 × 1/2	54,000
		1,50,000
June 2007		
Sales for April	1,08,000 × 1/2	54,000
Sales for May	1,74,000 × 1/2	87,000
		1,41,000

Illustration 15:

From the following budget data, forecast the cash position at the end of April, May and June 2008:

Month	*Sales*	*Purchase*	*Wages*	*Miscellaneous expenses*
	Rs.	*Rs.*	*Rs.*	*Rs.*
February	1,20,000	84,000	10,000	7,000
March	1,30,000	1,00.000	12,000	8,000
April	80,000	1,04,000	8,000	6,000
May	1,16,000	1,06,000	10,000	12,000
June	88,000	80,000	8,000	6,000

Additional information:

Sales: 20% realised in the month of sales, discount allowed 2%. Balance realised equally in two subsequent months:

Purchase: These are paid for in the month following the months of supply.

Wages: 25% paid in arrears following month.

Miscellaneous expenses: paid a month in arrears.

Rent: Rs. 1,000 per month paid quarterly in advance due in April.

Income Tax: First instalment of advance tax Rs. 25,000 due on or before 15th June.

Income from investments: Rs. 5,000 received quarterly, in April. July etc.

Cash in hand: Rs. 5,000 on 1st April 2008.

Solution:

Cash Budget

for Three Months Ended 30th June, 2008

	April	*May*	*June*
Receipts:	*Rs.*	*Rs.*	*Rs.*
Opening balance	5,000	5,680	—
Receipt from debtors	1,15,680	1,06,736	95,648
Income from investment	5,000	—	—
	1,25,680	1,12,416	95,648

Payments:			
Creditors	1,00,000	1,04,000	1,06,000
Wages	9,000	9,500	8,500
Rent	3,000	—	—
Miscellaneous expenses	8,000	6,000	12,000
Income tax	—	—	25,000
Opening balance	—	—	(–) 7,084
	1,20,000	1,19,500	1,58,684
Closing balance	5,680	(–)7,084	(–) 62,936

Notes:

Collection from debtors		Wages	
April:	*Rs.*		*Rs.*
20% of 80,000	16,000	25% of 12,000	3,000
Less: 2% discount	320	*Add:* 75% of 8,000	6,000
	15,680		9,000
Add: 40% of 1,20,000 + 1,30,000	1,00,000		
	1,15,680		
May			
20% of 1,16,000	23,200	20% of 8,000	2,000
Less: 2% of 1,16,000	464	*Add:* 75% of 10,000	7,500
	22,736		9,500
Add: 40% of 1,30,000 + 80,000	84,000		
	1,06,736		
June			
20% of 88,000	17,600	25% of 10,000	2,500
Less: 2% discount	352	*Add:* 75% of 8,000	6,000
	17,248		8,500
Add: 40% of 80,000 + 1,16,000	78,400		
	95,648		

Illustration 16:

The following data pertains to Mr. Y for the month budgeted for November 2008:

	Rs.
Direct materials used	847
Beginning finished goods inventory	?
Ending finished goods inventory	94
Direct manufacturing labour	389
Manufacturing overhead	?
Cost of goods manufactured	1,878
Cost of goods sold	?
Cost of goods available for sale	1,949

Prepare the cost of goods sold budget for the month of Nov. 2008 by filling the missing figures.

Solution:

	Rs.
Direct material used	847
Beginning Finished goods inventory	71
Ending finished goods inventory	94
Direct manufacturing labour	389
Manufacturing overhead	642
Cost of goods manufactured	1878
Cost of foods sold	1855
Cost of goods available for sale	1949

As we know that cost of goods manufactured is the aggregate of Direct material. Direct manufacturing labour and manufacturing overhead.

∴ Rs. 1878 = Rs. 847 + 389 + Manufacturing overhead

∴ Rs. 1878 – 847 – 389 = Manufacturing overhead

∴ Rs. 642 = Manufacturing overhead.

Cost of goods available for sale = Cost of goods manufactured + Opening balance of finished goods.

Rs. 1,949 – Rs. 1,878 + Opening balance of finished goods

Rs. 1,949 + Rs. 1,878 = Opening balance of finished goods

Rs. 71 = Opening balance of finished goods.

Cost of goods sold = Cost of goods manufactured + Opening balance of finished goods – Closing balance of finished goods

Cost of goods sold + Rs. 1878 + Rs. 71 – Rs. 94

Cost of goods sold = Rs. 1,875

Cost of goods sold budget for the month of November 2008

	Rs.
Direct material used	847
Direct manufacturing labour	389
Manufacturing overhead	642
Cost of goods manufactured	1,878
Add: Opening balance of finished goods	71
Cost of goods available for sale	1,949
Less: Closing stock of finished goods	94
Cost of goods sold	1855

ZERO BASE BUDGETING (ZBB)

Zero base budgeting (ZBB) is a method of budgeting whereby all activities are revaluated each time budget is formulated and every item of expenditure in the budget is fully justified. That is, ZBB involves starting from scratch or zero.

In traditional budgeting, departmental managers need justify only increases over the prior year's budget known as incremental budgeting. This implies that what is already being spent is automatically sanctioned. Under the ZBB concept, each department's functions are reviewed completely and all expenditures, rather than only the increases, must be approved.

Also in some departments, ascertainment of budgeted costs is easier than other departments. For example, in production departments, it is easier to determine costs of inputs to achieve a level of budgeted output. But, in other departments such as accounts, personnel, research and development, it is difficult to even identify the output, and therefore equally greater difficult to determine the cost of input to sustain (unidentifiable) output. Consequently, the budgets of previous year tend to be subjectively increased as the next year budgeted expenditure. However, the previous year's budgets may be inefficient and adjusting merely new year's budgets to the previous year's budget may result in wastage. ZBB overcomes this problem, to a certain extent. ZBB rejects the traditional view of annual budgeting as an incremental process which takes into account current expenditure plus an estimate of next year's expenditure to arrive at the next budget. Instead the projected expenditure for existing programmes should start from base zero with each year's budgets being compiled as if the programmes were being launched for the first time.

Application of ZBB

ZBB involves the following stages (steps):

(1) Each separate activity of the organisation is identified and called a decision package. A decision package is a document that identifies and describes a specific activity in such a manner that management can (*i*) evaluate it and rank it against other activities competing for limited resources and (*ii*) decide whether to approve or disapprove it.

(2) Each decision package must be justified, i.e., it should be enquired into whether a decision package promotes the coals of an enterprise.

(3) If justified, then the cost of minimum efforts needed to sustain each decision package is determined.

(4) Alternatives for each decision package are considered in order to select better and cheaper options for the package.

(5) Incremental decision package are also justified and costed in the above manner. These incremental packages describe the costs and benefits of additional work that would be done above that required by the base package for the minimum amount of work needed to carry out the activity.

(6) Managers rank their decision packages in order of priority for resource allocation.

(7) Resources are allocated to the packages.

Advantages of ZBB

(1) It represents a move towards allocation of resources by need and benefit and thus results in more efficient allocation of resources.

(2) It identifies and eliminates wastage and obsolete operations.

(3) It ensures that the best possible methods of performing jobs are used and that new ideas emerge.

(4) It creates a questioning attitude rather than one which accepts that current practices represent value for money.

(5) It leads to increased staff involvement which may lead to improved motivation and greater interest in the job.

(6) It increases communication and coordination within the organisation.

(7) Managers become more aware of the costs of inputs which helps them to identify priorities.

(8) The documentation of decision packages provides management with a deep, coordinated knowledge of all organisation's activities.

(9) It is useful especially for service departments where it can be difficult to identify output.

Disadvantages of ZBB

(1) The cost involved in preparing a vast number of decision packages in a large firm are very high.

(2) It is very time-consuming and a large amount of additional paper work is involved.

(3) Managers develop fear and feel threatened by ZBB and therefore may oppose new ideas and changes.

(4) The ranking of decision packages and allocation of resources is subjective to a certain degree, which can result in departmental conflict.

(5) Administration and communication of ZBB process may become critical problems because more managers become involved in this process than in most budgeting and planning procedures and these problems are further compounded in large organisations.

PERFORMANCE BUDGETING

The concept of performance budgeting is used extensively in the Government and Public sector undertakings. A performance budget is essentially a projection of the Government activities and expenditure thereon for the budget period. It shows budgeted expenses classified by functions and activities and wherever practical, units cost also. In comparison to other budget forms, the objectives of performance budgeting are to provide a closer linkage between planning and action and to provide a more common basis for review, control and reporting.

The basic issues involved in the preparation of performance budgets are that of developing work programmes and performance expectations by assigning responsibilities necessary for the attainment of the goals of objectives of the enterprise. It also involves establishment of well defined centres of responsibility, establishment of targets for each responsibility centre in terms of physical units so that actual performance can be measured against the same, forecasting the amount of expenditure required to meet physical plan laid down and evaluation of actual with both physical targets and monetary targets performance.

THEORY QUESTIONS

1. Define "budget" and "budgetary control." Give a description of two important budgets.
   (*a*) Define budgetary control and explain its objectives.
   (*b*) Define how functional budgets are built up, taking any one specific example.
3. Explain the meaning of a business budget. How does it serve as an instrument of control?
4. Discuss the mode of operation of systems of budgets and budgetary control.
5. What do you understand by budgetary control? Explain the mechanism that would lead to effective control.
6. What are the advantages arising out of the budgetary control system? What do you think are the essentials of an effective budgetary control system?
7. Discuss the objectives and limitations of budgetary control.

8. Define budgetary control and discuss the objectives of introducing a budgetary control system in an organisation.
9. Discuss the cardinal features and objectives of budgetary control.
10. Explain the difference between a forecast and a budget. Give examples to illustrate the differences between:
    (*a*) Fixed budget.
    (*b*) Flexible budget, and
    (*c*) Functional budget.
11. What are functional budgets. Which functional budgets are most commonly used by management?
12. Define budgetary control and distinguish it from standard costing. Discuss the inter-relationship between budgetary control and the standard costing system.
13. Discuss briefly the procedure for the preparation of a sales budget.
14. What do you understand by a "flexible budget"?
15. What is a sales budget? How is it prepared?
16. Describe briefly the fundamental functions of business budget.
17. Explain the concept of a flexible budget. How is it prepared?
18. What is flexible budget? How does the sales forecast differ from the sales budget?
19. What do you understand by 'Flexible Budget"? How is it prepared? Distinguish between fixed budgeting and flexible budgeting.
20. Explain the following:
    (*a*) Zero Base Budgeting
    (*b*) Master Budget
21. List the important functional budgets prepared by a business.
22. Distinguish between budget and forecast. What is a cash budget? What are its uses?
23. State the important features of zero base Budgeting.
24. Distinguish between fixed and flexible budget.

EXERCISES AND PROBLEMS

1. Prepare a flexible budget for overheads on the basis of data given below. Ascertain the overhead rates at 50, 60 and 70 per cent capacity.

	At 50% capacity Rs.	*At 60% capacity Rs.*	*At 70% capacity Rs.*
Variable overheads:			
Indirect material		6,000	
Indirect labour		18,000	
Semi-variable overheads:			
Electricity (40% fixed, 60% variable)		30,000	
Repairs and maintenance (80% fixed 20% variable)		3,000	
Fixed overheads:			
Depreciation		16,500	
Insurance		4,500	
Salaries		15,000	
Total overheads		93,000	

Estimated direct labour hours — 1.86,000

(*Ans.:* Overhead rates
Capacity level 50% = Rs. 0.55
Capacity level 60% = Re 0.50
Capacity level 70% = Re 0.46

2. The budgeted cost of a factory specialising in the production of a single product at the optimum capacity of 6,400 units per annum amounts Rs. 1,76,048 as detailed below:

Fixed cost		Rs. 20,688
Variable costs:		
Power	Rs. 1,440	
Repairs etc.	1,700	
Miscellaneous	540	
Direct material	49,280	
Direct labour	1,02,400	1,55,360
		1,76,048

Having regard to possible impact on sales turnover by market trends the company decided to have a flexible budget with a production target of 3,200 and 4,800 units (the actual quantity proposed to be produced being left to a later date before commencement of the budget period). Prepare a flexible budget for production levels at 50% and 75% capacity.

Assume selling price per unit is maintained at Rs. 40 as at present, indicate the effect on net profit.

Administration, selling and distribution expenses continue as Rs. 3,600.

(*Ans.:* Net profit.
(*a*) 100%. Rs. 75,352
(*b*) 75% Rs. 51,192
(*c*) 50% Rs. 26,032.

3. Draw up a flexible budget for overhead expenses on the basis of the following data and determine the overhead rates at 70%, 80% and 90% plant capacity levels.

	At 80% capacity
Variable overheads:	
Indirect labour	12,000
Indirect material	4,000
Semi-variable overheads:	
Power (30% Fixed. 70% variable)	20,000
Repairs & maintenance (60% fixed, 40% variable)	2,000
Fixed overheads:	
Depreciation	11,000
Insurance	3,000
Others	10,000
Total overheads	62,000
Estimated direct labour hours	1,24,000 hrs.

(*Ans.:* Overhead rate per direct labour hour
(*a*) 70% – Re. 0.5359
(*b*) 80% – Re. 0.5000
(*c*) 90% – Re. 0.4720

4. From the following information relating to 2007 and conditions expected to prevail in 2008, prepare a budget for 2008. State the assumptions you have made.

2007 Actuals	Rs.	
Sales	1,00,000	(40,000 units)
Raw materials	53,000	
Wages	11,000	
Variable overheads	16,000	
Fixed overheads	10,000	

2008 prospects			
Sales	1,50,000		(60,000 units)
Raw materials	5%	Price increase	
Wages	10%	Increase in wage rate	
	5%	Increase in productivity	
Additional plant		One lathe, Rs. 25,000	
		One drill, Rs. 12,000	

(*Ans.:* Budget for 2008 — Rs. 11,539)

5. Goodluck Ltd. is currently operating at 75% units capacity. In the past two years, the level of operations were 55% and 65% respectively. Presently, the production is 75,000 units. The company is planning for 85% capacity level during 2007-08. The cost details are as follows:

	55% Rs.	*65%* Rs.	*75%* Rs.
Direct Materials	11,00,000	13,00,000	15,00,000
Direct Labour	5,50,000	6,50,000	7,50,000
Factory Overhead	3,10,000	3,30,000	3,50,000
Selling Overhead	3,20,000	3,60,000	4,00,000
Administrative Overheads	1,60,000	1,60,000	1,60,000
	24,40,000	28,00,000	31,60,000

Profit is estimated @ 20% on sales.

The following increase in costs are expected during the year.

	In percentage
Direct Materials	8
Direct Labour	5
Variable Factory Overheads	5
Variable Selling Overheads	8
Fixed Factory Overheads	10
Fixed Selling Overheads	15
Administrative Overheads	10

Prepare flexible budget for the period 2007-2008 at 85% level of capacity. Also ascertain profit and contribution.

(*Ans.:* Total costs at 85%, Rs. 37,85,200; Profit Rs. 9,46,300; Contribution Rs. 14,57,300)

6. The following data are available in a manufacturing company for a yearly period.

	Rs. (lakhs)
Fixed expenses:	
Wages and salaries	9.5
Rent, rates and taxes	6.6
Depreciation	7.4
Sundry administrative expenses	6.5

Semi-variable expenses at 50% of capacity:	
Maintenance and repairs	3.5
Indirect labour	7.9
Sales department salaries, etc.	3.8
Sundry administrative salaries	2.8
Variable expenses (at 50% of capacity):	
Materials	21.7
Labour	20.4
Other expenses	7.9
Total cost	98.0

Assume that the fixed expenses remain constant for all levels of production: semi-variable expenses remain constant between 45% and 65% of capacity, increasing by 10% between 65% and 80% capacity and by 20% between 80% and 100% capacity.

Sales at various levels are:	*Rs. (lakhs)*
50% capacity	100
60% capacity	120
75% capacity	150
90% capacity	180
100% capacity	200

Prepare a flexible budget for the year and forecast the profit at 60%, 75%, 90% and 100% capacity.

(*Ans.:* Profit at 60% Rs. 12,00,000; at 75% Rs. 25,20,100; 90% Rs. 38,40,000; 100% Rs. 48,40,000)

7. Prepare a production budget for each month and a summarised production cost budget for the six-month period ending 31st December, 2008 from the following data of product X:

(*i*) The units to be sold for different months are as follows:

July 2008	1,100
August	1,100
September	1,700
October	1,900
November	2,500
December	2,300
January 2009	2,000

(*ii*) There will be no work-in-progress at the end of any month.

(*iii*) Finished units equal to half the sales for the next month will be in stock at the end of each month (including June 2008).

(*iv*) Budgeted production and production cost for the year ending 31st December, 2008 are as follows:

Production (units)	22,000
Direct material per unit	10.00
Direct wages per unit	4.00
Total factory overhead apportioned to product	88,000

(*Ans.:* Total production cost Rs. 1,98,000)

8. A company is drawing its production plan for the year 2007-08 in respect of two of its products 'Gamma' and 'Delta.' The company's policy is not to carry any closing *WIP* at the end of any month. However, its policy is to hold a closing stock of finished goods at 50% of the anticipated quantity of sales of the succeeding month. For the year 2007-08, the company's budgeted production is 20,000 units of 'Gamma' and 25,000 units of 'Delta.' The following is the estimated cost data:

Particulars	*Gamma* *Rs.*	*Delta* *Rs.*
Direct Materials per unit	50	80
Direct Labour per unit	20	30
Other Manufacturing expenses apportionable to each type of product based on production	2,00,000	3,75,000

The estimated units to be sold in the first 7 months of the year 2007-08 are as under:

Particulars	*April*	*May*	*June*	*July*	*Aug.*	*Sept.*	*Oct.*
Gamma	900	1,100	1,400	1,800	2,200	2,200	1,800
Delta	2,900	2,900	2,500	2,100	1,700	1,700	1,900

You are required to:

(*a*) prepare a production budget showing month-wise number of units to be manufactured:

(*b*) present a summarised production cost budget for the half-year ending 30.9.2007.

(***Ans.:*** Budgeted production, Gamma total 10,050 units, Delta total 13,300 units, total production cost Gamma Rs. 8,04,000, Delta Rs. 16,62,500.)

Responsibility Accounting, Divisional Performance Measurement and Transfer Pricing

DECENTRALISATION

In small organisations, decision-making and management of the business are often done by a single individual. However, in a large organisation, especially organisations engaged in manufacturing/undertaking multiple products and activities, successful management of it by the top management becomes more difficult. In order to overcome this difficulty, the large organisation may be decentralised or divisionalised. When the decision authority is delegated to managers, they, in turn are held responsible for the consequences of their decision-making. The process of delegating decision authority and responsibility in an organisation is known as *decentralisation*. In any organisation, in fact, some authority can be found delegated to the lower level management. In this way, almost every organisation can be said to be 'decentralised.' However, decentralisation is found in case of companies producing multiple products. Divisions in companies mean different things in different companies. In some companies, divisions are organised on the basis of product lines whereas in some decentralised companies, divisions may be created on the basis of geographical areas. Also, the term decentralisation or divisionalisation refers to those situations where individual managers of decentralised sub-units are given responsibility for profit and not just costs or revenues. In decentralised organisations, the top management handles broad corporate policies, establishes long range plans, raises capital and conducts other coordinating activities.

An example of divisionalised (decentralised) organisational structure is displayed in Figure 27.1. It can be noticed that different divisions have been created in terms of products made in each division in this particular decentralised company and these divisions are responsible for all the operations relating to their respective products. Divisional managers will have decision-making authority for their divisions and thus maybe free to set selling prices, choose which market to sell in, make product mix and output decisions and also make purchasing decisions. Some functions (activities) like research and development, industrial relations and general administration may be centralised with the top management which may have a responsibility for providing services to all of the divisions.

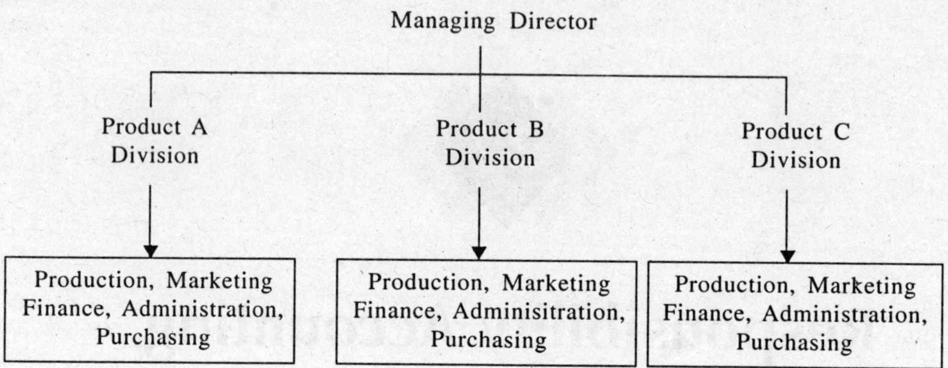

Fig. 27.1 Divisionalised Organisational Structure

ADVANTAGES OF DIVISIONALISATION

A number of advantages are found with the divisionalisation/decentralisation of an organisation:

(1) Top management becomes free from detailed involvement in day-to-day operations and enables them to devote their time and efforts to strategic planning, policy formulation, overall coordination and direction.

(2) It improves the decision-making process and leads to more informed decisions in the organisation because the managers who are directly involved in the day-to-day running of business and are familiar with the situation, make decisions.

(3) Speedier decisions can be made as decisions can be taken on the spot by the manager without any need of sending to/getting information from the top management.

(4) Managers can rapidly respond to changes in the market, competition, opportunities available due to non-existence of administrative bottlenecks in their organisation which can increase the profitability of the overall company.

(5) Experience of decision-making at the divisional level provides the divisional managers better career training.

(6) Decentralisation enhances the motivation and efficiency of the divisional managers as they find their status increased with wider responsibilities and greater freedom to manage their activities and more control over the factors which determine their performances.

(7) Divisionalisation may be more helpful in building good labour-management relations as the divisional managers will be able to maintain personalised contact with the employees.

DISADVANTAGES OF DIVISIONALISATION

There are some disadvantages of divisionalisation. They are listed as follows:

(1) Different divisions are likely to compete unreasonably and they may take action which may increase their profits but only at the expense of other divisions. This may adversely affect cooperation and harmony between divisions and in turn, the profitability of the

entire company may suffer. For example, two managers competing in a common product market may engage in price cutting to win customers. As a result, the overall company profits may be less than the profits that could have been if the price cutting has not occurred.

(2) There will be duplication of various assets and costs in the different operating divisions. For example, each division might have separate sales force and administrative office staff, but centralisation of these personnel could save money.

(3) A further argument against divisionalisation is that top management loses some control by delegating decision-making to divisional managers. It is argued that a series of control reports is not as effective as detailed knowledge of a company's activities.

RESPONSIBILITY CENTRE

A responsibility centre may be defined *as an area of responsibility which is controlled by an individual.* A responsibility centre is an activity such as the department over which a manager exercises responsibility. Responsibility areas may be departments (drilling or maintenance department), product lines (chemicals or fertilisers), territories (North or South) or any other type of identifiable unit or combination of units. The specific types of responsibility areas depend on the nature of the firm and its activities. It is relatively easy to identify activities with specific managers. A plant manager is in charge of a plant and is usually responsible for producing budgeted quantities of specific products within budgeted cost limits. A sales manager is responsible for getting orders from customers and so on. In most cases, it is relatively easy to identify activities with specific managers. However, in some cases, it is not a simple task to isolate the responsibilities of managers.

TYPES OF RESPONSIBILITY CENTRES

Responsibility centres can be classified by the scope of responsibility assigned and decision-making authority given to individual managers. The following are the four common types of responsibility centres:

1. Cost Centre

A cost or expense centre is a segment of an organisation in which the managers are held responsible for the cost incurred in that segment but not for revenues. Responsibility in a cost centre is restricted to cost. For planning purposes, the budget estimates are cost estimates; for control purposes, performance evaluation is guided by a cost variance equal to the differences between the actual and budgeted costs for a given period. Cost centre managers have control over some or all of the costs in their segment of business, but not over revenues. *Cost centres are widely used forms of responsibility centres.* In manufacturing organisations, the production and service departments are classified as cost centre. Also, a marketing department, a sales region or a single sales representative can be defined as a cost centre. Cost centres may vary in size from a small department with a few employees to an entire manufacturing plant. In addition, cost centres may exist within other cost centres. For example, a manager of a manufacturing plant organised as a cost centre may treat individual departments within the plant as separate cost centres, with the department managers reporting directly to the plant manager. Cost centre managers are responsible for the costs that are controllable by them and their subordinates. However, which costs should be charged to cost centres is an important question in evaluating cost centre managers.

2. Revenue Centre

A revenue centre is a segment of the organisation which is primarily responsible for generating sales revenue. A revenue centre manager does not possess control over cost, investment in assets, but usually has control over some of the expenses of the marketing department. The performance of a revenue centre is evaluated by comparing the actual revenue with budgeted revenue and actual marketing expenses with budgeted marketing expenses. The marketing manager of a product line or an individual sales representative are examples of revenue centres.

3. Profit Centre

A profit centre is a segment of an organisation whose manager is responsible for both revenues and costs. Managers of profit centres have control over both costs and revenues. In a profit centre, the manager has the responsibility and the authority to make decisions that affect both costs and revenues (and thus profits) for the department or division. The main purpose of a profit centre is to *earn profit.* Profit centre managers aim at both the production and marketing of a product. The performance of the profit centre is evaluated in terms of whether the centre has achieved its budgeted profit. A division of the company which produces and markets the products may be called a *profit centre*. Such a divisional manager determines the selling price, marketing programmes and production policies. Profit centres make managers more concerned with finding ways to increase the centre's revenue by increasing production or improving distribution methods. The manager of a profit centre does not make decisions concerning the plant assets available to the centre. For example, the manager of the sporting goods department does not make the decisions to expand the available floor space for the department.

Mostly profit centres are created in an organisation in which they (profit divisions) sell products or services outside the company. In some cases, profit centres may be selling products or services within the company. For example, repairs and maintenance department in a company can be treated as a profit centre if it is allowed to bill other production departments for the services provided to them. Similarly, the data processing department may bill each of that company's administrative and operating departments for providing computer-related services.

An example of a profit centre in a departmental store having different retail departments is displayed in Figure 27.2.

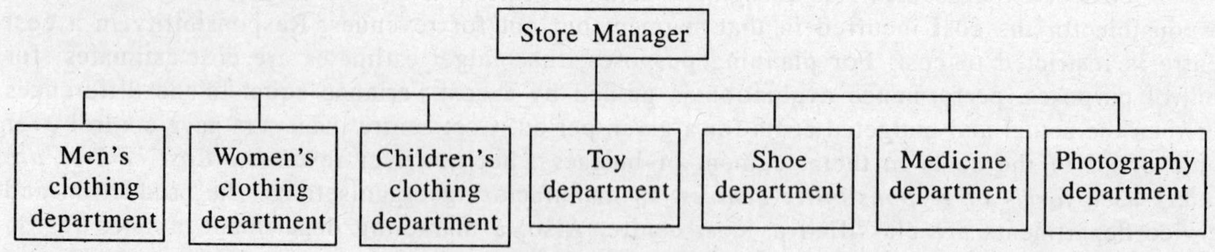

Fig. 27.2 Profit Centre

4. Investment Centre

An investment centre is responsible for both profits and investments. The investment centre manager has control over revenues, expenses and the amounts invested in the centre's assets. He also formulates the credit policy which has a direct influence on debt collection and the inventory policy which determines the investment in inventory. The manager of an investment centre has more authority and responsibility than the manager of either a cost centre or a profit centre.

Besides controlling costs and revenues, he has investment responsibility too. Investment on assets responsibility means the authority to buy, sell and use divisional assets.

RESPONSIBILITY ACCOUNTING

The term *'responsibility accounting'* refers to an accounting process that reports how well managers (of responsibility centres) have fulfilled their responsibility. Also known as activity or profitability accounting, it is an information system that personalises control reports by accumulating and reporting cost and revenue information according to defined responsibility areas within a company. Responsibility accounting systems are tailored to the organisation structure so that revenue and costs are accumulated and reported by centres of responsibility within the organisation. The responsibility accounting system recognises various decision centres throughout an organisation and traces costs (as well as revenues, assets, and liabilities, where relevant) to the individual managers who are primarily responsible for making decisions above these variables. The responsibility accounting system makes the following important assumptions:

(1) The areas of responsibility are defined for which managers should be held responsible.

(2) Managers are only charged with the items and responsibility over which they can exercise a significant degree of direct control.

(3) Managers should actively participate in establishing the goals or budgets against which their performance is measured.

(4) Goals defined for each area of responsibility should be attainable with efficient and effective performance.

(5) Control (performance) reports should contain significant information related to each area of responsibility.

(6) Responsibility centre managers should try to accomplish the budgets and objectives established for their respective areas of responsibility.

Responsibility accounting is closely related with the goal of controllability. Accordingly, in responsibility accounting, these elements in a certain area of activity are identified which are controllable and then a person is given the responsibility for managing such elements. Responsibility accounting implies that individuals in an organisation should be made responsible for only those elements which they can control. Obviously, they cannot be responsible for those items which they cannot control. They should also not claim any authority over those revenues which are not the result of their actions and performances. For instance, a foreman in a production department can be held responsible only for direct material and direct labour costs, because these are the costs which are controllable by him. On the other hand, divisional manager of the production division can be held accountable for all direct and indirect costs incurred in his division. Generally, those decision makers who are placed higher in the authority hierarchy, are held responsible for a greater number of activities and financial elements. In the long run, however, all costs are controllable by someone in the organisation.

RESPONSIBILITY PERFORMANCE REPORTING

Responsibility performance reporting implies the reporting phase of responsibility accounting. Responsibility reporting has two purposes:

(*i*) To determine the degree of performance in the area of responsibility for which the responsibility manager is directly responsible.

(*ii*) To formulate measures to improve the performance of the responsibility centre manager.

The responsibility reporting should be suitable and relevant with respect to content, frequency of reporting and level of details required. In order to provide relevant contents in the report, only those items that are controlled by the particular responsibility centre manager should be reported. Frequency of reporting and the quantum of details in the report can be decided in terms of requirements. Usry and Hammer[1] have mentioned the following as characteristics of responsibility reporting:

(1) Reports should fit the organisation chart, that is, the report should be addressed to the individual responsible for the items covered by it, who, in turn will be able to control those costs under his jurisdiction. Managers must be educated to use the results of the reporting system.

(2) Report should be prompt and timely. Prompt issuance of a report requires that cost records be organised so that information is available when it is needed.

(3) Reports should be issued with regularity. Promptness and regularity are closely tied up with the mechanical aids used to assemble and issue reports.

(4) Reports should be easy to understand. Often they contain accounting terminology that managers with little or no accounting training find it difficult to understand, and vital information may be incorrectly communicated. Therefore, accounting terms should be explained or modified to fit the user. Top management should have some knowledge of the kind of items chargeable to an account as well as the methods used to compute overhead rates, make cost allocations and analyse variances.

(5) Reports should convey sufficient but not excessive details. The amount and nature of the details depend largely on the management level receiving the report. Reports to the management should neither be flooded with immaterial facts or so condensed that management lacks vital information essential to carry out its responsibilities.

(6) Reports should give comparative figures, *i.e.,* a comparison of actual with budgeted figures or of predetermined standards with actual results and the isolation of variances.

(7) Reports should be analytical. Analysis of underlying papers such as time tickets, scrap tickets, work orders and materials requisitions provide reasons for poor performance which might have been due to power failure, machine breakdown, an inefficient operator, poor quality of materials or many other similar factors.

(8) Reports for the operating management should, if possible, be stated in physical units as well as in terms of money since monetary information may give a foreman, not trained in the language of the accountant, a certain amount of difficulty.

(9) Reports may tend to highlight departmental efficiencies and inefficiencies, results achieved, future goals or targets.

Illustration 1:

Nicefit manufactures ready-made garments by a simple process of cutting the clothes in various shapes and sewing the corresponding pieces together to form the finished products.

The Sewing Department and the Cutting Department report to the Production Manager who along with the Engineering Manager reports to the Director — Manufacturing. The Sales Manager, Publicity Manager and the Credit Manager report to the Managing Director of the Company.

The Accounts Department reports the following for the last quarter of 2008:

1. Milton E. Usry and Lawrence H. Hammer, *Cost Accountings, Planning and Control.* South Western Publishing Co., pp. 300-301.

	Budgeted (Rs.)	*Actual (Rs.)*
Bad Debt Losses	5,000	3,000
Cloth used	31,000	36,000
Advertising	4,000	4,000
Audit fees	7,500	7,500
Credit Reports	1,200	1,050
Sales Representatives:		
Travelling Expenses	9,000	10,200
Sales Commission	7,000	7,000
Cutting Labour	6,000	6,600
Thread	500	450
Sewing Labour	17,000	18,400
Credit Dept. Salaries	8,000	8,000
Cutting Utilities	800	700
Sewing Utilities	900	950
Director — Marketing:		
Salaries & Admn. Exp.	20,000	21,400
Production Engineering Expenses	13,000	12,200
Sales Management Office Expenses	16,000	15,700
Production Manager Office Expenses	18,000	17,000
Director — Manufacturing: Salaries & Admn. Expenses	21,000	20,100

Using the above data, prepare responsibility accounting reports for the Director — Marketing, the Director — Manufacturing and the production manager.

Solution:

Responsibility Accounting Reports

	Budgeted Rs.	*Actual* Rs.	*Variance* Rs.	
For the Production Manager				
Cutting Department:				
Cloth	31,000	36,000	5,000	(Unfavourable)
Cutting labour	6,000	6,600	600	(Unfavourable)
Cutting Utilities	800	700	100	(Favourable)
Total Cutting Dept. (A)	37,800	43,300	5,700	(Unfavourable)
Sewing Department:				
Thread	500	450	50	(Favourable)
Sewing Labour	17,000	18,400	1,400	(Unfavourable)
Sewing Utilities	900	950	50	(Unfavourable)
Total Sewing Dept (B)	18,400	19,800	1,400	(Unfavourable)
Total (A + B)	56,200	63,100	6,900	(Unfavourable)
For the Director — Manufacturing				
Production Department*	56,200	63,100	6,900	(Unfavourable)
Production Engineering Expenses	13,000	12,200	800	(Favourable)
Production Manager — Office Expenses	18,000	17,000	1,000	(Favourable)
Total	87,200	92,300	5,100	(Unfavourable)

(*As per Responsibility Accounting Report of the Production Manager)

For the Director — Marketing

	Rs.	Rs.	Rs.	
Sales Representatives:				
Travelling Expenses	9,000	10,200	1,200	(Unfavourable)
Sales commission	7,000	7,000	—	
Total (A)	16,000	17,200	1,200	(Unfavourable)
Sales Management:				
Office Expenses (B)	16,000	15,700	300	(Favourable)
Advertising (C)	4,000	4,000	—	
Credit Department:				
Salaries	8,000	8,000	—	
Credit Reports	1,200	1,050	150	(Favourable)
Bad Debt Losses	5,000	3,000	2,000	(Favourable)
	14,200	12,050	2,150	
Total (A + B + C + D)	50,200	48,950	1,250	(Favourable)

Illustration 2:

A manufacturing company has five plants A, B, C, D and E. Each plant has a forming, cleaning and packing department.

Each level of management has responsibility over costs incurred at its level.

The budget for the current year has been set up as follows: *(Rs. '000)*

Plant	*Budgeted cost (Rs.)*
A	67,500
B	61,250
C	54,200
D	67,500
E	67,500

Budgeted information for Plant C is as follows:

Plant Manager's office	Rs. 1,175
Forming departments	Rs. 15,000
Cleaning department	27,725
Packing department	10,300

Budgeted information for Plant C forming department is as follows:

Direct materials	4,167
Direct labour	7,500
Factory overhead	3,334

The following additional budgeted data are available:

President office	8,125
Vice-President, Marketing	10,000
Vice-President, Manufacturing Office	2,084

The following actual costs are incurred during the year:

Plant	*Actual cost*
A	63,825
B	62,150

C	54,238
D	65,550
E	68,400

The actual cost for Plant C (Forming Department) were as follows:

Direct materials	Rs. 167	Under budget
Direct labour	2,000	Under budget
Factory overhead	167	Over budget

Actual costs for Plant C (Plant Manager) were:

Plant Manager's Office	1,238
Cleaning Department	28,750
Packing Department	11,250
Forming Department	13,000

Actual costs for the President's level were:

President, Office	8,188
Vice-President, Marketing	14,900
Vice-President, Manufacturing	3,16,658

Prepare a responsibility report for the year showing the details of the budgeted, actual and variance amounts for the following areas:

Level 1 Forming department, Plant C
Level 2 Plant Manager, Plant C
Level 3 Vice-President, Manufacturing
Level 4 President

Solution:

Responsibility Report

(Rs. '000)

	Budgeted (Rs.)	*Actual (Rs.)*	*Variance (Rs.)*
President (level 4)	8,125	8,188	63
President's office	10,000	14,900	4,900
Vice-President, Manufacturing	3,20,034	3,16,658	(3,376)
Total controllable costs	3,38,159	3,39,745	1,587
Vice-President, Manufacturing: (level 3)			
Vice-President, Manufacturing Office	2,084	2,495	412
Plant A	67,500	63,825	(3,675)
Plant B	61,250	62,150	900
Plant C	54,200	54,238	(38)
Plant D	67,500	65,550	(1,950)
Plant E	67,500	68,400	900
Total controllable costs	3,20,034	3,16,658	(3,376)
Plant Manager, Plant C (level 2)			
Plant manager's office	1,175	1,238	63
Forming department	15,000	13,000	(2,000)
Cleaning department	27,725	28,750	1,025
Packing department	10,300	11,250	950
Total controllable costs	54,200	54,238	38

Forming department, Plant C (level 1)			
Direct materials	4,167	4,000	(167)
Direct labour	7,500	5,500	(2,000)
Factory overhead	3,334	3,500	167
Total controllable costs	15,000	13,000	(2,000)

MEASURING DIVISIONAL PERFORMANCE

Performance measurement is aimed in respect of all responsibility centres. Whether dealing with a cost, profit or investment centre, performance can only be evaluated by comparing results with something. Probably the best way to encourage managers to act in the firm's best interests is to measure their performance in relation to budgeted results. The following techniques can be used to measure the performance of a division:

(1) Variance Analysis: Variance analysis may be: (*i*) cost variance analysis and (*ii*) revenue variance analysis. As stated earlier, performance of a cost centre can be evaluated using cost variance analysis, *i.e.,* by comparing the actual costs with the standard costs. Standard costs display the costs the cost centre should have incurred, given their actual activity. Any variance between the actual costs and standard costs require corrective action by the management. On measuring the performance (in terms of incurrence of costs) attempts are made to minimise the costs of the cost centre.

Measuring the performance of the cost centre only in terms of cost incurred without relating to benefits achieved by the centre is not considered fair by many companies. Therefore, most companies use both financial (cost) data and non-financial measures (units produced, number of customers attended etc.) in performance measurement.

Decoster *et al.*[2] observes:

"It is difficult to assess the effectiveness and efficiency of a cost centre, even with a budget, because the financial impact of decisions is measured only by costs. There is no corresponding financial measure of what the cost centre accomplished. If not done carefully, the analysis of a cost centre may lead to the assumption that the best cost centre is the one that spreads the least. This attitude ignores benefits contributed by the cost centre to the overall firm."

Revenue variance analysis can be used in evaluating the performance of a revenue centre. If actual sales (revenues) are different from budgeted sales, they become the primary focus of management attention. While evaluating the performance of a revenue centre, costs incurred are not used as a *yardstick*.

(2) Division Contribution Margin: Division contribution margin is defined as the total division revenue less the direct costs of the division. This measure of performance emphasises the contribution of each division to overall company profit. In this measure, all revenues and costs traceable to the division are included and all common, indirect costs of the company are excluded. The reason is that operating expenses directly traceable to or incurred for the sole benefit of a specific division are generally subject to the control of the divisional manager. Indirect costs are incurred for the benefit of the entire company and are thus not subject to the control of individual division managers.

The direct contribution margin is the most useful profit measure for comparing divisional performances, for making resources allocation decisions and for overall corporate planning and

2. Don T. Decoster, *Management Accounting, A Decision Emphasis,* John Wiley and Sons, 1988, p. 547.

policy decisions. Top management of the company often uses the direct contribution margin to decide in which divisions additional investments should be made and in this decision, it will surely prefer those divisions which are giving the greatest contribution margin.

The contribution margin analysis can also be used to decide the discontinuance of a division or a certain operation. If a specific division or department provides a contribution margin, the division should not be eliminated but retained, although the allocation of indirect costs results in a net loss for that division.

(3) Division Net Profit: The division net profit is the most appropriate profit measure for the evaluation of a division's performance. This analysis can be used to judge the performance of a profit centre as both cost and revenue data measured in financial terms are available. Division net profit is obtained after considering related revenues, direct costs and a part of indirect costs incurred for the benefit of the division. Direct costs are easily identified with and traced to the division benefited. Indirect costs like salaries of company executives, officers, office staff, accounts staff are not identifiable with specific division and therefore should be allocated using an equitable and reasonable basis of allocation of indirect costs. There are many methods of cost allocation available and no single method can be considered superior under all circumstances. Hence the determination of divisional profit, that is, its performance, can itself be reliable if it includes a part of indirect costs.

The division net profit criterion is useful in the sense that a division manager becomes aware of the full costs incurred for the entire company and allocated full costs to the specific division. This may inspire the division manager to take measures to control costs and to improve the profitability of the division.

It is claimed that while measuring the performance of a profit division, it is better to use a measure of divisional revenue less divisional costs and a divisional revenue less divisional controllable costs should be used to measure the performance of the divisional manager. When fixed costs are considered and allocated to divisions, the resulting direct profit figure is more a measure of the division's performance rather than the divisional manager's performance.

On the contrary, controllable profit (divisional revenue – divisional controllable costs) is a much better measure of the divisional manager's performance as it considers all costs — fixed or variable — which are within his control. The full cost can be suitable to measure a division's performance but not the performance of a divisional manager because then he is held responsible for some costs (allocated fixed costs) which is not controllable by him and which he cannot influence directly or indirectly.

Roland Fox *et*[3] *al.* observe:

"If the performance of the manager is being assessed, then it would seem reasonable to base that assessment only on costs and revenues that are controllable by him. Thus, apart from those service costs, that are clearly identifiable with the activities of an individual division, the expenses of the central head office should not be included, even if the absence of an administrative centre would cause additional expenses in the division. The vast majority of central expenses are uncontrollable by the divisional management and their joint nature makes any allocation arbitrary and unfair. However, if the performance of the division is being evaluated, then it is perfectly reasonable to allocate all the operating expenses of the head office, together with the cost of say short-term financing undertaken by it, although the usual caveats regarding the decision value of such indirect costs should be observed by the top management."

3. Roland Fox, *Decision-making: A Management Accounting Perspective*, Butterworth Heinemann, 1990, p. 349.

(4) Return of Investment (ROI): This measure expresses divisional profit as a percentage of the firm's investment in the division and is similar to the widely accepted *'return on capital employed'* measure used in the external analysis and interpretation of accounts:

This is calculated as:

$$\text{ROI} = \frac{\text{Divisional Profit}}{\text{Divisional Investment}}$$

$$= \frac{\text{Net Profit}}{\text{Sales}} \times \frac{\text{Sales}}{\text{Investment}}$$

(Net Profit margin) (Assets Turnover)

The ROI ratio can be divided into other ratios such as net profit margin and the asset turnover as shown above. The net profit margin is the result of the firm's pricing policy and its cost control. It is a measure of the relationships among sales, expenses, volume and profit.

The assets turnover shows the amounts of sales generated by the assets available and whether a division has over- or under-utilised its assets. Thus, for analysis purposes, the basic formula of ROI is broken down into the product of return on sales and investment turnover and will appear as follows:

$$\text{ROI} = \frac{\text{Divisional Profit}}{\text{Divisional Investment}} = \frac{\text{Divisional Net Profit}}{\text{Divisional Sales}} \times \frac{\text{Divisional Sales}}{\text{Divisional Investment}}$$

(Net Profit Margin) (Asset Turnover)

The above expanded version will produce the same ROI because divisional sales cancels out the denominator in the first factor and the numerator in the second factor. However, the expanded version of the ROI formula is very useful for analysis and decision purposes. This is clear from the following example:

Illustration 3:

A merchandising firm sells its goods through department stores and discount houses which it has set up for operating the sales. The ROI of both businesses is 20 per cent and has the following data:

	Department Stores) (Rs.)	*Discount Warehouses (Rs.)*
Divisional profit	20,000	32,000
Divisional Investment	1,00,000	1,60,000
Divisional Sales	2,00,000	4,80,000

Calculation:

Departmental Stores

$$\text{Overall ROI} = \frac{\text{Divisional Profit}}{\text{Divisional Investment}}$$

$$= \frac{\text{Rs. } 20{,}000}{\text{Rs. } 1{,}00{,}000}$$

$$= 20\%$$

$$\text{Expanded ROI} = \frac{\text{Divisional Profit}}{\text{Divisional Sales}} \times \frac{\text{Divisional Sales}}{\text{Divisional Investment}}$$

$$= \frac{\text{Rs. } 20{,}000}{\text{Rs. } 2{,}00{,}000} \times \frac{\text{Rs. } 2{,}00{,}000}{\text{Rs. } 1{,}00{,}000}$$

$$= 10\% \times 2 = 20\%$$

Discount Warehouses

$$\text{Overall ROI} = \frac{\text{Divisional Profit}}{\text{Divisional Investment}}$$

$$= \frac{\text{Rs. } 32{,}000}{\text{Rs. } 1{,}60{,}000}$$

$$= 20\%$$

$$\text{Expanded ROI} = \frac{\text{Divisional Profit}}{\text{Divisional Sales}} \times \frac{\text{Divisional Sales}}{\text{Divisional Investment}}$$

$$= \frac{\text{Rs. } 32{,}000}{\text{Rs. } 4{,}80{,}000} \times \frac{\text{Rs. } 4{,}80{,}000}{\text{Rs. } 1{,}60{,}000}$$

$$= 6.67\% \times 3 = 20\%$$

It can be observed that the Department Store earns higher profit per rupee of sales but only turns over capital (assets) employed only twice. In case of Discount Houses, the sales volume generated is thrice of the assets therein and thus capital turnover is 3. However, profit earned per rupee of sales is lower which is only 6.67 as compared to 10% of the Department Stores.

The ROI formula recognises that the absolute size of divisional operating profit alone does not provide a basis for measuring its performance, but rather the relation between the division's net income and the assets used in the generation of that income. For example, the fact that division A has net income of Rs. 50,000 does not necessarily mean that it was more successful than Division B which has profit of Rs. 40,000. The differences between these profit levels could be attributable entirely to a difference in the investment size of divisions. In such a situation, ROI proves to be a good measure of performance of a division. For example, assuming that the investment in Division A and B are Rs. 2,00,000 and Rs. 1,00,000 respectively, the ROI can better indicate their comparative performances.

$$\text{ROI} = \frac{\text{Divisional Profit}}{\text{Divisional Investment}}$$

$$\text{Division A} = \frac{\text{Rs. } 50{,}000}{\text{Rs. } 2{,}00{,}000} = 25\%$$

$$\text{Division B} = \frac{\text{Rs. } 40{,}000}{\text{Rs. } 1{,}00{,}000} = 40\%$$

Thus, using ROI, it is proved that Division B is more efficient and has made more profit than Division A.

ROI can be increased by any of the following actions, all other factors being held constant:

(1) An increase in sales price or sales volume.

(2) A decrease in operating costs (fixed or variable).

(3) A reduction in divisional investment.

ROI has the following advantages:

(1) It relates net income to investments made in a division giving a better measure of divisional profitability.

(2) It can be used as a basis for other ratios which are useful for analytical purposes.

(3) It is easy to understand as it is based on financial accounting measurement.

(4) It may be used for interfirm comparisons, provided that the firms whose results are being compared are of comparable size and of the same industry.

ROI has the following limitations:

(1) Satisfactory definition of profit and investment are difficult to find. Profit has many concepts such as profit before interest and tax, profit after interest and tax, controllable profit, profit after deducting all allocated fixed costs. Similarly, the term investment may have many connotations such as gross book value, net book value, historical cost of assets, current cost of assets, assets including or excluding intangible assets.

(2) While comparing ROI of different companies, it is necessary that the companies use similar accounting policies and methods in respect of valuation of stocks, valuation of fixed assets; apportionment of overheads, treatment of research and development expenditure etc.

(3) ROI may influence a divisional manager to select only investments with high rates of return (*i.e.*, rates which are in line or above his target ROI). Other investments that would reduce the division's ROI but could increase the value of the business may be rejected by the divisional manager. It is likely that another division may invest the available funds in a project that might improve its existing ROI (which may be lower than a division's ROI which has rejected the investment) but which will not contribute as much to the enterprise as a whole. These types of decisions are sub-optimal and can distort an enterprise's overall allocation of resources and can motivate a manager to make under-investing in order to preserve his division's ROI.

Suppose a division's ROI is 25%.

$$\text{ROI} = \frac{\text{Profit Rs. } 1{,}00{,}000}{\text{Investment Rs. } 4{,}00{,}000} \times 100$$

Suppose there is an opportunity to make additional investment of Rs. 2,00,000 which will give 20% ROI. This investment is acceptable to the company because the company requires a minimum 15% ROI for this type of investment. This investment lowers the division's ROI to 23.3% calculated as follows:

$$\text{New ROI} = \frac{\text{Rs. }1,00,000 + \text{Rs. }40,000}{\text{Rs. }4,00,000 + \text{Rs. }2,00,000} \times 100$$

$$= 23.3\%$$

A comparison of old ROI (25%) with the new ROI (23.3%) would imply that performance has declined. Consequently, a divisional manager might decide not to make such an investment.

(5) Residual Income (RI)

Residual income can be defined as the *net income of a division,* less the 'imputed' *capital charge on the assets used by the division.* The capital charge is the minimum acceptable rate of return and is calculated by applying this required (or target) rate of return to the division's investment base. Theoretically, rate of return should be the division's cost of capital; in most cases, however, it is a cut-off rate based on the firm's objectives and strategies and will be somewhat higher than the divisional cost of capital. RI is calculated as

RI = Divisional Profit – (Per cent capital charge × Divisional Investment)

The 'divisional profit' and 'divisional investment' are as they are defined in ROI. Using the data given in the above example, *i.e.* divisional profit Rs. 1,00,000, investment Rs. 4,00,000 and further assuming capital charge of 15%, the RI will be Rs. 40,000 calculated as follows:

RI = Rs. 1,00,000 – (15% × Rs. 4,00,000)
= 1,00,000 – 60,000
= Rs. 40,000

Residual income from the additional investment of Rs. 2,00,000 will be

RI = Rs. 40,000 – (15% of Rs. 2,00,000)
= Rs. 10,000

Therefore, after making additional investment, the total residual income of the division will be Rs. 50,000, *i.e.*

RI = Profits 1,00,000 + 40,000 – (15% × (Rs. 4,00,000 + 2,00,000)
= (1,40,000 – 90,000)
= Rs. 50,000

Thus, the additional investment increases residual income, appropriately improving the measure of performance, whereas the use of ROI has worsened the measure of performance as it gives the overall lower ROI.

RI has following advantages:

(1) It avoids sub-optimal decisions as investments are not rejected merely because they lower the divisional manager's ROI.

(2) It maximises growth of the company and increases shareholders' wealth by accepting opportunities which earn a rate of return in excess of the cost of capital.

(3) The cost of capital charge on divisional investments ensures that divisional managers are aware of the opportunity cost of funds.

(4) Charging each division with the company's cost of capital ensures that decisions taken by different divisions are compatible with the interests of the organisation as a whole.

The following are the weaknesses of RI:

(1) Like the ROI, it is difficult to have a satisfactory definition of 'divisional profit' and 'divisional investment.'

(2) It may be difficult to calculate the accurate cost of capital. Also, the decision has to be taken to use company's cost of capital or specific divisional cost of capital. The former enhances divisional goal congruency and the later reflects each division's level of risk.

(3) Identifying controllable and uncontrollable factors at divisional level may be difficult.

To conclude about the measures for divisional performance evaluation, the following summary is prepared:

Measures	*Cost Centre*	*Revenue Centre*	*Profit Centre*	*Investment Centre*
1. Cost variance	✔	✔	✔	✔
2. Revenue variance analysis	—	✔	✔	✔
3. Contribution margin	—	—	✔	✔
4. Return on investment (ROI)	—	—	—	✔
5. Residual income	—	—	—	✔
6. Flexible budgeting	✔	✔	✔	✔
7. Standard costing or Expenses budgeting	✔	—	✔	✔
8. Profit Budgeting	—	—	✔	✔
9. Net profit margin (Profit/sales)	—	—	✔	✔
10. Assets turnover (Sales/Investment)	—	—	—	✔

NON-FINANCIAL MEASURES OF PERFORMANCE

ROI and RI both are recognised as important measures for evaluating the performance of a division. However, these and other financial measures are not considered fully adequate to evaluate the performance of a responsibility centre. Also, these techniques are short-term measures and division managers may be tempted, therefore, to derive short-term benefits (through using these measures) at the expense of long-run benefits of the company. Hence, it has been argued that additional non-financial measures should be used to evaluate a division's performance besides using both these techniques.

The additional non-financial measures or multiple measures of performance are market share, customer's complaints, personnel turnover ratios, personnel training and development, product or service quality, delivery reliability, minimisation of wastages and losses etc. These non-financial measures are vital to the success of a division and also to the overall success of a firm. Also, financial and non-financial goals and targets are often included as a part of a divisional manager's plan and responsibility. By informing the lower-level managers about the significance of non-financial measures and goals and long-run factors as well, top management can duly minimise the tendency to overemphasise ROI and RI. It is rightly claimed that any financial measures like ROI and RI have drawbacks while evaluating divisional performance, since it is virtually impossible to capture in one financial measure all the variables that measures the success of a division. For example, two divisional managers having equal amounts of investments in their respective divisions, may also have similar measures. However, this does not surely mean that their performances are also equal. For example, one division might have provided excellent customer service and thereby has created customer goodwill and reputation for the company. The other division might have done very poorly in the area of customer service. Likewise, a specific division may have invested on providing training, education, job enrichment and development, whereas some other division might have totally neglected these activities. Obviously, difference in the different divisions on account of non-performance of these and similar activities will not enter into ROI and RI calculated for different divisions.

Earlier, little attention was given to non-financial performance measurements. But recently, wider recognition and greater attention has been given for the development of non-financial measures to assess the performance of a division. Kaplan and Atkinson[4] suggest using factors like product quality, service, cleanliness, sales volume, personnel training and cost control to evaluate the performance of a division or overall company.

Johnson and Kaplan[5] have emphasised the importance of non-financial measures and comment in the following manner:

"More important than attempting to measure monthly or quarterly profits is measuring and reporting a variety of non-financial indicators. The indicators should be based on the company's strategy and include key measures of manufacturing, marketing and R and D systems. For example, a company emphasising quality could measure internal failure indicators — scrap, network, part-per-million defect rates, unscheduled machine down-time and external failure indicators — customer complaints, warranty expenses and service calls. Rather than attempting to extract such information from a system designed primarily to satisfy external reporting and auditing requirements, we should design systems consistent with the technology of the organisation, its product strategy and its organisation structure."

Colin Drury[6] also advises considering other measures of performance in the following words:

"ROI and Residual Income cannot stand alone as a measure of divisional performance. Short-run profitability is only one of the factors contributing to a company's long-run objectives. Return on investment and residual income are short-run concepts that deal only with the past year, whereas managerial performance measures should focus on future results that can be expected because of present actions. Divisional performance measurement should also measure those other factors that are critical to the success of the organisation. In particular, the performance measure should support the corporate objectives and the competitive strategies of the organisation."

TRANSFER PRICING

In divisionalised companies, where profit or investment centres are created, there is likely to be inter-divisional transfer of goods or services and these internal transfers create the problem of transfer pricing. A *transfer price* is that notional value at which goods and services are transferred between divisions in a decentralised organisation. Transfer prices are normally set for intermediate products which are goods and services that are supplied by the selling division to the buying

4. R.S. Kaplan and Atkinson, *Advanced Management Accounting*, Prentice Hall, 1989.
5. H.T. Johnson and R.S. Kaplan, *Relevant Lost — The Rise or Fall and Management Accounting*, Harvard Business School Press, 1987.
6. Colin Drury, *Management and Cost Accounting*, Chapman and Hall, 1992, p. 743.

division. The goods that are produced by the buying division and sold to the outside world are known as *final products*.

A question arises as to how the transfer of goods and services between divisions should be priced. The price charged to the inter-divisional transfer of goods and services is revenue to the selling division and cost to the buying division. Therefore, the price charged will affect the profit of both divisions: benefit (revenue) to one division can be created only at the expense of the other division. For example, the selling division will benefit from charging higher prices for such transfer of goods and services. However, for the buying divisions, this will result into higher costs. The transfer prices, thus, can have impact on the evaluation of each division's performance and measures applied for such measurements of performance. While determining transfer prices, a number of criteria should be carefully followed:

(*i*) Transfer prices should help in the accurate measurement of divisional performance (profitability) measurement.

(*ii*) Transfer prices should motivate the divisional managers into maximising the profitability of their divisions and making decisions that are in the best interests of the organisations as a whole.

(*iii*) Transfer prices should ensure that divisional autonomy and authority is preserved. The main purpose of decentralisation is to enable divisional managers to exercise greater autonomy and to measure the overall results achieved on a profit centre or investment centre. It is, therefore, not proper to give divisional managers authority by one hand by placing them in charge of divisional operations and to remove that authority by dictating transfer prices that affect the performance of the division.

(*iv*) Transfer prices should allow goal congruence to take place, which in effect means that the objectives of divisional managers are compatible with the objectives of the overall company.

(*v*) A transfer pricing system, if properly established, can check multinational companies which may try to manipulate transfer prices between countries in order to minimise the overall tax burden.

It can be said that the problem of suitable transfer prices arises only when divisions do business with one another. One way to eliminate the need to establish transfer prices is to eliminate all transactions among divisions. The problem with this solution is that it would forgo for the company and the divisions the very substantial scale economies that come as a result of being able to centralise certain corporate functions while simultaneously achieving the benefits of decentralisation. On the other hand, the greater the number of transfers relative to the volume of a division's operations, the less independent it becomes and the more meaningless it is to establish separate divisions with profit and investment responsibilities.

METHODS OF TRANSFER PRICING

Broadly, there are three bases available for determining transfer prices, but many options are also available within each base. These methods are:

(1) Market Prices.

(2) Cost-Based Prices

- (*a*) Variable cost
- (*b*) Actual full cost
- (*c*) Full cost plus profit margin
- (*d*) Standard full cost

(3) Negotiated Prices
(4) Dual Prices

(1) Market-Based Prices

Market prices refer to a price in an intermediate market between independent buyers and sellers. When there is a competitive external market for the transferred product, market prices work well as transfer prices. When transferred goods are recorded at market prices, divisional performance is more likely to represent the real economic contribution of the division to total company profits. If the goods cannot be bought from a division within the company, the intermediate product would have to be purchased at the current market price from the outside market. Divisional profits are therefore likely to be similar to the profits that would be calculated if the divisions were separate organisations. Consequently, divisional profitability can be compared directly with the profitability of similar companies operating in the same type of business. Managers of both buying and selling divisions are indifferent between trading with each other or with outsiders. No division can benefit at the expense of another division. In the market price situation, top management will not be tempted to intervene.

The opportunity cost approach also signals that the correct transfer price is the market price. Since the selling division can sell all that it produces at the market price, transferring internally at a lower price would make the division worse off. Similarly, the buying division can always acquire the intermediate goods at the market price, so it would be unwilling to pay more for an internally transferred goods. Since the minimum transfer price for the selling division is the market price and the maximum price for the buying division is also the market price, the only possible transfer price is the market price.[7]

The market price can be used to resolve conflicts among the buying and selling divisions. From the company's viewpoint, market price is optimal so long as the selling division is operating at full capacity. The market price does not allow any gains or losses in efficiency of the selling division. It saves administrative costs as the use of competitive market prices are free from any dispute, argument and bias.

However, there are some problems using the market price approach.

Firstly, finding a competitive market price may be difficult if such a market does not exist. Catalogue price may only vaguely relate to actual sales prices. Market prices may change often. Also, internal selling expenses may be less than that would be incurred if the products were sold to outsiders. Further, the fact that two responsibility centres are part of one company, indicates that there may be some advantages from being part of one company and not being two separate companies dealing with each other in the market. For example, there may be more certainty about the internal division's product quality or delivery reliability. Or the selling division may make a specialised product for which there are no substitutes in the market. Hence, it may not be possible to use market prices.

Another problem with market prices can occur when a selling division is not operating at full capacity and can sell its products. To illustrate this point, assume that material used by Division A in a company are being purchased from outside market at Rs. 20 per unit. The same materials are produced by Division B. If Division B is operating at full capacity, say of 50,000 units, and can sell all its products to either Division A or to outside buyers, then the use of transfer price of Rs. 20 per unit (market price) has no effect on Division B's income or total company

7. Ron R. Hanen and Maryanne M. Mowen, *Management Accounting,* South Western Publishing Co., 1992, p. 871.

profit. Division B will earn revenues of Rs. 20 per unit on all its production and sales, regardless of who buys its product and Division A will pay Rs. 20 per unit, regardless of whether it purchases the materials from Division B or from an outside supplier. In this situation, the use of market price as the transfer price is appropriate.

However, if Division B is not operating at full capacity and unused capacity exists in that division, the use of market price may not lead to maximisation of total company profit. To illustrate this point, assume that Division B has unused capacity of 30,000 units and it can continue to sell only 50,000 units to outside buyers. In this situation, the transfer price should be set to motivate the manager of Division A to purchase from Division B if the variable cost per unit of product of Division B is less than the market price. If the variable costs are less than Rs. 20 per unit but the transfer price is set equal to the market price of Rs. 20, then the manager of Division A is indifferent as to whether materials are purchased from Division B or from outside suppliers, since the cost per unit to Division B would be the same, Rs. 20. However, Division A's purchase of 20,000 units of materials from outside suppliers at a cost for Rs. 20 per unit would not maximise overall company profit, since this market price per unit is greater than the unit variable cost of Division B, say Rs. 10. Hence, the intracompany transfer could save the company the difference between the market price per unit and Division B's unit variable expenses. This savings of Rs. 10 per unit would add Rs. 2,00,000 (20,000 units × Rs. 10) to overall company profits.

(2) Cost-Based Prices

When external markets do not exist or are not available to the company or when information about external market prices is not readily available, companies may decide to use some forms of cost-based transfer pricing system.

As stated earlier, cost-based transfer prices may be in different forms such as variable cost, actual full cost, full cost plus profit margin, standard full cost.

(a) Variable Cost: Variable cost-based pricing approach is useful when the selling division is operating below capacity. The manager of the selling division will generally not like this transfer price because it yields no profit in that division. In this pricing system, only variable production costs are transferred. These costs are direct materials, direct labour and variable factory overheads. Variable cost has the major advantage of encouraging maximum profits for the entire firm. By passing only variable costs to the next division, production and pricing decisions are based on cost-volume-profit relationships for the firm as a whole. The obvious problem is that selling division is left holding all its fixed costs and operating expenses. That division is now a loss division, no near a profit centre.[8]

(b) Actual Full Cost: In actual full cost approach, transfer price is based on the total product cost per unit which will include direct materials, direct labour and factory overheads. When full cost is used for transfer pricing, the selling division cannot realise a profit on the goods transferred. This may be a disincentive to the selling division. Further, full cost transfer pricing can provide perverse incentives and distort performance measures. A full cost transfer price would have shut down the chances of any negotiation between divisions about setting transfer prices.

(c) Full Cost Plus Profit Margin: Full cost plus mark up (or profit margin) overcomes the weaknesses of full cost transfer pricing system. The full cost plus price include the allowed cost of the item plus a mark up or other profit allowance. With such a system, the selling division obtains a profit contribution on units transferred and hence benefits if performance is measured on

8 Lane K. Anderson and Harold M. Sollenberger, *Management Accounting,* South-Western Publishing Co. 1992, p. 174.

the basis of divisional operating profits. However, the manager of the buying division would naturally object that his costs (and hence reported performance) are adversely affected.

The basic question in full cost plus mark up is 'what should be the percentage of mark up.' It can be suggested that the mark up percentage should cover operating expenses and provide a target return on sales or assets.

(d) Standard Costs: In actual cost approaches, there is a problem of measuring cost. Actual cost does not provide any incentive to the selling division to control cost. All product costs are transferred to the buying division. While transferring actual costs, any variances or inefficiencies in the selling division are passed along to the buying division. The problem of isolating the variances that have been transferred to subsequent buyer divisions become extremely complex. To promote responsibility in the selling division and to isolate variances within divisions, standard costs are usually used as a basis for transfer pricing in cost-based systems.

Whether transferring at differential cost or full costs, standard costs where available, are often used as the basis for the transfer. This encourages efficiency in the selling division because inefficiencies are not passed on to the buying division. Otherwise, the selling division can transfer cost inefficiencies to the buying division. Use of standard costs reduce risk to the buyer. The buyer knows that standard costs will be transferred and avoids being charged with the supplier's cost over-run.[9]

(3) Negotiated Prices

Negotiated prices are generally preferred as a middle solution between market prices and cost-based prices. Under negotiated prices, the managers involved act much the same as the managers of independent companies. Negotiation strategies may be similar to those employed when trading with outside markets. If both divisions are free to deal either with each other or in the external market, the negotiated price will likely be close to the external market price. If all of a selling division's output cannot be sold in the external market (that is, a portion must be sold to the buying division), the negotiated price will likely be less than the market price and the total margin will be shared by the divisions.

Negotiated prices avoid mistrusts, bad feelings and undesirable bargaining interests among divisional managers. Also, it provides an opportunity to achieve the objectives of goal congruence, autonomy and accurate performance evaluation. The overall company is beneficiary if selling and buying divisions can agree upon some mutually transfer prices. Negotiated transfer prices are considered as a vital integrating tool among divisions of a company which is necessary to achieve goal congruence. If negotiations help ensure goal congruence, the top management has little temptation to intervene between divisions. The agreed prices also can be used for performance measurement without creating any friction. The use of negotiated prices is consistent with the concept of decentralised decision-making in the divisionalised firms.

However, negotiated prices have the following disadvantages:

(1) A great deal of management effort, time and resources can be consumed in the negotiating process.

(2) The final emerging negotiated prices may depend more on the individual manager's ability and skill to negotiate than on the other factors. Thus, performance measures will be distorted leading to incorrect evaluation of divisional performance.

(3) One divisional manager having some private information may take advantage of another divisional manager.

9. Sidney Davidson *et al. Management Accounting,* The Dryden Press, 1988, p. 683.

(4) Dual Prices

Under dual prices of transfer pricing, selling division sells the transferred goods at a profit using full cost profit margin. But the transfer price for the buying division is the *variable cost*. The difference in transfer prices for the two divisions could be accounted for by a special centralised account. This system would preserve cost data for the subsequent buyer department, and would encourage internal transfers by providing a profit on such transfers for the selling divisions.

Dual prices give motivation and incentive to selling divisions as goods are transferred at a profit or mark up. Variable cost can be considered as the most appropriate base for the buying division. The buying division will buy from a division within the company unless the outside price is less than the variable cost. This dual pricing system has the functions of motivating both the selling division and buying division to make decisions that are consistent with the overall goals of decentralisation — goal congruence, accurate performance measurement, autonomy and adequate motivation to divisional manager.

In conclusion, no particular transfer pricing system can be suggested for all decentralised companies as no one transfer price will be helpful to them in achieving all their goals and objectives. The divisionalised companies should first determine their goals and priorities before selecting a transfer pricing. Anderson and Sollenberger[10] have presented their evaluation of different transfer pricing approaches as follows:

	Goal Congruence	*Performance evaluation*	*Autonomy*	*Administrative cost*
1. Market Price	Good	Very Strong	Very strong	Low, if available
2. Cost-based prices:				
(*i*) Actual full cost	Poor	Poor	Poor	Very low
(*ii*) Full cost plus profit percentage	Poor	Average	Average	Low
(*iii*) Variable cost	Strong	Very poor	Poor	Often low
3. Negotiated prices	Strong	Strong	Strong to Poor	High
4. Dual prices	Strong (Variable Cost)	Strong (Market Price)	Poor	High

Illustration 4:

Division A and B are both considering an outlay on new investment projects.

	Division A	*Division B*
Investment outlay	Rs. 1,00,000	Rs. 1,00,000
Net return on the new investment	Rs. 16,000	Rs. 11,000
Current ROI	18%	11%

The company's cost of capital is 13%. Should the project be accepted or rejected?

Solution:

(i) Using Ratio

$$\text{ROI on New Investment} = \frac{\text{Net Return}}{\text{New investment}}$$

10. Lane K. Anderson and Harold M. Sollenberger, *Managerial Accounting*, South-Western Publishing Co., 1992, p. 719.

$$\text{Division A} = \frac{\text{Rs. } 16{,}000}{\text{Rs. } 1{,}00{,}000} \times 100 = 16\%$$

$$\text{Division B} = \frac{\text{Rs. } 11{,}000}{\text{Rs. } 1{,}00{,}000} \times 100 = 11\%$$

Division A should reject the new investment as its ROI is 16% which is less than the current ROI of 18%. Division B can accept the investment as its current ROI of 11% is equal to the new ROI on new investments.

(ii) Using RI

	Division A	*Division B*
Investment	Rs. 1,00,000	Rs. 1,00,000
Net Income on new Investment	16,000	11,000
Less: Imputed Cost of capital 13%	(13,000)	(13,000)
Residual income	3,000	(2,000)

Division A should accept the investment; it will make RI of Rs. 3,000 and Division B should reject it because it will give a loss of Rs. 2,000.

Illustration 5:

The following information relates to budgeted operation of Division X of a manufacturing company:

	(Rs.)
Sales (50,000 units of Rs. 8)	4,00,000
Less: Variable costs @ Rs. 6 per unit	3,00,000
Contribution margin	1,00,000
Less: Fixed costs	75,000
Divisional profit	25,000

The amount of divisional investment is Rs. 1,50,000 and the minimum desired rate of return on the investment is the cost of capital of 20%.

Required:

(i) Calculate divisional expected ROI

(ii) Calculate divisional expected RI

(iii) Comment on the results of *(i)* and *(ii)*

(iv) The divisional manager has the opportunity to sell 10,000 units at Rs. 7.50 per unit. Variable cost per unit would be the same as budgeted, but fixed costs would increase by Rs. 5,000. Additional investment of Rs. 20,000 would also be required. If the manager accepts the special order, by how much and in what direction would his residual Income change?

Solution:

(i) $\text{ROI} = \frac{\text{Rs. } 25{,}000}{\text{Rs. } 1{,}50{,}000} \times 100\% = 16.7\%$

(*ii*) RI = Divisional profit – Minimum desired rate of return
= Rs. 25,000 – (20% × Rs. 1,50,000)
= 25,000 – 30,000
RI = (Rs. 5,000)

(*iii*) The desired rate of return is 20% but the division X is expecting to achieve an ROI of 16.7%. The expected profit of Rs. 25,000 is less than Rs. 30,000 minimum return required, resulting in the negative of Rs. 5,000 residual income.

(*iv*) Opportunity to sell additional 10,000 units.

	Original budget Rs.	*Additional budget Rs.*	*Total Rs.*
Sales	4,00,000	75,000	4,75,000
Less: Variable costs	3,00,000	60,000	3,60,000
Contribution	1,00,000	15,000	1,15,000
Less: Fixed costs	75,000	5,000	80,000
Divisional profit	25,000	10,000	35,000
Less: Cost of capital (20%)	30,000	4,000	34,000
Residual income	(5,000)	6,000	1,000

The target residual income changes from a negative balance of Rs. 5,000 to a positive one of Rs. 1,000 as a result of the new opportunity to sell 10,000 units. This is due to the fact that Rs. 10,000 expected profit from additional order is offset by a further Rs. 4,000 cost of capital, thereby increasing residual income by Rs. 6,000.

Illustration 6:

A company has two divisions, A and B. Division A manufactures a component which is used by Division B to produce a finished product. For the next period, output and costs have been budgeted as follows:

	Division A Rs.	*Division B Rs.*
Component Units	50,000	—
Finished Units	—	50,000
Total variable costs	2,50,000	6,00,000
Fixed costs	1,50,000	2,00,000

The fixed costs are separable for each division. You are required to advise on the transfer price to be fixed for Division A's component under the following circumstances:

(1) Division A can sell the component in a competitive market for Rs. 10 per unit. Division B can also purchase the component from the open market at that price.

(2) As per the situation described in (1) above, and further assuming that Division B currently buys the component from an external supplier at the market price of Rs. 10 and there is reciprocal agreement between the external supplier and another Division C, within the group. Under this agreement, the external supplier agrees to buy one product unit from Division C, at a profit of Rs. 4 per unit to that division, for every component which Division B buys from the supplier.

Solution:

1. Transfer Price = Incremental (marginal) cost + opportunity costs of the company due to not being able to use the components in the next most profitable way.
= Rs. 5 + Rs. 5 (contribution foregone by transferring internally as opposed to selling in the open market)
= Rs. 10

The transfer price of Rs. 10 is equal to the market price of the component which is also Rs. 10.

2. Transfer price = Marginal cost + Contribution + Profit foregone by Division C as division B will acquire its units from Division A in place of external supplier.
= Rs. 5 + Rs. 5 + 4
= Rs. 5 + Rs. 9 (Rs. 9 is the opportunity cost to the whole company)
= Rs. 14.

The transfer price of Rs. 14 should result in the manager of Division B continuing to buy from the external supplier at the market price of Rs. 10. However, the transfer price of Rs. 14 is appropriate from the viewpoint of the organisation as a whole, since if the component is transferred internally, not only will Division A forego an external profit of Rs. 5, but Division C will also forego an external profit of Rs. 4. It is assumed that Division C could not achieve the same profit by selling elsewhere.

Illustration 7:

A company has two divisions, A and B. The division A is currently operating at full capacity. It has been asked to supply its product to division B. Division A sells its products to its regular customers for Rs. 30 each. Division B (currently operating at 50% capacity) is willing to pay Rs. 20 each for the component produced by division A (this represents the full absorption cost per component at division A).

The components will be used by division B in supplementing its main product to conform to the need of special order.

As per the contract terms of sales, the buyer calls for reimbursement of full cost to division B plus 10%.

Division A has a variable cost of Rs. 17 per component. The cost per unit of division B subsequent to the buying part from Division A is estimated as follows:

Purchased parts — outside vendors	Rs. 90
Purchased part — Division A	Rs. 20
Other variable costs	Rs. 50
Fixed overheads and administration	Rs. 40
	Rs. 200

The company uses return on investment in the measurement of division and the division manager's performance.

Required:

(*a*) As manager of Division A, would you recommend sales of your output to Division B at the stipulated price of Rs. 20.

(*b*) Would it be in the overall interest of the company for Division A to sell its output to Division B?

(*c*) Suggest an alternative transfer price and show how could it lead to goal congruence?

Solution:

(*a*) As manager of Division A, sales of Rs. 20 per unit to Division B should not be recommended. The division is already operating at its full capacity and the market is presumably absorbing all its output at Rs. 30 per unit. The internal transfer made to Division B, hence, would reduce its profits (by Rs. 10 per unit) as well as the ROI.

(*b*) Decision analysis (whether to transfer part from Division A to Division B at Rs. 20 per unit or not)

Particulars	*Sold externally (Rs.)*	*Transferred to Division B (Rs.)*
Sale price (Division A)	30.00	
Sale price (Division B) (Rs. 200 + 10%)		220.0
Less: relevant on incremental cost:		
For part of Division A	17.0	17.0
Purchased parts from outside	—	90.0
Other valuable costs	—	50.0
Profit per unit	13.0	63.0

It will be in the overall interest of the company that the transfer takes place as it would increase the firm's profit by Rs. 50 per unit.

(*c*) Dual price basis of effecting transfer is the most appropriate. In this case, the relevant transfer price will be Rs. 30 (sale) so far as Division A is concerned and Rs. 20 (purchase) so far as Division B is concerned. It will keep the profits of Division A unaffected and will facilitate the utilisation of idle capacity of Division B and also increase its profit:

Sale price (Rs. 210 + 10%)	Rs. 231
Less: costs (Rs. 90 + 50)	Rs. 140
	91

Illustration 8:

The Hillman Enterprises has two divisions, A and B. Division A produces a computer circuit that is used in the finished product of Division B. The cost of producing the circuit are variable costs of Rs. 40 per circuit and fixed costs of Rs. 10 per circuit. The part is sold in the highly competitive computer market for Rs. 70 per circuit.

Uptil now, Division B bought 60% of the output of Division A at a negotiated price of Rs. 65 per circuit. But because of overemphasis on divisional welfare rather than company welfare, a new transfer pricing method must be developed. The suggestion was to add 35% to the total cost of the circuit when transferring to Division B. Another suggestion was to use the variable costs of Rs. 40 per circuit in arriving at a transfer price.

You are required, using the above information and suggestions, to determine the gross profit per finished unit for Division B according to the five principal transfer pricing methods. Pertinent data of Division B, in addition to the transfer price of the circuit, there are additional processing and marketing costs of Rs. 100 per unit. The selling price of the finished product of Division B is Rs. 200 per unit.

Solution:

Division B	*Per Unit (Rs.)*
Selling Price	200
Less: processing and marketing cost	100
	100

New transfer price suggested = Total cost + 35%
= 50 + 17.50 = Rs. 67.50

Gross profit under different transfer pricing methods

(*i*) Negotiated price = 100 – 65 = Rs. 35 per unit

(*ii*) Variable cost = 100 – 40 = Rs. 60 per unit

(*iii*) Cost plus = 100 – 67.50 = Rs. 32.50 per unit

(*iv*) Market price = 100 – 70 = Rs. 30 per unit

(*v*) Dual pricing = In dual pricing selling Division A will price at Rs. 67.50 per unit and buying division B will price at Rs. 40/- per unit, therefore gross profit for Division B under Dual pricing will be Rs. 100 – 40 = Rs. 60 per unit.

Under dual pricing system, the buying department is charged the variable cost of unit and selling division is credited with cost plus some profit allowance.

THEORY QUESTIONS

1. What is decentralisation? What are the advantages of decentralisation?
2. Explain the concept of responsibility centres.
3. How will you measure the performance of cost and revenue division?
4. Describe and compare the main performance measures that have been suggested to measure the divisional performance.
5. Profit, Return on Investment and Residual Income have stood the test of time and are widely used for measuring the performance of a division. Describe the strengths and weaknesses of these measures of performance.
6. Outline problems in defining and measuring capital employed in a division.
7. Explain the rationale of using an interest charge while measuring the performance of a division.
8. "In ROI, there is lack of consensus on the definition of numerator and denominator both." Explain.
9. It has been argued that full cost is an inappropriate basis for setting transfer prices. Outline the objections which can be levied on this basis.
10. Distinguish between a cost centre, a profit centre and an investment centre.
11. How is performance generally measured in a cost centre, and investment centre?
12. What are some of the problems in using division profit as an evaluation measure?
13. When comparing various divisions, why it is important that the divisions should have the same or similar accounting methods?

14. List the components of ROI equation, tell how they are related and identify an action a manager can take regarding each component to improve ROI.
15. How is residual income defined? What is the major advantage of using residual income in performance evaluation versus ROI?
16. What is a transfer price? Under what conditions are transfer prices necessary?
17. Using the criteria for evaluating transfer prices, evaluate each of the following transfer prices:
    (*i*) Market prices
    (*ii*) Full cost
    (*iii*) Full cost plus mark up
    (*iv*) Negotiated price
18. Explain a dual transfer price. What are the advantages and disadvantages of using such a pricing system?
19. What is the disadvantage of negotiated transfer prices when no intermediate market exists for the producing division?
20. What are net profit margin and asset turnover? Explain how these concepts can improve the evaluation of an investment centre.
21. What disadvantages are shared by ROI and residual income? What can be done to overcome this problem?
22. Identify three cost based transfer prices. What are the disadvantages of cost-based transfer prices? When might it be appropriate to use these prices?
23. Name three performance measures useful in evaluating investment centres?
24. Why should the factors under the control of the investment centre manager (revenue, expenses and invested assets) be considered in the computation of ROI?
25. What are two ways of expessing ROI?
26. In a decentralised company in which the divisions are organised as investment centres, how could a division be considered the least profitable, even though it earned the largest amount of operating income?
27. How does the use of ROI facilitate comparability of divisions of decentralised companies?
28. When is the negotiated pricing preferred over the market price approach in setting transfer prices?
29. When using negotiated pricing approach to transfer pricing, within what range should the transfer price be established?
30. "The ROI measure may be used in favour of divisions with older plant and equipment." Explain.
31. Why are market based transfer prices considered optimal under many circumstances?
32. Why do companies often use prices other than market prices for inter-divisional transfers?
33. Division A has no external markets. It produces a product that is used by Division B. Division B cannot purchase this product from any other source. What transfer pricing system would you recommend for the inter-divisional sale of the product? Why?
34. "Evaluation of a division's performance is different from evaluating the performance of the divisional manager." Explain this statement giving reasons.
35. "In computing ROI, there are problems both with regard to the numerator and the denominator." Point out these problems and give your considered view thereon.
36. "The use of market prices for transfer pricing may lead to dysfunctional decisions by some employees."
37. Many firms use cost plus negotiated transfer prices even though they do not lead to optimal results for individual products. Why?
38. What do you understand by divisional performance? In what manner is divisional performance measured and compared?

EXERCISES AND PROBLEMS

1. A company has two divisions, X and Y and evaluates its manager on the ROI criterion. Budget for the next year are as follows:

	X (Rs.)	*Y (Rs.)*	*Total (Rs.)*
Investment	12,00,000	10,00,000	22,00,000
Revenue	6,00,000	3,00,000	9,00,000
Operating expenses	(3,00,000)	(2,00,000)	(5,00,000)
Profit	3,00,000	1,00,000	4,00,000

A new investment opportunity has arisen and could be adopted by either division. It requires an investment of Rs. 2,00,000 and promises annual operating profits of Rs. 40,000.

Required:

(*i*) Which division (X or Y) would accept the new project? Why?

(*ii*) If an RI criterion with minimum ROI of 18% were in use, which division (X or Y) would accept the new project? Why?

(*iii*) With minimum ROI of 18% should the new project be adopted from the viewpoint of the company as a whole? Why?

2. A company has two department stores, which are organised as divisions. One store is at Kanpur where business activity is declining. The other store is in Bangalore, located in an area of the city that is expanding rapidly. Results of operations for each store for 2009 are shown as follows:

	Bangalore (Rs.)	*Kanpur (Rs.)*
Sales	39,00,000	17,50,000
Total costs	27,62,000	15,70,000
Average current assets	5,87,500	1,65,000
Average long-term assets	40,62,500	9,62,000
Minimum desired rate of return	15%	10%

Required:

(*i*) ROI for each division

(*a*) Compute the return on sales
(*b*) Compute the asset turnover
(*c*) Compute the ROI

(*ii*) Residual income for each division

(*a*) Compute residual income
(*b*) Compute the residual income percentage

3. Reese Company has two divisions A and B. Invested assets and condensed income statement data for each division for the past year ended December 31 are as follows:

	Division A (Rs.)	*Division B (Rs.)*
Sales	3,125,000	5,100,000
Cost of goods sold	2,500,000	4,000,000
Operating expenses	150,000	590,000
Invested assets	2,500,000	3,000,000

Required:

(*i*) Prepare condensed income statements for the past year for each division.

(*ii*) Using the expanded expression, determine the profit margin, investment turnover, and rate of return on investment for each division.

(*iii*) If management desires a minimum rate of return of 12%, determine the residual income for each division.

4. The following information relate to the operating performance of two divisions of a company:

	Division A (*Rs.*)	*Division B* (*Rs.*)
Operating Profit	4,00,000	6,00,000
Total Assets (based on acquisition cost)	4,00,000	7,50,000
Total Assets (based on current replacement cost)	6,00,000	8,00,000

(*a*) Compute the return on investment (ROI) of each division, using total assets stated at acquisition cost as the investment base.

(*b*) Compute the ROI of each division, using total assets based on current replacement cost as the investment base.

(*c*) Which of the two measures do you think gives the better indication of operating performance? Explain your reasoning.

Activity-Based Costing

MEANING OF ACTIVITY-BASED COSTING (ABC)

The Activity-Based Costing (ABC) is a costing system which focuses on activities performed to produce products. ABC is that costing in which costs are first traced to activities and then to products. This costing system assumes that activities are responsible for the incurrence of costs and products create the demands for activities. Costs are charged to products based on individual product's use of each activity. In traditional product costing system, costs are, first, traced not to activities but to an organisational unit, such as department or plant and then to products. It means under both, ABC and traditional costing system, the second and final stage consists of tracing costs to the product.

ABC aims at identifying as many costs as possible to be subsequently accounted as direct costs of production. Any cost that is traced to a particular product, via., its consumption of activity becomes direct cost of the product. For instance, in conventional costing system, cost of setup and adjustment time is considered as factory overhead and subsequently assigned to different products on the basis of direct labour hours. But, in ABC, setup and adjustment time is determined for each product and its costs are directly charged to each product. Thus, by emphasing activities, ABC tries to ascertain the factors that cause each major activity, cost of such activities and the relationship between activities and products produced. The relationship between activities and products has been show in Figure 28.1.

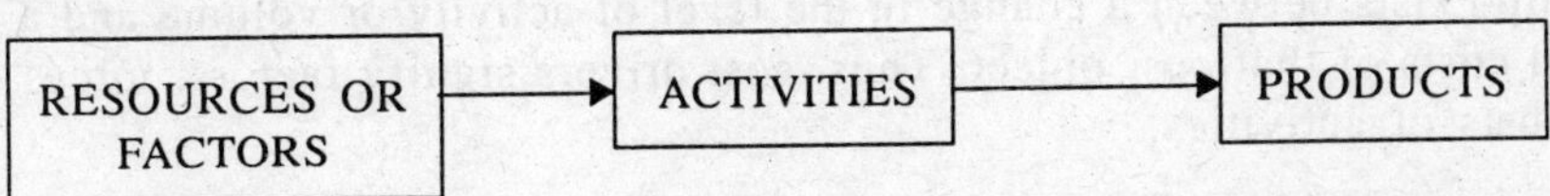

Fig. 28.1 ABC Process

STAGES AND FLOW OF COSTS IN ABC

As stated earlier, there are two primary stages in ABC — first, tracing costs to activities; second, tracing activities to products. The different steps in the two stages of ABC are explained below:

Step 1 Identify the main activities in the organisation.

Examples include: materials handling, purchasing, receipt, despatch, machining, assembly and so on.

Step 2 Identify the factors which determine the costs of an activity. These are known as cost drivers.

Examples include: number of purchase orders, number of orders delivered, number of set-ups and so on.

Step 3 Collect the costs of each activity. These are known as cost pools and are directly equivalent to conventional cost centres.

Step 4 Charge support overheads to products on the basis of their usage of the activity, expressed in terms of the chosen cost driver(s). For example, if the total costs of purchasing were Rs. 2,00,000 and there were 1,000 Purchase orders (the chosen cost driver), products would be charged Rs. 200 per purchase order. Thus a batch generating 3 purchase orders would be charged 3 × Rs. 200 = Rs. 600 for Purchasing overheads.

COST DRIVERS

An activity is a unit of work. If you go to a restaurant for lunch/dinner, a waiter or waiters might perform the following units of work:

- Seat customer and offer menu
- Take your order
- Send orders to kitchen
- Bring food
- Replenish beverages
- Determine and bring bill
- Collect money and give change
- Clear table

Each of these is an activity and the performance of each activity consumes resources that cost money. To manage activities and their costs, it is necessary to understand how costs respond to cost drivers, the factors that cause or influence costs.

A cost driver is an activity which generates cost. A cost driver is a factor, such as the level of activity or volume, that causally affects costs (over a given time span). That is, a cause-and-effect relationship exists between a change in the level of activity or volume and a change in the level of the total costs of that cost object. Thus, cost drivers signify factors, forces or events that determine the costs of activities.

ACTIVITY COST DRIVERS

Activity cost drivers are specific units of work (activities) performed to serve customer needs that consume costly resources. The customer may be outside the organisation, such as a client of an advertising firm or inside the organisation, such as an accounting office that receives maintenance services. Because the performance of activities consumes resources and resources cost money, the performance of activities drives cost. In a manufacturing organisation the following are examples of some activity cost derivers (see Fig. 28.2).

Activity Cost Drivers

1. Number of receiving orders for the receiving department.
2. Number of purchase orders for the cost of operating the purchase department.
3. Number of despatch orders for the despatch department.
4. Number of units.
5. Number of setups.
6. Amount of labour cost incurred.
7. Value of materials in a product.
8. Number of materials handling hours.
9. Number of inspections.
10. Number of schedule changes.
11. Number of parts received per month.
12. Number of machine hours used on a product.
13. Number of set up hours.
14. Number of direct labour hours.
15. Number of sub-assemblies.
16. Number of vendors.
17. Number of purchasing and ordering hours.
18. Number of units scrapped.
19. Number of labour transactions.
20. Number of customer orders processed.
21. Number of parts.
22. Number of employees.

Fig. 28.2 Cost Drivers

It should be understood that direct costs do not need cost drivers as they can he traced directly to a product. Direct costs are themselves cost drivers. However, all other factory or manufacturing costs need cost drivers. The cost driver of variable costs is the level of activity or volume whose change causes the variable costs to change proportionately.

Costs that are fixed in the short run have no cost drivers in the short run but may have cost drivers in the long run. For instance, costs of testing personal computers (which comprise costs of testing department equipment and staff costs) may not change with changes in the volume of production. Therefore, these costs would be fixed in the short run. In the long run, however, an organisation may need to increase/decrease testing department's equipment and staff to the levels needed to support future production volumes. So, in the long run, volume of production or activity becomes cost drivers of these testing and staff costs.

CLASSIFICATION OF ACTIVITIES IN MANUFACTURING ORGANISATIONS

As stated earlier, activities are identified and classified into different categories or segments of the production process. The grouping of activities is preferably done using the different levels at which activities are performed. Broadly, activities are classified into one of four activity categories:

1. Unit level Activities.
2. Batch level Activities.
3. Product level Activities.
4. Facility level Activities.

Unit level activities are those activities which are performed each time a unit is produced. They are repetitive activities. For example, direct labour hours, machine hours, power are used each time a unit is produced. Direct materials and direct labour activities are also unit level activities, although they are not overhead costs. Costs of unit level activities vary with the number of units produced.

Batch level activities are those activities which are performed each time a batch of goods or products is produced. The costs of batch level activities vary with the number of batches but are fixed with respect to the number of units in each batch. Machine setups, inspections, production scheduling, materials handling are examples of batch level activities which are related to batches but not to individual products.

Product level activities are those activities which are performed to support the production of each different type of product. Maintenance of equipment, engineering charges, testing routines, maintaining bills of materials, handling materials are some examples of batch-level activities.

Facility-level activities are those which are needed to sustain a factory's general manufacturing process. These activities are common to a variety of products and are most difficult to link to product specific activities. Examples of facility level activities are factory management, maintenance, security, plant depreciation.

Several additional examples of the costs driven by activities at each above level are presented in Fig. 28.3.

Activity Level	Reason for Activity	Examples of Activity Cost
1. Unit level	Performed for each unit of product produced or sold	• Cost of raw materials • Cost of inserting a component • Utilities cost of operating equipment • Some costs of packaging • Sales commissions
2. Batch level	Performed for each batch of product produced or sold	• Cost of processing sales order • Cost of issuing and tracking work order • Cost of equipment setup • Cost of moving batch between workstations • Cost of inspection (assuming same number of units inspected in each batch)
3. Product level	Performed to support each different product that can be produced	• Cost of product development • Cost of product marketing such as advertising • Cost of specialized equipment • Cost of maintaining specialized equipment.

4. Facility level	Performed to maintain general manufacturing capabilities	• Cost of maintaining general facilities such as buildings and grounds • Cost of nonspecialised equipment • Cost of maintaining non-specialised equipment • Cost of real property taxes • Cost of general advertising • Cost of general administration such as the plant manager's salary

Fig. 28.3 Activity Levels and Associated Activity Costs

Source: Wayne J. Morse, James R. Davis, AI. L. Hartgraves, *Managerial Accounting, A Strategic Approach,* South Western College Publishing, 2000, p.54.

In ABC system, facility level activities and costs are treated as period cost as they are found difficult to assign to different products. The costs associated with the first three categories — unit level, batch level, product level — are assigned lo products, using cost drivers that reflect the cause and effect relationship between activity consumption and cost.

COMPARING ABC WITH CONVENTIONAL COSTING SYSTEM

In traditional costing system, overhead costs are assumed to be influenced by only units produced. It means, in traditional costing system, costs of batch level, product level and facility level activities are fixed costs, that is, costs of these do not vary as production volume changes. Unit-based cost systems apportion fixed overhead to individual products and variable overhead are directly assigned to products using the base of number of units produced.

In ABC, variable overhead is appropriately traced to individual products. The costs incurred as the units are produced have been traditionally treated as variable overhead. But when fixed overheads are apportioned on the basis of units made, as in traditional costing, such apportionment is likely to be arbitrary and also may not reflect activities and cost actually consumed by the products. ABC improves product costing procedure (as compared to traditional costing) because it recognises that many so-called fixed overhead costs vary in proportion to changes other than production units. It means, under ABC, the other two level activities — batch level and product level — are assumed to influence fixed overhead costs and batch level and product level, thus, are accepted as nonunit-based cost drivers. By establishing the link between these cost drivers and fixed overhead costs, they are finally traced to individual products. Figure 28.4 presents an overview of product cost determination under traditional costing and ABC system.

It can be observed that both the costing systems follow a two stage allocation procedure. In traditional costing, in the first stage, overhead costs are allocated to production departments. But in ABC, in the first stage, overhead costs are assigned to each major activity and not to departments. In traditional costing, overheads are pooled/collected department-wise. But, in ABC, many activity-based cost pools or cost centres are created. In traditional costing, overhead costs of service departments are allocated/reapportioned to production departments and therefore in this costing system finally only fewer cost pools exist. But ABC creates separate cost pools for service activities as well and overhead costs of these service activities (service departments) are assigned directly to specific products through applying cost driver rates. Thus, in ABC, there is no need to allocate/reapportion overheads of service departments.

The fundamental differences in the conventional and ABC cost systems are summarised in Fig. 28.5.

TRADITIONAL COSTING AND ACTIVITY-BASED COSTING SYSTEM

(a) Traditional Product Costing System

Stage 1: Overheads assigned to production departments **Stage 2: Overheads allocated to products**

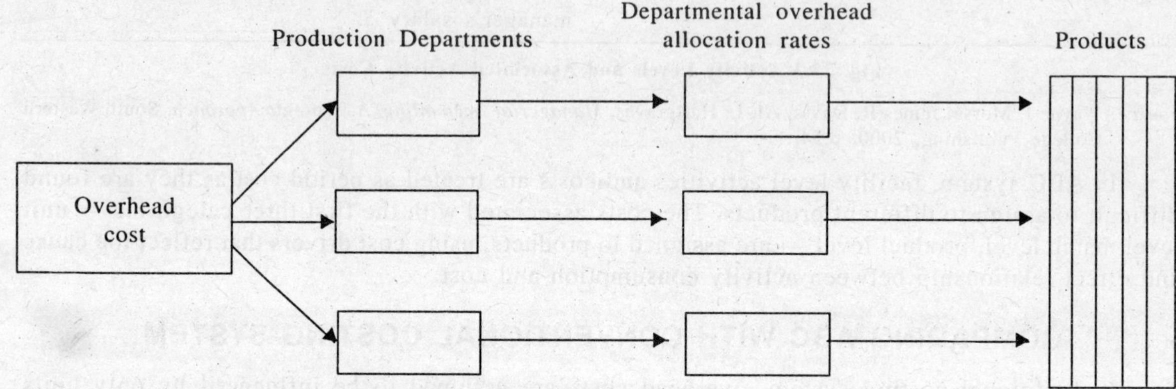

(b) Activity-based Product Costing System

Stage 1: Overheads assigned to cost centres/ cost pools **Stage 2: Overheads assigned to products using cost driver rates**

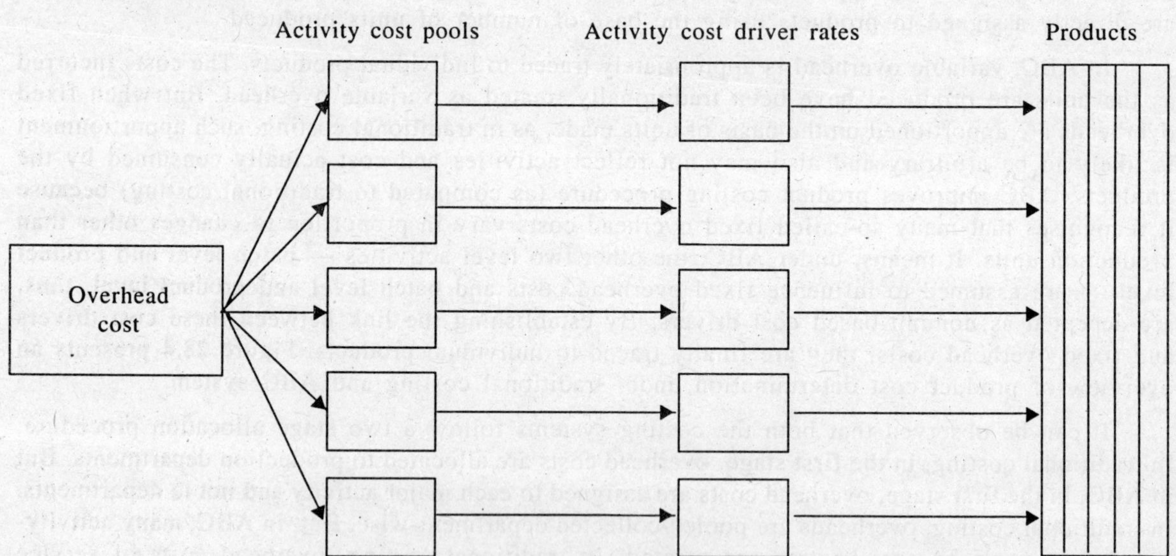

Fig. 28.4 Comparison of Traditional and Activity-Based Costing Systems

Source: J. Innes and F. Mitchell, *Activity-Based Costing: A Review with Case Studies,* 1990, CIMA, U.K.

	Conventional	ABC
Cost pools	One or a limited number	Many, to reflect different activities
Applied rate	Volume-based, financial	Activity-based, non-financial
Suited for	Labour-intensive, low-overhead companies	Capital-intensive, product-diverse, high-overhead companies
Benefits	Simple, inexpensive	Accurate product costing, possible elimination of non-value-added activities

Fig. 28.5 Conventional and ABC System

ADVANTAGES OF ABC

The following are the advantages of ABC:

1. ABC brings accuracy and reliability in product cost determination by focussing on cause and effect relationship in the cost incurrence. It recognises that it is activities which cause costs, not products and it is product which consume activities.

2. In advanced manufacturing environment and technology where support functions overheads constitute a large share of total costs, ABC provides more realistic product costs.

3. ABC identifies the real nature of cost behaviour and helps in reducing costs and identifying activities which do not add value to the product. With ABC, managers are able to control many fixed overhead costs by exercising more control over the activities which have caused these fixed overhead costs. This is possible since behaviour of many fixed overhead costs in relation to activities now become more visible and clear.

4. ABC uses multiple cost drivers, many of which are transaction based rather than product volume. Further, ABC is concerned with all activities within and beyond the factory to trace more overheads to the products.

5. ABC traces costs to areas of managerial responsibility, processes, customers, departments besides the product costs.

6. ABC improves greatly the manager's decision making as they can use more reliable product cost data. ABC helps usefully in fixing selling prices of products as more correct data of product cost is now readily available.

7. ABC produces reliable and correct product cost data in case of greater diversity among the products manufactured such as low-volume products, high-volume products. Traditional costing system is likely to bring errors and approximation in product cost determination due to using arbitrary apportionment and absorption methods.

8. ABC provides cost driver rates and information on transaction volumes which are very useful to management for cost management and performance appraisal of responsibility centres. Cost driver rates can be used advantageously for the design of new products or existing products as they indicate overhead costs that are likely to be applied in costing the product.

DEMERITS OF ABC

The following arc the demerits of ABC:

1. ABC has numerous cost pools and multiple cost drivers and therefore can be more complex than traditional product costing systems. It can prove costly to manage ABC system.
2. Some difficulties emerge in the implementation of ABC system, such as selection of cost drivers, assignment of common costs, varying cost driver rates etc.
3. ABC has different levels of utility for different organisations such as large manufacturing firm can use it more usefully than the smaller firms. Also, it is likely that firms depending on cost-plus pricing can take advantages from ABC as it gives accurate product cost. But those firms who use market based prices may not favour ABC. The level of technology and manufacturing environment prevailing in different firms also affect the application of ABC.

The decision to use ABC is comparing costs and benefits relating to this system. The advantages to a company of ABC system depends on many factors such as level of competition, number of products manufactured and product diversity. It can be claimed that those companies who operate in a more competitive environment, are in dire need of correct product cost data for taking sound decisions with regard to determination of selling prices and taking better cost management measures. Whether a company manufactures and sells smaller number or larger number of products, influence the operation of ABC system and the degree of sophistication in the system. The complexity of product mix plays a vital role in determining whether the cost of two or more activities can be combined and traced to a product by means of a single cost driver and still these costs can be assigned to products accurately. There is a need to increase the number of activity centres, cost pools and cost drivers in order to achieve the goal of more accurate product costs.

Example:

S. Chand & Co., a leading publisher, publishes two versions of a textbook. One is paperback and the other is hard bound. Management is considering publishing only the higher quality book. The firm assigns its Rs. 5,00,000 of overhead to the two types of books. The overhead is composed of Rs. 2,00,000 of utilities and Rs. 3,00,000 of quality control inspectors' salaries. Some additional data follow:

	Paperback	**Hard Bound**
Revenues	Rs. 16,00,000	Rs. 14,00,000
Direct costs	Rs. 12,50,000	Rs. 6,00,000
Production (units)	5,00,000	3,50,000
Machine hours	42,500	7,500
Inspections	2,500	12,500

Required:

(*a*) Compute the overhead cost that should be allocated to each type of textbook using cost drivers appropriate for each type of overhead cost.

(*b*) The firm has used machine hours to allocate overhead in the past. Should the publisher stop producing the paperback books? Explain why management was considering this action and what its decision should be.

Solution:

(a)	Paperback	Hard Bound	Total
Machine hours	42,500	7,500	50,000
Rate per MH (Rs. 2,00,000 ÷ 50,000)	× Rs. 4	× Rs. 4	× Rs.4
Utility cost	Rs. 1,70,000	Rs. 30,000	Rs. 2,00,000
Number of inspections	2,500	12,500	15,000
Rate per inspection (Rs. 3,00,000 ÷ 15,000)	Rs. 20	× Rs. 20	× Rs. 20
Quality inspection cost	Rs. 50,000	Rs. 2,50,000	Rs. 3,00,000
Total traceable overhead costs	Rs. 2,20,000	Rs. 2,80,000	Rs. 5,00,000

(b) Income calculation using machine hours to allocate utilities and inspection hours to allocate inspectors' salaries to products:

Using the traditional cost driver (machine hours), the following results had been achieved, given a Rs. 10 charge (Rs. 5,00,000 ÷ 50,000) per MH:

	Paperback	Hard Bound
Revenue	Rs. 16,00,000	Rs. 14,00,000
Direct costs	Rs. 12,50,000	Rs. 6,00,000
Overhead	Rs. 4,25,000	Rs. 75,000
Total costs	Rs. 16,75,000	Rs. 6,75,000
Margin	Rs. (75,000)	Rs. 7,25,000

The reason paperbacks were erroneously thought to be unprofitable was caused by the method of allocating overhead. The firm should continue producing paperbacks as shown in the following calculations:

	Paperback	Hard Bound
Revenue	Rs. 16,00,000	Rs. 14,00,000
Direct costs	Rs. 12,50,000	Rs. 6,00,000
Overhead	Rs. 2,20,000	Rs. 2,80,000
Total costs	Rs. 14,70,000	Rs. 8,80,000
Margin	Rs. 1,30,000	Rs. 5,20,000

ABC IN SERVICE ORGANISATIONS

The discussion of ABC so far has focussed on manufacturing companies where important cost components like direct material and direct labour can be traced to individual products. Therefore indirect costs are likely to be a much smaller proportion of total costs in such manufacturing companies. In service organisations, most of the costs are treated fixed and indirect, and therefore irrelevant for most decisions. No attempt is made to make profitability analysis in service organisations. There is a greater need of using ABC in service companies. Kaplan and Coopen[1] suggest that service companies are ideal candidates for ABC, even more than manufacturing companies.

1. R.S. Kaplan and R. Cooper, *Cost and Effect: Using Integrated Systems to Drive Profitability and Performance*, Harvard Business School Press, 1998.

Earlier, service organisations were government-owned or operated in highly regulated, protected and non-competitive environment. Thus, service organisations were not under any pressure to improve profitability by eliminating non-value added or non-profit activities. The prices of services were simply increased to cover cost increases. No efforts was made to design a cost system that accurately measures the costs and profitability of individual services.

However, due to privatisation, deregulation and increasing competition, the service organisations need to have cost and management accounting systems which can help them to accurately measure cost and resulting profitability for their services, customers and markets. Therefore, ABC would prove advantageous to service organisations to understand their cost base and to make decisions on value-added/non-value added activities. Kaplan and Cooper illustrate the use of ABC in banks for product and customer profitability analysis. The following are some of the activities and cost drivers in bank as identified by Kaplan and Cooper.[2]

Activity	Cost Driver
Provide ATM services	No. of ATM transactions
Clear debit items	No. of debits processed
Clear credit items	No. of credit processed
Issue cheque books	No. of cheque books issued
Computer processing	No. of computer transactions
Prepare statements of account transactions	No. of statements issued
Administer mortgages	No. of mortgages maintained

Drury and Tayles[3] after making survey of UK Companies have concluded that service organisations are more likely to implement ABC systems. They found that 51% of the financial and service organisations surveyed, compared with 15% of manufacturing organisations, had implemented ABC.

THEORY QUESTIONS

1. What is Activity-Based Costing? Why is it needed?
2. What is a cost driver? What is the role of cost driver in tracing costs to products?
3. Explain the steps in applying Activity-Based Costing (ABC) in a manufacturing company.
4. How are activities grouped in a manufacturing company?
5. Distinguish between activity-based costing and traditional costing system.
6. What are the benefits of activity-based costing?
7. Define unit level activities, batch level activities, product level activities.
8. "Overhead costs are source of product cost distortion." Do you agree? Explain.
9. What are the four basic steps required for activity-based costing?
10. Give the criterion for choosing cost drivers for allocating costs to products.
11. Why are conventional product-costing systems more likely to distort product costs in highly automated plants? How do activity-based costing systems deal with such a situation?
12. "Activity-based costing systems yield more accurate product costs than conventional systems because they use more cost drivers to assign support costs to products." Do you agree with this statement? Explain.
13. What are unit level activities? Batch level activities? Product-level activities? Facility-level activities?

2. R.S. Kaplan and R. Cooper, Ibid.
3. Colin Drury and M. Tayles, *Cost Systems Design and Profitability Analysis in UK Companies,* Chartered Institute of Management Accountants, 2000.

14. "Attributing direct costs and absorbing overhead costs to the product/service through an activity-based costing approach will result in a better understanding of the true cost of final output." You are required to explain and comment on the above statement.
15. What is an activity-based approach to designing a costing system?
16. Describe four levels of cost hierarchy.
17. What are the key reasons for product cost differences between traditional costing systems and ABC systems?
18. "ABC systems only apply to manufacturing companies." Do you agree? Explain.
19. "Activity-based costing is the wave of the present and the future. All companies should adopt it." Do you agree? Explain.
20. The following are six cost pools established for a company using activity-based costing. The pools are related to the company's product using cost drivers:

Cost Pools:

(*a*) Inspection of raw materials.
(*b*) Production equipment repairs and maintenance.
(*c*) Raw materials storage.
(*d*) Plant heat, light, water and power.
(*e*) Finished product quality control.
(*f*) Production line setups.

Required:

For each of the preceding cost pools, identify a possible cost driver.

APPENDIX

CASES

1. A condensed balance sheet and other financial data for Alpha Company appear below:

Alpha Company
Balance Sheet as on December 31, 2008

	Rs.
Assets	
Current Assets	1,00,000
Plant Assets	1,40,000
Total Assets	2,50,000
Liabilities and Equity	
Current Liabilities	1,00,000
Long-term Liabilities	75,000
Total Liabilities	1,75,000
Common Equity	75,000
Total Liabilities and Equity	2,50,000

Income Statement Data

Net Sales	3,75,000
Interest Expense	4,000
Net Income	22,500

The following account balances existed at December 31, 2007: Total Assets Rs. 2,00,000; Equity Rs. 65,000. The tax rate is 35 per cent.

Industry norms as of December 31, 2008 were:

Debt-equity ratio	1.75
Profit margin	0.12
Return on total assets	0.15
Return on common equity	0.30
Total asset turnover	1.71

Calculate and evaluate the following ratios for Alpha Company as of December 31, 2008:

(*a*) Debt-equity ratio
(*b*) Profit margin
(*c*) Return on total assets
(*d*) Return on common equity
(*e*) Total asset turnover

2. A company's financial statements appear below:

Balance Sheet as on December 31, 2007

	Rs.	Rs.
Assets		
Current Assets:		
Cash	1,00,000	
Marketable Securities	2,00,000	
Inventory	3,00,000	
Total Current Assets		6,00,000
Non-current Assets:		
Plant Assets		5,00,000
Total Assets		11,00,000
Liabilities and Equity:		
Current Liabilities	2,00,000	
Long-term Liabilities	1,00,000	
Total Liabilities		3,00,000
Common Equity		
(@ Rs. 10 per share, 10,000 shares)	1,00,000	
Premium on Common equity	5,00,000	
Retained Earnings	2,00,000	
Total Equity		8,00,000
Total Liabilities and Equity		11,00,000

Income Statement for the year ended December 31, 2007

	Rs.
Net Sales	1,00,00,000
Cost of Goods Sold	60,00,000
Gross Profit	40,00,000
Operating Expenses	10,00,000
Income before Taxes	30,00,000
Income Taxes (50% rate)	15,00,000
Net Income	15,00,000

Additional information available is a market price of Rs. 1,500 per share of equity and total dividends of Rs. 6,00,000 for 2007 and Rs. 2,50,000 of inventory as of December 31, 2006. Compute the following ratios:

(*a*) Current ratio
(*b*) Quick ratio
(*c*) Inventory turnover
(*d*) Average age of inventory
(*e*) Debt-equity ratio
(*f*) Book value per share
(*g*) Earnings per share
(*h*) Price-earnings ratio
(*i*) Dividends per share
(*j*) Dividend payout

3. Mr. Jaipal, was working as a Technical Manager in a Public Ltd. Co., took voluntary retirement with a view to start a small-scale unit in high grade ferrous metallic products. He took the assistance of one of his friends, who was an industrial consultant and prepared the project and submitted to the bankers. The project was accepted by the bankers and extended 80% of the project cost. The cost of the entire project was Rs. 25 lakhs. With the bank assistance and with his own resources the unit was started on Jan. 4, 2007. His son Mr. Jeevan who was doing his technical course, on completion of his course joined his father and converted their firm into a Pvt. Ltd. Co. Thereupon they wanted to expand the business. In order to do so, once again they approached their Bankers for additional funds on 1st February 2009, and submitted the following financial statements of their company drawn on 31st December, 2008.

Profit & Loss A/c

	Rs.		*Rs.*
To Cost of production	40,00,000	By Sales	50,00,000
" Gross profit	10,00,000		
	50,00,000		50,00,000
To Establishment Expenses	7,00,000	By Gross profit	10,00,000
" Depreciation	1,50,000		
" Net profit	1,50,000		
	10,00,000		10,00,000

Balance Sheet as at 31-12-2008

	Rs.		*Rs.*
Share capital	5,00,000	Building	8,00,000
Secured Loan	20,00,000	Machinery	14,00,000
Trade creditors	5,00,000	Stock	8,00,000
Bills payable	3,00,000	Debtors	2,50,000
		Cash in hand	20,000
		Cash at Bank	30,000
	33,00,000		33,00,000

The banker after going through the financial statements of the company submitted to them, have turned down the proposal for providing additional funds. Thereafter they are approaching you, as a financial consultant. What are your analysis and interpretation of the financial statement submitted by the company and how do you help the company to get over the difficulty?

4. Data taken from the financial statement of a manufacturer, follow (amounts in lakhs). The company has acquired another company, in Year 2.

For the year		*Year 2*	*Year 3*	*Year 4*
		Rs.	*Rs.*	*Rs.*
Net income before interest and income taxes		248	328	370
Cash flow from Operations		120	230	217
Interest Expense		43	36	30
On December 31	*Year 1*	*Year 2*	*Year 3*	*Year 4*
Long-term Debt	57	380	206	200
Total Liabilities	418	995	977	1,016
Total Shareholders' Equity	867	955	1,106	1,277

Required:

(a) Compute the long-term debt ratio and the debt-equity ratio at the end of Year 2, Year 3, and Year 4.

(b) Compute the cash flow from operations to total liabilities ratio and the interest coverage ratio for Year 2 through Year 4.

(c) How has the long-term liquidity risk of the company changed over this three-year period?

5. Data taken from the financial statements of Sun Microsystems, a computer manufacturer, appear as follows (amounts in lakhs):

(Rupees)

For the Year	*Year 6*	*Year 7*	*Year 8*
Revenues	3,589	4,309	4,690
Cost of Goods sold	1,963	2,518	2,753
Net income	173	157	196
Cash flow from operations	508	336	355

On December 31	*Year 5*	*Year 6*	*Year 7*	*Year 8*
Cash and Marketable Securities	834	1,220	1,139	883
Accounts Receivable	515	504	627	853
Inventories	224	179	256	295
Prepayments	228	245	250	274
Total Current Assets	1,801	2,148	2,272	2,305
Accounts Payable	212	236	271	364
Bank Loans	80	133	129	117
Other Current Liabilities	421	470	547	667
Total Current Liabilities	713	839	947	1,148

Required:

(*a*) Compute the current and quick ratios on December 31 of each year.

(*b*) Compute the cash flow from operations to current liabilities ratio and the accounts receivable, inventory, and accounts payable turnover ratios for Year 6, Year 7, and Year 8.

(*c*) How has the short-term liquidity risk of Sun Microsystems changed during the three-year period?

6. On December 15, 2007, the Accountant of ABC Company gave the Managing Director, a copy of an estimated year-end balance sheet for the company, containing the following figures:

Assets	*Rs.*
Cash	3,00,000
Accounts receivable	1,20,000
Inventories	1,80,000
Plant and equipment (net)	9,00,000
Total assets	15,00,000
Liabilities and Equity	
Accounts payable	3,00,000
Long-term debt	1,00,000
Common equity	8,00,000
Retained earnings	3,00,000
Total liabilities and equity	15,00,000

The Managing Director was concerned that the quick ratio was so low and asked the accountant to suggest some way of improving this ratio in the two weeks remaining before the end of the year.

Required:

(*a*) Calculate the quick ratio.

(*b*) What suggestion probably would be the easiest to implement? Would carrying out this suggestion impose any costs on the company?

7. Anderson Ltd. and Johnson Ltd. are doing business in a country in which generally accepted accounting principles are followed and the income tax rate is 25 per cent. The two companies offer the same general line of products to the same potential customers.

The following data were taken from the 2007 financial statements of these two companies:

	Anderson Ltd. *Rs.*	*Johnson Ltd.* *Rs.*
Cash	8,000	24,000
Accounts receivable	17,000	19,200
Inventories	27,200	29,568
Prepaid expenses	2,000	4,000
Property and equipment	1,00,000	2,20,000
Accumulated depreciation	(62,400)	(57,152)
Total	91,800	2,39,616
Current liabilities	20,000	40,000
Long-term debt — 6 per cent	40,000	—
Long-term debt — 9 per cent	—	20,000
Common equity	31,800	1,79,616
Total	91,800	2,39,616
Sales	2,04,000	4,60,800
Cost of goods sold	(1,63,200)	(3,54,816)
Other expenses	(22,440)	(46,080)
Interest	(2,400)	(1,800)
Income taxes	(3,990)	(14,526)
Net Income	11,970	43,578

Anderson's long-term debt was obtained about 10 years earlier. Its low interest rate constituted a subsidy from a state funding agency. Johnson's long-term debt also arose about 10 years before 2007, but it was a straight financial-market transaction, with no government subsidy.

All sales in both companies are on account and there are only minor seasonal variations in sales.

(*a*) Compare the current debt-paying ability of the two firms. To what extent can the inventories be looked upon as a means of paying debts due in 30 days? In 60 days?

(*b*) Compare the profitability of the two firms. What factors account for the difference?

(*c*) Compare the long-term debt-paying ability of the two firms.

8. The following information relates to the operations of the North Trading Company for the three year period ended 31st December 2007:

Profit and Loss Accounts

	2007 *Rs.*	*2006* *Rs.*	*2005* *Rs.*
Net sales	10,00,000	9,00,000	8,00,000
Cost of goods sold	6,00,000	5,50,000	5,45,000
Gross profit	4,00,000	3,50,000	2,55,000
Selling and administrative expenses	3,00,000	2,75,000	2,20,000
Net profit before tax	1,00,000	75,000	35,000
Tax at 50%	50,000	37,500	17,500
Net profit after tax	50,000	37,500	17,500
Dividends	30,000	25,000	10,000
Net increase in retained earnings	20,000	12,500	7,500

Balance Sheets

	2007 *Rs.*	*2006* *Rs.*	*2005* *Rs.*
Assets			
Land and buildings	5,00,000	4,50,000	4,25,000
Plant and equipment (net)	4,50,000	5,00,000	4,10,000
Stocks (at cost)	6,35,000	6,00,000	5,20,000
Debtors	4,25,000	4,10,000	4,40,000
Bank balance	40,000	55,000	63,000
	20,50,000	20,15,000	18,58,000
Shareholders' equity and liabilities			
Ordinary share capital @ Rs. 10 per share fully paid	6,00,000	6,00,000	6,00,000
Share premium account	1,25,000	1,25,000	1,25,000
Retained earnings	5,32,000	5,12,000	5,00,000
12% debentures	2,00,000	2,00,000	2,00,000
Creditors	4,96,000	4,93,000	3,90,000
Accrued expenses	15,000	17,000	9,000
Taxation	52,000	43,000	24,000
Provision for dividends	30,000	25,000	10,000
	20,50,000	20,15,000	18,58,000

Required:

From the foregoing information, calculate the following ratios for the years 2006 and 2007 (assume that all sales are on a credit basis and the year is of 360 days):

(*a*) The current ratio
(*b*) The acid-test ratio
(*c*) The average stock turnover
(*d*) The average collection period for debtors
(*e*) The shareholders' equity ratio
(*f*) The return on capital employed
(*g*) The earnings per share.

Evaluate the liquidity position of the company at the end of 2007 as compared with 2006.

9. The 2008 Balance Sheet and Income statement for Omex Limited are given below. *Compute* the financial ratios for Omex as per the table following the financial statements. *Evaluate* Omex's performance with reference to the standards:

Omex Limited Balance Sheet, December 31, 2008

Liabilities and Equity	*Rs.*
Equity capital	1,00,00,000
Reserves and Surplus	2,25,00,000
Long-term Debt	1,25,00,000
Short-term Bank Borrowing	1,50,00,000
Trade creditors	1,00,00,000
Provisions	50,00,000
Total	7,50,00,000

Assets	*Rs.*
Fixed Assets (Net)	3,00,00,000
Current Assets:	
Cash and Bank	50,00,000
Receivables	1,50,00,000
Inventories	2,00,00,000
Prepaid Expenses	25,00,000
Others	25,00,000
Total	7,50,00,000

Omex Limited Income Statement for the Year Ended December 31, 2008

	Rs.
Net sales	9,50,00,000
Cost of Goods Sold	7,20,00,000
Gross Profit	2,30,00,000
Operating Expenses	1,05,00,000
Operating Profit	1,25,00,000
Non-operating Surplus	26,00,000
Profit before Interest and Tax	1,51,00,000
Interest	50,00,000
Profit before Tax	1,01,00,000
Tax	50,00,000
Profit after Tax	51,00,000
Dividends	18,00,000
Retained Earnings	33,00,000

Omex (To be calculated)	*Standard*
Current Ratio	1.5
Acid-Test Ratio	0.80
Debt-Equity Ratio	1.5
Times Interest Covered Ratio	3.5
Inventory Turnover Ratio	4.0
Average Collection Period	60 days
Total Assets Turnover Ratio	1.0
Net Profit Margin Ratio	6%
Return on Investment	10%
Return on Equity	12%

10. Here are the income statements and balance sheets of A Company and B Company, taken from their annual reports for the year ended December 31, 2007.

Income Statement for the year 2007

	A Company Rs.	*B Company* Rs.
Sales	80,00,000	70,00,000
Cost of goods sold	60,00,000	47,00,000
Selling, general and administrative expenses	12,00,000	19,00,000
Interest on debt	—	70,000
Income before taxes	8,00,000	3,30,000
Income taxes	3,90,000	1,60,000
Net income	4,10,000	1,70,000
Dividends declared	1,00,000	70,000

Condensed Balance Sheets as of December 31, 2007

Assets	*A Company* Rs.	*B Company* Rs.
Cash	3,00,000	3,00,000
Accounts receivable	8,00,000	6,50,000
Inventory	13,00,000	8,50,000
Net plant and equipment	21,00,000	15,00,000
Total assets	45,00,000	33,00,000
Liabilities and Equity		
Accounts payable	7,10,000	4,00,000
Taxes payable	3,90,000	1,60,000
Long-term debt	—	14,00,000
Common equity	22,00,000	8,00,000
Retained earnings	12,00,000	5,40,000
Total liabilities and equity	45,00,000	33,00,000

On the basis of the available information, which do you consider to be (1) more liquid? (2) more solvent? (3) more profitable? Explain your conclusions.

11. Ram and Shyam each carry on business as wholesalers of the same product. Their respective accounts for the year ended 31st December 2007 are as follows:

Profit and Loss Accounts

	Ram		*Shyam*	
	Rs.	*Rs.*	*Rs.*	*Rs.*
Sales		1,44,000		1,40,000
Cost of sales:				
Opening stocks	28,000		3,200	
Purchases	1,24,000		1,21,600	
	1,52,000		1,24,800	
Closing stocks	32,000	1,20,000	4,800	1,20,000
Gross profit		24,000		20,000

Selling expenses	7,200		2,800	
Administrative expenses	8,160	15,360	9,500	12,300
Net profit		8,640		7,700

Balance Sheets as at 31 December 2007

	Ram *Rs.*	*Shyam* *Rs.*
Freehold property	20,000	14,000
Fixtures and fittings	21,750	13,840
Motor vehicles	12,000	6,000
	53,750	33,840
Stocks	32,000	4,800
Debtors	28,800	11,200
Bank	8,950	11,360
	1,23,500	61,200
Capital	1,08,000	30,800
Creditors	15,500	30,400
	1,23,500	61,200

Notes:

(*a*) All sales are on credit.

(*b*) The amounts of debtors and creditors have not changed significantly over the year.

(*c*) All fixed assets are at written-down value.

Required:

Compare the profitability and financial position of the two businesses by:

(*a*) Calculating suitable ratios for each business;

(*b*) Commenting on the significance of the results of your calculations.

12. A Company and B Company maintain dominant market shares in the athletic footwear market. A Company places somewhat greater emphasis on the performance characteristics of footwear while B company places somewhat greater emphasis on the fashion characteristics of its footwear. Exhibit below presents comparative balance sheets for A Company and B Company at the end of Year 2007 and Year 2008. Exhibit 2 presents an income statement for each firm for Year 2008. Cash flows from operations for Year 2008 were Rs. 255 million for A Company and Rs. 173 million for B Company. The income tax rate is 35 per cent. On the basis of this information and appropriate financial statement ratios, which company is:

(*a*) more profitable?

(*b*) less risky in terms of short-term liquidity?

(*c*) less risky in terms of long-term solvency?

EXHIBIT 1
A Co. and B Co.
Comparative Balance Sheets

(Amount in millions)

	A Co.		*B Co.*	
	Year 2007 *Rs.*	*Year 2008* *Rs.*	*Year 2007* *Rs.*	*Year 2008* *Rs.*
Assets:				
Cash	519	216	79	84
Accounts Receivable	703	1,053	457	532
Inventories	470	630	514	625
Prepayments	78	147	77	96
Total Current Assets	1,770	2,046	1,127	1,337
Property, Plant and Equipment (net)	406	555	131	165
Other Assets	198	542	134	147
Total Assets	2,374	3,143	1,392	1,649
Liabilities and Shareholders' Equity				
Accounts Payable	211	298	282	171
Bank Loans	131	429	27	69
Other current liabilities	220	381	87	266
Total Current Liabilities	562	1,108	396	506
Long-term Debt	12	10	134	132
Other Non-current Liabilities	59	60	15	21
Total Liabilities	633	1,178	545	659
Common equity	3	4	1	1
Additional Paid-in capital	108	122	267	168
Retained Earnings	1,630	1,839	1,182	1,424
Treasury Stock	—	—	(603)	(603)
Total Shareholders's Equity	1,741	1,965	847	990
Total Liabilities and Shareholders' Equity	2,374	3,143	1,392	1,649

EXHIBIT 2

A Co. and B Co.
Comparative Income Statements

(Amounts in millions)

	For Year 2008	
	A Co. *Rs.*	*B. Co.* *Rs.*
Sales revenue	4,761	3,280
Expenses:		
Cost of Goods Sold	2,865	1,966
Selling and Administrative	1,222	889
Interest	24	17
Income Taxes	250	154
Total Expenses	4,361	3,026
Net Income	400	254

13. You are financial adviser to a retailing company, A Co. Ltd. You obtain the accounts of their main competitor operating in the same market, B Co. Ltd., and extract the comparison shown below:

Balance Sheets as at 31st March 2008

	A Co. Ltd.			*B Co. Ltd.*		
	Rs. (000)	*Rs. (000)*	*Rs. (000)*	*Rs. (000)*	*Rs. (000)*	*Rs. (000)*
Fixed assets						
Land and buildings		381			286	
Fixtures and fittings		342			218	
Vehicles		62			59	
			785			563
Current assets						
Stocks		96			122	
Trade debtors	166			124		
Cash	9			6		
		271			252	
Current liabilities						
Overdraft		20			21	
Trade creditors	132			97		
Accruals	48			42		
		200			160	
			71			92
			856			655
Shareholders's funds						
Share capital		470			350	655
Capital reserves		35			65	
Profit and loss account		287			185	
			792			600
10% Debentures			64			55
			856			655

Profit and Loss Accounts for the year ended 31 March 2008

	A Co. Ltd		*B Co. Ltd.*	
	Rs. (000)	*Rs. (000)*	*Rs. (000)*	*Rs. (000)*
Sales (on credit)		570		747
Cost of sales				
Opening stock	92		102	
Purchases (on credit)	381		588	
	473		690	
Closing stock	96		122	
		377		568
Gross profit		193		179
Distribution costs	60		64	
Administration costs	29		31	
		89		95
		104		84
Interest charges		8		9
Net profit		96		75
Taxation		45		37
		51		38
Dividend		37		24
Retained profit for the year		14		14

Upon analysing this information, you observe that it reveals significant differences between the companies.

Required:

(*a*) Calculate and identify the key differences in profitability and in working capital management as between the two companies.

(*b*) Based upon the analysis at (a) above, recommend actions which the management of A Co. Ltd. should consider in order to improve their financial performance.

(*c*) State any reservations you may have about drawing conclusions from the comparative analysis of the two companies.

14. The Konrath Company is considering extending credit to the Hawk Company. It is estimated that sales to the Hawk Company would amount to Rs. 2 million each year. The Konrath Company is a wholesaler that sells throughout the mid-west. The Hawk Company is a retail chain operation that has a number of stores in the mid-west. The Konrath Company has had a gross margin of approximately 60 per cent in recent years and expects to have a similar gross margin on the Hawk Company order. The Hawk Company order is approximately 15 per cent of the Konrath Company's present sales. Recent statements of the Hawk Company are given below.

Hawk Company
Balance Sheet as of December 31

(000,000 omitted)

	Rs. 2008	Rs. 2009	Rs. 2010
Assets			
Current Assets:			
Cash	2.6	1.8	1.6
Government Securities (Cost)	0.4	0.2	—
Accounts and Notes Receivable (Net)	8.0	8.5	8.5
Inventories	2.8	3.2	2.8
Prepaid Assets	0.7	0.6	0.6
Total Current Assets	14.5	14.3	13.5
Property, Plant and Equipment (Net)	4.3	5.4	5.9
Total Assets	18.8	19.7	19.4
Equities			
Current Liabilities:			
Notes Payable	3.2	3.7	4.2
Accounts Payable	2.8	3.7	4.1
Accrued Expenses and Taxes	0.9	1.1	1.0
Total Current Liabilities	6.9	8.5	9.3
Long-term debt: 6%	3.0	2.0	1.0
Total Liabilities	9.9	10.5	10.3
Shareholders' Equity	8.9	9.2	9.1
Total Equities	18.8	19.7	19.4

Hawk Company
Income Statement for the year ended December 31

(000,000 omitted)

	Rs. 2008	Rs. 2009	Rs. 2010
Net Sales	24.2	24.5	24.9
Cost of Goods sold	16.9	17.2	18.0
Gross Margin	7.3	7.3	6.9
Selling expenses	4.3	4.4	4.6
Administrative expenses	2.3	2.4	2.7
Total expenses	6.6	6.8	7.3
Earning (Loss) before Taxes	0.7	0.5	(0.4)
Income Taxes	0.3	0.2	(0.2)
Net Income	0.4	0.3	(0.2)

Hawk Company
Statement of Changes in Financial Position
for the year ended December 31

(000,000 omitted)

	Rs. 2008	*Rs.* 2009	*Rs.* 2010
Sources of Funds			
Net Income (loss)	0.4	0.3	(0.2)
Depreciation	0.4	0.5	0.5
Funds from Operations	0.8	0.8	0.3
Sale of Building	0.2	—	—
Sales of Treasury Stock	—	0.1	0.1
Total Sources	1.0	0.9	0.4
Uses of Funds:			
Purchase of Property, Plant, and Equipment	1.2	1.6	1.0
Dividends	0.1	0.1	—
Retirement of Long-term Debt	—	1.0	1.0
Total Uses	1.3	2.7	2.0
Net Increase (Decrease) in Working Capital	(0.3)	(1.8)	(1.6)

I. Calculate for the year 2010 the following ratios:

(*a*) Return on total assets

(*b*) Acid-test ratio

(*c*) Profit margin

(*d*) Current ratio

(*e*) Inventory turnover

II. As part of the analysis to determine whether Konrath should extend credit to Hawk, assume that the ratios below were calculated from Hawk Company statements. For each ratio, indicate whether it is favourable, unfavourable, or neutral statistic in the decision to grant Hawk credit. Briefly explain your choice in each case.

	2008	*2009*	*2010*
(*a*) Return on total assets	1.96%	1.12%	(0.87)%
(*b*) Profit margin	1.69%	0.99%	(0.69)%
(*c*) Acid-test ratio	1.73/1	1.36/1	1.19/1
(*d*) Current ratio	2.39/1	1.92/1	1.67/1
(*e*) Inventory turnover (times)	4.41	4.32	4.52
(*f*) Equity relationships:			
Current liabilities	36.0%	43.0%	48.0%
Long-term liabilities	16.0	10.5	5.0
Shareholders	48.0	46.5	47.0
	100.0%	100.0%	100.0%
(*g*) Asset relationships:			
Current assets	77.0%	72.5%	69.5%
Property, plant and equipment	23.0%	27.5%	30.5%
	100.0%	100.0%	100.0%

III. Would you grant to Hawk Company? Support your answer with facts given in the problem.

IV. What additional information, if any, would you want before making a final decision?

15. The Managing Director and seven divisional heads of ABC Ltd. spent a long weekend at a hill station resort debating company goals. They concluded that ABC Ltd. had multiple goals and that the performance of senior managers should be assessed in terms of all of them.

The goal identified were:

(*i*) To generate a higher financial return for shareholders.

(*ii*) To maintain a high market share.

(*iii*) To increase productivity annually.

(*iv*) To offer excellent after sales service.

(*v*) To offer an up-to-date product range of high quality.

(*vi*) To be known as caring employers.

(*vii*) To acknowledge social responsibilities.

You as the Management Accountant of ABC Ltd. are required to set out briefly with reasons, suitable measures of performance for each of the stated goals.

16. Pawan Kumar has just joined as a manager at the XYZ manufacturing company at Hyderabad. The company makes the jewel cases. Earlier, before joining this company, Pawan Kumar worked hard for fifteen years in production engineering. Now, Pawan Kumar would be reporting directly to his managing director, Rakesh.

On a day, Rakesh advised Pawan Kumar to prepare and present an analysis of impact of new automated machines in place of the old machines. The new machines would reduce direct labour costs considerably and also there would be efficiency gains in direct materials. Overheads like depreciation and insurance will increase. The Managing Director desired savings in other costs such as supervision, maintenance, materials handling and quality inspection.

Pawan Kumar visited the accounting department to check accounting records and behaviour of different type of costs when the new machine was purchased.

Required:

(*i*) Identify the areas as referred to in the above paragraphs, about which Pawan Kumar should be knowledgeable.

(*ii*) Explain the importance of areas identified in point (i) above for a manager like Pawan Kumar in a large sized manufacturing firm.

17. During the early 2008, ProSoft Corporation developed and marketed business applications software for minicomputers, achieving a significant market share and a secure position in the industry. After maturing at this level of success, the company's mission became less clear. Further, software development for minicomputers was seen as costly with little value to the company, as the market for major business applications was saturated and the minor applications had limited markets.

In order to maintain ProSoft's market share, management decided to enter the growing personal computer field. While major programming would be required to make the company's existing software compatible with personal computers (PCs), management viewed the commitment of all personnel to this project as critical to the continued growth of ProSoft.

After weeks of executive strategy sessions regarding product specifications, management imposed the task deadlines and set the date for the introduction of its first PC product, an accounting package for general ledger, accounts payable, and accounts receivable applications. Three months prior to the introduction date, ProSoft began an advertising and dealer promotion campaign announcing the new product and setting the introduction date. Several technical problems arose during development, but the staff believed that a few time-saving measures would enable them to complete the package in time to meet the announced date. Management felt considerable pressure to meet this date as ProSoft had previously missed an announced date and suffered the consequences.

Two weeks before the announced date, ProSoft's marketing personnel learned that an updated version of the PC operating software that ProSoft's new package was designed to interact with was to be released shortly. The marketing staff knew that features could quickly be added to ProSoft's new product to take advantage of the new features in the operating software; however, there would not be time to field test the programme changes. The technical personnel warned the marketing staff of the dangers of releasing a product without proper field testing, but these warnings were not heeded. Management, with encouragement from the marketing staff, made the decision to incorporate the features necessary to take advantage of the new operating software and introduce the product on the scheduled date.

Not long after ProSoft despatched the first lots of its new software, customers began to complain about processing problems in the accounts payable and accounts receivable modules. Very quickly, it was determined that portions of ProSoft's new package were not compatible with the updated operating software. To correct the problem, the company had to rewrite the software and manuals and replace all existing product. The technical personnel were not dedicated to the development of the next PC product, and this problem fragmented their efforts. The revised product was not available for three months, causing a loss of sales. The financial impact of the Rs. 50 crores error on the company with annual profits of Rs. 40 crores was devastating.

Required:

(*a*) Identify the steps in the general decision-making process.

(*b*) Using the steps identified in Requirement (*a*), describe the weaknesses in ProSoft's decision-making process.

(*c*) Recommend changes to correct the weaknesses identified in requirement (*b*).

18. A Bangalore-based Stamping plant, was one of the largest and most modern stamping plants in India. It began producing parts for Compro's model cars in 2007.

A stamping line consisted of a series of presses. The first press cut sheets of metal to the desired size. Each subsequent press performed bending, punching, or shaping operations. After the metal was passed through the last press in the line, it was bonderised and dispatched to the different assembly plants.

The company had a large toolroom capable of producing smaller dies and many of the other tools and specially designed jigs and fixtures required by the extensive production equipment used in the plant. In the early part of 2008, the toolroom was operating at considerably less than capacity and this was a source of concern to the plant manager.

In March 2008, Mr. Ram, the plant manager, called a meeting to discuss what should be done about the toolroom. Attending the meeting were Shyam, the Controller, Ghanshyam, the Manager of Purchasing, and Mohan, the Toolroom Manager.

Following discussion took place in the meeting.

Ram: It seems to me we have to develop a policy for deciding what tools and dies we should make ourselves and which ones we should buy. At the present time, we have a lot of excess capacity in the toolroom.

Ghanshyam: It seems to me that we should make those tools and dies on which we can make an adequate profit, say 10% over cost. If the purchase price of a die or tool is less than our cost plus 10%, we should buy it. Otherwise, we should make it, if we have capacity.

Mohan: If I had to meet the overhead costs in this plant, I'd never make anything. The other producers don't have the overhead that we have. They don't have our training programme, company newspapers, engineers, and accountants. Also, their pay scales are considerably less than ours. As a result, they can outbid me every time. I think we should make any tool or die as along as my variable costs are less than the purchase price.

Shyam: I can't agree with that position. All of your costs, except material, are fixed. If we follow your policy, we would decide all make-or-buy decisions in favour of making. We could fill the toolroom with parts on which we would be losing our shirts. It seems to me that we should produce nothing unless our total costs are less than the purchase price.

Ram: I would be a little worried about Mohan's suggestion too. How do we know that we are making the most profitable items? Also, what we do when the toolroom reaches capacity? Do we just fill the toolroom with everything until we use up its capacity and then buy everything else? If we did this, the decision as to whether we should make or buy an item would depend on the timing of the purchase order. Today, we have capacity, so we make it; tomorrow, our capacity is committed, so we buy it. How do we know that today's part isn't a lot more profitable than yesterday's?

Ghanshyam: I certainly disagree with Mohan, I have to keep our vendors reasonably happy; otherwise, we'll be in trouble when we need them.

Ram: We aren't getting anywhere here, we need to utilize our toolroom capacity. We need to produce the parts that earn us the most money. It would be better to have a proposed policy that will meet these two objectives.

Required:

Recommend a make-or-buy policy for the Bangalore-based Stamping Plant. In this recommendation, be sure to include the following:

(*a*) The policy to be followed where excess capacity exists in the toolroom.
(*b*) The policy to be followed when there is no excess capacity in the toolroom.
(*c*) A workable definition of capacity — that is to say, if the policies for (*a*) and (*b*) are different, how can the Manager of Purchasing know whether capacity exists or not?
(*d*) Details as to what should be included in costs if the policy includes the use of cost data.
(*e*) An explanation telling why your policy will not result in filling the toolroom with unprofitable parts.

19. Crunchy Chips India (CCI) Ltd. is specially frozen food processor located in Punjab State of India. Since its founding in 2008, CCI has enjoyed a loyal clientele that is willing to pay premium prices for the high-quality frozen food it prepares from specialised recipes. In the last two years, the company has experienced rapid sales growth in its operating region and has had many enquiries about supplying its products on a national basis. To meet this growth, CCI expanded its processing capabilities which resulted in increased production and distribution costs. Furthermore, CCI has been encountering pricing pressures from competitors outside its normal marketing region.

Because CCI desires to continue its expansion, Raghvendra, Chief Executive Officer, has engaged a consulting firm to assist CCI in determining its best course of action. The consulting firm recommended instituting a standard costing system that would also facilitate a flexible budgeting system to better accommodate the changes in demand that can be expected when serving an expanding market area. Raghvendra met with his management team and explained the consulting firm's recommendations. Raghvendra then assigned the task of establishing standard costs to his management team. After discussing the situation with the respective staffs, the management team met to review the matter.

Rakesh, purchasing manager, advised that meeting expanded production would necessitate obtaining basic food supplies from other than CCI's traditional sources. This would entail increased raw material and other costs and might result in lower-quality supplies. Consequently, these increased costs would need to be made up by the processing department if current costs are to be maintained or reduced.

Ramesh, processing manager, countered that the need to accelerate processing cycles to increase production, coupled with the possibility of receiving lower-grade supplies, could be expected to result in a slip in quality and a greater product rejection rate. Under these circumstances, per unit labour utilisation could not be maintained or reduced and forecasting future unit labour content would become very difficult.

Rajiv, production engineer, advised that if equipment is not properly maintained and thoroughly cleaned at prescribed daily intervals, the quality and unique taste of the frozen-food products would probably be affected.

Johnson, Vice-president of Sales, stated that if quality could not be maintained, CCI could not expect to increase sales to the levels projected.

When Raghvendra was apprised of the problems encountered by his management team, he advised them that if agreement could not be reached on the appropriate standards, he would arrange to have them set by the consulting firm and everyone would have to live with the results.

Required:

(*i*) List the major advantages of using a standard costing system.

(*ii*) Identify those who should participate in setting standards, and describe the benefits of their participation in the standard-setting process.

(*iii*) What could be the consequences if Raghvendra, Chief Executive Officer, has the standards set by outside consulting firm?

20. Raghvendra, Manager of Electronics Division in Electronics Company discussed with the Division's Controller, Somender some issues recently brought to his attention. The discussion between the two was as follows:

Raghvendra: Somender, you have been my controller for 10 years. You should be able to answer to some of the problems that are coming to our notice. Our division has Engineers, Production Managers and Marketing Managers who are no longer comfortable with our Cost Accounting System. Customer demand is forcing to create new technology with increased capability. However, prices of our products are decreasing regularly. Yet, some Managers are saying that these costs are useless and they do not reflect the difference in product features such as colour, capabilities, packaging and services. Does our Cost Accounting System really allow us to determine product line profitability accurately?

Somender: I notice that in aggregate our product costing are accurate. What we report on our balance sheet and income statement is much on target. However, I am not confident that our cost assignment procedures allow us to make strong statements about individual product profitability. Many of the costs are assigned using assumed relationship and may not reflect a cause and effect relationship.

Raghvendra: If what you are saying is right, how can we rely on individual costing for decision making? For example, can we use them to help us price our products and determine the right product mix. Can these costs be used to help us improve product designs?

Somender: The points you are making are good. But there is a difference between decision and accuracy. If the costs are not assigned correctly, using them for pricing and design decisions could be harmful. We do not know the real cost of product differences and real cost differences between distribution channels and customers.

Raghvendra: Somender, something must be done. Can we improve the accuracy of our product costing. We must know how much each product is costing. It is also vital to have accurate cost information about our distribution channels and customers. It seems important that we need to learn more about costs and then make decisions relating to those cost. Understanding the nature of cost is fundamental to good management.

Required:

I. What is meant by product costing accuracy?

II. How will increasing accuracy of product costing improve decision making?

III. Why does Somender feel that the division's product costs are not very accurate?

IV. Is assigning cost accurately as important for services as it is for tangible products?

21. Arcadia has its headquarters in New Delhi and factory in Mumbai, Bangalore and Chennai, all of which produce the same product. The operations of the Chennai factory have been unprofitable for a number of years. The lease on the Chennai building will expire at the end of this year, and Arcadia's management has decided to cease operations there rather than renew the lease. This factory's machinery and equipment will be sold. Arcadia expects the proceeds from the sale of these assets will exceed their book value by an amount just adequate to cover the termination costs.

Prior to the decision to close the Chennai plant, Arcadia's management had prepared the following projection of operating results for the next year:

	Total	*Mumbai*	*Bangalore*	*Chennai*
Sales revenue (Rs.)	43,00,000	22,00,000	14,00,000	7,00,000
Fixed costs:				
Factory	11,00,000	5,60,000	2,80,000	2,60,000
Selling and administrative	3,50,000	2,10,000	1,10,000	30,000
Variable costs	14,50,000	6,65,000	4,25,000	3,60,000
Headquarter costs	5,00,000	2,25,000	1,75,000	1,00,000
Total operating expense	34,00,000	16,60,000	9,90,000	7,50,000
Operating income (loss) before taxes (Rs.)	9,00,000	5,40,000	4,10,000	(50,000)

Headquarter costs are divided among the factories in proportion to their labour costs and will remain Rs. 5,00,000 in total even after the Chennai factory is closed.

Arcadia would like to continue serving the customer now being served by the Chennai factory, if it can do so economically. Accordingly, management is considering the following alternatives, all based on the assumption that the selling price remains Rs. 25 a unit:

Alternative 1

Close the Chennai factory and expand the operations of the Bangalore factory by using space presently idle there. This move would result in the following changes in operations at the Bangalore factory:

(*a*) Sales revenue would increase by 50 per cent.

(*b*) Factory fixed costs would increase by 20 per cent.

(*c*) Selling and administrative fixed costs would increase by 10 per cent.

(*d*) Average variable costs would be Rs. 8 a unit.

Alternative 2

Close the Chennai factory and enter into a long-term contract with an independent manufacturer to serve the area's customers. This manufacturer would pay Arcadia a royalty of Rs. 4 a unit, based on an estimate of 30,000 units being sold.

Alternative 3

Close the Chennai factory and discontinue serving its present customers.

Prepare an analysis to help management decide which of these three alternatives is the most desirable for Arcadia.

22. Mr. Karan Mehta operates a small machine shop. He manufactures one *'standard product'* which is available from many other similar businesses and also manufactures another product referred to as 'universal.' His accountant prepared the annual income statement given as below:

	Universal Product Rs.	*Standard Product Rs.*	*Total Rs.*
Sales	5,00,000	2,50,000	7,50,000
Material	1,00,000	80,000	1,80,000
Labour	2,00,000	90,000	2,90,000
Depreciation	63,000	36,000	99,000
Power	7,000	4,000	11,000
Rent	60,000	10,000	70,000
Heat and light	6,000	1,000	7,000
Other expenses	4,000	9,000	13,000
	4,40,000	2,30,000	6,70,000
Net profit	60,000	20,000	80,000

The depreciation charges are for machines used in the respective product lines. The power charge is apportioned on the estimate of power consumed. The rent is for the building space which has been leased for ten years at Rs. 70,000 per year. The rent and heat and light are apportioned to the product lines based on amount of floor space occupied. All other costs are current expenses and are identified with the product line causing them.

A customer of 'universal product' has asked Karan Mehta if he would manufacture 5000 special units for him. Mr. Karan Mehta is working at capacity and would have to give up some other business in order to take this special order. Though he cannot reduce universal product orders already agreed to, he could reduce the output of his standard product by about one-half for one year while producing the specially requested universal product. The customer is willing to pay Rs. 70 for each part. The material cost will be Rs. 20 per unit and the labour will be Rs. 36 per unit. Mr. Karan Mehta will have to spend Rs. 20,000 for a special device which will be discarded when the job is done.

Required:

I. Calculate and present the following costs related to the 5,000 units universal product order:

(*a*) Incremental cost of the order
(*b*) Full cost of the order
(*c*) Opportunity cost of accepting the order
(*d*) Sunk costs related to the order.

II. Should Karan Mehta accept the special order? Explain your answer.